THE INSECTS
Structure and Function

THE INSECTS
Structure and Function

Third Edition

R. F. CHAPMAN

HARVARD UNIVERSITY PRESS
CAMBRIDGE, MASSACHUSETTS, 1982

QL
463
.C48
1982 / 58,950

ISBN 0-674-87535-4

Library of Congress Catalog Card Number 81-85964

Printed in Hong Kong

PREFACE TO THE THIRD EDITION

It is ten years since the first edition of *The Insects* was published. During that period the volume of entomological literature has increased to such an extent that it is now quite impossible for one individual to encompass it all. In the same period there has been a strong movement away from 'traditional' teaching of zoology. 'Entomology' is now only rarely taught as a subject in Britain.

These facts may seem to provide good reasons for not attempting to revise this book, but to some degree they encouraged me to make the attempt. In these days of specialisation, the need to consider the organism as a whole remains; it is even more important to try to draw the threads together to show how they contribute to the whole.

The second reason which stimulated me was the widespread acceptance which the book has gained outside Britain, in the United States and the Developing Countries where insects are important and will continue to be so. I felt an obligation to bring the book more up-to-date so that the students who make use of it have an entrée to more recent developments, which are both important and exciting.

The degree of rewriting has varied, depending on the extent to which research has advanced in the last ten years. Consequently some chapters have been entirely rewritten, others have undergone minor changes, but I have attempted to bring them all up-to-date. I have not attempted any major reorganisation apart from the omission of the chapter on diapause and the extension of the final chapter to include defensive substances as well as pheromones.

I must express my gratitude to Elizabeth Bernays who has contributed very significantly to the revision, and to the publishers for their helpfulness and understanding. Numerous colleagues at the Centre for Overseas Pest Research have helped with various aspects and to them I give my thanks.

A note on classification

The work of Manton (1964, 1977) provides strong evidence that the subclass Apterygota as it has been widely accepted by entomologists is an artificial assemblage of orders some of which differ so much from the insects proper that there is no justification for including them in the Class Insecta. Information on these Orders is retained in this book, but a classification based on Manton's work is adopted:

Superclass   **HEXAPODA**
     Class   **COLLEMBOLA***
     Class   **PROTURA***
     Class   **DIPLURA***
     Class   **INSECTA**

      Subclass   **APTERYGOTA**
        Order   Archaeognatha (including the family Machilidae)
        Order   Thysanura (including the family Lepismatidae)

         } These Orders were previously both included in the Order Thysanura*

* These groups were previously classified as Orders of the Subclass Apterygota

      Subclass   **PTERYGOTA**
The classification of Pterygota used here is that widely used in entomological texts.

See:

MANTON, S. M. (1964). Mandibular mechanisms and the evolution of arthropods. *Phil. Trans. R. Soc.* B, **247**: 1–183.

MANTON, S. M. (1977). *The Arthropods. Habits, functional morphology, and evolution*. Clarendon Press, Oxford.

PREFACE

My own interest in insects started from a behavioural—cum—ecological approach, but the need to try to understand what the insects were doing and how they were doing it extended my interests to morphology and physiology. This brought with it the realisation that in order fully to appreciate any problem, be it basically morphological, physiological or ecological, a broad understanding of the insect is essential. I have adopted this point of view in teaching entomology to first degree and postgraduate students.

Although there are a number of admirable textbooks dealing with the morphology, physiology and natural history of insects, none of these, perhaps advisedly, makes any real attempt to bring the different approaches together. In this book I have tried to fill the gap, bringing morphology and physiology together and relating these studies to the behaviour of the insect under natural conditions. It is not intended that the book should be comprehensive, but it is hoped that it gives a general picture of what makes an insect tick, at least as far as present-day knowledge allows.

The arrangement of the chapters and sections reflects my own line of thinking. One could justify almost any arrangement, and I hope that the brief introductions to each chapter will serve to link sections whose relationships may not otherwise be apparent. At the end of each introductory section I have included a list of some of the more important reviews on each topic. In addition to these, other references are included in the text only where a point is not fully dealt with in the reviews or if it is subject to controversy. In most chapters some more recent references are included not only for the value of the work which they contain, but also because they give the most up-to-date entry to the literature. The sources of the illustrations are given since the inability to trace the origin of an illustration is a common cause of annoyance.

I am indebted to many people for help and advice given in the course of preparing the manuscript, but the chief sufferers have undoubtedly been my family. Their forbearance and understanding have been quite overwhelming; without them the book would certainly not have been completed. In addition my wife has made the very real contribution of checking and criticising the whole manuscript.

My friend Dr. Lena Ward has offered the most valuable criticisms which have added materially to the book, and this is also true of Mr. T. E. Hughes who has read many chapters and contributed in many other ways from his wealth of zoological knowledge. Others who have offered valuable advice are Dr. J. W. L. Beament, Mr. J. W. Charter and Dr. L. Rathbone. Not least in this category are my students who all too frequently have picked up a glib statement or an inconsistency when I thought they were dozing. Despite these combined efforts and my own, I am afraid that errors will remain. These, of course, are my own responsibility.

CONTENTS

SECTION A

The Head, Ingestion and Utilisation of the Food

CHAPTER I

THE HEAD AND ITS APPENDAGES

The characteristic feature of arthropods, including the insects, is a hard, jointed exoskeleton or cuticle. This consists of a series of hard plates, the sclerites, which may simply be joined to each other by membranes giving flexibility, or may be closely articulated together so as to give a more precise movement of one sclerite on the next.

Insects and other arthropods are built up on a segmental plan. Each segment basically has a dorsal sclerite, the tergum, joined to a ventral sclerite, the sternum, by lateral membranous areas, the pleura. Arising from the sternopleural region on each side is a jointed appendage. In the insects such segments are grouped into three units, the head, thorax and abdomen, in which the various basic parts of the segments may be lost or greatly modified. Typical walking legs are only retained on the three thoracic segments. In the head the appendages are modified for feeding purposes and in the abdomen they are lost, except that some may be modified as the genitalia and in Apterygota some pregenital appendages are retained.

The insect head is a strongly sclerotised capsule joined to the thorax by a flexible membranous neck. It bears the mouthparts, comprising the labrum, mandibles, maxillae and labium, and also important sense organs. On the outside it is marked by grooves most of which indicate ridges on the inside, and some of these inflexions extend deep into the head, fusing with each other to form an internal skeleton. These structures serve to strengthen the head and provide attachments for muscles as well as supporting and protecting the brain and foregut.

The head is derived from the primitive pre-oral archecerebrum and a number of post-oral segments. Embryological evidence shows that the mandibles, maxillae and labium are derived from typical appendages so that the head includes at least three post-oral segments and it is generally believed that there is also a premandibular segment, although there are no corresponding appendages in the adult. Apart from this there is much controversy concerning the inclusion of other segments in the head and the extent of the archecerebrum (Snodgrass, 1960).

The main sense organs on the head are a pair of compound eyes, typically three ocelli and a pair of antennae. The latter are very variable in form and functions, but are usually concerned with mechanoreception and chemoreception.

The mouthparts consist of upper and lower lips and two pairs of jaw-like structures, the mandibles and maxillae. In many insects which feed by biting off fragments of food and chewing them up these structures retain their jaw-like form, but in many which are fluid feeders various elements of the mouthparts become tubular for sucking up the food, while others may be stylet-like, serving to pierce the tissues of the host plant or animal.

Important works dealing generally with the insect head are DuPorte (1957), Matsuda (1965) and Snodgrass (1960). The form and functioning of the antennae is reviewed by Schneider (1964), while mouthparts are most fully dealt with in various specialist books and papers on specific insects (p. 19). Bitsch and Denis (1973) give a wide-ranging account of head and mouthpart anatomy.

1.1 Head

1.1.1 Orientation

The orientation of the head with respect to the rest of the body varies. The hypognathous condition with the mouthparts in a continuous series with the legs is probably primitive (Fig. 1). This orientation occurs mostly in vegetarian species living in open habitats. In the prognathous condition the mouthparts point forwards and this is found in carnivorous species which actively pursue their prey, and in larvae, particularly of Coleoptera, which use their mandibles for burrowing. Finally, in Heteroptera and Homoptera there is the opisthorhynchous condition in which the elongate proboscis slopes backwards between the front legs.

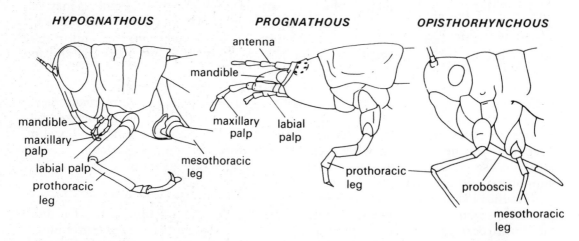

Fig. 1 Different positions of the head and mouthparts relative to the rest of the body. Hypognathous—grasshopper; prognathous—beetle larva; opisthorhynchous—aphid

1.1.2 Grooves of the head

The head is a continuously sclerotised capsule with no outward appearance of segmentation, but it is marked by a number of grooves. Commonly all these grooves are called sutures, but Snodgrass (1960) recommends that the term suture should be retained for grooves marking the line of fusion of two formerly distinct plates. Grooves with a purely functional origin are called sulci. The groove which ends between the points of attachment of maxillae and labium at the back of the head is generally believed to represent the line of fusion of the maxillary and labial segments and it is therefore known as the postoccipital suture. The remaining grooves on the head indicate only the presence of strengthening ridges on the inside and hence should be called sulci. Since they are functional mechanical developments to resist the various strains imposed on the head capsule, the sulci are variable in position in different species and any one of them may be completely absent. However, the needs for strengthening the head wall are similar in the majority of insects, so some of the sulci are fairly constant in occurrence and position.

The most constant is the epistomal (frontoclypeal) sulcus, which acts as a brace between the anterior mandibular articulations (Fig. 2). At each end of this sulcus is a pit, the anterior tentorial pit, which marks the position of a deep invagination to form the anterior arm of the tentorium (p. 9). The lateral margins of the head above the mandibular articulations are strengthened by a submarginal inflexion, the subgenal sulcus, which is generally a continuation of the epistomal sulcus to the postoccipital suture. The part of the subgenal sulcus above the mandible is called the pleurostomal sulcus, the part behind the mandible is the hypostomal sulcus. Another commonly occurring groove is the circumocular sulcus, which strengthens the rim of the eye and may develop into a deep flange protecting the inner side of the eye. Sometimes this sulcus is connected to the subgenal sulcus by a vertical subocular sulcus which, with the circumocular sulcus, acts as a brace against the pull of the mandibular muscles arising on the top of the head. The circumantennal sulcus strengthens the head at the point of insertion of the antenna, while running across the back of the head, behind the compound eyes, is the occipital sulcus.

Immature insects nearly always have a line along the dorsal midline of the head dividing into two lines on the face so as to form an inverted Y (Fig. 2). There is no

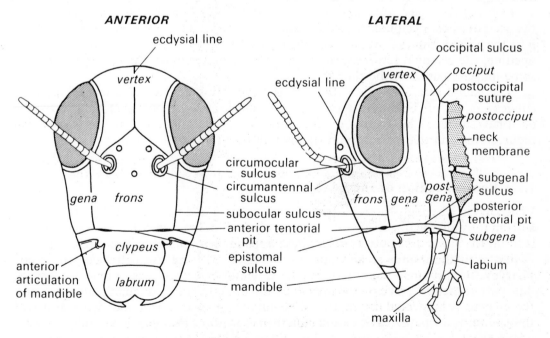

Fig. 2 The common lines or grooves on the insect head and the areas which they define. Names of areas are italicised (modified after Snodgrass, 1960)

groove or ridge associated with this line, which is simply a line of weakness, continuous with that on the thorax, along which the cuticle splits when the insect moults. It is therefore called the ecdysial cleavage line, but has commonly been termed the epicranial suture. The anterior arms of this line are very variable in their development and position (Snodgrass, 1947) and in Apterygota they are reduced or absent. The ecdysial cleavage line may persist in the adult insect and sometimes the cranium is inflected along this line to form a true sulcus.

Other ecdysial lines may be present on the ventral surface of the head of larval insects (Hinton, 1963).

1.1.3 Areas of the head

The different areas of the head defined by the sulci are given names for descriptive purposes, but they do not represent primitive sclerites. Since the sulci are variable in position, so too are the areas which they delimit. The front of the head, the frontoclypeal area, is divided by the epistomal sulcus into the frons above and the clypeus below (Fig. 2). It is common to regard the arms of the ecdysial cleavage line as delimiting the frons dorsally, but this is not necessarily so (Snodgrass, 1960). From the frons muscles run to the pharynx, the labrum and the hypopharynx; from the clypeus arise the dilators of the cibarium (see below). The two groups of muscles are always separated by the frontal ganglion and its connectives to the brain (Fig. 3) and Snodgrass (1947) believes that on the basis of the muscles frons and clypeus can be distinguished even in the absence of the epistomal sulcus. DuPorte (1946) does not believe that the muscles are necessarily so constant in their origins.

Dorsally the frons continues into the vertex and posteriorly this is separated from the occiput by the occipital sulcus. The occiput is divided from the postocciput behind it by the postoccipital suture, while at the back of the head, where it joins the neck, is an opening, the occipital foramen, through which the alimentary canal, nerve cord and some muscles pass into the thorax.

The lateral area of the head beneath the eyes is called the gena, from which the subgena is cut off below by the subgenal sulcus, and the postgena behind by the occipital sulcus. The region of the subgena above the mandible is called the pleurostoma and that part behind the mandible is the hypostoma.

1.1.4 Ventral region of the head

Ventrally, in a hypognathous insect, the head is extended by the mouthparts with the labrum forming the upper lip anteriorly, the mandibles and maxillae laterally and the labium, the lower lip, posteriorly. These appendages enclose a cavity, the pre-oral cavity, with the mouth at its upper end (Fig. 3). Behind the mouth is the hypopharynx, the proximal membranous part of which is continuous with the pharynx. The part of the pre-oral cavity enclosed by the proximal part of the hypopharynx and the clypeus is known as the cibarium. Behind the hypopharynx and between it and the labium is a smaller cavity known as the salivarium, into which the salivary duct opens.

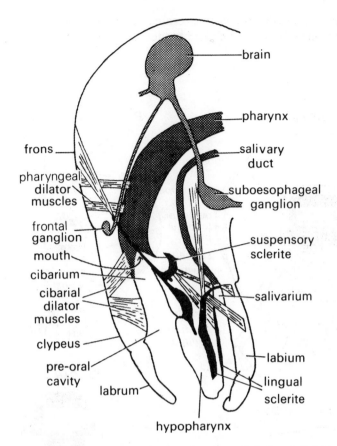

Fig. 3 Diagrammatic vertical longitudinal section through the head of a biting insect showing the pre-oral cavity and the musculature of the hypopharynx (after Snodgrass, 1947)

1.1.5 Modifications of the head

The most marked differences in the structure of the head capsule occur at the back of the head. Typically the hypostomal sulci bend upwards posteriorly and are continuous with the postoccipital suture (Fig. 4A). The posterior ventral part of the head capsule is membranous and is completed by the labium. In some insects, however, the hypostomata of the two sides meet in the midline below the occipital foramen to form a hypostomal bridge which is continuous with the postocciput. This is particularly well-developed in Diptera (Fig. 4B). In other cases, Hymenoptera and the water bugs *Notonecta* and *Naucoris*, a similar bridge is formed by the postgenae, but the bridge is separated from the postocciput by the postoccipital suture (Fig. 4C).

Where the head is held in the prognathous position the lower ends of the postocciput fuse and extend forwards to form a median ventral plate, the gula (Fig. 4D), which may be a continuous sclerotisation with the labium. Often the gula is reduced to a narrow strip by enlargement of the postgenae and sometimes the postgenae meet in the midline, so that the gula is obliterated. The median ventral suture which is thus formed at the point of contact of the postgenae is called the gular suture (but see Hinton, 1963).

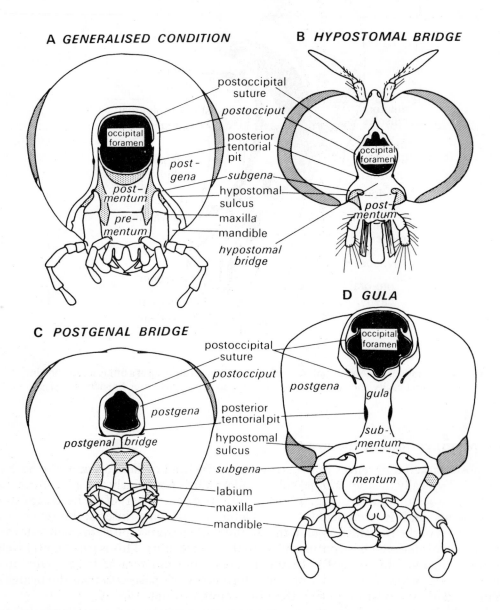

Fig. 4 Modifications occurring at the back of the head. A. Generalised condition. B. *Deromyia* (Diptera) with a hypostomal bridge. C. *Vespula* (Hymenoptera) with a postgenal bridge. D. *Epicauta* (Coleoptera) with a gula. Membranous areas stippled, compound eyes cross-hatched (after Snodgrass, 1960)

1.1.6 Tentorium

The tentorium consists of two anterior and two posterior apodemes which form the internal skeleton of the head, serving as a brace for the head and for the attachment of muscles. The anterior arms arise from the anterior tentorial pits, which in Apterygota and Ephemeroptera are ventral and medial to the mandibles. In Odonata, Plecoptera and Dermaptera the pits are lateral to the mandibles, while in most higher insects they are facial at either end of the epistomal sulcus (Snodgrass, 1960). DuPorte (1946), however, believes the anterior tentorial pits to lie on the sulcus between the frons and the gena.

The posterior arms arise from pits at the ventral ends of the postoccipital suture and they unite to form a bridge running across the head from one side to the other. In Pterygota the anterior arms also join up with the bridge (Fig. 5), but the development of the tentorium as a whole is very variable (Snodgrass, 1935). Sometimes a pair of dorsal arms arise from the anterior arms and they may be attached to the dorsal wall of the head by short muscles.

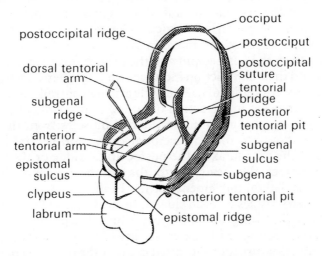

Fig. 5 Diagram of the tentorium and its relationship with the grooves and ridges of the head. Greater part of head capsule cut away (after Snodgrass, 1935)

In Machilidae (Archaeognatha) the posterior bridge is present, but the anterior arms do not reach it, while in Lepismatidae the anterior arms unite to form a central plate near the bridge and joined to it by very short muscles. In *Tomocerus* (Collembola) two branching anterior tentorial arms are present, while the posterior arms are long and unite above the hypopharynx. In addition, the tendons joining the transverse mandibular and maxillary muscles (Fig. 12A) form square plates which are linked together and with the posterior tentorial arms by fibrous connectives. These structures, together with extensions from the mandibular tendon, form a complex endoskeleton in the head. *Campodea* (Diplura) has no anterior tentorial arms, but the posterior arms are long and again unite over the hypopharynx. Transverse tendons are also present, but they are simpler than in *Tomocerus*. The association of the tentorium with the hypopharynx in these entognathous animals (p. 15) is probably connected with the feeding movements and protrusibility of the hypopharynx.

Manton (1964) indicates that the basic elements occurring in the head endophragmal skeleton are homologous throughout the insects; other authors have believed the structure in entognathous animals to be mesodermal in origin.

1.2 Neck

The neck or cervix is a membranous region which gives freedom of movement to the head. It extends from the occipital foramen at the back of the head to the prothorax, and possibly represents the posterior part of the labial segment together with the anterior part of the prothoracic segment. Laterally in the neck membrane are the cervical sclerites. Sometimes there is only one, as in Ephemeroptera, but there may be two or three. In *Schistocerca* (Orthoptera) the first lateral cervical sclerite, which articulates with the occipital condyle at the back of the head, is very small. The second sclerite articulates with it by a ball and socket joint allowing movement in all planes. Posteriorly it meets the posterior cervical sclerite and movement at this joint is restricted to the vertical plane. Finally the posterior cervical sclerite connects with the prothoracic episternum, relative to which it can move in all planes.

Muscles arising from the postocciput and the pronotum are inserted on the cervical sclerites (Fig. 6A) and their contraction increases the angle between the sclerites so that the head is pushed forwards (Fig. 6B). A muscle arising ventrally and inserted on to the first cervical sclerite may aid in retraction or lateral movements of the head. Running through the neck are longitudinal muscles, dorsal muscles from the antecostal ridge (p. 154) of the mesothorax to the postoccipital ridge, and ventral muscles from the sternal apophyses of the prothorax to the postoccipital ridge or the tentorium. These muscles serve to retract the head on to the prothorax, while their differential contraction will cause lateral movements of the head.

Schistocerca has 16 muscles on each side of the neck, each of which is innervated by several axons, often including an inhibitory fibre (Shepheard, 1973). This polyneuronal innervation, together with the versatility of the cervical articulations and the complexity of the musculature, permits movement of the head in a highly versatile and accurately controlled manner.

1.3 Antennae

All insects possess a pair of antennae, but they may be greatly reduced, especially in larval forms. This is also true of Collembola and Diplura, but not of Protura.

1.3.1 Antennal structure

The antenna consists of a basal scape, a pedicel and a flagellum. The scape is inserted into a membranous region of the head wall and pivoted on a single marginal point, the antennifer (Fig. 8A), so it is free to move in all directions. Frequently the flagellum is divided into a number of similar annuli joined to each other by membranes so that the flagellum as a whole is flexible. The term segmented should be avoided with reference

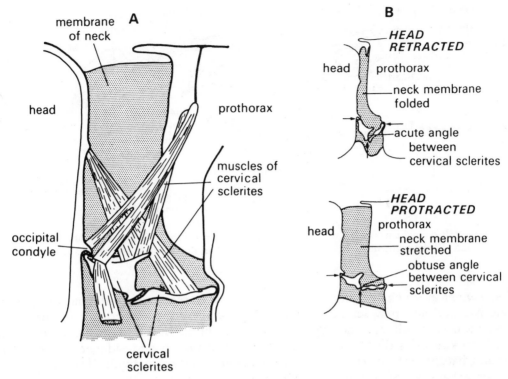

Fig. 6 A. The neck and cervical sclerites of a grasshopper seen from the inside (from Imms, 1957). B. Diagrams showing how a change in the angle between the cervical sclerites retracts or protracts the head. Arrows indicate points of articulation

to the flagellum of Pterygota since the annuli are not regarded as equivalent to leg segments (Schneider, 1964).

In Pterygota and Thysanura the antennae are moved by levator and depressor muscles arising on the anterior tentorial arms and inserted into the scape, and by flexor and extensor muscles arising in the scape and inserted into the pedicel (Fig. 7A) (Imms, 1940). There are no muscles in the flagellum and the nerve which traverses the flagellum is purely sensory. This is the annulated type of antenna.

In Collembola and Diplura the musculature at the base of the antenna is similar to that in Pterygota, but, in addition, there is an intrinsic musculature in each unit of the flagellum (Fig. 7B), and, consequently, these units are regarded as true segments. Five muscles run from the base of each segment to the base of the next and produce various movements, but in the more distal segments the muscles are reduced and all but one of them may be absent. This type of antenna is called segmented.

1.3.2 Growth of the antenna

In many hemimetabolous and ametabolous insects the number of annuli in the antennal flagellum increases during postembryonic life. Thus, the first instar larva of *Dociostaurus* (Orthoptera) has antennae with 13 annuli, while in the adult there are 25.

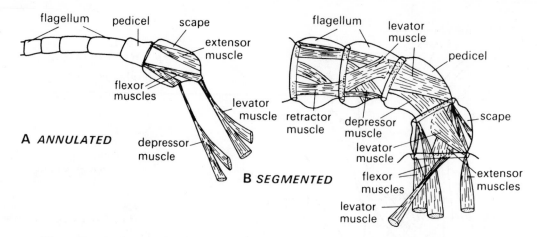

Fig. 7 Proximal parts of (A) the annulated antenna of *Locusta* (Orthoptera) in lateral view, and (B) the segmented antenna of *Japyx* (Diplura) in dorsal view (after Imms, 1940)

The manner in which new annuli are added varies. In segmented antennae the growth zone is apical and new segments arise from the most distal segment; in annulated antennae new annuli are added basally by division of the most proximal annulus of the flagellum known as the meriston. In orthopteroid insects and Odonata some of the annuli adjacent to the meriston, and derived from it, may also divide. They are known as meristal annuli. At each moult in *Periplaneta* (Dictyoptera) the meriston divides to produce 4–14 new annuli and each meristal annulus may divide once.

In cockroaches some loss of distal annuli also occurs, especially at the time of the moult when the antenna is brittle. As a result, there is no record of *Periplaneta* with more than 170 annuli, though the potential maximum, based on the numbers of new annuli formed in the meristal region, is over 260 (Schafer and Sanchez, 1973).

1.3.3 Variation in form of antennae

The form of the antenna varies considerably depending on its precise function (Fig. 8). Sometimes the modification produces an increase in surface area; for instance, the surface area of the pectinate antenna of a male *Bombyx* (Lepidoptera) (comparable with Fig. 8C) is 29·0 mm^2; without the branches it would only be 4·8 mm^2 (Schneider, 1964). The partial significance of this is probably to permit the presence of more sensilla. Very long antennae, such as occur in the cockroach, are possibly associated with their use as feelers.

Sexual dimorphism in the antennae is common, the antennae of the male often being more complex than those of the female. This often occurs where the male is attracted to or recognises the female by her scent (p. 860). Conversely, in chalcids scent plays an important part in host-finding by the female and in this case the female's antennae are more specialised than the male's (Richards, 1956).

The antennae of larval holometabolous insects are usually considerably reduced. The larval antennae of Neuroptera and Megaloptera contain a number of annuli, but in larval Coleoptera and Lepidoptera (Fig. 8F) the antennae are reduced to three simple

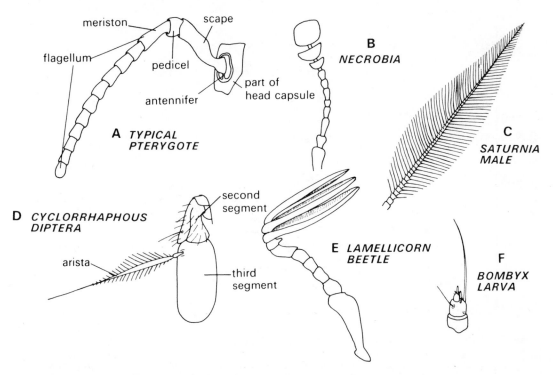

Fig. 8 Various types of antennae, not all the same scale

segments. In some larval Diptera and Hymenoptera the antennae are very small and may be no more than swellings of the head wall.

1.3.4 Functions of antennae

The antennae function primarily as sense organs and they bear a very large number of sensilla. Adult male *Periplaneta*, for instance, have about 250 000 sensilla on each antenna and male *Ostrinia* (Lepidoptera) about 8000. Usually there are several common types of sensillum on the antenna including trichoid hairs, basiconic and coeloconic pegs, plate organs and campaniform sensilla. Schneider (1964) gives a full list. The sensilla are often concentrated in particular regions and in *Melanoplus* (Orthoptera), for instance, there are no basiconic or coeloconic pegs on the proximal annuli; most of these sensilla are found on the annuli in the middle of the flagellum (Fig. 9). In Pieridae (Lepidoptera) most of the antennal sensilla are aggregated on the terminal club. The various types of sensilla function as tactile and odour receptors, contact chemoreceptors, hygroreceptors and temperature receptors.

The antenna as a whole is involved in the perception of sound by male mosquitoes and some other insects, and with the measurement of air speed. In these cases, movements of the flagellum are monitored by Johnston's organ, a chordotonal organ found in the pedical of insects with annulated antennae (p. 716). Callahan (1975)

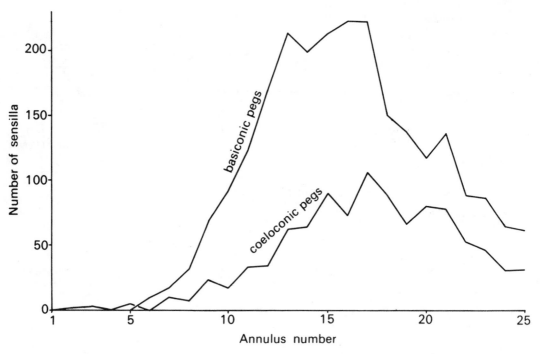

Fig. 9 Distribution of some sensilla on the flagellum of a male *Melanoplus*. 1 = most proximal annulus, 25 = most distal annulus (from data in Slifer *et al.*, 1959)

considers the whole structure of the antenna to be adapted for the perception of far infrared emissions from molecules. Critical electrophysiological support for the hypothesis is lacking and some evidence contradicts it (*e.g.* Floyd *et al.*, 1976).

Sometimes the antennae have other functions. The adult water beetle *Hydrophilus* submerges with a film of air over its ventral surface which it renews at intervals when it comes to the surface. At the surface the body is inclined to one side and a funnel of air, connecting the ventral air bubble to the outside air, appears between the head, the prothorax and the distal annuli of the antenna, which is held along the side of the head. The four terminal annuli of the antenna are enlarged and are clothed with hydrofuge hairs to facilitate the formation of the air funnel (Miall, 1922).

In the newly hatched larva of *Hydrophilus* the antennae assist the mandibles in masticating the prey. This is facilitated by a number of sharp spines on the inside of the antennae.

In fleas and Collembola the antennae are used in mating. Male fleas use the antennae to clasp the female from below and the inner surfaces bear large numbers of adhesive discs. These discs, about 5 μm in diameter, are set on stalks above the general surface of the cuticle and within each one there is a gland, presumably secreting an adhesive material. Species with sessile or semi-sessile females lack these organs (Rothschild and Hinton, 1968). In many Collembola the males have prehensile antennae with which they hold on to the antennae of the female and in *Sminthurides aquaticus* the male may be carried about by the female, holding on to her antennae, for several days.

1.4 Mouthparts

The mouthparts are the organs concerned with feeding, comprising the unpaired labrum in front, a median hypopharynx behind the mouth, a pair of mandibles and maxillae laterally, and a labium forming the lower lip. In Collembola, Diplura and Protura the mouthparts lie in a cavity of the head produced by the genae, which extend ventrally as oral folds and meet in the ventral midline below the mouthparts (Fig. 10). This is the entognathous condition (Manton, 1964). In the insects proper the mouthparts are not enclosed in this way, but are external to the head, the ectognathous condition (*e.g.* Fig. 1).

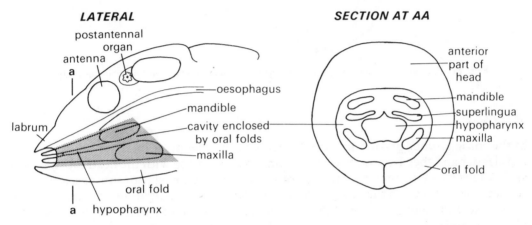

Fig. 10 Diagram to illustrate the entognathous condition of the mouthparts. In the lateral view the hatched area represents the cavity enclosed by the oral folds (modified after Denis, 1949)

The form of the mouthparts is related to diet, but two basic types can be recognised: (1) adapted for biting and chewing solid food, and (2) adapted for sucking up fluids. The biting and chewing form is considered to be primitive.

1.4.1 Biting mouthparts

Labrum

The labrum is a broad lobe suspended from the clypeus in front of the mouth and forming the upper lip. On its inner side it is membranous and may be produced into a median lobe, the epipharynx, bearing some sensilla (see Fig. 17). The labrum is raised away from the mandibles by two muscles arising in the head and inserted medially into the anterior margin of the labrum. It is closed against the mandibles by two more muscles arising in the head and inserted on the posterior lateral margins on two small sclerites, the tormae (Fig. 11). Differential use of these muscles can produce a lateral rocking movement of the labrum.

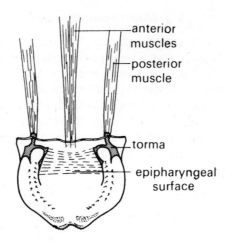

Fig. 11 The labrum from the posterior, epipharyngeal, surface (after Snodgrass, 1944)

Mandibles

In the entognathous groups and the Archaeognatha, the mandibles are relatively long and slender and they have only a single point of articulation with the head capsule. The mandible is rotated about its articulation by anterior and posterior muscles arising on the head capsule and on the anterior tentorial arms. The principal adductor muscles are transverse and ventral, those of the two sides uniting in a median tendon (Fig. 12A) (Manton, 1964).

In Lepismatidae and the Pterygota the mandibles are articulated with the cranium at two points, having a second more anterior articulation with the subgena in addition to the original posterior one (Fig. 12B). These mandibles are usually short and strongly sclerotised and often the biting surface is differentiated into a more distal incisor region and a proximal molar region, the mandibles of the two sides being asymmetrical so as to oppose each other in the midline. The development of incisor and molar areas varies with the diet. The mandibles of carnivorous insects are armed with strong shearing cusps; in grasshoppers feeding on vegetation other than grasses there is a series of sharp pointed cusps, while in grass-feeding species the incisor cusps are chisel-edged and the molar area has flattened ridges for grinding. These cusps may become worn down during feeding (Chapman, 1964).

The original anterior and posterior rotator muscles of Apterygota have become abductors and adductors in the Pterygota, the adductor becoming very powerful. The apterygote ventral adductor is retained in most orthopteroids and arises from the hypopharyngeal apophysis, but in Acrididae and the higher insects this muscle is absent (Fig. 12B), or, in insects with sucking mouthparts, may be modified as a protractor muscle of the mandible.

Maxillae

The maxillae occupy a lateral position on the head behind the mandibles. The proximal part of the maxilla consists of a basal cardo, which has a single articulation with the

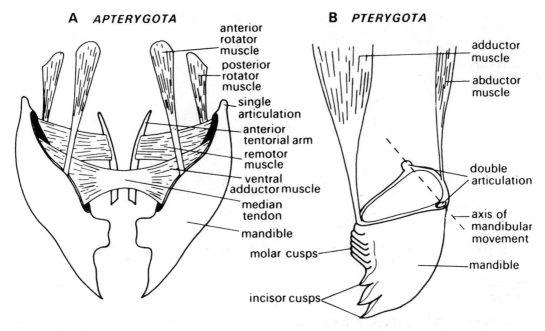

Fig. 12 Diagrams of the mandibles of (A) an apterygote, in which only some of the muscles are shown, and (B) a pterygote insect (after Snodgrass, 1935, 1944)

head, and a flat plate, the stipes, hinged to the cardo. Both cardo and stipes are loosely joined to the head by membrane so that they are capable of movement. Distally on the stipes are two lobes, an inner lacinea and an outer galea, one or both of which may be absent. More laterally on the stipes is a jointed, leg-like palp made up of a number of segments; in Orthoptera there are five (Fig. 13A).

The muscles of the maxilla are comparable with those of the mandible. Anterior and posterior rotator muscles are inserted on the cardo and a ventral adductor muscle arising on the tentorium is inserted on both cardo and stipes. Arising in the stipes are flexor muscles of lacinea and galea and a lacineal flexor also arises in the cranium, but neither lobe has an extensor muscle. The palp has levator and depressor muscles arising in the stipes and each segment of the palp has a single muscle causing flexing of the next segment (Fig. 13B).

The palps are sensory organs used to test the quality of the food. During feeding in the cockroach the whole maxilla makes rapid backwards and forwards movements at the side of the hypopharynx and at the same time the terminal lobes are moved. By this action particles of food are scraped back into the pre-oral cavity. The maxillary lobes are also used for cleaning antennae, palps and front legs, the appendage being drawn through the galeal pads, which work rapidly over its surface.

Labium

The labium is similar in structure to the maxillae, but with the appendages of the two sides fused in the midline so that they form a median plate. The basal part of the labium,

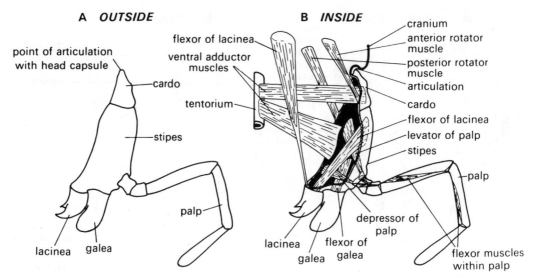

Fig. 13 Diagrams of the maxilla from the outside (A) and the inside (B) to show the musculature (after Snodgrass, 1935)

equivalent to the maxillary cardines and possibly including a part of the sternum of the labial segment, is called the postmentum. This may be subdivided into a proximal submentum and a distal mentum. Distal to the postmentum, and equivalent to the fused maxillary stipites, is the prementum. Terminally this bears four lobes, two inner glossae and two outer paraglossae, which are collectively known as the ligula. One or both pairs of lobes may be absent or they may be fused to form a single median process. A pair of palps arise laterally from the prementum, often being three-segmented (Fig. 14A).

The musculature corresponds with that of the maxillae, but there are no muscles to the postmentum. Muscles corresponding with the ventral adductors run from the tentorium to the front and back of the prementum; glossae and paraglossae have flexor muscles, but no extensors, and the palp has levator and depressor muscles arising in the prementum. The segments of the palp each have flexor and extensor muscles. In addition there are other muscles with no equivalent in the maxillae. Two pairs arising in the prementum converge on to the wall of the salivarium at the junction of labium with hypopharynx. A pair of muscles opposing these arises in the hypopharynx and the combined effect of them all may be to regulate the flow of saliva or to move the prementum (Fig. 3). Finally a pair of muscles arising in the postmentum and inserted into the prementum serves to retract or flex the prementum (Fig. 14B).

The prementum closes the pre-oral cavity from behind and the palpi, like the maxillary palpi, are mainly sensory in function.

Hypopharynx

The hypopharynx is a median lobe immediately behind the mouth. The salivary duct usually opens behind it, between it and the labium. Most of the hypopharynx is

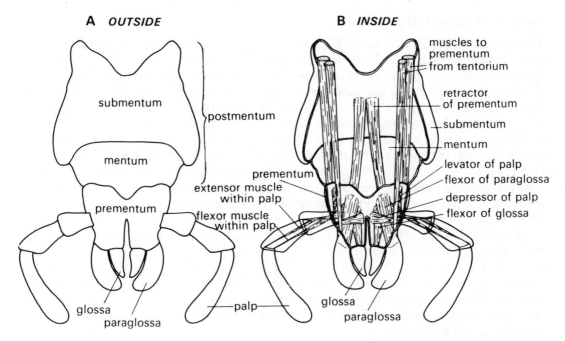

Fig. 14 Diagrams of the labium from the outside (A) and the inside (B) to show the musculature (after Snodgrass, 1944)

membranous, but the adoral face is sclerotised distally, and proximally contains a pair of suspensory sclerites which extend upwards to end in the lateral wall of the stomodaeum. Muscles arising on the frons are inserted into these sclerites, which distally are hinged to a pair of lateral lingual sclerites. These in turn have inserted into them antagonistic pairs of muscles arising on the tentorium and the labium. The various muscles serve to swing the hypopharynx forwards and back and in the cockroach there are two more muscles running across the hypopharynx which dilate the salivary orifice and expand the salivarium (Fig. 3).

In Apterygota, larval Ephemeroptera and Dermaptera there are two lateral lobes of the hypopharynx called the superlinguae (Fig. 15).

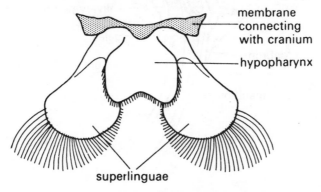

Fig. 15 The hypopharynx of a larval ephemeropteran showing the large superlinguae (after Snodgrass, 1935)

1.4.2 Sucking mouthparts

The mouthparts of insects which feed on fluids are modified in various ways to form a tube through which liquid can be drawn and the saliva injected. This results in elongation of some parts and often some of the typical structures are lost. In *Apis* (Hymenoptera) the galeae and labial palps form a tube round the elongate fused glossal tongue (Snodgrass, 1956). The proboscis of Lepidoptera is formed from the galeae, the rest of the mouthparts, apart from the labial palps, being reduced or absent (Eastham and Eassa, 1955). The Homoptera and Heteroptera have separate food and salivary canals between the opposed maxillae, which are styliform (Snodgrass, 1944), while in Diptera the food canal is formed between the labrum and labium and the salivary canal runs through the hypopharynx (Snodgrass, 1944). In addition the higher Diptera have specialised pseudotracheae in the labium. These are small tubes which connect to the exterior by pores and pass liquid food to the food canal.

   Associated with the production of a tube for feeding is the development of a pump for drawing up the fluids and a salivary pump for injecting saliva. Often the feeding pump is developed from the cibarium, which by extension of the lateral lips of the mouth becomes a closed chamber connecting with the food canal. The cibarial muscles from the clypeus enlarge so that a powerful pump is produced (Fig. 16). In Lepidoptera and Hymenoptera the cibarial pump is combined with a pharyngeal pump which has dilators arising on the frons.

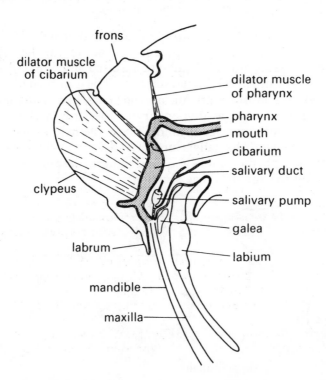

Fig. 16 Median vertical section of the head of a cicada showing the enlargement of the cibarial dilator muscles in the formation of a sucking pump (after Snodgrass, 1944)

REFERENCES

BITSCH, J. and DENIS, J. R. (1973). Morphologie de la tête des insectes. *in* Grassé, P.-P. (ed.), *Traité de Zoologie.* vol. 8. Masson et Cie., Paris.

CALLAHAN, P. S. (1975). Insect antennae with special reference to the mechanism of scent detection and the evolution of the sensilla. *Int. J. Insect Morphol. & Embryol.* **4**: 381–430.

CHAPMAN, R. F. (1964). The structure and wear of the mandibles in some African grasshoppers. *Proc. zool. Soc. Lond.* **142**: 107–121.

DENIS, R. (1949). Sous-classe des Aptérygotes. *in* Grassé, P.-P. (ed.), *Traité de Zoologie.* vol. 9. Masson et Cie., Paris.

DUPORTE, E. M. (1946). Observations on the morphology of the face in insects. *J. Morph.* **79**: 371–417.

DUPORTE, E. M. (1957). The comparative morphology of the insect head. *A. Rev. Ent.* **2**: 55–70.

EASTHAM, L. E. S. and EASSA, Y. E. E. (1955). The feeding mechanism of the butterfly *Pieris brassicae* L. *Phil. Trans. R. Soc.* B, **239**: 1–43.

FLOYD, M. A., EVANS, D. A. and HOWSE, P. E. (1976). Electrophysiological and behavioural studies on naturally occurring repellants to *Reticulitermes lucifugus*. *J. Insect Physiol.* **22**: 697–701.

HINTON, H. E. (1963). The ventral ecdysial lines of the head of endopterygote larvae. *Trans. R. ent. Soc. Lond.* **115**: 39–61.

IMMS, A. D. (1940). On the antennal musculature in insects and other arthropods. *Q. Jl microsc. Sci.* **81**: 273–320.

MANTON, S. M. (1964). Mandibular mechanisms and the evolution of Arthropods. *Phil. Trans. R. Soc.* B. **247**: 1–183.

MATSUDA, R. (1965). Morphology and evolution of the insect head. *Mem. Am. ent. Inst.* no. 4, 334 pp.

MIALL, L. C. (1922). *The natural history of aquatic insects.* MacMillan, London.

RICHARDS, O. W. (1956). Hymenoptera. Introduction and key to families. *Handbk Ident. Br. Insects* 6, part 1.

ROTHSCHILD, M. and HINTON, H. E. (1968). Holding organs on the antennae of male fleas. *Proc. R. ent. Soc. Lond.* **43**: 105–107.

SCHAFER, R. and SANCHEZ, T. V. (1973). Antennal sensory system of the cockroach, *Periplaneta americana*: Postembryonic development and morphology of the sense organs. *J. comp. Neur.* **149**: 335–354.

SCHNEIDER, D. (1964). Insect antennae. *A. Rev. Ent.* **9**: 103–122.

SHEPHEARD, P. (1973). Musculature and innervation of the neck of the desert locust, *Schistocerca gregaria* (Forskål). *J. Morph.* **139**: 439–464.

SLIFER, E. H., PRESTAGE, J. J. and BEAMS, H. W. (1959). The chemoreceptors and other sense organs on the antennal flagellum of the grasshopper, (Orthoptera: Acrididae). *J. Morph.* **105**: 145–191.

SNODGRASS, R. E. (1935). *Principles of insect morphology.* McGraw-Hill, New York.

SNODGRASS, R. E. (1944). The feeding apparatus of biting and sucking insects affecting man and animals. *Smithson. misc. Collns* **104**, no. 7, 113 pp.

SNODGRASS, R. E. (1947). The insect cranium and the "epicranial suture". *Smithson. misc. Collns* **107**, no. 7, 52 pp.

SNODGRASS, R. E. (1956). *Anatomy of the honey bee.* Constable, London.

SNODGRASS, R. E. (1960). Facts and theories concerning the insect head. *Smithson. misc. Collns* **142**: 1–61.

CHAPTER II
FEEDING

Insects feed on a very wide variety of animal, vegetable and dead organic materials. Some are virtually omnivorous, but the majority are more specific, being restricted to a particular category of food or even to a particular plant or animal. Food recognition involves sensilla on the mouthparts, which are distributed so as to monitor the food before and during feeding. Food preference is significant in ensuring that feeding occurs most commonly on the foods favouring survival and development. In phytophagous insects the chemical characteristics of the host-plants are particularly important in governing selection.

The food is eaten in discrete meals, which allows digestion to proceed most efficiently. The size of a meal is monitored by stretch receptors in the wall of the gut or the abdomen, but other changes are also involved in delaying further feeding until digestion is advanced.

A general account of feeding in insects is given by Brues (1946). Other more specialised reviews are as follows: food preference and selection: Chapman (1974), Friend and Smith (1977), Hocking (1971), Hsiao (1969, 1974), Mittelstaedt (1962), Mulkern (1967, 1969), Schoonhoven (1968, 1969, 1973), van Emden (1972), Wood (1973); venoms: Beard (1963), Edwards (1963); control of feeding: Barton Browne (1975), Bernays and Chapman (1974), Bernays and Simpson (1982), Gelperin (1971), Langley (1976), Stoffolano (1974); fungus feeding: Grassé (1949), Baker (1963); social insects: Richards (1953), Wheeler (1922).

2.1 Feeding habits

Any classification of feeding habits is arbitrary, but Brues (1946) recognises four fairly comprehensive categories: plant feeders, predators, scavengers and parasites.

Nearly half of the species of insects feed on plants and these may be further subdivided into those feeding on green plants (phytophagous) and those feeding on fungi (mycetophagous). Predominantly phytophagous groups of insects are: Orthoptera, Lepidoptera, Homoptera, Thysanoptera, Phasmida, Isoptera, Coleoptera (families Cerambycidae, Chrysomelidae and Curculionidae), Hymenoptera (Symphyta) and some Diptera. Most of these feed on higher plants, but, for instance, the aquatic larvae of Ephemeroptera and some Plecoptera and Trichoptera feed on algae. Fungus-feeding larvae are frequent amongst Diptera (particularly Mycetophilidae) and the habit also occurs in various Coleoptera. In many other insects fungi form at least a part of the diet. This is true in many dung-feeding insects and others, such as some termites, which cultivate their own fungi.

Some predators occur in most of the insect orders, some groups being entirely predaceous. Predominantly predaceous groups are: Odonata, Dictyoptera (Mantodea), Heteroptera (Reduviidae and others), larval Neuroptera, Mecoptera, Diptera (Asilidae and Empididae), Coleoptera (Adephaga, larval Lampyridae and Coccinellidae) and Hymenoptera (Sphecidae and Pompilidae). These feed mainly on other insects, but larval Lampyridae, for instance, prey on snails.

Saprophagous insects occur mainly in the higher insects with larvae differing from the adults. Decaying organic matter is a common source of food for many larval Diptera and Coleoptera. In this habitat fungi may also form an important part of the diet.

Parasites may live on the outside or inside their hosts. Amongst ectoparasites are all Siphonaptera, Anoplura and Mallophaga and some Dermaptera, Heteroptera, such as *Cimex* and some Reduviidae, and various Diptera—mosquitoes, Simuliidae, Ceratopogonidae, Tabanidae and the Pupipara for example. Many of these are bloodsucking, in many cases on vertebrates. Sometimes both sexes suck blood, as in Siphonaptera and tsetse flies, or only the females do so, as in Nematocera and Brachycera. In the latter instance the females also regularly feed on nectar, which is the only food of the males (Downes, 1958).

Internal parasites, most of which are parasitic only as larvae, include all the Strepsiptera, the Ichneumonoidea, Chalcidoidea and Proctotrupoidea amongst Hymenoptera and Bombyliidae, Cyrtidae, Tachinidae and some Sarcophagidae amongst Diptera.

In holometabolous insects larval food is often different from that of the adult; compare the caterpillar and the butterfly.

2.2 Sense organs associated with feeding

The compound eyes are often involved in locating food and they are particularly important in predators. Antennae are involved in the perception of odours and so may enable an insect, such as a locust, to locate a host-plant from a distance; they may also be involved in host recognition at close quarters. The tarsi of insects also bear contact chemoreceptors. These respond to food substances and so may play some role in feeding behaviour. This is especially obvious in blowflies and butterflies, where stimulation of the tarsi with sugar leads to proboscis extension. However, it is the sensilla of the mouthparts which are most important in food-selection; this is their prime or only role.

Orthoptera and Dictyoptera have large numbers of scattered mechanoreceptors and chemoreceptors on the exposed areas of the mouthparts. These do not differ in basic structure from other sensilla scattered over the whole body and may not be concerned primarily with feeding. In addition, there are groups of chemoreceptors specifically concerned with food selection and with monitoring quality of food. *Locusta* has four paired groups on the epipharyngeal face of the labrum (Fig. 17). There is a similar paired group on the hypopharynx and other less closely grouped sensilla on the galea and paraglossa. All these sensilla are conical in form, barely projecting above the surface of the cuticle. The tip of each maxillary and labial palp bears a group of short trichoid chemoreceptors. In an adult *Locusta* the total number of sensilla in these groups is about 3300, with a total of 15 000 neurones. All these are contact chemoreceptors, although they may perceive odours at high concentrations, so they

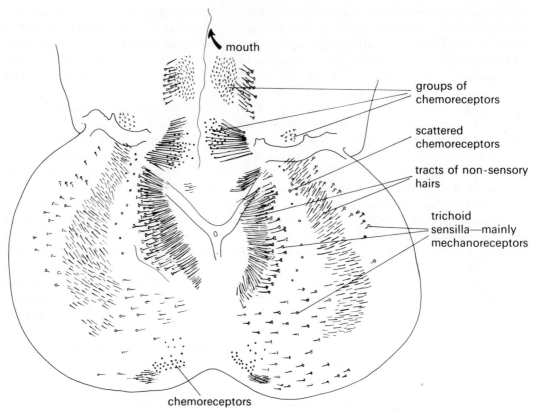

Fig. 17 Diagram of the inside of the labrum of a grasshopper showing the arrangement of sensilla and hair tracts

will normally function when they are in contact with the food or very close to it (Chapman and Thomas, 1978).

Caterpillars, by comparison, have many fewer sensilla and neurones concerned with host-plant selection. Apart from the antennae, the main sensilla are on the maxillae and in *Bombyx* and *Pieris* larvae the total number of neurones involved is only about 110 (Schoonhoven, 1973).

The tarsal chemoreceptors apparently play a more important part in fluid-feeding insects than they do in biting and chewing insects, but the mouthparts also bear numerous sensilla. *Phormia* (Diptera) has 240 trichoid sensilla on the outside of the labellar lobes and some of these are contact chemoreceptors. Others, called the interpseudotracheal pegs, are found on the lower surfaces of the labellar lobes between the pseudotracheae. There are about 40 on each side (Fig. 18) (Wilczek, 1967). In addition there are sensilla on the maxillary palps and in the cibarial cavity.

The piercing and sucking insects generally have only a few sensilla on the mouthparts. The plant-sucking bug *Dysdercus* has at the tip of the rostrum on each side 13 contact chemoreceptors and 6 to 8 mechanoreceptor sensilla. In mosquitoes the numbers of sensilla vary between the sexes. Female *Aedes* have two pairs of chemoreceptor sensilla on the tip of the labrum but there is none on the other stylets and the labral chemoreceptors are absent from males (Lee, 1974). Various types of sensilla, some of which are chemoreceptors, are present in the wall of the cibarium, and chemoreceptors are present on the maxillary palps.

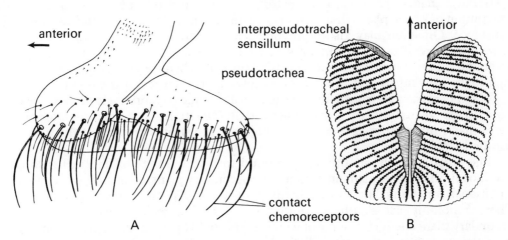

Fig. 18 Diagram of the labellum of *Phormia* (A) from the left showing the arrangement of trichoid sensilla and (B) from the ventral surface showing the positions of the inter-pseudotracheal sensilla (after Wilczek, 1967)

2.3 Finding and recognising the food

For some insects the problem of finding food does not arise since they are surrounded by an abundance of food from the time of hatching. This usually results from the oviposition habits of the parent. In many phytophagous species, for instance, the female oviposits on the plant which forms the larval food. Similarly amongst saprophagous and endoparasitic insects the female often lays her eggs in suitable detritus or in the appropriate host. The larvae of social insects are presented with food by the worker (p. 42) and are incapable of searching for it, but with these exceptions, food-finding must play an important part in the lives of many insects.

The initial attraction of insects to their food from a distance is often not very specific. Final recognition of the food usually occurs at closer quarters and involves different stimuli from those involved in attraction from a distance.

2.3.1 Food selection by phytophagous insects

The degree of specificity of insects to particular plants varies considerably. Some species, particularly amongst Homoptera and sawflies, are restricted to one particular plant species and are regarded as monophagous. *Coccus fagi* (Homoptera), for instance, only feeds on beech, and the larvae of the sawfly, *Xyela julii*, only on *Pinus sylvestris*. Some such species may feed on other plants if they are forced to do so, but others will die in the absence of the correct plant. Other insects are less restricted, but nevertheless feed on only a limited range of plants. They are called oligophagous. *Pieris rapae* (Lepidoptera), for instance, feeds only on Cruciferae and other plants which contain mustard oils. Finally there are polyphagous insects, which feed on a very wide range of plants, but even these show preferences for particular foods. *Schistocerca* is polyphagous.

Because plants are so variable in form vision can rarely be involved in specific recognition of a host-plant, though it may be important in locating a potential host from a distance. Olfaction may also be involved in attraction from a distance. Larvae of *Schistocerca* are attracted to the odour of a host-plant; if they have previously been without food for some time the insects turn upwind when they perceive the odour and then move upwind so that they progress towards the source of the odour.

Whether attraction from a distance is visual or olfactory, final selection of the host-plant occurs when the insect is in contact with it. Olfaction and contact chemoreception are of major importance at this time, though the physical characters of the plant may also be involved.

The sensilla on the mouthparts respond to a wide range of chemicals: those of nutritional value to the plant and others, the secondary plant chemicals, with no known nutritional function. The former include sugars and protein-forming amino acids. They commonly act as phagostimulants, promoting feeding activity by insects. Secondary plant chemicals, some of which are probably present in all plants, belong to a wide range of chemical classes: alkaloids, terpenoids, glycosides, non-protein amino acids and others. These compounds are believed to be concerned in the defence of the plants against herbivores, diseases and, in some cases, other plants (Fraenkel, 1969). The effect of any one of these chemicals on any one insect species may be to deter it from feeding or, sometimes, to promote feeding, or there may be no effect at all.

The insect sensilla respond to the sum of these nutrient and non-nutrient chemicals. How they respond will depend on the characteristics of the individual neurones and especially on the degree to which they are sensitive to particular substances. How the insect as a whole responds to the information perceived will depend on genetically governed processes within the central nervous sytem, so that a plant which appears distasteful to one insect can be a normal host-plant for another.

Locusta feeds on grasses and will normally reject all other kinds of plants. All the unacceptable plants contain secondary plant chemicals which deter feeding. These are generally absent from mature grasses, but they are present in grass seedlings, which consequently are only eaten in relatively small amounts. Sugars act as phagostimulants over a range of concentrations, but there is no evidence that the nutrient chemicals of host-plants play any significant role in selection (Bernays and Chapman, 1978). Host-plant selection is also dominated by the distribution of secondary plant chemicals acting as deterrents in other oligophagous species such as *Leptinotarsa* (Coleoptera). The members of this genus feed almost exclusively on Solanaceae; plants belonging to other families are rejected because of the chemicals they contain. However, the Solanaceae themselves are rich in alkaloids and the different species of *Leptinotarsa* are tolerant of different alkaloids, the distribution of which in different plants leads to host-plant specificity. *L. decemlineata*, for instance, is deterred by tomatine and rejects plants containing high concentrations; *L. haldemani* tolerates tomatine and accepts plants which contain it. Nutrient chemicals act as phagostimulants (Hsiao, 1974).

In other instances the secondary plant chemicals act as specific phagostimulants and little feeding occurs if they are absent. For instance, *Chrysolina* (Coleoptera) is stimulated to feed on *Hypericum* by the hypericin that it contains; *Plutella* (Lepidoptera) and *Pieris* feed on Cruciferae and they are stimulated to feed by mustard-oil glycosides. Nutrient chemicals act as phagostimulants, but in the whole plant are not effective unless mustard-oil glycosides are also present. Secondary plant chemicals belonging to other chemical groups have a deterrent effect on feeding, but their effects are offset by phagostimulants in the normal host-plants (Ma, 1972).

Although the alighting behaviour of aphids is affected by the colour of the substratum, this effect is non-specific, so hosts and non-hosts of similar appearance are landed on with equal frequency. Having landed the insect probes with its proboscis, just touching the surface or penetrating for a short distance. On a non-host the aphid soon takes off again after a few short probes; on a host it stays longer and makes longer probes. As in other insects there is interaction between the nutrient chemicals and the secondary plant chemicals, but their relative importance varies. *Brevicoryne brassicae* is oligophagous, feeding on Cruciferae. Colonisation and growth of this species depends on the presence of mustard-oil glycosides and sugars; it is relatively insensitive to amino acid levels. *Myzus persicae* is polyphagous and the amino acid levels play a major role in its host-plant selection; mustard oils are deterrent (van Emden, 1972).

2.3.2 Host finding and recognition by bark beetles

The bark beetles are generally specific in their choice of host plants, but there is no evidence of discrimination before landing on a tree. After landing the insects can differentiate between species and between healthy and unhealthy trees, selection being based on a balance of phagostimulant and deterrent chemicals, as in phytophagous insects. For instance, the bark of hickory contains 5-hydroxy-1, 4 naphthoquinone, known as juglone. This deters feeding by the elm bark beetle, *Scolytus mutistriatus*, but is tolerated by *S. quadrispinosus*, which attacks hickory. *S. multistriatus* is also deterred by a chemical in the bark of oak; elm bark extracts are accepted (Gilbert and Norris, 1968).

Dendroctonus brevicomis feeds on the bark of *Pinus ponderosa*. Once a female is established and feeding extensively she releases a pheromone with her frass. This is an alkane, 7-ethyl-5-methyl-6, 8-dioxabicyclo [3.2.1] octane, known as brevicomin. It attracts beetles of both sexes and its effects are enhanced by a terpene, myrcene, which is derived from the resin of the tree and is also present in the frass. Once males start to arrive, they too release a pheromone, frontalin (1, 5-dimethyl-6, 8-dioxabicyclo [3.2.1] octane), and this also contributes to the attraction and aggregation of other beetles on the tree. In this way, once a suitable host has been located a rapid build-up of beetles occurs (Wood, 1973). A similar complex of chemicals is involved in the aggregation of *Dendroctonus pseudotsugae* on Douglas fir (Rudinsky *et al.*, 1974) (p. 861).

2.3.3 Prey specificity and selection by predators

Some predaceous insects, particularly amongst Hymenoptera, are relatively specific in their choice of prey. *Philanthus* only catches bees, pompilid wasps only take certain spiders, and *Eumenes* only collects caterpillars, although of various species, for its nest. Other predators, such as asilids (Diptera), appear to take anything of a suitable size and exhibiting suitable behaviour, including even members of their own species.

Predators catch their prey either by sitting and waiting for it to come their way or by actively pursuing it. *Mantis* (Dictyoptera), for example, sits and waits for its prey and, as it has a very mobile head, the movements of the prey can be followed without the whole mantis moving. The eyes are large and wide apart enabling the mantis to judge its distance from the prey accurately. When striking at the prey, *Mantis* can compensate for the position of the head relative to the thorax, which is indicated by proprioceptive hairs at the front of the prothorax, and for deviation of the prey from the optical axis

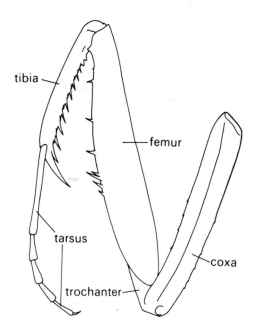

Fig. 19 Raptorial foreleg of a mantis

between the two eyes (Mittelstaedt, 1962). The front legs of the mantis are raptorial and armed with spines (Fig. 19). When the prey is within range it is caught and held by a rapid movement of the forelegs (extension only takes 30–60 ms) and then brought back to the mouth. In a comparable way some dragonfly larvae wait for their prey, lying concealed in the mud at the bottom of a pool and seizing the prey with the labial mask. This is a modification of the labium in which pre- and postmentum are elongated and the palps are modified to form grasping organs (Fig. 20). The mask can be extended in front of the head by an increase in blood pressure and the palps are used to catch the prey. By withdrawal of the mask the prey is carried back to the mandibles.

A few insects make traps in which they catch their prey. Ant lions (larval Myrmeleontidae, Neuroptera), for instance, dig pits one to two inches in diameter with sloping sides in dry sand and then bury themselves at the bottom with only the head exposed (Fig. 21). If an ant walks over the edge of such a pit it has difficulty in regaining the top because of the instability of the sides. In addition, the larva, by sharp movements of the head, flicks sand at the ant causing it to fall to the bottom of the pit and be captured.

Adult Odonata are active hunters, pursuing other insects in flight, and in order to facilitate catching, the thoracic segments are rotated forwards so as to bring the legs into an anterior position (Fig. 22). Tiger beetles hunt on the ground and have long legs, which increase their speed, and prognathous mouthparts with large mandibles.

The majority of hunters have well-developed eyes since only vision can give a sufficiently rapid directed response to moving prey. This reaction is usually not specific and the predator will pursue any moving object of suitable size. Thus dragonflies turn towards small stones thrown into the air and the wasp *Philanthus* orientates to a variety of moving insects of appropriate size, although it only catches bees. This subsequent recognition involves other senses and only if the insect has the smell of a bee does *Philanthus* attempt to capture it. Provided it has the appropriate smell the wasp will attack any insect of the right size, but, having caught it, stinging does not follow unless

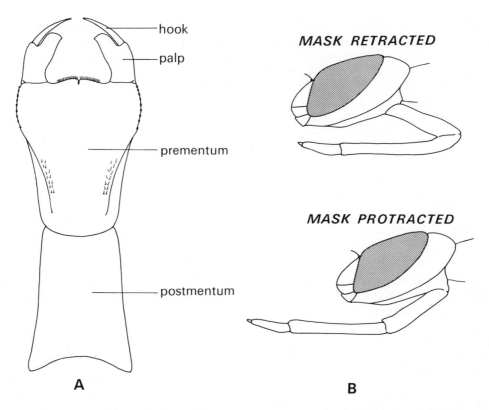

Fig. 20 A. The labial mask of a dragonfly larva. B. Lateral view of the head of a dragonfly larva showing the labial mask retracted and protracted (diagrammatic)

Fig. 21 Section through the pit made by an ant lion showing the larva lying in wait for its prey at the bottom of the pit

the insect really is a bee; other insects experimentally given the smell of a bee are released. This final recognition is presumably tactile. Comparable behaviour is probably common amongst other predators.

In predaceous larval forms with poorly developed eyes and often with subterranean habits, such as tabanid larvae, the finding of prey must be largely olfactory. *Dytiscus* (Coleoptera) also responds to chemical stimuli in the water, rather than the sight of prey.

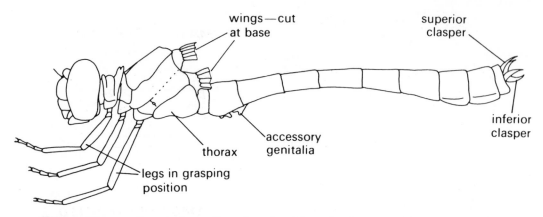

Fig. 22 Diagram of a male dragonfly to show the oblique development of the thorax bringing the legs into an anterior position which facilitates grasping the prey

Mechanical stimulation is sometimes important in finding prey and some dragonfly larvae depend on mechanoreceptors on the antennae or tarsi for this. *Notonecta* is able to locate prey trapped in the air–water interface as a result of the ripples which radiate from it, perceiving the vibrations with sensory hairs on the swimming legs. Amongst terrestrial insects the response of ant lions to their prey depends on mechanical stimulation from the falling sand as well as on vision.

Coccinellid (Coleoptera) larvae preying on aphids only respond to the prey on contact. They move across a leaf, searching to either side as they go, but after finding and eating an aphid they tend to remain in the same area by making numerous small turning movements. Since aphids usually occur in large numbers this is clearly an advantage and this type of behaviour is only suited to prey which is more or less sedentary and locally abundant.

2.3.4 Host finding and preferences of blood-sucking insects

In general the free-living blood-sucking insects, such as mosquitoes and tsetse flies, bite a wide range of hosts, although most are restricted to mammals and birds. Within this range tsetse flies, at least, show distinct preferences. *Glossina morsitans* feeds primarily on ungulates, which are essential for its continued existence, while man and reptiles are particularly important to *G. palpalis* (Fig. 23).

The less mobile blood-suckers are more specific. This is true to some extent of fleas, although here the specificity is largely ecological. Development of fleas usually occurs in the nest of the host and particular species tend to be restricted to a particular type of nest with a characteristic micro-environment. Nests may, for instance, be sub-terranean, on the surface of the ground or in trees. This clearly limits the type of host which a particular species of flea is likely to encounter, but, given the opportunity, most fleas will bite unusual hosts. Lice, on the other hand, which spend the whole of their life history on the host, are extremely host specific (Hopkins, 1950).

Perception of a host at a distance may arise from visual, olfactory or mechanical stimulation, depending on the species and the situation. *Glossina swynnertoni*, a tsetse fly inhabiting relatively open savannah, can see cattle moving 150 m away, but

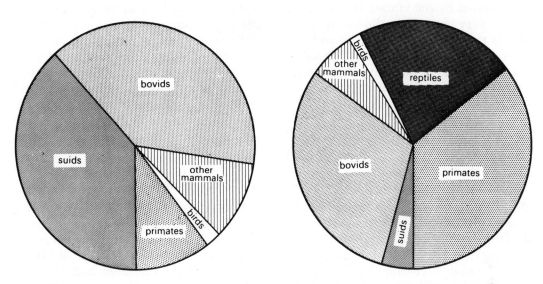

Fig. 23 The hosts of *Glossina morsitans* and *G. palpalis*. The angle subtended by each sector at the centre of the circle represents the proportion of flies feeding on each particular host (after Weitz, 1964)

G. medicorum, from dense forest and thicket, only reacts to a moving screen at distances under 10 m. Movement of a potential host increases the likelihood of the insect reacting to it. The smell of the host is also important in specific host recognition by tsetse flies (Vale, 1980). If an insect responds to the smell of a host by taking off and then orientating upwind it will fly into the vicinity of the source of smell. At closer quarters vision may become more important again (Buxton, 1955; Chapman, 1961). Mosquitoes react to hosts at a distance in similar ways (Kalmus and Hocking, 1960).

At closer quarters other factors also play a part in attraction (Hocking, 1971). In addition to smell, moisture and warmth are important to mosquitoes and settling depends on the nature of the surface. Mosquitoes settle more rapidly on rough than on smooth surfaces and often on dark rather than light ones. After settling, probing of the host tissues with the proboscis is induced by olfactory stimuli and also by the warmth of the host. ATP, which is present in high concentrations in the blood platelets, commonly acts as a phagostimulant in these insects (Friend and Smith, 1972, 1977).

2.3.5 Host-finding by internal parasites

In the majority of internal parasites the parent insect oviposits in a suitable host. Smell, and possibly also contact chemoreception, are involved in this. In some cases, however, the parent does not seek out the larval host, but oviposits or larviposits in places frequented by the host and the larvae make their own way on to the host when the occasion presents itself. For instance, the human warble fly, *Cordylobia anthropophaga*, oviposits in sand fouled with urine. The larvae hatch in a day or two and then remain inactive until the area is visited by a potential host, man or some other mammal. They are activated by the vibrations and warmth of the host and bore in through the skin.

In a very few insects the larvae act as the dispersive phase and reinfect new hosts. This is the case in Strepsiptera and the meloid beetles, both of which produce vast numbers of larvae known as triungulins. Strepsipteran triungulins escape from the female, which is an internal parasite, when the host is visiting a flower. They remain in the flower until another insect arrives and then jump on to it. If this is the correct host they remain clinging to it and, depending on the species, parasitise it or its offspring; if it is not the appropriate host they jump off again (Clausen, 1940). Some meloids find their hosts in essentially similar ways, while in others, parasitic in grasshoppers' eggs, the triungulins actively seek out the eggs.

2.4 Significance of food preferences

Most or all plants contain secondary plant chemicals, many of which affect growth, longevity or fecundity of insects if they are eaten in large amounts. For instance, growth of larval *Agrotis* (Lepidoptera) is inhibited by L-DOPA and by catechol, which act by reducing the amounts of food assimilated or converted to body tissues (Reese and Beck, 1976). Cyanide is released by some plants, such as *Trifolium*, *Pteridium* and *Manihot*, when their tissues are damaged, and since cyanide is a general respiratory poison these plants are toxic to most insects. It is an advantage if an insect avoids ingesting potentially harmful chemicals by exhibiting feeding preferences and in *Chortoicetes* (Orthoptera) the preferred food plants were the only ones in a range of plants tested which gave good survival and development (Bernays and Chapman, 1973).

Insects which habitually feed on plants containing specific secondary plant chemicals are able to tolerate, or even to utilise, these chemicals. Larvae of *Manduca* (Lepidoptera) feed on tobacco; they rapidly excrete the nicotine ingested. *Poekilocerus* (Orthoptera) feeds on *Calotropis*, which contains cardiac glycosides; it stores these and they contribute to the distastefulness of the insect to predators. Many similar examples are known (Rothschild, 1973). Duffey (1980) reviews the sequestration of plant natural products by insects.

2.5 Conditioning to food

Although food preferences of many species are relatively constant, some variation in food selection according to previous experience occurs in polyphagous species. Larvae of *Manduca* exhibit preferences for the plants they have been reared on, but if they are reared on artificial diet they have no preferences for particular host-plants and their tolerance of non-hosts is increased. This is also true if the insects are fed on tomato leaves containing the deterrent salicin; they then eat more dandelion or cabbage than insects reared on tomato without salicin. These changes involve changes within the central nervous system, but the sensitivity of chemoreceptor neurones is also altered by previous experience (Schoonhoven, 1969). There is some evidence that the food first eaten by a phytophagous insect conditions its subsequent behaviour so that it shows a preference for this food (Cassidy, 1978).

Locusta also becomes conditioned to take meals of a certain size. If small meals are habitually eaten due to restrictions in the amount of food available, subsequent meals are still small even when abundant food is present (Bernays and Chapman, 1972).

2.6 Feeding and ingestion

Once the insect has recognised its food as suitable it starts to feed. The processes by which food is ingested vary considerably.

2.6.1 Feeding by phytophagous insects

Typical plant-feeding insects with biting mouthparts bite off fragments of food and pass them back to the mouth with the aid of the maxillae while grasshoppers also help to guide the food into the mouth by holding it between their forelegs. Often such insects feed at the edge of a leaf, moving on towards the centre, and usually the more woody parts are avoided.

Fluid feeders may obtain their food from the cell sap or directly from distributive vessels. Aphids, for instance, usually tap the phloem. When an aphid lands it inserts its mouthparts into the plant tissue using the protractor and retractor muscles of the stylets in the head, probably aided by a clasping action of the labium. In the course of penetration through the leaf epidermis and parenchyma mechanical resistance is encountered and this to some extent affects selection of the feeding site. However, such resistance is probably partially overcome by the saliva dissolving the middle lamellae between the plant cells. The stylets penetrate the plant tissue in a series of back-and-forth movements. At the end of each slight withdrawal a drop of viscous saliva is secreted. A drop of watery saliva is injected into this and the stylets push through it so that a sleeve of salivary material is produced. By producing a succession of short lengths of sleeve at successive withdrawals a continuous sheath is formed surrounding the stylets from the point at which they penetrate the plant tissues almost to their tips.

The saliva of the sheath is mainly protein with about 10% phospholipid and conjugated carbohydrate. After secretion the molecules become held together by hydrogen bonds and further stabilised by disulphide bonds. Within the salivary glands such bonding does not occur, despite the fact that the various components mix together, because of strong reducing conditions and high levels of amino acids. After secretion, the amino acids diffuse away and free oxygen leads to bonding, aided by oxidising enzymes. Once formed, the sheath, which may take an hour to produce, is impermeable. Its function is uncertain, but it may serve to seal the stylets into cells containing fluid under pressure (Miles, 1972).

Species which feed on mesophyll inject watery saliva into each cell before sucking out the contents. Then the sheath is extended into a new cell before ingestion is resumed. With phloem feeders no more saliva is produced once the feeding site is reached unless the food canal in the stylets becomes blocked. If it does, a small amount of viscous saliva may be secreted to dislodge the blockage. Fluid food is pumped into the insect by the cibarial pump aided by the sap pressure of the plant, which drives sap into the food canal. The flow of sap is controlled by the aphid, and *Tuberolachnus* feeds faster if the concentration of nitrogen in the sap is low, while *Aphis fabae* feeds faster if it is attended by ants (Kennedy and Fosbrooke, 1973).

2.6.2 Feeding by predaceous insects

Having captured their prey some predaceous insects, such as the mantis, restrain the victim by sheer mechanical strength and then tear it to pieces with powerful mandibles, ingesting the whole insect. Many other forms, including Heteroptera and some Diptera (Asilidae), inject salivary secretions which kill the prey and then, following extra-intestinal digestion of the contents, ingest the digested remains and discard the cuticular shell. Predaceous Hymenoptera, which capture other animals and store them alive for use as food by the larvae, paralyse the victim by means of a venom injected via the sting.

2.6.3 Venoms of predaceous insects

The venoms injected by Heteroptera, such as *Platymerus*, are produced in the salivary glands, which are enlarged and have a muscular coat. Following penetration of the stylets into the prey, the venom is forcibly injected by a powerful salivary pump and then transported round the body of the victim in the haemolymph. Injection is followed by convulsive struggling, rapidly leading to tremors and then death. These venoms are non-specific, being toxic to a wide range of insects and their action is to cause a general lysis of the tissues so that nervous activity rapidly stops. Similar venoms are probably used by larval Neuroptera and by Asilidae and Empididae (Diptera) and Odonata (Beard, 1963; Edwards, 1963).

Hymenoptera which paralyse their prey inject the venom via the sting, which is a modified ovipositor. There is no real evidence that the wasp attempts to inject its venom into a nerve ganglion of the victim as is suggested in the literature, but localised stinging in particular regions of the prey probably indicates the presence of relatively weak spots in the integument at these points. These venoms also circulate in the haemolymph, but they do not kill the prey, only paralysing the musculature of the body wall, possibly by a neuromuscular block. The heart and alimentary canal continue rhythmic activity and the nervous system remains active, but, although such a state of paralysis may last for several months, degenerative changes set in and the insect eventually dies. The injected venom does not help to keep the prey 'fresh' for the larvae to feed on subsequently, but rather the prey is in the position of an insect deprived of food which can survive as long as its food reserves allow. These paralysing venoms may be very specific, affecting only one or a small number of species, so that injection into an inappropriate species has no effect. This indicates very specialised and specific chemical configurations for the venoms.

2.6.4 Feeding by blood-sucking insects

Mosquitoes and blood-sucking Heteroptera push the stylets of the proboscis into the host tissues with an initial thrust from the leg musculature. Further penetration is achieved mainly by the mandibular stylets, which are worked into the tissues by their protractor and retractor muscles. Tsetse flies, and some other blood-sucking species, have no mandibles, and a totally different mechanism of penetration is used. When a tsetse fly lands on its host it spreads its legs apart, grips the skin with its claws and braces itself so as to be able to exert a downward pressure. Then it lowers the haustellum and pierces the skin by the rasping action of the labella (Buxton, 1955).

Bugs, fleas and mosquitoes insert the stylets directly into capillaries and feed directly from the blood vessels. In these species the normal blood pressure of the host helps to force blood through the narrow food canal in the proboscis. Tabanids and tsetse flies, on the other hand, are pool feeders (Hocking, 1971). Feeding never follows the initial probe and the haustellum is partly withdrawn, the head moved and a new thrust made in a different direction. In this way the fly causes a local haemorrhage in the tissues and it drinks from the pool of blood which is produced. The whole process of feeding to repletion takes about two minutes in *Glossina morsitans*.

Blood-sucking insects inject saliva into the wound and often this saliva contains an anticoagulant. This prevents the blood from clotting in the wound and in the proboscis of the insect, but the saliva of some such insects, notably *Aedes aegypti*, contains no anticoagulant and the blood clots in the stomach within 15 minutes of feeding. The absence of an anticoagulant, however, does not impair feeding.

Blood is sucked up by the action of the cibarial pump and feeding continues until the insect is enormously distended; *Rhodnius* (Heteroptera) may increase its weight by more than six times in a 15-minute feed. The size of the meal in *Rhodnius* is limited by the extent to which the abdomen will enlarge, which is determined by the epicuticle. The abdominal cuticle consists only of undifferentiated endocuticle and strongly folded epicuticle and expansion can continue only until the epicuticle is smooth. Expansion is facilitated by plasticisation of the endocuticle so that it becomes less rigid at an early stage during the meal. This plasticisation is probably brought about by a neurosecretion which reaches the body wall through the abdominal nerves. It is only a temporary effect and decreases after feeding (Maddrell, 1966). Plasticisation probably results from a reduction in pH in the cuticle reducing the numbers of weak secondary bonds between the macromolecules (Reynolds, 1975).

2.7 Control of feeding

In most insects feeding is not continuous even under constant suitable conditions: bouts of active feeding alternate with periods without feeding (Fig. 24). This probably leads to more efficient digestion and utilisation of the food than if continuous feeding occurred, and it also conserves energy.

Feeding only begins when the insect is in a state of readiness to feed. Recently-fed insects fail to respond to food stimuli and their responsiveness increases with the time which has elapsed since the last meal. For example, larvae of *Schistocerca* do not

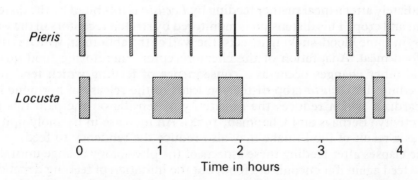

Fig. 24 Examples of the patterns of the feeding of larvae of *Pieris* and *Locusta*. Hatched areas indicate periods of feeding (after Ma, 1972; Blaney, Chapman and Wilson, 1973)

respond to the odour of food immediately after feeding, but four hours later most of them respond by moving upwind towards the source (Fig. 25). The mantis *Hierodula* does not respond to prey for the first eight hours after becoming satiated, but then it watches and strikes at potential prey at greater and greater distances. After 48 hours without food it makes head movements while the prey is still 18 cm away and strikes from a distance of 6 cm.

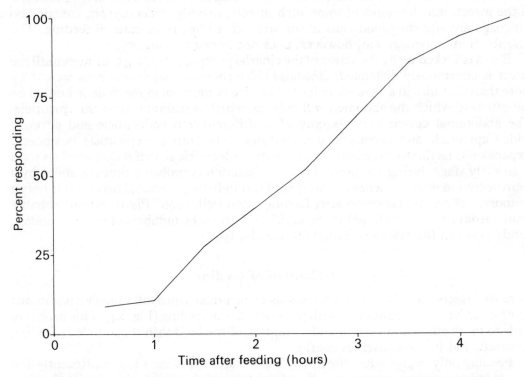

Fig. 25 Changes in responsiveness to the odour of grass by larvae of *Schistocerca* in relation to the period without food (after Moorhouse, 1971)

Immediately after a meal further feeding by *Locusta* is inhibited by the distension of the foregut and crop. This distension is monitored by stretch receptors in the wall of the foregut or, in some blood-sucking insects, the wall of the abdomen, which is distended by the blood meal. Adaptation of the chemoreceptors monitoring food quality also occurs and other changes occur as a consequence of feeding which tend to inhibit further feeding. In *Locusta* crop distension leads to the release of hormone from the corpora cardiaca which reduces the sensitivity of sensilla on the palp tips and also reduces activity (Bernays and Chapman, 1974). An increase in haemolymph osmotic pressure as a result of food intake may also reduce the tendency to feed.

As time elapses after feeding these aspects of the physiology change until the insect is ready to feed again if it encounters food, but the initiation of feeding depends on the stimulation of appropriate sensilla. In *Phormia* stimulation of the contact chemoreceptors of the tarsi by sugars leads to proboscis extension; this causes the labellar

chemoreceptors to touch the food and, if appropriate stimuli are perceived, ingestion
follows (Gelperin, 1971). As *Locusta* moves over a food plant the maxillary and labial
palps vibrate rapidly, bringing the sensilla at their tips into contact with the leaf surface.
If the stimulus indicates suitable food the head is lowered and the insect bites at an
edge. This releases the fluids within the plant and these flow over the inner surfaces of
the mouthparts to stimulate sensilla in the various groups (Fig. 17). If the stimulus is
appropriate, feeding follows.

Long-term changes in food intake are controlled by other factors (Stoffolano, 1974).

2.8 The timing of feeding activity and amount eaten

Feeding behaviour results from the summation of a series of internal and external
stimuli. Pupae do not feed at all and in Ephemeroptera, Lepidoptera and Oestridae
(Diptera) there are some species which do not feed as adults and often have reduced
mouthparts. Feeding does not occur in newly emerged insects and is reduced or
nonexistent during diapause (Fig. 26) and at the time of moulting (Fig. 27). Female
mosquitoes do not feed while they are producing eggs. The state of feeding is also
important and the tendency to feed is greatly reduced after a meal; it may even be
physically impossible as in *Rhodnius*, which only takes a single large meal in each larval
instar. Tsetse flies are not attracted to their hosts for two or three days after feeding and
phytophagous insects have a period of postprandial quiescence, during which feeding
activity, as well as other activities, is reduced.

There is often also some diurnal variation in feeding. This is, in part, directly
related to the existing environmental conditions, such as light and temperature, which
may be limiting, but, as with other activities, changes in these conditions may be

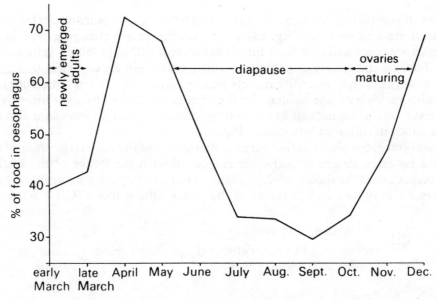

Fig. 26 Seasonal variation in the amount of feeding by adult female red locusts (after
Chapman, 1957)

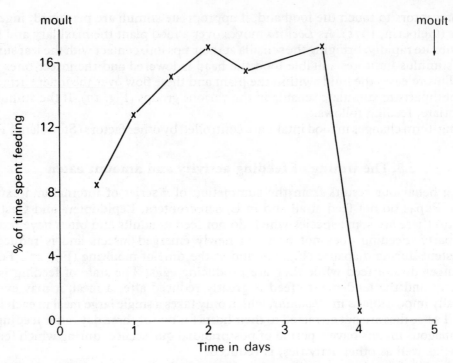

Fig. 27 Variations in the amount of time spent feeding by *Locusta* during the third larval instar (after Ellis, 1951)

important in stimulating feeding. *Nomadacris* (Orthoptera), for instance, feeds mainly in the morning and evening (Fig. 28) when conditions are changing rapidly. Many mosquitoes are crepuscular in their biting habits and, although biting is influenced by climatic factors, the timing appears to result partly from an endogenous rhythm of activity, changes of light intensity merely acting as time cues (Clements, 1963). Biting activity also varies with the habitat. In forest regions *Aedes africanus* bites by day at ground level, but is crepuscular in the canopy, and *Mansonia fuscopennata* also bites at different times in different situations (Fig. 29).

The amount eaten over a period varies with the size of the insect; the amount of food consumed by early instars is negligible compared with the intake of the final larval instar irrespective of the mode of feeding (Fig. 30). For comparative purposes it is usual to express the amount eaten in terms of the consumption index (C.I.), where

$$\text{C.I.} = \frac{\text{weight of food eaten}}{\text{mean weight of insect during feeding period} \times \text{duration of feeding period (days)}}$$

On an acceptable food the consumption index for fifth instar *Spodoptera* (Lepidoptera) larvae is 1·2–2·4, that is the insect eats up to 2·4 times its own weight per day (Waldbauer, 1968).

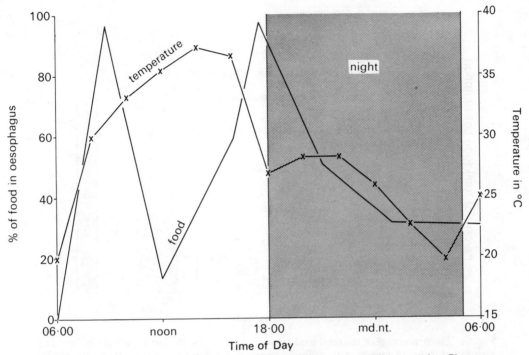

Fig. 28 Daily variation in the amount of feeding by adult male red locusts (after Chapman, 1957)

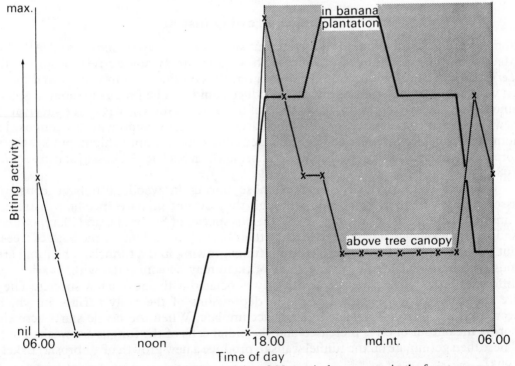

Fig. 29 Daily variation in the biting activity of *Mansonia fuscopennata* in the forest canopy and in a banana plantation (adapted from Haddow, 1961)

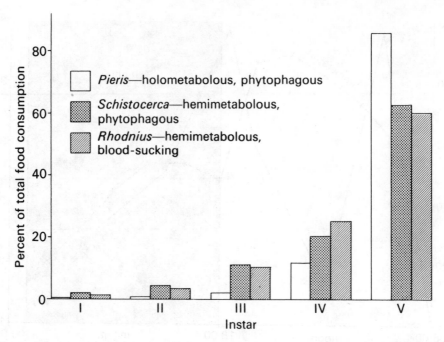

Fig. 30 The percentage of the total food consumption during the larval period consumed by each larval instar of insects with different types of development and feeding habits (after Waldbauer, 1968)

2.9 Fungus-growing insects

Some termites and ants grow fungi on specially prepared substrates. All the Macrotermitinae are fungus growers with an obligate symbiotic relationship with *Termitomyces*, a Basidiomycete. The worker termites produce a 'comb' of chewed wood on which the fungal hyphae grow and produce conidia. The fungus is eaten in small amounts by the workers and is fed to some of the larvae (Grassé, 1949). The survival of newly founded colonies depends on inoculation of the new comb with the fungus. In some genera conidia are carried by the winged adults on the nuptial flight, but in others foraging workers collect basidiospores and bring them back to the nest (Johnson *et al.*, 1981).

Other insects, especially some of those boring in wood, also have constant associations with particular fungi although they do not prepare specific substrates. Amongst these are the ambrosia beetles, various species of Scolytidae and Platypodidae and all Lymexylidae. These beetles make their tunnels in and under the bark of trees, but the bulk of their food is derived from fungi growing in the tunnels. The fungi are mostly rather specialised ones and some of them may be connected with a variety of different beetles while others are constantly associated with one or a few species. They are transmitted by the female beetle in depressions of the body surface in which secretions of oil from associated glands accumulate. When the beetle starts actively boring the output of oil is increased and the oidial cells of the fungus are washed out. These then germinate on the tunnel walls to produce a new growth of ambrosia (Baker, 1963).

2.10 Food storage

Many insects build up temporary internal stores of food in the fat body or, in fluid feeders, in the crop, but external storage is a characteristic of the social and subsocial insects. Many solitary Hymenoptera (Sphecoidea and Pompiloidea) build cells and provision them for the use of their larvae. Some, such as *Ammophila*, exhibit progressive provisioning of the nest. *Ammophila* excavates a hole in the ground, provisions it with a caterpillar and then lays an egg and closes the cell. The wasp then starts a new nest. Each morning on her first flight the female visits each nest, of which there may be three at any one time, and examines its state of provisions. If there is an ample supply she closes the nest and leaves it until the following day, but if there is not much food she brings a fresh supply. The female continues to bring food to the nest whenever it is required until the larva is well grown, when she puts in a final store and seals the nest for the last time. Other solitary wasps, like *Eumenes*, and solitary bees put a large stock of provisions into the nest at the time the egg is laid and this suffices for the whole of larval development, for the cell is never visited again. This type of provisioning is known as mass provisioning.

Honey ants, such as *Myrmecocystus*, store nectar and other sweet substances in the crops of certain workers known as repletes. These are fed sugars until their gasters become enormously distended and their movement is greatly restricted; they then remain hanging from the roof in special chambers in the nest. The sugar is regurgitated to other workers as it is required (Wheeler, 1926).

There are many other examples of food storage, but this becomes most significant in *Apis* with perennial colonies in temperate regions where there is a long period during which fresh food is unobtainable. *Apis* feeds on honey and pollen. Honey is derived from nectar, which has a variable composition but may consist of some 60 % water and a very high proportion of sugars, of which 40–50 % is sucrose. Only traces of protein are present. When nectar is collected the enzyme invertase is secreted on to it so that sucrose is broken down to glucose and fructose. On reaching the nest the forager gives its nectar to a house bee who has the task of reducing its water content to about 20 %. To achieve this the worker regurgitates a small drop of nectar from the honey stomach, manipulates it with the mandibles and then swallows it again, repeating this process some 80 or 90 times in 20 minutes. By this process water is evaporated and the nectar concentrated. When it has reached a suitable concentration the honey is put into a cell and used for food or is sealed up for use later.

Honey provides the carbohydrates and water for adults and larvae; protein is derived from pollen. Pollen collecting is facilitated by the pectinate hairs characteristic of Apoidea since the pollen grains tend to become caught up in these hairs. The bee may actively collect pollen, biting anthers so as to increase the amount released, or it may simply become dusted with pollen while in search of nectar. Pollen collected on the head region is brushed off with the forelegs and moistened with a little regurgitated nectar or honey before being passed back to the hind legs which also collect pollen from the abdomen using the combs on the inside of the legs (Fig. 31). The pollen on the combs of one side is then removed by the rake of the opposite hind leg and collects in the pollen press between the tibia and basitarsus. By closure of the press, pollen is forced outwards and upwards on to the outside of the tibia and is then held in place by the hairs and spines of the pollen basket. On returning to the nest the pollen is kicked off by the

INSIDE   *OUTSIDE*

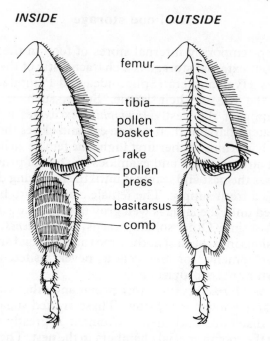

femur

tibia

pollen
basket

rake

pollen
press

basitarsus

comb

Fig. 31 The hind tibia and tarsus of the honey bee, from inside and outside, showing the pollen collecting apparatus (partly after Snodgrass, 1956)

middle legs into an empty cell, house bees break up the masses of pollen and pack it down and the cell is then capped or left open for current use (Butler, 1962).

2.11 Social feeding

Feeding of one insect by another sometimes occurs in non-social insects during courtship as in the presentation of food to the female empid (Diptera) by the male, but in general such behaviour occurs only in the social insects. Here there are often stages—larvae, soldiers or reproductive forms—which are incapable of feeding themselves and must be fed by the workers.

In wasps the larvae are fed on the masticated remains of other insects. Bees use honey and pollen, but also brood food, a secretion of the hypopharyngeal and mandibular glands of the workers containing protein derived from pollen. Brood food is fed to all larvae for the first three days after hatching and subsequently probably forms an important part of the diet of larvae destined to become queens. The quantity of food eaten also plays some part in queen determination (Butler, 1962). In a similar way queen determination in the ant *Myrmica* is related to feeding, larvae destined to become queens apparently having more protein in their diet. This varies with the physiological condition of the workers tending the larvae and possibly again involves glandular secretions by the workers (Weir, 1959).

Termites practise social feeding and in Calotermitidae proctodaeal feeding occurs. These insects produce two types of excrement, solid faeces and a liquid containing fragments of wood and intestinal flagellates (p. 71). Production of this second type of excrement is stimulated by other individuals placing their antennae on the dorsal or perianal region of the worker. Apart from any direct nutritive value this behaviour is important in renewing the intestinal fauna of newly moulted individuals because this fauna is lost each time a termite moults. This behaviour does not occur in Termitidae with no comparable intestinal fauna, although faeces may be eaten.

Trophallaxis

Often in the social insects a mutual exchange of food occurs, such behaviour being known as trophallaxis. When, for instance, an ant feeds a larva it receives from the larva a drop of salivary fluid, which may be so attractive to the worker that it solicits saliva from the larva without giving anything in return. This mutual exchange of food has been regarded as the basis of social systems in insects (Wheeler, 1922; Richards, 1953), but in the wasp *Vespula sylvestris* it has been shown that the larval saliva, although taken by the workers, is not especially attractive to them. It is probable that the secretion of saliva is a means whereby the larvae eliminate excess water, and its removal by the workers prevents the nest from becoming fouled. Thus in this insect, at least, typical trophallaxis does not occur, and if such a relationship ever existed it has become modified in the course of evolution (Brian and Brian, 1952).

REFERENCES

BAKER, J. M. (1963). Ambrosia beetles and their fungi, with particular reference to *Platypus cylindrus*, Fab. *Symp. Soc. gen. Microbiol.* **13**: 232–265.

BARTON BROWNE, L. (1975). Regulatory mechanisms in insect feeding. *Adv. Insect Physiol.* **11**: 1–116.

BEARD, R. L. (1963). Insect toxins and venoms. *A. Rev. Ent.* **8**: 1–18.

BERNAYS, E. A. and CHAPMAN, R. F. (1972). Meal size in nymphs of *Locusta migratoria*. *Entomologia exp. appl.* **15**: 399–410.

BERNAYS, E. A. and CHAPMAN, R. F. (1973). The role of food plants in the survival and development of *Chortoicetes terminifera* (Walker) under drought conditions. *Aust. J. Zool.* **21**: 575–592.

BERNAYS, E. A. and CHAPMAN, R. F. (1974). The regulation of food intake by acridids. *in* Barton Browne, L. (ed.), *Experimental analysis of insect behaviour*. Springer-Verlag, Berlin.

BERNAYS, E. A. and CHAPMAN, R. F. (1978). Plant chemistry and acridoid feeding behaviour. *in* HARBORNE, J. B. (ed.), *Biochemical aspects of plant and animal coevolution*. Academic Press, London.

BERNAYS, E. A. and SIMPSON, S. J. (1982). Control of food intake. *Adv. Insect Physiol.* **16**: 59–118.

BLANEY, W. M., CHAPMAN, R. F. and WILSON, A. (1973). The pattern of feeding of *Locusta migratoria* (L.) (Orthoptera, Acrididae). *Acrida* **2**: 119–137.

BRIAN, M. V. and BRIAN, A. D. (1952). The wasp, *Vespula sylvestris* Scopoli: feeding, foraging and colony development. *Trans. R. ent. Soc. Lond.* **103**: 1–26.

BRUES, C. T. (1946). *Insect dietary. An account of the food habits of insects*. Harvard University Press, Cambridge, Mass.

BUTLER, C. G. (1962). *The world of the honeybee*. Collins, London.

BUXTON, P. A. (1955). *The natural history of tsetse flies*. Lewis, London.

CASSIDY, M. D. (1978). Development of an induced food plant preference in the Indian stick insect, *Carausius morosus*. *Entomologia exp. appl.* **24**: 287–293.

CHAPMAN, R. F. (1957). Observations on the feeding of adults of the red locust (*Nomadacris septemfasciata* (Serville)). *Br. J. Anim. Behav.* **5**: 60–75.

CHAPMAN, R. F. (1961). Some experiments to determine the methods used in host-finding by the tsetse fly, *Glossina medicorum* Austen. *Bull. ent. Res.* **52**: 83–97.

CHAPMAN, R. F. (1974). *Feeding in leaf-eating insects*. Oxford Biology Reader no. 69, 16 pp.

CHAPMAN, R. F. and THOMAS, J. G. (1978). The numbers and distribution of sensilla on the mouthparts of Acridoidea. *Acrida* **7**: 115–148.

CLAUSEN, C. P. (1940). *Entomophagous insects*. McGraw-Hill, New York.

CLEMENTS, A. N. (1963). *The physiology of mosquitoes*. Pergamon Press, Oxford.

DOWNES, J. A. (1958). The feeding habits of biting flies and their significance in classification. *A. Rev. Ent.* **3**: 249–266.

DUFFEY, S. S. (1980). Sequestration of plant natural products by insects. *A. Rev. Ent.* **25**: 447–477.

EDWARDS, J. S. (1963). Arthropods as predators. *Viewpoints in Biology.* **2**: 85–114.

ELLIS, P. E. (1951). The marching behaviour of hoppers of the African migratory locust (*Locusta migratoria migratorioides* R. & F.) in the laboratory. *Anti-Locust Bull.* no. 7, 46 pp.

EMDEN, H. F. van (1972). Aphids as phytochemists. *in* Harborne, J. B. (ed.), *Phytochemical ecology*. Academic Press, London and New York.

FRAENKEL, G. (1969). Evaluation of our thoughts on secondary plant substances. *Entomologia exp. appl.* **12**: 473–486.

FRIEND, W. G. and SMITH, J. J. B. (1972). Feeding stimuli and techniques for studying the feeding of haematophagous arthropods under artificial conditions, with special reference to *Rhodnius prolixus*. *in* Rodriguez, J. G. (ed.), *Insect and mite nutrition*. North-Holland Publishing Co., Amsterdam and London.

FRIEND, W. G. and SMITH, J. J. B. (1977). Factors affecting feeding by bloodsucking insects. *A. Rev. Ent.* **22**: 309–331.

GELPERIN, A. (1971). Regulation of feeding. *A. Rev. Ent.* **16**: 365–378.

GILBERT, B. L. and NORRIS, D. M. (1968). A chemical basis for bark beetle (*Scolytus*) distinction between host and non-host trees. *J. Insect Physiol.* **14**: 1063–1068.

GRASSÉ, P.-P. (1949). Ordre des Isoptères ou termites. *in* Grassé, P.-P. (ed.), *Traité de Zoologie*. vol. 9. Masson et Cie., Paris.

HADDOW, A. J. (1961). Entomological studies from a high tower in Mpanga Forest, Uganda. VII. The biting behaviour of mosquitoes and tabanids. *Trans. R. ent. Soc. Lond.* **113**: 315–335.

HOCKING, B. (1971). Blood-sucking behaviour of terrestrial arthropods. *A. Rev. Ent.* **16**: 1–26.

HOPKINS, G. H. F. (1950). The host-associations of the lice of mammals. *Proc. zool. Soc. Lond.* **119**: 387–604.

HSIAO, T. H. (1969). Chemical basis of host selection and plant resistance in oligophagous insects. *Entomologia exp. appl.* **12**: 777–788.

HSIAO, T. H. (1974). Chemical influence on feeding behaviour of *Leptinotarsa* beetles. *in* Barton Browne, L. (ed.), *Experimental analysis of insect behaviour*. Springer-Verlag, Berlin.

JOHNSON, R. A., THOMAS, R. J., WOOD, T. G. and SWIFT, M. J. (1981). The inoculation of the fungus comb in newly founded colonies of some species of the Macrotermitinae (Isoptera) from Nigeria. *J. Nat. Hist.* **15**: 751–756.

KALMUS, H. and HOCKING, B. (1960). Behaviour of *Aedes* mosquitoes in relation to blood-feeding and repellants. *Entomologia exp. appl.* **3**: 1–26.

KENNEDY, J. S. and FOSBROOKE, I. H. M. (1973). The plant in the life of an aphid. *Symp. R. ent. Soc. Lond.* **6**: 129–140.

LANGLEY, P. A. (1976). Initiation and regulation of ingestion by haematophagous arthropods. *J. Med. Ent.* **13**: 121–130.

LEE, R. (1974). Structure and function of the fascicular stylets, and the labral and cibarial sense organs of male and female *Aedes aegypti* (L.) (Diptera, Culicidae). *Quaest. ent.* **10**: 187–215.

MA, Wei Chun (1972). Dynamics of feeding responses in *Pieris brassicae* Linn. as a function of chemosensory input: a behavioural, ultrastructural and electrophysiological study. *Meded. Landbouwhogeschool Wageningen* 1972, no. 11.

MADDRELL, S. H. P. (1966). Nervous control of the mechanical properties of the abdominal wall at feeding in *Rhodnius*. *J. exp. Biol.* **44**: 59–68.

MILES, P. W. (1972). The saliva of Hemiptera. *Adv. Insect Physiol.* **9**: 183–255.

MITTELSTAEDT, H. (1962). Control systems of orientation in insects. *A. Rev. Ent.* **7**: 177–198.

MOORHOUSE, J. E. (1971). Experimental analysis of the locomotor behaviour of *Schistocerca gregaria* induced by odour. *J. Insect Physiol.* **17**: 913–920.

MULKERN, G. B. (1967). Food selection by grasshoppers. *A. Rev. Ent.* **12**: 59–78.

MULKERN, G. B. (1969). Behavioural influences on food selection in grasshoppers (Orthoptera: Acrididae). *Entomologia exp. appl.* **12**: 509–523.

REESE, J. C. and BECK, S. D. (1976). Effects of allelochemics on the black cutworm, *Agrotis ipsilon*; effects of catechol, L-dopa, dopamine, and chlorogenic acid on larval growth, development, and utilization of food. *Ann. ent. Soc. Am.* **69**: 68–72.

REYNOLDS, S. E. (1975). The mechanism of plasticization of the abdominal cuticle in *Rhodnius*. *J. exp. Biol.* **62**: 81–98.

RICHARDS, O. W. (1953). *The social insects*. Macdonald, London.

ROTHSCHILD, M. (1973). Secondary plant substances and warning colouration in insects. *Symp. R. ent. Soc. Lond.* **6**: 59–83.

RUDINSKY, J. A., MORGAN, M. E., LIBBEY, L. M. and PUTNAM, T. B. (1974). Additional components of the Douglas fir beetle (Col., Scolytidae) aggregative pheromone and their possible utility in pest control. *Z. angew. Ent.* **76**: 65–77.

SCHOONHOVEN, L. M. (1968). Chemosensory bases of host plant selection. *A. Rev. Ent.* **13**: 115–136.

SCHOONHOVEN, L. M. (1969). Gustation and foodplant selection in some lepidopterous larvae. *Entomologia exp. appl.* **12**: 555–564.

SCHOONHOVEN, L. M. (1973). Plant recognition by lepidopterous larvae. *Symp. R. ent. Soc. Lond.* **6**: 87–99.

SNODGRASS, R. E. (1956). *Anatomy of the honey bee*. Constable, London.

STOFFOLANO, J. G. (1974). Control of feeding and drinking in diapausing insects. *in* Barton Browne, L. (ed.), *Experimental analysis of insect behaviour*. Springer-Verlag, Berlin.

VALE, G. A. (1980). Field studies of the responses of tsetse flies (Glossinidae) and other Diptera to carbon dioxide, acetone and other chemicals. *Bull. Ent. Res.* **70**: 563–570.

WALDBAUER, G. P. (1968). The consumption and utilisation of food by insects. *Adv. Insect Physiol.* **5**: 229–288.

WEIR, J. S. (1959). The influence of worker age on trophogenic larval dormancy in the ant *Myrmica*. *Insectes soc.* **6**: 271–290.

WEITZ, B. (1964). Feeding habits of tsetse flies. *Endeavour* **23**: 38–42.

WHEELER, W. M. (1922). *Social life among the insects*. Constable, London.

WHEELER, W. M. (1926). *Ants. Their structure, development and behaviour*. Columbia University Press, New York.

WILCZEK, M. (1967). The distribution and neuroanatomy of the labellar sense organs of the blowfly *Phormia regina* Meigen. *J. Morph.* **122**: 175–201.

WOOD, D. L. (1973). Selection and colonization of ponderosa pine by bark beetles. *Symp. R. ent. Soc. Lond.* **6**: 101–117.

CHAPTER III

THE ALIMENTARY CANAL

The alimentary canal comprises three regions, foregut, midgut and hindgut, various parts of which may become modified anatomically or physiologically to perform various functions. The foregut is commonly concerned with the storage of food and sometimes helps to fragment the food before it passes to the midgut. The latter, which in most insects is lined by a delicate membrane, is primarily concerned with the production of enzymes and the absorption of the products of digestion. In some fluid-feeding insects it is specialised, together with other parts of the gut, to facilitate the rapid elimination of water from the body. The hindgut conducts undigested food to the exterior via the anus, but also has other functions. In particular the rectum is involved in salt and water regulation.

The gut is innervated by motor nerves from the stomatogastric and central nervous systems which control the movements of the gut and the passage of food along it.

Various glands, associated with the mouthparts, function mainly in the production of saliva, but have other important roles as in the production of pheromones in social insects and silk in Lepidoptera.

A general account of the structure of the alimentary canal is given by Snodgrass (1935) and details of the fine structure of the cells are given by Smith (1968) and Berridge (1970). Richards and Richards (1977) review the structure and functions of peritrophic membranes. The evolution of the alimentary canal in bugs is reviewed by Goodchild (1966), and Miles (1972) surveys the structure of salivary glands and the functions of saliva in the Hemiptera.

3.1 General structure

The alimentary canal in insects is divided into three main regions: the foregut or stomodaeum, which is ectodermal in origin; the midgut or mesenteron, which is endodermal, and the hindgut or proctodaeum, which is again ectodermal. In many insects these regions are subdivided into various functional parts, of which the most usual are the pharynx, oesophagus, crop and proventriculus in the foregut, the caeca and ventriculus in the midgut, and pylorus, ileum and rectum in the hindgut (Fig. 32). The gut is supported in the body by muscles anteriorly and posteriorly, but elsewhere only by connective tissue and especially by tracheae which, in insects, form an important element of the connective tissue.

Usually the gut is a continuous tube running from the mouth to the anus, but in some insects which feed on a fluid diet containing little or no solid waste material the connection between the midgut and the hindgut is occluded. This is the case in some

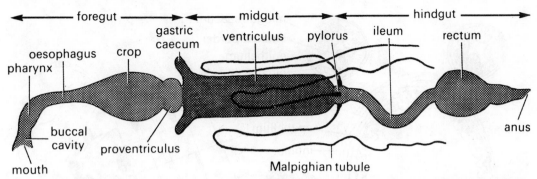

Fig. 32 Diagram showing the usual subdivisions and appendages of the alimentary canal
(after Snodgrass, 1935)

plant-sucking Heteroptera (Goodchild, 1963) and in larval Neuroptera which digest
their prey extra-orally. A similar modification occurs in the larvae of social
Hymenoptera with the result that the larvae never foul the nest; in this case a pellet of
faecal matter is deposited at the larva–pupa moult.

The length of the gut is roughly correlated with diet: insects feeding on a largely
protein diet tend to have a shorter gut than those feeding largely on carbohydrates, but
this is not always true.

3.2 Foregut

Since the foregut is ectodermal in origin it is lined with a layer of cuticle, known as the
intima, which is shed at each moult in the same way as the rest of the cuticle. The
foregut epithelium consists of flattened cells, and outside it is a layer of longitudinal
muscle and a layer of circular muscle, the latter often being relatively well developed
(Fig. 33). The circular muscles are not inserted into the epithelium but are continuous
all round the gut, so that their contraction leads to the development of even longitudinal
folding (Fig. 33). When the gut is distended with food these folds are flattened out. In
addition, especially in the proventriculus, there may be six or eight permanent
infoldings of the wall. The longitudinal muscles may be inserted into the circular
muscles or into the epithelium. Outside the muscle layers is a delicate connective tissue
sheath.

3.2.1 Pharynx

The pharynx is the first part of the foregut following on from the buccal cavity. Apart
from the typical foregut musculature the pharynx has a series of dilator muscles
inserted into it. These arise ventrally on the tentorium and dorsally on the frons and are
best developed in sucking insects, especially Lepidoptera and Hymenoptera, where the
pharyngeal pump is used to draw up fluids. They are also present in biting and chewing
insects and play a part in passing food back from the mouth to the oesophagus.

3.2.2 Oesophagus

The oesophagus is an undifferentiated part of the foregut serving to pass food back
from the pharynx to the crop.

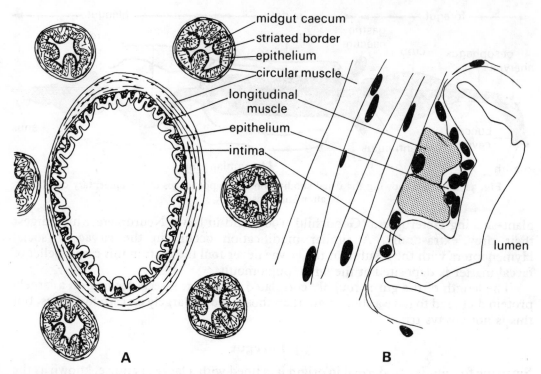

Fig. 33 A. Transverse section of foregut and midgut caeca of *Chorthippus*. B. Section of the foregut more highly magnified

3.2.3 Crop

The crop is an enlargement of the foregut in which food is stored. Usually it represents the posterior part of the oesophagus, but in some fluid feeders it is a lateral diverticulum. Frequently the crop is folded longitudinally and transversely when empty becoming distended when the insect feeds, but in *Periplaneta* the crop undergoes very little change in volume since when it does not contain food it is filled with air (Davey and Treherne, 1963).

In general, secretion and absorption do not occur in the crop, being limited by the impermeable intima. Digestion can occur, however, as a result of salivary enzymes passing back to the crop with the food and midgut enzymes being regurgitated from the midgut. Although the proventriculus acts as a valve limiting the backward movement of food, it does not prevent the regurgitation of fluids.

3.2.4 Proventriculus

The proventriculus is variously modified in different insects. In fluid feeders it is absent except for a simple valve at the origin of the midgut. A valve is also present in many other insects (Figs. 34, 35) and often the circular muscles form a sphincter at the entrance to the midgut.

In the cockroach and cricket the intima in the proventriculus is developed into six strong plates or teeth, which serve to break up the food (Fig. 34). The proventriculus as a whole controls the passage of food from the crop to the midgut (p. 59). In Acridoidea there are six longitudinal folds with small cuticular teeth, and here the proventriculus serves simply as a valve, retaining food in the crop while permitting the forward passage of enzymes.

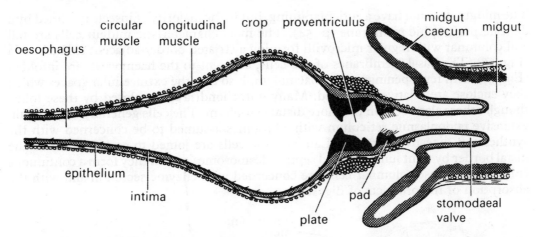

Fig. 34 Longitudinal section of the foregut of *Periplaneta* (after Snodgrass, 1935)

The proventriculus of the bee is very specialised (Fig. 35). An anterior invagination into the crop ends in four mobile lips each armed with a number of spines. Again the proventriculus controls the movement of food from the crop to the midgut, but it is also able to remove pollen from a suspension in nectar in the crop while nectar is retained. Writhing movements of the crop keep the pollen dispersed while the lips of the proventriculus make snapping movements in such a way that the spines strain off the

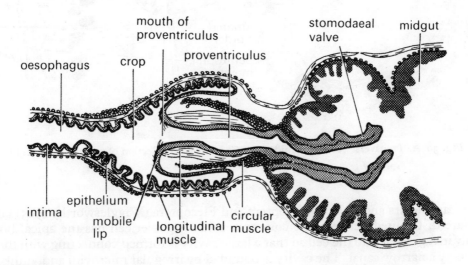

Fig. 35 Longitudinal section of the proventriculus of *Apis* (after Snodgrass, 1956)

grains of pollen and retain them. In this way a bolus of pollen is formed and then passed back through the proventriculus to the midgut. Nectar is retained in the crop for regurgitation and processing to form honey (p. 41).

3.3 Midgut

The midgut does not have a cuticular lining, but in the majority of insects it is lined by a delicate peritrophic membrane (p. 54). The most characteristic midgut cells are tall and columnar with regular microvilli forming a striated border adjacent to the lumen (Fig. 36). The basal membranes of the cells, adjacent to the haemocoel, are infolded (Fig. 37) with few openings to the haemolymph so that the extracellular spaces which they enclose are relatively isolated. Many mitochondria are enclosed by these folds, though others also occur in the more distal cytoplasm. The cells generally also contain extensive endoplasmic reticulum with ribosomes assumed to be concerned with the synthesis of digestive enzymes. Laterally the cells are joined to each other near the distal border by tight junctions and septate desmosomes so that they form a continuous epithelium. These columnar cells are concerned with enzyme secretion and with the absorption of the products of digestion.

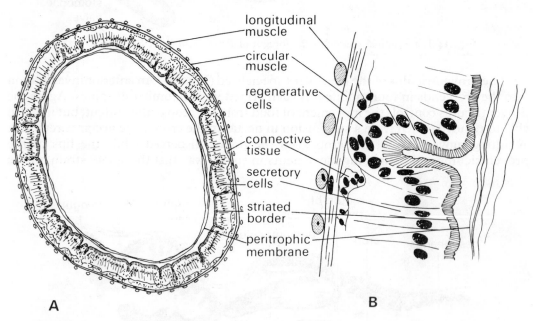

longitudinal muscle
circular muscle
regenerative cells
connective tissue
secretory cells
striated border
peritrophic membrane

A

B

Fig. 36 A. Transverse section of midgut of *Chorthippus*. B. Section of midgut more highly magnified

In caterpillars and in Ephemeroptera and Plecoptera (Wigglesworth, 1965) goblet cells are distributed between the columnar cells. A goblet cell has the apical border deeply invaginated into the cell so that a large cavity is formed connecting with the gut lumen by a narrow canal. The cavity is bounded by irregular microvilli and, unlike the microvilli of the columnar cells, these often contain elongate mitochondria. It is

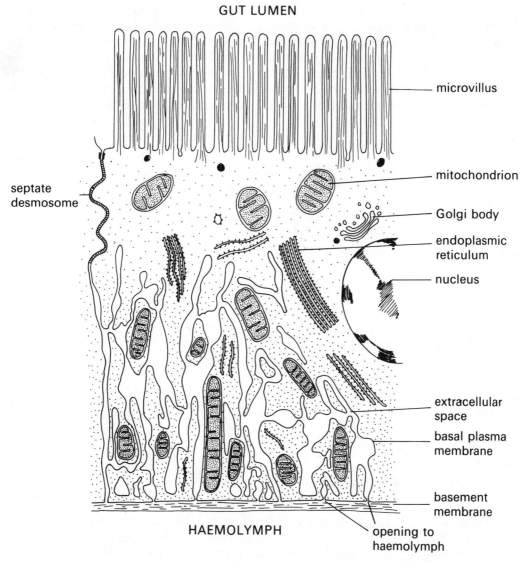

Fig. 37 Diagrammatic representation of the structure of a midgut cell (after Berridge, 1970)

possible that these cells are important in pumping excess potassium, derived from the food, out of the haemolymph (Smith, 1968; Wood *et al.*, 1969). They may also be concerned with deposit excretion. In *Tineola* (Lepidoptera) metals and dyes accumulate in the goblet cavity and in the cytoplasm of the cell. These substances are discharged at the following moult when the whole of the epithelium is renewed.

Midgut cells also play some part in excretion in *Rhodnius*. Here haemoglobin is broken down in the cells to haematin, a verdohaem pigment and biliverdin. The latter is accumulated and then discharged into the lumen of the gut for disposal.

When cells of the midgut break down, new ones are formed by the division and differentiation of regenerative cells (Fig. 36). These are small cells lying at the base of the epithelium either scattered or in groups (nidi) as in Orthoptera. Sometimes they occur at the bottom of folds or crypts in the epithelium and in many Coleoptera these crypts are visible as small papillae on the outside of the midgut (Fig. 38).

The muscle layers outside the epithelium are usually poorly developed, but the circular muscles lie adjacent to the epithelium, the reverse of the position in the foregut. The muscle layers are bounded by a delicate connective tissue sheath.

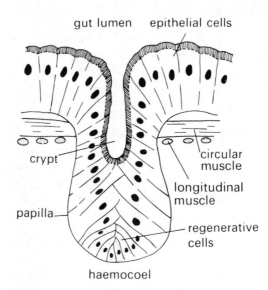

Fig. 38 Diagram of a midgut crypt extending through the muscle layer to form a papilla (after Snodgrass, 1935)

3.3.1 Anatomical differentiation

Anatomically the midgut is usually a simple tube, undifferentiated except for the presence of four, six or eight caeca at the anterior end. In some Diptera, however, the midgut is differentiated into an anterior cardiac chamber (Snodgrass, 1935; but called the proventriculus by other authors) and a long ventriculus, and in Heteroptera there are four regions, the last giving rise to numerous caeca which house bacteria.

The Homoptera and some Heteroptera feed on plant fluids. In order to obtain adequate nourishment large quantities of fluid must be ingested and modifications of the gut occur which provide for the rapid elimination of the excess water taken in. This is necessary in order to avoid excessive dilution of the haemolymph and to concentrate the food so as to facilitate enzyme activity. This problem is less acute in other fluid feeders because their needs are smaller. Those Lepidoptera, Hymenoptera and Diptera which feed on nectar as adults only need it for maintenance; growth is complete and the larval reserves often suffice for egg development so that only small amounts of fluid are taken in. This fluid is stored in the crop, which is lined by an impermeable cuticle and from which small quantities are passed back to the midgut as they are required. In this way over-dilution of the haemolymph resulting from the absorption of too much fluid is avoided. The volumes ingested by bugs are too large for this and the insects have no crop, but they do have a large rectum to which water is passed as quickly as possible.

The problem of excessive intake of water is most acute in the Cicadoidea feeding from the xylem of plants, since xylem contains small amounts of amino acids and relatively high concentrations of inorganic salts. Phloem contains higher concentrations of sugars and amino acids, so smaller amounts of fluid will supply adequate nutrients. Hence it is in the Cicadoidea that the most extensive elaboration of the midgut has developed ensuring the rapid elimination of excess water (Marshall and Cheung, 1974). The anterior midgut forms a thin-walled bladder which wraps round the posterior midgut and the proximal ends of the Malpighian tubules. The chamber formed within the folds of the anterior midgut is called the filter chamber. It is suggested that the Malpighian tubules produce a hypertonic fluid which is rich in potassium. This establishes an osmotic gradient from anterior midgut to filter chamber and then to the Malpighian tubules, so that water passes almost directly to the hindgut and absorption of nutrients takes place in the more central regions of the midgut (Fig. 39).

Fulgoroidea have the midgut enclosed in a sheath with oenocytes inside it and it is suggested that the sheath cells play an active role in limiting dilution of the haemolymph. An anterior, air-filled diverticulum of the midgut is not enclosed by the sheath and this may allow for the swallowing of air needed for expansion at each moult without damaging the sheath.

In plant-sucking Pentatomomorpha the midgut is divided into four regions, as in other Heteroptera. It is believed that the caeca of the fourth region actively remove water from the haemolymph so that excessive dilution does not occur, and between the third and fourth regions there is a constriction or a complete discontinuity which ensures the backward flow of this water to the rectum (Goodchild, 1963). Finally, in some bryocorine Miridae the anterior midgut makes contact with a large accessory salivary gland. After feeding a clear fluid is exuded from the mouthparts suggesting that water is withdrawn from the midgut to the salivary glands and then eliminated via the mouthparts.

The problem in blood-sucking insects is different. It is common for a large amount of blood to be ingested at one meal, but, since feeding is discontinuous and the bulk of the nutriment is in the blood corpuscles rather than in solution in the serum, the fluid contents can be eliminated with little loss of nutriment. In *Glossina*, for instance, water is removed from the blood in the anterior half of the midgut and very quickly eliminated via the Malpighian tubules so that a very clear urine may be passed while the insect is still feeding (see also p. 585).

3.3.2 Functional differentiation

Even if there is no anatomical differentiation of the midgut there may be functional differentiation. For instance, in nematoceran larvae absorption of different substances apparently occurs in different parts (Wigglesworth, 1942) (see p. 81) and this is also the case in the blowfly larva, where on histochemical grounds the midgut is divided into three regions and the middle part is further differentiated into five zones (Waterhouse, 1957). Similar differentiation occurs in larval Lepidoptera.

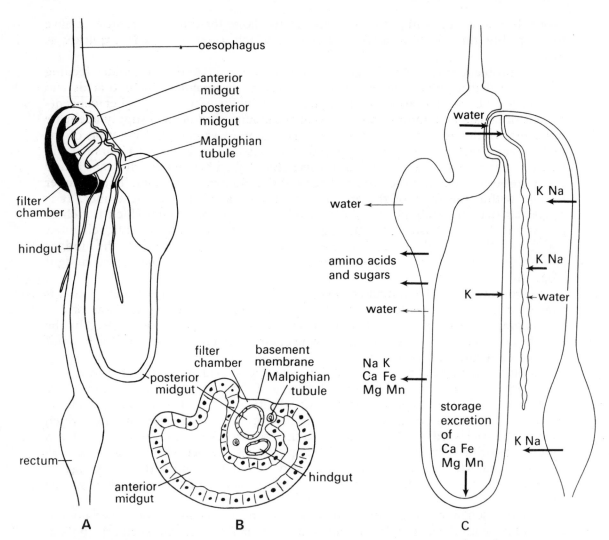

Fig. 39 Diagrams of the gut of a cercopid. A. General arrangement showing the filter chamber. B. Transverse section of the filter chamber. C. Postulated movements of water and solutes across the wall of the gut (after Snodgrass, 1935; Imms, 1957; Cheung and Marshall, 1973)

3.3.3 Peritrophic membrane

The peritrophic membrane forms a delicate lining layer to the midgut and is found in most insects, whether they eat solid food or feed only on fluids. It is apparently not present in many insects feeding on plant juices, notably the Homoptera and Heteroptera, while in Diptera it is only formed as a result of gut distension, usually following feeding. The membrane nearly always contains chitin and protein (Richards and Richards, 1977).

Two types of peritrophic membrane are recognised according to their modes of formation. In Diptera and some other orders, the membrane is secreted as a viscous fluid, commonly at the anterior end of the midgut. This fluid is forced through a mould or press formed by the stomodaeal invagination and the wall of the midgut so that it forms a tube which becomes the membrane. In *Anopheles* (Diptera) larvae the secretion differentiates to form fibrous layers after secretion. The first fibrous mat forms at the tips of the microvilli and then two more differentiate outside this. To form a satisfactory mould the cells of the invagination are large and turgid so that they press against the midgut wall (Fig. 40). They can be pulled away by longitudinal muscles, and spines at the tip of the invagination help to draw out the membrane during this movement. This type of membrane is formed continuously at a rate, in *Eristalis* (Diptera) larvae, of about 6 mm/h.

The second type of membrane is formed by delamination from the whole surface of the midgut. This type occurs in Orthoptera, Odonata, Coleoptera and Hymenoptera

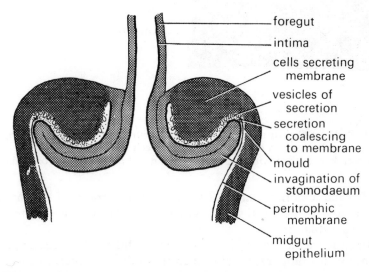

foregut
intima
cells secreting
 membrane
vesicles of
 secretion
secretion
 coalescing
 to membrane
mould
invagination of
 stomodaeum
peritrophic
 membrane
midgut
 epithelium

Fig. 40 Diagram of the junction of foregut and midgut in a dipteran showing the origin of the peritrophic membrane and the mould formed by the stomodaeal invagination and the midgut wall (modified from Wigglesworth, 1965)

and because of the mode of formation there are often several membranes lying one inside the other. In *Periplaneta* the membrane consists of a regular fibrillar network, usually with three systems of fibrils at 60° or 90° to each other, overlaid by, and sometimes continuous with, a less regular network. The pores in the network are up to 0·2 μm across and a thin, structureless film is stretched across them (Fig. 41A) (Mercer and Day, 1952). The fibrils forming the network are approximately 10nm in diameter and each strand of the net is made up of about four such fibrils.

It is possible that the microvilli of the midgut cells form a template on which the fibrils are laid down (Fig. 41B) so that a network is formed (Mercer and Day, 1952). The less regular networks could arise from fibrils laid down more distally on the microvilli and the amorphous matrix from the secretion of a second substance alternating with the secretion of fibrillar material. A period of secretion might be followed by a period in which material was elaborated, but not secreted, and in this way separate membranes would be formed. Wasp larvae form six such membranes in a day

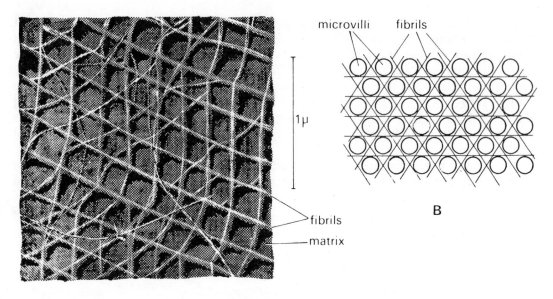

A

Fig. 41 A. Part of a fibrillar membrane from the peritrophic membrane of *Periplaneta*. B. Diagram of a surface section of a midgut epithelial cell showing the microvilli (in section) forming a template for the fibrils of the peritrophic membrane (after Mercer and Day, 1952)

and starved *Aeschna* (Odonata) larvae, two. In Dermaptera and Lepidoptera this mode of formation seems to occur together with that observed in Diptera so that the membranes have a dual origin.

The peritrophic membrane of insects eating solid food protects the midgut cells from abrasion, but it is apparently absent from adult Mecoptera, which also eat solid food, and is commonly present in fluid-feeders, where the problem of abrasion does not arise. Absorption may be facilitated if the products of digestion pass into the relatively static fluid outside the membrane from the faster moving liquid within the lumen. In the blowfly larva food passes through the gut, within the membrane, at the rate of about 50 mm/h, but the peritrophic membrane is only produced at about 5 mm/h so that the fluid between it and the epithelium is relatively still.

The membrane probably acts as a barrier to micro-organisms thus reducing infection of the tissues.

3.4 Hindgut

The hindgut is lined by a layer of cuticle which is thinner and more permeable than that of the foregut. The epithelium generally is thin, but the cells are more cuboid than in the foregut (Fig. 42) while those of the rectal pads are tall with a clear cytoplasm (Fig. 43). Except round the rectum the musculature is poorly developed, but where it is present the longitudinal muscles are usually external to the circular. Along the rectum the longitudinal muscles are often collected into strands opposite the gaps between adjacent rectal pads (Fig. 43).

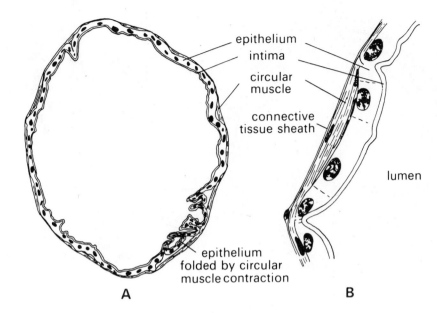

epithelium
intima
circular
muscle
connective
tissue sheath
lumen
epithelium
folded by circular
muscle contraction
A
B

Fig. 42 A. Transverse section of the ileum of *Chorthippus*. B. Section of ileum more highly magnified

3.4.1 Pylorus

The pylorus is the first part of the hindgut and from it the Malpighian tubules often arise. In some insects it forms a valve between the midgut and hindgut.

3.4.2 Ileum

In most insects the ileum is an undifferentiated tube running back to the rectum, but in some termites it forms a pouch in which the flagellates concerned with cellulose digestion live, and in larval Scarabaeoidea there is a comparable fermentation chamber in which the intima is produced into spines (see p. 71). In Heteroptera it is suggested that the ileum is concerned with the removal of water from the haemolymph (Goodchild, 1963) and in blowfly larvae certain cells are concerned in the excretion of ammonia (Waterhouse, 1957). The hormone proctodone is secreted by the cells of the ileum of *Ostrinia*.

3.4.3 Rectum

The rectum is often an enlarged sac and is thin walled except for certain regions, the rectal pads, which have a columnar epithelium. There are usually six rectal pads and they may extend longitudinally along the rectum or they may be papilliform as in Diptera. The cells of the rectal papillae of *Calliphora* (Diptera) enclose extensive intercellular sinuses which are separated from the gut lumen (Fig. 44) by cell junctions and which connect only indirectly with the haemocoel. The cell membranes bounding these spaces form a series of flattened sacs which are closely associated with

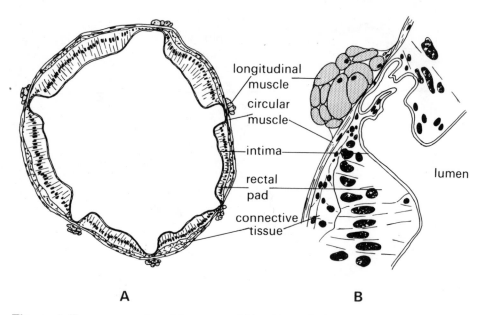

A   B

Fig. 43 A. Transverse section of the rectum of *Chorthippus*. B. Section of rectum more highly magnified

mitochondria. ATPase is localised in the infoldings which are a site of active ion transport. The apical membrane, beneath the cuticle lining the rectum, is infolded in a series of parallel leaflets. In Odonata and Orthoptera each pad consists of a single layer of cells (Fig. 43 B), but in Neuroptera, Lepidoptera and Hymenoptera there are two layers. The pads have a good tracheal supply indicating a high level of metabolism.

The rectum, and in particular the rectal pads, are important in the reabsorption of water, salts and amino acids from the urine (Ramsay, 1958). In addition in some aquatic insects, such as larval Anisoptera and Helodidae, there are tracheal gills in the rectum. In larval Anisoptera water is pumped in and out of the rectum so that the water round the gills is constantly renewed and by the forcible ejection of water the insect is able to propel itself forwards rapidly.

3.5 Innervation of the gut

The foregut is innervated from the frontal and ingluvial ganglia, from the intervening recurrent and oesophageal nerves and from the ingluvial nerve. Branches of these nerves also extend to the midgut. In *Schistocerca* the ingluvial ganglion is autonomous and exerts a major influence on movements of the proventriculus. The hindgut receives nerves from the last abdominal ganglion and in *Apis* the nerves extend to the midgut. The nerves of this system are associated with stretch receptors or run directly to the muscles of the gut, so that they are concerned in the control of gut movements. There is no evidence of chemoreceptors within the gut of insects.

3.6 Passage of food through the gut

Food is pushed back from the pharynx by the pharyngeal pump, aided by the cibarial pump when this is present, and subsequently passed along the gut by peristaltic

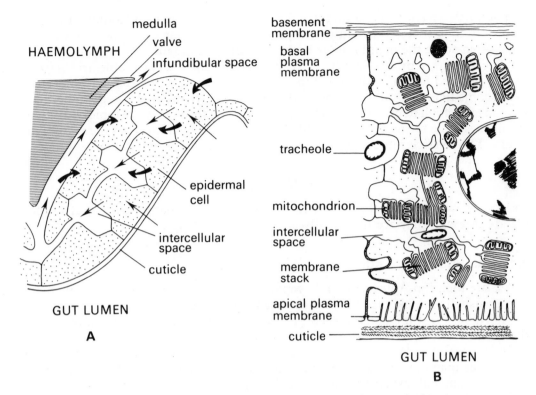

Fig. 44 Diagram of the organisation of the rectal papilla of *Calliphora*. A. Section through part of a papilla showing the direction of movement of water (thin arrows) and solutes (thick arrows). B. The structure of a single epidermal cell in a papilla (after Berridge, 1970)

movements. The movement of food from the crop to the midgut is controlled by the proventriculus and its associated sphincter. In *Periplaneta* the rate of emptying of the crop is inversely proportional to the concentration of food in it so that food in high concentration is passed back to the midgut very slowly. With dilute solutions the proventriculus opens more frequently and probably also wider and for a longer time than with concentrated solutions. When *Locusta* feeds after an interval of several hours without food, the food remains in the foregut while the insect is feeding. The contractions of the foregut which subsequently pass food back to the midgut are probably enhanced by a hormone from the corpora cardiaca which is released when the foregut becomes distended (Bernays and Chapman, 1974).

In the midgut the passage of food is aided by the peritrophic membrane which, as it moves down the gut, will carry the enclosed food with it. In some Diptera a rectal valve possesses spines which help to draw the peritrophic membrane backwards.

The movements of the hindgut are primarily concerned with the elimination of undigested material. In *Schistocerca* the ileum is usually thrown into an S-bend and at the point of inflexion the muscles constrict the gut contents causing the peritrophic membrane to bend and break. The separated posterior part of the membrane encloses a pellet of faecal material. When the insect is about to defaecate it elongates its abdomen, thereby straightening out the S-bend, and at the same time contractions of the posterior part of the ileum and the rectum force the pellet out of the anus (Goodhue, 1963). The faeces are thus enclosed in old peritrophic membrane, but this is not the case in all insects—in some the membrane is broken up in the hindgut.

The time taken by food in its passage through the gut is very variable. In *Periplaneta* food is retained longer in the gut if the insect is active or if it is starved—in a starved insect some food can still be found in the crop after two months. On the other hand a large meal or high temperature result in food passing through more rapidly. With food readily available the midgut can be filled in an hour and food reaches the rectum in six hours. The relative times vary very much from one insect to another.

3.7 Head glands

Associated with the mouthparts are the mandibular, maxillary, pharyngeal and labial glands although they are not usually all present together.

3.7.1 Mandibular glands

These are found in Apterygota, Dictyoptera, Isoptera, Coleoptera and Hymenoptera and are usually sac-like structures in the head opening near the bases of the mandibles. In *Apis* (Fig. 571) the glands are larger in the queen than in the worker and very small in the drone. In the queen they produce the pheromones concerned with colony control while in workers and in various species of ant they produce alarm pheromones (Wilson, 1971). The mandibular glands are particularly large in larval Lepidoptera where they are the functional salivary glands, but they are absent from adult Lepidoptera. In *Sphodromantis* (Dictyoptera) the glands produce an amylase (Mkhize and Kumar, 1972).

3.7.2 Maxillary glands

Maxillary glands are found in Protura, Collembola, Heteroptera and some larval Neuroptera and Hymenoptera. They are usually small, opening near the bases of the maxillae, and may be concerned with the lubrication of the mouthparts. In carnivorous Heteroptera they may play a part in producing the toxin which kills the prey (p. 34) (Edwards, 1963).

3.7.3 Pharyngeal glands

Pharyngeal glands (hypopharyngeal glands of Snodgrass, 1956) occur in Hymenoptera and are particularly well developed in worker honeybees. They are vestigial in the queen bee and absent from the male. There is one gland on each side of the head, each consisting of a long coiled tube to which large numbers of solid lobules are attached. The glands open at the base of the hypopharynx by separate ducts (Snodgrass, 1956). They produce brood food, with which young larvae are fed and which probably plays some part in caste determination (p. 42). It also provides a major part of the diet of laying queens and possibly also of drones (Ribbands, 1953). In addition the glands produce an invertase.

The pharyngeal glands of worker honeybees undergo changes in development which are associated with changes in the bees' behaviour. The newly emerged worker has poorly developed pharyngeal glands, but after feeding on pollen the glands become bigger and by the fifth day of adult life they start to produce brood food. At this time the worker acts as a nurse bee, feeding the young larvae. Subsequently, corresponding with the tendencies of older bees to leave the hive and forage for nectar and pollen, the pharyngeal glands retrogress. The secretion of invertase at first increases and then decreases in a way comparable with the secretion of brood food.

3.7.4 Labial glands

These glands are found in the majority of insects, although they are absent from some Coleoptera. They are large and extend back into the thorax. In most insects the labial glands are acinous glands (Fig. 45), but in Diptera, Lepidoptera and fleas they are tubular with the ducts swelling gradually to form the terminal glandular parts.

In larval Diptera the cells are enormous and contain polytene chromosomes as in *Drosophila*. Part of the gland may be differentiated to form a salivary reservoir, while in Heteroptera the gland consists of a number of separate lobes (Fig. 46).

In acinous glands there are two main types of cell. Large cells, called the central or zymogen cells, contain considerable amounts of rough endoplasmic reticulum. These cells are probably responsible for the production of salivary enzymes. In *Schistocerca* they may also secrete a mucoprotein or mucopolysaccharide, while in *Nauphoeta* (Dictyoptera) this function is carried out by separate cells, the secretory duct cells. Towards the outside of the acinus are the parietal cells (Fig. 45). Their function is unknown, but they may be concerned with the transfer of material from the haemolymph to the central cells for synthesis (Kendall, 1969). The cells forming the salivary duct possess microvilli along the border lining the duct lumen and their basal membranes are thrown into deep folds in close association with mitochondria. By analogy with similar cells in Diptera, these cells are presumed to resorb water and salts from the saliva. The production of saliva from acinous glands is under nervous control (House and Smith, 1980; Whitehead, 1973).

Cells with distinct secreting and reabsorptive functions are also present in tubular glands, but they form a continuous series and are differentiated on the basis of their fine structure (Ågren, 1975). These glands have no nerve supply and their secretory activity seems to be under hormonal control (Berridge and Prince, 1972).

Anteriorly the glands open into a narrow duct on each side and these join to a single median duct opening into the salivarium (Fig. 3). In fluid-feeding insects the salivarium is modified to form a pump. This has a rigid lower wall and a flexible upper one which can be drawn upwards by dilator muscles causing fluid to be sucked into the lumen; when the muscles relax, the upper wall springs down by virtue of its elasticity and forces saliva out. In some insects, at least, there are valves which ensure the forward flow of saliva.

3.7.5 Functions of the labial glands

In most insects the labial glands are the functional salivary glands. The saliva serves to lubricate the mouthparts, more is produced if the food is dry, and it also contains enzymes which start digestion of the food. The presence of particular enzymes is

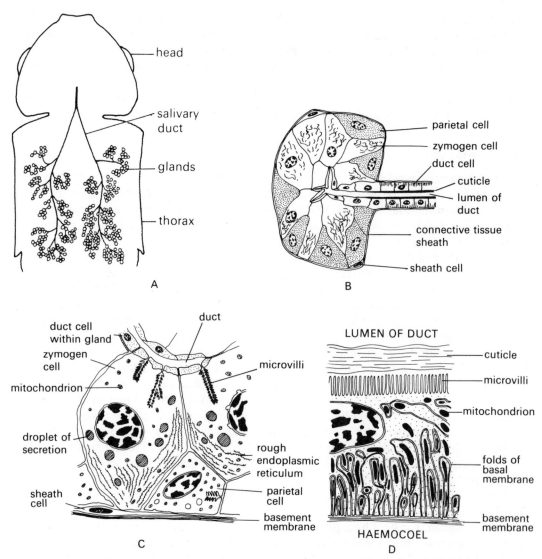

Fig. 45 Salivary glands of a locust. A. General arrangement. B. Section through an acinus. C. Structure of parietal and zymogen cells. D. Structure of a duct cell (after Albrecht, 1956; Kendall, 1969)

related to diet, but an amylase, converting starch to sugar, and an invertase, converting sucrose to glucose and fructose, are commonly present. Sometimes proteases and lipases are also present and in insects which digest their prey extra-intestinally these may be particularly important (p. 67). The saliva of some blood-sucking insects also contains an anticoagulant and if the salivary glands of *Glossina* are removed the blood eventually clots in the mouthparts. Not all blood-sucking insects have an anticoagulant (p. 35).

In larval Lepidoptera and Trichoptera the labial glands produce silk, which is used in the construction of larval shelters and the cocoon. The silk glands are cylindrical and the cells are characterised by the possession of large, branched nuclei. Silk consists of an inner tough protein, fibroin, enclosed by a water-soluble gelatinous protein, sericin. In *Bombyx* the fibrinogen, which on extrusion is denatured to fibroin, is secreted in the posterior part of the gland, while sericin is secreted in the middle regions. The ducts from these glands in Lepidoptera are joined by the duct from another small gland, Lyonnet's gland, which possibly lubricates the tube through which the silk passes. Finally, the silk is moulded to a thread as it passes through the silk press, which resembles a typical salivary pump.

Male scorpion flies, *Panorpa* (Mecoptera), have enlarged salivary glands and produce large quantities of saliva which are eaten by the female during copulation.

Plant-sucking Heteroptera and Homoptera produce two types of saliva, a viscous substance which hardens to form the sheath and a more fluid substance (Miles, 1972). In *Oncopeltus* (Heteroptera) the sheath material is produced in response to resistance encountered by the stylets during penetration of the leaf. If the leaf is tough the sheath is short and thick, but if the leaf is more easily penetrated the sheath is longer and thinner. It is secreted by the anterior and lateral lobes of the salivary glands (Fig. 46) and an oxidising substance comes from the accessory gland (Miles, 1960). The lipoprotein forming the sheath is exuded as the stylets are temporarily withdrawn during penetration and it gels in contact with air due to the formation of hydrogen bonds and disulphide bonds. Bonding does not occur within the salivary gland because of the reducing conditions and dielectric effects produced by companion materials. At the same time as these bonds are formed it is possible that a phenolase oxidises some substance such as DOPA, which is known to be present, to quinones and further bonding between the quinones produces the compact gelling of the sheath (Miles, 1964). As the stylets are pushed down again they punch a hole in the lump of sheath material, moulding it to their form, and by a repetition of this process as the stylets penetrate the leaf an elongate sheath is produced.

The function of the sheath is not clear, but the fact that it is open at the inner end suggests that it is not acting as a filter. It may serve to prevent loss of plant sap and loss of the more fluid saliva through the wound in the epidermis (Miles, 1959).

The more fluid saliva is produced in the posterior lobe of the glands and some of the mucoids it contains come from the accessory gland. In *Oncopeltus* it is secreted on to the

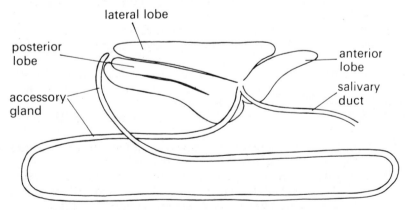

Fig. 46 Salivary gland of *Oncopeltus* (after Miles, 1960)

surface of a leaf before penetration starts and is then sucked back in by the bug. This presumably stimulates gustatory sense organs and is concerned with the selection of a feeding site. More saliva is secreted during feeding, but only if the food is not fluid, since the passage of fluid up the stylets inhibits the production of saliva. In more solid food the saliva digests starch and leaches the medium in which the bug is feeding.

In the aphid *Myzus*, which feeds from phloem, saliva is secreted during penetration of the stylets, but not while it is feeding, whereas in *Adelys*, feeding in parenchyma, salivary production is continuous. The saliva contains a pectinase which aids penetration by breaking down the middle lamellae of the plant cells, and in addition there are a number of amino acids and amides. *Aphis pomae* secretes relatively large amounts of alanine and glutamic acid, some aspartic acid, valine and serine and traces of leucine and histidine. It is suggested that these substances are unutilised dietary products from the haemolymph which are excreted in this way and which might be the cause of the injuries which aphid saliva causes to the plant (Auclair, 1963).

No sheath is produced by aquatic Heteroptera or Cimicomorpha in which the salivary glands produce a toxin killing and partially digesting the prey (p. 34).

In social insects the larval saliva is of great importance in trophallaxis (p. 43).

The labial glands of Collembola may have an excretory function.

REFERENCES

ÅGREN, L. (1975). Fine structure of the thoracic salivary gland of the male *Bombus lapidarius* L. (Hymenoptera, Apidae). *Zoon* **3**: 19–31.

ALBRECHT, F. O. (1956). The anatomy of the red locust, *Nomadacris septemfasciata* Serville. *Anti-Locust Bull.* no. 23, 9 pp. + figs.

AUCLAIR, J. L. (1963). Aphid feeding and nutrition. *A. Rev. Ent.* **8**: 439–490.

BERNAYS, E. A. and CHAPMAN, R. F. (1974). The regulation of food intake by acridids. *in* Barton Browne, L. (ed.), *Experimental analysis of insect behaviour*. Springer-Verlag, Berlin.

BERRIDGE, M. J. (1970). A structural analysis of insect absorption. *Symp. R. ent. Soc. Lond.* **5**: 135–151.

BERRIDGE, M. J. and PRINCE, W. T. (1972). The role of cyclic AMP and calcium in hormone action. *Adv. Insect Physiol.* **9**: 1–49.

CHEUNG, W. W. K. and MARSHALL, A. T. (1973). Studies on water and ion transport in homopteran insects: ultrastructure and cytochemistry of the cicadoid and cercopoid midgut. *Tissue & Cell* **5**: 651–669.

DAVEY, K. G. and TREHERNE, J. E. (1963). Studies on crop function in the cockroach (*Periplaneta americana* L.) I. The mechanism of crop-emptying. *J. exp. Biol.* **40**: 763–773.

EDWARDS, J. S. (1963). Arthropods as predators. *Viewpoints in Biology* **2**: 85–114.

GOODCHILD, A. J. P. (1963). Studies on the functional anatomy of the intestines of Heteroptera. *Proc. zool. Soc. Lond.* **141**: 851–910.

GOODCHILD, A. J. P. (1966). Evolution of the alimentary canal in the Hemiptera. *Biol. Rev.* **41**: 97–140.

GOODHUE, D. (1963). Some differences in the passage of food through the intestines of the desert and migratory locusts. *Nature, Lond.* **200**: 288–289.

HOUSE, C. R. and SMITH, R. K. (1980). Receptors mediating fluid secretion from the cockroach salivary gland. *in* Sattelle, D. B., Hall, L. M. and Hildebrand, J. G. (eds.), *Receptors for neurotransmitters, hormones and pheromones in insects*. Elsevier/North Holland Biomedical Press, Amsterdam.

IMMS, A. D. (1957). *A general textbook of entomology*. 9th edition, revised by Richards and Davies. Methuen, London.

KENDALL, M. D. (1969). The fine structure of the salivary glands of the desert locust *Schistocerca gregaria* Forskål. *Z. Zellforsch.* **98**: 399–420.

MARSHALL, A. T. and CHEUNG, W. W. K. (1974). Studies on water and ion transport in homopteran insects: ultrastructure and cytochemistry of the cicadoid and cercopoid Malpighian tubules and filter chamber. *Tissue & Cell* **6**: 153–171.

MERCER, E. H. and DAY, M. F. (1952). The fine structure of the peritrophic membranes of certain insects. *Biol. Bull. mar. biol. Lab., Woods Hole* **103**: 384–394.

MILES, P. W. (1959). The salivary secretions of a plant-sucking bug, *Oncopeltus fasciatus* (Dall.) (Heteroptera: Lygaeidae).—I. The types of secretion and their roles during feeding. *J. Insect Physiol.* **3**: 243–255.

MILES, P. W. (1960). The salivary secretions of a plant-sucking bug, *Oncopeltus fasciatus* (Dall.) (Heteroptera: Lygaeidae).—III. Origins in the salivary glands. *J. Insect Physiol.* **4**: 271–282.

MILES, P. W. (1964). Studies on the salivary physiology of plant bugs: the chemistry of formation of the sheath material. *J. Insect Physiol.* **10**: 147–160.

MILES, P. W. (1972). The saliva of Hemiptera. *Adv. Insect Physiol.* **9**: 183–255.

MKHIZE, S. B. V. and KUMAR, R. (1972). Histology and physiology of the mandibular glands in Dictyoptera. *J. Ent.* A **46**: 161–165.

RAMSAY, J. A. (1958). Excretion by the malpighian tubules of the stick insect, *Dixippus morosus* (Orthoptera, Phasmidae): amino acids, sugars and urea. *J. exp. Biol.* **35**: 871–891.

RIBBANDS, C. R. (1953). *The behaviour and social life of honeybees*. Bee research association, London.

RICHARDS, A. G. and RICHARDS, P. A. (1977). The peritrophic membranes of insects. *A. Rev. Ent.* **22**: 219–240.

SMITH, D. S. (1968). *Insect cells*. Oliver and Boyd, Edinburgh.

SNODGRASS, R. E. (1935). *Principles of insect morphology*. McGraw-Hill, New York.

SNODGRASS, R. E. (1956). *Anatomy of the honey bee*. Constable, London.

WATERHOUSE, D. F. (1957). Digestion in insects. *A. Rev. Ent.* **2**: 1–18.

WHITEHEAD, A. T. (1973). Innervation of the American cockroach salivary gland: neurophysiological and pharmacological investigations. *J. Insect Physiol.* **19**: 1961–1970.

WIGGLESWORTH, V. B. (1942). The storage of protein, fat, glycogen and uric acid in the fat body and other tissues of mosquito larvae. *J. exp. Biol.* **19**: 56–77.

WIGGLESWORTH, V. B. (1965). *The principles of insect physiology*. Methuen, London.

WILSON, E. O. (1971). *The insect societies*. Harvard University Press, Cambridge, Mass.

WOOD, J. L., FARRAND, P. S. and HARVEY, W. R. (1969). Active transport of potassium by the cecropia midgut. VI. Microelectrode potential profile. *J. exp. Biol.* **50**: 169–178.

CHAPTER IV

DIGESTION AND ABSORPTION

The alimentary canal is concerned primarily with the digestion and absorption of foodstuffs, and different parts of the gut are concerned with different aspects of these functions. In some insects, especially fluid feeders, digestion may begin before the food is ingested through the injection or regurgitation of enzymes on to the food, but in general digestion occurs largely in the midgut, where most of the enzymes are produced. These enzymes break down the complex substances in the food into more simple substances which can be absorbed and later assimilated. Most carbohydrates are degraded to monosaccharides, but in the majority of insects there is no enzyme which breaks down cellulose although this is commonly present in the diet. Some insects, notably the termites and wood-eating cockroaches, harbour micro-organisms which facilitate cellulose digestion. Proteins are broken down to polypeptides and amino acids. Fats may be absorbed unchanged, but they are often broken down to fatty acids and glycerol.

The enzymes carrying out these activities function optimally only within a limited range of pH and temperature.

Absorption in some cases is a passive process, but in others active transport occurs. Passive movement is only possible as long as the concentration in the gut exceeds that in the haemolymph, and in some cases there are special mechanisms which ensure that this is so. The absorption of water is particularly important in terrestrial insects, and the rectum plays an important part in removing water from the faeces.

The efficiency with which insects utilise their food is very variable, but most phytophagous insects digest and absorb only a relatively small proportion of the food they eat and the bulk is passed out unchanged as the faeces.

Digestion in insects generally is reviewed by Dadd (1970), Gilmour (1961), House (1974) and Wigglesworth (1965). Gooding (1975) reviews digestion in haematophagous insects and Miles (1972) considers the salivary enzymes of Hemiptera. Aspects of absorption are reviewed by Berridge (1970) and Treherne (1962, 1965, 1967).

4.1 Digestion

A large part of the food ingested by insects is macromolecular in the form of polysaccharides and proteins, and lipids are present as triglycerides, phospholipids and glycolipids. Only relatively small molecules can pass into the tissues and the larger molecules must be broken down into components of a suitable size before absorption occurs. Enzymes concerned with digestion are present in the saliva and in the secretions of the midgut. In addition, digestion may be facilitated by micro-organisms in the gut.

4.1.1 Extra-intestinal digestion

Since saliva contains enzymes, digestion often starts before the food is ingested. This is particularly true of fluid-feeding insects where enzymes are injected into the host. In many phytophagous Homoptera and Heteroptera a pectinase is injected in the fluid saliva. This enzyme causes disruption of the middle lamellae of the plant cell walls and so aids penetration of the tissues of the host-plant. An amylase is usually also present in these species. The aphids and mirids which feed from phloem apparently have no proteinases in the saliva; these are not necessary since the phloem contains a range of free amino acids, but bugs which feed from the mesophyll probably do produce salivary proteinases and lipases (Miles, 1972).

The saliva of carnivorous Heteroptera, such as *Platymerus*, contains hyaluronidase, which attacks the mucopolysaccharides of connective tissues and so acts as a spreading agent facilitating the entry of the other salivary enzymes, proteinase and phospholipase, into the host tissues. Enzymes are not present in the saliva of most haematophagous insects (Gooding, 1975). In other insects, such as Orthoptera, the salivary enzymes contribute to the early stages of digestion within the gut. An amylase is commonly present.

Extra-intestinal digestion also occurs in *Dytiscus* larvae. These have no salivary glands, so the midgut enzymes must be involved. The enzymes are injected into the prey through the mandibles, which are perforated by a narrow tube and when, in a short time, the contents of the prey have been digested the resulting fluid is withdrawn via the same route. A similar mode of feeding is employed by larval Neuroptera and Lampyridae.

Proteolytic enzymes persist in the excreta of larval blowflies and so the meat in which they live is partially liquified before it is ingested. Another instance of extra-intestinal digestion occurs in *Bombyx* where the moth on emergence secretes a protease which attacks the sericin of silk thus facilitating escape from the cocoon.

4.1.2 Internal digestion

Most digestion occurs in the midgut, in which the enzymes are secreted, but, because of the regurgitation of midgut juices, some also takes place in the crop. In Orthoptera the bulk of digestion occurs in the crop and this is reflected in the distribution of enzymes: in *Schistocerca* the greatest α-glucosidase activity occurs in the lumen of the foregut (Fig. 47), although in the tissues most activity is found in the midgut and caecal epithelia (Evans and Payne, 1964). Some α-glucosidase activity does occur in the foregut epithelium, but this is intracellular and the enzyme is probably not secreted into the lumen. Little digestion occurs in the hindgut apart from cellulose digestion in a few insects and in these micro-organisms rather than the insects' own enzymes, are responsible (p. 71).

Irrespective of whether an insect is carnivorous, herbivorous, parasitic or saprophagous, digestion of carbohydrates, proteins and lipids is involved. All these insects, regardless of their feeding habits, possess a range of enzymes in the midgut. But where the diet is specialised, the enzymes present are commonly adapted to it (Table 1): if an insect, like a larval blowfly, feeds on a primarily protein diet proteases are important, whereas in an adult, nectar-feeding lepidopteran they are absent. In aphids feeding on

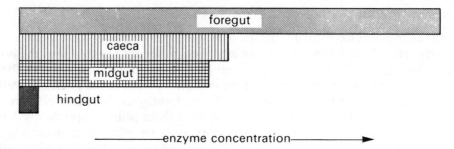

Fig. 47 Relative concentrations of α-glucosidase in different parts of the lumen of the alimentary canal of *Schistocerca* (modified after Evans and Payne, 1964)

Table 1

The midgut enzymes secreted by insects with different diets

(* indicates presence of enzyme) (Data from Wigglesworth, 1965)

Insect	Diet	Protease	Lipase	Amylase	Invertase	Maltase
Cockroach	omnivorous	*	*	*	*	*
Carausius	phytophagous	*	*	*	*	*
Lepidoptera						
larvae	phytophagous	*	*	*	*	*
adults	nectar	—	—	—	*	—
adults	non-feeding	—	—	—	—	—
Lucilia						
larvae	meat	*	*	—	—	—
Calliphora						
adults	sugars	weak	—	*	*	*
Glossina	blood	*	?	weak	—	—

phloem containing no polysaccharides or proteins the presence of amylase and proteinase has not been confirmed, but invertases do occur (Auclair, 1963).

Micro-organisms may produce enzymes which are utilised, directly or indirectly, by the insect. This is the case in cellulose and wax digestion (p. 74) and even in *Apis* the only enzymes produced by bacteriologically sterile bees are invertase, protease and lipase; the other carbohydrases normally present are produced by bacteria.

Carbohydrates

Carbohydrates are generally absorbed as monosaccharides so that, before they are absorbed, disaccharides and polysaccharides must be broken down to their component monosaccharides. This may be a complex reaction taking place partly in the gut wall and a variety of enzymes is involved. Different enzymes are usually necessary to hydrolyse different series of sugars, for instance those built up from glucose or from galactose, and different linkages, α or β, between the sugar residues also require different enzymes. Droste and Zebe (1974) have partially characterised seven carbohydrases from the gut of *Locusta*: α-1, 4-amylase, α-1, 6-amylase, α-glucosidase, β-glucosidase, trehalase, α-galactosidase and β-galactosidase.

Disaccharides. The common disaccharides maltose, trehalose and sucrose all contain a glucose residue which is linked to a second sugar residue by an α-linkage.

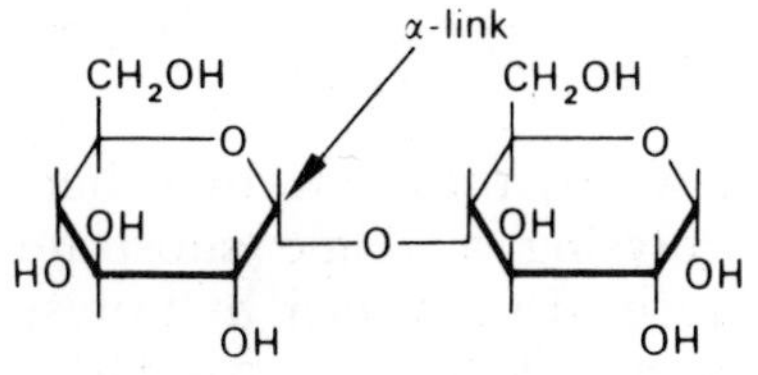

Glucose Glucose

MALTOSE

Glucose Glucose

TREHALOSE

Glucose Fructose

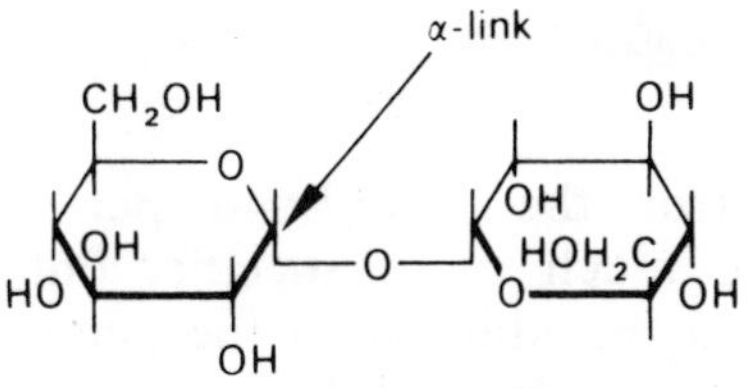

SUCROSE

All these are hydrolysed by an α-glucosidase (*i.e.* an enzyme attacking the α-link of a glucose residue) and this is the usual invertase found in insects although in *Calliphora* a β-fructosidase also occurs.

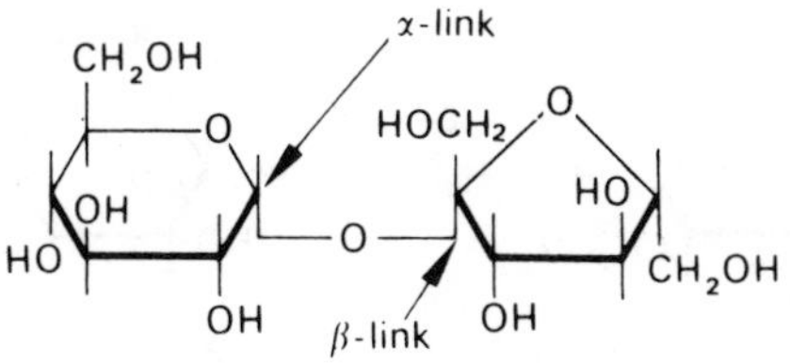

The naturally occurring β-glucosides (*e.g.* salicin, arbutin and cellobiose) are usually of plant origin and the highest β-glucosidase activity is found in phytophagous insects.

Glucose Glucose

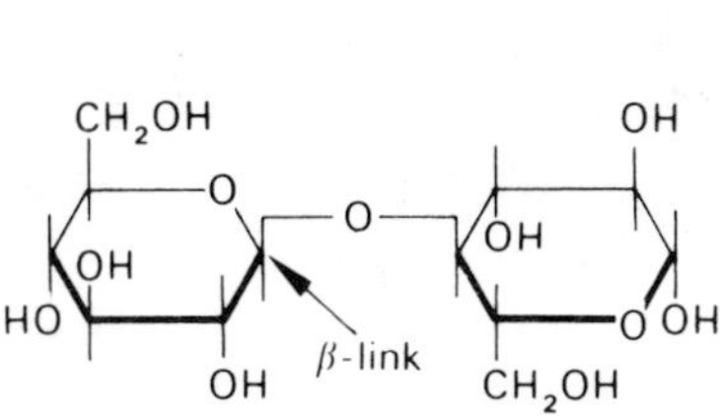

CELLOBIOSE

The glucosidases are the commonest glycosidases, but α-galactosidase, hydrolysing substances such as melibiose, is recorded from Diptera and *Schistocerca*, and β-galactosidase, hydrolysing lactose, is also present in *Schistocerca*.

Galactose   Glucose   Galactose   Glucose

MELIBIOSE   LACTOSE

Apart from the group/bond specificity shown by these enzymes there are others which are much more specific, only hydrolysing a single substrate. Thus in *Schistocerca*, in addition to the general α-glucosidase, which hydrolyses trehalose among other α-glucosides, there is probably a specific α-glucosidase which only hydrolyses trehalose (Evans and Payne, 1964).

In the hydrolysis of carbohydrates water is the typical acceptor for the sugar residues:

Sucrose   Glucose   Fructose

but other sugars may equally well act as acceptors with the formation of oligo-saccharides. Thus in the hydrolysis of sucrose other sucrose molecules may act as acceptors to form the trisaccharides glucosucrose and melezitose.

Glucose   Sucrose   Glucosucrose

Melezitose

These in turn may accept further glucose to form tetrasaccharides. This process is known as transglucosylation and a similar process occurs in the hydrolysis of maltose where, in addition, maltose is reformed by the glucose produced in hydrolysis acting as an acceptor in its turn (Payne and Evans, 1964).

With trehalose no transglucosylation occurs, perhaps because the relevant enzyme has a high degree of specificity for water as an acceptor as well as a high specificity to the substrate. In some aphids there appear to be two α-glucosidases with different acceptor specificities to different ends of the sucrose molecule. The effect of one is to add glucose to the C-4 of the glucose in sucrose to form glucosucrose, while the effect of the other is to add glucose to the C-3 of the fructose in sucrose to form melezitose, which is common in honeydew, the watery fluid continually excreted by feeding aphids (Auclair, 1963).

Polysaccharides. Starch is broken down to maltose, and glycogen to glucose, by the action of an amylase which specifically catalyses the hydrolysis of $1:4$-α-glucosidic linkages in polysaccharides, but there are two types of amylase working in different ways. An exoamylase splits off maltose residues from the ends of the starch molecule leading to a rapid increase in the concentration of maltose, while an endoamylase attacks bonds well within the starch molecule so that there is only a slow build-up of maltose to start with. The products are then further digested in the normal way by α-glucosidases.

Although many insects feed on plants and wood, only a minority of them have an enzyme, cellulase, capable of hydrolysing cellulose. Where there is no cellulase the insects must either feed on the cell contents without digesting the cell walls or they must rely on micro-organisms to digest the cellulose for them.

Amongst the larvae of wood-boring beetles various methods are adopted. Lyctids have no cellulase and feed only on the cell contents; Scolytidae have no cellulase, but do have a hemicellulase so that hemicelluloses, mixtures of pentosans, hexosans and polysaccharides, are attacked; finally, Anobiidae and Cerambycidae do possess a cellulase and can utilise the cell walls as well as the contents.

A cellulase has also been identified in *Ctenolepisma* (Thysanura) and in *Schistocerca* (Evans and Payne, 1964). The activity of the cellulase in *Schistocerca* is so slight that it can normally be of little value because the food passes through the alimentary canal too quickly, but if the insect is starved food already in the gut may be retained for several days and the cellulase might then have some effect. Cellulase acts by breaking cellulose down into cellobiose units, which are then further hydrolysed by a β-glucosidase.

Larval Scarabaeoidea have no cellulase although they feed on rotten wood, but the wood is retained in a pouch in the hindgut by branched spines arising from the intima. In the pouch the bacteria ingested with the wood continue to ferment it and as they die they in turn are digested by the insect's enzymes passing back from the midgut. The digested remains are absorbed through the wall of the pouch where, between the spines, the intima is very thin.

In some other wood-eating insects there is a permanent gut flora or fauna concerned with cellulose digestion. Thus, in the larvae of the beetle *Rhagium* there are cellulose fermenting bacteria, while in the cockroach *Cryptocercus* various flagellates are responsible for cellulose digestion. This is also true of the larvae, soldiers and workers of most wood-eating termites, but it is not true of Termitidae. The flagellates occur in vast numbers in an expansion of the hindgut and in workers of *Zootermopsis* (Isoptera) constitute about a third of the wet weight of the insect. They phagocytose fragments of wood which they hydrolyse to glucose, and in *Cryptocercus* the glucose is passed out into the gut of the insect and then, by contraction of the hindgut, it is forced forwards to the midgut for absorption. In *Zootermopsis*, however, the glucose is retained by the flagellates and the process of anaerobic fermentation continued with the ultimate release of carbon dioxide, hydrogen and organic acids, especially acetic. These acids are then used as a source of carbon by the insect (Grassé, 1949) and as a result of the activity of the flagellates some two-thirds of the food ingested is rendered assimilable.

Since the flagellates live in the hindgut they are lost at each moult when the intima is shed. In termites, however, the habit of proctodaeal feeding soon results in recolonis-ation of the intestine (p. 98). Many flagellates are damaged in the passage through the mandibles and proventriculus and are digested in the midgut, but the remainder pass on undamaged to the hindgut, where they stay. The passage through the gut takes about two hours. *Cryptocercus* is not a social insect, so recolonisation of the gut cannot occur by social feeding, and here a proportion of the flagellates move into the space which forms between the hindgut epithelium and the intima before the latter is shed. At the moult these flagellates, which may remain active or may encyst, are not lost, but form the nucleus of the population in the next instar.

The flagellates occurring in the insects are specific, and six orders of flagellates as well as certain families of the order Trichomonadina are composed entirely of gut-dwelling forms. The fauna is presumed to have originated in the cockroaches, since they are the older group. In *Cryptocercus* there are 13 genera and 25 species of flagellate. Two genera have free-living representatives, but the remainder are only found in the alimentary canals of insects. The genera *Oxymonas* and *Trichonympha* occur in termites as well as in the cockroach. Amongst the termites there is some specificity, some flagellate genera only occurring in certain genera of termites, but Grassé (1952) suggests that this is largely fortuitous and depends on the ethological isolation of the hosts. It is known that flagellates can be experimentally exchanged between termite species.

Proteins

Insects possess a series of proteases. A trypsin-like proteinase which breaks down protein to peptones and polypeptides is produced in the midgut. These, in turn, are acted on by peptidases, some of which occur in the gut lumen, but most of which are found in the epithelial cells indicating that most of the polypeptides are absorbed before being further digested. There are different types of peptidase: carboxypolypeptidase attacks the peptide chain from the —COOH end, provided tyrosine or other specific amino acids are present in the chain; aminopolypeptidase attacks the chain from the —NH$_2$ end; and dipeptidase hydrolyses all dipeptides.

Some insects are able to digest the inert animal proteins keratin and collagen. Keratin is the protein found in wool, hair and feathers. It consists of polypeptide chains, including sulphur-containing amino acids, which are linked together by disulphide bonds rendering the whole protein stable. Only the Mallophaga of birds, some dermestid larvae and some tineid larvae are able to digest it. *Tinea* (Lepidoptera) larvae utilise some 47 % of the wool ingested.

Tineola, at least, has a keratinase capable of digesting keratin under anerobic conditions. This releases cystine, which is probably reduced to cysteine by cystine reductase:—

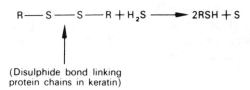

CYSTINE   CYSTEINE

and cysteine is further broken down by cysteine desulphydrase to form hydrogen sulphide. Both cysteine and hydrogen sulphide are reducing agents and will promote the breaking of the disulphide bonds in the keratin, so facilitating enzyme activity.

$$R-S-S-R + H_2S \longrightarrow 2RSH + S$$

(Disulphide bond linking protein chains in keratin)

They will also lower the redox potential (see p. 75) so that the very low potential characteristic of insects which digest keratin ($-200\,mV$ compared with up to $+200\,mV$ in other insects) is probably largely a consequence of, rather than an essential condition for, keratin digestion (Gilmour, 1965).

The larvae of *Hypoderma* (Diptera) and of some blowflies are known to produce a collagenase acting on the collagen of animal tissues. *Hypoderma* lays its eggs on hairs of the host and its larvae bore through the skin into the host tissues. Blowfly larvae are the cause of strike in sheep where, again, they live in live animal tissues, or they may live in carrion.

Lipids

Lipid is usually ingested mainly in the form of triglycerides. Digestion involves the production of smaller molecules of diglycerides, monoglycerides and free fatty acids.

Esterase attacks
here

CH$_2$O—CO—R

CHO —CO—R'

CH$_2$O—CO—R''

TRIGLYCERIDE

CH$_2$O—CO—R

CHO$_2$—CO—R'

CH$_2$O—PO—OCH$_2$—CH$_2$

Phosphatase   OH   HO—N(CH$_3$)$_3$
attacks here

PHOSPHOLIPID

A distinction is commonly made between lipases, which cleave insoluble glycerides of long-chain fatty acids, and esterases, which act on glycerides of short-chain acids, but the distinction is not absolute. Probably a number of esterases are present in insects, but it is not clear which enzymes are secreted into the gut lumen and which occur within the cells of the midgut (Dadd, 1970). Phosphatases, which probably contribute to the digestion of phospholipids, are produced by the midgut cells of *Periplaneta* (Cook *et al.*, 1969).

A specialised case of lipid digestion is the digestion of beeswax by larvae of the wax moth, *Galleria*. Honeycomb normally forms a large part of the diet of these larvae although they can survive without it. Beeswax, from which honeycomb is made, is a mixture of esters, fatty acids and hydrocarbons (see p. 109), and the larva of *Galleria* is able to utilise some 50% of the wax, mainly the fatty acids and some of the unsaponifiable material, but also some hydrocarbons. It is not known to what extent bacteria are important in digestion of the wax. Bacteriologically sterile larvae can digest stearic acid, hexadecyl alcohol and octadecyl stearate, but not the esters of myricyl alcohol, which form a large part of the wax. The insect is known to produce a lipase and possibly also lecithinase and cholinesterase, but it seems likely that most digestion of the esters and fatty acids results from the activities of the bacteria (Gilmour, 1961).

4.1.3 Enzyme activity

Enzymes only exhibit maximal activity under certain conditions, in which pH, redox potential and temperature play a large part.

pH

Enzymes exhibit maximum activity within a limited range of pH (Fig. 48) and so a buffering system is necessary in the gut to ensure efficient digestion. The pH of the foregut is greatly influenced by food and varies with the diet, since there is no appreciable buffering of the foregut contents. Thus with a cockroach fed on a protein diet the foregut pH is 6·3, fed with maltose it is 5·8 and with glucose 4·5–4·8. The more acid pH with the sugars results from micro-organisms producing organic acids.

The midgut is usually buffered so that pH is maintained relatively constant. In *Apis*

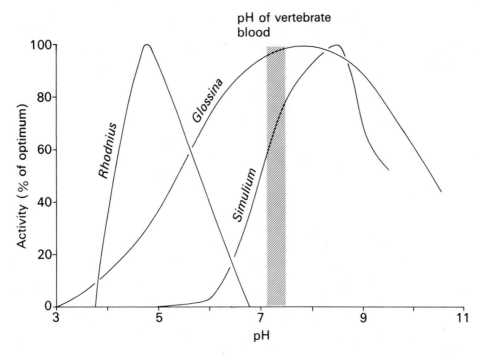

Fig. 48 Effect of pH on the proteolytic activity of midgut homogenates of various blood-sucking insects (after Gooding, 1975)

there are two buffering systems, one is a complex of organic acids and their salts having its maximum effect at pH 4·2, the other a series of mono- and di-hydrogen phosphates with a maximum effect at pH 6·8 (Fig. 49). These two systems tend to maintain the pH at about 6·3. In the cricket, grasshoppers and Lepidoptera larvae, however, phosphate has little buffering effect and here the main buffers are probably weak acids, including amino acids and their salts, and proteins. Mosquitoes have little buffering facility and after a blood meal the midgut pH rises to 7·3, the normal value for blood.

In the midgut the pH is usually in the range 6·0–8·0 (see Day and Waterhouse, 1953; House, 1974), but in larval Lepidoptera and Trichoptera pH 8·0–10·0 is usual. An alkaline pH is more usual in phytophagous insects than in carnivorous ones, but there are many exceptions. In *Periplaneta* and *Cydia* (Lepidoptera) pH is uniform throughout the midgut, but there may be localised differences in pH indicating differences in the activities of the different parts of the midgut. In *Lucilia* larva, for instance, the anterior and posterior ends of the midgut are weakly alkaline while the middle is strongly acid.

The hindgut is usually slightly more acid than the midgut, partly due to the secretions of the Malpighian tubules.

Redox potential

The redox potential is an important factor in digestion and absorption. It is a measure of the oxidising or reducing power of a substance expressed in terms of its tendency to

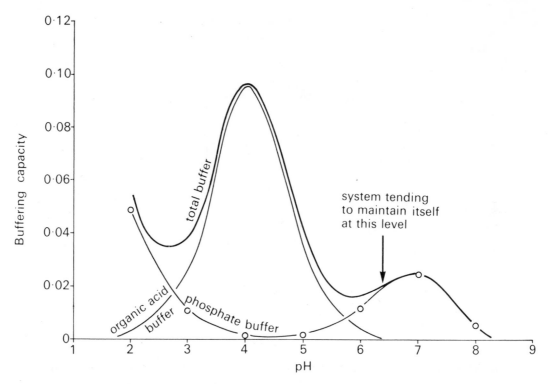

Fig. 49 The buffering capacity of the midgut contents of *Apis*. The measured pH of the midgut would be expected to bear some simple relationship to the buffering capacity (from Day and Waterhouse, 1953)

lose or gain electrons. A negative potential characterises a reducing substance, a positive potential an oxidising substance, while the greater the potential, positive or negative, the stronger the oxidising or reducing powers of the substance. Thus in *Tineola* a redox potential of − 200 mV in the midgut indicates very powerful reducing conditions. Usually the potential in the midgut is positive and it may reach as much as + 200 mV. In *Lucilia* larva the redox potential is positive throughout the gut whereas in *Blattella* (Dictyoptera) the hindgut contents have a negative potential.

Temperature

Enzyme activity increases with temperature and in *Schistocerca* the rate of increase in activity of α-glucosidase for a 10°C rise in temperature (Q_{10}) is 2·25. The greatest activity occurs at 45–50°C but only for short periods because enzymes are denatured at high temperatures, and long periods over 40°C result in inactivation of this enzyme. The optimum for long-term activity must be a balance between higher activity and more rapid denaturing at higher temperatures.

In *Tenebrio* (Coleoptera) larva changes of protease activity occur to compensate for changes in temperature. If the larva is transferred from 23°C to 13°C protease activity first falls and then increases, so that after ten days protease activity is twice as high as it was initially. On returning to 23°C, protease activity returns to its original level. Amylase activity shows no comparable compensating changes (Applebaum *et al.*, 1964).

4.1.4 Control of enzyme secretion

The level of enzyme activity in the gut lumen varies. Even in insects which feed at frequent intervals, like caterpillars and grasshoppers, enzyme activity fluctuates with the state of feeding. Protease activity persists at a lowered level in the gut lumen of *Melanoplus* during a period without food, but rises when food is ingested (Dogra and Gillott, 1971). A similar, but much more marked increase in enzyme activity follows feeding in insects which take only infrequent meals, such as *Rhodnius* (Fig. 50). Enzyme activity also changes with development and season; in *Bombyx* larva amylase activity doubles in the first six days of the fourth instar and *Apis* workers exhibit relatively little invertase activity in early spring and in autumn.

The changes in enzyme activity which occur indicate that synthesis or secretion of enzymes is regulated physiologically. Carbohydrases accumulate in the midgut epithelium of *Locusta* during periods of starvation (Droste and Zebe, 1974) suggesting that synthesis and secretion are independently regulated, but proteases are found in only small amounts in the epithelium and it is inferred that their synthesis and secretion are closely linked (Dogra and Gillott, 1971). Three possible regulatory mechanisms are known.

Enzyme secretion or production may be induced by the food or its products directly stimulating the midgut cells. This is called a secretagogue mechanism. Alternatively

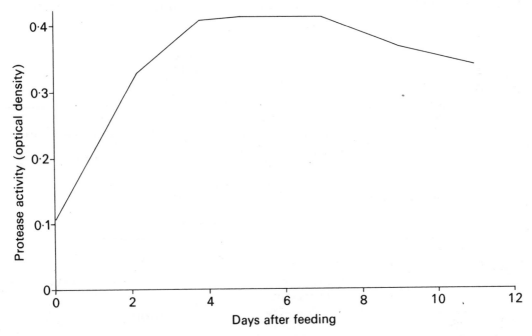

Fig. 50 Protease activity in the gut of male *Rhodnius* at various times after feeding (Persaud and Davey, 1971)

regulation may be under nervous or humoral control. Gooding (1975) concludes that in blood-sucking insects a secretagogue mechanism is most likely to occur. In *Tenebrio* and some other insects, however, the build up of protease is regulated by a secretion from the median neurosecretory cells (Dadd, 1970). In *Blatta* (Dictyoptera) secretion, but not synthesis, may be regulated in this way (Gordon, 1970). Regulation involving the nervous system alone seems unlikely to be important because of the long time which generally elapses between feeding and any increase in enzyme activity.

The evidence so far available suggests that the nature of the food, carbohydrate or protein, does not lead to the secretion only of more of the appropriate enzymes; probably all types of midgut enzymes are affected irrespective of the type of food.

The fate of enzymes in the alimentary canal is not known, but they are only rarely found in the hindgut.

4.2 Absorption

The products of digestion are absorbed in the midgut, especially in the more anterior parts including the caeca (Fig. 51). Absorption also occurs in the hindgut, especially in the rectum, but there is no evidence of absorption from the foregut, which has an impermeable cuticular lining (Treherne, 1967). The cells concerned with absorption are, at least in some cases, the same as those producing enzymes in a different phase of their cycle of activity. Phagocytosis of food particles does not occur: all the substances are absorbed in solution.

Absorption may be a passive or an active process. Passive absorption depends primarily on the relative concentrations of a substance inside and outside the gut, diffusion taking place from the higher to the lower concentration. In addition, in the

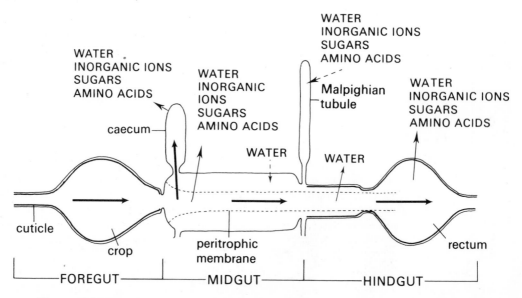

Fig. 51 Diagram of the movement of water and solutes into and out from the gut (after Berridge, 1970)

case of electrolytes, the tendency to maintain electrical equilibrium inside and outside the gut will interact with the tendency to diffuse down the concentration gradient. Active absorption depends on some metabolic process for movement of a substance against a concentration or electrical potential gradient. Movement of water involves movement from a solution of lower osmotic pressure to one of higher osmotic pressure.

4.2.1 Carbohydrates

Carbohydrates are mainly absorbed as monosaccharides and in *Periplaneta* and *Schistocerca* their absorption takes place in the midgut and especially in the midgut caeca. The process of absorption of the sugars resulting from the hydrolysis of more complex carbohydrates depends on diffusion from a high concentration in the gut to a low one in the haemolymph. This is facilitated by the immediate conversion of glucose to trehalose in the fat body which surrounds the gut so that the concentration of glucose in the blood never builds up. If, however, the concentration of glucose in the gut is very high diffusion occurs very rapidly at first and so the mechanism converting glucose to trehalose is unable to keep pace and glucose accumulates in the haemolymph. As a result the diffusion gradient across the wall of the gut is reduced and the rate of absorption falls off. In *Periplaneta* a very high concentration in the midgut is avoided by the rate of crop emptying, which is low when the concentration of sugar is high.

The conversion of glucose to trehalose, a disaccharide, involves an increase in molecular weight, so the possibility of diffusion back into the gut is reduced. Another factor favouring inward diffusion is the absorption of water, which results in an increased concentration of sugars in the gut and consequently a greater diffusion gradient.

Mannose and fructose are absorbed in a similar manner to glucose, but rather more slowly because their conversion to trehalose is less rapid and thus their concentration gradients across the gut wall are less marked.

In *Aedes* larva glycogen appears in the posterior midgut cells soon after glucose is ingested. It is possible that rapid conversion to glycogen might maintain a concentration gradient of glucose inwards from the gut lumen so that glucose diffuses in, but in *Phormia* and other dipterous larvae the concentration of glucose in the haemolymph is normally high, so glucose absorption must entail another, possibly active, process.

4.2.2 Proteins

It is presumed that, in general, proteins are absorbed after degradation to amino acids. Absorption takes place primarily from the midgut, and the caeca are especially important in the absorption of glycine and serine by *Schistocerca*, but amino acids passed out in the urine from the Malpighian tubules are also reabsorbed in the rectum (p. 588). Sometimes proteins are absorbed unchanged and then digested within the cells, and the midgut cells of *Rhodnius* and *Pediculus* (Siphunculata), for instance, are known to absorb haemoglobin unchanged.

The mode of absorption of amino acids depends to some extent on their relative concentrations in the food and the haemolymph. Some are present in higher concentrations in the food than in the haemolymph and these may be absorbed by passive diffusion. Others, such as glycine and serine in *Schistocerca*, are in higher concentration in the blood, but the absorption of water from the gut reverses the relative concentrations, and so again diffusion can account for their absorption. There is also evidence that a diffusion gradient may be maintained by the rapid metabolism of the absorbed amino acids. This is suggested by the accumulation of glycogen in the caecal cells of *Aedes* larva after it has been fed on casein, alanine or glutamic acid. It is, however, probable that the absorption of other amino acids depends on a specific, active mechanism rather than on diffusion alone. This probably varies from one insect to another, depending on the composition of the diet and the haemolymph.

4.2.3 Lipids

Very little is known about the absorption of fats, but it is possible that they are sometimes absorbed unchanged. The products of wax hydrolysis are absorbed in a phosphorylated form and dephosphorylation follows in the epithelium. It is suggested (Gilmour, 1961) that cholesterol is esterified as a preliminary to absorption.

Fat absorption takes place mainly in the midgut, for instance in the caeca in *Periplaneta*, the anterior midgut in *Aedes* larva, and the anterior and posterior midgut in blowfly larva; there is some evidence for the absorption of fats from the hindgut of adult Hymenoptera.

4.2.4 Water

Water is absorbed in various parts of the midgut: in *Schistocerca* and *Aedes* larva, for example, water is absorbed in the caeca, in *Glossina* in the anterior midgut and in *Lucilia* larva in the middle zone of the midgut. In addition, many insects reabsorb water from the urine via the rectal pads (p. 596), but where there is little need for water conservation, as in freshwater insects, Homoptera, Heteroptera and holometabolous larvae living on a fluid diet, reabsorption does not occur and the rectal pads may be absent (Waterhouse and Day, 1953). In *Carausius* some water from the urine is reabsorbed in the ileum.

Water may be absorbed passively if the osmotic pressure of the haemolymph exceeds that of the gut fluids. In *Lucilia* larva the acidity of the midgut coagulates the protein in the food. This reduces the osmotic pressure of the gut contents and so facilitates water absorption. The absorption of water is also linked to the uptake of inorganic ions and in this case the structure of the epithelia is important. In both the midgut and the rectal pads extensive intercellular spaces occur within the epithelia, the spaces being relatively isolated from the haemolymph (Fig. 44). In both tissues, mitochondria are closely associated with the infoldings of cell membranes and it is probable that ions are actively pumped from the cells into the intercellular spaces. As a result the osmotic pressure in these spaces is raised and water passes in passively from the gut lumen. The influx of water creates a positive hydrostatic pressure in the intercellular spaces and so water and ions pass into the haemolymph (Fig. 44). The continued supply of ions is necessary to maintain the osmotic pressure in the intercellular spaces. These ions may be derived from the gut lumen, from recycling within the epithelium or from the haemolymph (Berridge, 1970).

4.2.5 Inorganic ions

Inorganic ions are absorbed in the midgut and reabsorbed from the fluids in the rectum (see p. 587). There may be specific zones for the absorption of different ions in the midgut and in *Lucilia* larva there is a small zone in the centre of the midgut where iron is absorbed, while copper is absorbed in two small zones characterised by a mosaic of cuprophilic and lipophilic cells. Adult *Lucilia* absorb copper in the anterior and posterior parts of the midgut.

The potential of the rectal contents of *Schistocerca* is positive with respect to the haemolymph ($+15$ to $+30$ mV) so that anions (Cl^-) must undergo active absorption. Cations (Na^+, K^+) may be absorbed passively, but not in sufficient quantities to account for their concentrations in the haemolymph, suggesting that they too are absorbed actively. Potassium is absorbed about ten times more rapidly than sodium at the same rectal concentration, indicating selective permeability of the rectal wall (Phillips, 1964). All three ions (K^+, Na^+, Cl^-) may be taken up against very steep concentration gradients and this is not related to water uptake since the flux of water may be in the opposite direction. This may not always be true and in *Sialis* larva the active uptake of sodium ions appears to be linked to water uptake, while the potential difference between rectum and haemolymph is sufficient to account for the uptake of potassium. Similarly in *Aedes aegypti* larva sodium uptake from the rectum is active while potassium uptake is passive.

No storage of ions takes place in the rectal epithelium, at least in *Schistocerca*, and extrusion from the epithelium to the haemolymph must be active because sodium, for instance, is present in higher concentration in the haemolymph than in the epithelium (120 mEq compared with 57 mEq) and the epithelium is negatively charged with respect to the haemolymph (Phillips, 1964).

4.3 Efficiency of food utilisation

The efficiency with which food is utilised varies from insect to insect. In many fluid feeders there is little or no solid waste and the gut may be occluded as in larval Neuroptera. Utilisation in these insects must be very high. In aphids, on the other hand, utilisation is generally poor. A continuous flow of sap is taken from the plant and most of this is passed out at the anus as honeydew. Some 50–60% of the ingested nitrogen is removed from the sap but utilisation of sugars is usually low.

The utilisation of food is expressed in terms of approximate digestibility (A.D.) (Waldbauer, 1968).

$$\text{A.D.} = \frac{\text{Weight of food ingested} - \text{weight of faeces}}{\text{weight ingested}} \times 100$$

Approximate digestibility of food by leaf-eating insects is commonly poor. Fifth-instar larvae of *Schistocerca* utilise only 35% of the total dry weight of their food, but first-instar larvae use 78% (Davey, 1954). In lepidopterous larvae the figure is 25–40%. However, cellulose comprises a large proportion of the dry weight of the food, and specific components of the food are utilised to very different extents. The figures for the larva of *Phalera* (Lepidoptera) are:—

total leaves	35 %	starch	0 %
reducing sugars	74 %	lipids	63 %
non-reducing sugars	93 %	nitrogen	55 %

This species uses the sugars most effectively, but starch not at all. Some other species are able to utilise starch.

More recent work has tended to consider energy utilisation as being a more accurate measure of selective absorption than gross food utilisation. Thus the caterpillar of *Hyphantria* (Lepidoptera) utilises some 23 % of the food it ingests but assimilates 29 % of the calorific value of the ingested food (Gere, 1956) and the grasshopper *Orchelimum* assimilates 27 % of the calorific value of the food (Smalley, 1960).

Although high levels of utilisation will be efficient from the nutritional standpoint, this may be partly offset by other considerations. Thus Dadd (1960) obtained faster growth rates and better survival of *Schistocerca* and *Locusta* when large amounts of cellulose were added to an artificial diet and utilisation fell to 45–50 % as compared with 70–80 %. This suggests that mechanical factors, as well as the nutritional value of the food, are important.

REFERENCES

APPLEBAUM, S. W., JANKOVIĆ, M., GROZDANOVIĆ, J. and MARINKOVIĆ, D. (1964). Compensation for temperature in the digestive metabolism of *Tenebrio molitor* larvae. *Physiol. Zoöl.* **37**: 90–95.

AUCLAIR, J. L. (1963). Aphid feeding and nutrition. *A. Rev. Ent.* **8**: 439–490.

BERRIDGE, M. J. (1970). A structural analysis of insect absorption. *Symp. R. ent. Soc. Lond.* **5**: 135–151.

COOK, B. J., NELSON, D. R. and HIPPS, P. (1969). Esterases and phosphatases in the gastric secretion of the cockroach, *Periplaneta americana*. *J. Insect Physiol.* **15**: 581–589.

DADD, R. H. (1960). The nutritional requirements of locusts. I. Development of synthetic diets and lipid requirements. *J. Insect Physiol.* **4**: 319–347.

DADD, R. H. (1970). Digestion in insects. *in* Florkin, M. and Scheer, B. T. (eds.), *Chemical zoology*, vol. 5A. Academic Press, New York and London.

DAVEY, P. M. (1954). Quantities of food eaten by the desert locust, *Schistocerca gregaria* (Forsk.), in relation to growth. *Bull. ent. Res.* **45**: 539–551.

DAY, M. F. and WATERHOUSE, D. F. (1953). The mechanism of digestion. *in* Roeder, K. D. (ed.), *Insect physiology*. Wiley and Sons, New York.

DOGRA, G. S. and GILLOTT, C. (1971). Neurosecretory activity and protease synthesis in relation to feeding in *Melanoplus sanguinipes* (Fab.). *J. exp. Zool.* **177**: 41–50.

DROSTE, H. J. and ZEBE, E. (1974). Carbohydrasen und Kohlenhydratverdauung im Darmtrakt von *Locusta migratoria*. *J. Insect Physiol.* **20**: 1639–1657.

EVANS, W. A. L. and PAYNE, D. W. (1964). Carbohydrases of the alimentary tract of the desert locust, *Schistocerca gregaria* Forsk. *J. Insect Physiol.* **10**: 657–674.

GERE, G. (1956). Investigations concerning the energy turn-over of the *Hyphantria cunea* Drury caterpillars. *Opusc. zool. Bpest.* **1**: 29–32.

GILMOUR, D. (1961). *The biochemistry of insects.* Academic Press, New York and London.

GILMOUR, D. (1965). *The metabolism of insects.* Oliver and Boyd, Edinburgh.

GOODING, R. H. (1975). Digestive enzymes and their control in haematophagous arthropods. *Acta Trop.* **32**: 96–111.

GORDON, R. (1970). Synthesis and secretion of intestinal digestive enzymes in the adult female oriental cockroach, *Blatta orientalis*, with reference to the neuroendocrine system. *Ann. ent. Soc. Am.* **63**: 416–422.

GRASSÉ, P.-P. (1949). Ordre des Isoptères ou termites. *in* Grassé, P.-P. (ed.), *Traité de Zoologie*. vol. 9. Masson et Cie., Paris.

GRASSÉ, P.-P. (1952). La symbiose flagellés—termites. *in* Grassé, P.-P. (ed.), *Traité de Zoologie*. vol. 1. Masson et Cie., Paris.

HOUSE, H. L. (1974). Digestion. *in* Rockstein, M. (ed.), *The physiology of Insecta*. vol. 5. Academic Press, New York and London.

MILES, P. W. (1972). The saliva of Hemiptera. *Adv. Insect Physiol.* **9**: 183–255.

PAYNE, D. W. and EVANS, W. A. L. (1964). Transglycosylation in the desert locust, *Schistocerca gregaria* Forsk. *J. Insect Physiol.* **10**: 675–688.

PERSAUD, C. E. and DAVEY, K. G. (1971). The control of protease synthesis in the intestine of adults of *Rhodnius prolixus*. *J. Insect Physiol.* **17**, 1429–1440.

PHILLIPS, J. E. (1964). Rectal absorption in the desert locust, *Schistocerca gregaria* Forskål. II. Sodium, potassium and chloride. *J. exp. Biol.* **41**: 15–38.

SMALLEY, A. E. (1960). Energy flow of a salt marsh grasshopper population. *Ecology* **41**: 785–790.

TREHERNE, J. E. (1962). The physiology of absorption from the alimentary canal in insects. *Viewpoints in Biology*. **1**: 201–241.

TREHERNE, J. E. (1965). Active transport in insects. *in* Goodwin, T. W. (ed.), *Aspects of insect biochemistry*. Academic Press, London.

TREHERNE, J. E. (1967). Gut absorption. *A. Rev. Ent.* **12**: 43–58.

WALDBAUER, G. P. (1968). The consumption and utilisation of food by insects. *Adv. Insect Physiol.* **5**: 229–288.

WATERHOUSE, D. F. and DAY, M. P. (1953). Function of the gut in absorption, excretion, and intermediary metabolism. *in* Roeder, K. D. (ed.), *Insect Physiology*. Wiley & Sons, New York.

WIGGLESWORTH, V. B. (1965). *The principles of insect physiology*. Methuen, London.

CHAPTER V
NUTRITION

The food ingested and digested by the insect must fulfill its nutritional requirements for normal growth and development to occur. These requirements are complex and although most nutrients must be present in the diet some may be obtained from other sources. Some nutrients may be accumulated and carried over from earlier stages of development, others may be synthesised by the insect from different dietary constituents, while others may be supplied by micro-organisms. A number of amino acids, carbohydrates and vitamins, are essential for any development to occur; other nutrients, while not essential, are necessary for optimal development. The balance between different constituents is also important.

Carbohydrates are a common source of energy and, although not always essential, they are usually necessary for normal growth. Some ten amino acids are essential for tissue and enzyme production, but fats are usually essential only in very small quantities. A dietary source of sterols is necessary for all insects since they are unable to synthesise these compounds. Various vitamins are essential in the diet and a source of inorganic salts is also necessary.

In the absence or imbalance of certain requirements growth may not occur or may be impaired, or moulting may not occur. Colouration is also affected by some elements of the diet and in social Hymenoptera dietary differences are involved in caste determination. An adequate source of protein is essential for egg production.

All insects in the course of feeding and other activities become infested with micro-organisms, but in some species the micro-organisms are always present and may be essential for normal development. Sometimes they are housed in special cells and the biology of the insect is such that they are transferred from one generation to the next. Micro-organisms are usually present in insects with a restricted diet which is deficient in some essential nutrients and these are probably provided by the micro-organisms.

Insect nutrition is reviewed by Dadd (1963, 1970, 1973), Gilmour (1961) and House (1961, 1974) and many different aspects are discussed in Rodriguez (1972). Specific aspects are reviewed as follows: lipid metabolism by Gilbert (1967), choline metabolism by Bridges (1972), nutrient balance by House (1969) and the effects of feeding on reproduction by Johansson (1964). Micro-organisms in insects are discussed by Brooks (1963a, 1963b) and Musgrave (1964) and in Homoptera by Houk and Griffiths (1980).

5.1 Dietary requirements

Most insects have qualitatively similar nutritional requirements (Table 2) since the basic chemical composition of their tissues and basic metabolic processes are generally similar. Major differences in dietary requirements do occur, however, and these may reflect real differences in metabolism, or they may result from sufficient reserves being accummulated at a previous stage of development or from the ability of the insect or associated micro-organisms to synthesise certain nutrients (see p. 97).

Table 2

Qualitative nutritional requirements of the larvae of species with different feeding habits
(partly after Dadd, 1970; House, 1969)

	Anthonomus (plant tissues)	*Myzus* (plant sap)	*Blattella* (detritus)	*Phormia* (detritus)	*Agria* (other insects)
Amino acids					
arginine	+	+	±	+	+
histidine	+	+	+	+	+
isoleucine	+	+	+	+	+
leucine	+	+	+	+	+
lysine	+	+	+	+	+
methionine	+	+	−	+	+
phenylalanine	+	+	−	+	+
threonine	+	+	+	+	+
tryptophan	+	.	+	+	+
valine	+	+	+	+	+
others	.	±	.	+	±
Carbohydrates	+	+	+	−	±
Sterol	+	?	+	+	+
Fatty acids					
linoleic or linolenic	+	.	+	+	−
others	−	.	.	.	+
Nucleic acids	.	−	?	+	±
Salts	+	+	.	+	.
Vitamins					
biotin	−	+	−	+	+
folic acid	+	+	+	+	−
nicotinic acid	+	+	+	+	+
pantothenic acid	+	+	±	+	+
pyridoxine	.	.	.	+	.
riboflavin	+	+	±	+	+
thiamine	+	+	±	+	+
ascorbic acid	+	+	.	−	.
Choline	+	+	+	+	+
Inositol	+	+	+	+	−

+ essential   ? uncertain
− not needed   . not known
± not essential, but improves growth

5.1.1 Specific requirements

Carbohydrates

Carbohydrates serve as a source of energy and may be converted to fats for storage; they may also contribute to the production of amino acids. Consequently they often form an essential part of the diet and may be necessary in large amounts. *Schistocerca*, for instance, needs at least 20% sugar in an artificial diet for good growth (Fig. 52); *Tenebrio* fails to develop unless carbohydrate constitutes at least 40% of the diet, and growth is optimal with 70% carbohydrate. But carbohydrates are not always essential—they can be replaced by proteins or fats. This depends on the ability of the insect to convert the proteins and fats to intermediate products suitable for use in the cycles of energy transformation (p. 111) and the speeds with which these conversions take place. Some such conversion probably occurs in most insects and in some species may serve for the whole of energy production. In the diet of *Galleria*, carbohydrate can be entirely replaced by wax (Dadd, 1964), and this is also true in many Diptera, such as *Musca*. Larval *Phormia*, which normally live in necrotic tissues containing little carbohydrate, are adversely affected by any carbohydrate in the diet.

The utilisation of different carbohydrates depends on the ability to hydrolyse polysaccharides, the readiness with which different substances are absorbed and the possession of enzyme systems capable of introducing these substances into the metabolic processes. Some insects can use a very wide range of carbohydrates.

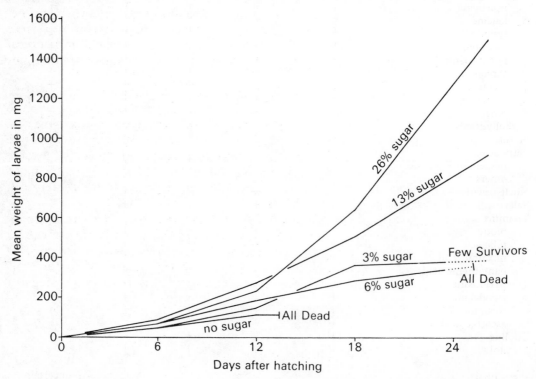

Fig. 52 The effect of various concentrations of sucrose in artificial diets on the growth of *Schistocerca* (after Dadd, 1960)

Tribolium (Coleoptera), for instance, uses starch, the alcohol mannitol, the trisaccharide raffinose, the disaccharides sucrose, maltose and cellobiose and the monosaccharides mannose and glucose among others. Other insects living in stored products and *Schistocerca* and *Locusta* are also able to utilise a wide range (Dadd, 1960), but many phytophagous insects, such as *Melanoplus*, are unable to utilise polysaccharides and some insects are only able to use a very restricted range of sugars. *Chilo* (Lepidoptera), for instance, only uses sucrose, maltose, fructose and glucose. The pentose sugars do not generally support growth and may be actively toxic, perhaps because they interfere with the absorption or oxidation of other sugars which are normally utilised (Lipke and Fraenkel, 1956).

There may be differences in the ability of larvae and adults to utilise carbohydrates. For instance, the larva of *Aedes* can use starch and glycogen, while the adult cannot.

Amino acids

Amino acids are required for the production of structural proteins and enzymes. They are commonly present in the diet as protein and the value of any ingested protein to an insect depends on the amino acid content of the protein and the ability of the insect to digest it. Consequently proteins or amino acids are always essential in the diet of developing insects and optimal growth requires a relatively high concentration (Fig. 53). Although some 20 amino acids are needed for protein production, only ten are essential in the diet; the others can be synthesised from these ten. The ten essential amino acids are arginine, lysine, leucine, isoleucine, tryptophan, histidine, phenylalanine, methionine, valine and threonine. There is some variation in these requirements by different insects. For instance, glycine is essential for several dipterous species, alanine for *Blattella* and proline for *Phormia*, but methionine is not essential in these insects.

In general, the absence of any one of these essential acids prevents growth. Although other amino acids are not essential, they are necessary for optimal growth to occur because their synthesis from the essential acids is energy consuming and necessitates the disposal of surplus fragments (Dadd, 1973). Consequently glutamic acid and aspartic acid are necessary in addition to the essential amino acids for good growth of *Bombyx* larvae and further improvement is obtained if alanine, glycine or serine are also present. Good growth of *Myzus persicae* depends on the presence of cysteine with glutamic acid, alanine or serine.

The interchangeability of amino acids depends to some extent on similarity of structure. Phenylalanine, a phenolic acid, is essential; tyrosine is not because it can be synthesised from phenylalanine, though it is often necessary for optimal growth. Similarly the sulphur-containing methionine is essential, and cystine and cysteine can be dispensed with if adequate methionine is available as a source from which they can be produced.

Phenylalanine

Tyrosine

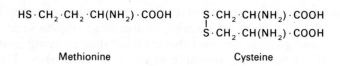

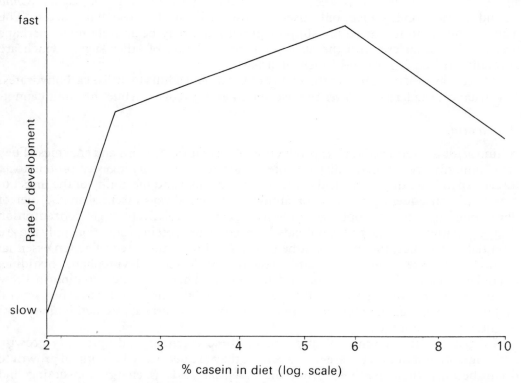

Fig. 53 The effect of different concentrations of casein on the rate of development of *Drosophila* larvae (modified after Sang, 1959)

Fatty acids

Fats are the chief form in which energy is stored and the ability to synthesise fats for storage is widespread, but, except for specific items in small amounts, they are not usually essential constituents of the diet. Only small quantities of fat are present in leaves, so it would not normally form an important source of energy in phytophagous insects and even in the wax moth, *Galleria*, beeswax is not an essential part of the diet although growth is improved when it is present (Dadd, 1964). The reserves of fat in the body are affected qualitatively and quantitatively by the fat in the diet (Friend, 1958), but this does not imply simple storage of the ingested fats; these are extensively changed before they are stored.

Linoleic acid is an essential requirement of some insects, such as *Ephestia* (Lepidoptera) and *Schistocerca*. It is concerned in the formation of lipid phosphatides and in its absence moulting is abnormal. A suboptimal amount of linoleic acid in the larval diet of *Ephestia* results in the wings being devoid of scales because the scales do not separate from the pupal cuticle; with no linoleic acid in the larval diet the insect fails to emerge. In many, but not all, insects linolenic acid can replace linoleic acid.

Lipogenic factors

Choline has two main functions in insects: in phosphatidyl cholines (lecithins), which are important in cell membranes, and in acetylcholine, essential for neural transmission. Some choline is probably necessary in the diet of all insects (Dadd, 1973), but it can be spared (see below) by structurally similar compounds. Dimethyl-aminoethanol, for instance, accelerates growth of *Drosophila* larvae on a diet containing suboptional amounts of choline. If insects can synthesise choline, they are unable to do so in amounts which are adequate for their requirements (Bridges, 1972).

Inositol is also a component of phospholipids and it is essential for most plant-feeding insects. It is not generally required by non-phytophagous insects.

Sterols

Nearly all insects need a dietary source of sterol for normal growth and reproduction, and the range of sterols used is limited to those essentially similar to cholesterol, with a hydroxyl group at position 3.

Cholesterol

Plant feeders amongst Orthoptera, Lepidoptera, Coleoptera, Diptera and Hymeno-ptera can use a variety of plant sterols, converting them to cholesterol or 7-dehydrocholesterol, whereas *Dermestes* (Coleoptera), feeding exclusively on animal material, can only use cholesterol and 7-dehydrocholesterol (Levinson, 1962).

A few insects have requirements for very specific sterols. *Drosophila pachea* in nature feeds only on the cactus *Lophocereus schotti* and requires the specific sterol, schottenol, from this plant. This cannot be replaced by cholesterol. Some aphids do not require a dietary source of sterol, but in these cases the material is probably provided by intracellular symbionts. There is no evidence that the insects are able to synthesise sterols (Dadd, 1970).

The amount of cholesterol required can be reduced by the inclusion of 22-dehydro-cholesterol or ∇^7-ergosterol in the diet, but these substances cannot entirely replace cholesterol. Such substances are called 'sparing' agents and it is probable that they can replace cholesterol where this only plays a structural role in other compounds, but that cholesterol itself is required for some specific metabolic role. This role is unknown. Cholesterol may be stored and this accounts for the reduced dietary requirements of older *Tenebrio* and *Calliphora* larvae.

Vitamins

Vitamins are organic substances, not necessarily chemically related to each other, which are required in small amounts in the diet since they cannot be synthesised. They mostly provide structural components of coenzymes.

The water soluble B vitamins thiamine, riboflavin, nicotinic acid, pyridoxine and pantothenic acid are essential to most insects (Table 2), while biotin and folic acid are also required by many (see *e.g.* Gilmour, 1961). Other vitamins may be specific requirements of particular insects. For instance, *Tenebrio* needs a source of carnitine, but this can be synthesised by *Dermestes* and *Phormia*. Other vitamins, although not essential, may promote growth; this is true of lipoic acid in *Hylemya* (Diptera).

In some insects some B vitamins are provided by associated micro-organisms (see p. 97). Thus *Stegobium* (Coleoptera) only needs thiamine and pyridoxine in its diet because riboflavin, nicotinic acid, pantothenic acid, folic acid, biotin and choline are supplied by intracellular symbionts.

Ascorbic acid (vitamin C) is not usually an essential dietary constituent, but it is widely distributed in insect tissues, indicating that it is synthesised. *Schistocera*, *Bombyx* and *Anthonomus* (Coleoptera), however, have a dietary requirement for ascorbic acid and this may be true for most, but not all, phytophagous insects (Dadd, 1963). In the absence of ascorbic acid *Schistocerca* undergoes abortive moults and dies. The level of ascorbic acid in the blood fluctuates and is minimal just after the moult in *Schistocerca* and it has a similar fluctuation in *Bombyx*.

β-carotene (provitamin A) is probably essential in the diet of all insects, since it is a component of the visual pigment (Dadd, 1973). It also has other functions. Normally the eggs of *Schistocerca* contain enough β-carotene to permit growth of the larvae, but in insects reared on a carotene-free diet from eggs already deficient in carotene growth is retarded and the moult delayed. In addition, the insects are smaller, lighter and less active than usual. β-carotene is commonly involved in the normal pigmentation of leaf-eating insects. Without it they do not develop their normal yellow or green colours and melanisation is also reduced.

There is increasing evidence that α-tocopherol (vitamin E) is required by many insects. Fertility of female *Cryptolaemus* (Coleoptera) and male *Acheta* (Orthoptera) depends on this material in the diet, and the fecundity of female *Plodia* (Lepidoptera) has also been shown to be related to the presence of dietary tocopherol (Dadd, 1973).

Nucleic acids

No insect with an absolute requirement for nucleic acids is known. Nucleic acids are normally synthesised, but a dietary supply improves the growth of most larval Diptera and some Coleoptera. Very few *Culex* (Diptera) larvae complete development if nucleic acid is not provided (Dadd and Kleinjan, 1977). Ribonucleic acid or its component nucleotides may be utilised. Of the nucleotides, *Culex* larvae require adenylic and thymidylic acids and either cytidilic or aridylic acid. DNA is not usually effective in place of RNA or the nucleotides.

Inorganic salts

A dietary source of inorganic salts is essential, but relatively little work on salt requirements has been carried out, because traces of salts are often present as impurities in other dietary factors. Their importance lies in the maintenance of an ionic balance suitable to the activity of living cells, as co-factors of some enzyme systems and as integral parts of others. *Schistocerca* develops on a diet containing only sodium, calcium, potassium, magnesium, chloride and phosphorus with other elements present only as impurities (Dadd, 1961a). Known essential trace elements are iron, copper, iodine, manganese, cobalt, zinc and nickel.

Most insects appear to be relatively insensitive to wide variations in levels and proportions of the different elements in the diet.

5.1.2 Balance of nutrients

Although some growth occurs with widely differing levels of nutrients, optimal growth requires the levels of different nutrients to be appropriately balanced. Larval *Agria* (Diptera), for instance, develop most rapidly to the final instar with relatively low levels of amino acids, but the effectiveness of these acids varies with the amounts of other nutrients present (Fig. 54). The concentration of RNA needed for optimal development of *Drosophila* is doubled if folic acid is not also present, and an increase in the dietary concentration of casein from 4% to 7% necessitates a doubling of the concentrations of nicotinic acid and pantothenic acid and a six-fold increase in folic acid for optimal growth. Requirements for thiamine and riboflavin remain unchanged. Nutrients also interact with non-nutrient chemicals in the diet: catechol, for instance, inhibits the growth of larval *Agrotis* (Lepidoptera) on a standard diet by reducing the efficiency with which assimilated food is converted to body tissues (Reese and Beck, 1976).

The optimal balance of nutrients probably varies continuously in relation to the state of development of the insect (Dadd, 1970). *Schistocerca* needs more carbohydrate in the later larval instars than in earlier ones and *Pyrausta* (Lepidoptera) larvae can develop without any carbohydrate for the first three instars. In this case the increased requirements in the later instars are associated with the accumulation of food reserves in the fat body. *Blattella* is able to develop as far as the third larval instar without inositol and young *Schistocerca* can survive without ascorbic acid, but these substances are required by the later instars. In these instances sufficient nutrients for the early instars are stored in the egg, but once these reserves have been used up a dietary supply is essential.

Protein is important for yolk production and the diet of the female insect may be modified to provide this protein. In virgin *Musca* females the ratio of sucrose to protein in the diet is 16:1, while in egg-laying females it is 7:1. In *Calliphora* food selection changes cyclically during yolk formation. During the early stages of egg development much protein is ingested and the intake of protein stimulates the corpora allata, which secrete a factor leading to increased carbohydrate intake during the period of yolk

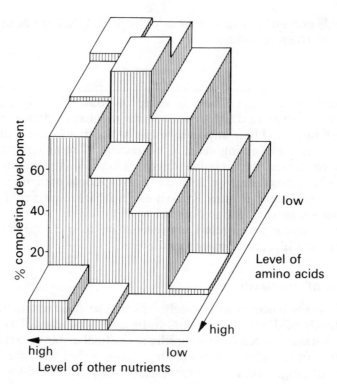

Fig. 54 Percentages of *Agria* larvae completing development in four days with amino acids present in different amounts and constituting different proportions of the diet (after House, 1969)

deposition in the egg. The removal of protein metabolites from the blood at this time leads to a reduction in corpus allatum activity and so to a lower carbohydrate intake (Strangways-Dixon, 1959) (but see Dethier, 1976).

5.1.3 Nutrition and body form

Colouration may be affected by nutrition either through the absence of some constituent of a pigment or through interference with pigment metabolism. The absence of β-carotene has both effects in *Schistocerca*. The carotene is an essential constituent of the yellow carotenoid giving the background colour, but in the absence of carotene melanisation is also reduced (Dadd, 1961b). *Aedes* larvae also lack pigmentation if there is no tyrosine and only a little phenylalanine in the diet.

If the diet is adequate qualitatively, but only available in limited amounts the resulting adults will be reduced in size. *Ephestia kühniella*, for instance, needs about 0·13 g of wholemeal flour for normal development. On smaller amounts, even as little as 0·04 g, the moths emerging are normal, but smaller (Norris, 1933). The proportions of the wings relative to the body may also be altered by the diet.

Differences in diet may lead to polymorphism. The chalcid *Melittobia* is parasitic on the wasp *Trypoxylon* and the first 12 to 20 larvae to develop within a host do so rapidly. The resultant adults emerge with short crumpled wings and proceed to mate and oviposit in the same host. Later larvae develop more slowly and give rise to fully-winged adults which leave the host. These differences are due to changes in the food supply from the host.

Dietary differences are often involved in polymorphism in the social Hymenoptera (Michener, 1961; Dietz, 1972). Some larvae of the honeybee, *Apis*, for instance, are fed by the workers in a qualitatively and quantitatively different way from the rest of the larvae and as a result they develop into queen bees (see p. 42). In the ant *Myrmica rubra* whether or not a larva becomes a queen depends on the treatment it receives early in the third instar. Of particular importance is the condition of the workers feeding the larvae. Workers in the spring (vernal) condition promote rapid growth of the larvae and these become workers, but if the larvae are fed by workers in the autumn (serotinal) condition their development is slow, they overwinter as larvae, and the larger ones amongst them develop into queens in the following spring (Weir, 1959). These differences result from differences in the food, in which the glandular secretions of the workers in various physiological conditions may be particularly important.

5.1.4 Nutrition and reproduction

The diet plays an important part in egg production by female insects (Johansson, 1964). For instance, *Leptinotarsa* (Coleoptera) females feeding on young potato plants with a high lecithin content produce 30–50 eggs in each batch; on older plants with a lower lecithin content only 8–20 eggs are laid, while feeding on *Solanum commersonii* instead of *S. edinense* prevents any egg production at all. In insects, such as some Lepidoptera, which do not feed as adults nutrients are stored by the larva and the larval diet is important in egg production. In the majority of insects, however, fecundity is largely related to adult nutrition, although food reserves derived from the larva may have some importance.

The need for protein for egg production is reflected in the sexual difference in feeding behaviour in many biting flies, such as mosquitoes and tabanids, where the female is blood-sucking and the male feeds exclusively on nectar. Some female mosquitoes lay no eggs until they have had a blood meal, these are known as anautogenous; others are autogenous and can lay their first batch of eggs without a blood meal. The protein for yolk production comes from the reserves in the fat body in autogenous *Culex pipiens* or from the flight muscles, which are degraded at this time; in autogenous *Aedes communis*. The differences between autogenous and anautogenous forms result from differences in regulation of activity of the corpora allata (Clements, 1963).

Nutritional factors other than protein influence egg production. For instance, the fecundity of the flea *Xenopsylla* is reduced by feeding on rats deficient in thiamine. *Culex* lays twice as many eggs per mg of blood after feeding on canary blood as compared with human blood and comparable results in *Aedes* are correlated with the level of isoleucine in the blood. These requirements may be such that a diet suitable for larval development is not optimal for reproduction. Thus in *Drosophila* fructose is important for egg production, but is of little importance to the larva.

The quantity of food is again important. In *Ephestia* the number of eggs laid is related to the amount of flour ingested as a larva and in *Cimex* (Heteroptera) the number of eggs laid increases with the size of the blood meal.

Dietary deficiencies may result in a disturbance of yolk synthesis (House, 1963). In

Rhodnius no yolk is deposited in the absence of a blood meal, because there is no protein to form yolk, but the effect may not always be a direct one. Protein synthesis is under endocrine control and failure to stimulate the corpora allata may result in a failure of protein synthesis despite adequate reserves. In *Calliphora* the corpora allata are stimulated by the ingestion of protein.

Even if eggs are produced their viability depends in part on the adult diet. The eggs of *Anthonomus* (Coleoptera) fail to hatch if there is no cholesterol in the adult diet and in *Musca* the number of eggs hatching is proportional to the amount of cholesterol in the diet.

5.1.5 Efficiency of conversion of food to tissue

The efficiency with which digested food is converted to body substance is expressed as the E.C.D.

$$\text{E.C.D.} = \frac{\text{weight gained by insect in given time}}{\text{weight of food ingested} - \text{weight of faeces}} \times 100$$

For phytophagous Orthoptera the dry weight E.C.D. varies from 13 to 39%, and for larval Lepidoptera from 14 to 69%, the latter generally being more efficient at conversion (Waldbauer, 1968). Species feeding on stored products are generally even less efficient.

5.2 Storage

Sometimes an essential nutrient is not required in the diet because sufficient reserves have been accumulated during an earlier feeding period. There are two important reserves of nutrients: the yolk in the egg and the fat body of the larva and adult.

Because of their relatively small size insect eggs cannot store major nutrients, such as glucose, in excess of the needs of the embryo, but minor nutrients, such as vitamins, may be present in sufficient quantity to accommodate the needs of the developing larva as well (Gordon, 1959). Not all the minor nutrients are stored to the same extent and while, for instance, there is a good deal of linoleic acid in the egg of *Blattella*, there is no thiamine.

Once these stores have been used up the insect needs a supply of the appropriate nutrients in the diet. Thus the egg of *Blattella* contains sufficient inositol for development as far as the third larval instar, while in the egg of *Schistocerca* there is enough β-carotene for normal growth throughout the whole of larval life, but if eggs are obtained from adults with a deficiency of carotene, no carotene is stored and it becomes an essential item in the larval diet (Dadd, 1961b).

Larger amounts of nutrients, including the major types, may be stored in larval and adult fat bodies. This is the case, for instance, in those Lepidoptera which do not feed as adults. Sufficient reserves are accumulated by the larva to supply the adult metabolic processes. Similarly, if locusts are fed on grass during the first two larval instars they can continue development up to the last larval instar without carbohydrate in the diet, because they have accumulated a sufficient quantity in the fat body (Dadd, 1963). Minor nutrients may also be stored and larval *Anthonomus* (Coleoptera) store sufficient choline and inositol to permit egg development even if these substances are absent from the adult diet.

In some cases nutrients are obtained from the degradation of tissues. Thus the nutrients required for egg development in autogenous mosquitoes (p. 93) and for the development of young in *Aphis* may be derived from the autolysis of flight muscles.

5.3 Micro-organisms

Many insects take in micro-organisms casually with their food, while others have a constant association with micro-organisms living either in the gut or intracellularly in various tissues.

5.3.1 Casual associations

Micro-organisms are almost inevitably ingested during feeding and so an intestinal flora is present in most insects. The alimentary canal of grasshoppers, for instance, is sterile when the insects hatch from the egg but soon acquires a bacterial flora, which increases in numbers and species throughout life. In general, insects with straight alimentary canals contain fewer micro-organisms than those with complicated guts with a range of pH, providing a number of different niches. The micro-organisms occurring in the gut in these cases of casual infection largely reflect what is present in the environment (Brooks, 1963a).

These casual associations with micro-organisms are important in the nutrition of some insects. Scarabaeoid larvae have a fermentation chamber in the hindgut in which decaying wood with its content of micro-organisms is retained. The micro-organisms continue to ferment the wood and without them the larvae would be unable to utilise the cellulose of the wood (p. 71). In other cases, although they are not essential, contamination of a diet with micro-organisms accelerates the rate of development. Thus larval *Hylemya* living on a sterile diet take 27 days to reach the pupal stage compared with 10 days on the same diet containing bacteria (Friend *et al.*, 1959). Such micro-organisms may make an otherwise unsuitable diet adequate by supplying essential vitamins or other substances. Friend *et al.* (1959) suggest that the onion bulb may provide only an inadequate diet for *Hylemya*, but the bacteria living in the tunnels made by the larva supply some essential substances which would otherwise be lacking and so enable the larva to survive.

Micro-organisms also assist with wax digestion in *Galleria* although the insect can survive without them.

5.3.2 Constant associations

In general, constant associations with micro-organisms occur in insects with a restricted diet deficient in certain essential nutrients, suggesting that the micro-organisms make good these deficiencies. Thus micro-organisms are found in insects feeding on wood, dry cereal, feather, hair and wool, in sap-feeding Heteroptera and Homoptera and in those blood-sucking insects which never feed on anything except blood. Those blood-sucking insects which at some stage partake of other food do not house micro-organisms. Thus symbionts are found in blood-sucking bugs and lice, and *Glossina* and Nycteribiidae, which are viviparous, amongst Diptera, but not in fleas, blood-sucking Nematocera or Tabanidae, since these have free-living larvae (Wigglesworth, 1952).

Micro-organisms are also found in cockroaches and some ants. These are omnivorous insects and hence in this instance the presence of micro-organisms is not correlated with a restricted diet. In the case of the cockroach, *Blattella*, however, it is suggested that in the normally rather poor diet the balance of amino acids is not optimal and a good deal of degradation and reformation takes place. For this, considerable amounts of riboflavin and pyridoxine are needed, often in excess of the amounts in the diet, and the micro-organisms supplement the dietary supply of these and other substances (Gordon, 1959).

Types of micro-organism

The most commonly occurring micro-organisms in insects are bacteria or bacterium-like forms which are found in Blattodea, Isoptera, Homoptera, Heteroptera, Anoplura, Mallophaga, Coleoptera, Hymenoptera and Diptera. In addition flagellates are found in wood-eating cockroaches and termites, yeasts in Homoptera and Coleoptera and an actinomycete in *Rhodnius*. In many cases the precise nature of the micro-organisms is not known.

Location in the insect body

In some insects the symbionts are free in the gut lumen. This is the case with the flagellates which live in the hindguts of wood-eating cockroaches and termites and with the bacteria living in the caeca of the last segment of the midgut in plant-sucking Heteroptera. In *Rhodnius*, *Actinomyces* lives in crypts between the cells of the anterior midgut.

Most micro-organisms are intracellular in various parts of the body. The cells housing the symbionts are known as mycetocytes and these may be aggregated together to form organs known as mycetomes.

Mycetocytes are large, polyploid cells occurring in many different tissues. Normally the micro-organisms are incorporated into them when the cells are first differentiated in the embryo, but sometimes the cells develop for a time before they are invaded. Most commonly the mycetocytes are scattered through the fat body, as they are in cockroaches and coccids, but in *Haematopinus* (Siphunculata) they are scattered cells in the midgut epithelium and in other insects they may be in the ovarioles or free in the haemolymph.

Mycetomes may originate in the gut wall, as in Anoplura and *Glossina*, where the mycetome is a ring of enlarged midgut cells, or in modified Malpighian tubules, as in some Coleoptera, but frequently they are independent of the gut. In *Calandra* (Coleoptera) larva the mycetome is a U-shaped structure well supplied with tracheae lying below the foregut, but not connected to it (Musgrave, 1964). Nycteribiidae have mycetomes in the abdomen and *Cimex* has a small mycetome near the gonads. In holometabolous insects the mycetomes are often only found in immature stages. At metamorphosis they fragment into mycetocytes which become lodged in adult organs, in the case of *Calandra* in the anterior midgut caeca.

The wood-eating cockroaches have two sets of symbionts: intestinal flagellates and intracellular bacteroids in the fat body. This situation also occurs in the termite *Mastotermes darwiniensis*, but the remainder of the wood-eating termites only retain the intestinal fauna.

The roles of micro-organisms in the insect

It is known that the intestinal flagellates of cockroaches and termites are concerned with the digestion of wood and that they release products which can be utilised by the insect (p. 72). In other cases it is presumed that the organisms provide essential nutrients, but this has only been shown conclusively in a few cases. The yeasts of *Stegobium* (Coleoptera) provide B vitamins and sterols, which may be secreted into the gut or released by the digestion of the micro-organisms. The symbionts of *Blattella* provide certain amino acids and possibly a tripeptide as well as B vitamins (see above). Blood is normally sterile and contains some of the B vitamins in smaller amounts than are required by insects. This deficiency is made good, at least in *Rhodnius* and *Triatoma* (Heteroptera), by the symbionts.

There is some evidence that the micro-organisms, particularly those in Homoptera and Heteroptera, are concerned with nitrogen metabolism (Tóth, 1952). This may result from the fixation of free nitrogen or by the breakdown of the insect's metabolic waste products, urea and uric acid, into nitrogenous compounds that can be used. Although it seems certain that the organisms can perform these functions *in vitro*, there is no proof that they do so when inside the host insect.

In the coccid *Stictococcus sjoestedti* the bacterium-like micro-organisms may be concerned with sex determination. In the mature insect, mycetocytes invade the ovary but only infect those oocytes to which they are adjacent. Consequently two types of eggs are produced: those with and those without micro-organisms. The eggs develop parthenogenetically and the uninfected eggs develop into males, while the infected ones give rise to females (Richards and Brooks, 1958).

The effect of loss of micro-organisms varies with the insect and will also depend on the diet available to the insect. *Rhizopertha* (Coleoptera) apparently suffers no loss from the absence of symbionts, *Calandra* is smaller and lighter in their absence, while *Rhodnius* deprived of its intestinal flora rarely reaches the adult stage. It appears that many insects can live equally well with or without their micro-organisms provided the diet is adequate. If, however, the diet is not adequate, as must often be the case, the micro-organisms become vital.

Transmission

Since these organisms are constantly associated with insects there must be some provision for their transfer from parent to offspring. There are essentially four different methods by which this is brought about (Brooks, 1963b).

In the cockroaches, and in *Mastotermes*, *Camponotus* (Hymenoptera) and some beetles, mycetocytes migrate to the ovary and the bacteria are surrounded and drawn into the oocyte by microvilli of the vitelline membrane. The oocytes of Homoptera are infected in a similar way, but the bacteria only enter the oocytes through the follicle cells at one end. Alternatively, micro-organisms from the female accessory glands may be smeared on to the outside of the egg as it is laid. The chorion and the micro-organisms are then eaten by the insect when it hatches. This occurs, for instance, in a number of Chrysomelidae and in this case the symbionts are able to survive on the outside of the chorion for longish periods. Some male bostrychid beetles transfer symbionts in the seminal fluid, but with this exception micro-organisms are always transmitted by the female.

Where the symbionts live in the gut other methods of infection are employed. Termites and some bugs exhibit behavioural adaptations facilitating transfer; in termites, for instance, proctodaeal feeding ensures that newly moulted individuals receive a fresh infection of flagellates (p. 72). Finally, reinfection may simply be a chance process as in the wood-eating cockroaches and *Rhodnius*. These insects live in restricted habitats already fouled and contaminated by their own excreta so that they readily pick up a fresh infection.

Symbionts may exhibit polymorphism with special transmission forms, perhaps stimulated to develop by the hormones of the insect (Richards and Brooks, 1958). The flagellates of termites and *Cryptocercus* have sexual stages which are related to the moulting cycles of the insect and transmission forms, concerned with the infection of oocytes, are described for several intracellular symbionts.

REFERENCES

BRIDGES, R. G. (1972). Choline metabolism in insects. *Adv. Insect Physiol.* **9**: 51–110.

BROOKS, M. A. (1963a). The microorganisms of healthy insects. *in* Steinhaus, E. A. (ed.), *Insect Pathology*. vol. 1. Academic Press, New York.

BROOKS, M. A. (1963b). Symbiosis and aposymbiosis in arthropods. *Symp. Soc. gen. Microbiol.* **13**: 200–231.

CLEMENTS, A. N. (1963). *The physiology of mosquitoes*. Pergamon Press, Oxford.

DADD, R. H. (1960). The nutritional requirements of locusts—III. Carbohydrate requirements and utilisation. *J. Insect Physiol.* **5**: 301–316.

DADD, R. H. (1961a). The nutritional requirements of locusts—V. Observations on essential fatty acids, chlorophyll, nutritional salt mixtures, and the protein or amino acid components of synthetic diets. *J. Insect Physiol.* **6**: 126–145.

DADD, R. H. (1961b). Observations on the effects of carotene on the growth and pigmentation of locusts. *Bull. ent. Res.* **52**: 63–81.

DADD, R. H. (1963). Feeding behaviour and nutrition in grasshoppers and locusts. *Adv. Insect Physiol.* **1**: 47–109.

DADD, R. H. (1964). A study of carbohydrate and lipid nutrition in the wax moth, *Galleria mellonella* (L.), using partially synthetic diets. *J. Insect Physiol.* **10**: 161–178.

DADD, R. H. (1970). Arthropod nutrition. *in* Florkin, M. and Scheer, B. T. (eds.), *Chemical zoology*. vol. 5. Academic Press, New York and London.

DADD, R. H. (1973). Insect nutrition: current developments and metabolic implications. *A. Rev. Ent.* **18**: 381–420.

DADD, R. H. and KLEINJAN, J. E. (1977). Dietary nucleotide requirements of the mosquito, *Culex pipiens*. *J. Insect Physiol.* **23**: 333–341.

DETHIER, V. G. (1976). *The hungry fly*. Harvard University Press, Cambridge, Mass.

DIETZ, A. (1972). The nutritional basis of caste determination in honey bees. *in* Rodriguez, J. G. (ed.), *Insect and mite nutrition*. North-Holland Publishing Co., Amsterdam and London.

FRIEND, W. G. (1958). Nutritional requirements of phytophagous insects. *A. Rev. Ent.* **3**: 57–74.

FRIEND, W. G., SALKELD, E. H. and STEVENSON, I. L. (1959). Nutrition of onion maggots, larvae of *Hylemya antiqua* (Meig.), with reference to other members of the genus *Hylemya*. *Ann. N.Y. Acad. Sci.* **77**: 384–393.

GILBERT, L. I. (1967). Lipid metabolism and function in insects. *Adv. Insect Physiol.* **4**: 70–211.

GILMOUR, D. (1961). *The biochemistry of insects*. Academic Press, New York and London.

GORDON, H. T. (1959). Minimal nutritional requirements of the German roach *Blattella germanica* L. *Ann. N.Y. Acad. Sci.* **77**: 290–351.

HOUK, E. J. and GRIFFITHS, G. W. (1980). Intracellular symbiotes of the Homoptera. *A. Rev. Ent.* **25**: 161–187.

HOUSE, H. L. (1963). Nutritional diseases. *in* Steinhaus, E. A. (ed.), *Insect Pathology*. vol. 1. Academic Press, New York.

HOUSE, H. L. (1969). Effects of different proportions of nutrients on insects. *Entomologia exp. appl.* **12**: 651–669.

HOUSE, H. L. (1974). Nutrition. *in* Rockstein, M. (ed.), *The physiology of Insecta*. vol. 5. Academic Press, New York and London.

JOHANSSON, A. S. (1964). Feeding and nutrition in reproductive processes in insects. *Symp. R. ent. Soc. Lond.* **2**: 43–55.

LEVINSON, Z. H. (1962). The function of dietary sterols in phytophagous insects. *J. Insect Physiol.* **8**: 191–198.

LIPKE, H. and FRAENKEL, G. (1956). Insect nutrition. *A. Rev. Ent.* **1**: 17–44.

MICHENER, C. D. (1961). Social polymorphism in Hymenoptera. *Symp. R. ent. Soc. Lond.* **1**: 43–56.

MUSGRAVE, A. J. (1964). Insect mycetomes. *Can. Ent.* **96**: 377–389.

NORRIS, M. J. (1933). Contributions towards the study of insect fertility.—III. Experiments on the factors influencing fertility of *Ephestia kühniella* Z. (Lepidoptera, Phycitidae). *Proc. zool. Soc. Lond.* 1933, 905–934.

REESE, J. C. and BECK, S. D. (1976). Effects of allelochemics on the black cutworm, *Agrotis ipsilon*; effects of catechol, L-dopa, dopamine, and chlorogenic acid on larval growth, development, and utilization of food. *Ann. ent. Soc. Am.* **69**: 68–72.

RICHARDS, A. G. and BROOKS, M. A. (1958). Internal symbiosis in insects. *A. Rev. Ent.* **3**: 37–56.

RODRIGUEZ, J. G. (ed.) (1972). *Insect and mite nutrition*. North-Holland Publishing Co., Amsterdam and London.

SANG, J. H. (1959). Circumstances affecting the nutritional requirements of *Drosophila melanogaster*. *Ann. N.Y. Acad. Sci.* **77**: 352–365.

STRANGWAYS-DIXON, J. (1959). Hormonal control of selective feeding in female *Calliphora erythrocephala* Meig. *Nature, Lond.* **184**: 2040–2041.

TÓTH, L. (1952). The role of nitrogen-active micro-organisms in the nitrogen metabolism of insects. *Tijdschr. Ent.* **95**: 43–62.

WALDBAUER, G. P. (1968). The consumption and utilization of food by insects. *Adv. Insect Physiol.* **5**: 229–288.

WEIR, J. S. (1959). The influence of worker age on trophogenic larval dormancy in the ant *Myrmica*. *Insectes soc.* **6**: 271–290.

WIGGLESWORTH, V. B. (1952). Symbiosis in blood-sucking insects. *Tijdschr. Ent.* **95**: 63–69.

CHAPTER VI

THE FAT BODY AND GENERAL METABOLISM

The fat body of insects is made up of cells resembling blood cells aggregated to form a rather irregular and diffuse tissue. It serves as a store for food reserves and, in some insects, for the storage of excretory materials. In a few it becomes modified as a light-producing organ. The fat body is of major importance as a centre in which many metabolic processes occur.

Metabolism involves, among other things, the utilisation of substances absorbed from the gut, their assimilation into the substance of the body or their oxidation to provide energy. Carbohydrates are the usual source of energy in insects, but in some species fats are utilised during flight. The carbohydrate is oxidised in a series of small steps so that the energy which is released can be conserved in high energy phosphate bonds. In this form the energy is made available to the insect for driving other metabolic and particularly synthetic processes, and as a source of muscular energy.

Food reserves are stored in insects as particular forms of fats and carbohydrates. These substances are synthesised from the food taken in and mechanisms are also available for their subsequent utilisation in energy or tissue production. Proteins, too, must be synthesised in the forms characteristic of the insect from the amino acids derived from the food.

Gilmour (1961, 1965) gives general accounts of insect biochemistry. Intermediate metabolism of carbohydrates is reviewed by Friedman (1970) and Wyatt (1967), of fats by Gilbert (1967) and Gilbert and O'Connor (1970), of steroids by Robbins et al. (1971) and Svoboda et al. (1975), and of nitrogenous compounds by Ilan and Ilan (1974) and Schoffeniels and Gilles (1970). Oxidative metabolism, especially in flight muscle, is reviewed by Bailey (1975), Hansford and Sacktor (1971) and Sacktor (1974, 1975). The control of metabolism is discussed in most of these papers and especially in Sacktor (1970). The anatomy and functioning of light organs is considered by Buck (1948), Carlson (1969), Lloyd (1971), McElroy (1965), McElroy et al. (1974) and Smith (1963). Keeley (1978) reviews the endocrine regulation of the fat body.

6.1 Fat body

The insect fat body consists of loosely aggregated or compact masses of cells enclosed in a membranous sheath and freely suspended in the haemocoel so that they are intimately bathed by the blood. The cells are arranged in irregular strands or sheets, but the arrangement is relatively constant within a species. Often there is a parietal layer of fat just beneath the body wall; less frequently a visceral layer ensheathes the gut (Fig. 55).

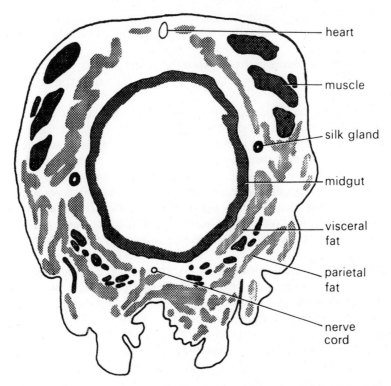

heart

muscle

silk gland

midgut

visceral fat

parietal fat

nerve cord

Fig. 55 Transverse section of *Pieris* larva to show the distribution of fat

6.1.1 Trophocytes

The greater part of the fat body is made up of cells called trophocytes. In the young larva these cells contain few inclusions and have rounded nuclei, but subsequently they become vacuolated and distended by stores of glycogen, fat or protein. The nuclei are compressed and become elongate or stellate and the cell boundaries may no longer be apparent, although they become visible again if the cell contents are depleted. At the time of metamorphosis in holometabolous insects, albuminoid granules appear in the trophocytes. They are usually regarded as the products of protein or lipoprotein synthesis, but Nair and George (1964) regard them as definite organelles concerned with fat synthesis.

The trophocytes are very like some blood cells and there may be a close relationship between the two. There is a good deal of evidence suggesting that blood cells enter and add to the substance of the fat body, and in the aquatic Heteroptera, for instance, the fat body increases in size throughout life by the inclusion of free adipohaemocytes (p. 798). In *Aleyrodes* (Homoptera) the cells of the fat body float freely in the haemolymph and there is no sharp distinction between them and the haemocytes.

The trophocytes accumulate reserves of food of which fat is the most usual, being stored in variable forms which depend, among other things, on the diet and the temperature of synthesis (p. 107). Carbohydrate in the fat body is usually in the form of glycogen, and protein may also be present. Protein is not usually stored in quantity in adult insects, but it does occur in the trophocytes of overwintering worker bees where it is used in the production of the salivary secretions with which larvae are fed in the following spring.

Food reserves usually increase throughout the larval period, especially in holometabolous insects, so that in the mature larva of *Apis*, for instance, the fat body comprises 33 % of the dry weight.

These food reserves are of particular importance to the insect during non-feeding periods, whether these are of short or long duration and whatever their cause. During long flights, for instance, the stores in the fat body provide a major source of energy and it is generally true that insects can go on flying until their reserves in the fat body are consumed (p. 277). They also enable the insect to survive periods of quiescence or diapause and usually, as a preliminary to diapause, extensive reserves are accumulated. For instance, the female *Culex* builds up her reserves in the autumn so that at the beginning of the winter they constitute about 30 % of the wet weight. By the end of the winter, however, they are severely depleted and only amount to about 6 % of the wet weight.

The reserves of larval holometabolous insects are largely used at metamorphosis when the adult tissues are built up. The fate of the fat body at this time is very variable. The cells generally survive, but in Hymenoptera and some higher Diptera their breakdown is almost complete (p. 486). The adult fat body is then rebuilt from the few remaining larval cells or from embryonic tissue. Egg production may also depend on reserves in the fat body, especially in insects which do not feed as adults, and it is often the case that the fat body is more prominent in female than in male insects.

6.1.2 Urate cells

Scattered amongst the trophocytes in the fat body of Collembola, *Blatta* and larval Apocrita are the urate cells, in which uric acid accumulates. In these animals the Malpighian tubules are absent or do not excrete uric acid and the accumulation in the urate cells may be regarded as a form of storage excretion. In some other insects, such as larval Lepidoptera, with fully functional Malpighian tubules, uric acid accumulates in some of the trophocytes during the larval instars and then is passed to the Malpighian tubules at pupation. The uric acid in the urate cells provides a store of nitrogen (see p. 583).

6.1.3 Mycetocytes

Mycetocytes are cells containing micro-organisms. In many insects, such as cockroaches, they are scattered through the fat body and the organisms they contain are responsible for the synthesis of nutritional elements (p. 97). In *Blaberus* (Dictyoptera), at least, the mycetocytes do not differ in structure from ordinary trophocytes and each bacterium is enclosed by a membrane (Walker, 1965).

6.1.4 Tracheal cells

Tracheal cells, which are characterised by having numbers of intracellular tracheoles, occur in the larva of the bot fly, *Gasterophilus*. They are very large cells, 350–400 μm in diameter, and almost completely fill the posterior third of the body (see Fig. 373). The larva of *Gasterophilus* spends part of its life attached to the wall of the stomach of a horse and during this period it contains haemoglobin. At first the haemoglobin is dispersed throughout the fat body, but later it becomes concentrated in the tracheal cells which differentiate from typical trophocytes. These cells, with the haemoglobin, appear to enable the larva to make better use of the intermittent supply of air brought to it as gas bubbles in the food of the horse (Keilin and Wang, 1946).

6.1.5 Other cells

In queen termites the fat body differs structurally and chemically from the fat body of other castes, including the larvae. The change from the larval structure occurs in *Kalotermes* when the queen is first fed entirely by other members of the colony, and at this time specialised cells develop (Grassé and Gharagozlou, 1963, 1964). The fat body of the queen contains little glycogen or fat, but is probably specialised for protein synthesis. This is in keeping with the high level of nitrogen in the secretions fed to it by other members of the colony and with the large amounts of protein required to produce the enormous numbers of eggs.

The larvae of phytophagous Diptera accumulate calcium in the fat body in the form of calcospherites.

6.2 Intermediate metabolism

Intermediate metabolism includes all the cellular reactions which are not immediately concerned with the release of energy. These reactions are concerned with the formation of special secretions and the synthesis and breakdown of cellular constituents. Only the better-known processes and substances will be considered.

6.2.1 Carbohydrate metabolism

Trehalose

Trehalose is a disaccharide derived from glucose via glucose-6-phosphate in the fat body. It occurs in all insects, though not necessarily at all stages, and it is commonly the most abundant sugar in the haemolymph. In *Schistocerca*, for instance, the trehalose concentration varies from 2 to 20 mg/ml while the glucose concentration does not exceed 2 mg/ml. At any one stage of development the concentration of trehalose in the haemolymph is relatively constant irrespective of the state of nutrition of the insect. This relative stability is the result of a balance between utilisation and synthesis: as trehalose is metabolised more is produced from glycogen, so the glycogen reserves in a non-feeding insect steadily decline (see Friedman, 1978).

The metabolic use of trehalose depends on its hydrolysis to glucose in the presence of trehalase. Trehalase occurs in the muscles and the glucose produced is utilised as a fuel for flight by *Phormia*, *Locusta* and *Periplaneta* (Fig. 56). A trehalase in the haemolymph is most active at times of moulting and makes glucose available for chitin synthesis and for other tissues which lack trehalase and so are unable to use trehalose directly. Finally, a trehalase occurs in the midgut epithelium and to a lesser extent in the lumen. Since trehalose is not found in higher plants or in vertebrates it is unlikely that

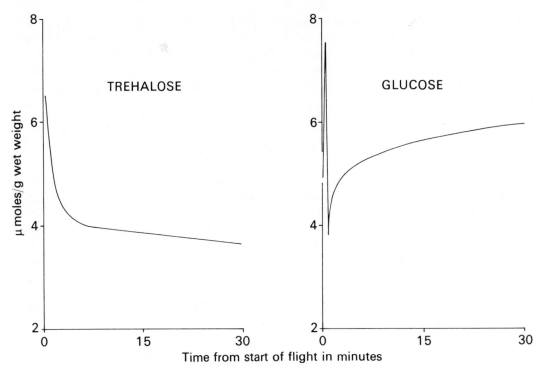

Fig. 56 Changes in the concentrations of trehalose and glucose in the thorax of *Phormia* during the first 30 minutes of flight (after Wyatt, 1967)

the major function of this enzyme in the midgut is digestion. Possibly the enzyme hydrolyses trehalose which diffuses out of the haemolymph into the midgut, the glucose so formed then tending to diffuse back into the haemolymph (see diagram p. 105).

Glycogen

Glycogen is a polysaccharide, forming the major energy reserve in many insects. Some glycogen may occur in most tissues, but commonly the main reserves are present in the fat body. Glycogen is synthesised during periods of active feeding and depleted at times of reduced feeding, as during a moult, over the pupal period, or during a period of diapause (Fig. 57). Synthesis may be directly from glucose, but it can also be derived from amino acids. For instance, when *Aedes* larva is fed on glycine and alanine, glycogen is rapidly deposited in the midgut cells. Utilisation of glycogen involves phosphorylation.

Chitin

Chitin, a constituent of insect cuticle, is a polymer of acetyl glucosamine units (p. 504). In *Schistocerca* it is formed during and just after a moult from carbohydrate reserves, of which trehalose is probably the most important. The synthesis of chitin possibly involves uridine triphosphate leading to the formation of uridine diphosphate

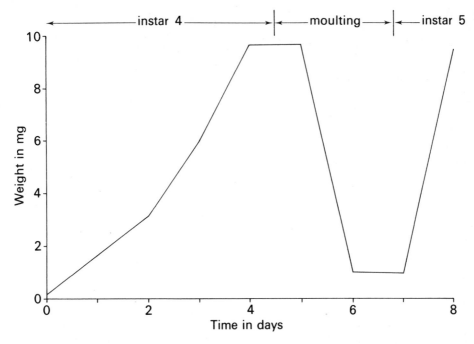

Fig. 57 Changes in the amount of glycogen stored by male *Bombyx* during the fourth instar and the early part of the fifth instar (after Wyatt, 1967)

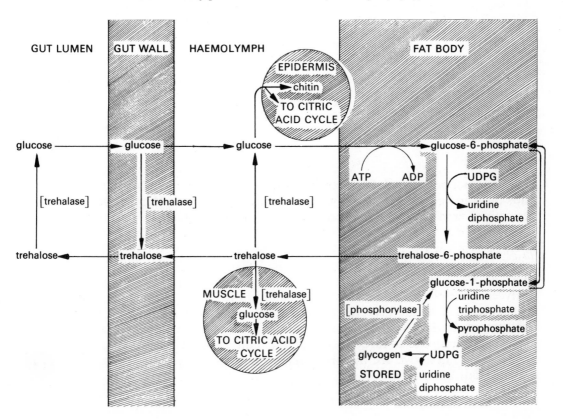

acetylglucosamine (UDPAG) followed by condensation to form chitin (Candy and Kilby, 1962).

Much of the cuticular material is digested by the moulting fluid and reabsorbed by the insect when it moults. The carbohydrate present in the old cuticle may thus be resynthesised and re-used in the new one.

6.2.2 Lipids

Lipids are not precisely defined substances, but they are mostly fatty acid esters (fatty acids form an homologous series with the general formula $C_nH_{2n+1}COOH$) and their derivatives, insoluble in water, but soluble in organic solvents.

Triglycerides and fatty acids

Most of the lipid in insect tissue is in the form of glycerides, predominantly triglycerides in the fat body and diglycerides in the haemolymph (Fig. 58). The fatty acids combined in the glycerides are usually long-chain acids, both saturated and unsaturated. In *Anthonomus* (Coleoptera) 23 fatty acids have been identified, varying in chain length from 6 to 20 carbon atoms, but palmitic and oleic acids comprise over 60 % of the total. These two are the predominant fatty acids in most insects. Stearic and linoleic acids are also important.

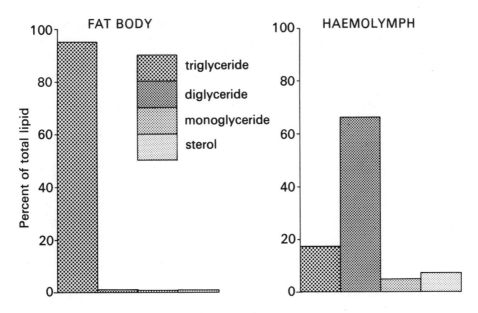

Fig. 58 Major lipid components of the fat body and haemolymph of the male pupa of *Hyalophora* (after Gilbert, 1967)

Fatty acids are obtained in the diet, but in phytophagous insects the lipid content of the food is low and fatty acid synthesis occurs in the fat body. Synthesis from short-chain acids is known to occur, as well as from carbohydrates and amino acids. In *Eurycotis* (Dictyoptera) synthesis first involves the production of even-numbered saturated fatty acids by the condensation of 2-carbon units (Bade, 1964). The saturated acids are then desaturated to give the unsaturated acids: thus, stearic is converted to oleic acid. Insects are apparently unable to synthesise polyunsaturated acids such as linoleic and linolenic acids. Consequently these acids are essential dietary constituents for many insects.

Fatty acids are accumulated in the fat body as triglycerides to provide reserves of energy, the advantage over carbohydrate reserves being that the lipid contains more potential energy and yields more metabolic water per unit weight. Hence lipid reserves are built up during active feeding periods and utilised during periods of non-feeding, as during diapause, over the pupal period or in embryogenesis. In *Locusta*, for instance, the lipid content of the egg falls by 32 % during embryonic development. Fatty acids also provide a major energy reserve for the flight muscles of Lepidoptera and Orthoptera. In these insects the lipid reserves become depleted during prolonged flight.

The mobilisation of lipid in the fat body entails the hydrolysis of triglycerides to diglycerides by a lipase. The diglycerides then associate with proteins to form lipoproteins and it is in this form that they enter the haemolymph. In the pupal haemolymph of *Hyalophora* (Lepidoptera) there are three lipoprotein classes, based on the molecular weight of the protein, including at least eight recognisably different lipoproteins (Gilbert and O'Connor, 1970). On entering muscle, the diglycerides are hydrolysed and the fatty acids progressively oxidised to produce acetyl-coenzyme A, which enters the citric acid cycle (see diagram below).

Fatty acids are also components of phospholipids in cell membrane. Little is known of the biosynthesis of phospholipids in insects (Gilbert, 1967).

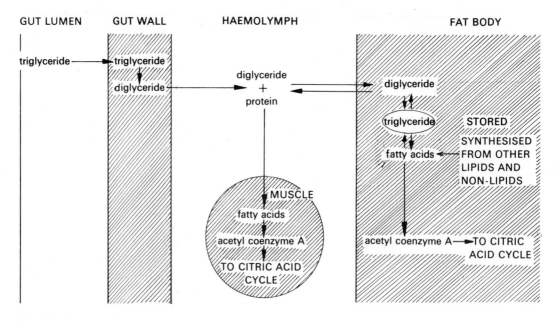

Sterols

All insects require a source of sterol and, in most cases, have a specific requirement for cholesterol. Sterols cannot be synthesised by insects, but phytophagous species are able to produce cholesterol from the commonly occurring phytosterols such as β-sitosterol. Cholesterol forms the starting point for the synthesis of the moulting hormones (ecdysones) (p. 827). Sterols are excreted as sulphates.

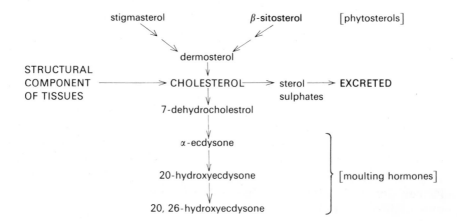

Waxes

Waxes are complex mixtures of lipids varying from species to species and even in different stages of the same species. In the cuticle of larval *Pteronarcys* (Plecoptera), for instance, triglycerides comprise 78 % of the wax and free fatty acids another 12 %; in the adult, free fatty acids make up nearly 50 %, sterols 18 % and hydrocarbons 12 %. Wax esters and triglycerides are also present. The wax in the cuticle provides the waterproofing layer (p. 592) and may also have some structural significance (Neville, 1975).

Very large amounts of wax are produced by coccids and related insects which cover themselves or their eggs with strands or plates of wax, while bees construct their larval cells of wax. Beeswax contains 12 % paraffins, 72 % esters and 13 % free long-chain fatty acids. The fat cells and oenocytes play a major part in the synthesis of beeswax and in the process material passes from the fat cells to the oenocytes and from both these to the wax glands in the abdomen.

6.2.3 Amino acid and protein metabolism

Amino acids

A good deal of amino acid synthesis occurs in the fat body. In *Schistocerca*, for instance, carbon from acetate is incorporated into glutamate, proline, aspartate and alanine in the fat body (Clements, 1959). Since these amino acids correspond with keto acids occurring in the citric acid cycle (*e.g.* glutamic with α-ketoglutaric, aspartic with oxaloacetic) and can be derived from the keto acids by transamination mechanisms, it is suggested that the intermediates of the citric acid cycle provide the carbon skeletons of these amino acids.

Transamination, the transfer of amino groups from an amino acid to a keto acid without the intermediate formation of ammonia and resulting in the formation of a second amino acid, occurs in a variety of tissues.

amino acid	keto acid		keto acid	amino acid
$CH(NH_2).COOH$	$CO.COOH$		$CO.COOH$	$CH(NH_2).COOH$
$\mid$	$\mid$	$\rightleftharpoons$	$\mid$	$\mid$
$CH_2.COOH$	CH_2		$CH_2.COOH$	CH_2
	$\mid$			$\mid$
	$CH_2.COOH$			$CH_2.COOH$
aspartic	α-ketoglutaric		oxaloacetic	glutamic

Insect tissues contain many transaminases and in *Bombyx*, for instance, 19 amino acids are known to act as donors in transamination reactions. The glutamate-aspartate conversion is the most widespread and the most active, being recorded from the nerve cord, the muscles, the gut wall and the Malpighian tubules as well as from the fat body. Activity is highest in the Malpighian tubules, while little or no transaminase activity occurs in the blood.

Keto acids (R.CO.COOH) such as pyruvic and oxaloacetic may be produced in transamination reactions and also by the oxidative deamination of amino acids, involving amino acid oxidases and glutamic dehydrogenase. These acids may be used in fat synthesis or as substrates in the citric acid cycle. In *Schistocerca* the fat body uses glycine and leucine as respiratory substrates and it is suggested that the fat body is important in transdeaminating amino acids and making them available for further metabolism by other tissues (Clements, 1959).

Glutamate plays a central role in the transfer of nitrogen from one compound to another. Ammonia is more actively incorporated into it and aspartate than into other amino acids and glutamate is also involved in the most active transamination reactions. Thus it serves to incorporate nitrogen into the system and then to distribute it. The general reactions of amino acids in insects can be summarised:

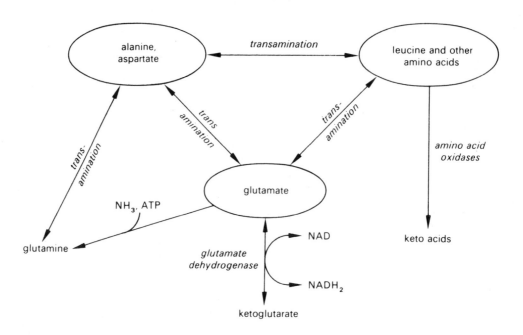

Protein synthesis

Amino acids are the units from which body proteins are synthesised. They are joined by peptide bonds to form peptides and further bonding of polypeptide chains produces proteins. By analogy with other organisms it is presumed that RNA acts as a template for protein synthesis, determining the order in which amino acids are linked.

Increased protein synthesis is often related to an increase in RNA. In *Tenebrio* the ratio RNA : DNA is high at the beginning of the pupal period when the adult tissues are forming. Subsequently the ratio falls, but then it rises again just before adult emergence when the adult cuticle is being produced.

Protein is an essential component of all cells and many special secretions. The midgut epithelium, for instance, produces the digestive enzymes and the silk gland of lepidopterous larvae elaborate the proteins of silk. Blood protein is produced in the cells of the fat body.

6.3 Respiratory metabolism

In general, carbohydrates such as glucose and glycogen form the initial substrates for oxidation and energy production. At normal body temperatures oxidation occurs as a series of small steps each facilitated by a specific catalyst or enzyme. By this means much of the free energy of the reaction can be conserved, whereas if the breakdown was direct most of this energy would be dissipated as heat. The first part of this breakdown is an anaerobic process known as glycolysis which occurs in the extra-mitochondrial cytoplasm. Glycolysis commonly leads to the formation of pyruvate, which is then oxidised within the mitochondria by the enzymes of the citric acid cycle (also known as the tricarboxylic acid or Krebs cycle) (see diagram, p. 113). The energy released in these reactions is finally conserved in a terminal oxidase system involving the cytochromes (see below).

6.3.1 Release and conservation of energy

Before sugars enter into metabolic reactions they are phosphorylated by the addition of a phosphate group. Their subsequent oxidation usually involves the removal of hydrogen, a process known as dehydrogenation. This results in structural changes in the molecule which are accompanied by a redistribution of the intrinsic energy in the system so that most of it is concentrated in a bond linking a phosphate radical to the rest of the system. In this way an energy-rich bond is created. By the process of dephosphorylation this bond energy is transferred to a molecule of adenosine diphosphate (ADP) converting it to adenosine triphosphate (ATP).

The hydrogen which is removed in dehydrogenation is not transferred directly to oxygen, but passes to some other hydrogen acceptor, which is usually NAD or nicotinamide-adenine dinucleotide phosphate (NADP). In accepting hydrogen these are converted to the reduced forms $NADH_2$ and $NADPH_2$. These in turn pass the hydrogen to flavoproteins (FP), which then become reduced (FPH_2), but α-glycerophosphate, formed in glycolysis, and succinate, formed in the citric acid cycle, transfer hydrogen directly to the flavoprotein. From the flavoproteins electrons (ε) are passed to the cytochrome system and H^+ ions are released into solution.

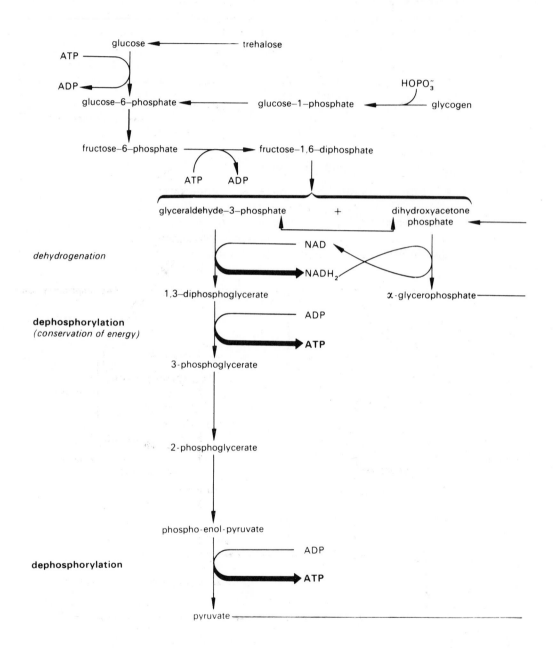

Glycolysis, occurring in the cytoplasm

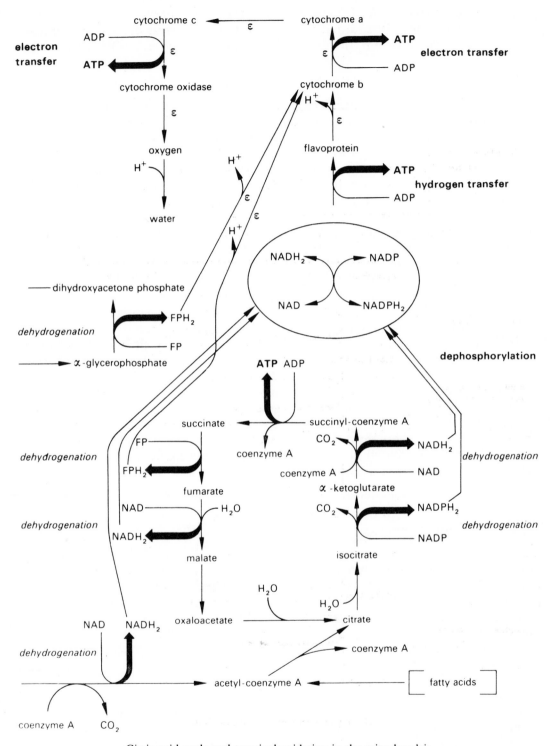

Citric acid cycle and terminal oxidation in the mitochondria

Cytochromes have a central iron atom which is capable of reversible oxidation and reduction by the removal or addition of electrons. Thus in the transfer of electrons from flavoprotein to cytochrome b, the first in the series, the reaction can be summarised:

$$FPH_2 + 2Fe^{+++} \rightarrow FP + 2Fe^{++} + 2H^+$$

The various cytochromes are arranged in a series of ascending redox potential (p. 75) from -0.1 volt at the flavoprotein to $+0.8$ volt at the oxygen. That is to say, each stage is a successively stronger oxidising agent than the previous one. This means, for instance, that cytochrome a will accept electrons more readily than cytochrome c, while the latter, being the stronger reducing agent, will give up its electrons more readily. Hence there is a smooth flow of electrons from the flavoprotein to oxygen, the final transfer from cytochrome a to oxygen being catalysed by cytochrome oxidase.

With the rise in the state of oxidation, free energy is liberated which serves to produce a high-energy bond linking phosphate to ADP with the production of ATP. The greater part of the energy of the reaction is conserved at this stage, but some ATP is also formed in the course of glycolysis and the citric acid cycle. In all, the oxidation of one molecule of glucose yields a net gain of 38 high-energy bonds combined in ATP. ATP is the only known source of energy which can be directly utilised in animal processes, but other nucleotide phosphates are concerned in energy conservation. These are inosine, guanosine, uridine and cytidine triphosphates.

In general, energy is produced as it is required and very little is stored in an immediately available form. Some energy can be stored in ATP, but the supply of the latter is limited because ADP, from which it is derived, is essential for the transfer of energy and so ADP and ATP must be continually recirculated. The store of energy can be increased by the transfer of the high-energy bonds to phosphagens, of which arginine is known to occur in insects, although only in low concentrations. It is most abundant in muscle, where the most urgent needs for large amounts of energy are to be expected. The energy stored in arginine phosphate is not immediately available, but can rapidly be transferred to ADP:

$$\text{ARGININE PHOSPHATE} + \text{ADP} \rightleftharpoons \text{ATP} + \text{ARGININE}$$

6.3.2 Utilisation of energy

The energy conserved during the respiratory processes is utilised in muscular activity (see p. 262), in biosynthesis and in other active mechanisms of the cell. It is probable that all the cells of the body possess an ATPase, an enzyme hydrolysing ATP, and it is presumed that this splits off a phosphate group and its high energy bond from ATP. The phosphate group may be transferred to various acceptor molecules, which are thus phosphorylated. The effect of phosphorylation is to activate the acceptor molecules so that they readily take part in reactions. For instance, glucose is activated by conversion to glucose-6-phosphate:

$$\text{GLUCOSE} + \text{ATP} \rightarrow \text{GLUCOSE-6-PHOSPHATE} + \text{ADP}$$

The energy thus provided also enables the glucose to be actively absorbed by a cell against a concentration gradient.

In Odonata and Orthoptera two phosphate groups, each with an associated high energy bond, may be split from ATP and the enzymes responsible for this are known as apyrases. Their activity is highly temperature dependent. The fibrillar flight muscles of Diptera and Hymenoptera (see p. 251) are more specialised, with an ATPase capable of splitting off only one phosphate group from ATP.

6.3.3 Respiration by flight muscles

During flight the energy output of flight muscle is increased 50- to 100-fold. In many insects this energy is derived from carbohydrate metabolism and the flight muscles possess a greatly enhanced α-glycerophosphate cycle. This cycle provides a shuttle by which nicotinamide-adenine dinucleotide (NAD) is rapidly regenerated from $NADH_2$ and the hydrogen is transferred to the mitochondrial oxidase system. The supply of NAD is potentially limiting for pyruvate production but the α-glycerophosphate cycle ensures that NAD is always available. Pyruvate and α-glycerophosphate never accumulate; they are transferred to the mitochondria and oxidised as quickly as they are produced.

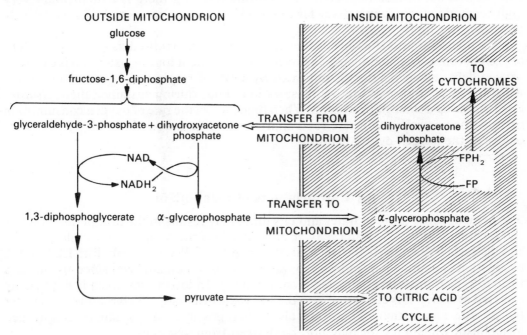

An enhanced level of α-glycerophospate dehydrogenase occurs in the flight muscles of all the insects investigated. Probably all insects use some carbohydrate as a fuel for flight (Sacktor, 1974), but migrant Orthoptera and Lepidoptera use fat to a greater extent and *Glossina* depends on proline as its main fuel in flight. Fatty acids enter the citric acid cycle after conversion to acetylcoenzyme A (p. 113). Proline is first transformed to glutamate and then deaminated to α-ketoglutaric acid, which occurs in the citric acid cycle. Other insects have the capacity to utilise proline or other amino acids, but only in *Glossina* and *Leptinotarsa* has amino acid oxidation been shown to be of general importance. *Glossina* is unusual in having very small reserves of glycogen and low concentrations of sugars in the haemolymph. In *Phormia* proline metabolism provides intermediates for the citric acid cycle in the first few seconds of flight before pyruvate oxidation becomes fully active (Sacktor, 1974; Kammer and Heinrich, 1978).

6.3.4 Anaerobic respiration

The supply of oxygen to the tissues via the tracheae is very efficient and even in flight, when oxidative processes are extremely active, the supply normally keeps pace with the rate at which the substrate is dehydrogenated and electrons transferred to the cytochromes. Thus it is unusual for oxidation to be incomplete, but anaerobic respiration may sometimes occur during flight (see p. 267) and insects can survive under anaerobic conditions for quite long periods.

In anaerobic respiration the breakdown of the substrate does not proceed beyond glycolysis. In vertebrates pyruvate, the end product of glycolysis, is reduced to lactate. Insect tissues other than flight muscle do have a lactic dehydrogenase, leading to the formation of two molecules of lactic acid for every molecule of glucose used, with a consequent net gain in energy. This system is known to occur in insects or tissues where oxygen is likely to be in short supply. Thus it is found in the leg muscle of *Belostoma*, an aquatic bug, and in the aquatic larva of *Chironomus* (Diptera). It also occurs in the femoral muscles of grasshoppers, where during jumping there is a momentary very high demand for energy in a tissue far removed from the spiracles and with a relatively poor oxygen supply.

When anaerobiosis does occur the end products are oxidised as soon as sufficient oxygen becomes available again. The oxygen requirement for this oxidation is called an oxygen debt and such a debt is indicated by a rate of respiration higher than normal when the insect returns to aerobic respiration. Thus during sustained flight *Schistocerca* builds up a small oxygen debt. When flight stops, the rate of oxygen consumption exceeds the normal resting rate for a short time while the products of glycolysis are oxidised (the oxygen debt is paid off) (Fig. 59).

6.4 End products of catabolism

The breakdown of carbohydrates and fats ultimately results in the production of water and carbon dioxide. The water may be eliminated via the Malpighian tubules (p. 595) and the carbon dioxide via the tracheal system (p. 542). Protein catabolism leads to the production of ammonia in addition to water and carbon dioxide and since ammonia is toxic to cells it must be eliminated from the body. In insects ammonia is not usually excreted as such but is converted into the less toxic uric acid, which requires less water for its safe elimination. There are also other possible end products of nitrogen metabolism which may, or may not, be derived from uric acid.

Uric acid

The synthesis of uric acid probably utilises glycine, glutamine and aspartate as substrates and involves formate, ribose-5-phosphate and ATP. The fat body is probably important in this synthesis but whether or not it is the only or even the most important tissue involved in the synthesis is not known.

Uric acid is also derived from the metabolism of purines such as adenine and guanine, which may be released during the breakdown of nucleic acid.

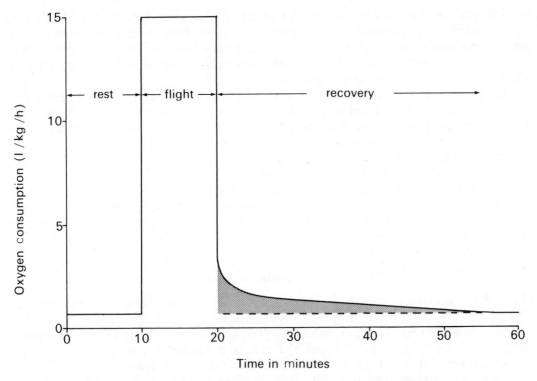

Fig. 59 Oxygen consumption of *Schistocerca* at rest and during flight showing the elevated consumption during flight and afterwards during the recovery from an oxygen debt (hatched area) (after Krogh and Weis-Fogh, 1951)

ADENINE ⟶ HYPOXANTHINE ⟶ XANTHINE ⟶ URIC ACID
⟶ (from) GUANINE

Other end products

Allantoin is excreted by aquatic insects, and uricase, which produces allantoin from uric acid, is present in Orthoptera, Coleoptera, Lepidoptera and Diptera. The larva of *Lucilia* accumulates uric acid in the tissues, but excretes allantoin and ammonia.

URIC ACID —URICASE→ ALLANTOIN —ALLANTOINASE→ ALLANTOIC ACID [—ALLANTOICASE→ UREA + GLYOXALIC ACID] ·?

Allantoic acid occurs in the excreta of larval and adult Lepidoptera and larval Hymenoptera, constituting 0·2–0·4 % of the wet weight of the excreta compared with 1–40 % of uric acid. It also comprises up to 25 % of the meconium, the waste products of pupal metabolism discharged when the adult emerges. Allantoic acid is produced from allantoin by the action of allantoinase.

Urea is commonly present in small amounts in the excreta of insects. Sometimes, as in *Rhodnius*, it may be derived directly from the diet, but in most cases it is synthesised by the insect. It is not certain if an allantoicase occurs by which urea might be derived from allantoic acid. In *Schistocerca* and some other insects there is some evidence for an ornithine cycle (see *e.g.* Gilmour, 1961) as in vertebrates, but in Diptera it is concluded that no ornithine cycle is present.

Ammonia is excreted in large amounts by the larvae of aquatic insects and blowflies. It is not derived from the breakdown of urea, but may be carried in a bound form to the excretory organs and there released by deamination. *Lucilia* (Diptera) larva has an adenosine deaminase with high activity in the gut and Malpighian tubules.

6.5 Metabolic rate

The rates at which metabolic processes proceed vary considerably but for resting insects oxygen consumption, used as a measure of metabolism, is greater in the adult than in the larva, while the pupal consumption is lower than either (Fig. 60). Even within these stages the rate is variable and in the pupa oxygen consumption is at first high, then falls off, but rises again before adult emergence (Fig. 61). The oxygen consumption of diapausing insects follows a similar pattern, being high during phases of morphogenesis, but low during the period of diapause development.

Activity results in sharp increases in metabolism. Thus in resting *Apis* energy is consumed at the rate of 38 J/kg/h; during flight the figure may be up to 48 times as high and in *Schistocerca* oxygen consumption increases by a factor of 25 or more during flight (Fig. 59). Usually larger insects have slightly lower metabolic rates than small ones.

Extrinsic factors also influence metabolism, and temperature is particularly important. Metabolism increases with temperature up to a maximum and then sharply declines at the upper lethal temperature (Fig. 60).

The respiratory quotient, $\dfrac{CO_2 \text{ output}}{O_2 \text{ input}}$, varies with the substrate which is being oxidised. If the substrate is completely oxidised, carbohydrate metabolism is associated with an R. Q. of 1·0 and fat metabolism with an R. Q. of 0·7. Thus a cockroach has an R. Q. of 1·0, but after several days' starvation, when it is using fat reserves, the R. Q. falls to 0·7. The respiratory quotient of *Drosophila* in sustained flight is 1·0, that of *Schistocerca* 0·7, suggesting the utilisation of carbohydrates and fats respectively.

6.6 Control of metabolism

Cell metabolism in many instances is controlled by hormones. Thus, hormones are known to be concerned in the control of growth and differentiation, cuticular tanning, development of the gonads, rate of heartbeat, diuresis, the mobilisation of energy

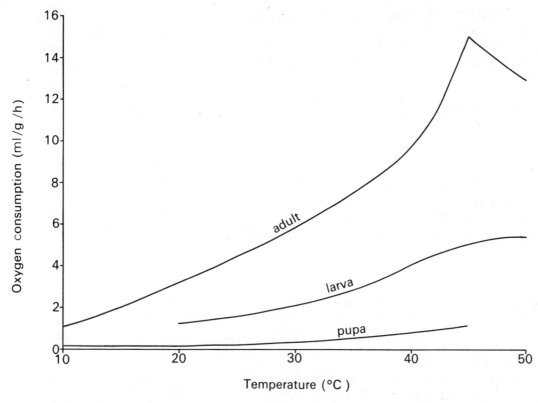

Fig. 60 Oxygen consumption of larval, pupal and adult *Calliphora vomitoria* showing the increase in consumption with temperature and, in adults, the sharp fall at the upper lethal temperature (data from Battelli and Stern, 1913)

reserves and the activity of the central nervous system. The mode of action of the hormones is not understood, but it is possible that they act directly on the cell nucleus so activating or depressing the activity of certain genes (see Chapter XXXIV).

Within the cell some regulation results from the structural organisation of the cell, some components being spatially isolated from others. Thus, part of the respiratory cycle occurs in the cytoplasm, part in the mitochondria, and the enzymes and substrates involved are effectively isolated from each other. The rates of enzyme reaction are regulated by the availability of substrate or coenzymes and by the accumulation of the products of enzyme activity.

Sacktor (1970) discusses the control of oxidative metabolism in insect flight muscle and suggests a series of events, following the arrival of a nerve impulse at the muscle, which may regulate the change from resting to the highly active state. It is envisaged that in the resting state a number of enzyme systems are inhibited and removal of this inhibition results in very high metabolic rates. In the fly these systems are:

1. phosphorylase and trehalase, which control the entrance of carbohydrates into the catabolic pathway (see diagram p. 105)

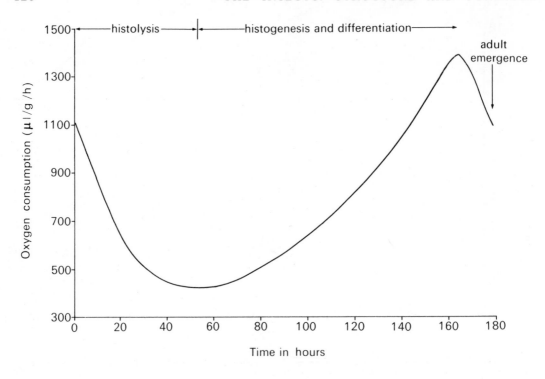

Fig. 61 Oxygen consumption of the pupa of *Galleria*. Not all insects show the fall in consumption just before adult emergence (from Wigglesworth, 1965)

2. phosphofructokinase, which limits the rate of glycolysis by controlling the rate of production of fructose-1, 6-diphosphate (see diagram p. 112)

3. mitochondrial oxidation of pyruvate and α-glycerophosphate (see diagram p. 115)

4. oxidation of proline to provide intermediates for the citric acid cycle (see p. 226)

The release of Ca^{++} ions from the sarcoplasmic reticulum by the arrival of the nerve impulse is believed to activate a phosphorylase kinase, the mitochondrial α-glycerophosphate dehydrogenase and ATPase. The first leads to the production of an active phosphorylase which catalyses the breakdown of glycogen making glucose available for fuel. ADP is produced from ATP by the ATPase, so reactions are not limited by lack of ADP as a phosphate acceptor and the change in balance of ATP and ADP may result in a shift in the energy charge such that phosphofructokinase is activated and the transformation of glucose to fructose-1, 6-diphosphate can proceed without interruption. Finally the activation of α-glycerophosphate dehydrogenase facilitates the oxidation of α-glycerophosphate and the regeneration of NAD required for pyruvate production (diagram p. 112). Consequently all these reactions can proceed at maximal rates and ATP is synthesised at the very high rate which results in the enormous power output of the muscles. This continues as long as Ca^{++} is made available by the arrival of nerve impulses at the muscle and ADP is generated from ATP by the ATPase.

6.7 Luminescence

A number of insects appear to luminesce, but in many cases this luminescence is due to bacteria. Self-luminescence, not involving bacteria, is only known to occur in a few Collembola, such as *Onychiurus armatus*, in the homopteran *Fulgora lanternaria*, in a few larval Diptera belonging to the families Platyuridae and Bolitophilidae, and in a relatively large number of Coleoptera, primarily in the families Lampyridae, Elateridae and Phengodidae. In these families luminescence may occur in both sexes or be restricted to the female; it also occurs in some larval forms.

The light-producing organs occur in various parts of the body. *Onychiurus* emits a general glow from the whole body, but in most beetles the light organs are relatively compact. They are often on the ventral surface of the abdomen. In male *Photuris* (Coleoptera) there is a pair of light organs in the ventral region of each of the sixth and seventh abdominal segments. In the female the organs are smaller and often only occur in one segment. The larvae have a pair of small light organs in segment eight, but these disappear at metamorphosis when the adult structures form. A review of the positions and anatomy of light organs in fireflies is given by Buck (1948). In *Fulgora* the light organ is in the head.

The light organs are generally derived from the fat body, but in *Bolitophila* (Diptera) they are formed from the enlarged distal ends of the Malpighian tubules.

6.7.1 Structure of a light-producing organ

The structure of the light organ or lantern of adult *Photuris* has been studied in detail by Smith (1963) and the following description is based on his account.

Each light organ consists of a number of large cells, the photocytes, lying just beneath the epidermis and backed by several layers of cells called the dorsal layer cells (Fig. 62). The cuticle overlying the light organ is transparent. The photocytes are so arranged that they form cylinders running at right angles to the cuticle, and within each cylinder are tracheae and nerves. Each trachea gives off branches at right angles and as these branches enter the region of the photocytes they break up into a number of tracheoles, which run between the photocytes parallel with the cuticle. The tracheoles are spaced 10 to 15 μm apart and since the photocytes are only about 10 μm thick the diffusion path for oxygen is short. The origin of the tracheoles is enclosed within a large tracheal end cell, the inner membrane of which, where it bounds the tracheoblast (p. 531), is complexly folded. In some species the end cells are only poorly developed.

The nerves entering the photocyte cylinder end as spatulate terminal processes between the plasma membranes of the end cell and the tracheoblast within which the tracheoles arise. There are two types of vesicles within the terminal process; large vesicles, about 100 nm across, resembling neurosecretory droplets, and smaller ones, 20–40 nm across, which are typical of the vesicles found in presynaptic positions and containing acetylcholine (p. 630).

The photocytes are packed with photocyte granules, each of which contains a cavity connecting with the outside cytoplasm via a neck. It is presumed that the reactants involved in light production are housed in these granules. Smaller granules also occur dorsally and ventrally. Mitochondria are sparsely distributed except where the cell adjoins the end cells and tracheoles. The dorsal layer cells also contain granules,

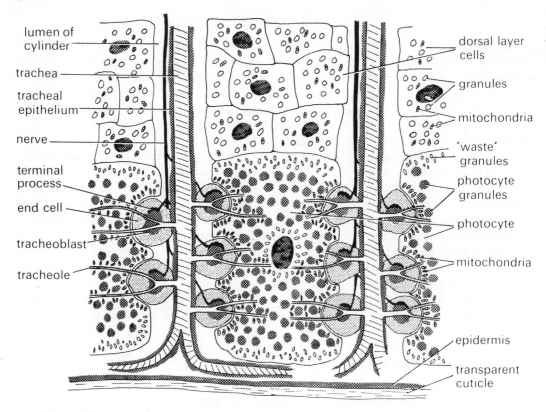

Fig. 62 Diagrammatic section through part of the light organ of *Photuris*. The tracheoles pass between the photocytes, but do not penetrate into the cells (based on Smith, 1963)

generally regarded as urate granules, and it has been supposed that the cells form a reflecting layer. There is, however, no evidence for this and it has also been suggested that the oxyluciferin irreversibly produced in light production (section 6.7.2) is stored in them.

In *Photinus* (Coleoptera) it is estimated that the two lanterns together contain about 15 000 photocytes forming some 6000 cylinders, each with 80–100 end cells.

The lanterns of larval fireflies contain the same elements, but their organisation is simpler. The tracheal system is diffuse and there are no tracheal end cells. Nerve endings occur on the photocytes, not separated from them by the tracheal end cells as in adult *Photuris*. In adult *Pteroptyx* (Coleoptera) and some other genera nerve endings occur on the photocytes as well as on the tracheal end cells.

6.7.2 Mechanism of light production

Basically, light is produced by the oxidation of luciferin, in the presence of the enzyme, luciferase. Luciferin is first activated by ATP in the presence of magnesium and luciferase to produce adenylluciferin. This is oxidised by an organic peroxide, again in the presence of luciferase, to form so-called excited adenyloxyluciferin, which decays

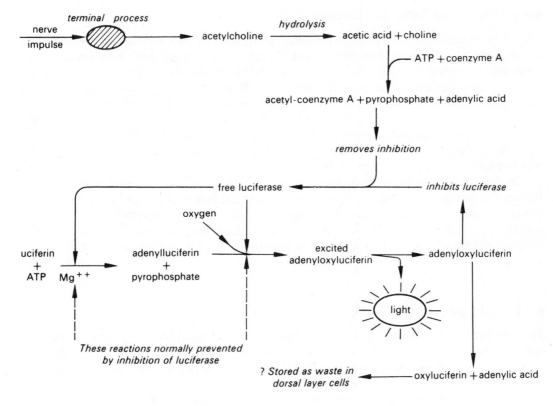

Scheme of the reactions involved in light production.

spontaneously to low energy adenyloxyluciferin with the production of light. The energy for this reaction is obtained directly from the oxidation process, not from the ATP, and it is released in one large step. The reaction is very efficient, some 98% of the energy involved being released as light.

The low energy adenyloxyluciferin produced inhibits further reaction, perhaps by becoming bound to the luciferase; pyrophosphate, however, removes the inhibition. It is suggested that when the light organ is stimulated by a nerve the acetylcholine released at the nerve ending (section 6.7.4) reacts with ATP and coenzyme A to yield pyrophosphate. This diffuses to the photocyte granules and stimulates the production of light by removing the inhibition of luciferase. During the reaction in the photocyte more pyrophosphate is released and this may spread through the cell, extending the reaction (Gilmour, 1961; McElroy, 1965).

6.7.3 Colour of light produced

In many insects the light produced by the light organs is yellow-green in colour, extending over a relatively narrow band of wavelengths, 520–650 nm in *Photinus* and *Lampyris* (Coleoptera). The light is blue-green in *Bolitophila*, white in *Fulgora*. *Phrixothrix* (Coleoptera) larvae and adult females have 11 pairs of green light organs on the thorax and abdomen, and a pair of red ones on the head.

6.7.4 Control of light production

The light organs of *Photuris* are innervated from the last two abdominal ganglia. The axons, acting via the end cells, supply small parts of each organ and these units can be stimulated to produce light independently of the rest of the organ. There is a long delay between the time of stimulation of the nerve and the production of light, suggesting that a chemical diffuses a certain distance before light is produced. Possibly the arrival of the nerve impulse at the nerve ending leads to the release of acetylcholine, which then diffuses out initiating the reaction in the photocytes (section 6.7.2). The flash produced by each unit is very short, but different units are usually out of phase, so the organ as a whole produces a relatively long flash.

In *Photinus* each flash from the whole organ lasts a few hundred milliseconds, flashes following each other at regular time intervals, but in some larval insects and in *Lampyris* and *Platyura* (Diptera) the light is emitted as a sustained glow. In these insects the end cells are less well-developed than they are in *Photinus* and the mechanism by which light production is controlled may be rather different (Carlson, 1969).

6.7.5 Light production in the field

In most luminous insects light production has sexual significance. Light signals are used in two basic ways in Lampyridae (Lloyd, 1971). In some species, such as *Lampyris*, the female is sedentary and attracts the male to herself; in other species, such as *Photuris* and *Photinus*, one sex, usually the male, flies around flashing in a specific manner. The male of *Photinus pyralis*, for instance, produces single short flashes at regular intervals. If he comes within three or four metres of a female she flashes in response, the delay between male and female flashes being characteristic of the species. The male then turns and moves towards the female and after five to ten exchanges of signals reaches the female and mates with her.

Sexual recognition depends on species-specific signals. The wavelength of light emitted is constant for a species and may differ between species, while flash duration and the interval between flashes is often characteristic (Fig. 63). For instance, the female of *P. pyralis* flashes in response to a male flash after an interval of two seconds; the males do not respond to flashes occurring after different time intervals. The females of *P. scintillans* respond to flashes lasting 0·13–0·16 seconds, but not to flashes of 0·20–0·34 seconds duration. Precise timing requires a very well-defined time marker and flashes begin or end with sharp transients which probably serve this function.

Certain species of fireflies, notably in South-east Asia, form male groups in which the individual insects flash in synchrony. It is probable that the flashing groups attract females (Lloyd, 1971). The males of these species, in isolation, can flash regularly with almost constant intervals between flashes. Buck and Buck (1968) observed one individual of *Pteroptyx* with a mean flash-cycle length of 557·3 ms and 95 % of all flash cycles fell within 5 ms of this mean. Synchrony is achieved when individual insects set their normal free-running flashing cycles by a single pacer signal.

The luminescence of *Bolitophila* larvae serves as a lure, attracting insects on which they feed into networks of glutinous silk threads.

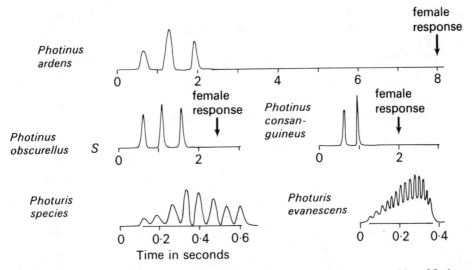

Fig. 63 Flash patterns of various fireflies. Heights of peaks show relative intensities of flashes (after Lloyd, 1971)

REFERENCES

BADE, M. L. (1964). Biosynthesis of fatty acids in the roach *Eurycotis floridana*. *J. Insect Physiol*. **10**: 333–342.

BAILEY, E. (1975). Biochemistry of insect flight. Part 2—fuel supply. *in* Candy, D. J. and Kilby, B. A. (eds.), *Insect biochemistry and function*. Chapman and Hall, London.

BATELLI, F. and STERN, L. (1913). Intensität des respiratorischen Gaswechsels der Insekten. *Biochem. Z*. **56**: 50–58.

BUCK, J. B. (1948). The anatomy and physiology of the light organ in fireflies. *Ann. N.Y. Acad. Sci*. **49**: 397–483.

BUCK, J. B. and BUCK, E. M. (1968). Mechanism of rhythmic synchronous flashing of fireflies. *Science* **159**: 1319–1327.

CANDY, D. J. and KILBY, B. A. (1962). Studies on chitin synthesis in the desert locust. *J. exp. Biol*. **39**: 129–140.

CARLSON, A. D. (1969). Neural control of firefly luminescence. *Adv. Insect Physiol*. **6**: 51–96.

CLEMENTS, A. N. (1959). Studies on the metabolism of insect fat body. *J. exp. Biol*. **36**: 665–675.

CLEMENTS, A. N. (1963). *The physiology of mosquitoes*. Pergamon Press, Oxford.

FRIEDMAN, S. (1970). Metabolism of carbohydrates in insects. *in* Florkin, M. and Scheer, B. T. (eds.), *Chemical Zoology*. vol. 5. Academic Press, New York and London.

FRIEDMAN, S. (1978). Trehalose regulation, one aspect of metabolic homeostasis. *A. Rev. Ent*. **23**: 389–407.

GILBERT, L. I. (1967). Lipid metabolism and function in insects. *Adv. Insect Physiol*. **4**: 70–211.

GILBERT, L. I. and O'CONNOR, J. D. (1970). Lipid metabolism and transport in arthropods. *in* Florkin, M. and Scheer, B. T. (eds.), *Chemical Zoology*. vol. 5. Academic Press, New York and London.

GILMOUR, D. (1961). *The biochemistry of insects*. Academic Press, New York and London.

GILMOUR, D. (1965). *The metabolism of insects*. Oliver and Boyd, Edinburgh.

GRASSÉ, P.-P. and GHARAGOZLOU, I. (1963). L'ergastoplasme et la genèse des protéines dans le tissu adipeux royal du termite à cou jaune. *C. r. hebd. Séanc. Acad. Sci., Paris*. **257**: 3546–3548.

GRASSÉ, P.-P. and GHARAGOZLOU, I. (1964). Sur une nouvelle sorte de cellules du tissu adipeux royal de *Calotermes flavicollis* (Insecte isoptère): l'endolophocyte. *C. r. hebd. Séanc. Acad. Sci., Paris*. **258**: 1045–1047.

HANSFORD, R. G. and SACKTOR, B. (1971). Oxidative metabolism of Insecta. *in* Florkin, M. and Scheer, B. T. (eds.), *Chemical Zoology*. vol. 6. Academic Press, New York and London.

ILAN, J. and ILAN, J. (1974). Protein synthesis in insects. *in* Rockstein, M. (ed.), *The physiology of Insecta*. vol. 4. Academic Press, New York and London.

KAMMER, A. E. and HEINRICH, B. (1978). Insect flight metabolism. *Adv. Insect Physiol.* **13**: 133–228.

KEELEY, L. L. (1978). Endocrine regulation of fat body development and function. *A. Rev. Ent.* **23**: 329–352.

KEILIN, D. and WANG, Y. L. (1946). Haemoglobin of *Gastrophilus* larvae. Purification and properties. *Biochem. J.* **40**: 855–866.

KILBY, B. A. (1963). The biochemistry of insect fat body. *Adv. Insect Physiol.* **1**: 112–174.

KROGH, A. and WEIS-FOGH, T. (1951). The respiratory exchange of the desert locust (*Schistocerca gregaria*), before, during and after flight. *J. exp. Biol.* **28**: 342–357.

LLOYD, J. L. (1971). Bioluminescent communication in insects. *A. Rev. Ent.* **16**: 97–122.

McELROY, W. D. (1965). Insect bioluminescence. *in* Rockstein, M. (ed.), *The physiology of Insecta*. vol. 1. Academic Press, New York.

McELROY, W. D., SELIGER, H. H. and DELUCA, M. (1974). Insect bioluminescence. *in* Rockstein, M. (ed.), *The physiology of Insecta*. vol. 2. Academic Press, New York and London.

NAIR, K. S. S. and GEORGE, J. C. (1964). A histological and histochemical study of the larval fat body of *Anthrenus vorax* Waterhouse (Dermestidae, Coleoptera). *J. Insect Physiol.* **10**: 509–517.

NEVILLE, A. C. (1975). *Biology of the arthropod cuticle*. Springer-Verlag, Berlin.

ROBBINS, W. E., KAPLANIS, J. N., SVOBODA, J. A. AND THOMPSON, M. J. (1971). Steroid metabolism in insects. *A. Rev. Ent.* **16**: 53–72.

SACKTOR, B. (1970). Regulation of intermediary metabolism, with special reference to the control mechanisms in insect flight muscle. *Adv. Insect Physiol.* **7**: 268–347.

SACKTOR, B. (1974). Biological oxidations and energetics in insect mitochondria. *in* Rockstein, M. (ed.), *The physiology of Insecta*. vol. 4. Academic Press, New York and London.

SACKTOR, B. (1975). Biochemistry of insect flight. Part 1—utilization of fuels by muscle. *in* Candy, D. J. and Kilby, B. A. (eds.), *Insect Biochemistry and function*. Chapman and Hall, London.

SCHOFFENIELS, E. and GILLES, R. (1970). Nitrogenous constituents and nitrogen metabolism in arthropods. *in* Florkin, M. and Scheer, B. T. (eds.), *Chemical Zoology*. vol. 5. Academic Press, New York and London.

SMITH, D. S. (1963). The organization and innervation of the luminescent organ in a firefly, *Photuris pennsylvanica* (Coleoptera). *J. Cell Biol.* **16**: 323–359.

SVOBODA, J. A., KAPLANIS, J. N., ROBBINS, W. E. and THOMPSON, M. J. (1975). Recent developments in insect steroid metabolism. *A. Rev. Ent.* **20**: 205–220.

WALKER, P. A. (1965). The structure of the fat body in normal and starved cockroaches as seen with the electron microscope. *J. Insect Physiol.* **11**: 1625–1631.

WIGGLESWORTH, V. B. (1965). *The principles of insect physiology*. Methuen, London.

WYATT, G. R. (1967). The biochemistry of sugars and polysaccharides in insects. *Adv. Insect Physiol.* **4**: 287–360.

CHAPTER VII
COLOUR

Some pigments play a vital role in metabolic processes and their production is often linked with other processes in the body. Several different classes of pigment exist and they are responsible for many of the colours of insects. Most whites, blues and metallic colours, on the other hand, result from the physical structure of the surface of the cuticle and not from pigments.

Short-term, reversible colour change resulting from the movement of pigments only occurs in a few insects, but long-term changes in the deposition of pigment commonly occur. These often result in the insect matching its background, and if the background undergoes a permanent alteration the colour of the insect may undergo a parallel evolutionary change.

The colour of many insects tends to conceal them from potential predators. Other insects have markings which help to frighten off predators, or they may have a conspicuous colouration associated with distastefulness so that predators soon learn to avoid them. Different species, which may or may not themselves be distasteful, may have a similar colouration to a distasteful species so that they benefit from the learned avoidance by predators of this particular colour pattern.

Colours are also important in intraspecific recognition, and sometimes excretory products are stored in a coloured form.

Animal colours are reviewed by Broughton (1965) and Fox and Vevers (1960). Aspects of insect colouration are considered by Fuzeau-Braesch (1972), Hinton (1976), Linzen (1974), Rowell (1971) and Ziegler and Harmsen (1969). The significance of colour is considered extensively by Cott (1957).

7.1 The nature of colour

Colour is produced from white light when some of the wavelengths are eliminated, usually by absorption, and the remainder are reflected or transmitted. The wavelengths of the reflected or transmitted component determine the colour which is seen (Fig. 64). If all wavelengths are reflected equally the reflecting surface appears white; if all are absorbed the appearance is black.

Differential reflection of light to produce colours occurs in one of two ways: the physical nature of the surface may be such that only certain wavelengths are reflected, or pigments may be present which, as a result of their molecular structure, absorb certain wavelengths and reflect the remainder. Colours produced by these methods are known, respectively, as physical (or structural) and pigmentary colours.

127

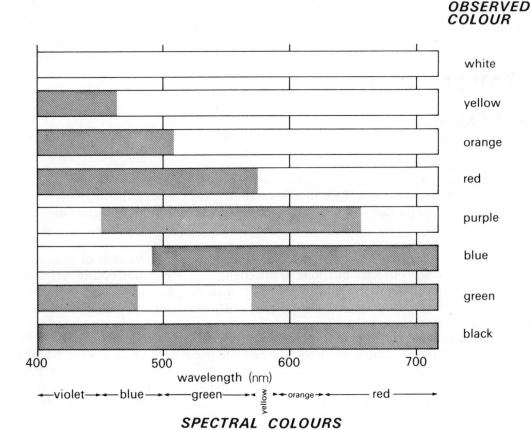

Fig. 64 Colour production by the elimination (*e.g.* absorption) of certain wavelengths from white light. Eliminated wavelengths are hatched, reflected wavelengths clear (from Fox, 1953)

7.2 Physical colours

Surface structures are mainly responsible for the production of whites, blues and iridescent colours. Such colours may be produced by scattering, interference or diffraction.

7.2.1 Scattering

Light may be scattered, that is, reflected in all directions, by irregularities of a surface or by granules just beneath it. If the irregularities or granules are large relative to the wavelength of light all the light is reflected and the surface appears white. Most whites in insects are produced in this way, although some white pigments also occur. Matt whites are produced by an even scattering of the light in all directions and in Lepidoptera, such as Pieridae, this results from deep longitudinal corrugations and fine, unordered striations on the surface of the scales (but see also p. 134). Pearly whites, such as occur in *Argynnis* (Lepidoptera), are produced by scattering from a number of thin, overlapping lamellae separated by airspaces. In butterflies the lamellae are the upper and lower laminae of overlapping scales (Mason, 1926).

If the granules near the surface are very small (0.6μm or less), with dimensions similar to the wavelengths of blue light, the short, blue waves are reflected while the longer wavelengths are not. This type of scattering is called Tyndall scattering and produces blue or green. It depends for its effect on an absorbing layer of dark pigment beneath the fine granules. In the absence of this layer the blue is masked by light reflected from the background.

Tyndall blues are uncommon in insects, but the blue of dragonflies is produced in this way, the dark background being provided by a brown–violet ommatin.

7.2.2 Interference

Interference colours result from the reflection of light from a series of superimposed surfaces separated by distances comparable with the wavelengths of light. As a result of this spacing some of the wavelengths reflected from successive surfaces will be in phase and so are reinforced, others are out of phase and are cancelled out. The net result is that only certain wavelengths are reflected and the surface appears coloured (Fig. 65). The wavelength of the reflected colour depends on the refractive index of the material and

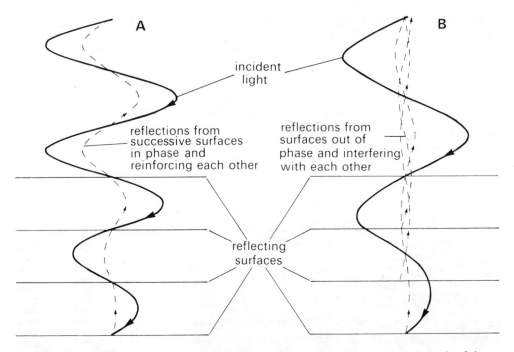

Fig. 65 Diagrammatic representation of colour production by interference. At each of the reflecting surfaces some light is reflected while the remainder is transmitted at a lower intensity (as indicated by the reduced amplitude). The diagram shows two components of incident white light, the wavelength of one of which (A) bears a simple relationship to the distance between the reflecting surfaces so that its reflections from these surfaces reinforce each other. The other component (B) has a wavelength unrelated to the distance between the surfaces so that its reflections interfere with each other (after Richards, 1951)

the distance between the reflecting surfaces. Viewing the surface from an oblique angle is equivalent to reducing the distance between successive surfaces so that the colour changes in a definite sequence as the angle of viewing becomes more oblique (Newton's series). This change in colour with the angle of viewing is called iridescence and is a characteristic of interference colours (Mason, 1923, 1927a, 1927b).

Interference colours are common in Lepidoptera, being produced by the scales. In *Uranio* the iridescent scales are hollow with an upper lamina composed of five to ten lamellae which produce colour by interference (Fig. 66). Viewed from immediately above, different scales appear green, blue or reddish-purple, depending on the spacing of the lamellae, changing to purple, orange and yellow-green when viewed obliquely. In *Lycaena* the iridescence is produced by the lower lamina of the scale seen through the grid-like upper surface (Mason, 1927a).

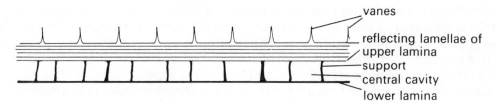

Fig. 66 Diagrammatic transverse section of a scale of *Uranio* (modified after Mason, 1927a)

The blue of *Morpho* (Lepidoptera) is produced by a different type of scale which consists of a flat basal plate carrying a large number of vertical vanes running parallel to the length of the scale on Y-shaped supports (Fig. 67). Each vane is made up of a number of delicate vertical lamellae supported by a series of vertical and obliquely horizontal mullions (thickenings). There are twelve horizontal mullions spaced about 0·19 μm apart and becoming thicker towards the base of the vane. Collectively the mullions of adjacent lamellae form a series of reflecting surfaces so spaced that a blue

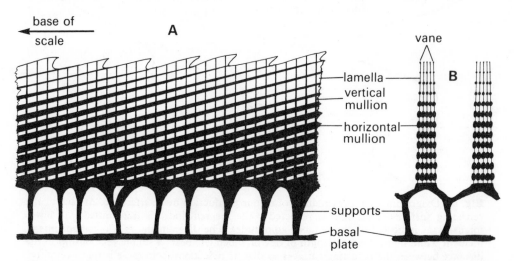

Fig. 67 A. Diagrammatic representation of a lateral view of part of an iridiscent scale of *Morpho*. B. Transverse section of part of the scale (after Anderson and Richards, 1942)

colour is produced by interference effects (Anderson and Richards, 1942).

In Scarabaeidae the reflecting layers are formed by lamellae in the exocuticle. These lamellae are produced by microfibrils with a common orientation. This orientation changes progressively in successive layers so that a helicoidal arrangement is produced within which any given orientation recurs at intervals (Neville, 1975). This arrangement confers on the cuticle certain optical properties, and the spacing between layers of microfibrils with the same orientation determines whether or not interference colours are produced. If the spacing between the reflecting surfaces is constant, specific colours are produced; impure colours are produced if the spacing increases regularly with increasing distance from the surface of the cuticle. In this way the bronze of *Potosia* and gold of *Plusiotis* are produced as interference colours. *Plusiotis* also lacks any black backing pigment in the cuticle; spectral purity is enhanced when such a layer is present.

Interference colours may also be produced by layers in the cuticle which are formed independently of the helicoidal layers of microfibrils. In *Hetororrhina* alternating layers of cuticle have different refractive indices, so they act as reflectors and a green colour is produced. *Smaragdesthes*, with a different spacing between the layers, is blue. In some tortoise beetles interference colours are produced by layers of cuticle immediately adjacent to the epidermis which are separated from each other by layers with a high water content.

Apart from colours of the (human) visible spectrum, ultraviolet may also be produced as an interference colour. This occurs in Pieridae. In *Eurema* certain scales possess reflecting lamellae about 55 nm thick separated by air gaps of about 80 nm. This system reflects light with a peak wavelength of 350 nm.

The brightness of the reflected colour increases with the number of reflecting surfaces and in *Aspidomorpha* there are 44 layers, while in *Plusiotis* the high degree of reflection results from a large amount of uric acid in the reflecting layers.

The iridescence of membranous insect wings is due to reflection from the surfaces of a series of cuticular layers.

7.2.3 Diffraction

A series of fine grooves or ridges separated by spaces corresponding with the wavelength of light will split white light into its component spectral colours. This is known as diffraction. Colours are produced by diffraction in at least 19 groups of beetles (Hinton, 1976) in which the spacings between the gratings vary from 0·8 to 3·3 μm. Diffraction gratings occur on the elytron where these are fully developed, or on the abdomen of Staphylinidae, so that the insects are iridescent in bright light. Scarabaeidae have rows of microtrichia along the gratings and the effect of these is to make the insects iridescent when viewed from one direction, but not from the opposite direction. The rib spacing of some lepidopteran scales is appropriate to produce diffraction colours, but their irregularity produces an overlap of spectra and so white light results. Diffraction colours are not produced in dim light and beetles which iridesce in bright light look black or brown at low light intensities.

7.3 Pigmentary colours

Pigmentary colours result from the molecular structure of certain compounds. Particularly important in the production of colour are double bonds, $C = C$, $C = O$,

$C = N$, and $N = N$, the number and arrangement of these being important. Particular groupings are also important. The —NH$_2$ and —Cl radicals, for instance, shift the absorptive region of a particular compound so that it tends to absorb longer wavelengths. The colour-producing molecule, known as the chromophore, is often conjugated with a protein molecule, forming a chromoprotein. The black and brown colours of insects often result from the colour of the cuticle; other pigments occur in the epidermal cells and sometimes in internal tissues.

7.3.1 Brown and black of cuticle

The black or brown colour of much insect cuticle is attributed to the pigment melanin, but, if the definition of melanin is restricted to compounds composed of polymerised indole rings, this is not entirely true. Hardening of the cuticle involves cross-linkages between the protein molecules, quinones providing the links (p. 507), and some darkening does result from this tanning process. However, hardening and darkening may be independent of each other. Thus, albino *Schistocerca* have a hard, but colourless cuticle and when a normal locust moults it exhibits some dark markings before it hardens. This suggests that darkening may involve some deposition of melanin.

Melanin synthesis, like sclerotisation (p. 523), involves tyrosine and dopaquinone:

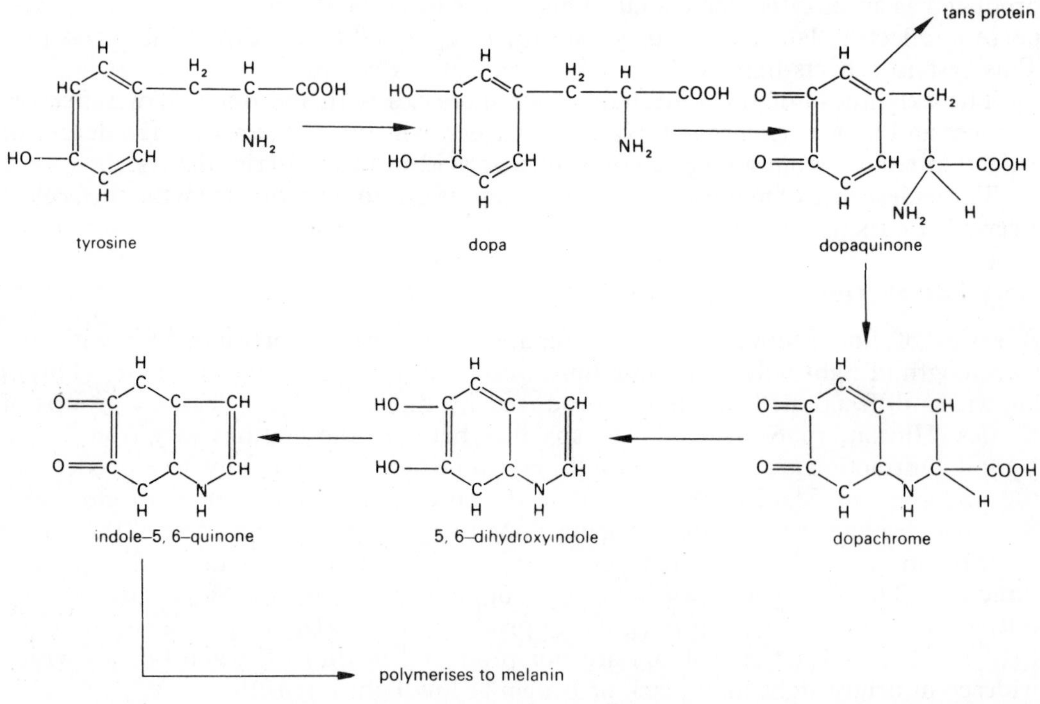

tans protein

tyrosine   dopa   dopaquinone

indole–5, 6–quinone   5, 6–dihydroxyindole   dopachrome

polymerises to melanin

It is possible that quinones are produced in excess of those needed in sclerotisation and the excess polymerise to melanin. Such polymerisation could take place round the quinones linking the proteins provided that these still have substitutable positions (Cottrell, 1964).

The dark colouring of cuticle is diffuse, but typically melanin occurs in a granular form. Dark granules, which may be melanin, do exist in the epidermis of *Carausius* and true melanin, in the chemical sense, is present in the cuticle of various flies (Fuzeau-Braesch, 1972).

7.3.2. Carotenoids

Carotenoids are a major group of pigments, soluble in fats and containing no nitrogen. They are built up from isoprene residues:

$$CH_2 \!=\!\!=\! C(CH_3) \!-\!\!-\! CH \!=\!\!=\! CH_2$$

isoprene

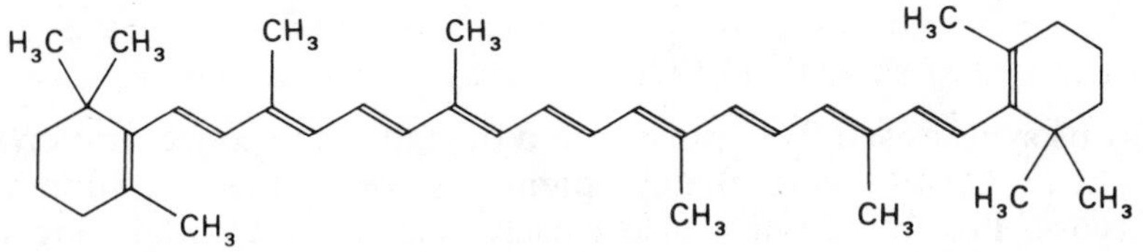

β-carotene

Carotenoids are of plant origin and are not synthesised by insects. There are two groups: the carotenes, and their oxidised derivatives—the xanthophylls. The latter may be obtained in the diet, but can also be produced by insects by the oxidation of carotene.

Yellow, orange and red are commonly produced by carotenoids, the colour depending largely on the form of the terminal isoprene residues—whether or not they form a closed ring and the degree of unsaturation.

The yellow of larval and mature adult *Schistocerca* is produced by β-carotene, which also occurs in internal organs, and in various insect secretions, such as the silk of *Bombyx* (Lepidoptera) and beeswax.

The red colour of *Coccinella* (Coleoptera) is due to α- and β-carotenes together with lycopene, and the latter also produces the red of *Pyrrhocoris* (Heteroptera). Astaxanthin, a xanthophyll, is produced from carotene in the cuticle of *Schistocerca* and contributes to the pink colour of the immature adult, although this is mainly due to ommochromes.

In grasshoppers of the genus *Oedipoda* carotenoid proteins produce the blue, red and yellow of the hindwings of different species.

In combination with a blue pigment, usually mesobiliverdin, carotenoids produce greens (green produced in this way is sometimes known as insectoverdin). The yellow component is β-carotene in *Carausius* (Phasmida) and *Schistocerca* blood, β-carotene and astaxanthin in the integument of solitary *Schistocerca* larvae, and lutein, a xanthophyll, in the larva of *Sphinx* (Lepidoptera).

The functions of carotenoids in cell metabolism are not known, but small quantities are probably concerned in the production of the visual pigment retinene (p. 653). Feltwell (1978) reviews the distribution of carotenoids in insects.

7.3.3 Pterines (pteridines)

The pterines are nitrogen-containing compounds, all having the same basic structure, but differing in the radicals attached to this nucleus (Ziegler-Günder, 1956; Ziegler and Harmsen, 1969).

xanthopterin   erythropterin

Pterines may be synthesised from purines and the fall in the concentration of uric acid in the pupa of *Drosophila* when the eye pigments are synthesised supports this (see Chefurka, 1965). Possibly flavins, also closely related compounds, are involved in pterine synthesis.

White (leucopterin), yellow (xanthopterin) and red (erythropterin) are commonly produced by pterines, xanthopterin being the most widely distributed. Other pterines, such as biopterin, fluoresce in ultraviolet light, although they do not appear coloured in daylight.

Pterines are important pigments in Lepidoptera. Leucopterin and xanthopterin are common in the wings of Pieridae, where they supplement the structural white. The yellow of the brimstone butterfly is due to chrysopterin, the brighter colour of the male resulting from its higher concentration, while the red of the orange-tip butterfly is due to erythropterin. The yellows of Hymenoptera are produced by crystalline granules of pterine in the epidermis overlying areas of metabolically inactive tissue (Fig. 74).

The pterines are also important eye pigments, occurring with ommochromes in the accessory pigment cells separating the ommatidia. In *Drosophila* five pterines have been isolated from the eye: two yellow compounds, another (isoxanthopterin) with a purple fluorescence, and two (including biopterin) with a blue fluorescence.

Pterines are important metabolically as cofactors of enzymes concerned in growth and differentiation and they may act as controlling agents in these processes. Their association with ommochromes arises because they are cofactors of the enzymes involved in ommochrome synthesis. The vitamin folic acid is possibly derived from pterines.

7.3.4 Ommochromes

The ommochromes are a group of pigments derived from the amino acid tryptophan via kynurenine and 3-hydroxykynurenine. Oxidative condensation of the 3-hydroxy-kynurenine gives rise to the ommochromes.

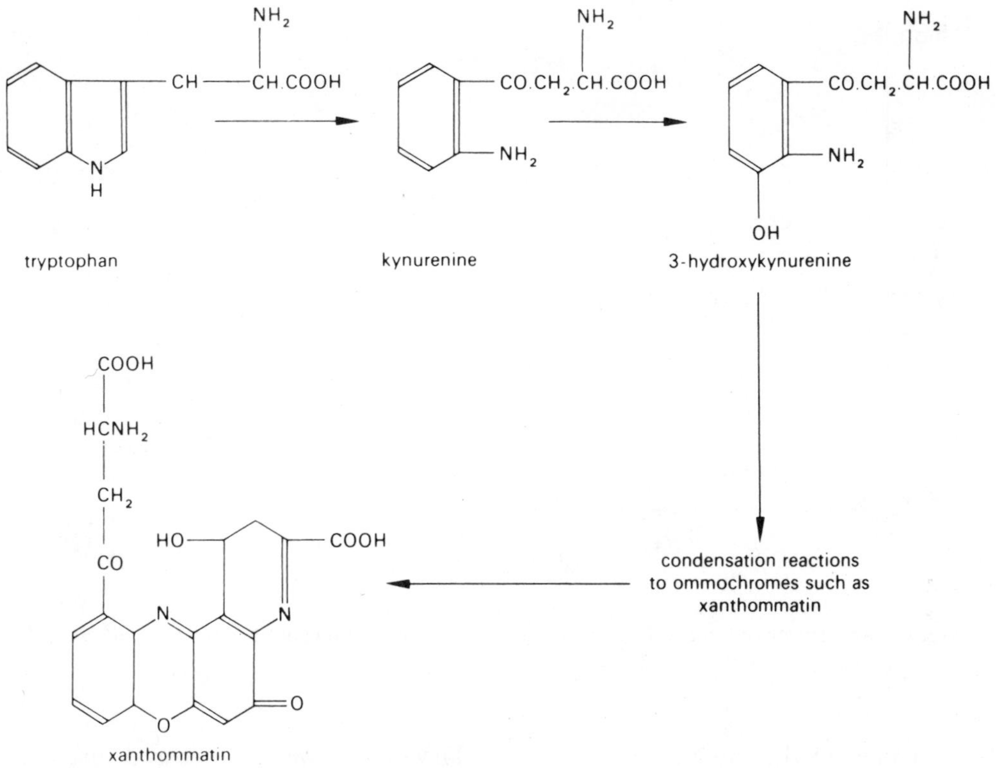

tryptophan   kynurenine   3-hydroxykynurenine

xanthommatin

condensation reactions
to ommochromes such as
xanthommatin

This condensation is coupled with the production of dopaquinone from dopa (p. 132), involving the same enzyme as in melanin formation. Dopaquinone acts as an electron acceptor, inducing the condensation (Gilmour, 1965).

Ommochromes are widely distributed in insects as masking pigments in the accessory cells of the eyes, serving to isolate the ommatidia, and usually associated with pterines (Fig. 70). The combined pigments provide a fairly uniform filter for all wavelengths from the near ultraviolet to about 600 nm, covering the whole of the visible spectrum for the fly (Fig. 68).

Yellow, red and brown body colours are produced by ommochromes in the epidermis. The pink of immature adult *Schistocerca* is due to a mixture of ommochromes which decreases in amount as the insect gets older. Red Odonata and probably also the reds and browns of nymphalid butterflies are due to ommochromes, while in blue Odonta a dark brown ommochrome provides the background for the production of Tyndall blue. Epidermal ommochromes sometimes directly underlie cuticular melanin; in these cases they do not contribute to the colour of the insect.

Ommochrome production is often associated with unusually high levels of tryptophan in the haemolymph. For instance, red faecal pellets containing ommochromes are produced by locusts during moulting or starvation. At these times tryptophan is likely to be liberated from proteins broken down during structural rearrangement or used for energy production. A transitory increase in tryptophan also occurs at metamorphosis in holometabolous insects (Fig. 69) and this is followed by the production of 3-hydroxykynurenine or of ommochromes. The accumulation of

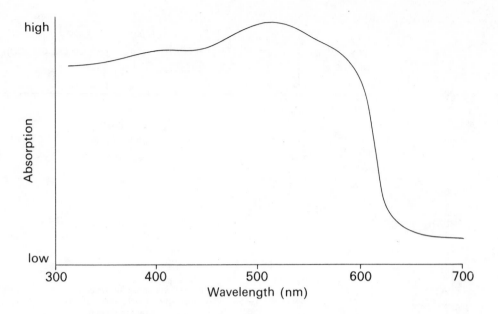

Fig. 68 Absorption of light of different wavelengths by pigment cells of the eye of *Calliphora*
(after Linzen, 1974)

ommochromes in the integument causes the larva of *Cerura* to turn red just before
pupation and it also produces the red colour of the meconium of Lepidoptera.
Tryptophan concentrations also increase before pupariation in *Phormia* and in this case
nearly all the amino acid is converted to xanthommatin, a screening pigment in the eyes
of the adult (Linzen, 1974).

7.3.5 Tetrapyrroles

There are two major classes of tetrapyrroles:
(i) the porphyrins, in which the pyrroles form a ring:

and (ii) the bilins, with a linear arrangement of the pyrroles:

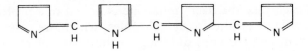

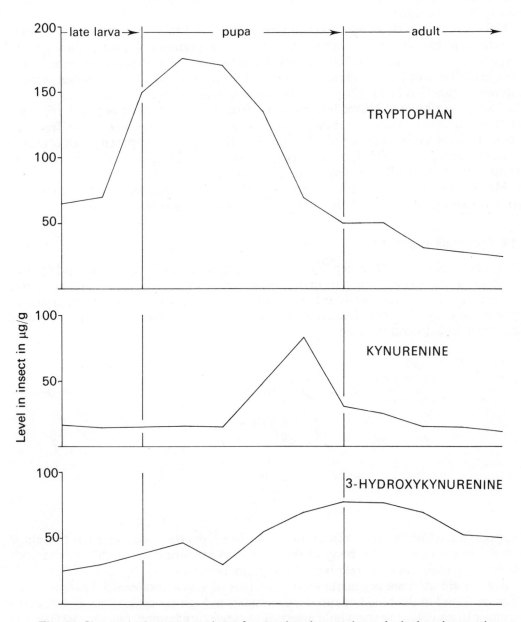

Fig. 69 Changes in the concentrations of tryptophan, kynurenine and 3-hydroxykynurenine during the development of adult *Phormia*. The rise in kynurenine coincides with the beginning of eye pigmentation (after Linzen, 1974)

A porphyrin with an atom of iron in the centre is called a haem molecule and this forms the basis of two important classes of compounds, the cytochromes and the haemoglobins. In each case the haem molecule is linked to a protein.

All insects are able to synthesise cytochromes, which are essential in respiration (p. 111), the different cytochromes differing in the forms of their haem groupings. Normally they are only present in small amounts and so they produce no colour, but where, as in flight muscle, they are present in high concentrations, they produce a reddish-brown colour.

Only a few insects, living in conditions subject to low oxygen tensions, contain haemoglobin and these are coloured red by the pigment showing through the integument. In *Chironomus* (Diptera) larva the haemoglobin is in solution in the blood, while in the larva of *Gasterophilus* (Diptera) it is in the fat body. Haemoglobin serves a respiratory function but perhaps also serves as a protein store (p. 489).

Bilins, bilirubin and biliverdin, may arise from the opening out of porphyrins as a result of oxidation. Typically they are blue or green. In *Chironomus* bilins from the haemoglobin of the larva accumulate in the fat of the adult and impart a green colour to the newly emerged fly. Similarly in *Rhodnius* the pericardial cells become green due to the accumulation of bilins derived from ingested haemoglobin.

Mesobiliverdin is commonly present combined with protein and in association with a yellow carotenoid produces the green colour of many insects.

7.3.6 Quinone pigments

The quinone pigments of insects fall into two categories: anthraquinones and aphins.

Anthraquinones are formed from the condensation of three benzene rings and three of these pigments, each produced by a different coccid, used to be important as commercial dyes. The best known is cochineal from *Dactylopius cacti*. The purified pigment is called carminic acid:

Carminic acid

The pigment, which is derived from the food-plant *Opuntia coccinellifera*, is present in globules in the eggs and fat body of the female, constituting up to 50% of the body weight. The male contains relatively little pigment.

Aphins are quinone pigments with a nucleus of seven condensed benzene rings. They are found in the blood of aphids, sometimes in high concentration, and impart a purple or black colour to the whole insect. Two series are known, one characteristic of *Aphis*, the other of *Tuberolachnus*.

7.3.7 Flavones (anthoxanthins)

These are plant pigments found in a few insects. They are responsible for the red colour of the bugs *Leptocoris* and *Lygaeus* and also occur in Lepidoptera. The yellow colour of the marbled white butterfly is due to a flavone obtained unaltered from the grass, *Dactylis glomerata*, on which it feeds.

The related anthocyanins, responsible for the colours of many plants, have not been identified certainly in insects.

7.4 The colours of insects

The colours of insects may result from a variety of structures and pigments. Very often several pigments are present together and in this case the observed colour will depend on the relative abundance and positions of the pigments, as in the eye colours of different mutants of *Drosophila* (Fig. 70).

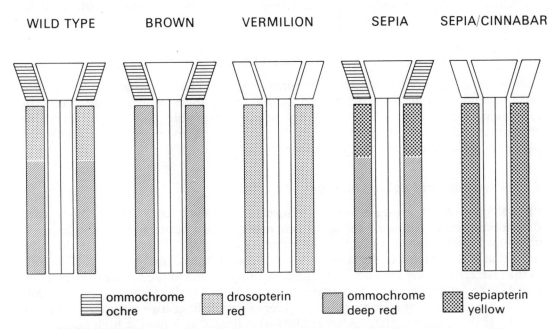

Fig. 70 Pigments present in the primary and secondary pigment cells of various *Drosophila* mutants (after Ziegler and Harmsen, 1969)

Black and browns result from sclerotised protein and melanin. Aphins produce a black or very dark purple colour in aphids, while iridescent purples, as in the purple emperor butterfly, result from interference effects.

Red is commonly produced by carotenoids (Coccinellidae, *Pyrrhocoris*), but may be due to pterines (orange-tip butterfly) or ommochromes (Odonata, probably the reds and browns of Nymphalidae, pink of immature *Schistocerca*). Pterines and ommochromes are also responsible for eye colours. Chironomid larvae may be red due to the presence of haemoglobin and some coccids have red quinone pigments. Orange-reds and coppery colours of many beetles are interference or diffraction colours.

Yellow is produced by pterines (brimstone butterfly, Hymenoptera) and carotenoids (locusts). Carotenoids also colour some secretions (silk, beeswax). Flavones may contribute to yellow, usually with other pigments. Brassy yellows are interference colours.

Green in Orthoptera and larval Lepidoptera is generally considered to be formed by a mixture of blue bile pigment with yellow β-carotene or astaxanthin, but it may be that a green bile pigment is primarily responsible (Rowell, 1971). Certainly a green bile pigment is present in adult Chironomidae. In Pieridae green is produced by the juxtaposition of yellow and black scales, while interference effects produce the metallic greens of beetles and Zygaenidae.

Blues are usually produced by interference phenomena (Lycaenidae) or by Tyndall scattering (Odonata). Blue pigments are uncommon, but *Oedipoda caerulescens* (Orthoptera) has a blue carotenoid in the wings.

White results primarily from scattering, sometimes associated with a white pigment, such as leucopterin in Lepidoptera.

7.5 Colour change

Colour changes are of two kinds: short-term reversible changes which do not involve the production of new pigment, and long-term changes which result from the formation of new pigments and are not usually reversible. Short-term reversible changes are called physiological changes. Colour changes involving the metabolism of pigments are called morphological colour changes.

7.5.1 Physiological colour change

Physiological colour change is unusual in insects. Tortoise beetles change colour when they are disturbed. Normally the beetles are brassy yellow or green, but they change to violet and finally brown-orange in less than one minute. The change is due to a reduction in the spacing of the lamellae which produce the normal interference colours of the insect, following a reduction in the state of hydration of the cuticle. Rehydration restores the original colour. The elytra of the hercules beetle, *Dynastes*, are normally yellow due to a layer of spongy, yellow-coloured cuticle beneath a transparent layer of cuticle. If the spongy cuticle becomes filled with liquid, as it does at high humidities, light is no longer reflected by it but passes through and is absorbed by black cuticle underneath. The insect now appears black. Probably these changes occur daily, the insect tending to be yellow in the daytime when it is feeding among leaves and dark at night, so that it is less conspicuous (Hinton, 1976).

Physiological colour changes which involve pigment movements are known to occur in *Carausius* (Phasmida), in the grasshopper *Kosciuscola*, and in a number of blue damselflies. All these insects become black at night due to the movement of dark pigment granules to a more superficial position in the cells (Fig. 563). In *Kosciuscola* the blue is produced by Tyndall scattering from small granules, less than 0·2 μm in diameter, composed mainly of white leucopterin and uric acid. At night the blue is masked by the dispersal of larger pigment granules amongst the small reflecting granules (Filshie *et al.*, 1975).

The change in *Kosciuscola* and the dragon flies is temperature dependent. The insects are always black below a temperature which is characteristic of the species but usually about 15°C. Above this there is a tendency to become blue, which in some species is enhanced by light (Veron, 1976). In these changes the epidermal cells are to some extent independent effectors, responding directly to stimulation. This is true of the change from black to blue in *Austrolestes* (Odonata), but the reverse change is controlled by a secretion released from the terminal abdominal ganglion (Veron, 1973). The significance of these changes is unknown, but they may be thermoregulatory. Dark insects absorb more radiation than pale ones (p. 760) so that they may warm up more rapidly in the mornings and become active earlier than would be the case if they remained pale.

7.5.2 Morphological colour change

Changes in the amount of pigment may be produced in many different ways in response to external or internal factors. The colours of grasshoppers and related insects tend to have a general resemblance to the prevailing colour of the environment, a phenomenon known as homochromy, and a change in the environment leads to a change in the colour of the insect. Thus *Acrida* (Orthoptera) changes from straw-yellow to green if put on to the appropriate background, some specimens changing in three days, but most taking rather longer. Such changes in the colour of the integument only occur at a moult, but this is not true of darkening, which can occur in the absence of moulting. Black grasshoppers are commonly found in Africa after bush fires and some individuals of *Phorenula werneriana* change from grey to coal black in two days. This change occurs in recently emerged and old adults, but only in bright sunlight. In diffuse light the change is much less marked and in general the contrast between incident and reflected light is an important factor in this type of colour change (Rowell, 1971). In *Mantis* (Dictyoptera) the green biliverdin breaks down in high light intensities forming products which are initially brown and subsequently become almost colourless (Passama-Vuillaume, 1965). Differences due to background colour also occur in other groups. Pierid pupae, for instance, may be dark or pale according to their surroundings.

Temperature is important in pigment development. Locusts bred at 40°C have very little pigmentation and are pale yellow with a few dark markings. At lower rearing temperatures the darkening becomes progressively greater and at 26°C the larvae are largely black with some yellow pattern (Goodwin, 1952). Similar changes occur in Lepidoptera and probably also in other insects.

Crowding influences colour in some insects. Locust larvae reared in isolation are green or fawn, while rearing in crowds produces yellow and black individuals. The colours and patterns change as the degree of crowding alters (Stower, 1959). The larvae of some Lepidoptera, such as *Plusia*, undergo comparable changes, some of them occurring in the course of an instar, but the most marked alterations occur only at moulting (Long, 1953).

Many changes occur in the course of development, the reasons for which are unknown. Thus the early larva of *Papilio demodocus* (Lepidoptera) is brown with a white band at the centre; the late larva is green with purple markings and a white lateral stripe. Some, at least, of these changes are under hormonal control and just before pupation the larva of *Cerura* (Lepidoptera) turns from green to red, the change being controlled by the moulting hormone.

Colour change is often associated with ageing and maturation. Male *Schistocerca* change from pink to yellow as they mature and *Mesopsis* (Orthoptera) slowly develops a black patch on the hind wings over a period of about six months, again possibly associated with maturation (Burtt and Uvarov, 1944). The male of the dragonfly *Brachythemis leucosticta* develops dark patches on the wings as it matures.

7.5.3 Seasonal colour change

In some insects there are marked differences in colour between successive generations correlated with seasonal changes in the environment. This is particularly well shown in some African butterflies such as *Precis octavia*, which is rusty red in the wet season and violet-blue in the dry. In butterflies from temperate regions the spring and summer generations often look different and in *Arachnia levana* they are quite distinct. The form which develops depends on the length of day to which the larvae are subjected. Larvae experiencing short days give rise to diapause pupae and adults of the spring form; larvae experiencing long days have no diapause in the pupa and the adults are of the summer form (Müller, 1955).

Insects of many orders exhibit a green/brown polymorphism, tending to be green in the wetter times of year and brown when the vegetation is dry. This is to be distinguished from other forms of homochromy which depend on levels of orange/ yellow and black pigments; in green morphs the production of ommochromes in the epidermis is largely or completely inhibited. High humidity is a major environmental factor leading to the development of the green morph (Rowell, 1971).

7.5.4 Long-term evolutionary changes

The best-known evolutionary colour changes are those associated with industrial melanism (Kettlewell, 1973). During the last 120 years there has been a marked increase in the incidence of melanism amongst moths, which is well shown by *Biston betularia*. The typical form is peppered black and white, while the melanic form *carbonaria* is almost entirely black. In 1848 form *carbonaria* was a rarity in the Manchester area, but by 1895 it constituted 95 % of the *B. betularia* population of this region. At the same time and subsequently it has spread through Britain, so that in 1958 the black form was known from all parts of Britain except the extreme west of England and the north of Scotland, often being the dominant form.

Biston betularia is a night-flying moth spending the day at rest on tree trunks. Originally the typical form blended well with its background of bark and lichens, but industrial pollution has blackened the bark and killed the lichens, so that over the past 150 years the background against which these moths rest has been completely altered and form *carbonaria* is now much better concealed than the typical form. Field experiments show that in a polluted wood birds take more typical forms than black forms. The effects of pollution are not restricted to industrial areas because the prevailing south-westerly winds drift dust over the greater part of the country so that even in the less industrialised east of England form *carbonaria* came to comprise at least 80 % of the population. Since the early 1960s, however, the typical form has tended to increase in numbers, apparently following reduced pollution due to the introduction of smokeless fuels. Hence at Cambridge the percentage frequency of *carbonaria* fell from 95 % during 1957–64 to 65 % in 1973. As well as increasing protection from predators, the form *carbonaria* has physiological advantages over other forms which are probably more important than the crypsis conferred by colour (Lees and Creed, 1975).

Some 70 to 100 of the 780 macrolepidoptera found in Britain are undergoing similar changes, but only those species which spend the day on backgrounds affected by pollution and which depend on concealment are involved. Similar changes are occurring elsewhere in Europe and North America, but they are not known from the tropics.

7.6 Significance of colour

The pigments of insects probably have some metabolic significance, but, in addition, the colours which they produce are of significance in the relations of the insect with other animals. Colour is frequently used as a defence against vertebrate predators and it may also be important in intraspecific recognition.

Colours are interpreted in terms of human vision, but their appearance, and hence significance, may be different for other animal groups. For instance, the male brimstone butterfly, which to us appears uniform yellow, has markings on the forewing which become visible in a photograph taken on film sensitive to ultraviolet (Nekrutenko, 1965). At least some insects are sensitive to ultraviolet, so the appearance of this butterfly to them might be quite different from its appearance to humans. Of the potential predators of insects, birds and probably also lizards are relatively less sensitive to light of short wavelength but more sensitive to long wavelengths, while insectivorous mammals are believed to be colour blind (Walls, 1942). This, however, only means that they may be unable to discriminate between light of different wavelengths, it tells us nothing of the range of wavelengths to which they are sensitive.

7.6.1 Concealment from predators

Colour often helps to conceal insects from predators (Cott, 1957). This may result simply from a general similarity of colour between the insect and its background (homochromy), as in grasshoppers which become black on burnt ground or green in fresh grass. Given the choice these insects are able to select a background of the appropriate colour and experiments on *Biston betularia* show that this resemblance and behaviour do afford the insects some protection from predators. Often homochromy is associated with some appropriate body form and behaviour as in Phasmidae and many mantids and grasshoppers.

Protection may also be afforded by obliterative shading. Objects are made conspicuous by the different light intensities which they reflect as a result of their form. Usually a solid object looks lighter on the upper side and darker beneath because of the effect of shadows (Fig. 71A), but by appropriate colouring this effect can be eliminated. The object is shaded in such a way (Fig. 71B) that when viewed in normal lighting conditions all parts of the body reflect the same amount of light so that it loses its solid appearance (Fig. 71C). Such countershading is well-known in caterpillars where the side towards the light is most heavily pigmented and the side normally in shadow has

UNSHADED	COUNTERSHADED	COUNTERSHADED
light	lateral lighting	light

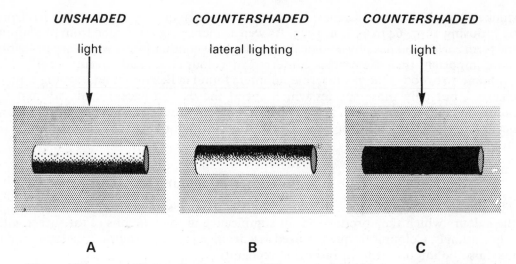

A	B	C

Fig. 71 Diagrams to illustrate the appearance of (A) an unshaded object in overhead light, (B) a countershaded object in lateral light and (C) a countershaded object in overhead light (after Cott, 1957)

least pigment. To be successful this type of pigmentation must be combined with appropriate behaviour patterns since if the larva were to sit with the heavily pigmented side away from the light it would become more, not less, conspicuous. Countershading with the appropriate behaviour does afford some protection from visual predators (de Ruiter, 1955).

Colour may also afford protection if the arrangement of colours is such as to break up the body form. This is disruptive colouration and is most efficient when some of the colour components match the background and others contrast strongly with it (Fig. 72). Disruptive colouration occurs, for instance, in moths such as *Xanthorhoë fluctuata*, which rests on tree trunks.

A	B	C

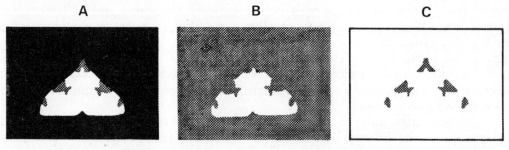

Fig. 72 Diagram of a moth with disruptive pattern on (A) an unsuitable background, (B) and (C) backgrounds blending with one of the insect colours and contrasting with the other (after Cott, 1957)

7.6.2 Advertisement

The colour patterns of some insects are used to attempt to intimidate predators or to deflect their attention to parts of the body which are least vulnerable. Eyespots play an important part in this behaviour and they are found in various positions on the wings of Lepidoptera and some other insects.

The peacock butterfly has one eyespot on the upper surface of each wing. These eyespots are primarily black, yellow and blue, surrounded by dark red. At rest the butterfly sits with its wings held up over its back, the upper surfaces of the forewings being juxtaposed so that the eyespots are concealed. If the insect is disturbed by visual or tactile stimuli it lowers the wings so that the eyespots on the forewings are displayed and then protracts the forewings so as to expose the hindwing eyespots. At the same time the insect makes a hissing sound by rubbing the anal veins of the forewings against the costal veins of the hindwings and a series of high frequency clicks by rubbing the wings against the body. The forewings are then retracted and partly raised and the sequence of movements repeated, sometimes for several minutes. While displaying, the body is tilted so that the wings are fully exposed to the source of stimulation and at the same time the insect turns so as to put the stimulus behind it (Blest, 1957). This display does release an innate escape response in birds and some birds learn to avoid peacock butterflies altogether, but in others the effectiveness of the display wanes.

Other experiments show that the attacks of birds are usually directed at eyespots so that these do serve, temporarily, to deflect attacks away from vulnerable parts. There is no sharp distinction between eyespots used for intimidation and those concerned with deflection. In general it may be that deflecting spots are smaller than those used in intimidation, but it is possible that some may serve either function depending on the nature and experience of the predator.

Other types of colour advertisement by insects are associated with distastefulness, so that predators learn to associate a particular colour pattern with distastefulness and so subsequently avoid taking insects displaying this pattern. Such patterns must be bold and readily recognisable and frequently involve red or yellow with black. Thus the black and yellow of the bee and wasp is associated with a sting and the red and dark green of the burnet moth with extreme distastefulness.

In experiments, toads learned to avoid bees, some after eating only one bee, others only after repeated trials, but after a week all of 33 toads had stopped eating bees. The distasteful association was remembered by the toads, so that when they were offered bees again two weeks after the original experiment very few of them would accept the food. Complete avoidance was soon re-established in spite of the fact that, apart from the bees, each toad had eaten only one mealworm during the whole experiment (Fig. 73) (Cott, 1957).

7.6.3 Mimicry

Predators learn to avoid distasteful insects with distinctive colours, but theoretically a predator must learn to avoid each individual species separately. If, however, the colour patterns of some species are similar to each other, learning to avoid one also produces an avoidance of the other, so it is an advantage for distasteful insects to look similar because in this way wastage is reduced. Thus various wasp species have the same basic black and yellow pattern, and burnet and cinnabar moths have comparable red markings on a dark green or black ground.

Resemblance of one species by another is called mimicry and the principle on which it is based may be extended to include species which are not distasteful or are only

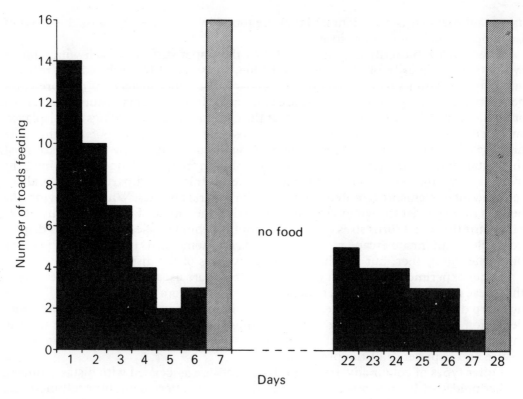

Fig. 73 The number of toads, out of 18, which accepted bees (black) on successive days and the number which accepted mealworms (hatched) when they would no longer take bees (after Cott, 1957)

mildly so. If a predator learns to avoid a particular pattern because the insect having it is distasteful it will subsequently avoid other species with the same pattern, even though they may not be distasteful. As a result of this, palatable species gain some advantage from a resemblance to distasteful ones. The distasteful species is called the model, those that resemble it in appearance are mimics (Rettenmeyer, 1970).

In this type of mimicry it is important that the mimic is uncommon relative to the model. If this were not the case a predator might learn to associate a particular pattern with palatability rather than distastefulness. This limits the numbers or distribution of a mimetic form, but such a limit may be circumvented by the mimic becoming polymorphic with each of the morphs resembling a different distasteful species. The best-known example of genetic polymorphism is that of the female *Papilio dardanus* (Lepidoptera), which has a large number of mimetic forms mimicking a series of quite different butterflies (Carpenter and Ford, 1933).

7.6.4 Intraspecific recognition

In some insects colour is important in the recognition of one sex by the other. Thus the male of *Hypolimnas misippus* (Lepidoptera) responds to the brown of the female wings by pursuing her, but his response is inhibited by the presence of white in the wings (Stride, 1957). Similar use of colour is known in other insects.

Some dragonflies exhibit territorial behaviour, a male in his home territory chasing off other males of the same species (p. 360). Threatening sign stimuli are employed in this behaviour and, for instance, the male of *Plathemis lydia* raises its abdomen so that its blue upper surface is displayed to other males. In the presence of the female the abdomen is depressed (Corbet, Longfield and Moore, 1960).

7.6.5 Storage excretion

Some pigments may be regarded as metabolic waste products and so their accumulation may be regarded as a form of storage excretion (see also p. 584). Pterines, for instance, may be derived from purines, such as uric acid. Similarly melanin production might be a method of disposing of toxic phenols arising from metabolism and it may be significant that melanin is often produced over metabolically active tissue such as muscle (Fig. 74).

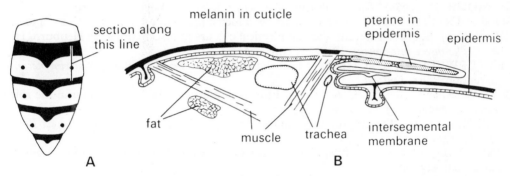

Fig. 74 A. The pigment pattern on the abdomen of *Vespa*. B. Longitudinal section through a tergite and associated tissues showing the distribution of pigments (from Wigglesworth, 1965)

Tryptophan in high concentrations reduces the rate of development of *Drosophila* and *Oryzaephilus* and it is noteworthy that ommochrome production follows the appearance of unusually high levels of tryptophan in the tissues (Linzen, 1974). It is reasonably certain that ommochrome synthesis represents a form of storage excretion, although the positive uses of ommochromes in colouration and as screening pigments indicate that storage excretion is not their sole function. A similar argument applies to pterines. Most insects, like *Nymphalis*, excrete most of the end product of the biologically active hydrogenated pterines; *Pieris*, on the other hand, synthesises much larger amounts and accumulates them in the wings, where they contribute to the colour (Ziegler and Harmsen, 1969).

REFERENCES

ANDERSON, T. F. and RICHARDS, A. G. (1942). An electron microscope study of some structural colours of insects. *J. appl. Phys.* **13**: 748–758.
BLEST, A. D. (1957). The function of eyespot patterns in the Lepidoptera. *Behaviour* **11**: 209–256.

BROUGHTON, W. B. (ed.) (1965). *Colour and Life*. Institute of Biology, London.

BURTT, E. D. and UVAROV, B. P. (1944). Changes in wing pigmentation during the adult life of Acrididae (Orthoptera). *Proc. R. ent. Soc. Lond.* A, **19**: 7–8.

CARPENTER, G. D. H. and FORD, E. B. (1933). *Mimicry*. Methuen, London.

CHEFURKA, W. (1965). Intermediary metabolism of carbohydrates in insects. *in* Rockstein M. (ed.), *The physiology of Insecta*. vol. 2. Academic Press, New York.

CORBET, P. S., LONGFIELD, C. and MOORE, N. W. (1960). *Dragonflies*. Collins, London.

COTT, H. B. (1957). *Adaptive coloration in animals*. Methuen, London.

COTTRELL, C. B. (1964). Insect ecdysis with particular emphasis on cuticular hardening and darkening. *Adv. Insect Physiol.* **2**: 175–218.

FELTWELL, J. (1978). The distribution of carotenoids in insects. *in* Harborne, J. B. (ed.), *Biochemical aspects of plant and animal coevolution*. Academic Press, London.

FILSHIE, B. K., DAY, M. F. and MERCER, E. H. (1975). Colour and colour change in the grasshopper, *Kosciuscola tristis*. *J. Insect Physiol.* **21**: 1763–1770.

FOX, D. L. (1953). *Animal biochromes and structural colours*. Cambridge University Press.

FOX, H. M. and VEVERS, G. (1960). *The nature of animal colours*. Sidgwick and Jackson, London.

FUZEAU-BRAESCH, S. (1972). Pigments and color changes. *A. Rev. Ent.* **17**: 403–424.

GILMOUR, D. (1965). *The metabolism of insects*. Oliver and Boyd, Edinburgh.

GOODWIN, T. W. (1952). The biochemistry of locust pigmentation. *Biol. Rev.* **27**: 439–460.

HINTON, H. E. (1976). Recent work on physical colours of insect cuticle. *in* Hepburn, H. R. (ed.), *The insect integument*. Elsevier, Amsterdam.

KETTLEWELL, H. B. D. (1973). *The evolution of melanism, a study of a recurring necessity*. Clarendon Press, Oxford.

LEES, D. R. and CREED, E. R. (1975). Industrial melanism in *Biston betularia*: the rôle of selective predation. *J. Anim. Ecol.* **44**: 67–83.

LINZEN, B. (1974). The tryptophan→ommochrome pathway in insects. *Adv. Insect Physiol.* **10**: 117–246.

LONG, D. B. (1953). Effects of population density on larvae of Lepidoptera. *Trans. R. ent. Soc. Lond.* **104**: 543–584.

MASON, C. W. (1923). Structural colours in feathers. II. *J. phys. Chem., Ithaca.* **27**: 401–447.

MASON, C. W. (1926). Structural colours in insects. I. *J. phys. Chem., Ithaca.* **30**: 383–395.

MASON, C. W. (1927a). Structural colours in insects. II. *J. phys. Chem., Ithaca.* **31**: 321–354.

MASON, C. W. (1927b). Structural colours in insects. III. *J. phys. Chem., Ithaca.* **31**: 1856–1872.

MÜLLER, H. J. (1955). Die Saisonformenbildung von *Arachnia lavana*, ein photoperiodisch gesteuerter Diapause-Effect. *Naturwissenschaften* **42**: 134–135.

NEKRUTENKO, Y. P. (1965). 'Gynandromorphic effect' and the optical nature of hidden wing-pattern in *Gonepteryx rhamni* L. (Lepidoptera, Pieridae). *Nature, Lond.* **205**: 417–418.

NEVILLE, A. C. (1975). *Biology of the arthropod cuticle*. Springer-Verlag, Berlin.

PASSAMA-VUILLAUME, M. (1965). Étude de l'irridiation lumineuse, facteur essentiel du brunissement de *Mantis religiosa* (L.). *C. r. hebd. Séanc. Acad. Sci., Paris.* **261**: 3683–3685.

RETTENMEYER, C. W. (1970). Insect mimicry. *A. Rev. Ent.* **15**: 43–74.

RICHARDS, A. G. (1951). *The integument of arthropods*. University of Minnesota Press, Minneapolis.

ROWELL, C. H. F. (1971). The variable coloration of the acridoid grasshoppers. *Adv. Insect Physiol.* **8**: 145–198.

RUITER, L. de (1955). Countershading in caterpillars. *Archs néerl. Zool.* **11**: 1–57.

STOWER, W. J. (1959). The colour patterns of hoppers of the desert locust (*Schistocerca gregaria* Forskål). *Anti-Locust Bull.* no. 32, 75 pp.

STRIDE, G. O. (1957). Investigations into the courtship behaviour of the male of *Hypolimnas misippus* L. (Lepidoptera, Nymphalidae), with special reference to the role of visual stimuli. *Br. J. Anim. Behav.* **5**: 153–167.

VERON, J. E. N. (1973). Physiological control of the chromatophores of *Austrolestes annulosus* (Odonata). *J. Insect Physiol.* **19**: 1689–1703.

VERON, J. E. N. (1976). Responses of Odonata chromatophores to environmental stimuli. *J. Insect Physiol.* **22**: 19–30.

WALLS, G. L. (1942). *The vertebrate eye.* Cranbrook Press, Michigan.

WIGGLESWORTH, V. B. (1965). *The principles of insect physiology.* Methuen, London.

ZIEGLER-GÜNDER, I. (1956). Pterine: Pigmente und Wirkstoffe im Tierreich. *Biol. Rev.* **31**: 313–348.

ZIEGLER, I. and HARMSEN, R. (1969). The biology of pteridines in insects. *Adv. Insect Physiol.* **6**: 139–203.

SECTION B

The Thorax and Movement

CHAPTER VIII

THE THORAX AND LEGS

The six-legged condition of insects is probably derived from some myriapod condition. The development of longer legs to facilitate fast running necessitates a reduction in the number of legs for functional efficiency and six is the smallest number which gives continuous stability during movement at a variety of speeds (see Chapter IX). Mechanical efficiency also requires the placing of these legs close together behind the head and it is believed that as a result of these mechanical and functional requirements the insect thorax was evolved (see Manton, 1953, 1977).

Independently of this, wings also developed on the thorax, so that it became the locomotor centre of the insect. Hence the skeleton of the thoracic segments is modified to give efficient support for the legs and wings and the musculature is adapted to produce the movements of the appendages. The legs themselves, starting from a typical walking leg, are also adapted to various functions with appropriate modifications in their form.

For general reviews of the morphology of the insect thorax and legs see Snodgrass (1935) and Matsuda (1970).

8.1 Segmentation

In larval holometabolous insects the cuticle is soft and flexible, or only partially sclerotised, and the longitudinal muscles are attached to the intersegmental folds (Fig. 75A). This represents a primitive condition comparable with that occurring in the annelids, and the segments delimited by the intersegmental folds are regarded as the primary segments. Insects with this arrangement move as a result of successive changes in the shapes of the thoracic and abdominal segments (p. 182), these changes of shape being permitted by the flexible cuticle.

When the cuticle is sclerotised the basic arrangement is believed to comprise dorsal and ventral plates associated with narrow intersegmental sclerites which develop in the intersegmental folds and have the longitudinal muscles attached to them (Fig. 75B). Clearly, such an arrangement permits very little movement and the intersegmental sclerites usually become fused with the segmental sclerites behind. The large sclerite on the dorsal surface of a segment is called the tergum, or, in the thorax, the notum, the groove of the intersegmental sclerite is the antecostal sulcus, and the narrow rim in front of the sulcus is called the acrotergite (Fig. 75C). An acrotergite never occurs at the front of the prothorax because the anterior part of this segment is involved in the neck (p. 10) and the muscles from the head pass directly to the acrotergite of the mesothorax.

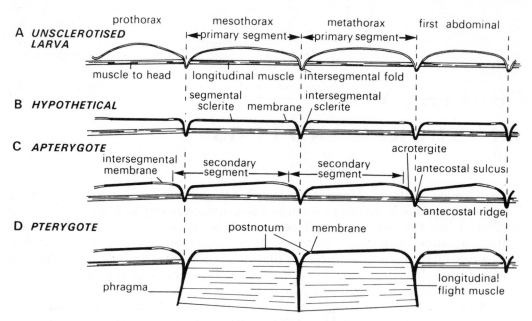

Fig. 75 Schematised diagrams showing changes in segmentation and the derivation of the postnotum and phragmata in pterygote insects. Sclerotised areas are indicated by a solid line, membranous areas by a double line

An area at the back of each segment remains membranous, forming a new intersegmental membrane. This does not correspond with the original intersegmental groove and so a secondary segmentation is superimposed on the first. Thus the visible segmentation of adult insects is, in fact, this secondary segmentation and may not correspond precisely with the larval segmentation (Snodgrass, 1935).

This basic condition occurs in the abdomen where this is sclerotised, in the meso- and meta-thoracic segments of larval insects with a sclerotised thorax, in the Apterygota and in adult Dictyoptera and Isoptera where the wings are not moved by indirect muscles (see p. 217). With this arrangement contraction of the longitudinal muscles produces telescoping of the segments.

8.2 Thorax

The thorax consists of three segments known, respectively, as the pro-, meso- and meta-thorax. In most insects all three segments bear a pair of legs, but this is not the case in larval Diptera, larval Hymenoptera Apocrita, some larval Coleoptera and a small number of adult insects which are apodous. In addition, winged insects have a pair of wings on the meso- and meta-thoracic segments and these two segments are then collectively known as the pterothorax.

8.2.1 Tergum

The tergum of the prothoracic segment is known as the pronotum. It is often small as it serves only for the attachment of the leg muscles, but in Orthoptera, Dictyoptera and

Coleoptera it forms a large plate affording some protection to the pterothoracic segments. The meso- and meta-nota are relatively small in wingless insects and larvae, but in winged insects they become modified for the attachment of the wings. In the majority of winged insects the downward movement of the wings depends on an upward distortion of the thorax (p. 217). This is made possible by a modification of the basic segmental arrangement. The acrotergites of the metathorax and the first abdominal segment extend forwards to join the tergum of the segment in front and in many cases become secondarily separated from their original segment by a narrow membranous region. Each acrotergite and antecostal sulcus is now known as a postnotum (Fig. 75D). There may thus be a mesopostnotum and a metapostnotum if the wings are more or less equally important in flight, but if only the hind wings are important, as in Orthoptera and Coleoptera, only the metapostnotum is developed. The Diptera on the other hand, using only the forewings for flight, have a well developed mesopostnotum, but no metapostnotum. To provide attachment for the large longitudinal muscles moving the wings the antecostal ridges at the front and back of the mesothorax and the back of the metathorax usually develop into extensive internal plates, the phragmata (Figs. 75D and 80). Which of the phragmata are developed again depends on which wings are most important in flight.

Various strengthening ridges develop on the tergum of a wing-bearing segment which are local adaptations to the mechanical stresses imposed by the wings and their muscles. The ridges appear externally as sulci (see p. 4) which divide the notum into areas. Often a transverse sulcus divides the notum into an anterior prescutum and a scutum, while a V-shaped sulcus posteriorly separates the scutellum (Fig. 76). These areas are commonly demarcated, but, because of their origins as functional units, plates of the same name in different insects are not necessarily homologous. In addition

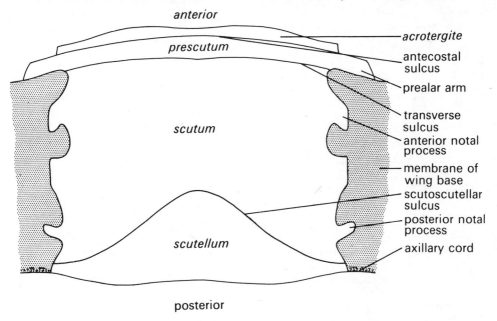

Fig. 76 Diagram showing the main features of the notum of a wing-bearing segment (from Snodgrass, 1935)

the lateral regions of the scutum may be cut off or there may be a median longitudinal sulcus. Commonly the prescutum connects with the pleuron by an extension, the prealar arm, in front of the wing, while behind the wing a postalar arm connects the postnotum to the epimeron. Laterally the scutum is produced into two processes, the anterior and posterior notal processes, which articulate with the axillary sclerites in the wing base (p. 210). The posterior fold of the scutellum continues as the axillary cord along the trailing edge of the wing.

8.2.2 Sternum

As on the dorsal surface, the primary sclerotisations are separate segmental and intersegmental plates and commonly in the thorax these remain separate. The intersegmental sclerite is produced internally into a spine and is called the spinasternum, while the segmental sclerite is called the eusternum (Fig. 80). Various degrees of fusion occur so that four basic arrangements may be found:

a) all elements separate—eusternum of prothorax; first spina; eusternum of mesothorax; second spina; eusternum of metathorax (see Fig. 77A. Notice that in the diagram eusternum is divided into basisternum and sternellum)

b) eusternum of mesothorax and second spina fuse, the rest remaining separate

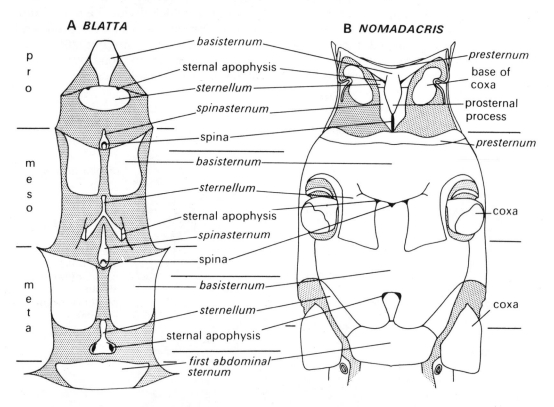

Fig. 77 Ventral view of the thorax of (A) *Blatta* (Dictyoptera) and (B) *Nomadacris* (Orthoptera) (after Snodgrass, 1935; Albrecht, 1956)

c) eusternum of prothorax and first spina also fuse so that there are now three main elements—compound prosternum; compound mesosternum; eusternum of metathorax

d) complete fusion of meso- and meta-thoracic elements to form a pterothoracic plate (Fig. 77B).

Arising from the eusternum are a pair of apophyses, the so-called sternal apophyses (Fig. 80). The origins of these on the sternum are marked by pits joined by a sulcus (Fig. 77B) so that the eusternum is divided into a basisternum and sternellum, while in higher insects the two apophyses arise together in the midline and only separate internally, forming a Y-shaped furca (Fig. 78). Distally the sternal apophyses are associated with the inner ends of the pleural ridges, usually being connected to them by short muscles. This adds rigidity to the thorax, while variation in the degree of contraction of the muscles makes this rigidity variable and controllable. The sternal apophyses also serve for the attachment of the bulk of the ventral longitudinal muscles, although a few fibres retain their primitive intersegmental connections with the spinasterna (Fig. 80).

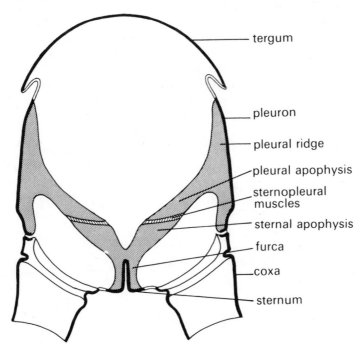

Fig. 78 Diagrammatic cross-section of a thoracic segment showing the pleural ridges and sternal apophyses (from Snodgrass, 1935)

Some insects have a longitudinal sulcus with an internal ridge running along the middle of the sternum. This is regarded by some authorities as indicating that the whole of the primitive sternum has become invaginated and that the apparent sternum in these insects is really derived from subcoxal elements (see Matsuda, 1963). The median longitudinal sulcus is known as the discrimen.

The sternum is attached to the pleuron by pre- and post-coxal bridges. The sternum of the pterothoracic segments does not differ markedly from that of the prothorax, but usually the basisternum is bigger, providing for the attachment of the large dorsoventral flight muscles.

8.2.3 Pleuron

The pleural regions are membranous in many larval insects, but typically become sclerotised in the adult. Basically there are probably three pleural sclerites, one ventral and two dorsal, which may originally have been derived from the coxa (Snodgrass, 1958). The ventral sclerite, or sternopleurite, articulates with the coxa and becomes fused with the sternum so as to become an integral part of it. The dorsal sclerites, anapleurite and coxopleurite, are present as separate sclerites in Apterygota and in the prothorax of larval Plecoptera (Fig. 79A). In other insects they are fused to form the pleuron, but the coxopleurite, which articulates with the coxa, remains partially separate in the lower pterygote orders forming the trochantin and making a second, more ventral articulation with the coxa (Fig. 79B).

Above the coxa the pleuron develops a nearly vertical strengthening ridge, the pleural ridge, marked by the pleural sulcus externally. This divides the pleuron into an anterior episternum and a posterior epimeron. The pleural ridge is particularly well developed in the wing-bearing segments, where it continues dorsally into the pleural wing process which articulates with the second axillary sclerite in the wing base (Fig. 79B).

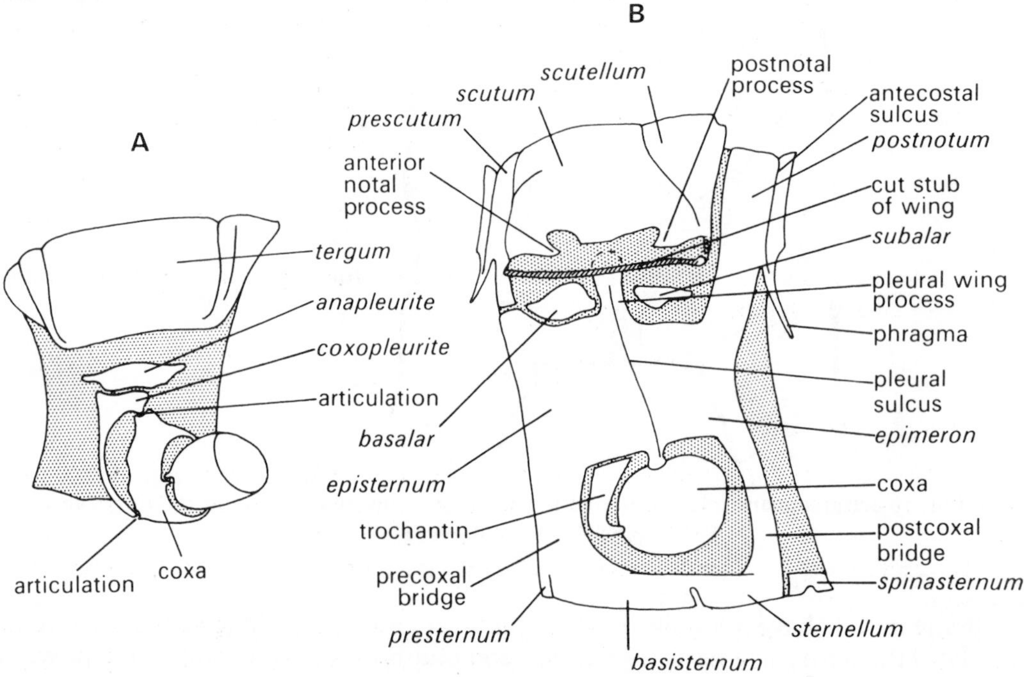

Fig. 79 A. Lateral view of the prothorax of *Perla* (Plecoptera). B. Diagrammatic lateral view of a typical wing-bearing segment. Anterior to left, membranous regions stippled (from Snodgrass, 1935)

In front of the pleural process in the membrane at the base of the wing and only indistinctly separated from the episternum are one or two basalar sclerites, while in a comparable position behind the pleural process is a well-defined subalar sclerite. Muscles concerned with the movement of the wings are inserted into these sclerites.

Typically there are two pairs of spiracles on the thorax. These are in the pleural regions and are associated with the mesothoracic and metathoracic segments. The mesothoracic spiracle often occupies a position on the posterior edge of the propleuron, while the smaller metathoracic spiracle may similarly move on to the mesothorax. The Diplura are exceptional in having three or four pairs of thoracic spiracles. *Heterojapyx*, for instance, has two pairs of mesothoracic and two pairs of metathoracic spiracles.

8.2.4 Muscles of the thorax

The longitudinal muscles of the thorax, as in the abdomen, run from one antecostal ridge to the next. They are relatively poorly developed in sclerotised larvae, in adult Odonata, Dictyoptera and Isoptera which have direct wing depressor muscles (p. 217), and also in secondarily wingless groups such as Siphonaptera. In these cases they tend to telescope one segment into the next, while the more lateral muscles rotate the segments relative to each other. In unsclerotised insects contraction of the longitudinal muscles shortens the segment.

In most winged insects, however, the dorsal longitudinal muscles are the main wing depressors and they are strongly developed (see p. 217; Fig. 80), running from phragma to phragma so that their contraction distorts the segments. The ventral longitudinal muscles run mainly from one sternal apophysis to the next in adult insects, producing some ventral telescoping of the thoracic segments.

Dorso-ventral muscles run from the tergum to the pleuron or sternum. They are primitively concerned with rotation or compression of the segment, but in winged insects they are important flight muscles (p. 217). In larval insects an oblique intersegmental muscle runs from the sternal apophysis to the anterior edge of the following tergum or pleuron, but in adults it is usually only present between prothorax and mesothorax.

The other important muscles of the thorax are concerned with movement of the legs and are dealt with separately (p. 170).

8.3 Legs

8.3.1 Basic structure

With the exception of apodous larval forms and a few specialised adults, all insects have three pairs of legs, one pair on each of the thoracic segments. Each leg consists typically of six segments, articulating with each other by mono- or di-condylic articulations set in a membrane, the corium. The six basic segments are coxa, trochanter, femur, tibia, tarsus and pretarsus (Fig. 81A).

The coxa is often in the form of a truncated cone and articulates basally with the wall of the thorax. There may be only a single articulation with the pleuron (Fig. 82A), in which case movement of the coxa is very free, but frequently there is a second articulation with the trochantin (Fig. 82B). This restricts movement to some extent, but because the trochantin is flexibly joined to the episternum the coxa is still relatively

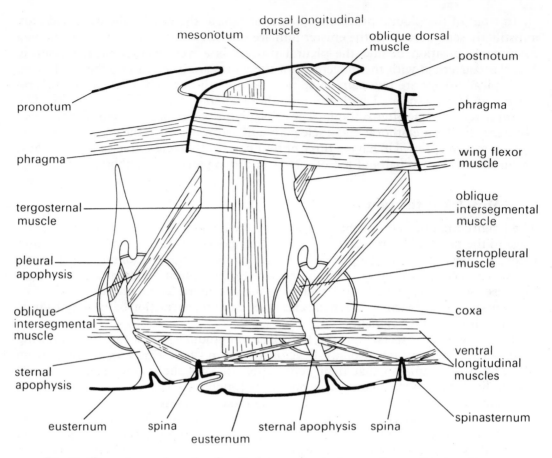

Fig. 80 The main muscles, other than the leg muscles, in the mesothorax of a winged insect (from Snodgrass, 1935)

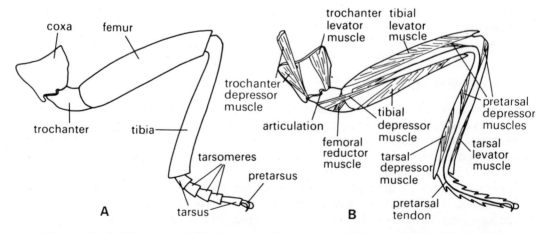

Fig. 81 Typical insect leg. A. External view. B. Internal arrangement showing the intrinsic muscles (after Snodgrass, 1927)

mobile. In some higher forms there are rigid pleural and sternal articulations limiting movement of the coxa to swinging about these two points (Fig. 82C). In the Lepidoptera the coxae of the middle and hind legs are fused with the thorax and this is also true of the hind coxae in Adephaga.

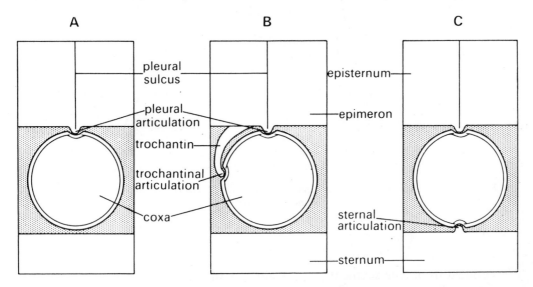

Fig. 82 Diagrammatic representations of different types of coxal articulation with the thorax. Membranous regions stippled (from Snodgrass, 1935)

The part of the coxa bearing the articulations is often strengthened by a ridge indicated externally by the basicostal sulcus which marks off the basal part of the coxa as the basicoxite (Fig. 83A). The basicoxite is divided into anterior and posterior parts by a ridge strengthening the articulation, the posterior part being called the meron. This is very large in Neuroptera, Mecoptera, Trichoptera and Lepidoptera (Fig. 83B), while in the higher Diptera it becomes separated from the coxa altogether and forms a part of the wall of the thorax.

The trochanter is a small segment with a dicondylic articulation with the coxa such that it can only move vertically (Fig. 84A). In Odonata there are two trochanters and this also appears to be the case in Hymenoptera, but here the apparent second trochanter is, in fact, a part of the femur.

The femur is often small in larval insects, but in most adults it is the largest and stoutest part of the leg. Often the femur is more or less fixed to the trochanter and in this case there are no muscles to move it, but sometimes a single muscle arising in the trochanter is able to produce a slight backward movement, or reduction, of the femur.

The tibia is the long shank of the leg articulating with the femur by a dicondylic joint so that it moves in a vertical plane (Fig. 84B and C). In most insects the head of the tibia is bent so that the shank can flex right back against the femur (Fig. 81).

In Protura, some Collembola and the larvae of holometabolous insects the tarsus is simple (Fig. 85A) or, in the latter, may be fused with the tibia. In most insects, however, it becomes subdivided into from two to five tarsomeres. These are

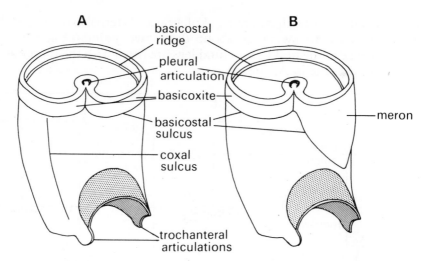

Fig. 83 Outer view of (A) typical insect coxa, and (B) coxa with a large meron (from Snodgrass, 1935)

differentiated from true segments by the absence of muscles (see Fig. 81). The basal tarsomere, or basitarsus, articulates with the distal end of the tibia by a single condyle (Fig. 84D), but between the tarsomeres there is no articulation; they are connected by flexible membrane so that they are freely movable. Levator and depressor muscles of the tarsus arise in the tibia and are inserted into the proximal end of the metatarsus.

The pretarsus consists of a single claw-like segment in Protura, some Collembola and many holometabolous larvae (Fig. 85A), but in the majority of insects it consists of a membranous base supporting a median lobe, the arolium, which may be membranous or partly sclerotised, and a pair of claws which articulate with a median process of the last tarsomere known as the unguifer. Ventrally there is a basal sclerotised plate, the unguitractor, and between this and the claws are small plates called auxiliae (Fig. 85B). In Diptera a membranous pulvillus arises from the base of each auxilia while a median empodium, which may be spine- or lobe-like, arises from the unguitractor (Fig. 85C). There is no arolium in Diptera other than Tipulidae. The development of the claws is variable. Commonly they are more or less equally well-developed, but in Thysanoptera they are minute and the pretarsus consists largely of the bladder-like arolium. In other groups the claws develop unequally and one may fail to develop altogether, so that in Mallophaga, for instance, there is only a single claw.

The muscles of the leg are described in Chapter IX.

8.3.2 Modifications of the basic pattern

The basic insect walking leg may be modified in various ways to serve a number of functions. Amongst these are jumping, swimming, digging, grasping, grooming and stridulation. Modifications associated with jumping and swimming are considered in Chapter IX.

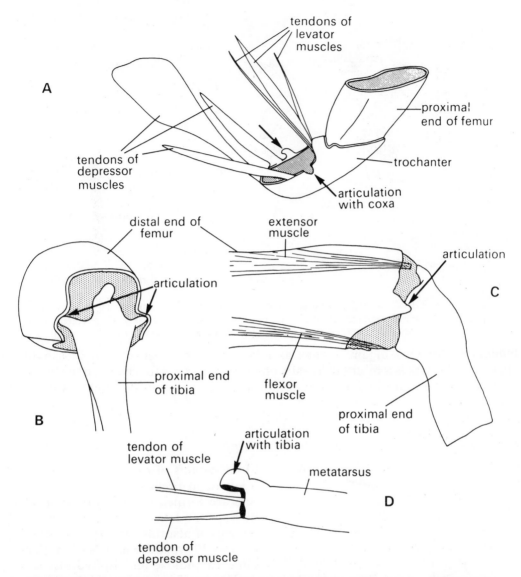

Fig. 84 Details of articulations of the leg joints. A. Articulation of trochanter with coxa and the muscles moving the trochanter. B and C. Articulation of tibia and femur, (B) end view, (C) side view. D. Articulation of tarsus with tibia (after Snodgrass, 1935, 1952)

Digging

Legs modified for digging are best known in the Scarabaeoidea and the mole cricket, *Gryllotalpa*. In *Gryllotalpa* the forelimb is very short and broad, the tibia and tarsomeres bearing stout lobes which are used in excavation. In the scarab beetles the femora are short, the tibiae are again strong and toothed, but the tarsi are often weakly developed. Larval cicadas are also burrowing insects. They have large, toothed fore

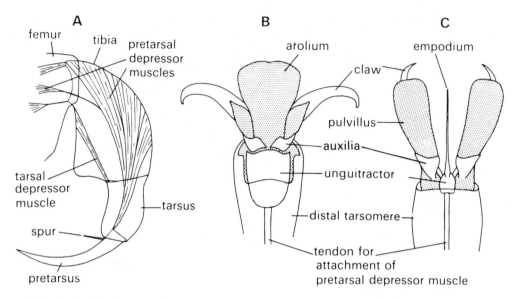

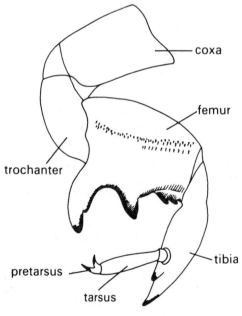

Fig. 85 A. Distal part of prothoracic leg of *Triaenodes* (Trichoptera) larva showing a primitive pretarsal segment. B. Pretarsus of *Periplaneta*, ventral view. C. Pretarsus of a dipteran, ventral view (after Tindall, 1964; Snodgrass, 1935)

femora, the principal digging organs, and the strong tibiae may serve to loosen the soil (Fig. 86). The tarsus is inserted dorsally on the tibia and can fold back. In the first instar larva it is three-segmented, but it becomes reduced in later instars and may disappear completely.

Fig. 86 Foreleg of a larval cicada (from Pesson, 1951)

Grasping

Modifications of the legs for grasping are frequent in predatory insects. Often pincers are formed by the apposition of the tibia on the femur and this occurs in the forelegs of mantids (Fig. 19), in some bugs such as Phymatidae and Nepidae, and in some Empididae and Ephydridae among the Diptera. In some Empididae the middle legs are modified in this way, while in *Bittacus* (Mecoptera) the fifth tarsomere folds back on the fourth.

The legs may be adapted for grasping in other ways and for other purposes. In the male *Dytiscus* (Coleoptera), for instance, the first three tarsomeres of the foreleg are enlarged to form a circular disc. On the inside this disc is set with stalked cuticular cups, most of which are very small, but two of which, on the basitarsus, are very much larger than the rest (Fig. 87A). A viscous secretion from a gland in the tarsus is discharged from these suckers so that they adhere to surfaces to which they are applied (Miall, 1922). The suckers are chiefly employed in holding the female during mating, but may also be used occasionally to grasp prey. Suckers are also possessed by the males of some other beetles belonging to the families Hydrophilidae, Carabidae, Cicindelidae, Meloidae and Silphidae.

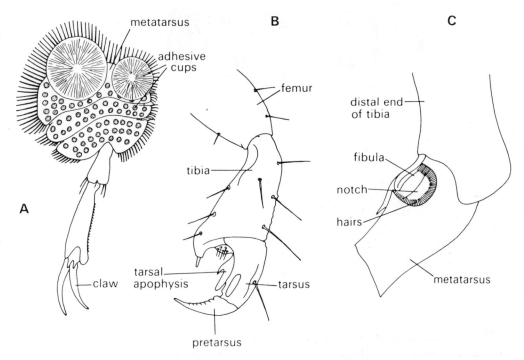

Fig. 87 A. Foretarsus of male *Dytiscus*. B. Leg of *Haematopinus* (Siphunculata). C. Toilet organ on the foreleg of *Apis* (after Miall, 1922; Séguy, 1951; Snodgrass, 1956)

The ability to hold on is also important in ectoparasitic insects. These usually have well-developed claws and frequently the legs are stout and short as in Hippoboscidae, Mallophaga and Siphunculata. In the latter two groups the tarsi are only one or two segmented and often there is only a single claw, which folds back against a projection of the tibia (Fig. 87B).

In free-living insects the claws are used to grip on to normally rough surfaces, while if the surface is very smooth a purchase can be obtained by the adhesion of the hairs on the arolia or pulvilli. In Orthoptera there are adhesive pads on the undersides of the tarsomeres, and in *Rhodnius* (Heteroptera) and some other Reduviidae there are specialised adhesive pads on the distal ends of the tibiae of the front and middle legs. These pads are closely set with about 5000 adhesive spines, which do not arise from sockets in the usual manner. Glandular cells in the epidermis open into the spines and presumably discharge at the tips, which are somewhat dilated and cut back (Fig. 88). The glands produce an oily secretion which forms a film on the surface and it is believed that the breakdown of this oil film causes the tips of the spines to adhere to the surface

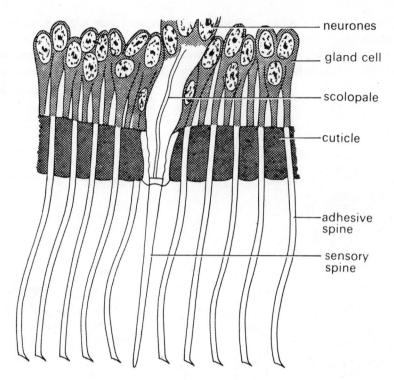

Fig. 88 Section through part of the adhesive organ of *Rhodnius* (after Gillett and Wigglesworth, 1932)

on which the insect is walking. Edwards and Tarkanian (1970), however, consider it likely that frictional forces together with meniscus forces, depending on the presence of aqueous or lipid films on the surface, account for the traction achieved by the insect. In this case no special secretion is necessary. The pads are used by the insect when it is walking up smooth surfaces on which the claws cannot obtain a grip.

Grooming

Insects commonly use the legs or mandibles to groom parts of the body, removing particles of detritus in the process. The eyes and antennae are often groomed, and so are the wings. Cockroaches clean their antennae by passing them through the mandibles, which chew lightly at the surface, but in most insects the forelegs are used for this purpose, often being cleaned themselves by the mandibles. Neuroptera and Diptera hold an antenna between the two forelegs, which are drawn forwards together towards the tip. Mosquitoes have a comb, consisting of several rows of setae, at the distal end of the fore tibia. The combs are scraped along the proboscis or antennae in rapid strokes (Goldman *et al.*, 1972). In many other insects each antenna is cleaned by the ipsilateral foreleg alone and the leg is often modified as a toilet organ (Jander, 1966). *Schistocerca* (Orthoptera) has a cleaning groove between the first and second pads of the first tarsomere. This is fitted over the lowered antenna and then drawn slowly along it by an upward movement of the head and extension of the leg (O'Shea, 1972). In *Apis* (Hymenoptera) there is a basal notch in the basitarsus lined with spinelike hairs. A flattened spur called the fibula extends down from the tip of the tibia in such a way that when the metatarsus is flexed against the tibia the fibula closes off the notch so as to form a complete ring (Fig. 87C). This ring is used to clean the antenna. First it is closed round the base of the flagellum and then the antenna is drawn through it so that the hairs clean the outer surface and the fibula scrapes the inner surface (Snodgrass, 1956).

A similar, though less well-developed organ, occurs in other Hymenoptera and some Coleoptera of the families Staphylinidae and Carabidae.

Lepidoptera have a mobile lobe called the strigil on the ventral surface of the fore tibia. It is often armed with a brush of hairs and is used to clean the antenna and possibly the proboscis (Callahan and Carlysle, 1971).

The hind legs of Apoidea are modified to collect pollen from the hairs of the body and accumulate it in the pollen basket (see p. 42).

Reduction of legs

Some reduction of the legs occurs in various groups of insects. Many Papilionoidea, for instance, have the anterior tarsi reduced, and the Nymphalidae are functionally four-legged, the front legs being held permanently withdrawn against the thorax. In the male nymphalid the tarsus and pretarsus of the foreleg are completely lacking, while in the female the tarsus consists only of very short segments. In the male of *Hepialus* (Lepidoptera), on the other hand, the hind leg lacks a tarsus.

More usually reduction of the legs is associated with a sedentary or some other specialised habit, such as burrowing, in which legs would be an encumbrance. Thus female coccids are sedentary and are held in position by the stylets of the proboscis. The legs are reduced, sometimes to simple spines, and in some species they are absent altogether. Similarly female Psychidae show varying degrees of reduction of the legs, some species being completely apodous; these insects never leave the bags constructed by their larvae. Legs are also completely absent from female Strepsiptera, which are parasitic in other insects.

Apart from the Diptera, all the larvae of which are apodous, legless larvae are usually associated with particular modes of life. There is a tendency for the larvae of leaf-mining Lepidoptera, Coleoptera and Tenthredinoidea to be apodous (see Hering, 1951). Parasitic larvae of Hymenoptera and Strepsiptera are apodous and in Meloidae the legs are greatly reduced. Finally in the social and semisocial Hymenoptera, in which the larvae are provided with food by the parent, apodous forms are also the rule.

REFERENCES

ALBRECHT, F. O. (1956). The anatomy of the red locust, *Nomadacris septemfasciata* Serville. *Anti-Locust Bull.* no. 23, 9 pp. + figs.

CALLAHAN, P. S. and CARLYSLE, T. C. (1971). A function of the epiphysis on the foreleg of the corn earworm moth, *Heliothis zea. Ann. ent. Soc. Am.* **64**: 309–311.

EDWARDS, J. S. and TARKANIAN, M. (1970). The adhesive pads of Heteroptera: a re-examination. *Proc. R. ent. Soc. Lond.* A, **45**: 1–5.

GILLETT, J. D. and WIGGLESWORTH, V. B. (1932). The climbing organ of an insect, *Rhodnius prolixus* (Hemiptera: Reduviidae). *Proc. R. Soc.* B, **111**: 364–376.

GOLDMAN, L. J., CALLAHAN, P. S. and CARLYSLE, T. C. (1972). Tibial combs and proboscis cleaning in mosquitoes. *Ann. ent. Soc. Am.* **65**: 1299–1302.

HERING, E. M. (1951). *Biology of leaf miners*. Junk, 's-Gravenhage.

JANDER, U. (1966). Untersuchungen zur Stammesgeschichte von Putzbewegungen von Tracheaten. *Z. Tierpsychol.* **23**: 799–844.

MANTON, S. M. (1953). Locomotory habits and the evolution of the larger arthropodan groups. *Symp. Soc. exp. Biol.* **7**: 339–376.

MANTON, S. M. (1977). *The Arthropoda. Habits, functional morphology and evolution*. Clarendon Press, Oxford.

MATSUDA, R. (1963). Some evolutionary aspects of the insect thorax. *A. Rev. Ent.* **8**: 59–76.

MATSUDA, R. (1970). Morphology and evolution of the insect thorax. *Mem. ent. Soc. Can.* no. 76, 431 pp.

MIALL, L. C. (1922). *The natural history of aquatic insects*. MacMillan, London.

O'SHEA, M. R. (1972). The antennal cleaning reflex in the desert locust, *Schistocerca gregaria* (Forsk.) *in* Hemming, C. F. and Taylor, T. H. C. (eds.), *Proceedings of the International study conference on the current and future problems of acridology*. Centre for Overseas Pest Research, London.

PESSON, P. (1951). Ordre des Homoptères. *in* Grassé, P.-P. (ed.), *Traité de Zoologie*. vol. 10. Masson et Cie., Paris.

SÉGUY, E. (1951). Ordre des Anoploures ou poux. *In* Grassé, P.-P. (ed.), *Traité de Zoologie*. vol. 10. Masson et Cie, Paris.

SNODGRASS, R. E. (1927). Morphology and mechanism of the insect thorax. *Smithson. misc. Collns* **80**, no. 1, 108 pp.

SNODGRASS, R. E. (1935). *Principles of insect morphology*. McGraw-Hill, New York.

SNODGRASS, R. E. (1952). *A textbook of arthropod anatomy*. Cornell Univ. Press, Ithaca.

SNODGRASS, R. E. (1956). *Anatomy of the honey bee*. Constable, London.

SNODGRASS, R. E. (1958). Evolution of arthropod mechanisms. *Smithson. misc. Collns* **138**, no. 2, 77 pp.

TINDALL, A. R. (1964). The skeleton and musculature of the larval thorax of *Triaenodes bicolor* Curtis (Trichoptera: Limnephilidae). *Trans. R. ent. Soc. Lond.* **116**: 151–210.

CHAPTER IX
LOCOMOTION

Mobility at some stage of the life history is a characteristic of all animals. They must move in order to find a mate, for dispersal and, in many cases, in order to find food. The success of insects as terrestrial animals is in part due to their high degree of mobility arising from the power of flight (see Chapter XIII), but more local movements by walking or swimming are also important. Most insects move over the surface of the ground by running or hopping, the power for these movements coming from the legs. The legs move in sequences which are varied at different speeds in such a way that stability is always maintained. Co-ordination of these movements involves central mechanisms, but segmental reflexes are also important.

The legs can only function in this way when the skeleton is rigid. In soft-bodied larval forms the muscles work against a hydrostatic skeleton maintained by the turgor pressure of the haemolymph. These forms crawl by extending the body anteriorly, obtaining a fresh purchase on the substratum and then drawing up the rest of the body. Some forms have abdominal appendages which assist in crawling.

Aquatic insects also use the legs in movement, the swimming legs being modified to expose a maximum area on the power stroke and a minimum on the return stroke. With other adaptations this ensures a maximal thrust on the backstroke so that the insect moves forwards. Larvae of aquatic Diptera which are legless move by lateral flexure of the whole body and larval Anisoptera use a method of jet propulsion.

Insect locomotion on land is reviewed by Hughes and Mill (1974) and Wilson (1966); Bowerman (1977) and Wendler (1966) consider control mechanisms. Aquatic locomotion is reviewed by Nachtigall (1974).

9.1 Walking

9.1.1 Movements of the leg

In describing the movements of the legs the following terms are used (Hughes, 1952).

Protraction—complete movement forwards of the whole limb relative to its articulation with the body

Promotion—the movement of the coxa resulting in protraction

Retraction—the backward movement of the leg between the time it is placed on the ground and the time it is raised

Remotion—the corresponding movement of the coxa

Adduction—the movement of the coxa towards the body

Abduction—the movement of the coxa away from the body

Levation—the raising of the leg or a part of the leg, part of protraction

Depression—lowering the leg, or a part of the leg. The terms levation and
    depression are to some extent interchangeable with:

Extension—an increase in the angle between two segments of the leg

Flexion—a decrease in the angle between two segments of the leg

The muscles which produce these movements fall into two categories: extrinsic,
arising outside the leg, and intrinsic, wholly within the leg and running from one
segment to the next. The coxa is moved by extrinsic muscles arising in the thorax and a
fairly typical arrangement is shown in Fig. 89 with promotor and remotor muscles
arising on the tergum, abductor and adductor muscles from the pleuron and sternum,
and rotator muscles also from the sternum. The functions of the muscles may vary,
depending on the activities of other muscles and also on the type of articulation. In *Apis*
(Hymenoptera), which has rigid pleural and sternal articulations, promotor and
remotor muscles from the tergum are absent.

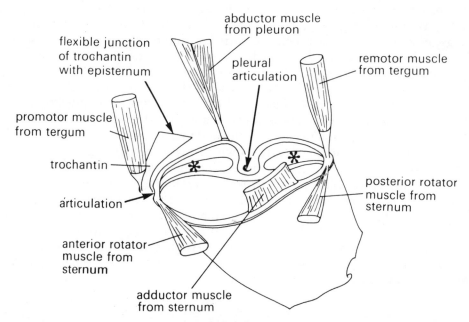

Fig. 89 Inner view of coxa showing the extrinsic leg muscles which move it. Muscles arising
from the points marked with asterisks and inserted at the wing base are omitted (from
Snodgrass, 1935)

In the pterothoracic segments, muscles (insertions marked with an asterisk in
Fig. 89) run from the coxae to the basalar and subalar sclerites. They are concerned
with movements of the wings as well as the legs.

The intrinsic musculature of the leg is much simpler than the coxal musculature,
typically consisting only of pairs of antagonistic muscles in each segment (Fig. 81B). In
Periplaneta (Dictyoptera) there are three levator muscles of the trochanter arising in the
coxa and three depressor muscles, two again with origins in the coxa and a third arising
on the pleural ridge and the tergum.

The femur is usually immovably attached to the trochanter, but the tibia is moved by extensor and flexor muscles arising in the femur and inserted into tendons from the membrane at the base of the tibia. Levator and depressor muscles of the tarsus arise in the tibia and are inserted into the top of the basitarsus, but there are no muscles within the tarsus moving the tarsomeres.

It is characteristic of the insects that the pretarsus has a depressor muscle, but no levator muscle. The fibres of the depressor occur in small groups in the femur and tibia, being inserted into a long tendon which arises on the unguitractor (Figs. 81B, 85B and C). Levation of the pretarsus results from the elasticity of its basal parts.

9.1.2 Mechanism of walking

The forces which act on the body to produce locomotion arise in various ways from the activities of the legs.

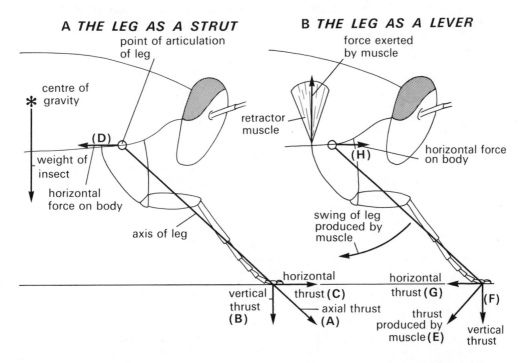

Fig. 90 A. Diagrammatic representation of a leg acting as a strut. The axial thrust (A) is exerted down the length of the leg by virtue of the weight of the insect. The size of the axial thrust depends, among other things, on how much of the weight is borne by the other legs. It can be resolved into vertical and horizontal components (B and C), but because the foot is held by friction with the substratum it does not move. Instead, an equal and opposite horizontal force (D) acts on the body and, in this case, tends to push it back unless balanced by other forces. B. Diagrammatic representation of a leg acting as a lever. Contraction of the retractor muscle tends to swing the leg back so that the foot exerts a thrust (E) on the ground. This can be resolved into vertical and horizontal components (F and G), but since the foot is held still by friction an equal and opposite horizontal force (H) acts on the body pushing it forwards. For a fuller consideration of the mechanics involved see Gray (1944)

A leg may act simply as a strut with the forces acting down it depending on its angle of inclination to the body and the weight of the insect (Fig. 90A). Equal and opposite forces will be exerted by the leg on the body. The force acting down the leg can be resolved into two components, horizontal and vertical, and because the leg is splayed out lateral to the body the horizontal force can be resolved into longitudinal and transverse components (Fig. 91). The relative sizes of the longitudinal and transverse components will vary according to the position of the leg. In Fig. 91 it is assumed that only three legs are on the ground (see p. 175) and it is clear that for most of its movement the strut effect of the foreleg tends to retard forward movement, while that of the middle and hind legs promotes forward movement. So long as all the longitudinal and lateral forces balance each other there will be no movement, but if the forces are not balanced the body will be displaced due to a fall in the centre of gravity.

A leg can also act as a lever, that is a bar on which external work is done so that it rotates about a fulcrum. This effect is produced by the extrinsic muscles which move the leg relative to the body and so lever the insect along (Fig. 90B).

The leg, however, is not a simple, rigid strut or bar. It also has intrinsic muscles which can exert forces on the body by flexing or extending the leg. If a leg is extended

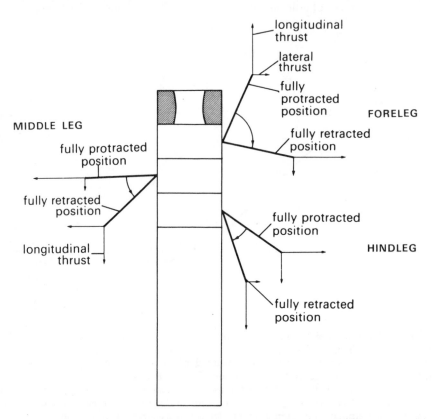

Fig. 91 Diagram to show the positions of the legs forming a typical triangle of support when fully protracted and fully retracted, together with the longitudinal and lateral components of the horizontal strut effect which the legs exert on the ground at these times. The forces acting on the body will be in the opposite directions (after Hughes, 1952)

anteriorly flexion of the joints will pull the body forwards (Fig. 92B), while in a leg directed backwards straightening the joints will push the body forwards (Fig. 92A).

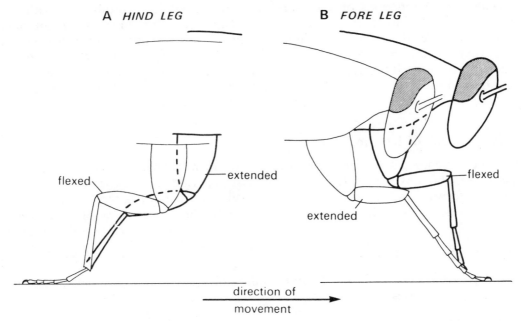

Fig. 92 Diagrams to show the effects of extension and flexion of the coxotrochanteral and femoro-tibial joints on the movement of the body, while the feet remain still. A. Extension of the hind leg pushes the body forwards. B. Flexion of the foreleg pulls the body forwards

When *Periplaneta* starts to move, the foreleg is fully protracted due to maximum promotion of the coxa and extension of all the leg segments. At this stage it exerts a strut action retarding forward movement. Retraction begins by remotion of the coxa, which produces a lever effect drawing the animal forwards, an effect which is added to by flexion of the trochanter on the coxa and the tibia on the femur. This phase continues until the leg is at right angles to the long axis of the insect. When it has passed this position it exerts a strut effect which, aided by extension of the leg, tends to push the insect forwards.

During protraction the leg is lifted and flexed so that it exerts no forces on the body. The promotor muscle of the coxa probably starts to contract before retraction is complete and so the change over from retraction to protraction is smooth. As the leg swings forwards it extends again, so that in each cycle of movement the intrinsic muscles undergo two phases of contraction and relaxation, while the extrinsic muscles only contract and relax once.

The tarsi of the middle and hind legs are always placed on the ground behind their coxae, so their longitudinal strut effect always assists forward movement (Fig. 91). The main propulsive forces of both pairs of legs are derived from extension of the trochanter on the coxa and of the tibia on the femur pushing the insect forwards.

The longitudinal forces produced by these movements are mostly such that the insect moves forwards. At the same time lateral forces are produced and when, for instance, the right foreleg is on the ground it tends to push the head to the left. This is partly balanced by the other legs, but there is some tendency for the head to swing from side to side during movement (see Hughes, 1952).

The precise functions of a muscle or a leg during locomotion vary with the orientation of the insect. For instance, when *Carausius* (Phasmida) is walking on a horizontal plane, the middle and hind legs provide most support and most of the propulsive force is provided by the hind legs; the forelegs have a largely sensory function. However, if the insect is suspended beneath a surface, all the legs are used to hold on and much of the power for movement comes from the middle legs (Cruse, 1976).

9.1.3 Patterns of leg movement

The rate of stepping determines the speed of movement of an insect. *Periplaneta* at top speed takes about 25 steps/s. Each step comprises a period of protraction, when the leg is swung forwards off the ground, and a period of retraction, as the leg moves back relative to the body with the foot on the ground. The rate of stepping is increased primarily by shortening the period of retraction; the period of protraction also shortens (Fig. 93) but less markedly, so that the ratio $\dfrac{\text{protraction time}}{\text{retraction time}}$ increases from about 0·3 at low speeds to 1·0 at high speeds. In *Carausius* protraction time is constant and only retraction time varies.

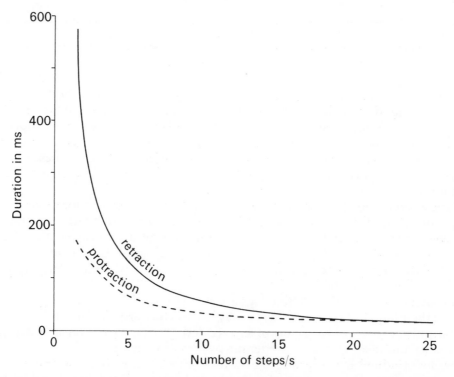

Fig. 93 Changes in duration of retraction and protraction times of a leg of *Periplaneta* in relation to the rate of stepping (after Delcomyn, 1971)

The pattern of stepping also varies with the speed of movement, but in general the movements of the two legs of a segment alternate and no leg is moved until the leg behind is in a supporting position. At low stepping rates most of the legs are on the ground most of the time and the legs are protracted singly in the sequence R3 R2 R1 L3 L2 L1 R3 etc. (where R and L indicate right and left, and 1, 2 and 3 the fore, middle and hind legs respectively) (Figs. 94A, 95A). At the highest stepping rates three legs, the fore and hind legs of one side and the middle leg of the other, are lifted more or less simultaneously, so that a triangle of support is formed by the other three legs. As one set

is protracted the other is retracted and *vice versa* in the sequence $\begin{matrix} R1 & L1 & R1 \\ L2 & R2 & L2 \\ R3 & L3 & R3 \end{matrix}$ etc.

(Figs 94B, 95B), the insect thus being supported on alternate triangles of legs. It never has less than three legs on the ground and can stop at any point without losing its stability since the three legs enclose the vertical axis through the centre of gravity. Stability is enhanced by the fact that the body is slung between the legs so the centre of gravity is low (Fig. 96). Patterns of leg movement approximating to alternating triangles of support are commonly observed in insects (Burns, 1973; Delcomyn, 1971).

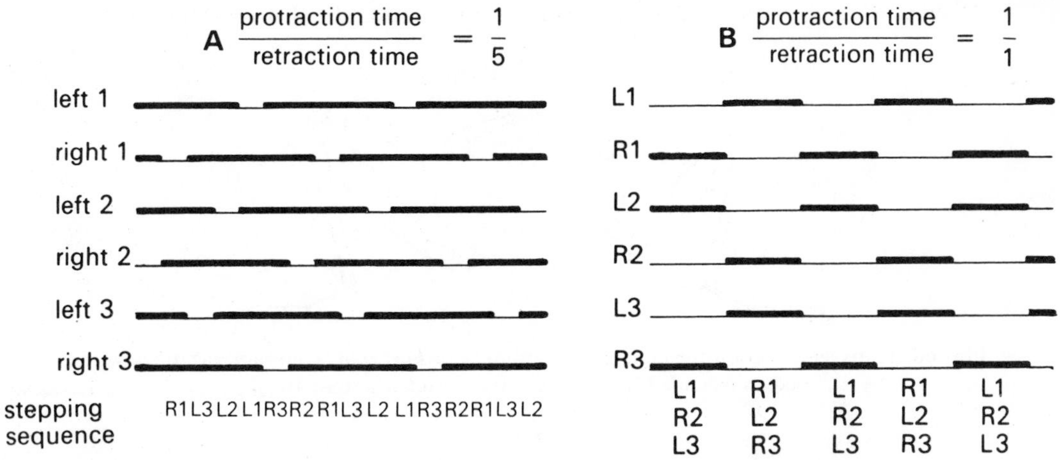

Fig. 94 Diagram showing the disposition of the legs with different protraction time: retraction time ratios. Thick lines indicate retraction with the foot on the ground, thin lines protraction with the foot in the air (modified after Hughes, 1952)

Other patterns of movement also occur. Thus *Petrobius* (Archaeognatha) moves the two legs of a segment together and this is also true of the climbing grasshopper *Tropidopola*. This insect is effectively quadrupedal, using only the anterior two pairs of legs, while the tip of the abdomen provides an additional point of support (Fig. 95C). At high speeds the legs are moved in the sequences $\begin{matrix} L1 & L2 & L1 \\ R1 & R2 & R1 \end{matrix}$ etc. At low speeds mantids are also functionally quadrupedal using only the posterior two pairs of legs, but the sequence of stepping is L3 L2 R3 R2 L3 etc., or $\begin{matrix} L3 & L2 & L3 \\ R2 & R3 & R2 \end{matrix}$ etc.

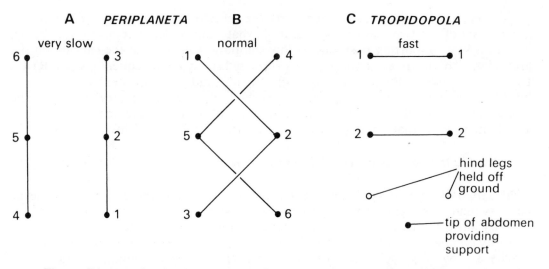

Fig. 95 Diagrams showing the order in which the feet are lifted (A) in *Periplaneta* at very low speeds, (B) in *Periplaneta* and most other insects at normal speeds, and (C) in *Tropidopola* at high speeds. Numbers indicate the sequence of stepping; points joined by straight lines indicate legs stepping together or in rapid succession (from Hughes and Mill, 1974)

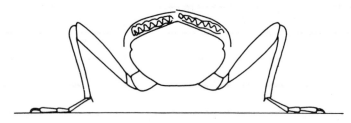

Fig. 96 Transverse section through the mesothorax of *Forficula* (Dermaptera) to show the body suspended between the legs (after Manton, 1953)

The speed of movement varies very greatly from one insect to another, but in general it is higher at higher temperatures. At 25°C *Periplaneta* moves at about 70 cm/s with top speeds up to 130 cm/s (see Hughes and Mill, 1974). Speed also depends to some extent on size: insects with longer legs can take longer paces, so that for the same frequency of pacing they will move further than smaller insects. Thus first instar larvae of *Blattella* (Dictyoptera) can move at about 3 cm/s, while adults are capable of speeds up to 20 cm/s.

9.1.4 Co-ordination of leg movements

The alternating movements of protraction and retraction are generated by a programme within the central nervous system. As a consequence levator and depressor muscles of the coxa contract in antiphase to produce stepping movements even when there is no sensory input (and see p. 257). The action of individual muscles, and of the leg as a whole, is however altered by the input from peripheral sensilla on the leg. Hairs at the base of the coxa, campaniform sensilla on the trochanter, the femoral chordotonal organs and tarsal receptors have all been shown to produce such a modulating effect (Bässler, 1977). Input from the sensilla influences individual muscles in the course of a step and may act over a longer period to modify the output from the rhythm generating system (Fig. 97). In this way the stepping movements are modified to suit the conditions in which the insect is moving.

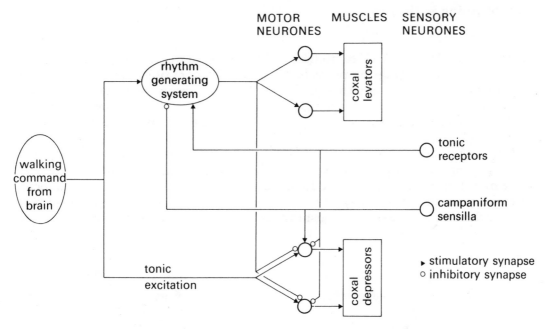

Fig. 97 Diagrammatic representation of the control of leg movement in cockroach walking (after Bowerman, 1977)

Some reflex inhibition of the muscles in the contralateral leg also occurs, so that, for instance, stimulation of the depressor muscles of one side inhibits the discharge to the depressor muscles on the other side of the segment. As a result of this the two legs of a segment are out of phase.

Clearly there must also be co-ordination between the segments to maintain stepping and control timing. This might involve intersegmental reflexes, but there is little evidence for their existence. Some measure of intersegmental co-ordination could arise from the perception by the sensilla of each leg of changing drag and gravitational effects resulting from the activities of the other legs, but there are good arguments suggesting that such explanations are not adequate and it seems certain that autonomous central nervous processes are involved (see Wendler, 1966; Wilson, 1966).

9.2 Jumping

Jumping normally involves some modification of the hind legs as in Orthoptera, Siphonaptera and Homoptera (see p. 181), but other mechanisms occur in Collembola,

Elateridae and *Piophila* (Diptera). In most cases jumping is a form of escape reaction. The power output required for such a jump is greater than that of any muscle, but it is achieved by the storage of energy derived from the relatively slow contraction of a muscle and then its sudden release to produce the jump. Energy is stored in the muscle itself and in the cuticle and its release is controlled independently of the muscle producing the power.

9.2.1 Jumping with legs

Orthoptera and jumping beetles

In Orthoptera, Halticinae (Flea beetles) and *Orchestes* (a weevil) the hind femora are greatly enlarged, housing the powerful extensor (levator) tibiae muscles, which in Orthoptera consist of two large masses of muscle fibres arising obliquely from the wall of the femur and inserted into a long, flat apodeme (Fig. 98). The jump in this case results from the sudden straightening of the femoro-tibial joint extending the tibia, which is also elongate.

Fifth instar larvae of *Locusta* (Orthoptera) can make long jumps of up to 70 cm, reaching a height of 30 cm. The power for the jump is provided by the sudden extension of the hind tibiae, which at rest are folded under the femora. Before a jump a locust raises the front part of the body and flexes the femoro-tibial joint. The tibiae of both sides are then suddenly extended, pushing against the ground and projecting the insect

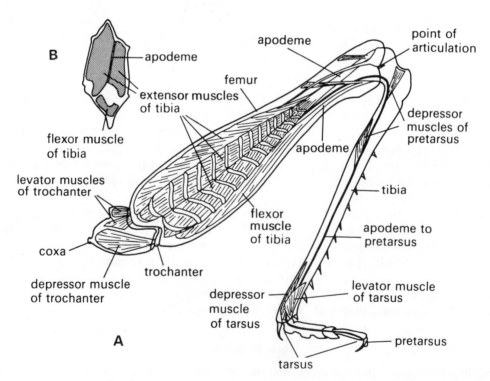

Fig. 98 Hind leg of a grasshopper showing (A) the musculature and (B) a transverse section of the femur (from Snodgrass, 1935)

into the air. The centre of gravity of the insect is close to the line joining the insertions of the metathoracic coxae, so little torque is produced when the legs extend and the insect moves through the air without rolling. The initial thrust exerted by the tibiae is directly downwards because just before the jump the flexed femur–tibia is rotated so that it is parallel with the ground. In the course of extension, however, a backward component develops pushing the insect forwards.

The measured take-off velocity in an adult locust weighing 3 g is 3·4 m/s. This can be resolved into horizontal and vertical components which will determine the length and height of the jump. The height increases with the angle of take-off, which is usually about 60°, and also with the distance through which the legs move (Hoyle, 1955).

The structure of the hind legs, and especially of the femoro-tibial joints, is adapted to permit the development of maximum force by the extensor tibiae muscles, the storage of the energy produced, and its rapid release resulting in the sudden extension of the tibiae. The power for the movement comes from the extensor tibiae muscles, which occupy much of the femur. Since they consist of a series of short fibres inserted obliquely into the apodeme (Fig. 98), they have a large cross-sectional area and can develop a force up to 1600N compared with only 70N by the flexor tibiae muscle. Just above the articulation with the tibia, the cuticle of the femur is heavily sclerotised forming a dark area known as the semilunar process (Fig. 99A). Beneath the articulation, the cuticle of the femur is thickened internally to form a process, known as Heitler's lump, over which the apodeme of the flexor tibiae slides. Finally, the form of the head of the tibia and the muscle insertions are such that the flexor muscle has a mechanical advantage over the extensor muscle (Fig. 99C) and a small movement of the head of the tibia produces a big movement of the distal end. This mechanical advantage varies with the position of the tibia, but is greatest, about 150:1, when the tibia is close up to the femur (Bennet-Clark, 1975).

Before a jump the tibia is flexed against the femur by the action of the flexor muscle. The axons to the extensor muscle remain silent (Fig. 100). Then, after an interval of 100–200 ms, both flexor and extensor muscles contract together. There is no movement of the tibia at this time because the mechanical advantage of the flexor muscle offsets the greater power of the extensor muscle. However, the distal end of the femur is distorted and energy is stored in the semilunar processes. Rapid extension of the tibia then occurs when the flexor muscles suddenly relax due to the inhibition of their motor input and to the activity of their inhibitory nerve supply (Fig. 100) (Heitler and Burrows, 1977; Heitler, 1977).

Homoptera

In the jumping Homoptera of the families Cercopidae, Cicadellidae, Membracidae and Psyllidae the jump is produced by a rotation of the leg on the coxo-trochanteral joint. Powerful muscles from the furca, pleuron and notum are inserted into a tendon from the edge of the trochanter and the coxa opens very widely to the thorax to permit the entry of these muscles. In psyllids the coxa is fused with the thorax and the position of the trochanteral articulations is altered so as to bring the femora parallel with the trunk.

Siphonaptera

The muscles producing the jumps of the flea are those of the femur which arise in the thorax. These muscles are so inserted relative to the point of articulation of the leg with

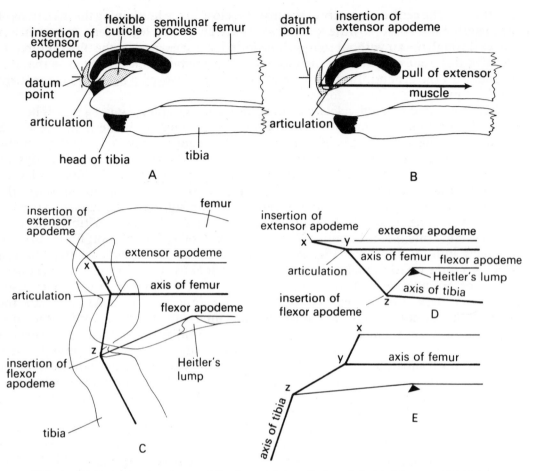

Fig. 99 Diagram showing the specialisations and functioning of the hind femoro-tibial joint of a locust. A. The semilunar process; the tibia is flexed, but the extensor muscle remains relaxed. B. The extensor muscle contracts at the same time as the flexor muscle. Because the insertion of the extensor apodeme is almost in line with the articulation, contraction of the extensor muscle causes distortion of the head of the femur, straining the semilunar processes. C. Diagram showing the position of Heitler's lump and arrangement of the apodemes. D and E. Changes in positions of apodemes and their insertions with the tibia flexed (D) and extended (E) (after Bennet-Clark, 1975; Heitler, 1977)

the thorax that they draw it up against a pad of resilin (p. 514) without rotating it. The energy produced is stored in the resilin and a slight sideways movement of the femoral muscle, produced by a laterally inserted muscle, causes the coxa to swing suddenly downwards as the tension in the system is released. This has the effect of projecting the insect into the air (Bennet-Clark and Lucey, 1967).

9.2.2 Mechanisms of jumping not involving legs

Collembola

Collembola jump using modified abdominal appendages. Arising from the posterior end of the fourth abdominal segment is a structure called the furca, which consists of a

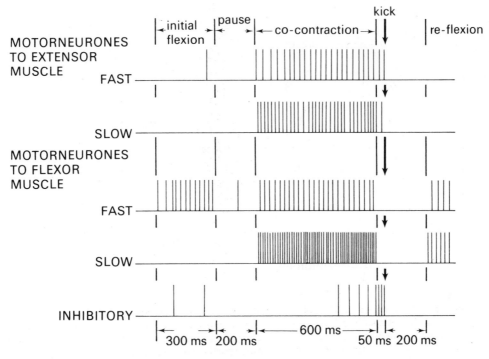

Fig. 100 Diagrammatic representation of the activity of the motorneurones controlling the extensor and flexor tibiae muscles of the hind leg of a locust in relation to a jump. Vertical lines represent action potentials (after Heitler and Burrows, 1977)

basal manubrium bearing a pair of rami, each divided into a proximal dens and a distal mucron (Fig. 101). The furca can be turned forwards and held flexed beneath the abdomen by a retinaculum on the posterior border of segment three (Fig. 101C). The jump is produced by the furca swinging back rapidly to the extended position so that it strikes the substratum and throws the animal into the air.

It is not certain how the sudden movement is produced and different mechanisms may be employed by different species. In *Allacma* Denis (1949) suggests that the furca is pulled round by flexor muscles distorting the cuticle at the base of the manubrium so that it is under tension. Once the furca is held by the retinaculum all the muscles relax, so that when the furca is released it springs back as the distorted cuticle assumes its normal shape again. Manton (1977) and Christian (1978), however, consider that the jump is produced by the powerful longitudinal muscles of the abdomen. Christian shows that extension of the furca is a direct result of the action of these muscles coupled, in at least some species, with a click mechanism (p. 219), but Manton considers it to be an indirect effect consequent upon a sudden increase in haemolymph hydrostatic pressure.

Other insects

Jumping as a result of the sudden release of tension previously developed also occurs in Elateridae and the larvae of various Diptera. Elaterids (click beetles) jump if they are turned on their backs and the jump serves as a means by which they can right

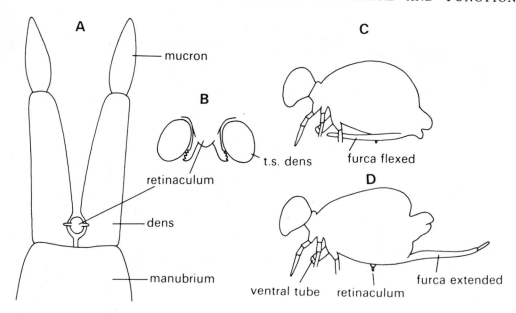

Fig. 101 Jumping in Collembola. A. Furca and retinaculum seen from below. B. Diagram showing the retinaculum holding the dentes. C and D. Diagrams of a collembolan with the furca in the flexed and extended positions. Jumping is produced by the swing from the flexed to the extended position (partly after Denis, 1949)

themselves. The insect first arches its back between the prothorax and the mesothorax so that it is supported anteriorly by the prothorax and posteriorly by the distal ends of the elytra with the middle of the body off the ground. This movement is produced by the median dorsal muscle and results in the withdrawal of a median prosternal peg from the pit in which it is normally at rest. A small process on the upper side of the peg catches on a lip on the anterior edge of the mesosternum, so that subsequent contraction of the massive prothoracic intersegmental muscle (Fig. 102) produces no movement but tension builds up in the muscle. Energy is stored within it and, possibly, in the associated cuticle. When the prosternal peg slips off its catch, this energy is released as rotational energy, both prothorax and the rest of the body rotating upwards, and as translational energy, the centre of gravity of both parts of the body being moved upwards with considerable velocity. This translational energy carries the insect into the air at an initial speed of about 2·5 m/s, the whole jumping action being complete in about 0·5 ms. This is a relatively inefficient process and only 60% of the energy expanded during the jump is used in lifting the beetle off the ground (Fig. 103) (Evans, 1972, 1973).

The larva of *Piophila* (Diptera) lives in cheese and in the last instar it is able to jump. It does this by bending the head back beneath its abdomen so that the mandibles engage in a transverse fold near the posterior spiracles. The longitudinal muscles on the outside of the loop so formed contract and build up a tension until suddenly the mandibles are released and the larva jerks straight striking the ground so that it is thrown into the air, sometimes as high as 20 cm. A similar phenomenon occurs in the larvae of some Clusiidae and Tephritidae, while in cecidomyid larvae anal hooks catch in a forked prosternal projection producing a leap in a similar way as *Piophila* by building up muscular tension and then suddenly releasing it.

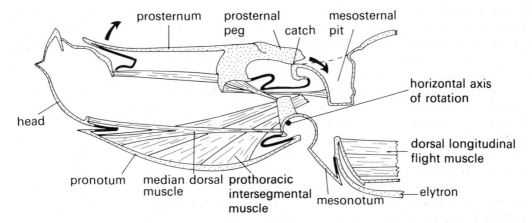

Fig. 102 Diagrammatic longitudinal section of the head and thorax of a click beetle, ventral side uppermost, with the prosternal peg withdrawn from the mesosternal pit. Arrows show direction of rotation of the head and prothorax about the horizontal axis which contributes to the jump. Sclerotised cuticle stippled, membranous cuticle black (after Evans, 1972)

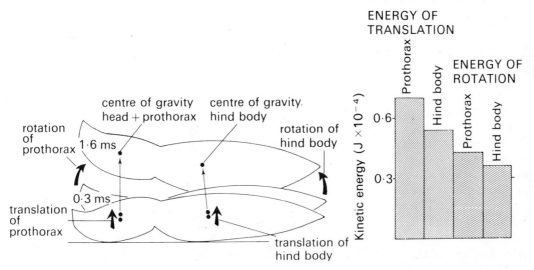

Fig. 103 Diagrams showing the movements of the body of a click beetle in the first 1.6 ms of a jump, starting with the insect at rest on its dorsal surface. Histogram shows the energy produced by the movements shown (after Evans, 1972, 1973)

9.3 Crawling

The larvae of many holometabolous insects move by changes in the shape of the body rather than by movements of the legs as in walking or running by adult insects. This type of locomotion can be differentiated as crawling. In the majority of crawling forms the cuticle is soft and flexible and does not, by itself, provide a suitable skeleton on which the muscles can act. Instead, the pressure of the haemolymph within the body provides a hydrostatic skeleton. Special muscles lining the body wall of caterpillars keep the body turgid and, because of the incompressibility of the body fluids, a change in the shape of one part of the body due to muscular contraction must be compensated by an opposite change in some other part. The place and form of these compensating changes will be controlled by the degree of tension of the muscles throughout the body.

Caterpillars typically have, in addition to the thoracic legs, a pair of prolegs on each of abdominal segments three to six and another pair on segment ten (Fig. 298). The prolegs are hollow cylindrical outgrowths of the body wall, the lumen being continuous with the haemocoel (Fig. 104). An apical area, less rigid than the sides, is known as the planta and it bears a row or circle of outwardly curved hooks, or crochets, with which the leg obtains a grip. Retractor muscles from the body wall are inserted into the centre of the planta so that when they contract it is drawn inwards and the crochets are disengaged. The leg is evaginated by turgor pressure when the muscles relax. On a smooth surface the prolegs can function as suckers. The crochets are turned up and the planta surface is first pressed down on to the substratum and then the centre is slightly drawn up so as to create a vacuum (Hinton, 1955).

Caterpillars move by serial contractions of the longitudinal muscles coupled with leg movements. The contractions start posteriorly and the anal claspers are lifted and moved forwards, followed by similar movements of the more anterior legs, the two legs of a segment moving together. Each segment is lifted by contraction of the dorsal

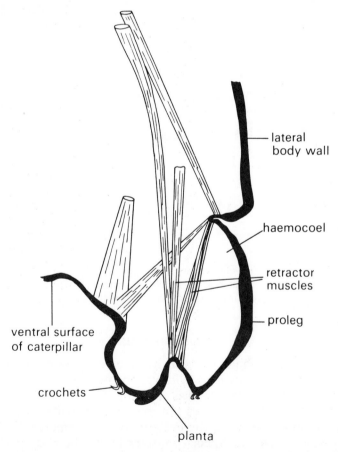

Fig. 104 Transverse section through part of an abdominal segment of a caterpillar showing the proleg (after Hinton, 1955)

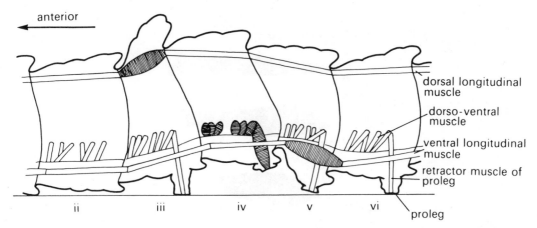

Fig. 105 Diagrammatic section through a caterpillar showing a wave of contraction which passes along the body from behind forwards and produces forward movement. Contracted muscles are shown hatched (modified from Hughes, 1965)

longitudinal muscles of the segment in front, while at the same time the prolegs are retracted (Fig. 105). Subsequently contraction of the ventral longitudinal muscles brings the segment down again and completes the forward movement as the legs are extended and obtain a fresh grip. As the wave of contraction passes forwards along the body at least three segments are in different stages of contraction at any one time. This calls for a high degree of co-ordination and it appears that control is largely a central nervous process, the muscles being stimulated by impulses passing down the nerve cord. It is probable, however, that this central control is modified by local reflexes involving the stretch receptors (see p. 728) (Weevers, 1965).

Many geometrid larvae have prolegs only on abdominal segments six and ten. These insects loop along, drawing the hind end of the body up to the thorax and then extending the head and thorax to obtain a fresh grip.

In the apodous larvae of Diptera a different method is used, although movement again depends on changes in the shape of the body as a result of muscles acting against the body fluids. The posterior segments of the body are often provided with prolegs (see Fig. 206) or with creeping welts (Fig. 300F). These are raised pads usually running right across the ventral surface of a segment and armed with stiff, curved setae, which may be distributed evenly or in rows or patches. Each welt is provided with retractor muscles (Hinton, 1955). In the larva of *Musca* there are locomotory welts on the anterior edges of segments six to twelve and also on the posterior edge of segment twelve and behind the anus.

In movement the anterior part of the body is lengthened and narrowed by the contraction of oblique muscles, while the posterior part maintains a grip with the prolegs or welts. Hence the front of the body is pushed forwards over, or through, the substratum. It is then anchored and the posterior part moved forwards by a wave of longitudinal shortening. The anterior region is anchored in the soil-dwelling larvae of Tipulidae, Bibionidae and Hepialidae (Lepidoptera), and probably in other burrowing forms, by the broadening of the body which accompanies shortening (Fig. 106), while in the larva of *Musca* crawling on a plane surface, anchorage is provided by the mandibles, which are thrust against the substratum until they are held by an irregularity of the surface (Hewitt, 1914).

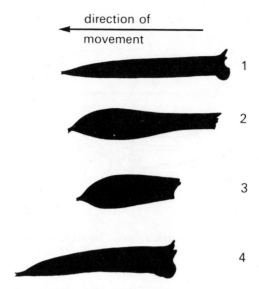

Fig. 106 Diagram of the movement of *Tipula* (Diptera) larva during locomotion through the soil (after Ghilarov, 1949)

9.4 Movements on the surface of water

Some insects are able to move on or in the film at the surface of water. Collembola, such as *Podura aquatica*, sometimes occur on the surface film in large numbers. These animals have hydrofuge cuticles which prevent them from getting wet, but the ventral tube on the first abdominal segment is wettable and anchors the insect to the surface, while the claws, which are also wettable, enable it to obtain a purchase on the water. These animals can spring from the water surface using the caudal furca in the same way as terrestrial Collembola (p. 181).

Gerris (Heteroptera) stands on the surface film and rows over the surface. All the legs possess hydrofuge properties distally, so they do not break the surface film. At the start of a power stroke, the forelegs are lifted off the surface and the long middle legs sweep backwards producing an indentation of the water surface which spreads backwards as a wave. The mesotarsus pushes against the wave giving extra impetus to the forward movement of the insect which continues as a glide as the middle legs protract off the water surface (Fig. 107). During retraction muscles inserted into the coxa and trochanter contract simultaneously, most of the power being provided by two muscles arising in the mesothorax and inserted into the trochanter. These muscles start to contract before movement of the leg begins, and the rapid acceleration of the leg suggests that some click mechanism following the build-up of energy might be operating (Bowdan, 1978). Steering may be achieved by the unequal contractions of the retractor muscles on the two sides and fast turning is produced by movement of the legs of one side while the legs of the other, towards which the insect is turning, remain still (Brinkhurst, 1959).

Stenus (Coleoptera) lives on grass stems bordering mountain streams in situations such that they fall into the water quite frequently. The beetle can walk on the surface of the water, but only slowly. More rapid locomotion is produced following the secretion

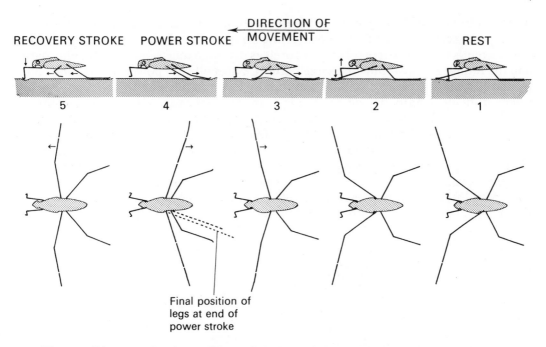

Fig. 107 Diagrams showing positions of the legs of *Gerris* during movement across the surface of water. Arrows show the directions of movement of the legs relative to the body; insect moving from right to left (from Nachtigall, 1974)

of chemicals from the pygidial glands opening beneath the last abdominal tergite. Five chemicals are released, of which the most important is probably a terpenoid called stenusin. This substance lowers the surface tension of the water and at the same time it makes the surface of the beetle hydrophobic, so drag is reduced as the insect is drawn through the water by the higher surface tension in front. It may move at up to 70 cm/s using its abdomen as a rudder (Schildknecht, 1977).

9.5 Movement under water

The activity of aquatic insects is affected by their respiratory habits (see Chapter XXIV). Permanently submerged forms which respire by gills or a plastron have a density greater than that of the water and can move freely over the bottom of their habitat. In swimming these must produce a lift force to take them off the bottom. Many other insects come to the surface to renew their air supply and submerge with a store of air, which tends to give them buoyancy. In swimming the buoyancy must be balanced or overcome by the forces of propulsion. A few insects, such as larval *Chaoborus* (Diptera) and *Anisops* (Heteroptera), can control their buoyancy so that they can remain suspended in mid water (p. 571, and see Teraguchi, 1975).

9.5.1 Bottom dwellers

Bottom-dwelling aquatic insects, such as *Aphelocheirus* (Heteroptera) and larval Odonata and Trichoptera, can walk over the substratum in the same way as terrestrial insects. The larva of *Limnephilus* (Trichoptera) basically uses an alternation of triangles of support (see p. 175), but because of the irregularity of the surface the stepping pattern tends to become irregular. The forelegs may step together instead of alternating and the hind legs may follow the same pattern. Normally the power for walking comes primarily from traction by the fore and middle legs and pushing by the hind legs, but under difficult conditions the hind legs may be extended far forwards outside the middle legs so that they help the other legs to pull the larva along (Tindall, 1963).

In the bottom-dwelling *Triaenodes* (Trichoptera) the larval case is built of plant material arranged in a spiral, the last whorl of which extends dorsally beyond the rest of the case (Fig. 108). The dorsal position is essential since otherwise the movements of the hind swimming legs are hindered, and in this position it also provides a certain amount of lift, carrying the case off the bottom. This lift is controlled by the movements of the legs, which tend to produce a downward thrust (Tindall, 1964).

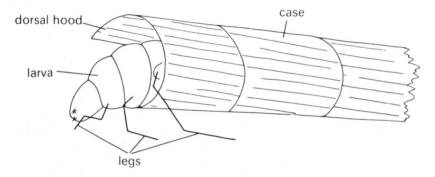

Fig. 108 Diagram of *Triaenodes* larva in its case (after Tindall, 1964)

Larval Anisoptera can walk across the substratum using their legs, but they are also able to make sudden escape movements by forcing water rapidly out of the branchial chamber (p. 561) so that the body is driven forwards. The branchial chamber is compressed by longitudinal and dorso-ventral contractions of the abdomen, the contractions being strongest in segments six to eight, in which the branchial chamber lies (see Fig. 364). Before this contraction the anal valves close and then open slightly leaving an aperture about 0·01 mm² in area. The contractile movement lasts about 0·1 s and water is forced through the anus at a velocity of about 250 cm/s propelling the larva forwards at 30–50 cm/s.

As the abdomen contracts the legs are retracted so as to lie along the sides of the body, offering a minimum of resistance to the forward movements (Hughes, 1958). Successive contractions may occur at frequencies up to 2·2/s, continuing for up to 15 s (Mill and Pickard, 1975). Co-ordination involves giant fibres running in the ventral nerve cord.

9.5.2 Free-swimming insects

Larval and pupal Diptera, larval and adult Heteroptera and adult Coleoptera form the bulk of free-swimming insects and, apart from the Diptera, most of these use the hind legs, sometimes together with the middle legs, in swimming. The hind tibiae and tarsi, and sometimes also those of the middle legs, are flattened antero-posteriorly to form a paddle, which is often increased in area by inflexible hairs or, as in *Gyrinus* (Coleoptera), by cuticular blades 1 μm thick and 30–40 μm wide (Fig. 109). In *Acilius* (Coleoptera) the hairs constitute 69 % of the total area of the hind tibiae and 83 % of the tarsi. The hind legs of these insects are relatively shorter than the hind legs of related terrestrial insects, but the tarsi are relatively longer.

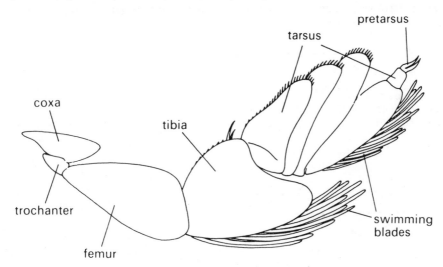

Fig. 109 Hind leg of *Gyrinus* (after Miall, 1922)

The point of attachment of the hind legs is displaced posteriorly compared with terrestrial insects and in dytiscids and gyrinids the coxae are immovably fused to the thorax. This limits the amount of movement at the base of the leg and the basal muscles are concentrated into two functional groups, a powerful retractor group and a weaker protractor group. Intrinsic muscles of the legs tend to be reduced and the movements of the distal parts of the legs during swimming are largely passive.

The two legs of a segment move together, contrasting with the alternating movement of the legs in terrestrial insects (p. 175), but *Hydrophilus* (Coleoptera) is an exception. This beetle uses the middle and hind legs in swimming, the middle leg of one side being retracted simultaneously with the hind leg of the opposite side, but out of phase with the contralateral middle leg.

Buoyancy

Many free-swimming insects are buoyant and when they stop swimming come to rest at the surface of the water in a characteristic position which results from the distribution of air stores on and in the body. Most forms float head down and *Notonecta* (Heteroptera), for instance, rests at an angle of 30° to the surface. As it kicks with its swimming legs this angle is increased to 55° so that the insect is driven down, but as it loses momentum during the recovery stroke of the legs it will tend to rise again

(Fig. 110A). If the driving movements of the legs are repeated rapidly, before the insect rises very much, the path may be straightened out and by controlling the rate of leg movement the insect can dive, move at a constant level or rise to the surface (Fig. 110B). The beat tends to be faster at higher temperatures and so movement becomes more uniform as the temperature rises (Popham, 1952). In *Dytiscus* the buoyancy effect is offset at faster speeds by using the middle and hind legs alternately, while *Hydrophilus* achieves the same effect by using the legs of the two sides out of phase. Hence these insects produce a continuous driving force which offsets their buoyancy.

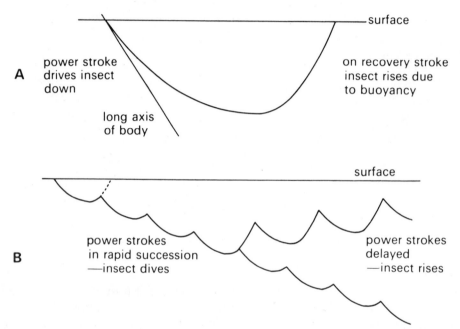

Fig. 110 Diagram of the path through water of an insect such as *Notonecta*. A. The path due to a single swimming stroke by the legs. B. Different paths produced by differences in the timing of successive strokes (after Popham, 1952)

Thrust

The thrust which pushes the insect down through the water is developed during retraction of the legs, but, because the insect is surrounded by the medium, protraction of the legs also produces forces. These tend to drive the insect backwards and if it is to move forwards the forward thrust produced on the backstroke must exceed the backward thrust produced on the forward, recovery stroke of the legs.

The thrust which a leg exerts in water is proportional to its area and the square of the velocity with which it moves. Hence to produce the most efficient forward movement a leg should present a large surface area and move rapidly on the backstroke, while presenting only a small surface and moving relatively slowly on the recovery stroke.

To achieve a large surface area during the backstroke the swimming legs of *Dytiscus* are straight with the fringing hairs, which are articulated at the base, spread to expose a maximum area (Fig. 111A and B). On the forward stroke, however, the femorotibial joint flexes so that the tibia and tarsus trail out behind (Fig. 111D–F). At the same time the tibia rotates through 45° so that the previously dorsal surface becomes anterior and the fringing hairs fold back. The tarsus, which articulates with the tibia by a ball and socket joint, rotates through 100° in the opposite direction. These movements are passive, resulting from the form of the legs and the forces exerted by the water, and they ensure that the tibia and tarsus are presented edge on to the movement, producing a minimum of thrust. Subsequently, at the beginning of the backstroke the leg and hairs extend passively to expose a maximum surface area again. There is no extensor tarsi muscle and the extensor tibiae is weak. The power for the stroke comes from the muscles moving the trochanter on the fixed coxa (Hughes, 1958).

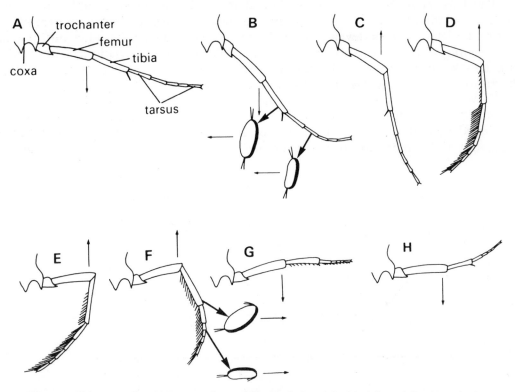

Fig. 111 Diagram showing successive positions of the right hind leg of *Dytiscus* during swimming. G, H, A and B show stages of retraction, C–F stages of protraction. Insets are cross-sections of the tibia and tarsus showing their orientation during retraction (B) and protraction (F). Small arrows indicate the directions of movement of the femur relative to the body of the insect (after Hughes, 1958)

Similar devices are employed by other insects for exposing a maximum leg area during the power stroke and a minimum during the recovery stroke. The swimming blades fringing the leg of *Gyrinus* (see Fig. 109) are placed asymmetrically so that they open like a venetian blind, turning to overlap and produce a solid surface during the power stroke. In the recovery stroke the tarsomeres collapse like a fan and are concealed in a hollow of the tibia, which in turn is partly concealed in a hollow of the femur. These changes decrease the area of the middle leg by 35 % and of the hind leg by 28 %.

The relative power developed on the forward and backward strokes also depends on the relative speeds of the strokes. In *Acilius* (Coleoptera) the backstroke is faster than the forward stroke, so that for a given leg area the forward thrust on the body exceeds the backward thrust. In *Gyrinus*, on the other hand, the backstroke is slower than the forward stroke, so that for a given area the backward thrust is greater than the forward thrust. Hence if the area of the legs of *Gyrinus* remained constant the insect would tend to move backwards and it is only because the reduction in area of the leg on the forward stroke reduces the backward thrust on the body that the net effect is to push the insect forwards.

The legs move in an arc and so lateral thrust is produced in addition to the longitudinal thrust (Fig. 112). In most insects, where the legs of the two sides move in phase, the lateral forces developed on the two sides balance each other out, but in *Hydrophilus*, where the legs are used alternately, there is some deviation to either side, although the lateral thrust of the hind leg on one side is largely balanced by the opposite lateral thrust of the contralateral middle leg.

Forward thrust is minimal at the beginning and end of each stroke (Fig. 112, leg at A and C), but when the legs are at right angles to the body the whole of the thrust developed is longitudinal (Fig. 112, leg at B). It is advantageous if the velocity of the leg is greatest at this point and is low at the beginning and end of the stroke so that the

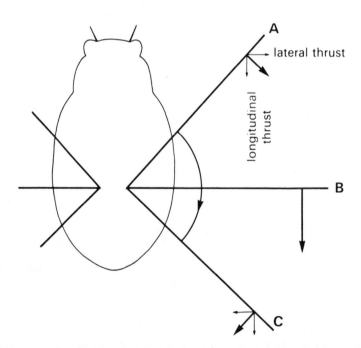

Fig. 112 Diagram of a water beetle showing the thrust exerted by the hind leg at different points of the power stroke. It is assumed that the velocity of the leg at A and C is only half its velocity at B, where, since the leg is at right angles to the body, only longitudinal thrust is produced. Equal and opposite forces act on the body (modified after Nachtigall, 1965)

lateral forces, which are produced mainly during these phases, are kept to a minimum. This is the case, at least in *Acilius* and *Gyrinus*. In the latter the leg is moving most rapidly when it is at an angle of 90–135° to the body. After this the velocity rapidly falls to zero.

Streamlining

Most aquatic insects are streamlined and dorso-ventrally flattened, so that they offer a minimum of resistance as they pass forwards through the water. *Acilius*, for instance, only creates about three times the resistance of an ideal streamlined body and deviations of up to 10° on either side do not markedly increase the resistance. There is, however, a marked increase in resistance if the insect turns broadside or ventral side to the direction of movement and this facilitates turning and braking. Turns are made by producing strokes of unequal amplitude on the two sides or, in making a sharp turn, the leg on the inside may be extended and kept still while the contralateral leg paddles.

Stability

The dorso-ventral flattening of many aquatic insects provides stability in the rolling and pitching planes (see p. 235). The control of yawing involves the eyes, antennae and possibly also receptors on the legs, these receptors acting so that any unequal stimulation as a result of deviation from a straight course is corrected for. The head ganglia are involved in these responses. In *Triaenodes* the long case (Fig. 108) acts as a rudder giving some stability in the pitching and yawing planes. Rolling may be controlled by the long, outstretched hind legs.

Speed

The speed of movement depends on the frequency with which strokes are made and the lengths and velocities of the strokes. *Gyrinus* can swim on the surface at up to 100 cm/s in short bursts, the hind leg making 50–60 strokes/s. Beneath the surface its speed rarely exceeds 10 cm/s. *Acilius*, making 3–10 strokes/s, can reach 35 cm/s, while *Triaenodes*, with hind legs making 13 strokes/s, only moves at about 1·7 cm/s because of the high drag effect of the larval case.

Other forms of swimming

Appendages other than the legs are sometimes used in swimming. Mosquito larvae when suspended from the surface film or browsing on the bottom can glide slowly along as a result of the rapid vibrations of the mouth brushes in feeding. In *Aedes communis* this is the normal method of progression. *Caraphractus cinctus* (Hymenoptera) parasitises the eggs of dytiscids, which are laid under water. The parasite swims jerkily through the water by rowing with its wings, making about two strokes per second. Larval Ephemeroptera and Zygoptera move by vertical undulations of the caudal filaments (Fig. 297) and the abdomen, while in the larva of *Ceratopogon* (Diptera) lateral undulations pass down the body from head to tail driving the insect through the water (Fig. 113A). Many other dipterous larvae flex and straighten the

A *CERATOPOGON*   B *AEDES*

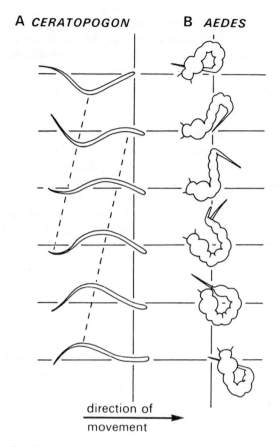

direction of
movement

Fig. 113 Diagrams showing successive positions in swimming of the larvae of (A) *Cerato-pogon* and (B) *Aedes*. Dashed lines indicate the movement of a lateral undulation along the body from front to back (from Nachtigall, 1965)

body alternately to either side, often increasing the thrust by a fin-like extension of the hind end. Mosquito larvae, for instance, have a fan of dense hairs on the last abdominal segment and as a result of the lateral flexing of the body move along tail first (Fig. 113B). The relative density of mosquito larvae is very close to that of water and its value affects their locomotion. Early instar larvae are usually less dense than the medium, so they rise to the surface when they stop swimming. This is also true of the pupae, but last instar larvae may be slightly denser and so they sink when they stop moving actively. The larvae of *Chaoborus* and other Diptera make similar movements to those of mosquito larvae. The mechanics of undulating propulsion are considered by Gray (1953).

REFERENCES

BÄSSLER, U. (1977). Sensory control of leg movement in the stick insect *Carausius morosus*. *Biol. Cybernetics* **25**: 61–72.

BENNET-CLARK, H. C. (1975). The energetics of the jump of the locust *Schistocerca gregaria*. *J. exp. Biol.* **63**: 53–83.

BENNET-CLARK, H. C. and LUCEY, E. C. A. (1967). The jump of the flea: A study of the energetics and a model of the mechanism. *J. exp. Biol.* **47**: 59–76.

BOWDAN, E. (1978). Walking and rowing in the water strider, *Gerris remigis* II. Muscle activity associated with slow and rapid mesothoracic leg movement. *J. comp. Physiol.* **123**: 51–57.

BOWERMAN, R. F. (1977). The control of arthropod walking. *Comp. Biochem. Physiol.* **56A**: 231–247.

BRINKHURST, R. O. (1959). Studies on the functional morphology of *Gerris najas* DeGeer (Hem. Het. Gerridae). *Proc. zool. Soc. Lond.* **133**: 531–559.

BURNS, M. D. (1973). The control of walking in Orthoptera I. Leg movements in normal walking. *J. exp. Biol.* **58**: 45–58.

CHRISTIAN, E. (1978). The jump of the springtails. *Naturwissenschaften* **65**: 495.

CRUSE, H. (1976). The function of the legs in the free walking stick insect, *Carausius morosus*. *J. comp. Physiol.* A, **112**: 235–262.

DELCOMYN, F. (1971). The locomotion of the cockroach *Periplaneta americana*. *J. exp. Biol.* **54**: 443–452.

DENIS, R. (1949). Sous-classe des Aptérygotes. *in* Grassé, P.-P. (ed.), *Traité de Zoologie*. vol. 9. Masson et Cie., Paris.

EVANS, M. E. G. (1972). The jump of the click beetle (Coleoptera: Elateridae)—a preliminary study. *J. Zool., Lond.* **167**: 319–336.

EVANS, M. E. G. (1973). The jump of the click beetle (Coleoptera: Elateridae)—energetics and mechanics. *J. Zool., Lond.* **169**: 181–194.

GHILAROV, M. S. (1949). *The peculiarities of the soil as an environment and its significance in the evolution of insects.* [in Russian]. Moskva, Leningrad.

GRAY, J. (1944). Studies in the mechanics of the tetrapod skeleton. *J. exp. Biol.* **20**: 88–116.

GRAY, J. (1953). Undulatory propulsion. *Q. Jl microsc. Sci.* **94**: 551–578.

HEITLER, W. J. (1977). The locust jump III. Structural specializations of the metathoracic tibiae. *J. exp. Biol.* **67**: 29–36.

HEITLER, W. J. and BURROWS, M. (1977). The locust jump I. The motor programme. *J. exp. Biol.* **66**: 203–219.

HEWITT, C. G. (1914). *The house-fly, Musca domestica Linn.* Cambridge University Press.

HINTON, H. E. (1955). On the structure, function, and distribution of the prolegs of the Panorpoidea, with a criticism of the Berlese–Imms theory. *Trans. R. ent. Soc. Lond.* **106**: 455–545.

HOYLE, G. (1955). Neuromuscular mechanisms of a locust skeletal muscle. *Proc. R. Soc. B,* **143**: 343–367.

HUGHES, G. M. (1952). The co-ordination of insect movements. I. The walking movements of insects. *J. exp. Biol.* **29**: 267–284.

HUGHES, G. M. (1958). The co-ordination of insect movements. III. Swimming in *Dytiscus*, *Hydrophilus*, and a dragonfly nymph. *J. exp. Biol.* **35**: 567–583.

HUGHES, G. M. (1965). Locomotion: terrestrial. *in* Rockstein, M. (ed.), *The physiology of Insecta.* vol 2. Academic Press, New York.

HUGHES, G. M. and MILL, P. J. (1974). Locomotion: terrestrial. *in* Rockstein, M. (ed.), *The physiology of Insecta.* vol. 3. Academic Press, New York.

MANTON, S. M. (1953). Locomotory habits and the evolution of the larger arthropodan groups. *Symp. Soc. exp. Biol.* **7**: 339–376.

MANTON, S. M. (1977). *The Arthropoda. Habits, functional morphology and evolution.* Clarendon Press, Oxford.

MIALL, L. C. (1922). *The natural history of aquatic insects.* MacMillan, London.

MILL, P. J. and PICKARD, R. S. (1975). Jet-propulsion in anisopteran dragonfly larvae. *J. comp. Physiol.* **97**: 329–338.

NACHTIGALL, W. (1965). Locomotion: swimming (hydrodynamics) of aquatic insects. *in* Rockstein, M. (ed.), *The physiology of Insecta*. vol. 2. Academic Press, New York.

NACHTIGALL, W. (1974). Locomotion: mechanics and hydrodynamics of swimming in aquatic insects. *in* Rockstein, M. (ed.), *The physiology of Insecta*. vol. 3. Academic Press, New York.

POPHAM, E. J. (1952). A preliminary investigation into the locomotion of aquatic Hemiptera and Coleoptera. *Proc. R. ent. Soc. Lond.* A, **27**: 117–119.

SCHILDKNECHT, H. (1977). Protective substances of arthropods and plants. *Scripta Varia* **41**: 59–107.

SNODGRASS, R. E. (1935). *Principles of insect morphology*. McGraw-Hill, New York.

TERAGUCHI, S. (1975). Correction of negative buoyancy in the phantom larva, *Chaoborus americanus*. *J. Insect Physiol.* **21**: 1659–1670.

TINDALL, A. R. (1963). The skeleton and musculature of the thorax and limbs of the larva of *Limnephilus* sp. (Trichoptera: Limnephilidae). *Trans. R. ent. Soc. Lond.* **115**: 409–477.

TINDALL, A. R. (1964). The skeleton and musculature of the larval thorax of *Triaenodes bicolor* Curtis (Trichoptera: Limnephilidae). *Trans. R. ent. Soc. Lond.* **116**: 151–210.

WEEVERS, R. de G. (1965). Proprioceptive reflexes and the co-ordination of locomotion in the caterpillar of *Antheraea pernyi* (Lepidoptera). *in* Treherne, J. E. and Beament, J. W. L. (eds.), *The physiology of the insect central nervous system*. Academic Press, London.

WENDLER, G. (1966). The co-ordination of walking movement in arthropods. *Symp. Soc. exp. Biol.* **20**: 229–250.

WILSON, D. M. (1966). Insect walking. *A. Rev. Ent.* **11**: 103–122.

CHAPTER X
THE WINGS

The success of insects as terrestrial animals is at least partly due to their ability to fly. Typically, adult insects have two pairs of wings articulating with the thorax and consisting of flattened lobes of the integument supported by hollow veins. The wings are modified in various ways and often the fore wings are hardened and serve to protect the hind wings. In some insects the two pairs of wings are to some extent independent of each other in flight, but this appears to be relatively inefficient and most insects tend to become functionally two-winged either by the loss of one pair of wings or by coupling the wings on each side so that they function as one. At the bases of the wings small sclerites articulate with the thorax, permitting not only the movements of the wings in flight, but also enabling them to be folded back over the body when at rest. At the base of the wings are sensilla concerned with the control of wing movements and in the Diptera the hind wing has become wholly modified as a sense organ. The muscles moving the wing fall into two classes; those directly inserted into the base of the wing and others which move the wings indirectly by distorting the thorax.

The structure of the wings is considered by Comstock (1918) and Snodgrass (1935), wing coupling in Panorpoidea by Tillyard (1918), and various aspects, including the articulation of wings, by Pringle (1957). The terminology used for venation and parts of the wing is that of Wootton (1979).

10.1 Occurrence and structure of wings

Fully developed and functional wings occur only in adult insects, although the developing wings may be present in the larvae. In hemimetabolous larvae they are visible as external pads (p. 478), but they develop internally in holometabolous forms (p. 482).

The Ephemeroptera are exceptional in having two fully winged instars. The final larval instar moults to a subimago, which resembles the adult except for having fringed and slightly translucent wings and rather shorter legs. It is able to make a short flight, after which it moults and the adult stage emerges. In the course of this moult the cuticle of the wings is shed with the rest of the cuticle.

The fully developed wings of all insects appear as thin, rigid flaps arising dorsolaterally from between the pleura and nota of the meso- and meta-thoracic segments. Each wing consists of a thin membrane supported by a system of tubular veins. The membrane is formed by two layers of integument closely apposed, while the veins are formed where the two layers remain separate and the cuticle is more heavily sclerotised (Fig. 114). Within each of the major veins is a nerve and a trachea, and since

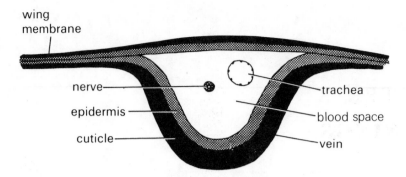

Fig. 114 Diagrammatic section through part of a wing including a transverse section of a vein

the cavities of the veins are connected with the haemocoel the haemolymph can circulate round the wing (see Fig. 531).

On the anterior margin of the wing in some groups is a pigmented spot, the pterostigma (Fig. 118). This is present on both pairs of wings of Odonata and on the forewings of many Hymenoptera, Psocoptera, Megaloptera and Mecoptera. The mass of the pterostigma is greater than that of an equivalent area of adjacent wing and its inertia influences the movement of the whole wing membrane. In Odonata it reduces wing flutter during gliding, thus raising the maximum speed at which gliding can occur. In smaller insects it provides some passive control of the angle of attack of the wing (p. 226) during flapping flight, giving enhanced efficiency at the beginning of the wing stroke without the expenditure of additional energy (Norberg, 1972).

The wing folds along certain well-defined lines, which are functionally of two types: flexion-lines, along which bending of the wings occurs in flight, and fold-lines, along which the wings fold when at rest.

The veins and folds have functional significance and it is not always possible to homologise structures between groups of insects or to derive them from some ancestral arrangement (Wootton, 1979).

10.1.1 Venation

In many fossil insects the venation consists of an irregular network known as the archedictyon. A similar arrangement is exhibited by some present-day insects, as in the reticulum of veins occurring in the wings of Odonata and at the base of the forewings of Tettigonioidea and Acridoidea (Fig. 115). In most living insects, however, the venation consists of a number of well-marked longitudinal veins running along the length of the wing and connected by a variable number of cross-veins. There is a tendency for the wings of lower orders of insects to fold in a fan-like manner with the veins alternately on the crests or in the troughs of folds (Fig. 116B). A vein on a crest is called convex (indicated by + in Fig. 116), while a vein in a trough is called concave (− in Fig. 116). The basic longitudinal veins which can be distinguished in most modern insects are, from the leading edge of the wing backwards:

Costa (abbreviated to C) on or just behind the leading edge
Subcosta (Sc)
Radius (R)

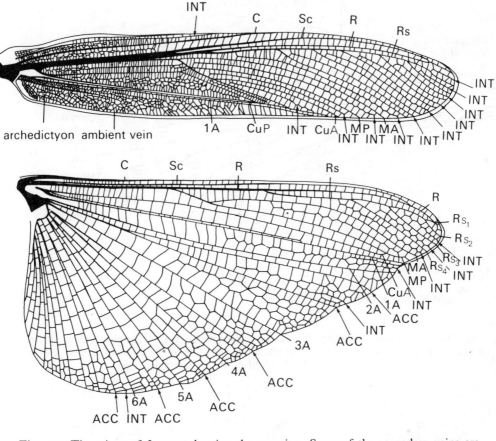

Fig. 115 The wings of *Locusta* showing the venation. Some of the secondary veins are indicated by arrows. INT = intercalary vein, ACC = accessory vein (after Ragge, 1955)

Radial Sector (Rs), regarded as a major branch of R in the widely-used Comstock–
  Needham system,

Anterior media (MA) ⎫ Media (M) where the
Posterior media (MP) ⎬ two cannot be distinguished
Anterior cubitus (CuA) ⎫
Posterior cubitus (CuP) ⎬ Cu_1 and Cu_2 in the Comstock–Needham system
Anal veins (1A, 2A, *etc.*) ⎭

Any of these veins may branch, the branches then being given subscripts 1, 2, 3, etc as in
Fig. 116A. The more usual cross-veins are also shown in Fig. 116A. In some very small
insects the venation may be very greatly reduced and in the Chalcidoidea, for instance,
only the subcosta and part of the radius are present (Fig. 117). Conversely, an increase
in the venation may occur by the branching of existing veins to produce accessory veins
or by the development of additional, intercalary veins between the existing ones, as in
the hind wing of Orthoptera (Fig. 115). Large numbers of cross-veins are also present
in some forms as in the Neuroptera.

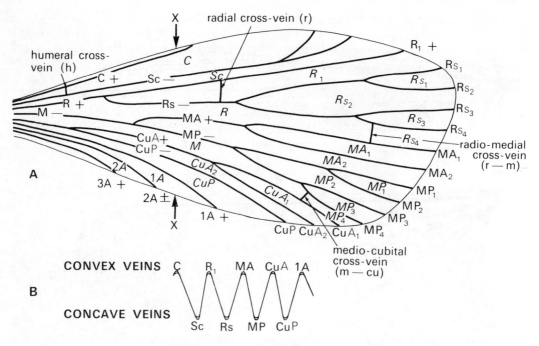

Fig. 116 A. Diagram of the hypothetical basic wing venation showing also the main cross-veins and the names of the cells (italicized). B. Section X-X in (A) showing the concave and convex veins with the depth of pleating greatly exaggerated

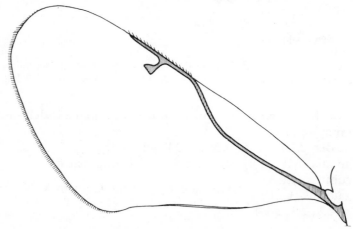

Fig. 117 Forewing of *Perilampus* (Hymenoptera) showing extreme reduction of venation (after Clausen, 1940)

10.1.2 Wing folds

Insect wings are subject to passive deformation in flight, but the presence of flexion-lines ensures that this deformation is localised and contributes most effectively to the functioning of the wing as an aerofoil. Two flexion-lines are of widespread occurrence.

These are the median flexion-line, which runs just behind the Media, and the claval furrow, which usually lies along CuP (Fig. 118). Flexion along these lines produces the Z-shaped profile of the forewing of a locust during the upstroke (p. 224), giving maximum aerodynamic efficiency and probably also limiting the extent of passive deformation of the distal parts of the wing. Comparable functions are performed in other insects (Wootton, 1979).

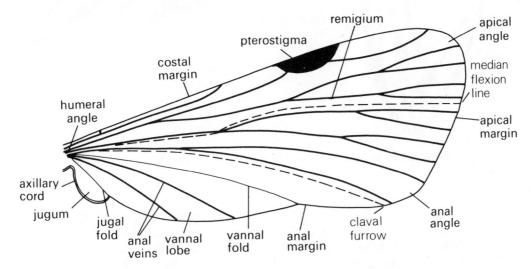

Fig. 118 Diagram illustrating some of the features of the wing

When at rest, the wings are held over the back and in most insects this involves longitudinal folding of the wing membrane and sometimes also transverse folding. In most Neoptera a jugal fold is present just behind vein 3A on the forewings. It is sometimes also present on the hindwings, but where the anal area of the hind wing is large, as in Orthoptera and Dictyoptera, the whole of this part may be folded under the anterior part of the wing along the vannal fold (Fig. 118). In addition, in these insects the anal area is folded like a fan along a number of fold-lines.

Folding is produced by a muscle arising on the pleuron and inserted into the third axillary sclerite in such a way that when it contracts the sclerite pivots about its points of articulation with the posterior notal process and the second axillary sclerite. As a result the distal arm of the third axillary sclerite rotates upwards and inwards, so that finally its position is completely reversed. The anal veins are articulated with the sclerite in such a way that when the sclerite moves they are carried with it and become flexed over the back of the insect. The rest of the wing is pulled back by the vannal region. Extension of the wings probably results from the contraction of muscles attached to the basalar sclerite or, in some insects, to the subalar sclerite.

The wings of Coleoptera and Dermaptera fold transversely as well as longitudinally so that they can be accommodated beneath the elytra. This transverse folding necessitates a modification of the venation and in Coleoptera there is a discontinuity between the proximal and distal parts of the veins (Fig. 119). The folding results automatically from the structure and flexibility of the veins.

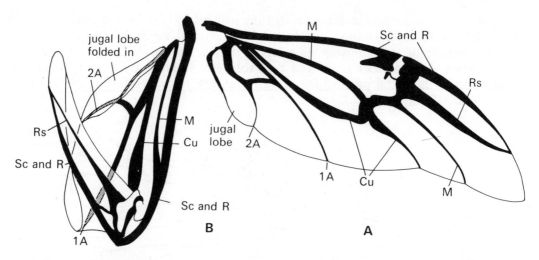

Fig. 119 Wing folding in *Melolontha* (Coleoptera). A. Wing extended. B. Wing folded (from Jeannel, 1949)

Sometimes the wings are held in the folded position by being coupled together or fastened to the body. For instance, in Psocoptera the costal margin of the hind wing is held by a fold on the pterostigma of the fore wing. The elytra of Coleoptera are held together by their tongueing and grooving, but they are also held to the body by a median longitudinal groove in the metathorax which holds the reflexed inner edges of the elytra. Dermaptera have rows of spines on the inside edge of the elytron which catch into combs on the metathorax, while many aquatic Heteroptera have a peg on the mesothorax which fits into a pit in the margin of the hemelytron. Symphyta have specialised lobes, the cenchri, on the metanotum which engage with rough areas on the undersides of the fore wings to hold them in place.

10.1.3 Areas of the wing

In order to give maximum efficiency and support to the wing during flight the longitudinal veins tend to be concentrated towards the anterior margin of the wing. The region containing the bulk of the veins in front of the claval furrow is called the remigium (Fig. 118). The area behind the claval furrow is called the clavus except in hindwings in which this area is greatly expanded, when it is known as the vannus. Finally the jugum is cut off by the jugal fold where this is present (Wootton, 1979). In some Diptera there are three separate lobes in this region of the wing base (Fig. 120), known from proximally outwards as the thoracic squama, alar squama and alula. There is some confusion in the terminology and homologies of these lobes, but it appears that the thoracic squama is derived from the posterior margin of the scutellum, the alar squama represents the jugum and the alula is a part of the claval region which has become separated off from the rest. Some Coleoptera have a lobe called an alula folded beneath the elytron. It appears to be equivalent to the jugum.

The wing margins and angles are also named (Fig. 118). The leading edge of the wing is called the costal margin, the trailing edge is the anal margin and the outer edge is

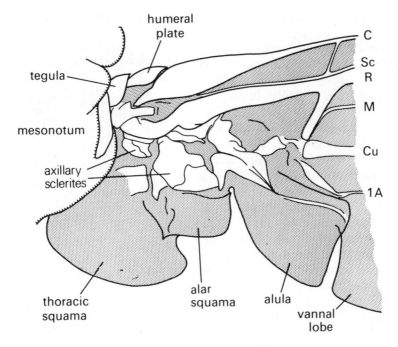

Fig. 120 Base of the right wing of a tabanid showing the arrangement of the various structures (after Oldroyd, 1949)

the apical margin. The angle between the costal and apical margins is the apical angle, that between the apical and anal margins is the anal angle, while the angle at the base of the wing is called the humeral angle.

The veins divide the area of the wing into a series of cells which are most satisfactorily named after the vein forming the anterior boundary of the cell (Fig. 116A). A cell entirely surrounded by veins is said to be closed, while one which extends to the wing margins is open.

10.2 Modifications of the wings

10.2.1 The wing membrane

Typically the wing membrane is semitransparent as it is in Odonata and Hymenoptera. Such wings often exhibit iridescence as a result of their structure (see p. 131), but sometimes, in addition, the wings are patterned by pigments contained in the epidermal cells. This is true in some Mecoptera and Tephritidae, while in many insects which have the fore wing hardened, such as Orthoptera and Coleoptera, the fore wing is wholly pigmented.

10.2.2 Hairs and scales on the membrane

The surface of the wing membrane is often set with small non-innervated spines called microtrichia. Typically, trichoid sensilla (p. 708) are confined to the veins, but in

Trichoptera comparable hairs, known as macrotrichia clothe the whole of the wing membrane.

In Lepidoptera the wings are clothed in scales. These vary in form from typical hair-like structures to flat plates (Fig. 121A) and they usually cover the body as well as the wings. A flattened scale consists of two lamellae with an airspace between, the inferior lamella, that is the lamella facing the wing membrane, being smooth, the superior lamella usually with longitudinal and transverse ridges. The two lamellae are supported by internal struts called trabeculae (Fig. 121B). The scales are set in sockets of the wing membrane so that they are inclined to the surface and overlap each other to form a complete covering. In primitive Lepidoptera their arrangement on the wings is random, but in Papilionoidea, for instance, they are arranged in rows.

Pigments in the scales are responsible for the colours of many Lepidoptera, the pigment being in the wall or the cavity of the scale. In other instances physical colours result from the structure of the scale

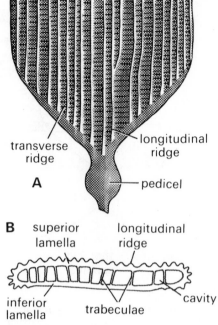

Fig. 121 A. Basal half of a typical lepidopteran scale. B. Transverse section of a scale (after Bourgogne, 1951)

(see Figs. 66, 67). Some specialised scales are associated with glands (p. 857), while the scales may also be important in smoothing the air-flow over the wings and body. On the body they are important as an insulating layer helping to maintain the high temperature of the thorax (p. 759).

Scales also occur on the wing veins and body of Culicidae and on the wings of some Psocoptera and a few Trichoptera and Coleoptera.

10.2.3 Wing form

In Odonata, Isoptera, Mecoptera and male Embioptera the two pairs of wings are similar in form, roughly shaped like elongate triangles, but in most other groups of insects one or other of the wings becomes modified from this basic form. Thus the hind wings of Plecoptera, Dictyoptera and Orthoptera have large vannal lobes and so they are generally much more extensive than the fore wings (Fig. 115). Sometimes the hind wings have a projection from the hind margin as in swallow-tailed butterflies and some Lycaenidae, while in the Nemopteridae the hind wings are slender ribbons trailing out behind the insect (Fig. 122A). The hind wings are similarly modified in some Zygaenidae.

Sometimes the hind wings are very small, as in Ephemeroptera, Hymenoptera and male coccids, while in some Ephemeroptera, such as *Cloeon*, and some male coccids they are absent altogether. In Diptera the hind wings are modified to form the halteres

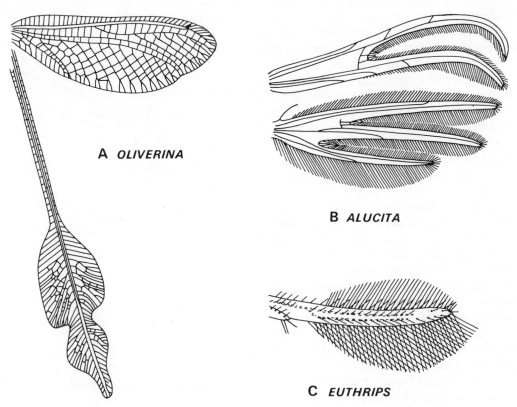

Fig. 122 A. Wings of *Oliverina* (Neuroptera) (after Comstock, 1918). B. Wings of *Alucita* (Lepidoptera) (from Bourgogne, 1951). C. Forewing of *Euthrips* (Thysanoptera) (from Pesson, 1951)

(p. 212), while in male Strepsiptera the fore wings form similar dumb-bell-shaped structures.

Sometimes the outline of the wings is irregular, as in *Polygonia c-album* (Lepidoptera) where it serves to break up the outline of the resting insect. In the plume moths, Pterophoridae and Orneodidae, the wings are very deeply cleft and divided into a number of lobes fringed with scales (Fig. 122B). Wing fringes are common in Lepidoptera and Culicidae and in some Tinaeoidea they are so extensive as to greatly increase the effective area of the wing. The wings of very small insects are often reduced to straps with one or two supporting veins and long fringes of hairs (Fig. 122C). This occurs in Thysanoptera, in Trichogrammatidae and Mymaridae amongst the Hymenoptera and in some of the small Staphylinoidea amongst the Coleoptera.

Some insects have both pairs of wings reduced and they are said to be brachypterous or micropterous. This occurs, for instance, in some Orthoptera and Heteroptera. The completely wingless, or apterous, condition is also widespread. Winglessness occurs as a primitive condition in the Apterygota, while the ectoparasitic orders Mallophaga, Anoplura and Siphonaptera are secondarily wingless. Wingless species are also widespread in most other orders, but apparently do not occur in Odonata or

Ephemeroptera. Sometimes both sexes are wingless, but frequently the male is winged and only the female is apterous. This is the case in coccids, Embioptera, Strepsiptera, Mutilidae and some Chalcididae. In the ants and termites only the reproductive caste is winged and here the wings are shed after the nuptial flight, breaking off by a basal suture so that only a wing scale remains (Fig. 123). The break is achieved in different ways, but termites frequently rest the wing on the ground and then break it off by twisting the wing base. After loss of the wings the flight muscles degenerate.

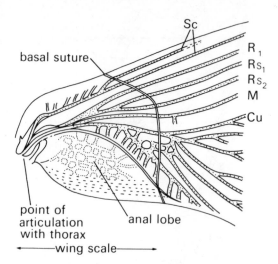

Fig. 123 Wing base of a termite showing the basal suture at which the distal part of the wing breaks off (from Grassé, 1949)

Quite commonly the development of the wings varies within a species either geographically or seasonally. Such wing polymorphism occurs in various groups, but is particularly well known in Homoptera and Heteroptera. For instance, *Gerris lacustris* (Heteroptera) is bivoltine in Britain and the overwintering generation is largely macropterous, that is fully winged, while the summer generation contains a relatively high proportion of micropterous individuals. In this case the wing length is determined largely by the environment and to a lesser extent by genetic segregation (see *e.g.* Brinkhurst, 1959, 1963; Lees, 1961; Young, 1965).

10.2.4 The protective function of the fore wings

The fore wings of many insects become more fully sclerotised than the hind wings and serve to protect the latter when they are folded up at rest (Fig. 124). Fore wings modified in this way are known as elytra or tegmina. Leathery elytra occur in Orthoptera, Dictyoptera and Dermaptera, while in Heteroptera only the basal part of the wing is hardened, such wings being known as hemelytra (Fig. 125). The basal part of the hemelytron may be subdivided into regions by well-marked veins and in mirids where the development is most complete, the costal margin of the wing is cut off as a proximal embolium and distal cuneus, the centre of the wing is the corium, and the anal region is cut off as the clavus. In lygaeids only the corium and the clavus are differentiated.

The elytra of Coleoptera are very heavily sclerotised and the basic wing venation is lost, although it may be indicated internally by the arrangement of tracheae. The two surfaces of the elytron are separated by a blood space (Fig. 126), across which run cuticular columns, the trabeculae, arranged in longitudinal rows and marked externally by rows of striations. Primitively there are eight such striae, although the number may be increased in some Adephaga. The elytra of beetles do not overlap in the midline, but meet and are held together by a tongued and grooved joint, while in some Carabidae, Curculionidae and Ptinidae they are fused together so that they cannot open and in

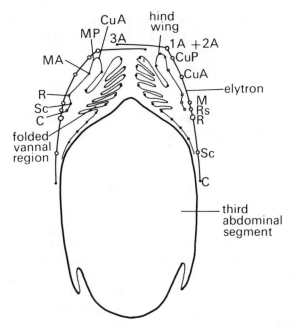

Fig. 124 Transverse section through the abdomen of *Dociostaurus* (Orthoptera) showing the hindwings folded beneath the elytra (from Uvarov, 1966)

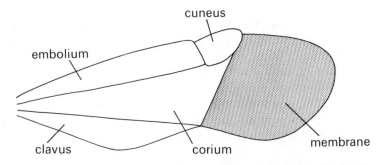

Fig. 125 Forewing of a mirid (Heteroptera) (after Comstock, 1918)

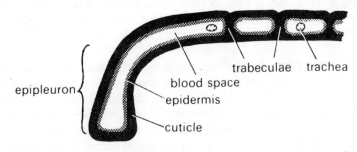

Fig. 126 Diagrammatic transverse section through part of an elytron of a beetle

these species the hind wings are also atrophied. At the sides the elytra are often reflexed downwards, the vertical part being called the epipleuron and the horizontal part the disc.

10.2.5 Sound production

In various groups of insects the wings are modified for sound production and they may be retained for this function when they are no longer used in flight (see Chapter XXVIII).

10.3 Wing coupling

The wings of most insects are moved by distortions of the thorax (see p. 217) and, because they are so closely associated, the movements of each of the thoracic segments must influence the other. Hence it is impossible for the fore and hindwings to beat completely independently of each other and in Orthoptera and Odonata, where the wings are not otherwise linked, both pairs of wings vibrate with the same frequency and with the hind wing beat consistently more advanced than the forewing beat (see Fig. 145). Such mechanical linking of the wings also involves the timing of the nerve impulses to the flight muscles.

The two-winged condition is apparently more efficient than the four-winged and in the majority of insects the mechanical coupling of the wings is supplemented, and possibly made more precise, by an anatomical coupling of the fore and hind wings so that they move together as a single unit.

This wing coupling may take various forms, but in many species involves lobes or spines at the wing base. A primitive arrangement is found in some Mecoptera of the family Choristidae in which there is a jugal lobe at the base of the fore wing and a humeral lobe at the base of the costal margin of the hind wing. Both lobes are set with setae, those on the humeral lobe being termed frenular bristles (Fig. 127A), and, although they do not firmly link the wings, they overlap sufficiently to prevent the wings moving out of phase. From this the types of coupling occurring in other Mecoptera, Neuroptera, Trichoptera and Lepidoptera can be derived (see Tillyard, 1918).

In some of the older forms of Trichoptera only the jugum is present on the fore wing; it lies on top of the hind wing and so the coupling mechanism is not very efficient. However, the Hepialidae have a strong jugal lobe which lies beneath the costal margin of the hind wing so that this is held between the jugum and the rest of the fore wing (Fig. 127B). This is called jugate wing coupling. In Micropterygidae the jugum is folded under the fore wings and holds the frenular bristles. This is jugo-frenate coupling.

Many other Lepidoptera have the frenulum well developed and engaging with a catch or retinaculum on the underside of the fore wing so that the wings are firmly coupled. This is frenate coupling. Female noctuids, for instance, have from two to 20 frenular bristles and a retinaculum of forwardly directed hairs on the underside of the cubital vein (Fig. 127C); in the male the frenular bristles are fused together to form a single stout spine and the retinaculum is a cuticular clasp projecting down from the radial (Tillyard, 1918) or subcostal (Bourgogne, 1951) vein (Fig. 127D). Thysanoptera

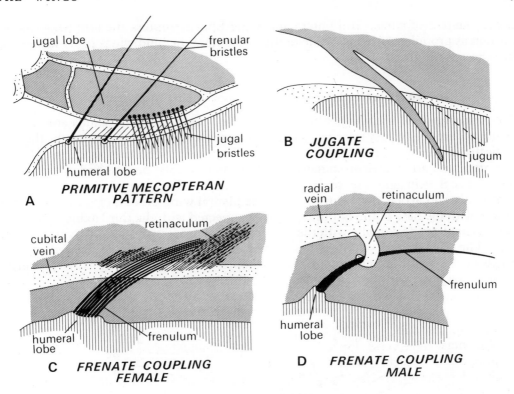

Fig. 127 Wing coupling mechanisms involving the jugal and humeral regions of the wings. A. Primitive mecopteran pattern in *Taeniochorista* (Mecoptera). B. Jugate coupling in *Charagia* (Lepidoptera). C. Frenate coupling in female *Hippotion* (Lepidoptera). D. Frenate coupling in male *Hippotion* (Lepidoptera). All diagrams represent the mechanisms as seen from below with the attachment to the thorax immediately to the left. Membrane of the forewing shown diagonally hatched, that of the hindwing with vertical hatching (after Tillyard, 1918)

have the wings coupled in a comparable way by hooked spines at the base of the hind wing catching a membranous fold of the fore wing.

The wings of the Papilionoidea and some Bombycoidea are coupled by virtue of an extensive area of overlap between the two. This is known as amplexiform wing coupling. A similar arrangement occurs in some Trichoptera, often together with some other method of coupling.

Other insects have the wings coupled by more distal modifications which hold the costal margin of the hind wing to the anal margin of the fore wing. Thus Hymenoptera have a row of hooks, the hamuli, along the costal margin of the hind wing which catch into a fold of the fore wing; Psocoptera have a hook at the end of CuP of the fore wing which hooks on to the hind costa; and Heteroptera have a short gutter edged with a brush of hairs on the underside of the clavus which holds the costal margin of the hind wing. Homoptera exhibit a variety of modifications linking the anal margin of the fore wing to the costal margin of the hind wing (see Pesson, 1951).

Other insects have become functionally two-winged by the reduction or complete loss of one pair of wings. In Diptera and some Ephemeroptera the fore wings alone function as propulsive organs, while in the Coleoptera the hind wings provide most of the power for flight.

10.4 Articulation of the wings with the thorax

The basal region of the wing, where it joins the thorax, is membranous and in this membrane are the axillary sclerites, which permit the wing to move freely on the thorax. Typically there are three axillary sclerites (Fig. 128). The first is in the dorsal membrane and articulates proximally with the anterior notal process and distally with the subcostal vein and the second axillary sclerite. The second extends to both membranes and articulates ventrally with the pleural wing process (see Fig. 131) and distally with the base of the radius. It is also connected with the third axillary sclerite, which articulates proximally with the posterior notal process and distally with the anal veins. The third axillary sclerite is Y-shaped with a wing flexor muscle inserted into the crutch of the Y. In Hymenoptera and Orthoptera there is a fourth axillary sclerite between the posterior notal process and the third axillary sclerite.

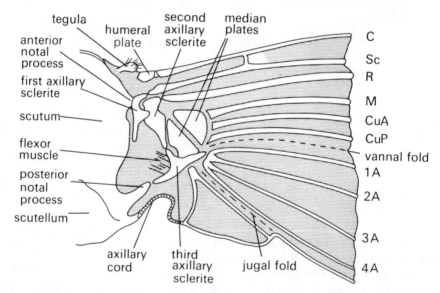

Fig. 128 Diagram of the articulation of a wing with the thorax (modified after Snodgrass, 1935)

In addition to the axillary sclerites there are other plates in the wing base. Connected with the third axillary, and perhaps representing a part of it, may be one or two median plates from which the media and the cubitus arise. At the base of the costa is a humeral plate and often, proximal to it, is another plate derived from the edge of the articular membrane and called the tegula. In Lepidoptera the tegula is very large and overlaps the wing base; it is also well-developed in Hymenoptera and Diptera (Fig. 120). The tegula only rarely occurs in association with the hind wing.

All present-day insects other than Ephemeroptera and Odonata are able to fold their wings back over the body when at rest. It might be expected that this folding would be associated with greater complexity of the sclerites at the wing base and that in Ephemeroptera and Odonata the arrangement would be simpler. The wing base of Ephemeroptera is very similar to that in other insects (see Snodgrass, 1935), but Odonata have only two large plates hinged to the tergum and supported by two arms from the pleural wing process. The plates are called the humeral and axillary plates.

Although the movement of the wings on the thorax involves some condylic movement at the pleural process, a great deal of movement is permitted by the presence of resilin ligaments, such as the wing hinge ligament of Orthoptera (see p. 514). In this way the problems of friction and lubrication which would occur at a normal articulation moving at the high frequency of the wings are avoided. The wings of Hymenoptera and Diptera are suspended by two opposing ligaments (Neville, 1965).

10.5 Sensilla on the wings and the haltere

The macrotrichia along the veins are probably mechanoreceptors responding to touch and possibly to the flow of air over the wings in flight. At the base of the wing are several groups of campaniform sensilla (p. 711), generally three groups on the underside of the subcosta and three on the dorsal side of the radius (Fig. 129 and see Pringle, 1957). These groups are not always well defined and in Acrididae, Blattodea and Plecoptera the radial groups are absent altogether. More distally on the veins are other scattered campaniform sensilla, but these are large and circular, so that, unlike those in the basal groups, they can have no directional sensitivity. The sensilla in the groups are oval, all those in a group being similarly orientated, so that they are sensitive to distortions of the wing base in particular planes. The number of sensilla in each group varies, there being more in more highly manoeuverable species. Thus *Apis* has about 700 campaniform sensilla at the base of each fore wing, while *Panorpa* (Mecoptera) has only about 60. Some of these sensilla, at least, are concerned in the control of stability in flight (see p. 235).

In addition to the campaniform sensilla there are up to four chordotonal organs at the base of each wing. One of these is inserted into the costa, arising proximally at the wing base, while the others run obliquely across the radial, medial and sometimes also the cubital veins.

Most insects do not have internal proprioceptors connected with the wings or their muscles, but in Orthoptera each wing has a stretch receptor and a chordotonal organ in the thorax associated with the wing base. The two organs of a mesothoracic wing of *Schistocerca*, for example, arise together on the mesophragma. The stretch receptor extends to just behind the subalar, while the chordotonal organ is attached a little more ventrally (Gettrup, 1962). The stretch receptor is already present in the third instar and appears to be homologous with the abdominal stretch receptors. These organs have been identified in acridids, gryllids and tettigoniids, but not in a gryllotalpid or a blattid. They are concerned with the control of wing movement (see p. 232).

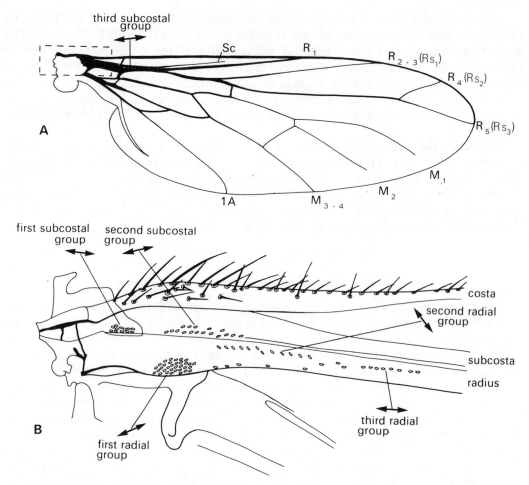

Fig. 129 Distribution of groups of campaniform sensilla at the base of the wing of *Empis* (Diptera). A. Whole wing showing, enclosed within the broken line, the position of the area enlarged in B. Arrows indicate the orientation of the long axes of the sensilla (after Pringle, 1957). Labels in brackets give the names of the veins according to the system of Wootton (1979)

Halteres

The hind wings of the Diptera are modified to form the halteres, which are sense organs concerned with the maintenance of stability in flight (see p. 238). Each haltere consists of a basal lobe, a stalk and an end knob which projects backwards from the end of the stalk so that its centre of gravity is also behind the stalk. The whole structure is rigid except for some flexibility of the ventral surface near the base which allows some freedom of movement, while the cuticle of the end knob is thin but kept distended by the turgidity of large vacuolated cells inside it. The haltere is larger in less specialised forms such as *Tipula*; in *Calliphora* it is only 0·7 mm long.

On the basal lobe of the haltere are groups of campaniform sensilla which can be homologised with the groups at the base of a normal wing (see Pringle, 1948, 1957). Dorsally there are two large groups of sensilla: the basal and scapal plates (Fig. 130). In *Calliphora* there are about 100 sensilla in each group. The sensilla of the basal plate are orientated with their long axes at about 30° to the axes of the longitudinal rows in which they are arranged; the sensilla of the scapal plate are parallel with the axis which passes through the main point of articulation and the centre of gravity of the haltere (indicated as the long axis of the haltere in Fig. 130). Near the basal plate is a further small group of campaniform sensilla known as Hicks papillae. These are set below the surface of the haltere and are orientated parallel with its long axis. There is also a single round, so-called undifferentiated papilla near the scapal plate. On the ventral surface there is another scapal plate with about 100 sensilla and a group of ten Hicks papillae. These are orientated parallel with the long axis of the haltere.

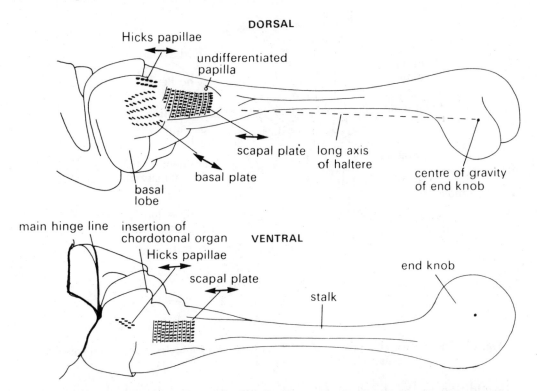

Fig. 130 Dorsal and ventral views of the halteres of *Lucilia* showing the basal groups of sensilla. The orientation of the campaniform sensilla is indicated by the arrows (after Pringle, 1948)

Also attached to the ventral surface is a large chordotonal organ orientated at about 45° to the long axis of the haltere. A smaller chordotonal organ runs vertically across the base.

These sensilla react to the forces acting at the base of the haltere during flight. They perceive the vertical movements of the haltere and also the torque produced by lateral turning movements of the fly (p. 240).

10.6 Muscles associated with the wings

A number of muscles are inserted directly into the sclerites of the wing base; they are called the direct wing muscles (Fig. 131). One of these, arising on the pleuron and inserted into the third axillary sclerite, flexes the wing backwards and in Diptera this muscle may be assisted by another inserted into the first axillary sclerite. Extension of the wing from the flexed position is produced by one or more muscles inserted into the basalar. These muscles arise on the episternum, the sternum and the coxa. Another muscle, arising on the meron, is inserted into the subalar, accompanied in gryllids, Trichoptera and Lepidoptera by a second muscle from the epimeron. The basalar and subalar muscles extend and depress the wing. Odonata have two muscles arising from the episternum inserted into the humeral plate and two from the edge of the epimeron inserted into the axillary plate.

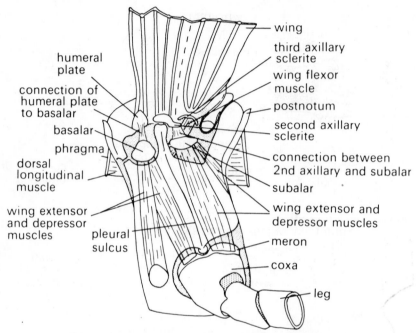

Fig. 131 Lateral view of the thorax showing the direct wing muscles. The pleural region is assumed to be transparent (after Snodgrass, 1935)

In addition to the direct muscles there are other muscles which, although not directly associated with the wings, move the wings as a result of the distortions which they produce in the shape of the thorax (see p. 217). These are the indirect flight muscles. The most important indirect flight muscles are the dorsal longitudinal muscles and the tergosternal muscles (see Fig. 133) of which there may be two or more pairs. These muscles are usually well developed, while the oblique dorsal muscles, which run from the postphragma to the scutum are often small or absent altogether. In Diptera and Cicadidae, however, the oblique dorsal muscle becomes almost vertical by extension of the postphragma and in these groups it is well developed.

REFERENCES

BOURGOGNE, J. (1951). Ordre des Lépidoptères *in* Grassé, P.-P. (ed.), *Traité de Zoologie.* vol. 10. Masson et Cie., Paris.

BRINKHURST, R. O. (1959). Alary polymorphism in the Gerroidea (Hemiptera-Heteroptera). *J. Anim. Ecol.* **28**: 211–230.

BRINKHURST, R. O. (1963). Observations on wing-polymorphism in the Heteroptera. *Proc. R. ent. Soc. Lond.* A, **38**: 15–22.

CLAUSEN, C. P. (1940). *Entomophagous insects.* McGraw Hill, New York.

COMSTOCK, J. H. (1918). *The wings of insects.* Comstock Publishing Co., New York.

GETTRUP, E. (1962). Thoracic proprioceptors in the flight systems of locusts. *Nature, Lond.* **193**: 498–499.

GRASSÉ, P.-P. (1949). Ordre des Isoptères ou termites. *in* Grassé, P.-P. (ed.), *Traité de Zoologie.* vol. 9. Masson et Cie., Paris.

JEANNEL, R. (1949). Ordre des Coléoptèroïdes. *in* Grassé, P.-P. (ed.), *Traité de Zoologie.* vol. 9. Masson et Cie., Paris.

LEES, A. D. (1961). Clonal polymorphism in aphids. *Symp. R. ent. Soc. Lond.* **1**: 68–79.

NEVILLE, A. C. (1965). Energy and economy in insect flight. *Sci. Prog., Lond.* **53**: 203–220.

NORBERG, R. A. (1972). The pterostigma of insect wings an inertial regulator of wing pitch. *J. comp. Physiol.* **81**: 9–22.

OLDROYD, H. (1949). Diptera. 1. Introduction and key to families. *Handbk Ident. Br. Insects* 9, part 1.

PESSON, P. (1951). Ordre des Thysanoptera. *in* Grassé, P.-P. (ed.), *Traité de Zoologie.* vol. 10. Masson et Cie., Paris.

PRINGLE, J. W. S. (1948). The gyroscopic mechanism of the halteres of Diptera. *Phil. Trans. R. Soc.* B, **233**: 347–384.

PRINGLE, J. W. S. (1957). *Insect flight.* Cambridge University Press.

RAGGE, D. R. (1955). *The wing-venation of the Orthoptera Saltatoria.* British Museum, London.

SNODGRASS, R. E. (1935). *Principles of insect morphology.* McGraw-Hill, New York.

TILLYARD, R. J. (1918). The panorpoid complex. 1. The wing-coupling apparatus, with special reference to the Lepidoptera. *Proc. Linn. Soc. N.S.W.* **43**: 286–319.

UVAROV, B. P. (1966). *Grasshoppers and locusts.* vol. 1. Cambridge University Press.

WOOTTON, R. J. (1979). Function, homology and terminology in insect wings. *Syst. Ent.* **4**: 81–93.

YOUNG, E. C. (1965). The incidence of flight polymorphism in British Corixidae and description of the morphs. *J. Zool.* **146**: 567–576.

CHAPTER XI

MOVEMENT AND CONTROL OF THE WINGS

Insects fly by beating their wings up and down and only a few large species are known to glide for any distance between wing strokes. Some of the movements of the wing are produced by muscles directly inserted into the wing base, but others result from distortions of the thorax produced by muscles not directly associated with the wings. In some insects, such as the Diptera, all the wing movements are produced by such indirect muscles. The movement is aided by the elasticity of the wing hinge, the flight muscles and the thorax itself and this elasticity may result in the wings clicking automatically into the up or down positions after the muscles have pulled them into a position which is unstable.

The frequency with which the wings vibrate varies considerably. In some insects with a low wingbeat frequency each cycle is produced by a nervous impulse and the oscillating rhythm of the flight muscles results from oscillation in the motor neurones driving the muscles. The basic oscillation is modified by the input from peripheral sensilla. In Hymenoptera and Diptera, in which the wings commonly vibrate at over 100 Hz, there is no direct relationship between nervous stimuli and muscle contraction. A steady flow of nerve impulses keeps the muscles activated, but the frequency of muscle contraction is a function of the muscles and the resonant frequency of the thorax.

The movements of the wing during the stroke are complex and the twisting of the wings is particularly important because this controls the aerodynamic forces which are produced and which propel the insect through the air. In larger insects flight depends on steady state aerodynamic principles, but in small insects non-steady state principles may apply.

Normally when the insect is in contact with the ground, the activity of the nerve cells controlling flight is inhibited, but once the tarsi lose touch with the substratum the inhibition is removed. During flight the insect tends to deviate from a steady path, but peripheral sensory mechanisms enable it to correct for such deviations.

Flight in general is reviewed by Pringle (1957, 1968, 1974) and aerodynamic aspects are considered by Nachtigall (1976) and Weis-Fogh (1976).

11.1 Mechanisms of wing movement

The up and down movements of the wings are produced by direct and indirect wing muscles but they also involve the elasticity of the thorax, the wing base and the muscles themselves.

11.1.1 Movements produced by the muscles

In all insects the upward movement of the wings is produced by indirect dorso-ventral muscles inserted into the tergum of the segment bearing the wing. By contracting they pull the tergum down and hence also move down the point of articulation of the wing with the tergum. The effect of this is to move the wing membrane up, with the pleural process acting as a fulcrum (Fig. 132A, 133A). The muscles producing this movement are not always homologous. In many insects they arise on the sternum or the coxae, but in Auchenorrhyncha and Psyllidae the tergosternal muscles are small and are functionally replaced as wing elevators by the oblique dorsal muscles. These arise on the postphragma and so are normally obliquely longitudinal (Fig. 80), but in the groups mentioned the phragma extends ventrally carrying the origins of the muscles with it so that they come to exert their pull vertically instead of horizontally (see Pringle, 1957).

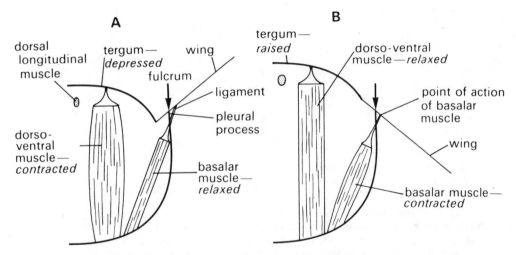

Fig. 132 Diagrammatic cross-section of the thorax illustrating the wing movements in an insect, such as a dragonfly, in which the direct wing muscles cause depression of the wings

The downward movement of the wings in Odonata and Blattaria is produced by direct muscles inserted into the basalar and subalar sclerites, which are connected to the axillary sclerites by ligaments (see Fig. 131). Hence contraction of these muscles exerts a pull on the wings outside the fulcrum of the pleural process and so pulls the wings down (Fig. 132B).

In Diptera and Hymenoptera the downward movement is produced by the dorsal longitudinal indirect muscles. Because the dorsum of the pterothorax is an uninterrupted plate, without membranous junctions (see Fig. 75D), contraction of the dorsal longitudinal muscles cannot produce a telescoping of the segments as in the abdomen. Instead, the centre of the tergum becomes bowed upwards (Fig. 133D) and so the tergal articulation of the wing is also moved up and the wing membrane flaps down (Fig. 133C). At the same time the anterior and posterior notal processes become approximated because of the hinging of the scutellum to the scutum (see Fig. 136), and this also assists in the movement of the wing (Pringle, 1957).

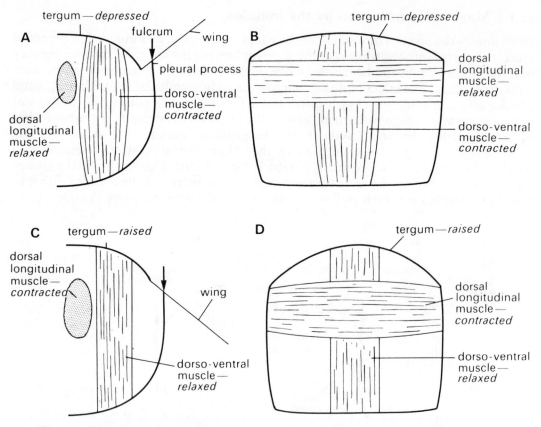

Fig. 133 Diagrams illustrating the movements of the wings in an insect, such as a fly, in which both up and down movements of the wing are produced by indirect muscles. A and C. Cross-sections of the thorax. B and D. Views of the wing-bearing segment from the inside showing, in D, the shortening and bowing of the tergum produced by contraction of the dorsal longitudinal muscles

In Coleoptera and Orthoptera the downward movement is produced by the direct and indirect muscles acting together. The direct muscles are then dual purpose since they are also concerned in twisting the wing during the course of the stroke (see p. 224).

A number of the muscles moving the wings arise in the coxa, which is itself moveable. Whether these muscles move the legs or the wings appears to be determined by the activity of other muscles and the position of the appendages: if the wings are closed the muscles move the legs, but in flight with the legs in the flight position (p. 232) the wings are moved.

11.1.2 Movement due to elasticity

The capacity to store elastic energy and subsequently to release it at high rates is an essential feature of the flight mechanism of most insects (Weis-Fogh, 1976). In *Schistocerca* (Orthoptera), and probably in other insects, much of the energy involved in the upstroke is stored as elastic forces for use in the downstroke. This is possible because the aerodynamic forces produced at this time act in the same direction as the wing movement so assisting its movement. Thus the muscles have only to overcome the forces of inertia of the wing and elasticity of the wing base, and as a result some 86 % of the energy they produce is stored for use in the downstroke.

The elasticity of the system results partly from the pad of resilin which forms the main wing hinge (see Fig. 328). The elastic properties of this pad are almost perfect and so all but 3 % of the energy imparted to it when it is stretched in the upward movement of the wings is available for pulling the wing down.

The elasticity of the flight muscles is also important. These muscles are characterised by a greater resistance to stretch compared with other muscles due to the elastic properties of the contractile system. The sarcolemma seems to add little to the elasticity of the muscle (Buchthal *et al.*, 1957).

Contraction of the indirect flight muscles distorts the thorax and so the elastic properties of the thorax as a whole are also significant factors in wing movement. Figure 134 shows diagrammatically the manner in which the movement of the wings involves a lateral movement of the wall of the thorax. This movement is resisted by the elasticity of the thorax, which is largely due to the sternopleural articulation and, to a lesser extent, the tergopleural articulation. In the mesothorax of Coleoptera and the metathorax of Hymenoptera the pleural and sternal apophyses are fused and so lateral stiffness of the thorax is considerable and constant. However, in other insects the apophyses are joined by a muscle and lateral stiffness can be regulated by alterations in its tension.

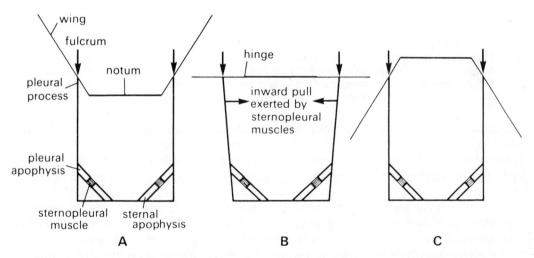

Fig. 134 Diagrammatic cross-section of the insect thorax illustrating the distortion of the thorax produced by wing movement. A. Wings stable in the up position. B. Unstable position due to the inward pull of the sternopleural muscles. C. Wings stable in the down position

As a result of this lateral stiffness the position of the wings is unstable for much of the stroke and they will tend to return automatically either to the fully up or fully down positions (Fig. 134), these being the only stable positions. Thus in flight the wings are moved by the muscles to the position of maximum instability (Fig. 134B) and then they will swing into the up or down position as a result of the thoracic elasticity. This arrangement is called a 'click' mechanism.

In an insect the wing articulation is more complex than in the diagrams, but the method of working is basically the same. Thus in *Sarcophaga* (Diptera) both dorsoventral and dorsal longitudinal indirect flight muscles produce a lateral extension of the notum, exerting forces outwards, while the pleural process is pulled inwards by the sternopleural muscle. Hence the system XYZ in Figure 135 is only stable at the extreme ends of the stroke (Fig. 135A and C).

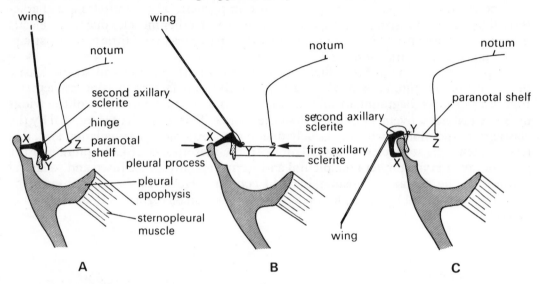

Fig. 135 Diagrammatic section through the wing base of a fly illustrating the click mechanism in the wing movement. A. Wing stable in the up position. B. Unstable position with the system XYZ in a straight line and under pressure between the arrows. C. Wing stable in the down position (partly from Pringle, 1957)

Contraction of the dorsal longitudinal muscles of *Sarcophaga* lowers the scutellum, which is hinged to the scutum. This raises the anterior end of the scutellar lever, which arises from the side of the scutellum (Fig. 136), and this pushes the first axillary sclerite up until it reaches the unstable position (Fig. 135B), when the forces exerted at X and Z cause the wing to click into the stable down position (Fig. 135C). In raising the wings the scutellar lever pulls the first axillary sclerite down to the position of maximum instability and then the wing automatically clicks up. Click mechanisms have been demonstrated in Orthoptera, Diptera, Coleoptera and possibly Odonata.

In *Sarcophaga* the upstroke is limited by the scutellar lever hitting against the pleural sclerites. This increases efficiency in flight since it eliminates the necessity of doing work in stopping the movement. The lower limit of the wing stroke is more variable. It is determined by the nature of the articulation between the first and second axillary sclerites, which can be varied to some extent by the direct muscles altering the lateral tension. In *Schistocerca* the movement of the wings may be stopped by the contraction of antagonistic muscles before the wingstroke is complete. Thus the dorsal longitudinal muscles may start to contract before the end of the upstroke. This requires a greater muscular output than is necessary in *Sarcophaga*.

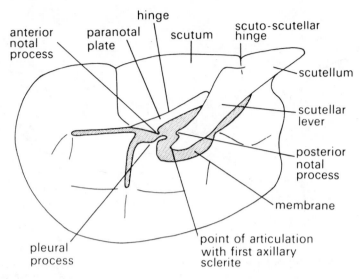

Fig. 136 Lateral view of the thorax of *Sarcophaga* (from Pringle, 1957)

11.2 Movements of the wings

11.2.1 Stroke plane

The wings do not make simple up and down movements, but in the course of each cycle they also move backwards and forwards to some extent. As a result, the tip of the fore wing of *Schistocerca* moves in an ellipse relative to the body (Fig. 137), moving forward and down on the downstroke, and up and back on the upstroke. In some other insects, such as bees and flies, the wing tip traces a more complex figure relative to the body (Nachtigall, 1976). The upstroke is faster than the downstroke and when the insect is moving the wing tip follows an irregular path through the air (Fig. 137).

The plane in which the wings vibrate relative to the body is called the stroke plane and in *Schistocerca* this is at a more or less constant angle of 30° to the long axis of the body. In *Apis* and many other insects the plane is variable and when a bee hovers the stroke plane almost coincides with the horizontal plane through the long axis of the body (p. 230). Differences in the plane of movement of the two sides produce turning movements.

11.2.2 Amplitude of wingbeat

The amplitude of the wing stroke, measured in the stroke plane, is often within the range 70–130°. Greater amplitudes are associated with greater power output and are regarded as occurring most frequently at the beginning of flight, when high lift forces are necessary to raise the insect off the ground. In *Drosophila* (Diptera) an increase in amplitude from 90° to 140° is associated with a change in the stroke plane, but in *Apis* the amplitude varies independently of stroke plane. Variation in the amplitude of wingbeat on the two sides of the body may be used in steering, the insect turning away from the side of greatest amplitude.

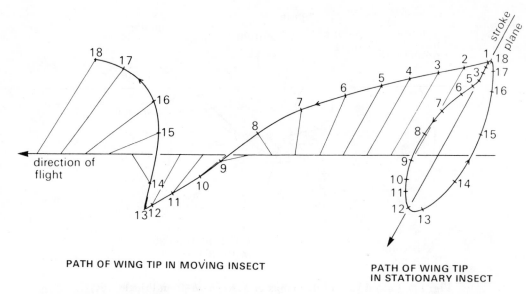

PATH OF WING TIP IN MOVING INSECT

PATH OF WING TIP
IN STATIONARY INSECT

Fig. 137 Movement of the tip of the forewing of *Schistocerca*. The ellipse on the right shows
the movement relative to the body of the insect, while the irregular curve shows the path of the
wing-tip as the insect moves through the air. The numbers indicate the positions of the wing at
regular time intervals throughout the stroke and the lines joining the wing-tip path to the flight
axis show the angle which the long axis of the wing makes with the body at different stages of·
the stroke (after Jensen, 1956)

Wings whose primary function is protective, such as the elytra of beetles and
tegmina of grasshoppers, beat with lower amplitudes since they are not the primary
power producers. The fore wings of *Locusta*, for instance, move through 70–80°
compared with 110–130° for the hind wings, and the elytra of *Oryctes* (Coleoptera) have
an amplitude of only about 20°, nearly all the power coming from the hind wings.

11.2.3 Wingbeat frequency

The high power output needed to lift an insect into the air and propel it forwards is
achieved primarily by the high frequency of contraction of the flight muscles (p. 263)
leading to high wingbeat frequencies. Wingbeat frequency is controlled in one of two
ways depending on the nature of the muscles driving the wings: in insects with
synchronous flight muscles (p. 249) frequency depends on the rate of firing of the
motorneurones to the muscle; in insects with asynchronous flight muscles (p. 251) the
frequency is determined by the mechanical properties of the thorax, the flight muscles
and the wing articulations. In general, insects with synchronous flight muscles have
relatively low wingbeat frequencies, up to about 50 Hz; insects with asynchronous
flight muscles often have higher frequencies, usually over 100 Hz and extending to at
least 600 Hz, in *Aedes*, and perhaps 1000 Hz, in *Forcipomyia* (Diptera). Coleoptera and
some large Heteroptera are unusual in having asynchronous muscles but relatively low
wingbeat frequencies. Frequencies are generally higher in small insects (Fig. 138),
although the relationship between size and frequency varies from group to group and is
also affected by physiological and environmental parameters.

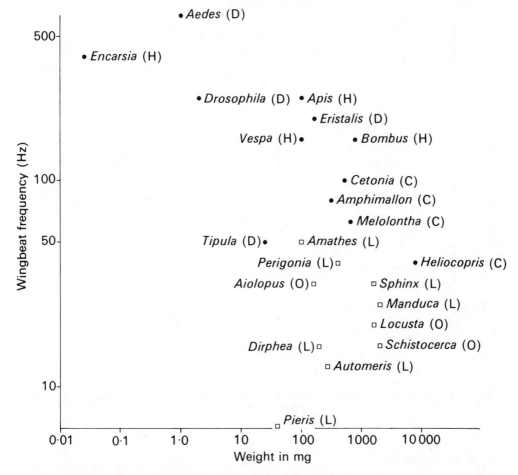

Fig. 138 Relationship between wingbeat frequency and weight in various insects.□—insects with synchronous muscles, ●—insects with asynchronous muscles. C—Coleoptera, D—Diptera, H—Hymenoptera, L—Lepidoptera, O—Orthoptera (mainly after Weis-Fogh, 1973; Bartholomew and Casey, 1978)

Adult age affects wingbeat frequency. In *Chortoicetes* (Orthoptera), for instance, wingbeat frequency increases from 15–20 Hz soon after moulting to 25–35 Hz about ten days later. The co-ordination of activity of the flight motorneurones is fully established five days after ecdysis and subsequent changes relate to the development of the flight muscles and the cuticle (p. 275) (Altman, 1975). Comparable changes occur in other insects. In *Drosophila* the wingbeat frequency increases with temperature (Fig. 139), but in Hymenoptera temperature has no effect. The wingbeat frequency of *Schistocerca* is constant within the range 25–35°C, but alters at lower and higher temperatures (and see Casey, 1980).

An increase in wingbeat frequency gives greater power output and in *Schistocerca* increased lift may be achieved in this way, but except at take-off and landing changes in frequency are apparently not generally used to control power output.

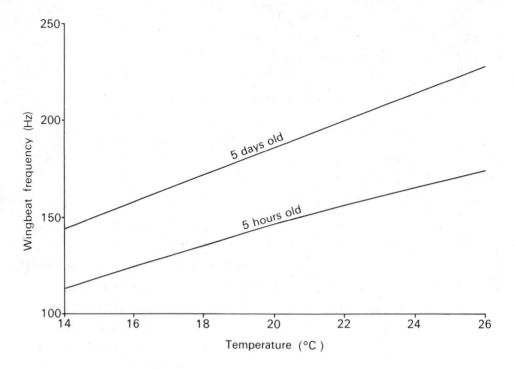

Fig. 139 Variation with age and temperature of the wingbeat frequency of *Drosophila* (from Chadwick, 1953)

11.2.4 Wing twisting

In addition to variations in the form of the wingbeat, the wing may twist in different ways in different phases of the stroke thereby altering the forces which it exerts. In many insects the twisting is produced by two direct flight muscles, the basalar muscle, which pronates the wing, that is it pulls down the leading edge, and the subalar muscle, which supinates the wing causing the ventral surface to face obliquely forwards by pulling down the trailing edge. Since these muscles also act as direct wing depressors they are active only during the downstroke, when the balance between them determines the degree of pronation of the wing. In addition there is some passive bending of the wing on the downstroke as a result of its flexibility and this is evident in the hind wing of the locust, which always assumes a smooth camber. During the upstroke, when the direct muscles are inactive, the twisting of the wing is entirely passive. In *Sarcophaga* wing twisting results automatically from the relative movements of the first and second axillary sclerites (see Pringle, 1957).

The wings undergo a regular sequence of changes in twisting, being fully pronated during most of the downstroke with, in *Schistocerca*, a posterior flap coming forwards towards the end of the movement (Fig. 140). In the upstroke the wing is supinated and Z-shaped in cross-section. Essentially similar twisting occurs in *Phormia* (Diptera) and in *Apis* (Nachtigall, 1976).

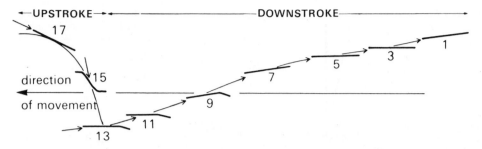

Fig. 140 Changes in the twisting of the mid-section of the forewing of *Schistocerca* in the course of a single stroke. The relative size of the wing is greatly exaggerated for clarity. Short arrows indicate the direction of the relative wind and the numbers correspond with those showing the wing-tip positions in figures 137 (after Jensen, 1956)

11.3 Aerodynamics

To a large extent steady-state aerodynamics, with the wing acting as an aerofoil, can account for the performances of most insects when flying forwards, but non-steady-state aerodynamics, depending on the creation of air circulation (vortices) round the wing, also apply and in some very small insects must play a major role in lift production (Pringle, 1974; Weis-Fogh, 1976).

11.3.1 Flapping flight

The steady state forces acting on the wing vary throughout the wingbeat due to changes in the twisting of the wings and changes in the velocity of the relative wind. The relative wind is the movement of the air relative to the wing. It has two major components: one due to the airspeed of the insect and a second due to the velocity of the wing in the stroke plane. The relative wind may be regarded as the resultant of these two forces (Fig. 141).

The forces which the relative wind exerts on the wing depend on the angle at which it strikes the chord of the wing. This angle, known as the angle of attack, may be either positive or negative (Fig. 141A,B). Because of the twisting of the wing the angle of attack varies along its length, while the twisting also modifies the angle of attack at any one point in the course of the wingbeat (Figs. 140, 142). Thus in *Schistocerca* the angle of attack at the mid-point of the wing is positive and fairly constant throughout the downstroke, but becomes negative during the upstroke.

Lift

The force which the relative wind exerts on the wing can be resolved into two components, the lift and the thrust. The lift is the vertical force produced. In order to keep the insect steady in the air, the lift force must roughly equal the weight of the insect. Lift becomes minimal during the upstroke of the wings, but, in *Schistocerca*, because of the adjustment of the angle of attack, it never becomes negative, that is the wings as a whole never produce a force pushing the insect down (Fig. 143). Because of their bigger area and greater amplitude of movement the hind wings produce more lift than the fore wings, about 71 % of the total, and because of the adjustment of the angle

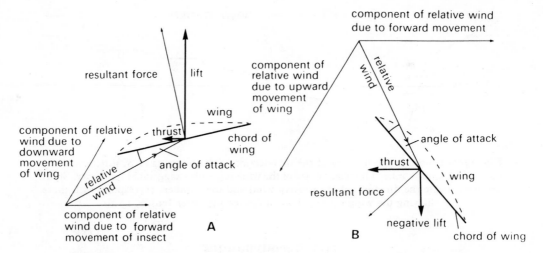

Fig. 141 Diagrams illustrating the forces acting at the mid-point of the wing at different phases of the wingbeat corresponding roughly with positions 7 and 15 in Fig. 140. A. Downstroke of wing with positive angle of attack. B. Upstroke of wing with negative angle of attack. The lengths and thicknesses of the arrows have no significance in indicating the strengths of the forces

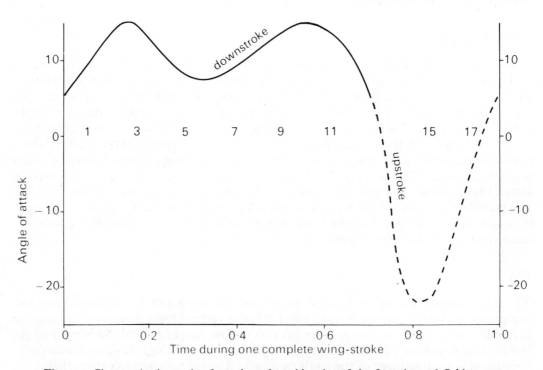

Fig. 142 Changes in the angle of attack at the mid-point of the forewings of *Schistocerca* during a single cycle of movement of the wings. Since the angle of attack varies along the length of the wing, no negative lift is produced by the wing as a whole (see Fig. 143). Numbers along the zero axis indicate intervals corresponding with those in Fig. 140 (after Jensen, 1956)

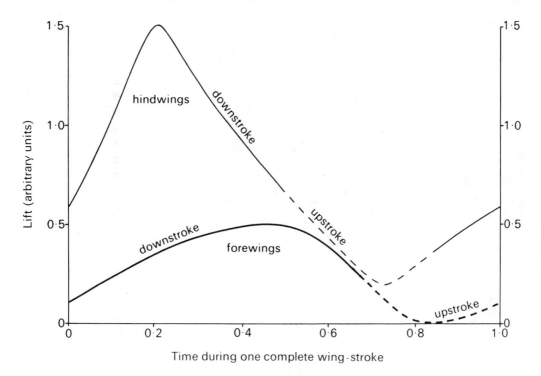

Fig. 143 Changes in the lift produced by the wings of *Schistocerca* during a wing-stroke (after
Jensen, 1956)

of attack 20% of the total lift is produced during the upstroke of the wings. The
resulting variation in lift in the course of a wingbeat leads to a cycle of vertical
displacements of the insect as it flies along so that instead of following a horizontal path
it loops up and down (Fig. 144).

Lift is also produced by the action of the relative wind on the body as distinct from
the wings, but the force is insignificant compared with that produced by the wings,
amounting to less than 1/20th of the total lift in *Schistocerca* (Jensen, 1956). In
Drosophila lift is proportional to the body angle (p. 237) (Vogel, 1966).

Thrust

In order to move forwards the insect must also produce a horizontal force known as the
thrust. This must be sufficiently great to overcome the drag forces which resist the
motion of the insect through the air. Drag results partly from the profile of the insect,
i.e. the area which it presents to the air, but largely from an induced drag due to the
development of vortices at the wing tips which dissipate much of the kinetic energy of
the wings as heat. These vortices result from the mixing of air at different pressures
from the two sides of the wing.

The thrust, like lift, varies in the course of wingbeat and the hind wing of
Schistocerca produces thrust maximally in the middle of the downstroke and again in
the upstroke (Fig. 145). This variation results in slight changes in the forward speed of
the insect in the course of a wingbeat.

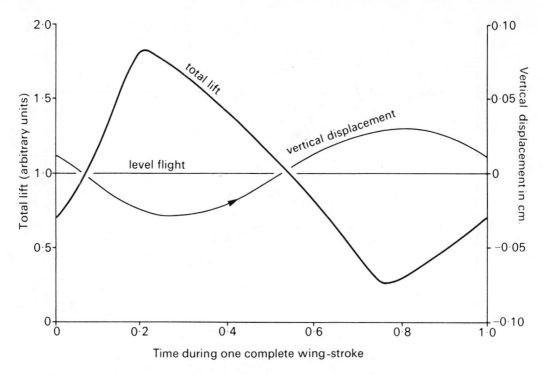

Fig. 144 Changes in the total lift and associated vertical displacements of *Schistocerca* during a wing-stroke. There is a time lag between the period of maximum lift and the corresponding rise of the insect (after Jensen, 1956)

Propelling the insect forwards requires relatively little energy compared with that needed to keep it in the air and in *Schistocerca* the average thrust is only 7 % of the average lift.

A steady-state pattern of air circulation cannot exist during wing accelerations or when the angle of attack is changing rapidly. Weis-Fogh (1973) has described a 'fling' mechanism which operates in the flight of *Encarsia* and observations on larger insects indicate that a similar phenomenon may be widespread in generating high lift forces (Cooter and Baker, 1977).

The chalcid wasp *Encarsia* has a wing span of about 1·3 mm. The wingbeat frequency is about 400 Hz: At the top of the upstroke the wings clap together and then by very rapid promotion the leading edges of the wings separate (are flung apart) while the posterior parts remain in contact. Air is sucked into the increasing gap between the upper surfaces of the wings creating bound vortices round the edges (Fig. 146). Immediately after the 'Fling', the wings separate completely, each carrying a bound vortex with it. As a consequence of the fling an appropriate air circulation exists over the wings from the start of the down stroke and lift equal to the body weight is produced almost from the beginning.

Evidence also exists for a fling mechanism in other, larger insects, and Weis-Fogh (1976) suggests that the requisite circulation of air round the wings may be produced in other ways in other insects.

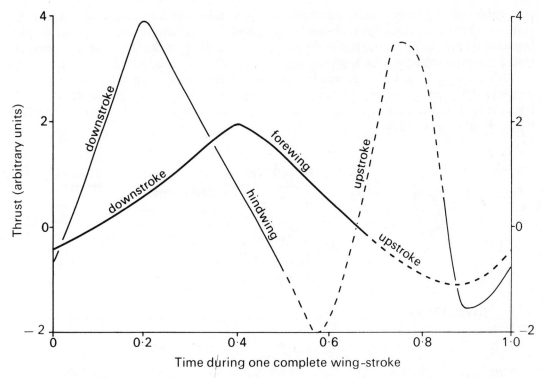

Fig. 145 Changes in the thrust produced by the wings of *Schistocerca* during a wing-stroke (after Jensen, 1956)

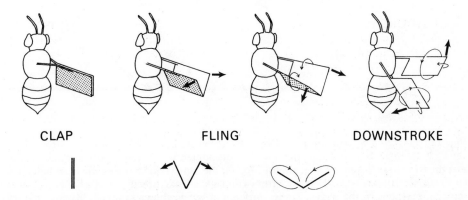

Fig. 146 Diagrammatic representation of the fling mechanism in *Encarsia*. Upper row shows movement of the wings, lower row the cross-section at the midpoint of the wings. Heavy arrows show wing movements, thin arrows air movements. Under side of wing stippled (after Weis-Fogh, 1973)

11.3.2 Hovering

Many insects are able to hover. Sometimes this behaviour is particularly associated with feeding, as in *Macroglossum* (Lepidoptera), or with mating, as in swarms of some flies (p. 351), and often it occurs before landing, enabling the insect to land on a particular spot. In large beetles, hawk moths, bees and wasps hovering employs steady-state aerodynamic principles with the body almost vertical and the stroke plane almost horizontal (Fig. 147). At the top and bottom of each wing stroke the wing is rotated so that a positive angle of attack giving substantial lift is maintained throughout.

Other insects employ non-steady-state aerodynamics during hovering. *Encarsia* employs the 'fling' mechanism to produce lift (see above) and in syrphids, which hover with the body horizontal, vortices are created by sudden changes in the form of the wing (Weis-Fogh, 1973, 1976).

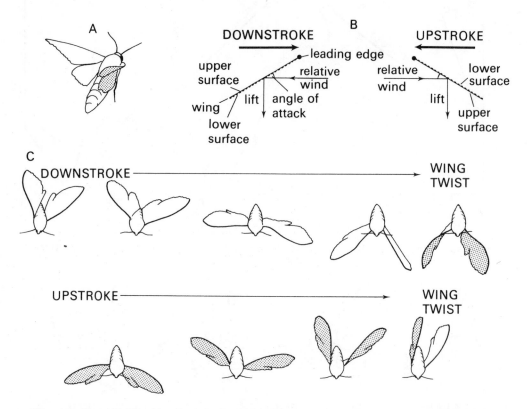

Fig. 147 Hovering by *Manduca*. A. Dorso-lateral view, body almost vertical, strokeplane almost horizontal. B. Lift production on the morphological 'up' and 'down' strokes. Notice that the wing has twisted through almost 180° on the 'up-stroke' to bring the morphological lower surface uppermost. C. Sequence from a film taken from directly above a hovering insect showing positions of the wings. Under surfaces of wings shown stippled, leading edge of forewing thicker (after Weis-Fogh, 1973)

11.3.3 Gliding

Occasionally insects are seen to glide with the wings outstretched. This behaviour has been observed in Odonata, Orthoptera and Lepidoptera and ranges from a pause in wing movement lasting only a fraction of a second to prolonged glides lasting many seconds. The ability to glide depends on the maintenance of a high lift/drag ratio produced by having the wings at a suitable angle to the airflow (drag is the force opposing the movement of the body and acting in the direction of the airflow). The lift/drag ratio varies with the angle of attack and is at a maximum for various Lepidoptera at an angle of attack of 5 to 15° (Fig. 148). The scales on the wings contribute to the lift but do not affect drag and so enable butterflies to glide for longer than would be possible without them (Nachtigall, 1976).

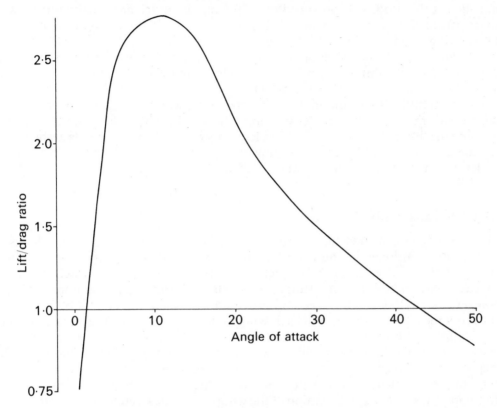

Fig. 148 Lift/drag ratio in relation to the angle of attack of the wings of a Lepidopteran in gliding flight (after Nachtigall, 1976)

During a glide the insect expends very little energy and it is suggested that the inability of dragonflies to fold their wings is a secondary adaptation to gliding. Locusts are able to lock their fore wings in an outstretched position (Neville, 1965) and this may facilitate gliding. Short glides by *Locusta* are described by Baker and Cooter (1979).

11.4 Control of wingbeat

11.4.1 The initiation of wing movements

In most insects the wings start to beat as a result of loss of tarsal contact with the substratum and in the locust this occurs when the insect jumps into the air. When the legs are touching the ground movement of the wings is inhibited, contact probably being perceived through the proprioceptors of the legs. The wings may also be induced to beat by various shock stimuli.

11.4.2 Maintenance of wing movements

The loss of tarsal contact with the substratum is sufficient to maintain the movement of the wings of *Drosophila* as well as initiating it, but in most other insects flight soon stops unless the insect receives further stimulation. This is provided by the movement of wind against the head. A wind speed of only 2 m/s is sufficient to maintain the wing movements of *Schistocerca* and since this is less than the flight speed of the insect the relative wind produced in flight will provide sufficient stimulus. Air movement is perceived in locusts by hair beds on the face (Fig. 465). In Diptera the wind is perceived by movements of the third antennal segment relative to the second, probably involving Johnston's organ (p. 716) (Hollick, 1941).

These stimuli also result in the legs being drawn up close to the body in a characteristic manner. Thus in locusts stimulation of the hair beds causes the fore legs to assume the flight position, but the hind legs only do so when the sensilla at the base of the wing are stimulated by the wing movement. Diptera hold their legs in the flight position when their antennae are stimulated in flight.

11.4.3 Nervous control of wing movements

The basic rhythm of muscular contractions involved in the flight of the locust is inherent and continues in the complete absence of nervous input from peripheral sensilla. This rhythm is probably generated by interneurones, which drive the motorneurones in both locusts (Burrows, 1975b) and dragonflies (Simmons, 1977b). However, the rhythm is reinforced and provided with a fine adjustment by input from the stretch receptors at the base of each wing. The axon of a forewing stretch receptor has a complex of branches in all three thoracic ganglia, while that from a hind wing stretch receptor has branches in the meso- and meta-thoracic ganglia. These branches synapse with dendrites of the flight motor neurones without any intervening interneurones so that monosynaptic pathways are present between sensillum and effector muscles (Fig. 149). Elevation of the wing causes the stretch receptors to fire and their input inhibits the activity of motorneurones to the levator muscles and excites the motorneurones to the depressor muscles (Fig. 150). Hence the stretch receptors regulate the amplitude of the upstroke and the precise times at which the depressor motorneurones fire (Burrows, 1975a).

Despite the complexity of the flight movements of the locust each of the muscles comprises only a small number of units, each of which is controlled by a motorneurone with its perikaryon in a specific position in the ganglion (Bentley, 1970). The first basalar muscle consists of only a single unit, the second basalar and subalar muscles have two units and the dorsal longitudinal muscles five. In dragonflies the muscles have rather more units; the second basalar muscles which in these insects are major wing depressors are controlled by ten motorneurones (Simmons, 1977a).

The force exerted by a muscle can be increased either by increasing the number of units which are active or by increasing the strength of the pull exerted by each unit. Although the units of the flight muscles are only innervated by fast axons (p. 255) they are caused to contract more strongly if, instead of being stimulated by a single nerve impulse, they are stimulated by two impulses following close together, the time between the impulses probably being determined by the relative refractory period of

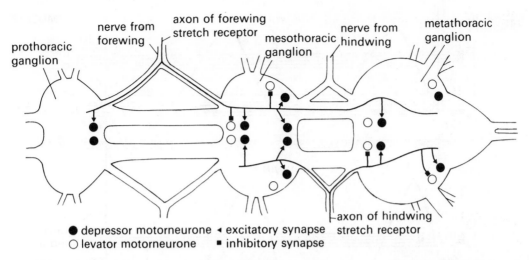

● depressor motorneurone ◄ excitatory synapse
○ levator motorneurone ■ inhibitory synapse

Fig. 149 Connections of the axons from two of the stretch receptors at the base of the wings with some of the motorneurones which drive the flight muscles of a locust (after Burrows, 1975a)

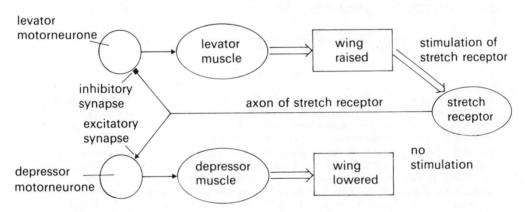

Fig. 150 Diagram of the monosynaptic feed-back loop between a stretch receptor at the base of the wing of a locust and the motorneurones driving the flight muscles (after Burrows, 1975a)

the nerve and the muscle membrane (Wilson, 1964). This provides a means by which graded information can be transmitted to muscles despite the all-or-nothing code of the nervous system (p. 624). Thus when the insect is producing only low lift forces the second basalar muscle and some units of the dorsal longitudinal muscle of the hind wing may be inactive, whereas in producing high lift forces all the units come into action and the forces exerted by the individual units are increased by double firing of the motorneurones (Fig. 151).

The twisting of the wings by the controller muscles is precisely timed by the pattern of motor impulses to the muscles (Fig. 151). In the locust, only in the case of one muscle, the mesothoracic subalar muscle, is the firing of the motor nerve very variable in its timing and this is the muscle which varies the twisting of the fore wing to control

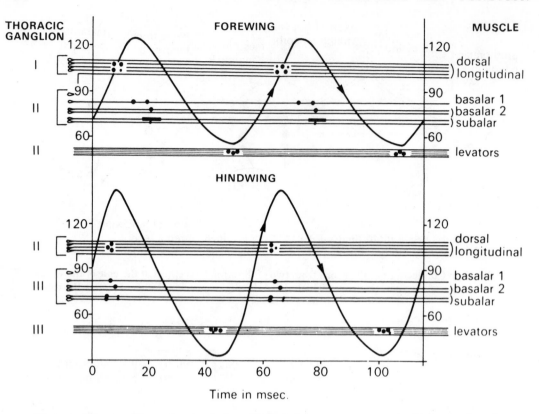

Fig. 151 Diagram illustrating the timing of firing of motorneurones to the flight muscles of fore and hind wings in relation to the wingbeat cycle. Each neurone is shown by a horizontal line with its origin in the appropriate ganglion on the left-hand side. Each dot on a line represents a nerve impulse occurring at that time; a small dot indicates that an impulse may or may not occur, a large dot that it always occurs. The heavy bar on the motorneurone to the forewing subalar muscle indicates that firing occurs within this period, but not at a precisely fixed time as with the other units. The heavy curve and the numbers along the ordinate indicate the angular displacement of the wings in degrees; 90° indicates wing horizontal, above 90° wings up, below 90° wings down (after Wilson and Weis-Fogh, 1962)

lift (Wilson and Weis-Fogh, 1962). The precise co-ordination of the other neurones does not arise from a fixed pattern of connections between them since they can function in sequences other than that involved in flight (Wilson, 1962).

The problem of control of the wingbeat is different in insects in which the wingbeat is produced by asynchronous muscles. Here also the muscles must act in a precise sequence, but this sequence is not directly related to nervous input and the timing of firing of the motorneurones does not coincide with a particular phase of the wingbeat cycle. The nervous input to the flight muscles serves only as a general stimulator maintaining the muscle contractions. Control of the movements is exerted by the muscles which control the mechanical properties of the thorax; an increase in the lateral stiffness of the thorax produces an increased wingbeat frequency, while a decrease in stiffness leads to a reduced frequency. These changes only take effect over a number of cycles of wing movement; there is no stroke-by-stroke control and such precise control is unnecessary because the insect only travels a very short distance in the course of a single wingbeat (Wilson and Wyman, 1963).

11.5 Stability in flight

Because of the variations in the forces acting on it during flight, there is a tendency for an insect to deviate from a steady path. This instability may involve rotation about any of the three major axes passing through the centre of gravity of the body (Fig. 152). Rotation about the long axis of the body is called rolling, rotation about the horizontal, transverse axis is pitching, and rotation about the vertical axis is yawing. To some extent such deviations may be corrected for passively through the shape of the body and form of the wingbeat, but insects also have the capacity to make active changes in the aerodynamic forces acting on the body in order to maintain a steady flight.

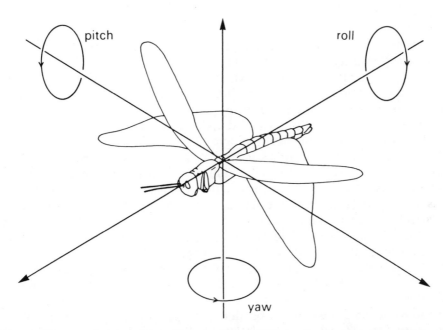

Fig. 152 Diagram showing the main axes about which an insect may rotate due to its instability in flight (after Weis-Fogh, 1956)

11.5.1 Passive stability

Some degree of passive stability about the rolling axis results from the wing insertions being above the centre of gravity. Some stability in yaw is achieved if the maximum thrust is delivered when the wings are in front of the centre of gravity of the insect; this appears to be the case in flies, for instance. The long abdomen of insects such as dragonflies and locusts acts as a rudder giving stability about yawing and pitching axes.

In *Muscina* (Diptera) stability in roll is conferred by changes in stroke amplitude following changes in the body angle. These changes alter the line of action of the forces acting on the body in such a way that the insect is restored to its original orientation (Pringle, 1968).

11.5.2 Active maintenance of stability

Deviations from a steady path are perceived by various sensilla and the nervous input from these exerts a controlling influence on the wingbeat so that the deviation is corrected. Of primary importance in this respect is Johnston's organ in the antenna (p. 716), the hair beds on the front of the head (p. 709) and the sensilla at the base of the wings (p. 211). The halteres of Diptera are of fundamental importance in this order and they are considered separately.

Rolling

Vision plays an important part in the control of rolling. Odonata and Orthoptera, and probably also other insects, have a dorsal light reaction by which they align the head so that the dorsal ommatidia receive maximal illumination. To produce a dorsal light reaction a number of ommatidia must be illuminated, but the response does not depend on stimulation of a particular part of the eye since it is still apparent if the most dorsal ommatidia, which are normally concerned in the response, are covered. The response is improved by stimulation of the ocelli (p. 670) (Goodman, 1965; and see Taylor, 1981).

Since normally most light comes from the sun or the sky overhead the dorsal light reaction ensures that the head is usually held in a vertical position. In Odonata, where the head is loosely articulated to the thorax, the head also tends to stay in a vertical plane due to its own inertia, but this is not the case in the locust where the head and thorax are broadly attached so that rolling by the thorax is immediately transmitted to the head. As a result, a locust flying in complete darkness is unable to orientate in this plane and will fly upside down or at any other angle (Fig. 153).

The dorsal light reaction gives stability to the head, and the rest of the body is aligned with the head. Any deviation from this alignment is signalled by proprioceptors between the head and the thorax. In *Schistocerca* there are hair beds on the cervical sclerite and hairs along the anterior border of the pronotum which are involved in this orientation (p. 710). Unequal stimulation of the sensilla on the two sides due to a turning of the thorax relative to the head leads to differential twisting of the wings so that the thorax is brought back into alignment again (but see Taylor, 1981).

If insects controlled rolling exclusively by a dorsal light reaction they would sometimes have a tendency to fly at unusual angles. This might occur, for instance, with the sun low in the sky just before sunset. That this does not occur indicates that other stimuli are also important. *Schistocerca* also orientates to the horizon, keeping it transversely across the eyes with the upper ommatidia more brightly illuminated than the lower ones. The orientation is accurate and the insect can follow a slow change of $5°$ so that it is able to perceive any tendency to roll. This and the dorsal light reaction give *Schistocerca* good control of rolling (Goodman, 1965).

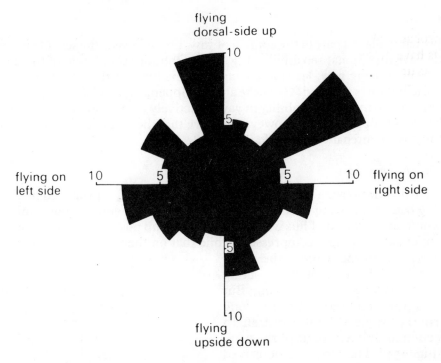

Fig. 153 Diagram showing the orientation of a locust in a series of observations made when it was flying in complete darkness. The figures indicate the percentage frequency with which orientation occurred in each sector (based on Goodman, 1965)

Pitching and lift control

When flying steadily insects tend to keep the body at a more or less constant angle with the horizontal. In locusts this body angle is usually 6–7°. Any tendency to pitch is counteracted by changes in the twisting of the fore wing so that the forces which it exerts are modified, but even if locusts are subjected experimentally to changes of up to 15° in body angle they are able to keep the lift force more or less constant. This constancy is achieved by regulating the twist of the fore wing during the downstroke so that the amount of lift which it produces is altered. There is no regulation of the upstroke or of the hind wing in any phase. Thus an increase in body angle will increase the angle of attack of the hind wings on the downstroke so that they produce more lift, but this is compensated for by a reduction in the lift produced by the fore wings and so the total lift force remains constant. In addition the balance between the fore and hind wings is disturbed resulting in a tendency for the insect to pitch forwards and so to counteract the imposed change in body angle. The twisting of the fore wing in this compensating reaction and in the control of pitch is regulated by the campaniform sensilla at the bases of the wings. There is no evidence for a comparable lift-control reaction in *Drosophila* (Vogel, 1966).

In Diptera the halteres are important in controlling pitching, but it is also probable that Johnston's organ in the antenna exerts some controlling influence over the wing movements.

Yawing

Vision probably plays a part in the control of yaw, but in locusts the sensilla in the facial hair beds have directional sensitivity (Fig. 463). Oblique stimulation of these sensilla, such as occurs during yaw, leads to a change in the form of the wingbeat so that the original orientation is restored (Gewecke and Philippen, 1978). Camhi (1970) considers that the insect also maintains stability in yaw by actively using the abdomen as a rudder; Gewecke and Philippen (1978), however, believe that the abdomen is used in steering, but not in the maintenance of stable flight.

Sensilla at the wing base

In the normal vibration of a wing a twisting-force, or torque, is produced in the cuticle at the wing base. If the wing were to move up and down in a vertical plane only vertical torque would be produced. Thus with the wing in the up position the cuticle at the base on the upper side would be compressed, while that on the ventral side was stretched,

and *vice versa* with the wing in the down position; all the forces would be acting parallel with the long axis of the wing. But because of the complexity of the wing movement the torque will differ in strength and direction in different parts of the wing stroke (Fig. 154). The torque is perceived by the sensilla, and particularly the campaniform sensilla, of the wing base. These sensilla are arranged in groups, all those within a group having a similar orientation (see Figs. 129, 130), so that each group will respond maximally to torque in a particular direction and, if the sensitivity of the sensilla is appropriately adjusted, they may respond only once during a wing cycle. It is possible that any tendency for the insect to deviate from a stable orientation would result in differential changes in the stimulation of these sensilla, which could thus exert a controlling influence on the wingbeat to correct for the deviation. This is certainly the case in the control of lift and pitching in *Schistocerca*, but the situation is best understood in the halteres of Diptera, which are specialised organs of stability.

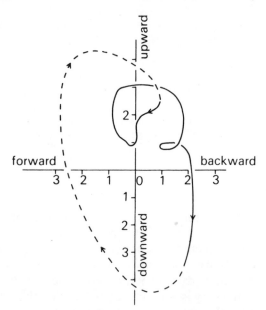

Fig. 154 Graph of the magnitude, in g/cm, and the direction of the torque in the basal veins of the forewing of *Schistocerca* during one stroke. Solid line indicates downstroke, broken line upstroke (based on Jensen, 1956).

Halteres

The halteres vibrate with the same frequency as the fore wings, but in antiphase. Their movement is less complex than that of the wings because of their structure and the nature of their articulation with the thorax. The centre of gravity of the haltere lies in the end knob (see Fig. 130), so when the haltere vibrates it swings forwards until the long axis passing through the hinge and the centre of gravity is at right angles to the long axis of the body. As a result, the haltere vibrates in a vertical or near vertical plane without making the complex fore and aft movements of the wing. Hence the forces acting at the base of the haltere and stimulating the campaniform sensilla are limited to a vertical plane when the haltere is oscillating with the insect in steady flight, and dorsal and ventral torques oscillate with the same frequency as the vibration of the halteres (Fig. 155B). These torques are perceived by the dorsal and ventral scapal plates, which are believed to maintain a constant amplitude of oscillation of the haltere.

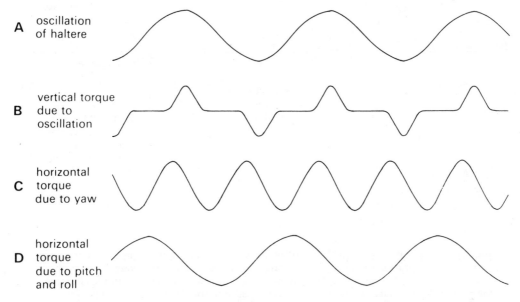

A oscillation of haltere

B vertical torque due to oscillation

C horizontal torque due to yaw

D horizontal torque due to pitch and roll

Fig. 155 Diagrams showing oscillation of the torques occurring at the base of a haltere as a result of vibration of the haltere and turning movements of the insect (after Pringle, 1948)

The path of the end knob during vibration represents an arc of a circle about the long axis of the insect and the haltere may thus be regarded as a gyroscope whose axis of rotation corresponds with the long axis of the insect. As in a gyroscope the moving halteres possess inertia, tending to maintain a fixed orientation in space so that if the insect rotates about any of its axes torques will be produced at right angles to the stroke plane. In yawing, the haltere on the outer side of the rotation will tend to swing back relative to the insect, while that on the inside will swing forwards (Fig. 156). The campaniform sensilla respond to compression forces along their long axes and bending the haltere forwards will compress the campaniform sensilla of the basal plate, while bending backwards will extend and stimulate the chordotonal organ. A single haltere can distinguish the direction and rate of yawing by the relative timing of the impulses from these two sets of sensilla, while there may, in addition, be central summation of the input from the halteres of the two sides. Stimulation of the halteres by yawing leads to a reflex modification of the twisting of the fore wings on the downstroke so that the deviation is corrected and the insect maintains a steady path.

Rolling and pitching also produce torque at the bases of the halteres at right angles to the stroke plane, but the torques are differentiated from yaw by the timing and

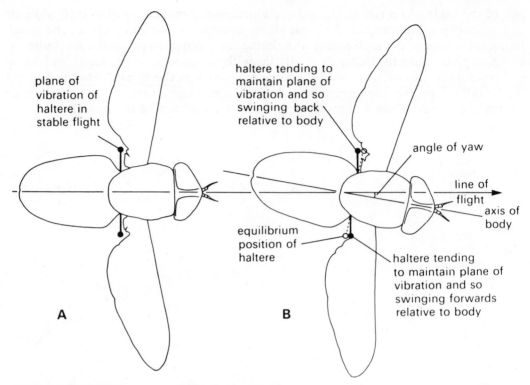

Fig. 156 Diagrams to illustrate the action of the halteres. A. In stable flight the halteres swing outwards and vibrate in a plane with their long axes at right angles to the long axis of the body. B. If the insect makes a yawing movement the halteres have a tendency to continue vibrating in their original plane and a horizontal torque is created at the base of the haltere. If the yaw is not corrected the halteres rapidly assume the equilibrium position

frequency of their oscillation. Yawing produces a torque which oscillates at twice the frequency of vibration of the halteres (Fig. 155C), pitching and rolling produce torques which oscillate with the same frequency as the halteres (Fig. 155D). Although the torques generated by pitching and rolling are identical, the two movements are differentiated by the fact that in pitching the torques produced by the two halteres are in phase while in rolling they are in antiphase. Summation in the thoracic ganglion would enable the insect to distinguish instability in these two planes and to adjust the wing twisting to correct for the instability. This adjustment of the wings does occur and the halteres are important in controlling stability in all planes (Pringle, 1948, 1957).

11.5.3 Control of flight speed

Flight speed relative to the ground may be controlled by an optomotor reaction with a tendency to keep images moving over the eye from front to back at a certain speed (p. 667). In addition, air speed is measured and regulated by the antennae, at least in *Apis, Calliphora* and locusts. In flight the antennae are held horizontally and directed forwards. Movement through the air tends to push the flagellum backwards relative to the insects, but the insect compensates for this deflection by swinging the pedicel forwards. At higher air speeds the compensation is greater and so the antennae are pointed more directly forwards (Fig. 157). Vibrations of the flagellum are produced by the flapping of the wings and these vibrations stimulate Johnston's organ. Different scolopidia are stimulated depending on the position of the flagellum and it is probably on this basis that airspeed is determined (Gewecke, 1974).

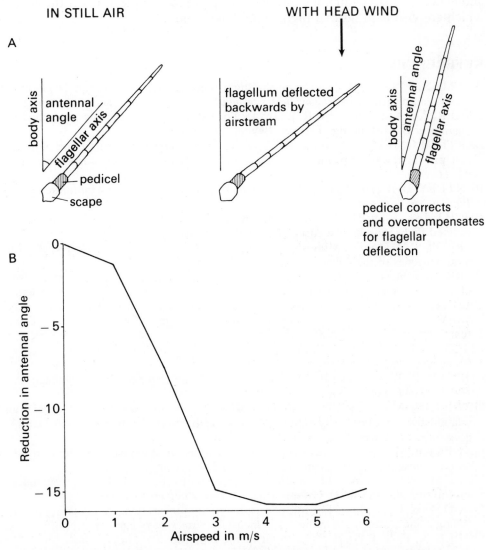

Fig. 157 A. Diagrams showing the changes in the position of an antenna resulting from a head wind. B. Changes in the antennal angle associated with increasing air-speed (after Gewecke, 1974)

11.6 Landing

During flight the legs of an insect are held close to the body (p. 232), but before landing the legs obviously must be extended so that the insect lands on its feet. In *Lucilia* extension of the legs results from visual stimuli. Particularly important in producing leg extension is a marked contrast in the stimulation of adjacent ommatidia and a rapid change in the illumination of successive ommatidia. Such changes might occur as the insect approaches a surface since the angular movement will increase as it gets closer and details with contrasting shadows will become more apparent. In addition, to produce the leg movements a relatively large number of ommatidia must be stimulated and hence the insect will not continually respond to small features of the environment which are visible in normal flight (Goodman, 1960).

REFERENCES

ALTMAN, J. S. (1975). Changes in the flight motor pattern during the development of the Australian plague locust, *Chortoicetes terminifera*. *J. comp. Physiol.* **97**: 127–142.

BAKER, P. S. and COOTER, R. J. (1979). The natural flight of the migratory locust, *Locusta migrateria* L. II. Gliding. *J. comp. Physiol.* **131**: 89–94.

BARTHOLOMEW, G. A. and CASEY, T. M. (1978). Oxygen consumption of moths during rest, pre-flight warm-up, and flight in relation to body size and wing morphology. *J. exp. Biol.* **76**: 11–25.

BENTLEY, D. R. (1970). A topological map of the locust flight system motor neurons. *J. Insect Physiol.* **16**: 905–918.

BUCHTHAL, F., WEIS-FOGH, T. and ROSENFALCK, P. (1957). Twitch contractions of isolated flight muscle of locusts. *Acta physiol. Scand.* **39**: 246–276.

BURROWS, M. (1975a). Monosynaptic connexions between wing stretch receptors and flight motoneurones of the locust. *J. exp. Biol.* **62**: 189–219.

BURROWS, M. (1975b). Co-ordinating interneurones of the locust which convey two patterns of motor commands: their connexions with flight motoneurones. *J. exp. Biol.* **63**: 713–733.

CAMHI, J. M. (1970). Yaw-correcting postural changes in locusts. *J. exp. Biol.* **52**: 519–531.

CASEY, T. M. (1980). Flight energetics and heat exchange of gypsy moths in relation to air temperature. *J. exp. Biol.* **88**: 133–145.

CHADWICK, L. E. (1953). The motion of the wings. *in* Roeder, K. D. (ed.), *Insect physiology*. Wiley and Sons, New York.

COOTER, R. J. and BAKER, P. S. (1977). Weis-Fogh clap and fling mechanism in *Locusta*. *Nature, Lond.* **269**: 53–54.

GEWECKE, M. (1974). The antennae of insects as air-current sense organs and their relationship to the control of flight. *in* Browne, L. Barton (ed.), *Experimental analysis of insect behaviour*. Springer-Verlag, Berlin.

GEWECKE, M. and PHILIPPEN, J. (1978). Control of the horizontal flight-course by air-current sense organs in *Locusta migratoria*. *Physiol. Ent.* **3**: 43–52.

GOODMAN, L. J. (1960). The landing responses of insects. 1. The landing response of the fly, *Lucilia sericata*, and other Calliphorinae. *J. exp. Biol.* **37**: 854–878.

GOODMAN, L. J. (1965). The role of certain optomotor reactions in regulating stability in the rolling plane during flight in the desert locust, *Schistocerca gregaria*. *J. exp. Biol.* **42**: 385–408.

HOLLICK, F. S. J. (1941). The flight of the dipterous fly *Muscina stabulans* Fallén. *Phil. Trans. R. Soc.* B, **230**: 357–390.

JENSEN, M. (1956). Biology and physics of locust flight. III. The aerodynamics of locust flight. *Phil. Trans. R. Soc.* B, **239**: 511–552.

NACHTIGALL, W. (1976). Wing movements and the generation of aerodynamic forces by some medium-sized insects. *Symp. R. ent. Soc. Lond.* **7**: 31–47.

NEVILLE, A. C. (1965). Energy and economy in insect flight. *Sci. Prog., Lond.* **53**: 203–220.

PRINGLE, J. W. S. (1948). The gyroscopic mechanism of the halteres of Diptera. *Phil. Trans. R. Soc.* B, **233**: 347–384.

PRINGLE, J. W. S. (1957). *Insect flight.* Cambridge University Press.

PRINGLE, J. W. S. (1968). Comparative physiology of the flight motor. *Adv. Insect Physiol.* **5**: 163–227.

PRINGLE, J. W. S. (1974). Locomotion: flight. *in* Rockstein, M. (ed.), *The physiology of Insecta.* vol. 3. Academic Press, New York.

SIMMONS, P. (1977a). The neuronal control of dragonfly flight I. Anatomy. *J. exp. Biol.* **71**: 123–140.

SIMMONS, P. (1977b). The neuronal control of dragonfly flight II. Physiology. *J. exp. Biol.* **71**: 141–155.

TAYLOR, C. P. (1981). Contribution of compound eyes and ocelli to steering of locusts in flight. *J. exp. Biol.* **93**: 1–18.

VOGEL, S. (1966). Flight in *Drosophila*. 1. Flight performance of tethered flies. *J. exp. Biol.* **44**: 567–578.

WEIS-FOGH, T. (1956). Biology and physics of locust flight. II. Flight performance of the desert locust (*Schistocerca gregaria*). *Phil. Trans. R. Soc.* B, **239**: 459–510.

WEIS-FOGH, T. (1973). Quick estimates of flight fitness in hovering animals, including novel mechanisms for lift production. *J. exp. Biol.* **59**: 169–230.

WEIS-FOGH, T. (1976). Energetics and aerodynamics of flapping flight: a synthesis. *Symp. R. ent. Soc. Lond.* **7**: 48–72.

WILSON, D. M. (1962). Bifunctional muscles in the thorax of grasshoppers. *J. exp. Biol.* **39**: 669–677.

WILSON, D. M. (1964). Relative refractoriness and patterned discharge of locust flight motor neurons. *J. exp. Biol.* **41**: 191–205.

WILSON, D. M. and WEIS-FOGH, T. (1962). Patterned activity of co-ordinated motor units, studied in flying locusts. *J. exp. Biol.* **39**: 643–667.

WILSON, D. M. and WYMAN, R. J. (1963). Phasically unpatterned nervous control of dipteran flight. *J. Insect Physiol.* **9**: 859–865.

CHAPTER XII
THE MUSCLES

Since much of the work on insect muscles has been concerned with flight muscles, it is convenient to consider muscles in general in this section. All the muscles of insects are built on a similar plan, with elongate cells housing the contractile elements and, in many cases, inserted into the integument at either end. The internal arrangement of the muscle cells, however, varies in different muscles and wing muscles often have characteristic forms. Shortening of the muscles involves the filaments of which they are composed sliding between each other. The muscles are stimulated to contract by the arrival of nerve impulses which cause local changes in the electrical properties of the muscle membrane and induce chemical changes within the cell. Usually one nerve impulse causes one contraction, but in specialised muscles which can oscillate at high frequency the muscles may contract several times as a result of a single nervous impulse. The speed with which these muscles oscillate depends on their mechanical properties and on the structures to which they are attached. The output of power by flight muscles may be very high and the associated metabolic rate is higher than in any other tissue. In order to maintain such a high level of metabolism the supply of oxygen and fuel must be adequate and insects are adapted anatomically, physiologically and biochemically to ensure that this is the case.

All aspects of insect muscle are reviewed in Usherwood (1975) and specialist papers on fibrillar flight muscle are contained in Tregear (1977). The neural control of insect muscles is reviewed by Hoyle (1974) and neuro-muscular transmission by Usherwood (1969, 1974). Flight metabolism and biochemical aspects of muscular activity are reviewed by Bailey (1975), Kammer and Heinrich (1978) and Sacktor (1970, 1974, 1975).

12.1 Structure

12.1.1 Basic muscle structure

Each muscle is made up of a number of fibres, which are long, usually multinucleate, cells running the whole length of the muscle. Each fibre is bounded by the sarcolemma, which comprises the plasma membrane of the cell plus the basement membrane (Smith, 1961). The cytoplasm of the fibre is called sarcoplasm and the endoplasmic reticulum, which is not connected to the plasma membrane, is known as the sarcoplasmic reticulum. The plasma membrane is deeply invaginated into the fibre, often as regular radial canals between the Z and the H bands (see below); this system of invaginations is called the transverse tubular, or T, system. It is associated with vesicles of the sarcoplasmic reticulum (Fig. 158). When the two systems are very close the space

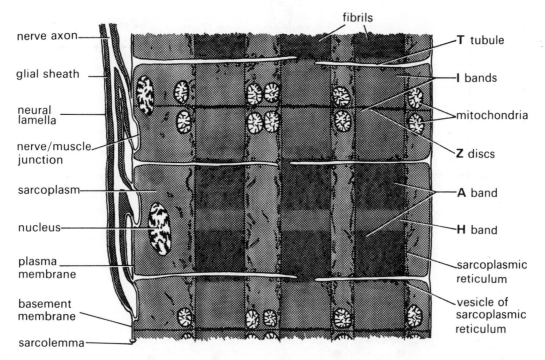

Fig. 158 Diagram of a lateral view of part of a muscle fibre showing the arrangement of the major constituents

between their membranes is occupied by electron-dense material and the arrangement is called a dyad. In *Philosamia* (Lepidoptera) the T-system is extensive and about 70 % of the muscle plasma membrane is within the system (Piek, 1975). This may be a common phenomenon. The nuclei occur in different positions in the cell in different types of muscle.

The characteristic feature of muscle cells is the presence of myofibrils (fibrils) embedded in the sarcoplasm and extending continuously from one end of the fibre to the other. The arrangement of the fibrils varies, but they are always in close contact with the mitochondria, which are sometimes known as sarcosomes.

The fibrils in their turn are composed of molecular filaments consisting mainly of two proteins: myosin and actin (see Fig. 165). The myosin filaments are stouter and are made up of numerous myosin molecules. These are elongate structures with two globular 'heads' at one end, and in each sarcomere (see below and Fig. 165) all the molecules in one half are aligned in one direction, while all those in the opposite half are aligned in the opposite direction (Fig. 159). The myosin molecules are probably arranged round a core of another protein, paramyosin, with their heads arranged in a helix (Squire, 1977). The thick filaments are each surrounded by a number of thin, actin filaments (Fig. 160A), which consist of two chains of actin molecules twisted round each other. The actin filaments are orientated in opposite directions on the two sides of a Z-line (Fig. 159). At this line actin flaments are joined together, overlapping each other and held by an amorphous material (Fig. 161) (Ashhurst, 1977). All the

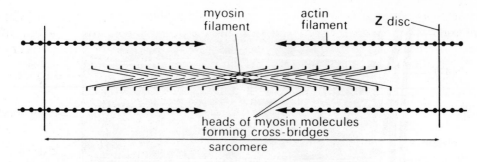

Fig. 159 Diagrammatic representation of the orientations of the actin and myosin molecules and filaments in a muscle (after Huxley, 1965)

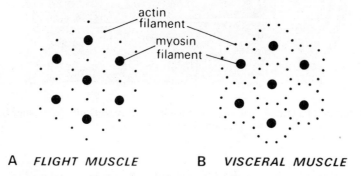

A   *FLIGHT MUSCLE*   B   *VISCERAL MUSCLE*

Fig. 160 Diagrams showing the arrangement of the muscle filaments in (A) flight muscle and (B) visceral muscle (after Smith *et al.*, 1966)

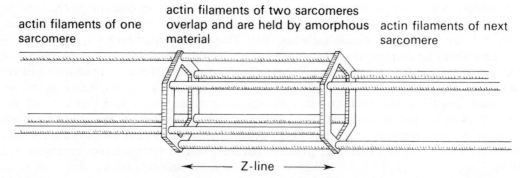

Fig. 161 Diagrammatic representation of the way in which actin filaments from adjacent sarcomeres overlap to form the Z-line. It is probable that the filaments become associated in pairs to produce a triangular arrangement within the line rather than the hexagonal one illustrated (Ashhurst, 1977)

filaments in a fibre are aligned with each other so that the joints between the ends of the actin filaments form a distinct line, known as the Z-line, running across the whole fibre. The unit of the muscle between two Z-lines is called a sarcomere. On either side of each Z-line actin filaments extend towards, but do not reach, the centre of the sarcomere. The myosin filaments do not normally reach the Z-lines, although there is some controversy concerning the presence of a connection with the Z-lines in fibrillar muscle (see Elder, 1975; Ashhurst, 1977). Hence each sarcomere has a lightly staining band at each end and a darkly staining band in the middle known respectively as the isotropic, I, and anisotropic, A, bands. In the centre of the A band, where actin filaments are absent, is the rather paler H zone. Other bands may also be present and changes occur when the muscle contracts (see Figs. 165, 166).

The actin and myosin filaments are linked at intervals by cross-bridges formed from the 'heads' of the myosin molecules which carry an ATPase. These cross-bridges provide structural and mechanical continuity along the whole length of the muscle fibre (Huxley, 1965). Further proteins, tropomyosin and troponin A and B, are also present in small quantities in the contractile elements. Troponin A acts as a receptor for Ca^{++} ions (see p. 253) (Ebashi, 1972).

The muscle fibres are collected into units of 10–20 fibres separated from neighbouring units by a tracheolated membrane. Each muscle consists of one or a few such units and, for instance, there are five in the dorsal longitudinal flight muscles of *Schistocerca*. Each muscle unit may have its own nerve supply independent of all the others, and in this case it is the basic contracting unit of the muscle, but in other cases several muscle units may have a common innervation and so function together as the motor unit.

Innervation

The nervous supply to a muscle consists of a small number of large axons. Basically each unit is innervated by a fast axon and a slow axon (p. 255) and sometimes also by an inhibitory axon (p. 254). Such multiple innervation is called polyneuronal. Within the unit each muscle fibre receives endings from the fast axon, and some may also be innervated by the slow axon (Fig. 162). In the jumping muscle of the locust about 40 % of the fibres receive branches from both axons, but in the flight muscles of Odonata, Orthoptera, Diptera and Hymenoptera only fast axons are present. Sometimes different parts of a muscle serve different functions and in this case the two parts have separate nerve supplies. Thus the posterior part of the basalar muscle of *Oryctes* is concerned only with wing depression and has only a fast innervation, but the anterior part also controls wing twisting and its innervation is complex, consisting of up to four axons, one of which is inhibiting (Ikeda and Boettiger, 1965).

Characteristically in insects there are many nerve endings spaced at intervals of 30–80 μm along each fibre (Fig. 162). Where a fibre has a double innervation it is probable that both axons have endings in the same terminals (see Fig. 403).

Oxygen supply

Since muscular contraction requires metabolic energy the muscles have a good tracheal supply and this is particularly true of the flight muscles, where often the respiratory

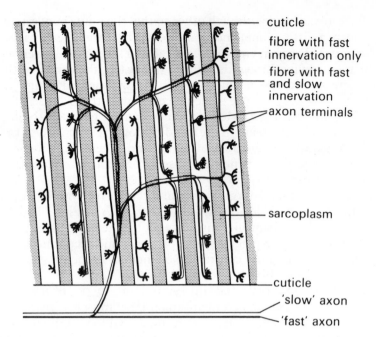

Fig. 162 Diagram illustrating the innervation of a typical muscle unit. All the fibres receive branches of the fast axon, while some also have endings from the slow axon (from Hoyle, 1974)

system is specialised to maintain the supply of oxygen to the muscles during flight (see p. 534). In most muscles the tracheoles are in close contact with the outside of the muscle fibre. This provides an adequate supply of oxygen to relatively small muscles or those whose oxygen demands are not high, but in the flight muscles of many insects the tracheoles indent the muscle membrane becoming functionally, but not anatomically, intracellular within the muscle fibre.

Muscle insertion

Skeletal muscles are fixed at either end to the integument, spanning a joint in the skeleton so that contraction of the muscle moves one part of the skeleton relative to the other. Typically such muscles are said to have an origin in a fixed or more proximal part of the skeleton, and an insertion into a distal, movable part, but these terms become purely relative in the case of muscles with a dual function (see p. 218) (Wilson, 1962). In many cases muscles are attached to invaginations of the cuticle called apodemes.

At the point of attachment of the muscle fibre to the epidermis, the plasma membranes interdigitate and are held together by desmosomes. Within the epidermal cell, microtubules run from the desmosomes to hemidesmosomes on the outer plasma membrane, and from each hemidesmosome a dense attachment fibre passes to the epicuticle through a pore canal. In earlier studies the microtubules and attachment fibres were not separated and were called tonofibrillae. Only actin filaments reach the terminal plasma membrane of the muscle fibre, inserting into the dense material of desmosomes or hemidesmosomes (Fig. 163).

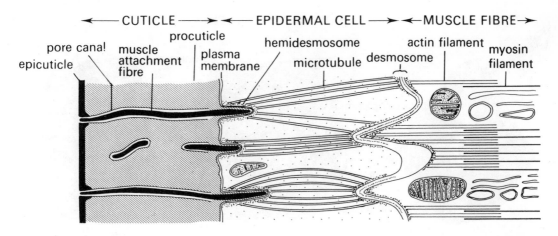

Fig. 163 Diagrammatic representation of the attachment of a muscle fibre to the integument
(after Caveney, 1969)

The muscle attachment fibres are not digested by moulting fluid and so during moulting they retain their attachment to the old cuticle across the exuvial space between the new and old cuticles. As a result, the insect is able to continue its activities after apolysis during the development of the new cuticle. The connections to the old cuticle are broken at about the time of ecdysis (Lai-Fook, 1967).

Muscle attachment fibres which extend to the epicuticle can only be produced at a moult and most muscles appear to form their attachments at this time. Muscle attachment can occur later on, however, if cuticle production continues in the post-ecdysial period, but in this case the attachment fibres are only connected to the newly formed procuticle and do not reach the epicuticle (Hinton, 1963).

12.1.2 Variations in structure

The structure of muscles varies in different parts of the body. Two broad categories can be distinguished: skeletal muscles, which are attached at either end to the cuticle and move one part of the skeleton relative to another, and visceral muscles, which move the viscera and have only one or, more commonly, no attachment to the body wall. Skeletal muscles can be differentiated functionally into synchronous and asynchronous, or fibrillar, muscles. Fibrillar (asynchronous) muscle fibres only occur in the flight muscles of Thysanoptera, Psocoptera, Homoptera, Heteroptera, Hymenoptera, Coleoptera and Diptera and in the tymbal muscles of Cicadidae (p. 691). All other muscles are synchronous muscles, that is they exhibit a direct relationship between contraction and motorneurone activity.

Synchronous skeletal muscles

In synchronous muscles the form and arrangement of the fibrils is very variable. Tubular muscles have the myofibrils arranged radially round a central core of cytoplasm containing the nuclei. This arrangement is common in leg and trunk muscles

A *TUBULAR*   **B** *CLOSE-PACKED*   **C** *FIBRILLAR*

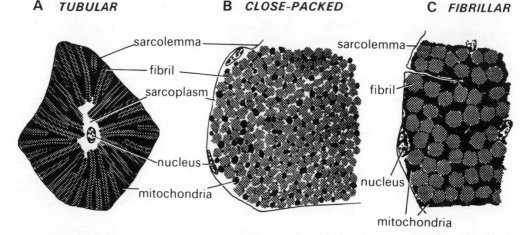

Fig. 164 Transverse sections of flight muscle fibres, all to approximately the same scale. A. Tubular muscle of *Enallagma* (Odonata) (after Smith, 1965). B. Part of a close-packed fibre of *Locusta* (based on Bücher, 1965). C. Part of a fibrillar fibre of *Tenebrio* (based on Smith, 1961)

and also occurs in the flight muscles of Odonata and Dictyoptera (Fig. 164A). In close-packed muscles, on the other hand, the fibrils are only $0.5-1.0\,\mu$m in diameter and are packed throughout the whole fibre. The nuclei are flattened and peripheral. Fibres of this type occur in some larval insects and in Apterygota and form the flight muscles of Orthoptera, Trichoptera and Lepidoptera (Fig. 164B).

The abundance and arrangement of mitochondria is related to the activity of the muscles. In the tubular and close-packed flight muscles of Odonata and Orthoptera they are large and numerous, occupying about 40% of the fibre volume. In other muscles they are generally smaller and they may occur in pairs on either side of a Z-line or be scattered irregularly between the fibres. Fibres with abundant mitochondria may be coloured pink by the high cytochrome content.

The development of the sarcoplasmic reticulum is correlated with the mechanical properties of the muscle, and in particular with the rates of relaxation of fibres. In muscles which tend to maintain a sustained contraction, such as the locust extensor tibiae muscle and the accessory flight muscles of Diptera, it is poorly developed. On the other hand, in the fast-contracting sound-producing muscles of male *Neoconocephalus* (Orthoptera) the sarcoplasmic reticulum comprises 19% of the total fibre volume. A characteristic of synchronous flight muscles, whether they are tubular or close-packed, is that the distance from the sarcoplasmic reticulum to the myofibrils is short, generally less than $0.5\,\mu$m, and in very fast-contracting muscle is even shorter. In moths with a high wingbeat frequency none of the myosin filaments is more than about $10\,\mu$m from the nearest element of the sarcoplasmic reticulum (Elder, 1975). This close proximity facilitates the rapid movement of Ca^{++} ions during contraction and relaxation (p. 253).

Sarcomere length in synchronous muscles ranges from about $3\,\mu$m to $9\,\mu$m, but in flight muscles is usually about $3-4\,\mu$m. The I band usually constitutes 30–50% of the resting length of the sarcomere, although *in situ* the extent of muscle shortening may be much less than this. For instance, the I bands of locust flight muscle constitute about

20 % of the sarcomere length, but during flight the muscle shortens by only about 5 %. Fibre diameter is commonly greater in close-packed muscle than in tubular muscle; up to 100 μm in the former compared with 10–30 μm in the latter.

Asynchronous (Fibrillar) skeletal muscles

Fibrillar muscles are characterised by the large size of the fibrils, up to 5 μm in diameter, with a corresponding increase in the diameters of the fibres, which range from 30 μm in carabid beetles to 1·8 mm in *Rutilia* (Diptera). The fibrils, with nuclei scattered between them, are distributed through the entire cross-section of the fibre (Fig. 164C).

The plasma membrane is invaginated in a T-system as in other muscles and in *Polistes* (Hymenoptera) the T-tubules are aligned with the H band, but in the fibrillar muscles of *Tenebrio* (Coleoptera) and *Megoura* (Homoptera) the system is more complex and less regular. In these insects invaginations of the plasma membrane are produced by indenting tracheoles and from these invaginations fine tubules of plasma membrane extend in to entwine each fibril. Associated with the T-system are vesicles of the sarcoplasmic reticulum, but this differs markedly in its development from the sarcoplasmic reticulum of other muscles since it consists only of a number of unconnected vesicles scattered without reference to the sarcomere pattern.

Mitochondria are large, as in all flight muscles, and occupy 30–40 % of the fibre volume. Almost the whole surface of each myofibril may be in direct contact with mitochondria. These may be regularly arranged, as between the Z and H bands in *Polistes*, or without any regular arrangement, as in *Calliphora*. The mitochondria increase in size and number over the first few days of adult life and in *Drosophila*, at least, this is paralleled by an increase in wingbeat frequency (Figs. 139, 180). Subsequently, as flight activity declines so does the size of the mitochondria (Rockstein and Bhatnagar, 1965; Kammer and Heinrich, 1978).

Fibrillar muscles may contain only a few fibres because these are so big. Thus the dorsal longitudinal flight muscles of Muscidae consist of only six fibres. Further, sarcomere length is short, only one or two microns in *Tenebrio*, and the I band makes up less than 10 % of this. In some cases the myosin filaments taper towards the Z-line and may be attached to it (Elder, 1975), so that there is no distinct I band.

Visceral muscles

The activity of visceral muscles is often irregular, or slow and rhythmic, contrasting with the more rapid, precise movements of skeletal muscle. Some visceral muscles have the capacity for supercontraction (p. 255).

Visceral muscles differ in structure from skeletal muscles in several respects. Adjacent fibres are held together by desmosomes, which are absent from skeletal muscle, and in some cases the fibres may branch and anastomose. Further, each fibre is uninucleate and the contractile material is not grouped into fibrils but packs the whole of the fibre. As in other muscles it consists of thick and thin filaments, presumably representing myosin and actin, but the filament array is different, often having a ring of ten to twelve actin filaments round each myosin filament (Fig. 160B). A T-system with a regular arrangement is present in *Periplaneta*, but in *Carausius* and *Ephestia*

(Lepidoptera) it is irregularly disposed. The sarcoplasmic recticulum is poorly developed; mitochondria are small and often few in number (Miller, 1975).

The muscles appear striated due to the alignment of the filaments. They therefore resemble skeletal muscle but contrast with the visceral muscle of vertebrates, which is not striated. The Z and H bands are irregular and sarcomere length is very variable in different visceral muscles. The sarcomeres are short, about 3 μm, in cardiac muscle, but may be as long as 10 μm in other visceral muscles.

Visceral muscles may be innervated from the stomatogastric nervous system or from the ganglia of the ventral nerve cord, but sometimes they are without any innervation. This is the case, for instance, in the heart of *Anopheles* (Diptera) larvae (p. 789).

12.2 Control of muscular contraction

12.2.1 Excitation of the muscle

With the exception of some visceral muscles, muscles are stimulated to contract by the arrival of a nerve impulse at the nerve/muscle junctions (Fig. 404). Where the junction involves excitation of a skeletal muscle it is almost certain that L-glutamate is the chemical transmitter across the synaptic gap and this may also be true with visceral muscles (Miller, 1975). However, receptor sites for L-glutamate on the muscle membrane are not restricted to the synaptic region and excitation of the muscles by L-glutamate in the haemolymph is theoretically possible. Perhaps the L-glutamate in the haemolymph is present in a bound form, or there is some diffusion barrier between the haemolymph and the synapses. This problem remains unresolved (Usherwood, 1974; Usherwood and Cull-Candy, 1975). It is probable that, as with acetylcholine at a central nervous synapse (p. 630), the transmitter substance is present in synaptic vesicles at the nerve ending. Some spontaneous discharge of transmitter substance into the synaptic gap normally occurs, but the rate of release of the vesicles is greatly enhanced by the arrival of the nerve impulse (Usherwood, 1974).

As in a nerve, there is a difference in electrical potential across the muscle membrane so that it has a resting potential of 30-70 mV, the inside being negative with respect to the outside. Since the magnitude of the potential is not always what would be expected from the ionic concentrations in the muscle and the surrounding haemolymph, it is possible that the fluid in the tubules of the T-system, rather than the haemolymph in general, determines the size of the potential and that its composition differs from that of the haemolymph (Piek, 1975). The arrival of the excitatory transmitter substance at the postsynaptic membrane on the muscle surface causes a change in permeability leading to an influx of sodium ions and a rise (that is a depolarisation) in the muscle membrane potential. Subsequently an increase in the permeability to potassium ions leads to their movement out from the muscle and so the potential falls to its original level (p. 627). The short-lived increase in potential produced by these changes is called the postsynaptic potential and it is suggested that changes in the relative permeability to sodium and potassium determine its size (Hoyle, 1974). The postsynaptic potential spreads from the synapse but decreases rapidly; its effect is therefore localised and in order to stimulate the whole fibre a large number of nerve endings are necessary.

It is probable that the invaginations of the T-system convey the changes in potential deep into the muscle and close to the fibrils. This is important since activation of the fibrils involves chemical transmission within the fibres and the diffusion of a chemical from the surface membrane to the central fibrils would involve a considerable delay in contraction. The T-system greatly reduces this delay by bringing the plasma membrane to within a few microns of each fibril.

12.2.2 Activation of the muscle fibre

Activation of the contractile mechanism involves the release of calcium from the sarcoplasmic reticulum and it is presumed that this occurs where the T-system and sarcoplasmic reticulum form dyads. The calcium binds to both the actin and the myosin filaments (Lehman, 1977) and its effect is to activate an ATPase in the myofilaments. In the resting muscle this activity is inhibited by a protein, called troponin B, in the actin filament, but in the presence of Ca^{++} ions the inhibition is removed; other proteins, troponin A and tropomyosin, are also involved in this process (Aidley, 1975).

The effect of the ATPase is to break down ATP to ADP with the release of energy which is used in muscle contraction. It is believed that the actin and myosin filaments first become linked together by the cross-bridges and that movement of these links with subsequent breaking and recombination causes the actin filaments to slide further between the myosin filaments so that the sarcomere, and hence the muscle, shortens (see Huxley and Hanson, 1960, and Huxley and Huxley, 1964, for discussion of the possible mechanisms of movement). Relaxation of the muscle possibly involves the sequestration of calcium ions so that ATPase activity is suppressed. Each cycle of contraction and relaxation of the muscle is associated with calcium release and sequestration.

In fibrillar muscle the picture is rather different. The muscles start to contract in response to a burst of motor nerve impulses, which presumably results in the release of Ca^{++} ions from the sarcoplasmic reticulum. However, subsequent muscle oscillations are not related directly to nervous stimulation (p. 261) and occur at a constant concentration of calcium within the fibre. After the initial activation, the muscle is maintained in an active state by rapid changes in length and tension which result from the mechanical properties of the muscle itself and the resonant characteristics of the thorax (p. 262, and Pringle, 1977; Tregear, 1975).

12.2.3 Changes in muscle banding during shortening

As a result of the sliding of the filaments during muscle contraction the I bands shorten and may disappear as the myosin approaches the Z-lines (Fig. 165). Hence the length of the I band in relaxed muscle is roughly proportional to the degree of shortening which the sarcomere can undergo. Some muscles may shorten by as much as 50% of their length, while flight muscles may shorten by as little as 1%.

As the I band is obliterated by the myosin filaments the H band also disappears as the ends of the actin filaments approach each other (Fig. 165). Ultimately the actin filaments from the two ends of a sarcomere may come to overlap each other so that another dark band, C_m, forms. Extreme contractions may cause crumpling of the myosin filaments at the Z-line so that a dark band, C_z, is formed.

Some visceral muscles have the capacity of supercontraction, the sarcomeres

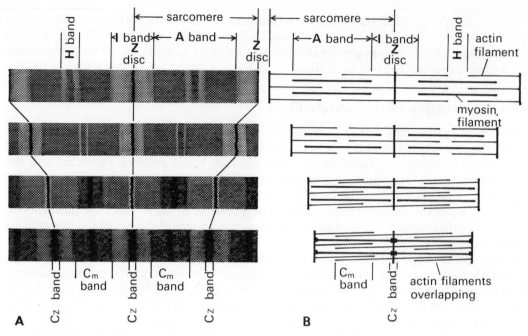

Fig. 165 A. The appearance of a muscle fibre in various states of contraction. B. Diagrams showing the presumed arrangement of the muscle filaments in positions corresponding to (A) (after Smith, 1965)

shortening by more than half their length. In these muscles the myosin filaments pass through pores in the Z-line so that they project into the adjacent sarcomeres (Fig. 166). This may be made possible by the cross-bridges on a myosin filament linking with the actin filaments of the next sarcomere as it passes through the Z-line pores (Osborne, 1967).

12.2.4 Inhibition of muscle contraction

In addition to the normal excitatory innervation, some fibres of some muscles have an inhibitory nerve supply. Inhibitory axons are known to run to some leg muscles in locusts and cockroach.

At an inhibitory nerve/muscle junction a neural transmitter, probably γ-amino-butyric acid (GABA), is released and causes a change in permeability at the postsynaptic membrane, but, unlike the process occurring at an excitatory synapse, this results in an influx of chloride ions. As a result the membrane potential becomes even more negative, the membrane is hyperpolarised, and the tension exerted by the fibre decreases (Hoyle, 1974; Usherwood, 1974).

12.2.5 Control of visceral muscles

In visceral muscles which are innervated the principles of muscle control are the same as in skeletal muscles. L-glutamate may be involved as a neurotransmitter, but it is

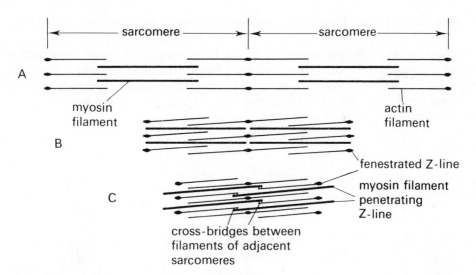

Fig. 166 Diagrammatic representation of the probable mechanism of supercontraction in a visceral muscle. A. Fully relaxed muscle; B. Partially contracted; C. Supercontracted (after Osborne, 1967)

conceivable that different transmitters are involved in different muscles (Usherwood, 1974). Axons containing neurosecretory material are known to be associated with various visceral muscles in a number of insects (Miller, 1975) and it is possible that these muscles are controlled via the neurosecretory system.

There is no clear picture of how the activity of muscles which have no innervation is controlled (p. 794).

12.3 Patterns of muscular contraction

Insects have only small numbers of fibres as motor units in their muscles compared with vertebrates. Consequently precision and flexibility of movement is achieved not by employing different numbers of fibres but by changes in the strengths of contraction of individual fibres. This fine control is effected through the polyneuronal innervation of the muscles (p. 247). Stimulation via the different axons effects contraction in different ways and interaction between these inputs gives a very high degree of flexibility.

Most behavioural activities result from the co-ordinated activity of sets of muscles. This is most obvious in locomotion which involves the oscillation of an appendage such as a leg or a wing and the control of some of these movements is described.

12.3.1 Fast and slow axons

The size of the muscle twitch produced by the arrival of an excitatory nerve impulse varies depending on whether stimulation occurs via the fast or slow axons. It must be understood that the terms 'fast' and 'slow' do not refer to the speed of conduction of the impulse, but to the size of postsynaptic potential, and hence muscle twitch, that is produced. It is probable that the difference resides in the amount of neurotransmitter released at the nerve/muscle junction following the arrival of the impulse (Usherwood, 1974).

Stimulation via the fast axon releases a large amount of neurotransmitter and produces a postsynaptic potential of constant size with a brief, powerful contraction of the muscle (Fig. 167A). Contractions tend to fuse if the rate of stimulation exceeds 10 per second and with 20–25 stimuli per second the muscle undergoes a smooth, maintained contraction: it is in a state of tetanus.

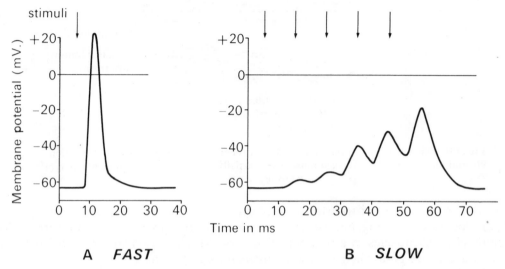

Fig. 167 Electrical changes at the muscle membrane following stimulation by (A) fast and (B) slow axons (after Hoyle, 1974)

A single impulse from the slow axon, on the other hand, releases a small amount of neurotransmitter and produces only a small postsynaptic potential followed by a very small twitch. With increasing frequency of impulses the velocity and force with which the muscle contracts increases progressively and the response is said to be graded (Fig. 167B). In the extensor tibiae muscles of the locust, for instance, less than five impulses per second produce no response in the muscle, 15–20 impulses per second produce muscle tonus, and stimulation by over 70 impulses per second produces rapid extension of the tibia. The speed of response increases up to an impulse frequency of 150 per second.

12.3.2 Muscular control in the intact insect

Very little information is available about the manner in which muscular control is achieved in the intact insect. Some indication of the variability and complexity of the control systems is apparent from studies on the use of the coxal muscles of *Periplaneta* during walking (Iles and Pearson, 1971; Pearson, 1972; Pearson and Iles, 1971). Each of the meso- and metathoracic coxae has four depressor muscles (Fig. 168). Two of these (136 and 137) are innervated only by a fast axon which also goes to parts of the other two muscles (135d′, e′). These parts are also innervated by a slow axon and this also supplies parts of the muscle (135d and e) which have no fast nerve supply. The muscle

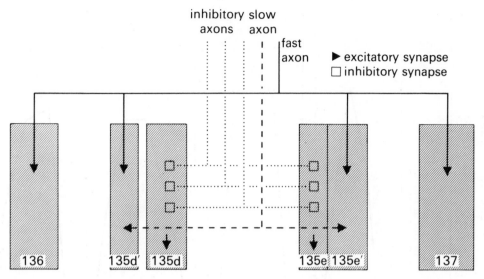

Fig. 168 Diagrammatic representation of the motorneurones to the mesothoracic coxal depressor muscles of *Periplaneta*. Muscle units are numbered as in text (after Pearson and Iles, 1971)

fibres in these parts also receive inhibitory axons, one of which goes to most of the fibres, the distribution of the others being more restricted.

During slow walking only the slow axon is active and so only the muscles numbered 135 are active in coxal depression, and the strength and speed of contraction depends on the frequency of nerve firing. When the coxa is moved at more than 10 cycles per second the activity of the slow axon is reinforced by activity of the fast axon, which also brings in muscles 136 and 137. It is presumed that the inhibitory axons fire at the end of contraction and so ensure complete and rapid relaxation as the antagonistic muscle contracts. The presence of three separate inhibitors, perhaps innervating different fibres in the muscles, gives increased flexibility to the system, but the situation is complicated by the fact that they also innervate other muscles.

The control of muscle activity in jumping by the locust and the control of stridulation in grasshoppers provide other examples of the interaction between fast, slow and inhibitory axons (Figs. 100, 448) (and see Hoyle, 1975).

When only a fast axon is present some grading of the strength of contractions is produced by impulses following each other in rapid succession. This occurs, for instance, in the double firing of the axon to the second basalar muscle of *Schistocerca* (p. 232), which may result in the muscle more than doubling the amount of work which it does. The extra force exerted varies with the timing of the second impulse relative to the first and in the basalar muscle at 40°C the force is maximal when the second stimulus follows about 8 ms after the first (Neville and Weis-Fogh, 1963).

12.3.3 Oscillation of antagonistic pairs of muscles

Skeletal muscles usually occur in antagonistic pairs, *e.g.* the extensor and flexor muscles of the tibia. Commonly these muscles are mutually inhibited by a central

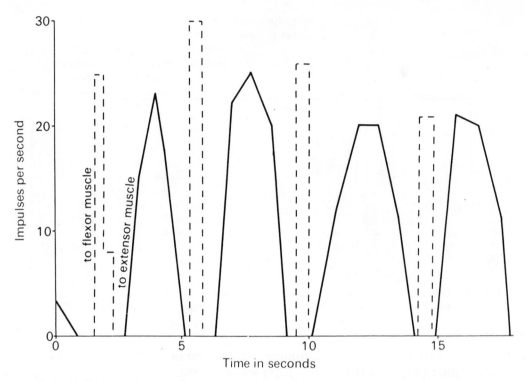

Fig. 169 Diagram showing the frequency of firing from the slow axons to the extensor and flexor tibiae muscles of the hind leg of *Schistocerca* during slow walking. There is complete reciprocal inhibition of the two muscles (after Hoyle, 1964)

control so that as one contracts the other relaxes and *vice versa* (Fig. 169), but sometimes in faster movements one muscle may be maintained in a continual state of mild contraction, while the other alternately contracts and relaxes so that the appendage is moved (Fig. 170). In this case either the flexor or the extensor may act as the driver (Hoyle, 1964). This mechanism may increase the speed at which repeated movements can occur since the continually contracting antagonist helps to restore the position of the limb rapidly on relaxation of the driver. Further, the driver itself does not relax fully in these circumstances, so a shorter time is needed for it to develop the necessary force on contraction than would be the case if it became fully relaxed (Hoyle, 1974).

Sometimes a muscle is opposed only by the elasticity of the cuticle. Thus depression of the pretarsus is produced by a muscle, but extension results entirely from the elasticity of the cuticle at the base of the segment.

12.3.4 Oscillation of flight muscles

The high wingbeat frequencies necessary for flight are produced by the rapid oscillation of pairs of antagonistic muscles (see Fig. 133) and this is achieved despite the relatively low rate of shortening of about 40 mm/s in *Schistocerca* and only 11 mm/s in *Sarcophaga*. Three factors combine to reduce the duration of the muscle twitch and so

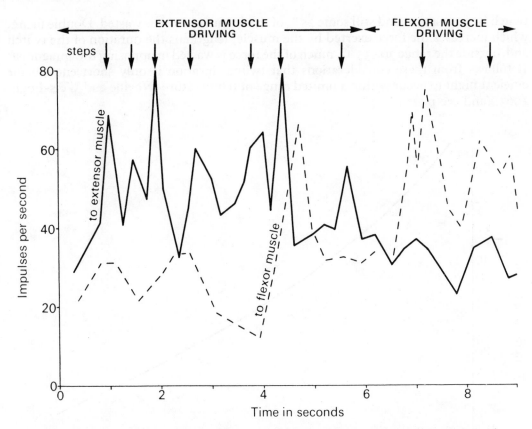

Fig. 170 Graph showing the frequency of firing from the slow axons to the extensor and flexor tibiae muscles of the hind leg of *Schistocerca* which sometimes occurs during fairly rapid walking. There is a continuous discharge to both muscles with first the extensor and then the flexor acting as the driver (after Hoyle, 1964)

to make flight possible; these are the loading of the muscle, the temperature of the muscle and the very slight contraction necessary to move the wing.

A maximum rate of shortening is achieved if the tension and loading of the muscle are maximal at the beginning of its stroke. Loading of the flight muscles involves the inertia of the wings, elastic loading due to the straining of the thorax (p. 219), the mechanical leverage of the wings, which changes in the course of a stroke, damping of the movement of the wings by the air, and elastic loading due to the stretching of the antagonistic muscle. The first three of these factors are high during the first part of the stroke and so a high rate of muscle contraction is favoured.

The duration of each muscle twitch is also influenced by temperature (Fig. 171). In *Schistocerca* contraction and relaxation of the metathoracic dorsal longitudinal muscle takes 59 ms at 22°C; a cycle of movement of the wings takes about the same time. Thus in flying at 22°C about 50 % of the work done by the metathoracic dorsal longitudinal muscle would be wasted due to interaction with the antagonistic muscle. It is therefore not surprising that sustained flight does not occur at such a temperature. Sustained flight is only observed above 24°C, at which temperature the duration of the muscle twitch is about 49 ms and still some 25 % of the output of work is wasted. Double firing, which increases the force exerted by the muscle, lengthens the duration of the twitch and, outside the range 30–35°C, much of the force is wasted in opposing the antagonist. It follows from these considerations that twitch duration is only short enough for efficient flight to occur within a limited range of temperature (Neville and Weis-Fogh, 1963) (and see p. 273).

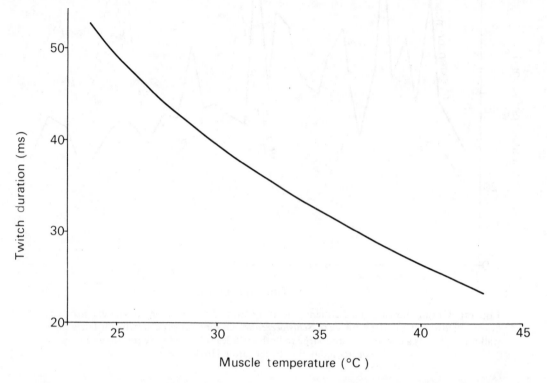

Fig. 171 The duration of single twitches of the flight muscle of *Schistocerca* at different temperatures (after Neville and Weis-Fogh, 1963)

Finally, the flight muscles are inserted in such a way (see Figs. 132, 133) that only a very small contraction is necessary to produce a large movement of the wing: the flight muscles of *Sarcophaga*, for instance, only shorten by 1 or 2 % in the course of a wingstroke. As a result the muscle twitch is brief despite the low rate of shortening.

Synchronous muscles

Each contraction of the flight muscles of Odonata, Orthoptera and Lepidoptera is produced by the arrival of a nerve impulse (Fig. 172A) and the muscles are described as synchronous. Most insect skeletal muscles are of this type. Usually the wingbeat frequency of insects with synchronous flight muscles is low, not more than about 25 beats/second, but in some instances it is much higher, reaching 100 Hz in *Hemaris*, the bee hawk moth.

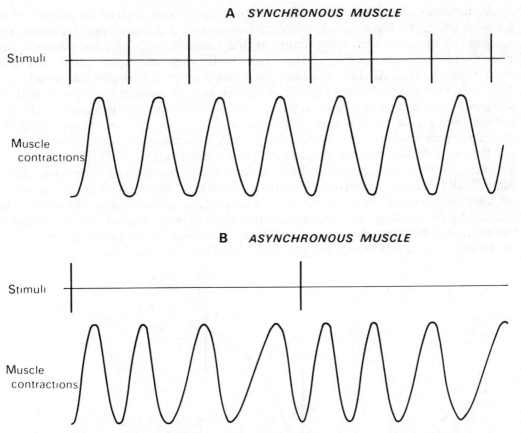

Fig. 172 Relationship between nervous stimulation and muscle contraction in (A) synchronous muscle and (B) asynchronous muscle, such as the tymbal muscle of *Platypleura*

Asynchronous muscles

In insects which possess fibrillar muscles the wingbeat frequency is often in excess of 100 Hz and it is a characteristic of these muscles that several contractions follow the arrival of each nerve impulse. The tymbal muscle of *Platypleura* (Homoptera) is also a fibrillar muscle and in this case four contractions follow one nerve impulse (Fig. 172 B). The frequency of contraction of the flight muscle of *Oryctes* is independent of the frequency of stimulation, which only affects the amplitude of the contraction. These muscles in which the ratio of contractions to stimuli differs from the normal 1 : 1 ratio are said to be asynchronous.

Asynchronous muscles can contract and relax at very high frequencies, but high frequency stimulation via the motor nerve causes them to contract tetanically. A nerve impulse is necessary to initiate contractions, but subsequent contractions are products of the muscles themselves and are said to be myogenic. Further nervous stimulation is necessary only to maintain the level of activity of the muscles, perhaps through the release of calcium from the vesicles of the reduced sarcoplasmic reticulum (Smith, 1965; and see p. 251).

Asynchronous muscles occur only in oscillating systems such as the thorax. Here the contraction of a flight muscle moves the wings and at the same time lengthens the antagonistic muscles. This lengthening at first takes place slowly, but occurs much more rapidly towards the end of the stroke if the wing movement involves a click mechanism (p. 219). At the same time the active muscle at first shortens slowly and then, following the click, very rapidly. These sudden changes in length will produce corresponding changes in tension in the muscle, a sudden increase in length produces a sudden increase in tension and *vice versa*, and it is an intrinsic property of the contractile proteins of fibrillar muscle that a sudden change in tension is followed, after a delay, by a further change (Fig. 173) (Jewell and Ruegg, 1966). Thus a sudden increase in tension due to stretching is followed by a further rise in tension, and a delayed fall follows a sudden drop in tension. Since the flight muscles are antagonists a decrease in tension in one corresponds to an increase in tension in the other. The increased tension acting on a pliant system will produce movement and as a result of this the muscles alternately contract and relax, the rate of oscillation being determined by the mechanical and elastic properties of the thorax and the muscles.

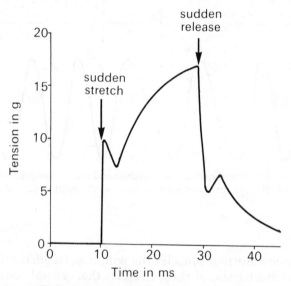

Fig. 173 The effect of sudden small changes of length on the tension developed by fibrillar muscle. Initial tension = 0 (from Pringle, 1965)

The precise relationship between muscle length and tension varies with the temperature, and the muscles of *Oryctes*, for instance, only produce maximum work at the resonant frequency of the system when they are at 40°C. Thus the thoracic temperature is of considerable importance in insects with asynchronous flight muscles and this accounts for the period of warming up by muscular activity (p. 274) which commonly precedes flight.

12.4 Energetics of muscle contraction

The tension exerted by insect muscles is not exceptional. For instance, the mandibular muscles of various insects exert tensions of 3·6–6·9 g/cm², and the extensor tibiae muscle of *Decticus* (Orthoptera) 5·9 g/cm² compared with the values of 6–10 g/cm² in man. The force exerted by a muscles is proportional to its cross-sectional area and, in general, this is not very great in insects, but in some muscles, such as the extensor tibiae of a locust, a considerable cross-sectional area is achieved by an oblique insertion of the muscle fibres into an apodeme (see Fig. 98A). As a result, this muscle can exert a force of up to 15 N (1·5 kg/m/s²).

Flight demands a great deal of power to lift the insect off the ground and drive it forwards. The forces exerted by flight muscles are in no way unusual, but the high power output is achieved by their high frequencies of contraction.

Because of chemical and mechanical inefficiencies only a small proportion of the energy expended by the muscles is effectively available. About 80% of the energy consumed by the muscles is wasted as heat, and of the mechanical work performed by the muscles only about one half may be aerodynamically useful. Consequently only 5–10% of the energy consumed by the flight muscles contributes to flight and their energy consumption is correspondingly large to make good the deficiency.

The metabolic rates of insects in flight are often 50–100 times higher than their resting rates and for most insects investigated fall between 12 and 60 W/N (Kammer and Heinrich, 1978). This compares with rates of 1–4 W/N in active small mammals and 24 W/N in hummingbirds. Calculations of the power expended on lift range from about 0·8 W/N for *Schistocerca* in forward flight to 2·3 W/N in *Drosophila* and 3·9 W/N in *Bombus* (Hymenoptera) while hovering (Weis-Fogh, 1976). Hovering requires a greater output of energy because the insect is not assisted by the aerodynamic forces which normally act on it by virtue of its forward momentum.

12.4.1 Fuels for flight

The fuels providing energy for flight vary in different insects. Hymenoptera and Diptera commonly use carbohydrates; locusts, aphids and migratory Lepidoptera depend mainly on fats but use carbohydrates during the early stages of flight; and some Diptera and possibly Coleoptera use amino acids. Initially fuel reserves within the flight muscles themselves are utilised, but these are limited and further supplies of fuel are drawn from elsewhere.

Carbohydrates

Trehalose in the haemolymph forms an important carbohydrate reserve in many insects (p. 103), although in *Apis* glucose is more important. Glycogen in the fat body is withdrawn during flight by *Drosophila* and *Culex* (Diptera), while sugars in the crop of *Tabanus* (Diptera) and the honey stomach of *Apis* are sources of fuel in these insects. In general all these carbohydrates are transported in the blood as trehalose.

During flight by *Calliphora* trehalose is maintained at a more or less constant level in the haemolymph by release from the fat body (and see Fig. 56). By contrast, the trehalose content of the haemolymph of *Locusta* falls rapidly during the first 20–30 minutes of flight and then reaches a stable level (Fig. 174). At this time the insect switches to fat as its main fuel and the rate of utilisation of carbohydrate drops from about 120 μg/min to 10 μg/min (Jutsum and Goldsworthy, 1976). In *Calliphora* the production of trehalose from the fat body is controlled by a hyperglycaemic hormone released from the corpora cardiaca.

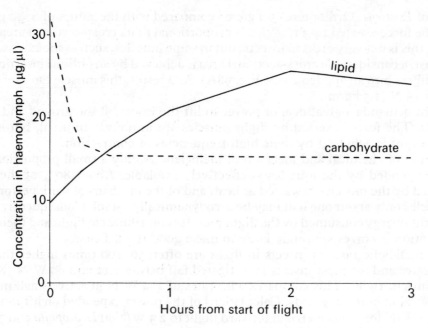

Fig. 174 Changes in the concentrations of carbohydrates and lipids in the haemolymph of *Locusta* in the course of flight (after Jutsum and Goldsworthy, 1976)

The very rapid oxidation of carbohydrate in insect flight muscle demands a special mechanism. Glycolysis (p. 111) occurs in the extramitochondrial cytoplasm and the first oxidation reaction to occur is the removal of hydrogen from glyceraldehyde phosphate and its transfer to nicotinamide adenine dinucleotide (NAD). The supply of NAD is limited, so the reduced form (NADH$_2$) must be reoxidised as quickly as possible, but in the process the hydrogen must be transferred to the mitochondria in which the cytochrome system is housed. A cytoplasmic α-glycerophosphate de-hydrogenase appears to be particularly important in this reaction, catalysing the oxidation of NADH$_2$ by dihydroxyacetone phosphate to produce NAD and α-glycerophosphate, which now contains the hydrogen. The α-glycerophosphate passes into the mitochondria and is then oxidised, giving up the hydrogen to the cytochrome system and reforming dihydroxyacetone phosphate, which is thus made available for further oxidation of the extramitochondrial NADH$_2$ (see diagram, p. 115). The oxidation of α-glycerophosphate proceeds at a very high rate, more than ten times as fast as with most other substrates, and there is a correspondingly high rate of transfer of hydrogen to the cytochrome system. This mechanism is believed to account for the greater part of the oxygen uptake during the first part of flight, but subsequently the importance of α-glycerophosphate may be reduced, perhaps because the availability of phosphate is limited since it is employed in the phosphorylation of ADP. In this case NADH$_2$ is oxidised by a malic dehydrogenase and oxidation in the citric acid cycle becomes more important.

High levels of α-glycerophosphate dehydrogenase do not occur in all the insects examined, but in most cases the activity is higher in flight muscle than in leg muscle

(Table 3). The highest levels occur in those insects which use carbohydrate as the principal fuel.

Table 3

Relative activity of α-glycerophosphate dehydrogenase in flight and leg muscles of different insects. Activity in rat skeletal muscle = 1
(after Sacktor, 1974)

Insect	Flight muscle	Leg muscle
Locust	3·3	0·7
Cockroach	1·0	0·6
Mantis	0·2	0·02
Waterbug	1·0	0·3
Blowfly	24·6	—
Bee	14·0	—
Cockchafer	2·1	—
Hawk moth	0·7	—

Lipids

Fat is more suitable than carbohydrate as a reserve for insects which make long flights because it produces twice as much energy per unit weight. Thus a gram of fat yields 39 000 J, but a gram of carbohydrate yields only 17 000 J, while glycogen, a common carbohydrate reserve, is strongly hydrated so that it is eight times heavier than isocaloric amounts of fat. Thus an insect can store large amounts of energy more readily as fat and 85 % of the energy stored by the locust is in this form (Weis-Fogh, 1952). Fat has the further possible advantage over carbohydrate that it produces approximately twice as much water on combustion so the effects of water loss during prolonged flight may be offset.

Fats are stored in the fat body, usually as triglycerides, but they are released into the haemolymph as diglycerides and transported as lipoprotein. In locusts their release into the haemolymph is apparent within 5 minutes of the start of flight and the concentration more than doubles. This release is initiated by the adipokinetic hormone from the glandular lobes of the corpora cardiaca (Jutsum and Goldsworthy, 1976). The same hormone may also act on the flight muscles causing them to utilise lipids instead of carbohydrates (Robinson and Goldsworthy, 1977).

The high concentration of lipid in the haemolymph probably speeds up diffusion into the flight muscles. Within the mitochondria the fats enter the tricarboxylic acid cycle as acetyl-coenzyme A (p. 108) condensing with oxaloacetate to form citrate. In locust muscle the condensing enzyme catalysing this reaction is 130 times more active than the same enzyme in frog gastrocnemius muscle and so a ready supply of substrate for oxidation is maintained (see Neville, 1965).

Amino acids

Oxidation of amino acids may occur to a minor extent in the flight muscle of most insects, but in a few species amino acids provide the major fuel for flight. The most completely studied example is *Glossina* (Diptera) (see Bursell, 1975). In this insect proline is the primary fuel for flight, but the initial reserve of proline is small, sufficient to last for about two minutes while flight can continue for up to eight minutes. The enzyme systems of the flight muscle mitochondria are not sufficiently well developed to use carbohydrates, lipids or other amino acids efficiently and it is probable that proline is synthesised during flight. Proline is first converted to glutamate, which then undergoes transamination with pyruvate to produce alanine and α-ketoglutarate. The latter enters the tricarboxylic acid cycle while the former could provide a substrate for the resynthesis of proline (Hargrove, 1976).

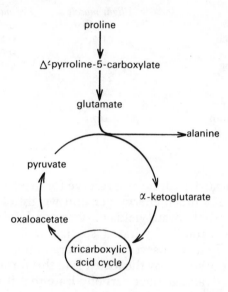

Utilisation of proline may be an adaptation to blood-sucking, since in other blood-sucking flies the rate at which mitochondria oxidise proline is greater than in most other species. However, the phytophagous beetle *Leptinotarsa* also uses proline as a fuel in flight.

12.4.2 Control of metabolism in flight

The nerve impulse which initiates contraction of the flight muscles activates the fibrillar ATPase by the release of Ca^{++} from the sarcoplasmic reticulum. This calcium also promotes the breakdown of glycogen stored in the muscle and the activity of the enzyme glycerol-3-phosphate dehydrogenase (GPDH), one of the enzymes involved in the α-glycerophosphate shuttle. As a consequence, utilisation of carbohydrate proceeds at a fast rate (Fig. 175) (see Sacktor, 1970).

In locusts and some other insects information from the brain leads to the release of adipokinetic hormone from the corpora cardiaca, but this release is inhibited if the carbohydrate concentration in the haemolymph is high. The hormone causes the release of diglycerides from the fat body and these are transported in the haemolymph to the muscles. At the same time, it is suggested that the hormone affects the enzyme

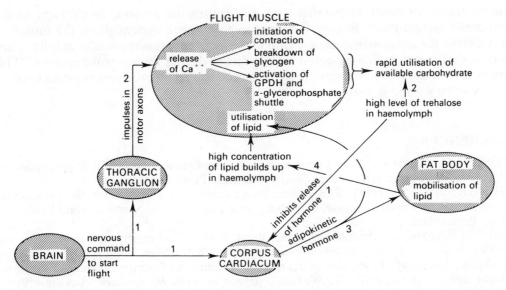

Fig. 175 Diagram of the mechanisms involved in the mobilisation and utilisation of fuel in an insect using at first carbohydrate and then lipid as the main source of energy during flight

system of the muscles so that the utilisation of lipid is favoured (Jutsum and Goldsworthy, 1976).

12.4.3 Oxygen supply

During flight insects incur little or no oxygen debt (p. 116) and rates of oxygen consumption are very high. The locust flight muscles, for instance, use some 80 litres O_2/kg/h and for other insects consumption may exceed 400 litres O_2/kg/h. The special adaptations of the thoracic tracheal system enable these demands to be met. In the locust, pterothoracic ventilation produces a supply well in excess of the needs, and the specialised system of tracheae and tracheoles in the muscles (p. 534) ensures that the oxygen reaches the site of consumption. Other than in Odonata and blattids, tracheoles indent the flight muscle fibres and approach very close to the mitochondria so that tissue diffusion is reduced to a minimum. It is calculated that the muscles have a safety factor of two or three with respect to their oxygen supply.

In Odonata and blattids, on the other hand, tracheoles remain superficial to the muscle fibres and these fibres, with a radius of about 10 μm are believed to be approaching the limiting size for the efficient diffusion of oxygen in sufficient quantities (Weis-Fogh, 1964).

12.4.4 Elasticity of muscle

Not all the energy used during muscle contraction need be derived directly from the combustion of fuels; energy may be stored in elastic elements of flight muscle. Flight muscles, and especially fibrillar muscles, have a much higher elasticity than other muscles. Some of this elasticity is attributed to the sarcolemma, but the greater part is due to elastic elements in parallel with the contractile system, or perhaps to the contractile system itself. Energy is stored in this elastic system when the muscle is stretched by the antagonistic muscle and, in the locust depressor muscles at least, when work is done on the wing by aerodynamic forces during the upstroke (p. 219). This energy is then used when the muscle shortens and as a result much energy which would otherwise be wasted is used.

REFERENCES

AIDLEY, D. J. (1975). Excitation–contraction coupling and mechanical properties. *in* Usherwood, P. N. R. (ed.), *Insect muscle*. Academic Press, London.

ASHHURST, D. E. (1977). The Z-line: its structure and evidence for the presence of connecting filaments. *in* Tregear, R. T. (ed.), *Insect flight muscle*. North-Holland Publishing Co., Amsterdam.

BAILEY, E. (1975). Biochemistry of insect flight. Part 2. Fuel supply. *in* Candy, D. J. and Kilby, B. A. (eds.), *Insect biochemistry and function*. Wiley, New York.

BÜCHER, Th. (1965). Formation of the specific structural and enzymic pattern of the insect flight muscle. *in* Goodwin, T. W. (ed.), *Aspects of insect biochemistry*. Academic Press, London.

BURSELL, E. (1975). Substrates of oxidative metabolism in dipteran flight muscle. *Comp. Biochem. Physiol.* **52**: 235–238.

CAVENEY, S. (1969). Muscle attachment related to cuticle architecture in Apterygota. *J. Cell Sci.* **4**: 541–559.

EBASHI, S. (1972). Calcium ions and muscle contraction. *Nature, Lond.* **240**: 217–218.

ELDER, H. Y. (1975). Muscle structure. *in* Usherwood, P. N. R. (ed.), *Insect muscle*. Academic Press, London.

HARGROVE, J. W. (1976). Amino acid metabolism during flight in tsetse flies. *J. Insect Physiol.* **22**: 309–313.

HINTON, H. E. (1963). The origin and function of the pupal stage. *Proc. R. ent. Soc. Lond.* A, **38**: 77–85.

HOYLE, G. (1964). Exploration of neuronal mechanisms underlying behaviour in insects. *in* Reiss, R. F. (ed.), *Neural theory and modeling*. Stanford University Press.

HOYLE, G. (1974). Neural control of skeletal muscle. *in* Rockstein, M. (ed.), *The physiology of Insecta*. vol. 4. Academic Press, New York.

HOYLE, G. (1975). The neural control of skeletal muscles. *in* Usherwood, P. N. R. (ed.), *Insect muscle*. Academic Press, London.

HUXLEY, H. E. (1965). The mechanism of muscular contraction. *Scient. Am.* **213**, no. 6: 18–27.

HUXLEY, H. E. and HANSON, J. (1960). The molecular basis of contraction in cross-striated muscles. *in* Bourne, G. H. (ed.), *The structure and function of muscle*. vol. 1. Academic Press, London.

HUXLEY, A. F. and HUXLEY, H. E. (1964). A discussion on the physical and chemical basis of muscular contraction. *Proc. R. Soc.* B, **160**: 434–542.

IKEDA, K. and BOETTIGER, E. G. (1965). Studies on the flight mechanism of insects.—III. The innervation and electrical activity of the basalar fibrillar flight muscle of the beetle, *Oryctes rhinoceros. J. Insect Physiol.* **11**: 791–802.

ILES, J. F. and PEARSON, K. G. (1971). Coxal depressor muscles of the cockroach and the role of peripheral inhibition. *J. exp. Biol.* **55**: 151–164.

JEWELL, B. R. and RÜEGG, J. C. (1966). Oscillatory contraction of insect fibrillar muscle after glycerol extraction. *Proc. R. Soc.* B, **164**: 428–459.

JUTSUM, A. R. and GOLDSWORTHY, G. J. (1976). Fuels for flight in *Locusta*. *J. Insect Physiol*. **22**: 243–249.

KAMMER, A. E. and HEINRICH, B. (1978). Insect flight metabolism. *Adv. Insect Physiol*. **13**: 133–228.

LAI-FOOK, J. (1967). The structure of developing muscle insertions in insects. *J. Morph*. **123**: 503–528.

LEHMAN, W. (1977). The dual system of calcium-activation in arthropod muscles. *in* Tregear, R. T. (ed.), *Insect flight muscle*. North-Holland Publishing Co., Amsterdam.

MILLER, T. A. (1975). Insect visceral muscles. *in* Usherwood, P. N. R. (ed.), *Insect muscle*. Academic Press, London.

NEVILLE, A. C. (1965). Energy and economy in insect flight. *Sci. Prog., Lond*. **53**: 203–220.

NEVILLE, A. C. and WEIS-FOGH, T. (1963). The effect of temperature on locust flight muscle. *J. exp. Biol*. **40**: 111–121.

OSBORNE, M. P. (1967). Supercontraction in the muscles of the blowfly larva: an ultrastructural study. *J. Insect Physiol*. **13**: 1471–1482.

PEARSON, K. G. (1972). Central programming and reflex control of walking in the cockroach. *J. exp. Biol*. **56**: 173–193.

PEARSON, K. G. and ILES, J. F. (1971). Innervation of coxal depressor muscles in the cockroach, *Periplaneta americana*. *J. exp. Biol*. **54**: 215–232.

PIEK, T. (1975). Ionic and electrical properties. *in* Usherwood, P. N. R. (ed.), *Insect Muscle*. Academic Press, London.

PRINGLE, J. W. S. (1965). Locomotion: flight. *in* Rockstein, M. (ed.), *The physiology of Insecta*. vol. 2. Academic Press, New York.

PRINGLE, J. W. S. (1977). The mechanical characteristics of insect fibrillar muscle. *in* Tregear, R. T. (ed.), *Insect flight muscle*. North-Holland Publishing Co., Amsterdam.

ROBINSON, N. L. and GOLDSWORTHY, G. J. (1977). A possible site of action for adipokinetic hormone on the flight muscle of locusts. *J. Insect Physiol*. **23**: 153–158.

ROCKSTEIN, M. and BHATNAGAR, P. L. (1965). Age changes in size and number of the giant mitochondria in the flight muscle of the common housefly (*Musca domestica* L.). *J. Insect Physiol*. **11**: 481–491.

SACKTOR, B. (1970). Regulation of intermediary metabolism, with special reference to the control mechanisms, in insect flight muscle. *Adv. Insect Physiol*. **7**: 267–347.

SACKTOR, B. (1974). Biological oxidations and energetics in insect mitochondria. *in* Rockstein, M. (ed.), *The physiology of Insecta*. vol. 4. Academic Press, New York.

SACKTOR, B. (1975). Biochemistry of insect flight. Part I. Utilization of fuels by muscle. *in* Candy, D. J. and Kilby, B. A. (eds.), *Insect biochemistry and function*. Wiley, New York.

SMITH, D. S. (1961). The structure of insect fibrillar flight muscle. *J. biophys. biochem. Cytol*. **10**, suppl. 123–158.

SMITH, D. S. (1965). The organisation of flight muscle in an aphid, *Megoura viciae* (Homoptera). With a discussion of the structure of synchronous and asynchronous striated muscle fibres. *J. Cell Biol*. **27**: 379–393.

SMITH, D. S., GUPTA, B. L. and SMITH, U. (1966). The organization and myofilament array of insect visceral muscles. *J. Cell Sci*. **1**: 49–57.

SQUIRE, J. M. (1977). The structure of insect thick filaments. *in* Tregear, R. T. (ed.), *Insect flight muscle*. North-Holland Publishing Co., Amsterdam.

TREGEAR, R. T. (1975). The biophysics of fibrillar flight muscle. *in* Usherwood, P. N. R. (ed.), *Insect muscle*. Academic Press, London.

TREGEAR, R. T. (1977). *Insect flight muscle*. North-Holland Publishing Co., Amsterdam.

USHERWOOD, P. N. R. (1969). Electrochemistry of insect muscle. *Adv. Insect Physiol*. **6**: 205–278.

USHERWOOD, P. N. R. (1974). Nerve-muscle transmission. *in* Treherne, J. E. (ed.), *Insect neurobiology*. North-Holland Publishing Co., Amsterdam.

USHERWOOD, P. N. R. (1975). *Insect muscle*. Academic Press, London.

USHERWOOD, P. N. R. and CULL-CANDY, S. G. (1975). Pharmacology of somatic nerve-muscle synapses. *in* Usherwood, P. N. R. (ed.), *Insect Muscle*. Academic Press, London.

WEIS-FOGH, T. (1952). Fat combustion and metabolic rate of flying locusts (*Schistocerca gregaria* Forskål). *Phil. Trans. R. Soc.* B, **237**: 1-36.

WEIS-FOGH, T. (1964). Diffusion in insect wing muscle, the most active tissue known. *J. exp. Biol.* **41**: 229-256.

WEIS-FOGH, T. (1976). Energetics and aerodynamics of flapping flight: a synthesis. *Symp. R. ent. Soc. Lond.* **7**: 48-72.

WILSON, D. M. (1962). Bifunctional muscles in the thorax of grasshoppers. *J. exp. Biol.* **39**: 669-677.

CHAPTER XIII
FLIGHT ACTIVITY

The mechanisms by which insects fly have been discussed in the previous chapters (Chapters X, XI and XII); in this chapter the functions of flight and the factors limiting and stimulating flight activity are considered. For physiological reasons flight only occurs under particular conditions, being limited by factors of the external and internal environment. The functioning of the flight muscles is particularly important in this respect and for these to work properly body temperature must be sufficiently high. Often the flight muscles are not fully developed until some time after emergence and during this period of development flight activity is restricted. Even when conditions are favourable for flight, insects do not necessarily fly unless they are stimulated to take off. Many external factors may promote take-off and it is probable that sometimes internal factors are responsible. Once in flight various stimuli will induce an insect to land, the precise stimuli depending on the habits and behaviour of the insect.

Flight activity may be concerned with routine behaviour such as feeding and reproduction, or it may take the form of a dispersal flight or migration from the habitat, during which these other activities are suppressed. The direction of migration is controlled by the insect in some cases, but where the insects fly in winds whose speed exceeds their own speed through the air, direction is determined mainly by the wind. Return migrations sometimes occur, the return movement occasionally being made by the original migrants, but in other cases by members of a later generation. The distances flown vary from a few metres to thousands of kilometres, but in general the function of migratory flights is the same, the invasion of new habitats.

Major publications on flight and migration are those of Dingle (1978), C. Johnson (1969) and Rainey (1976).

13.1 Factors limiting flight activity

Flight only occurs within a limited range of conditions, being inhibited by various external and internal factors, the external factors presumably acting through the peripheral sensilla. These factors are separated below, but it must be remembered that the insect responds to the whole complex of its environment, external and internal, although at various times different factors may become dominant.

13.1.1 External limiting factors

Light

The flight activity of many insects is limited by light intensity and Lewis and Taylor (1965) conclude that this is the major factor controlling times of flight. For instance, many day-flying insects, such as butterflies and Hymenoptera, are not active in the dark and aphids will not take off when the intensity falls below 200 lux. On the other hand, many Orthoptera, moths, Neuroptera, Trichoptera and Nematocera are essentially nocturnal and do not fly when it is light. In some instances these differences in behaviour are known to be coupled with morphological and physiological adaptations, as in the eyes of Lepidoptera (p. 646), and probably can be correlated with the development of different senses. Thus day-flying predators and flower- and leaf-eating insects rely to a large extent on sight, while crepuscular and nocturnal forms depend largely on scent to find their food or a mate (p. 859).

Wind-speed

Most insects tend to fly only when the wind-speed is relatively low and if the wind-speed is high over long periods flight occurs mainly during lulls (Fig. 176). It appears in part that take-off is inhibited by high winds, although after a time aphids will take off in spite of the wind (p. 279). In addition, insects in flight tend to land when the wind-speed increases and this behaviour probably involves an optomotor reaction (p. 667). If the insect is flying high above the ground, however, it may be unable to distinguish the pattern of features on the ground or their images may move so slowly over the eye that they do not evoke a response from the insect. In these circumstances wind-speed is unlikely to be limiting and the insects will remain airborne in the highest winds (Kennedy, 1951).

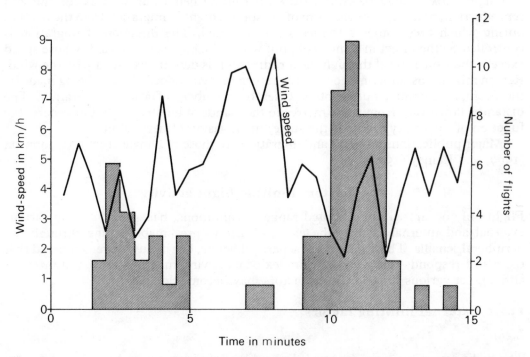

Fig. 176 The number of *Nomadacris* seen flying in successive half-minutes in relation to wind-speed (after Chapman, 1959a)

Humidity

It is doubtful if flight is ever completely inhibited, in the sense that it is physically impossible, by the humidity of the environment, but in some cases there is a correlation between humidity and the continuity of flight. In laboratory experiments the longest flights made by *Schistocerca* occur at high humidities (Weis-Fogh, 1952) and field observations on both *Schistocerca* and *Nomadacris* also suggest that the most continuous flight is observed at high humidities (Chapman, 1959a; Waloff, 1953). The flight of *Aphis*, however, is not shortened at low humidities.

Temperature

Environmental temperature is of the greatest importance as a factor limiting flight, but since it exerts its effect largely through the body temperature of the insect it is considered with other internal limiting factors.

13.1.2 Internal limiting factors

Temperature

The body temperature of an insect is of overriding importance in limiting flight and all insects have a minimum body temperature below which flight is quite impossible. Figure 177 shows the percentage of field observations at various air temperatures

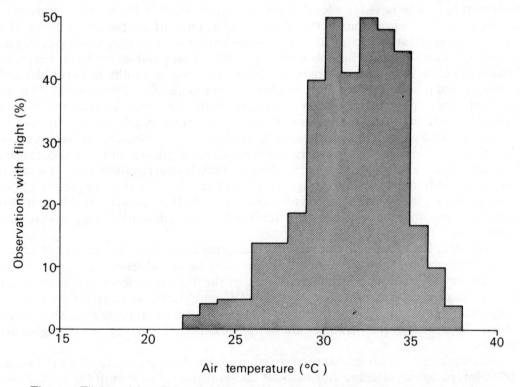

Fig. 177 Flight activity of *Nomadacris* in relation to air temperature (after Chapman, 1959a)

during which *Nomadacris* is observed in flight. Very occasional short spontaneous flights are also observed at 19°C. The limiting air temperatures for flight are therefore about 19°C and 38°C, with peak flight activity between 29° and 35°C. Comparable ranges are known for other insects and in the laboratory the lowest air temperature at which *Schistocerca* flies for any length of time is 22°C; no sustained flight occurs above 38°C (Weis-Fogh, 1956). It is probable that at the lower temperatures quoted, body temperature is much the same as air temperature, but at higher temperatures the insects are probably several degrees hotter than the figures given because their temperature is raised by radiation from the sun and by muscular activity.

In *Culex* the minimum air temperature for flight is 15°C, but the Arctic *Aedes punctor* can fly at 2.5°C. Limiting body temperatures are probably some degrees higher.

The lower temperature limits for flight activity are related to the physiology of the flight muscles. Thus the length of time taken for the completion of a flight muscle twitch at temperatures below 24°C is so long that flight of *Schistocerca* is extremely inefficient and only above 30°C is the twitch sufficiently short for really sustained flight to occur (p. 260). Also, the apyrases, enzymes concerned in the utilisation of energy, are only efficient at high temperatures (p. 114), and in insects with asynchronous flight muscles the power output is maximal only within a limited range of temperatures, with an optimum at about 40°C in *Oryctes* (Coleoptera) (p. 262). Thus the lower limit for flight is set by the inefficiency of the muscles at these temperatures.

Many insects, including locusts and some Hymenoptera, raise their body temperature when the air temperature is low by basking in the sun and in this way body temperature may be raised to a level at which flight is possible. Body temperature may also be raised by contractions of the flight muscles, but without the insect flying. If a locust is disturbed at a temperature which is too low for flight, it sometimes vibrates its wings, *i.e.* fans, so that flight becomes possible. Comparable preflight warm-up behaviour occurs in a number of insects. It is common in some moths, in Syrphidae and in *Bombus* and is associated with low amplitude movements of the folded wings. During preflight warm-up the pattern of nerve impulses to the flight muscles is quite different from that in flight so that antagonistic muscles contract synchronously instead of alternately. In Sphingidae the rate of heat production is dependent on frequency of vibration and increases with temperature throughout warm-up until the appropriate body temperature is reached (Fig. 178); then the muscles start to alternate, but without any change in frequency. This change, resulting from the altered firing pattern of the motorneurones, is dependent on the temperature of the thoracic ganglia. There is also some evidence that *Bombus* can produce heat without muscular contractions (see Kammer and Heinrich, 1978).

The upper limit for flight may be set by the upper lethal temperature. For instance, sustained flight of *Schistocerca* in the laboratory is not observed at air temperatures above 38°C. Because of the heat output by the flight muscles, body temperature in these experiments is probably close to 45°C and clearly any further increase in temperature would approach dangerously close to the lethal limit (p. 769). Hence sustained flights at high temperatures are not to be expected, although short flights are possible.

A flying locust has no special mechanism to prevent it from overheating (Church, 1960), but in Sphingidae and *Bombus* heat loss is regulated so that in flight the body temperature is independent of air temperature (p. 764).

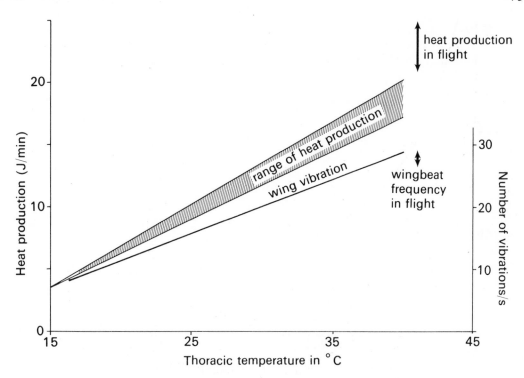

Fig. 178 Rate of wing vibration and heat production during preflight warm-up by *Manduca* (from Kammer and Heinrich, 1978)

Muscle development

For a time after emergence the flight pattern of adult insects is not fully developed and this period is known as the teneral period. Thus adult locusts usually remain with the larvae for a week to ten days after becoming adult. At first they are unable to fly, then they begin to make short flights, which get progressively longer until the full flight pattern is developed. In other insects the teneral period may be much shorter, a matter of hours in aphids, and its length is proportional to temperature (Fig. 179).

The initial inability to fly may be partly related to the softness and incompleteness of the cuticle. In most insects a period of an hour or two is required after emergence for the hardening of the cuticle to occur (p. 522) and during this period no flight is possible. Complete development of the cuticle may take some time after this (p. 522), but probably much more important in limiting flight is the degree of development of the flight muscles, which in many insects are known to undergo extensive changes during the first few days of adult life. Thus in *Locusta* the flight muscle mitochondria increase in size over the first eight days of adult life (Fig. 180) and there are corresponding changes in the enzyme systems with increases of glycerol-1-phosphate oxidase and α-glycerophosphate dehydrogenase, both essential enzymes in the flight mechanism (p. 264). During the same period the number of myofibrils increases from about 30 to approximately 1000 in each muscle fibre and the number of filaments in each fibril is doubled (Bücher, 1965).

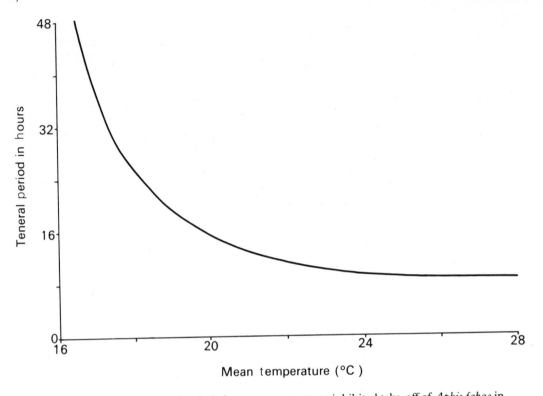

Fig. 179 The mean teneral periods from emergence to uninhibited take-off of *Aphis fabae* in relation to air temperature (from C. Johnson, 1965)

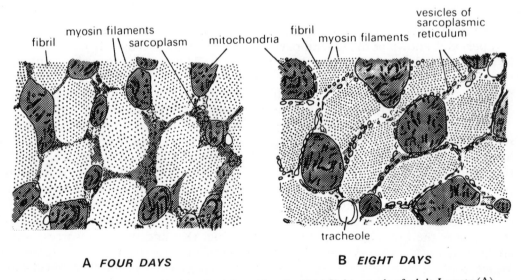

A *FOUR DAYS*   **B** *EIGHT DAYS*

Fig. 180 Cross-sections of parts of the dorsal longitudinal flight muscle of adult *Locusta* (A) four days and (B) eight days after emergence. Notice the larger mitochondria and increased number of filaments in B (after Bücher, 1965)

Similar changes occur in other insects. In *Apis* the muscles are fully developed after about 20 days and only after this are the bees able to make long flights (Herold and Borei, 1963). Similarly in *Glossina* (Diptera) the changes extend over several days and it is possible that in some holometabolous insects the delay in development of the muscles reflects a limitation of the reserves available during the pupal period (Bursell, 1961). In Lepidoptera, on the other hand, the flight muscles are almost fully developed at eclosion.

Other fully winged insects may be unable to fly at any stage because the wing muscles never develop fully and some corixids are polymorphic with regard to the development of flight muscles. In the flightless forms the full number of muscle fibrils is present, but they are thin and white compared with the large, yellowish muscles of flying forms. The differences in colour probably reflect differences in mitochondrial development and hence in the concentrations of cytochrome present (Young, 1965).

In many insects after the teneral development there is a period of extensive flight activity, followed by a further period of reduced activity, which may be associated with the breakdown, or autolysis, of the flight muscles. This usually occurs in aphids within two or three days of emergence, depending on when the insects settle down on a host plant. If they do not settle down the muscles, and the capacity to fly, are retained. The breakdown involves the dissolution of the fibrils of all the large direct and indirect wing muscles. The sarcolemma remains, but the nuclei become pycnotic and scattered through the cytoplasm. This breakdown is accompanied by an increase in the size of the fat body, and embryos in the reproductive ducts resume their development, which is inhibited during the flight period (B. Johnson, 1957, 1959).

A similar process occurs in a variety of other insects belonging to different orders, for example, *Dysdercus* (Heteroptera), *Leptinotarsa* (Coleoptera), *Aedes* (Diptera), winged termites generally, and *Acheta* (Orthoptera). In *Leptinotarsa* and the Scolytidae some degree of histolysis of the flight muscles takes place at the beginning of diapause; they then regenerate when diapause ends (C. Johnson, 1974). In some cases, at least, muscle degeneration is induced by the increasing titre of juvenile hormone associated with oogenesis (Davis, 1975).

Output of motorneurones

Apart from the changes taking place in the flight muscles of locusts in the first few days after the final moult, changes also occur in the pattern of firing of the motorneurones which control them. In *Chortoicetes* the alternating pattern of antagonistic muscles is established by the time of the moult, but the activity of individual muscles is rather irregular and variable. The fully developed pattern is not established until 3–6 days after moulting and at this time stable adult flight is possible. Subsequently the frequency of firing increases, producing a characteristic increase in wingbeat frequency from 15–20 Hz on the first day after moulting to 25–30 Hz by day ten (Altman, 1975).

Availability of fuel

Flight can only occur as long as there is fuel to drive the muscles. Experiments suggest that, on average, fuel in *Schistocerca* is sufficient for about ten hours of uninterrupted flight, although this period could be greatly prolonged if flight were intermittent with periods of feeding in between. Flight might also be prolonged if periods of active flight were interspersed with glides on rising air currents and certainly some flights are much longer than the experimental figures suggest is possible. For instance, it is estimated that a swarm of locusts which moved from the Canary Isles to southern Britain must have been in the air for some 60 hours.

Various estimates of flight range, based on performance on flight mills in still air, are available for other insects (Hocking, 1953). For instance, the range of *Aedes* species is estimated at roughly 20–50 km, and for various *Simulium* (Diptera) species at over 100 km, but it is doubtful if these figures bear very much relationship to performances in the field.

Apart from its effect in some migrations it is doubtful if the availability of fuel ever limits flight. Migrants often use fat as a fuel because it provides more energy per unit weight (p. 265).

State of feeding

Feeding often reduces activity and there is some evidence that this applies to the flight activity of *Nomadacris* in the field (Chapman, 1959a). *Glossina* tends to remain inactive after a blood meal, only becoming active again when the meal is well digested, but conversely migrating locusts often feed as they progress and in *Ascia* (Lepidoptera) a series of short feeding flights leads into migration (p. 285).

State of maturity

The state of maturity may not, in general, limit short-range flight, but there is some evidence that gravid females of *Nomadacris* do not fly readily and tend to drop down into the vegetation when disturbed. In many insects, such as aphids, locusts and *Ascia*, the long-range migratory flights occur mainly in the immediate post-teneral period before the insect becomes mature, although migration by mature locusts does occur.

13.2 Factors promoting take-off

It does not follow that, if conditions are suitable for flight, flight necessarily occurs. The occurrence of flight depends on the interaction of internal and external factors. Insects which fly in search of food or to migrate may exhibit an increased tendency to fly if take-off has been inhibited; the threshold for external stimuli is thus lowered and they may then take-off spontaneously. This is the case with aphids which are inhibited from taking off by sustained relatively high winds; after a time they take off despite the wind. The same may be true in predaceous insects such as Asilidae which move their perch from time to time if no potential prey appears. Spontaneous flight activity of *Glossina*, and probably of other species of Diptera, varies through the day and comparable changes in responsiveness to stimuli leading to flight also occur. This endogenous circadian activity plays a major part in controlling flight in the field, although environmental factors such as temperature are also significant (Brady and Crump, 1978).

Many different stimuli may cause an insect to start flying and it commonly appears that a change in stimulation rather than the absolute level of stimulation is important. Sometimes strong stimuli may lead to take-off when conditions are unsuitable for sustained flight and in this case the insect lands almost immediately.

Light and visual stimulation

There is some evidence that flight may be initiated in some insects by light of a particular intensity. Thus *Anax* (Odonata) is probably stimulated to take off by a certain low light intensity (Corbet, Longfield and Moore, 1960) and in *Calliphora* the frequency of take-off increases with the light intensity above a low level (Digby, 1958a). On the other hand in some insects a change in light intensity appears to provide an important stimulus. Thus in locusts bursts of flying are often seen following changes in light intensity on an intermittently cloudy day, either an increase or a decrease in intensity apparently being effective, although it is impossible to separate the effects of light and temperature in these cases (Chapman, 1959a; Waloff and Rainey, 1951). Night flight in a number of species starts at about half-an-hour after sunset irrespective of other conditions and it is probable that in this instance the rapid decrease in light intensity promotes take-off (Roffey, 1963; Waloff, 1963) (Fig. 186).

Visual stimuli other than changes in intensity may promote take-off in some predatory and parasitic insects. Experiments indicate that movement of an object in the visual field of *Glossina* causes the fly to take off and approach the host (p. 30). Similarly the parasitic fly *Pachyophthalmus*, which detects the nest of its host *Eumenes* (Hymenoptera) by pursuing the wasp, normally sits on some vantage point and is stimulated to fly by any insect flying within about two feet. Pursuit only ensues if the passing insect is *Eumenes*, otherwise the fly lands again (Chapman, 1959b). Many Asilidae and dragonflies catch their prey by darting out from a vantage point on which they sit until an insect comes sufficiently close (Corbet, Longfield and Moore, 1960; Oldroyd, 1964).

Wind-speed

It is believed that high winds inhibit take-off, causing the insect to cling more strongly to its perch. This is true in aphids, but only over short periods; if the high wind persists the aphids take off regardless of its speed. This suggests some degree of adaptation to the high winds, and experimental work on *Calliphora* shows that this does occur in this insect. After a sudden increase in wind-speed take-off is less frequent, but gradually the number taking off increases in spite of the high wind (Fig. 181). In *Calliphora* it has been suggested that wind-speeds below 0.7 m/s have a stimulating effect and increase the numbers of flies taking off, but at higher speeds the numbers taking off decrease (Fig. 182) (Digby, 1958b).

A sudden fall in wind-speed leads to a sharp increase in the numbers of insects taking off and in *Calliphora* the number taking off is greater than would be expected from the simple relationship between wind-speed and flight activity indicated above (Fig. 182). This suggests that the fall in wind-speed is itself important, irrespective of the speed of the wind. Kennedy (1951) concludes that this is also true in *Schistocerca*. Conversely, in locusts there is an occasional suggestion that sudden strong gusts of wind stimulate take-off, but this could arise from the sudden cooling effects produced by the wind rather than being a direct effect of the wind. Temperature changes may also follow more normal changes in wind-speed and it is possibly these, rather than the wind itself, which promote take-off (Chapman, 1959a).

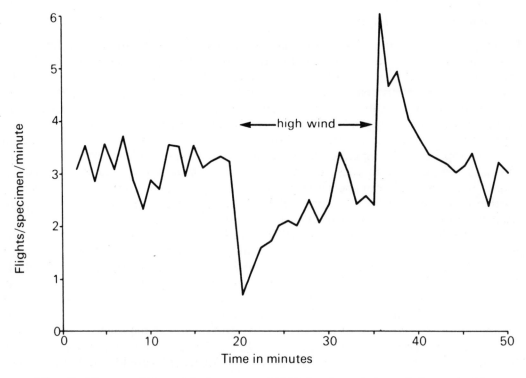

Fig. 181 The mean flight activity in a group of *Calliphora* in a wind-speed of 0·5 m/s with a short period of 3·0 m/s (after Digby, 1958b)

Humidity

There are some suggestions from field work that the flight of locusts may be initiated by an increase in humidity, such as might be caused by a moist wind blowing from a wet to a dry area, but there is no general agreement on this point (see *e.g.* Davey, 1959).

Smell

Some insects are stimulated to take off when they perceive particular smells, take-off being followed by an upwind orientation which takes the insect to the source of the smell. Field and laboratory experiments indicate that the smell of the host stimulates take-off by *Glossina medicorum* (Chapman, 1961), and this may also be true in some other blood-sucking insects. In a similar way some male moths are stimulated to take off by a pheromone produced by the female (p. 859).

Temperature

Activity is promoted by sharp changes in temperature (p. 769) and there is good evidence that this applies also to flight activity in the field. Often under these circumstances temperature changes are accompanied by changes in wind-speed or light

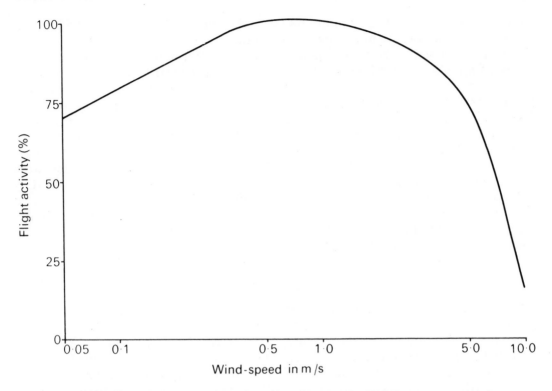

Fig. 182 Flight activity of *Calliphora* in relation to wind-speed. The figures are expressed as a percentage of the activity at 0·5 m/s and show the activity 30 minutes after a change from this level (after Digby, 1958b)

intensity and it is impossible to separate the effects of the different stimuli with certainty (Chapman, 1959a). In *Calliphora*, an increase in temperature at the rate of 5 °C/minute at first reduces take-off, but subsequently more flights occur at the higher temperature (Digby, 1958a).

Other stimuli

Many different stimuli may promote take-off in various insects. Disturbance by other animals, for instance, may sometimes be important and the flight responses of locusts to each other may simply be a special case of this. Thus an individual locust may be stimulated to take off by the mechanical agitation of its fellows or, visually or aurally, by the passage of other locusts overhead.

13.3 Stimuli leading to landing

Very little is known of the factors which cause an airborne insect to land, but landing at any time must depend on whether or not the insect has the opportunity to do so, and can only occur if the insect is close to the ground and can control its own movements.

Since sustained flight only occurs under certain conditions a change resulting in adverse conditions will lead to landing by the insect. This will occur, for instance, if the temperature falls below the minimum for flight and similarly landing will follow quickly if take-off occurs in suboptimal conditions.

On the other hand, insects often land although the environmental conditions remain suitable for flight, and landing may be promoted by special stimuli appropriate to the particular insect. For instance, a food-collecting bee is stimulated to approach and land on a flower with the appropriate smell and colour. However, since it may only just have taken off from a similar flower the landing clearly results from a change in the responses of the insect itself. This is seen in aphids and some other insects where the positive phototactic reactions which are important at take-off become weaker or even reversed so that the insect moves towards the vegetation. The change in behaviour is regarded as arising through a change in a central nervous balance mechanism which is modified by different inputs (Kennedy and Booth, 1963a). Flight itself influences this balance so that after a period of flight an aphid is more ready to settle down on a leaf and the longer the period of flight the more readily will it settle. Settling is said to be induced by flying (Kennedy and Booth, 1963b).

13.4 Speed of flight

The speed of an insect in flight can be measured in terms of its movement relative to the ground, its ground-speed, or its movement relative to the air, its air-speed. Ground-speed depends on the air-speed of the insect, the speed of the wind and the orientation of the insect relative to the wind. If air-speed is greater than wind-speed the insect can orientate at any angle to the wind and make headway (Fig. 183A), although its path relative to the ground, known as its track, will not generally coincide with the direction in which it is heading (its course). If the air-speed is less than wind-speed the insect will move downwind irrespective of its course (Fig. 183B).

Laboratory and field observations on *Schistocerca* indicate that it has an air-speed of 15–20 km/h, the speed being greatest soon after take-off and subsequently falling to a steady level. Experiments on a flight mill indicate air-speeds of about 9 km/h for *Apis* and various Tabanidae and speeds of 3–4 km/h for *Aedes*. Field observations suggest

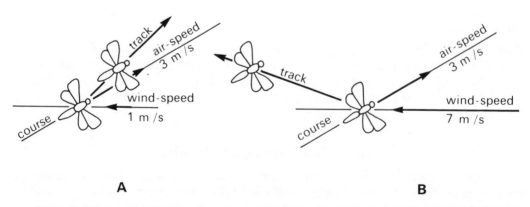

A   **B**

Fig. 183 Diagrams showing the interrelationships between course, track and wind direction (A) where the air-speed of the insect exceeds wind-speed and (B) where the air-speed is less than the wind-speed

air-speeds of the same order, with maximum speeds over short distances of approximately double these figures (Hocking, 1953).

If the insect is moving downwind its ground-speed may exceed its air-speed, but in upwind orientation the converse must be true. There is evidence that insects can regulate their ground-speed by adjusting the air-speed to some extent and this is most obvious in some hovering insects such as syrphids, *Apis* and *Macroglossum* (Lepidoptera) and in others, such as some Diptera and Ephemeroptera, which form swarms (p. 351). These insects are able to remain stationary over one spot despite changes in wind-speed and this involves balancing the air-speed against the wind-speed. The insect maintains its station by means of a visual fix on some feature of the environment.

Adjustment of air-speed also occurs in forward progression into the wind. For instance, in still air *Aedes* has an air-speed of 17 cm/s; in a wind of 33 cm/s the air-speed is increased to 49 cm/s, so the ground-speed is only slightly less than in still air, falling to about 16 cm/s. Further increase in wind-speed is compensated by an increased air-speed and so the insect is able to maintain its forward movement against the wind, although with a gradually decreasing ground-speed (Fig. 184). Observations on *Ascia* and locusts also suggest that air-speed is regulated to maintain a fairly constant ground-speed despite changes in the velocity of the wind (Kennedy, 1951; Nielsen, 1961).

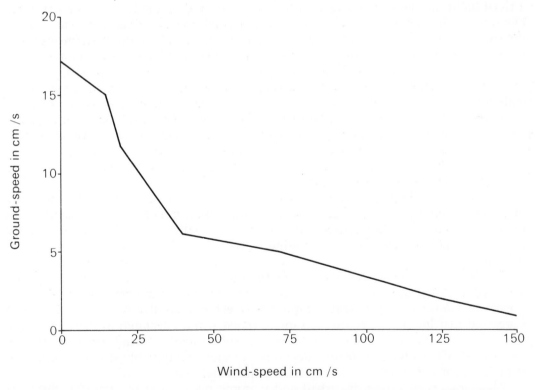

Fig. 184 The ground-speed of *Aedes aegypti* when flying into winds of varying force. Air-speed is adjusted so that ground-speed does not fall as quickly as would otherwise be expected (from Clements, 1963)

This regulation is believed to involve an optomotor reaction, the insect preferring to perceive the movement of images of the background across the eye from front to back at a certain moderate rate (p. 667). There is also evidence that air-speed may be perceived through the stimulation of Johnston's organ in the antennae and that changes in stimulation lead to modifications in the amplitude of wingbeat (p. 241).

13.5 Types of flight

Flight activity is broadly divided into two categories: trivial flight, which is concerned with feeding and mating, and migration, in which these vegetative activities are suppressed and flight behaviour dominates. There is no clear separation between the two types of flight and one may grade into the other. For instance, in termites the migration of winged reproductives away from the nest leads to the finding of a mate. Conversely, the trivial feeding flights of *Ascia* gradually become longer until the insect is migrating. Either type of flight may lead to dispersal, but migration, which frequently carries the insect beyond the confines of its habitat, is probably more important in this respect.

13.5.1 Trivial flights

Trivial flights are local movements concerned with finding food, a mate or a suitable oviposition site, or with escaping from a potential enemy. Thus they show great diversity in their length and orientation. They may involve no more than flitting from flower to flower within a limited habitat, or they may involve movements over some metres as in the attraction of some male moths to the scent of females (p. 859). In other cases the trivial flight may lead to no displacement at all, as in the mating swarms of male mosquitoes and Ephemeroptera (p. 351) and the territorial behaviour of some male dragonflies. For instance, the males of *Tholymis tillarga* (Odonata) fly up and down a narrow stretch of water driving off other males, and despite a good deal of flight activity there is no effective displacement of the individual, although his behaviour does lead to some dispersion of the species by driving others away from his stretch of water (Corbet, Longfield and Moore, 1960).

Vision is important in many cases of trivial flight. For instance, the colour and size of flowers are important in attracting bees and butterflies, and predatory insects, such as Odonata, and blood-sucking insects may orientate visually to their food (p. 28). Visual means may also be employed in finding a mate, as in *Hypolimnas* (Lepidoptera) (p. 146).

Smell also plays a part in flight orientation, the insect orientating to a wind carrying some specific smell as in the mating behaviour of some moths and host-finding by some species of *Glossina* (p. 31). Water vapour may act in a similar way and it has been suggested that locusts move upwind into a moist wind. Although in these cases the odour stimulates take-off and governs the subsequent upwind orientation, the mechanism of orientation probably depends on vision and possibly also on mechanical stimulation of the antennae, or, in locusts, the facial hair beds (p. 710).

Most insects fly when disturbed and in some insects special types of flight are associated with this escape reaction. Solitary *Schistocerca*, for instance, 'rocket' into the air and then crash down again very quickly. Often an escaping insect flies on an erratic course with frequent sharp turns or high-speed climbs (Callahan, 1965), or, as in the case of some moths pursued by bats, high-speed power dives to the ground. The stimuli evoking these responses are probably normally visual or mechanical, and some night-flying moths are able to perceive and react to the sounds emitted by bats (p. 727).

13.6 Migration

In the course of the adult life of many, perhaps most, insects there is a phase during which flight activity dominates over all other forms of behaviour. The flight occurring during this period is called migration. Often it is the immediate post-teneral flight and in many insects migration is restricted to a short period, only a few days at most in aphids and 15–30 hours in *Ascia*. Following this the insect matures and only trivial flights occur, or the flight muscles may break down so that no further flight is possible (p. 277). Sometimes, however, migration follows a prolonged period of diapause and usually in such cases the movement is additional to an immediate post-teneral migration. *Eurygaster* (Heteroptera), for instance, migrates to and from its place of aestivation, only maturing when it finally settles in its breeding grounds. Finally, a number of insects also migrate when they are mature. This is true, for instance, of some locust movements, some instances of migration by *Catopsilia* (Lepidoptera) (Williams, 1958) and some migrations of dragonflies (Corbet, Longfield and Moore, 1960), but again in these species migration is more commonly an immediate post-teneral flight.

Migration is regarded as a dispersal mechanism and always includes females but not necessarily males, depending on the mating behaviour of the species. The migration of *Schistocerca* involves both sexes, and in *Eurygaster* the outward flight to the aestivation quarters includes both sexes but only the females return to the breeding grounds. In *Rhyacionia* (Lepidoptera) only the females migrate, having been fertilised before they start, while the migrations of aphids involve parthenogenetic females.

13.6.1 Direction of migration

The direction of migration is strongly influenced by wind-speed and direction (Fig. 183). Wind-speed increases with the height above the ground so that, for all insects, there is a layer of air close to the ground in which their air-speed exceeds the wind-speed, while at higher levels the converse is true. The layer of relatively low wind-speeds is called the boundary layer and its thickness varies with different insects having different air-speeds, with the presence and form of vegetation, and with the wind-speed (Taylor, 1974). Within the boundary layer an insect can orientate and make progress in any direction, but at higher levels the wind-speed exceeds the air-speed and displacement will be predominantly downwind irrespective of the orientation of the insect.

Migration within the boundary layer

The migrations of some insects are made largely or entirely within the boundary layer and hence their direction is controlled by the insect. Thus *Ascia monuste* in Florida flies low, only 1–4 m above the ground, and it tends to fly in situations sheltered from the wind. Moreover, it is a strong flier and can make headway against a wind of 10 km/h, so its movement is not much affected by wind direction. Flights from the coastal colonies are directed to the north and to the south at the same time and it is suggested that in this case the direction of migration is determined by the behaviour immediately before migration. At this time the insect feeds at flowers and the colonies of flowers extend in a north-south direction along the coast. Hence there is some tendency for feeding flights to be similarly orientated and as intervals between feeding become longer and the insects start to migrate they continue the tendency to fly in a northerly or southerly direction. Subsequently the direction may become fixed by a sun compass reaction or by orientation to polarised light (p. 663). In this way the main trend of the migration is fixed, but the insects follow landmarks, such as roads and the coastline, when these head in the right general direction (Nielsen, 1961). Similar phenomena probably direct the migrations of queen wasps and *Bombus* along the coast of Finland in the spring (Mikkola, 1978).

The migrations of *Melolontha* (Coleoptera) also occur within the boundary layer. In this case the beetles fly from their site of emergence to woodland up to two miles distant. The initial orientation is visual, involving fixation on the highest visible point in the woodland, but again this appears to be supplemented by orientation to the sun or the pattern of polarised light from the sky. This orientation is remembered by the insect and serves to direct it on the return course to the breeding grounds (Schneider, 1962). Thus in species migrating within the boundary layer it appears that a variety of factors may be involved in the initial orientation, but this subsequently becomes fixed with reference to the sun or the pattern of polarised light.

Daytime migration outside the boundary layer

During the daytime the air above the ground is commonly turbulent as a result of thermals rising from the ground as it is heated by the sun. Many insects, especially smaller ones, are carried upwards beyond the limits of their boundary layers by these thermals and then are transported by the wind.

In order to support an insect the velocity of a convection current must exceed the sinking speed of the insect and such velocities commonly occur at certain times. Rainey (1958) estimated a sinking speed for locusts with the wings outstretched of about 1 m/s and in one observation obtained evidence for some 50 up-gusts per square kilometre with a velocity equivalent to or greater than this. In Canada vertical velocities of up to 8 m/s are recorded (Wellington, 1945) and these currents would be capable of supporting relatively large insects. Convection due to the heating of the ground by the sun will be of great importance in carrying insects high into the air; this is primarily a diurnal phenomenon, dying down in the evening as the ground cools. Hence many insects will be carried upwards into the air and occasional records are obtained of insects at 3000 m; at midday, with convection approaching its maximum, half the population of *Oscinella* (Diptera) in Britain is normally above 400 m.

These up-currents are not continuous, but have down-draught zones between them. Hence insects may not, in general, remain airborne due to convection for very long periods and convection will not necessarily result in the insects being transported over long distances. It will, however, distribute them over a considerable area because of the turbulent movement of the air in the up-currents.

The upper limit of flight of day-flying locust swarms corresponds closely with the limit of convective air movement (Fig. 185) and it is probable that this also applies to other insects not aggregated into swarms.

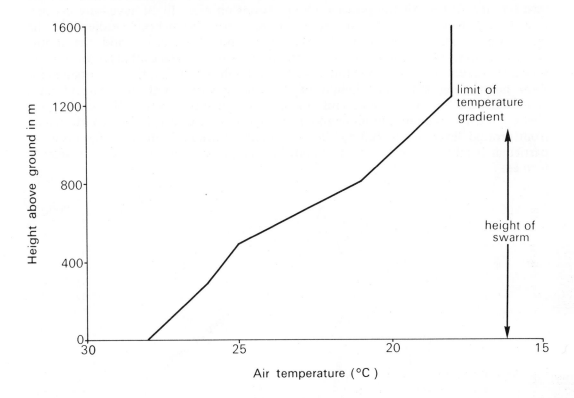

Fig. 185 The height of a cumuliform swarm of *Schistocerca* in relation to the temperature gradient above the ground (based on Rainey, 1958)

Because of their relatively limited capacity for flight it is probable that most long-range migration by small insects takes place outside the boundary layer during the daytime (Taylor, 1974). This is not to say that the insect plays a purely passive role. Its original launching into the air is an active movement different from that seen in trivial flights. Aphids, for instance, climb steeply due to a positive phototactic reaction to the shorter wavelengths of light. If, after being carried upwards by convection currents the insects keep flying, they will be transported downwind, perhaps over considerable distances.

Apart from small insects such as aphids, thrips and *Oscinella*, some larger insects also migrate outside the boundary layer during the day. Locusts are an obvious example (p. 291), but butterflies are often recorded flying in large numbers at heights which must be well beyond their boundary layer. Even species which normally migrate within the boundary layer are sometimes seen flying outside it. For instance, *Ascia monuste* in Argentina has been observed migrating at all levels up to 1500 m. At the lower levels the insects were variously orientated to the wind, but the higher flights were all downwind (Hayward, 1953; C. Johnson, 1969).

Migration at night

At night, in the absence of radiation, the thermals die away and insects depend on their own activity to carry them upwards. Observations on night flight have only become possible by using radar and the main species which have been studied are the grasshopper *Aiolopus*, the locusts *Chortoicetes* and *Schistocerca*, and the moths *Choristoneura* and *Heliothis* (Schaefer, 1976). All these species take off in large numbers soon after sunset (Fig. 186) and climb steadily to a ceiling, which is then maintained for some hours (Fig. 187). The height of the ceiling varies with species and local conditions, but for *Schistocerca* and *Aiolopus* is sometimes over 1000 m, while for *Choristoneura* it is commonly about 200 m. Sometimes the insects extend continuously from ground level to the ceiling, but on other occasions high densities occur at particular heights with relatively few above or below, so a discrete layer of insects is formed.

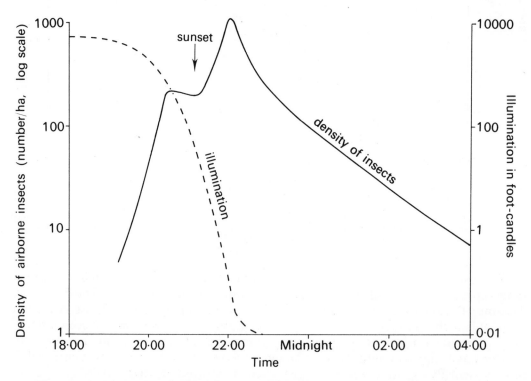

Fig. 186 Aerial density of *Choristoneura* at different times during the night showing the extensive take-off soon after sunset (after Schaefer, 1976)

Since these insects are flying so high, they are normally outside their boundary layer and are displaced downwind. On some occasions the insects, although they have no contact with each other, have a common orientation, often downwind. Consequently displacement may occur at the speed of the wind or even faster and in the course of a night insects may travel 100 km or more.

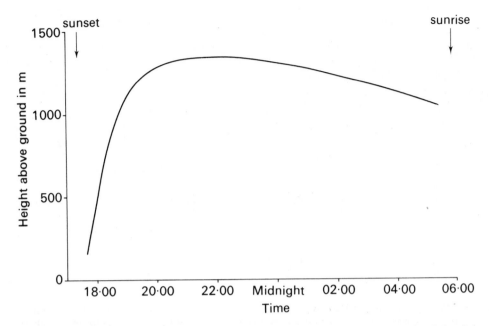

Fig. 187 Maximum height of flight (ceiling) of *Aiolopus* throughout one night (after Schaefer, 1976)

13.6.2 Return movements

Few insects are known to make return migrations comparable with those made by birds, but evidence is accumulating which indicates that such movements are not uncommon. In many instances the return flight is not made by the initial migrants, but by members of a subsequent generation, a reflection of the general brevity of the life of adult insects.

The best documented example of a return migration is that of *Danaus plexippus*, the American monarch butterfly. In the summer months this insect is found right across the United States and extending into southern Canada (Fig. 188A). The adult, however, can survive only for short periods at low temperatures and requires constant access to nectar, which is not available in the northern winter. Hence it is unable to overwinter in the more northern parts of its range. In the autumn it moves south into areas beyond the range of the cold air masses or into areas in which, as in the Gulf of Mexico, the cold air is moderated by warm-water currents (Fig. 188B).

The southward movement begins in July in the northern parts of the range, reaching its climax in September and finally fading out in October. Flight is usually within 5 m of the ground, within the boundary layer, although higher flights are made to avoid obstacles. On the way south the butterflies roost in trees, clustering together on cold nights and remaining in the roosts until the temperature rises above about 13 °C.

In the warmer parts of the overwintering range (Fig. 188B) the insects remain free-flying and breeding occurs, but in some localities in Florida and California which are within the range of the cold northern air masses the butterflies roost in dense colonies in the trees, flitting out on warm days to feed on nectar.

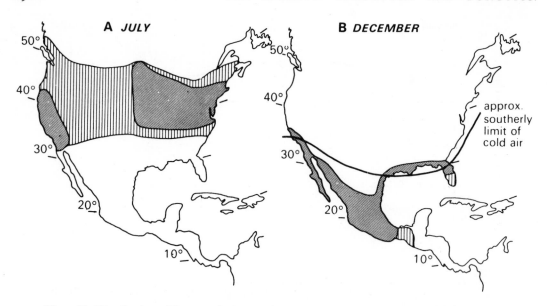

Fig. 188 Distribution of *Danaus plexippus* in North America in (A) July and (B) December. Vertical hatching indicates low densities, diagonal hatching high densities (after Urquhart, 1960)

In February and March as the temperature rises the colonies start to break up and a return movement to the north begins. The individuals leaving the Californian colonies are the same as those which flew south in the autumn and this may also be true of some individuals from Florida, but here some winter breeding is known to occur, so at least some of the individuals flying north are the offspring of those that originally came south. The return to the extreme north of the range takes about two months (Urquhart, 1960).

Outward and return movements by the same individual are also known in a few other insects. For instance, *Agrotis infusa* (Lepidoptera) in Australia moves to the mountains in the summer, so avoiding the excessive aridity of the plains, and returns to the plains to breed in the autumn. The pentatomids *Eurygaster integriceps* and *Aelia rostrata* make similar movements in middle eastern countries, but here it is believed that the movements are purely fortuitous, depending on the prevailing winds at the time of migration so that many insects are lost and never return to their breeding grounds (Brown, 1965). The two-way movement of *Hippodamia convergens* (Coleoptera) is believed to occur in a similar way (Hagen, 1962).

In many other instances the return movement is made by members of a subsequent generation and not by the original insects. For instance, *Vanessa atalanta* (Lepidoptera) in Britain is generally observed moving in a northerly direction in spring and, after breeding, in a southerly direction in the autumn (Fig. 189), and evidence is accumulating for comparable movements in other Lepidoptera in Europe and elsewhere (see Williams, 1958). These movements commonly involve orientation with respect to the sun (Baker, 1969).

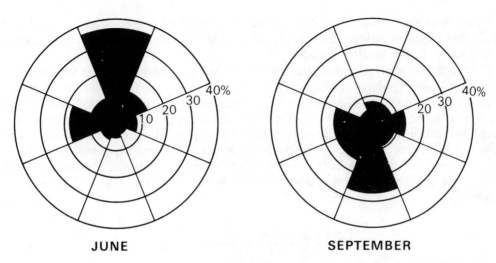

JUNE **SEPTEMBER**

Fig. 189 The direction of flight of *Vanessa atalanta* in Britain in June and September. Expressed as a percentage of the total numbers of observations (based on Williams, 1951)

13.6.3 Locust migration

Locust migrations are conspicuous because they involve swarms consisting of enormous numbers of individuals which move over hundreds of kilometres. There are many locust species, but the best known is *Schistocerca gregaria*, which extends across north and central Africa to the Middle East, Arabia and India. Swarms of *Schistocerca* commonly have an area of over 10 km² and big swarms may extend over 250 km². This involves vast numbers of insects and a swarm with an area of 20 km² was estimated to contain 1 000 000 000 locusts. The distance moved by such swarms is very variable, but is often 30–40 km/day and not infrequently 100 km/day.

Swarms in flight may be roughly classified into two types depending on their form. They may be flat with all the locusts flying within a few metres of the ground or they may extend upwards in a towering form to over 1000 m above the ground. These types are called stratiform and cumuliform swarms respectively. In the first the locusts are highly concentrated with densities usually between one and ten locusts per cubic metre, but in cumuliform swarms the insects are much more widely dispersed and density ranges from 0·001–0·1 locusts/m³ (Waloff, 1972).

A single swarm may occur in either of these forms at different times since the differences arise from differences in the air currents in the swarm. Stratiform swarms are formed when there is no marked temperature gradient above the ground, indicating the absence of convective up-currents, but cumuliform swarms occur where there is a marked temperature gradient and associated convection. The convection currents in this case carry the locusts upwards, but they will only do so provided they exceed the sinking speed of the locusts. Up-gusts of sufficient velocity to do this may occur with a frequency of 50/km² and they are probably responsible for the towering pillars of locusts often seen in cumuliform swarms. The top of such a swarm is close to the limit of the temperature gradient in the air, this being associated with the limit of convective air movements (Fig. 185).

Small swarms, with an area of less than one square kilometre, are often stratiform even in turbulent conditions and this probably reflects some difference in the behaviour of the locusts in the smaller group.

Photographic analysis shows that, although in any one part of the swarm all the locusts tend to be similarly orientated, in the swarm as a whole the locusts are randomly orientated with respect to each other. It might be expected that this randomness, together with the disruptive effects of air turbulence would lead to the dispersal of the swarm, but it is found that at the edge of the swarm all the locusts are heading towards the body of insects (Fig. 190) and so the cohesion of the swarm is maintained. It is believed that whenever a locust heads out of the swarm it turns and flies back in again, possibly reacting to visual and auditory stimuli provided by the swarm (Haskell, 1960; Waloff, 1972).

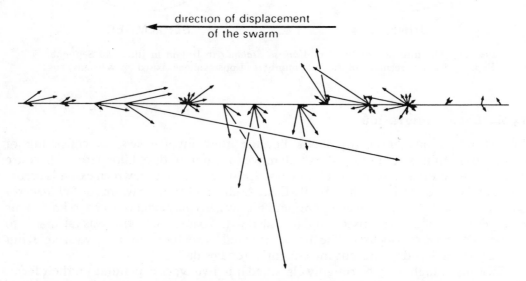

Fig. 190 Diagram illustrating the orientations of individual locusts in a swarm, based on a series of photographs taken at intervals as the swarm passed overhead. The length of each arrow is proportional to the number of locusts orientated in the direction shown (from Haskell, 1960)

Since the locusts in a swarm are randomly orientated, the swarm will inevitably tend to be displaced downwind. Other directions are possible if orientation is co-ordinated instead of random and there are many reports in the literature of swarms flying into the wind, but these reports have yet to be substantiated by critical analysis. Where critical methods have been employed it is found that swarm displacement is downwind (Fig. 191) (Rainey, 1963). The speed with which the locusts move downwind is very variable and is usually less than half the wind-speed. This is due in part to the fact that flight is intermittent, with locusts continually landing and taking off, so that although the swarm as a whole is continually airborne the individual locusts are only in the air for a part of the time. It is rare for the whole of a swarm to be airborne for any length of time. The slow downwind progress of swarms could also result from a preponderance of upwind orientation by the locusts.

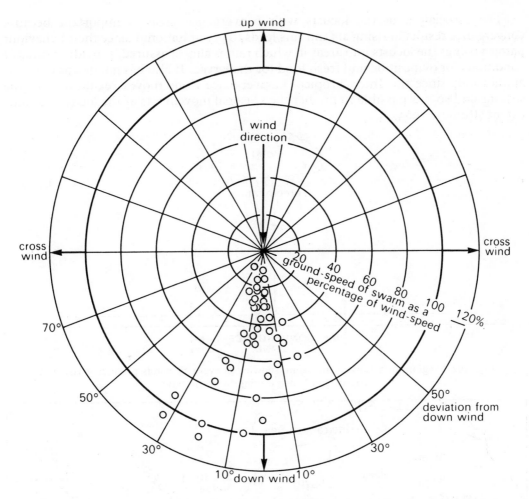

Fig. 191 Direction and speed of displacement of 49 desert locust swarms in relation to wind
(after Rainey, 1963)

The effect of downwind displacement is to bring the locusts into convergence areas, that is areas in which there is a net excess of inflowing air over outflowing air across the boundaries (Fig. 192). Often these areas are somewhat ephemeral, but some are more permanent and one of these, the Inter-Tropical Convergence Zone between winds originating on either side of the Equator, is of particular importance in the biology of *Schistocerca*. The convergent winds tend to carry locust swarms into the convergence zones and once there they tend to remain, so swarms accumulate and this is especially true in the Inter-Tropical Convergence Zone (Fig. 193). Swarms may continue to fly when in these zones, but the irregularity of the winds tends to limit displacement. For instance, there is a record of a swarm in the Sudan in June, 1955 which flew 150 km in two days, but at the end of this time it had undergone no net displacement because of the irregularity of its movements.

The association of the locusts with convergence areas is important because convergence results in rising air and this leads to precipitation. Hence their behaviour pattern brings the locusts into areas in which rain is almost assured, providing suitable conditions for oviposition and fresh food for the larvae. It also has important practical applications since the Inter-Tropical Convergence Zone moves regularly over the seasons and so it is possible to predict the seasonal movements of the locusts to some extent (Rainey, 1963).

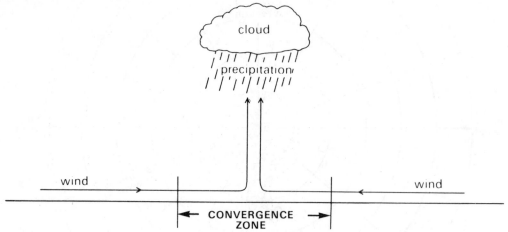

Fig. 192 Diagram of a convergence zone showing convergent winds producing rising air currents and hence leading to precipitation

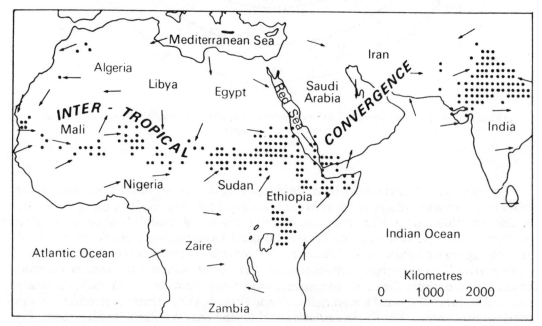

Fig. 193 The distribution of swarms of *Schistocerca* (●) in July 1954 in relation to the Inter-Tropical Convergence Zone. Arrows indicate the general wind direction at mid-day 900 m above the ground (after Rainey, 1963)

Swarms of locusts usually migrate in the daytime although their flight sometimes continues into the night, but solitary locusts also migrate extensively at night. Solitary migratory locusts, *Locusta*, for instance, make seasonal movements from the semi-desert areas surrounding the Niger flood plain into the plain, recolonising the semidesert areas again in a later generation following the onset of the rainy season. The movement to the plain appears to be a downwind movement into a moister, more clement region.

13.6.4 Mass flights

Although migration of small numbers of insects occurs and is probably more common than it appears to be, migration frequently involves mass flights. Aphid migration, for instance, commonly involves very large numbers often reaching two daily peaks, one in the morning and a second in the afternoon (Fig. 194). The numbers of aphids in the air at any one time depend primarily on the numbers of insects becoming adult, the length of the teneral period and the presence or absence of limiting weather conditions. Aphids emerging in the morning with the temperature rising have a short teneral period and fly in the afternoon, but those emerging in the afternoon are inhibited from taking off by

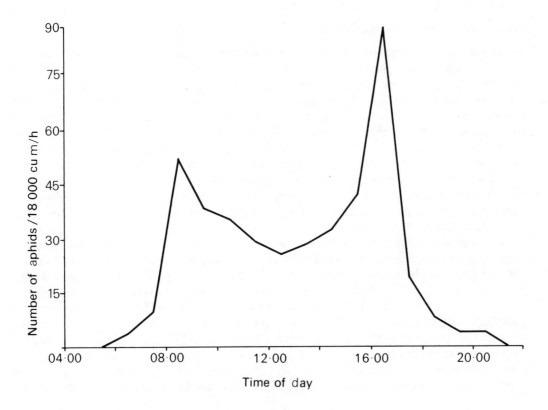

Fig. 194 Daily changes in the density of *Aphis fabae* in the air above a bean crop (after C. Johnson and Taylor, 1957)

the low light intensity and temperature of the evening. These all leave together the following morning when light and temperature become suitable and, together with others emerging and completing the teneral period overnight, they provide the morning peak of numbers. It is important to notice here that the two peaks arise from the activity of different individuals and not from changes in the activity of the same aphids (C. Johnson and Taylor, 1957).

Similarly in *Aedes taeniorrhynchus* adult emergence reaches a peak between 09.00 and 12.00 hours, but flight is inhibited by the light intensity until 18.00 hours when it is getting dark, so all the insects take off together in a mass flight (Nielsen, 1958). Probably in many insects with a short teneral period mass exodus on migration follows mass adult emergence and limiting flight conditions as in these examples. In some cases emergence is synchronised by a diapause (p. 833). The mass flights of some other insects appear to result largely from some common reaction to the environment since emergence may take place over a relatively long period. For instance, winged termites and ants accumulate in the nest, only flying when particular weather conditions prevail. Possibly some social factor is also relevant in these insects.

In locusts the synchronising of take-off arises from the gregarious behaviour of the insects which at some earlier period have aggregated as a response to environmental conditions.

13.6.5 Beginning of migration

Migration is to be regarded as an evolved adaptation and not a reaction to current adversity. This is suggested by the fact that migration in many cases is not immediately referable to prevailing adverse conditions, but commonly begins before these conditions are met. *Danaus*, for instance, begins to move south before the onset of cold weather (p. 289), and locust swarms leave their habitats while food supplies are still abundant. Sometimes the movements may involve all the individuals of every generation as in *Danaus* or a population may show genetically determined polymorphism with some individuals in every generation migrating as in *Dysdercus* (Heteroptera) (Fig. 196). In these cases the onset of migration may be spontaneous, not involving environmental signals. In other cases, however, migration is facultative and only occurs in certain generations, sometimes again involving polymorphism, which in this case is controlled by the environment.

In the case of facultative migration the insect must be put into a state of readiness to migrate by environmental factors. This state of readiness may be simply a physiological and behavioural phenomenon, but it may also involve the production of fully winged forms in an otherwise flightless population. Possibly in some cases photoperiod provides the stimulus for such development and photoperiod is known to affect wing polymorphism in aphids. In corixids, temperature and the availability of food may be important in controlling the development of flying forms (Young, 1965). Crowding also appears to be of some importance, possibly because over a long term it tends to be correlated with food shortage. Thus crowding stimulates the production of winged forms in aphid populations and the mass migrations of locusts are associated with crowding.

The stimuli which initiate take-off when the insects are in a state of readiness to migrate are considered above (Section 13.2).

13.6.6 Displacement as a result of migration

The displacements resulting from migration are extremely variable from species to species and even within a species, the distance moved depending on the speed of flight, the duration and frequency of single flights and the duration of the migratory period. The southerly movement of *Danaus plexippus* in the autumn involves a migration of over 1600 km for the individuals in the north of the range and one marked individual was recovered in Mexico 2800 km from its origin in Ontario four months previously. The rate of movement was probably faster than this would suggest since another recovery had travelled 1700 km in 18 days, an average speed of almost 100 km per day (Urquhart, 1960).

These movements are made largely within the boundary layer as are those of *Ascia* which, in Florida, migrates from 16 to 150 km, the longer distances occurring where more insects are involved in the migration.

With insects moving outside the boundary layer displacements are equally variable. Many insects may not be displaced particularly far because of the pattern of convection currents, but some may be carried on the wind for considerable distances and Gressitt *et al.* (1962) collected a number of terrestrial insects in mid-Pacific, a pyralid and a pentatomid being 500 km or more from the nearest land. It is not certain that these insects were airborne for the whole of this distance, but it is quite probable since it is known that Lepidoptera may be carried as much as 3000 km on the wind (French, 1965). On the other hand the wind-borne movements of *Eurygaster* only extend over 20–30 km (Brown, 1965).

Locust swarms may remain in one place without effective displacement (see above), but conversely there are records of swarms moving from northern Arabia to the Niger Republic, some 3500 km, in a month (Rainey, 1963). Solitary *Locusta* fly for distances of up to 300 km in and around the Niger flood plain (Davey, 1959).

Many migratory movements are on a much smaller scale than these figures would suggest and for instance the dispersal flights of termites and ants may extend over distances of 100 m or less.

13.6.7 End of migration

Although migration may occasionally come to an end because the insects are exhausted such evidence as is available suggests that this is usually not the case. Various environmental factors may ultimately be responsible, but the readiness to react to these factors probably depends on some physiological changes within the insect so that signals which evoked no response during migration now produce a reaction. Thus in aphids there is some neurophysiological relationship between flight and settling with settling becoming more prolonged and stable after longer flights (p. 282).

The stimuli promoting landing behaviour in an insect ready to respond are variable and appropriate to the particular insect. Aphids respond to leaves reflecting relatively long light wavelengths, *Ascia* to the smell of salt marshes in which it breeds (Nielsen, 1961), and *Melolontha* to the trees to which its flight is directed.

When the migration is an immediate post-teneral flight it is often followed by maturation. It is unlikely that maturation is the immediate cause of the end of migration, but the two phenomena are clearly related, perhaps hormonally, since maturation is known to be under hormonal control (p. 838) (Rankin, 1978).

13.6.8 Control of migratory behaviour

Migratory behaviour is probably regulated by hormones. In *Oncopeltus*, and probably in *Danaus* and *Leptinotarsa*, flight behaviour is stimulated by intermediate titres of juvenile hormone (Rankin, 1978). After the final moult the titre of juvenile hormone is low. Subsequently it increases more quickly in insects exposed to long day-lengths than in insects exposed to short days (Fig. 195). There is correspondingly a short period of flight in long days, when the hormone titre is at an intermediate level, and a longer period of flight in short days. At higher concentrations of juvenile hormone oogenesis occurs and flight comes to an end. If the insect is deprived of food or given food of poor quality the hormone titre declines and this again is associated with a period of more sustained flights.

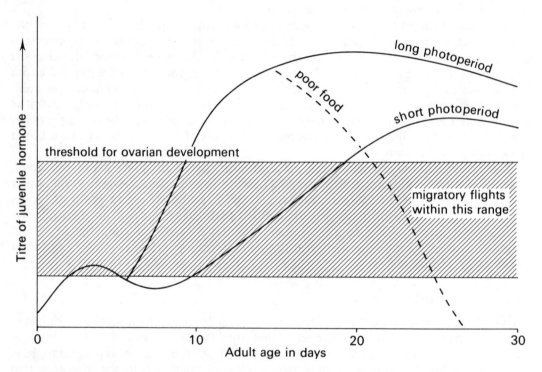

Fig. 195 Control of migratory flight activity by juvenile hormone as in *Oncopeltus*. The juvenile hormone titre varies with the age of the insect and also depends on the daylength and food quality. When the titre is within the shaded area extensive flights are promoted. At higher titres oogenesis begins and long flights stop (after Rankin, 1978)

These changes induced experimentally parallel those observed in the field in North America. A period of northward migration during short days in spring is followed by oogenesis and the development of a non-migrant population in the summer. A southerly migration occurs in the shortening days of autumn.

13.6.9 Significance of migration

The probable long-term advantage of migration is that it enables a species to keep pace with changes in the location of its habitats (Southwood, 1962). This is suggested by the fact that migration is most fully developed in insects living in temporary habitats; those living in stable habitats have much less tendency to migrate. This can be illustrated by reference to the British Anisoptera. Six species live in streams which are regarded as permanent habitats and none of these migrates, 14 species occupy only slightly less permanent lakes and canals and six of them (43 %) migrate, while of 19 species living in relatively temporary pools ten (53 %) migrate.

The impermanence of a habitat may result from a number of causes. Often seasonal climatic changes make a habitat untenable for part of a year. In north temperate regions the winter is the unfavourable period, while in the tropics many insects are unable to survive the dry season in an active form. In these cases suitable and unsuitable conditions alternate in a regular sequence, but in other cases climatic changes may occur in an irregular manner. A habitat may also become untenable because of ecological changes, as in the progress of an ecological succession where, for instance, open grassland may be replaced by scrub. Or the habitat itself may be ephemeral in the case of species breeding in flowers or fungi or carrion. Finally in some cases the impermanence of the habitat may arise through alterations in the requirements of the insect at different stages in the life cycle: Acrididae, for instance, have different requirements for feeding and for oviposition.

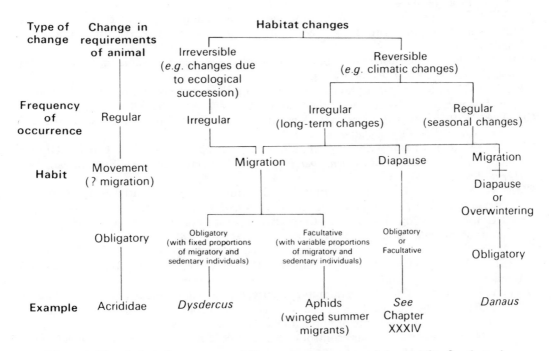

Fig. 196 The relation of movement and diapause to environmental change (after Southwood, 1962)

An unfavourable period arising through the impermanence of the habitat may be survived either by migration to some other more suitable habitat or by diapause. If the change in habitat is reversible, as with seasonal changes, diapause may be an advantage since it does not subject the insect to the possibility of completely failing to find a suitable habitat as may occur with migration (Dingle, 1978). Sometimes a migration precedes diapause, carrying the insect to a suitable site in which to survive. This occurs, for instance, in *Eurygaster*, in thrips which leave the vegetation to overwinter under the bark of adjacent trees, and in *Danaus*. Where changes in the habitat are irregular migration has a clear advantage over diapause. The interrelationships of the various types of migration, dispause and environmental change are summarised in figure 196.

REFERENCES

ALTMAN, J. S. (1975). Changes in the flight motor pattern during the development of the Australian plague locust, *Chortoicetes terminifera*. *J. comp. Physiol.* **97**: 127–142.

BAKER, R. R. (1969). The evolution of the migratory habit in butterflies. *J. Anim. Ecol.* **38**: 703–746.

BRADY, J. and CRUMP, A. J. (1978). The control of circadian activity rhythms in tsetse flies: environment or physiological clock. *Physiol. Ent.* **3**: 177–190.

BROWN, E. S. (1965). Notes on the migration and direction of flight of *Eurygaster* and *Aelia* species (Hemiptera, Pentatomoidea) and their possible bearing on invasions of cereal crops. *J. Anim. Ecol.* **34**: 93–108.

BÜCHER, T. (1965). Formation of the specific structural and enzymic pattern of the insect flight muscle. *in* Goodwin, T. W. (ed.), *Aspects of insect biochemistry*. Academic Press, London.

BURSELL, E. (1961). Post-teneral development of the thoracic musculature in tsetse flies. *Proc. R. ent. Soc. Lond.* A, **36**: 69–74.

CALLAHAN, P. S. (1965). A photoelectric–photographic analysis of flight behaviour in the corn earworm, *Heliothis zea*, and other moths. *Ann. ent. Soc. Am.* **58**: 159–169.

CHAPMAN, R. F. (1959a). Observations on the flight activity of the red locust, *Nomadacris septemfasciata* (Serville). *Behaviour* **14**: 300–334.

CHAPMAN, R. F. (1959b). Some observations on *Pachyophthalmus africa* Curran (Diptera: Calliphoridae), a parasite of *Eumenes maxillosus* De Geer (Hymenoptera: Eumenidae). *Proc. R. ent. Soc. Lond.* A, **34**: 1–6.

CHAPMAN, R. F. (1961). Some experiments to determine the methods used in host-finding by the tsetse fly, *Glossina medicorum* Austen. *Bull. ent. Res.* **52**: 83–97.

CHURCH, N. S. (1960). Heat loss and the body temperatures of flying insects. I. Heat loss by evaporation of water from the body. *J. exp. Biol.* **37**: 171–185.

CLEMENTS, A. N. (1963). *The physiology of mosquitoes*. Pergamon Press, Oxford.

CORBET, P. S., LONGFIELD, C. and MOORE, N. W. (1960). *Dragonflies*. Collins, London.

DAVEY, J. T. (1959). The African migratory locust (*Locusta migratoria migratorioides* Rch. and Fem., Orth.) in the Central Niger delta. Part two. The ecology of *Locusta* in the semi-arid lands and seasonal movements of populations. *Locusta* **7**: 1–180.

DAVIS, N. T. (1975). Hormonal control of flight muscle histolysis in *Dysdercus fulvoniger*. *Ann. ent. Soc. Am.* **68**: 710–714.

DIGBY, P. S. B. (1958a). Flight activity in the blowfly, *Calliphora erythrocephala*, in relation to light and radiant heat, with special reference to adaptation. *J. exp. Biol.* **35**: 1–19.

DIGBY, P. S. B. (1958b). Flight activity in the blowfly, *Calliphora erythrocephala*, in relation to wind speed, with special reference to adaptation. *J. exp. Biol.* **35**: 776–795.

DINGLE, H. (ed.) (1978). *Evolution of insect migration and diapause.* Springer-Verlag, New York.

FRENCH, R. A. (1965). Long range dispersal of insects in relation to synoptic meteorology. *Proc. XIIth. Int. Congr. Ent.* 418–419.

GRESSITT, J. L., COATSWORTH, J., and YOSHIMOTO, C. M. (1962). Air-borne insects trapped on "Monsoon expedition". *Pacif. Insects* **4**: 319–323.

HAGEN, K. S. (1962). Biology and ecology of predaceous Coccinellidae. *A. Rev. Ent.* **7**: 289–326.

HASKELL, P. T. (1960). The sensory equipment of the migratory locust. *Symp. zool. Soc. Lond.* **3**: 1–23.

HAYWARD, K. J. (1953). Migration of butterflies in Argentina during the spring and summer of 1951–52. *Proc. R. ent. Soc. Lond.* A, **28**: 63–73.

HEROLD, R. C. and BOREI, H. (1963). Cytochrome changes during honeybee flight muscle development. *Devl. Biol.* **8**: 67–79.

HOCKING, B. (1953). The intrinsic range and speed of flight of insects. *Trans. R. ent. Soc. Lond.* **104**: 223–345.

JOHNSON, B. (1957). Studies on the degeneration of the flight muscles of alate aphids—I. A comparative study of the occurence of muscle breakdown in relation to reproduction in several species. *J. Insect Physiol.* **1**: 248–256.

JOHNSON, B. (1959). Studies on the degeneration of the flight muscles of alate aphids—II. Histology and control of muscle breakdown. *J. Insect. Physiol.* **3**: 367–377.

JOHNSON, C. G. (1965). Migration. *in* Rockstein, M. (ed.), *The physiology of Insecta.* vol. 2. Academic Press, New York.

JOHNSON, C. G. (1969). *Migration and dispersal of insects by flight.* Methuen, London.

JOHNSON, C. G. (1974). Insect migration: aspects of its physiology. *in* Rockstein, M. (ed.), *The physiology of Insecta.* vol. 3. Academic Press, New York.

JOHNSON, C. G. and TAYLOR, L. R. (1957). Periodism and energy summation with special reference to flight rhythms in aphids. *J. exp. Biol.* **34**: 209–221.

KAMMER, A. E. and HEINRICH, B. (1978). Insect flight metabolism. *Adv. Insect Physiol.* **13**: 133–228.

KENNEDY, J. S. (1951). The migration of the desert locust (*Schistocerca gregaria* Forsk.). *Phil. Trans. R. Soc.* B, **235**: 163–290.

KENNEDY, J. S. and BOOTH, C. O. (1963a). Free flight of aphids in the laboratory. *J. exp. Biol.* **40**: 67–85.

KENNEDY, J. S. and BOOTH, C. O. (1963b). Co-ordination of successive activities in an aphid. The effect of flight on the settling responses. *J. exp. Biol.* **40**: 351–369.

LEWIS, T. and TAYLOR, L. R. (1965). Diurnal periodicity of flight by insects. *Trans. R. ent. Soc. Lond.* **116**: 393–479.

MIKKOLA, K. (1978). Spring migrations of wasps and bumble bees on the southern coast of Finland (Hymenoptera, Vespidae and Apidae). *Ann. ent. Fenn.* **44**: 10–26.

NIELSEN, E. T. (1958). The initial stage of migration in salt-marsh mosquitoes. *Bull. ent. Res.* **49**: 305–313.

NIELSEN, E. T. (1961). On the habits of the migratory butterfly *Ascia monuste* L. *Biol. Meddr.* **23**: 1–81.

OLDROYD, H. (1964). *The natural history of flies.* Weidenfeld and Nicolson, London.

RAINEY, R. C. (1958). Some observations on flying locusts and atmospheric turbulence in eastern Africa. *Q. Jl R. met. Soc.* **84**: 334–354.

RAINEY, R. C. (1963). Meteorology and the migration of desert locusts. Applications of synoptic meteorology in locust control. *Anti-Locust Mem.* no. 7, 115 pp.

RAINEY, R. C. (ed.) (1976). Insect flight. *Symp. R. ent. Soc. Lond.* **7**: 1–287.

RANKIN, M. A. (1978). Hormonal control of insect migratory behaviour. *in* Dingle, H. (ed.), *Evolution of insect migration and diapause.* Springer-Verlag, New York.

ROFFEY, J. (1963). Observations on night flight in the desert locust (*Schistocerca gregaria* Forskål). *Anti-Locust Bull.* no. 39, 32 pp.

SCHAEFER, G. W. (1976). Radar observations of insect flight. *Symp. R. ent. Soc. Lond.* **7**: 157–197.

SCHNEIDER, F. (1962). Dispersal and migration. *A. Rev. Ent.* **7**: 223–242.

SOUTHWOOD, T. R. E. (1962). Migration of terrestrial arthropods in relation to habitat. *Biol. Rev.* **37**: 171–214.

TAYLOR, L. R. (1974). Insect migration, flight periodicity and the boundary layer. *J. Anim. Ecol.* **43**: 225–238.

URQUHART, F. A. (1960). *The monarch butterfly.* University of Toronto Press.

WALOFF, Z. (1953). Flight in desert locusts in relation to humidity. *Bull. ent. Res.* **43**: 575–580.

WALOFF, Z. (1963). Field studies on solitary and *transiens* desert locusts in the Red Sea area. *Anti-Locust Bull.* no. 40, 93 pp.

WALOFF, Z. (1972). Orientation of flying locusts, *Schistocerca gregaria* (Forsk.), in migrating swarms. *Bull. ent. Res.* **62**: 1–72.

WALOFF, Z. and RAINEY, R. C. (1951). Field studies on factors affecting the displacements of desert locust swarms in eastern Africa. *Anti-Locust Bull.* no. 9, 1–50.

WEIS-FOGH, T. (1952). Fat combustion and metabolic rate of flying locusts (*Schistocerca gregaria* Forskål). *Phil Trans. R. Soc.* B, **237**: 1–36.

WEIS-FOGH, T. (1956). Biology and physics of locust flight. II. Flight performance of the desert locust (*Schistocerca gregaria*). *Phil. Trans. R. Soc.* B, **239**: 459–510.

WELLINGTON, W. G. (1945). Conditions governing the distribution of insects in the free atmosphere. III. Thermal convection. *Can. Ent.* **77**: 44–49.

WILLIAMS, C. B. (1951). Seasonal changes in flight direction of migrant butterflies in the British Isles. *J. Anim. Ecol.* **20**: 180–190.

WILLIAMS, C. B. (1958). *Insect migration.* Collins, London.

YOUNG, E. C. (1965). Flight muscle polymorphism in British Corixidae: ecological observations. *J. Anim. Ecol.* **34**: 353–390.

SECTION C

The Abdomen, Reproduction and Development

CHAPTER XIV

THE ABDOMEN

The insect abdomen is more obviously segmental in origin than either the head or the thorax, consisting of a series of similar segments, but with the posterior segments modified for mating and oviposition. The musculature of the anterior segments is fairly uniform and it is concerned primarily with compressing and distending the abdomen in ventilatory movements. In general the abdominal segments are without appendages except for those concerned with reproduction and a pair of terminal, usually sensory, cerci. Pregenital appendages are, however, present in Apterygota and in many larval insects. Aquatic larvae often have segmental gills, while many holometabolous larvae, especially amongst the Diptera and Lepidoptera, have lobe-like abdominal legs called prolegs. It is not clear whether or not these are serially homologous with the thoracic legs.

All aspects of the insect abdomen are reviewed in detail by Matsuda (1976). The general structure is considered by Snodgrass (1935), and for a discussion on the origins of abdominal appendages see Hinton (1955).

14.1 Segmentation of the abdomen

14.1.1 Number of segments

The basic number of segments in the abdomen is eleven plus the postsegmental telson which bears the anus, although Matsuda (1976) regards the telson as a twelfth segment. Only in adult Protura and the embryos of some hemimetabolous insects is the full complement visible. In all other instances some degree of reduction has taken place. The telson, if it is present at all, is generally represented only by the circumanal membrane, but larval Odonata are exceptional in that three small sclerites surrounding the anus may represent the telson.

In general, more segments are visible in the more generalised hemimetabolous orders than in the more specialised holometabolous insects. Thus in Acrididae all eleven segments are visible (Fig. 197A) whereas in Muscidae only segments 2–5 are visible and segments 6–9 are telescoped within the others (Fig. 197B). Collembola are exceptional in having only six abdominal segments, even in the embryo.

The definitive number of segments is present at hatching in all hexapods except Protura. All the segments differentiate in the embryo and this type of development is called epimorphic. In Protura, on the other hand, the first instar larva hatches with only eight abdominal segments plus the telson; the remaining three segments are added at subsequent moults, arising behind the last abdominal segment, but in front of the telson (Fig. 198). This type of development is called anamorphic.

305

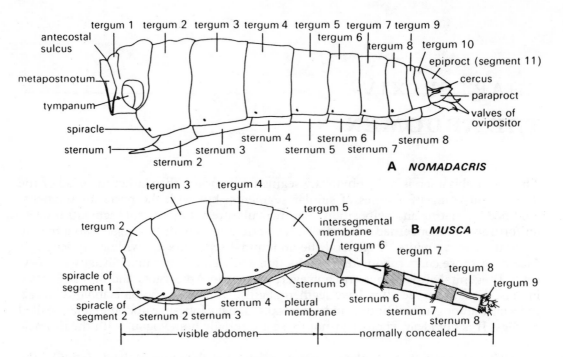

Fig. 197 Lateral view of the abdomen of (A) female *Nomadacris* and (B) female *Musca* with the terminal segments extended (after Albrecht, 1956; and Hewitt, 1914)

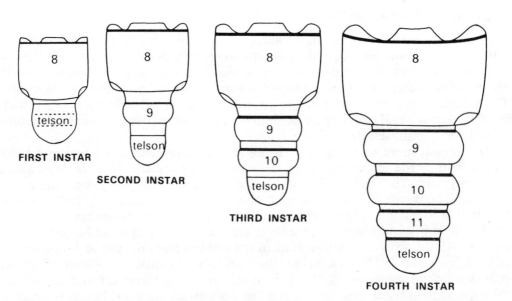

Fig. 198 Diagram illustrating the anamorphic development of the terminal abdominal segments of a proturan (from Denis, 1949)

In general, the abdomen is clearly marked off from the thorax, but this is not the case in Hymenoptera, where the first abdominal segment is intimately fused with the thoracic segments and is known as the propodeum. The waist of Hymenoptera Apocrita is thus not between the thorax and abdomen, but between the first abdominal segment and the rest of the abdomen. Often segment 2 forms a narrow petiole connecting the two parts. The swollen part of the abdomen behind the waist is called the gaster (Fig. 199).

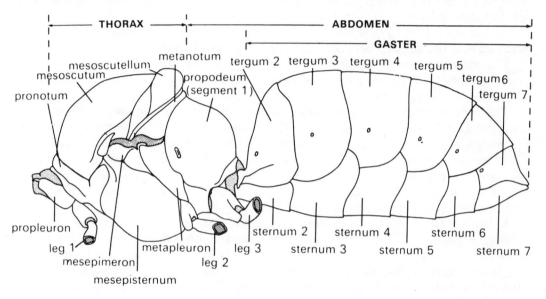

Fig. 199 Lateral view of the thorax and abdomen of *Apis* (after Snodgrass, 1956)

14.1.2 Structure of abdominal segments

A typical abdominal segment, such as the third, consists of a sclerotised tergum and sternum joined by membranous pleural regions (Fig. 202). In many holometabolous larvae, however, there is virtually no sclerotisation and the abdomen consists of a series of membranous segments. This is true in many Diptera and Hymenoptera, some Coleoptera and most lepidopterous larvae. In these the only sclerotised areas are small plates bearing trichoid sensilla, while in others, such as larval Thysanoptera, the membrane is studded with small sclerotised plaques. Even where well-developed terga and sterna are present these may be divided into a number of small sclerites as in the larva of *Calosoma* (Coleoptera) (Fig. 200).

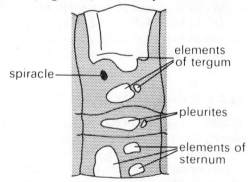

Fig. 200 Lateral view of an abdominal segment of a larva of *Calosoma* (after Snodgrass, 1935)

In other insects, however, the extent of sclerotisation may be increased by sclerites in the pleural regions (Fig. 200), and these pleural sclerites sometimes bear appendages. The styli of Thysanura (p. 312) and the gills of Ephemeroptera arise from such plates. Sometimes the tergum, sternum and pleural elements fuse to form a complete ring and this is true in the genital segments of many male insects, in segment 10 of Odonata, Ephemeroptera and Dermaptera and segment 11 of Machilidae.

Typically the posterior part of each segment overlaps the anterior part of the segment behind (Fig. 201), the two being joined by a membrane, but segments may fuse together, wholly or in part. For instance, in Acrididae the terga of segments 9 and 10 fuse together (Fig. 197), while in some Coleoptera the second sternum fuses with the next two and the sutures between them are largely obliterated.

The more anterior segments have a spiracle on either side. This may be set in the pleural membrane (Fig. 200), or in a small sclerite within the membrane, or on the side of the tergum (Fig. 197) or sternum.

The reproductive opening in male insects is usually on segment 9, while in the majority of female insects the opening of the oviduct is on or behind segment 8 or 9. The Ephemeroptera and Dermaptera are unusual in having the opening behind segment 7. These genital segments may be highly modified, in the male to produce copulatory apparatus (p. 361) and in the females of some orders to form an ovipositor. This may be formed by the sclerotisation and telescoping of the posterior abdominal segments, or it may involve modified abdominal appendages (p. 378).

In front of these genital segments the abdominal segments are usually unmodified, although segment 1 is frequently reduced or absent. Behind them segment 10 is usually developed, but segment 11 is often represented only by a dorsal lobe, the epiproct, and two lateroventral lobes, the paraprocts. In Plecoptera, Blattidae and Isoptera the epiproct is reduced and fused with the tergum of segment 10, while in most holometabolous insects segment 11 is lacking altogether and segment 10 is terminal.

Modifications of the terminal abdominal segments often occur in aquatic insects and are concerned with respiration (see Chapter XXIV). In some larval Diptera segment 8 may become long and thin, forming a respiratory siphon; this development is most marked in *Eristalis*, where segment 8 forms a telescopic tube. In mosquito larvae the siphon is a dorsal projection from segment 8 and in *Mansonia* the siphon is modified for piercing plant tissues. A similar modification of the terminal abdominal segment occurs in the larva of the syrphid *Chrysogaster*.

In *Nepa* and *Ranatra* (Heteroptera) the spiracles are not on a siphon, but air is conveyed to the terminal abdominal spiracles while the insect is under water by a tube formed from two processes held together by fine hooks.

14.1.3 Musculature

Where the cuticle of the abdomen is largely membranous, as in many holometabolous larvae, most longitudinal muscles run from one primitive intersegmental fold to the next (Fig. 75), but in well-sclerotised insects a secondary segmentation becomes superimposed on this primary pattern with the intersegmental sclerites fusing with the anterior ends of the following terga and sterna (p. 154) to produce antecostal ridges. In most insects the dorsal and ventral longitudinal muscles are in two series, external and internal (Fig. 201). The internal muscles run from one antecostal ridge to the next and

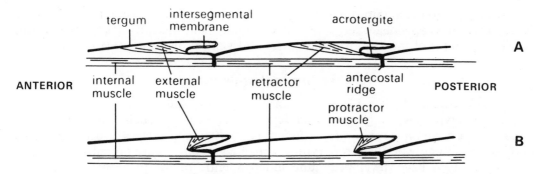

Fig. 201 Diagram of the dorsal longitudinal musculature in an abdominal segment. A. Typical arrangement of external and internal muscles, both acting as retractors. B. Origin of external muscle shifted posteriorly so that it acts as a protractor (from Snodgrass, 1935)

so retract the segments within each other. The external muscles are much shorter and only extend from the posterior end of one segment to the anterior end of the next and, because of the degree of overlap between the segments, the origins may be posterior to the insertions (Fig. 201B). Hence they may act as protractor muscles, extending the abdomen, and their efficiency is sometimes improved by the development of apodemes so that their pull is exerted longitudinally instead of obliquely. If such a protractor mechanism is absent extension of the abdomen results from the flexibility of the cuticle and the pressure of blood in the abdomen. In the grasshopper the external dorsal muscles are so placed that they produce some lateral twisting of the abdomen.

There are also lateral muscles which usually extend from the tergum to the sternum, but sometimes arise or are inserted into the pleuron. They are usually intrasegmental, but sometimes cross from one segment to the next. Their effect is to compress the abdomen dorso-ventrally. Dilation of the abdomen often results from its elasticity and from blood pressure, but in some insects some of the lateral muscles function as dilators. This occurs when the tergal origins of the muscles are carried ventrally by extension of the terga, while the sternal insertions may also be carried dorsally on apodemes (Fig. 202B).

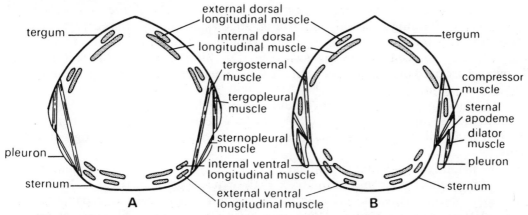

Fig. 202 Diagrammatic transverse sections of an abdominal segment. A. Typical arrangement of the muscles. B. Lateral muscles differentiated into compressor and dilator muscles (from Snodgrass, 1935)

In addition to the longitudinal and lateral muscles others are present in connection with abdominal appendages, especially the genitalia, and the spiracles (p. 538), while transverse bands of muscle form the dorsal and ventral diaphragms (p. 786).

14.2 Abdominal appendages

Insects are generally believed to have been derived from some myriapod-like ancestor with a pair of typical walking legs on each segment. Typical legs, such as are found on the thorax, never occur on the abdomen of insects, but various appendages do occur and some of these are probably derived from typical appendages. Others are probably secondary structures which have developed quite independently of the primitive appendages.

14.2.1 Primitive appendages

The appendages of segment 11 form a pair of structures called cerci, which arise from the membranes between the epiproct and the paraprocts, and even where segment 11 is absent the cerci may be present, appearing to arise from segment 10.

Cerci are present and well-developed in the Apterygota and the hemimetabolous orders other than the hemipteroids. In holometabolous insects their development varies and they may be reduced or completely absent (see Matsuda, 1976). They may be simple, unsegmented structures as in Orthoptera (Fig. 203A), or annulated as in Dictyoptera (Fig. 203B). They may be very short and barely visible or form long filaments as long or longer than the body as in Thysanura, Ephemeroptera and Plecoptera. Even within a group, such as the Acridoidea, the range of form of the cerci is considerable (Uvarov, 1966).

The cerci usually function as sense organs, being set with large numbers of trichoid sensilla with a complex articulation at the base. Thus they are sensitive to tactile stimuli and to air movement and sometimes act as sound receptors (p. 708).

Sometimes the cerci differ in the two sexes of a species, suggesting that they play a role in copulation. Thus the cerci of female *Calliptamus* (Orthoptera) are simple cones, but in the male they are elongate, flattened structures with two or three lobes at the apex armed with strong inwardly directed points. There is similar dimorphism in Embioptera, where the male cerci are generally asymmetrical with the basal segment of the left cercus forming a clasping organ (Fig. 203C) and amongst the earwigs the cerci form powerful forceps which are usually straight and unarmed in the female, but incurved and toothed in the male (Fig. 203D). Similar forceps-like cerci in the Japygidae are used in catching prey. In some holometabolous insects they form part of the external genitalia.

In larval Zygoptera the cerci are modified to form the two lateral gills (see Fig. 363), while in the ephemeropteran *Prosopistoma* the long, feather-like cerci, together with the median caudal filament, can be used to drive the insect forwards by beating against the water.

The primitive segmental appendages are not known to persist on segment 10, but those of segments 8 and 9 may be modified as the external genitalia (p. 361). In the more anterior segments many insects have appendages, but it is generally agreed that they are derived from segmental appendages only in the Apterygota. The first abdominal appendages are well developed in the embryo of insects belonging to a number of groups. They are known as pleuropodia (p. 422), but they do not persist after hatching.

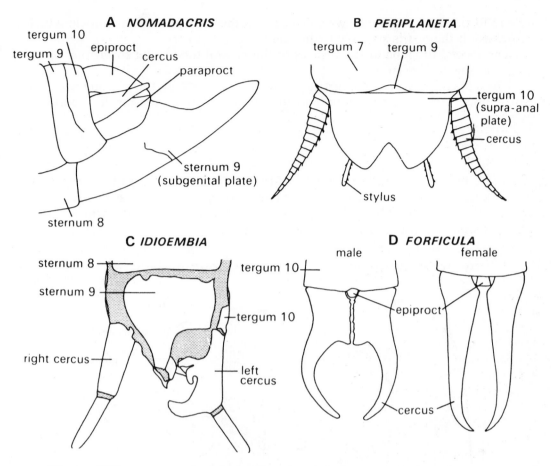

Fig. 203 Different types of cerci. A. *Nomadacris* (Orthoptera)—lateral view of tip of abdomen of male. B. *Periplaneta* (Dictyoptera)—dorsal view of the tip of the abdomen of male. C. *Idioembia* (Embioptera)—ventral view of tip of abdomen of male. D. *Forficula* (Dermaptera)—male and female forceps (cerci) (after various authors)

Collembola

The Collembola have pregenital appendages on three abdominal segments. From the first segment a median lobe projects forwards and down between the last pair of legs (see Fig. 101C, D). This is known as the ventral tube and at its tip are a pair of eversible vesicles which in many Symphypleona are long and tubular. The unpaired basal part of the ventral tube is believed to represent the fused coxae of the segmental appendages and the vesicles are thus coxal vesicles. The vesicles are everted by blood pressure from within the body and are withdrawn by retractor muscles.

The ventral tube appears to have two functions. In some circumstances it functions as an adhesive organ enabling the insect to walk over smooth or steep surfaces. To facilitate this on a dry surface the vesicles are moistened by a secretion from cephalic glands opening on to the labium and connecting with the ventral tube by a groove in the cuticle in the ventral midline of the thorax. The ventral tube also enables Collembola to adhere to the surface film on water since it is the only part of the cuticle which is wettable; all the rest is strongly hydrofuge.

The second function of the vesicles of the ventral tube is the absorption of water from the substratum (p. 597).

The appendages of the third and fourth segments of the abdomen of many Collembola form the retinaculum and the furca, which are used in locomotion (see p. 180).

Protura

There are pairs of appendages on each of the first three segments of the abdomen of Protura. At their most fully developed they are two segmented with an eversible vesicle at the tip (Fig. 204A). The appendages are moved by extrinsic and intrinsic muscles, which include a retractor muscle of the vesicle.

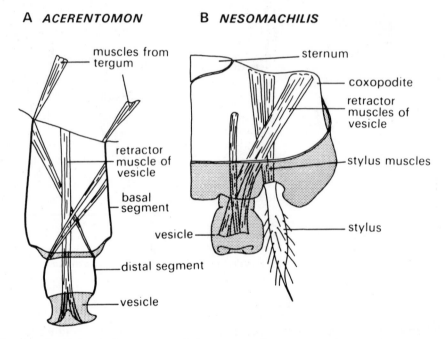

A ACERENTOMON   **B NESOMACHILIS**

Fig. 204 A. Abdominal appendage of *Acerentomon* (Protura). B. Abdominal appendage of *Nesomachilis* (Archaeognatha). The sternum and coxopodite are seen from the inside (from Snodgrass, 1935)

Archaeognatha, Thysanura and Diplura

On abdominal segments 2–9 of Machilidae, 7–9 or 8–9 of Lepismatidae, 1–7 of Japygidae and 2–7 of Campodeidae there are pairs of small, unjointed styli, each inserted on a basal sclerite which is believed to represent the coxa (Fig. 204B). Since similar styli are present on the coxae of the thoracic legs of *Machilis* (Archaeognatha) these styli are regarded as coxal epipodites.

Associated with the styli, but occupying a more median position, are eversible vesicles. These are present on segments 1–7 of Machilidae and 2–7 of *Campodea* (Diplura), but in Lepismatidae and Japygidae there are generally fewer or none. The vesicles evert through a cleft at the posterior margin of the segment, being forced out by blood pressure (Fig. 205). The retractor muscles of the vesicles arise close together on the anterior margin of the sternum. As in the Collembola, these vesicles can absorb water from the substratum (Drummond, 1953).

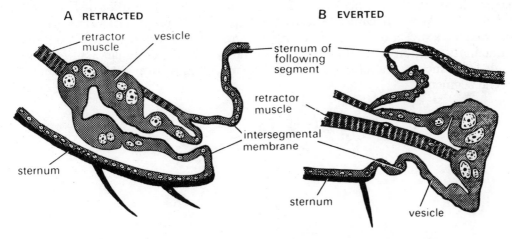

Fig. 205 Sections through an eversible vesicle of *Campodea*. (A) retracted and (B) everted (after Drummond, 1953)

14.2.2 Secondary appendages

Appendages are absent from the pregenital segments of adult insects other than Apterygota, but are widely present in the larvae of holometabolous insects and, as gills, in diverse aquatic larval forms. Some authorities regard these appendages as being derived from primitive segmental appendages (see *e.g.* Snodgrass, 1935), but it is probably more reasonable to regard most of them as secondary developments (Hinton, 1955) and this point of view is taken here.

Gills are present on the abdominal segments of the larvae of many aquatic insects. Ephemeroptera usually have six or seven pairs of plate-like or filamentous gills (Fig. 297) which are moved by muscles and may play a direct role in gaseous exchange, but perhaps are more important in maintaining a flow of water over the body (p. 562). Gill tufts may also be present on the first two or three abdominal segments, or in the anal region of larval Plecoptera. The larva of *Sialis* (Megaloptera) has seven pairs of five-segmented gills, each arising from a basal sclerite on the side of the abdomen (Fig. 208A), and a similar terminal filament arises from segment 9. Similar, but unsegmented gills are present in other larval Megaloptera and in some larval Coleoptera. Larval Trichoptera have filamentous gills in dorsal, lateral and ventral series.

Leg-like outgrowths of the body wall, known as prolegs, are common features of the abdomen of holometabolous larvae. These appendages are expanded by blood pressure and moved mainly by the normal muscles of the adjacent body wall together with others inserted at the base of the proleg and a retractor muscle extending to the sole or planta surface (see Fig. 104). Frequently the prolegs are armed distally with spines or crochets which grip the substratum and sometimes, when prolegs are not developed, their position is occupied by a raised pad armed with spines. Such a pad is called a creeping welt and is clearly comparable with a proleg (Fig. 300).

Creeping welts and prolegs are present in many dipterous larvae, some of which have several prolegs on each segment (Fig. 206) while others have creeping welts which extend all round the segment. The larvae of a number of families of Diptera have abdominal suckers which may be derived from prolegs. Thus the larva of the psychodid *Maruina* has a sucker on each of abdominal segments 1–8 and these enable the larva to maintain its position along the sides of waterfalls, and in another larva, of *Horaiella*, a single large sucker, bounded by a fringe of hairs, extends over the ventral surface of several segments.

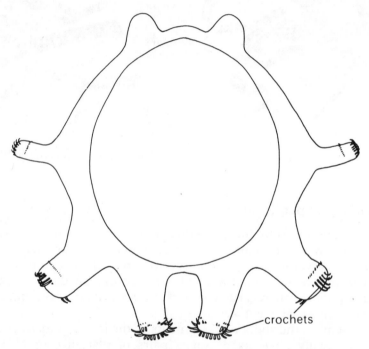

Fig. 206 Cross-section of an abdominal segment of a tabanid larva showing numerous prolegs, including dorsal and lateral pairs (after Hinton, 1955)

Larval Blepharoceridae, which live in fast-flowing streams and waterfalls, have a sucker on each of abdominal segments 2–7. Each sucker has an outer flaccid rim with an incomplete anterior margin. The central disc of the sucker is supported by close-packed sclerotised rods and in the middle a hole leads into an inner chamber with strongly sclerotised walls and an extensive folded roof (Fig. 207). Muscles inserted into the roof and the rim of the sclerotised walls of the inner chamber increase the volume of the chamber when they contract and if at the same time the rim of the sucker is pressed

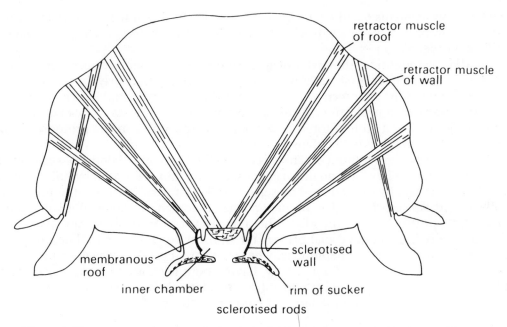

retractor muscle
of roof

retractor muscle
of wall

membranous
roof

inner chamber

sclerotised
wall

rim of sucker

sclerotised rods

Fig. 207 Transverse section through the sixth abdominal segment of a blepharocerid larva
showing the ventral sucker (after Hinton, 1955)

down on to the substratum a partial vacuum is created so that the sucker adheres to the
surface.

Even if a well-formed sucker is not present many dipterous larvae can produce a
sucker-like effect by raising the central part of the ventral surface while keeping the
periphery in contact with the substratum, the sucker being sealed and made effective by
a film of moisture.

Finally, in a few larval Diptera prolegs may be used for holding prey. The larva of
Vermileo lives in a pit in dry soil and feeds in the same way as an ant lion (p. 29). It lies
ventral side up and prey which fall into the pit are grasped against the thorax by a
median proleg on the ventral surface of the first abdominal segment.

Thus prolegs are present in many different families of Diptera and have a variety of
functions. Hinton (1955) suggests that prolegs have evolved separately in at least
twenty-seven different groups within the order.

Well-developed prolegs are also a feature of lepidopterous larvae, which usually
have a pair on each of abdominal segments 3–6 and 10 (Fig. 298). Embryological
evidence suggests that these prolegs may be serially homologous with the thoracic legs,
but the bulk of other evidence is opposed to this suggestion (Hinton, 1955). The prolegs
are armed distally with crochets (Fig. 104), which may form a complete ring, but
climbing forms have the prolegs pointed mesally with a median row of crochets so that
they are suited for grasping twigs. Climbing caterpillars occur in several families
including the Geometridae and Sphingidae.

The number of prolegs in lepidopterous larvae varies. Megalopygidae have prolegs
on segments 2–7 and 10, but those on segments 2 and 7 have no crochets. More
frequently the number of prolegs is reduced and in Geometridae there are usually only

two pairs, on segments 6 and 10. Prolegs are completely absent from some leaf-mining larvae and from the free-living Eucleidae, some of which, however, have weak ventral suckers on segments 1–7.

In some Notodontidae the anal prolegs are modified for defensive purposes. Thus in *Cerura* they are slender projections which normally point posteriorly, but if the larva is touched the tip of the abdomen is flexed forwards and a slender pink process is everted from the end of each projection. At the same time the larva raises its head and thorax from the ground and emits formic acid from a ventral gland in the prothorax. This reaction is presumed to be a defensive display.

Digitiform prolegs without crochets occur on the first eight abdominal segments of larval Mecoptera. They have no intrinsic musculature, but are moved by differences in blood pressure and by the action of muscles on adjacent parts of the ventral body wall. Prolegs without crochets also occur on the abdomen of larval Symphyta and particularly in the Tenthredinoidea. The number varies from six to nine pairs.

Larval Trichoptera have anal prolegs on segment 10 (Fig. 208B). Their development varies, but in the Limnephilidae, where they are most fully developed, there are two basal segments with a terminal claw, having both levator and depressor muscles. These appendages, together with a dorsal and two lateral retractile papillae on the first abdominal segment, enable the larva to hold on to its case.

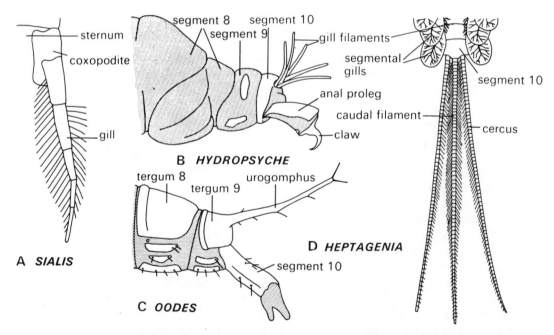

Fig. 208 Abdominal appendages of pterygote larvae. A. *Sialis* gill, dorsal view. B. *Hydropsyche* (Trichoptera) lateral view of terminal abdominal segments showing gills and anal proleg. C. *Oodes* (Coleoptera) lateral view of terminal abdominal segments showing urogomphus. D. *Heptagenia* (Ephemeroptera) dorsal view of terminal abdominal segments showing gills, cerci and median caudal filament (mainly from Snodgrass, 1935)

14.2.3 Other appendages

Apart from the segmentally arranged prolegs and gills some insects have other abdominal appendages, commonly in the form of a median process from the last segment. Thysanura and Ephemeroptera have a median caudal filament which resembles the two cerci (Fig. 208D). Larval Zygoptera have a median terminal gill on the epiproct, while in larval Sphingidae a terminal spine arises from the dorsum of segment 10. In larval mosquitoes and chironomids a group of four papillae surrounds the anus (see Fig. 384). These papillae are concerned with salt regulation (p. 589).

Some larval Coleoptera have a pair of processes called urogomphi, which are outgrowths of the tergum of segment 9 (Fig. 208C). They may be short spines or multiarticulate filaments and they may be rigid with the tergum or arise from the membrane behind it so that they are mobile. Jeannel (1949) regards them as homologous with cerci, but see Crowson (1960).

Aphids have a pair of tubes, known as cornicles, projecting from the dorsum of segment 6. Each cornicle has a terminal opening which is normally closed by a flap of cuticle controlled by an opener muscle and the whole structure can be moved by a muscle inserted at the base so that the cornicle can be pointed forwards. Lipid-filled cells are expelled through the terminal opening and in *Myzus* myristic acid is the principal lipid expelled. It is generally considered that these cornicles have a defensive function, but this is questioned by Lindsay (1969).

REFERENCES

ALBRECHT, F. O. (1956). The anatomy of the red locust, *Nomadacris septemfasciata* Serville. *Anti-Locust Bull.* no. 23, 9 pp.

CROWSON, R. A. (1960). The phylogeny of Coleoptera. *A. Rev. Ent.* **5**: 111–134.

DENIS, R. (1949). Sous-classe des Aptérygotes. *in* Grassé, P.-P. (ed.), *Traité de Zoologie*. vol. 9. Masson et Cie., Paris.

DRUMMOND, F. H. (1953). The eversible vesicles of *Campodea* (Thysanura). *Proc. R. ent. Soc. Lond.* A, **28**: 145–148.

HEWITT, C. G. (1914). *The house-fly, Musca domestica Linn.* Cambridge University Press.

HINTON, H. E. (1955). On the structure, function, and distribution of the prolegs of the Panorpoidea, with a criticism of the Berlese–Imms theory. *Trans. R. ent. Soc. Lond.* **106**: 455–545.

JEANNEL, R. (1949). Ordre des Coléoptéroïdes. *in* Grassé, P.-P. (ed.), *Traité de Zoologie*. vol. 9. Masson et Cie., Paris.

LINDSAY, K. L. (1969). Cornicles of the pea aphid, *Acyrthosiphon pisum*; their structure and function. A light and electron microscope study. *Ann. ent. Soc. Am.* **62**: 1015–1021.

MATSUDA, R. (1976). *Morphology and evolution of the insect abdomen*. Pergamon Press, Oxford.

SNODGRASS, R. E. (1935). *Principles of insect morphology*. McGraw-Hill, New York.

SNODGRASS, R. E. (1956). *Anatomy of the honey bee*. Constable, London.

UVAROV, B. P. (1966). *Grasshoppers and locusts*. vol. 1. Cambridge University Press.

CHAPTER XV

THE REPRODUCTIVE SYSTEM

The male and female reproductive systems generally consist of paired gonads connected to a median duct leading to the gonopore. Accessory glands are often present which in the male are usually concerned with spermatophore formation and sperm maintenance and in the female provide a glue for sticking the eggs to the substratum or provide the substance for a complex egg-case. The female has, in addition, a spermatheca for storing sperm after copulation.

Each gonad typically consists of a series of tubes, each with a germinal area at the tip containing the primordial sex cells. From these, spermatogonia or oogonia are produced, which can be seen in successive stages of development as they pass down the tube. Each secondary spermatogonium gives rise to four spermatozoa, but only a single oocyte is formed from each secondary oogonium. In some cases the oocyte is connected with trophic tissue, a primary function of which is the synthesis of RNA which is then transferred to the oocyte; in other cases the oocyte is independent of trophic cells and synthesises its own RNA. Protein yolk is derived from protein in the haemolymph, the female insect producing specific yolk proteins which are preferentially absorbed. The process of yolk formation is generally controlled by the corpora allata. An extremely large egg cell is produced, enclosed in a shell and passed to the oviduct. If conditions are adverse, oocytes may be resorbed.

Insects are not always sexually mature when they have completed the final moult to the adult stage and in species with an adult diapause there may be a considerable delay before mature sex cells are produced. Hence it is necessary to distinguish between becoming adult and becoming sexually mature.

General reviews of insect reproduction are given by Engelmann (1970) and de Wilde and de Loof (1973a), while the structure of reproductive organs is described by Snodgrass (1935). The fine structure of insect sperm is reviewed by Baccetti (1972) and Phillips (1970). For reviews of aspects of oogenesis see Hagedorn and Kunkel (1979), Engelmann (1979), Telfer (1975) and Telfer and Smith (1970). Control of reproduction is reviewed by de Wilde and de Loof (1973b), and nutritional aspects are considered by Johansson (1964). Bell and Bohm (1975) discuss oocyte resorption.

MALE

15.1 Anatomy of male internal reproductive organs

The male reproductive organs typically consist of a pair of testes connecting with paired seminal vesicles and a median ejaculatory duct (Fig. 209). In most insects there

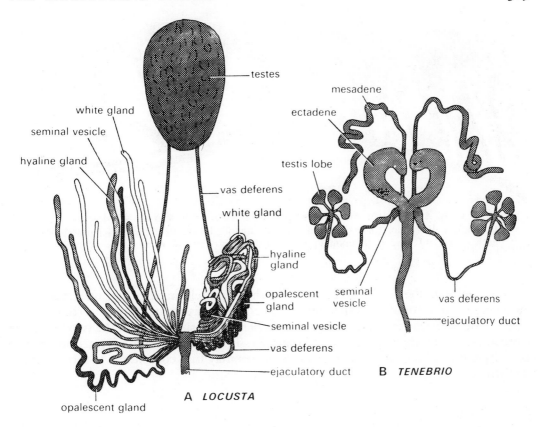

Fig. 209 Male reproductive system of (A) *Locusta,* with the accessory glands in their normal position on the right and separated on the left, and (B) *Tenebrio* (from Uvarov, 1966; Imms, 1957)

are also a number of accessory glands which open into the vasa deferentia or the ejaculatory duct.

Testis

The testes may lie above or below the gut in the abdomen and are often close to the midline. Usually each testis consists of a number of testis tubes or follicles. Sometimes, as in Coleoptera Adephaga, there is only a single follicle, in lice there are two, while in Acrididae there may be over 100. In other cases, as in Lepidoptera, the follicles are incompletely separated from each other (Fig. 210B), and the testes of Diptera consist of simple, undivided sacs, although these may be regarded as single follicles. Sometimes the testis consists of a series of lobes each of which consists of a number of follicles. Thus in the cerambycid *Prionoplus* each testis comprises 12 to 15 lobes each with 15 follicles (and see Fig. 209B). The testes of Apterygota are often undivided sacs, but it is not certain in this case that they are strictly comparable with the gonads of other insects since the germarium occupies a lateral position in the testis instead of being terminal.

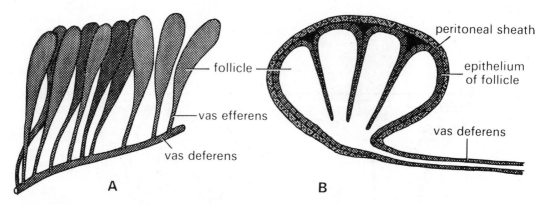

Fig. 210 A. A series of testis follicles opening independently into the vas deferens as in Orthoptera. B. Section through a testis in which the follicles are incompletely separated from each other and have a common opening to the vas deferens, as in Lepidoptera (from Snodgrass, 1935)

The walls of the follicles consist of a thin epithelium standing on a basement membrane and in some cases the epithelium consists of two layers of cells (Snodgrass, 1935). The follicles are bound together by a peritoneal sheath and if the two testes are close to each other they may be bound together. This occurs in some Hymenoptera and Lepidoptera, and in some of the latter the testes may fuse completely to form a single median structure.

Vas deferens

From each testis follicle a fine, and usually short, vas efferens connects with the vas deferens (Fig. 210A), which is a tube with a fairly thick bounding epithelium, a basement membrane and a layer of circular muscle outside it. The vasa deferentia run backwards to lead into the distal end of the ejaculatory duct and often they are dilated to form the seminal vesicles (Fig. 209B). In other cases, as in Acrididae, the seminal vesicles are separate diverticula arising from the ejaculatory duct (Fig. 209A), while in some Diptera there is a common median seminal vesicle.

Ejaculatory duct

The ejaculatory duct, which leads to the aedeagus (p. 361), is ectodermal in origin and is lined with cuticle. Often at least a part of the wall is muscular, but the ejaculatory duct in *Apis* is entirely without muscles (Snodgrass, 1956).

Where a complex spermatophore is produced the ejaculatory duct is also complex. Thus in *Locusta* (Orthoptera) the ejaculatory duct consists of upper and lower ducts connected via a funnel-like constriction (Fig. 211A). The lumen of the upper part of the duct is a vertical slit bounded laterally by columnar epithelium (Fig. 211D). In the funnel the cuticle forms a series of ridges, usually nine, on either side. These curve upwards posteriorly as they run back to meet in the dorsal midline and they project so that they almost completely divide the lumen (Fig. 211C). The lumen of the lower duct is circular and leads to the ejaculatory sac and spermatophore sac (Fig. 211A, B).

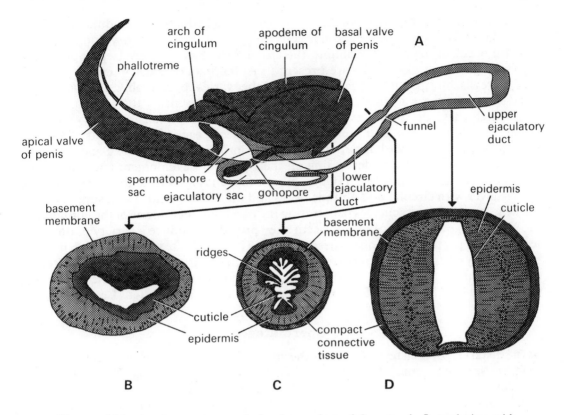

Fig. 211 Male copulatory organ and ejaculatory duct of *Locusta*. A. Lateral view with musculature removed. B. Transverse section of lower ejaculatory duct. C. Transverse section of funnel. D. Transverse section of upper ejaculatory duct (after Gregory, 1965)

Scattered muscle fibres are present in the wall of the upper duct but are absent elsewhere (Gregory, 1965).

The ejaculatory duct of *Oncopeltus* (Heteroptera) is also extremely complex, being specialised for the erection of the penis (Bonhag and Wick, 1953).

Ephemeroptera have no ejaculatory duct and the vasa deferentia lead directly to the paired genital openings. Dermaptera, on the other hand, have paired ejaculatory ducts, although in some species one of the ducts remains vestigial. Thus in *Forficula* the right-hand ejaculatory duct is fully functional while the left-hand duct is vestigial (Popham, 1965).

Accessory glands

The male accessory glands open into the vasa deferentia or the distal end of the ejaculatory duct. They may be ectodermal in origin, when they are known as ectadenia, and in this case they open into the ejaculatory duct. Ectadenia occur in Coleoptera and possibly other groups, but lack of embryological information makes this uncertain. Glands of mesodermal origin, mesadenia, are found in Orthoptera and in some cases, *Tenebrio* (Coleoptera) for instance, both ectadenia and mesadenia are present

(Fig. 209B). In some cases the epidermal cells of the main ducts are glandular, but there are no discrete glands. Such glandular cells line part of the ejaculatory duct in *Musca* and also occur in the tubes leading to the ejaculatory duct in many Lepidoptera. No accessory glands or gland cells are present in Apterygota or Palaeoptera.

Where discrete glands are present their number varies considerably. In *Schistocerca* and *Locusta* there are 15 pairs of accessory glands, not counting the seminal vesicles with which they are closely associated (Fig. 209), and *Periplaneta* has a very large number. In *Schistocerca*, and probably in other insects, each gland consists of a single layer of epithelial cells with microvilli extending into the lumen of the gland. The fine structure of the cells varies depending on their stage of development and also on the nature of the secretion produced (Odhiambo, 1969, 1971). Outside the epithelium is a muscle layer with circular and oblique fibres and the whole gland is well supplied with tracheae, some of the tracheoles penetrating the basement membrane of the epithelium.

Where large numbers of glands occur they probably produce a variety of different secretions. A primary function of these secretions is to facilitate sperm transfer (p. 367), but they may also act as barriers to further insemination, either physically or by altering the behaviour of the female. In some cases the secretions may have some nutritional value for the female (p. 375), or they may accelerate oocyte maturation (Leopold, 1976).

15.2 Spermatogenesis

At the distal end of each testis follicle is the germarium, in which the germ cells divide to produce spermatogonia (Fig. 212). In Orthoptera, Dictyoptera, Homoptera and Lepidoptera, the spermatogonia probably obtain nutriment from a large apical cell with which they have cytoplasmic connections, while in Diptera and Heteroptera (Bonhag and Wick, 1953) there is a comparable apical complex consisting of a syncytium with numerous nuclei. In Diptera the transfer of mitochondria from this complex to the spermatogonia has been observed (Carson, 1945).

These apical connections are soon lost and the spermatogonia associate with other cells which form a cyst around them (Fig. 212). One, or sometimes more, spermatogonia are enclosed in each cyst and, in *Prionoplus*, there are initially two cyst-cells round each spermatogonium. The cyst-cells may be spermatogonia which lack adequate nutrition and therefore fail to continue their normal development. They may supply nutriment to the developing sperm and, in *Popillia* (Coleoptera), the sperm at one stage

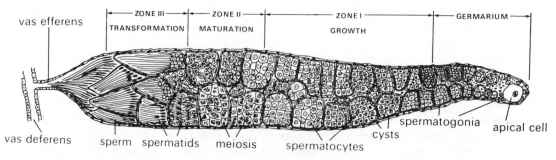

Fig. 212 Diagram of a testis follicle showing the stages of development of the sperm (from Wigglesworth, 1965)

have their heads embedded in the cyst-cells, this perhaps facilitating the transfer of nutrients (J. Anderson, 1950). In Heteroptera large cells with irregular nuclei, called trophocytes, are scattered amongst the cysts.

As more spermatogonia are produced they push those which have developed earlier down the follicle; a range of development is therefore present in each follicle with the earliest stages distally in the germarium and the oldest in the proximal part of the follicle adjacent to the vas deferens. Three zones of development are commonly recognised below the germarium (Fig. 212):

I a zone of growth, in which the primary spermatogonia, enclosed in cysts, divide and increase in size to form spermatocytes

II a zone of maturation and reduction, in which each spermatocyte undergoes the two meiotic divisions to produce spermatids

III a zone of transformation, in which the spermatids develop into spermatozoa, a process known as spermiogenesis.

Since, in general, all the cells in a cyst are derived from a single primary spermatogonium they remain synchronised in their subsequent development. The number of sperm which a cyst ultimately produces depends on the number of spermatogonial divisions which occur and this is fairly constant for a species. In Acrididae there are between five and eight spermatogonial divisions and Melanoplus, which typically has seven divisions before meiosis, usually has 512 sperm per cyst. Normally four spermatozoa are produced from each spermatocyte, but in many coccids the spermatids which possess heterochromatic chromosomes degenerate so that only two sperm are formed from each spermatocyte and 32 are present in each cyst (Nur, 1962). In Sciara (Diptera) only one spermatid is formed from each spermatocyte because of the unequal distribution of chromosomes and cytoplasm which occurs at the meiotic divisions (Phillips, 1966).

Biochemical changes occur in the course of spermatogenesis. The repeated cell divisions entail the synthesis of large amounts of DNA and RNA, but the synthesis of DNA stops before meiosis occurs, while RNA synthesis continues into the early spermatid. Subsequently no further synthesis occurs and the RNA is eliminated first from the nucleus and then from the cell as the nucleus elongates. The reduction in RNA synthesis is associated with a rise in the production of an arginine-rich histone which forms a complex with DNA stopping it from acting as a primer for RNA synthesis. It is suggested that this mechanism insulates the genetic material during transit from one generation to the next (Bloch and Brack, 1964; Das, et al., 1964; Muckenthaler, 1964).

The time taken for the completion of spermatogenesis varies, but in Melanoplus the period is about 28 days, the spermatogonial divisions occupying eight or nine days and spermiogenesis ten (Muckenthaler, 1964). In most insects meiosis is complete before the final moult and in insects which do not feed as adults spermatogenesis may be complete before the adult emerges (Fig. 213).

15.2.1 Structure of mature spermatozoa

The mature sperm of most insects are filamentous in form, often about 300 μm long and less than a micron in diameter, while the sperm of Drosophila (Diptera) may be as much as 1·7 mm long. The head and tail of the sperm are of approximately the same diameter (Fig. 214). The cell wall of the sperm is a typical three-layered membrane, but in some

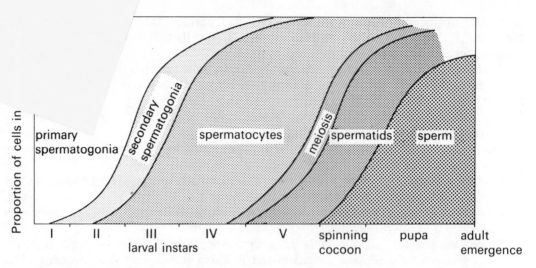

Fig. 213 Spermatogenesis in *Bombyx* showing the proportion of germ cells in each stage at different periods during the development of the insect (after Engelmann, 1970)

species it is coated on the outside by a layer of glycoprotein known as the glycocalyx. In fleas this is about 13 nm thick, and in grasshoppers about 30 nm; the cell membrane proper is about 10 nm thick. The glycocalyx is made up of rods at right angles to the surface of the sperm. Lepidopteran sperm have a series of projections running along their length. These projections are made up of thin laminae stacked parallel with the surface membrane. They become rearranged in the ejaculatory duct to form a complete coating all round the sperm (see Baccetti, 1972).

The greater part of the head region is occupied by the nucleus (Fig. 214). In the mature sperm of most species the nucleus is homogeneous in appearance, but sometimes, as in the grasshopper *Chortophaga*, it has a honeycomb appearance. The DNA is apparently arranged in strands parallel with the long axis of the sperm. In front of the nucleus is the acrosome. This is a membrane bound structure of glycoprotein with, in most insects, a granular extra-acrosomal layer and an inner rod or cone. Sperm of Neuroptera have no acrosome and occasional species with no acrosome occur in other orders. The acrosome is probably concerned with attachment of the sperm to the egg and possibly also with lysis of the egg membrane, thus permitting sperm entry. Mature sperm do not have a centriole, although this is present during spermiogenesis, but most insect sperm do have a centriole adjunct. This consists of a mass of ribonucleoprotein, usually in granular form, which develops at the back end of the nucleus. It is best developed in the spermatid and progressively declines in extent as development proceeds.

Immediately behind the nucleus the axial filament, or axoneme, arises. In most cases this consists of two central tubules with a ring of nine doublets and nine accessory tubules on the outside (Fig. 214). The central tubules are surrounded by a sheath and are linked radially to the doublets. Some unusual exceptions to this $9 + 9 + 2$ arrangement occur. Protura have 12 or 14 doublets with no other tubules, while accessory tubules are lacking in Collembola, Japygidae, Mecoptera and Siphonaptera. Psocoptera, Mallophaga, Anoplura, Thysanoptera and many bugs have two axial

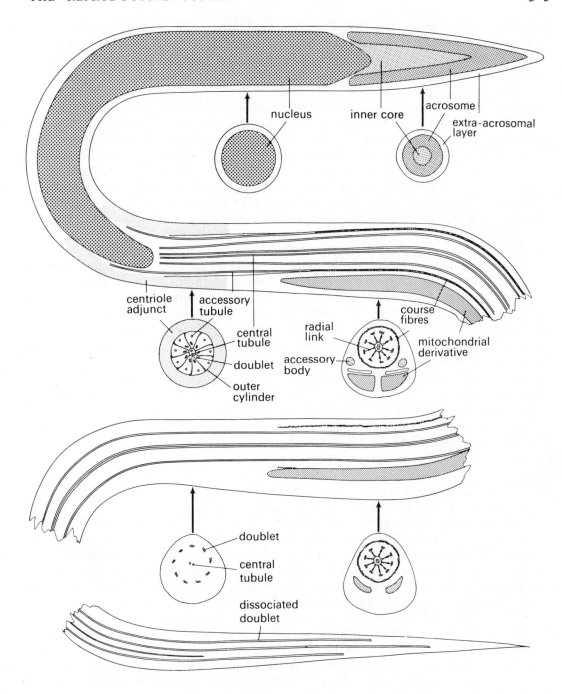

Fig. 214 Diagram showing the structure of a sperm in longitudinal section with representative transverse sections at the points shown. The anterior end shown in the upper half of the figure comprises only a small proportion of the total length

filaments in the sperm tail, while in *Sciara* (Diptera) there are 70–90 doublets, each with an associated accessary tubule, arranged in a spiral which encloses the mitochondrial derivative posteriorly. It is presumed that the axial filament or the equivalent structure causes the undulating movements of the tail which drive the sperm forwards.

The sperm of Pterygota have two mitochondrial derivatives (p. 329) which flank the axial filament. Within these the cristae become arranged as a series of lamellae projecting in from one side of the derivative and at right angles to its long axis. The matrix of the derivative is occupied by a paracrystalline material. Sperm of Mecoptera and Trichoptera and species of some other orders have only one mitochondrial derivative, while phasmids have none at all. In this case respiration is entirely anaerobic. More or less normal mitochondria persist in the sperm of Apterygota except that they fuse together and become elongated. There are three such mitochondria in the sperm tail of Collembola, and two in Diplura and Machilidae.

The sperm of coccids, which occur in bundles, lack all the typical organelles. In *Parlatoria* the nucleus is apparently represented by an electron opaque core with no limiting membrane. Mitochondrial derivatives are absent, but Robison (1966) suggests that the homogeneous cytoplasm of the sperm is a mitochondrial product and serves as a store of energy so that mitochondria themselves are not necessary. Each sperm has 45–50 microtubules about 20 nm in diameter in a spiral round a central mass of chromatin. These run the whole length of the sperm and may be concerned with its mobility, replacing the typical axial filament.

In Kalotermitidae and Rhinotermitidae there is no flagellum at all. The sperm of *Reticulitermes* is spherical with no acrosome, but it has a few normal mitochondria. There are also two short axial filaments, but these do not protrude from the body of the sperm. It is presumed that this sperm is non-motile. Non-motile sperm also occur in the dipteran family Psychodidae and in *Eosentomon* (Protura).

Sperm bundles

In a number of insects sperm are grouped together in bundles for at least some part of their existence and sometimes the bundles persist even after transference of the sperm to the female. The sperm of *Thermobia* normally occur in pairs, the two individuals being twisted round each other, and although their plasma membranes remain distinct an electron opaque substance is visible between them where they are close together. In addition, a continuous membrane appears to be present round both spermatozoa in some places (Bawa, 1964). Pairs of sperm also occur in some Coleoptera.

Coccids have much more specialised sperm bundles. In these insects each cyst commonly produces 32 sperm and these may become separated into two bundles of about 16 sperms. Each bundle becomes enclosed in a membranous sheath and the cyst wall degenerates. The bundles of *Pseudococcus* are much longer than the sperm, which occupy only the middle region, and the head-end of the bundle has a corkscrew-like form, which may be involved in locomotion (Nur, 1962). The sperm bundles of *Parlatoria*, on the other hand, are only the same length as the sperm, which are all orientated in the same direction within the bundle. Movement of the bundle results from the combined activity of the sperm within (Robison, 1966).

In some Orthoptera and Odonata different types of sperm bundle, known as spermatodesms, are formed. The spermatodesms of tettigoniids comprise about ten sperm anchored together by their acrosomes. These bundles are released from the testis and the sperm heads then become enclosed in a muff of mucopolysaccharide secreted by the gland cells of the duct. In acridids the whole structure is completed within the testis cyst and may include all the sperm within it. The spermatids come to lie with their heads orientated towards a cyst cell and extracellular granular material round the acrosome of each coalesces to form a cap in which the heads of all the sperm are embedded (Szöllösi, 1974). The spermatodesms of Acrididae persist until they are transferred to the female.

15.2.2 Sperm capacitation

In a number of species sperm undergo changes after they are transferred to the female spermatheca and in some cases, at least, these changes are essential before the sperm can fertilise an egg. This process of maturation of sperm within the female is known as capacitation. In *Sciara* part of the mitochondrial derivative is sloughed off and at this time the sperm becomes motile. In coccids the sperm, which were previously in bundles, become separated, while in Lepidoptera and other groups changes occur in the glycocalyx.

15.2.3 Spermiogenesis

The spermatid which is formed after meiosis is typically a rounded cell containing the normal cell organelles. Subsequently it becomes modified to form the sperm and this process of spermiogenesis entails a complete reorganisation of the cell. It is convenient to consider separately each organelle of the mature sperm.

Acrosome

The acrosome is derived, at least in part, from Golgi material, which in spermatocytes is scattered through the cytoplasm in the form of dictyosomes. There may be 30 or 40 of these in the cell and they consist of several pairs of parallel membranes with characteristic vacuoles and vesicles (Fig. 215A). After the second meiotic division the dictyosomes in *Acheta* fuse to a single body called the acroblast, which consists of 6–10 membranes forming a cup with vacuoles and vesicles both inside and out (Fig. 215B).

In the later spermatid a granule, called the pro-acrosomal granule, appears in the cup of the acroblast and increases in size. The acroblast migrates so that the open side faces the nucleus and then the granule, associated with a newly developed membrane, the interstitial membrane, moves towards the nucleus and becomes attached to it (Fig. 215C). As the cell elongates the acroblast membranes migrate to the posterior end of the spermatid and are sloughed off together with much of the cytoplasm and various other cell inclusions. The pro-acrosomal granule then forms the acrosome, becoming cone-shaped and developing a cavity in which an inner cone is formed (Fig. 215D) (Kaye, 1962).

In *Gelastocoris* (Heteroptera) the pro-acrosome is formed from the fusion of granules in the scattered Golgi apparatus and no acroblast is formed. This may also be the case in Acrididae (F. Payne, 1966).

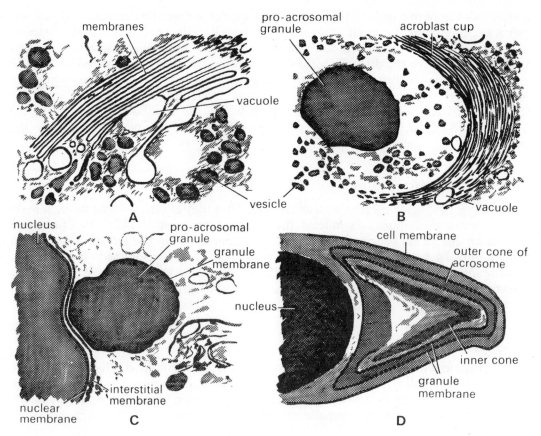

Fig. 215 Development of the acrosome of *Acheta*. A. A dictyosome. B. Acroblast with pro-acrosomal granule. C. Pro-acrosomal granule attached to the nucleus. D. Acrosome of a mature spermatozoon. Not all to same scale (after Kaye, 1962)

Nucleus

In the early spermatid of grasshoppers the nucleus appears to have a typical interphase structure with the chromosome fibrils unorientated. In *Chorthippus* each of the fibrils, which constitute the basic morphological units of the chromosomes, is about 20 nm in diameter and is made up of two subunits about 10 nm in diameter. The nucleus becomes very long and narrow and as it does so the chromosome fibrils become aligned more or less parallel with its long axis. The 10 nm microfibrils appear to separate into 4 nm fibrils and at the same time the non-histone protein, which in *Acheta* is largely in granules in the nucleoplasm, disappears from the nucleus (see above). The 4 nm fibrils appear to form an anastomosing network when the nucleus is seen in cross-section and as the nucleus elongates and narrows the nucleoplasm between them is progressively reduced until finally the whole of the nucleus appears to consist of a uniformly dense material (Dass and Ris, 1958). A similar linear arrangement of the chromosomes occurs in other groups but in several species the fibrils become thicker rather than thinner. In *Acheta* Kaye and McMaster-Kaye (1966) suggest that the nucleus at this time does not consist wholly of chromatin, but also contains thin fibres containing non-histone protein.

Mitochondria

In the spermatid the mitochondria fuse to form a single large body, the nebenkern, which consists of an outer limiting membrane and a central pool of mitochondrial components. The nebenkern separates into two mitochondrial derivatives which are associated with the developing axial filament immediately behind the nucleus and which elongate to form a pair of ribbon-like structures. At the same time the internal structure of the mitochondrion is reorganised so that the cristae form a series of parallel lamellae along one side and the matrix is replaced by paracrystalline material.

Centriole and axial filament

Young spermatids contain two centrioles composed, as in most cells, of nine triplets of tubules and orientated at right angles to each other. One gives rise to the axial filament, but ultimately both disappear. The tubules of the axial filament grow out from the centriole and are initially enclosed within a cup-shaped vesicle. They elongate to extend finally throughout the length of the tail of the sperm. The accessory tubules arise from tubule doublets, appearing first as side arms, which become C-shaped and then separate off and close up to form cylinders (Phillips, 1970).

15.2.4 Control of spermatogenesis

The factors which regulate spermatogenesis are not well understood (see review by Dumser, 1980). There is no strong evidence to indicate that hormones are generally involved (Engelmann, 1970), but in some moths the moulting hormone facilitates the process by increasing the permeability of the wall of the testis to some macromolecular factor (de Wilde and de Loof, 1973b). The corpora allata do, however, regulate maturation of the accessory glands and may affect other aspects of maturation and reproductive behaviour (see Chapter XXXIV).

15.3 Transfer of sperm to the seminal vesicle

In some Heteroptera, in *Chortophaga* (Orthoptera), and possibly in other insects, the sperm make a complex circuit of the testis follicle before they leave the testis, moving in a spiral path to the region of the secondary spermatocytes and then turning back and passing into the vas deferens. In *Chortophaga* the movement occurs after the spermatodesm is released from the cyst, but in the heteropteran *Leptocoris* the sperm are still enclosed in the cyst. In this case the displacement starts while the spermatids are still differentiating and is at least partly due to the elongation of the cyst which occurs during the development of the sperm (M. Payne, 1934).

The fate of the cyst-cells is variable. In *Prionoplus* they break down in the testis (Edwards, 1961), but in *Popillia*, although the sperm escape from the cysts as they leave the testis, the cyst-cells accompany the sperm in the seminal fluid into the bursa of the female. Here they finally break down and it is suggested that they release glycogen which is used in the maintenance of the sperm (J. Anderson, 1950).

The sperm are inactive in the vas deferens and are carried along by peristaltic movements of the wall of the tube (M. Payne, 1933, 1934). They remain immobile in the seminal vesicle, where they are often very tightly packed and in some cases, as in *Apis*, the heads of the sperm are embedded in the glandular wall of the vesicle.

FEMALE

15.4 Anatomy of female internal reproductive organs

The female reproductive system consists of a pair of ovaries, which connect with a pair of lateral oviducts. These join to form a median oviduct opening posteriorly into a genital chamber. Sometimes the genital chamber forms a tube, the vagina, and this is often developed to form a bursa copulatrix for reception of the penis. Opening from the genital chamber or the vagina is a spermatheca for the storage of sperm, and frequently a pair of accessory glands is present (Fig. 216).

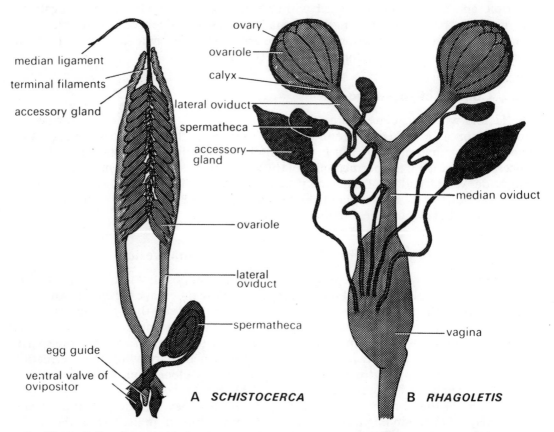

Fig. 216 Female reproductive systems of (A) *Schistocerca* and (B) *Rhagoletis* (Diptera) (partly after Snodgrass, 1935)

Ovary

The ovaries lie in the abdomen above or lateral to the gut. Each consists of a number of egg-tubes, or ovarioles, comparable with the testis follicles in the male. Development of the oocytes takes place in the ovarioles.

The number of ovarioles is roughly constant within a species, although in locusts it is affected by the treatment of the parental population. Thus *Schistocerca* reared from parents bred in a crowd have an average of 96 ovarioles in the two ovaries, while others after three generations of breeding in isolation have about 116 (Uvarov, 1966). There is also evidence of geographical variation in the numbers of ovarioles in African grasshoppers (Phipps, 1962) and within the Acridoidea some families tend to have more than others. Pyrgomorphidae, for instance, tend to have more ovarioles than Gomphocerinae of the same size. In general larger species have more ovarioles than small ones; thus the small British grasshoppers commonly have a total of eight ovarioles, the larger locusts about 100.

Similar variation occurs in other orders. *Calliphora* (Diptera) has about 100 ovarioles in each ovary, *Drosophila* 10–30, while the viviparous Diptera, *Melophagus*, *Hippobosca* and *Glossina* have only two in each ovary. Some viviparous aphids exhibit extreme reduction in the number of ovarioles, having only one functional ovary with a single ovariole. At the other extreme are the queens of some species of termite: *Eutermes* has over 2000 ovarioles in each ovary. Most Lepidoptera have only four ovarioles on each side.

The ovaries of Collembola are not composed of ovarioles, but are sac-like with a lateral germarium from which files of oocytes are produced. The ovaries are probably not homologous with those of pterygote insects.

Other than in the Diptera there is no sheath enclosing the ovary as a whole, but each ovariole has a wall which, frequently at least, is made up of two layers: an outer ovariole sheath and an inner tunica propria (Fig. 219A). The external sheath is a cellular network of modified fatty tissue. The cells of this net are rich in lipids and glycogen and are metabolically active, but there is no evidence that they are directly concerned with oocyte development. Tracheoles also form part of the external sheath, but they do not penetrate it and all the oxygen utilised by the ovariole diffuses in from these elements. In *Periplaneta* mycetocytes (p. 96) are present in the sheath, but there are no muscle fibres such as are present in the sheaths of *Bombyx* (Lepidoptera) and *Drosophila* (King and Aggarwal, 1965).

The tunica propria is an elastic membrane containing fine fibrils. It surrounds the whole of the ovariole and the terminal filament. During the early stages of development it increases in thickness, but subsequently during vitellogenesis, when the oocytes enlarge rapidly, it becomes stretched and very thin. It is possibly a secretion of the terminal filament and follicle cells. The tunica propria has a supporting function, and in addition, because of its elasticity, it plays a part in ovulation (section 15.7) (Bonhag and Arnold, 1961). Amoeboid cells in the space between the ovariole sheath and the tunica propria may be concerned with repairing the latter if it is damaged (Koch and King, 1966).

Distally each ovariole is produced into a long terminal filament consisting of a syncytial core bounded by the tunica propria. Usually the individual filaments from each ovary combine to form a suspensory ligament and sometimes the ligaments of the two sides merge into a median ligament (Fig. 216A). The ligaments are inserted into the body wall or the dorsal diaphragm and so suspend the developing ovaries in the haemocoel.

Proximally the ovariole narrows to a fine duct, the pedicel, which connects with the oviduct. In the immature insect the lumen of the ovariole is cut off from the pedicel by an epithelial plug (Fig. 219B), but this is destroyed at the time of the first ovulation and subsequently is replaced by a plug of follicular tissue (p. 346).

The ovarioles may enter the oviduct in a linear sequence and so if there are only a few, as in some Apterygota and Ephemeroptera, they may appear to be segmental. This arrangement is probably of no particular significance and is not apparent in insects with a larger number of ovarioles (Fig. 216A). In other groups, such as the Lepidoptera and Diptera, the ovarioles open together into an expansion of the oviduct known as the calyx (Fig. 216B).

Oviducts

The oviducts are tubes with walls of a single layer of cuboid or columnar cells standing on a basement membrane and with a muscle layer outside. In Acridoidea a part of the wall is glandular. Usually the two lateral oviducts join a median oviduct which is ectodermal in origin and hence is lined with cuticle, but the Ephemeroptera are exceptional in having the lateral oviducts opening separately by two gonopores. The median oviduct is usually more muscular than the lateral ducts, with circular and longitudinal muscles. It opens at the gonopore which, in Dermaptera, is ventral on the posterior end of segment 7, but in most other groups opens into a genital chamber invaginated above the sternum of segment 8 (Fig. 217A). Sometimes the genital chamber becomes tubular and is then effectively a continuation of the oviduct through segment 9. This continuation is called the vagina and its opening the vulva. It is often not distinguishable in structure from the oviduct, but its anterior end, and the position of the true gonopore, is marked by the insertion of the spermatheca (Snodgrass, 1935).

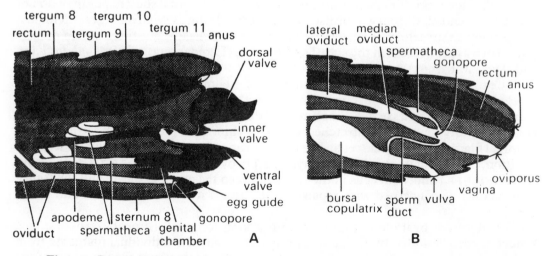

Fig. 217 Diagrammatic sagittal sections of the end of the abdomen of (A) *Locusta* and (B) a ditrysian lepidopteran (from Uvarov, 1966; Imms, 1957)

Frequently the vagina is developed to form a pouch, the bursa copulatrix, which receives the penis, while in viviparous Diptera the anterior part of the chamber is enlarged to form the uterus, in which larval development occurs (p. 437).

Most female Lepidoptera are unusual in having two reproductive openings. One on segment 9 serves for the discharge of eggs and is known as the oviporus, while the other on segment 8 is the copulatory opening, the vulva. The latter leads to the bursa copulatrix which is connected with the oviduct by a sperm duct (Fig. 217B).

Two openings also occur in the water beetles *Agabus*, *Ilybius* and *Hydroporus*, but here both openings are terminal with the opening of the bursa copulatrix immediately above the vaginal opening (Jackson, 1960).

Spermatheca

A spermatheca, which serves for the storage of sperm from the time the female is impregnated until the eggs are fertilised, is present in most female insects. Sometimes two are present, as in *Blaps* (Coleoptera) and *Phlebotomus* (Diptera), and most of the higher flies have three (Fig. 216B). In the lower orders of insects, as in Orthoptera, the spermatheca opens into the genital chamber independently of the oviduct (Fig. 217A), but where the genital chamber forms a vagina the spermathecal opening becomes internal and is effectively within the oviduct (Fig. 217B).

The spermatheca is ectodermal in origin and is lined with cuticle. Typically it consists of a storage pouch with a muscular duct leading to it, and often there is an associated gland, or the spermathecal epithelium may itself be glandular, producing secretions which probably provide nutrients for the sperm.

Accessory glands

Female accessory glands often arise from the genital chamber or the vagina, but in Acrididae they are simply anterior extensions of the lateral oviducts (Fig. 216A). Where such glands are apparently absent the walls of the oviducts may be glandular, and this is the case in Pyrgomorphidae (D. Anderson, 1965). Often the glands produce a substance for attaching the eggs to the substratum during oviposition and hence they are often called colleterial glands, but there are frequent instances of specialised functions which have been most fully investigated in *Periplaneta*. In this insect the eggs are laid in an ootheca consisting of a tanned, cuticle-like substance, which is produced by the accessory glands. The two glands open into the genital chamber and each consists of a mass of branched tubules lined with cuticle. The cuticle is secreted by epidermal cells, but opening between these are the gland cells. These differ in different parts of the glands and in the left gland, which is larger than the right, three types are recognisable, but all of them possess a structure called the end-apparatus which forms the secreting surface of the cell. It consists of an invagination of the free margin lined with radially directed microvilli projecting into it (Fig. 218). In the most distal cells (Type 4 of Brunet, 1952) the ends of the microvilli are free, but in the more proximal types 2 and 3 they end in a dense feltwork. The type 4 cells occupy the bulk of the gland and they, perhaps together with the type 2 cells, produce the protein from which the ootheca is formed. In addition this gland produces a β-glucoside of protocatechuic acid and an oxidase, the latter possibly from the type 2 cells. The type 4 cells may become

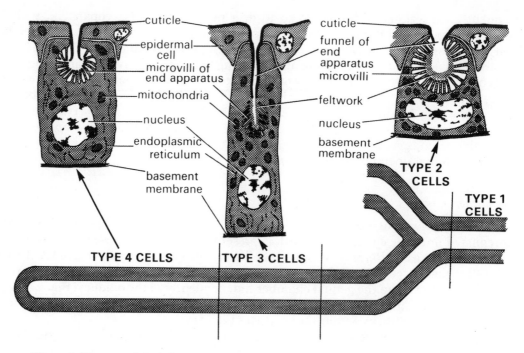

Fig. 218 Diagram of the left colleterial gland of *Periplaneta* showing the different types of secretory cells and their positions in the gland (based on Brunet, 1953; and Mercer and Brunet, 1959)

inactive after a time and they may be replaced by the type 3 cells. The right-hand gland has two types of secretory cell, both of which are columnar with a tubular end-apparatus. It secretes a β-glucosidase which liberates protocatechuic acid from its β-glucoside when the secretions of the two glands mix in the genital chamber. The protocatechuic acid is oxidised to a quinone by the oxidative enzymes and this tans the protein to produce a cuticle-like structure (p. 523) (Brunet, 1952; Mercer and Brunet, 1959).

The frothy secretions which form the eggpods of grasshoppers and the gelatinous sheath of *Chironomus* (Diptera) eggs are also produced by the accessory glands. In *Hydrophilus* (Coleoptera) the accessory glands produce silk, which forms the cocoon in which the eggs are laid. The cocoon is moulded to the shape of the abdomen with the aid of the forelegs, then the abdomen is withdrawn and the eggs are laid. Finally the cocoon is sealed off and remains floating on the surface of the water. It is equipped with a silken 'mast' about an inch high, which serves a respiratory function (Fig. 243A).

Glands associated with the genitalia perform a variety of functions in female Hymenoptera. The poison used by Pompilidae and others to paralyse their prey, and that used in a defensive manner by *Apis* and various ants, is derived from such glands. Another gland may serve to lubricate the ovipositor, while in many ants pheromones used in marking trails are produced by glands discharging via the sting (p. 858).

15.5 Oogenesis

Each ovariole consists of a distal germarium in which oocytes are produced from oogonia, and a more proximal vitellarium in which the oocytes grow as yolk is deposited in them. The vitellarium in a mature insect forms by far the greater part of the ovariole.

The germarium contains prefollicular tissue (see below) and the stem line oogonia and their derivatives. The stem line oogonia are derived directly from the original germ cells (p. 428), and in *Drosophila* there are only one or two of these in each ovariole (Chandley, 1966; Koch and King, 1966). When they divide, one of the daughter cells retains the function of the stem line cell, while the other becomes a definitive oogonium and develops into an oocyte. Oocytes pass back down the ovariole, enlarging as they do so, and as each oocyte leaves the germarium it is clothed by the prefollicular tissue which forms the follicular epithelium. At first this may be two- or three-layered, but ultimately it comes to consist of a single layer of cells. Oocyte growth continues and the follicular epithelium keeps pace by cell division, so that its cells become cuboid or columnar. In *Drosophila* the number of follicle cells round each oocyte increases from an initial figure of about 80 to about 1200. Subsequently, during yolk deposition, growth of the oocyte is very rapid, but at this time the follicle cells do not divide and they become stretched over the oocyte as a flattened, squamous epithelium. Nuclear division may continue without cell division so that the cells become binucleate or endopolyploid and this may have the effect of maintaining a suitable ratio of genetic material to actively synthesising cytoplasm in these relatively large cells.

As the oocyte grows the nucleus also increases in size, due largely to the production of more karyolymph, while the strands forming the chromosomes are dispersed and lose their basophilic staining properties. The nucleus is now known as the germinal vesicle and at first it increases in size as rapidly as the oocyte, but during yolk deposition the oocyte grows much more rapidly and the germinal vesicle becomes relatively smaller (Seshacher and Bagga, 1963).

Typically each ovariole contains a linear series of oocytes in successive stages of development with the most advanced in the most proximal position at the greatest distance from the germarium (Fig. 219). An oocyte with its surrounding follicular epithelium is termed a follicle and successive follicles are separated by interfollicular tissue derived from the prefollicular tissue. The number of follicles in a mature ovariole is variable between species, but roughly constant for a species. Thus *Schistocerca* commonly has about 20 follicles in each ovariole and this number is present even in senile females which have oviposited several times, suggesting that more oocytes are produced as the older ones are ovulated. In *Oncopeltus* there are often eight follicles per ovariole and in *Drosphila* six, while *Melophagus* has only one follicle in each ovariole at any one time.

In most insects the meiotic divisions are not completed in the ovary and oocytes usually leave the ovarioles in the metaphase of the first maturation division. This, however, is not true of viviparous species such as *Hemimerus* (Dermaptera) or in *Cimex* (Heteroptera) and related species in which fertilisation takes places in the ovary; in these, maturation of the oocytes is completed in the ovary.

15.5.1 Types of ovariole

There are two broad categories of ovarioles: panoistic, in which there are no special nurse cells, and meroistic, in which nurse cells, or trophocytes, are present. Further, there are two types of meroistic ovariole: telotrophic, in which all the trophocytes are terminal in the germarium, and polytrophic, in which trophocytes accompany each oocyte and are enclosed within the follicle.

Panoistic

Panoistic ovarioles, which have no speciliased nurse cells, are found in the more primitive orders of insects, the Thysanura, Odonata, Plecoptera, Orthoptera and Isoptera. Amongst the holometabolous insects only Siphonaptera have ovarioles of this type. The prefollicular tissue may be cellular, but sometimes, as in *Thermobia* (Thysanura) (Fig. 219A) it consists of small scattered nuclei in a common cytoplasm.

Telotrophic

Telotrophic ovarioles are characterised by the presence of trophic tissue as well as oogonia and oocytes in the germarium. This arrangement is found in Heteroptera and many Coleptera Polyphaga. The trophic cells are derived, with the oocytes, from the oogonia, but their subsequent development varies. In *Oncopeltus* the trophic tissue can be divided into three zones (Fig. 219B):

1. in which the cells are distinct, but probably connected to each other by intercellular bridges (see below). Cell division occurs in this zone and the cells pass to Zone 2.

2. in which the cell boundaries are lost and the nuclei, often bigger than in Zone 1, aggregate in clusters.

3. in which the nuclei are bigger still, probably as a result of endomitosis, and occupy the periphery of the ovariole so that a mass of cytoplasm, forming the trophic core, remains in the centre. Nuclei migrate from the periphery into the core and some of them fuse to form giant nuclei, but ultimately they all break down, releasing their contents into the cytoplasm.

In Coleoptera with telotrophic ovarioles the trophic cells do not divide in the adult, although endomitosis probably occurs. The cells do not break down to form a trophic core but form a syncytium in which they are connected by intercellular bridges.

Proximal to the trophic tissue are the oocytes and prefollicular tissue and, as in other types of ovariole, oocytes become clothed by follicle cells as they leave the germarium. Each oocyte is connected to the germarium by a cytoplasmic nutritive cord which extends to the trophic core, elongating as the oocyte passes down the ovariole. Finally, at the time of vitellogenesis, the nutritive cord breaks and the follicle cells form a complete layer round the oocyte. In Coleoptera the nutritive cords are much finer than in Heteroptera and they may disappear as the follicles are completed.

Polytrophic

Polytrophic ovarioles have trophocytes enclosed in the follicles with each oocyte (Fig. 219C, 221). They occur in Dermaptera, lice and throughout the holometabolous

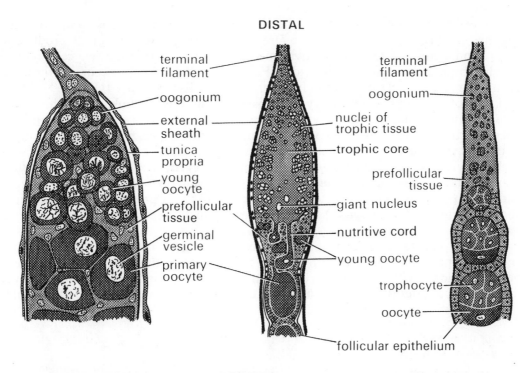

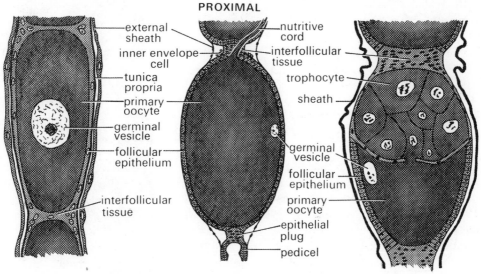

Fig. 219 Diagrams illustrating the structure of the distal region of the ovariole, including the germarium (above) and a proximal part with well-developed oocyte (below) in (A) panoistic, (B) telotrophic and (C) polytrophic ovarioles (from Bonhag, 1958; Davey, 1965)

orders, except for the Siphonaptera. The distal end of the germarium is occupied by the oogonia, of which there are about 50 in *Drosophila*. An oogonium divides to produce an oocyte and a trophocyte, but the division is incomplete so that the two cells remain attached by a narrow cytoplasmic bridge. Further divisions usually occur and these too are incomplete, so that a complex of interconnecting cells is produced (Fig. 220). These divisions of the trophocytes are synchronised by cues, as yet unknown, which pass through the cytoplasmic bridges. The number of trophocytes associated with each oocyte is characteristic for each species, although in those species with larger numbers of trophocytes some variation may occur. Dermaptera have only one trophocyte with each oocyte, *Aedes* and *Melophagus* (Diptera) seven, *Drosophila* and *Dytiscus* (Coleoptera) 15, *Apis* and *Bombus* (Hymenoptera) 48 and *Carabus* (Coleoptera) 127. In addition to oocytes and trophocytes, prefollicular tissue is present in the germarium and in *Anisolabis* (Dermaptera) the prefollicular nuclei are scattered in a common cytoplasm.

As each oocyte with its trophocytes leaves the germarium the oocyte always occupies a proximal position with respect to the base of the ovariole. All the cells become enclosed within a common epithelial layer, which soon becomes flattened over the trophocytes, but is thicker, with cuboid cells, round the oocyte. A fold of follicular

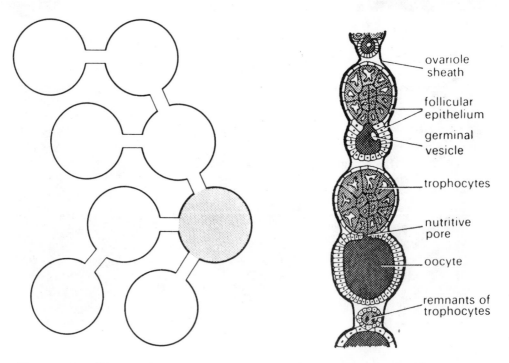

ovariole
sheath

follicular
epithelium

germinal
vesicle

trophocytes

nutritive
pore

oocyte

remnants of
trophocytes

Fig. 220 (*left*) Diagram showing the interconnections of the oocyte (stippled) and the trophocytes at the 8-cell stage in *Drosophila*. Each cell will divide again to produce the final, 16-cell, stage. The oocyte always occupies the most posterior position, to the right in the diagram (after King, 1964)

Fig. 221 (*right*) Diagram of part of an ovariole of *Bombus*, a polytrophic ovariole in which the trophocytes are in a separate follicle from the oocyte (after Hopkins and King, 1966)

epithelium pushes inwards separating oocyte from trophocytes except for a median pore (Fig. 219C). In Neuroptera, Coleoptera and Hymenoptera the trophocytes are pinched off in a separate follicle from the beginning (Fig. 221).

At first the trophocytes are bigger than the oocyte and the trophocyte nuclei enlarge considerably. In *Drosophila* the trophocyte nuclei increase in volume about 2000-fold and the chromosomes undergo eight or nine doublings to produce polytene chromosomes. Unlike the earlier cell divisions these mitoses are not synchronised in the different trophocytes of one follicle. The chromosomal strands do not adhere together, but form a tangled mass in the nucleus. In *Drosophila* the trophocytes adjacent to the oocyte have larger nuclei, and their chromosomes undergo one more replication than the anterior (distal) trophocytes. Subsequently they lose their DNA, but the anterior cells do not. In most cases the whole genome is replicated to an equal extent, but there is also evidence for selective replication of those elements of the system which are particularly important in development of the oocyte (Telfer, 1975).

During the interphase before the beginning of trophocyte formation, the nucleus in some species produces an extrachromosal DNA body. This occurs in *Dytiscus*, for instance, and the DNA body is passed to the presumptive oocyte at each cell division. Similar structures are produced in the oocytes of a number of species with panoistic ovarioles. An increase in the DNA content of these bodies occurs up to the early stages of meiosis, but then they fragment and ultimately disappear.

15.5.2 Functions of trophic tissue

The principal function of the trophic tissue of meriostic ovarioles, and possibly of DNA bodies when they are present, is to supply RNA to the oocyte in the relatively large quantities necessary for its subsequent rapid growth. The trophocytes are the primary source of ribosomal and transfer RNA for the oocyte and relatively little is synthesised in the oocyte nucleus in polytrophic ovarioles; in panoistic ovarioles, on the other hand, the oocyte nucleus is often the only source of RNA.

The movement of material into the oocyte from the trophocytes is an active one along an electrical potential gradient, the resting potential of the oocyte being positive with respect to the trophocytes. It is possible that this difference in potential is responsible for the movement into the oocyte since there is evidence that initially cytoplasmic streaming does not occur. At this stage ribosomes and centrioles, as well as RNA, are carried to the oocyte. Subsequently the trophocytes collapse and at this time much of their cytoplasm and a variety of organelles, sometimes including the nuclei, passes to the oocyte. In *Drosophila* this final movement involves a substantial transfer of RNA, but in *Hyalophora* this is unimportant compared with the earlier supply from active trophocytes.

15.5.3 Vitellogenesis

Vitellogenesis, the deposition of yolk in the oocyte, occurs in the more proximal parts of the ovariole and it results in a very rapid increase in size. In *Drosophila* the oocyte volume increases about 100 000 times during the course of its development, which takes about three days after leaving the germarium, and in *Nomadacris* (Orthoptera) the oocytes grow from less than two millimetres to over six millimetres long in about a week. Normally vitellogensis is largely restricted to the terminal oocyte nearest the oviduct, the following oocyte remaining relatively small until the first is discharged from the ovariole. Hence there is an interval between successive ovulations (p. 345) which is determined by the rate of vitellogenesis.

In some insects, such as those Lepidoptera which do not feed as adults, Ephemeroptera and Plecoptera, vitellogenesis is completed in the late larva or pupa. In most cases, however, a period of maturation is required in the adult before the eggs are ready to ovulate. Commonly this period is only a matter of days, but in cases of adult diapause it may be very prolonged (p. 834). Hence it is necessary in insects to differentiate between becoming adult and becoming sexually mature. Having matured, successive ovulations occur at regular intervals.

The yolk may be broadly categorised as protein yolk, which is a protein–carbohydrate complex and lipid yolk, while in some insects glycogen is also present in granules between the other yolk bodies. The protein yolk is most abundant and forms the richest deposit of protein in the oocyte. The different types of yolk have different origins and will be dealt with separately.

Protein yolk

The protein which forms the protein yolk is derived from proteins in the blood. In *Hyalophora* (Lepidoptera) the haemolymph of the female contains a protein which is not present in the male and this is absorbed preferentially by the oocyte, becoming 20–30 times more concentrated in the yolk than in the blood. The other blood proteins are also absorbed, but to a much lesser extent and it may be that there is selective adsorption of the proteins on some component of the uptake system, such as the oocyte membrane. Sexual differences in the blood proteins are known to occur in Orthoptera and some Lepidoptera and such differences may reflect the development of special proteins in the females for yolk synthesis. These proteins are synthesised in the fat body.

At the time of vitellogenesis in *Hyalophora*, *Panorpa* (Mecoptera), *Aedes* and *Calliphora* the follicle epithelium retracts from the surface of the oocyte and gaps appear between the follicle cells. Thus there is a free access of haemolymph to the surface of the oocyte since the only potential barrier, the tunica propria, is permeable to large molecules. The follicle cells secrete material into these gaps and the blood proteins undergo some concentration in them, possibly as a result of binding by the secretion. It is presumed that the proteins are released from this bound state at the vitelline membrane and are then taken up by pinocytosis, pinosomes appearing in the cell membrane at points indicated by a series of bristle-like striations on the inside (Fig. 222). In *Aedes* the number of pinosomes present at any one time during vitellogenesis is 15 times as high as during the period before vitellogenesis and in *Hyalophora* a 10 μm^2 patch of surface produces 2.5×10^5 pinocytotic vesicles in 24 h (Telfer and Smith, 1970). The pinosomes become cut off as vesicles, which fuse together, ultimately becoming crystalline and forming the yolk spheres. In *Hyalophora* it is estimated that about 1 000 000 vesicles are required for the formation of each yolk sphere. Since each vesicle is bounded by an element of the cell membrane there must be a rapid turnover in this membrane with rapid production to make good the loss. Within the oocyte the cortical region immediately below the surface comes to contain a high

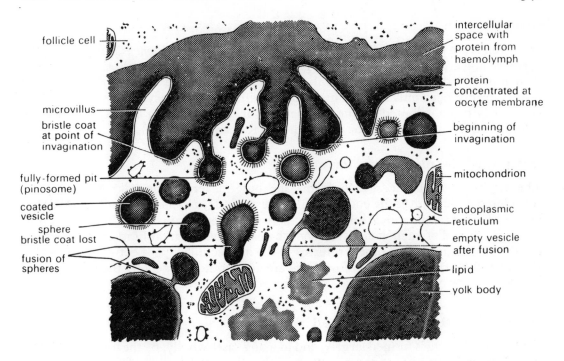

follicle cell

intercellular space with protein from haemolymph

protein concentrated at oocyte membrane

microvillus

bristle coat at point of invagination

beginning of invagination

fully-formed pit (pinosome)

mitochondrion

coated vesicle

endoplasmic reticulum

sphere bristle coat lost

empty vesicle after fusion

fusion of spheres

lipid

yolk body

Fig. 222 Diagram illustrating the uptake of protein by micropinocytosis and its subsequent incorporation into yolk bodies in the oocyte of *Aedes* (after Roth and Porter, 1964)

concentration of vesicles. This region also contains tubules with diameters of 30–45 nm, which may be the residues of vesicles that have injected their contents into yolk spheres. Below the cortex is a layer of cytoplasm containing many mitochondria. This stratification persists until the chorion is formed.

The oocyte itself synthesises protein during this period, but this synthesis is concerned with maintenance processes in the oocyte rather than with yolk production.

Lipid yolk

In *Pyrrhocoris*, and probably in other insects, lipid yolk is derived from lipid stored in the fat body. The quantity of lipid in the fat body decreases as that in the oocytes increases (Martin, 1969). It is also possible that in some species with meroistic ovarioles lipid is obtained early in development from the trophocytes. Within the oocyte, vesicles of the Golgi apparatus become filled with lipid, grow and ultimately develop into the lipid yolk bodies. The nature of the lipid may vary in the course of development and often at first only phospholipid droplets are present. Subsequently droplets having a triglyceride core and phospholipid sheath are found and finally only homogeneous triglyceride bodies remain. It is suggested that these represent successive stages in the development of the lipid yolk and that the phospholipid is utilised in the synthesis of the yolk platelets (Seshacher and Bagga, 1963).

Glycogen

Glycogen is not present in all insect oocytes. In *Anisolabis* and *Bombus*, sugars from the haemolymph are metabolised to form glycogen in the trophocytes and the glycogen is then transferred to the oocyte (Bonhag, 1956; Hopkins and King, 1966). In other insects the glycogen only appears in the oocyte after the trophocytes have degenerated and it may be contributed by the follicle cells or, as in *Panorpa* and *Apis*, it may be synthesised from glucose in the oocyte itself (Ramamurty, 1968).

15.5.4 Vitelline membrane formation

The vitelline membrane, which forms the outer layer of the oocytes, is usually considered to develop at the end of vitellogenesis. In *Hyalophora* (Lepidoptera) a thin membrane is present much earlier, but it is increased in thickness from $0.2\ \mu$m to $1.5\ \mu$m at the end of vitellogenesis. In some cases it may be a modification of the oocyte plasma membrane, but in others it forms in the intercellular space between the oocyte and the follicle cells. Droplets of material are contributed largely by the follicle cells, but also by the oocyte, and these condense to form the membrane.

15.5.5 Formation of the egg-shell

The shell of the egg is formed largely, and in many cases wholly, by the follicle cells, but in Acrididae a secretion of the common oviduct is added to that of the follicle cells.

The part of the shell secreted by the follicle cells is known as the chorion and this typically consists of two layers, an inner endochorion and an outer exochorion. In *Rhodnius*, at least, the endo- and exo-chorion are not chemically homogeneous and their development entails the production of a series of secretions. First, in the production of the endochorion, a polyphenol is secreted in droplets over the vitelline membrane and this is followed by a protein, which subsequently becomes tanned and resistant due to the addition of more polyphenol, which also forms another layer of droplets outside the protein. Then follows an amber-coloured layer, produced by the addition of oil to tanned protein, which cements a second layer of protein to the rest. This layer is not produced uniformly, but is deposited more rapidly at the edges of the follicle cells than at their centres, so that pits appear in the chorion opposite each cell. This protein also becomes tanned, but less strongly than the inner layer.

The exochorion of *Rhodnius* is added during a second phase of secretion by the follicle cells and, unlike the endochorion, it is not modified after its production. First a layer of soft lipoprotein is added to the outside of the endochorion and again more is added round the edges of the follicle cells so that the pits are accentuated. Subsequently a uniformly thin layer of resistant lipoprotein is added to complete the chorion. As in many eggs, the outside of the chorion is marked with a series of hexagons, which are the imprints of the follicle cells which produce it (Beament, 1946a).

Specialised parts of the chorion in *Rhodnius* involve the same secretions as produce the more generalised regions, but the secretions are produced in different amounts and some may be omitted altogether. Thus there are rings of cells in the follicular epithelium which by differential secretion produce the cap, the junction of the cap with the rest of the chorion, and the micropyles and aeropyles (Fig. 223, and see Beament, 1947). The cells forming the junction, for instance, produce no exochorion, while the

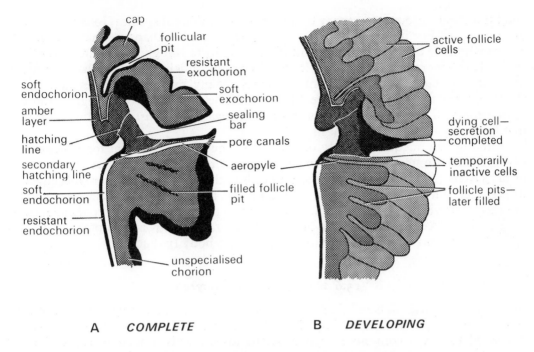

cap
follicular pit
resistant exochorion
soft endochorion
amber layer
hatching line
secondary hatching line
soft endochorion
resistant endochorion
soft exochorion
sealing bar
pore canals
aeropyle
filled follicle pit
unspecialised chorion

active follicle cells
dying cell— secretion completed
temporarily inactive cells
follicle pits— later filled

A   *COMPLETE*   B   *DEVELOPING*

Fig. 223 Section through the chorion of the egg of *Rhodnius* at the junction of the cap with the main shell. A. Completed chorion. B. Chorion in process of secretion by the follicle cells (after Beament, 1946b)

aeropyles are deep follicular pits comparable with the shallower pits produced by all the other follicle cells.

Telfer and Smith (1970) describe the laying down of a series of fibrous lamellae in the chorion of *Hyalophora*. The chorion probably has a fibrous basis in other insects, but this has only been observed in a few species.

In Acrididae the common oviduct secretes an extrachorion over the outside of the exochorion. It is produced as a layer of uniform thickness, but starts to shrink while the eggs are still in the oviduct and continues to do so after they are laid. Shrinkage is not even and so islands of extrachorion remain, contributing to the typical pattern of sculpturing on the outside of the egg (Hartley, 1961).

15.5.6 Control of oogenesis

In many insects oogonia continue to be produced in the adult and there is no apparent limit to the number which can be produced but in *Oncopeltus*, for instance, oogonial division is completed in the larva and so the adult germarium contains only oocytes and trophic tissue. In either case vitellogenesis occurs in the adult and is regulated by the conditions experienced by it at that stage. This is not true of all insects, however, and many Lepidoptera emerge with all their oocytes fully developed and are capable of mating and ovipositing shortly afterwards.

The development of mature oocytes is dependent on suitable environmental conditions and various factors may be important for different species (Johansson, 1964; Norris, 1964). For instance, in many insects with an adult diapause maturation only occurs when the daylength is long and the temperature is high. Adequate nutrition is probably of general importance and in the absence of sufficient food or a lack of protein many insects fail to produce mature oocytes. Many mosquito species and *Cimex* (Heteroptera), for instance, require a blood meal before they produce eggs, although mosquitoes will live for long periods on a diet of sugars. In *Schistocerca* the presence of mature males accelerates oogenesis.

Although an adequate supply of protein in the diet is essential for oogenesis to occur, the environmental phenomena generally exert their influence via the neurosecretory system. The median neurosecretory cells of the brain have two possible effects: a direct effect on protein synthesis, including the synthesis of yolk protein, and an indirect effect via the corpora allata. The hormone produced by the corpora allata may have a direct effect on metabolism, but in *Schistocerca* it controls the uptake of protein by the oocyte and vitellogenin synthesis in the fat body (p. 840).

15.6 Resorption of oocytes

In a number of insects, belonging to the orders Thysanura, Dermaptera, Orthoptera, Heteroptera, Diptera, Hymenoptera and Coleoptera, oocytes in the ovarioles may be destroyed and their contents resorbed by the insect. This process of resorption, or oosorption, most commonly occurs under adverse conditions, but some degree of resorption is evident even in insects under apparently optimal conditions. Resorption may occur when an oocyte is at any stage of development, but it is most commonly observed in terminal oocytes during vitellogenesis. In extreme cases the terminal oocytes of all the ovarioles may be resorbed, in other cases only some oocytes are destroyed while those in most of the ovarioles continue to develop normally. Resorption provides a mechanism for making optimal use of available nutrient so that only eggs with an adequate quantity of yolk are laid; they have the greatest chance of survival (Bell and Bohm, 1975).

During resorption the yolk spheres break down and protein and lipid yolk disappear from the oocyte. It is probable that vitellogenins are returned unchanged to the haemolymph as a consequence of their release from the yolk spheres and an increase in permeability of the oocyte membrane. The role of the follicle cells is not clear, but they become folded on each other as the oocyte shrinks and finally the whole follicle collapses to form a resorption body, which persists at the base of the ovariole. In locusts the resorption body is frequently coloured orange due to the accumulation of lipids (Lusis, 1963).

In *Machilis* and *Diadromus* (Hymenoptera) resorption is known to occur after the chorion is formed, but the mechanism by which yolk is withdrawn through the chorion is not known.

Lack of food often leads to resorption, both quantity and quality of food being important. In *Culicoides barbosai* (Diptera) the number of oocytes which develop for a second oviposition is proportional to the size of the blood meal taken by the insect, and in *Locusta* the percentage of oocytes resorbed is inversely proportional to the quantity of food eaten (Fig. 224). Low levels of protein in the food also lead to oocyte resorption. In *Cimex* the absence of fertilisation has the same effect, while in *Schistocerca* less

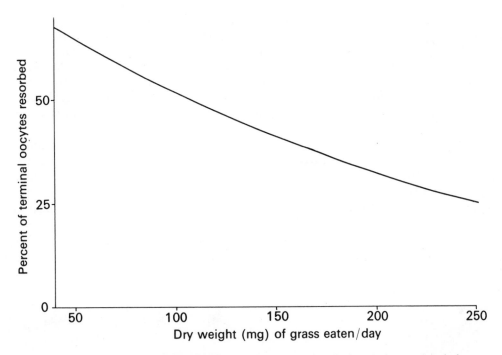

Fig. 224 Changes in the number of terminal oocytes resorbed by female *Locusta* in relation to the amount of grass eaten daily (after McCaffery, 1975)

resorption occurs if the females are in the presence of mature males. Lack of suitable oviposition sites causes mosquitoes to resorb terminal oocytes, though mature eggs are retained, and in parasitic Hymenoptera resorption may occur in the absence of a suitable host. Resorption has been observed to be more frequent in older females compared with young ones in a number of insects.

Juvenile hormone is generally involved in the control of vitellogenesis (p. 838) and the lack of this hormone is associated with resorption, at least when this affects all the developing oocytes. The control mechanism involved when only some of the oocytes regress is not clear, but it is possible that competition between oocytes for the available hormone or some other factor is involved. In some species, at least, it is clear that resorption is not a direct response to a lack of vitellogenins in the haemolymph. The production of juvenile hormone is regulated via the brain and so the extent of resorption depends on the sum of the relevant inputs which are integrated within the brain.

15.7 Ovulation

The passage of the oocyte into the oviduct, a process known as ovulation, involves escaping from the follicular epithelium and the breakdown of the epithelial plug at the entrance to the pedicel. In *Periplaneta* the elasticity of the tunica propria helps to force the oocyte into the oviduct, where it may be stored temporarily before oviposition. In species where the external ovariole sheath contains muscle fibres these probably assist the movements of the oocyte. Sometimes, as in Orthoptera, all the ovarioles ovulate simultaneously, but in other cases, as in viviparous Diptera, they function alternately or in sequence. In Lepidoptera, which commonly lay large batches of eggs although possessing a total of only eight ovarioles, the oocytes may accumulate in the very long pedicels until a large number is present. Similarly in some parasitic Hymenoptera, such as *Apanteles*, large numbers of eggs may be stored, in this case in the lateral oviducts, thus enabling the insect to lay a large number of eggs quickly when it finds a suitable host (Flanders, 1942).

The elasticity of the tunica propria causes it to fold up after the oocyte is shed and this pulls the next oocyte down into the terminal position. The empty follicle epithelium of the first oocyte usually persists, but it becomes greatly folded and compressed and comes to form a new plug at the entrance to the pedicel (Fig. 225). The compressed follicle epithelium is known as a corpus luteum and sometimes the corpora lutea of two or three successive ovulations may be present together despite the fact that they break down progressively (Singh, 1958). In *Melophagus* much of the debris from the follicle cells and trophocytes is passed out of the ovariole when this contracts after ovulation, so only a small relic of the follicle epithelium persists. In this case the

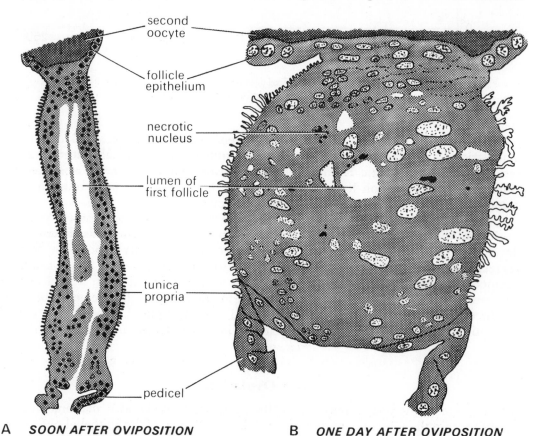

second
oocyte

follicle
epithelium

necrotic
nucleus

lumen of
first follicle

tunica
propria

pedicel

A   *SOON AFTER OVIPOSITION*   B   *ONE DAY AFTER OVIPOSITION*

Fig. 225 The corpus luteum formed by the empty follicle cells of *Locusta*. A. Soon after oviposition. B. 24 hours later. Not to same scale (after Singh, 1958)

ovariole contraction is slow and is not completed until the next oocyte is well developed (Saunders, 1964).

REFERENCES

ANDERSON, D. S. (1965). Observations on female accessory glands of some Acridoidea, with particular reference to *Pyrgomorpha dispar* I. Bolivar. *Ent. mon. Mag.* **101**: 16–17.

ANDERSON, J. M. (1950). A cytological and histological study of the testicular cyst-cells in the Japanese beetle. *Physiol. Zoöl.* **23**: 308–316.

BACCETTI, B. (1972). Insect sperm cells. *Adv. Insect Physiol.* **9**: 316–397.

BAWA, S. R. (1964). Electron microscope study of spermiogenesis in a fire-brat insect, *Thermobia domestica* Pack. I. Mature spermatozoon. *J. Cell Biol.* **23**: 431–446.

BEAMENT, J. W. L. (1946a). The formation and structure of the chorion of the egg in an hemipteran, *Rhodnius prolixus*. *Q. Jl microsc. Sci.* **87**: 393–439.

BEAMENT, J. W. L. (1946b). The waterproofing process in eggs of *Rhodnius prolixus* Stähl. *Proc. R. Soc. B*, **133**: 407–418.

BEAMENT, J. W. L. (1947). The formation and structure of the micropylar complex in the egg-shell of *Rhodnius prolixus* Stähl. (Heteroptera Reduviidae). *J. exp. Biol.* **23**: 213–233.

BELL, W. J. and BOHM, M. K. (1975). Oosorption in insects. *Biol. Rev.* **50**: 373–396.

BLOCH, D. P. and BRACK, S. D. (1964). Evidence for the cytoplasmic synthesis of nuclear histone during spermiogenesis in the grasshopper *Chortophaga viridifasciata* (De Geer). *J. Cell Biol.* **22**: 327–340.

BONHAG, P. F. (1956). The origin and distribution of periodic acid—Schiff-positive substances in the oocyte of the earwig, *Anisolabis maritima* (Géné). *J. Morph.* **99**: 433–463.

BONHAG, P. F. (1958). Ovarian structure and vitellogenesis in insects. *A. Rev. Ent.* **3**: 137–160.

BONHAG, P. F. and ARNOLD, W. J. (1961). Histology, histochemistry and tracheation of the ovariole sheaths in the American cockroach, *Periplaneta americana* (L.). *J. Morph.* **108**: 107–129.

BONHAG, P. F. and WICK, J. R. (1953). The functional anatomy of the male and female reproductive systems of the milkweed bug, *Oncopeltus fasciatus* (Dallas) (Heteroptera: Lygaeidae). *J. Morph.* **93**: 177–283.

BRUNET, P. C. J. (1952). The formation of the ootheca by *Periplaneta americana* II. The structure and function of the left colleterial gland. *Q. Jl microsc. Sci.* **93**: 47–69.

CARSON, H. L. (1945). A comparative study of the apical cell of the insect testis. *J. Morph.* **77**: 141–155.

CHANDLEY, A. C. (1966). Studies on oogenesis in *Drosophila melanogaster* with ³H-thymidine label. *Expl Cell Res.* **44**: 201–215.

DAS, C. C., KAUFMANN, B. P. and GAY, H. (1964). Histone–protein transition in *Drosophila melanogaster*. I. Changes during spermatogenesis. *Expl Cell Res.* **35**: 507–514.

DASS, C. M. S. and RIS, H. (1958). Submicroscopic organisation of the nucleus during spermiogenesis in the grasshopper. *J. biophys. biochem. Cytol.* **4**: 129–132.

DAVEY, K. G. (1965). *Reproduction in the insects*. Oliver and Boyd, Edinburgh.

DUMSER, J. B. (1980). The regulation of spermatogenesis in insects. *A. Rev. Ent.* **25**: 341–369.

EDWARDS, J. S. (1961). On the reproduction of *Prionoplus reticularis* (Coleoptera, Cerambycidae), with general remarks on reproduction in the Cerambycidae *Q. Jl microsc. Sci.* **102**: 519–529.

ENGELMANN, F. (1970). *The physiology of insect reproduction*. Pergamon Press, Oxford.

ENGELMANN, F. (1979). Insect vitellogenin: identification, biosynthesis and role in vitellogenesis. *Adv. Insect Physiol.* **14**: 49–108.

FLANDERS, S. E. (1942). Oosorption and ovulation in relation to oviposition in the parasitic Hymenoptera. *Ann. ent. Soc. Am.* **35**: 251–266.

GREGORY, G. E. (1965). On the initiation of spermatophore formation in the African migratory locust, *Locusta migratoria migratorioides* Reiche and Fairmaire. *J. exp. Biol.* **42**: 423–436.

HAGEDORN, H. H. and KUNKEL, J. G. (1979). Vitellogenin and vitellin in insects. *A. Rev. Ent.* **24**: 475–505.

HARTLEY, J. C. (1961). The shell of acridid eggs. *Q. Jl. microsc. Sci.* **102**: 249–255.

HOPKINS, C. R. and KING, P. E. (1966). An electron-microscopical and histochemical study of the oocyte periphery in *Bombus terrestris* during vitellogenesis. *J. Cell Sci.* **1**: 201–216.

IMMS, A. D. (1957). *A general textbook of entomology.* 9th edition, revised by Richards and Davies. Methuen, London.

JACKSON, D. J. (1960). Observations on egg-laying in *Ilybius fuliginosus* Fabricius and *I. ater* Degeer (Coleoptera: Dytiscidae), with an account of the female genitalia. *Trans. R. ent. Soc. Lond.* **112**: 37–52.

JOHANNSON, A. S. (1964). Feeding and nutrition in reproductive processes in insects. *Symp. R. ent. Soc. Lond.* **2**: 43–55.

KAYE, J. S. (1962). Acrosome formation in the house cricket. *J. Cell Biol.* **12**: 411–431.

KAYE, J. S. and McMASTER-KAYE, R. (1966). The fine structure and chemical composition of nuclei during spermiogenesis in the house cricket. I. Initial stages of differentiation and the loss of nonhistone protein. *J. Cell Biol.* **31**: 159–179.

KING, R. C. (1964). Studies on early stages of insect oogenesis. *Symp. R. ent. Soc. Lond.* **2**: 13–25.

KING, R. C. and AGGARWAL, S. K. (1965). Oogenesis in *Hyalophora cecropia*. *Growth* **29**: 17–83.

KOCH, E. A. and KING, R. C. (1966). The origin and early differentiation of the egg chamber of *Drosophila melanogaster*. *J. Morph.* **119**: 283–303.

LEOPOLD, R. A. (1976). The role of male accessory glands in insect reproduction. *A. Rev. Ent.* **21**: 199–221.

LŪSIS, O. (1963). The histology and histochemistry of development and resorption in the terminal oocytes of the desert locust, *Schistocerca gregaria*. *Q. Jl microsc. Sci.* **104**: 57–68.

MARTIN, J. S. (1969). Lipid composition of fat body and its contribution to the maturing oocytes in *Pyrrhocoris apterus*. *J. Insect Physiol.* **15**: 1025–1045.

McCAFFERY, A. R. (1975). Food quality and quantity in relation to egg production in *Locusta migratoria migratorioides*. *J. Insect Physiol.* **21**: 1551–1558.

MERCER, E. H. and BRUNET, P. C. J. (1959). The electron microscopy of the left colleterial gland of the cockroach *J. biophys. biochem. Cytol.* **5**: 257–262.

MUCKENTHALER, F. A. (1964). Autoradiographic study of nucleic acid synthesis during spermatogenesis in the grasshopper, *Melanoplus differentialis*. *Expl Cell Res.* **35**: 531–547

NORRIS, M. J. (1964). Environmental control of sexual maturation in insects. *Symp. R. ent. Soc. Lond.* **2**: 56–65.

NUR, U. (1962). Sperms, sperm bundles and fertilisation in a mealy bug, *Pseudococcus obscurus* Essig. (Homoptera: Coccoidea). *J. Morph.* **111**: 173–199.

ODHIAMBO, T. R. (1969). The architecture of the accessory reproductive glands of the male desert locust. 4. Fine structure of the glandular epithelium. *Phil. Trans. R. Soc. B,* **256**: 85–114.

ODHIAMBO, T. R. (1971). The architecture of the accessory reproductive glands of the male desert locust. 5: ultrastructure during mating. *Tissue & Cell.* **3**: 309–324.

PAYNE, F. (1966). Some observations on spermatogenesis in *Gelastocoris oculatus* (Hemiptera) with the aid of the electron microscope. *J. Morph.* **119**: 357–381.

PAYNE, M. A. (1933). The structure of the testis and movement of sperms in *Chortophaga viridifasciata* as demonstrated by intravitam technique. *J. Morph.* **54**: 321–345.

PAYNE, M. A. (1934). Intravitam studies on the hemipteran, *Leptocoris trivittatus*. A description of the male reproductive organs and the aggregation and turning of the sperms. *J. Morph.* **56**: 513–531.

PHILLIPS, D. M. (1966). Observations on spermiogenesis in the fungus gnat *Sciara coprophila*. *J. Cell Biol.* **30**: 477–497.

PHILLIPS, D. M. (1970). Insect sperm: their structure and morphogenesis. J. Cell Biol. **44**: 243–277.

PHIPPS, J. (1962). The ovaries of some Sierra Leone Acridoidea (Orthoptera) with some comparisons between East and West African forms. *Proc. R. ent. Soc. Lond.* A, **37**: 13–21.

POPHAM, E. J. (1965). The functional morphology of the reproductive organs of the common earwig (*Forficula auricularia*) and other Dermaptera with reference to the natural classification of the order. *J. Zool.* **146**: 1–43.

RAMAMURTY, P. S. (1968). Origin and distribution of glycogen during vitellogenesis of the scorpion fly, *Panorpa communis*. *J. Insect Physiol.* **14**: 1325–1330.

ROBISON, W. G. (1966). Microtubules in relation to the motility of a sperm syncytium in an armored scale insect. *J. Cell Biol.* **29**: 251–265.

ROTH, T. F. and PORTER, K. R. (1964). Yolk protein uptake in the oocyte of the mosquito *Aedes aegypti* L. *J. Cell Biol.* **20**: 313–332.

SAUNDERS, D. S. (1964). Age-changes in the ovaries of the sheep ked, *Melophagus ovinus* (L.) (Diptera: Hippoboscidae). *Proc. R. ent. Soc. Lond.* A, **39**: 68–72.

SESHACHAR, B. R. and BAGGA, S. (1963). A cytochemical study of oogenesis in the dragonfly *Pantala flavescens* (Fabricius). *Growth* **27**: 225–246.

SINGH, T. (1958). Ovulation and corpus luteum formation in *Locusta migratoria migratorioides* Reiche and Fairmaire and *Schistocerca gregaria* (Forskål). *Trans. R. ent. Soc. Lond.* **110**: 1–20.

SNODGRASS, R. E. (1935). *Principles of insect morphology*. McGraw-Hill, New York.

SNODGRASS, R. E. (1956). *Anatomy of the honeybee*. Constable, London.

SZÖLLÖSI, A. (1974). Ultrastructural study of the spermatodesm of *Locusta migratoria migratorioides* (R.F.): acrosome and cap formation. *Acrida* **3**: 175–191.

TELFER, W. H. (1975). Development and physiology of the oocyte–nurse cell syncytium. *Adv. Insect Physiol.* **11**: 223–319.

TELFER, W. H. and SMITH, D. S. (1970). Aspects of egg formation. *Symp. R. ent. Soc. Lond.* **5**: 117–134.

UVAROV, B. P. (1966). *Grasshoppers and locusts*. vol. 1. Cambridge University Press.

WIGGLESWORTH, V. B. (1965). *The principles of insect physiology*. Methuen, London.

WILDE, J. DE and LOOF, A. DE (1973a). Reproduction. *in* Rockstein, M. (ed.), *The physiology of Insecta*. vol. 1. Academic Press, New York.

WILDE, J. DE and LOOF, A. DE (1973b). Reproduction—endocrine control. *in* Rockstein, M. (ed.), *The physiology of Insecta*. vol. 1. Academic Press, New York.

CHAPTER XVI

MATING BEHAVIOUR AND THE TRANSFER OF SPERM TO THE FEMALE

Mating behaviour may be defined broadly as the events surrounding the insemination of the female by the male. Typically this involves a whole sequence of events which are not always clearly separable from each other, but which it is convenient to treat separately. Before mating can occur the sexes must come together and this may be facilitated by scent or sound, both of which can be specific and carry over considerable distances. Vision is important in some day-flying insects and the swarming behaviour which occurs in some species leads to aggregation for mating. The attractants which result in the meeting of the sexes may be specific, but sometimes, particularly with visual attraction, this is not so and further recognition is required. In specific recognition a variety of signals, including visual and chemical ones, are used. Commonly aggregation results in a number of males courting a single female and this may lead to aggression between the males, but in some insects male aggression results in the setting up of territories which facilitate undisturbed mating.

The exchange of signals at close range which results in the male and female adopting positions to allow coupling and sperm transfer is known as courtship. In some cases this occurs very rapidly, but in others courtship is more prolonged and a sequence of events is apparent. Courtship behaviour is often under the control of the corpora allata in those insects which remain sexually immature for a time after becoming adult.

The male genitalia consist essentially of claspers for holding the female and an intromittent organ for sperm transfer. In more primitive insects sperm are transferred to the female in a structure known as the spermatophore, which is produced by the male, but in many groups sperm are transferred directly via a long penis. The spermatophore is usually placed or formed in the copulatory pouch of the female and from here the sperm pass to the spermatheca, where they are stored until the eggs are fertilised. In direct insemination the sperm may be deposited directly in the spermatheca.

Females are generally unreceptive of males after copulation and in many species the change to unreceptiveness is due to substances produced in the male accessory glands. Other material from the male glands may provide protein for oogenesis, speed up oocyte maturation and induce oviposition.

General accounts of reproduction in insects are given by Davey (1965) and Engelmann (1970). Swarming behaviour in Diptera is reviewed by Downes (1969) and the hormonal control of reproductive behaviour by Barth and Lester (1973) and Truman and Riddiford (1974). Spieth (1974) reviews courtship behaviour in *Drosophila*. Scudder (1971) discusses the homologies of the male genitalia, and functions of the accessory glands, including spermatophore production, are reviewed by Leopold (1976).

MATING

16.1 Aggregation

For mating to occur it is obvious that male and female must be in the same place and various devices are employed by one or other sex for attracting the other. Scent is commonly emitted by female insects to attract males, and since these scents, or pheromones, are carried by air currents and are perceived at very low concentrations they are effective over relatively long distances and, at least in Lepidoptera, large numbers of males may be attracted to a single female. Female scents are also produced by, for example, some cockroaches, Coleoptera, Hymenoptera and Isoptera. Less commonly attractant scents are emitted by male insects. These scents are usually highly specific (Chapter XXXV).

Sound also carries for long distances and is equally effective during the day or at night and it is used by various insects to attract other members of the species. Sound production is particularly important in cicadas and Orthoptera (Chapter XXVIII) where, except in a few geographically separated species, different species have characteristic songs. These may be attractive to both sexes, and acridids of either sex tend to move into a stridulating group of the same species. This is also true of cicadas, and in North America, where three species of *Magicicada* may occur in a single locality, the species are aggregated and sexually isolated from each other by their specific songs. Amongst most Orthoptera only males stridulate, but in some Acrididae both sexes do so, male and female responding to each other as they approach.

Vision is often employed by day-flying insects when searching for a mate, but, unlike scents and sounds, distance perception is usually not specific. The males of the butterfly *Hypolimnas*, for example, fly up towards anything moving which is of a size appropriate to the female, and *Eumenis* (Lepidoptera) is attracted by any dark object with a fluttering flight. A non-specific response also occurs in many Diptera and probably in other insects. Vision is occasionally employed in mating at night by insects, mainly beetles of the families Lampyridae and Elateridae, which exhibit luminescence. Both sexes or the female only may be luminous and the characteristics of the light, such as wavelength and frequency of flashing, are specific (p. 124).

Sometimes a particular reaction to the environment tends to bring about aggregation and in some species this behaviour plays an important part in mating. Males of *Andrena flavipes* (Hymenoptera) are attracted by the scent of the area in which the females nest and outside these areas, even quite close to them, the males fail to recognise the females (Butler, 1965). Comparably the male of *Culicoides nubeculosus* (Diptera), although it does not feed on blood, is attracted to the same host as the female, and mating may follow.

16.1.1 Swarming

Swarming behaviour, in which a group of insects remains more or less stationary, flying over one spot, is a special instance of insects showing a common reaction to a feature of the environment. Swarming is best known in the Diptera, occurring in many Nematocera, in some species of Tabanidae and Stratiomyidae and occasionally in members of other families. It also occurs in many Trichoptera, and some Lepidoptera, Plecoptera and Ephemeroptera.

Swarming does not involve any gregarious reaction on the part of the insects, but results from a common response to some visual marker by a number of individual insects. Hence a swarm may contain from one to several hundred insects. Usually the marker is some feature which contrasts with its background; in *Culicoides nubeculosus* it may be a dark patch of damp sand or a cow pat, or in *C. riethi* a light patch. Often swarms form over tall objects and in forest swarms may occur over the tops of tall trees. The marker need not always be below the insect: *Serromyia* forms swarms beneath the tips of branches silhouetted against the sky.

The insects maintain their positions relative to the marker visually, flying into the wind and adjusting their air-speed so as to remain in one place, or allowing themselves to drift back slightly and then flying forwards again. Their ability to hold station in the wind depends on their flying strength and *Tabanus thoracinus* can maintain its position against a 5 km/h wind without difficulty, while a 3 km/h wind disperses a swarm of *Culicoides*. The insects often do not hover in a stationary position even under ideal conditions, but perform a 'dance', making up and down or side to side movements within the swarm. The height at which swarms develop varies, but frequently they are between two and ten feet above the marker. In high winds the swarms may be nearer the ground and if the marker is a solid object they may develop on its lee side.

In the tropics swarms commonly occur in the twilight after sunset or before sunrise, but in temperate regions swarming may be conspicuous at other times of day, twilight swarming perhaps being limited by low temperatures. Various species form swarms at particular times. Thus over high forest in Uganda mosquitoes swarm at dusk rather than dawn, being most abundant about half-an-hour after sunset (Haddow and Corbet, 1961). The common *Mansonia fuscopennata* first appears in numbers about 15 minutes after sunset and *M. aurita* about five minutes later, but despite these characteristic differences in arrival time all the mosquito species stop swarming about 40 minutes after sunset. Tabanids on the other hand swarm mainly in the morning. *Tabanus thoracinus* appears within a few minutes of Nautical twilight, when the sun is 12° below the horizon and only the general outlines of objects are visible, and disappears after 25 minutes when *T. insignis* is just arriving (Corbet and Haddow, 1962). Tabanids in temperate regions may, however, swarm late in the morning after sunrise, while *Culicoides* often swarms in the afternoon. Swarms at this time of day may persist for an hour or more, but crepuscular swarms are, of necessity, much shorter-lived and often persist for 15 minutes or less.

The timing of crepuscular swarms is related to light intensity, but the times of appearance of mosquito swarms are very precise and do not always occur at particular intensities. Possibly in the evening the sharp fall in intensity acts as a stimulus, provided the level is below a threshold intensity, which may differ for different species, but it is not certain that all species react in a similar way (see *e.g.* Nielsen and Nielsen, 1958). Swarming activity stops when the light intensity falls below a certain very low level. In morning swarms the converse may be true, swarms forming when light intensity rises above a threshold, but at this time low temperature may also be a limiting factor.

Because of their mode of formation swarms of Diptera are not always monospecific, although they commonly are so as a result of specific responses to markers or to specific differences in the time of flight. As a consequence swarms can provide some measure of interspecific isolation (Downes, 1969). The swarms observed by Haddow and Corbet

(1961), however, always contained several species of mosquitoes and sometimes small tipulids and other insects. The majority of dipteran swarms consist only of males, but mixed swarms are recorded in some species of *Mansonia*, *Ceratopogon* and *Bezzia*, while in *Serromyia* and a few mosquito and empid species wholly female, as well as male, swarms occur.

The swarms provide foci in which the sexes meet and mate, although mating has not been observed in the swarms of some species, giving rise to doubts about the significance of the habit. It is probable that females respond to visual markers in the same way as males and there is no evidence of their being attracted to the swarm as such. When a female enters a swarm mating occurs quickly and the pair drop down to the ground. Subsequently the male returns, but the mated female does not, so that the male dominance in the swarm persists.

In mosquitoes and related insects sexual recognition at close range within the swarm involves perception of the sounds produced by the flying female (p. 718), while in several other families of Diptera, such as the Bibionidae, Simuliidae and Tabanidae, the eyes of the male are specialised and sexual recognition depends on visual cues. No special adaptations for sexual recognition are known in Trichoceridae and some other families of Diptera which form swarms.

Mating of swarming species can occur outside the swarm, but this presumably depends on chance meetings between the sexes since these species are not known to produce long-range sex attractants.

Swarming in honeybees is a quite different process, which commonly results from overcrowding in the hive. A brief account of the causes and consequences of swarming is given by Simpson (1974) and of the mechanisms involved in swarm cohesion and displacement by Avitabile *et al.* (1975).

16.2 Recognition and courtship

Before mating can occur it is necessary for each participant to behave in a manner which permits copulation. This involves the exchange of signals which indicate the appropriateness of species, sex and, on the part of the female, readiness to mate. This exchange of signals may begin when the insects are widely separated from each other, leading to aggregation. The continuation of this behaviour at close range is distinguished as courtship.

In some cases, as in *Ammophila* (Hymenoptera) and *Musca* (Diptera), there is no obvious courtship behaviour, males simply leaping onto objects of appropriate size and form and attempting to copulate. Even here elements of recognition are involved, though the whole process occurs very rapidly and a sequence of events is not apparent. Other insects such as *Drosophila*, have more extended periods of precopulatory behaviour and it is usually these insects which are referred to as displaying courtship behaviour.

16.2.1 Mechanisms of courtship

Courtship involves a variety of different mechanisms and senses in different insects. Visual displays are used by many species and often their markings serve to emphasise their movements. For instance, the movements of the wings which male sepsids perform in front of the females are made more conspicuous by the black wing tips. The male *Hypolimnas*, having been attracted non-specifically, recognises the female by virtue of her brown colour, the effect of which is enhanced by the contrasting margin of black. White inhibits pursuit by the male (Stride, 1957). In *Drosophila* the initial approach of the male to the female is also visual, but specific recognition involves tapping with the fore legs. If the stimulus, presumably a chemical one, is not appropriate courtship is broken off at this point. In *Eumenis* the male bows towards the female so that her antennae are brought into contact with his alary scent glands (p. 864), while in many Lepidoptera the sex pheromones which attract males to females also lead to attempts at copulation when they are present in high concentrations. Hearing may be important, as in grasshoppers in which the male hops excitedly round the female singing his courtship song at the end of which he leaps onto her back (p. 697).

In many species courtship involves a sequence of signals and responses and different kinds of signal may be employed at different stages of the sequence. For instance the male of *Drosophila subobscura* orientates towards the female and taps her with his fore legs, while the female stands still (Fig. 226). The visual and tactile

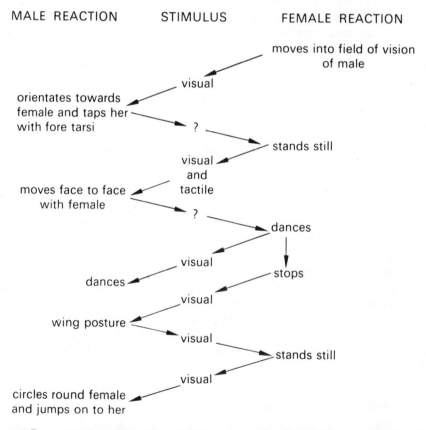

Fig. 226 Representation of the interactions between male and female *Drosophila subobscura* during courtship (after Brown, 1965)

stimuli which she presents cause the male to extend his proboscis and move face to face with her. She continues to stand still and he taps her head, whereupon both begin to dance. The dance consists of a series of side to side steps in which the two insects remain facing each other. In the course of this the male gradually opens his wings and when the dance stops he spreads his wings in an attitude called wing posturing. The wings are raised at right angles to the body with the leading edge down and this posture prompts the female to stand still. Then the male circles her and finally jumps on her, attempting to copulate at the same time (Brown, 1965). Comparable sequences of events are known to occur in other insects, such as crickets (see *e.g.* Alexander, 1961) and *Nasonia* (Hymenoptera) (Barrass, 1960). These sequences, though common, are not fixed behaviour patterns. Signals later in a sequence do not occur in a rigid order and mating can occur when only a part of the pattern has been completed (Spieth, 1974).

Courtship feeding

In some insects feeding has a special role in courtship. In *Byrsotria* and some other cockroaches the male turns away from the female after the initial approach and opens his wings. This exposes a gland on the metanotum and incites the female to climb onto his back and feed on the secretion of this gland. When she is in this position the male is able to copulate with her.

The bug *Stilbcoris* feeds on fig seeds and an adult male usually carries a seed impaled on his proboscis. He approaches a female from behind and presents the seed to her so that she can see it and so that it comes into contact with her antennae. By flexing his legs the male vibrates the seed, alternating periods of stillness with periods of vibration, and at the same time he injects saliva into the seed. This makes it more acceptable to the female, who now investigates it and may insert her proboscis into it. If she does the male slowly approaches her until he is able to grasp her and copulate. The female continues to feed on the seed. Males which do not have a seed do not normally attempt to court (Carayon, 1964).

Courtship feeding also occurs amongst the wasps of the subfamily Thynninae. In some genera the females feed themselves while they are copulating, but in others the male carries the wingless female to a feeding site and feeds her either directly from his mouth or by first regurgitating food on to his abdomen or a leaf. The female feeds from the regurgitated drops with her reduced mouthparts. In yet other species the male collects nectar and honeydew in a cavity beneath his head where the food is held by hairs. The food bolus may be larger than the head of the insect and the female is fed from it without being transported to the feeding ground (Given, 1954). Various Diptera, such as *Rivellia* and some Sepsidae also regurgitate a drop of fluid and pass this to the female before mating.

In predaceous species courtship feeding may provide a distraction for the female so that the male himself is not eaten. Some male empids catch prey and then present this to the female, who feeds on it while he copulates with her. In other species this behaviour is ritualised and the male presents the female with an inanimate object, such as a petal, wrapped in a silken cocoon, or even with an empty cocoon. The male of *Panorpa* secretes drops of saliva on to the surface of a leaf. These harden and are eaten by the female while the male copulates with her.

16.2.2 Functions of courtship

The principal function of courtship is to facilitate copulation with an appropriate partner, but courtship does not always lead to successful copulation. Where mating involves a relatively indiscriminate attempt at mounting by an aggressive male he commonly assaults the wrong species or sex. In such cases the attempt inevitably fails, the recipient of the attack sometimes attempting to repel the assault by kicking, or by wing flicking. Where courtship is more extended a variety of signals may indicate an inappropriate species or sex before the active male attempts to copulate. For instance in *Drosophila* tapping the partner with the foreleg indicates whether or not the species and sex is appropriate; if it is not, courtship is broken off. Homosexual behaviour is particularly common when females are scarce. Sometimes the assaulting male is simply kicked off by the other, as in locusts, but sometimes more specific stimuli inhibit the activity of the aggressor. Thus *Drosophila* males when assaulted flick their wings in the same way as unreceptive females, this behaviour inhibiting the advances of other males.

Even if the male courts an appropriate female courtship is not always successful. Females are completely non-receptive for a time after the final moult and again after oviposition. To avoid copulation a non-receptive virgin female *Drosophila* flicks her wings and twists the abdomen sideways, while a female which has already copulated extrudes the terminal abdominal segments. These activities not only prevent the male from copulating, but also inhibit his courtship to some extent.

In *Drosophila*, and perhaps in many other insects, the female typically does not respond positively to the first bout of courtship and two or more sequences are necessary before she will mate. Such delayed responses have suggested that one function of courtship is to overcome the 'coyness' of the female. Barrass (1976), however, considers that although courtship stimulates the female and leads to her adopting an appropriate posture for copulation there is no evidence of any cumulative stimulatory effect on the female.

It is possible that, in some cases, courtship serves to bring the male himself into a state of readiness to copulate. This is suggested by the behaviour of the male of *Gomphocerus* (Orthoptera), which may fail to copulate successfully with a singing and receptive female, but after courting her is able to mate immediately with a second female without or with only a brief courtship (Loher and Huber, 1966).

16.2.3 Control of courtship behaviour

There is relatively little information on the control of courtship behaviour, but the evidence indicates that there may be marked differences in control mechanisms between species.

In the males of many species courtship behaviour first occurs soon after the final moult and is independent of hormonal regulation. This is true in the grasshoppers *Gomphocerus* and *Syrbula*, but in *Schistocerca* mating behaviour is regulated by a hormone from the corpora allata. No reproductive behaviour occurs after allatectomy. In *Locusta* mating behaviour occurs in the absence of corpora allata, but the intensity of the behaviour is increased by their presence. These differences between species probably reflect basic differences in the biology of the insects. Where maturation occurs without delay following the final moult no special control is necessary, but in species exhibiting delay between moulting and maturation some control is obviously essential.

Male sexual behaviour in the dung fly *Scathophaga* is also regulated by the corpora allata.

Male courtship behaviour is much more precisely controlled in *Gryllus*, which only courts a female when a spermatophore is present in the genitalia or the seminal vesicles contain semen. The information is conveyed to the brain via the ventral nerve cord and presumably mechanical stimuli are involved.

In female insects the corpora allata are more intimately involved in regulating sexual receptivity. For instance, *Aedes* females are completely unreceptive after emergence, but after one or two days, when the corpora allata release juvenile hormone into the haemolymph, they become receptive. Application of a juvenile hormone mimic to the flies immediately after emergence causes them to become receptive much sooner than is usual. Apart from controlling receptivity the same hormone also controls other aspects of courtship behaviour in female *Gomphocerus*; allatectomised females do not stridulate in response to the male song (p. 702). In female *Hyalophora* calling behaviour in which the pheromone glands are protruded is controlled by a hormone from the corpora cardiaca. No calling behaviour occurs after these glands have been removed. On the other hand in *Diploptera*, *Gryllus* and a number of moths female reproductive behaviour is independent of the endocrine system.

Courtship behaviour is often associated with the development of specific signalling systems or with stridulation in female *Gomphocerus* (see above) and the production of sex attractant and aphrodisiac pheromones in many species. In female cockroaches pheromone production is regulated by the corpora allata and after allatectomy females are no longer attractive because they produce no pheromone. In the intact insect the corpora allata and pheromone production are switched off while females are carrying oothecae (p. 841). This type of control is lacking in insects which mature soon after emergence (Barth and Lester, 1973; Truman and Riddiford, 1974).

16.3 Pairing

Courtship behaviour culminates in the male and female coming together, one sex commonly mounting on the back of the other. Copulation may occur immediately or the insects may remain paired for a time before copulating. Various positions are adopted which are characteristic of the species (Fig. 227). In cockroaches, and some gryllids and tettigoniids the female climbs on to the back of the male (Fig. 227C), and Alexander (1964) considers this to be the primitive condition since it occurs in the lower orders of insects. Another common position is with the male on the female (Fig. 227A); this occurs, for instance in Tabanidae and this is often regarded as the primitive position because the male is considered to be the active partner with the female needing coercion (Richards, 1927). Sometimes, as in Acrididae, although the male sits on top of the female his abdomen is twisted underneath her (the false male above position: Fig. 227B). The abdomen of the male is also twisted under the female in insects, such as *Panorpa*, which lie side by side at the start of copulation. Sometimes the insects pair end to end (Fig. 227E, F and G) and often in this case the terminal segments of the male are twisted through 180°. This occurs, for instance, in some Heteroptera (Fig. 231B) and in Tipulidae. In some tettigoniids and a few Diptera the end-to-end position is achieved with the male on his back, while in Culicidae male and female lie with their ventral surfaces in contact (Fig. 227D).

There is considerable diversity in the positions assumed during copulation by

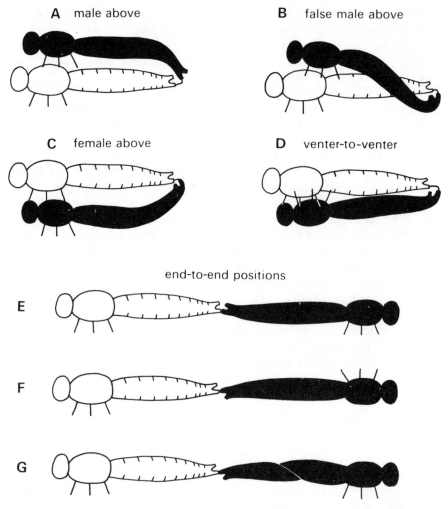

A   male above   **B**   false male above

C   female above   **D**   venter-to-venter

end-to-end positions

E

F

G

Fig. 227 Different positions assumed by the male and female during copulation, male black, female white. A. Male above (*e.g.* some Diptera). B. False ·male above (*e.g.* Acrididae). C. Female above (*e.g.* some Orthoptera). D. Venter-to-venter (*e.g.* Diptera, Culicidae—hypopygium inverted, cf. Fig. 229). E. End-to-end, male abdomen not twisted (*e.g.* some Hymenoptera). F. End-to-end, male inverted (*e.g.* some Tettigonioidea). G. End-to-end, male abdomen twisted (*e.g.* some Heteroptera, cf. Fig. 231) (based on Richards, 1927)

insects within any one order. Thus all the above positions are to be seen in various families of Diptera. The same is true of Orthoptera except for the male above and venter-to-venter positions, while in Heteroptera only the female above and venter-to-venter positions do not occur. On the other hand Ephemeroptera always adopt the female above position and mantids the false male above.

Once the genitalia of male and female are linked the insects may alter their positions and it is common among Orthoptera and Diptera for an end to end position to be adopted at this time.

Usually in pairing the male grasps the female with his feet. In *Aedes aegypti*, for instance, the insects lie with their ventral surfaces adjacent and the male holds the hind legs of the female in a hollow of the distal tarsomere by flexing back the pretarsus. His middle and hind legs push up the female abdomen until genital contact is established and then his middle legs may hook on to the wings of the female, while his hind legs hang free. Some male Hymenoptera, such as *Ammophila*, hold the female with the mandibles instead of, or, in some species, as well as, the legs.

In some insects the appendages are modified for grasping the female. Thus the fore legs of *Dytiscus* and some other beetles bear suckers (p. 165). *Hoplomerus* (Hymenoptera) has spines on the middle femora which fit between the veins on the wings of the female. In *Osphya* (Coleoptera) the male hind femora are modified to grip the abdomen and elytra of the female. A few groups, such as Collembola and fleas, have the antennae modified for holding the female.

The dragonflies are exceptional in their manner of holding the female. At first the male grasps the thorax of the female with his second and third pairs of legs, while the first pair touch the basal segments of her antennae. He then flexes his abdomen forwards and fits two pairs of claspers on abdominal segment 10 into position on the female. This completed he lets go with his legs and the two fly off 'in tandem'. The claspers consist of superior and inferior pairs and in Anisoptera the superior claspers fit round the neck of the female while the inferior claspers press down on top of her head (Fig. 228A). In most Zygoptera the claspers grip a dorsal lobe of the pronotum and in some Coenagriidae they appear to be cemented on by a sticky secretion, but this may be produced incidentally during sperm transfer (Corbet, 1962).

16.4 Male aggression

If females are scarce the competition between males may lead to aggression. This is not always clearly separated from attempts to mate with other males, but certainly occurs in some Hymenoptera and in grasshoppers which have a specific song which is sung if a male intrudes during courtship (p. 698). The males sing against each other in the rivals duet until the intruder retires. In crickets actual fighting occurs whenever they meet and not only in the presence of a female. The contestants rear up, lash each other with their antennae or kick with their hind legs. The longer the fight goes on the fiercer it gets, the insects stridulating and grappling with each other and one may be thrown on to its back, but mutilation is rare. If a group of male crickets is in a restricted area they rapidly establish a hierarchy which is stable over short periods. The position of an individual in the hierarchy depends on his age, how recently he has copulated, or been in isolation, whether or not he occupies a crevice, and on his dominance in recent bouts of fighting (Alexander, 1961).

Territory

If male crickets are not confined to a small space in which fighting is frequent each insect tends to remain in a particular burrow or crevice on many successive nights. In and around this burrow he becomes dominant and so a small territory is established. This has the effect of reducing the numbers of encounters between males, so that they sing the normal mating song more frequently at times appropriate to attract the

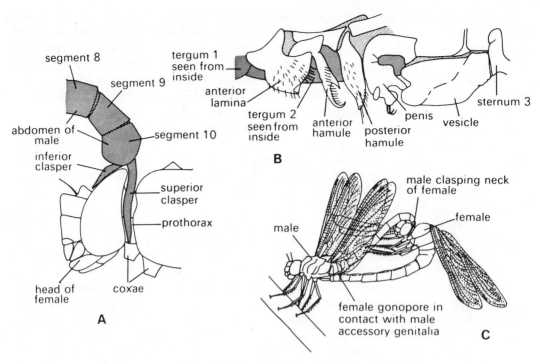

Fig. 228 Mating in Odonata. A. Position of the male claspers round the neck of female *Aeschna* during pairing (after Tillyard, 1917). B. Male accessory genitalia of *Onychogomphus*, terga of left side removed (based on Chao, 1953). C. Male and female *Aeschna in copula* (after Longfield, 1949)

females. Further, the territorial habit disperses the males over a bigger area and this makes for maximum size and continuity of the acoustic field to which the female is attracted. Finally, once the female is within the territories she is able to localise the position of a calling male more easily than if the males are all together in a confined space (Alexander, 1961).

Territorial behaviour with similar functions is exhibited by the sphecid *Sphecius*. Most males of this species emerge before the females and each male establishes a territory, usually at a site where emergence holes are already numerous, driving off intruders of other species and sometimes grappling with males of its own species. There is some tendency for the boundaries between adjacent territories to be learned, so that the amount of grappling is reduced and a single male occupies the same territory for a week or more. If a receptive, unfertilised female enters the territory the male follows her and mates with her. As a result of this behaviour males are spread over a maximum area, increasing the chances of a female finding a mate, while at the same time interference by other males during mating is reduced (Lin, 1963). Territoriality is also known in some other sphecids (Alcock, 1975).

Territorial behaviour also occurs in some dragonflies. Males fly over particular stretches of water, clashing with intruders, so that individual territories are established. These may be very temporary, different territories being occupied on successive days, but often the boundaries are learned by the insects, so there is a tendency for clashes to be avoided. In some cases fighting has been replaced by ritualised behaviour involving sign stimuli. For instance, *Plathemis* displays the bluish-white upper surface of its abdomen to other males, which fly off with the abdomen depressed, and in *Perithemis* the amber-coloured wings provide the stimulus. The effect of this behaviour may be to reduce disturbance by other insects during mating and subsequent oviposition; it also leads to dispersal of the species within and away from the habitat (Corbet, 1962; Corbet, Longfield and Moore, 1960).

SPERM TRANSFER

16.5 External reproductive organs of the male

The external reproductive organs of the male are concerned in coupling with the female genitalia and with the intromission of sperm. They are known collectively as the genitalia.

In most cases after the initial pairing the male holds the female with claspers. These claspers may be derived from the cerci, as in Dermaptera and many Orthoptera, or from the paraprocts, as in Zygoptera and some Tridactyloidea, or they may be appendages of the ninth abdominal segment. In many Plecoptera, and occasionally in other orders, there are no claspers, the sexes simply being held together by the fit of the intromittent organ into the female bursa. Claspers are also absent in Apterygota where the spermatophores are deposited outside the female (p. 366). Sometimes the organs used for seizing the female are different from those finally used to hold her. This is the case in some Lepidoptera and cockroaches which begin copulation with the female mounted on the back of the male and then move to an end to end position. The initial grip is achieved with the hooked left phallomere, but the right phallomere and other structures are subsequently involved (Fig. 232). In these cases the genitalia of the two sides are asymmetrical, and this is also true of Embioptera (Fig. 203) and some Heteroptera.

No intromittant organ is present in Collembola or Diplura and Thysanura have only a simple penis. In these groups the sperm are not transferred directly to the female. Paired penes are present in Ephemeroptera and some Dermaptera, but in the majority of Pterygota there is a single median intromittent organ usually called the aedeagus. This is protected against external injury in various ways. Often the terminal abdominal sternum forms a protection as in Fulgoridae. In many Endopterygota protection is afforded by withdrawal of the genital segment within the preceding abdominal segments.

Many male Diptera have the terminal abdominal segments rotated so that the relative positions of the genitalia are altered. In Culicidae, some Tipulidae, Psychodidae, Mycetophilidae and some Brachycera segment 8 and the segments behind it are rotated through 180° soon after adult emergence. Thus the aedeagus comes to lie above the anus instead of below it and the hindgut is twisted over the reproductive duct (Fig. 229A). The rotation may occur in either a clockwise or an anticlockwise direction. In *Calliphora*, and probably in all Schizophora, the terminal segments have rotated through 360° so that the genitalia are in their normal positions, but the movement is indicated by some asymmetry of the preceding sclerites and by the ejaculatory duct looping right round the gut (Fig. 229 B). This rotation occurs in the pupa and the degree of torsion between different segments varies in different groups.

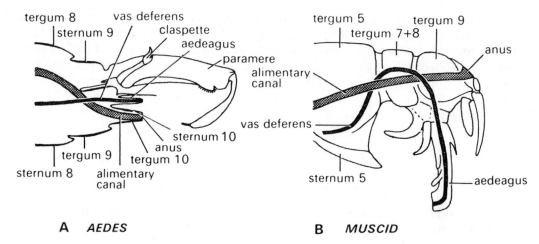

A AEDES   **B MUSCID**

Fig. 229 Diagrams illustrating torsion of the terminal segments of male Diptera. A. *Aedes* with the ninth and following segments rotated through 180°. B. A muscid with the terminal segments rotated through 360° as indicated by the twisting of the vas deferens over the alimentary canal (from Séguy, 1951)

Amongst the Syrphidae a total twist of 360° is achieved by two segments rotating through 90° and one through 180° so that there is an obvious external asymmetry. Temporary rotation of the genital segments during copulation occurs in some other insects, such as Heteroptera (Fig. 231).

There is considerable variation in structure and terminology of the genitalia in different orders (see Tuxen, 1956, for terminology) and the problems of homologising the different structures are outlined by Scudder (1971). According to Snodgrass (1957) the basic elements are derived from a pair of primary phallic lobes which are present in the posterior ventral surface of segment 9 (Fig. 230A). They are commonly regarded as representing limb buds and the structures arising from them as derived from typical appendages. Snodgrass (1957), however, believes that they may represent ancestral penes. These phallic lobes divide to form an inner pair of mesomeres and outer

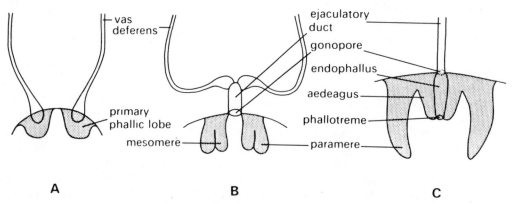

A   **B**   **C**

Fig. 230 Diagrams illustrating the origin and development of the phallic organ (after Snodgrass, 1957)

parameres, collectively known as the phallomeres (Fig. 230B). The mesomeres unite to form the aedeagus, the intromittent organ. The inner wall of the aedeagus, which is a continuation of the ejaculatory duct, is called the endophallus, and the opening of the duct at the tip of the aedeagus is the phallotreme (Fig. 230C). The true gonopore is at the junction of the ejaculatory duct and endophallus and hence is internal, but in many insects the endophallic duct is eversible and so the gonopore assumes a terminal position during copulation. The parameres develop into claspers, which are very variable in form. They may be mounted with the aedeagus on a common base called the phallobase and in many insects these basic structures are accompanied by secondary structures on segments 8, 9 or 10. The term phallus is used by Snodgrass (1957) to mean the parameres together with the aedeagus, but is often used to mean the aedeagus alone; penis is sometimes used instead of phallus.

The Odonata differ from all other insects in having the intromittent organs on abdominal segments 2 and 3. Appendages which are used to clasp the female are present on segment 10, but the genital apparatus on segment 9 is rudimentary. A depression on the ventral surface of segment 2 forms the genital fossa, which opens posteriorly into a vesicle derived from the anterior end of segment 3. In Anisoptera the vesicle connects with a three-segmented penis and laterally there are various accessory lobes which guide and hold the tip of the female abdomen during intromission; the whole complex is termed the accessory genitalia (Figs. 22 and 228B). Sperm are transferred to the vesicle from the terminal gonoduct by bending the abdomen forwards. This may occur before the male grasps the female, as in *Libellula*, or after he has grasped her, but before copulation, as in *Aeschna*. The possible origins of the accessory genitalia are discussed by Corbet (1962).

16.6 Copulation

Copulation involves the linking of the male and female genitalia to form a firm connection between the two insects. While they are joined in this way the male transfers sperm to, or inseminates, the female, the sperm passing via the aedeagus. The details of copulation vary from group to group depending on the structure of the genitalia, and only a few examples are given.

In Acrididae the tip of the male's abdomen is twisted below the female and the edges of the epiphallus, a plate on top of the genital complex, grip the sides of the sub-genital plate of the female and draw it down into the anal depression of the male. The male uses his cerci to grip the female's abdomen and the aedeagus is inserted between the ventral valves of the ovipositor.

The male of *Oncopeltus* mounts the female, the genital capsule is rotated through 180°, mainly by muscular action, and the parameres grasp the ovipositor valves. Following insertion of the aedeagus the insects assume an end to end orientation in which they are held together mainly by the aedeagus (Fig. 231). An end to end position is also taken up by *Blattella* (Dictyoptera), but at first the female climbs on the back of the male, who engages the hook on his left phallomere on a sclerite in front of the ovipositor. Then, in the end to end position, the lateral hooks on either side of the anus and a small crescentic sclerite take a firm grip on the ovipositor (Fig. 232).

Copulation in Odonata involves the male flexing his abdomen so that the head of the female touches his accessory genitalia; she then brings her abdomen forwards beneath

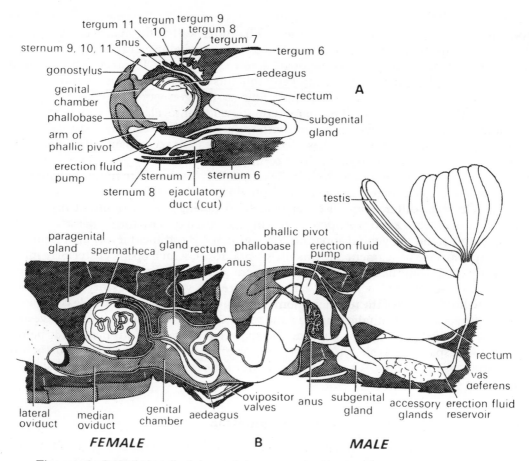

Fig. 231 A. Sagittal section of the genital capsule of a male *Oncopeltus* with the aedeagus retracted. B. Sagittal section of the posterior ends of copulating *Oncopeltus*. Notice the inversion of the male genital capsule and the insertion of the aedeagus into the spermatheca (after Bonhag and Wick, 1953)

her so as to make contact with the accessory genitalia (Fig. 228C). Some species, such as *Crocothemis*, copulate and complete sperm transfer in flight and in these copulation is brief, lasting less than 20 s. Many species, however, settle before copulating and in these the process may last for a few minutes or an hour or more (Corbett, 1962).

The duration of copulation in other insects is equally variable. In various mosquitoes the process is complete within a few seconds (Clements, 1963), while in *Oncopeltus* the insects may remain coupled for five hours, in *Locusta* for eight to ten hours, and in *Anacridium* (Orthoptera) for up to 60 hours. Insemination is completed much more rapidly than this: in *Locusta* sperm reach the spermatheca within two hours of the start of copulation and in *Hetaerina* (Odonata) sperm transfer takes about 7·5 s in a copulation lasting some three minutes.

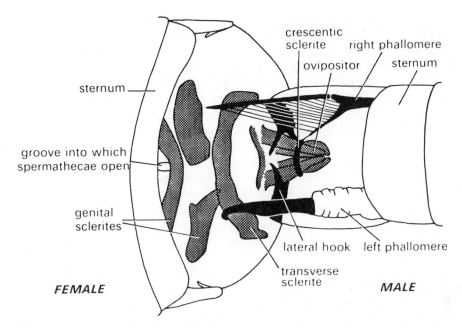

Fig. 232 Ventral view of the terminal abdominal segments of male and female *Blattella* showing the manner in which the male genitalia clasp the female. The insects are represented in the end-to-end position with the subgenital plates and endophallus of the male removed. Female sclerites shaded, male sclerites black (after Khalifa, 1950b)

16.7 Insemination

In the insects the transfer of sperm to the female is a quite separate process from fertilisation of the eggs, which in some cases does not occur until some months after insemination. During this interval the sperm are stored in the spermatheca. Sperm may be transferred in a spermatophore produced by the male, or they may be passed directly into the spermatheca without a spermatophore being produced.

16.7.1 Spermatophore

The primitive method of insemination in insects involves the production by the male of a spermatophore, a capsule enclosing the sperm. Spermatophores are produced by the Apterygota, Orthoptera, Dictyoptera, some Heteroptera, all the Neuroptera except Coniopterygidae, some Trichoptera, Lepidoptera, some Hymenoptera and Coleoptera and a few Diptera Nematocera and *Glossina* (Davey, 1965; Gadzama and Happ, 1974; Pollock, 1970).

Structure and transmission

In Collembola the male deposits spermatophores on the ground quite independently of the females. Sometimes spermatophores are produced in aggregations of Collembola, so there is a good chance of a female finding one and inserting it into her reproductive opening, but in other cases the male grasps the female by her antennae and leads her over the spermatophore. The spermatophores of *Campodea* are also produced in the absence of the female and, like those of Collembola, each one consists of a globule 50–70 μm in diameter mounted on a peduncle 50–100 μm high (Fig. 233A). The globule has a thin wall which encloses a granular fluid, floating in which are from one to four bundles of sperm. The sperm can survive in a spermatophore for two days. A male may produce some 200 spermatophores in a week, but at least some of these will be eaten by himself and other insects.

Lepisma (Thysanura) males also deposit spermatophores on the ground, but in this case in the presence of the females. By side to side movements of his abdomen a male spins silk threads over the female so that her movements are restricted and she is guided over the spermatophore, which she inserts into her genital duct. In *Machilis* sperm droplets are deposited on a thread. Then the male twists his body round the female and with his antennae and cerci guides her genitalia into positions in which they can pick up the droplets (Schaller, 1971).

In the Pterygota spermatophores are passed directly from the male to the female. Basically a spermatophore consists of a gelatinous protein capsule formed from the secretions of the male accessory glands. Two or more layers may be visible in the capsule and embedded in it are one or two sacs containing sperm. A single sperm sac is present in Grylloidea and Trichoptera; two are present in Tettigonioidea and *Sialis*. The outer gelatinous mass is prolonged into a neck and the sperm sacs may open on this (Fig. 233B) or they may be completely enclosed within the capsule. The whole structure is commonly of the order of two millimetres long.

In phasmids, gryllids and tettigoniids only the neck of the spermatophore penetrates the female ducts, the body of the structure remains outside and is liable to be eaten by the female or other insects. In Dictyoptera the body of the spermatophore, although still outside the female ducts, is protected by the enlarged subgenital plate of the female.

The spermatophore is specialised in some Acrididae to form a tube which is effectively a temporary elongation of the intromittent organ (Fig. 233C). It consists of two basal bladders in the ejaculatory and sperm sacs of the male (Fig. 211) leading to a tube which is differentiated into proximal and distal parts and extends into the bulb of the spermatheca. In *Locusta* the whole structure is 35–45 mm long, while the tube is only some 0·3 mm in diameter.

Most other insects practise internal fertilisation and where a spermatophore is retained it is deposited directly into the bursa copulatrix of the female, and may be formed there as in Lepidoptera and Trichoptera. In these instances it is suggested that the spermatophore forms a plug which prevents loss of sperm from the female while they are in transit to the spermatheca (Davey, 1960). The structure of the spermatophore may be simplified in accordance with its altered function and in *Rhodnius* it consists only of a pear-shaped mass of transparent mucoprotein with an apical slit containing the sperm. There is no sperm sac.

Mating plugs, which are distinct from spermatophores, are produced in a number of insects. Thus in mosquitoes belonging to the genera *Anopheles*, *Aedes* and *Psorophora* a plug, formed from the accessory gland secretions of the male, is deposited in the genital chamber of the female. In *Psorophora* the plug is almost completely dissolved within 24 h. A comparable structure present in some Lepidoptera, such as *Amauris* and

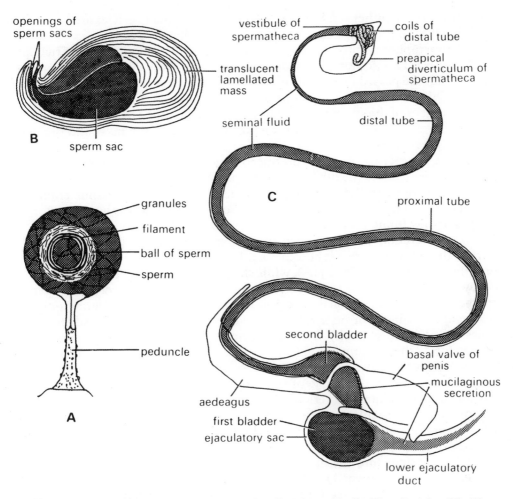

Fig. 233 Spermatophores. A. *Campodea* (after Bareth, 1964). B. *Blattella* (after Khalifa, 1950b). C. *Locusta* (after Gregory, 1965)

Acraea, is called the spermatophragma or sphragis and it effectively prevents further mating by the female. Similarly, the bursa of *Apis* is occluded for some hours after the nuptial flight by a plug of mucus and often with detached parts of the male genitalia.

Spermatophore production

In gryllids and tettigoniids the spermatophore is produced before the male meets a female and these insects will only court when they carry a spermatophore. Other insects produce the spermatophore during copulation from secretions of the accessory glands. In *Rhodnius* the secretion becomes gelatinous as a result of a sharp change in pH from 7·0 in the transparent accessory gland to 5·5 in the spermatophore sac which moulds its form. The spermatophore sac is formed by the endophallus and part of the aedeagus which is inverted. The spermatophore of *Blattella* is formed in a pouch of the ejaculatory duct from three secretions produced in different glands. A milky secretion is surrounded by two others and sperm from the two seminal vesicles are injected into the middle layer to form two separate sperm sacs (Khalifa, 1950b).

The spermatophore is produced within the female in Lepidoptera and Trichoptera. Thus in *Galleria* (Lepidoptera) the aedeagus extends into the ductus bursae so that the male secretions are passed directly into the bursa copulatrix. First a yellow secretion is produced. This hardens and is followed by a white secretion which forms a mass in the bursa and the neck of the spermatheca, this part being moulded by the penis. Sperm are injected with other secretions into the vacuolated centre of the mass and the penis is withdrawn (Khalifa, 1950a).

In *Locusta* the spermatophore is produced largely in the male, although the ducts of the female serve to mould the tubular part. Its production begins within two minutes of copulation starting with the secretions of some of the accessory glands entering the ejaculatory duct. The secretions build up and so are forced down the ejaculatory duct and through the funnel (Fig. 211), the shape of which produces a series of folds moulding the secretions into a cylinder. A white semi-fluid secretion is then forced into the core of the cylinder so that it becomes a tube. This is enlarged in the ejaculatory sac to form the first bladder (Fig. 234A), while the part remaining in the ejaculatory duct, and known at this time as the reservoir tube, ultimately forms the second bladder in the sperm sac. At this stage seminal fluid is passed into the rudimentary spermatophore and then a separate cylinder of material is formed and pushed into the bladder, where it becomes coiled up (Fig. 234B). This will form the distal tube and a further series of secretions forms the proximal tube (Fig. 234C). As the last part of the proximal tube enters the bladder it draws the wall of the reservoir tube with it, so that this becomes invaginated, and finally the whole of the tube except for the tip is pushed inside the bladder by a mucilaginous secretion (Fig. 234D).

At this time the ejaculatory sac starts to contract and so squeezes the tube of the spermatophore out of the bladder, while the pressure of mucilage in the ejaculatory duct forces the tip backwards through the gonopore, which is now open, and out through the aedeagus into the duct of the spermatheca (Fig. 234E, F). This process involves the tube being turned inside out and finally the second bladder is everted and moulded in the sperm sac (see Gregory, 1965, for a full account of this process). In *Gomphocerus* the tube is not turned inside out, but elongates by expansion (Hartmann, 1970).

Transfer of sperm to the spermatheca

Immediately following the transfer of the spermatophore the sperm migrate to the spermatheca, where they are stored. Sometimes they are able to escape from the sperm sac through a pore, but in other cases, where the sperm sac is completely enclosed within the spermatophore, they escape as a result of the spermatophore rupturing. In Lepidoptera and *Sialis* the inside of the bursa copulatrix is lined with spines or bears a toothed plate, the signum dentatum, to which muscles are attached. The spermatophore is gradually abraded by movements of the spines until it is torn open. In *Rhodnius* the first sperm reach the spermatheca within about 10 minutes of the end of mating, while in *Acheta* transfer takes about an hour, and in *Zygaena* (Lepidoptera) 12–18 h.

Although there is some evidence that the sperm move actively towards the spermatheca, guided by a chemical stimulus or a flow of fluid from the spermatheca, the

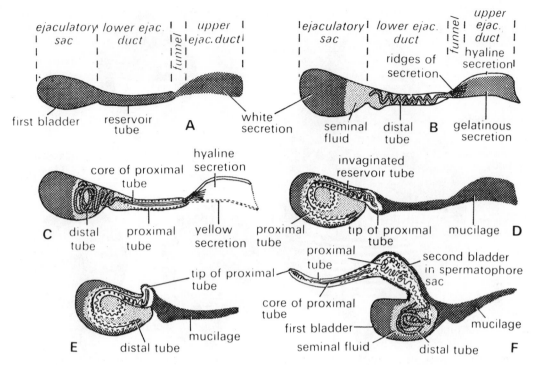

Fig. 234 Stages in spermatophore formation in *Locusta*. The parts of the male ducts in which the processes occur are indicated along the top (see Figs, 211, 233) (after Gregory, 1965)

bulk of evidence suggests that their movement is passive. In *Acheta* the sperm are held in the body of the spermatophore, which remains external to the female, and the spermatophore is specialised to force the sperm out into the female ducts. An outer reservoir of fluid, the evacuating fluid, with a low osmotic pressure is separated by an inner layer with semipermeable properties from an inner proteinaceous mass called the pressure body, which has a high osmotic pressure (Fig. 235A). When the spermatophore is deposited fluid passes from the evacuating fluid into the pressure body because of the difference in osmotic pressure. The pressure body swells producing a transparent material which forces the sperm out of the ampulla and down the tube of the spermatophore into the spermatheca (Fig. 235B–D). In *Locusta*, also, the sperm in the spermatophore are initially outside the female, in this case in the first bladder of the spermatophore. From here they are pumped along the spermatophore by contractions of the ejaculatory sac, first appearing in the spermatheca about 90 minutes after the start of copulation.

In many insects the spermatophore is placed in the bursa copulatrix of the female and the transfer of sperm to the spermatheca is probably brought about by the contractions of the female ducts. An opaque secretion from the male accessory glands of *Rhodnius* injected into the bursa with the spermatophore induces rhythmic contractions of the oviducts, probably by way of a direct nervous connection from the bursa to the oviducal muscles. The contractions cause shortening of the oviduct, and, it is suggested, cause the origin of the oviduct in the bursa to make bite-like movements in

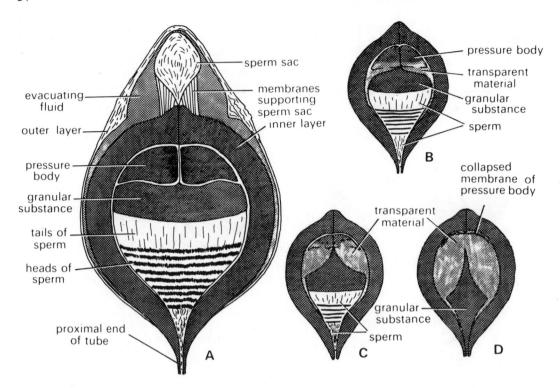

Fig. 235 A. Horizontal section through the ampulla of the spermatophore of *Acheta*. B, C, D. Stages in the evacuation of the spermatophore. The outer layer and evacuating fluid are not represented (after Khalifa, 1949)

the mass of semen in the bursa so that sperm are taken into the oviduct. As this process continues the more anterior sperm are forced forwards along the oviduct and are passed into the spermathecae (Davey,1958). Similar control over the movement of sperm to the spermatheca may occur in other insects (Leopold, 1976).

Fate of the spermatophore

In some female insects the spermatophore is ejected some time after fertilisation. *Blattella* and *Rhodnius*, for instance, drop the old spermatophores some 12 and 18 h respectively after copulation. The female *Sialis* pulls the spermatophore out and eats it and this commonly happens in Dictyoptera, where the post-copulatory behaviour often keeps the female occupied for a time to ensure that the sperm have left the spermatophore before she eats it. In some grasshoppers, such as *Gomphocerus*, the spermatophore is ejected by muscular contraction of the spermathecal duct.

The spermatophore is dissolved by proteolytic enzymes in other insects, such as Lepidoptera and Trichoptera, and in many Trichoptera only the sperm sac remains one or two days after copulation. In *Galleria* digestion is complete in ten days, but the neck of the spermatophore persists. The spermatophore of *Locusta* breaks when the two sexes separate, either where the tube fits tightly in the spermathecal duct or at its origin with the bladders in the male. The part remaining in the male is ejected within about two hours by the contractions of the copulatory organ, while in the female the distal tube disappears, presumably being dissolved within a day, but the proximal tube dissolves much more slowly, and persists for several days until it is ejected, probably by contractions of the spermathecal duct. In *Chorthippus* the activity of the enzyme-secreting cells is controlled by the corpora allata (Hartmann and Loher, 1974).

16.7.2 Direct insemination

Various groups of insects have dispensed with a spermatophore and sperm are transferred directly to the female ducts, and often into the spermatheca, by the penis, which may be long and flagelliform for this purpose. Such direct insemination occurs, for instance, in some members of the orders Heteroptera, Mecoptera, Trichoptera, Hymenoptera, Coleoptera and Diptera.

Direct insemination occurs in *Aedes aegypti* and in this insect the paraprocts expand the genital orifice of the female while the aedeagus is erected by the action of muscles attached to associated apodemes. The aedeagus only penetrates just inside the female opening, where it is held by spines which engage with a valve of the spermatheca. A stream of fluid from the accessory glands is driven along the ejaculatory duct and into the female by contractions of the glands and sperm are injected into the stream by the contractions of the seminal vesicles. Thus a mass of semen is deposited inside the atrium of the female and from here the sperm are transferred to the spermatheca (Spielman, 1964). The sperm of *Drosophila* are similarly deposited in the vagina and then pass to the spermatheca.

Oncopeltus has a long penis which reaches into the spermatheca and deposits sperm directly into it (Fig. 231B). Erection of the phallus in this insect is a specialised mechanism involving the displacement of an erection fluid into the phallus from a reservoir in the ejaculatory duct. The fluid is forced back from the reservoir by pressure exerted by the body muscles, and this pressure is maintained throughout copulation. At the end of the ejaculatory duct the fluid is forced into a vesicle and then pumped into the phallus (Bonhag and Wick, 1953). In those Coleoptera and Hymenoptera with a long penis, erection is probably produced by an increase in blood pressure resulting from the sudden contraction of the abdominal walls.

16.7.3 Haemocoelic insemination

In some Cimicoidea the sperm, instead of being deposited in the female reproductive tract, are injected into the haemocoel. A good deal of variation occurs between the species practising this method and they can be arranged in a series showing progressive specialisation (Hinton, 1964). In *Alloeorhynchus flavipes* the penis enters the vagina, but a spine at its tip perforates the wall of the vagina so that the sperm are injected into the haemocoel. They are not phagocytosed immediately, but disperse beneath the integument and later collect under the peritoneal membrane surrounding the ovarioles. Their movements are possibly directed chemotactically. The sperm adjacent to the lowest follicle penetrate the follicular epithelium and fertilise the eggs via the micropyles.

Primicimex shows a further separation from the normal method of insemination. Here the left clasper of the male penetrates the dorsal surface of the abdomen of the female, usually between tergites 4 and 5 or 5 and 6. The clasper ensheathes the penis and sperm are injected into the haemocoel. They accumulate in the heart and are distributed round the body with the blood. Many are phagocytosed by the blood cells, but those that survive are stored in two large pouches at the base of the oviducts. The holes made in the integument by the claspers become plugged with tanned cuticle.

In other species the sperm are not injected directly into the haemocoel, but are received into a special pouch called the mesospermalege or organ of Ribaga or Berlese, which is believed to be derived from blood cells. Other genera have a cuticular pouch, called the ectospermalege, for the reception of the clasper and the penis. There may be one or two ectospermalegia and their positions vary, but in *Afrocimex* they are situated in the membrane between segments 3 and 4 and segments 4 and 5 on the left-hand side. *Xylocoris galactinus* has a mesospermalege for the reception of sperm immediately beneath the ectospermalege (Fig. 236). It is formed from vacuolated cells surrounding a central lacuna into which the sperm are injected and from here they move down a solid core of cells, forming the conducting lobe, into the haemocoel. Finally they arrive at the conceptacula seminis at the bases of the lateral oviducts, where they accumulate. In *Cimex* this migration takes about 12 h and after the female takes her next blood meal the sperm are carried intracellularly in packets to the overies through special conduit cells. At the base of each ovariole they accumulate in a corpus seminalis derived from the follicular cells (Davis, 1964).

In *Anthocoris* and *Orius* temporary perforation of the integument does not occur because a copulatory tube opens on the left between the sternites of segments 7 and 8 and passes to a median sperm pouch, where the sperm accumulate. From here the mesospermalege forms a column of conducting tissue along which the sperm pass to the oviducts, so that they are never free in the haemocoel (Fig. 237).

In all these examples some sperm are digested by blood cells or by phagocytes in the mesospermalege. It is suggested that they are of nutritional value and perhaps

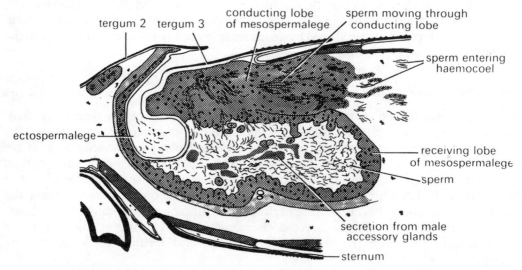

Fig. 236 Longitudinal section through the ectospermalege and mesospermalege of *Xylocoris galactinus* taken about an hour after copulation (after Carayon, 1953a)

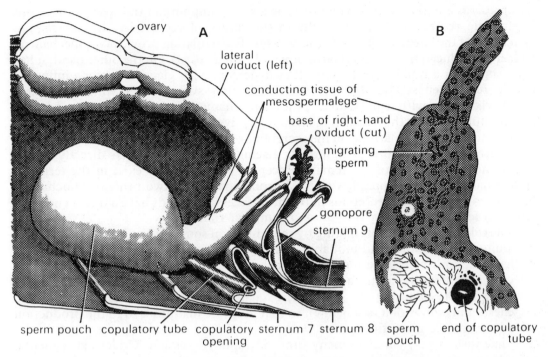

Fig. 237 A. Diagram of the internal reproductive organs of *Orius*. B. Longitudinal section of part of the mesospermalege showing the sperm pouch and conducting tissue (after Carayon, 1953b)

haemocoelic insemination and its associated digestion of sperm facilitates more prolonged survival of the recipients in the absence of food (Hinton, 1964), but this has been questioned by other authorities (see Leopold, 1976).

In Strepsiptera sperm also pass into the haemocoel to fertilise the eggs, but they do so via the genital canals of the female (see Fig. 281).

16.8 Post-copulatory behaviour

The behaviour of insects immediately following copulation is as variable as that immediately preceding it. In *Oecanthus* (Orthoptera) and some blattids the female remains feeding on the metanotal gland of the male for some time. This behaviour prevents her from eating the spermatophore. The female mantid may eat the male and sometimes she starts feeding before copulation. The effect of eating the head of the male is to release copulatory behaviour by the removal of inhibitory centres. The female is also known to eat the male in *Carabus auratus* and the ceratopogonid *Johannesenomyia*.

Following insemination it is common for females to reject further attempts at mating. In species which mate only once in their lifetime this lack of receptivity then persists for the remainder of their lives; in species exhibiting multiple mating receptivity is subsequently regained. In some species the loss of receptivity is regulated directly through the nervous system. For instance, females of *Nauphoeta* and

Gomphocerus are unreceptive while there is a spermatophore in the spermatheca, but cutting the ventral nerve cord results in the return of receptivity. In *Chorthippus* distension of the lateral oviducts by the oocytes after ovulation provides the mechanical trigger for reduced receptivity (Hartmann and Loher, 1974). On the other hand, it has been shown in a number of Diptera that male accessory gland secretions influence female receptiveness. In *Aedes* receptivity is first switched off when the bursa copulatrix is filled with seminal fluid. This is a mechanical effect relayed via the nervous system. Subsequently the female remains unreceptive for the rest of her life as a result of a substance, known as matrone, in the secretions of the male accessory glands. Matrone passes from the bursa copulatrix into the haemolymph and then acts directly on the central nervous system of the female. Receptor sites probably exist in the terminal abdominal ganglion (Leopold, 1976). Matrone consists of two proteins (Fuchs and Hiss, 1970). In *Glossina* secretions of the male accessory glands have a direct chemical effect on female receptivity (Gillott and Langley, 1981).

The relevance of multiple mating by the females of some species is not clear since in mosquitoes and acridids and probably in many other insects a single mating provides sufficient sperm to fertilise most of the eggs which a female produces. A possible selective advantage lies in the fact that mating with several different males increases the diversity of the offspring. In addition, in a number of insects mating stimulates oogenesis and oviposition (see below), so that multiple matings lead to the production of more eggs in a given time.

Male insects may copulate many times in rapid succession. Under experimental conditions a male *Nasonia* has mated 154 times in four and a half hours, and a male of *Aedes aegypti* mated 30 times in 30 minutes. Although in the field such excessive copulation is unlikely to occur, multiple copulation by males must be common. When copulations follow each other in rapid succession only some of them result in successful insemination because the supply of sperm is limited. Thus of seven copulations performed by a male *Aedes* only four resulted in insemination of the female, but further insemination occurred on subsequent days as fresh sperm were produced (and see Jones and Wheeler, 1965). In species which produce a spermatophore the availablity of material for the spermatophore may also be limiting. *Galleria* males which copulated within three hours of a previous copulation produced only small spermatophores, in some cases devoid of sperm. A normal spermatophore is produced after about 12 hours (Khalifa, 1950a).

16.9 Effects of male accessory glands on oogenesis and oviposition

In grasshoppers belonging to the subfamilies Cyrtacanthacridinae, Catantopinae and Pyrgomorphidae several spermatophores are produced during a period of copulation. *Melanoplus* produces about seven and *Schistocerca* six at each normal mating. These spermatophores are simple sac-like structures quite different from those of *Locusta* and related species (Pickford and Padgham, 1973). A large proportion of the soluble protein in these spermatophores is absorbed by the female and passed into the oocytes, so that there is a direct contribution of protein from the male accessory glands to the developing oocytes (Friedel and Gillott, 1977). A single spermatophore contains sufficient sperm to fertilise several batches of eggs and it is possible that mating after the first oviposition is more important in maintaining fecundity than in maintaining fertility (Leahy, 1973).

In some other insects the spermatophores are digested within the female genital tracts and it is known that in *Galleria* the components are absorbed by the female. Some Orthoptera and Neuroptera eat the spermatophores. It is probable that in these cases the contents and substance of the spermatophores have nutritional value for the female, but this has not been proved (Leopold, 1976).

The rate of oogenesis is increased by accessory gland material in a number of grasshoppers, cockroaches, moths and some other insects. It is not clear whether the secretion has a direct effect on the oocytes resulting from its nutritional value or if it has an indirect effect and acts through the female endocrine system.

In *Melanoplus* secretions of the male accessory gland induce oviposition, acting via the neurosecretory cells of the brain (Friedel and Gillott, 1976). Similar control of oviposition probably occurs in other insects, but in most cases the direct effect on oviposition has not been certainly differentiated from an indirect effect resulting from the speeding up of oogenesis.

REFERENCES

ALCOCK, J. (1975). Territorial behaviour by males of *Philanthus multimaculatus* (Hymenoptera: Sphecidae) with a review of territoriality in male sphecids. *Anim. Behav.* **23**: 889–895.

ALEXANDER, R. D. (1961). Aggressiveness, territoriality, and sexual behaviour in field crickets (Orthoptera: Gryllidae). *Behaviour* **17**: 130–223.

ALEXANDER, R. D. (1964). The evolution of mating behaviour in arthropods. *Symp. R. ent. Soc. Lond.* **2**: 78–94.

AVITABILE, A., MORSE, R. A. and BOCH, R. (1975). Swarming honey bees guided by pheromones. *Ann. ent. Soc. Am.* **68**: 1079–1082.

BARETH, C. (1964). Structure et dépôt des spermatophores chez *Campodea remyi*. *C. r. hebd. Séanc. Acad. Sci., Paris* **259**: 1572–1575.

BARRASS, R. (1960). The courtship behaviour of *Mormoniella vitripennis* Walk. (Hymenoptera: Pteromalidae.) *Behaviour* **15**: 185–209.

BARRASS, R. (1976). Inhibitory effects of courtship in the wasp *Nasonia vitripennis* and a new interpretation of the biological significance of courtship in insects. *Physiol. Ent.* **1**: 229–234.

BARTH, R. H. and LESTER, L. J. (1973). Neuro-hormonal control of sexual behaviour in insects. *A. Rev. Ent.* **18**: 445–472.

BONHAG, P. F. and WICK, J. R. (1953). The functional anatomy of the male and female reproductive systems of the milkweed bug, *Oncopeltus fasciatus* (Dallas) (Heteroptera: Lygaeidae). *J. Morph.* **93**: 177–283.

BROWN, R. G. B. (1965). Courtship in the *Drosophila obscura* group. II. Comparative studies. *Behaviour* **25**: 281–323.

BUTLER, C. G. (1965). Sex attraction in *Andrena flavipes* Panzer (Hymenoptera: Apidae), with some observations on nest-site restriction. *Proc. R. ent. Soc. Lond.* **40**: 77–80.

CARAYON, J. (1953a). Organe de Ribaga et fécondation hémocoelienne chez les *Xylocoris* du groupe *galactinus* (Hemipt. Anthocoridae). *C. r. hebd. Séanc. Acad. Sci., Paris* **236**: 1099–1101.

CARAYON, J. (1953b). Existence d'un double orifice génital et d'un tissu conducteur des spermatozoides chez les Anthocorinae (Hemipt. Anthocoridae). *C. r. hebd. Séanc. Acad. Sci., Paris* **236**: 1206–1208.

CARAYON, J. (1964). Un cas d'offrande nuptiale chez les Hétéroptères. *C. r. hebd. Séanc. Acad. Sci., Paris* **259**: 4815–4818.

CHAO, H.-F. (1953). The external morphology of the dragonfly *Onychogomphus ardens* Needham. *Smithson. misc. Collns.* **122**, no. 6: 1–56.

CLEMENTS, A. N. (1963). *The physiology of mosquitoes.* Pergamon Press, Oxford.

CORBET, P. (1962). *A biology of dragonflies.* Witherby, London.

CORBET, P. S. and HADDOW, A. J. (1962). Diptera swarming high above the forest canopy in Uganda, with special reference to Tabanidae. *Trans. R. ent. Soc. Lond.* **114**: 267–284.

CORBET, P. S., LONGFIELD, C. and MOORE, N. W. (1960). *Dragonflies.* Collins, London.

DAVEY, K. G. (1958). The migration of spermatozoa in the female of *Rhodnius prolixus* Stal. *J. exp. Biol.* **35**: 694–701.

DAVEY, K. G. (1960). The evolution of spermatophores in insects. *Proc. R. ent. Soc. Lond.* A, **35**: 107–113.

DAVEY, K. G. (1965). *Reproduction in the insects.* Oliver and Boyd, Edinburgh.

DAVIS, N. T. (1964). Studies on the reproductive physiology of Cimicidae (Hemiptera)— I. Fecundation and egg maturation. *J. Insect Physiol.* **10**: 947–963.

DOWNES, J. A. (1969). The swarming and mating flight of Diptera. *A. Rev. Ent.* **14**: 271–298.

ENGELMANN, F. (1970). *The physiology of insect reproduction.* Pergamon Press, Oxford.

FRIEDEL, T. and GILLOTT, C. (1976). Male accessory gland substance of *Melanoplus sanguinipes*: an oviposition stimulant under the control of the corpus allatum. *J. Insect Physiol.* **22**: 489–495.

FRIEDEL, T. and GILLOTT, C. (1977). Contribution of the male-produced proteins to vitellogenesis in *Melanoplus sanguinipes*. *J. Insect Physiol.* **23**: 145–151.

FUCHS, M. S. and HISS, E. A. (1970). The partial purification and separation of the protein components of matrone from *Aedes aegypti*. *J. Insect Physiol.* **16**: 931–939.

GADZAMA, N. M. and HAPP, G. M. (1974). The structure and evacuation of the spermatophore of *Tenebrio molitor* L. (Coleoptera: Tenebrionidae). *Tissue & Cell* **6**: 95–108.

GILLOTT, C. and LANGLEY, P. A. (1981). The control of receptivity and ovulation in the tsetse fly, *Glossina morsitans. Physiol. Ent.* **6**: 269–281.

GIVEN, B. B. (1954). Evolutionary trends in the Thynninae with special reference to feeding habits of Australian species. *Trans. R. ent. Soc. Lond.* **105**: 1–10.

GREGORY, G. E. (1965). The formation and fate of the spermatophore in the African migratory locust, *Locusta migratoria migratorioides* Reiche and Fairmaire. *Trans. R. ent. Soc. Lond.* **117**: 33–66.

HADDOW, A. J. and CORBET, P. S. (1961). Entomological studies from a high tower in Mpanga Forest, Uganda. V. Swarming activity above the forest. *Trans. R. ent. Soc. Lond.* **113**: 284–300.

HARTMANN, R. (1970). Experimentelle und histologische Untersuchungen der Spermatophorenbildung bei der Feldheuschrecke *Gomphocerus rufus* L. (Orthoptera, Acrididae). *J. Morph. Tiere* **68**: 140–176.

HARTMANN, R. and LOHER, W. (1974). Control of sexual behaviour pattern 'secondary defence' in the female grasshopper, *Chorthippus curtipennis. J. Insect Physiol.* **20**: 1713–1728.

HINTON, H. E. (1964). Sperm transfer in insects and the evolution of haemocoelic insemination. *Symp. R. ent. Soc. Lond.* **2**: 95–107.

JONES, J. C. and WHEELER, R. E. (1965). Studies on spermathecal filling in *Aedes aegypti* (Linnaeus). I. Description. *Biol. Bull. mar. biol. Lab., Woods Hole* **129**: 134–150.

KHALIFA, A. (1949). The mechanism of insemination and the mode of action of the spermatophore in *Gryllus domesticus. Q. Jl microsc. Sci.* **90**: 281–292.

KHALIFA, A. (1950a). Spermatophore production in *Galleria mellonella* L. (Lepidoptera). *Proc. R. ent. Soc. Lond.* A, **25**: 33–42.

KHALIFA, A. (1950b). Spermatophore production in *Blattella germanica* L. (Orthoptera: Blattidae). *Proc. R. ent. Soc. Lond.* A, **25**: 53–61.

LEAHY, M. G. (1973). Oviposition of virgin *Schistocerca gregaria* (Forskål) (Orthoptera: Acrididae) after implant of the male accessory gland complex. *J. Ent.* A, **48**: 69–78.

LEOPOLD, R. A. (1976). The role of male accessory glands in insect reproduction. *A. Rev. Ent.* **21**: 199–221.

LIN, N. (1963). Territorial behaviour in the cicada killer wasp, *Sphecius speciosus* (Drury) (Hymenoptera: Sphecidae). I. *Behaviour* **20**: 115–133.

LOHER, W. and HUBER, F. (1966). Nervous and endocrine control of sexual behaviour in a grasshopper (*Gomphocerus rufus* L., Acridinae). *Symp. Soc. exp. Biol.* **20**: 381–400.

LONGFIELD, C. (1949). *The dragonflies of the British Isles* Warne, London.

NIELSEN, E. T. and NIELSEN, H. T. (1958). Observations on mosquitoes in Iraq. *Ent. Meddr.* **28**: 282–321.

PICKFORD, R. and PADGHAM, D. E. (1973). Spermatophore formation and sperm transfer in the desert locust, *Schistocerca gregaria* (Orthoptera: Acrididae). *Can. Ent.* **105**: 613–618.

POLLOCK, J. N. (1970). Sperm transfer by spermatophores in *Glossina austeni* Newstead. *Nature, Lond.* **225**: 1063–1064.

RICHARDS, O. W. (1927). Sexual selection and allied problems in the insects. *Biol. Rev.* **2**: 298–364.

SCHALLER, F. (1971). Indirect sperm transfer by soil arthropods. *A. Rev. Ent.* **16**: 407–446.

SCUDDER, G. G. E. (1971). Comparative morphology of insect genitalia. *A. Rev. Ent.* **16**: 379–406.

SEGUY, E. (1951). Ordre des Diptères. in Grassé, P.-P. (ed.), *Traité de Zoologie*, vol. 10. Masson et Cie., Paris.

SIMPSON, J. (1974). *The reproductive behaviour of European honeybee colonies.* Central Association of Bee-Keepers, Ilford, England.

SNODGRASS, R. E. (1957). A revised interpretation of the external reproductive organs of male insects. *Smithson. misc. Collns.* **135**, no. 6, 60 pp.

SPIELMAN, A. (1964). The mechanics of copulation in *Aedes aegypti*. *Biol. Bull. mar. biol. Lab., Woods Hole* **127**: 324–344.

SPIETH, H. T. (1974). Courtship behaviour in *Drosophila*. *A. Rev. Ent.* **19**: 385–405.

STRIDE, G. O. (1957). Investigations into the courtship behaviour of the male of *Hypolimnas misippus* L. (Lepidoptera, Nymphalidae), with special reference to the role of visual stimuli. *Br. J. Anim. Behav.* **5**: 153–167.

TILLYARD, R. J. (1917). *The biology of dragonflies.* Cambridge University Press.

TRUMAN, J. W. and RIDDIFORD, L. M. (1974). Hormonal mechanisms underlying insect behaviour. *Adv. Insect Physiol.* **10**: 297–352.

TUXEN, S. L. (1956). *Taxonomist's glossary of genitalia in insects.* Monksgaard, Copenhagen.

CHAPTER XVII

OVIPOSITION AND THE EGG

In some insects the female has no special structures associated with egg-laying, but in others the posterior part of the abdomen or some posterior abdominal appendages are modified to form an ovipositor. This enables the female to insert her eggs into special situations, within plant or animal tissue, for instance, instead of simply depositing them on a surface. The eggs may be laid singly or in masses and in some species they are deposited in special protective structures called oothecae formed from secretions of the female accessory glands. The oviposition site selected by the female is usually characteristic for the species and is of some importance since the survival of the egg and the availability of food for the larva when it hatches depend on her choice. The selection of the site involves a general attraction to some particular area and then a specific reaction which determines the precise spot at which the egg is laid within this area.

Insect eggs are relatively large because they contain a great deal of yolk. The shell of the egg is often complex and contains cavities connecting with the outside air by a number of small holes or, in some cases, through an open network. This system facilitates gaseous exchange all round the surface of the egg and in some cases, where the eggs of terrestrial insects are liable to flooding, it may function as a plastron. Water loss from the egg is restricted by a layer of wax on the inside of the shell and sometimes a second wax layer is formed in an embryonic cuticle. Many insect eggs absorb water during development and so may increase considerably in size. One or more small holes are present in the shell, passing right through it to permit the entry of sperm.

The structure of the female genitalia is reviewed by Scudder (1961, 1971) and Snodgrass (1935). Hinton (1981) reviews the literature on all aspects of insect eggs and water regulation is discussed by Edney (1977).

17.1 Female genitalia: the ovipositor

The gonopore of the female insect is usually situated on or behind the eighth or ninth abdominal segment, but the Ephemeroptera and Dermaptera are exceptional in having the gonopore behind segment 7. In many orders there are no special structures associated with oviposition, although sometimes the terminal segments of the abdomen are long and telescopic forming a type of ovipositor (Fig. 197B). Such a structure is found in some Lepidoptera, Coleoptera and Diptera. In *Musca* the telescopic section is formed from segments six to nine and normally, when not in use, it is telescoped within segment five. This species has the sclerites of the ovipositor reduced to rods. In other species, as in tephritids, the tip of the abdomen is hardened and forms a sharp point, which enables the insect to place its eggs in small holes and crevices.

Other insects have an ovipositor of a quite different form derived from the appendages of abdominal segments eight and nine. Such a structure is present in Thysanura, some Odonata, Orthoptera, Homoptera, Heteroptera, Thysanoptera Terebrantia and Hymenoptera. Scudder (1961) has attempted to rationalise the terminology associated with the ovipositor and his terms will be used together with the more generally used terminology of Snodgrass (1935).

Scudder (1961) believes *Lepisma* to possess a basic form of the ovipositor from which the ovipositors of other insects can be derived. At the base of the ovipositor on each side are the coxae of segments 8 and 9. These are known as the first and second gonocoxae (first and second valvifers of Snodgrass, 1935) (Fig. 238). Articulating with each of these plates is a slender process which curves posteriorly. These are the first and second gonapophyses (valvulae of Snodgrass, 1935) and they form the shaft of the ovipositor. In *Lepisma* the second gonapophyses of the two sides are united, so that the shaft comprises three elements fitting together to form a tube down which the eggs pass. At the base of the ovipositor there is a small sclerite, the gonangulum, which is attached to the base of the first gonapophysis and articulates with the second gonocoxa and the tergum of segment 9. The gonangulum probably represents a part of the coxa of segment 9. It is not differentiated in *Petrobius* (Archaeognatha).

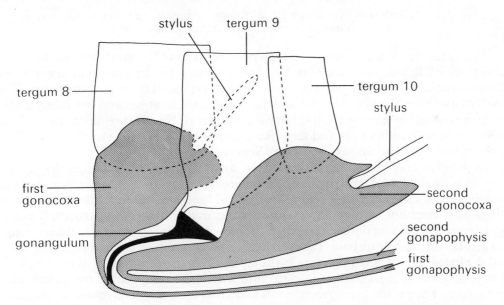

Fig. 238 Inner view of the genital segments of *Lepisma*. The forms and positions of some basal sclerites of the ovipositor have been slightly modified in order to show their inter-relationships more clearly. Styli occur on other segments and are not an essential part of the ovipositor (after Scudder, 1961)

In some Thysanura and in the Pterygota an additional process is present on the second gonocoxa. This is the gonoplac (third valvula of Snodgrass, 1935). It may or may not be a separate sclerite and may form a sheath round the gonapophyses. The

gonoplacs are well developed in the Orthoptera, where they form the dorsal valves of
the ovipositor with the second gonapophyses enclosed within the shaft as in tettigoniids
(Fig. 239) or reduced as in the gryllids. Throughout the Orthoptera the gonangulum is
fused with the first gonocoxa.

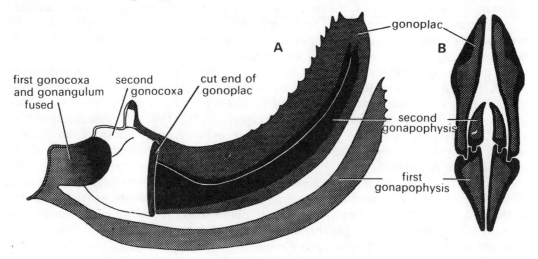

Fig. 239 The ovipositor of a tettigoniid. A. Lateral view with one gonoplac removed. B.
Transverse section (from Snodgrass, 1935)

The Homoptera, Heteroptera and Thysanoptera have the gonangulum fused with
tergum 9, while the gonoplac may be present or absent. In Pentatomomorpha and
Cimicomorpha the development of the ovipositor is related to oviposition habit. If the
insect oviposits in plant or animal tissue the valves are sclerotised and lanceolate and the
anterior strut of the gonangulum is heavily sclerotised. Species laying on leaf surfaces,
however, have membranous and flap-like gonapophyses and the anterior strut of the
gonangulum is membranous or absent (Scudder, 1959).

In the Hymenoptera the first gonocoxae are usually absent, although they may be
present in Chalcidoidea, and the second gonapophyses are united. In the Symphyta and
parasitic groups the ovipositor retains its original function, but in Aculeata it forms the
sting. This does not involve any major modifications of the basic structure, but the
eggs, instead of passing down the shaft of the ovipositor, are ejected from the opening of
the genital chamber at its base. In *Apis* the first gonapophyses are known as the lancets
and the fused second gonapophyses as the stylet. This forms an inverted trough, which
is enlarged into a basal bulb (Fig. 240) into which the reservoir of the poison gland
discharges. The poison gland, sometimes known as the acid gland, consists of a pair of
tubular glands with a common duct leading to the poison reservoir. Another accessory
gland, the alkaline gland, discharges at the base of the sting. Its function is unknown,
but it may be concerned with lubrication of the sting.

Sensilla on the ovipositor

The terminal abdominal segments, and the ovipositor where one is present, have an
array of sensilla in which mechanoreceptors usually predominate. In the moth *Chilo*,

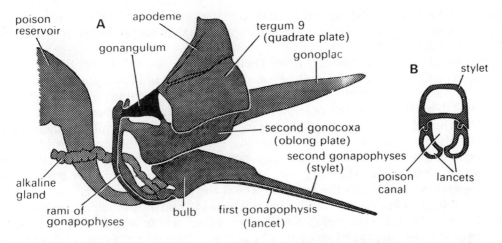

Fig. 240 Structure of the sting of a worker *Apis*. A. Lateral view. B. Transverse section through the shaft (after Snodgrass, 1956)

which lacks an appendicular ovipositor, the genital opening is surrounded by a ring of long mechanoreceptors with only four contact chemoreceptors. Similar arrangements occur in other moths. In *Musca* there are rings of mechanoreceptors on the posterior margins of abdominal segments 6 and 7, and other sensilla on sclerotised plates surrounding the gonopore. Most of these are mechanoreceptors, but a few contact chemoreceptors and olfactory receptors are also present (Hooper *et al.*, 1972). A similar arrangement occurs in other cyclorrhaphan flies (Behan and Ryan, 1977; Rice, 1976).

The valves of the ovipositor of locusts possess large numbers of trichoid mechanoreceptors, campaniform sensilla and contact chemoreceptors (Rice and McRae, 1976; Thomas, 1965).

17.2 Oviposition

17.2.1 Oviposition habits

The selection of a suitable oviposition site by the female is of great importance since it must ensure that the eggs are adequately protected from the environment and that the correct food will be available for the relatively immobile larvae when they hatch.

In many cases the eggs are laid in or on the food of the larvae. Tenthridinidae, Thysanoptera and some Homoptera insert their eggs in the tissues of the host plant. In this way the eggs are protected from extremes of temperature and desiccation, and perhaps to some extent from predators. Such behaviour may be modified to suit the ecological requirement of the species. For instance, *Muellerianella* (Homoptera) feeds specifically on *Holcus* and the eggs of the spring generation are laid in the tissues of *Holcus*, but *Holcus* is an annual grass and does not overwinter and the eggs of the second generation, which survive the winter, are laid in *Juncus*. When the larvae hatch in spring they move from the *Juncus* to *Holcus* to feed (Claridge and Wilson, 1978). Many other phytophagous species, notably among the Lepidoptera and Heteroptera, lay their eggs on the surface of the larval food plant. For instance, *Pieris brassicae* lays its eggs on crucifers and *Papilio machaon* lays eggs preferentially on *Peucedanum*; these are the principal larval foods. The eggs are cemented to the leaf with accessory gland secretions and are commonly placed on the undersurface, where they are protected from extremes of heat and desiccation.

It is usual for parasitic insects to lay their eggs in or on their hosts. Bethylidae lay their eggs on the outside of the body of larval Lepidoptera and Coleoptera and the wasp larvae puncture the cuticle and feed externally after hatching. Some Tachinidae (Diptera) deposit eggs on the outside of the host and the larvae bore in through the cuticle of the host when they hatch. Other members of the same family lay their eggs in the host tissues and this is common amongst parasitic Hymenoptera with a well-developed ovipositor. In some instances, notably in *Rhyssa*, which parasitises the larvae of *Sirex* (Hymenoptera), the insect can locate and oviposit in its host by boring down with its ovipositor through the wood in which the host is burrowing.

Saprophagous insects commonly lay their eggs in or on the decaying materials eaten by the larvae. *Orthellia* (Diptera), for instance, makes a hole with its ovipositor in the surface of a freshly deposited cow pat. The hole is enlarged by pressing outwards with the ovipositor and a group of 25–35 eggs is laid in the cavity so formed (Fig. 241A).

In many other species the eggs are not laid on the larval food, but are put in situations from which the larvae can readily find food. The eggs of stick insects, for instance, drop to the ground amongst the vegetation and the newly hatched larvae make their own way back to the food. Acrididae and some other insects, such as *Psila rosae* (Diptera), lay their eggs in the ground in the region of the host plant, while some moths, such as *Spodoptera littoralis*, lay their eggs in situations from which the larvae disperse on silken threads to food plants. The significance of these different strategies is not always apparent, but it is assumed that they offer some adaptive advantage which offsets the lack of immediate contact with the food.

Predaceous insects nearly always lay their eggs in the habitat of the prey, rather than directly on the prey. The eggs of *Chrysopa* (Neuroptera) are laid on leaves, but raised on stalks which may be up to 15 mm high. The stalk is produced as a viscous material which hardens in air as the insect draws it out. As a result of this habit the larvae are likely to hatch close to a source of food and at the same time the stalk removes the eggs

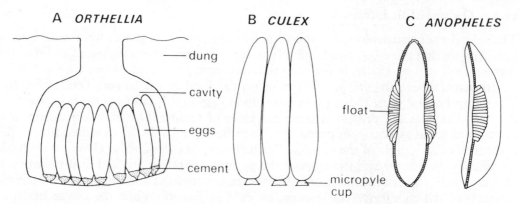

Fig. 241 A. Eggs of *Orthellia* in a cavity in cow-dung (after Hinton, 1960). B. Eggs of *Culex* showing the hydrophilic micropyle cup. C. Eggs of *Anopheles*, ventral and lateral views (after Marshall, 1938)

from the immediate vicinity of other predators moving on the leaf surface. Those syrphids and coccinellids which feed on aphids also oviposit on the leaves on which the prey is feeding. The predaceous tettigoniid *Meconema* lays its eggs into crevices in bark or fungi growing on the bark of the trees in which it feeds. The eggs of most tiger beetles are laid in soil in areas likely to provide prey for the larvae as they lie in wait in burrows: in a few species the eggs are laid in the twigs of woody plants and from these situations the larvae catch other insects, probably mainly ants, moving up and down the twigs.

In some parasitic species the female oviposits in an area frequented by the host rather than on the host itself. The eggs of Trigonalidae are laid on leaves and must be eaten by a caterpillar or sawfly larva infected with an ichneumon or tachinid parasite which is the host of the trigonalid larva. Because of the wastage which occurs these insects produce large numbers of eggs; several thousand in a few days are recorded (Clausen, 1940). Meloid eggs are deposited near the host nesting or oviposition sites and the larvae search for the host. Meloids also produce large numbers of eggs.

Cordylobia (Diptera) also lays its eggs away from the host, while *Dermatobia*, the human warble fly, oviposits on other insects, especially mosquitoes, which then transport the eggs to the host. The female fly waits at a pool and as a mosquito emerges from the pupa she will capture it and lay a group of about 15 eggs on its abdomen. Such an association in which an animal of one species provides transport for another species is known as phoresy.

Insects with aquatic larvae show a similar range of variation in their oviposition behaviour. *Culex*, for instance, lands on the water and constructs a raft of 150–300 eggs between the hind tarsi, which lie flat on the surface. The eggs float in an upright position because the micropyle cup at one end is hydrophilic and the rest of the chorion is hydrophobic (Fig. 241B). Other mosquito species, such as *Anopheles*, lay their eggs singly on the surface and the position in which the eggs float, ventral surface uppermost, is determined by the presence of air-filled floats in the chorion (Fig. 241C). The eggs of dragonflies are also sometimes laid on the surface, either being dropped from above or washed off by the tip of the abdomen touching the water, but in this case the eggs slowly sink to the bottom. In other cases, as in *Chironomus*, the eggs are laid in a string which is anchored at the surface (Fig. 243). Other insects with aquatic larvae lay their eggs in floating vegetation. This is true of *Nepa*, which lays its eggs so that their respiratory horns (p. 397) remain above the water. Various species of Zygoptera also lay their eggs in surface vegetation such as *Potamogeton* and *Myriophyllum*.

Some species submerge to lay their eggs. This occurs in some Zygoptera which lay their eggs in the submerged parts of water plants. The female of *Hetaerina*, for instance, submerges to a depth of about 10 cm and may remain submerged for nearly an hour while she lays her eggs in the roots of *Salix* (Bick and Sulzbach, 1966). Aquatic beetles also oviposit under water. Some, such as *Agabus*, lay their eggs on aquatic plants, the female in this species laying a row of eggs inside the leaf sheath (Jackson, 1958). *Ilybius* (Coleoptera) lays its eggs in the tissues of aquatic plants, making an incision to place the eggs amongst the airspaces in the plant (Jackson, 1960). The mymarid *Caraphractus* swims under water in order to parasitise the eggs of these beetles (Jackson, 1966).

Some aquatic insects oviposit in positions over or near water enabling the larvae readily to find their way to it. Some dragonflies and Trichoptera lay their eggs in or on emergent vegetation, so that the larvae tend to drop into the water when they hatch.

Aedes, on the other hand, lays its eggs on the ground near water in places liable to flooding and the eggs do not hatch until such flooding occurs.

The social insects are exceptional in laying their eggs in nests constructed to house the developing larvae.

17.2.2 Oothecae

Although in the majority of insects the eggs are simply glued on to, or inserted into, the substratum, a number of species lay their eggs in oothecae formed by secretions of the female accessory glands.

Characteristic oothecae are produced by the Dictyoptera. *Blatta*, for instance, lays its eggs in two rows, each of eight eggs, inside a capsule which becomes tanned as it is formed (p. 333) (Fig. 242A). Along the top of the capsule is a crest containing cavities which connect via small pores with the outside and thus facilitate respiration by the eggs. Roth (1968) reviews the structure of oothecae in the Blattaria.

Acrididae lay their eggs in egg pods in the ground. A pod consists of a mass of eggs under the ground held together by a frothy secretion and sometimes also enclosed by a layer of the same substance. The hole above the egg-mass is plugged by more froth (Fig. 242B,C). The eggs within the mass are arranged irregularly in the Pyrgomorphidae and Cyrtacanthacridinae (Fig. 242B) but are in regular rows in the Acridinae and Truxalinae (Fig. 242C). Some species produce pods with only a few

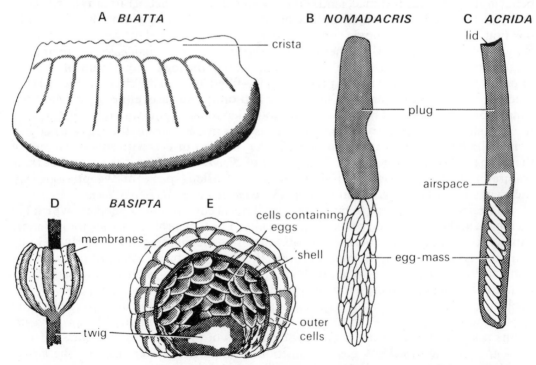

Fig. 242 A. Ootheca of *Blatta* (after Ragge, 1965). B and C. Egg pods of *Nomadacris* and *Acrida* (after Chapman and Robertson, 1958). D. Ootheca of *Basipta*. E. Transverse section of the ootheca of *Basipta* (after Muir and Sharp, 1904)

eggs; *Badistica*, for instance, lays between one and six, while at other extreme *Phymateus* has been recorded to lay over 200 eggs in a pod.

The tortoise beetles also produce oothecae. The form and complexity of the ootheca varies from species to species, but *Basipta* attaches its ootheca to the stem of its food plant. The theca is formed of a large number of lamellae produced from an accessory gland secretion which is compressed into a plate-like form as it is extruded between the terminal sclerites of the abdomen. The lamellae are placed so as to form an open cup, the interior of which is occupied by about 30 cells also formed by the lamellae (Fig. 242D, E). An egg is placed in each cell as it is formed and round the outside of the cup the lamellae are plastered firmly together to form a hard 'shell' with looser lamellae outside it (Muir and Sharp, 1904).

The heteropteran *Plataspis* forms a type of ootheca, laying its eggs in two rows and then covering them with hard elongate pellets of a secretion produced by specialised cells in the intestine. *Coptosoma* (Heteroptera) covers its eggs with an irregular layer of cement which traps pockets of air in deep follicular pits.

Amongst aquatic insects *Hydrophilus* constructs a silken cocoon with a mast (Fig. 243A, and see p. 334), while in many groups the eggs are enclosed in a gelatinous matrix. For instance, *Chironomus dorsalis* produces a structure in which the eggs loop backwards and forwards round the circumference of the matrix while a pair of fibres, which anchor the mass to the surface, run through the centre (Fig. 243B). Other species of chironomids and Trichoptera lay their eggs in masses or strands of gelatinous material.

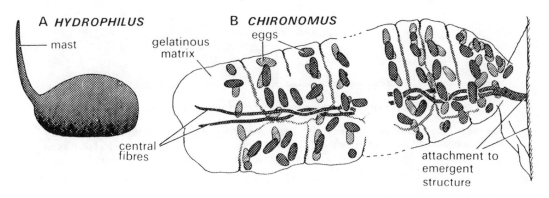

Fig. 243 A. Egg cocoon of *Hydrophilis* (after Miall, 1922). B. Egg-rope of *Chironomus*

17.2.3 Choice of oviposition site

Two phases can be recognised in the selection of an oviposition site. The first, or initial selection is based on a general reaction to the environment and this is followed by a final selection which depends on more specific responses.

Initial selection of a site involves various factors and pre-oviposition behaviour may be important, as in locusts and grasshoppers. These insects tend to bask in warm spots on bare ground and often they oviposit at the basking site (Popov, 1958). Their choice is also influenced by the availability of suitable vegetation on which to feed and roost.

Thus *Nomadacris* oviposits largely in areas where the vegetation has been burnt leaving the ground bare, but more eggs are laid, and later more larvae are present, adjacent to stands of unburnt grass than in extensive areas of bare ground (Fig. 244). Finding an area in which to oviposit may involve visual or olfactory stimuli. The olive fly, *Dacus oleae*, recognises olive trees by the colour of the foliage and once on a tree the flies are retained by the chemical or physical characteristics of the leaves and branches. The olive fruit is recognised from a distance by its colour and size (Prokopy and Haniotakis, 1976). Attraction of *Psila* to its host depends initially on non-specific visual signals at wavelengths around 560 nm (Städler, 1977). On the other hand, gravid females of *Delia brassicae* (Diptera) ovipositing on crucifers are attracted by the odour of allylisothio-cyanate, which contributes to the characteristic odour of crucifers.

Some parasitic Hymenoptera localise their hosts by the chemicals produced in the faeces or present in the cuticle of the plant on which the host is feeding. For example,

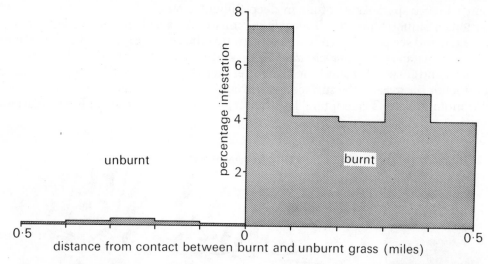

Fig. 244 The distribution of early instar larvae of *Nomadacris* in relation to a boundary between burnt and unburnt ground. The distribution of larvae at this stage can be taken as an indication of the distribution of the egg pods (after Symmons and Carnegie, 1959)

contact with the frass of *Heliothis zea* by the female braconid *Microplitis* causes the female to examine the immediate neighbourhood with her antennae. This behaviour is stimulated by a mixture of methylhentriacontanes (long-chain hydrocarbons), which are probably derived from the food, and increases the chances of finding a host. *Cardiochiles* is induced to search for the larvae of *Heliothis virescens* by similar compounds, especially 11-methylhentriacontane, but 13-methylhentriacontane, which is most active for *Microplitis*, has little effect. Such differences confer some degree of specificity in host-finding by the two parasites (Lewis *et al.*, 1977; Vinson *et al.*, 1975). *Cheiloneurus*, which is a hyperparasite of parasites of scale insects, is induced to probe by the chemical and physical features of the cuticle of the scale irrespective of whether or not it is parasitised (Weseloh and Bartlett, 1971).

Having arrived in the vicinity of an appropriate oviposition site, final selection depends on further stimulation, which very often involves contact chemoreception. Oviposition is often induced by specific key chemicals, but in some cases it may depend on a balance between such oviposition stimulants and inhibitors in the same way that feeding by phytophagous insects is often regulated (Jermy and Szentesi, 1978, and see p. 26). These stimuli are often perceived by tarsal chemoreceptors. In a number of butterflies the foretarsi of the female have more contact chemoreceptors than those of the male and many species drum on the leaf surface with their foretarsi. It is generally believed that this is part of the recognition process (Calvert, 1974; Ma and Schoonhoven, 1973).

The females of crucifer-feeding insects, such as *Pieris*, *Plutella* and *Delia* are stimulated to oviposit by glucosinolates, such as sinigrin, which are characteristic of these plants. In the case of *Delia*, allylisothiocyanate acts as a synergist with sinigrin, so that the insect lays many more eggs when perceiving both chemicals (Städler, 1978). The spruce budworm moth, *Choristoneura*, is stimulated to oviposit by α- and β-pinene and other chemicals acting when the insect is on the host tree.

The physical characteristics of a leaf also influence oviposition by phytophagous species. In *Choristoneura* the shape of the needle is an important recognition feature. *Chilo*, which lays its eggs in groups, does not oviposit on hairy leaves (Roome *et al.*, 1977), whereas *Plathypena* (Lepidoptera), which lays its eggs singly, lays more eggs on hairy or rough surfaces (Pedigo, 1971).

Amongst the parasitic Hymenoptera *Venturia* responds to a chemical produced by larvae of *Anagasta* by making stabbing movements with its ovipositor. In this case the chemical is produced as a pheromone by the moth larvae and regulates their behaviour (p. 865). Host proteins and amino acids induce oviposition in other parasites (Lewis *et al.*, 1977).

Although mosquitoes are attracted to water they do not always oviposit once they have reached it. Oviposition depends, at least to a large extent, on the stimuli received by tarsal sensilla when the insect lands on the surface. *Aedes aegypti* and *Culex* reject water with a high salt content, the rejection possibly being based on the high osmotic pressure of saline solutions. In some species, although not these two, pH is also important (Hudson, 1956).

17.2.4 Regulation of oviposition density

It is important for a species to avoid excessive oviposition at one oviposition site since this would lead to competition between the offspring. Parasitic insects can discriminate parasitised from non-parasitised hosts and generally avoid ovipositing in the former. In *Venturia* discrimination is probably effected on the basis of a secretion or metabolite from eggs of its own species. A freshly parasitised host is not discriminated against, but it can be distinguished from an unparasitised host within a few hours of being attacked. Recognition probably depends on stimulation of chemoreceptors in the ovipositors of the parasite in the course of probing in the host (Ganesalingam, 1974).

Avoidance of overcrowing is also important in phytophagous insects. *Dacus* will not oviposit in an olive which has already been attacked; it is deterred by the olive juice escaping from a previous oviposition puncture (Haniotakis and Voyadjoglou, 1978). *Pieris brassicae* avoids ovipositing on damaged host-plant leaves, which might indicate the presence of feeding larvae, but is also deterred by the presence of eggs already on the leaf. This response depends partly on the visual stimuli presented by the eggs, but also on their odour (Rothschild and Schoonhoven, 1977) (but see Traynier, 1979).

In some cases it is an advantage to the insect to lay large numbers of eggs in one place. First instar larvae of *Zonocerus variegatus* (Orthoptera) occur in dense groups and are aposematic and distasteful. The dense groups result from aggregation of the adults for oviposition: it is possible that a pheromone which attracts gravid females is produced during oviposition. Oviposition by *Lucilia* is stimulated by contact with other flies; a pheromone is involved. The high density of larvae which results probably utilises the host tissues more effectively than is possible by small numbers of larvae (Browne *et al.*, 1969).

17.2.5 Mechanisms of oviposition

In the majority of species which lack an appendicular ovipositor eggs are simply deposited on a surface or, if the terminal segments of the abdomen are elongated or telescopic, they may be inserted into crevices. In some cases, however, specialised structures are involved in the oviposition process. Many Asilidae, for instance, have spine-bearing plates called acanthophorites at the tip of the abdomen. These push aside the soil as the insect oviposits so that the tip of the abdomen can be inserted and then, when the abdomen is withdrawn, the soil falls back and covers the eggs (Oldroyd, 1964). The beetle *Ilybius* has two finely toothed blades which form an ovipositor. The points of these blades are pushed into the surface of a suitable plant and then worked upwards by a rapid, rhythmic, saw-like action so that a tongue of plant tissue is cut away at the sides. An egg is laid in the hole beneath the blades and is covered by the tongue of plant tissue when the blades are withdrawn (Jackson, 1960).

Species which possess an ovipositor derived from the appendages of segments 8 and 9 penetrate tissues by a sliding movement of the valves relative to each other similar to that in the sting of *Apis* (see below). In an ichneumon the tip of the abdomen is turned down at the start of oviposition so that the valves point ventrally instead of posteriorly (Fig. 245). The gonapophyses then work their way into the host tissue, or through the wood in which the host is boring in the case of *Rhyssa*, by rapid to and fro movements. The gonoplacs do not enter the wound, but become deflected outside it. In this way *Rhyssa* can bore through 3 cm of wood in 20 minutes.

In *Apis*, although the ovipositor now forms a sting, the manner of functioning is essentially the same as in the ichneumon. When the insect is about to sting, the basal parts of the apparatus swing up due to an upward movement of the anterior end of sternum 7, while the shaft of the sting is depressed by muscles (Fig. 246A, B). The initial thrust which pushes the tip of the valves into the host is produced by the downward deflection of the abdomen, but subsequently penetration results from the movements of the lancets on the stylet. These movements are produced by protractor and retractor muscles running from either end of the second gonocoxa to the quadrate plate (see Fig. 240), which represents the lateral part of tergum 9. The quadrate plate is free to move because the central part of the tergum is membranous and the alternate contractions and relaxations of the muscles from the gonocoxa make it move backwards and forwards (Fig. 246 C, D). This movement causes the gonangulum to rock on its articulation with the second gonocoxa (Fig. 246 C, D, point X) and so moves the lancet relative to the stylet. The movements of the lancets of the two sides are out of phase and

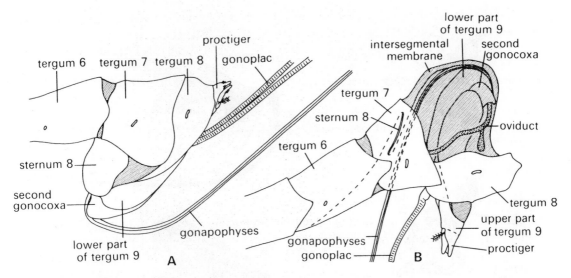

Fig. 245 Basal part of the ovipositor of *Megarhyssa* (Hymenoptera). A. At rest. B. Positions of abdominal sclerites and ovipositor during oviposition. Membranes stippled (after Snodgrass, 1935)

as they push into the wound they are held by their barbed tips. Hence the retractor muscles, instead of extracting the lancets from the wound, tend to depress the anterior ends of the second gonocoxae and so to restore the sclerites to their original positions, at the same time pushing the stylet into the wound. Successive thrusts carry the sting progressively deeper.

Poison is also injected by the action of the lancets since the poison reservoir itself has no muscles. Each lancet bears a concave valve which fits in the shaft of the sting (Fig. 246E). The movements of these valves as the lancets move in and out push poison along the shaft of the sting and out through a cleft near the tip of the lancets (Snodgrass, 1956).

In the Acrididae the action of the valves is quite different, involving an opening and closing movement of the dorsal and ventral valves rather than a sliding movement (Fig. 247). These movements are produced by muscles inserted on to an apodeme at the base of the valves, together with others inserted directly into the valves. The insect starts to dig a hole by raising the body on the first two pairs of legs and arching the tip of the abdomen downwards so that it presses more or less vertically on the ground. The opening movement of the valves scrapes particles of the substratum sideways and upwards and pressure is exerted down the abdomen so that the valves slowly dig a hole. As the hole deepens the abdomen lengthens by the unfolding and stretching of the intersegmental membranes between segments 4 and 5, 5 and 6, and 6 and 7. The membranes are specialised to permit stretching, having a lamellated endocuticle under a thin epicuticle, which is folded at right angles to the long axis of the body. As the abdomen lengthens these folds become smoothed out and the endocuticle stretches. The intersegmental membranes of the male do not stretch to the same extent as in the mature female, nor do those of the immature female, indicating that some change occurs during maturation. The change is controlled by the corpora allata and it is

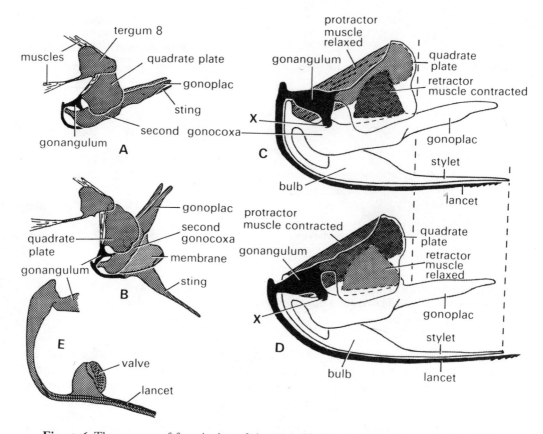

Fig. 246 The manner of functioning of the sting of *Apis*. A. Sting in retracted position. B. Sting protracted. C and D. Movements of lancet resulting from backwards and forwards movement of quadrate plate rocking the gonangulum on its articulation X. E. Basal part of lancet showing valve (after Snodgrass, 1956)

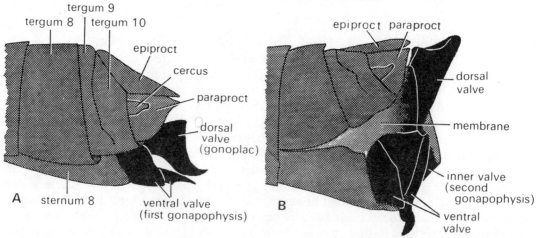

Fig. 247 Showing the manner in which the ovipositor valves of *Schistocerca* open. A. Valves closed. B. Valves open (after Thomas, 1965)

probable that hydrogen bonding between the protein chains in the cuticle is reduced by an enzyme from the epidermis (Tychsen and Vincent, 1976).

The extension of the abdomen may be very considerable. For instance, the abdomen of *Anacridium* stretches from 3.5 to 10.0 cm length and *Schistocerca* can dig to a depth of 14 cm. During digging the ventral valves of the ovipositor lever the abdomen downwards while the upper valves push soil away and effect the excavation. The pull exerted by the ventral valves is transmitted to the abdomen through the membranes connecting them with it and this results in the extension of the intersegmental membranes between segments 4 and 7 (Vincent, 1975).

At intervals during digging the female partly withdraws her abdomen and the walls of the hole are smoothed and compacted by small movements of the ovipositor valves together with twisting movements of the abdomen. Even in a suitable soil a female frequently abandons a hole and starts to dig again, but when a suitable hole has been constructed the process of oviposition proper begins. Just before an egg is laid the female pumps more air into the tracheal system by rapid movements of the head and then, with the thoracic spiracles closed, forces the air backwards so that the abdomen becomes turgid. It remains turgid until the egg is laid, then the head moves forwards again and the pressure is released. Eggs are passed out micropylar end first and the abdomen is slowly withdrawn as more eggs are laid. When all the eggs have been laid the frothy plug is formed in the upper part of the hole and finally, after withdrawing her abdomen, the female scrapes soil over the top of the hole with her hind tibiae. The whole process may take about two hours, of which egg-laying occupies some 20 minutes.

17.2.6 Control of oviposition

The readiness to oviposit is influenced by mating. A female *Bombyx*, for example, lays all her eggs within 24 h of mating whereas a virgin female retains most of her eggs for some days. An essentially similar change of behaviour occurs in insects belonging to many different orders. In some cases the increased tendency to oviposit following mating may occur indirectly as a result of the stimulus provided to oocyte maturation (p. 838), but certainly in some cases oviposition is affected directly. This is true in moths in which the oocytes are mature at the time of adult emergence.

Mating may produce this effect through male accessory gland secretions. In *Bombyx* these diffuse from the bursa copulatrix through the haemolymph of the female and promote spontaneous activity in the motorneurones to the muscles which regulate the extrusion and positioning of the egg. This activity persists for about 24 h and so spans the time during which oviposition is completed (Yamaoka and Hirao, 1977). In *Hyalophora*, on the other hand, the sperm appear to interact with the bursa copulatrix and cause it to release a substance into the haemolymph which in turn leads to the release of a hormone from the intrinsic cells of the corpora cardiaca. This hormone is responsible for switching on oviposition behaviour (Truman and Riddiford, 1974). The male accessory gland secretion of *Melanoplus* probably acts via the neurosecretory cells in the brain of the female to induce oviposition (Friedel and Gillott, 1976).

Once oviposition behaviour has been switched on by blood-borne factors following mating the act of egg-laying is controlled via the sensory system. Various senses are involved in locating an oviposition site (see section 17.2.3) and the final placement of eggs depends on stimulation of the sensilla on the ovipositor. In *Bombyx* the eggs are normally laid close together in a single layer; if the trichoid mechanoreceptors on the anal papillae are damaged the eggs are deposited in uneven clumps. In the intact insect the information from the hairs is relayed to the brain (Fig. 248) and from the brain a command to motorneurones arising in the terminal abdominal ganglion leads to contractions of the oviducts so that eggs are deposited and to movements of the abdomen which result in the eggs being spread evenly over a surface (Yamaoka and Hirao, 1971, 1977). Presumably in other insects egg-laying is normally a response to appropriate mechanical and perhaps chemical stimulation of sensilla on the ovipositor.

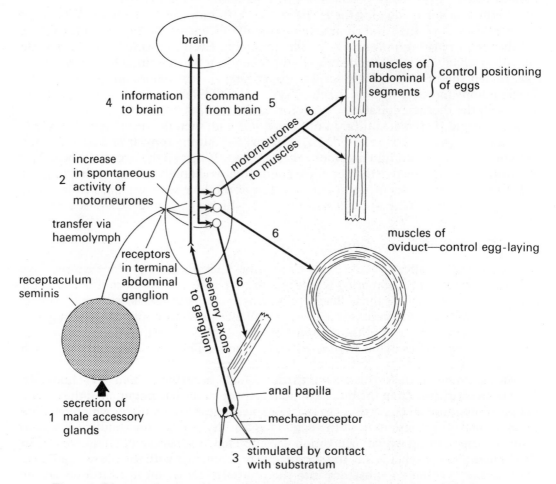

Fig. 248 Diagram showing the events controlling oviposition in the silkmoth, *Bombyx*. Numbers indicate the sequence of events (after Yamaoko and Hirao, 1971, 1977)

17.3 The egg

17.3.1 Structure

Typically insect eggs are very large since they contain a great deal of yolk. The egg of Acrididae, for instance, may be 8 mm long and 1 mm in diameter and the eggs of smaller insects, such as *Musca*, are often a millimetre long. Some parasitic Hymenoptera, however, whose larvae develop internally in the fluids of other insects produce small eggs containing very little yolk. Thus the eggs of Platygasteridae, which parasitise cecidomyid larvae, are 0·02–0·10 mm long and those of Mymaridae, which are laid in the eggs of other insects, 0·06–0·25 mm long.

Insect eggs occur in a variety of forms. Commonly, as in Orthoptera and many Hymenoptera, they are sausage shaped (Fig. 249A). Sometimes they are conical, as in *Pieris* (Fig. 249B), or rounded, as in many moths and Heteroptera. In the eggs of some Diptera, and the Nepidae extensions of the chorion form one or more horns (Fig. 249D), while the eggs of many parasitic Hymenoptera have a projection called a pedicel at one end. The eggs of *Encyrtus* (Hymenoptera) are unusual in consisting of two bladders connected by a tube (Fig. 249C). During the process of oviposition the contents of the egg pass from the proximal to the distal bladder and the proximal bladder is lost. It is suggested that this may facilitate the entry of the egg into a host through a relatively small hole.

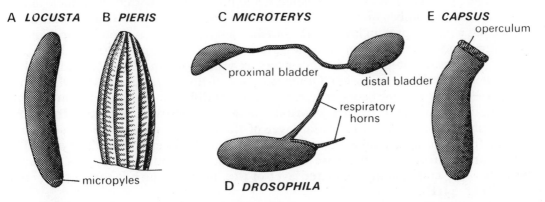

Fig. 249 Various forms of eggs. A. *Locusta*. B. *Pieris*. C. *Microterys* (Hymenoptera). D. *Drosophila*. E. *Capsus* (Heteroptera). Not all to same scale (after various authors)

At the time of oviposition the cytoplasm of the egg forms a bounding layer, the periplasm, and an irregular reticulum within the yolk. The zygote nucleus usually occupies a posterior position. Round the outside of the ovum are the vitelline membrane and the chorion, or 'shell', with a layer of wax on the inside (Fig. 250). Later in the course of development the serosal cuticle is formed. It incorporates the vitelline membrane on the outside and consists of a chitinous endocuticle, sometimes called the white cuticle, with an epicuticle having a second wax layer. In the greater part of the epicuticle, which is sometimes known as the yellow cuticle, the wax layer is beneath a fibrous layer (Slifer and Sekhon, 1963).

Structure of the chorion

The chorion is a complex structure produced by the follicle cells while the egg is in the ovary (p. 342). The outer surface is often sculptured, frequently with a pattern which is basically hexagonal and reflects the form of the follicle cells. In other cases the surface

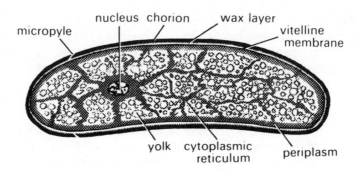

Fig. 250 Diagram of the structure of an egg at the time of oviposition

may be ribbed or ridged and pitting also occurs, resulting from uneven laying down of the chorion by the follicle cells (Fig. 223B).

In *Rhodnius* the chorion is completed while the oocyte is within the follicle and is formed from a number of chemically distinct layers. This is also true in *Carausius*, which has a tanned protein layer on the outside, a layer of fibrous protein impregnated with lime, and a layer of lipoprotein (Wigglesworth and Beament, 1950). In the eggs of some species two anatomically distinct layers are present and these are sometimes called the endochorion and exochorion. Other eggs lack distinct layers, and even where they are present they are not necessarily comparable in different species (Hinton, 1969).

Usually some part of the chorion contains extensive airspaces. In *Tetrix* (Orthoptera), for instance, the basal layer of the chorion is a continuous sheet and arising from this are a number of struts with airspaces between them (Fig. 251A). The struts are buttressed at the base and branch at their outer ends, the branches anastomosing and forming the outer layer of the chorion, which is thus a perforated sheet (Fig. 251B).

Other insects have a more complex arrangement. In the egg of *Musca* there are extensive airspaces in the outer and inner meshworks of the chorion (Fig. 251C, D) and these are connected by fine pores, the aeropyles, which run through the otherwise solid middle layer (Fig. 251C, E). The outer meshwork is absent over the greater part of the egg of *Calliphora*, but is present between the hatching lines (Fig. 252).

The outer surface of the chorion is strongly hydrophobic in *Musca* and *Calliphora*, but in *Tetrix* and *Delia* (Diptera) the outer layers are readily wetted. There is a continous basal layer adjacent to the oocyte in *Calliphora*, *Rhodnius* and *Nepa* as it is in *Tetrix*, but in the Muscinae this layer is perforated (see Hinton and Cole, 1965, and other papers by Hinton).

The eggs of some species have a cap, or operculum, which is joined to the body of the egg along a line of weakness facilitating hatching (Fig. 249E). A cap is present in Cimicomorpha and, in *Rhodnius*, its structure differs from that of the rest of the chorion although the same elements are involved. The soft endochorion is much thinner than elsewhere on the egg, but the amber layer is much thicker and the follicular pits have slit-like openings and do not extend through the soft endochorion (Fig. 223A). The cap is joined to the rest of the chorion by the sealing bar, which is formed from a very thin layer of resistant endochorion and a thick amber layer. There is a line of weakness where the sealing bar meets the cap (Beament, 1946a, 1947). Some pentatomids appear

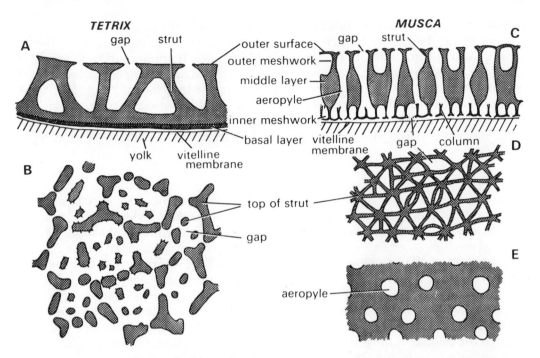

Fig. 251 The structure of the chorion of *Tetrix* and *Musca*. *Tetrix*: A. Transverse section. B. View of the surface. *Musca*: C. Transverse section. D. View of the surface. E. Horizontal section through the middle layer (after Hartley, 1962; Hinton, 1960)

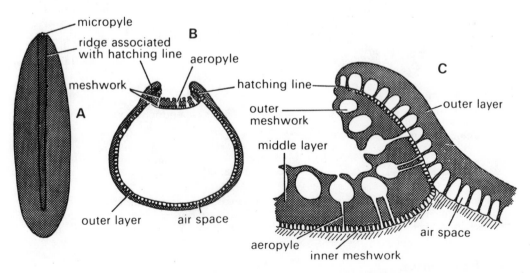

Fig. 252 Structure of the egg of *Calliphora*. A. Dorsal view showing hatching lines. B. Cross-section through the middle of the egg. C. Detail of section though one of the hatching lines (based on Anderson, 1960; Hinton, 1960)

to have a cap, but this has the same structure as the rest of the chorion and is not joined to it by a sealing bar. A cap is present in the eggs of *Carausius*, Embioptera and the lice.

The eggs of some Diptera have hatching lines, which are lines of weakness along which the egg splits when the larva emerges. In *Musca* and *Calliphora* these take the form of two ridges which run longitudinally along the length of the egg (Fig. 252A). Along these lines the inner layer of the chorion extends outwards so that each ridge contains two inner layers which are back to back (Fig. 252C). In *Calliphora* the surface of the chorion between the hatching lines differs from that elsewhere (Hinton, 1960).

Micropyles

Since the chorion is laid down in the ovary some provision is necessary to allow the subsequent entry of the sperm. This takes the form of the micropyles, which are funnel-shaped canals passing right through the chorion. Most dipterous eggs have only a single terminal micropyle, while Acrididae commonly have 30 or 40 arranged in a ring at the posterior end of the egg (Fig. 253C,D). In most Cimicomorpha the micropyles are present near the junction of the cap with the body of the egg, but there are no micropyles in the eggs of Cimicoidea, which are fertilised in the ovary (p. 371). The Pentatomomorpha have micropylar processes projecting from the chorion and in *Oncopeltus* each consists of a cup on a stem (Fig. 253A,B). The micropylar canal passes through the middle of the process and through the chorion and it is surrounded by an open reticulum enclosing airspaces. There may be from two to several hundred such processes, depending on the species.

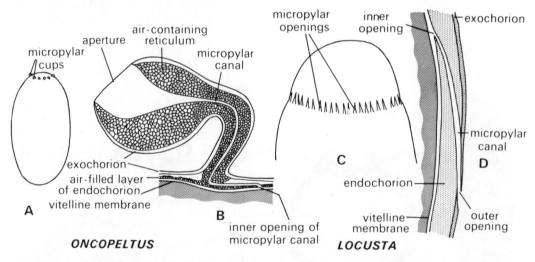

Fig. 253 A and B. *Oncopeltus*: Whole egg and longitudinal section through a micropylar process (after Southwood, 1956). C and D. *Locusta*: posterior end of egg and longitudinal section through the chorion along the length of a micropylar canal (after Roonwal, 1954)

17.3.2 Respiration

Some gaseous exchange takes place through the solid chorion of most insect eggs laid out of water, but the rate of diffusion of oxygen through this substance is not adequate to meet the demands of the developing embryo. Hence the majority of terrestrial insect eggs have a series of air-filled cavities in the inner layers of the chorion which connect with the outside air through a series of aeropyles. The aeropyles may be widely distributed as in *Musca* or restricted to a limited area as in *Calliphora*, where they occur only between the hatching lines, and *Ocypus* (Coleoptera), which has an equatorial band of functional aeropyles. In *Rhodnius* they are restricted to a ring just below the cap (Fig. 223). In other cases the cavities of the inner part of the chorion extend to the surface to facilitate gaseous exchange. Thus there is a small pore on the surface of the egg of *Carausius* at which the reticular inner chorion is exposed, and the respiratory horns of some Diptera and the Nepidae serve the same function of connecting the inner layer of air with the atmosphere outside while at the same time restricting the area through which rapid loss of water can occur (Fig. 254). This is also true of the smaller respiratory horns of the Pentatomomorpha (Fig. 253B).

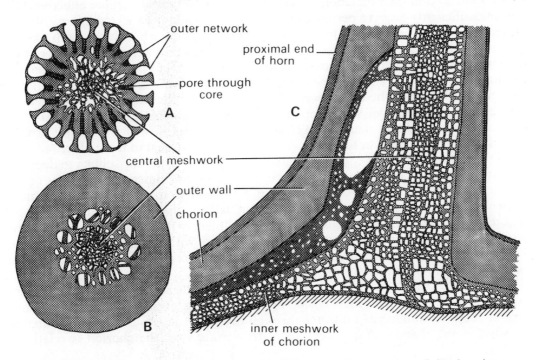

Fig. 254 Structure of the respiratory horn of *Nepa*. A. Cross-section of distal region. B. Cross-section of proximal region. C. Longitudinal section of the base of a horn showing its connection with the chorion (after Hinton, 1961)

In all these cases there is a layer of air in the inner chorion which entirely or largely surrounds the ovum and which is connected to the outside air. This layer may have direct access to the ovum through pores in the innermost sheet of the chorion, but in most species, as in *Calliphora*, this sheet is imperforate. The chorion itself, however, is formed from a meshwork of fibrils with interstices of 2–5 nm, so oxygen can pass through this sheet although its movement will be impeded (Hinton, 1969).

Special provision for respiration by the eggs is made in the oothecae of cockroaches. In *Blattella* small cavities occur above each egg in the crest of the ootheca. These cavities connect with the outside air and a narrow duct leads down to a point above each egg at which the chorion is expanded to form an open meshwork. Each egg thus has a connection with the outside air (Wigglesworth and Beament, 1950).

The eggs of some terrestrial insects which are laid in the soil and other similar situations are subject to periodic flooding. Some eggs can survive this because the chorion, with its hydrophobic characteristics, maintains a layer of air round the egg into which gas from the surrounding water may diffuse. Thus the chorion acts as a plastron (p. 563), but the effectiveness of a plastron depends on the area available for gaseous exchanges, that is on the extent of the air/water interface. In the eggs of Lepidoptera and most Heteroptera, *Rhodnius*, for example, the air/water interface is too small to be of significance, but the eggs may survive flooding by virtue of the fact that they can survive a great reduction in their metabolic rate. The plastron of *Ocypus* is more effective, but still not sufficiently large to permit continued development, but in *Calliphora*, where the plastron occurs between the hatching lines, and in *Musca*, where it covers the whole egg, normal development continues if the egg is immersed in well-aerated water. The respiratory horns of many dipteran eggs also form an efficient plastron if the eggs are flooded and this is true also in the eggs of Nepidae, which are essentially terrestrial in their respiration since the horns normally project above the surface of the water.

The surface tension of water contaminated with organic acids and other surface active substances is lower than that of clean water, and the ease with which a plastron is wetted, and hence ceases to function, is inversely proportional to the surface tension. Thus the plastron of insect eggs which are laid in organic materials subject to flooding needs to have a high resistance to wetting if it is to continue functioning in spite of the low surface tension. It must also be able to withstand wetting by raindrops which, momentarily, may exert a pressure approaching half an atmosphere. Hence, although eggs in dung and similar situations can rarely be subject to flooding by more than a few centimetres of water, they possess a plastron capable of withstanding flooding by clean water to a much greater depth, and in some cases their resistance is greater than that exhibited by the plastron of some aquatic insects (p. 563; Hinton, 1969).

Eggs which are laid in water, such as those of dragonflies, obtain their oxygen from that dissolved in the water. The chorion in these eggs is generally without any obvious system of spaces and oxygen diffuses through the solid material. This is presumably because, in the absence of any need to restrict water loss, the chorion is relatively porous.

17.3.3 Water regulation

Water loss

Insect eggs are subject to water loss just as the postembryonic stages are. The rate of water loss is often very low, especially in eggs of species which do not take up water during development. In *Rhodnius*, for instance, water is lost at a rate of $3\,\mu g/cm^2/h/mmHg$ from the egg compared with $12\,\mu g/cm^2/h/mmHg$ from adults. However, in eggs laid in damp places, where water uptake is possible, the rate of water loss may be much higher, $60\,\mu g/cm^2/h/mmHg$ in *Phyllopertha*, and the permeability of the chorion may vary in the course of development (Fig. 256).

In most eggs the chorion itself is not waterproof and at the time of oviposition water loss from the egg is limited by a layer of wax on the inside of the chorion. This is secreted by the oocyte at about the time it leaves the follicle and, in *Rhodnius*, it is complete over the micropyles where it is supported by the vitelline membrane. The wax has the characteristics of a monolayer (p. 510) with a critical temperature above which the monolayer breaks down and water loss increases sharply (Fig. 255; Beament, 1946b). The critical temperature for the eggs of *Rhodnius* is 42·5°C, and for the eggs of *Lucilia* (Diptera) and *Locustana* (Orthoptera) 38°C and 55–58°C respectively. Below this temperature water loss from the eggs of *Rhodnius* is negligible even in dry air, but not all insect eggs are as waterproof as this. The eggs of *Musca*, for instance, only develop at high humidities and even at 80% relative humidity only 15% of the eggs survive to hatching.

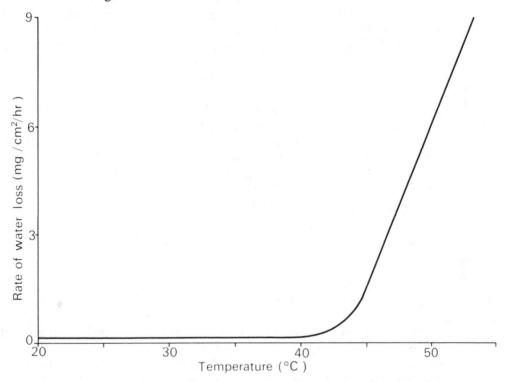

Fig. 255 Graph showing the relationship of temperature to water loss from the egg of *Rhodnius* in a dry atmosphere (after Beament, 1946b)

A second layer of wax is laid down, at least in *Rhodnius* and various Orthoptera, in the serosal cuticle. In *Melanoplus* and *Locustana* this layer is between the serosal endocuticle and an outer fibrous network. In the Orthoptera this seconday wax layer replaces the layer on the inside of the chorion since the latter probably becomes broken after a few days by the increase in size of the egg. The rate of evaporation from the egg of *Locustana* at 35°C and 60% relative humidity drops from 0·35–0·54 mg/egg/24 h at oviposition, when only the primary wax layer is present, to 0·11–0·36 mg/egg/24 h five days later when the serosal cuticle and secondary wax layer are completed all over the egg except for the hydropylar area (see below). When this region is also sealed off the evaporation rate falls to 0·03–0·04 mg/egg/24 h (Matthée, 1951), but in some other species the rate of loss is higher during the later stages of embryonic development. The egg of *Aedes* is not fully waterproofed until the serosal cuticle, presumably including the wax layer, is formed.

In some instances there is a suggestion that the chorion itself provides some resistance to desiccation. For instance, the inner chorion of *Aedes*, which resists desiccation, is thicker and darker than that in the non-resistant eggs of *Culex*, and some tropical grasshoppers, such as *Tropidiopsis*, which survive the dry season in the egg stage have thick, tough chorions. A thick chorion and a reduction in the number of respiratory horns is also a characteristic of the eggs of heteropteran species which are laid in exposed situations subject to desiccation (Southwood, 1956).

Under natural conditions water loss is normally restricted by the particular microenvironment of the oviposition site selected by the female. Thus many eggs are laid in crevices in bark or in the soil where transpiration will be restricted; or they may be in plant or animal tissues, where because of the moist environment little or no water loss occurs. Sometimes the insect creates a micro-environment for its eggs by depositing them in an ootheca, such as that of the cockroaches and mantids, which, even if it does not possess a waterproofing wax layer, will limit transpiration by restricting air movement round the eggs. In the Acrididae the eggs are protected from desiccation to some extent by being some distance below the surface of the ground. In addition, in some tropical species which survive the dry season in the egg, the egg mass is enclosed in a layer of very hard, tough froth, as in *Cataloipus*, or has a conspicuous dark lid at the top of the plug, as in *Acrida* (Fig. 242C). These formations do not occur in species with different life cycles, suggesting that they have some role in the prevention of water loss from the egg.

Absorption of water

The eggs of *Rhodnius*, and probably of many other Heteroptera and Lepidoptera which are laid in dry, exposed situations, develop without any uptake of water, but the eggs of many insect species absorb water from the environment in the course of development. This occurs in both terrestrial and aquatic insects and has been recorded, for example, in *Ocypus*, *Phyllopertha* and *Dytiscus* (Coleoptera), in *Notostira* and *Nepa* (Heteroptera), in *Culex* (Diptera) and in various Orthoptera. It results in a considerable increase in volume and weight (Fig. 256).

In some species, such as *Notostira* and *Gryllulus* (Orthoptera), water is absorbed over the whole of the egg, but at least in the Acrididae a specialised structure, the hydropyle, appears to have a dominant role in the uptake of water. It consists of a thickened region of the serosal epicuticle over a layer of endocuticle which is thinner than elsewhere (Fig. 257) and the area of contact between the two layers is greatly increased by interdigitation. There is no secondary wax layer over the hydropyle of eggs of *Locustana* and *Melanoplus*, but numerous epicuticular filaments (p. 510), not found in other parts of the serosal cuticle, are present. It is presumed that water is taken up by the porous material on the outside of the hydropyle and held at the interface with the endocuticle, which forms a semipermeable membrane.

A type of hydropyle is also present in *Nepa*, but no such structure is present in the

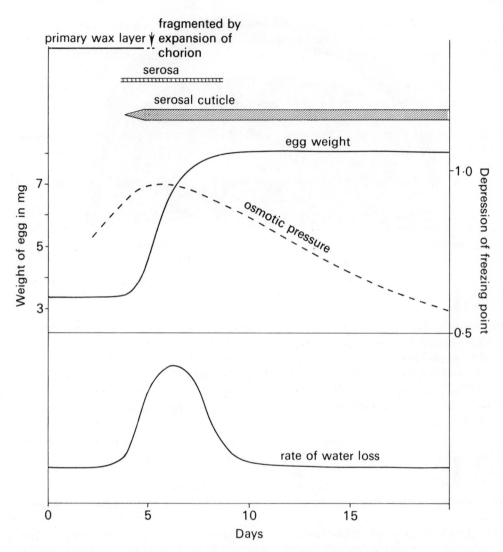

Fig. 256 Diagram showing the events associated with water uptake by the egg of a grasshopper (based on Lees, 1976)

egg of *Deraeocoris* (Heteroptera). In the latter water may be taken up through the posterior end of the egg, which is embedded in plant tissue, or through the projecting anterior end (Hartley, 1965).

The uptake of water usually occurs over a limited period of development which varies from species to species. For instance, it occurs before there has been any significant development in *Camnula*, during early embryonic development in *Locusta*, and after blastokinesis in *Melanoplus differentialis* (Edney, 1977). Immediately after oviposition no water is taken up. Then follows a period of rapid uptake, followed by a further period in which no marked change in water content occurs (Fig. 256). In the eggs of Acrididae the initial failure to absorb water is due to the presence of the primary

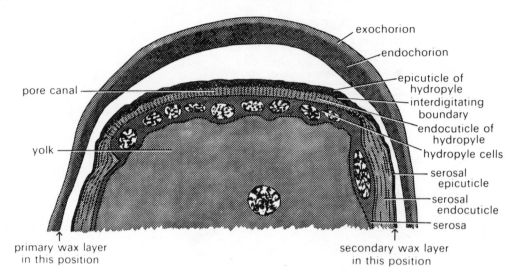

Fig. 257 Section through the posterior end of the egg of *Locusta* showing the hydropyle (based on Roonwal, 1954)

wax layer in the chorion. This forms a barrier to the osmotic uptake of water and is equally effective in preventing water loss.

The period of water uptake begins at the time the serosa is completed and the serosal cuticle is first laid down (p. 416). During the initial stages water uptake probably occurs only at the posterior end of the egg, where the hydropyle becomes differentiated as the serosal cuticle thickens. The increase in volume resulting from water uptake produces cracking of the chorion and the primary wax layer must be disrupted. This leads to a great increase in permeability of the chorion and at the same time initiates mobilisation of the yolk so that the osmotic pressure within the egg increases. These two factors combined lead to a rapid uptake of water (Fig. 256).

Following blastokineses in *Chortoicetes* the osmotic pressure of the yolk falls, contributing to, but not wholly accounting for, the reduction in water intake. This reduction may also be a consequence of the completion of the serosal cuticle and the secondary wax layer or of the reduction in stress on the egg membranes so that they become less permeable (Edney, 1977; Lees, 1976). The eggs remain capable of taking up water during this period if they are subject at any stage to water loss.

In *Teleogryllus* the mechanism may be different. Here it is supposed that the chorion remains permeable and that water uptake is prevented initially, despite a high internal osmotic pressure, by the hydrostatic pressure within the egg. Subsequently the structure of the inner chorion changes so that the egg is enabled to increase in volume due to the osmotic intake of water. The resulting increase in hydrostatic pressure may then be responsible for preventing further water uptake (Browning, 1969). The chorion in *Teleogryllus* is thicker than that of *Chortoicetes* and other acridids even though the egg is smaller; the difference in the mechanism of water regulation may be associated with this difference in structure. In Heteroptera it is suggested that water uptake by the eggs of *Notostira* does not begin until osmotically active substances are produced within the egg, while water uptake by the eggs of *Phyllopertha* stops following a modification of the chorion which makes it waterproof.

REFERENCES

ANDERSON, D. S. (1960). The respiratory system of the egg-shell of *Calliphora erythrocephala*. *J. Insect Physiol.* **5**: 120–128.

BEAMENT, J. W. L. (1946a). The formation and structure of the chorion of the egg in an hemipteran, *Rhodnius prolixus*. *Q. Jl microsc. Sci.* **87**: 393–439.

BEAMENT, J. W. L. (1946b). The waterproofing process in eggs of *Rhodnius prolixus* Stähl. *Proc. R. Soc.* B, **133**: 407–418.

BEAMENT, J. W. L. (1947). The formation and structure of the micropylar complex in the egg-shell of *Rhodnius prolixus* Stähl. (Heteroptera Reduviidae). *J. exp. Biol.* **23**: 213–233.

BEHAN, M. and RYAN, M. F. (1977). Sensory receptors on the ovipositor of the carrot fly (*Psila rosae* (F.)) (Diptera: Psilidae) and the cabbage root fly (*Delia brassicae* (Wiedemann)) (Diptera: Anthomyiidae). *Bull. ent. Res.* **67**: 383–389.

BICK, G. H. and SULZBACH, D. (1966). Reproductive behaviour of the damselfly, *Hetaerina americana* (Fabricius) (Odonata: Calopterygidae). *Anim. Behav.* **14**: 156–158.

BROWNE, L. B., BARTELL, R. J. and SHOREY, H. H. (1969). Pheromone-mediated behaviour leading to group oviposition in the blowfly *Lucilia cuprina*. *J. Insect Physiol.* **15**: 1003–1014.

BROWNING, T. O. (1969). The permeability of the shell of the egg of *Teleogryllus commodus* measured with the aid of tritiated water. *J. exp. Biol.* **51**: 397–405.

CALVERT, W. H. (1974). The external morphology of foretarsal receptors involved with host discrimination by the nymphalid butterfly, *Chlosyne lacinia*. *Ann. ent. Soc. Am.* **67**: 853–856.

CHAPMAN, R. F. and ROBERTSON, I. A. D. (1958). The egg pods of some tropical African grasshoppers. *J. ent. Soc. sth. Afr.* **21**: 85–112.

CLARIDGE, M. F. and WILSON, M. R. (1978). Oviposition behaviour as an ecological factor in woodland canopy leaf hoppers. *Entomologia exp. appl.* **24**: 301–309.

CLAUSEN, C. P. (1940). *Entomophagous insects.* McGraw-Hill, New York.

EDNEY, E. B. (1977). *Water balance in land arthropods.* Springer-Verlag, Berlin.

FRIEDEL, T. and GILLOTT, C. (1976). Male accessory gland substance of *Melanoplus sanguinipes*: an oviposition stimulant under the control of the corpus allatum. *J. Insect Physiol.* **22**: 489–495.

GANESALINGAM, V. K. (1974). Mechanism of discrimination between parasitized and unparasitized hosts by *Venturia canescens* (Hymenoptera: Ichneumonidae). *Entomologia exp. appl.* **17**: 36–44.

HANIOTAKIS, G. E. and VOYADJOGLOU, A. (1978). Oviposition regulation in *Dacus oleae* by various olive fruit characters. *Entomologia exp. appl.* **24**: 387–392.

HARTLEY, J. C. (1962). The egg of *Tetrix* (Tetrigidae, Orthoptera), with a discussion on the probable significance of the anterior horn. *Q. Jl microsc. Sci.* **103**: 253–259.

HARTLEY, J. C. (1965). The structure and function of the egg-shell of *Deraeocoris ruber* L. (Heteroptera, Miridae). *J. Insect Physiol.* **11**: 103–109.

HINTON, H. E. (1960). Plastron respiration in the eggs of blowflies. *J. Insect Physiol.* **4**: 176–183.

HINTON, H. E. (1961). The structure and function of the egg-shell in the Nepidae (Hemiptera). *J. Insect Physiol.* **7**: 224–257.

HINTON, H. E. (1969). Respiratory systems of insect egg shells. *A. Rev. Ent.* **14**: 343–368.

HINTON, H. E. (1981). *Biology of insect eggs.* 3 vols. Pergamon Press, Oxford.

HINTON, H. E. and COLE, S. (1965). The structure of egg-shell of the cabbage root fly, *Erioischia brassicae*. *Ann. appl. Biol.* **56**: 1–6.

HOOPER, R. L., PITTS, C. W. and WESTFALL, J. A. (1972). Sense organs on the ovipositor of the face fly, *Musca autumnalis*. *Ann. ent. Soc. Am.* **65**: 577–586.

HUDSON, B. N. A. (1956). The behaviour of the female mosquito in selecting water for oviposition. *J. exp. Biol.* **33**: 478–492.

JACKSON, D. J. (1958). Egg-laying and egg-hatching in *Agabus bipustulatus* L., with notes on oviposition in other species of *Agabus* (Coleoptera: Dytiscidae). *Trans. R. ent. Soc. Lond.* **110**: 53–80.

JACKSON, D. J. (1960). Observations on egg-laying in *Ilybius fuliginosus* Fabricius and *I. ater* Degeer (Coleoptera: Dytiscidae), with an account of the female genitalia . *Trans. R. ent. Soc. Lond.* **112**: 37–52.

JACKSON, D. J. (1966). Observations on the biology of *Caraphractus cinctus* Walker (Hymenoptera: Mymaridae), a parasitoid of the eggs of Dytiscidae (Coleoptera) III. The adult life and sex ratio. *Trans. R. ent. Soc. Lond.* **118**: 23–49.

JERMY, T. and SZENTESI, Á. (1978). The role of inhibitory stimuli in the choice of oviposition site by phytophagous insects. *Entomologia exp. appl.* **24**: 458–471.

LEES, A. D. (1976). The role of pressure in controlling the entry of water into the developing eggs of the Australian plague locust *Chortoicetes terminifera* (Walker). *Physiol. Ent.* **1**: 39–50.

LEWIS, W. J., JONES, R. L., NORDLUND, D. A. and GROSS, H. R. (1977). Kairomones and their use for management of entomophagous insects. *Colloq. Int. C.N.R.S.* no. 265: 455–469.

MA, W. C. and SCHOONHOVEN, L. M. (1973). Tarsal contact chemosensory hairs of the large white butterfly *Pieris brassicae* and their possible rôle in oviposition behaviour. *Entomologia exp. appl.* **16**: 343–357.

MARSHALL, J. F. (1938). *The British mosquitoes.* British Museum, London.

MATTHÉE, J. J. (1951). The structure and physiology of the egg of *Locustana pardalina* (Walk). *Bull. Dep. Agric. For. Un. S. Afr.* no. 316: 83 pp.

MIALL, L. C. (1922). *The natural history of aquatic insects.* MacMillan, London.

MUIR, F. and SHARP, D. (1904). On the egg-cases and early stages of some Cassididae. *Trans. ent. Soc. Lond.* 1904, 1–23.

OLDROYD, H. (1964). *The natural history of flies.* Weidenfeld and Nicolson, London.

PEDIGO, L. P. (1971). Ovipositional response of *Plathypena scabra* (Lepidoptera: Noctuidae) to selected surfaces. *Ann. ent. Soc. Am.* **64**: 647–651.

POPOV, G. B. (1958). Ecological studies on oviposition by swarms of the desert locust (*Schistocerca gregaria* Forskål) in Eastern Africa. *Anti-Locust Bull.* no. 31, 70 pp.

PROKOPY, R. J. and HANIOTAKIS, E. G. (1976). Host detection by wild and lab-cultured olive flies. *Symp. Biol. Hung.* **16**: 209–214.

RAGGE, D. R. (1965). *Grasshoppers, crickets and cockroaches of the British Isles.* Warne, London.

RICE, M. J. (1976). Contact chemoreceptors on the ovipositor of *Lucilia cuprina* (Wied.), the Australian sheep blowfly. *Aust. J. Zool.* **24**: 353–360.

RICE, M. J. and McRAE, T. M. (1976). Contact chemoreceptors on the ovipositor of *Locusta migratoria* L. *J. Aust. ent. Soc.* **15**: 364.

ROOME, R. E., CHADHA, G. K. and PADGHAM, D. (1977). Choice of oviposition site by *Chilo*, the Sorghum stem-borer. *IOBC/WPRS Bulletin* 1977(3), 115–121.

ROONWAL, M. L. (1954). The egg-wall of the African migratory locust, *Locusta migratoria migratorioides* Reiche and Frm. (Orthoptera, Acrididae). *Proc. natn. Inst. Sci. India.* **20**: 361–370.

ROTH, L. M. (1968). Öothecae of the Blattaria. *Ann. ent. Soc. Am.* **61**: 83–111.

ROTHSCHILD, M. and SCHOONHOVEN, L. M. (1977). Assessment of egg load by *Pieris brassicae* (Lepidoptera: Pieridae). *Nature, Lond.* **266**: 352–355.

SCUDDER, G. G. E. (1959). The female genitalia of the Heteroptera: morphology and bearing on classification. *Trans. R. ent. Soc. Lond.* **111**: 405–467.

SCUDDER, G. G. E. (1961). The comparative morphology of the insect ovipositor. *Trans. R. ent. Soc. Lond.* **113**: 25–40.

SCUDDER, G. G. E. (1971). Comparative morphology of insect genitalia. *A. Rev. Ent.* **16**: 379–406.

SLIFER, E. H. and SEKHON, S. S. (1963). The fine structure of the membranes which cover the egg of the grasshopper, *Melanoplus differentialis*, with special reference to the hydropyle. *Q. Jl microsc. Sci.* **104**: 321–334.

SNODGRASS, R. E. (1935). *Principles of insect morphology.* McGraw-Hill, New York.

SNODGRASS, R. E. (1956). *Anatomy of the honey bee.* Constable, London.

SOUTHWOOD, T. R. E. (1956). The structure of the eggs of the terrestrial Heteroptera and its relationship to the classification of the group. *Trans. R. ent. Soc. Lond.* **108**: 163–221.

STÄDLER, E. (1977). Host selection and chemoreception in the carrot rust fly (*Psila rosae* F., Dipt. Psilidae): extraction and isolation of oviposition stimulants and their perception by the female. *Colloq. Int. C.N.R.S.* no. 265: 357–372.

STÄDLER, E. (1978). Chemoreception of host plant chemicals by ovipositing females of *Delia* (*Hylemya*) brassicae. *Entomologia exp. appl.* **24**: 711–720.

SYMMONS, P. and CARNEGIE, A. J. M. (1959). Some factors affecting breeding and oviposition of the red locust, *Nomadacris septemfasciata* (Serv.). *Bull. ent. Res.* **50**: 333–353.

THOMAS, J. G. (1965). The abdomen of the female desert locust (*Schistocerca gregaria* Forskål) with special reference to the sense organs. *Anti-Locust Bull.* no. 42, 20 pp.

TRAYNIER, R. M. M. (1979). Long-term changes in the oviposition behaviour of the cabbage butterfly, *Pieris rapae*, induced by contact with plants. *Physiol. Ent.* **4**: 87–96.

TRUMAN, J. W. and RIDDIFORD, L. M. (1974). Hormonal mechanisms underlying insect behaviour. *Adv. Insect Physiol.* **10**: 297–352.

TYCHSEN, P. H. and VINCENT, J. F. V. (1976). Correlated changes in mechanical properties of the intersegmental membrane and bonding between proteins in the female adult locust. *J. Insect Physiol.* **22**: 115–125.

VINCENT, J. F. V. (1975). How does the female locust dig her oviposition hole? *J. Ent.* A, **50**: 175–181.

VINSON, S. B., JONES, R. L., SONNET, P. E., BIERL, B. A. and BEROZA, M. (1975). Isolation, identification and synthesis of host-seeking stimulants for *Cardiochiles nigriceps*, a parasitoid of tobacco budworm. *Entomologia exp. appl.* **18**: 443–450.

WESELOH, R. M. and BARTLETT, B. R. (1971). Influence of chemical characteristics of the secondary scale host on host selection behaviour of the hyperparasite *Cheiloneurus noxius* (Hymenoptera: Encyrtidae). *Ann. ent. Soc. Am.* **64**: 1259–1264.

WIGGLESWORTH, V. B. and BEAMENT, J. W. L. (1950). The respiratory mechanisms of some insect eggs. *Q. Jl microsc. Sci.* **91**: 429–452.

YAMAOKA, K. and HIRAO, T. (1971). Rôle of nerves from the last abdominal ganglion in oviposition behaviour of *Bombyx mori*. *J. Insect Physiol.* **17**: 2327–2336.

YAMAOKA, K. and HIRAO, T. (1977). Stimulation of virginal oviposition by male factor and its effect on spontaneous nervous activity in *Bombyx mori*. *J. Insect Physiol.* **23**: 57–63.

CHAPTER XVIII
EMBRYOLOGY

Development from egg to adult is a continuous process, but it is convenient to deal with development in the egg in this chapter and with postembryonic development in Chapters XX and XXI.

The insect egg is fertilised as it passes down the oviduct at the time of oviposition. Sperm entry initiates maturation of the oocyte and the subsequent development of the egg. The zygote nucleus divides and the daughter nuclei migrate to the periphery of the egg to form a layer of cells surrounding the yolk. Part of this cell layer becomes thickened to form the band from which the embryo develops and then gastrulation occurs, as a result of which an inner layer of cells is formed over the band. The details of gastrulation vary and the process is not immediately comparable with gastrulation in other animals. The embryo becomes cut off from the surface of the egg by extra-embryonic membranes, which break and disappear when the embryo undergoes more or less extensive movements in the yolk. These movements bring the embryo to its final position with the yolk now enclosed within the body wall.

The ectoderm forms the body wall, which invaginates to form the tracheal system, and the stomodaeum and proctodaeum; the nervous system and sense organs are also ectodermal in origin. The mesoderm may at first form coelomic sacs, but these break down to form muscles and the circulatory and reproductive systems. The germ cells from which the sex cells are ultimately derived are differentiated early in development, sometimes after only a few nuclear divisions. The midgut is formed by the growth of two centres anteriorly and posteriorly. Physiological changes accompany the morphological developments.

A general account of insect embryology is given by Counce and Waddington (1972). Sander (1976) discusses the regulation of embryogenesis.

18.1 Fertilisation

Within the spermatheca the sperm of most insects become active and the spermatodesms, in which up till now they have been aggregated, break down. They may remain alive in the spermatheca for months or, in the case of *Apis* queens, years, and hence require some nutriment. This may be provided initially in the seminal fluid from the male or from the degenerating cells of the testis cysts (p. 329), but probably further nutriment is supplied in most cases from the spermathecal glands.

Fertilisation does not occur until the eggs are about to be laid and as each egg passes down the oviduct a few sperm are released from the spermatheca. It is not clear how this is brought about, although in some insects in which the spermatheca has compressor muscles it is likely that a few sperm are forced out each time these muscles contract. In other instances sudden pulses of haemolymph pressure due to contractions of the body musculature may be responsible, while in *Nasonia* it is suggested that the sperm are activated in the spermatheca by a change of pH due to a secretion from the spermathecal gland and that they then actively swim from the spermatheca (King, 1962). The release of sperm from the spermathecae in Hymenoptera must be closely regulated since fertilised eggs give rise to females and unfertilised eggs to males.

The orientation of the egg in the oviduct often facilitates sperm entry. Thus in *Drosophila* the egg is orientated so that the single micropyle comes opposite the opening of the ventral receptacle of the oviduct, which is filled with sperm. Comparable orientations occur in other insects.

Having reached the egg the sperm of *Periplaneta* swim in a curving path towards the surface and this tends to carry them into the funnel-shaped micropyles. The final entry into the egg probably involves a chemotactic response.

It is usually stated that several sperm penetrate each oocyte and where this happens fertilisation is effected by one of the sperms while the rest degenerate. The evidence, however, is conflicting and Hildreth and Luchesi (1963) conclude that in *Drosophila* it is usual for only one sperm to enter each egg.

In a few insects fertilisation occurs while the oocytes are still in the ovary. This is true of the Cimicoidea, which practise haemocoelic insemination (p. 371), and also of *Aspidiotus*, in which the sperm become attached to large cells which proliferate in the common oviduct and then migrate to the pedicels.

18.2 Maturation of the oocytes

In most insects meiosis of the oocyte is initiated by sperm entry. In *Drosophila* the sperm head, after entering the oocyte, migrates towards the centre of the egg and resolves into a vesicular nucleus. During this period the oocyte undergoes its first meiotic division; the second is not completed until some five minutes after the egg is laid. A few minutes later the mitotic spindles of the male and female pronuclei fuse together and the first mitotic division occurs. The polar nuclei resulting from the meiotic divisions of the oocyte fuse together and later degenerate (Fahmy, 1952).

18.3 Cleavage and formation of the blastoderm

18.3.1 Cleavage and the blastoderm

After oviposition the zygote nucleus of an insect egg starts to divide, the first division occurring within about 30 minutes of zygote formation in *Dacus* (Diptera). Nuclear division is not accompanied by cell division, but each daughter nucleus is accompanied by a halo of cytoplasm and each such unit of nucleus and cytoplasm may be called an energid. The first few, up to about eight, divisions of the daughter nuclei are synchronised, synchrony perhaps being facilitated by the fact that they are in cytoplasmic continuity. During interphase periods the cytoplasm of the energids increases at the expense of the cytoplasmic reticulum.

The energids move apart as they divide (Fig. 258A) and become arranged in a layer within the yolk, bounding a spherical or elongate mass of yolk which roughly corresponds with the form of the egg. In the eggs of hemimetabolous insects the nuclei

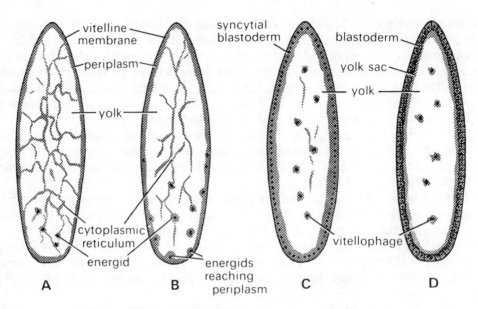

Fig. 258 Diagram illustrating the formation of the blastoderm

at this time are more superficial than those of holometabolous insects and this may be connected with the amount of cytoplasm in the egg. The eggs of most hemimetabolous insects contain little cytoplasm and the periplasm is thin, while eggs of holometabolous insects have much more cytoplasm and a thick periplasm.

Migration of the energids continues until they reach and enter the periplasm (Fig. 258B), but the point at which they do this varies, being at the posterior end of the egg in *Locusta*, for instance, but near the equator in *Panorpa*. In the higher Diptera their arrival at the periplasm appears to be synchronised, but in other cases this is not so.

The mechanism by which the energids move out to the periplasm is not understood. In *Calliphora* the centriole always leads during the movement and after division each nucleus rotates so that the centriole again assumes a leading position. This suggests that the nucleus itself is controlling the movement in some way, but in other species, *Pieris*, for example, cytoplasmic strands precede the energids to the periplasm.

Within the periplasm, which is commonly invaded after about the eighth cleavage, nuclear division continues, but is often no longer synchronised. Synchronous division does continue in *Dacus*, however, while in *Apis*, *Calandra* (Coleoptera) and *Calliphora* waves of mitoses pass along the egg from one end to the other. The nuclei spread all round the periphery of the egg (Fig. 258C) and at the same time, at least in Diptera, the periplasm thickens due to the addition of cytoplasm from the reticulum, which becomes vacuolated.

In *Drosophila* folds of the plasma membrane develop between adjacent nuclei in the periplasm, retracting at each nuclear division. Finally, however, the folds extend beyond the nuclei and join together internally, so that the undivided mass of yolk becomes surrounded by a layer of cells called the blastoderm (Fig. 258D) in which adjacent cells are held together by desmosomes (Mahowald, 1963b). As the cell walls form, the nuclei increase in size and a nucleolus becomes apparent for the first time. At first the nuclei are near the outer walls of the cells, but later they move inwards, their previous positions becoming occupied by complexes of granular and agranular membranes, ribosomes and mitochondria (Mahowald, 1963a). In *Dacus* and *Drosophila* the inner cell walls of the blastoderm cut off an inner undivided layer of cytoplasm. This anucleate layer is called the yolk sac (Fig. 258D). Subsequently it becomes nucleated due to invasion by some of the vitellophages, but finally it is digested with the yolk in the midgut.

Cleavage of this type, in which only the peripheral layer of cytoplasm divides, is known as superficial cleavage.

Mitotic activity during this period of development is very high, but the time taken to complete a mitotic cycle is greater in the more primitive groups, such as Orthoptera, where it may take some hours, than in more advanced groups such as Lepidoptera and Diptera. Amongst the Lepidoptera a complete mitotic cycle normally takes less than an hour, while in *Drosophila* at 25°C it takes only about ten minutes. This rapid division necessitates a rapid multiplication of the chromatin material and this is made possible by the large amount of DNA stored in the cytoplasm during oogenesis (p. 339). Thus in *Drosophila*, although nuclear multiplication in the first 13 hours of development exceeds 1000 with a corresponding increase in nuclear DNA, the total DNA content of the egg only increases five times. Presumably the cytoplasmic DNA is broken down to some extent before being incorporated in the nuclei.

18.3.2 Vitellophages

In many insects only some of the energids migrate to the surface to form the blastoderm, the rest remain behind in the yolk to form the yolk cells, or vitellophages. Thus in *Dacus* about 38 of 128 energids remain in the yolk to form the primary vitellophages and their subsequent division increases their number to about 300. Commonly the vitellophages begin to separate after the sixth or seventh divisions and become marked by the large size of the nucleus, which increases through endomitotic division of the chromosomes. In most orders some cells migrate back from the blastoderm to form secondary vitellophages and in Dictyoptera, some Lepidoptera and Nematocera all the vitellophages apparently have this secondary origin. There is some evidence that vitellophages are derived from some of the pole cells (p. 427) and in *Dacus* some tertiary vitellophages are formed from the proliferating anterior midgut rudiment.

The vitellophages have a variety of functions. They are concerned with the breakdown of yolk at all stages of development and later, when the yolk is enclosed in the midgut, they may form part of the midgut epithelium. They are also involved in the formation of new cytoplasm and are responsible for the contractions of the yolk, producing the local liquefactions which are necessary for this.

In the eggs of Orthoptera, Lepidoptera and Coleoptera the yolk may become temporarily divided by membranes into large masses or spherules containing one or more vitellophages. These yolk spherules are first formed close to the embryo and under the serosa, but ultimately extend throughout the yolk.

18.3.3 Other types of cleavage

The superficial pattern of cleavage occurring in most insects is determined by the large amount of yolk present, but in species with less yolk other forms of cleavage occur. The eggs of Collembola contain relatively little yolk and early cleavage is complete. Each cell produced consists of a mass of yolk in the centre of which is an island of cytoplasm containing the nucleus (Fig. 259A). In *Isotoma* cleavage is equal, so that cells of similar size result, but in *Hypogastrura* cleavage is unequal with the formation of micro- and macro-meres. Total cleavage continues to about the 64-cell stage, when the nuclei in their islands of cytoplasm migrate to the surface and become cut off from the yolk by cell boundaries. A blastoderm is thus formed and subsequent cleavage becomes superficial (Fig. 259B). Some nuclei remain in the yolk forming the vitellophages and the original boundaries within the yolk disappear leaving a single central mass.

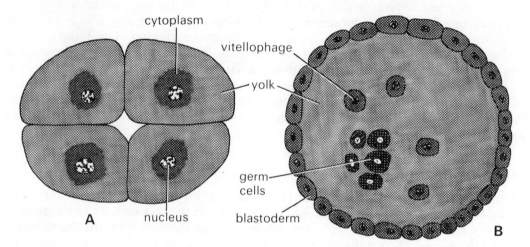

Fig. 259 A. Eight-cell stage in the development of *Isotoma* showing total cleavage. B. Blastoderm stage of *Isotoma* (from Johannsen and Butt, 1941)

An unusual form of cleavage also occurs in the small eggs of some parasitic Hymenoptera (p. 440).

18.3.4 Control of cleavage and blastoderm formation

The initial stages of cleavage and migration are controlled by a cleavage centre situated somewhere in the future head region. In general the cleavage centre is not recognisable morphologically, but it is characterised as the region into which the zygote nucleus moves before dividing and from which the energids subsequently move out. The cleavage centre is probably activated by sperm entry.

In most insects the major axes of the embryo are determined before the egg is laid. Thus the end of the egg which is anterior while the egg is in the ovary becomes the head end of the embryo and the dorsal surfaces similarly correspond. This association presumably results from the position of some other orientating factor intimately associated with the oocyte. Thus in *Drosophila* the embryonic head always forms at the end of the egg which was adjacent to the nurse cells irrespective of this orientation with respect to the parent. The follicle cells are also variously differentiated (*e.g.* p. 339) and these too may have a role in determining polarity. The dorso-ventral axis in *Drosophila* is probably determined by factors outside the follicle and, in most insects, the germinal vesicle is situated towards the dorsal side of the oocyte (Gill, 1964).

Changes probably occur in the cytoplasm between the time of maturation and blastoderm formation. At first the periplasm appears to inhibit further division of the polar bodies, but it does not have this inhibiting effect on the nuclei of the blastoderm later on. Despite these and other effects of the cytoplasm it is nevertheless true that the genes play an active role in controlling development from a very early stage (Waddington, 1956).

18.4 Early development of the embryo

18.4.1 Formation of the germ band

In most insect eggs the blastoderm initially forms a uniformly thin layer of cuboid cells all over the yolk. Subsequently as a result of aggregation of the cells so that they become columnar, it becomes thicker in the ventral region of the egg. This thickening is the embryonic primordium, or germ band, which develops into the future embryo, while the rest of the blastoderm remains extra-embryonic (Fig. 260). Sometimes, as in Mallophaga and *Apis* the whole blastoderm is thick but subsequently becomes thinner except at the germ band, while in some Lepidoptera the blastoderm is differentiated into germ band and extra-embryonic tissue from the time of its first appearance.

Initially, in eggs containing little cytoplasm, as in most hemimetabolous insects, the germ band may be a small disc or streak of tissue over the posterior end of the egg. In holometabolous insects it is more extensive and in dipteran eggs, which contain a

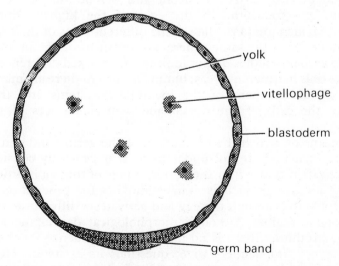

Fig. 260 Diagrammatic transverse section of a developing egg showing the ventral thickening which forms the germ band

relatively small amount of yolk, almost the whole of the blastoderm forms the germ band and there is very little extra-embryonic tissue (Fig. 261 and 263B). The germ band is differentiated into a broad head region, the protocephalon, and a narrow 'tail', the protocorm (Fig. 262A). Where the germ band is short relative to the whole egg embryonic development usually involves the differentiation of additional tissue posteriorly. Where the germ band is large all the parts of the larval body are represented from the outset.

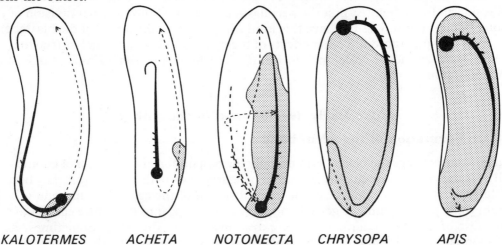

KALOTERMES   ACHETA   NOTONECTA   CHRYSOPA   APIS

Fig. 261 Diagrams showing the extent of the germ band (shaded), the position of the embryo prior to katatrepsis (solid black, showing position of protocephalon, gnathal and thoracic appendages), and the movement of the embryo at katatrepsis (arrow). In all cases the embryo finally comes to lie on the ventral surface of the egg (to the right) with its head at the anterior (upper) pole

In a typical hemimetabolous insect the midventral cells of the germ band are the presumptive midgut (Fig. 263A). In front and behind this are the presumptive stomodaeum and proctodaeum. In the eggs of the higher Diptera and some Lepidoptera and Hymenoptera the fate of the different parts of the egg is much more precisely determined, but the same general arrangement of presumptive areas exists (Fig. 263B). Preliminary studies do not indicate any marked differences in ultrastructure between the cells in different areas, but in *Drosophila* there are marked differences in the degree of development of the membrane systems and the numbers of mitochondria in the cells of the dorsal and ventral surfaces of the blastoderm (Mahowald, 1963a).

The mechanisms by which the production of the germ band and its subsequent development are regulated are not understood. It is generally considered (Counce, 1972) that an activation centre near the posterior pole of the egg is brought into action by the arrival of a cleavage nucleus. This stimulates the production of a substance which diffuses forwards through the egg and activates a differentiation centre in the prospective thoracic region. Although morphological development is often most advanced in the prothorax there is no physiological evidence for the existence of a differentiation centre and Sander (1976) questions its existence. He supposes that differentiation is effected in response to specific signals from the yolk/cytoplasm system underlying the blastoderm.

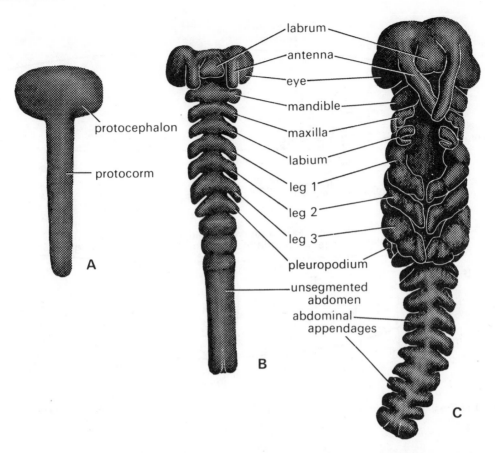

labrum
antenna
eye
mandible
maxilla
labium
leg 1
leg 2
leg 3
pleuropodium
unsegmented abdomen
abdominal appendages

protocephalon

protocorm

A

B

C

Fig. 262 Early stages in the development of *Ornithacris* showing the whole embryo with the embryonic membranes removed

18.4.2 Gastrulation

Gastrulation is the process by which the mesoderm and endoderm are invaginated within the ectoderm. In insects there is no deep invagination as in other animals, but an inner layer of cells is formed by the cells initially lying along the midline of the germ band. In most insects the cells along the midline become columnar and then migrate inwards so that a mid-ventral groove is formed. These cells are progressively overgrown by more lateral cells spreading inwards. At the same time the invaginated cells proliferate to form an inner layer (Fig. 264). In some beetles, as in *Clytra*, the invagination is so marked that it is at first almost tubular (Fig. 264A), while in *Apis* a broad middle plate sinks in without rolling up and the ectoderm grows inwards to cover it (Fig. 264B). The inner layer which is formed in this way comprises the mesoderm with a midgut rudiment anteriorly and posteriorly.

In the Diptera the latter part of gastrulation has a superficial resemblance to the process in other animals with the invagination of the posterior midgut rudiment deep into the yolk. Mesodermal invagination begins along the ventral surface, but extension

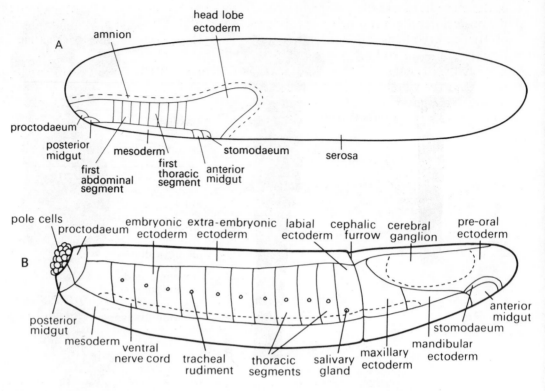

Fig. 263 The presumptive larval areas on the blastoderm of (A) *Acheta* and (B) *Dacus*

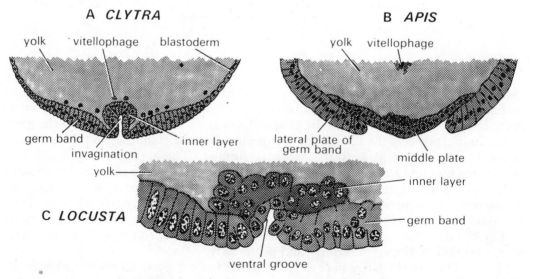

Fig. 264 Different types of gastrulation. A. Invagination in *Clytra* (Coleoptera). B. Overgrowth in *Apis*. C. Proliferation in *Locusta* (from various sources)

of the mesoderm and the ectoderm which comes to cover it pushes the invagination of the posterior midgut rudiment and the proctodaeum anteriorly along the dorsal surface of the embryo (Fig. 265A,B). Invagination of the proctodaeum then carries the posterior midgut rudiment deep into the yolk (Fig. 265C).

Finally, in *Isotoma* all the cells of the blastoderm divide tangentially to form an inner layer over the whole of the inside (Fig. 272). Later the inner layer cells migrate to the region of the germ band so that the extra-embryonic region comes to consist of a single layer of cells (Jura, 1972).

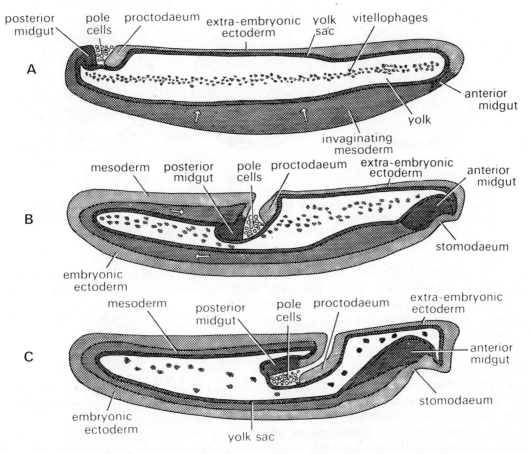

Fig. 265 Diagrammatic sagittal sections through the embryo of *Dacus*. A. Eight hours after laying. B. Nine hours after laying. C. Twelve hours after laying. Arrows indicate the movements of the mesoderm (after Anderson, 1962)

18.4.3 Formation of embryonic membranes

The germ band usually does not remain exposed at the surface of the yolk, but becomes covered by one or more embryonic membranes. Soon after its formation folds appear at the periphery of the germ band (Fig. 266A) and these extend ventrally beneath the embryo until they meet and fuse in the ventral midline (Fig. 266B). Thus the embryo lies on the dorsal surface of a small cavity, the amniotic cavity, bounded by a thin membrane, the amnion. The membrane round the outside of the yolk is now called the serosa, and amnion and serosa may remain connected where the embryonic folds fuse (Fig. 266B) or they may become completely separated, the embryo sinking into the yolk so that yolk penetrates between amnion and serosa (Fig. 266C). No further cell division occurs in the serosa, but endomitosis may occur so that the nuclei become very large and, in *Gryllus* (Orthoptera), they contain four times as much DNA as the nuclei in the germ band.

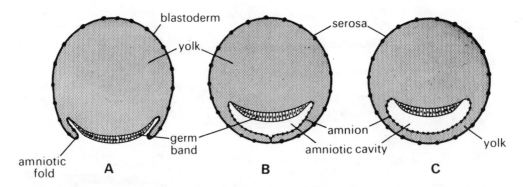

Fig. 266 Diagram illustrating the development of the amniotic cavity. A. Lateral folds beginning to grow over germ band. B. Lateral folds meet beneath germ band. C. Amnion and serosa separated, embryo immersed in yolk

The embryo of *Machilis* (Archaeognatha) does not become cut off in an amniotic cavity but is invaginated within the yolk, while the extra-embryonic membranes are differentiated into a zone of cells with small nuclei adjacent to the embryo and a zone of cells with large nuclei over the rest of the egg (Fig. 267). From their superficial resemblance to amnion and serosa these zones are called proamnion and proserosa. In *Lepisma* the amnion-like cells are restricted to the membrane lining the invagination, while in *Ctenolepisma* the amnio-serosal folds fuse as they do in pterygote insects.

In the Cyclorrhapha the embryo occupies the whole egg from the beginning of development and in these insects the amnion is vestigial and the serosa absent.

After completion of the amnion and serosa further embryonic membranes are produced in tettigoniids from a thickening of the serosa in front of the head known as the indusium. This sinks in from the serosa and becomes separated into outer and inner

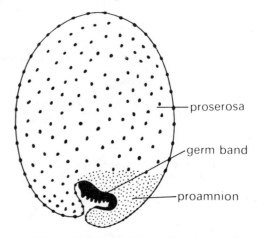

Fig. 267 Early stages of the invagination of the germ band in *Machilis* (from Johannsen and Butt, 1941)

layers which push between the serosa and the yolk, surrounding the egg except at the anterior pole. The outer layer of the indusium persists until the larva emerges, but the inner layer assumes the role of the serosa in other groups and, after fusing with the amnion, is broken during katatrepsis (see below). A similar structure is present in *Siphanta* (Homoptera) and, less well-developed, in a few other insects.

In Orthoptera the serosa secretes a cuticle to the outside and in tettigoniids this is supplemented by a second layer secreted by the inner indusial membrane. A subserosal layer is produced by Coleoptera, while in *Isotoma* two successive cuticles are formed all round the outside of the egg.

18.5 Movements of the embryo

18.5.1 Basic movements

The early embryos of most hemimetabolous orders are small relative to the size of the egg and in many of these groups the embryo makes extensive movements during development. In Dictyoptera, Dermaptera and Isoptera the germ band is initially on the dorsal surface of the egg near its posterior pole. In most cases as the germ band lengthens it extends onto the ventral surface and the head moves to a more posterior position (Fig. 268). In other hemimetabola the movements are more marked and the embryo becomes immersed within the yolk (Fig. 269). The posterior end of the germ band is flexed upwards into the yolk, so that the embryo comes to lie with its head-end towards the posterior pole of the egg. These movements are known as anatrepsis and comparable displacements of the embryo occur in Ephemeroptera, Odonata, most Orthoptera and hemipteroid insects.

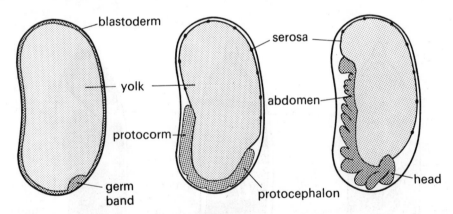

Fig. 268 Early stages in the development of the embryo of *Zootermopsis*, an example of an embryo developing superficially on the yolk. The amnion, not shown, covers the outer surface of the embryo

Following the period of elongation and development of the appendages, the amnion and serosa, which enclose these embryos, fuse and rupture close to the head. The embryonic membranes now pull back from the embryo leaving it exposed on the surface of the yolk (Fig. 268). Where the embryo is already on the ventral surface of the egg, as in some Dictyoptera, it stays where it is, but where, as in other groups, the embryo has developed on the dorsal side of the egg with its head towards the posterior pole, it now moves round to lie with its head towards the anterior pole (Fig. 261, 269). This movement is known as katatrepsis. The term blastokinesis is sometimes used synonymously with katatrepsis, but it is also used to refer to all the movements of the embryo within the egg, including both anatrepsis and katatrepsis.

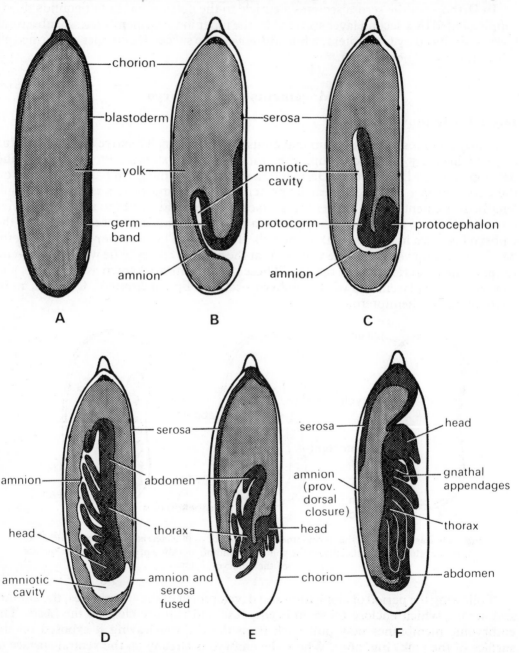

Fig. 269 Stages in the embryonic development of *Agrion* (from Johannsen and Butt, 1941)

In holometabolous insects the embryo elongates and differentiates with its head towards the anterior pole of the egg and the extensive movements which occur in many hemimetabolous groups do not take place. In some Coleoptera, such as *Dytiscus* and *Tenebrio*, the embryonic membranes fuse and rupture, and the embryo shortens rapidly, but without changing its position. Shortening also occurs in embryos of other holometabolous insects but the fate of the embryonic membranes varies (see below).

Lepidoptera are unusual amongst holometabolous insects in making extensive movements during embryogenesis. The movements are called blastokinesis though they differ entirely from the movements occurring during blastokinesis in hemimetabolous insects (Anderson, 1972).

18.5.2 Dorsal closure

One effect of katatrepsis in many insects is to reverse the relative positions of embryo and yolk. At first the embryo lies on or in the yolk, but when the movements are completed the yolk is contained within the embryo. This results from the formation of the dorsal wall of the embryo and in this process two phases can be recognised. The first, or provisional, dorsal closure is formed by the extra-embryonic membranes as a result of katatrepsis; later the provisional tissue is replaced by the embryonic ectoderm which grows upwards to form the definitive dorsal closure.

Various methods are employed to achieve the dorsal closure. In Orthoptera katatrepsis results in the yolk becoming enclosed by the amnion and serosa (Fig. 270A). As the ectoderm grows up to replace this provisional closure amnion and serosa shrink and become confined to an antero-dorsal region where finally the serosa invaginates into the yolk in the form of a tube (Fig. 271). This is the secondary dorsal organ and it is ultimately digested in the midgut.

Where no marked katatrepsis occurs the dorsal closure is produced by re-arrangement of the embryonic membranes even though the embryo itself remains relatively static. In *Leptinotarsa* (Coleoptera) and other Chrysomelidae the amnion breaks and grows up inside the serosa (Fig. 270B). Later it is replaced by the ectoderm while the serosa remains intact round the outside. In *Chironomus* amnion and ectoderm grow dorsally together so that the ectoderm forms the dorsal closure at an early stage while the amnion forms a membrane all round the outside (Fig. 270C). The serosa is invaginated and destroyed. Similar growth of the membranes occurs in Lepidoptera and Tenthredinidae, but the serosa also persists so that a layer of yolk is present all round the embryo, held between the amnion and serosa (Fig. 270D). This provides the first meal for larval Lepidoptera when they hatch.

18.5.3 Dorsal organ

As the definitive dorsal closure develops the membranes forming the provisional closure are invaginated into the midgut and destroyed. The temporary structure which the membranes form during this process is known as the secondary dorsal organ (Fig. 271) and it is necessary to differentiate it from the primary dorsal organ, which is most fully developed in the eggs of Collembola. In *Isotoma* the primary dorsal organ first appears at the anterior pole of the egg after the formation of the inner layer (Fig. 272). The ectodermal cells at this point are deep and become vacuolated,

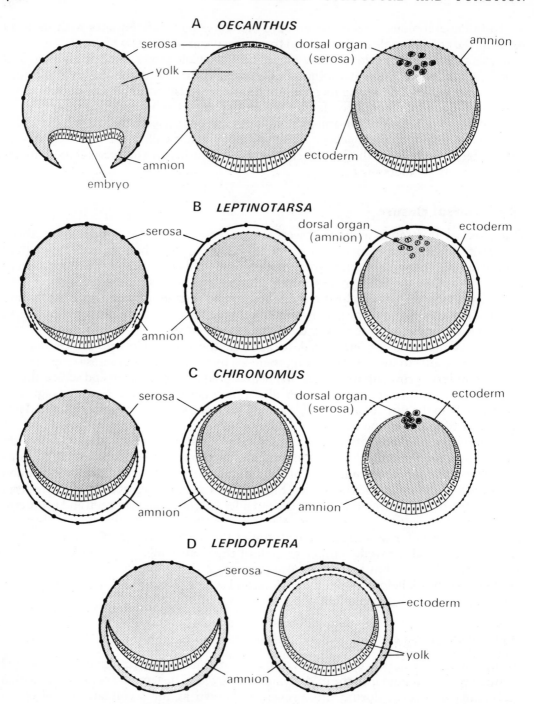

Fig. 270 Diagrams illustrating the dorsal closure and the fate of the embryonic membranes in (A) *Oecanthus* (Orthoptera), (B) *Leptinotarsa* (Coleoptera), (C) *Chironomus* (Diptera) and (D) a lepidopteran. The earliest stages figured on the left of the diagram can be derived from stage B or C in Fig. 266 (from Imms, 1957)

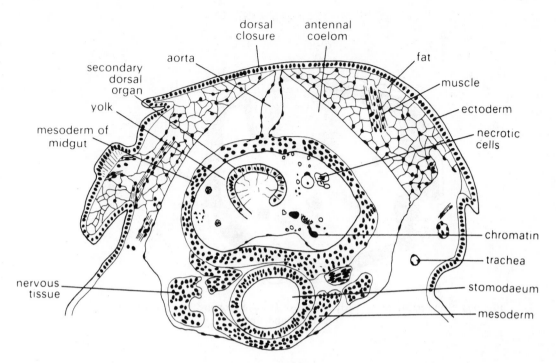

Fig. 271 Transverse section of the dorsal half of an embryo of *Ornithacris* after completion of the definitive dorsal closure

suggesting a glandular function. From the organ a series of tendrils grow out. In *Isotoma* these remain short, but in *Tetradontophora* they extend outwards so as to invest the developing embryo (Jura, 1972). In this species the dorsal organ also produces quantities of extra-embryonic fluid. At the time of the dorsal closure of the embryo the primary dorsal organ passes into the alimentary canal and is digested. Similar, but less well-developed structures, are formed in the early embryos of some beetles and *Apis*.

18.6 Development of organ systems

18.6.1 Appendages

The whole outer wall of the embryo represents the ectoderm and by outgrowths of the wall the appendages are formed. In front of the stomodaeum is the labrum and on either side on the protocephalon are the antennal rudiments (Fig. 262B). The protocorm becomes segmented and, in the lower orders, each segment extends laterally to form the rudiment of an appendage. Immediately behind the protocephalon are the rudiments of the mandibles, maxillae and labium. The latter arises in series with the rest as a pair of limbs which later fuse in the midline to form the definitive labium.

The appendages of the next three segments form the walking legs. These grow longer and become folded and grooved where later they will become segmented (Fig. 262C). By contrast the abdominal appendages disappear except that in some insects the appendages of segments 8 and 9 contribute to the ovipositor and those on

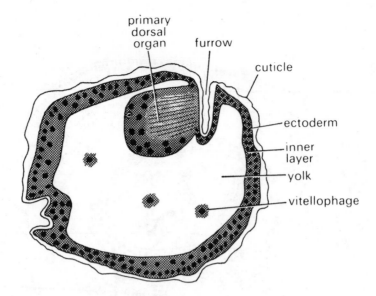

Fig. 272 Section through an early embryo of *Isotoma* showing the primary dorsal organ (from Johannsen and Butt, 1941)

segment 11 form the cerci. In Orthoptera and some other orders the appendages of the first abdominal segment also persist for a time (Fig. 274). They are known as the pleuropodia and in Orthoptera have a distal area in which the cells become very large and secrete an enzyme which digests the serosal endocuticle. They then degenerate, becoming torn off when the insect hatches. They probably serve the same purpose in *Belostoma* (Heteroptera), where they sink into the body so that only the tip of each cell projects from a bowl-shaped cavity. They reach their greatest development just before hatching.

In *Hesperoctenes* (Heteroptera) the egg has no yolk or chorion since it develops within the female parent, nutriment being obtained from the parent via a pseudo-placenta (p. 434) formed from the pleuropodia. These grow and fuse together to form a membrane which completely covers the embryo and which makes contact with the wall of the oviduct.

The pleuropodia assume a variety of forms in Coleoptera, but in Dermaptera, Hymenoptera and Lepidoptera they are only ever present as small papillae which soon disappear (Hussey, 1927).

18.6.2 Nervous system

The central nervous system arises as a thickening of the ectoderm on either side of the midline. The ectodermal cells divide tangentially cutting off large cells called neuroblasts, which then divide several times in the same plane so as to form a column of nerve cells at right angles to the surface (Fig. 273). Usually there are four or five columns of cells on either side of the midline and a median row which forms the median

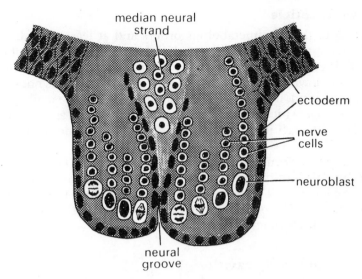

median neural
strand

ectoderm

nerve
cells

neuroblast

neural
groove

Fig. 273 Section through the developing ventral nerve cord showing the neuroblasts with their daughter cells (from Johnnsen and Butt, 1941)

neural strand. In *Pieris* and *Musca* the daughter cells of the neuroblasts do not divide again, but in *Apis* and *Calandra* they undergo lateral divisions.

As the embryo segments the ganglia become differentiated. Three paired groups of neuroblasts corresponding with the protocerebrum, deutocerebrum and tritocerebrum (p. 610) develop in the protocephalon and in addition, when the full complement of segments is present, 17 postoral ganglia may be recognisable: three in the gnathal segments, three in the thorax and eleven in the abdomen. The first three always fuse to form the suboesophageal ganglion and some fusion of abdominal ganglia always occurs, but the further extent of fusion varies, depending on the species (p. 614).

The optic lobes which come to be associated with the protocerebrum arise separately from the nervous ganglia and contain no neuroblasts, although similar large cells are present. In Orthoptera they are formed by delamination from the ectodermal thickening which forms the eye, but in Hymenoptera and Coleoptera they develop from an ectodermal invagination arising outside the eye rudiment.

The nervous system is enclosed within a sheath which secretes the neural lamella (p. 621). The sheath cells are probably ectodermal in origin, being derived from some of the outer ganglion cells (see Ashhurst, 1965, for references).

The ganglia of the stomatogastric system are formed from the ectoderm of the stomodaeum, and sensory structures arise from local modifications of the epidermis.

18.6.3 Other ectodermal structures

The tracheal system arises as paired segmental invaginations which become T-shaped. The arms of the T in adjacent segments fuse to form the longitudinal trunks and further invaginations from these develop into the finer branches of the system.

Oenocytes (p. 503) are cut off from the epidermis of all the abdominal segments except possibly the last two.

18.6.4 Embryonic cuticle

Insects belonging to the hemimetabolous orders and at least some belonging to the Neuroptera, Trichoptera, Lepidoptera and Coleoptera, secrete a cuticle soon after blastokinesis. This embryonic cuticle soon separates from the epidermis and the first instar cuticle is laid down in its place, but the embryonic cuticle is not shed, remaining round the embryo until it hatches. The significance of the embryonic cuticle is unknown and the stage which possesses it is usually regarded as representing the true first larval instar, although it is not counted as such in the designation of the larval instars (p. 455).

A very thin cuticle is formed in Acrididae, *Carausius* and *Dysdercus* (Heteroptera) before the embryonic cuticle just described and a similar cuticle is present in *Hyalophora* (Lepidoptera). This thin cuticle separates from the epidermis when the embryonic cuticle proper is formed, so that the latter is strictly the second embryonic cuticle (Louvet, 1974, Dorn and Hoffman, 1981).

18.6.5 Mesoderm and body cavities

The mesoderm is derived from the inner layer (p. 413) forming two lateral strands which run the length of the body and are joined across the midline by a thin sheet of cells. In the lower orders the lateral strands become segmented and the somites separate off from each other, but in Lepidoptera and Hymenoptera the somites remain connected together. Amongst the Cyclorrhapha there is a tendency for the mesoderm to remain unsegmented as in *Dacus*, in which the strands of mesoderm only become segmented as they differentiate into the definitive structures associated with the ectoderm. The mesoderm in the protocephalon arises *in situ* in the lower orders, but moves forwards from a postoral position in the more advanced groups.

Cavities, which represent the coelom, appear in the blocks of mesoderm (Fig. 274). These cavities result from the development of clefts in the somites in *Carausius* and *Formica* (Hymenoptera), but by the block rolling up to enclose a cavity in *Locusta* and *Sialis*. In the Heteroptera the coelomic sacs remain open to the epineural sinus, while in Diptera the coelomic cavities are not formed.

Where they are most fully developed a pair of coelomic cavities is present in each segment of the protocorm, while in the protocephalon pairs of cavities develop in association with the premandibular and antennal segments. Sometimes one or two more pairs are present in front of the antennae. Subsequently in Orthoptera and Coleoptera the thoracic and abdominal cavities become confluent forming a tube on either side.

At the same time as the coelom is forming, the primary body cavity develops as a space between the upper surface of the embryo and the yolk. This cavity is called the epineural sinus and in Orthoptera and *Pediculus* (Siphunculata) it is bounded dorsally by a special layer of cells forming the yolk cell membrane (Fig. 274).

Soon the walls of the coelomic sacs break down as the mesoderm which forms them differentiates to form muscles and other tissues. As a result the coelomic cavities and the epineural sinus become confluent. So the body cavities of those insects which develop coelomic cavities is a mixocoel, although it is usually called a haemocoel. Some of the coelomic sacs, particularly those associated with the antennae, may be quite large and make a significant contribution to the final cavity.

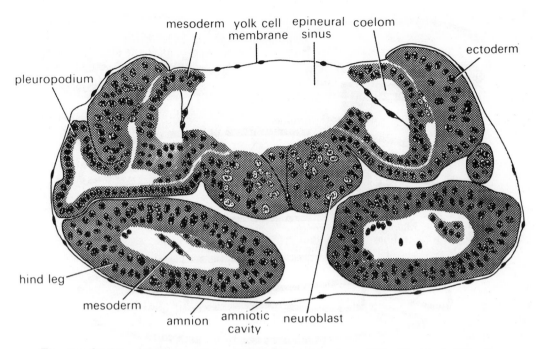

Fig. 274 Slightly oblique transverse section of an early embryo of *Ornithacris*. At this stage the embryo is completely immersed in the yolk

After katatrepsis when the midgut is formed the mesoderm extends dorsally between the body wall and the gut so that the body cavity is also extended until finally it completely surrounds the gut.

The outer walls of the coelomic sacs form the somatic muscles, the dorsal diaphragm, the pericardial cells and the suboesophageal body. The latter is found in the Orthoptera, Plecoptera, Isoptera, Mallophaga, Coleoptera and Lepidoptera and consists of a number of large binucleate cells in the body cavity and closely associated with the inner end of the stomodaeum. The cells become vacuolated and usually disappear at about the time of hatching, but in Isoptera they persist until the adult stage is reached. It is usually assumed that these cells are concerned with nitrogenous excretion, but Kessel (1961) suggests that they are concerned with the breakdown of yolk.

The inner walls of the coelomic sacs form the visceral muscles, and the gonads, fat body and blood cells are also mesodermal in origin (see *e.g.* Ullmann, 1964). The heart is formed from special cells, the cardioblasts, originating from the upper angle of the coelomic sacs, while the aorta is produced by the approximation of the median walls of the two antennal coelomic sacs (Fig. 271).

18.6.6 Alimentary canal

The foregut and hindgut arise early in development as ectodermal invaginations, the stomodaeum and proctodaeum (Fig. 275). These invaginations carry the anterior and posterior rudiments of the midgut into the embryo. These rudiments then extend to

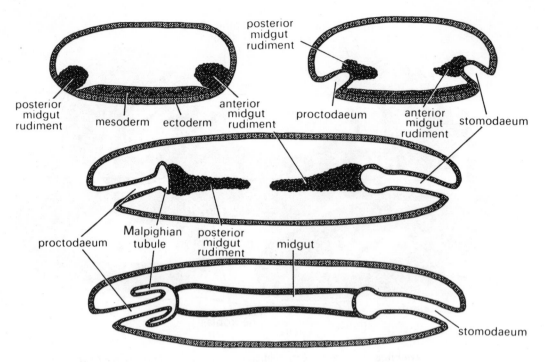

Fig. 275 Diagrams illustrating the development of the midgut (after Henson, 1946)

form longitudinal strands of tissue ventrally beneath the yolk. From these strands midgut tissue spreads out over the surface of the yolk, eventually completely enclosing it (Fig. 275).

The Malpighian tubules arise from the tip of the proctodaeum. Usually only two or three pairs develop in the embryo, but others may be produced during larval development (p. 461, and Savage, 1956).

18.6.7 Reproductive system

In the Diptera and some Coleoptera and Hymenoptera the cells destined to form the germ cells in the gonads are differentiated at the very start of embryonic development. At the posterior end of the egg is an area of cytoplasm, the pole plasm, which is differentiated from the rest and contains granules, called polar granules, rich in RNA. These granules differentiate during oogenesis. In *Drosophila* they first become apparent as small bodies which make contact with the mitochondria and increase in size. After fertilisation contact with the mitochondria is lost.

Cleavage nuclei move into the pole plasm and become surrounded by the polar granules which tend to coalesce. In Nematocera the numbers of energids which migrate into the pole plasm are constant for a species: one in *Miastor* and *Wachtliella*, two in *Sciara* and six in *Culex*. However, in most of the Cyclorrhapha studied the number is variable, between three and eleven in *Drosophila*, for example. The invading nuclei divide to produce eight pole cells in *Miastor* and about 40 in *Drosophila*. These may be outside the blastoderm or, as in *Dacus*, in a circular polar opening of the blastoderm (Fig. 263B).

The pole plasm appears to prevent the elimination of chromatin from the nucleus which occurs in other parts of the egg in these insects. In *Wachtliella* the cleavage nuclei contain some 40 chromosomes. After the third division one of the nuclei moves into the pole plasm, while the rest move towards the periphery elsewhere. At the next division the nucleus in the pole plasm divides normally, but in the others, although all the chromosomes start to move towards the poles of the mitotic spindle, only eight chromosomes in each half of the spindle complete the journey. The remainder return to the equator, agglomerate in large complexes and then degenerate (Geyer-Duszyńska, 1959). This elimination probably arises as a result of some defect of the centromeres. Two more chromosomes are eliminated from the somatic cells of the male embryo at the seventh division.

The elimination of whole chromosomes from the somatic cells is known to occur in Cecidomyidae, Sciaridae and some Chironomidae, but even in *Drosophila* and *Calliphora* one of the chromosomes of the somatic nuclei loses a terminal segment. The chromosomes which are retained in the germ cells appear to be essential for oogenesis (Geyer-Duszyńska, 1959), and Painter (1966) suggests that they serve to increase the ribosome-forming capacity of the nurse cells. In some other insects, such as *Drosophila*, the same end is achieved by endomitosis in the nurse cells (p. 339).

In the Nematocera all the pole cells migrate in to form the germ cells in the gonads, but in Cyclorrhapha only a proportion of them do so, the rest becoming vitellophages or contributing to the midgut epithelium. Some of these cells migrate in through the blastoderm before gastrulation, but others do so only during or after gastrulation and during this process they are carried forwards and invaginated with the proctodaeum (Fig. 265). Controversy exists as to which of these cells form the germ cells, some authorities maintaining that the early migrating group is involved, others that the cells from the proctodaeum are responsible (see Anderson, 1972; Counce, 1972).

The early separation of the germ cells results in a very direct cell lineage from the gametes of one generation to the gametes of the next, in isolation from the structural cells of the body (Fig. 276). This presumably helps to ensure the integrity of the genetic system by reducing the possibility of abnormal divisions.

The germ cells also differentiate during blastoderm formation in Dermaptera, Psocoptera and Homoptera, but in some groups of insects they are not recognisable quite so early in development, appearing at about the time the mesoderm differentiates. In *Locusta* they first appear in the walls of the coelomic sacs in abdominal segments 2 and 5. Later they condense to a single group and become associated with ridges of mesoderm. There is some evidence that the development of these genital ridges is induced by the germ cells, but the bulk of existing work does not support this. The germ cells become enclosed by the mesoderm and increase in number before they become separated into columns by the ingrowth of the mesoderm. These columns form the germaria of the ovarioles or the testis follicles. The mesoderm thickens ventrally and gives rise to solid strands of cells in which cavities appear to form the lateral ducts. The median ducts arise from ectodermal invaginations.

In Orthoptera the mesodermal accessory glands of the male are formed from hollow ampullae which are remnants of the coelomic sacs of abdominal segment 10. The ampullae become divided into separate glands by the ingrowth of the walls.

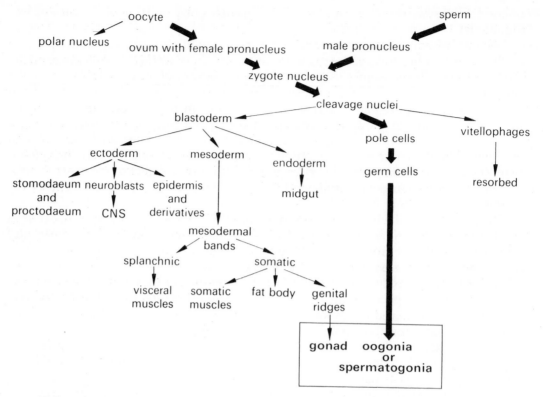

Fig. 276 Cell lineage during development, illustrating the early segregation and specialisation of the genital cells (based on Anderson, 1962)

18.7 Metabolic changes and control of organ development

Oxygen uptake by the egg increases throughout development as the embryo increases
in size, while the respiratory quotient, which at first equals one, soon falls to a low level.
This suggests that at first the small carbohydrate reserves of the egg are used and that
subsequently fat is the main metabolic substrate. It has been calculated that in the egg
of a grasshopper 75 % of the oxygen uptake is concerned in the oxidation of fat.

The total nitrogen content of the egg remains constant throughout development,
but its distribution varies, increasing in the embryo at the expense of the yolk. During
embryogenesis the concentration of free amino acids at first increases due to the rapid
breakdown of yolk reserves, probably by cathepsin-type enzymes which increase in
activity to a maximum during this period (Kuk-Meiri *et al.*, 1966). These amino acids
are used in the synthesis of proteins in the embryo and their concentration falls as the
rate of protein synthesis increases (Chen, 1966). Changes in other substances during
embryogenesis are reviewed by Agrell and Lundquist (1973).

The mechanisms which control later development, including organogeny, are not
clear. In general it is true that the ectoderm is self-differentiating, but that mesodermal
development after the inital spreading out of the inner layer is induced by relatively
undifferentiated ectoderm. There is also some evidence for the induction of some

organs by others: of the midgut by the splanchnic mesoderm, the anterior midgut by the stomodaeum, and ocelli by the wing buds. The eyes and optic lobes appear to have reciprocal inducing effects.

The embryonic moults are not, apparently, regulated by the endocrine system although this is fully developed at the time of moulting (Doane, 1972; but see Lagueux et al., 1979).

18.8 Duration of embryonic development

The times which insects take to complete their embryonic development vary considerably. Thus at 30°C the complete development of *Culex* takes about 30 hours compared with 82 hours in *Ostrinia* (Lepidoptera), five days in *Oncopeltus*, 15 days in *Schistocerca* and 43 days in *Ornithacris* (Orthoptera).

The duration of development decreases as temperature increases and conversely the rate of development increases in a more or less linear manner with increasing temperature except at the extreme ends of the range for development (Fig. 277). Development is not completed if the temperature exceeds a certain level, often in the range 35–40°C, nor below a certain level, which in *Oncopeltus* is about 14°C and in *Cimex* about 13 C. Some development does occur at lower temperatures, however, and in *Oncopeltus* some morphogenesis occurs even at 5 C. In addition to these

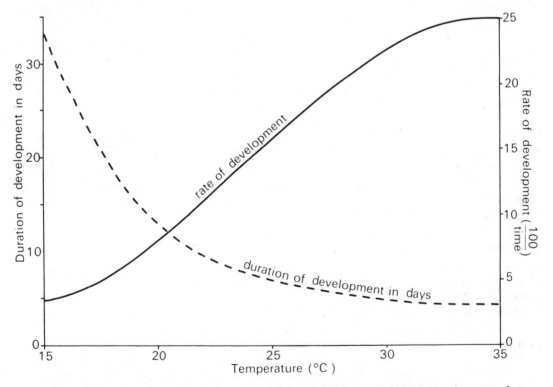

Fig. 277 The duration of the embryonic period and the rate of embryonic development of *Oncopeltus* in relation to temperature (from Richards, 1957)

developmental thresholds there is another temperature below which hatching of the fully developed embryo will not occur (p. 450).

It is thus necessary to distinguish between the threshold temperature for some development, below which no differentiation occurs, the threshold for full development, and the hatching threshold. These distinctions are not always clear in the literature and in particular the thresholds for full development and hatching may be lumped as the developmental–hatching threshold or simply the hatching threshold (Richards, 1957). This, however, can obscure the differences between different processes and the three thresholds are best considered separately.

Above the minimum temperature for full development the total heat input (temperature × time) necessary to produce full development and hatching is constant whatever the temperature. Thus in *Schistocerca* full development requires 224 degree days above a theoretical minimum for full development of 15°C. For instance, at 30°C development takes about 15 days [(30–15°) × 15 days = 225 degree days] and at 20°C about 45 days [(20 − 15°) × 45 days = 225 degree days]. In *Schistocerca* this relationship also holds with fluctuating temperatures, including periods below the minimum for full development, but in *Oncopeltus* and some other insects this is not entirely true because, although the development of *Oncopeltus* is not completed at temperatures below 14°C, some development does occur. Hence periods of low temperature do have an influence on the total number of degree days above 14°C necessary for development (Richards, 1957, and see Howe, 1967).

Humidity also influences egg development in some species and in *Lucilia* there is a linear relationship between the time of development and saturation deficit. Many eggs must absorb water before they can complete their development (p. 400), while if there is sufficient moisture in the environment to prevent death through desiccation, but not enough for development to continue, the eggs may remain quiescent for some time. Under such circumstances the eggs of *Schistocerca* develop to the beginning of katatrepsis and will then remain quiescent and viable for up to six weeks. At any time during this period development will proceed if more water becomes available.

In some species the embryonic period is greatly prolonged by an egg diapause and as an extreme example the diapause eggs of *Locustana* may survive for over three years. Diapause occurs at different stages of development in different species: just after blastoderm formation in *Austroicetes* (Orthoptera), before katatrepsis in *Melanoplus*, and in the fully developed embryo in *Lymantria* (Lepidoptera).

REFERENCES

AGRELL, I. P. S. and LUNDQUIST, A. M. (1973). Physiological and biochemical changes during insect development. *in* Rockstein, M. (ed.), *The physiology of Insecta*. vol. 1. Academic Press. New York.

ANDERSON, D. T. (1962). The embryology of *Dacus tryoni* (Frogg.) [Diptera, Trypetidae (= Tephritidae)], the Queensland fruit-fly. *J. Embryol. exp. Morph.* **10**: 248–292.

ANDERSON, D. T. (1972). The development of holometabolous insects. *in* Counce, S. J. and Waddington, C. H. (eds.), *Developmental systems: insects*. vol. 1. Academic Press. London.

ASHHURST, D. E. (1965). The connective tissue sheath of the locust nervous system: its development in the embryo. *Q. Jl microsc. Sci.* **106**: 61–74.

CHEN, P. S. (1966). Amino acid and protein metabolism in insect development. *Adv. Insect Physiol.* **3**: 53–132.

COUNCE, S. J. (1972). The causal analysis of insect embryogenesis. *in* Counce, S. J. and Waddington, C. H. (eds.), *Developmental systems: insects*. vol. 2. Academic Press, London.

COUNCE, S. J. and WADDINGTON, C. H. (eds.) (1972). *Developmental systems: insects*. 2 vols. Academic Press, London.

DOANE, W. W. (1972). Role of hormones in insect development. *in* Counce, S. J. and Waddington, C. H. (eds.), *Developmental systems: insects*. vol. 2. Academic Press, London.

DORN, A. and HOFFMANN, P. (1981). The 'embryonic moults' of the milkweed bug as seen by the S.E.M. *Tissue & Cell* **13**: 461–473.

FAHMY, O. G. (1952). The cytology and genetics of *Drosophila subobscura* VI. Maturation, fertilisation and cleavage in normal eggs and in the presence of the *cross-over suppressor* gene. *J. Genet.* **50**: 486–506.

GEYER-DUSZYŃSKA, I. (1959). Experimental research on chromosome elimination in Cecidomyidae (Diptera). *J. exp. Zool.* **141**: 391–447.

GILL, K. S. (1964). Epigenetics of the promorphology of the egg in *Drosophila melanogaster*. *J. exp. Zool.* **155**: 91–104.

HENSON, H. (1946). The theoretical aspect of insect metamorphosis. *Biol. Rev.* **21**: 1–14.

HILDRETH, P. E. and LUCHESI, J. C. (1963). Fertilisation in *Drosophila*. 1. Evidence for the regular occurence of monospermy. *Devl Biol.* **6**: 262–278.

HOWE, R. W. (1967). Temperature effects on embryonic development in insects. *A. Rev. Ent.* **12**: 15–42.

HUSSEY, P. B. (1927). Studies on the pleuropodia of *Belostoma flumineum* Say and *Ranatra fusca* Palisot de Beauvois, with a discussion of these organs in other insects. *Entomologica am.* **7**: 1–81.

IMMS, A. D. (1957). *A general textbook of entomology*. 9th edition, revised by Richards and Davies. Methuen, London.

JOHANNSEN, O. A. and BUTT, F. H. (1941). *Embryology of insects and myriapods*. McGraw-Hill, New York.

JURA, C. (1972). Development of apterygote insects. *in* Counce, S. J. and Waddington, C. H. (eds.), *Developmental systems: insects*. vol. 1. Academic Press, London.

KESSEL, R. G. (1961). Cytological studies on the suboesophageal body cells and pericardial cells in embryos of the grasshopper, *Melanoplus differentialis differentialis* (Thomas). *J. Morph.* **109**: 289–321.

KING, P. E. (1962). The structure and action of the spermatheca in *Nasonia vitripennis* (Walker) (Hymenoptera: Pteromalidae). *Proc. R. ent. Soc. Lond.* A, **37**: 73–75.

KUK-MEIRI, S., LICHTENSTEIN, N., SHULOV, A. and PENER, M. P. (1966). Cathepsin-type proteolytic activity in the developing eggs of the African migratory locust, (*Locusta migratoria migratorioides* R. and F.). *Comp. Biochem. Physiol.* **18**: 783–795.

LAGUEUX, M., HETRU, C., GOLTZENE, F., KAPPLER, C. and HOFFMANN, J. A. (1979). Ecdysone titre and metabolism in relation to cuticulogenesis in embryos of *Locusta migratoria*. *J. Insect Physiol.* **25**: 709–723.

LOUVET, J.-P. (1974). Observation en microscopie électronique des cuticules édifiées par l'embryon, et discussion du concept de "mue embryonnaire" dans le cas du phasme *Carausius morosus* Br. (Insecta, Phasmida). *Z. Morph. Tiere* **78**: 159–179.

MAHOWALD, A. P. (1963a). Ultrastructural differentiations during formation of the blastoderm in the *Drosophila melanogaster* embryo. *Devl Biol.* **8**: 186–204.

MAHOWALD, A. P. (1963b). Electron microscopy of the formation of the cellular blastoderm in *Drosophila melanogaster*. *Expl Cell Res.* **32**: 457–468.

PAINTER, T. S. (1966). The role of the E-chromosomes in Cecidomyiidae. *Proc. natn. Acad. Sci. U.S.A.* **56**: 853–855.

RICHARDS, A. G. (1957). Cumulative effects of optimum and suboptimum temperatures on insect development. *in* Johnson, F. H. (ed.), *Influence of temperature on biological systems*. Amer. Physiol. Soc.

SANDER, K. (1976). Specification of the basic body pattern in insect embryogenesis. *Adv. Insect Physiol.* **12**: 125–238.

SAVAGE, A. A. (1956). The development of the Malpighian tubules of *Schistocerca gregaria* (Orthoptera). *Q. Jl microsc. Sci.* **97**: 599–615.

ULLMANN, S. L. (1964). The origin and structure of the mesoderm and the formation of the coelomic sacs in *Tenebrio molitor* L. (Insecta, Coleoptera). *Phil. Trans. R. Soc.* B, **248**: 254–277.

WADDINGTON, C. H. (1956). *Principles of embryology*. Allen and Unwin, London.

CHAPTER XIX

UNUSUAL TYPES OF DEVELOPMENT

Sometimes eggs are retained by the female after they are fertilised, so that they start to develop before they are laid. If this period of internal development is extended the larva may hatch within the parent and in a few species it is nourished by her, so that finally the female gives birth to a fully developed larva ready to pupate. In other instances eggs which are deficient in yolk are nourished via special placenta-like structures in the ducts of the female or in the haemocoel. Thus viviparity in insects takes various forms.

Amongst parasitic insects eggs sometimes give rise to a number of larvae instead of just one. This is known as polyembryony.

Eggs will develop without being fertilised, and sometimes such parthenogenesis is a normal occurrence. The sex of the offspring then depends on the behaviour of the chromosomes at meiosis and, in general, haploid eggs are male, diploid eggs female. A disadvantage of parthenogenesis is that it reduces the genetic variability of the species, but in some cases this is overcome by an alternation of parthenogenetic and bisexual generations.

A few insects mature precociously and start to produce offspring while they are still larvae or pupae. This is known as paedogenesis.

Viviparity in insects is documented by Hagan (1951) and, in the Diptera, by Keilin (1916). Parthenogenesis is reviewed by Soumalainen (1962) and White (1954, 1964), male haploidy by Whiting (1945), and sex determination by Kerr (1962). Ivanova-Kasas (1972) reviews polyembryony.

19.1 Viviparity

The eggs of some insects are fertilised in the ovary or upper oviduct and in some of these species they are retained within the body of the female for some time before being laid. As a result the eggs start to develop while they are still within the parent and in *Cimex*, which practises haemocoelic insemination (p. 371), the embryo has almost reached the stage of blastokinesis by the time the egg is laid. In some other species internal development proceeds until the stage of hatching or even beyond, and such species are said to be viviparous.

19.1.1 Ovoviviparity

Many species retain the eggs in the genital tracts until the larvae are ready to hatch, hatching occurring just before or as the eggs are laid. All the nourishment for the embryo is present in the egg and no special nutritional structures are developed.

433

Viviparity of this sort is called ovoviviparity and it differs from normal oviparity only in the retention of the eggs.

Ovoviviparity occurs spasmodically in various orders of insects: Ephemeroptera, Dictyoptera, Psocoptera, Homoptera, Thysanoptera, Lepidoptera, Coleoptera and Diptera, being particularly widespread in the last group from which the following examples are drawn. Sometimes a species of *Musca* which is normally oviparous will retain its eggs and deposit larvae, but numerous other Diptera, particularly the Tachinidae, are always ovoviviparous. In these the eggs are retained in the median oviduct which becomes enlarged as the uterus during gestation. Ovoviviparous tachinids produce large numbers of eggs as do many oviparous Diptera, but in other ovoviviparous species, such as *Sarcophaga*, small numbers of relatively large eggs are produced at each ovulation and in *Musca larvipara* only one large egg is produced at a time. This lower rate of egg production probably reflects the greater protection afforded to eggs carried by the female compared with eggs deposited in the environment.

The increased size of the eggs permits the accumulation of more nutriment so that the embryo may develop beyond the normal hatching stage and larvae are born in a late stage of development. In *Hylemya strigosa*, for instance, the larva passes through the first instar and moults to the second instar in the egg, casting the first instar cuticle immediately after hatching. In *Termitoxenia* development in the uterine egg goes even further. The egg hatches immediately it is laid, giving birth to a fully developed third instar larva, which pupates a few minutes later, so that in this insect the larva never feeds as a free-living insect.

19.1.2 Viviparity

In some insects in which the eggs are retained after fertilisation the embryos receive nourishment directly from the parent in addition to or instead of that present in the yolk. Such insects are regarded as truly viviparous and some anatomical adaptations are present in the parent or egg which facilitate the exchange of nutriment. Viviparous species commonly produce fewer offspring than related oviparous species and this may be associated with a reduction in the number of ovarioles. Thus *Melophagus* and *Glossina* (Diptera) have only two ovarioles on each side, while in the related, oviparous, *Musca* there are about 70 ovarioles in each ovary. Similarly amongst the viviparous Dermaptera *Hemimerus* has 10–12 ovarioles on each side, but only about half these are functional. *Arixenia* (Dermaptera) has only three ovarioles on each side.

Sometimes the eggs are retained and development occurs in the ovariole, as in *Hemimerus*, the aphids and Chrysomelidae. In other insects, such as the viviparous Diptera, the vagina is enlarged to form a uterus. In Strepsiptera and a few parthenogenetic Cecidomyidae the eggs develop in the haemocoel of the parent.

Hagan (1951) recognises three main categories of viviparity and his scheme is followed.

Pseudoplacental viviparity

Insects exhibiting pseudoplacental viviparity produce eggs, containing little or no yolk, which are retained by the female and are presumed to receive nourishment via embryonic or maternal structures called pseudoplacentae. There is, however, no physiological evidence relating to the importance of these structures. Viviparous development continues up to the time of hatching, but the larvae are free-living.

In *Hemimerus* the fully developed oocyte has no chorion or yolk, but is retained in the ovariole during embryonic development. The oocyte is accompanied by a single nurse cell and enclosed by a follicular epithelium one cell thick. At the beginning of development the follicle epithelium becomes two or three cells thick and at the two ends thickens still more to form the anterior and posterior maternal pseudoplacentae (Fig. 278A). As the embryo develops it comes to lie in a cavity, the pseudoplacental cavity, produced by the enlargement of the follicle, but it becomes connected with the follicle by cytoplasmic processes extending out from the cells of the amnion and, later, of the serosa (Fig. 278B). Further, some of the embryonic cells form large trophocytes which come into contact with the anterior maternal pseudoplacenta. The follicle epithelium and pseudoplacentae show signs of breaking down and this is taken to indicate that nutriment is being drawn from them.

Later in development the serosa spreads all round the embryo and, with the amnion, enlarges anteriorly to form the foetal pseudoplacenta (Fig. 278C). By this time the dorsal closure is complete except anteriorly, where the body cavity is open to an extra-embryonic cavity, the cephalic vesicle. It is presumed that nutriment passes from the pseudoplacenta to the fluid in the cephalic vesicle and then is free to circulate into and round the embryo. The heart is probably functional at this time thus aiding the circulation.

The eggs of aphids also develop in the ovarioles and have no chorion. At first nutriment is received via the nutrient cords since aphids have telotrophic ovarioles (p. 336), but later a dominant role is played by the follicle cells. In *Macrosiphum* the follicle epithelium separates from the developing egg, but retains a connection posteriorly (Fig. 279). Through this connection reserve materials and symbionts are passed to the embryo, but the growth of the blastoderm restricts and finally severs the link. Possibly there is later some direct transfer of nutriment across the serosa from the follicle cells since the length of the egg increases by about 30 times in the course of development.

Pseudoplacental viviparity is also known to occur in a psocopteran, *Archipsocus*, in which the serosa is an important trophic organ, and in the Polyctenidae (Heteroptera) in which first the serosa and then the pleuropodia are important (p. 422).

Viviparity in Dictyoptera

The position of the cockroaches with regard to viviparity is anomalous. Fundamentally all cockroaches are oviparous, laying their eggs in an ootheca (Fig. 242A), which is extruded from the genital ducts. In some species the ootheca may be carried projecting from the genital opening, but in *Periplaneta* it is finally dropped some time before the eggs hatch. Other species such as *Blattella* continue to carry the ootheca externally until the time of hatching. Some others extrude the ootheca, but then withdraw it into the body again where it is held in a median brood sac, which extends beneath the rest of the reproductive system. In this case the ootheca may be poorly developed and as the eggs increase in size they come to project beyond the ootheca. In most species the increase in size results only from the absorption of water, but in *Diploptera*, in which the eggs increase in length by five or six times during embryonic development, there is also an increase in dry weight, indicating that some nutriment is obtained from the parent after ovulation.

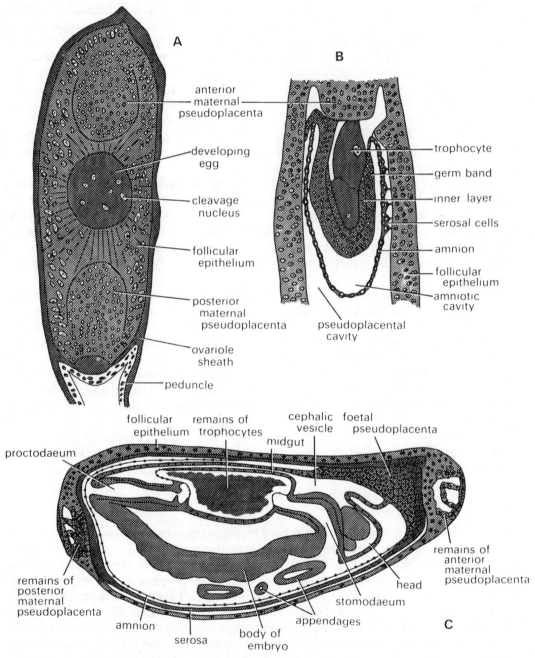

Fig. 278 Stages in the development of *Hemimerus*. A. Early cleavage. B. Fully developed germ band. C. End of blastokinesis (from Hagan, 1951)

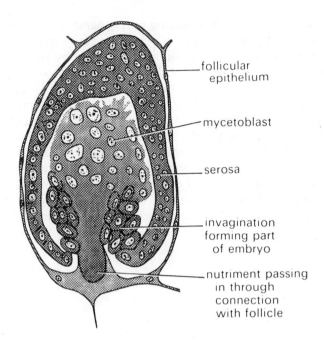

follicular
epithelium

mycetoblast

serosa

invagination
forming part
of embryo

nutriment passing
in through
connection
with follicle

Fig. 279 Section through an early embryo of *Macrosiphum* (from Hagan, 1951)

It is not certain how *Diploptera* embryos obtain their nutriment, but it is possible that the pleuropodia function as pseudoplacentae. This is suggested by the fact that the pleuropodia are long hollow tubes which extend outside the serosal cuticle and lie beneath the chorion. Similar long pleuropodia occur in some other cockroaches, such as *Leucophaea*, which are not thought to obtain further nutriment from the parent after ovulation (Roth and Willis, 1958).

Adenotrophic viviparity

In adenotrophic viviparity fully developed eggs with chorions are produced and passed to the uterus where they are retained. Embryonic development follows as in ovoviviparity, but when the larva hatches it remains in the uterus and is nourished by special maternal glands. Parturition occurs when the larva is fully developed and pupation follows within a short time, there being no free-living feeding phase. This type of viviparity only occurs in *Glossina* and the Pupipara.

In *Glossina* each ovary has only two ovarioles and these function in a sequence: first one ovariole on the right produces a mature oocyte, then one on the left, then the second on the right, and so on. Only one mature oocyte is produced at a time. It is fertilised in the uterus and embryonic development proceeds rapidly lasting three or four days at 25°C (Denlinger and Ma, 1974; Tobe and Langley, 1978). The larva hatches in the uterus, on the ventral wall of which is a small pad of glandular cells with a cushion of muscle beneath and other muscles running to the ventral body wall. This structure is known as the choriothete and it is responsible for removing the chorion and the cuticle of the first instar larva. It undergoes cyclical development, degenerating during the later stages of larval development and starting to regenerate just before larviposition, so that it is fully developed by the time the next larva is ready to hatch. The choriothete adheres to the chorion and when this is split longitudinally by an egg-burster (p. 453) it is pulled off by the action of the muscles of the choriothete, becoming folded up against the ventral wall of the uterus. The cuticle of the first instar larva is pulled off in the same way. When the second instar moults its cuticle is not shed immediately but it is subsequently split by the growth of the third instar. The cast cuticles are expelled by the female at parturition (Bursell and Jackson, 1957).

The larva feeds in the uterus on the secretion of specialised accessory glands, known as milk glands. The milk contains approximately equal dry weights of lipids and proteins plus amino acids, with very little else. Its production is cyclical, beginning just before a larva hatches and then continuing until the third instar is well-developed (Fig. 280). These changes in production are reflected in changes in the development of the milk glands.

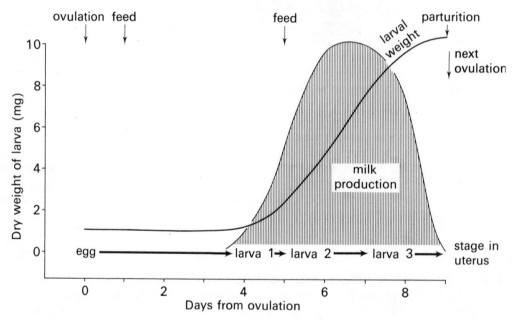

Fig. 280 Diagram showing the development of larval *Glossina* in the uterus of the female in relation to the cycle of milk production and feeding. A feed may occur on any day up to day 6, but feeding after this is unusual (after Denlinger and Ma, 1974)

The nutrients in the milk are derived from the blood meals taken by the parent fly. Most flies feed on the first day of pregnancy and then after an interval of three or four days. A relatively large proportion of the amino acids in the first feed are incorporated into lipids and are retained until the larva starts feeding actively. Amino acids from a second feed are probably utilised more or less directly by the larva and there is little lipid synthesis (Langley and Pimley, 1979). The adult fly does not usually feed in the later stages of pregnancy when the large larva occupies most of the space in the abdomen.

The larval respiratory system opens by a pair of posterior spiracles in the first two instars, but in the third instar larva the system is much more specialised. The terminal segment of the abdomen bears two heavily sclerotised lobes each of which is crossed by three longitudinal bands of perforations leading into the tracheal system. Each of these perforations is guarded by a valve which permits air to be drawn into the system but not to be forced out. In addition to these openings in the polypneustic lobes the second instar spiracles on the insides of the lobes remain open because the second instar cuticle is not shed. Also as a result of this, the tracheal system is lined by two layers of cuticle, the second instar cuticle being broken only at the inner ends of the system.

Indirectly acting dorso-ventral muscles produce a piston-like movement in a specialised part of the tracheal system in the polypneustic lobes and it is suggested that this movement sucks air in through the valved perforations and forces it forwards between the two linings of the tracheae. An exhalent current flows through the loose second instar linings and out through the second instar spiracles. The respiratory muscles contract 15–25 times per minute (for details see Bursell, 1956). By this means the larva is able to draw air in through the genital opening of the parent, but this mechanism can only function while the second instar cuticle persists, a period of four or five days at the beginning of the third larval instar. In the earlier instars oxygen may be obtained, at least partly, by diffusion from the female tracheal system which invests the uterus, while in the late third instar the valves in the polypneustic lobes disappear and a two-way airflow through the perforations is possible.

The hindgut of the larva is occluded at its connection with the midgut and again at the anus, so that waste materials from the midgut are not voided and the hindgut forms a reservoir for nitrogenous waste. This arrangement prevents the larva from fouling the female ducts.

Following parturition the larva moves to a suitable site for puparium formation; it does not feed during the short period for which it is active. Maturation of the next oocyte occurs during pregnancy and ovulation follows about 30 minutes after parturition. In this way maximum fecundity is achieved. For a discussion of the possible endocrine control of reproduction in *Glossina* see Tobe and Langley (1978).

As far as is known the development of the Pupipara does not differ in essentials from that of *Glossina* outlined above, but there is no evidence for a complex air circulation similar to that which occurs in the larva of *Glossina*.

Haemocoelous viviparity

Haemocoelous viviparity differs from the other forms of viviparity in that development occurs in the haemocoel of the parent female. This type of development occurs throughout the Strepsiptera and in some larval Cecidomyidae which reproduce paedogenetically (p. 446).

Female Strepsiptera have two or three ovarial strands on either side of the midgut, but there are no oviducts and mature oocytes are released into the haemocoel by the rupture of the ovarian walls. In *Stylops* the eggs contain very little yolk, but some is present in other genera such as *Acroschismus*. Sperm enter through the genital canals which open in the ventral midline of the female (Fig. 281) and fertilisation and development continue in the haemocoel with a direct transfer of nutriment from the

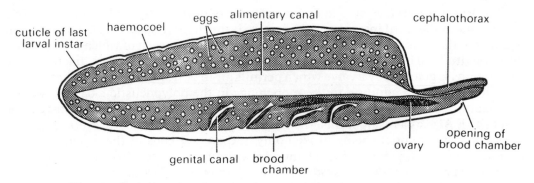

Fig. 281 Sagittal section through a female strepsipteran (from Clausen, 1940)

haemolymph to the embryo. The larvae hatch and find their way to the outside through the genital canals (Hagan, 1951).

In *Miastor* (Diptera) the eggs are similarly liberated into the haemocoel from simple sacs. The developing egg is nourished via nurse cells, which arise independently of the oocyte (cf. p. 338), and later via the serosa, which becomes thickened and vacuolated. When the larvae hatch they feed on the tissues of the female and any unhatched eggs, finally escaping through a rupture in the wall of the parent.

19.2 Polyembryony

Sometimes an egg instead of giving rise to a single larva may produce two or more, this process being called polyembryony. It occurs occasionally in Acridoidea and probably in other groups, but in some endoparasitic insects it is a regular phenomenon. This is true, for instance, in *Halictoxenos* (Strepsiptera), a parasite of *Halictus*; in *Aphelopus theliae* (Hymenoptera), a parasite of *Thelia* (Homoptera); in *Platygaster* (Hymenoptera), a parasite of Cecidomyidae; and in several genera of Encyrtidae and Ichneumonidae which parasitise the eggs and larvae of Lepidoptera. In all these cases the eggs of the parasite are small and relatively free from yolk, nutriment being derived from the host tissues in which they are situated.

When the oocyte of *Platygaster hiemalis* matures two polar bodies are produced. They fuse together and the polar nucleus increases in size to form a paranuclear mass. Some of the cytoplasm in the egg is associated with the paranuclear mass and forms the trophamnion, the remainder is associated with the fusion nucleus and forms the embryonic region. The trophamnion surrounds the embryonic region and the paranuclear mass divides. At the same time cleavage occurs in the embryonic region, but after the second division the whole region divides into two so that two embryos are produced (Fig. 282). Nutriment is passed to the embryo from the host via the trophamnion, but later the paranuclear masses are absorbed and the trophamnion is represented by a very thin membrane. In *P. vernalis* several divisions of the embryonic region occur so that eight embryos are produced from each egg.

A somewhat similar, but more extensive, process occurs in *Litomastix* (Hymenoptera) a parasite of the moth *Plusia*. Three polar bodies are produced when the oocyte matures; two of these fuse to form the polar nucleus and the third

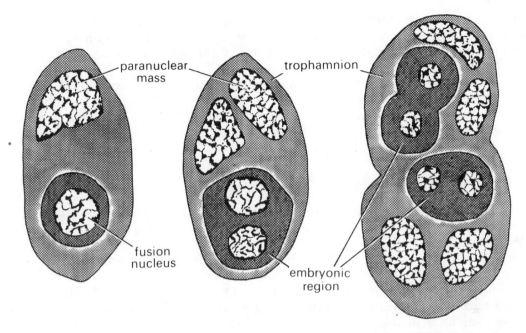

Fig. 282 Stages in the early development of *Platygaster hiemalis* showing the formation of two embryonic regions from a single egg (from Johannsen and Butt, 1941)

degenerates (Fig. 283A). The zygote nucleus and its associated cytoplasm divides to form two blastomeres, which become surrounded by the trophamnion. By further division (Fig. 283B) over 200 blastomeres are produced, some of them becoming spindle-shaped and pushing between the others to form nucleated inner membranes which divide the embryonic region into 15–20 primary embryonic masses each containing up to 50 blastomeres (Fig. 283C). These cells continue to divide and the

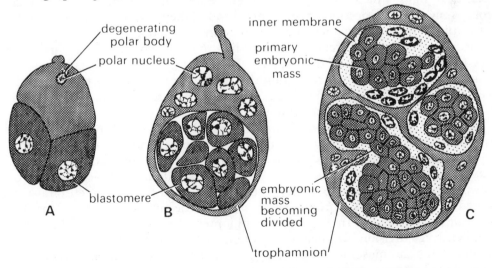

Fig. 283 Early stages in the development of the polygerm of *Litomastix* (from Johannsen and Butt, 1941)

embryonic masses are further divided into secondary and tertiary embryonic masses by ingrowths of the inner layer and the trophamnion. Finally the tertiary masses, which may become separated from each other, divide to form embryos of which 1000 or more may be derived from one egg.

The effect of polyembryony is to increase the reproductive potential of the insect, but the net effect is not always much greater than in related monembryonic species because polyembryonic forms tend to lay fewer eggs. Polyembryony may facilitate survival of the species during its relatively long life as a parasite while it is subjected to the reactions of the host (Clausen, 1940).

19.3 Parthenogenesis

Sometimes eggs develop without being fertilised and this phenomenon is known as parthenogenesis. Occasional parthenogenesis, resulting from the failure of a female to find a mate, is probably widespread, while in a number of insects parthenogenesis is a normal means of reproduction. It has been recorded from all the insect orders except Odonata, Dermaptera, Neuroptera and Siphonaptera.

The sex of the offspring developing from an unfertilised egg is dependent on the sex-determining mechanism of the insect and the behaviour of the chromosomes at the meiotic division of the oocyte nucleus. In the majority of insects the female is homogametic (XX) and the male heterogametic (XY or XO), but the Lepidoptera are exceptional with the females having the heterogametic constitution (see Kerr, 1962, for review of sex-determination). Hence the unfertilised eggs of most insects can contain only X-chromosomes since any Y-chromosome must come from the male. Whether the egg contains one or two X-chromosomes, that is, whether it is haploid or diploid, depends on the behaviour of the chromosomes at meiosis. Sometimes no reduction division occurs or reduction is followed by doubling of the chromosome number so that the diploid and XX composition of the egg is maintained. These eggs will give rise only to females. Eggs which undergo a normal reduction division and in which no chromosome doubling occurs remain haploid and, if they develop at all, become males. Such haploid males are characteristic of some insect groups.

Parthenogenesis may be classified according to the behaviour of the chromosomes at the maturation division of the oocyte:

haplo-diploidy—A normal reduction division occurs in the oocyte, fertilised eggs developing into females, unfertilised eggs into males. This is characteristic of Hymenoptera and some smaller groups.

apomictic (ameiotic) parthenogenesis—No reduction division occurs so that the offspring have the same genetic constitution as the mother and all are female. This is of common occurrence in blattids, aphids, tenthredinids and curculionids.

automictic (meiotic) parthenogenesis—A normal reduction division occurs, but is followed by the fusion of two nuclei so that the diploid number of chromosomes is restored. Often the female pronucleus fuses with the second polar nucleus, or two cleavage nuclei may fuse. In *Solenobia* (Lepidoptera) two pairs of nuclei fuse after the second cleavage division. *Moraba* (Orthoptera) is exceptional in having a pre-meiotic doubling of the chromosomes followed by a normal division so that the diploid number is restored. This type of parthenogenesis, in which only females are produced, occurs in phasmids, coccids and psychids.

An alternative classification based on the sex of the offspring produced as a result of parthenogenesis is as follows:

arrhenotoky—Only males are produced.

thelytoky—Only females are produced.

amphitoky—Individuals of either sex may be produced.

19.3.1 Arrhenotoky

Facultative arrhenotoky, in which the eggs may or may not be fertilised, is characteristic of a few groups of insects and has probably arisen only four or five times. It occurs throughout the Hymenoptera, in some Thysanoptera, the Coccidae Iceryini, some Aleyrodidae and the beetle *Micromalthus*. In all of these the unfertilised, haploid eggs, produce males.

In the Hymenoptera the female determines whether or not an egg is fertilised by controlling the release of sperm from the spermatheca as the eggs pass down the oviduct. The stimuli prompting the female to withhold sperm are largely unknown, but in *Apis* the season and the size of the brood cell in which the female is ovipositing are relevant. In the parasitic Hymenoptera the size of the host is often important, relatively more unfertilised eggs being laid in small hosts (see *e.g.* Shaumar, 1966). For a discussion of male haploidy in Hymenoptera see Kerr (1962), White (1954) and Whiting (1945).

The coccid *Icerya purchasi* is of interest in that, apart from a few haploid males, the adult population consists entirely of hermaphrodites which are diploid with diploid ovaries, but which also have haploid testes. No true females occur. When the larva giving rise to an hermaphrodite hatches from the egg all the cells are diploid, but after a time haploid nuclei appear in the gonad. They form a core from which the testis develops surrounded by the ovary. Oocytes undergo a normal reduction division, but the spermatocytes, as in normal haploid males, do not. The hermaphrodites are normally self-fertilising, but they can be fertilised by the occasional males. Cross-fertilisation between the hermaphrodites does not occur. The few eggs which are not fertilised develop into males.

19.3.2 Thelytoky

Thelytokous parthenogenesis probably occurs occasionally in many species of insect and is known to occur in a number of species of Acrididae, for instance (Hamilton, 1955). Unmated females of *Schistocerca* live for much longer than mated females, but lay about the same number of eggs. Nearly all of these start to develop, but only about 25 % hatch and further heavy mortality occurs in the first larval instar. Thus the viability of unfertilised eggs is much less than that of fertilised eggs, but nevertheless *Schistocerca* has been reared parthenogenetically for six generations. It appears that the only eggs to survive are those in which the chromosomes double after meiosis. Unmated cockroaches also live longer than mated females, but they produce fewer eggs with poor viability (Roth and Willis, 1956). In *Bombyx* the tendency for sporadic parthenogenesis to occur varies in different strains.

In other insects thelytoky is a regular occurrence and, for instance, in *Carausius* and some Thysanoptera males are extremely rare, the whole population normally reproducing parthenogenetically. Sometimes, as in some Psychidae and Coccidae, a parthenogenetic race exists together with a normal bisexual race. Thus *Lecanium* (Homoptera) has one race consisting entirely of females which reproduce apomictically and another race which is bisexual and exhibits facultative thelytoky. In this case fertilised eggs may become males or females while unfertilised eggs develop automictically and so produce females. Commonly such races occur in different areas and in the weevil *Otiorrhynchus dubius*, for instance, a parthenogenetic race occurs in northern Europe and a bisexual race in central Europe. In general parthenogenesis occurs more commonly in the north than further south and in the genus *Otiorrhynchus* 78% of the species occurring in Scandinavia reproduce parthenogenetically, while only 28% of those occurring in the Austrian Alps do so.

Constant thelytoky occurs in a few Lepidoptera, such as the psychid *Solenobia*, and this raises the question of sex determination since the females of Lepidoptera are heterogametic. Thelytoky in these insects may result from the passage of the X-chromosome to the polar body at maturation so that only the Y-chromosome remains in the egg; or two polar nuclei may fuse to give a female XO or XY constitution, while the egg nucleus degenerates. A completely different explanation supposes that the females are homozygous, YY, and so can give rise only to females (Soumalainen, 1962; White, 1954).

An unusual type of thelytoky, known as gynogenesis, occurs in the form *mobilis* of *Ptinus clavipes* (Coleoptera). The form *mobilis* exists only as triploid females which reproduce parthenogenetically, but the development of eggs is triggered by healthy sperm of *P. clavipes* or, less successfully, of *P. pusillus* (see Sanderson, 1961, for refs.).

Thelytoky occurs in many different and unrelated insects and is believed to have arisen on a large number of occasions. It may result from apomixis or automixis and its probable advantages over reproduction involving fertilisation are that the female spends all her time in feeding and reproduction, no time is lost in finding a mate, and, since the whole of the population is female, the reproductive potential is much greater than if half the population are males. These advantages are, however, offset by the absence of genetic recombination which normally occurs at mating. Thus the long-term effect of thelytoky, in many cases at least, is to prevent a species from adapting to environmental changes, so that it is destined to die out or to return to bisexuality (Soumalainen, 1962; White, 1954).

19.3.3 Alternation of generations

A number of insects combine the advantages of parthenogenesis with the advantages of bisexual reproduction by an alternation of generations. This occurs, for instance, in the Cynipidae, which are commonly bivoltine, a generation of parthenogenetic females alternating with a bisexual generation. *Neuroterus lenticularis* (Hymenoptera) forms galls on the underside of oak leaves in which the species overwinters. Females emerge in the spring and lay eggs. The eggs of some females undergo meiosis but, since in the absence of males they cannot be fertilised, they remain haploid and so give rise to males; other females produce eggs in which no reduction division occurs and which give rise only to females. In this way the bisexual generation arises, the insects emerging from catkin galls in early summer. After mating, the females of this generation lay eggs which are fertilised and which produce the females of the following spring generation.

Aphids have a more complex alternation of generations with several partheno-genetic generations occurring during the summer (Fig. 284). Sometimes, as in *Aphis fabae*, an alternation of host plants also occurs. The first generation emerges on spindle in spring from overwintering eggs. It consists entirely of females, the fundatrices, which may or may not produce wingless generations of fundatrigeniae before a winged generation, the migrantes, appears. These migrate to a bean plant and produce wingless alienicolae, of which there may be many successive generations, but ultimately these produce the sexuparae, some of which are winged and return to the spindle while others are wingless. The former produce females, the latter winged males which then join the females; they mate and winter eggs are produced. All these generations except for the last reproduce parthenogenetically and consist entirely of females. In some species, such as *Tetraneura*, only one class of sexuparae is produced and these individuals give birth to both male and female sexual forms, an instance of amphitoky.

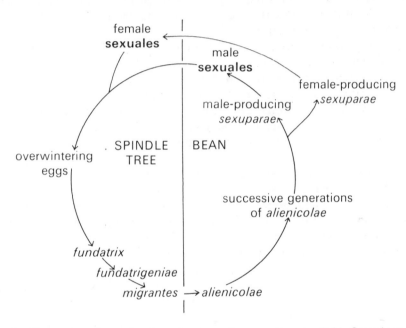

Fig. 284 Alternation of sexual and parthenogenetic generations in *Aphis*. Sexual generation in bold type; wholly female parthogenetic generations in italics (from Imms, 1957)

Female aphids are produced apomictically (but see Lees, 1966), while males result from the loss of an X-chromosome to a polar body at meiosis, although no reduction of the autosomes occurs. Thus an egg acquires the XO constitution of the male. The production of males is ultimately under environmental control, but how the environment controls chromosome behaviour is not known (Lees, 1966).

Spermatogenesis in male aphids is characteristic, ensuring that all the eggs produced are female. At the first meiotic division two kinds of spermatocytes are produced: some with an X-chromosome and some without. The latter degenerate and so only the former undergo the second meiotic division and only one type of sperm, containing an X-chromosome, is produced. Hence the fertilised eggs can only be female.

The aphids reproduce very rapidly, combining the advantages of parthenogenesis with viviparity and paedogenesis, so that successive generations are extensively telescoped. In the tropics, where conditions are continuously favourable, parthenogenesis may continue indefinitely without the intervention of a sexual generation.

An alternation of generations may also occur in Cecidomyidae (see below).

19.4 Paedogenesis

Sometimes immature insects mature precociously and are able to reproduce, this phenomenon being known as paedogenesis. It arises from an unusual hormonal balance (p. 835) and most insects reproducing paedogenetically are also parthenogenetic and viviparous. Development of the offspring which are produced paedogenetically usually begins in the larval insect, but these insects may be grouped according to the stage which gives birth to the offspring.

In *Miastor* and *Micromalthus* the larvae give birth to other larvae or, occasionally, lay eggs. Paedogenesis occurs in *Miastor* only under very good or poor nutritional conditions. Young larvae are set free in the body cavity of the paedogenetic larva and they feed on the maternal tissues, eventually escaping through the body wall of the parent. Under average nutritional conditions normal adults are produced.

Micromalthus has five reproductive forms: adult males, adult females, male-producing larvae, female-producing larvae, and larvae producing males and females. The species has a complex heteromorphosis (Fig. 285). The form emerging from the egg is a triungulin and this moults to an apodous larva which can develop in one of three ways. It can develop through a pupa to a normal adult female, or it can moult to a larval form which gives rise paedogenetically to a male, or to a paedogenetic larva which produces triungulins. Male-producing larvae lay a single egg containing a young embryo, but the egg adheres to the parent and when the larva hatches it eats the parent larva. If, for some reason the parent larva is not eaten, it subsequently produces a small brood of female larvae (Pringle, 1938; Scott, 1941).

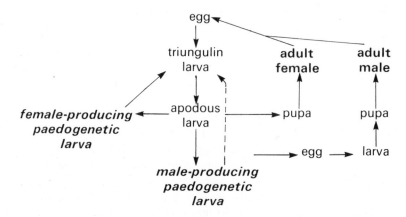

Fig. 285 Diagram of the life history of *Micromalthus*. Reproductive forms in bold type; paedogenetically reproducing larvae italicised (based on Pringle, 1938)

In the cecidomyids *Tekomyia* and *Henria* pupal forms give birth to larvae. The larvae of these insects are of two types: one type produces a pupa and, ultimately, a normal adult; the other forms a hemipupa, a rounded structure with, in *Henria*, vestiges of wings and legs. A brood of larvae, commonly between 30 and 60 of them, escapes from the hemipupa by rupturing the cuticle (Wyatt, 1961). Wyatt (1963) also suggests that pupal paedogenesis occurs in *Heteropeza* (*Oligarces*). Larvae are released into the haemocoel of the parent larva, but they escape from a form which he interprets as a hemipupa in which they can survive, if the conditions are moist, for up to 18 months. Paedogenesis is the normal method of reproduction in these insects and although normal adults may be produced it is not certain that they are capable of producing viable offspring.

Paedogenesis also occurs in aphids. Although the young are not born until the aphid has reached the adult stage, their development may begin before she is born while she is still in the ducts of the grandparental generation. Development of the offspring continues through the larval life of the parent.

The bug *Hesperoctenes* is an example of a paedogenetic form in which fertilisation occurs. Some last instar larvae are found with sperm in the haemocoel as a result of haemocoelic insemination (p. 371). These sperm fertilise the eggs which develop in the ovaries of the larva.

REFERENCES

BURSELL, E. (1956). The polypneustic lobes of the tsetse larva (*Glossina*, Diptera). *Proc. R. Soc.* B, **144**: 275–286.

BURSELL, E. and JACKSON, C. H. N. (1957). Notes on the choriothete and milk gland of *Glossina* and *Hippobosca* (Diptera). *Proc. R. ent. Soc. Lond.* A, **32**: 30–34.

CLAUSEN, C. P. (1940). *Entomophagous insects*. McGraw-Hill, New York.

DENLINGER, D. L. and MA, W.-C. (1974). Dynamics of the pregnancy cycle in the tsetse *Glossina morsitans*. *J. Insect Physiol.* **20**: 1015–1026.

HAGAN, H. R. (1951). *Embryology of the viviparous insects*. Ronald Press Co., New York.

HAMILTON, A. G. (1955). Parthenogenesis in the desert locust (*Schistocerca gregaria* Forsk.) and its possible effect on the maintenance of the species. *Proc. R. ent. Soc. Lond.* A, **30**: 103–114.

IMMS, A. D. (1957). *A general textbook of entomology*. 9th edition, revised by Richards and Davies. Methuen, London.

IVANOVA-KASAS, O. M. (1972). Polyembryony in insects. *in* Counce, S. J. and Waddington, C. H. (eds.), *Developmental systems: insects*. Academic Press, London.

JOHANNSEN, O. A. and BUTT, F. H. (1941). *Embryology of insects and myriapods*. McGraw-Hill, New York.

KEILIN, D. (1916). Sur la viviparité chez les Diptères et sur les larves de Diptères vivipares. *Archs Zool. exp. gén.* **55**: 393–415.

KERR, W. E. (1962). Genetics of sex determination. *A. Rev. Ent.* **7**: 157–176.

LANGLEY, P. A. and PIMLEY, R. W. (1979). Storage and mobilisation of nutriment for uterine milk synthesis by *Glossina morsitans*. *J. Insect Physiol.* **25**: 193–197.

LEES, A. D. (1966). The control of polymorphism in aphids. *Adv. Insect Physiol.* **3**: 207–277.

PRINGLE, J. A. (1938). A contribution to the knowledge of *Micromalthus debilis* LeC. (Coleoptera). *Trans. R. ent. Soc. Lond.* **87**: 271–286.

ROTH, L. M. and WILLIS, E. R. (1956). Parthenogenesis in cockroaches. *Ann. ent. Soc. Am.* **49**: 195–204.

ROTH, L. M. and WILLIS, E. R. (1958). An analysis of oviparity and viviparity in the Blattaria. *Trans. Am. ent. Soc.* **83**: 221–238.

SANDERSON, A. R. (1961). The cytology of a diploid bisexual spider beetle, *Ptinus clavipes* Panzer and its triploid gynogenetic form *mobilis* Moore. *Proc. R. Soc. Edinb.* **67**: 333–350.

SCOTT, A. (1941). Reversal of sex production in *Micromalthus*. *Biol. Bull. mar. biol. Lab., Woods Hole.* **81**: 420–431.

SHAUMAR, N. (1966). Anatomie du système nerveux et analyse des facteurs externes pouvent intervenir dans le determinisme du sexe chez les Ichneumonidae Pimplinae. *Annls Sci. nat. Zool.* **8**: 391–493.

SOUMALAINEN, E. (1962). Significance of parthenogenesis in the evolution of insects. *A. Rev. Ent.* **7**: 349–366.

TOBE, S. S. and LANGLEY, P. A. (1978). Reproductive physiology of *Glossina*. *A. Rev. Ent.* **23**: 283–307.

WHITE, M. J. D. (1954). *Animal cytology and evolution.* Cambridge University Press.

WHITE, M. J. D. (1964). Cytogenetic mechanisms in insect reproduction. *Symp. R. ent. Soc. Lond.* **2**: 1–12.

WHITING, P. W. (1945). The evolution of male haploidy. *Q. Rev. Biol.* **20**: 231–260.

WYATT, I. J. (1961). Pupal paedogenesis in the Cecidomyiidae (Diptera).—I. *Proc. R. ent. Soc. Lond.* A, **36**: 133–143.

WYATT, I. J. (1963). Pupal paedogenesis in the Cecidomyiidae (Diptera).—II. *Proc. R. ent. Soc. Lond.* A, **38**: 136–144.

CHAPTER XX

HATCHING AND POSTEMBRYONIC DEVELOPMENT

When the larva is fully developed within the egg it escapes by rupturing the egg membranes and sometimes it has some special device which assists this process. In the course of hatching or immediately afterwards many insects shed an embryonic cuticle.

Once it has hatched the larva begins to feed and grow, but since the cuticle will only stretch to a limited extent growth is punctuated by a series of moults. The number of moults which occurs is variable, but is generally less in more advanced insects. In general, weight increases progressively, but linear measurements may increase in a series of steps corresponding with the moults, or more or less continuously if the cuticle is membranous, as it is in many larvae. It is common for different parts of the body to grow at different rates, so simple mathematical relationships often do not hold. Growth of the epidermis and internal organs may entail an increase in cell size or an increase in cell number.

Growth from larva to adult usually involves some degree of metamorphosis. In many insects the larval form is tied to that of the adult by morphogenetic considerations, but in others a pupal instar interposed between the last larval instar and the adult has permitted a great divergence of form and habitat between larva and adult. In these a great variety of larval forms occurs. Sometimes the larva changes its habits during the life history and there is a corresponding change of form, a phenomenon known as heteromorphosis.

Postembryonic development of the nervous system is reviewed by Edwards (1969). Lawrence (1973) discusses the possible mechanisms by which the development of cuticular patterns is regulated.

HATCHING

20.1 Escape from the egg

20.1.1 Hatching stimuli

The fully developed larva within the egg escapes by rupturing the vitelline membrane, the serosal cuticle when it is present (p. 417), and the chorion. The stimuli which promote hatching are largely unknown and in many cases insects appear to hatch whenever they are ready to do so. Even in these instances, however, it is possible that some external stimulus influences hatching.

In a few cases specific hatching stimuli are known. These vary, but are relevant to the insect concerned. The eggs of some *Lestes* (Odonata) species hatch when they are wetted provided the temperature is above a certain level. *Aedes* eggs hatch when immersed in deoxygenated water, the lower the oxygen tension the greater the percentage hatching (Fig. 286), but the responsiveness varies with age. The larvae are most sensitive soon after development is complete and will then hatch even in aerated water (Fig. 287), but if they are not wetted for some time they will only hatch at very low oxygen tensions. The low oxygen tension is perceived by a sensory centre in the head or thorax and maximum sensitivity coincides with a period of maximum activity of the central nervous system as indicated by the concentration of acetylcholine. Low oxygen tension has completely the opposite effect on the hatching of *Agabus* larvae, which only occurs in oxygenated water (Jackson, 1958).

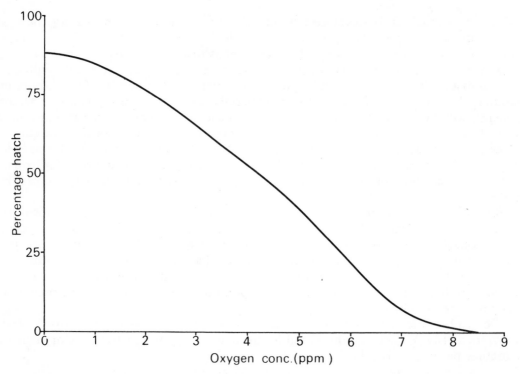

Fig. 286 The percentage of eggs of *Aedes* which hatch in water containing different concentrations of dissolved oxygen after incubation at 90–100% relative humidity (from Clements, 1963)

Amongst terrestrial insects the eggs of *Dermatobia* (Diptera) are stimulated to hatch by the warmth of host (p. 383), while in grasshoppers the mechanical disturbance produced by one larva hatching activates other, unhatched larvae in the egg pod so that they all hatch within a short time (Uvarov, 1966).

Suitable temperatures are necessary for all insect eggs to hatch and there is a threshold temperature below which hatching does not occur. This temperature varies in different insects, but is about 8°C for *Cimex*, 13°C for *Oncopeltus* and 20°C for *Schistocerca*. It is independent of the threshold temperature for full embryonic

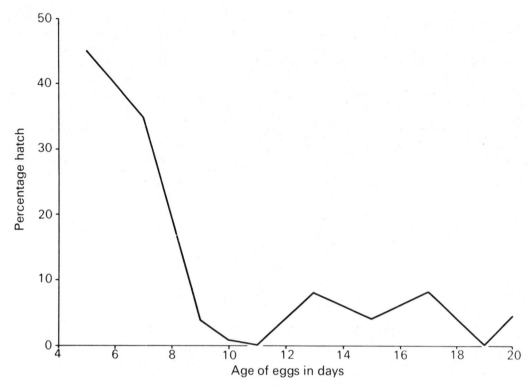

Fig. 287 The percentage of *Aedes* eggs of different ages which hatch under sub-optimal conditions, that is in aerated water. Only newly developed larvae hatch under these conditions, larvae which have remained some time in the egg require anaerobic conditions to induce them to hatch (after Judson *et al.*, 1965)

development, which may be either higher, as in *Cimex* (13°C), or lower, as in *Schistocerca* (about 15°C). The failure to hatch at low temperatures may be related to the inactivity of the larva. Newly emerged *Schistocerca* larvae, for instance, are not normally active below about 17°C and their activity remains sluggish below 24°C (Hussein, 1937), and *Cimex* is not normally active below 11°C. Further, temperatures must be sufficiently high for the enzyme digesting the serosal cuticle to function efficiently (see below).

The larvae of *Schistocerca* hatch mainly at about dawn. This is not an immediate response to the changing temperature of the surrounding soil, but results from an entrainment of activity to the 24-hour cycle of temperature changes during the last days of embryonic development (Padgham, 1981).

20.1.2 Mechanism of hatching

Most insects force their way out of the egg by exerting pressure against the inside of the shell, which comprises the serosal cuticle and the chorion. The volume of the body is increased by swallowing the extra-embryonic fluid and in some cases by swallowing air which diffuses through the shell. Then waves of muscular contraction pump haemolymph forwards and result in the head and thoracic regions being pressed tightly against the inside of the shell. In acridids these muscular waves are interrupted periodically by a sudden simultaneous contraction of the abdominal segments which causes a sudden increase in pressure in the anterior region. Within the neck and thorax are accessory muscles, some of which degenerate soon after hatching and which prevent expansion of the lateral and ventral body wall (Fig. 288B) but permit expansion dorsally of the neck membrane. This is developed into a pair of lobes, the cervical ampullae, which are inflated by the increase in pressure (Fig. 288A) and which serve to focus the pressure on a limited area of the shell. If the shell does not split, the ampullae are withdrawn and a further series of posterior – anterior waves of contraction follows, ending with another sudden abdominal contraction. It is one of these sudden contractions which ultimately ruptures the shell (Bernays, 1971a, 1972a).

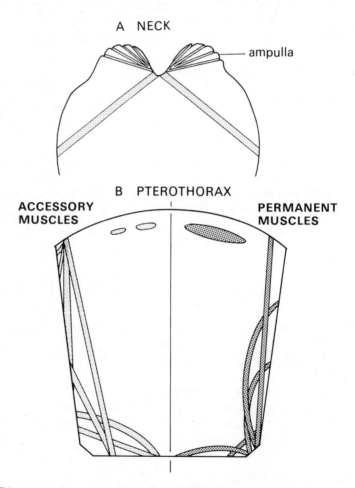

Fig. 288 Diagrammatic cross-sections through (A) the neck and (B) the pterothorax of a newly hatched first instar larva of *Schistocerca* showing the accessory muscles. All the muscles associated with the ampullae break down after hatching. In the pterothorax some muscles (right) persist throughout life while others (left) break down after the final moult (after Bernays, 1972a, 1972b)

Special muscles which break down soon after hatching are known to occur in *Acheta* as well as in acridids and may occur in other groups of insects. Muscles which are functional only at the time of the moult are known in other insects (p. 518).

In acridids the chorion is split transversely above the ampullae; in *Agabus* the split is longitudinal while in other cases it varies in position depending on where the pressure is exerted. In some species the split occurs along a predetermined line of weakness in the structure of the chorion. The egg of *Calliphora* has a pair of hatching lines running longitudinally along its length (Fig. 252) and in Heteroptera a hatching line runs round the egg where the cap joins the body of the egg shell (Fig. 223). *Aedes* has a line of weakness in the serosal cuticle and a split in the chorion follows this passively, perhaps because the serosal cuticle and chorion are closely bound (Judson and Hokama, 1965). In Acrididae, and probably in *Carausius* and in the Heteroptera which have a thick serosal cuticle, hatching is aided by an enzyme which digests the serosal endocuticle in the two days before hatching movements begin. The enzyme is produced by the pleuropodia, which are not covered by the embryonic cuticle and so they secrete it directly into the extra-embryonic space.

In a number of insects hatching is aided by cuticular structures, usually on the head, known as egg bursters. These are on the head of the embryonic cuticle of Odonata, Orthoptera, Heteroptera, Neuroptera and Trichoptera, but on the cuticle of the first instar larva in Nematocera, Carabidae and Siphonaptera. Their form varies, but in the pentatomids they are in the form of a T- or Y-shaped central tooth. Often, as in the fleas, mosquitoes and *Glossina*, the tooth is in a membranous depression which can be erected by blood pressure (Fig. 289A,B). In *Agabus* the egg burster is in the form of a spine on either side of the head, while in Cimicomorpha a row of spines runs along each side of the face from near the eye to the labrum (Fig. 289C). *Polyplax* (Siphunculata) has a pair of spines with lancet-shaped blades arising from depressions above them,

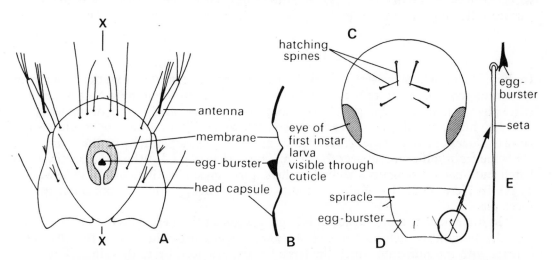

Fig. 289 Egg-bursters. A. The head of a first instar larva of *Aedes*. B. Diagrammatic vertical section through (A) along the line XX. C. Head of the embryonic cuticle of *Rhinocoris* (Heteroptera). D. Dorsal view of the eighth abdominal segment of the first instar larva of *Tenebrio*. E. Seta and egg-burster spine on (D) enlarged (after Marshall, 1938; Southwood, 1956; van Emden, 1946)

while in *Pediculus* (Siphunculata) there are five pairs of these blades and in *Haematopinus* nine or ten pairs.

Many Polyphaga have egg bursters on the thoracic or abdominal segments of the first instar larva (van Emden, 1946). For instance, in *Meligethes* there is a tooth on each side of the mesonotum and metanotum, while larval tenebrionids have a small tooth on either side of the tergum of these and the first eight abdominal segments (Fig. 289D,E).

It is not clear how these various devices function and Jackson (1958) believes that in *Agabus*, the egg of which has a soft chorion, they are no longer functional. In other cases they appear to be pushed against the inside of the shell until finally they pierce it and then a slit is cut by appropriate movements of the head. The larva of *Dacus* (Diptera) uses its mouth hooks in a similar way, repeatedly protruding them until they tear the chorion (Anderson, 1962). The blades in *Polyplax* and the spines in *Cimex* are used to tear the vitelline membrane, the chorion then being broken by pressure (Sikes and Wigglesworth, 1931).

Larval Lepidoptera gnaw their way through the chorion and after hatching they continue to eat the shell until only the base is left. In *Pieris brassicae*, where the eggs are laid in a cluster, a newly hatched larva may also eat the tops off adjacent unhatched eggs (David and Gardiner, 1962).

When the egg is enclosed in an ootheca the larva escapes from this after leaving the egg. In the Blattodea the ootheca is split open before hatching by the swelling of the eggs as they absorb water. Acridids, still enclosed in the embryonic cuticle, wriggle through the froth of the plug (Fig. 242). The head is thrust forwards through the substrate by an elongation of the abdomen, the tip of which is pressed against the substrate to give a point of support while the cervical ampullae are withdrawn. Then, when elongation is complete, the cervical ampullae are expanded to give a purchase while the abdomen is drawn up. By repeating this cycle the larva digs its way to the soil surface following the line of least resistance offered by the plug (Bernays, 1971b).

20.2 Intermediate moult

In those insects which possess an embryonic cuticle this separates from the underlying epidermis some time before hatching, but it is not shed, so when the larva hatches it is still a pharate first instar (p. 466). The embryonic cuticle is shed during or immediately after hatching and this process is commonly known as the intermediate moult. As the larva of *Cimex* or a louse emerges from the egg it swallows air and, by further pumping, splits the embryonic cuticle over the head. The cuticle is shed as the larva continues to hatch and finally it remains attached to the empty egg shell (Sikes and Wigglesworth, 1931). In Heteroptera the embryonic cuticle is attached inside the chorion at two or three places.

The intermediate moult in acridids begins as the larva emerges on the surface of the soil, the activities which lead to ecdysis being triggered by the lack of the all-round contact with the substrate which the larva has experienced up to that time. The larva swallows air and in this way increases its volume by about 25 %. Soon after the start of swallowing, waves of shortening and lengthening pass along the body of the larva causing it to move forwards within the apolysed, but still intact, embryonic cuticle. It maintains its forward position within the embryonic cuticle by backwardly directed spines on the abdominal sternites, and as a result of these movements the embryonic cuticle is pulled taught over the head and thorax and finally splits mid-dorsally. The first instar larval cuticle expands so that the insect swells out of the embryonic cuticle, which is worked backwards. It is held at the tip of the abdomen by two spiney knobs, called brustia, at the bases of the cerci so that the hind legs can be withdrawn and then finally it is kicked off the abdomen by the hind legs (Bernays, 1972b).

POSTEMBRYONIC DEVELOPMENT

The life history of an insect is divided into a series of stages, each separated from the next by a moult. The form which the insect assumes between moults is known as an instar, that which follows the intermediate moult being the first instar, which later moults to the second instar, and so on until at a final moult the adult or imago emerges. No further moults occur except in the Apterygota (p. 829).

20.3 Numbers of instars

Primitive insects usually have more larval instars than advanced species. Thus *Ephemera* and *Stenonema* (Ephemeroptera) moult 30 and 40–45 times respectively, while Heteroptera commonly have five larval instars and Nematocera only four. Even within a group of related insects there is variation and amongst the Acridoidea the Pyrgomorphidae have five or more larval instars while the Gomphocerinae, which are also usually smaller, have four.

The number of larval instars through which a species passes is not absolutely constant. In the Orthoptera, in which the female is bigger than the male, she commonly has an extra larval instar, while larvae emerging from small eggs grow slowly and have an additional instar. *Nomadacris* may have six, seven, or occasionally eight larval instars depending on the treatment of the parents (Albrecht, 1955). In *Plusia* and some other Lepidoptera, larvae reared in isolation may pass through five, six or seven instars, while nearly all of those reared in a crowd have only five (Long, 1953).

20.4 Growth

20.4.1 Weight

There is a progressive increase in weight throughout the larval instars and usually the rate of increase is greater in the later instars (Fig. 290). In Schistocerca the rate of increase in weight is greater in the female than in the male and her final weight is greater. From a hatching weight of about 18 mg the male grows to a weight of about 1400 mg on emergence and the female to about 1800 mg (Davey, 1954).

Typically the weight increases steadily throughout a stage of development and then falls slightly at the time of moulting due to the loss of the cuticle and the loss of some water, which is not replaced because the insect is not feeding. Following the moult the weight rapidly increases above its previous level (Fig. 290). In some aquatic insects the decrease in weight at the moult does not occur, but, conversely, there is a sharp increase due to the absorption of water, either through the cuticle or via the alimentary canal (Fig. 291).

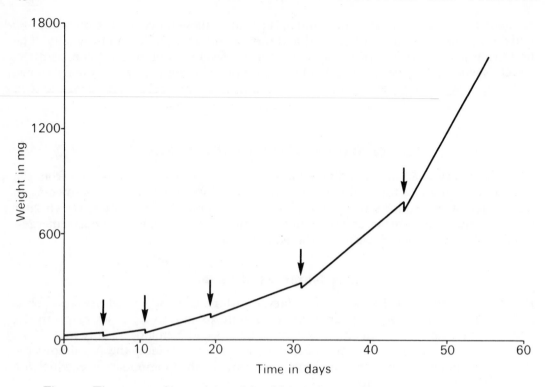

Fig. 290 The pattern of increase in weight of female *Locusta*. The times of the moults are indicated by arrows (after Clarke, 1957)

In blood-sucking insects, such as *Rhodnius*, which only feeds once during each instar, the pattern of growth is different. During the non-feeding period of each instar there will be a slow, steady loss in weight due to water loss and respiration, but feeding is accompanied by a sharp increase in weight followed by a fairly rapid fall as water is eliminated. There is, of course, a net increase in weight from one instar to the next.

The final weight of the adult insect varies according to the conditions under which the larva develops. Rapid development at high temperatures results in adults which are relatively light in weight. This occurs in *Dysdercus* (Heteroptera), for instance, but in this species an even greater reduction in weight is produced if the larvae do not have water for drinking. Crowding, possibly through its effect on the rate of development, also influences the adult size, insects from crowds being smaller than others bred in isolation. For instance, in one experiment on *Locusta*, Gunn and Hunter-Jones (1952) obtained adult females weighing 1·5 g from larvae reared in isolation, while others from larvae reared in crowds weighed only 1·2 g. Where isolation is correlated with the production of an extra larval instar the difference in weight may be even more marked. Finally, adult weight may be influenced by the food on which the larva is nourished. This is particularly well illustrated in phytophagous insects such as *Melanoplus* in which the weight of females varies from 140 mg to 320 mg depending on the food available (Pfadt, 1949).

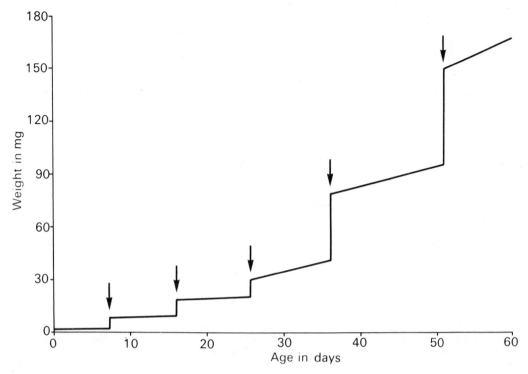

Fig. 291 The pattern of increase in weight of *Notonecta* (Heteroptera). Arrows indicate the times of the moults (from Wigglesworth, 1965)

20.4.2 Growth of the cuticle

Fully sclerotised cuticle does not expand, so growth of sclerotised parts only occurs when an insect moults and a new, soft cuticle is produced and expanded. Consequently the growth of hard parts occurs in a series of steps (Fig. 292). Membranous regions can expand, however, both by the pulling out of folds and by stretching the cuticle itself. Thus a structure with a wholly membranous cuticle, or one, such as the abdomen of *Locusta*, in which the membranes are extensive, may grow continuously (Fig. 292). Other regions in which there is rather less membrane show an intermediate type of growth with some extension occurring in the course of each instar together with a marked increase at each moult.

The extent to which sclerotised parts of the body increase in size from instar to instar varies. Dyar's law suggests that various parts of the body increase in linear dimensions by a ratio which is constant for the species (often about 1·4) and Przibram's rule suggests that the ratio by which cuticular structures increase in length at each ecdysis is constant, 1·26. However, Brown and Davies (1972) have shown that only a minority of the 74 cuticular structures of *Ectobius* which they studied fit these 'rules', which may be regarded as a guide to the order of magnitude of increase to be expected, but which are not rigidly applicable in all cases.

Different parts of the body grow at different rates when compared with some standard such as body length. If the rate of growth of the part, such as head width, is the

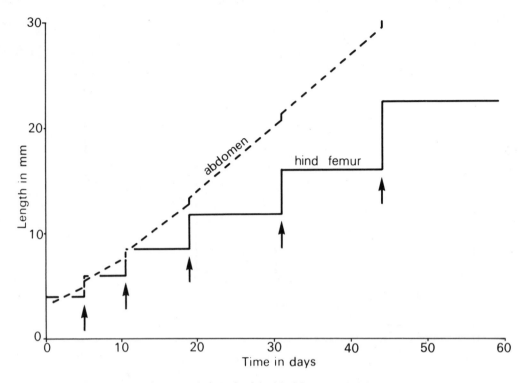

Fig. 292 The pattern of increase in length of the hind femur and abdomen of *Locusta*. Arrows indicate the times of the moults (after Clarke, 1957)

same as that of the standard, growth is said to be isometric; if the rate is different from the standard, growth is said to be allometric. If the part in question grows relatively faster than the standard, it exhibits positive allometry, while slower growth is negative allometry. For instance, in *Hemimerus* the meriston with the meristal annuli grows faster than the antenna as a whole, so that in the adult it contributes a greater proportion of the length than in the earlier instars (Fig. 293). Conversely the five apical segments grow more slowly than the whole antenna, so their final contribution is proportionately less than their original one.

The straight line relationship between two parts on a log./log. plot as illustrated in Figure 293 will only occur if the growth rates are consistent, but this is not always the case. In the first instar of *Dysdercus* the mesothorax grows at roughly the same rate as the body as a whole, but subsequently its growth is more rapid; the seventh abdominal segment grows slowly in the early instars, but very much faster in the final instar as the genitalia develop (Fig. 294). In none of the segments is growth relative to the body as a whole uniform throughout larval life (Blackith *et al.*, 1963). Similar variations in the rate of growth occur in *Ectobius* (Brown and Davies, 1972).

20.4.3 Growth of the tissues

The form of the cuticle depends on the epidermis, and growth of the epidermis may occur through an increase in cell number or an increase in cell size. Cell numbers

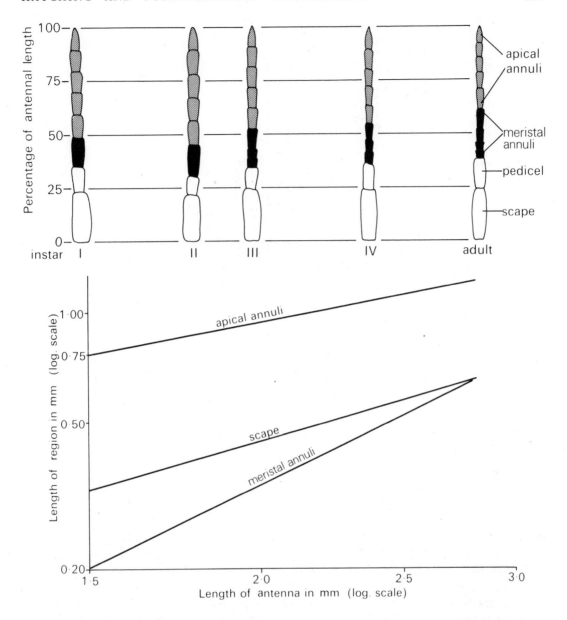

Fig. 293 Allometric growth in the antenna of *Hemimerus*. The diagram at the top illustrates the changes in the relative proportions of the different regions of the antenna in different instars. The graph shows these changes plotted against changes in the length of the antenna as a whole (after Davies, 1966)

increase just before moulting in many insects (p. 516), but in larval Cyclorrhapha the increase in size during larval life results, entirely from an increase in the size of the epidermal cells. In this case the nuclei also increase in volume as a consequence of becoming polytene (Fig. 295). This results in an increase in the amount of DNA present in each nucleus (Pearson, 1974). The number of cells in the epidermis

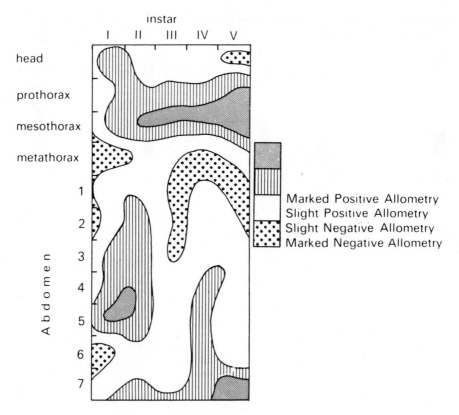

Fig. 294 Diagram showing the growth rates of different parts of the body of *Dysdercus* relative to the growth of the body as a whole in different larval instars (after Blackith *et al.*, 1963)

influences the numbers of setae which may develop on the cuticle (Lawrence, 1966a; Spickett, 1963; Wigglesworth, 1954).

As with the epidermis, increase in the size of an internal organ may result from an increase in cell size or in cell number. In the central nervous system of hemimetabolous insects growth does not involve new neurones except in the brain. In the terminal abdominal ganglion of *Acheta*, for example, there are about 2100 neurones at all stages of development, but these increase in volume. On the other hand the number of glial cells in the ganglion increases from about 3400 in the first instar to 20 000 in the adult and the volume of the ganglion is increased 40-fold. Neuroblasts, giving rise to new neurones, only persist in the brain after hatching in *Acheta*, but in *Gryllotalpa* they are also present in the segmental ganglia in the early stages of postembryonic development. In most holometabolous insects there is extensive reconstruction of the nervous system at metamorphosis and undifferentiated neuroblasts persist through the larval period up to this time (p. 422) (Edwards, 1969).

The nervous system and fat body of *Aedes* grow by an increase in cell number, but most other tissues in this insect and in *Drosophila* have a constant number of cells and grow by cell enlargement. This enlargement is accompanied by endomitosis and occurs, for instance, in the salivary glands, abdominal muscles and Malpighian tubules.

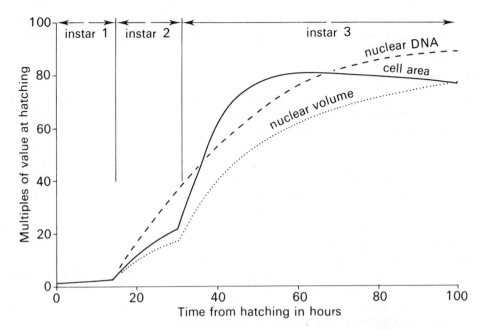

Fig. 295 Increase in epidermal cell area, nuclear volume and DNA content during development of the larva of *Calliphora*. Increase in each parameter is expressed in multiples of the initial value at the time of hatching (after Pearson, 1974)

In the midgut both processes occur; the epithelial cells enlarge, but ultimately break down during secretion and each is replaced by two or more small cells derived from the regenerative cells. In some other insects the whole of the midgut epithelium is replaced at intervals by the regenerative cells (p. 52). Oenocytes may be produced progressively, as in the water bugs, or the same cells may persist throughout larval life, becoming progressively bigger; in the last instar larva of *Drosophila* the oenocytes may be 80 μm in diameter. From this scant amount of data there is a general impression that tissues which are destroyed at metamorphosis grow by cell enlargement while those that persist in the adult grow by cell multiplication. Cell enlargement is perhaps less wasteful of time and energy than cell division.

The development of the Malpighian tubules varies. Henson (1944) differentiates between primary tubules, which arise as outpushings from the proctodaeum in the embryo, and secondary tubules, which develop later and largely post-embryonically. There are four primary tubules in *Blatta*, while some other insects have six. *Schistocerca* has six primary tubules, but twelve more are added before the larva hatches and more develop in each instar up to the adult (Fig. 376). Secondary tubules appear as buds at the beginning of each instar, but after their initial development they increase in length without further cell division as a result of an increase in cell size (Savage, 1956). The number of tubules similarly increases in each instar in *Carausius* and *Forficula*, and, in the latter, elongation of the existing tubules results partly from an increase in cell size, but also from rearrangement of the cells. At first each tubule consists of five rows of cells, but these later become rearranged to form two rows and so the tubule quickly trebles in length. In other insects, such as *Dysdercus* and *Pieris*, no increase in the number of Malpighian tubules occurs, but an increase in length again involves an increase in cell size and, particularly in *Pieris*, cell rearrangement.

20.4.4 Growth rate

The rate at which insects grow is influenced by the environment, and temperature is particularly important (p. 766). Within the limits of temperature which permit growth, development generally proceeds more rapidly at higher temperatures. Thus in *Dysdercus* the time from hatching to adult emergence is 49 days at 20°C, 35 days at 25°C and 25 days at 30°C. Humidity may also affect the rate of development. For instance, the larval development of *Locusta* occurs most rapidly between 60 and 70% relative humidity and mortality is also minimal within this range (Hamilton, 1950).

Availability of food is also important. If food is not available or is present in small quantities an insect may survive without growing for long periods. Thus a mosquito larva may survive for several months, although normally its development is complete in a few days, and the larvae of many blood-sucking bugs can survive for months without a meal, growth being initiated only when they feed (p. 829). The rate of development may be influenced by the type of food and *Plusia* develops more rapidly on dandelion than on dock (Long, 1953). In the laboratory increased amounts of glucose or amino acid in the diet of *Pseudosarcophaga* (Diptera) reduce its rate of development (and see Fig. 54) and also alter the effect of temperature on growth. Thus with no glucose in the diet the larva grows faster at 30°C, but with 2·25% glucose development is more rapid at 20°C (House, 1966).

Crowding tends to increase the rate of development quite apart from changes which may be induced in the number of instars. Crowded larvae of *Plusia*, for instance, develop in 75–80% of the time taken by isolated larvae and this reflects the fact that the crowded insects spend 25% more time feeding.

20.4.5 Control of growth

Larval growth is characterised by periodic moults and to some extent internal changes are correlated with the moulting cycle. Moulting is initiated by the growth and moulting hormone and at larval moults the effect of this hormone is modulated by the juvenile hormone so that larval genes are stimulated and hence larval characters are produced (p. 831).

While hormones exert an overall controlling influence, local factors, presumably chemical, control the form of particular areas. For instance, epidermal cells often show a distinct polarity, secreting cuticle in a form which gives an obvious anterior–posterior pattern. In the first instar larva of *Schistocerca* the cuticular plates associated with each epidermal cell on the sides of the abdominal sternites are produced into backwardly pointing spines; similarly, in *Oncopeltus* a row of spines marks the posterior end of the area of cuticle secreted by each of the cells forming the abdominal sternites; the scales of Lepidoptera grow out with a particular orientation. Experimental manipulation suggests that the polarity of the cells within a body segment is produced by a gradient of some diffusable substance. Similar gradients occur in each abdominal segment and probably also in the thoracic segments and legs. No chemical gradient has yet been discovered, although the results of transplant experiments are consistant with its existence (Lawrence, 1973).

In addition to having a particular orientation, cuticular structures are dispersed in regular patterns characteristic of the species. For instance, the abdominal tergites of larval *Rhodnius* bear a number of evenly-spaced sensilla. At each moult these increase in number, new sensilla being formed in the biggest gaps between the existing sensilla. This is consistent with the hypothesis that a determining substance present in the epidermis is absorbed by existing sensilla, but accumulates between them if they become widely spaced due to growth of the epidermis. If this concentration exceeds a certain threshold the development of a new sensillum is initiated. The development of sensilla on the adult cuticle of *Oncopeltus* can be accounted for in a similar way (Lawrence and Hayward, 1971).

Where two or more integumental features are present in an integrated pattern they may be controlled by the same substance. In *Rhodnius*, for instance, it is suggested that a differentiating substance in high concentration produces the sensilla and that the same substance in low concentration initiates the development of dermal glands, which are thus arranged round each sensillum. Where the integumental features are not arranged in an integrated manner, as with the hairs and scales on the abdomen of *Ephestia*, two determining substances might be involved (Lawrence, 1973).

There is relatively little information on the control of growth of internal organs, but some of these show cyclical activity which coincides with the moult. In the cells of the fat body of *Rhodnius*, for instance, there is a marked increase in the concentration of RNA and the number of mitochondria just before a moult and only at this time are the ventral abdominal intersegmental muscles fully developed (p. 518). In insects in which the Malpighian tubules increase in number, mitosis and development of new tubules are phased with respect to the moult. On the other hand, in locusts, protein synthesis is continuous in various internal organs.

20.5 Types of development

During larval development there is usually no marked change in body form, each successive instar being essentially similar to the one preceding it, but the degree of change from last instar larva to adult varies considerably and may be very marked. This change is called metamorphosis (Snodgrass, 1954; Wigglesworth, 1965) and it is possible to define it in physiological terms as the change which accompanies a moult in the absence of the juvenile hormone (p. 831). In morphological terms Snodgrass (1954) relates metamorphosis to the loss of adaptive features peculiar to the larva and this is a reflection of the degree of ecological separation of the larva from the adult. The term metamorphosis is sometimes applied to all the changes occurring in the life history, from egg to adult (see *e.g.* Imms, 1957), but it is better not to use it in this wide sense.

The insects can be grouped in three categories, ametabolous, hemimetabolous or holometabolous, according to the extent of the change at metamorphosis. Ametabolous insects have no metamorphosis, the adult form resulting from a progressive development of the larval form. This is characteristic of the Apterygota, in which the larvae emerge from the egg in a form which essentially resembles the adult apart from its small size and lack of development of genitalia. At each moult the larva grows bigger and the genitalia develop. Adults and larvae live in the same habitat.

In hemimetabolous insects the larvae hatch in a form which generally resembles the adult except for its small size and lack of wings and genitalia (Fig. 296), but in addition they usually show some other features which are characteristic of the larva and which do not occur in the adult. At the final moult these features are lost. The Orthoptera, Isoptera, Heteroptera and Homoptera are commonly regarded as hemimetabolous. Snodgrass (1954) calls these groups ametabolous or paurometabolous, that is with a very slight metamorphosis, but a quantitative analysis of growth changes in *Dysdercus* shows a gradual transformation through the larval instars and a sharp discontinuity at the moult from larva to adult. This discontinuity applies not to typical adult features

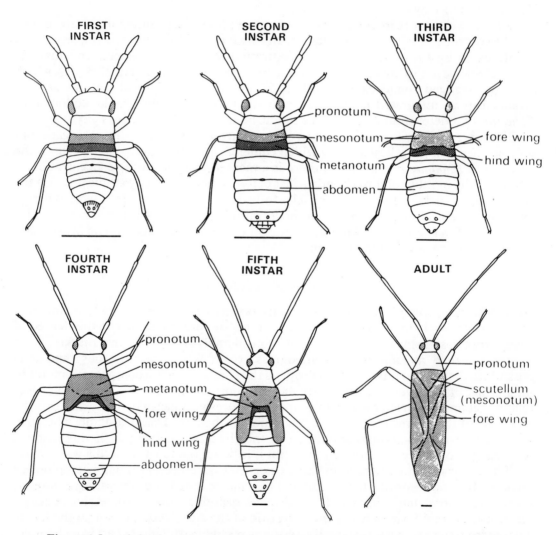

Fig. 296 Larval development of a hemimetabolous insect. The larva and adult stages of *Cyllecoris* (Heteroptera). The horizontal line under each stage represents 0.5 mm (after Southwood and Leston, 1959)

such as the wings and genitalia, but to other features which are not regarded as typically adult (Blackith *et al.*, 1963). There is thus quantitative evidence of a metamorphosis and one of the changes which occurs at this time in *Rhodnius* is the loss of the larval cuticle with its stellate folds and abundant plaques bearing sensilla and its replacement by the adult cuticle, which has transverse folds, a few sensilla and no plaques (Lawrence, 1966b; Locke, 1959).

The Plecoptera, Ephemeroptera and Odonata have aquatic larvae and the typically larval adaptations are much more marked than in the previous groups. Hence these forms undergo a more conspicuous metamorphosis involving, among other things, the loss of the gills (Fig. 297). The general body form, nevertheless, resembles that of the adult and these insects are also regarded as hemimetabolous.

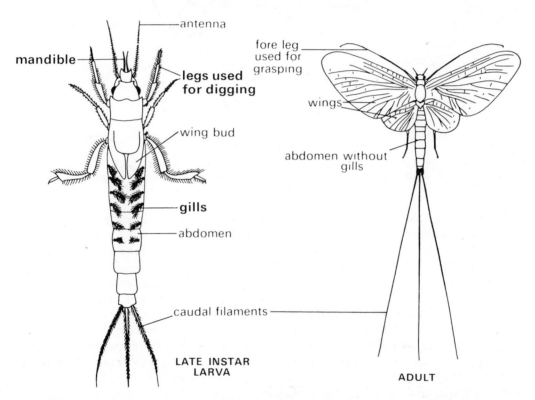

Fig. 297 Late larval instar and adult of *Ephemera*, a hemimetabolous insect showing conspicuous adaptive features in the larva. These features are indicated in heavy type (after Macan, 1961; Kimmins, 1950)

Finally, in holometabolous insects the larvae are quite unlike the adults and a pupal instar is present between the last larval instar and the adult (Fig. 298). The pupa is characteristic of holometabolous development, which occurs in all the Neuroptera, Trichoptera, Lepidoptera, Coleoptera, Hymenoptera, Diptera and Siphonaptera, in the Thysanoptera and Aleyrodidae, and in male Coccidae. The extensive differences between larval and adult structures are associated with the separation of larval and adult habitats. There is, however, no fundamental difference between the metamorphosis of

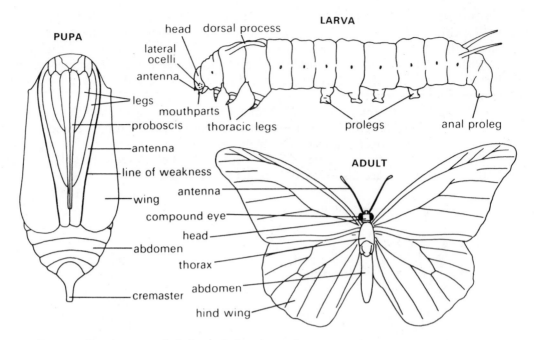

Fig. 298 Development of a holometabolous insect. Larva (lateral view), pupa (ventral view) and adult (dorsal view) of *Danaus* (Lepidoptera) (after Urquhart, 1960)

hemimetabolous insects and that of holometabolous insects, both being associated with a moult in the absence of juvenile hormone (p. 831).

Some difficulties in terminology arise because of variation in the intervals between different events in the moulting cycle. The term 'moult' as commonly used includes two distinct processes: apolysis, the separation of the epidermis from the cuticle; and ecdysis, the casting of the old cuticle after the production of a new one (p. 518). The terminology which has usually been applied to different stages, such as first instar larva, or pupa, refers to the outward appearance of the insect between ecdyses (Fig. 299), but Hinton (*e.g.* 1971) considers that each stage naturally extends from apolysis to apolysis. The importance of this distinction becomes apparent when extreme examples are considered. For instance, in cyclorrhaphan Diptera the cuticle of the last larval instar forms the puparium and from this the adult emerges (p. 475). There is nevertheless a normal pupal stage, which is always enclosed within the old larval cuticle. Some moths which diapause as adults do so within the pupal cuticle, so that they appear to be pupae although, in fact, they are adults. A stage which remains within the cuticle of a preceding stage is called a pharate instar.

It is most important that this pharate stage is recognised, especially in relation to the physiology and behaviour of insects. In exopterygote (hemimetabolous) insects and most endopterygote (holometabolous) larval stages the pharate stage remains relatively short (Fig. 299A), but it is often extended at the larval–pupal moult and pupal–adult moult (adult emergence) (Fig. 299B). The Cyclorrhapha represent an extreme condition (Fig. 299C).

In practice, however, the pharate stage is not always readily recognised and the

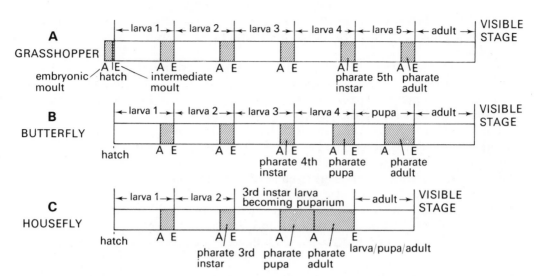

Fig. 299 Diagram showing the visible stages of development and the times of apolysis (A) and ecdysis (E), defining the pharate periods, in an exopterygote insect (grasshopper) and two endopterygotes (butterfly and housefly)

more usual terminology, with each stage extending from ecdysis to ecdysis, has been retained in this book, but reference is made to the pharate condition where it is known to occur.

20.6 Types of larvae

It is convenient, for descriptive purposes, to group the insect larvae into broad categories based on their general appearance. Larvae of hemimetabolous insects essentially resemble the adults and they are sometimes called nymphs to distinguish them from the more radically different larvae of holometabolous insects. The most conspicuous difference between hemimetabolous and holometabolous larvae is in the development of the wings. In the former the wings develop as external buds which become larger at each moult, finally enlarging to form the adult wings (Fig. 296). In the latter, however, the wings develop in invaginations beneath the larval cuticle and so are not visible externally (Fig. 311). The invaginations are finally everted so that the wings become visible externally when the larva moults to a pupa (Fig. 298). The separation of the forms exhibiting these types of development as nymphs and larvae respectively, however, suggests some basic difference between the two where none exists and the term nymph in this context is therefore better avoided.

There are many different larval forms amongst the holometabolous insects. The least modified with respect to the adult is the oligopod larva (but see also Chen, 1946). This is a hexapodous form with a well-developed head capsule and mouthparts similar to the adult, but no compound eyes. Two forms of oligopod larvae are commonly recognised: a campodeiform larva, which is well sclerotised, dorso-ventrally flattened and is usually a long-legged predator with a prognathous head (Fig. 300A); and a scarabaeiform larva, which is fat with a poorly sclerotised thorax and abdomen, and which is usually short-legged and inactive, burrowing in wood or soil (Fig. 300B). Campodeiform larvae occur in the Neuroptera, Trichoptera, Strepsiptera and some Coleoptera, while scarabaeiform larvae are found in the Scarabaeoidea and some other Coleoptera.

A second basic form is the polypod larva. This, in addition to the thoracic legs, has abdominal prolegs. It is generally poorly sclerotised and is a relatively inactive form living in close contact with its food (Fig. 300C). The larvae of Lepidoptera, Mecoptera and Tenthredinidae are of the polypod type.

The third basic form is the apodous larva, which has no legs and is very poorly sclerotised. Several different forms can be recognised according to the degree of sclerotisation of the head capsule:

eucephalous—with a well-sclerotised head capsule (Fig. 300D). Found in Nematocera, Buprestidae, Cerambycidae and Aculeata.

hemicephalous—with a reduced head capsule which can be retracted within the thorax (Fig. 300E). Found in Tipulidae and Brachycera.

acephalous—without a head capsule (Fig. 300F). Characteristic of Cyclorrhapha.

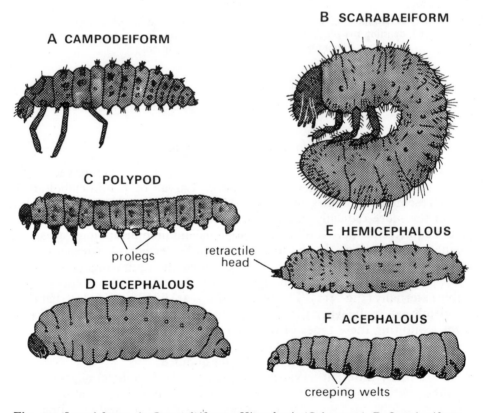

Fig. 300 Larval forms. A. Campodeiform—*Hippodamia* (Coleoptera). B. Scarabaeiform—*Popillia*. C. Polypod—*Neodiprion* (Hymenoptera). D. Eucephalous—*Vespula* (Hymenoptera). E. Hemicephalous—*Tanyptera* (Diptera). F. Acephalous—*Musca* (after Peterson, 1960, 1962; Hewitt, 1914)

Amongst the parasitic Hymenoptera the first instar larva hatches as a type known as a protopod larva. The protopod larva has many different forms and is often quite unlike a normal insect (see Fig. 302 and Clausen, 1940). These larvae hatch from eggs which contain very little yolk and some authorities regard them as embryos which hatch precociously (Chen, 1946), but others believe them to be specialised forms adapted to their peculiar environment (Snodgrass, 1954).

20.7 Heteromorphosis

In most insects development proceeds through a series of essentially similar larval forms leading up to metamorphosis, but sometimes successive instars have quite different forms, and development which includes such marked differences is termed heteromorphosis. (Hypermetamorphosis is commonly used for this type of development, but this implies the use of metamorphosis in the broad sense, referring to change of form throughout the life history.) Heteromorphosis is common in predaceous and parasitic insects in which a change in habit occurs during the course of larval development. Two types of heteromorphosis occur, one in which the eggs are laid in the open and the first instar larva searches for the host, and a second in which the eggs are laid in or on the host.

In the first type the first instar larva is an active form which, in Strepsiptera, for instance, is a campodeiform larva known as a triungulin (Fig. 301A). The triungulin attaches itself to a host when the latter visits a flower in which the larva is lurking. Subsequently it becomes an internal parasite and loses all trace of legs, while

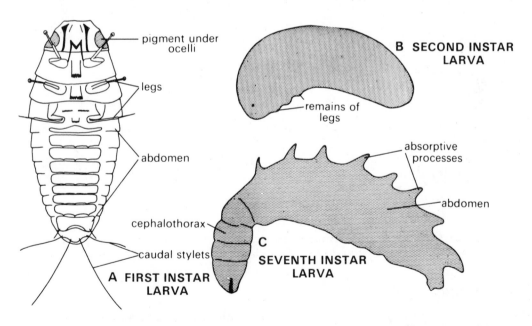

Fig. 301 Heteromorphosis. Larval stages of *Corioxenos* (Strepsiptera). A. Ventral view of the free-living first instar larva. B and C. Lateral views of older parasitic larvae (from Clausen, 1940)

developing a series of dorsal projections which increase its absorptive area. Later, in the sixth and seventh instars it develops a cephalothorax (Fig. 301B,C).

A basically similar life history with an active first instar larva followed by inactive parasitic stages occurs in Mantispidae (Neuroptera), Meloidae and some Staphylinidae (Coleoptera), Acroceridae, Bombyliidae and Nemestrinidae (Diptera), Perilampidae and Eucharidae (Hymenoptera) and Epipyropidae (Lepidoptera) (Clausen, 1940; Snodgrass, 1954).

The second type of heteromorphosis occurs in some endoparasitic Diptera and Hymenoptera. The first instar larva of *Cryptochaetum* (Diptera) has a pair of finger-like terminal processes which in the later instars develop into very long respiratory processes and greatly alter the appearance of the larva. A more marked heteromorphosis occurs in those Hymenoptera which hatch as protopod larvae. The braconid *Helorimorpha*, for instance, has a big head, a small unsegmented body and a tapering tail in the first instar (Fig. 302B). The third instar larva, on the other hand, is a fairly typical hymenopterous larva (Fig. 302C). In the Platygasteridae the first instar larva is even more specialised with an anterior cephalothorax bearing rudimentary appendages, a segmented abdomen and various tail appendages (Fig. 302A).

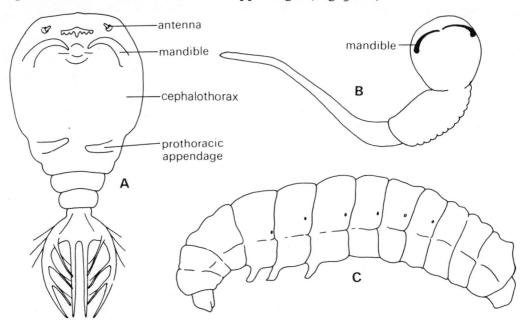

Fig. 302 Larvae of parasitic Hymenoptera. A. First instar larva of *Platygaster instricator*. B. First instar larva of *Helorimorpha*. C. Mature larva of *Helorimorpha* (from Snodgrass, 1954)

REFERENCES

ALBRECHT, F. O. (1955). La densité des populations et la croissance chez *Schistocerca gregaria* (Forsk.) et *Nomadacris septemfasciata* (Serv.); la mue d'adjustement. *J. Agric. trop. Bot. appl.* **11**: 109–192.

ANDERSON, D. T. (1962). The embryology of *Dacus tryoni* (Frogg.) (Diptera, Trypetidae (= Tephritidae)), the Queensland fruit-fly. *J. Embryol. exp. Morph.* **10**: 248–292.

BERNAYS, E. A. (1971a). Hatching in *Schistocerca gregaria* (Forskål) (Orthoptera: Acrididae). *Acrida* **1**: 41–60.

BERNAYS, E. A. (1971b). The vermiform larva of *Schistocerca gregaria* (Forskål): form and activity (Insecta: Orthoptera). *Z. Morph. Tiere* **70**: 183–200.

BERNAYS, E. A. (1972a). The muscles of newly hatched *Schistocerca gregaria* larvae and their possible functions in hatching, digging and ecdysial movements (Insecta: Acrididae). *J. Zool., Lond.* **166**: 141–158.

BERNAYS, E. A. (1972b). The intermediate moult (first ecdysis) of *Schistocerca gregaria* (Forskål) (Insecta: Orthoptera). *Z. Morph. Tiere* **71**: 160–179.

BLACKITH, R. E., DAVIES, R. G. and MOY, E. A. (1963). A biometric analysis of development in *Dysdercus fasciatus* Sign. (Hemiptera: Pyrrhocoridae). *Growth* **27**: 317–334.

BROWN, V. and DAVIES, R. G. (1972). Allometric growth in two species of *Ectobius* (Dictyoptera: Blattidae). *J. Zool., Lond.* **166**: 97–132.

CHEN, S. H. (1946). Evolution of the insect larva. *Trans. R. ent. Soc. Lond.* **97**: 381–404.

CLARKE, K. U. (1957). On the increase in linear size during growth in *Locusta migratoria* L. *Proc. R. ent. Soc. Lond.* A, **32**: 35–39.

CLAUSEN, C. P. (1940). *Entomophagous insects*. McGraw-Hill, New York.

CLEMENTS, A. N. (1963). *The physiology of mosquitoes*. Pergamon Press, Oxford.

DAVEY, P. M. (1954). Quantities of food eaten by the desert locust, *Schistocerca gregaria* (Forsk.), in relation to growth. *Bull. ent. Res.* **45**: 539–551.

DAVID, W. A. L. and GARDINER, B. O. C. (1962). Oviposition and the hatching of the eggs of *Pieris brassicae* (L.) in a laboratory culture. *Bull. ent. Res.* **53**: 91–109.

DAVIES, R. G. (1966). The postembryonic development of *Hemimerus vicinus* Rehn & Rehn (Dermaptera: Hemimeridae). *Proc. R. ent. Soc. Lond.* A, **41**: 67–77.

EDWARDS, J. S. (1969). Postembryonic development and regeneration of the insect nervous system. *Adv. Insect Physiol.* **6**: 97–137.

EMDEN, F. I. van (1946). Egg-bursters in some more families of polyphagous beetles and some general remarks on egg-bursters. *Proc. R. ent. Soc. Lond.* A, **21**: 89–97.

GUNN, D. L. and HUNTER-JONES, P. (1952). Laboratory experiments on phase differences in locusts. *Anti-Locust Bull.* no. **12**: 1–29.

HAMILTON, A. G. (1950). Further studies on the relation of humidity and temperature to the development of two species of African locusts—*Locusta migratoria migratorioides* (R. & F.) and *Schistocerca gregaria* (Forsk.). *Trans. R. ent. Soc. Lond.* **101**: 1–58.

HENSON, H. (1944). The development of the Malpighian tubules of *Blatta orientalis* (Orthoptera). *Proc. R. ent. Soc. Lond.* A, **19**: 73–91.

HEWITT, C. G. (1914). *The house-fly, Musca domestica Linn*. Cambridge University Press.

HINTON, H. E. (1971). Some neglected phases in metamorphosis. *Proc. R. ent. Soc. Lond.* C, **35**: 55–64.

HOUSE, H. L. (1966). Effects and interactions of varied levels of temperature, amino acids, and a vitamin on the rate of larval development in the fly *Pseudosarcophaga affinis*. *J. Insect Physiol.* **12**: 1493–1501.

HUSSEIN, M. (1937). The effect of temperature on locust activity. *Bull. Minist. Agric. Egypt. tech. scient. Serv.* no. 184, 55 pp.

IMMS, A. D. (1957). *A general textbook of entomology*. 9th edition, revised by Richards and Davies. Methuen, London.

JACKSON, D. J. (1958). Egg-laying and egg-hatching in *Agabus bipustulatus* L., with notes on oviposition in other species of *Agabus* (Coleoptera: Dytiscidae). *Trans. R. ent. Soc. Lond.* **110**: 53–80.

JUDSON, C. L. and HOKAMA, Y. (1965). Formation of the line of dehiscence in aedine mosquito eggs. *J. Insect Physiol.* **11**: 337–345.

JUDSON, C. L., HOKAMA, Y. and HAYDOCK, I. (1965). The physiology of hatching of aedine mosquito eggs: some larval responses to the hatching stimulus. *J. Insect Physiol.* **11**: 1169–1177.

KIMMINS, D. E. (1950). Ephemeroptera. *Handbk Ident. Br. Insects* 1, part 9.

LAWRENCE, P. A. (1966a). Development and determination of hairs and bristles in the milkweed bug, *Oncopeltus fasciatus* (Lygaeidae) (Hemiptera). *J. Cell Sci.* **1**: 475–498.

LAWRENCE, P. A. (1966b). The hormonal control of the development of hairs and bristles in the milkweed bug, *Oncopeltus fasciatus* Dall. *J. exp. Biol.* **44**: 507–522.

LAWRENCE, P. A. (1973). The development of spatial patterns in the integument of insects. *in* Counce, S. J. and Waddington, C. H. (eds.), *Developmental systems: insects.* Academic Press, London.

LAWRENCE, P. A. and HAYWARD, P. (1971). The development of a simple pattern: spaced hairs in *Oncopeltus fasciatus. J. Cell Sci.* **8**: 513–524.

LOCKE, M. (1959). The cuticular pattern in an insect, *Rhodnius prolixus* Stal. *J. exp. Biol.* **36**: 459–477.

LONG, D. B. (1953). Effects of population density on larvae of Lepidoptera. *Trans. R. ent. Soc. Lond.* **104**: 543–584.

MACAN, T. T. (1961). A key to the nymphs of the British species of Ephemeroptera. *Freshwater Biol. Assoc. Sci. Publ.* no. 20, 63 pp.

MARSHALL, J. F. (1938). *The British mosquitoes.* British Museum, London.

PADGHAM, D. E. (1981). Hatching rhythms in the desert locust, *Schistocerca gregaria. Physiol. Ent.* **6**: 191–198.

PEARSON, M. J. (1974). The abdominal epidermis of *Calliphora erythrocephala* (Diptera) I. Polyteny and growth in the larval cells. *J. Cell Sci.* **16**: 113–131.

PETERSON, A. (1960). *Larvae of insects. Part II. Coleoptera, Diptera, Neuroptera, Siphonaptera, Mecoptera, Trichoptera.* Columbus, Ohio.

PETERSON, A. (1962). *Larvae of insects. Part I. Lepidoptera and plant infesting Hymenoptera.* Columbus, Ohio.

PFADT, R. E. (1949). Food plants as factors in the ecology of the lesser migratory grasshopper, *Melanoplus mexicanus* (Sauss.) *Bull. Wyoming agric. Exp. Stn.* no. 290, 51 pp.

SAVAGE, A. A. (1956). The development of the Malpighian tubules of *Schistocerca gregaria* (Orthoptera). *Q. Jl microsc. Sci.* **97**: 599–615.

SIKES, E. K. and WIGGLESWORTH, V. B. (1931). The hatching of insects from eggs and the appearance of air in the tracheal system. *Q. Jl microsc. Sci.* **74**: 165–192.

SNODGRASS, R. E. (1954). Insect metamorphosis. *Smithson. misc. Collns.* **122**, no. 9, 124 pp.

SOUTHWOOD, T. R. E. (1956). The structure of the eggs of the terrestrial Heteroptera and its relationship to the classification of the group. *Trans. R. ent. Soc. Lond.* **108**: 163–221.

SOUTHWOOD, T. R. E. and LESTON, D. (1959). *Land and water bugs of the British Isles.* Warne, London.

SPICKETT, S. G. (1963). Genetic and developmental studies of a quantitative character. *Nature, Lond.* **199**: 870–873.

URQUHART. F. A. (1960). *The monarch butterfly.* University of Toronto Press.

UVAROV, B. P. (1966). *Grasshoppers and locusts*, vol. 1. Cambridge University Press.

WIGGLESWORTH, V. B. (1954). *The physiology of insect metamorphosis.* Cambridge University Press.

WIGGLESWORTH, V. B. (1965). *The principles of insect physiology.* Methuen, London.

CHAPTER XXI

METAMORPHOSIS

The changes which occur in the transformation of the larva to the adult may be more or less extensive depending on the degree of difference between the larva and the adult. Where the larva and adult are similar metamorphosis is relatively slight, but if the larva differs markedly from the adult a pupal instar may precede the adult. The pupa is probably to be regarded as the equivalent of the last larval instar of hemimetabolous insects and is a prerequisite for the greater divergence of larval and adult forms, permitting the larva to invade entirely new habitats. During the pupal period reconstruction of the tissues takes place involving particularly the eversion and growth of the wings and the development of the flight muscles.

Since the pupa is generally immobile and therefore vulnerable most insects pupate in a concealed cell or cocoon and they employ various means of escaping from this when they emerge as adults. Adult eclosion is often synchronised.

Insect pupae and their significance are considered by Hinton (1946, 1948, 1963), the morphological aspects of metamorphosis by Snodgrass (1954), the biochemical aspects by Agrell and Lundquist (1973) and Thomson (1975), and the physiological aspects by Wigglesworth (1964). Gehring and Nothiger (1973) review the development of imaginal discs in *Drosophila*.

21.1 The pupa

21.1.1 Form of the pupa

In the pupa of holometabolous insects all the features of the adult become recognisable and the pupa shows a greater resemblance to the adult than to the larva. At the larva–pupa moult the wings and other features which have been developing internally in the larva are everted and so become visible although they are not fully expanded to the adult form (Fig. 298). In some pupae the appendages are free from the body and this condition is known as exarate, but in many others the appendages are glued down to the body by a secretion produced at the larva–pupa moult. This is the obtect condition and obtect pupae are usually more heavily sclerotised than are exarate pupae. A further differentiation can be made on the presence or absence of articulated mandibles in the pupa. When articulated mandibles are present, the decticous condition, they have apodemes which fit closely inside the mandibular apodemes of the adult (Fig. 303) and hence they can be moved by the mandibular muscles of the pharate adult. The alternative condition with immobile mandibles is known as adecticous.

Decticous pupae are always exarate. They occur in Megaloptera, Neuroptera, Trichoptera and some Lepidoptera. Some adecticous pupae are also exarate as in

473

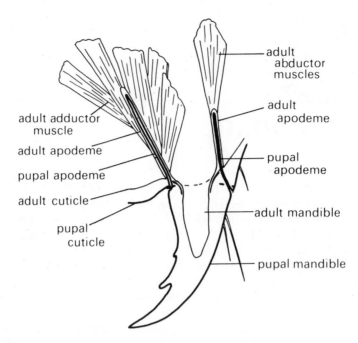

Fig. 303 Diagrammatic section through a mandible of a decticous pupa showing the pupal apodemes inside the adult apodemes (after Hinton, 1946)

Cyclorrhapha, Siphonaptera and most Coleoptera and Hymenoptera, but others are obtect. Most Lepidoptera, Nematocera, Brachycera, Staphylinidae, some Chrysomelidae and many Chalcidoidea have obtect, adecticous pupae.

Prepupa

The last instar larva is often quiescent for two or three days before the ecdysis to a pupa and in some cases the insect is a pharate pupa for a part of this time. This stage is sometimes known as a prepupa, but it does not usually represent a distinct morphological stage. A separate morphological stage known as the prepupa does exist in Thysanoptera and male Coccidae. In these insects the prepupa is a quiescent instar following the last larval instar and it is succeeded by a second, quiescent, pupal instar.

21.1.2 Protection of the pupa

The pupa of most insects is an immobile and hence vulnerable stage and a majority of insects pupate in a cell or cocoon which affords them some protection. Many larval Lepidoptera construct an underground cell in which to pupate, cementing particles of soil with a fluid secretion. *Cerura* (Lepidoptera) constructs a chamber of wood fragments glued together to form a hard enclosing layer and some coleopterous larvae pupate in cells in the wood in which they bore. Many larvae produce silk, which may be used to hold other structures, such as leaves, together to form a chamber for the pupa, while in other species a cocoon is produced wholly from silk (Fig. 304B). Silken cocoons are produced by Bombycoidea amongst the Lepidoptera and by Siphonaptera, Trichoptera and some Hymenoptera.

In *Antheraea* cocoon formation takes about two days. It follows gut purging, in which the larva expels the gut contents by a series of waves of contraction passing along the abdomen from front to back. Subsequently the larva enters an active wandering phase, which ends when it finds a suitable site in which to pupate. The first phase of cocoon formation is the construction of a scaffold of silk threads between leaves of the foodplant and the production of a stalk which attaches the cocoon to the leaf petiole. Subsequent behaviour consists of a series of cycles in which the insect weaves loops of silk by figure-of-eight movements of the head to construct one end of the cocoon and then turns through 180° to form the other end. After a period of about 14 h, by which time a complete layer of silk has been produced, the insect turns from one end of the cocoon to the other at much shorter intervals (5 min as compared with 80 min at 23°C) and at the same time it coats the inside of the cocoon with a liquid from the anus containing crystals of calcium oxalate. This liquid accumulates in the hindgut after purging and the calcium oxalate is produced by the Malpighian tubules (Lounibos, 1976). The hydration of the silk by the secretion promotes cross-linking, tanning, of the silk protein sericin and the wall of the cocoon becomes stiff and coloured yellow-brown. This period of impregnation of the cocoon lasts for about an hour. After it, more silk is added to the inside of the cocoon, but the cycles of spinning are interrupted by periods of inactivity which become longer until the larva becomes completely quiescent (Lounibos, 1975).

The behaviour sequence starting with gut purging is initiated by ecdysone production in the absence of the juvenile hormone (p. 829; Fig. 553).

An exceptional protective structure is produced by the larvae of cyclorrhaphous Diptera from the cuticle of the last instar larva. Procuticle is laid down throughout the last larval instar and at the end of this stage the larva rounds off and the outer part of the cuticle is tanned (p. 522) to form a rigid ovoid structure. The larva moults to the pupa, but its newly tanned and shaped cuticle remains unshed round the outside of the pupa, forming a protective structure known as the puparium (Fig. 304C). A thin membrane which adheres to the inside of the tanned cuticle probably represents the inner, untanned part of the larval cuticle, but alternatively, it is suggested that the larva undergoes an additional moult within the puparium to produce the pupa, and the thin membrane represents the cast cuticle from this moult (Whitten, 1957).

A few insects form unprotected pupae. These are particularly well known in the Nymphalidae and Pieridae, where the pupae are suspended from a silk pad. These exposed pupae exhibit homochromy (p. 143) whereas protected pupae are normally brown or very pale in colour.

21.1.3 Pupae of aquatic insects

The behaviour of aquatic insects on pupation varies considerably. Some larvae, such as the aquatic Arctiidae, Syrphidae and *Hydrophilus*, leave the water and pupate on land, but many others, particularly the aquatic Diptera, pupate in the water. Sometimes the pupae are fastened to the substratum. For instance, the pupae of Blepharoceridae have ventro-lateral pads on the abdomen with which they hold to stones, while Simuliidae construct open cocoons attached to stones and rocks (Fig. 304A). The pupa projects

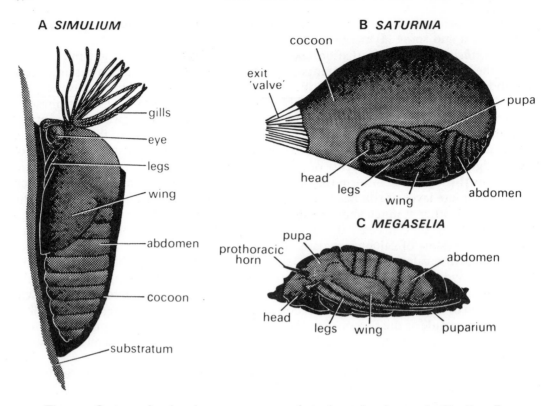

Fig. 304 Cocoons of various insects cut away to show the enclosed pupa. A. *Simulium*. B. *Saturnia*. C. Puparium of *Megaselia* (Diptera) (after various authors)

from the open end of the cocoon, which is constructed more strongly in faster flowing water than it is in a weak current. Chironomidae pupate in the larval tubes or imbedded in the mud, while *Acentropus* (Lepidoptera) forms a silken cocoon with two chambers separated by a diaphragm. The pupa is in the lower chamber, which is air-filled. In all these species oxygen is obtained from that dissolved in the water.

Other aquatic pupae obtain oxygen from the air, either directly or indirectly. The pupae of most Culicidae and Ceratopogonidae are free-living and active. They are buoyant so that, undisturbed, they rise to the surface and respire via prothoracic respiratory horns (Fig. 305). If disturbed their activity drives them downwards and the anal paddles assist in this movement. The pupae of some Culicidae and Ephydridae have their respiratory horns imbedded in the tissues of aquatic plants, obtaining their oxygen via the aerenchyma (p. 558).

21.1.4 Significance of the pupa

The pupa is indicative of the broad differences which occur between larval and adult forms of holometabolous insects. It is a stage during which major internal reconstruction may occur, but possibly its greatest importance is in permitting the full development of the wings. The internal development of the wings within the larva is

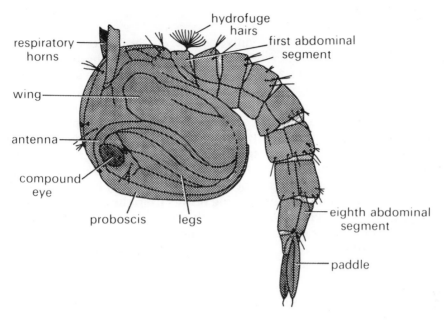

Fig. 305 The pupa of a mosquito (after Marshall, 1938)

restricted by lack of space and this problem becomes more acute as the insect approaches the adult condition and the flight muscles also increase in size. Thus development can only be completed after the wings are everted and for this reason two moults are necessary in the transformation from larva to adult. At the first, from larva to pupa, the wings are everted and grow to some extent. Further growth occurs and the adult cuticle is laid down at the pupa–adult moult (Hinton, 1963).

Two moults may also be necessitated by extensive modification to the muscular system which occur at this time. Commonly all the muscles of the adult thorax are different from those of the larva and they are not attached to the pupal cuticle. It has been suggested that muscles will only develop in an appropriate form and length if they have a mould in which to do so. The pupa provides a mould for the adult muscles.

The importance of the pupa in wing development and associated changes is emphasised by the absence of a pupal instar in the life histories of female Strepsiptera and Coccidae, which are wingless and larviform. The males in these groups are winged and have a pupal instar.

The pupa is probably best regarded as equivalent to and derived from the last larval instar of hemimetabolous insects, but for a summary of this and other points of view see Hinton (1963) and Thomson (1975).

21.2 Development of adult features

Adult features may appear at the final moult, but commonly they undergo a progressive development through the larval instars. This is most obvious in hemimetabolous insects, but is equally true of many features of holometabolous insects.

21.2.1 Hemimetabolous insects

Epidermal mitosis and expansion only occurs at the time of a moult and in hemimetabolous insects a progressive development of the wing buds occurs at each moult. Apart from their small size the wing buds differ from the adult wings in being continuous sclerotisations with the terga and pleura; the basal region of the wing is not membranous and no accessory sclerites are present. These appear at the final moult.

In general the wings arise in such a way that the lateral margins of the wing buds become the costal margins of the adult wings (Fig. 296), but in Odonata the buds arise in an erect position, the margin nearer the midline ultimately becoming the costal margin (Fig. 306). The wing buds of Acrididae originate as simple outgrowths of the terga as in Heteroptera, but at the antepenultimate moult they become twisted into the position found in the Odonata. This twisting results from the lower epidermis growing more rapidly than the upper. At the final moult the wings twist back so that the costal margin of the folded wings is ventral in position.

In *Locusta* and dragonflies all the flight muscles are present in the larva, although some are histologically distinct, lacking striations and presumably being nonfunc-

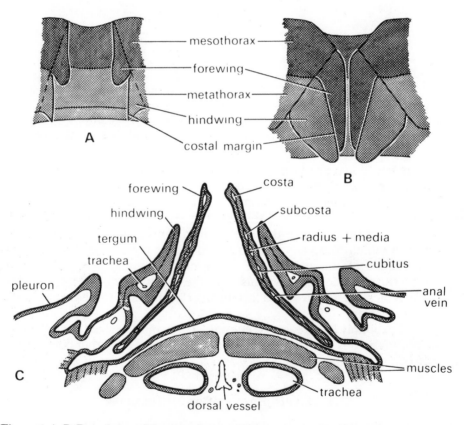

Fig. 306 A, B. Dorsal view of the pterothorax of (A) young and (B) older larvae of a dragonfly showing the wing buds. C. Transverse section though the dorsal part of the metathorax of a dragonfly larva (from Comstock, 1918)

tional. These muscles increase in size in various ways throughout the larval period. In Orthoptera they grow by the division of the existing elements; in Cicadellidae and some other Homoptera free myoblasts are incorporated into existing rudiments, while in *Bathylus* (Homoptera) both fibre division and myoblast incorporation occur. The incorporation of free myoblasts apparently takes place through a localised gap in the sarcolemma (Hinton, 1959; Tiegs, 1955). Further changes occur in the muscles in the young adult (p. 275). The phragmata to which the dorsal longitudinal flight muscles are attached become progressively bigger at each moult (Thomas, 1954).

Although accessory wing sclerites are not developed in the larva, the muscles which become attached to them in the adult are attached to appropriate positions on the larval cuticle. For instance, in *Locusta* the promotor–extensor muscle of the mesothoracic wing is inserted into the first basalar sclerite, but the equivalent muscle of the metathoracic wing is inserted into both basalar sclerites. In the larvae, although the sclerites are not developed, the muscle in the mesothorax has one point of attachment to the pleural cuticle, while that in the metathorax is attached at two points (Thomas, 1954).

The genitalia develop progressively by modification of the terminal abdominal segments (Fig. 307).

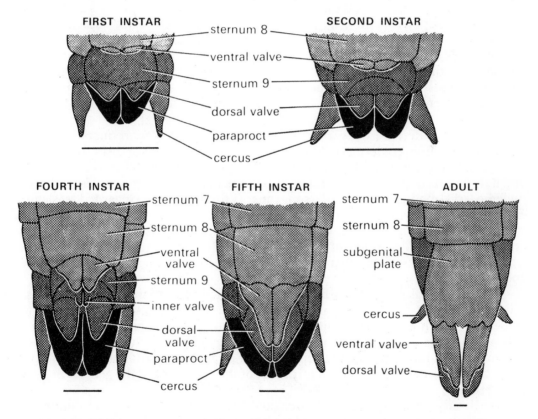

Fig. 307 Ventral view of the tip of the abdomen of various instars of the female *Eyprepocnemis* (Orthoptera) showing development of the genitalia. Horizontal bars under each figure represent 0.5 mm. (after Jago, 1963)

21.2.2 Holometabolous insects

The development of adult features in holometabolous insects varies in the degree of modification of larval features which is involved. In Neuroptera and Coleoptera, where the larvae have some resemblance to the adults, relatively little reconstruction occurs, but in Diptera the tissues are almost completely rebuilt following histolysis and phagocytosis of the larval tissues. It is generally agreed that phagocytes are not involved in the initial breakdown, but only attack tissue which is in the process of being histolysed.

Appendages

The development of adult appendages, including the mouthparts and antennae, may begin in the early larval instars and rudiments are commonly present in the embryo. If the adult appendage does not differ markedly from that of the larva it may be formed by a proliferation of the tissue within and at the base of the larval organ. This occurs in the legs of *Pieris*, for instance. Soon after the larva enters its final instar the epidermis becomes separated from the cuticle except at points of muscle attachment, so that it is free to thicken and fold. The first thickening, well supplied with tracheae, develops at the junction of the second and third leg joints (Fig. 308A) and from this a wave of cell multiplication spreads out (Fig. 308B,C). As a result of the increase in area the epidermis becomes folded and a particularly large fold develops basally. Later, when the epidermis expands to form the pupal leg, this basal fold is divided by a longitudinal septum to form the femur and tibia. Epidermis from the more proximal parts of the larval leg forms the coxa and trochanter, and more distal tissue forms the tarsus. Further differentiation continues in the pupa to produce the adult leg (Fig. 308E) (Kim, 1959).

Where the difference between larval and adult organs is more marked the adult tissues develop from epidermal thickenings called imaginal buds or discs. In Diptera all the main adult features develop in this way (Fig. 309) and since the production of adult organs is thus restricted to small groups of cells the remainder of the epidermis is free to undergo larval modifications (Anderson, 1964). The discs may be regarded as islands of embryonic tissue which remain undifferentiated until they give rise to the adult structures. They do not produce cuticle in the larva and the cells may continue to divide at all times, being independent of, or reacting in a different way to, the hormonal system which regulates growth in other parts of the epidermis (Schneiderman and Gilbert, 1964).

The imaginal disc commonly becomes invaginated beneath the larval epidermis. In this way a cavity, the peripodial cavity is formed (Fig. 310A,B). It is lined with epidermis known as the peripodial membrane and as the imaginal disc enlarges the appendage forms and evaginates into the cavity (Fig. 310C). As the appendage grows it becomes folded inside the cavity until finally, at pupation, the rudiment is everted and the peripodial membrane comes to form part of the epidermis of the general body wall (Fig. 310D,E).

The details of development of the imaginal discs vary from one insect to another and from organ to organ. Where an appendage is present in the larva as well as the adult the imaginal disc is closely associated with the larval structure. Thus in *Pieris* the adult antenna is first apparent in the first larval instar as an epidermal thickening at the base of

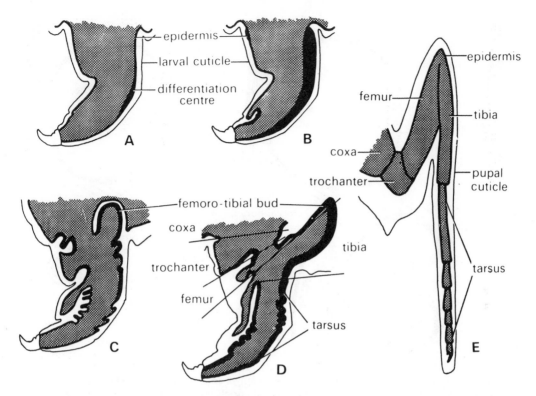

Fig. 308 Development of the adult leg in *Pieris*. A. Section through a leg of a last instar larva three hours after moulting. B. One day after moulting. C. Three days after moulting. D. Just before pupation. E. Section though a leg of a pupa. In (D) the presumptive areas of the adult leg are indicated (after Kim, 1959)

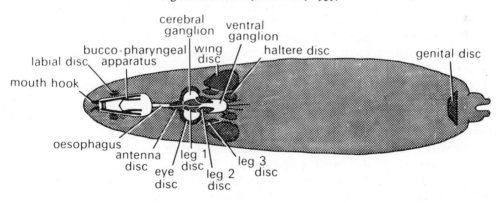

Fig. 309 Imaginal discs of a mature larva of *Drosophila* seen from the ventral surface (after Bodenstein, 1950)

the larval antenna. The cells divide and in the succeeding instars an invagination is produced which pushes upwards deep into the larval head. In the fifth larval instar the adult antennal tissue grows more quickly than the peripodial membrane, so that it is thrown into folds and towards the end of the instar the larval antenna starts to

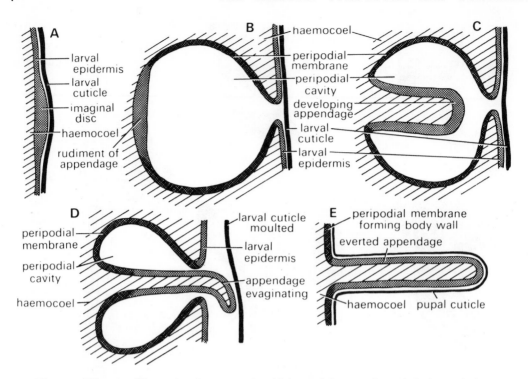

Fig. 310 Diagrams illustrating the manner in which an adult appendage of a holometabolous insect may develop in a cavity beneath the larval cuticle. A–C. In the developing larva. D. Larva in the process of moulting. E. Pupa with appendage everted

degenerate and is invaded by imaginal cells. When the peripodial cavity, which opens by a slit on the front of the epidermis of the head, evaginates, the antenna is carried to the outside and the peripodial membrane now forms a part of the wall of the head. The maxilla develops in an essentially similar way, but very little development of the labium takes place until the fifth instar (Eassa, 1953).

The wings also develop from imaginal discs. In some Coleoptera they form as simple evaginations of the epidermis beneath the larval cuticle, but more usually they develop in peripodial cavities. In *Pieris* the imaginal disc is already apparent in the embryo and it invaginates in the second and third larval instars (Fig. 311). In the fourth instar the wing starts to develop as an evagination within the peripodial cavity, finally becoming everted at the larva–pupa moult. In *Drosophila*, on the other hand, invagination of the peripodial cavity is complete before the larva hatches, but the wing thickening does not develop until the second instar, growing more extensively in the third instar and becoming evaginated at the moult to the pupa.

The internal development of the wings is complex, involving great expansion and the formation of the veins. The development of a wing of *Drosophila* is used as an example. When the puparium is formed the wing projects backwards as a hollow cylinder of cells. The upper and lower surfaces come together except along certain lines which remain as lacunae (Fig. 312A,B) and where they meet their basement membranes may fuse to form a central membrane, but this soon disappears. There are four

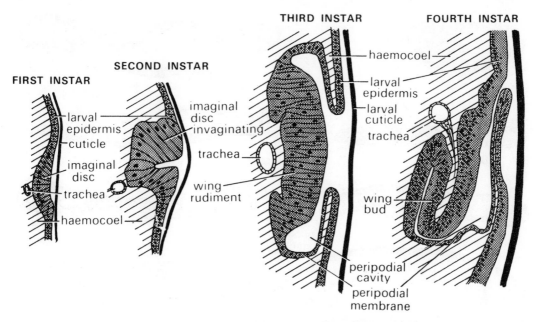

Fig. 311 Sections through the developing wing bud in the first four larval instars of *Pieris* (from Comstock, 1918)

lacunae running along the length of the wing rudiment, the second dividing into two distally. A nerve and a trachea enter the second lacuna, and at about this stage, some six hours after the formation of the puparium, the pupal cuticle is laid down. Afer this the upper and lower surfaces of the wing are forced apart by an increase in blood pressure (Fig. 312C,D). The cells at first become stretched across the gap as narrow threads connecting the two surfaces, but finally these connections are broken except at the margins. A less extensive inflation occurs in *Tenebrio* and *Habrobracon* (Hymenoptera). Perhaps the inflation has the effect of expanding the newly formed pupal cuticle to the greatest possible extent so that the development of the adult wing can proceed.

Following the inflation, the wing contracts again. The epidermal layers on the two sides first become apposed round the edges (Fig. 312E) and then the contraction spreads inwards so that a flat double membrane is produced (Fig. 312F). During this process the definitive wing veins are formed along lines where the two epidermal layers remain separated (Fig. 312G). The veins are at first wide channels, but ultimately they become narrower as the membrane continues to expand. Cell division proceeds actively, especially above the veins, so that here the cells become crowded and columnar, while elsewhere they are flattened. The fully developed wing finally secretes the adult cuticle (Fig. 312H) (Waddington, 1941).

Epidermis

When the imaginal appendages are everted from the peripodial cavities at the time of pupation the peripodial membrane contributes to the general epidermis of the adult body wall (Fig. 310). The extent to which the larval epidermis is replaced varies. In

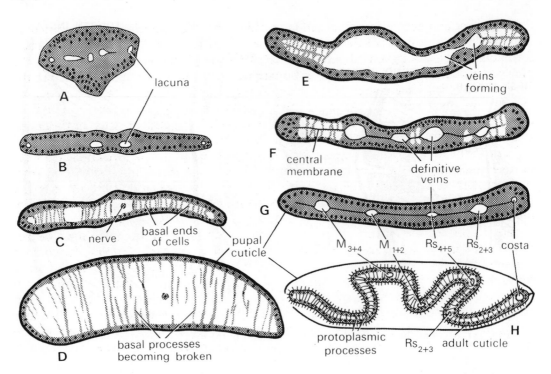

Fig. 312 Diagrammatic transverse sections of a developing wing of *Drosophila*. A, B. Successive stages in the resting larva before pupation. C–G. Further stages in the pupa. H. Pharate adult (after Waddington, 1941)

Coleoptera there is no extensive replacement, but in Hymenoptera and Diptera the epidermis is completely renewed from imaginal discs. The epidermis of the head and thorax are formed by growth from the imaginal appendage discs, while the abdominal epithelium is formed from special imaginal discs. In *Drosophila* most abdominal segments have pairs of dorsal, ventral and spiracular discs which expand to form the adult epidermis. As they do so the larval cells are sloughed off into the body cavity and are phagocytosed.

Muscles

The muscular system usually undergoes extensive modification at metamorphosis and the muscles fall into five categories according to their fate at this time:

1. Larval muscles may pass unchanged into the adult. This applies to some abdominal muscles.

2. Existing larval muscles are reconstructed.

3. Larval muscles may be destroyed and not replaced.

4. Larval muscles are destroyed, but are replaced in the adult by new muscles.

5. New muscles, not represented in the larva, may be formed.

In general larval muscles are histolysed and adult muscles rebuilt in the pupa, but the precise timing varies because some larval muscles have specific functions in pupal development and are destroyed much later than some other muscles. For instance, in *Drosophila* most muscles of the head and thorax start to break down before puparium formation and are fragmented before the larva pupates, but the dilator muscles of the pharynx remain unchanged until after pupation. They apparently are important in the evagination of the head region of the insect at pupation and after this they degenerate. In addition, one pair of muscles persists in each abdominal segment for about half the pupal period. It is suggested that they help to establish the segmentation of the pupal abdomen by telescoping each segment into the preceding one.

The first sign of muscle degeneration is liquefaction of the peripheral parts of the fibre. This is followed by a separation of the fibrils and in *Ephestia* phagocytes penetrate the sarcolemma and assist the destruction. The sarcolemma breaks down and the muscles separate from their attachments and fragment, the remains being consumed by phagocytes.

New muscles are always formed by free myoblasts, but muscles may be reconstructed in two ways. In the Neuroptera and Coleoptera the larval muscles contain two sets of nuclei, the functional larval nuclei and other small nuclei which are scattered through the cytoplasm. At metamorphosis the small nuclei multiply and, with associated cytoplasm, form myocytes. These migrate into the body of the muscle and associate in strands to form new fibres. In Diptera and some Hymenoptera, on the other hand, myoblasts which originate outside the larval muscle are concerned in the production of adult muscle, adhering to the outside or penetrating the sarcolemma in order to form new fibres.

Sometimes, as in *Simulium* and chironomids, the adult muscles are already present in the larva as rudimentary non-functional fibres. The dorsal longitudinal muscles in *Simulium*, for instance, are only about four microns in diameter in the first larval instar. They grow throughout the larval period and their nuclei increase in number. During the pharate pupal period they become divided up to produce the definitive number of fibres and at this time also myofibrils appear for the first time. They continue to grow until some time after the final moult (Hinton, 1959).

Alimentary canal

The alimentary canal is extensively remodelled at metamorphosis in species which have different larval and adult diets. In larval Lepidoptera, for instance, the midgut occupies most of the body cavity (Fig. 313A), but in the adult the midgut is small and there is a large crop and rectal sac (Fig. 313B). This change is associated with the change from leaf–feeding, with continuous access to food, to fluid–feeding, with the need to store nectar in the crop between feeds and the requirement to digest and absorb only sugars (Table 1). The meconium is stored in the large rectal sac. In Coleoptera the reconstruction of the stomodaeum and proctodaeum is carried out by the renewed activity of the larval cells without any accompanying cell destruction, but in Lepidoptera and Diptera new structures develop from imaginal rings, which are proliferating centres at the inner ends of the foregut and hindgut. The larval cells are sloughed into the body cavity.

The midgut is probably completely renewed in all holometabolous insects, usually being reformed from the regenerative cells at the base of the epithelium (p. 52). These cells proliferate and form a layer round the outside of the larval cells which thus come to lie in the lumen of the new alimentary canal. Sometimes this process occurs twice, once

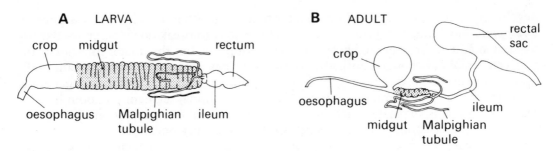

Fig. 313 Diagram showing the change in the form of the alimentary canal at metamorphosis in a moth

on the formation of the pupa and again when the adult tissues are forming and it is suggested that the special pupal midgut enables the insect to digest the sloughed remains of the larval midgut so that these can be assimilated and used in the reconstruction.

Malpighian tubules

Sometimes the larval Malpighian tubules pass unchanged to the adult, or slight modifications may occur as in the Lepidoptera. Here the larval tubules have a cryptonephridial arrangement (p. 577), but at metamorphosis the parts associated with the rectum are histolysed while the more proximal parts form the adult tubules (Srivastava and Khare, 1966). In Coleoptera the tubules are rebuilt from special cells in the larval tubules, while in Hymenoptera the larval tubules break down completely and are replaced by new ones developing from the tip of the proctodaeum.

Fat body

The fate of the fat body at metamorphosis depends on the degree of reconstruction of the other tissues. Where, as in Coleoptera, many larval tissues remain unchanged the fat body shows little depletion, but where reconstruction is extensive the fat body may be almost or completely destroyed. It is then reformed in the adult from the few remaining larval fat cells or, as in *Musca*, from mesenchyme cells on the inside of the imaginal discs.

Other systems

In general the tracheal system shows little change other than the development of new branches to accommodate the particular needs of the adult, such as the supply to the flight muscles, and the elimination of some specifically larval elements. In cyclorrhaphous Diptera, however, an extensive reconstruction occurs. The pupal tracheal system consists of four main tracheal trunks which extend into the head and as far as the anterior segments of the abdomen from the thoracic spiracle. From these main trunks tufts of fine, unbranched tracheae arise and each ends in several tracheoles which became tightly coiled about a third of the way through the puparial period (Fig. 314). Up to this time the developing adult flight muscles are still very short and their

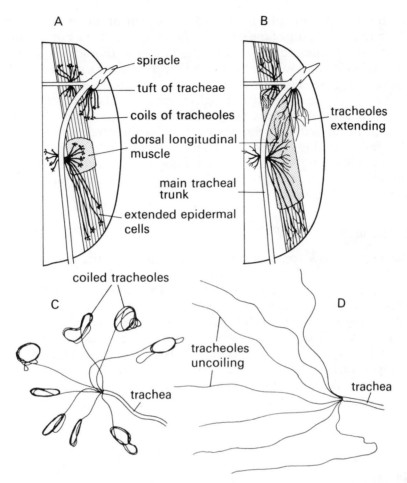

Fig. 314 A, B. Diagrams of half the thorax of the pharate adult of *Calliphora* (A) three days and (B) four days after pupariation showing the pupal tracheal supply to the developing dorsal longitudinal flight muscle. C, D. Diagrams of a tuft of tracheoles arising from the end of a trachea showing the tracheoles coiled (day 3) and uncoiled (day 4) (after Houlihan and Newton, 1979)

development is not dependent on an oxygen supply. Subsequently, however, they elongate rapidly and the tracheoles uncoil, extending with the muscles fibres (Fig. 314) whose metabolic processes at this time are at least partially dependent on aerobic respiratory processes. Subsequently the adult tracheal supply develops from tracheoblasts largely independently of the pupal supply, but it remains fluid-filled until about three hours before emergence. The filling of the adult tracheae with air corresponds with a sharp increase in oxygen consumption, partly associated with increased metabolic activity in the tissues and partly with an increase in movements by the fly (Houlihan and Newton, 1979).

The circulatory system undergoes little change from larva to adult.

In most holometabolous insects, particularly those that are more specialised, the central nervous system becomes more concentrated at metamorphosis. This concentration is accompanied by a forward movement of the more posterior ganglia resulting from the shortening of the interganglionic connectives. For instance, the larva of *Pieris* has, in addition to the head ganglia, three thoracic and eight separate abdominal ganglia. In the adult the meso- and meta-thoracic ganglia are fused with the first two abdominal ganglia to form a compound ganglion close behind the prothoracic ganglion. The next three abdominal ganglia remain separate, but the last three fuse together to form another compound ganglion. In the course of these changes the perineurium is histolysed and the neural lamella digested, the former being re-developed from remaining glial cells. The nerve cells increase in number and this involves an accompanying increase in the numbers of glial cells (Heywood, 1965).

The higher Diptera are exceptional in having a more concentrated central nervous system in the larva than in the adult.

Biochemical changes

During the pupal period oxygen consumption at first falls and then rises again, following a characteristic U-shaped curve (Fig. 61). This is associated with changes in the enzyme systems regulating energy release. In *Calliphora* the activity of lactate dehydrogenase is high two days after pupariation, but falls sharply about midway through the puparial period, while citrate synthase and glycerophosphate dehydrogenase increase (Fig. 315). These changes indicate a switch from predominantly anaerobic catabolic processes to aerobic processes corresponding with the time at which the pupal tracheal system forms a well-developed air supply to the developing muscles (Fig. 314). A comparable change in the relative emphasis of anaerobic and

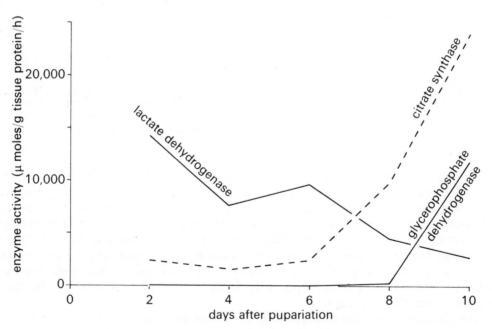

Fig. 315 Activity of different enzymes at different times after puparial formation in *Calliphora* (after Beenakkers *et al.*, 1975)

aerobic metabolic pathways occurs after completion of about two thirds of the pupal period of *Philosamia* (Lepidoptera) (Beenakkers *et al.*, 1975).

The proteins necessary for the production of new adult tissues and enzyme systems are synthesised primarily from amino acids, though there may be some synthesis by reorganisation of peptides from larval proteins without total degradation to amino acids. The components of the adult proteins are derived partly from the histolysis of larval tissues and partly from proteins built up and stored in the larva for this specific purpose. At least in some insects stored proteins provide the major source of amino acids for adult protein synthesis; and in *Calliphora* a single protein, known as calliphorin, comprises over 60 % of the total protein in the body at the beginning of metamorphosis. This protein is synthesised in the fat body and stored in the haemolymph and in the third instar larva at the end of feeding it comprises 75 % of the haemolymph proteins with a weight of about 7 mg in an insect weighing about 120 mg. Many other proteins which are qualitatively important are present in the haemolymph, but in many insects, as in *Calliphora*, one, two or three proteins form the bulk of the haemolymph protein. For instance in *Pieris* a single large-molecular-weight protein similar to calliphorin forms 50 % of larval protein. It is possible that haemoglobin, which forms 40 % of the plasma protein of *Chironomous* larva, also functions primarily as a storage protein in this insect and that its respiratory function (p. 570) is of secondary importance. After the cessation of feeding in *Calliphora* larva the calliphorin is taken up into the fat body, which comes to form 50 % of the wet weight of the larva. Subsequently the protein is degraded into its component amino acids and is used in building adult proteins; some is also used in energy metabolism. By the time of adult eclosion most of the calliphorin has been destroyed (Thomson, 1975). Ribosomal RNA, which is concerned in protein synthesis, increases during histogenesis and is at a maximum during differentiation (Fig. 316).

The waste products of pupal metabolism are discharged as the meconium when the adult emerges. Uric acid accumulates throughout the pupal period, but especially during histolysis, while in Lepidoptera and Hymenoptera allantoic acid comprises an appreciable part of the nitrogenous waste of the pupa. In *Phormia* (Diptera), urea accumulates during the development of the adult, suggesting that it is the end product of nitrogen metabolism in this insect.

21.2.3 Control of metamorphosis

The development of adult characters is controlled by hormones (p. 830), but while the growth and moulting hormone causes the epidermis to adopt adult features it does not order the development of particular parts of the body. Some degree of determination of the adult tissues may be apparent in the embryo, the presumptive adult areas coinciding with the presumptive larval areas (Anderson, 1966), but in *Drosophila* some lability of the adult tissues persists up to the time of pupation and even later (Waddington, 1956). More detailed features are not determined until after the more basic characters. For instance, the outline of the wing pattern of *Philosamia* (Lepidoptera) is determined before the details of the pattern.

There is some evidence that the various organs each have a differentiation centre which orders their development. For instance, in the leg of *Pieris* a basal thickening appears as an area of rapid cell division (Fig. 308) and mitosis spreads outwards from

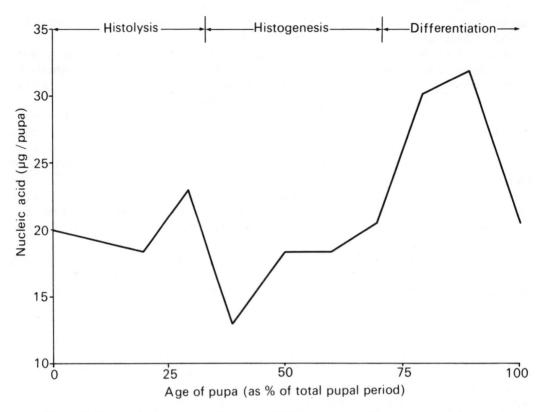

Fig. 316 Changes in the amount of ribosomal RNA present in different stages of the pupal instar of *Calliphora* (from Agrell and Lundquist, 1973)

this point (Kim, 1959). Similarly the eye of *Aedes* begins as a thickening at the back of the future eye region from which a wave of mitosis passes forwards and a thickening, the optic placode, develops in an area which is already physiologically delimited. It is suggested that development of the optic placode is initiated by some factor which spreads forwards from the posterior region, while in the final larval instar a wave of ommatidial differentiation also starts at the back of the eye and spreads forwards (White, 1961). Finally, the pattern on the wings of *Ephestia* is determined in a regular sequence which again might be due to the spread of some factor from a differentiation centre in the middle of the wing (Wigglesworth, 1965).

21.3 Adult emergence

The escape of the adult insect from the cuticle of the pupa or, in hemimetabolous insects, of the last larval instar is known as eclosion. The thorax of the enclosing cuticle splits along a line of weakness, which in the pupa is often T-shaped. In order to produce the split the adult increases its volume by swallowing air and then further increases its thoracic volume by pumping blood forwards from the abdomen. In Lepidoptera and Diptera with an obtect pupa the mouth is sealed by a strongly sclerotised plate so that the adult insect cannot suck air directly into its gut. However, although some of the spiracles of the pharate adult connect with the pupal spiracles others do not, but open beneath the pupal cuticle. It is thus possible for the insect to pump air out of the tracheal system into the space between the adult and pupal cuticles and this air can be swallowed so as to increase the volume of the body (Hinton, 1946).

Having split the cuticle the adult pulls itself out, expanding the wings by pumping blood through them. In many insects the newly emerged adult hangs so that the force of gravity assists the unfolding of the wings.

21.3.1 Escape from the cocoon

Where the pupa is enclosed in a cell or cocoon the adult also has to escape from this. Sometimes the pharate adult is sufficiently mobile to make its escape while still within the pupal cuticle. This is the case in species with decticous pupae which use the pupal mandibles, actuated by the adult muscles, to bite through the cocoon. Sometimes, as in Trichoptera, the adult mouthparts are non-functional and the sole function of the adult mandibular muscles is to work the pupal mandibles at emergence; subsequently they degenerate. The pupa moves away from the cocoon before the adult emerges and this is facilitated by the freedom of the appendages together with backwardly directed spines on the pupal cuticle which assist forward movement.

In species with adecticous pupae other methods are employed in escaping from the cocoon. In Monotrysia and primitive Ditrysia the pupa works its way forwards with the aid of backwardly directed spines on the abdomen, forcing its way through the wall of the cocoon with a ridge or tubercle known as a cocoon cutter on the head. The pupa does not escape completely from the cocoon, but is held with the anterior part sticking out by forwardly directed spines on the ninth and tenth abdominal segments. With the pupal cuticle fixed in this way the adult is able to pull against the substratum and so drag itself free more readily. Cocoon cutters are also present in Nematocera although in this group they are usually multiple structures.

In many insects with adecticous pupae the adult emerges from the pupa while it is still in the cocoon, making its final escape later, often while its cuticle is still soft and unexpanded. This is true of the higher Ditrysia, whose escape is facilitated by the flimsiness of the cocoon or the presence of a valve at one end of the cocoon through which the insect can force its way out while the ingress of other insects is prevented. The cocoon of *Saturnia* is of this type (Fig. 304B), while in Megalopygidae a trap door is present at one end. Some Lepidoptera produce secretions which soften the material of the cocoon. *Cerura*, for instance, produces from its mouth a secretion containing pottassium hydroxide which softens one end of its cell of agglutinated wood chips. This enables the insect to push its way out protected by the remnants of the pupal cuticle.

The silkmoths *Bombyx* and *Antheraea* produce a proteinase which softens the silk wall of the cocoon sufficiently for the adults to push their way out. In *Antheraea* the proteinase is secreted on to the surface of the galeae two days before eclosion. The secretion dries forming a semicrystalline encrustation. At the time of eclosion a liquid is secreted from labial glands opening by a single median pore just below the mouth. This liquid dissolves the enzyme and wets the inside of the cocoon. It contains potassium and functions as a buffer solution keeping the enzyme solution at a pH of about 8·5. The enzyme digests the sericin coating of the silk so that the fibroin threads are readily separated (Kafatos and Williams, 1964). A few Noctuidae also produce softening secretions.

Cyclorrhaphous Diptera have a special structure called the ptilinum, an eversible sac at the front of the head which assists in their escape from the puparium (Fig. 317). It can be expanded in the newly emerged fly by blood forced into the head from the thorax and abdomen and is then withdrawn again by muscles which force blood back to the thorax. The pressure of the ptilinum on the puparium splits off the cap of the latter and, if the puparium is buried in the soil, the ptilinum is also used by the fly to dig its way to the surface. Once the fly has hardened the ptilinum is no longer eversible and the muscles associated with it degenerate. Its position is indicated in the mature fly by the ptilinal suture.

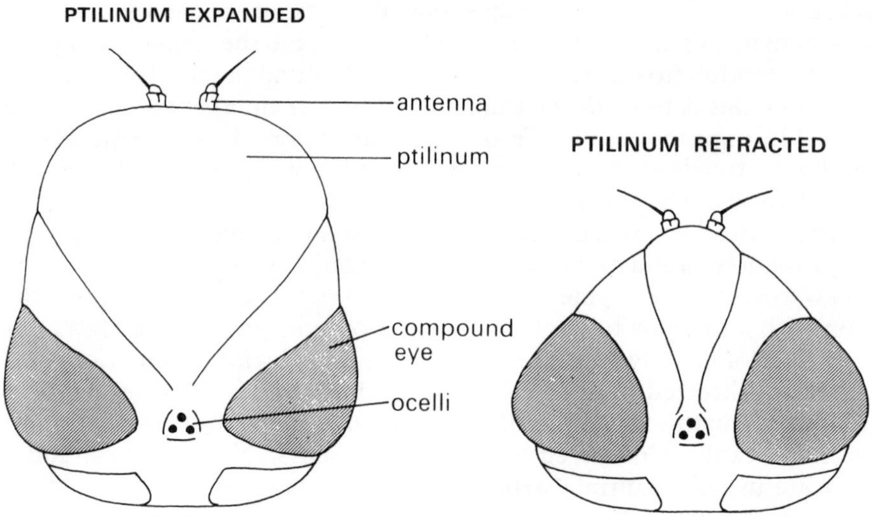

Fig. 317 Dorsal view of the head of a cyclorrhaphous fly showing the ptilinum expanded and retracted

The degree of hardening which these insects undergo before escaping from the cocoon varies. In some, most of the cuticle remains soft until after eclosion, but some parts, particularly those involved in locomotion, harden beforehand. Thus, in *Calliphora*, the legs and apodemes harden, so do the bristles which protect the soft cuticle, and such specialised parts as the halteres, antennae and genitalia. The remainder of the cuticle does not harden until after it is expanded when the insect is free (p. 524, and see Cottrell, 1964). In Lepidoptera, however, the body does not expand greatly after emergence and here hardening of the cuticle is extensive before the insect emerges from the cocoon, although the wings remain limp.

Other insects emerge from the pupa and harden fully before making their escape from the cocoon and they may have specialised features to assist this. Coleoptera and Hymenoptera use their mandibles to bite their way out. Some weevils of the subfamily Otiorrhynchinae have on the outside of the mandible an appendage, known as the false mandible (Fig. 318A), which is used in escaping from the cocoon and then, in most species, falls off. Amongst the Cynipidae which do not feed as adults, escape from the host in which the larva pupated is the sole function of the adult mandibles.

The cuticle of fleas also hardens before they escape from their cocoons and they may remain in the cocoon for some time after emergence. Their escape is stimulated by mechanical disturbances and in many species is facilitated by a cocoon cutter on the frons. In *Trichopsylla* the cocoon cutter is deciduous (Fig. 318B, C). Finally in the males of Strepsiptera the mandibles are used to cut through the cephalothorax of the last larval instar in which they pupate. The larval cephalothorax is earlier extruded through the cuticle of the host so that the adult insect can easily escape (Hinton, 1946).

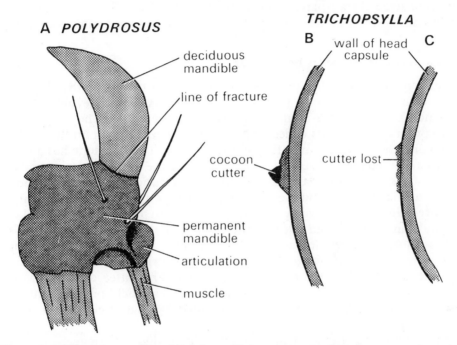

Fig. 318 A. The right mandible of *Polydrosus* (Coleoptera) at the time of emergence from the pupa. B. Front of the head of *Trichopsylla* showing the cocoon cutter. C. Front of the head of *Trichopsylla* after the loss of the cocoon cutter (after Hinton, 1946)

21.3.2 Emergence of aquatic insects

Of the insects which pupate under water some emerge under water and swim to the surface, while in others the pupa rises to the surface before the adult emerges. In the Blepharoceridae the adult undergoes some degree of hardening within the pupal cuticle, so that as soon as it emerges it rises to the surface and is able to fly *Simulium* and *Acentropus* also emerge beneath the surface, but come up in a bubble of air. In *Acentropus* this is derived from the air in the cocoon, while *Simulium* pumps air out into the gap between the pupal and adult cuticles. Thus the adult emerges into a bubble of air and is able to expand its wings before rising to the surface.

The pupae of Culicidae are buoyant, while some other insects, such as *Chironomus*, whose pupae are normally submerged, increase their buoyancy just before emergence by forcing air out beneath the pupal cuticle or increasing the volume of the tracheal system. Aided by backwardly directed spines these pupae then escape from their cocoons or larval tubes and rise to the surface. Many Trichoptera swim to the surface as pharate adults, the middle legs of the pupae of these species being fringed to facilitate swimming and the insect may continue to swim at the surface until it finds a suitable object to crawl out on. In other Trichoptera the pharate adults crawl up to the surface, while the last instar larvae of Odonata and Plecoptera crawl out onto emergent vegetation so that the adult emerges above the water. Larval Ephemeroptera also come to the surface, but the form which emerges is a subimago, not the imago. The subimago resembles the imago, but its legs and caudal filaments are shorter and the wings are translucent instead of transparent and are fringed with hairs. The subimago flies off as soon as it emerges, but settles a short distance away and soon moults to the imago.

21.3.3 Control of eclosion behaviour

The control of eclosion behaviour has been studied in the silkmoths *Antheraea* and *Hyalophora* and in *Manduca* by Truman and his associates (see Reynolds *et al.*, 1979, for references). About three hours before eclosion the eclosion hormone is released from the corpora cardiaca. Its concentration in the haemolymph rapidly builds up to a maximum and then declines over the next few hours. The hormone has a number of effects: it acts directly on the ventral nerve cord to release the pre-eclosion and eclosion behaviour of the moth; it causes plasticisation of the cuticle of the wings; and it leads ultimately to the release of bursicon. The patterns of motorneurone activity which produce pre-eclosion and eclosion behaviour are built-in programmes in the abdominal ganglia and can be produced even in the isolated abdominal nerve cord (Truman, 1978). Pre-eclosion behaviour consists of a set number of abdominal rotations and lasts about 30 minutes in *Hyalophora*; it is followed by a period of quiescence of about the same length and then by the eclosion behaviour. The latter consists of waves of abdominal contraction and 'shrugging' of the wing bases which continues until eclosion is complete. Eclosion behaviour is then inhibited by higher centres in the central nervous system.

At the time of emergence wing spreading behaviour is triggered via the sub-oesophageal ganglion, but it is inhibited by contact stimuli until the moth has escaped from the cocoon or, in the case of *Manduca*, has dug its way to the soil surface and come to rest on a vertical perch. Tonic contraction of the abdomen forces blood into the wings and wing spreading begins. The start of this activity triggers the release of the hormone bursicon from the neurohaemal organs associated with the abdominal ganglia and this leads first to a further increase in the plasticity of the wing cuticle and then to tanning (Truman and Endo, 1974) (p. 524). This sequence of events is summarized in Fig. 319. Bursicon also produces plasticisation of the cuticle of *Calliphora* at the time of eclosion (Reynolds, 1976).

21.3.4 Timing of emergence

It is important that the emergence of species is timed so that the life history is synchronised with suitable environmental conditions and so that the meeting of the two sexes is facilitated. Synchrony with the environment results from the common reaction

PRE-ECLOSION

1. Eclosion hormone produced in neurosecretory cells of brain.
2. Eclosion hormone released into blood from corpora cardiaca.
3. Eclosion hormone
    (a) triggers pre-eclosion and eclosion behaviour patterns in abdominal ganglia
    (b) triggers bursicon release
    (c) causes plasticisation of wing cuticle
4. Motor sequences to abdominal muscles lead to pre-eclosion and eclosion behaviour sequences.
5. Eclosion occurs.

POST-ECLOSION

6a. Eclosion leads to triggering of wing spreading behaviour by suboesophageal ganglion.
6b. Wing spreading and bursicon release inhibited during digging.
7. Wing spreading programme in thoracic ganglia released when insect free and in vertical position.
8. Bursicon release follows start of wing spreading.
9. Bursicon leads to further plasticisation of wing cuticle and then to tanning.

Fig. 319 Summary of the sequence of events and their control in *Manduca*

to the environment of the members of the species. Temperature is particularly important since to a large extent it governs the rate of development and the activity of the insect. Often a diapause is involved and in long-lived species a diapause may also be important in synchronising emergence so that the sexes meet.

It is common for male insects to emerge as adults a little before the females, although the difference is not great. This is often the case with locusts (Hamilton, 1936) and mosquitoes (Clements, 1963), for instance, and it probably reflects, in part, the smaller size of many male insects.

Apart from these general seasonal effects many insects emerge mainly at particular times of day, often at night or in the early morning. This may have some adaptive significance in giving the insect some degree of protection against predators while it is vulnerable in the period before it is able to fly. Thus in Britain, the last instar larvae of *Anax* (Odonata) which are ready to moult leave the water between 20.00 and 21.00 hours and by 23.00 hours most adults have emerged and are expanding their wings. The timing of emergence of *Sympetrum* (Odonata) and most tropical dragonflies is similar, although some temperate species emerge during the day, perhaps because activity is limited by low temperature at night.

Moths are also known to emerge at particular times of day, the timing being controlled by photoperiod or temperature cycles and differing from species to species. For instance, with a cycle of 17 h light: 7 h dark *Hyalophora* escapes from the pupal shell in the first hours of the light period, while *Antheraea pernyi* does so towards the end of the light period (Truman and Riddiford, 1970). The emergence of *Manduca* is also affected by light, but is regulated more effectively by an increase in temperature of 3 to 5°C. This is to be expected since the insect pupates beneath the soil surface (Lockshin *et al.*, 1975). The behaviour of the moths is entrained to the light or temperature cycles after a few days of exposure, so that they emerge at the normal time even under constant conditions. The emergence of *Drosophila* occurs mainly in the first three or four hours of a 12 h light: 12 h dark regime and it is probable that the time of emergence of many insects is determined by light or temperature cycles. In silkmoths the brain itself is photosensitive and induces eclosion by releasing the eclosion hormone at a particular phase of the diurnal cycle (Truman and Riddiford, 1970).

Aedes taeniorhynchus also emerges at particular times of day, but different broods emerge at different times depending on the temperature during the pupal period. The synchrony within a brood is brought about by a tendency of the larvae to pupate at about sunset.

REFERENCES

AGRELL, I. P. S. and LUNDQUIST, A. M. (1973). Physiological and biochemical changes during insect development. *in* Rockstein, M. (ed.), *The physiology of Insecta*. vol. 1. Academic Press, New York.

ANDERSON, D. T. (1964). The embryology of *Dacus tryoni* 3. Origins of imaginal rudiments other than the principal discs. *J. Embryol. exp. Morph.* **12**: 65–75.

ANDERSON, D. T. (1966). The comparative embryology of the Diptera. *A. Rev. Ent.* **11**: 23–46.

BEENAKKERS, A. M. T., VAN DEN BROEA, A. T. M. and DE RONDE, T. J. A. (1975). Development of catabolic pathways in insect flight muscles. A comparative study. *J. Insect Physiol.* **21**: 849–859.

BODENSTEIN, D. (1950). The postembryonic development of *Drosophila*. *in* Demerec, M. (ed.), *Biology of Drosophila*. Wiley & Sons, New York.

CLEMENTS, A. N. (1963). *The physiology of mosquitoes*. Pergamon Press, Oxford.

COMSTOCK, J. H. (1918). *The wings of insects*. Comstock Publishing Co., New York.

COTTRELL, C. B. (1964). Insect ecdysis with particular emphasis on cuticular hardening and darkening. *Adv. Insect Physiol.* **2**: 175–218.

EASSA, Y. E. E. (1953). The development of imaginal buds in the head of *Pieris brassicae* Linn. (Lepidoptera). *Trans. R. ent. Soc. Lond.* **104**: 39–50.

GEHRING, W. J. and NÖTHIGER, R. (1973). The imaginal discs of *Drosophila*. *in* Counce, S. J. and Waddington, C. H. (eds.), *Developmental systems: insects*. vol. 2. Academic Press, London.

HAMILTON, A. G. (1936). The relation of humidity and temperature to the development of three species of African locusts—*Locusta migratoria migratorioides* (R. and F.), *Schistocerca gregaria* (Forsk.), *Nomadacris septemfasciata* (Serv.). *Trans. R. ent. Soc. Lond.* **85**: 1–60.

HEYWOOD, R. B. (1965). Changes occurring in the central nervous system of *Pieris brassicae* L. (Lepidoptera) during metamorphosis. *J. Insect Physiol.* **11**: 413–430.

HINTON, H. E. (1946). A new classification of insect pupae. *Proc. zool. Soc. Lond.* **116**: 282–328.

HINTON, H. E. (1948). On the origin and function of the pupal stage. *Trans. R. ent. Soc. Lond.* **99**: 395–409.

HINTON, H. E. (1959). How the indirect flight muscles of insects grow. *Sci. Prog., Lond.* **47**: 321–333.

HINTON, H. E. (1963). The origin and function of the pupal stage. *Proc. R. ent. Soc. Lond.* A, **38**: 77–85.

HOULIHAN, D. F. and NEWTON, J. R. L. (1979). The tracheal supply and muscle metabolism during muscle growth in the puparium of *Calliphora vomitoria*. *J. Insect Physiol.* **25**: 33–44.

JAGO, N. D. (1963). Some observations on the life cycle of *Eyprepocnemis plorans meridionalis* Uvarov, 1921, with a key for the separation of nymphs at any instar. *Proc. R. ent. Soc. Lond.* A, **38**: 113–124.

KAFATOS, F. C. and WILLIAMS, C. M. (1964). Enzymatic mechanism for the escape of certain moths from their cocoons. *Science* **146**: 538–540.

KIM, C.-W. (1959). The differentiation centre inducing the development from larval to adult leg in *Pieris brassicae* (Lepidoptera). *J. Embryol. exp. Morph.* **7**: 572–582.

LOCKSHIN, R. A., ROSETT, M. and SROKOSE, K. (1975). Control of ecdysis by heat in *Manduca sexta. J. Insect Physiol.* **21**: 1799–1802.

LOUNIBOS, L. P. (1975). The cocoon spinning behaviour of the Chinese oak silkworm, *Antheraea pernyi. Anim. Behav.* **23**: 843–853.

LOUNIBOS, L. P. (1976). Initiation and maintenance of cocoon spinning behaviour by saturniid silkworms. *Physiol. Ent.* **1**: 195–206.

MARSHALL, J. F. (1938). *The British mosquitoes.* British Museum, London.

REYNOLDS, S. E. (1976). Hormonal regulation of cuticle extensibility in newly emerged adult blowflies. *J. Insect Physiol.* **22**: 529–534.

REYNOLDS, S. E., TAGHERT, P. H. and TRUMAN, J. W. (1979). Eclosion hormone and bursicon titres and the onset of hormonal responsiveness during the last day of adult development in *Manduca sexta* (L). *J. exp. Biol.* **78**: 77–86.

SCHNEIDERMAN, H. A. and GILBERT, L. I. (1964). Control of growth and development in insects. *Science* **143**: 325–333.

SNODGRASS, R. E. (1954). Insect metamorphosis. *Smithson. misc. Collns* **122**, no. 9, 124 pp.

SRIVASTAVA, U. S. and KHARE, M. K. (1966). The development of Malpighian tubules and associated structures in *Philosamia ricini* (Lepidoptera, Saturnidae). *J. Zool.* **150**: 145–163.

THOMAS, J. G. (1954). The post-embryonic development of the dorsal part of the pterothoracic skeleton and certain muscles of *Locusta migratoria migratorioides* (Reiche & Fairm.). *Proc. zool. Soc. Lond.* **124**: 229–238.

THOMSON, J. A. (1975). Major patterns of gene activity during development in holometabolous insects. *Adv. Insect Physiol.* **11**: 321–398.

TIEGS, O. W. (1955). The flight muscles of insects—their anatomy and histology; with some observations on the structure of striated muscle in general. *Phil. Trans. R. Soc.* B, **238**: 221–348.

TRUMAN, J. W. (1978). Hormonal release of stereotyped motor programmes from the isolated nervous system of the cecropia silkmoth. *J. exp. Biol.* **74**: 151–173.

TRUMAN, J. W. and ENDO, P. T. (1974). Physiology of insect ecdysis: neural and hormonal factors involved in wing-spreading behaviour of moths. *J. exp. Biol.* **61**: 47–55.

TRUMAN, J. W. and RIDDIFORD, L. M. (1970). Neuroendocrine control of ecdysis in silkmoths. *Science* **167**: 1624–1626.

WADDINGTON, C. H. (1941). The genetic control of wing development in *Drosophila. J. Genet.* **41**: 75–139.

WADDINGTON, C. H. (1956). *Principles of embryology.* Allen and Unwin, London.

WHITE, R. H. (1961). Analysis of the development of the compound eye in the mosquito, *Aedes aegypti. J. exp. Zool.* **148**: 223–239.

WHITTEN, J. M. (1957). The supposed pre-pupa in cyclorrhaphous Diptera. *Q. Jl microsc. Sci.* **98**: 241–249.

WIGGLESWORTH, V. B. (1964). The hormonal regulation of growth and reproduction in insects. *Adv. Insect Physiol.* **2**: 247–336.

WIGGLESWORTH, V. B. (1965). *The principles of insect physiology.* Methuen, London.

SECTION D

The Cuticle, Respiration and Excretion

CHAPTER XXII
THE INTEGUMENT

The integument is the outer layer of the insect, comprising the epidermis (hypodermis) and the cuticle. The cuticle is a characteristic feature of arthropods and is, to a large extent, responsible for the success of insects as terrestrial animals. It affords support and protection through its rigidity and hardness and is of primary importance in restricting water loss from the body surface. It is secreted by the epidermis and oenocytes and consists of a number of layers serving different functions.

As first secreted the cuticle is soft and flexible, but the outer part subsequently becomes hardened by a process known as tanning or sclerotisation, which involves the production of chemical bonds between the protein chains which make up a large part of the cuticle. Another important constituent of cuticle is chitin, which acts as a packing, conserving the amount of protein used. The whole of the cuticle does not become hardened since flexible joints must occur between the hard plates for the insect to be able to move and in some joints a specialised rubber-like cuticle, resilin, is present.

The hardened cuticle by itself is not particularly waterproof. The waterproofing is provided by a thin but complex epicuticle which is secreted to the outside. The shape of the epicuticle also determines the form of the cuticle and especially its surface appearance.

Since hard cuticle will not expand, it limits growth. Hence it is necessary for the insect to shed the existing cuticle from time to time and replace it with another which, before it hardens, is sufficiently flexible to permit some expansion. To conserve as much material as possible the untanned parts of the old cuticle are digested by moulting fluid and resorbed. The new cuticle is laid down, at least in part, before the old one is shed and the first layer to be produced is a layer of the epicuticle which protects the newly developing cuticle from digestion by the moulting fluid. Wax secretion is advanced by the time the old cuticle is shed so that water loss is restricted even at this time. The old cuticle is ruptured along lines of weakness by outward pressure exerted by the insect. This and the subsequent expansion of the new cuticle may involve swallowing air or water and the presence of special muscles which degenerate soon after the moult.

The whole of the life history of the insect is geared to the moulting cycle and co-ordination of the various aspects of moulting involves a number of hormones.

The books by Hepburn (1976) and Neville (1975) review many aspects of the insect cuticle. Andersen (1979) reviews the biochemistry of insect cuticle and Jungreis (1979) and Reynolds (1980) the physiology and behaviour associated with moulting.

22.1 Epidermis

22.1.1 Epidermal cells

The epidermis is the outer cell layer of the insect. It is one cell thick with cell densities ranging from about 3000/mm² in the trachea of *Rhodnius* to 11 000/mm² in the sternal area of larval *Tenebrio*. In larval *Manduca* with a flexible and extensible cuticle, cell density decreases from about 9000/mm² soon after ecdysis to 3000/mm² a few days later (Wielgus and Gilbert, 1978). In most insects cell density increases as a result of mitosis at the onset of the moulting cycle (Fig. 330), but in larval Cyclorrhapha, where no mitosis occurs in the epidermis, the density of cells decreases throughout larval life. The depth of the cells at right angles to the surface of the epidermis also changes through development. In *Rhodnius* the cells are columnar immediately after moulting, but subsequently become squamous until the insect feeds; after this they become deeper again. The epidermal cells of larval *Manduca*, which feeds continuously, grow throughout the instar and become progressively deeper in the days following ecdysis.

The epidermal cells are held together near their apices by zonulae adhaerens and lower down by gap junctions and septate junctions (Satir and Gilula, 1973). The gap junctions probably provide a pathway for the movement of low molecular weight substances between the epidermal cells and could form the anatomical link necessary for the integration of activity of the cells in different parts of the body (p. 463). Ecdysone reduces the resistance to the transfer of ions from one epidermal cell to the next in the period just before mitosis occurs (Caveney, 1976).

During and just after a moult the cells may have long cytoplasmic processes on the outside extending into the pore canals of the cuticle (p. 510), but these processes may be withdrawn as the cuticle matures.

Some of the epidermal cells are specialised to form sense organs (Chapters XXIX, XXX) or glands. In many species the secretions of these glands are important in intra- or interspecific communication (Chapter XXXV), but they may also contribute to the cuticle. In *Rhodnius*, for example, they produce the cement layer (p. 510), while in all dipterous larvae there are peristigmatic glands, surrounding the spiracles. They are usually single, large cells with intracellular ducts opening to the outside near the edges of the spiracles. Their secretion, which is produced continuously, is responsible for the hydrofuge properties of the cuticle surrounding the spiracles and prevents the entry of water into the tracheal system.

22.1.2 Basement membrane

The epidermal cells stand on a basement membrane consisting of an amorphous granular material, probably a mucopolysaccharide, which in some species has collagen fibres embedded in it (Neville, 1975). It forms a continuous sheet and at points where muscles are attached it is continuous with the sarcolemma. In *Rhodnius* the basement membrane of the fourth instar larva is about 0·15 μm thick, but six days after feeding it thickens to about 0·5 μm. This thickening is produced by plasmatocytes which at this time aggregate on the basement membrane and actively take up material from the haemolymph by pinocytosis. The pinocytotic vesicles fuse to form large inclusions which change in their staining properties and then are discharged to contribute to the membrane. The role of the epidermal cells in the normal production of basement membrane is not clear, though they have the capacity to produce it. The thickening serves to strengthen the basement membrane sheet when it serves as a base for the forces used in moulding the new epicuticle which is produced soon afterwards (Wigglesworth, 1973a). The epidermal cells are anchored to the basement membrane by hemidesmosomes.

22.1.3 Oenocytes

The oenocytes are often large cells, more than 100 μm in diameter, in a group on either side of each abdominal segment. In Ephemeroptera, Odonata and Heteroptera, among others, the oenocytes remain close to their point of origin in the epidermis, lying between the bases of the epidermal cells and the basement membrane (Fig. 331); in Lepidoptera and Orthoptera they form clusters in the body cavity; while in Homoptera, Hymenoptera and some Diptera they are dispersed and embedded in the fat body. These cells may be formed continously, or a new generation of cells may be produced at each moult, or, in holometabolous insects, there may be separate larval and adult generations. They show cycles of development which in immature insects are associated with the moulting cycle and they are probably concerned with the production of the lipids in the cuticle (Wigglesworth, 1976). They may also be concerned with the synthesis of ecdysone (p. 823).

22.2 Basic structure of cuticle

The cuticle is a secretion of the epidermis and covers the whole of the outside of the body as well as lining ectodermal invaginations such as the stomodaeum and proctodaeum and the tracheae. It is differentiated into two major regions: an inner region, up to 200 μm thick, which contains chitin and forms the bulk of the cuticle, and the thin outer epicuticle which contains no chitin and is only 1–4 μm thick.

   The chitinous cuticle as it is first secreted is known as procuticle, but subsequently the outer part often becomes tanned or sclerotised to form exocuticle while the inner undifferentiated part is called endocuticle (Fig. 320). Between the two there may be a region of hardened, but not fully darkened cuticle which is fuchsinophil (fully sclerotised cuticle does not stain readily) and such a layer is called mesocuticle.

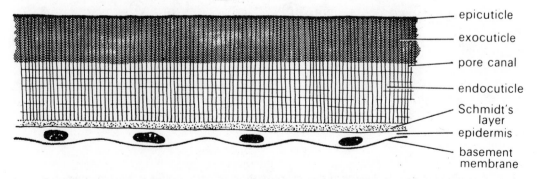

epicuticle

exocuticle

pore canal

endocuticle

Schmidt's layer

epidermis

basement membrane

Fig. 320 Diagrammatic representation of a section of mature cuticle and epidermis

22.2.1 Procuticle

Chitin

Chitin is a characteristic constituent of insect procuticle, commonly comprising 20–50 % of the dry weight. It is a polysaccharide made up largely of N-acetylglucosamine, but also probably containing some glucosamine (Rudall, 1963). The sugar residues are linked by 1–4 β linkages so that they form a chain in which all the residues are orientated in the same direction (*e.g.* in the following diagram C1 is always at the left-hand end of the sugar residue).

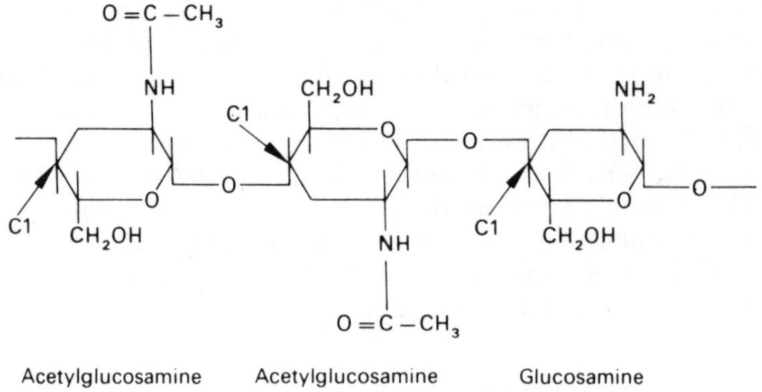

| Acetylglucosamine | Acetylglucosamine | Glucosamine |

Adjacent chitin chains are held together by hydrogen bonds to form microfibrils, and hydrogen bonds probably also link the oxygen atoms of adjacent acetylglucosamine residues. Neighbouring chains run in opposite directions (*i.e.* with the C1 atoms at opposite ends of the molecules) and the suggested linkages are as follows:

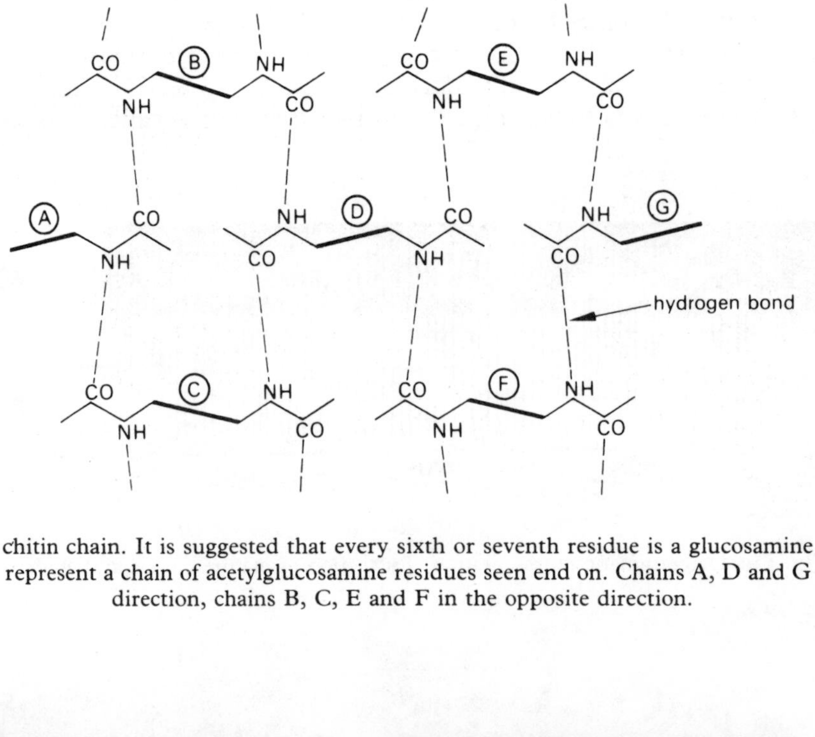

Part of a chitin chain. It is suggested that every sixth or seventh residue is a glucosamine residue. Thick lines represent a chain of acetylglucosamine residues seen end on. Chains A, D and G run in one direction, chains B, C, E and F in the opposite direction.

Part of previous diagram seen in face view and with linkages distorted so that chains C and D are in the same plane.

The microfibrils are about 2·8 nm in diameter and are embedded in a protein matrix. At any one level in the cuticle they lie parallel to each other in the plane of the cuticle, but the orientation is often different in successive levels. In most insects the microfibrils in the outer parts of the procuticle, which subsequently becomes the exocuticle, rotate anticlockwise through a fixed angle in successive levels so that their arrangement is helicoidal and a series of thin lamellae is produced (Fig. 321A). This is called lamellate cuticle. The inner procuticle may also be lamellate throughout, or layers with helicoidally arranged microfibrils may alternate with layers in which the microfibrils are uniformly orientated. Wholly lamellate cuticle is found in Apterygota and larval and pupal Lepidoptera, Diptera and Coleoptera. Where helicoidal and unidirectional layers alternate, all the unidirectional layers may have the same orientation (Fig. 321B), as in locusts and cockroaches, or they may have different orientations (Fig. 321C), as in beetles and bugs. In some such cases the intervening layers of helicoidal cuticle are very thin, so that the orientation appears to change suddenly from one layer to the next. This is called a pseudo-orthogonal arrangement (Neville, 1975). The endocuticle contains a higher proportion of lamellate cuticle in larval insects than in adults of the same species.

The alternate production of helicoidally arranged and unidirectional layers of microfibrils has a circadian periodicity in most species. In locusts, cuticle laid down at night has microfibrils with a helicoidal arrangement whereas that produced in the

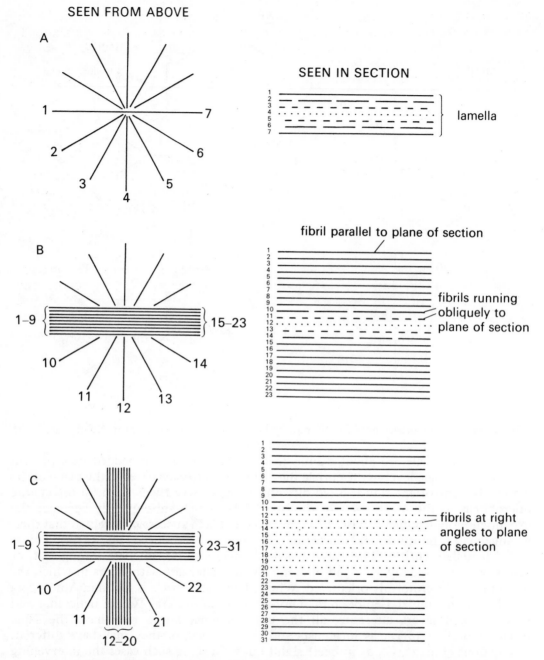

Fig. 321 Diagrams showing the arrangement of chitin microfibrils in cuticle. Numbers indicate successive layers in the cuticle with, on the left, the orientation of microfibrils in successive layers as seen in transparency, and, on the right, the appearance of the fibrils in sections of the cuticle running parallel to the fibrils in layer 1. A. A helicoidal arrangement producing a single lamella. B. Two layers with uniformly orientated microfibrils separated by a single lamella with a helicoidal arrangement. C. Layers of unidirectional fibrils at right angles to each other and separated by layers with a helicoidal arrangement

daytime has them uniformly orientated. Such daily growth layers are found in larval and adult Exopterygota and in adult Endopterygota. In some cases, however, shortage of food may limit cuticle production so that growth layers may not be produced regularly (Neville, 1975).

Chitin in insect cuticle is always associated with protein perhaps being bound to it by covalent bonds (Andersen, 1979).

Protein

Proteins are the major constituents of insect cuticle. Cuticle from any one part of an insect contains several different proteins and these may differ from the proteins in the cuticle of other parts of the same insect. The proteins of soft cuticle generally contain more aspartic acid, glutamic acid, histidine, lysine and tyrosine and are more hydrophilic than those of hard cuticles.

Hardening of cuticle is primarily a consequence of cross-linking between the protein molecules so that they form a rigid matrix. The process of cross-linking is called tanning or sclerotisation and the cuticle is then said to be sclerotised. The process involves the production of N-acetyldopamine, which forms links between the protein chains. The precise manner in which this is achieved is not certain, but there is good evidence that the links are made with the β-carbon atom on the side chain:

N-acetyldopamine   linking proteins

Evidence for this process has been found in a number of insects (Andersen and Barrett, 1971) and in *Schistocerca* it is probably the major mechanism involved in sclerotisation (Andersen, 1974). However, in other insects it is probable that some proteins become linked directly to the aromatic ring of N-acetyldopamine quinone in a process known as quinone tanning:

N-acetyldopamine quinone   linking proteins

It is possible that in some Diptera N-β-alanyldopamine replaces N-acetyldopamine either in β-sclerotisation or quinone tanning (Andersen, 1979). β-sclerotisation produces a colourless cuticle, but quinone tanning causes the cuticle to darken.

The N-acetyldopamine forms links with amino groups in the protein, but most of the amino groups are already involved in the peptide linkages,—CO.NH—, between adjacent amino acids forming the protein chain. Consequently, the only amino groups available for tanning are the terminal groups of the chains and those associated with dibasic acids, usually lysine. In the dibasic acid only one of the amino groups is involved in a peptide linkage, leaving the other available for tanning.

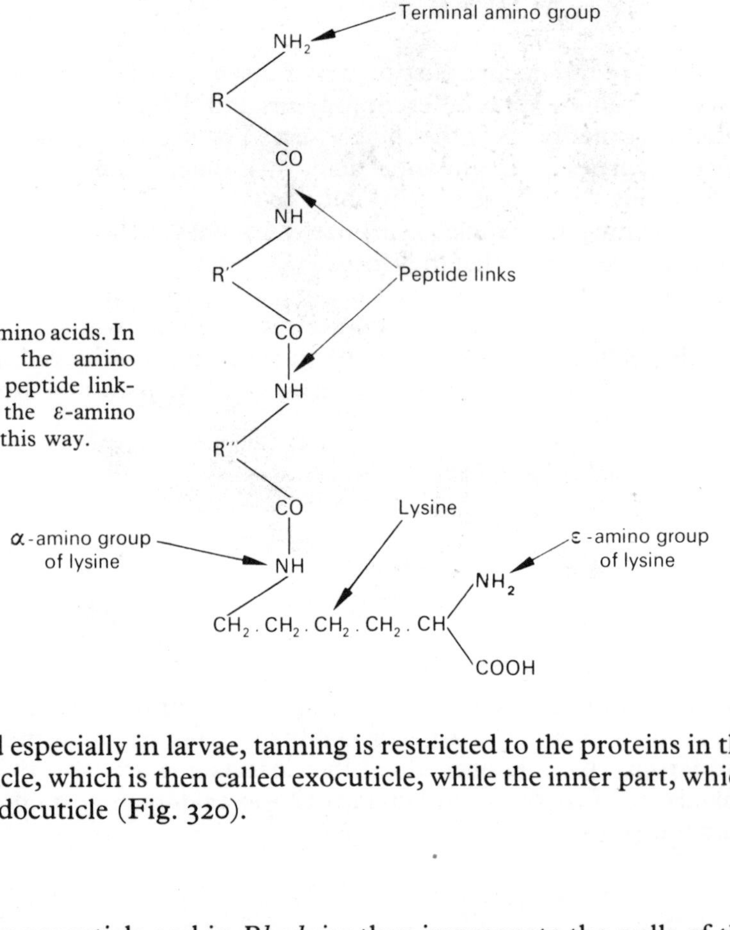

Diagram of chain of 4 amino acids. In the monobasic acids the amino groups are involved in peptide linkages, but in lysine the ε-amino group is not bound in this way.

Terminal amino group — NH_2

R

CO

NH

R'

Peptide links

CO

NH

R''

CO

Lysine

α-amino group of lysine — NH

$CH_2 . CH_2 . CH_2 . CH_2 . CH$

NH_2 — ε-amino group of lysine

COOH

In many insects, and especially in larvae, tanning is restricted to the proteins in the outer part of the procuticle, which is then called exocuticle, while the inner part, which lacks tanning, is the endocuticle (Fig. 320).

Lipid

Lipids are present in the procuticle and in *Rhodnius* they impregnate the walls of the pore canals and are present in layers at intervals of o·5—1·0 μm. These lipid layers are dispersed when the insect feeds and the cuticle stretches, but more layers are laid down with the new cuticle (Wigglesworth, 1976).

22.2.2 Epicuticle

The epicuticle is made up of several layers. The thickest layer is the inner epicuticle immediately outside the procuticle. It is o·5 μm to 2·0 μm thick. Outside it is a very thin outer epicuticle, only about 18 nm thick, and outside this again is a wax layer of variable thickness. Some insects have a thin 'cement' layer outside the wax (Fig. 322). The

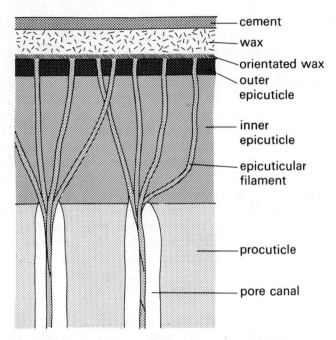

cement
wax
orientated wax
outer epicuticle
inner epicuticle
epicuticular filament
procuticle
pore canal

Fig. 322 Diagrammatic representation of a section through the epicuticle

terminology used here is that of Weis-Fogh (1970); in earlier studies the inner and outer epicuticles are not usually separated from each other and are known as the cuticulin layer, while Locke (*e.g.* 1976) refers to the outer epicuticle alone as cuticulin.

Inner epicuticle

This layer is chemically complex and is known to consist primarily of tanned lipoproteins. During its production phenolic substances and phenoloxidase are also present. These are probably concerned with tanning the proteins. Phenoloxidase persists as an extracellular enzyme in mature cuticle, producing further tanning if the epicuticle is damaged.

Outer epicuticle

This is a very thin trilaminar membrane. It is a highly polymerised lipid with the lipid chains orientated at right angles to the surface (Weis-Fogh, 1970), and it probably also has a protein component (Locke, 1976). Polyphenols and phenoloxidase take part in its formation (Locke and Krishnan, 1971).

This layer is believed to be inextensible, setting a limit on any extension of the procuticle which may occur during growth or other activities (pp. 389, 515).

Wax

The wax of the epicuticle consists of long chain hydrocarbons and the esters of fatty acids and alcohols. It is possible that the molecules adjacent to the cuticulin are strongly orientated as a result of their polar, hydrophilic groups being adsorbed on to the surface of the cuticulin so that they form a layer only one molecule thick and hence called a monolayer (p. 594). The monolayer may be in a liquid phase which is continually being moved and replaced; experiments on *Phormia* (Diptera) show that such movements can occur, since an oil film can spread over the whole surface of an insect within 15 minutes. The molecules of the monolayer are very close together and inclined at an angle so that their packing is as close as possible (Fig. 388) and the spaces between them are extremely small (Beament, 1964). This provides the waterproof layer of the cuticle since water molecules are unable to pass between the close-packed wax molecules. Due to their orientation the molecules also present a row of aliphatic groups to the outside and these are partly responsible for the hydrofuge properties of the insect cuticle. Outside the monolayer the wax molecules are randomly orientated.

In some species the wax forms a bloom on the outside of the cuticle and, in a few, very large quantities are produced. This is the case with some Fulgoroidea and scale insects, and the larva of *Calpodes*. Bees secrete large quantities of beeswax, which is used in the production of the larval cells.

Cement

The cement is a very thin layer outside most of the wax, perhaps consisting of tanned protein with lipids or of a shellac-like substance. It may serve to protect the underlying wax, but where the cuticle expands, as it does in the larvae of holometabolous insects, the cement might be in the form of an open meshwork which provides a reservoir of lipids to replace lost surface lipids. It is not produced by all insects.

22.2.3 Pore canals and epicuticular filaments

Running through the cuticle at right angles to the surface are very fine pore canals (Fig. 322). They extend from the epidermis to the inner epicuticle and, at least early in the development of the cuticle, they contain cytoplasmic extensions of the epidermal cell at a density of about 15 000/mm^2. In adult beetles and bugs the pore canals are more abundant in the outer procuticle, and some 30 pore canals per cell in the outer region may join to a single canal lower down. The canals are one micron or less in diameter.

In *Rhodnius* the pore canals are circular in cross-section, but in many species they have a flattened ribbon-like form, the plane of flattening being parallel with the microfibres in each layer of the cuticle. As the microfibres in successive layers change direction the canal also rotates, so that it has the form of a twisted ribbon (Fig. 323).

It is presumed that the cytoplasmic threads within the canals are subsequently withdrawn and the canals may be filled by chitin and protein with the chitin microfibres orientated along the canal. Whether they are filled or not, the canals contain a central filament formed from fused epicuticular filaments.

Epicuticular filaments run from the wax layer through the epicuticle and into the pore canals (Fig. 322). In many insects several filaments converge on each pore canal, but in *Rhodnius* there is only one to each canal (Wigglesworth, 1976). Each filament is about 6 nm in diameter and extends down the pore canal to the surface of the epidermis. They possibly consist of tanned protein and may be concerned with the transport of lipids from the epidermal cells to the surface of the cuticle (Locke and Krishnan, 1971).

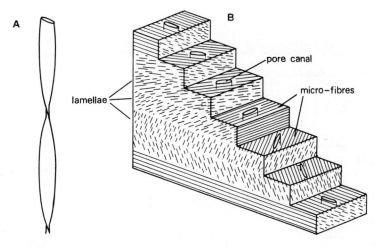

Fig. 323 A. Diagrammatic representation of a twisted ribbon pore canal. B. Diagrammatic section through a segment of cuticle showing microfibres of successive lamellae running in different directions and pore canals orientated parallel to the fibres (based on Neville *et al.*, 1969)

22.3 Different types of cuticle

The cuticle varies in nature in different parts of the body. The most obvious difference is between the hard, rigid cuticle of the sclerites and the flexible cuticle of the membranes between them.

22.3.1 Rigid cuticle

Rigid cuticle is produced as a result of tanning in the outer part of the procuticle to form exocuticle, but the extent of tanning, and hence the hardness of the cuticle, varies. In larval *Schistocerca* the exocuticle of the sclerites is sharply differentiated from the endocuticle, which never tans. In the adult, on the other hand, tanning continues for weeks after the final ecdysis and the whole of the procuticle is ultimately tanned. In the fully hardened larva the mandibles are much more heavily tanned than other parts of the cuticle; they are also heavily tanned in the adult, but to no greater degree than some other parts of the body. The dorsal mesothorax is particularly heavily tanned in association with its function in flight (Fig. 324) (Andersen, 1974).

22.3.2 Membranous cuticle

The sclerites are joined by flexible arthrodial membranes. In these the procuticle remains untanned (Fig. 325), but it also differs quantitatively from the cuticle of the sclerites in containing proteins with a different amino acid composition (p. 507). The extent of the membrane and the method of articulation of the two adjacent sclerites determines the degree of movement which can occur at the joint. Sometimes, as between abdominal segments, the membrane is extensive and there is no point of contact between adjacent sclerites, so that movement is unrestricted (Fig. 326A). More usually the sclerites make contact with each other to form true articulations and the

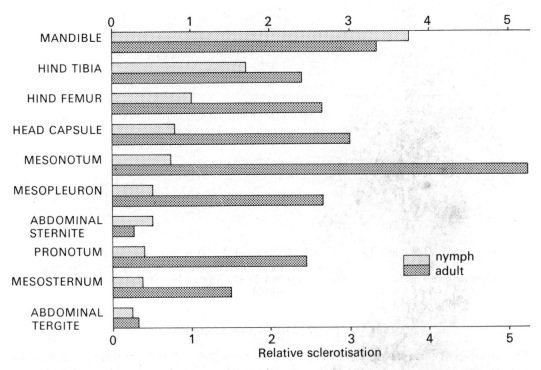

Fig. 324 Amounts of sclerotisation of cuticle from different parts of the body of a mid-fifth instar nymph and a 10-day-old adult locust. Sclerotisation is based on the amounts of ketocatechols released when the cuticle is hydrolysed (based on Andersen, 1974)

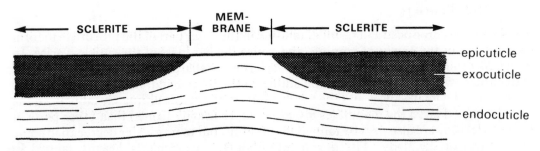

Fig. 325 Diagrammatic section through the cuticle showing a flexible membranous region between two rigid sclerites

joints are called monocondylic or dicondylic depending on whether there are one or two points of articulation. Monocondylic articulations, such as that of the antenna with the head, permit considerable freedom of movement, whereas dicondylic articulations, which occur at many of the leg joints, give more limited, but much more precise movements. The articular surfaces may lie within the membrane (instrinsic), as in most leg joints (Fig. 326B), or they may lie outside it (extrinsic), as, for instance, in the mandibular articulations (Fig. 326C).

Apart from membranous areas, exocuticle is also absent along the ecdysial lines of larval hemimetabolous insects. The cuticle along these lines consists only of

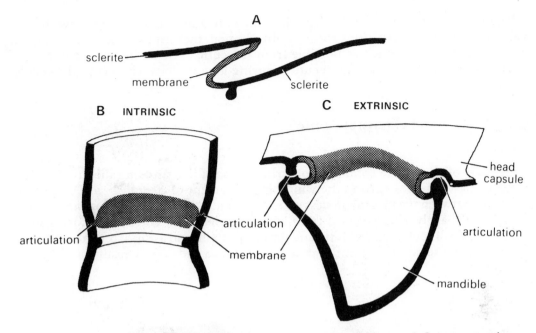

Fig. 326 Diagrams of different types of joints between sclerotised areas. A. Intersegmental. Extensive membrane with no articulation between sclerites. B. Dicondylic leg joint with intrinsic articulations. C. Dicondylic articulation of mandible with head capsule. Extrinsic articulations. Edges of sclerotised regions shown black, membrane hatched (from Snodgrass, 1935)

undifferentiated procuticle and epicuticle (Fig. 327), so that they constitute lines of weakness along which the cuticle splits at ecdysis (p. 518).

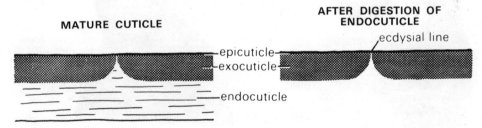

Fig. 327 Diagrammatic section of the cuticle transverse to an ecdysial line. Moulting fluid digests the endocuticle leaving the cuticle held together only by the epicuticle, producing a line of weakness

In many larval holometabolous insects the greater part of the cuticle remains undifferentiated (Dennell, 1946; Locke, 1960; Way, 1950) and somewhat extensible. This facilitates growth, it also permits movement by changes in body form (p. 183), and it is important for the conservation of materials. The bulk of the undifferentiated cuticle is digested and resorbed at moulting, while sclerotised parts are lost. Hence an unsclerotised cuticle is more economic for a larval form which moults several times.

Collembola moult continuously even when they are adult and, in keeping with this, their cuticle contains very little exocuticle. In addition, they eat their exuviae (p. 519) so that they conserve as much as possible from the cuticle. Some insects are known to utilise material from unsclerotised cuticle during long periods without food (Neville, 1975).

22.3.3 Elastic and extensible cuticle

Resilin

Some parts of the cuticle contain a colourless, rubber-like protein called resilin. It is found in elastic hinges such as the wing-hinge ligament of *Schistocerca* (Orthoptera) which lies between the pleural process and the second axillary sclerite (Fig. 328A). The ligament is sharply differentiated from adjacent sclerotised cuticle and consists of a ventral region of tough, dense chitin and fibrous protein, and a dorsal region containing layers of resilin separated by chitinous lamellae, with a pad of pure resilin on the inside (Fig. 328B).

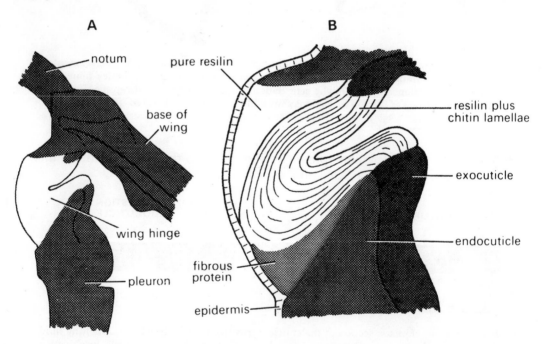

Fig. 328 A. Transverse section through the thoracic wall of *Schistocerca* showing the base of the wing and the wing hinge. B. Section through the wing hinge enlarged (modified after Andersen and Weis-Fogh, 1964)

Resilin contains amino acids, which provide the links between the protein chains. These linkages are produced continuously as the resilin is laid down and so the process contrasts with the linking of protein in sclerotisation (p. 522), which occurs some time after the protein is laid down (Neville, 1963). The amino acid sequence in resilin is such as to prevent other cross-links occurring, since these would impair the rubber-like properties.

Like rubber, resilin can be stretched under tension and stores the energy involved so that when the tension is released it returns immediately to its original length. In the locust between one-quarter and one-third of the recoil energy of the wing away from its equilibrium position is due to the elasticity of the wing-hinge ligament. Elsewhere resilin is found in the clypeo-labral spring which keeps the labrum pressed against the mandibles, while in beetles, where there are no inspiratory muscles, inspiration is produced by resilin ligaments between the terga and sterna.

Plasticisation of cuticle in Rhodnius

Rhodnius larvae normally take only one very large blood meal in each instar, which results in considerable distension of the abdomen, so that its surface area is increased about four times and the cuticle becomes considerably thinner. This distension is facilitated by a plasticisation of the abdominal procuticle due to a lowering of pH. In unplasticised cuticle the pH is above 6, whereas in plasticised cuticle it is less than 6. This change disrupts weak bonding between the protein and chitin microfibrils so that they can slide with respect to each other. Plasticisation is apparent within two minutes of the start of feeding and the pumping activity associated with food intake initiates the process. Information is passed via stretch receptors to the central nervous system and via neurosecretory axons directly to the epidermal cells which regulate the pH in the cuticle. The increase in size associated with plasticisation is to a large extent reversible and the abdomen slowly shrinks to approach its original size as the meal is digested and excreted (see Reynolds, 1975, for refs.). This cuticle only contains about 11 % of chitin, and the proteins are low in aspartic acid and glutamic acid, but high in alanine and histidine. The low levels of amino acids with bulky side-chains may facilitate sliding of the molecules (Hackman, 1975).

Stretching of cuticle in locusts

Locusts and grasshoppers lay their eggs in the ground, often extending the abdomen to more than twice its normal length by stretching some of the intersegmental membranes. This process is described on p. 389.

22.4 Moulting

Growth is limited by the cuticle, which normally undergoes only a limited amount of stretching, so that for any marked increase in size to occur the cuticle must be shed and replaced. Casting the cuticle is commonly known as moulting, but it involves a sequence of events beginning with the separation of the old cuticle from the underlying epidermal cells. This is called apolysis by Jenkin and Hinton (1966), although some authors use 'moulting' in a restricted sense to include only this process. Moulting (in the broad sense) ends with the shedding of the remnants of the old cuticle, and this is known as ecdysis. After ecdysis the cuticle is expanded and chemically modified and in most insects extensive deposition of new cuticle continues in the intermoult period. The timing of events is illustrated in Fig. 329.

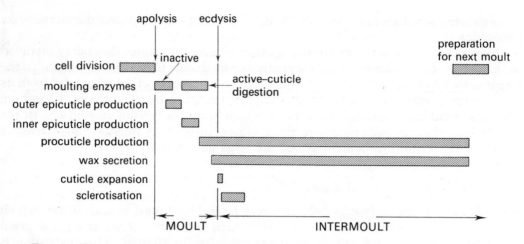

Fig. 329 Diagram showing the sequence of events in moulting and cuticle production. The timing of apolysis relative to cell division and the degree of overlap between procuticle and cell division vary in different insects

22.4.1 Changes in the epidermis

The onset of moulting is usually first indicated by changes in the epidermal cells, which divide and so become close-packed and columnar in form. In *Rhodnius*, at least, cell destruction accompanies cell division and continues for a time after cell division stops, being dependent on the level of juvenile hormone in the blood. There is, nevertheless, a net increase in the number of cells per unit area (Fig. 330), so that when these are flattened the overall area of the epidermis, and hence of the cuticle which they subsequently produce, is increased. An increase in size does not always involve cell division and in the larvae of cyclorrhaphous Diptera growth takes place solely as a result of the cells increasing in size. In *Lucilia* (Diptera) larva the cells increase in area by a factor of 20 between the first and third instars.

22.4.2 Separation of the cuticle from the epidermis (Apolysis)

Perhaps as a result of the changes in cell shape, a tension is generated at the surface of the epidermal cells which results in their separating from the cuticle (Fig. 331B) (Passonneau and Williams, 1953). On the other hand, in *Podura* (Collembola) the outer plasma membrane of the epidermal cells forms small out-pushings which separate off as vesicles and form a foam which lifts off the cuticle (Noble-Nesbitt, 1963).

22.4.3 Digestion of the old endocuticle

At least in some species changes occur in the cuticle before apolysis in preparation for its subsequent digestion. In the larva of *Calpodes* electron-dense droplets are secreted during the production of the last layers of procuticle. These exuvial droplets are probably inactive precursors of the moulting enzymes (Locke and Krishnan, 1973) and in *Manduca* larva chitinase is present in the cuticle in an inactive form (Bade, 1974).

In many species at least some of the moulting enzymes are secreted into the space, known as the exuvial space, between the epidermis and the cuticle after apolysis. In *Podura* the enzymes are produced as granules and in various Lepidoptera they are described as forming a gel. Initially the enzymes are inactive and they remain in this state until the outer epicuticle of the new cuticle is formed. This is of great importance since otherwise the moulting enzymes would digest the newly formed procuticle as well as the old cuticle.

Activation of the moulting enzymes is probably associated with the active transport of potassium into the exuvial space accompanied by a bulk flow of water, which occurs when the outer epicuticle is complete. The ionic composition of this fluid may also serve to buffer the enzyme systems against pH changes during the subsequent digestion of cuticle (Jungreis, 1978). At this time the exuvial droplets, when they are present, dissolve.

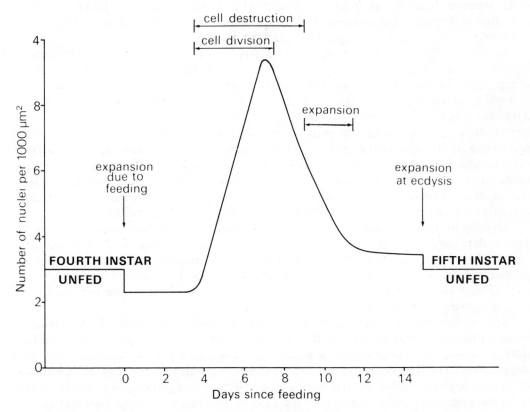

Fig. 330 The change in nuclear density (as an indication of cell density and size) in the tracheal epithelium of *Rhodnius*. Expansion and cell destruction decrease the density, cell division increases it. In this instance most expansion takes place before ecdysis (after Locke, 1964)

The moulting fluid contains a chitinase and at least one proteinase (Bade and Shoukimas, 1974; Katzenellenbogen and Kafatos, 1971). These enzymes digest all the unsclerotised cuticle except for the ecdysial membrane (see below), but they have no effect on the exocuticle or on the muscle and nerve connections to the old cuticle. These persist so that the insect is still able to move and receive stimuli from the environment, but they are finally broken at ecdysis by the muscular activity of the insect. The products of digestion of the cuticle are absorbed, it is said through the integument, and up to 90 % of the materials present in the cuticle may be conserved in this way.

As a result of the activity of the moulting fluid the cuticle becomes very thin and weak along the ecdysial lines (Fig. 327). These vary in position, but in the locust there is a ⅄ -shaped line on the head, the ecdysial cleavage line (p. 5), and a median dorsal line on the thorax.

22.4.4 Ecdysis

When the moulting fluid and the products of digestion of the moulting fluid are resorbed the old cuticle consists of little more than epicuticle and exocuticle and it is quite separate from the new cuticle (Fig. 331E). Usually ecdysis follows as soon as digestion is complete, but sometimes the old cuticle may be retained for some time and the insect so enclosed is referred to as pharate (p. 466).

In *Teleogryllus* a preparatory phase of activity loosens the old cuticle and culminates in splitting it; this activity lasts about two hours and is followed by ecdysis proper, the escape from the old cuticle, which takes about 20 minutes at 25°C. Each of these phases is made up of a sequence of relatively simple motor activities which follow each other in a more or less definite order. Carlson (1977) recognises seven motor programmes in the preparatory phase and 30 in the ecdysial phase (Fig. 332). Each programme occurs in bursts of activity separated by periods of quiescence and the level of expression of each rises to a peak and then declines as the frequency of bursts and the number of muscle units active is changed. The sequence of activities is controlled largely endogenously by the central nervous system, but feedback from peripheral sensilla can prolong activities, or cause them to stop when their function has been fulfilled.

Usually in the preparatory phase the insect swallows air or water, which swells the gut so that haemolymph pressure is increased. In *Schistocerca* the blood volume is highest just before ecdysis and the high blood volume also increases haemolymph pressure (Lee, 1961). Then by muscular action the blood is pumped into a particular part of the body, often the thorax, so that this expands and exerts pressure on the old cuticle causing it to split along its lines of weakness.

Special muscles may be concerned in these pumping movements. In *Rhodnius* the ventral intersegmental muscles of the abdomen develop just before a moult, are used during ecdysis to pump blood forwards by contracting the abdomen, and then degenerate, to re-develop again just before the next moult. Similarly in adult blowflies there are specialised muscles in the abdomen which persist during the period of escape from the puparium and expansion of the new cuticle and then break down (Fig. 333) (Cottrell, 1962a). The special abdominal muscles are internal to the definitive muscles and extend from the front edge of one presumptive sclerite to the front edge of the next, so that, since they are not yet hardened, the sclerites are buckled when the muscles contract and the abdominal cavity is reduced in volume. Comparable muscles occur in Lepidoptera, Orthoptera and probably in other groups (and see p. 452).

Having split the old cuticle the insect draws itself out, usually the head and thorax first, followed by the abdomen and appendages. Many insects suspend themselves freely from a support so that their emergence from the old cuticle is aided by the force of

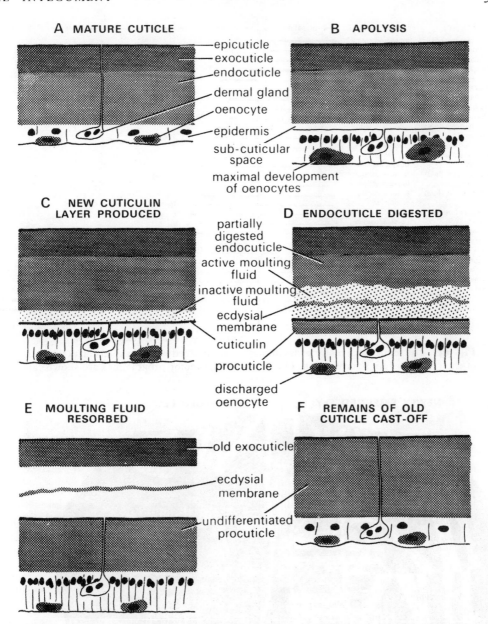

A MATURE CUTICLE

- epicuticle
- exocuticle
- endocuticle
- dermal gland
- oenocyte
- epidermis

B APOLYSIS

- sub-cuticular space
- maximal development of oenocytes

C NEW CUTICULIN LAYER PRODUCED

D ENDOCUTICLE DIGESTED

- partially digested endocuticle
- active moulting fluid
- inactive moulting fluid
- ecdysial membrane
- cuticulin
- procuticle
- discharged oenocyte

E MOULTING FLUID RESORBED

F REMAINS OF OLD CUTICLE CAST-OFF

- old exocuticle
- ecdysial membrane
- undifferentiated procuticle

Fig. 331 Diagrammatic representation of the changes occurring in the integument during the moulting cycle

gravity. All the cuticular parts are shed, including the intima of fore- and hind-gut, the endophragmal skeleton and the linings of the tracheae except for some delicate parts which may break off. The old cuticle is referred to as the exuviae.

Immediately after emergence the new cuticle is still unexpanded and soft, so that it provides the insect with little support. Probably the blood acts as a hydrostatic skeleton, since its volume is still high, and in *Calliphora* it constitues 30 % of the body weight at

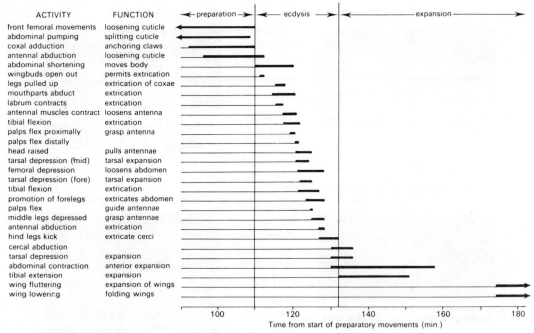

Fig. 332 The sequence of motor programmes involved in ecdysis and expansion of the cuticle of the cricket before sclerotisation. Only some of the motor programmes are shown (after Carlson, 1977)

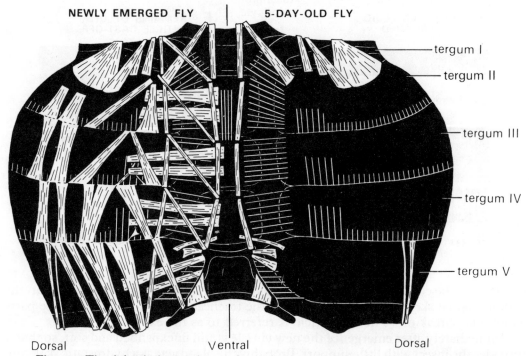

Fig. 333 The abdominal musculature of a newly emerged *Sarcophaga* (left) and a 5-day old fly (right). The abdomen has been split along the dorsal midline, laid out flat and viewed from the inside (after Cottrell, 1962a)

this time. After expansion is complete the blood volume is reduced so that it comprises only about 10% of the body weight (p. 806).

Some parts of the skeleton may be hard before ecdysis. Usually this pre-ecdysial hardening is restricted to small parts of the cuticle such as the claws, which are essential for the insect to hold on with, but it is more extensive in Cyclorrhapha and those Lepidoptera which have to escape from a pupal cell or cocoon (p. 475).

22.5 Cuticle formation

22.5.1 Formation of the epicuticle

The first step in the production of the new cuticle is the secretion of the outer epicuticle as patches at the tips of microvilli of the epidermal cells. The patches grow at their margins and coalesce to form a continuous layer over the whole of the epidermis. Apart from the lipids and proteins which form the structure of this layer, polyphenols and phenoloxidase are produced at the same time and so the proteins are probably stabilised from the beginning (Locke, 1976; Locke and Krishnan, 1971). The surface pattern of the cuticle is produced as the outer epicuticle is formed, being moulded by the underlying epidermal cells, which develop temporary vacuoles distally. The vacuoles and intercellular spaces disappear as the inner epicuticle is laid down (Wigglesworth, 1976).

At the same time as the outer epicuticle is produced the ecdysial membrane forms from the last few lamellae of the old procuticle, which become tanned by the polyphenols and phenoloxidase involved in stabilising the new outer epicuticle. Locke and Krishnan (1971) suggest that formation of the ecdysial membrane is simply a consequence of the presence of these chemicals, and that it has no functional significance. In *Calpodes* the ecdysial membrane becomes fenestrated when the ecdysial droplets dissolve and this permits the free access of moulting fluid to the more distal procuticle (Locke and Krishnan, 1973).

The inner epicuticle is secreted when the outer epicuticle is complete and the apical surfaces of the epidermal cells withdraw slightly. It is discharged in vesicles, which coalesce to form a discrete layer, and in *Calpodes* phenoloxidase is secreted at the same time. Polyphenols, however, are not present until about the time of ecdysis and so tanning of this layer does not take place until some time after its production (Locke and Krishnan, 1971).

Shortly before ecdysis wax is secreted onto the surface of the new cuticle, and the layer adjacent to the cuticulin forms the orientated monolayer (p. 594). In the cockroach, at least, the orientation of the molecules in the monolayer is dependent on the water-saturated layer of cuticulin beneath. The cuticulin adsorbs the hydrophilic polar groups, so that the hydrofuge aliphatic groups are towards the outside. Tanned cuticulin has a very high affinity for the polar groups and so tanning is also important in the production and maintenance of the hydrofuge monolayer (Beament, 1960). Wax secretion is well advanced at ecdysis, but even so, in *Tenebrio*, the rate of water loss during the first 24 hours after ecdysis is four to six times as high as normal, due to the incompleteness of wax production, which continues to a greater or lesser extent through the intermoult period. It is possible that the wax is transported to the surface in the epicuticular filaments (Locke and Krishnan, 1971).

The lipids of the epicuticle are secreted by and probably elaborated in the epidermal cells, but most of them probably originate in the oenocytes and are then liberated into the spaces between epidermal cells (Wigglesworth, 1976).

Soon after ecdysis a layer of cement produced by the dermal glands is formed over the surface of the wax in some species.

22.5.2 Production of procuticle

Production of procuticle begins after the inner epicuticle is laid down. The chitin microfibrils are produced at plaques on the surface membrane of the epidermal cells. At the same time protein is laid down in the interstices. Some of it is probably taken up from the haemolymph, while some is synthesised *de novo* in the epidermal cells (Andersen, 1979). The zone of deposition of new cuticle is distinct and is sometimes called Schmidt's layer. The precise nature of this zone is not known (Neville, 1975).

Although the deposition of procuticle begins before ecdysis it is, in some species at least, a continuous process and material continues to be added to the cuticle until the next moult when cuticle digestion begins. In *Calpodes*, and probably in other insects, the rate of cuticle deposition is greater during the intermoult period than during the moult (Fig. 334). In general new cuticular material is added as new lamellae adjacent to the epidermis, but in some cases additional proteins and lipids may be added to earlier layers via the pore canals.

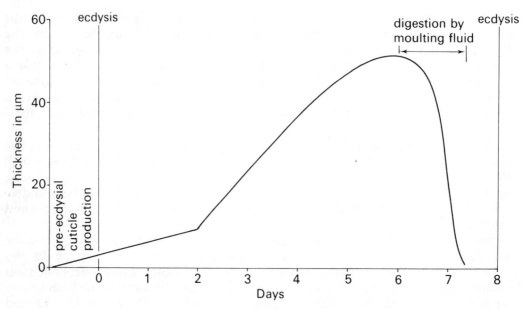

Fig. 334 Changes in the thickness of the endocuticle of a caterpillar during the final instar (based on Locke, 1970)

22.5.3 Hardening the cuticle

Apart from the larvae of many endopterygote insects, the cuticle in most species consists of areas of hardened cuticle linked by areas of flexible cuticle. Some hardening takes place before ecdysis, but the bulk occurs soon afterwards when expansion of the new cuticle is completed. The process of hardening involves the development of cross-links between protein chains and is known as tanning or sclerotisation. This commonly involves N-acetyldopamine (p. 507), which is derived from tyrosine. The concentration of this amino acid in the haemolymph increases just before ecdysis and it is taken up by haemocytes. From it dopamine is produced and in the epidermal cells this is acetylated to N-acetyldopamine, which is transported into the cuticle. Proteins may be linked by oxidation of the β-carbon atom of the side chain of the N-acetyldopamine or by oxidation of the hydroxyl groups on the phenolic ring to form N-acetyldopamine quinone, which then reacts with free amino groups on the protein chains (p. 507).

As the cuticle hardens it usually also darkens. This darkening may simply result from quinone tanning, but it may also involve the polymerisation of excess quinones to form melanin.

In the larva of *Calpodes* a phenoloxidase responsible for quinone production is produced as an integral part of the procuticle as it is laid down, but the polyphenols which it oxidises are only produced at about the time of ecdysis, so it is only at this time that sclerotisation begins. The phenoloxidases are incorporated into the cuticle only in areas destined to become sclerotised (Locke and Krishnan, 1971).

It is probably true that, as in *Schistocerca*, only procuticle produced before ecdysis is sclerotised in larval insects. Procuticle which is produced subsequently remains undifferentiated, so that the insects come to have distinct exo- and endocuticles. In the adult locust, however, where cuticle deposition continues for more than 20 days, sclerotisation continues for a similar period and so the whole thickness of the cuticle of the sclerites becomes stabilised. As in *Calpodes*, sclerotisation in the larva is regulated by the availability of substrate since the activity of the enzyme involved in cross-linking does not vary significantly during the instar. In the larva N-acetyldopamine is produced by the epidermal cells only for the first day after ecdysis, whereas in the adult it is formed continuously. This control is effected by the haemocytes, which take up tyrosine from the haemolymph for only a limited period at the larval moult (Andersen, 1974).

Membranous regions remain untanned apart from the epicuticle and it is clear that the extent of tanning is regulated by the epidermal cells responsible for producing the cuticle.

Vincent and Hillerton (1979) consider that cuticular hardening is due primarily to physical bonding between molecules following controlled dehydration of the cuticle; they believe that covalent cross-links between the protein molecules are relatively unimportant. Andersen (1981) considers the converse to be true.

22.6 Expansion of the new cuticle

In the later stages of ecdysis and immediately afterwards the insect expands the new cuticle before it hardens. This often involves swallowing air or water. In the blowfly air is pumped into the gut by the pharyngeal muscles, producing a steady increase in blood pressure (Fig. 335), while at the same time simultaneous contractions of the abdominal and ptilinal muscles produce transient increases in pressure. The expansion results partly from the opening out of deep folds in the new cuticle and partly from the pulling out of minor wrinkles in the epicuticle (Fig. 336). It is probably facilitated by a plasticisation of the procuticle of the presumptive sclerites, perhaps due to a temporary reduction in the linking between the molecules of the cuticle before tanning begins (Cottrell, 1962b) (see also p. 494). As a result of these processes the hind femur of *Schistocerca* increases in length by about 35 % over the period from hatching to final hardening of the cuticle of the first instar larva, but the dimensions of the epicuticle do not change (Bernays, 1972).

As the procuticle expands it also becomes thinner, partly due to stretching and partly to dehydration. Some changes in the orientation of chitin microfibrils may occur. In the wing of the butterfly *Aglais* they have a helicoidal arrangement when the cuticle is first laid down, but when the wing is expanded they are orientated parallel with the veins.

The high pressure does not expand the membranous regions between the sclerites because the presumptive sclerites are held tightly together by accessory muscles (see Fig. 333 and 288B).

22.7 Control of moulting and cuticle production

Ecdysone is the major hormone concerned with moulting (p. 828). It initiates apolysis and cuticle production, exerting its effects by inducing specific enzyme activities. Growth and division of the epidermal cells are not directly induced by ecdysone though they are linked with its activity. It is possible that another hormone acts as a trigger for

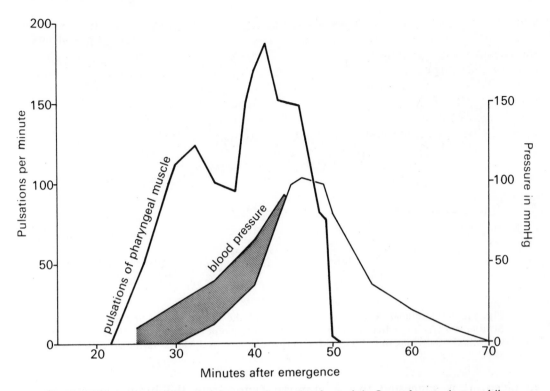

Fig. 335 The rate at which the pharyngeal muscle of an adult *Sarcophaga* pulsates while pumping air into the gut during the period of expansion after emergence. This produces an increase in blood pressure and further transient increases are produced by the simultaneous contraction of ptilinal and abdominal muscles. The hatched area indicates the range of fluctuation of blood pressure induced by these muscular efforts (after Cottrell, 1962a)

ecdysis and cuticle expansion (Carlson and Bentley, 1977) as it is known to in the eclosion of moths (p. 844). In this case the hormone acts on the central nervous system and releases a built-in programme of motor activities. In the moulting of *Teleogryllus* there are four discrete programmes which follow in sequence: preparation, ecdysis, expansion and eating the exuviae. Each programme involves a series of specific motor activities (Fig. 332) which, in general, progress without input from the peripheral nervous system, though their duration and strength may be affected by sensory input. Finally bursicon acts to plasticise and then to initiate sclerotisation of the cuticle. Its release occurs as soon as the insect is free to expand. For instance, in *Sarcophaga* bursicon is not released until the newly emerged fly has finished digging through the soil in which the puparium is formed (Cottrell, 1964) and in silkmoths its release follows as soon as the insect escapes from the cocoon and starts to expand (p. 494). Bursicon probably acts by controlling membrane permeability so that the substrates associated with tanning are taken up from the haemolymph by the epidermal cells.

After the moult further cuticle deposition occurs. It is not clear how this is regulated. In some larval Lepidoptera it is believed that very low concentrations of ecdysone govern the process, but in *Manduca* there is evidence that ecdysone is not

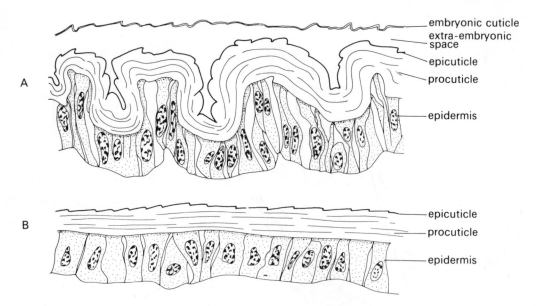

A

B

Fig. 336 Longitudinal sections of the cuticle of the femur of the first instar larva of *Schistocerca* (A) immediately before the embryonic moult (ecdysis) and (B) after ecdysis, showing the flattening out of the folds and the reduction in thickness of the procuticle (after Bernays, 1972)

involved. It is suggested that a humoral factor from the brain regulates cuticle production by causing the fat body to synthesise or release precursors of cuticular proteins (Wielgus and Gilbert, 1978). The secretion of wax by *Calpodes* larvae is controlled by a hormone released from the corpus allatum–corpus cardiacum complex. This hormone is only effective when it is present with ecdysone (Locke, 1965).

22.8 Functions of the cuticle

The cuticle is one of the features of insects which is primarily responsible for their success. It plays an important part in supporting the insect, an essential requirement of terrestrial animals. Further, the presence of hard, jointed appendages makes accurate movements possible with a minimum of muscle, thus effecting an economy of muscle, and, by lifting the body off the ground, facilitating rapid movement. Flight depends on the possession of rigid wings and in insects the cuticle provides the rigidity.

Protection is also provided by the cuticle. Some insects, such as adult beetles, have hardened heavily sclerotised cuticles which make them difficult for predators to catch or parasites to parasitise. Protection from the physical environment is also afforded. Again in beetles, the upper cuticle of the abdomen, protected by the elytra, is very thin, but the cuticle of the ventral surface, exposed and subject to abrasion by the substratum, is very thick. The cuticular lining of the fore- and hind-guts also protects the epidermis from abrasion by the food, while the wax layer is of great importance in the restriction of water loss (p. 592).

Finally, parts of the cuticle are modified to form sense organs (pp. 708, 736, 748) and its physical structure is also often important in the production of colour (p. 128).

REFERENCES

ANDERSEN, S. O. (1974). Cuticular sclerotization in larval and adult locusts, *Schistocerca gregaria. J. Insect Physiol.* **20**: 1537–1552.

ANDERSEN, S. O. (1979). Biochemistry of insect cuticle. *A. Rev. Ent.* **24**: 29–61.

ANDERSEN, S. O. (1981). The stabilization of locust cuticle. *J. Insect Physiol.* **27**: 393–396.

ANDERSEN, S. O. and BARRETT, F. M. (1971). The isolation of ketocatechols from insect cuticle and their possible rôle in sclerotization. *J. Insect Physiol.* **17**: 69–83.

ANDERSEN, S. O. and WEIS-FOGH, T. (1964). Resilin. A rubberlike protein in arthropod cuticle. *Adv. Insect Physiol.* **2**: 1–66.

BADE, M. L. (1974). Localization of moulting chitinase in insect cuticle. *Biochem. Biophys. Acta* **372**: 474–477.

BADE, M. L. and SHOUKIMAS, J. J. (1974). Neutral metal chelator-sensitive protease in insect moulting fluid. *J. Insect Physiol.* **20**: 281–290.

BEAMENT, J. W. L. (1960). Wetting properties of insect cuticle. *Nature, Lond.* **186**: 408–409.

BEAMENT, J. W. L. (1964). The active transport and passive movement of water in insects. *Adv. Insect Physiol.* **2**: 67–130.

BERNAYS, E. A. (1972). Changes in the first instar cuticle of *Schistocerca gregaria* before and associated with hatching. *J. Insect Physiol.* **18**: 897–912.

CARLSON, J. R. (1977). The imaginal ecdysis of the cricket (*Teleogryllus oceanicus*) I. Organization of motor programs and roles of central and sensory control. *J. comp. Physiol.* A, **115**: 299–317.

CARLSON, J. R. and BENTLEY, D. (1977). Ecdysis: neural orchestration of a complex behavioural performance. *Science* **195**: 1006–1008.

CAVENEY, S. (1976). The insect epidermis: a functional syncytium. *in* Hepburn, H. R. (ed.), *The insect integument.* Elsevier, Amsterdam.

COTTRELL, C. B. (1962a). The imaginal ecdysis of blowflies. Observations on the hydrostatic mechanisms involved in digging and expansion. *J. exp. Biol.* **39**: 431–448.

COTTRELL, C. B. (1962b). The imaginal ecdysis of blowflies. Evidence for a change in the mechanical properties of the cuticle at expansion. *J. exp. Biol.* **39**: 449–458.

COTTRELL, C. B. (1964). Insect ecdysis with particular emphasis on cuticular hardening and darkening. *Adv. Insect Physiol.* **2**: 175–218.

DENNELL, R. (1946). A study of an insect cuticle: the larval cuticle of *Sarcophaga falculata* Pond. (Diptera). *Proc. R. Soc. B,* **133**: 348–373.

HACKMAN, R. H. (1975). Expanding abdominal cuticle in the bug *Rhodnius* and the tick *Boophilus. J. Insect Physiol.* **21**: 1613–1623.

HEPBURN, H. R. (ed.) (1976). *The insect integument.* Elsevier, Amsterdam.

JENKIN, P. M. and HINTON, H. E. (1966). Apolysis in arthropod moulting cycles. *Nature, Lond.* **211**: 871–872.

JUNGREIS, A. M. (1978). The composition of larval–pupal moulting fluid in the tobacco hornworm, *Manduca sexta. J. Insect Physiol.* **24**: 65–73.

JUNGREIS, A. M. (1979). Physiology of moulting in insects. *Adv. Insect Physiol.* **14**: 109–183.

KATZENELLENBOGEN, B. S. and KAFATOS, F. C. (1971). Inactive proteinases in silkmoth moulting gel. *J. Insect Physiol.* **17**: 823–832.

LEE, R. M. (1961). The variation of blood volume with age in the desert locust (*Schistocerca gregaria* Forsk.). *J. Insect Physiol.* **6**: 36–51.

LOCKE, M. (1960). The cuticle and wax secretion in *Calpodes ethlius* (Lepidoptera: Hesperiidae). *Q. Jl microsc. Sci.* **101**: 333–338.

LOCKE, M. (1961). Pore canals and related structures in insect cuticle. *J. biophys. biochem. Cytol.* **10**: 589–618.

LOCKE, M. (1964). The structure and formation of the integument in insects. *in* Rockstein, M. (ed.), *The physiology of Insecta.* vol. 3. Academic Press, New York.

LOCKE, M. (1965). The hormonal control of wax secretion in an insect, *Calpodes ethlius* Stoll (Lepidoptera: Hesperiidae). *J. Insect Physiol.* **11**: 641–658.

LOCKE, M. (1970). The moult/intermoult cycle in the epidermis and other tissues of an insect *Calpodes ethlius* (Lepidoptera: Hesperiidae). *Tissue & Cell* **2**: 197–223.

LOCKE, M. (1976). The role of plasma membrane plaques and Golgi complex vesicles in cuticle deposition during the moult/intermoult cycle. *in* Hepburn, H. R. (ed.), *The insect integument.* Elsevier, Amsterdam.

LOCKE, M. and KRISHNAN, N. (1971). The distribution of phenoloxidases and polyphenols during cuticle formation. *Tissue & Cell* **3**: 103–126.

LOCKE, M. and KRISHNAN, N. (1973). The formation of the ecdysial droplets and the ecdysial membrane in an insect. *Tissue & Cell* **5**: 441–450.

NEVILLE, A. C. (1963). Growth and deposition of resilin and chitin in locust rubber-like cuticle. *J. Insect Physiol.* **9**: 265–278.

NEVILLE, A. C. (1975). *Biology of the arthropod cuticle.* Springer-Verlag, Berlin.

NEVILLE, A. C., THOMAS, M. G. and ZELAZNY, B. (1969). Pore canal shape related to molecular architecture of arthropod cuticle. *Tissue & Cell* **1**: 183–200.

NOBLE-NESBITT, J. (1963). The cuticle and associated structures of *Podura aquatica* at the moult. *Q. Jl microsc. Sci.* **104**: 369–392.

PASSONNEAU, J. V. and WILLIAMS, C. M. (1953). The moulting fluid of the cecropia silkworm. *Q. Jl microsc. Sci.* **30**: 545–560.

REYNOLDS, S. E. (1975). The mechanism of plasticization of the abdominal cuticle in *Rhodnius. J. exp. Biol.* **62**: 81–98.

REYNOLDS, S. E. (1980). Integration of behaviour and physiology in ecdysis. *Adv. Insect Physiol.* **15**: 475–595.

RUDALL, K. M. (1963). The chitin/protein complexes of insect cuticles. *Adv. Insect Physiol.* **1**: 257–314.

SATIR, P. and GILULA, N. B. (1973). The fine structure of membranes and intercellular communication in insects. *A. Rev. Ent.* **18**: 143–166.

SNODGRASS, R. E. (1935). *Principles of insect morphology.* McGraw-Hill, New York.

VINCENT, J. F. V. and HILLERTON, J. E. (1979). The tanning of insect cuticle—a critical review and a revised mechanism. *J. Insect Physiol.* **25**: 653–658.

WAY, M. J. (1950). The structure and development of the larval cuticle of *Diataraxia oleracea* (Lepidoptera). *Q. Jl microsc. Sci.* **91**: 145–182.

WEIS-FOGH, T. (1970). Structure and formation of insect cuticle. *Symp. R. ent. Soc. Lond.* **5**: 165–185.

WIELGUS, J. J. and GILBERT, L. I. (1978). Epidermal cell development and control of cuticle deposition during the last larval instar of *Manduca sexta. J. Insect Physiol.* **24**: 629–637.

WIGGLESWORTH, V. B. (1973a). Haemocytes and basement membrane formation in *Rhodnius. J. Insect Physiol.* **19**: 831–844.

WIGGLESWORTH, V. B. (1973b). The role of the epidermal cells in moulding the surface pattern of the cuticle in *Rhodnius* (Hemiptera). *J. Cell Sci.* **12**: 683–705.

WIGGLESWORTH, V. B. (1976). The distribution of lipid in the cuticle of *Rhodnius. in* Hepburn, H. R. (ed.), *The insect integument.* Elsevier, Amsterdam.

CHAPTER XXIII

THE TRACHEAL SYSTEM AND RESPIRATION IN TERRESTRIAL INSECTS

Gaseous exchange in insects is carried on through a system of internal tubes, the tracheae, the finer branches of which extend to all parts of the body and may become functionally intracellular in muscle fibres. Thus oxygen is carried directly to its sites of utilisation and the blood is not concerned with gas transport. The tracheae open to the outside through segmental pores, the spiracles, which generally have some closing mechanism which permits water loss from the respiratory surfaces to be kept to a minimum. The spiracles open in response to a low concentration of oxygen or a high concentration of carbon dioxide in the tissues.

Diffusion alone can account for the gaseous requirements of the tissues of most insects at rest, but in larger insects or during activity demands on oxygen are greater. To meet these demands the insect pumps air in and out of the tracheal system by expanding and collapsing air-sacs, which are enlarged parts of the tracheae whose volume can be changed by movements of the body. These movements are controlled by endogenous rhythms within the central nervous system.

In some insects which have low oxygen requirements the spiracles may open in such a way as to permit the entry of oxygen, but they prevent the exit of water and carbon dioxide except in occasional bursts. This is regarded as a water conserving mechanism. In some insects living in moist environments, where water loss is not a problem, gaseous exchange may take place through the permeable cuticle.

Insect respiration is reviewed by Buck (1962), Keister and Buck (1964) and Miller (1964, 1966). The anatomy of the tracheal system is reviewed by Whitten (1972).

23.1 The tracheal system

23.1.1 Tracheae

The tracheae are the larger tubes of the tracheal system, running inwards from the spiracles and usually breaking up into finer branches, the smallest of which are about 2 μm in diameter. Tracheae are formed by invaginations of the ectoderm and so are lined by a cuticular intima which is continuous with the rest of the cuticle (Fig. 337). A spiral thickening of the intima runs along each tube, each ring of the spiral being called a taenidium. The taenidia prevent the collapse of the trachea if the pressure within is reduced. The intima consists of outer epicuticle (p. 508) with a protein/chitin layer beneath it. In the taenidia the protein/chitin cuticle is differentiated as mesocuticle or exocuticle. The chitin microfibrils in the taenidia run round the trachea and prevent its collapse, while between the taenidia they are parallel with the long axis of the trachea. A layer of resilin may be present beneath the epicuticle (Whitten, 1972).

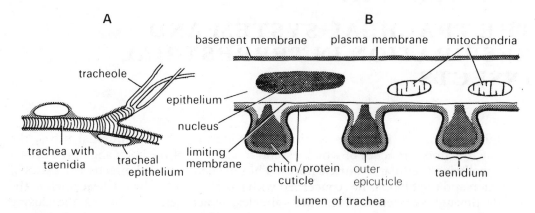

Fig. 337 A. Small part of the tracheal system showing tracheae, with taenidial thickenings, and tracheoles (from Wigglesworth, 1954). B. Longitudinal section of tracheal wall; body cavity above, lumen of trachea below

23.1.2 Air-sacs

In places the tracheae are expanded to from thin-walled air-sacs (Fig. 343), in which the taenidia are absent or poorly developed and often irregularly arranged. Consequently, the air-sacs will collapse under pressure and they play a very important part in ventilation of the tracheal system (p. 544) as well as having other functions (p. 551). Air-sacs are widely distributed along the main tracheal trunks of many insects.

23.1.3. Tracheoles

At various points along their length, and especially distally, the tracheae give rise to finer tubes, the tracheoles. There is no sharp distinction between tracheae and tracheoles, but the latter are always intracelluar and retain their cuticular lining at moulting, which is not usually true of tracheae. Proximally the tracheoles are about $1\,\mu m$ in diameter, tapering to about $0.1\,\mu m$. They are formed in cells called tracheoblasts, which are derived from the epidermal cells lining the tracheae (Fig. 338). The intima of tracheoles is some 16–20 nm thick and may consist only of outer epicuticle. It is thrown into taenidial ridges, but, unlike the taenidia of tracheae, these ridges are not filled with chitin/protein matrix (Edwards *et al.*, 1958). The intima stands on a membrane, which may be a deep in-tucking of the plasma membrane (Whitten, 1972), and outside this are the cytoplasm and plasma membrane of the tracheoblast.

The tracheoles are very intimately associated with the tissues and in fibrillar muscle,

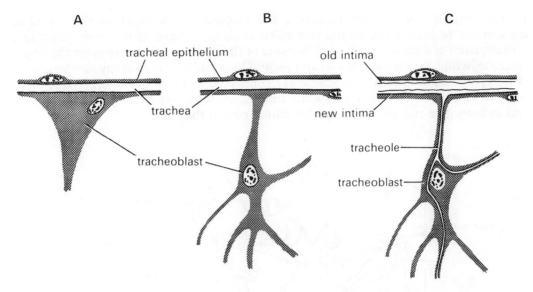

Fig. 338 The development of a tracheole. A. Tracheoblast developing from tracheal epithelial cell. B. Tracheoblast with extensive cytoplasmic processes. C. Tracheole develops within tracheoblast and connects with the trachea at the moult (after Keister, 1948)

for instance, they may indent the muscle plasma membrane and penetrate deep into the fibre (Fig. 339), but it is probable that they never become truly intracellular. Distally the tracheoles end blindly or they may anastomose.

23.1.4 Distribution of the tracheal system

The tracheal system arises externally at the spiracles and in some Collembola and the Archaeognatha the tracheae from each spiracle form a series of unconnected tufts.

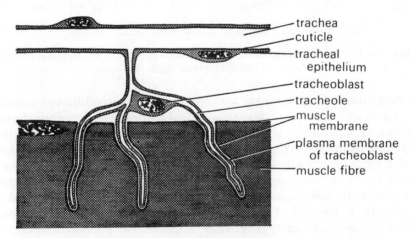

Fig. 339 Diagrammatic representation of tracheoles indenting the membrane of a muscle fibre to become functionally intracellular within the fibre

In the majority of insects, however, the tracheae from neighbouring spiracles anastomose to form longitudinal trunks running the length of the body (Fig. 340). Usually there is a lateral trunk on either side of the body and these are often the largest tracheae, while, in addition, dorsal and ventral longitudinal trunks may also be present (Fig. 341). The longitudinal tracheae are connected to those of the other side of the body by transverse commissures, while smaller branches extend to the various tissues and in turn give rise to the tracheoles which run to the cells.

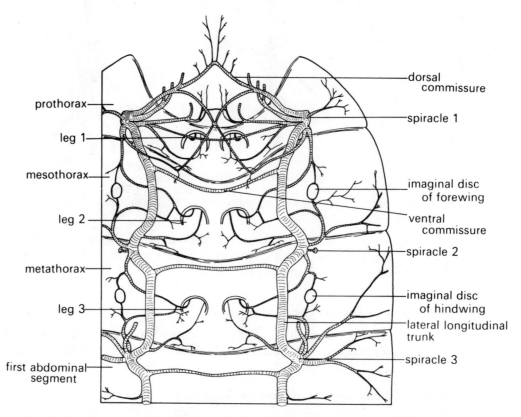

Fig. 340 Tracheation of the thorax and first abdominal segment of a caterpillar, dorsal view (from Snodgrass, 1935)

The arrangement of the tracheal system varies between different insects, but in general the heart and dorsal muscles are supplied by branches from the dorsal trunks, the alimentary canal, gonads, legs and wings from the lateral trunks and the central nervous system from the ventral trunks or transverse commissures. The head is supplied with air from spiracle 1 through two main tracheal branches on each side, a dorsal branch to the antennae, eyes and brain and a ventral branch to the mouthparts and their muscles. In *Schistocerca*, at least, the tracheal system of the head is largely isolated from that in the rest of the body by the small bore of some interconnecting tubes and the occlusion of others (Fig. 342). This ensures a good and direct supply of air to the brain and major sense organs and since the exhalent trunk from the head supplies the thoracic ganglia these also have a good air supply (Miller, 1960c).

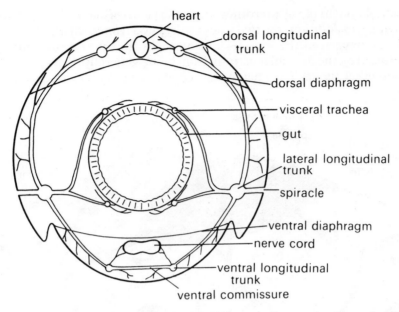

Fig. 341 Diagrammatic cross-section of the abdomen of an orthopteran showing the principal tracheae and tracheal trunks (from Snodgrass, 1935)

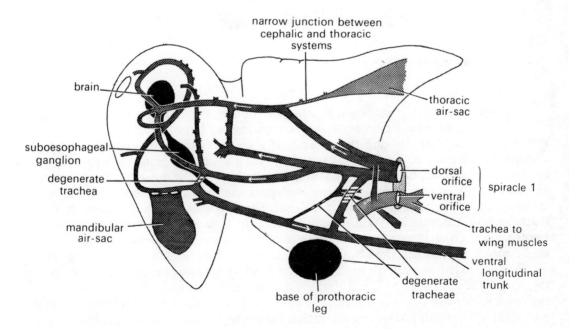

Fig. 342 Diagram of the main tracheae to the head of *Schistocerca*. Arrows indicate the probable direction of air-flow resulting from abdominal ventilation (after Miller, 1960c)

The tracheal system of the pterothorax (p. 154) in *Schistocerca* in similarly isolated (Fig. 343), while, in addition, the two sides are isolated from each other. This ensures a good supply of oxygen to the muscles during flight, but it also prevents the carbon dioxide produced by the muscular activity from being generally distributed throughout the body, and other tissues from being starved of oxygen by the excessive demands of the muscles.

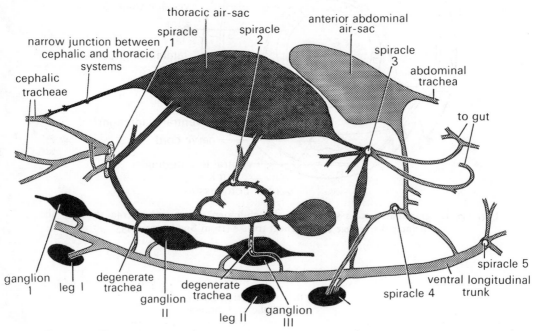

Fig. 343 Diagram of the pterothoracic tracheal system of *Schistocerca* (after Miller, 1960c)

The tracheal supply to the flight muscles follows a similar pattern in all larger insects. Each muscle has a primary supply consisting of a large tracheal trunk or air-sac running alongside or through the muscle. If a trachea forms the primary supply it widens to an air-sac beyond the muscle (Fig. 344). From the primary supply, small, regularly spaced tracheae arise at right angles, running into the muscle. These form the secondary supply and they are often oval proximally, permitting some degree of collapse, and taper regularly to the distal end. Finer branches pass in turn from these tracheae into the muscles (Weis-Fogh, 1964a). In Odonata the terminal tracheolar branches run alongside and between the muscle fibres, but in close-packed and fibrillar flight muscle they indent the fibre membrane and are functionally internal (Fig. 339).

To some extent the distribution and abundance of tracheae reflect the demands for oxygen by different tissues. Small changes may occur within an instar. For instance, in the event of damage to the epidermis the epidermal cells produce cytoplasmic threads which extend towards and ultimately attach themselves to the nearest tracheole. These cytoplasmic threads which may be 150 μm long, are contractile and drag the tracheole to the region of the oxygen deficient tissue (Fig. 345). The normal distribution of tracheoles in the epidermis might arise in a similar way (Wigglesworth, 1959). Changes

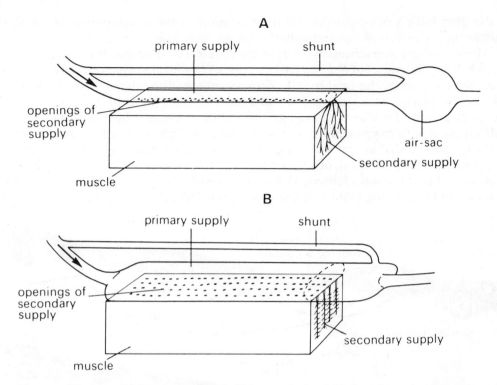

Fig. 344 Diagram of the tracheal supply to flight muscles in which the primary supply is (A) a trachea, or (B) an air-sac. Arrows indicate the inward flow of air (modified after Weis-Fogh, 1964a)

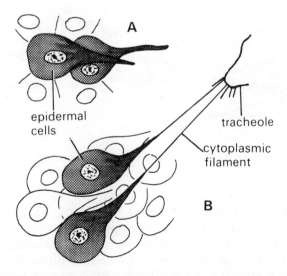

Fig. 345 A. Two epidermal cells sending out processes in the direction of a tracheole. B. Cytoplasmic filaments from epidermal cells attached to a tracheole and drawing it towards the cells (after Wigglesworth, 1959)

in the distribution of tracheoles occur in relation to the development of the flight muscles in the pupae of cyclorrhaphan Diptera (Fig. 314).

Major changes in tracheation occur at the moult. For instance, the relative volume of tracheae in the ovaries of *Schistocerca* increases 18 times at the penultimate moult and a further 16 times at the final moult. Between moults the relative volume decreases because the ovary continues to grow, and similar changes occur in the testes and male accessory glands. Thus as the tissue grows within an instar it becomes relatively less well supplied with oxygen and possibly shortage of oxygen stimulates mitosis in the tracheal cells, so that at the moult new tracheae are formed. New tracheae arise as outgrowths, mainly terminal, of columns of cells from the existing tracheal epithelium (Fig. 346). They develop a lumen, which subsequently becomes lined with cuticle and connects to the existing system at the next moult (Wigglesworth, 1954).

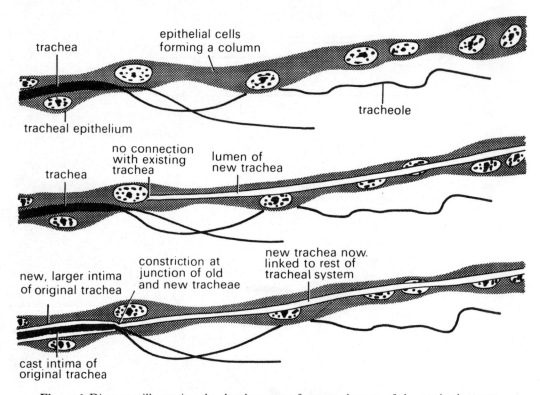

Fig. 346 Diagrams illustrating the development of a new element of the tracheal system (derived from Wigglesworth, 1954)

At least partly related to altered oxygen demands, the tracheal system varies with the state of development and becomes more complex at each moult. This may involve changes in the functional spiracles as well as in tracheation. For instance, the first instar larva of *Sciara* (Diptera) is metapneustic, the second instar is propneustic and the fourth instar hemipneustic (see below). Each new system is built round that of the preceding instar, but on a larger scale and with new extensions (Fig. 346) (Keister, 1948).

23.2 Spiracles

The spiracles are the external openings of the tracheal system. They are lateral in position, usually on the pleura, and, except in *Japyx* (Diplura) with two pairs on the metathorax, there is never more than one pair of spiracles on a segment. Often each spiracle is contained in a small, distinct sclerite, the peritreme.

23.2.1 Number and distribution

The largest number of spiracles found in insects is ten pairs, two thoracic and eight abdominal, and the respiratory system may be classified on the basis of the number and distribution of the functional spiracles (Keilin, 1944).

Polypneustic—at least 8 functional spiracles on each side
    Holopneustic—10 spiracles: 1 mesothoracic, 1 metathoracic, 8 abdominal—as in bibionid larvae
    Peripneustic—9 spiracles: 1 mesothoracic, 8 abdominal—as in cecidomyid larvae
    Hemipneustic—8 spiracles: 1 mesothoracic, 7 abdominal—as in mycetophilid larvae
Oligopneustic—1 or 2 functional spiracles on each side
    Amphipneustic—2 spiracles: 1 mesothoracic, 1 post-abdominal—as in psychodid larvae
    Metapneustic—1 spiracle: 1 post-abdominal—as in culicid larvae
    Propneustic—1 spiracle: 1 mesothoracic—as in dipterous pupae
Apneustic—no functional spiracles—as in chironomid larvae.
Apneustic does not imply that the insect has no tracheal system, but that the tracheae do not open to the outside. In numerous insects the first spiracle is on the prothorax, but is mesothoracic in origin (Hinton, 1966). Where less than ten functional spiracles are present the others, nevertheless, persist. These 'non-functional' spiracles are open at the time of ecdysis and permit the cast intima to be shed (p. 541).

Amongst other hexapod groups some Diplura, such as *Japyx*, have 11 pairs of spiracles, including four pairs on the thorax, while the sminthurids (Collembola) have only a single pair of spiracles between the head and prothorax and from these tracheae extend, without anastomoses, to all parts of the body. Most Collembola have no tracheae at all.

23.2.2 Structure

In its simplest form, found in some Apterygota, the spiracle is a direct opening from the outside into a trachea, but generally the visible opening leads into a cavity, the atrium, from which the tracheae arise. In this case the opening and the atrium are known collectively as the spiracle. Often the walls of the atrium are lined with hairs which filter out dust (Fig. 347). In some Diptera, Coleoptera and Lepidoptera the spiracle is covered by a sieve plate containing large numbers of small pores, which in the fifth instar larva of *Bombyx* (Lepidoptera) measure $6 \mu m \times 3 \mu m$. These sieve plates also serve to prevent the entry of dust or, especially in aquatic insects, water into the tracheal system.

The spiracles of most terrestrial insects have a closing mechanism which is important in the control of water loss (Fig. 389). The closing mechanism may consist of one or two movable valves in the spiracular opening itself or it may be internal, closing off the atrium from the trachea by means of a constriction.

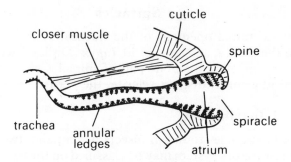

Fig. 347 Longitudinal section of the spiracle of a louse, *Haemotopinus*, showing the dust-catching spines and ledges (after Webb, 1948)

Spiracle 2 in grasshoppers is in the membrane between the meso- and meta-thorax. It is closed by two movable semi-circular valves which are unsclerotised except at the hinge and are thickened basally to form a pad into which a muscle is inserted (Fig. 348). This muscle, by pulling down on the valves, causes them to rotate and so to close. The spiracle normally opens by virtue of the elasticity of the surrounding cuticle, but in flight it opens wider as a result of the slight separation of the mesepimeron and metepisternum. These two sclerites which surround the spiracle are normally held together by an elastic bridge, but when the basalar and subalar muscles contract the sclerites are pulled apart. This movement is transmitted to the spiracle largely through the ligament connecting the metepisternum to the anterior valve and the effect is to make the spiracle open wide (Fig. 348) (Miller, 1960b).

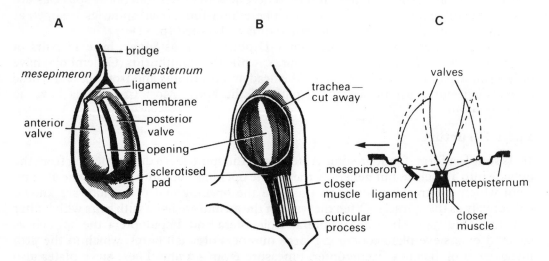

Fig. 348 The second thoracic spiracle of a locust. A. External view. B. Internal view. C. Diagrammatic transverse section showing how movement (indicated by arrow) of the mesepimeron causes the valves to open wide (after Miller, 1960b)

This 'one muscle' type of spiracle is usually present on the thorax, but in Orthoptera spiracle 1 has both opener and closer muscles. This spiracle is on the membrane between the pro- and mesothorax, and consists of a fixed anterior valve and a movable posterior valve. It is unusual in having two orifices which lead directly from the external opening. A scelerotised rod runs along the free edge of the posterior valve, passing between the orifices and running round the ventral one (Fig. 349). The closer muscle arises on a cuticular inflexion beneath the spiracle and is inserted into a process of the sclerotised rod, while the opener muscle, also from the cuticular inflexion, is inserted on to the posterior margin of the posterior valve. When the insect is at rest and the closer muscle relaxes the spiracle opens some 20–30% of its maximum as a result of the elasticity of the cuticle; the opener muscle plays no part. Contraction of the opener muscle occurs with slow, deep ventilatory movements and this results in the spiracle opening fully (Miller, 1960b).

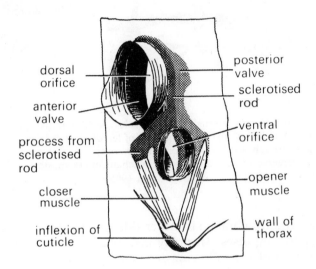

Fig. 349 The first thoracic spiracle of a locust, internal view (modified after Snodgrass, 1935; and Miller, 1960b)

Closure of abdominal spiracles usually involves a constriction method. Commonly the atrium is pinched between two sclerotised rods, or in the bend of one rod, as the result of the contraction of a muscle. Opening may involve a muscle (Fig. 350A), an elastic ligament (Fig. 350B) or the elasticity of the cuticle (Fig. 350C). In other instances the atrium or trachea is bent so that the lumen is occluded.

23.2.3 Control of spiracle opening

The spiracles are normally open for the shortest time necessary for efficient respiration in order to keep water loss from the tracheal system to a minimum. Spiracle closure results from the sustained contraction of the closer muscle, while opening commonly results from the elasticity of the surrounding cuticle when the closer muscle is relaxed. The muscle is controlled by the central nervous system, but may also respond to local chemical stimuli which interact with the central control.

The motorneurones to the spiracle muscles in each segment arise in the ganglion of the same segment or that immediately in front. The axons pass along the median nerve

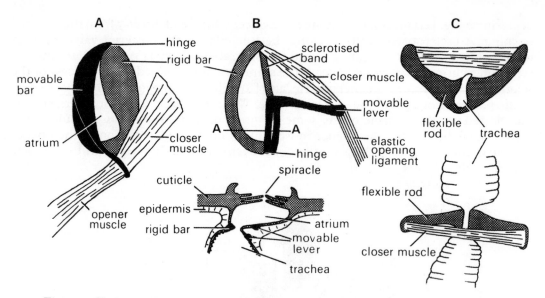

Fig. 350 Closing mechanisms internal to the spiracles. A. Abdominal spiracle of *Dissosteira* (Orthoptera) (from Snodgrass, 1935). B. Spiracle of lepidopterous larva; inner view above, horizontal section through AA below (from Imms, 1957). C. Constricting mechanism of trachea of flea; transverse section through the mechanism above, dorsal view below (after Wigglesworth, 1965)

and then bifurcate, sending a branch to either side, so that the two spiracles receive the same pattern of motor impulses. In many insects a sensory nerve passes from each spiracle to the ganglion of the following segment.

The closer muscle is caused to contract by a stream of impulses from the central nervous system, but the frequency of the impulses, which determines the degree of contraction, may be altered by various factors acting on the central nervous system. Of particular importance are a high level of carbon dioxide and a low level of oxygen (hypoxia) in the tissues and both these conditions will arise while the spiracles are closed, due to the production of carbon dioxide and the utilisation of oxygen in respiration. Both conditions lead to a reduction in impulse frequency and so to spiracle opening, probably by stimulating an interneurone which inhibits the spiracle motor neurone. In 'two muscle' spiracles the impulse frequency to the opener muscle is increased by high carbon dioxide levels and hypoxia.

The frequency of motor impulses to the opener muscle is also affected by the water balance of the insect, possibly acting through the concentration of a particular ion. If the insect is desiccated the impulse frequency rises and the spiracles remain closed longer; with excess hydration the converse is true and so the rate of water loss is increased.

Carbon dioxide also acts directly on the closer muscle of 'one muscle' spiracles, interfering with neuromuscular transmission so that the junction potential falls, muscle tension is reduced and the spiracle opens (Hoyle, 1960). The carbon dioxide has some other, internal, effect on the muscle, not concerned with neuromuscular transmission, and this also results in a reduction in tension.

The threshold of the peripheral response to carbon dioxide is set by the frequency of motor impulses from the central nervous system. The lower the impulse frequency, the lower is the threshold to carbon dioxide. In the adult dragonfly the impulse frequency is reduced by hypoxia and high carbon dioxide concentrations, and completely inhibited by flight, so that under these conditions the spiracles tend to open more frequently. Desiccation and high temperature increase the impulse frequency, so that the peripheral threshold to carbon dioxide is raised and the spiracles open less frequently.

'Two muscle' spiracles do not respond to peripheral stimulation and are controlled entirely by the output from the central nervous system·(Miller, 1960b).

Spiracle 2 of *Schistocerca* acts independently of the nervous system in its response to potassium. Concentrations of potassium above 30 mM/litre cause the closer muscle to contract even when it is isolated from the nervous system (Hoyle, 1961). Normally the concentration in the blood is not as high as this, but it may be exceeded as a result of desiccation and also at the moult. Consequently at these times the spiracles remain closed for most of the time, opening only when the concentration of carbon dioxide is high, and thus water loss is restricted. Such sustained muscular contraction due to high concentrations of potassium does not occur in other muscles.

23.3 Moulting the tracheal system

The cuticular lining of the tracheae is cast at each moult, and a new, larger intima is formed in its place. The longitudinal trunks break at predetermined points, the nodes, between adjacent spiracles and the old lining is drawn out through the spiracles and shed with the rest of the exuviae. In early *Sciara* larvae, with a relatively simple tracheal system, the whole of the cuticular lining is shed, but in older larvae with a more complex system the linings of the finest branches are persistent (Keister, 1948). In *Rhodnius* the linings of the tracheoles are never shed (Wigglesworth, 1954). Instead, when a new tracheal lining is formed it pinches in on the old lining at the origin of the tracheoles. At the point of constriction the old cuticle breaks and the new tracheal intima becomes continuous with the original tracheole lining, but a marked discontinuity is apparent (Fig. 351).

Where the number of functional spiracles is reduced, the 'non-functional' spiracles persist and facilitate the shedding of the tracheal intima so that this can occur even in apneustic insects. The 'non-functional' spiracles may be visible as faint scars on the cuticle and from each scar a strand of cuticle connects with the longitudinal trachea. At each moult new cuticle is laid down round this thread in the form of a tube opening to the outside and through this the old intima is withdrawn. Subsequently the tube closes and forms the cuticular thread connecting the new intima with the outer cuticle. Similar ecdysial tubes are formed next to functional spiracles when the structure of the spiracles is so complex that it does not permit the old intima to be drawn through it. This occurs, for instance, in Elateridae, Scarabaeidae and some Diptera (Hinton, 1947).

23.3.1 Pneumatisation

Immediately following ecdysis, and in the embryonic insect, the tracheal system is liquid-filled. Subsequently the liquid is replaced by gas, a process known as

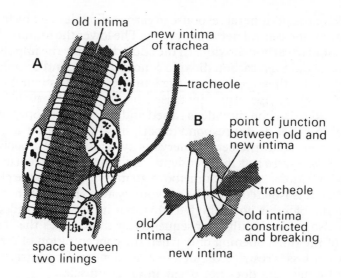

Fig. 351 A. Showing the development of a new tracheal intima at the moult and its junction with the original lining of a tracheole. B. The junction of trachea and tracheole enlarged (after Wigglesworth, 1954)

pneumatisation, but this gas does not enter via the spiracles. It usually appears first in a main tracheal trunk and then spreads rapidly through the system so that this becomes completely gas-filled in 10–30 minutes. The gas is probably forced out of solution in the liquid by physical forces resulting from the active resorption of liquid from the trachea together with the change in the surface properties from hydrophile to hydrofuge which occurs when the cuticle is tanned. These forces lead to the rupture of the liquid column and the appearance of gas in its place.

In most insects, but not in *Sciara*, some liquid normally remains in the endings of the tracheoles. During periods of high energy consumption the liquid is withdrawn from the system and air is drawn further into the tracheoles. At other times the liquid is secreted again and the air retreats. The level of liquid in the tracheoles represents the balance between the forces of capillarity and forces resulting mainly from imbibition by colloidal substances in the tracheoblast cytoplasm. These, in turn, are influenced by changes in the osmotic pressure of the tissues and so are related to metabolism. Similar forces may be responsible for the initial withdrawal of liquid from the tracheae after moulting (Buck and Keister, 1955).

23.4 Gaseous exchange

From the spiracles oxygen passes through the tracheal system to the tissues and ultimately must reach the mitochondria in order to play a part in oxidative processes. Carbon dioxide follows the reverse path. There are thus two distinct phases in the transport of gases, one through the tracheal system, known as air-tube diffusion, and one through the tissues in solution in the cytoplasm, known as tissue diffusion (Weis-Fogh, 1964b).

23.4.1 Diffusion

The rate of diffusion of a gas depends on a number of factors. It is inversely proportional to the square root of the molecular weight of the gas, so that in air, oxygen, with a molecular weight of 16, diffuses 1·2 times faster than carbon dioxide, molecular weight 28. Diffusion also depends on the differences in concentration of the gas at the two ends of the system and in the absence of a difference in concentration there is no net movement of gas. The change in concentration, or partial pressure (p), with distance (x), that is the concentration gradient, is expressed as $\frac{\delta p}{\delta x}$. Finally the permeability of the substrate, in this case air or the tissues, through which the gas is diffusing affects the rate of diffusion. This factor is expressed in terms of the permeability constant, P, which is the flow of a substance through unit area per unit time when the concentration gradient is unity.

Hence the volume (J) of a given gas transported by diffusion at NTP can be represented by the equation

$$J = -P\frac{\delta p}{\delta x} \text{ (Weis-Fogh, 1964b).}$$

The permeability constant for different substrates varies widely. That for oxygen in air at 20°C is 11 ml/min/cm²/atm/cm whereas in water $P = 3\cdot4 \times 10^{-5}$ and in frog muscle $1\cdot4 \times 10^{-5}$ ml/min/cm²/atm/cm. Hence oxygen in air diffuses more than 100 000 times faster than in water or the tissues, so that although, in the insect, the path of oxygen through the tracheal system is very much longer than its path through the tissues, perhaps 10 000 times as long, it will take over 10 times as long for the gas to diffuse from the tracheole endings to the mitochondria, than from the spiracles to the tracheole endings.

Thus the length of the tissue diffusion path is likely to be a factor limiting the size of tissues and, in particular, of flight muscles with a high requirement for oxygen. With a partial pressure difference between the tracheole and the mitochondrion of 5 % of an atmosphere a tracheole 1 μm in diameter would serve a muscle 7–15 μm in diameter if the oxygen uptake of the muscle was 1·5–3·0 ml/g/min, a level of uptake achieved in flight muscle (p. 267). Hence a muscle fibre in which the tracheoles are restricted to the outside of the fibres cannot exceed about 20 μm in diameter. The fibres of the flight muscles of dragonflies are of this type and are approaching their theoretical maximum size. On the other hand, if the tracheoles indent the muscle so as to become functionally internal, as they do in fibrillar muscle (p. 251), the muscle fibres can become much larger. In *Musca* (Diptera), for instance, the indenting tracheoles are only separated by distances of 3–5 μm, so that although individual fibres may be over one millimetre in diameter, they are well within the size limits imposed by tissue diffusion (Weis-Fogh, 1964b).

The inward diffusion of oxygen from the spiracles depends on the partial pressure within the tracheoles being lower than in the outside air and this will arise from the passage of oxygen into the tissues when it is utilised. A drop of 2 % of an atmosphere is sufficient to ensure that enough oxygen diffuses to the tissues and a 5 % drop ensures an adequate supply even to the extremities of the limbs. Such a difference also provides sufficient oxygen, by diffusion alone, for the flight muscles of small insects such as *Drosophila* (Diptera), but in larger insects diffusion by itself cannot meet the demands of highly active tissues.

Because of its greater solubility, the permeability constant of carbon dioxide in the tissues is 36 times greater than that for oxygen, so that despite its higher molecular weight, carbon dioxide travels more quickly than oxygen through the tissues for the same difference in partial pressure. Hence a system capable of bringing an adequate supply of oxygen to the tissues will also suffice to take the carbon dioxide away.

Carbon dioxide is more soluble and is present in higher concentrations in the tissues than oxygen. Thus some carbon dioxide, instead of passing directly into the tracheal system, might diffuse outwards through the tissues and enter the tracheae near the spiracles or pass out directly through the integument (p. 551). Such a shunt system is, however, unlikely to be of great importance if an adequate tracheal system exists because diffusion is so much more rapid in the gas phase. Carbonic anhydrase is present in insect tissues, but its role is not clear.

The exchange of gases between the tracheal system and the tissues is partly limited by the walls of the tracheae and tracheoles. The whole system may be permeable, with no marked difference between tracheoles and tracheae, but since the tracheoles are more closely associated with the tissues they will, in general, be more important than the tracheae in the transfer of oxygen to the tissues. The rate of exchange of gases also varies with the surface area through which they are diffusing. In some insects, the summed cross-sectional area of the tracheal system at different distances from the spiracles is believed to remain constant. Distally this area is made up of many small tubes, proximally of a few large ones, so that the circumference or wall area/unit length is much greater distally than proximally. Although in *Bombyx* larva the summed cross-sectional area of the tracheoles is less than that of the tracheae, the wall area/unit length of the tracheoles is nevertheless greater (Buck, 1962). Since this is so, it again follows that the tracheoles are generally a more important site of gaseous exchange with the tissues than are the more proximal tracheae.

23.4.2 Ventilation

In large, active insects diffusion alone does not bring sufficient oxygen to the tissues to meet their requirements and it is supplemented by convection produced by changes in the volume of the tracheal system. This is known as ventilation. Most tracheae are circular in cross-section and resist any change in form, but some, such as the longitudinal trunks of *Dytiscus* (Coleoptera) larvae, are oval in cross-section and are subject to collapse. The collapse of a trachea forces air out of the tracheal system, while its subsequent expansion sucks air in again. But changes in shape of the trachea only produce small volume changes. Much larger changes, and hence better gaseous exchange, are produced by the alternating collapse and expansion of air-sacs.

Compression of the system, causing expiration, results indirectly from muscular contractions, usually of the abdomen. These contractions lead to increased haemolymph pressure and movements of organs which press on the air-sacs, causing them to collapse. Expansion of the air-sacs and inspiration result from the reduction of pressure due to the muscular or elastic expansion of the abdomen. Changes in abdominal volume may be produced in various ways. In Heteroptera and Coleoptera the tergum moves up and down (Fig. 352A); in Odonata, Orthoptera, Hymenoptera and Diptera both tergum and sternum move (Fig. 202, 352B) and this movement may be associated with telescoping movements of the abdominal segments (Fig. 352C); in Lepidoptera the movement is complex and involves movements of the pleural regions as well as terga and sterna.

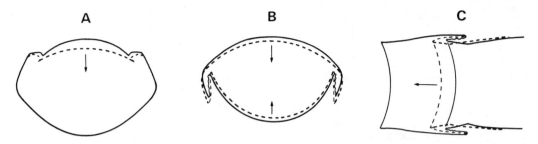

Fig. 352 Diagrammatic representations of types of abdominal ventilatory movements. Dashed lines indicate the contracted positions, arrows the directions of movement. (A) and (B) in transverse section, (C) in longitudinal section (from Snodgrass, 1935)

Alternate movements of compression and expansion pump air out from and in to the tracheal system through the spiracles. Air may flow in and out of each of the spiracles and such a movement of air is called a tidal flow. In many insects, however, opening and closing of certain spiracles is synchronised with the ventilatory pumping movements of the abdomen, so that air is sucked in through some spiracles and pumped out through others and a directed flow of air is produced. This is a more efficient form of ventilation than tidal flow since the 'dead' air, trapped in the inner parts of the system by tidal movements, is removed. In most insects the flow of air is from front to back and in *Schistocerca* spiracle movements are always coupled with ventilatory movements. In many insects, however, the two activities may become uncoupled so that they are not always synchronised (Miller, 1971) and the coupling may even be modified so as to produce a reversal of the airstream (Miller, 1973). In *Schistocerca* spiracles 1, 2 and 4 are open during inspiration, and then they close and spiracle 10 opens for expiration. When the insect is more active expiration takes place through spiracles 5 to 10. The spiracles for inspiration open immediately after the expiratory spiracles have closed and remain open for about 20 % of the cycle while air is drawn in. Then they close and for a short time all the spiracles are closed (Fig. 353A). The abdomen starts to contract while the spiracles are still closed, so that the air in the tracheae is under pressure, this is known as the compression phase. Then the expiratory spiracles open and air is forced out. The expiratory spiracles are only open for some 5–10 % of the cycle. During activity the frequency of ventilation and spiracular movements is increased. The times for which the spiracles open remain the same, but the period of closure is reduced and the compression phase eliminated (Fig. 353B) (Miller, 1960b).

Ventilation in large insects, such as locusts, is continuous, although there may be periods of a minute or more without ventilation. After periods of activity abdominal ventilation is supplemented by other types of ventilation and in *Schistocerca* these involve protraction and retraction of the head on the prothorax, neck ventilation, and movement of the prothorax on the mesothorax, prothoracic ventilation (Miller, 1960a). These movements primarily ventilate the head, so that they may be of considerable importance. The normal level of abdominal ventilation in *Schistocerca* pumps about 40 litres air/kg/h through the body, about 5 % of the air being exchanged at each

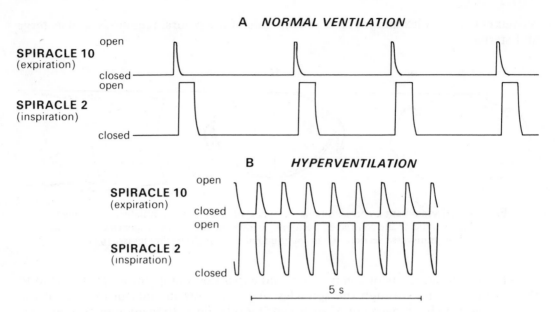

Fig. 353 Diagram illustrating the activity of the spiracles of *Schistocerca* in ventilation. A. Normal ventilation. B. Hyperventilation (after Millar, 1960b)

movement, but this can be raised to 150 litres, with an exchange of about 20 % of the volume at each stroke. Neck and prothoracic ventilation provide a further 50 litres air/kg/h. In *Dytiscus* 60 % of the air is renewed with each compression and expansion.

Ventilation in flight

A stationary insect uses 0·6–3·0 litres O_2/kg/h, whereas in flight the figure rises to 15–180 litres O_2/kg/h, a 30- to 100-fold increase and the demands of the flight muscles themselves may increase up to 400-fold. During the flight of *Schistocerca* abdominal ventilation increases in frequency and amplitude, but still only supplies about 150 litres air/kg/h, which is not sufficient to supply the needs of the flight muscles. However, the distortion of the thorax, and in particular the raising and lowering of the notal sclerites, produces large volume changes in the extra-muscular air-sacs of the pterothoracic tracheal system (Fig. 343), while changes in the volumes of the muscles themselves compress the intramuscular air-sacs. This pterothoracic ventilation produces an airflow of about 350 litres air/kg/h, which is adequate for the needs of the flight muscles.

When *Schistocerca* starts to fly the pattern of opening of the spiracles also alters (Fig. 354). At first spiracles 1 and 4 to 10 close and then they open and close rhythmically, being synchronised with abdominal ventilation so that there is a good flow of air to the brain and the sense organs. Increased abdominal ventilation may also improve the blood circulation and hence the fuel supply to the flight muscles. Spiracles 2 and 3 remain wide open throughout flight and although they show some incipient closures after a time these do not affect the airflow through the spiracles. These spiracles supply the flight muscles, and since the tracheal system of these muscles is

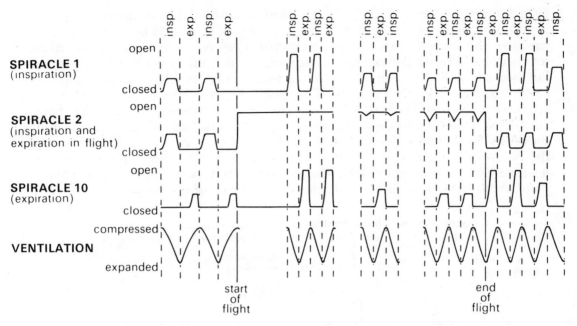

Fig. 354 Diagram illustrating the activity of some spiracles of *Schistocerca* synchronised with ventilatory movements during flight (after Miller, 1960c)

largely isolated and the spiracles remain open all the time, there is a tidal flow of air in and out of them (Miller, 1960c).

Thoracic pumping is also important in flight in Odonata and probably in Lepidoptera and Coleoptera, although in these two groups abdominal pumping is also important since the abdominal system is widely connected to the thoracic tracheal system. In Hymenoptera and Diptera changes in the thoracic volume during flight are not very large and abdominal pumping is of greater importance in maintaining the air supply to the flight muscles (Weis-Fogh, 1964a).

Control of ventilation

As in the control of spiracles, ventilatory movements are initiated by the accumulation of carbon dioxide and, to a lesser extent, the lack of oxygen, acting directly on centres in the ganglia of the central nervous system. Each abdominal ganglion produces rhythmical sequences of impulses controlling the movements, and the rhythm, once started, is autonomous. In *Schistocerca* and *Periplaneta* the metathoracic ganglion acts as a pacemaker and overrides the rhythms of the other ganglia (Farley *et al.*, 1967; Lewis *et al.*, 1973).

In normal ventilation, involving only dorso-ventral movements, expiration is produced by tergosternal muscles innervated by motorneurones from the ganglion of the corresponding segment. Inspiration is produced by muscles inserted low on the tergum (Fig. 202) and innervated by axons in branches from the median ventral nerve (p. 616). The perikarya of these motorneurones are in the ganglion of the preceding segment, so that the alternation of inspiratory and expiratory movements is controlled from different segments (Fig. 355). Coordination is achieved by an interneurone, one in each ventral connective (cell 2 in Fig. 356), which originates in the metathoracic ganglion and extends to the last abdominal ganglion. Action potentials in the interneurone activate the expiratory motorneurones (cell 4) via a small segmental interneurone (cell 3) and probably have a weak inhibitory effect on the inspiratory motorneurones (cell 5 in Fig. 356). The latter are more strongly inhibited by the interneurone (cell 3). The pacemaker (cell 1 in Fig. 356) in the metathoracic ganglion is considered to produce bursts of impulses of relatively constant duration which inhibit the otherwise continuously active interneurones. Hence inspiration only occurs when the interneurones (cell 2) are inhibited (Fig. 356), so that the inspiratory motor-neurones fire as a result of their endogenous activity and inhibit the expiratory motorneurones via a small interneurone (cell 6) (Lewis *et al.*, 1973).

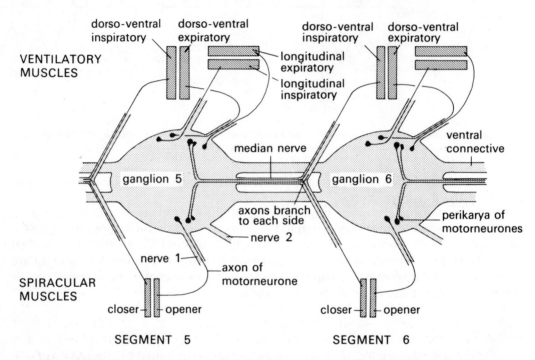

Fig. 355 Diagrammatic representation of the motor control of abdominal ventilation (top half) and spiracular closure (lower half) in *Schistocerca*. The positions of the perikarya within a ganglion are only approximations (based on Lewis *et al.*, 1973)

The rate of ventilation is altered by reducing the interval between inspiratory bursts and is affected by sensory input from various sources. Centres sensitive to carbon dioxide are present in the head and thorax of *Schistocerca* and these modify the activity of the pacemaker, while the output is also modified by high temperature and nervous excitation generally. Proprioceptors may play some part in the maintenance of the frequency of ventilation (Miller, 1960a; Farley and Case, 1968).

The coordination of the spiracles with the ventilatory movements is brought about by motor patterns derived from the ventilatory centres.

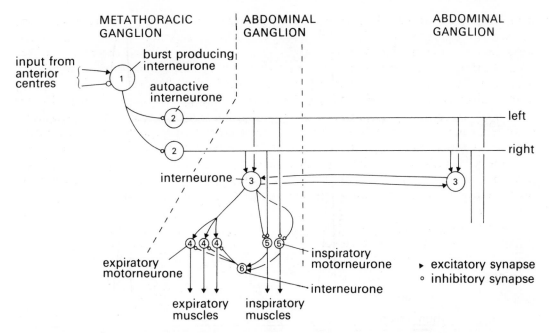

Fig. 356 Diagram of the connections between neurones in the central nervous system involved in the control of ventilation in a locust (after Lewis *et al.*, 1973)

23.4.3 Cyclic release of carbon dioxide

In some quiescent insects carbon dioxide is not released continuously from the spiracles, but is produced in bursts followed by long intervals in which very little carbon dioxide is liberated, although the uptake of oxygen is continuous. This occurs during the diapause of some lepidopterous larvae and pupae, in some Coleoptera, and in immature and senile locusts. In *Hyalophora* pupae the period between bursts of carbon dioxide release may be as much as seven hours (Fig. 357), while in locusts the interburst period is only about three minutes and the bursts are synchronised with ventilatory movements (Hamilton, 1964). During the bursts of carbon dioxide release the spiracles are wide open, while during the interburst period they repeatedly open very slightly and then close again, a phenomenon known as fluttering.

Cyclic release of carbon dioxide is usually observed when the oxygen requirements of an insect are low but the oxygen in the tracheae is used up faster than it enters through the spiracles. At the end of a burst in *Hyalophora* pupa oxygen comprises about 18 % of the gas in the tracheae. The spiracles close tightly and as the oxygen is used up the pressure in the tracheae which is already below atmospheric pressure, falls by about 3·5 mmHg. At the same time there is a small increase in the proportion of carbon dioxide present. In response to the low oxygen content of the tracheal air and tissues the spiracles open slightly, 5–10 % of their maximum, and because of the low pressure in the tracheal system air rushes in. The bulk influx of air prevents the outward diffusion of carbon dioxide, which therefore accumulates in the tracheae and the tissues. The influx of air temporarily increases the amount of oxygen present, so that the spiracles

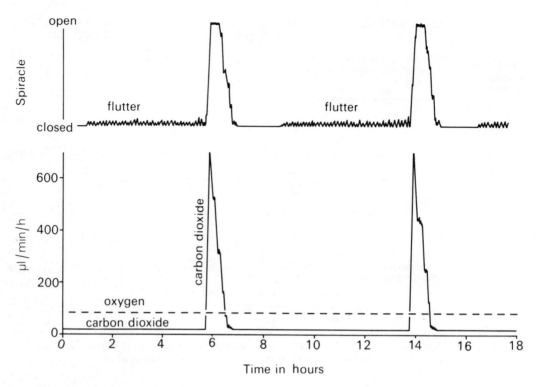

Fig. 357 Diagram to show the cyclic release of carbon dioxide and the associated activity of the spiracles. Oxygen uptake remains almost constant (from Miller, 1964)

close again, and the repeated lowering and raising of the oxygen level leads to the fluttering movement of the spiracle valves.

Slowly, in the course of the interburst period, carbon dioxide accumulates. Most of it is in the tissues, and in the pupa of *Agapema* (Lepidoptera) 90 % of the carbon dioxide produced during the interburst is retained in the tissues. Nevertheless the concentration in the tracheal system rises and ultimately it reaches a level which promotes spiracle opening. In *Hyalophora* this occurs when the gas in the tracheae contains more than 6 % carbon dioxide then the spiracles open wide, releasing a burst of carbon dioxide. The bulk inward movement of air, while preventing the outward flow of carbon dioxide and carrying in oxygen also carries in a large volume of nitrogen and the inflow of this gas must be matched by its outward diffusion (Buck, 1962; and see Kanwisher, 1966).

The cyclic release of carbon dioxide may not, in itself, be important, but the prolonged periods of closure of the spiracles are important because they result in the restriction of water loss from the tracheal system. Kanwisher (1966) suggests that as a result of this mechanism water loss from the pupa of *Hyalophora* does not greatly exceed the production of metabolic water and the pupa only loses 5 % of its weight over a four-month period. The cyclic release of CO_2 is not observed in pupae living in a moist environment, while in *Schistocerca* it is often associated with a lack of moisture (Hamilton, 1964).

23.4.4 Cutaneous respiration

Some gaseous exchange takes place through the cuticle of most insects, but this does not usually amount to more than a few percent of the total movement of gas. On the other hand, Protura and most Collembola have no tracheal system and must depend on cutaneous respiration together with transport from the body surface to the tissues by the haemolymph. Cutaneous respiration is also important in eggs (p. 396), aquatic insects, coupled with an apneustic tracheal system (p. 559), and endoparasitic insects. Cutaneous respiration without an associated apneustic tracheal system can only suffice for very small insects with a large surface/volume ratio.

The impermeability of most insect cuticles to oxygen arises from the epicuticle, but not from the wax layer which renders the cuticle impermeable to water (Buck, 1962). The permeability to carbon dioxide may be rather greater and the loss of this gas through the intersegmental membranes may be appreciable.

23.5 Other functions of the tracheal system

Apart from respiration the tracheal system has a number of other functions. The whole system, and in particular the air-sacs, lowers the specific gravity of the insect. In aquatic insects, but not in terrestrial ones, it also gives some degree of buoyancy and in the larvae of *Chaoborus* (Diptera) the tracheae form hydrostatic organs enabling the buoyancy to be adjusted (Teraguchi, 1975).

Air-sacs, being collapsible, allow for the growth of organs within the body without any marked changes in body form. Thus at the beginning of an instar the tracheal system of *Locusta* (Orthoptera) occupies 42 % of the body volume. By the end of the instar it only occupies 3.8 %, due to the growth of the other organs causing compression of the air-sacs (Clarke, 1957). The air-sacs also permit changes in gut volume as a result of feeding. In *Locusta* the increase in crop volume following a meal is accompanied by a corresponding decrease in the volume of the thoracic air-sacs (Bernays and Chapman, 1973).

When adult *Drosophila* emerge the air-sacs are collapsed, but subsequently they expand and at the same time there is a marked reduction in blood volume. Availability of oxidisable substrate, rather than shortage of oxygen, is likely to be a limiting factor in the activity of flight muscles and the air-sacs may indirectly improve the fuel supply by permitting a reduction in blood volume with a consequent increase in the concentration of fuels (Wigglesworth, 1963). Possibly intramuscular ventilation, causing marked changes in the volumes of the flight muscles, may also improve the blood supply to the muscles (Weis-Fogh, 1964b).

In some noctuids (Lepidoptera) tracheae form a reflecting tapetum beneath the eye (p. 647), and tympanic organs are usually backed by an air-sac which, being open to the outside air, allows the tympanum to vibrate freely with a minimum of damping (p. 718).

Expansion of the tracheal system may assist in inflation of the insect after a moult. Thus in dragonflies, spiracle closure, preventing the escape of gas from the tracheae, accompanies each muscular effort of the abdomen during expansion of the wings (Miller, 1964).

Some insects, such as *Aeschna* (Odonata), have an extensive development of air-sacs, apparently having no respiratory function, round the pterothoracic musculature.

They probably serve an insulating function, helping to maintain the temperature of the flight muscles (Church, 1960).

An important general function of tracheae and tracheoblasts is in acting as connective tissue, binding other organs together (Edwards, 1960).

Finally, the tracheal system may be involved in defence mechanisms. In the cockroach *Diploptera* quinones which probably have a defensive function can be forcibly expelled from the second abdominal spiracle (Roth and Stay, 1958) and in *Gromphadorrhina* (Dictyoptera) sounds are produced by forcing air out through the spiracles.

REFERENCES

BERNAYS, E. A. and CHAPMAN, R. F. (1973). The regulation of feeding in *Locusta migratoria*: internal inhibitory mechanisms. *Entomologia exp. appl.* **16**: 329–342.

BUCK, J. (1962). Some physical aspects of insect respiration. *A. Rev. Ent.* **7**: 27–56.

BUCK, J. and KEISTER, M. (1955). Further studies of gas-filling in the insect tracheal system. *J. exp. Biol.* **32**: 681–691.

CHURCH, N. S. (1960). Heat loss and body temperatures of flying insects. II. Heat conduction within the body and its loss by radiation and convection. *J. exp. Biol.* **37**: 186–212.

CLARKE, K. U. (1957). On the role of the tracheal system in the post-embryonic growth of *Locusta migratoria* L. *Proc. R. ent. Soc. Lond.* A, **32**: 67–79.

EDWARDS, G. A. (1960). Insect micromorphology. *A. Rev. Ent.* **5**: 17–34.

EDWARDS, G. A., RUSKA, H. and HARVEN, E. de (1958). The fine structure of insect tracheoblasts, tracheae and tracheoles. *Arch. Biol.* **69**: 351–369.

FARLEY, R. D. and CASE, J. F. (1968). Sensory modulation of ventilative pacemaker output in the cockroach, *Periplaneta americana*. *J. Insect Physiol.* **14**: 591–601.

FARLEY, R. D., CASE, J. F. and ROEDER, K. D. (1967). Pacemaker for tracheal ventilation in the cockroach, *Periplaneta americana* (L.). *J. Insect Physiol.* **13**: 1713–1728.

HAMILTON, A. G. (1964). The occurrence of periodic and continuous discharge of carbon dioxide by male desert locusts (*Schistocerca gregaria* Forskål) measured by an infra-red gas analyser. *Proc. R. Soc.* B, **160**: 373–395.

HINTON, H. E. (1947). On the reduction of functional spiracles in the aquatic larvae of the Holometabola, with notes on the moulting process of spiracles. *Trans. R. ent. Soc. Lond.* **98**: 449–473.

HINTON, H. E. (1966). Respiratory adaptations of the pupae of beetles of the family Psephenidae. *Phil. Trans. R. Soc.* B, **251**: 211–245.

HOYLE, G. (1960). The action of carbon dioxide gas on an insect spiracular muscle. *J. Insect Physiol.* **4**: 63–79.

HOYLE, G. (1961). Functional contracture in a spiracular muscle. *J. Insect Physiol.* **7**: 305–314.

IMMS, A. D. (1957). *A general textbook of entomology*. 9th edition, revised by Richards and Davies. Methuen, London.

KANWISHER, J. W. (1966). Tracheal gas dynamics in pupae of the cecropia silkworm. *Biol. Bull. mar. biol. Lab., Woods Hole* **130**: 96–105.

KEILIN, D. (1944). Respiratory systems and respiratory adaptations in larvae and pupae of Diptera. *Parasitology* **36**: 1–66.

KEISTER, M. L. (1948). The morphogenesis of the tracheal system of *Sciara*. *J. Morph.* **83**: 373–424.

KEISTER, M. and BUCK, J. (1964). Respiration: some exogenous and endogenous effects on rate of respiration. *in* Rockstein, M. (ed.), *The physiology of Insecta*. vol. 2. Academic Press, New York.

LEWIS, G. W., MILLER, P. L. and MILLS, P. S. (1973). Neuro-muscular mechanisms of abdominal pumping in the locust. *J. exp. Biol.* **59**: 149–168.

MILLER, P. L. (1960a). Respiration in the desert locust. I. The control of ventilation. *J. exp. Biol.* **37**: 224–236.

MILLER, P. L. (1960b). Respiration in the desert locust. II. The control of the spiracles. *J. exp. Biol.* **37**: 237–263.

MILLER, P. L. (1960c). Respiration in the desert locust. III. Ventilation and the spiracles during flight. *J. exp. Biol.* **37**: 264–278.

MILLER, P. L. (1964). Respiration—aerial gas transport. *in* Rockstein, M. (ed.), *The physiology of Insecta.* vol. 3. Academic Press, New York.

MILLER, P. L. (1966). The regulation of breathing in insects. *Adv. Insect Physiol.* **3**: 279–344.

MILLER, P. L. (1971). Rhythmic activity in the insect nervous system I. Ventilatory coupling of a mantid spiracle. *J. exp. Biol.* **54**: 587–597.

MILLER, P. L. (1973). Spatial and temporal changes in the coupling of cockroach spiracles to ventilation. *J. exp. Biol.* **59**: 137–148.

ROTH, L. M. and STAY, B. (1958). The occurrence of *para*-quinones in some arthropods, with emphasis on the quinone-secreting tracheal glands of *Diploptera punctata* (Blattaria). *J. Insect Physiol.* **1**: 305–318.

SNODGRASS, R. E. (1935). *Principles of insect morphology.* McGraw-Hill, New York.

TERAGUCHI, S. (1975). Correction of negative buoyancy in the phantom larva, *Chaoborus americanus. J. Insect Physiol.* **21**: 1659–1670.

WEBB, J. E. (1948). The origin of the atrial spines in the spiracles of sucking lice of the Genus *Haematopinus* Leach. *Proc. zool. Soc. Lond.* **118**: 582–587.

WEIS-FOGH, T. (1964a). Functional design of the tracheal system of flying insects as compared with the avian lung. *J. exp. Biol.* **41**: 207–227.

WEIS-FOGH, T. (1964b). Diffusion in insect wing muscle, the most active tissue known. *J. exp. Biol.* **41**: 229–256.

WHITTEN, J. M. (1972). Comparative anatomy of the tracheal system. *A. Rev. Ent.* **17**: 373–402.

WIGGLESWORTH, V. B. (1954). Growth and regeneration in the tracheal system of an insect, *Rhodnius prolixus* (Hemiptera). *Q. Jl microsc. Sci.* **95**: 115–137.

WIGGLESWORTH, V. B. (1959). The role of the epidermal cells in the migration of tracheoles in *Rhodnius prolixus* (Hemiptera). *J. exp. Biol.* **36**: 632–640.

WIGGLESWORTH, V. B. (1963). A further function of the air sacs in some insects. *Nature, Lond.* **198**: 106.

WIGGLESWORTH, V. B. (1965). *The principles of insect physiology.* Methuen, London.

CHAPTER XXIV

RESPIRATION IN AQUATIC AND ENDOPARASITIC INSECTS

Aquatic insects obtain oxygen directly from the air or from air dissolved in the water. The former necessitates some semi-permanent connection with the surface or frequent visits to the surface, but the frequency of surfacing may be reduced by increasing the size of the store of air with which they submerge. Insects which obtain air from the water nearly always retain the tracheal system so that the oxygen comes out of solution into the gaseous phase. This is important because the rate of diffusion in the gas phase is very much greater than in solution in the haemolymph. Often gaseous exchange takes place through thin-walled gills well supplied with tracheae, but in other cases a thin, permanent film of air is present on the outside of the body. The spiracles open into this film so that oxygen can readily pass from the water into the tracheae.

Like aquatic insects, endoparasitic insects may obtain their oxygen directly from the air outside the host or from that in the surrounding host tissues.

Insects rarely have respiratory pigments, but haemoglobin is present in a few aquatic and endoparasitic insects. It may provide a short-term store of oxygen or facilitate recovery from a period of oxygen lack.

For a general account of respiration see Wigglesworth (1965). Crisp (1964) and Thorpe (1950) review plastron respiration, while Hinton (1968) reviews the structure and functioning of spiracular gills, and (1976) respiration in marine insects.

24.1 Aquatic insects obtaining oxygen from the air

The majority of aquatic insects obtain their oxygen from the air and this usually necessitates periodic visits to the surface of the water to renew the gases in the tracheal system. A few insects, however, maintain a semi-permanent connection with the air via a long respiratory siphon or through the aerenchyma of certain aquatic plants.

Problems facing all insects which come to the surface are those of breaking the surface film when they surface and of preventing the entry of water into the spiracles when they submerge. The ease with which this is accomplished depends on the surface properties of the cuticle, and in particular its resistance to wetting. When a liquid rests on a solid or a solid dips into a liquid, the liquid/air interface meets the solid/air interface at a definite angle which is constant for the substances concerned. This angle, measured in the liquid, is known as the contact angle (Fig. 358). A high contact angle indicates that the surface of the solid is only wetted with difficulty and such surfaces are said to be hydrofuge. Under these conditions the cohesion of the liquid is greater than its adhesion to the solid, and so when an insect whose surface properties are such that

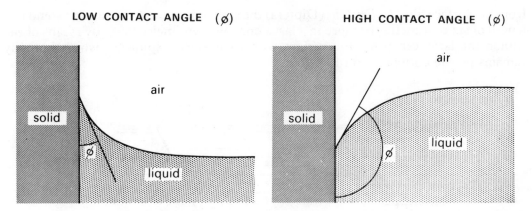

Fig. 358 Diagrams to illustrate low and high contact angles

the contact angle is high comes to the surface, the water falls away leaving the body dry (Holdgate, 1955).

The whole surface of the cuticle may possess hydrofuge properties, so that it is not readily wetted at all, or these properties may be restricted to the region around the spiracles, while the rest of the cuticle is easily wetted. In dipterous larvae, for instance, perispiracular glands (p. 502) produce an oily secretion in the immediate neighbour-hood of the spiracle. Often hydrofuge properties round the spiracle are associated with hairs, as in *Notonecta* (Heteroptera), or valves, as in mosquito larvae, which close when the insect dives, but open at the surface (Fig. 359), being spread out by the surface tension.

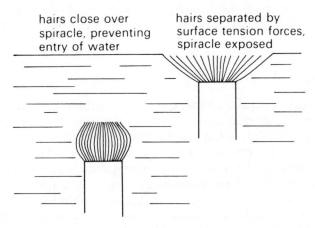

Fig. 359 Diagrams to show the movements of hydrofuge hairs surrounding a spiracle when the insect is submerged and at the surface. The movement of the hairs is entirely passive, depending on physical forces acting between the hairs and the water (modified after Wigglesworth, 1965)

In many of these insects only the posterior spiracles are functional and they are often carried on a siphon, as in larval Ephydridae and Culicidae, so that only the posterior part of the body penetrates the surface film, the rest remaining submerged, suspended from the surface film. In *Eristalis* (Diptera) the siphon is telescopic and can extend to a length of six centimetres or more in a larva only one centimetre long. By means of the siphon the larva can reach the surface with its posterior spiracles, while the body remains on the bottom mud (Fig. 360).

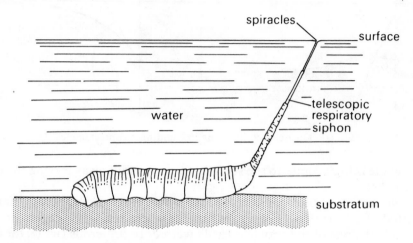

Fig. 360 Larva of *Eristalis* with the respiratory siphon partly extended (after Imms, 1947)

An increase in the number of functional spiracles often occurs in the last instar larva since this stage is commonly less strictly aquatic than earlier instars, leaving the water in order to pupate or, in hemimetabolous insects, to facilitate adult emergence. The number of functional spiracles never decreases from one instar to the next (Hinton, 1947).

24.1.1 Air stores

Some insects, such as mosquito larvae, can remain submerged only for as long as the supply of oxygen in the tracheae lasts, but some other insects have an extra-tracheal air store, carrying a bubble of air down into the water when they dive. The spiracles open into this bubble, so that it provides a store of air additional to that contained in the tracheal system, enabling the insects to remain submerged for longer periods than would be possible without it. The position of the store is characteristic for the species; in *Dytiscus* it is beneath the elytra, and removal of the hind wings, by increasing the space beneath the elytra, enables the insect to remain submerged for longer periods. In *Notonecta* air is held by long hydrofuge hairs on the ventral surface as well as in a store under the wings and in a thin film held by small bristles over the dorsal surface of the fore wing. The related *Anisops* (Heteroptera) has ventral and subelytral stores supplemented by oxygen loosely associated with haemoglobin in large tracheal cells just inside the abdominal spiracles (p. 488).

The air store also gives the insect buoyancy, so that as soon as it stops swimming or releases its hold on the vegetation, the insect floats to the surface. The position of the store is such that the insect breaks the surface suitably orientated to renew the air.

Dytiscus, for instance, comes to the surface tailfirst and renews the subelytral air from the posterior end of the elytra (and see p. 189).

24.1.2 Physical gills

When an insect dives, the gases in its air store are in equilibrium with the gases dissolved in the water, assuming that this is saturated with air. Normally at the dive the bubble would contain approximately 21 % oxygen and 79 % nitrogen, while the water, because of the differing solubilities of the gases, will contain 33 % oxygen, 64 % nitrogen and 3 % carbon dioxide. Carbon dioxide is very soluble, so there is never very much in the bubble.

Within a short period after diving the proportion of oxygen in the bubble is reduced, since the oxygen is utilised by the insect, and so there is a corresponding increase in the proportion, and hence partial pressure, of nitrogen. This will disturb the equilibrium between the gases in the bubble and those in solution and movements of gases will occur tending to restore the equilibrium. Oxygen will tend to pass into the bubble from the surrounding medium, because the oxygen tension in the bubble is reduced, while nitrogen tends to pass out of the bubble into solution, because the nitrogen tension in the bubble is increased. Thus more oxygen will be made available to the insect than was originally present in the bubble, which is, in fact, acting as a gill.

This effect is enhanced by the fact that the oxygen passes into the bubble about three times more readily than nitrogen passes out into solution, so that there is a tendency for equilibrium to be restored by the movement of oxygen into the bubble rather than nitrogen out. As a result of this the insect is able to remain submerged for longer periods than would be the case if it depended solely on the oxygen initially available in its store.

The nitrogen, as a non-respiratory gas, is essential for the air bubble to act as a gill, since in its absence there is no change in partial pressure as the oxygen is utilised. For this reason an insect with a bubble of pure oxygen in water saturated with oxygen does not survive for very long.

With small, inactive insects at low temperatures, that is when the rate of utilisation of oxygen is low, the air store may be sufficiently efficient as a gill for the insect to remain submerged for a long time. Thus *Hydrous* (Coleoptera) can remain submerged for some months during the winter (de Ruiter *et al.*, 1952), but in larger, more active insects, with higher oxygen requirements, the bubble lasts for only a short time and the insect must come to the surface more frequently. If the temperature is above about 15°C oxygen is utilised by *Notonecta* so much more rapidly than it enters the bubble that the gill effect is of negligible importance and the insect soon surfaces to replenish its airstore. At 10°C, however, it remains submerged for twice as long as would otherwise be possible and below 5°C it can survive for a very long period without access to the surface (Popham, 1962).

The efficiency of the bubble as a gill depends on the oxygen content of the water adjacent to the gill. In water devoid of oxygen, or containing only a very little, the gas will tend to pass out of the bubble into solution and will be lost to the insect. Even if the oxygen tension in the water exceeds that in the bubble, the amount entering the bubble will depend on the difference in tension. Hence the higher the oxygen tension of the outside water, the more effective will the bubble be as a gill, and this must be true of any type of gill. Consequently the frequency with which an insect visits the surface will depend on the oxygen tension of the water (Fig. 361). If the water is still, that adjacent to the bubble will soon be depleted of oxygen, and some insects direct a stream of water over the bubble so that this accumulation of 'spent' water does not occur. *Naucoris* (Heteroptera), for instance, holds on to the vegetation and makes swimming movements with its back legs so that a current is created, the movement apparently being stimulated by a high concentration of carbon dioxide in the tracheal system (de Ruiter *et al.*, 1952).

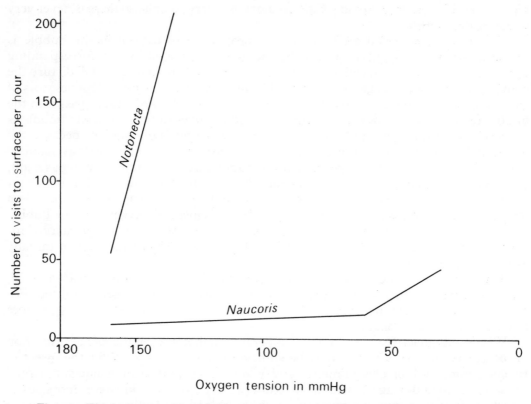

Fig. 361 The frequency with which insects using an air bubble as a physical gill visit the surface at different oxygen tensions. *Naucoris* at 20°C, *Notonecta* at 17°C (data from de Ruiter *et al.*, 1952)

24.1.3 Insects obtaining oxygen via the tissues of aquatic plants

A number of insects obtain oxygen by thrusting their spiracles into the aerenchyma of aquatic plants. This habit occurs in larval *Donacia* (Coleoptera) and *Chrysogaster* (Diptera), the larvae and puparia of *Notiphila* (Diptera) and the larvae and pupae of the mosquito *Mansonia*. With the exception of *Mansonia*, all of these live in mud containing very little free oxygen (Varley, 1937). The functional spiracles are at the tip of a sharp pointed post-abdominal siphon in larval forms (Fig. 362) and on the anterior thoracic horns of the pupae.

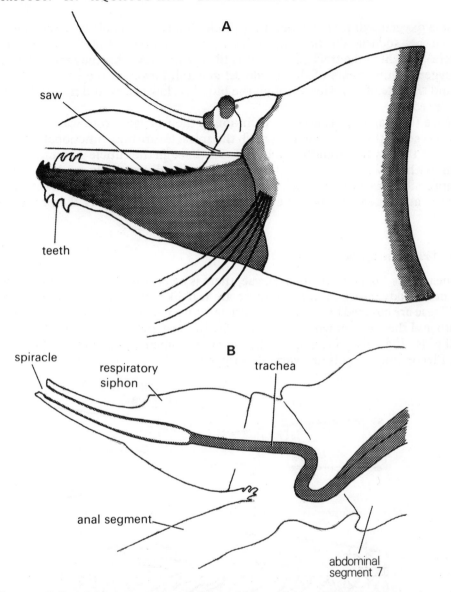

Fig. 362 A. Postabdominal respiratory siphon of *Mansonia* larva. B. Section of posterior end of larva to show tracheae and the terminal spiracle (after Keilin, 1944)

24.2 Insects obtaining oxygen from the water

In all insects living in water some inward diffusion of oxygen from the water takes place through the cuticle and in many larval forms gaseous exchange takes place solely in this way. Cutaneous diffusion depends on the permeability of the cuticle and a lower oxygen tension in the tissues as compared with the water. In many larval forms the cuticle is relatively permeable and in *Aphelocheirus* (Heteroptera), for instance, the cuticle of the last instar larva is about four times as permeable as that of the adult (Thorpe and Crisp, 1947b).

Some oxygen will pass through the cuticle into the blood of the insect and in very small larvae, such as the first instar larvae of *Simulium* (Diptera) and *Chironomus* (Diptera), in which the tracheal system is filled with fluid, this may meet the whole of the oxygen requirements of the insect. In general, however, the blood circulation is poor and the rate of diffusion through the blood is slow and would not suffice for most larger insects.

Hence the majority of insects which obtain their oxygen from water have a closed tracheal system, that is a system in which the spiracles are non-functional. Under these conditions the oxygen from the water diffuses through the cuticle and into the tracheal system within which it can rapidly diffuse round the body to the tissues. An incompressible tracheal system is essential for this type of gas movement to occur, otherwise as oxygen was used the tracheae would collapse under the pressure of the water.

24.2.1 Tracheal gills

In some insects, such as *Simulium* larvae, there is a network of tracheoles close beneath the general body cuticle, but often there are leaf-like extensions of the body forming gills. These are covered by a very thin cuticle with a network of tracheoles immediately beneath and they are known as tracheal gills. In most Zygoptera larvae there are three caudal gills (Fig. 363); Trichoptera larvae have filamentous abdominal gills, while in larval Plecoptera the gills are variable in position.

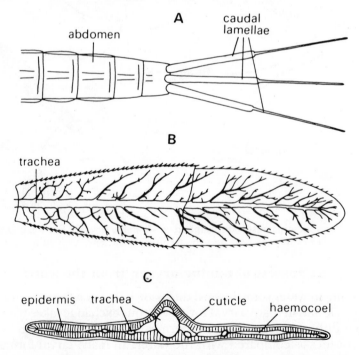

Fig. 363 Tracheal gills (caudal lamellae) of larval Zygoptera. A. Dorsal view of the posterior end of the abdomen of the larva of *Coenagrion*. B. Lateral view of one lamella (after Gardner, 1960). C. Transverse section of a caudal lamella of *Synlestes* (after Tillyard, 1917)

Larval Anisoptera have gills in the anterior part of the rectum, which is known as the branchial chamber (Fig. 364). Water is drawn in and out over the gills by muscular pumping which results largely from the activity of muscles unconnected with the gut. Contraction of dorso-ventral muscles in the abdomen reduces the volume, primarily by drawing up the sterna of segments 5 to 7. The haemocoel in the posterior part of the abdomen is isolated from the rest of the body by a muscular diaphragm across the fifth abdominal segment and as a result pressure is exerted on the branchial chamber. Water is forced out through the partially open anus and drawn in again when the volume of the abdomen is restored partly by the elasticity of the cuticle and partly by contraction of muscles in the diaphragm and in a transverse subintestinal muscle. During inspiration the anal valves are wide open (Fig. 365). A muscular prebranchial valve presumably prevents water from moving forwards into the midgut (Mill and Pickard, 1972; Pickard and Mill, 1972).

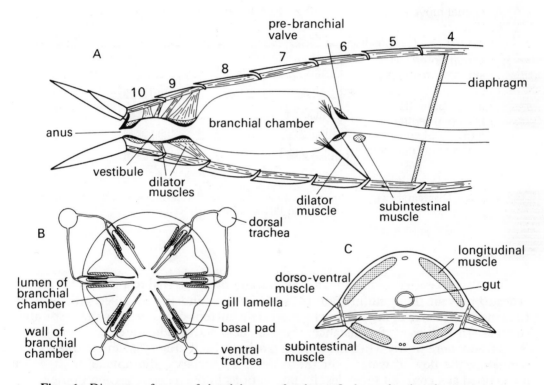

Fig. 364 Diagrams of parts of the abdomen of a dragonfly larva showing the structures concerned with rectal ventilation. A. Longitudinal section. Numbers refer to abdominal segments. B. Diagrammatic cross-section of branchial chamber. C. Transverse section of abdominal segment 6 showing the subintestinal muscle and dorso-ventral muscles (after Mill and Pickard, 1972; Tillyard, 1917)

Some 85 % of the water in the rectum is renewed at each cycle of compression and relaxation and the frequency of pumping in *Aeschna* varies from about 25 to 50 cycles per minute. At the higher rates the interval between inspiration and expiration is reduced (Hughes and Mill, 1966).

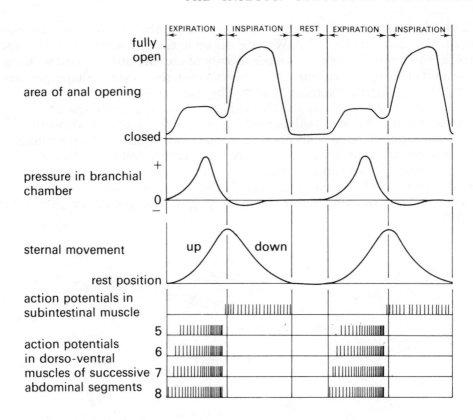

Fig. 365 Diagram showing the timing of events in rectal ventilation by a dragonfly larva (after Mill and Pickard, 1972)

It is also necessary to maintain a flow of water over external respiratory surfaces in order to prevent the accumulation of 'spent' water, and the so-called gills of many Ephemeroptera are, in fact, fans which create a current of water over the respiratory surfaces. In *Ephemera*, for instance, the gills beat actively in water containing little oxygen and more slowly when the oxygen tension is high (Fig. 366) and in this way, by regulating the flow of water over the respiratory surfaces, the uptake of oxygen is maintained at a constant level despite fluctuations in the oxygen tension in the water. When the oxygen content of the water is very low, however, the uptake does fall off (Eriksen, 1963). In *Ephemera* a good deal of gaseous exchange takes place through the gills, but in *Cloeon* they function almost entirely as paddles.

In general, although a good deal of gaseous exchange may take place through tracheal gills and in *Agrion* (Odonata) larva 32–45 % of the oxygen absorbed normally takes this route, the insects are able to survive without the gills under normal oxygen tensions. Where the oxygen tension of the water is low, however, they are of importance since they considerably increase the area available for gaseous exchange.

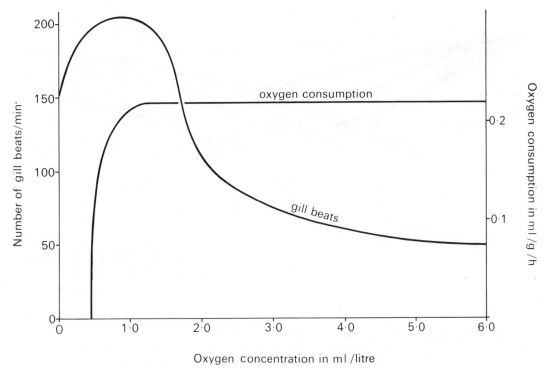

Fig. 366 The relationships of gill beat and oxygen uptake in the larva of *Ephemera* to the oxygen content of the water (after Eriksen, 1963)

24.2.2 Plastron respiration

Some insects have specialised structures which hold a permanent thin film of air on the outside of the body in such a way that an extensive air water interface is present for gaseous exchange. Such a film of gas is called a plastron (Thorpe, 1950) and the tracheae open into it so that oxygen can pass directly to the tissues.

The volume of the plastron is constant and usually small since it does not provide a store of air, but acts as a gill. The constant volume is maintained by various hydrofuge devices spaced very close together so that water only penetrates between them when under considerable pressure. Excess external pressures which may develop during the normal life of the insect are resisted. Such pressures may develop through the utilisation of oxygen from the plastron so that the internal pressure is reduced, or through the insect being in deep water and therefore subjected to high hydrostatic pressure.

In adult insects the plastron is held by a very close hair pile in which the hairs resist wetting as a result of their hydrofuge properties and their orientation. The most efficient resistance to wetting would be achieved by a system of hairs lying parallel with the surface of the body (Thorpe and Crisp, 1947a). *Aphelocheirus* approaches this condition in possessing hairs which are bent over at the tip (Fig. 367B); in other insects,

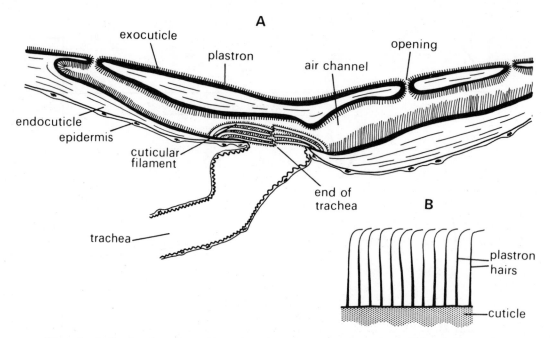

Fig. 367 A. Section through a spiracular rosette of *Aphelocheirus* showing the junction of the trachea with the system of channels in the cuticle. B. Part of the plastron highly enlarged, showing the form of the hairs (after Thorpe and Crisp, 1947a)

such as *Elmis* (Coleoptera) the hairs are sloping (Fig. 368B). The ability to withstand collapse depends on the hairs being slightly thickened at the base and also on their close packing. As a system of closely packed hairs is compressed the hairs become pressed together so that their overall resistance to compression increases.

In the adult *Aphelocheirus* the plastron covers the ventral and part of the dorsal surface of the body. The hairs which hold the air are 5–6 μm high and about 0·2 μm in diameter. They are packed very close together, about 2 500 000 mm^2 and are able to withstand a pressure of about 400 kN/m^2 before they collapse. Hence this is an extremely stable plastron which would only be displaced by water at excessive depths. The spiracles open into the plastron by small pores along a series of radiating canals in the cuticle (Fig. 367A). These canals are lined with hairs so that the entry of water into the tracheal system is prevented. The basal rate of oxygen utilisation at 20°C is about 6 μl/h/individual and this is readily provided by the plastron, so that, except in water poor in oxygen, the insect need never come to the surface.

The plastrons of other insects are generally less efficient than that of *Aphelocheirus* since they have a less dense hair pile from which the air is more readily displaced. However, a number of insects with a hair density of $3 \times 10^4 - 1 \cdot 5 \times 10^5$/mm^2, such as *Elmis*, have plastrons which are usually permanent and adequate for the needs of the insect. In these cases the more permanent plastron is often supplemented by a less permanent macroplastron. This consists of a thicker layer of air outside the plastron and held by longer hairs than the plastron, as in *Hydrophilus* (Coleoptera) (Fig. 368A), or by the erection of the plastron hairs, as in *Elmis* (Fig. 368B). The macroplastron is an

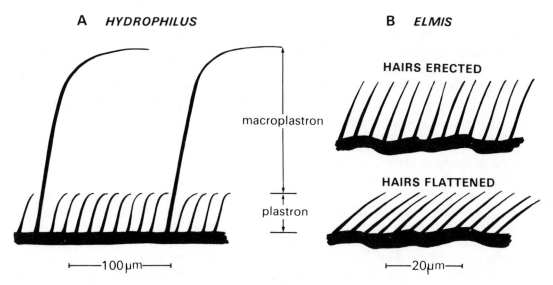

Fig. 368 Diagrams of the arrangement of hairs in (A) *Hydrophilus* and (B) *Elmis*, showing the mode of formation of a macroplastron (based on data in Thorpe and Crisp, 1949)

air store and acts as a physical gill. Consequently it is progressively reduced in size and finally eliminated, leaving only the plastron. The hairs holding the macroplastron are relatively long and flexible, so that as the gas bubble is reduced they tend to clump, leaving patches of exposed cuticle which would be liable to wetting. To avoid this these insects groom their hair pile and in *Elmis* there are brushes on the legs for this purpose. These brushes are also used in capturing air bubbles and adding them to the macroplastron. Insects which only have a plastron do not make grooming movements of this type.

As with any form of gill, the water adjacent to the plastron tends to become depleted of oxygen. *Phytobius relatus* (Coleoptera) offsets this by directing a current of water over the plastron with its middle legs, while in *Aphelocheirus* and *Elmis*, both of which live in fast-flowing streams, the movement of the water obviates any such activity on the part of the insect.

A plastron forms an essential part of the respiratory apparatus of many insect eggs (p. 396) and also of the pupae of many aquatic insects. In the latter the plastron is held by spiracular gills (see below).

24.3 Insects subject to occasional submersion

It is relatively common for terrestrial insects to fall into water, but in general this does not occur sufficiently regularly for special respiratory adaptations to have developed. Insects living close to the edge of water are, however, subject to more frequent alternations of submersion and emergence and so tend to be adapted for respiration in air or water. This is the situation with insects which live intertidally, where submersion occurs regularly, and at the edges of streams where submersion is much less regular.

Some intertidal beetles, such as *Bledius* and *Dichirotrichus*, effectively avoid submergence by living in burrows and crevices where sufficient air is trapped to enable them to survive aerobically for several hours. If they do become submerged they become quiescent as a result of anoxia. The time for recovery when returned to air is then proportional to the period of anoxia (Evans *et al.*, 1971).

The lice living on aquatic mammals live in the layer of air trapped in the fur, so that these, too, probably encounter no peculiar respiratory problems (Hinton, 1976).

24.3.1 Spiracular gills

A spiracular gill consists of an extension of the cuticle surrounding a spiracle and bearing a plastron connected to the spiracle by aeropyles. In water the plastron provides a large gas/water interface for diffusion, while in air the interstices of the gill provide a direct route for the entry of oxygen, and water loss is limited because the gill opens into the atrium of the spiracle. Thus, in air, water loss through the spiracles is scarcely greater than in terrestrial insects (Hinton, 1968).

Spiracular gills occur in the pupal stages of many flies and beetles living intertidally or at the edges of streams. They also occur in the larvae of a few Coleoptera and in *Canace* (Diptera). Where they occur in pupae, the basal structure of the gill is modified to permit respiration by the pharate adult (Fig. 369).

The spiracular gills of most dipteran pupae are prothoracic and connect with the prothoracic spiracles. In *Taphrophila*, for example, there is a single gill on each side with eight branches (Fig. 369). The whole gill is about 1·5 mm long. In Simuliidae there are also two prothoracic gills. In this case each has at least two main branches and in some species there is abundant secondary branching. In the pupae of Psephenidae (Coleoptera), however, the gills are associated with the abdominal spiracles and in *Psephenoides volatilis* they are on abdominal segments two to seven. Each gill has between four and ten long slender branches, which maintain their shape in water because two of their sides consist of very thick cuticle and these two sides are held apart by stout cuticular struts. Abdominal spiracular gills also occur in the larvae of beetles of the genera *Torridincola*, *Sphaerius* and *Hydroscapha*.

The form of the plastron differs in different insects. In *Simulium*, *Eutanyderus* (Diptera) and many other species it is held by hydrofuge cuticular struts running at right angles to the surface of the gill. These struts branch at the apices and the branches of adjacent struts anastomose to form an open network. An extensive air/water interface thus exists in the interstices of the network. In these insects the plastron extends all over the gills and connects with the atrium of the spiracle at the base of each gill.

In the tipulid *Taphrophila* the spiracular atrium extends into each gill and its branches, and where the atrium meets the wall of the gill it opens to the outside through a series of small pores, the aeropyles, about 4 μm in diameter (Figs. 369, 370). The atrium is flattened in cross-section with the two walls connected by cuticular struts so that it does not collapse even if the gills dry, and the hydrofuge properties of the struts prevent the entry of water into the atrium. Running from each aeropyle, on the outside of the gill, is a shallow canal about 4 μm wide which is crossed at intervals of about 1·0 μm by cuticular bridges about 0·5 μm wide (Fig. 371). The lining of the canals is strongly hydrofuge, so that in water each canal holds a long cylinder of air, known as a plastron line, which is not easily displaced because of the cuticular bridges. The air is not displaced by the pressure of ten feet of water, although the pupae are not normally found below two feet. The plastron lines provide a relatively large air/water interface over which gaseous exchange occurs.

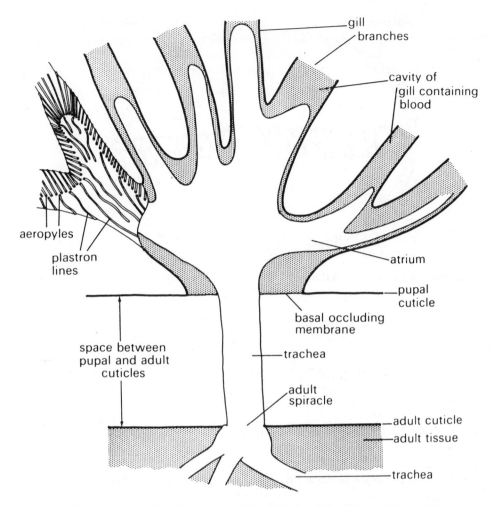

Fig. 369 The spiracular gill of the pharate adult of *Taphrophila*. The two left-hand branches represent the gill as seen from the outside, while the remainder represents a section to show the internal arrangement (modified after Hinton, 1957)

For the plastron to function efficiently it is important that the gills are turgid when the insects are submerged. In many species of tipulid and in *Psephenoides* the gills are rigid, but in other species the turgor is maintained by the high osmotic content of the gills which results from the haemolymph and epidermal cells which they contain. At the pupa/adult apolysis the pupal cuticle becomes separated from the adult, but the lining and blood of the gills are not withdrawn. Instead they become cut off from the rest of the tissues by the basal occluding membrane (Fig. 369). The epithelium within the gills disintegrates and the cells form loose irregular clusters in the middle of the gill. This isolated tissue is important because it is able to repair damage to the surface of the gill, forming cuticular plugs in any holes which are produced, and this facility is retained even after the gills have been strongly desiccated. Repairs to the gills are important because a damaged gill loses its high internal osmotic pressure and so becomes flaccid and inefficient when in the water.

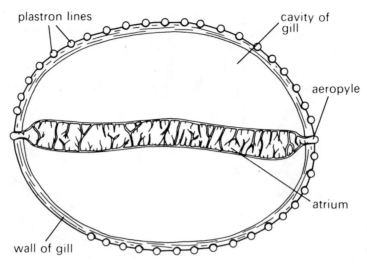

Fig. 370 Transverse section through a branch of a gill of pupal *Taphrophila* (after Hinton, 1957)

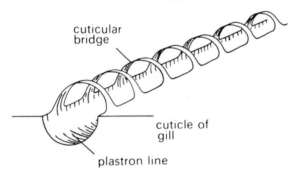

Fig. 371 Diagram of the cuticular bridges across a plastron line on the gill of *Taphrophila* (after Hinton, 1957)

In *Simulium* pupa the gills are fully expanded in water because they have an opening at the base into which water can freely pass. At the base of each gill in the newly ecdysed pupa is a thin membrane which bursts due to the intake of water resulting from the high internal osmotic pressure. This provides the opening for subsequent water movement in or out of the gill, ensuring that the shape of the gill is independent of the hydrostatic pressures exerted on it.

The efficiency of a plastron depends on its surface area. In spiracular gills the area of the interface varies from $1.5 \times 10^4 \ \mu m^2$/mg net body weight in the pupa of *Eutanyderus* to $1.9 \times 10^6 \ \mu m^2$/mg net weight in the pupa of *Simulium*. These areas are presumably large enough to permit efficient absorption of oxygen from well-aerated water. As with other plastrons, the plastron of a spiracular gill resists displacement by high hydrostatic pressures.

24.4 Respiration in endoparasitic insects

Endoparasitic insects employ various methods of obtaining oxygen, generally comparable with those used by aquatic insects. The majority of endoparasites obtain some oxygen by diffusion through the cuticle from the host tissues. In many ichneumonid and braconid (Hymenoptera) larvae the tracheal system of the first instar is liquid-filled and even when it becomes gas-filled the spiracles remain closed until the last instar. Thus these insects and the young larvae of most parasitic Diptera depend entirely on cutaneous diffusion. In braconid larvae the hindgut is everted through the anus to form a caudal vesicle. This is variously developed in different species, but in some, such as *Apanteles*, it is relatively thin-walled and closely associated with the heart (Fig. 372), so that oxygen passing in is quickly carried round the body. In these insects the vesicles are responsible for about a third of the total gaseous exchange.

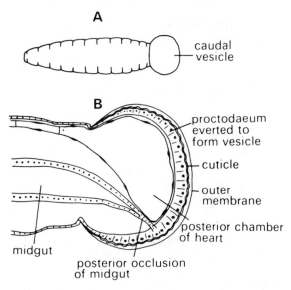

Fig. 372 A. Larva of *Apanteles* showing the caudal vesicle. B. Longitudinal section of the vesicle (from Wigglesworth, 1965)

When the tracheal system becomes air-filled, networks of tracheoles may develop immediately beneath the cuticle, thus facilitating the diffusion of gases away from the surface. In *Cryptochaetum iceryae* (Diptera), a parasite of scale insects, there are two caudal filaments, which in the third instar larva are ten times as long as the body and are packed with tracheae. Often these filaments get entangled with the host tracheae and so provide an easy path for the transfer of oxygen (Thorpe, 1930).

Other insects, and particularly older, actively growing larvae, with greater oxygen requirements communicate with the outside air either through the body wall of the host or via its respiratory system. The majority of these insects are metapneustic or amphipneustic, using the posterior spiracles to obtain their oxygen. Chalcid (Hymenoptera) larvae are connected to the outside from the first instar onwards by the hollow egg pedicel, which projects through the body wall of the host. The posterior spiracles of the larva open into the funnel-shaped inner end of the pedicel and so make contact with the outside air. Many tachinid (Diptera) larvae, parasitic in other insects, tap the tracheal supply or pierce the body wall of the host, perforating the epidermis from within with their posterior spiracles. The host epidermis is stimulated to grow and spreads round the larva, almost completely enclosing it, and secreting a thin, cuticular membrane over its surface. The larva of *Melinda* (Diptera), parasitic in snails, respires by sticking its posterior spiracles out through the respiratory opening of the snail.

Parasites of vertebrates also often use atmospheric air. The larva of *Cordylobia* (Diptera) bores into the skin and produces a local swelling, but it always retains an opening to the outside into which the posterior spiracles are thrust. Similarly in the larva of the warble fly, *Hypoderma*, the warble opens to the outside, but in this case the larva bores its way out to the surface from within the host tissues (Keilin, 1944).

24.5 Haemoglobin

The majority of insects have no respiratory pigments, but a few have haemoglobin in solution in the blood. The best known examples are the aquatic larvae of *Chironomus* and related insects, the aquatic bug *Anisops* and the endoparasitic larvae of *Gasterophilus* (Diptera).

The haemoglobin of *Chironomus* has a molecular weight of 31 400, that of *Gasterophilus* is about 34 000. This is about half the molecular weight of vertebrate haemoglobin and indicates that it contains only two haem groups. It has a much higher affinity for oxygen than vertebrate haemoglobin, being 50 % saturated at tensions of less than 1·0 mm of oxygen, compared with 27 mm. The haemoglobin of *Anisops* is different, however, having only a low affinity for oxygen, associated with the fact that it becomes unloaded during a dive even in well-aerated water.

Chironomus

Chironomus larvae live in burrows in the mud under stagnant water which is commonly poor in oxygen. A flow of water may be directed through the burrow by dorso-ventral undulating movements of the body and the current so produced provides food and oxygen. During such periods of irrigation the haemoglobin in the blood is fully saturated with oxygen and apparently has no function, but during the intervals between them the oxygen of the surrounding medium is quickly used up. The haemoglobin has a high affinity for oxygen and only dissociates when the tension in the tissues is very low as is soon the case during the pauses between irrigation movements. At this time the haemoglobin dissociates and gives up its oxygen to the tissues. Thus the haemoglobin provides a small store of oxygen for these periods, but the store only lasts for about nine minutes and since the pauses often last longer than this, respiration during the rest of the time is anaerobic.

Haemoglobin in *Chironomus* is more important in facilitating rapid recovery from this oxygen lack when irrigation movements are resumed. The haemoglobin is able to take up oxygen and pass it to the tissues more quickly than is possible by simple solution in the haemolymph and this is especially true when the oxygen content of the water itself is low. Under these conditions the haemoglobin is continuously taking up oxygen from the water and transferring it to the tissues, so that it never becomes fully saturated with oxygen. It thus makes muscular activity more aerobic, and hence more efficient, than would be the case if physical solution alone was involved and it also permits filter feeding, which does not occur under anaerobic conditions, to continue at low oxygen tensions (Walshe, 1950). It may be that the respiratory function of haemoglobin in *Chironomus* is secondary and its primary function is as a protein store (p. 489).

Anisops

When *Anisops* dives it carries with it a small ventral air-store which is continuous with air under the wings. All the spiracles open into the air-store and the spiracles of abdominal segments 5–7 are very large and covered by sieve plates. From the atria of these spiracles several tracheae arise, branching repeatedly to form 'trees', the terminal branches of which indent large tracheal cells filled with haemoglobin. This haemo-globin is oxygenated when the bug is at the surface and deoxygenated during a dive, the supply of oxygen released at this time enabling the insect to remain submerged for longer than would otherwise be possible, while at the same time affecting its buoyancy.

When the insect first dives it is buoyant because of its ventral air-store, but as the store is used up this buoyancy is reduced until the density of the insect is roughly the same as water and it is able to float in mid water. This phase is maintained by the steady release of oxygen from the tracheal cells resulting from the reduction of partial pressure of oxygen in the store. After about five minutes, however, the haemoglobin is fully unloaded and the insect, now with a tendency to sink, swims to the surface and renews its air-store (Miller, 1966).

Gasterophilus

The third instar larva of *Gasterophilus* is an internal parasite in the stomach of the horse. In the early instars the larvae contain haemoglobin dissolved in the blood, but in the third instar this becomes concentrated in large tracheal cells (p. 102). Running from the posterior spiracles are four pairs of tracheal trunks which taper and give off short branches at intervals along their lengths. Each branch breaks up into numerous tracheoles which are functionally, if not structurally, within a tracheal cell (Fig. 373).

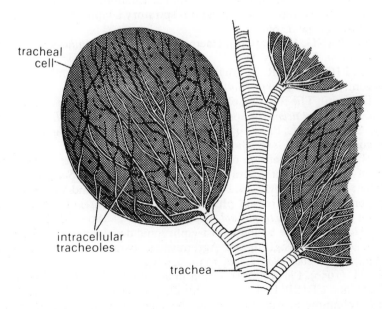

Fig. 373 Tracheal cells arising from a trachea in the larva of *Gasterophilus* (after Keilin, 1944)

Within the stomach of the horse the larva receives only an intermittent supply of air in gas bubbles with the food, and the haemoglobin of the tracheal cells enables the larva to take up more oxygen than is needed for its immediate requirements, to be used later when air is no longer available. The haemoglobin thus facilitates a more efficient use of the oxygen supply, but the store it provides is very small, lasting, at most, for four minutes (Keilin and Wang, 1946).

REFERENCES

CRISP, D. J. (1964). Plastron respiration. *Recent Prog. Surf. Sci.* **2**: 377–425.

ERIKSEN, C. H. (1963). Respiratory regulation in *Ephemera simulans* (Walker) and *Hexagenia limbata* (Serville) (Ephemeroptera). *J. exp. Biol.* **40**: 455–468.

EVANS, P. D., RUSCOE, C. N. E. and TREHERNE, J. E. (1971). Observations on the biology and submergence behaviour of some littoral beetles. *J. Mar. Biol. Assoc. U.K.* **51**: 375–386.

GARDNER, A. E. (1960). A key to the larvae of the British Odonata. *in* Corbet, P. S., Longfield, C. and Moore, N. W. *Dragonflies*. Collins, London.

HINTON, H. E. (1947). On the reduction of functional spiracles in the aquatic larvae of the Holometabola, with notes on the moulting processes of spiracles. *Trans. R. ent. Soc. Lond.* **98**: 449–473.

HINTON, H. E. (1957). The structure and function of the spiracular gill of the fly *Taphrophila vitripennis*. *Proc. R. Soc.* B, **147**: 90–120.

HINTON, H. E. (1968). Spiracular gills. *Adv. Insect Physiol.* **5**: 65–162.

HINTON, H. E. (1976). Respiratory adaptations of marine insects. *in* Cheng, L. (ed.), *Marine insects*. North-Holland Publishing Co., Amsterdam.

HOLDGATE, M. W. (1955). The wetting of insect cuticles by water. *J. exp. Biol.* **32**: 591–617.

HUGHES, G. M. and MILL, P. J. (1966). Patterns of ventilation in dragonfly larvae. *J. exp. Biol.* **44**: 317–334.

IMMS, A. D. (1947). *Insect natural history*. Collins, London.

KEILIN, D. (1944). Respiratory systems and respiratory adaptations in larvae and pupae of Diptera. *Parasitology* **36**: 1–66.

KEILIN, D. and WANG, Y. L. (1946). Haemoglobin of *Gastrophilus* larvae. Purification and properties. *Biochem. J.* **40**: 855–866.

MILL, P. J. and PICKARD, R. S. (1972). Anal valve movement and normal ventilation in aeshnid dragonfly larvae. *J. exp. Biol.* **56**: 537–543.

MILLER, P. L. (1966). The function of haemoglobin in relation to the maintenance of neutral bouyancy in *Anisops pellucens* (Notonectidae: Hemiptera). *J. exp. Biol.* **44**: 529–544.

PICKARD, R. S. and MILL, P. J. (1972). Ventilatory muscle activity in intact preparations of aeshnid dragonfly larvae. *J. exp. Biol.* **56**: 527–536.

POPHAM, E. J. (1962). A repetition of Ege's experiments and a note on the efficiency of the physical gill of *Notonecta* (Hemiptera-Heteroptera). *Proc. R. ent. Soc. Lond.* A, **37**: 154–160.

RUITER, L. de., WOLVEKAMP, H. P., TOOREN, A. J. van, and VLASBLOM, A. (1952). Experiments on the efficiency of the "physical gill" (*Hydrous piceus* L., *Naucoris cimicoides* L., and *Notonecta glauca* L.). *Acta physiol. pharmac. néerl.* **2**: 180–213.

THORPE, W. H. (1930). The biology, post-embryonic development, and economic importance of *Cryptochaetum iceryae* (Diptera: Agromyzidae) parasitic on *Icerya purchasi* (Coccidae: Monophlebini). *Proc. zool. Soc. Lond.* 1930, 929–971.

THORPE, W. H. (1950). Plastron respiration in aquatic insects. *Biol. Rev.* **25**: 344–390.

THORPE, W. H. and CRISP, D. J. (1947a). Studies on plastron respiration. I. The biology of *Aphelocheirus* [Hemiptera, Aphelocheiridae (Naucoridae)] and the mechanism of plastron retention. *J. exp. Biol.* **24**: 227–269.

THORPE, W. H. and CRISP, D. J. (1947b). Studies on plastron respiration. II. The respiratory efficiency of the plastron in *Aphelocheirus*. *J. exp. Biol.* **24**: 270–303.

THORPE, W. H. and CRISP, D. J. (1949). Studies on plastron respiration. IV. Plastron respiration in the Coleoptera. *J. exp. Biol.* **26**: 219–260.

TILLYARD, R. J. (1917). *The biology of dragonflies*. Cambridge University Press.

VARLEY, G. C. (1937). Aquatic insect larvae which obtain oxygen from the roots of plants. *Proc. R. ent. Soc. Lond.* A, **12**: 55–60.

WALSHE, B. M. (1950). The function of haemoglobin in *Chironomus plumosus* under natural conditions. *J. exp. Biol.* **27**: 73–95.

WIGGLESWORTH, V. B. (1965). *The principles of insect physiology*. Methuen, London.

CHAPTER XXV

EXCRETION AND SALT
AND WATER REGULATION

The activities of the cell are carried out most efficiently within a narrow range of conditions. It is therefore important that the environment within the cell and in the animal in general should be kept as nearly uniform as possible. This involves the maintenance of a constant level of salts and water and osmotic pressure in the haemolymph and the elimination of toxic nitrogenous wastes derived from protein and purine metabolism and of other toxic compounds which may be absorbed from the food. In these activities the excretory system plays an essential part.

In most insects the Malpighian tubules and the rectum are concerned in excretion and salt and water regulation. Water and salts and excretory products pass into the Malpighian tubules from the haemolymph and controlled resorption takes place in the rectum. Waste nitrogen is usually excreted as uric acid since this is relatively non-toxic and insoluble. It can therefore be excreted with a minimum of water and the terrestrial insect is thus able to conserve water. Sometimes nitrogenous end products are stored in some relatively non-toxic form rather than being passed out of the body.

Terrestrial insects are subject to water loss from the respiratory and excretory systems, freshwater insects to an excessive intake of water and brackish water insects may be subject to osmotic loss of water. The changes in water content will be accompanied by alterations in salt concentrations and the latter are also affected by the ionic concentrations of the food ingested. Terrestrial insects use various devices for gaining water, while some freshwater insects can absorb salts from the environment, but, in general, regulation in the different environments primarily involves differences in the amounts of water and salts resorbed in the rectum.

Various aspects of excretion and water balance are reviewed by Berridge (1970), Edney (1977), Maddrell (1971), Stobbart and Shaw (1974) and Wharton and Richards (1978). Machin (1979) reviews the uptake of atmospheric water.

25.1 Excretory organs

The typical insect excretory system consists of the Malpighian tubules, intestine and rectum. The intestine and rectum are described in Chapter III.

25.1.1 Malpighian tubules

The Malpighian tubules are long, thin, blindly ending tubes arising from the gut near the junction of midgut and hindgut (Fig. 32) and lying freely in the body cavity. In some insects, such as *Necrophorus* (Coleoptera), the tubules clearly arise from the midgut, while in caterpillars they arise from the anterior hindgut. They may open independently into the gut or may join in groups at an ampulla or a more tubular ureter which then enters the gut (Fig. 377A). In *Carausius* (Phasmida) there are three distinct groups of Malpighian tubules; superior and inferior tubules arising at the junction of midgut and hindgut, and lateral tubules opening into the midgut. The different tubules show some histological differentiation and the inferior tubules are dilated distally (Fig. 383).

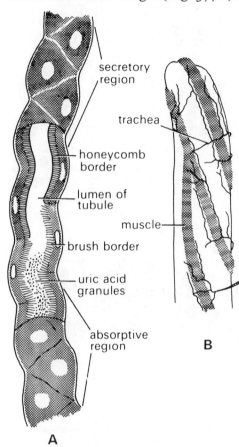

Fig. 374 A. Part of a Malpighian tubule of *Rhodnius* showing the junction of the more distal, secretory region of cells with honeycomb borders with the proximal region of absorptive cells with brush borders. B. End of a Malpighian tubule of *Apis* showing the spiral muscle strands and the tracheal supply
(from Wigglesworth, 1965)

The wall of the tubule is one cell thick with one or a few cells encircling the lumen. The cells stand on a tough basement membrane outside which, in Orthoptera and some other insects, are strands of muscle forming wide spirals round the tubule (Fig. 374B). The Malpighian tubules of *Rhodnius* and Lepidoptera and Diptera in general have no muscles other than a series of circular and longitudinal muscles proximally, while those of Coleoptera and Neuroptera have a continuous muscular sheath. These muscles produce writhing movements of the tubules in the haemolymph ensuring a maximum of contact with the blood and at the same time, perhaps, improving the movement of fluid into the tubules themselves. Outside the muscles is a peritoneal sheath formed from tracheoblasts.

The principal cell type in the wall of the tubule has the free margins of the cell produced into closely packed microvilli (Fig. 375A). These form the so-called honeycomb border. Mitochondria are abundant in and just below the microvilli. The plasma membrane of the basal regions of the cell is deeply invaginated and the endoplasmic reticulum is often well-developed. These are probably the main secretory cells of the tubule.

In some insects this type of cell predominates throughout the length of each tubule, but in some, *Rhodnius* for example, a different type of cell occurs proximally. This has more widely dispersed microvilli (Fig. 375B), forming a brush border and varying in length at different times from 7 μm to 40 μm. The infoldings of the basal membrane are less complex than in the more distal cells and mitochondria tend to be concentrated in the basal region. Some of these cells are concerned with resorption of some solutes from

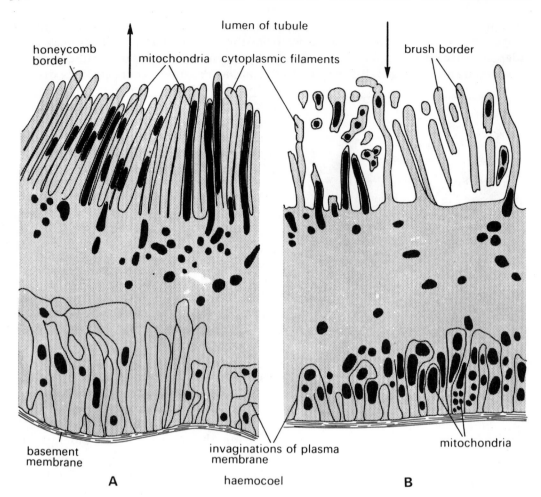

Fig. 375 A. Section of a cell from the distal region of a Malpighian tubule of *Rhodnius* showing the regular cytoplasmic filaments of the honeycomb border. B. Section of a cell from the proximal region showing the irregular filaments of the brush border. Some of the filaments are cut in transverse section. Arrows indicate the direction of secretion (after Wigglesworth and Salpeter, 1962)

the fluid secreted into the tubule more distally. Maddrell (1978) has shown that although the cells of the proximal part of the tubule are uniform in ultrastructure they differ in their functions.

Small numbers of another cell type sometimes occur scattered irregularly between the commonly occurring cells. They appear to secrete acid mucopolysaccharide, but may also have other functions.

Malpighian tubules are absent from Collembola and aphids, and represented only by papillae in Diplura, Protura and Strepsiptera, but they are present in all other insects, varying in number from two in coccids to about 250 in *Schistocerca*. The number may increase during post-embryonic development (Fig. 376; and see p. 461).

Because of the large number of tubules usually present their overall surface area in large, facilitating an exchange of materials with the haemolymph. In *Periplaneta*, with 60 tubules, their total surface area is about 132 000 mm².

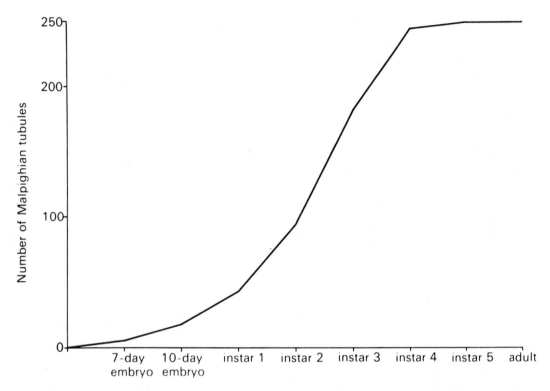

Fig. 376 The numbers of Malpighian tubules at the end of each stage of development of *Schistocerca* (from data in Savage, 1956)

In many Coleoptera and larval Lepidoptera the distal parts of the Malpighian tubules are closely associated with the rectum, forming a convoluted layer over its surface (Fig. 377A) (Ramsay, 1964; Saini, 1964). This is known as a cryptonephridial arrangement of the tubules. Commonly, as in *Tenebrio*, the tubules form a single layer, but in caterpillars they pass beneath the muscle layer of the rectum and then double back on themselves to form a more convoluted outer layer. Inner and outer layers of tubules are separated by a double membrane of thin cells and outside the outer layer is a single membrane, called the perinephric membrane, and the muscles of the rectum (Fig. 377B). The perinephric membrane is relatively impermeable, but in *Tenebrio*, at least, it is not fused with the alimentary canal anteriorly but forms a close-fitting sleeve, so that water can seep out from the enclosed perirectal cavity into the haemocoel, but movement in the opposite direction is unlikely to occur. The cavity enclosed by the perinephric membrane may be divided by other membranes, but it is assumed that these do not form effective barriers. At intervals the tubules are attached to the

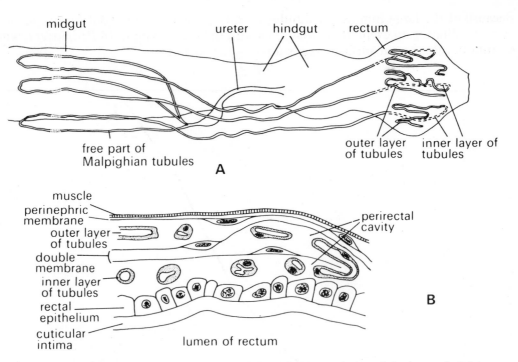

Fig. 377 Cryptonephridial arrangement of the Malpighian tubules of the larva of *Aglais urticae* (Lepidoptera). A. General arrangement showing the close association of the distal ends with the rectum. B. Section of rectum and associated tubules (from Wigglesworth, 1965)

perinephric membrane by specialised cells called leptophragmata over which, in *Tenebrio*, the outer lamina of the perinephric membrane is domed.

The cryptonephridial arrangement in *Tenebrio* is concerned with improving the uptake of water from the rectum (p. 57). In larval Lepidoptera it may be primarily concerned with ionic regulation.

25.1.2 Nephrocytes

Nephrocytes are cells which take up from the haemocoel foreign chemicals of relatively high molecular weight which the Malpighian tubules may be incapable of dealing with. They take up dyes and colloidal particles but not bacteria. Some nephrocytes are usually present on the surface of the heart, when they are known as pericardial cells (Fig. 526), others lie on the pericardial septum or the aliform muscles. In larval Odonata they are scattered throughout the fat body and in *Pediculus* (Siphunculata), in addition, form a group on either side of the oesophagus. In larval Cyclorrhapha they form a conspicuous chain running between the salivary glands (Fig. 378).

In the larva of *Calliphora* there are 12–14 pericardial cells on each side of the posterior part of the heart. These are large cells 140–200 μm in diameter. In front of them the heart is coated by hundreds of smaller pericardial cells, 25–60 μm in diameter. Each cell is held by a meshwork of connective tissue strands continuous with its own basement membrane and that of the adjacent heart or pericardial septum. The

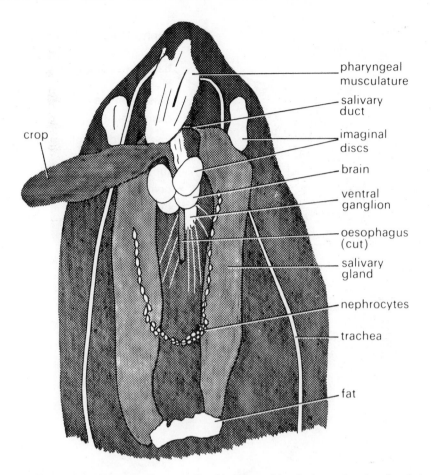

crop

pharyngeal
musculature

salivary
duct

imaginal
discs

brain

ventral
ganglion

oesophagus
(cut)

salivary
gland

nephrocytes

trachea

fat

Fig. 378 Dissection of the anterior part of a third instar blowfly larva showing the chain of nephrocytes between the salivary glands. Oesophagus cut just behind brain

organelles in the larger cells are in concentric zones with the nucleus in the centre (Fig. 379). The plasma membrane is invaginated to form a labyrinthine network, but on the outside the folds are held together by desmosome-like structures, so that the outer layer of the cell is more or less smooth and the basement membrane does not line the invaginations. Coated vesicles arise from the invaginations and are associated with intracellular tubular elements. Inside this zone is a vacuolar region containing vacuoles of several different types, including lysosomes, and inside this is a layer rich in rough endoplasmic reticulum and Golgi bodies (Crossley, 1972). In *Calliphora* the cells are uninucleate, but in mosquitoes and *Panorpa* they each have two nuclei.

The basement membrane and desmosomes form a barrier which limits the size of the molecule absorbed, but the pericardial cells of *Rhodnius* can absorb haemoglobin. Absorption involves the coated vesicles associated with the outer labyrinth. The foreign substances taken up are degraded within the cells and may then be returned to the haemolymph. In addition, the nephrocytes probably release lysozymes into the haemolymph and these may be important in the resistance of the insect to disease.

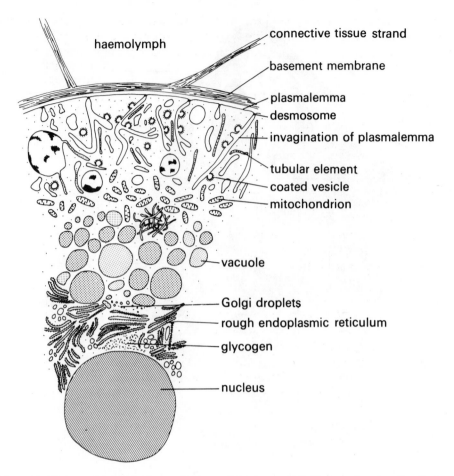

Fig. 379 Diagram of a part of a nephrocyte of the larva of *Calliphora* showing the distinct zonation of the organelles (after Crossley, 1972)

25.1.3 Excretion by the midgut

In some insects the cells of the midgut are known to have a role in regulation of the haemolymph content, both of inorganic ions and organic molecules. Most work has been carried out on Lepidoptera.

The larva of *Hyalophora* feeds on leaves of *Viburnum*, which contain very large amounts of potassium. It maintains a relatively low haemolymph potassium concentration by actively pumping potassium into the midgut. The goblet cells probably carry out this function (p. 50). Regulation of calcium concentration in the haemolymph appears to be a principal function of the pupal midgut of *Bombyx* (Waku and Suminoto, 1971), which develops following destruction of the larval cells and contains only one cell type. Calcium appears in the cells as granules which are subsequently discharged into the lumen.

The midgut of larval *Bombyx* is capable of excreting some acid dyes (Nijhout, 1975), and in *Tineola* metals and dyes accumulate in the goblet cells and are discharged at the following moult. This capacity suggests that these cells are able to excrete relatively large organic molecules which may be absorbed if they are present in the food. The midgut probably performs a similar function in a number of other insects (Waterhouse and Day, 1953).

25.1.4 Other organs occasionally concerned in excretion

In Collembola, where the Malpighian tubules are absent, glands in the head which open at the base of the labium may be concerned in excretion. These consist of an upper saccule followed by a coiled labyrinth and have a gland opening into the outlet duct (Fig. 380). They take up dyes from the haemolymph and it is suggested that they may have an excretory function.

The labial glands of *Antheraea* (Lepidoptera) secrete a potassium-rich saliva at the time of emergence. A principal function of this secretion is to dissolve and buffer the cocoonase (p. 491), but it also lowers the haemolymph concentration of potassium and reduces the haemolymph volume by about 15 %. Production of large amounts of saliva by *Hyalophora* and *Calliphora* soon after emergence may be of primary importance in fluid reduction (Maddrell, 1971).

In *Blattella* and a few other cockroaches uric acid accumulates in a part of the male accessory glands, where it is stored temporarily and then poured out over the spermatophore during copulation (Roth and Dateo, 1965).

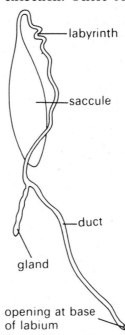

Fig. 380 Labial glands of a collembolan (from Wigglesworth, 1965)

25.2 Nitrogenous excretion

25.2.1 Excretory products

Ammonia is the primary end product of nitrogen metabolism, but it is highly toxic except in extreme dilutions. Consequently ammonia is only excreted in any quantity by insects with an ample supply of water, such as those living in fresh water and others, like blowfly larvae, which live in extremely moist environments (Table 4). Ammonia comprises a relatively large proportion of the nitrogen excreted by *Periplaneta*, which stores uric acid in the fat body (Mullins and Cochran, 1973).

For most terrestrial insects water conservation is essential and the loss by excretion must be reduced to a minimum. Hence it is necessary to produce a less toxic substance than ammonia so that less water is required for its safe elimination. The substance produced is uric acid, which, in addition to being relatively harmless, is also highly insoluble. As a result it tends to crystallise out of solution and can be retained as a solid, non-toxic waste substance for long periods. Further, uric acid contains less hydrogen

Table 4

The distribution of nitrogen in the excreta of insects

(expressed as a percentage of the total nitrogen in the excreta)

Insect	Uric acid	Urea	Ammonia	Allantoin	Amino acids	Protein	
Rhodnius	90	+	—	—	+	—	Wigglesworth, 1931
Bombyx larva	86	—	—	—	—	—	Wigglesworth, 1965
Attacus	81	trace	1–8	—	9	—	Prosser and Brown, 1961
Aedes	47	12	6	—	4	11	Clements, 1963
Anopheles	42	9	8	—	5	9	Clements, 1963
Culex	47	8	10	—	5	10	Clements, 1963
Lucilia larva	—	—	90	10	—	—	Stobbart and Shaw, 1974
Aeschna larva	8	—	74	—	—	—	Staddon, 1959
Sialis larva	—	—	90	—	—	—	Staddon, 1955
Dysdercus larva	—	12	—	61	13	6	Berridge, 1965

per atom of nitrogen than any other nitrogenous end product produced by animals and since hydrogen may be derived from water this means that less water is needed in its production.

NH_3	NH_2 — CO — NH_2	(uric acid structure)
AMMONIA	UREA	URIC ACID
H:N 3:1	H:N 2:1	H:N 1:1

Because of these various advantages, most insects excrete 80–90% of their waste nitrogen as uric acid (Table 4), although it has the possible disadvantage of containing more carbon per atom of nitrogen than urea.

Uric acid is often present as the free acid, which, for instance, constitutes 80–90% of the uratic spheres formed in the Malpighian tubules of *Rhodnius*. In larval *Tinea* (Lepidoptera) ammonium urate occurs, while in the meconium of *Deilephila* (Lepidoptera) a good deal of potassium urate is present. Sodium and calcium urates may also occur.

Other substances may occasionally form the bulk of the nitrogenous waste, reflecting the circumstances of the particular insect. *Dysdercus* (Heteroptera), for instance, excretes a great deal of allantoin but no uric acid, although the latter is present in the haemolymph. Allantoic acid is often present in quantity in the meconium of Lepidoptera and more nitrogen may be excreted in this form than as uric acid (Razet, 1956). Urea is commonly present, but only in relatively small amounts.

Apart from these end products of metabolism, other nitrogen-containing substances are sometimes present in the excreta. Thus in *Glossina* (Diptera), arginine and histidine from the blood of the host are excreted unchanged after absorption. These are substances with high nitrogen contents which would require a considerable expenditure of energy if they were to be metabolised along the normal pathways. Smaller amounts of other amino acids and proteins may be lost through not being fully resorbed in the rectum. Apart from ammonia, *Periplaneta* excretes some derivatives of tryptophan (Mullins and Cochran, 1973).

25.2.2 Excretion from the Malpighian tubules

The products of nitrogenous excretion are, in most insects, eliminated from the haemolymph via the Malpighian tubules. The movement into the tubules is probably passive, the rate depending on the size of the molecule and the rate of fluid secretion (Maddrell and Gardiner, 1974). As a consequence urea passes into the tubules more rapidly than uric acid. Since fluid secretion is an osmotic process dependent on the active movement of potassium, the outward movement of urea and uric acid are related to potassium excretion.

Subsequently, in the more proximal parts of the system, water and salts are resorbed to a greater or lesser extent and uric acid or a urate may precipitate out. In *Rhodnius*, and other insects in which the tubules have an anatomical differentiation, this process is initiated in the proximal parts of the Malpighian tubules, uratic spheres first appearing at the bases of the filaments of the brush border. In *Carausius* the bulk of the uric acid appears only in the rectum since the whole of the tubules are concerned with secretion, while in dipterous larvae uric acid may appear throughout the tubules, suggesting either a change in the direction of secretion by the cells or the interspersion of different types of cell throughout the tubule. The separation of the uratic spheres is accompanied by a change in pH from weakly alkaline to weakly acid (Fig. 383). A continuous flow of water down the Malpighian tubules to the rectum carries the uric acid with it, so that ultimately the nitrogenous waste is excreted with the faeces via the anus.

25.2.3 Storage excretion

Waste materials may be retained in the body in a harmless form instead of being passed out with the urine. This is known as storage or deposit excretion. It is observed in Collembola, which lack Malpighian tubules, in the larva of *Apis*, where excretion would foul the cell in which it lives, and in embryonic insects, where normal excretion is not possible. In these instances uric acid accumulates in the fat body, although in the egg of *Schistocerca* it is present in the yolk before the fat body has differentiated (Moloo, 1973).

Although *Periplaneta* has Malpighian tubules they are not involved in the excretion of uric acid. Instead this accumulates in the fat body when there is ample nitrogen in the diet. The store is depleted if the insect feeds on a diet deficient in nitrogen and it is possible that symbionts are involved in the metabolism of the uric acid (Cochran, 1979).

Even in insects which have normally functional Malpighian tubules, uric acid may accumulate in unspecialised cells in various tissues. It occurs, for instance, in the ordinary fat body cells of *Culex* (Diptera) and in the fat and epidermal cells of caterpillars. In these cases the uric acid may be the end product of metabolism of the individual cells. Subsequently, in the pupa, it is transferred to the Malpighian tubules and excreted with the meconium. Uric acid also accumulates in the epidermis of *Rhodnius* during moulting, being removed after each moult is completed.

In *Dysdercus* permanent deposits of uric acid accumulate in the epidermis and contribute to the colour pattern of the insect. The progressive increase in uric acid throughout life accounts for the increase in the extent of the white markings in later instars of this insect (Berridge, 1965). Similarly in *Pieris* (Lepidoptera) 80 % of the uric acid produced during the pupal instar is stored, mainly in the scales of the wings, and the pterines (p. 134) are also stored in this way (Harmsen, 1966).

Larvae of phytophagous Diptera accumulate calcospherites in the fat, while *Rhodnius* stores iron from the haemoglobin in the gut epithelium and bilin in the nephrocytes. Nephrocytes in general accumulate particles of colloidal proportions (p. 578). The goblet cells in the midgut of caterpillars accumulate heavy metals as sulphides (p. 50).

25.3 Excretion of ingested organic molecules

In the course of feeding, insects may ingest potentially toxic materials and some of these may be absorbed. It is vital that the insect is able to deal with such materials. This may involve chemical detoxification or excretion. The way in which the insect excretes them depends on the molecular size. Large molecules and colloidal particles are ingested by nephrocytes in which they may be metabolised (p. 578). Other rather smaller molecules may be actively secreted by the Malpighian tubules. This is true of the alkaloid nicotine, which is actively secreted by the tubules of larval *Manduca* and *Pieris*, but not by the adults of these species (Maddrell and Gardiner, 1976). Some organic anions are also actively secreted by the Malpighian tubules of *Rhodnius* (Maddrell and Gardiner, 1975); the mechanism is different from that concerned with the removal of alkaloids from the haemolymph.

In addition to these active processes, molecules enter the Malpighian tubules down concentration gradients. The rate of diffusion depends on the molecular weight of the compound and the rate of fluid movement down the tubule. As a consequence of this diffusion disaccharides and amino acids, as well as potentially harmful compounds, are lost from the haemolymph (Fig. 381). Even molecules as large as inulin diffuse into the tubules, although at a relatively low rate. The useful compounds are resorbed from the fluid in the hindgut, principally in the rectum. The importance of this system is that harmful molecules which unexpectedly enter the haemolymph are disposed of without the necessity of a special system to deal with each one (Maddrell, 1971).

25.4 Maintenance of haemolymph ionic levels

25.4.1 Terrestrial insects

The balance of salts in the haemolymph of terrestrial insects is likely to be disturbed by salts absorbed in the food. This intake is balanced by output via the Malpighian tubules and subsequent selective resorption in the rectum. Many insects are able to regulate the

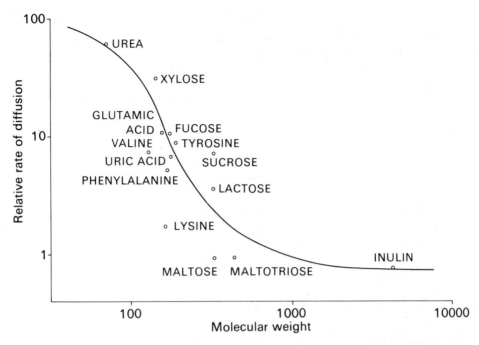

Fig. 381 The relative rates of diffusion into the Malpighian tubules of *Rhodnius* of organic substances of different molecular weight. The rate of diffusion is expressed as the ratio of each substance in the tubule fluid relative to that in the haemolymph at a constant rate of fluid production (after Maddrell and Gardiner, 1974)

composition of the haemolymph despite substantial alterations in the diet and in most the ionic composition of the haemolymph differs widely from that of the food (Table 5), indicating efficient regulation. The osmotic pressure of the haemolymph is also maintained at a relatively stable level. To some extent this regulation may involve differential absorption from the midgut, but no information is available on this. It appears that regulation is brought about largely by the excretory system.

The fluid which passes into the Malpighian tubules is iso-osmotic with the haemolymph, but it does not have the same ionic composition. The concentration of potassium is never less than six times as high in the tubules as in the haemolymph and a small increase in the haemolymph concentration results in a big increase in the tubule concentration. All the other inorganic ions, apart from phosphate, are present in concentrations proportional to, but lower than that in the haemolymph (Table 6), and this is generally true also of sugars, amino acids and urea. The potassium is actively secreted into the tubule and this is probably true also of the sodium, despite its lower concentration in the tubules. In *Rhodnius* active transport of chloride ions also occurs. Other substances pass passively into the tubules, which indiscriminately remove all soluble substances of low molecular weight (Ramsay, 1958; Maddrell, 1971).

The composition of the tubule fluid may vary according to the food and state of feeding. This variation is particularly marked in insects, such as *Rhodnius*, which take large meals at infrequent intervals. Immediately after a blood meal the urine of this insect consists of water and salts with only a little uric acid. Then, as the amount of uric

Table 5

The ionic composition of the diet in relation to that of the haemolymph in some terrestrial insects

(after Shaw and Stobbart, 1963)

Diet and insect	mEq/l or/kg wet weight			
	Na	K	Ca	Mg
Human blood	87·0	51·1	3·0	2·5
Rhodnius	164·0	6·0	—	—
Horse blood	84·8	31·4	1·7	3·3
Gasterophilus larva	175·0	11·5	5·7	32·0
Lettuce leaves	13·0	86·2	—	—
Periplaneta	113·0	25·6	—	—
Privet leaves	46·4	152·1	824·5	39·9
Carausius	8·7	27·5	16·2	142·0
Carrot leaves	25·6	176·9	214·5	35·6
Papilio larva	13·6	45·3	33·4	59·8
Potato leaves	trace	144·5	128·6	85·9
Leptinotarsa	3·5	65·1	47·5	188·3
Ribes leaves	trace	249·1	271·2	53·6
Pteronidea larva	1·6	43·4	17·5	60·5

Table 6

Comparison of osmotic pressures and ionic concentrations in haemolymph, Malpighian tubules and rectum

(after Stobbart and Shaw, 1974; Concentrations are in mEq/l)

		Osmotic pressure*	Na	K	Cl
TERRESTRIAL					
Carausius	haemolymph	171	11	18	87
	tubule	171	5	145	65
	rectum	390	18	327	—
Schistocerca	haemolymph	214	108	11	115
	tubule	226	20	139	93
	rectum	433	1	22	5
Rhodnius	haemolymph	206	174	7	155
	tubule	228	114	104	180
	rectum	358	161	191	—
FRESHWATER					
Aedes aegypti (larva)	haemolymph	138	87	3	—
	tubule	130	24	88	—
	rectum	12	4	25	—

* expressed as the equivalent solution of NaCl

acid increases the fluid becomes first cloudy and then of a creamy consistency. At the same time the proportions of other constituents decline (Fig. 382).

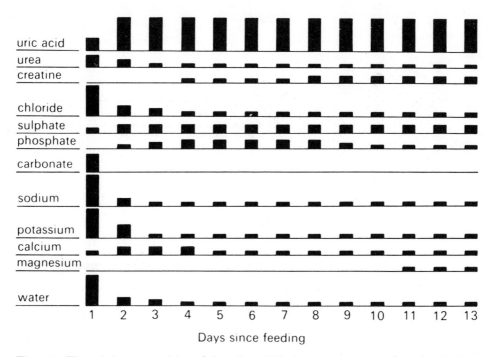

Fig. 382 The relative composition of the urine of *Rhodnius* on successive days after feeding (from Wigglesworth, 1965)

Subsequently, water, salts and organic molecules are selectively resorbed from the urine. In *Rhodnius* some resorption takes place in the proximal region of the Malpighian tubules as well as in the rectum (p. 78), but in *Carausius* only the rectum is involved. The role of the hindgut between the origin of the Malpighian tubules and the rectum is unknown, but there is some evidence of solute absorption in *Periplaneta* and of fluid absorption in locusts (see Maddrell, 1971).

The rectum appears to have a major role in resorption of water, ions and specific organic molecules from the secretion of the Malpighian tubules in all insects. It is probable that there is active uptake of potassium, and possibly of other ions, which compensates for the active secretion of potassium in the Malpighian tubules. In *Carausius* about 95 % of the sodium and 80 % of the potassium in the tubule fluid may be resorbed. The uptake of amino acids which pass passively into the tubule fluid may also be active.

The cuticle lining the rectum may limit the size of molecules which can be absorbed since in the locust at least, it is impermeable to molecules with a radius greater than 0·6 nm. As a consequence glucose passes readily through it, but trehalose does so only at a low rate. The effect of this relatively impermeable membrane is to protect the rectal cells from the high concentrations of toxic materials which may develop in the rectum as a result of water absorption (Maddrell, 1971).

The secretion and absorption of substances into and from the excretory systems of *Rhodnius* and *Carausius* is summarised diagrammatically in Fig. 383.

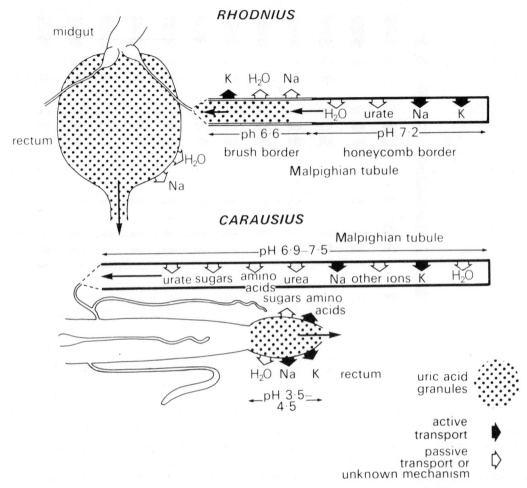

Fig. 383 Diagrammatic representation of the movement of inorganic ions and organic molecules into and out from the excretory system of *Rhodnius* and *Carausius* (modified after Stobbart and Shaw, 1974)

Calcium often crystallises out in the Malpighian tubules as calcium carbonate or oxalate. This usually occurs in a particular part of the tubule and in *Carausius*, with a very high level of calcium in its diet (Table 5), involves the expanded terminal regions of the inferior tubules. In this insect the calcium carbonate is later resorbed into the haemolymph and deposited in the chorion of the eggs when these are produced. In the larva of *Cerambyx* (Coleoptera) the calcium carbonate passes forwards through the alimentary canal and is ejected through the mouth to form an operculum to the burrow in which the larva lives.

25.4.2 Freshwater insects

Freshwater insects tend to lose salts to the medium as a result of excretion and the permeability of the cuticle, but the amount lost by excretion is reduced to a very low level by resorption from the rectum. Sodium, potassium and chloride are known to be resorbed, the process being an active one in the case of sodium and chloride, at least, and being regulated in relation to the composition of the haemolymph (Stobbart and Shaw, 1974). The resorption of salts, but not of water, leads to the production of a rectal fluid which is hypotonic to the haemolymph. However, despite the almost complete resorption of the major ions the osmotic pressure of the rectal fluid may still be as much as 60% of that of the haemolymph. It is possible that this relatively high osmotic pressure is due to the presence of ammonia, probably as ammonium carbonate, which is secreted directly into the rectum.

Some salts will be gained from the food, but, in addition, some larvae are able to take up salts from very dilute solutions. This is true, for instance, of the larvae of *Aedes*, *Culex* and *Chironomus* in which the uptake occurs through the anal papillae. This is an active process and sodium, potassium, chloride and phosphate are known to be taken up in this way. Normal *Aedes aegypti* larvae are able to maintain a steady state in a medium containing only 6 μM/l of sodium, indicating that they are able to take up salt from extremely dilute solutions. The size of the anal papillae is greater in larvae from more dilute solutions (Fig. 384), the increased surface area presumably facilitating salt uptake. Salts are also taken up by the rectal gills of larval Anisoptera, but not all freshwater insects have this ability, and larval *Sialis*, for instance, are unable to take up chloride.

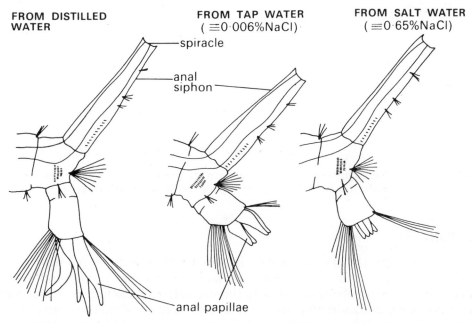

FROM DISTILLED WATER

FROM TAP WATER (≡0·006%NaCl)

FROM SALT WATER (≡0·65%NaCl)

spiracle

anal siphon

anal papillae

Fig. 384 Posterior end of larval *Culex pipiens* reared in different media showing the variation in size of the anal papillae (from Wigglesworth, 1965)

Some freshwater insects are able to offset changes in ionic concentrations in the haemolymph by compensating changes in the non-electrolyte fraction. Probably amino acids are produced from haemolymph proteins in sufficient quantity to maintain the osmotic pressure.

The ability of freshwater insects to regulate the composition and osmotic pressure of the haemolymph is good over the range of conditions to which they are normally subjected, but in hypertonic media the haemolymph rapidly becomes isotonic with the medium and regulation breaks down (Fig. 385, *Aedes aegypti*). Apparently they are unable to produce a fluid in the rectum which is hypertonic to the haemolymph.

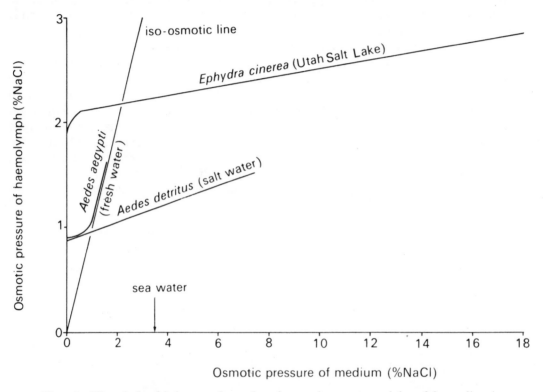

Fig. 385 The relationship between haemolymph osmotic pressure and that of the medium in some freshwater and salt-water larvae (from Shaw and Stobbart, 1963)

25.4.3 Salt-water insects

Many salt-water insects live in habitats in which the salinity varies widely. *Aedes detritus*, for instance, occurs in salt marshes, and *Coelopa frigida* (Diptera) breeds in *Laminaria* washed up on the shore. In both these situations the salinity varies according to the degree of inundation and desiccation. The salinity of the salt pans in which *Ephydrella* (Diptera) lives varies seasonally from 300 to 1200 mM NaCl (Marshall and Wright, 1974). In keeping with these environmental variations, salt-water insects are able to tolerate very wide fluctuations in the salinity of the bathing medium ranging from fresh water to salinities well in excess of that of sea water (Fig. 386). *Ephydra cinerea* (Diptera) is quite exceptional, living in the Utah Salt Lake, which has a salinity equivalent to a 20% sodium chloride solution (over 3M NaCl).

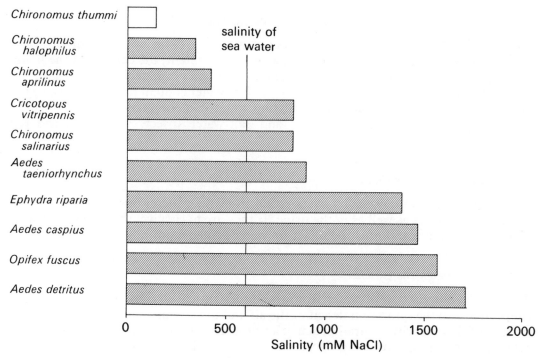

Fig. 386 The ranges of salinity tolerated by some salt-water dipterous larvae. *Chironomus thummi* is a freshwater species included for comparison (after Foster and Treherne, 1976)

Those insects which are able to tolerate salinities greater than in sea water regulate the ionic composition of the haemolymph so that the osmotic pressure changes very little over wide ranges of environmental salinity. This is the case in *Aedes detritus* and *Ephydra*, for example (Fig. 385). Others, like *Limnephilus affinus* (Trichoptera), regulate relatively poorly but can tolerate a 3-fold increase in haemolymph osmotic pressure (Foster and Treherne, 1976).

Insects living in salt water tend to gain salts with the diet and lose water osmotically. Ingestion of salts is reduced in *Bledius* by selecting food of the lowest available salinity. *Limnephilus affinis* drinks only 3–7% of its body weight per day compared with about 50% by freshwater insects, but the rate of drinking by *Aedes taeniorhynchus* remains more or less constant irrespective of the osmotic concentration of the medium (Bradley and Phillips, 1977b).

Salt-water insects get rid of excess ions and conserve water by excreting a urine which is hypertonic to the haemolymph. In *Aedes* fluid is secreted into the Malpighian tubules; this involves the active movement of potassium. Subsequently some resorption occurs in the anterior rectum, but then a hypertonic fluid is secreted into the posterior rectum. This involves the active secretion of sodium, potassium, magnesium and chloride ions. In this way the haemolymph osmotic pressure is regulated, but there is a net loss of potassium, which may be offset by active uptake from the medium via the anal papillae (Bradley and Phillips, 1977a).

25.5 Water regulation

The water content of insects varies from about 50 to 90 % of the body weight, but since this includes the cuticle, with a relatively low water content, the content of the living tissues is higher than this. Reduction of the water content ultimately leads to death, and *Rhodnius* and *Tenebrio*, for instance, die when their water content falls from about 75 to 60 %. The problems of insects in regulating water content vary according to their habitat and so terrestrial, freshwater and salt-water insects will be considered separately.

25.5.1 Terrestrial insects

Terrestrial insects lose water by evaporation from the general body surface and the respiratory surfaces as well as in the urine. If they are to survive, these losses must be kept to a minimum and must be offset by water gained from other sources.

Water loss through the cuticle

The rate of evaporation of water from the insect cuticle at constant temperature is proportional to the saturation deficit of the air and to the wind speed. In still air local pockets of air with a low saturation deficit accumulate round the insect, so reducing the rate of evaporation. In many species evaporation through the cuticle is largely independent of temperature up to a certain point known as the transition temperature but above this, in most insects, water is lost rapidly and continuously until the insect dies (Fig. 387). The transition temperature is usually well above the normal environmental temperatures which the insect is likely to meet. Some species, such as *Rhodnius* and *Pieris* pupae, have two transition temperatures (Fig. 387), while in *Periplaneta* the rate of water loss is proportional to temperature with no transition (Edney, 1977). The transition temperature is relatively low and ill-defined early in an instar, becoming sharper and higher subsequently. The increase in permeability which results from heating an insect above its transition temperature is permanent.

Water loss through the cuticle is restricted by the lipids of the epicuticle. A widely held view is that there is a layer of uniformly orientated wax molecules on the outside of the outer epicuticle. These molecules form a film one molecule thick, and hence called a monolayer, with their polar groups adsorbed on to the surface of the tanned cuticulin and the acetyl groups towards the outside. It is suggested (Beament, 1964) that the long chain molecules stand at an angle of about 25° to the perpendicular from the cuticle and are close-packed so that there are no spaces between them through which water could escape (Fig. 388A). Apart from being adsorbed on to the surface they are stabilised by van der Waals forces. The molecules of wax outside the monolayer are believed to be randomly orientated.

At the transition temperature it is supposed that the van der Waals forces are overcome and the molecules become thermally agitated, vibrating about a mean verticle

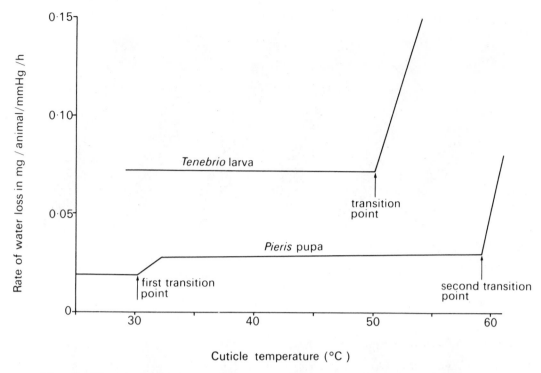

Fig. 387 The relationship between the rate of water loss through the cuticle and temperature in *Tenebrio* larvae and *Pieris* pupae (after Beament, 1959)

position so that spaces appear between them and water is able to escape (Fig. 388B). In species with higher transition temperatures the wax molecules are longer and so are more strongly bound by van der Waals forces; higher temperatures are therefore required to break the forces. Where two transition temperatures exist there may be a second monolayer on the outer surface of the wax.

However, the presence of a monolayer has not been proved and an alternative view is that impermeability is conferred by the lipids present throughout the outer epicuticle. It is not supposed that these exhibit any preferred orientation, but at the transition temperature they undergo a change in their crystalline structure which leads to an increase in permeability (Edney, 1977).

It is also possible that the epidermal cells are concerned with regulating the permeability of the integument (Berridge, 1970) and Treherne and Willmer (1975) have demonstrated that in *Periplaneta* a factor from the brain and corpus cardiacum results in a higher rate of water loss, presumably by altering the permeability of the integument.

Water loss from the respiratory surfaces

The respiratory surfaces, being permeable, are a potential source of water loss. The loss from this source is reduced by the invagination of the respiratory surfaces as the tracheal system (p. 539) and further by the spiracles, which are opened for the

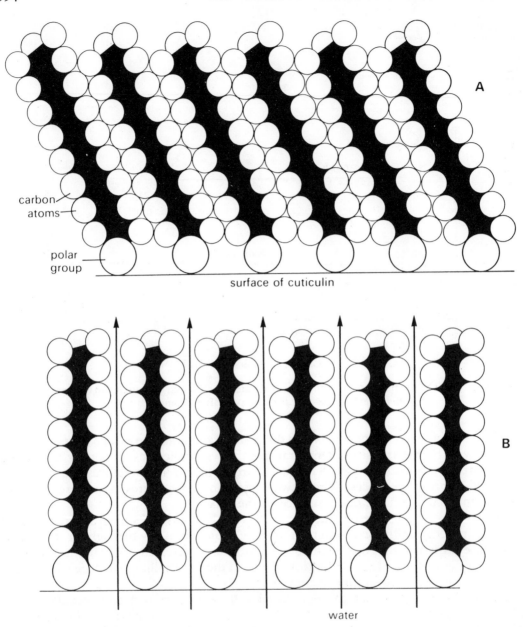

Fig. 388 Diagrammatic representation of the molecules of the wax monolayer providing the waterproofing layer of the insect cuticle. A. Molecules orientated at about 25 ° to the vertical with carbon atoms of adjacent chains interfitting so that there are no gaps between them. B. Molecules in the vertical position leaving gaps through which water can escape (after Beament, 1964)

minimum time consistent with efficient respiration (see Sections 23.2.3 and 23.4.3). The efficiency of the spiracles in this respect is demonstrated when they are kept open constantly, as they are in an atmosphere of 5 % carbon dioxide (Fig. 389). Under these conditions the loss of water is excessive.

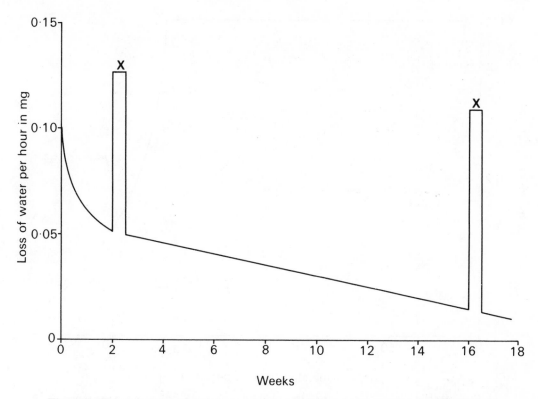

Fig. 389 The rate of water loss from starved *Tenebrio* larvae. At the points indicated by X the spiracles were kept open in 5 % carbon dioxide (after Wigglesworth, 1965)

The rate of water loss through the spiracles may be low in comparison with loss through the cuticle when the insect is at rest, but it is higher when the insect is actively ventilating the tracheal system. For instance, in *Glossina* loss through the spiracles accounts for 25 % of the water loss of a resting fly, but when the fly becomes active this figure increases to about 60 %. Similarly, 65 % of water loss by flying *Schistocerca* is through the spiracles; very little is lost by this route in the resting insect.

At low humidities water loss is reduced in *Glossina* and some other insects by closure of the spiracles (Edney, 1977).

Water loss in excretion

The major source of water loss is in the urine and faeces, the amount of water which is ultimately lost depending on the rate at which fluid is secreted by the Malpighian tubules and the extent to which it is resorbed in the rectum. By regulating the activity of these two processes the insect is able to maintain its water balance at an appropriate level. This effect is most obvious in insects, such as *Rhodnius* and *Glossina*, which take liquid meals at relatively long intervals. For a period after feeding the rate of fluid excretion is very high (Fig. 390) but this falls as the insect eliminates the excess liquid. The percentage of the blood meal eliminated by *Glossina* at this time is reduced in insects which had previously been desiccated and so their water balance is restored. A

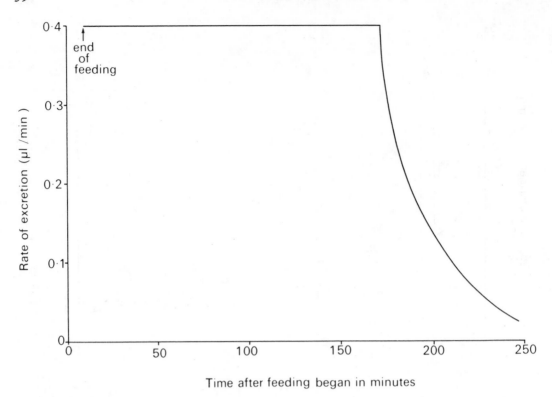

Fig. 390 The rate of excretion of *Rhodnius* immediately after feeding (after Maddrell, 1964)

similar but much less extreme pattern occurs in other insects, much wetter faeces being produced in the period immediately after feeding.

The rate of fluid production by the Malpighian tubules is enhanced by the diuretic hormone (p. 843). In *Rhodnius* this increases the rate of secretion by about 1000 times, so that it reaches a level of 3·3 μl/cm^2/min in the period just after feeding. This high rate is dependent on the rate of potassium secretion (p. 585) and so entails a potentially considerable loss of ions from the haemolymph, which is offset by the active resorption of potassium and chloride in the most proximal part of the Malpighian tubules. As a result, a copious urine which is hypotonic to the haemolymph is produced (Maddrell, 1978).

The resorption of water from the rectum is an osmotic process dependent on the active secretion of ions into the extracellular compartments external to the rectum (Fig. 44; p. 59). Regulation of this process ensures that the insect conserves or eliminates water according to its state of hydration. A locust feeding on wet food produces faeces with a water content of about 80 %; this is reduced to 25 % when the insect feeds on dry food in a dry habitat.

Insects living in very dry environments, such as *Tenebrio* larvae, can reduce the water content of the faeces to about 15 %. This involves the cryptonephridial arrangement of the Malpighian tubules (Fig. 377), which effectively provides two water-absorbing systems in series with each other. First water passes from the lumen of the rectum into the perirectal cavity, and then from the perirectal cavity into the

Malpighian tubules. In both cases the movement is osmotic. The high osmotic pressure in the perirectal cavity is achieved largely by a non-electrolyte contained within the cavity, while that in the Malpighian tubules results from the increased movement of potassium and chloride ions from the haemolymph through the leptophragmata (p. 578) without an associated influx of water from the haemolymph. Presumably the water which enters the upper parts of the Malpighian tubules from the rectum is subsequently passed into the haemolymph more proximally (Maddrell, 1971; Edney, 1977).

Fluid-feeding insects may have the problem of rapidly eliminating excess fluid. In discontinuous feeders, such as *Rhodnius*, this may be achieved physiologically (see above), but in plant-sucking bugs, where the intake of fluid is more or less continuous, the structure of the alimentary canal is modified to deal with the excess water (p. 53).

Gain of water

To offset the inevitable loss by transpiration and excretion water must be obtained from other sources. Most insects normally obtain sufficient water with their food and may select food with a high water content (Chapman, 1957). Others, with an efficient regulatory mechanism, require very little water, and food with a moisture content of only 1 % is sufficient for the needs of *Tenebrio* larvae, for instance. There is also a suggestion that, if the moisture content of the food is very low, some insects may consume more food than needed in order to extract the water from it. Thus *Ephestia* (Lepidoptera) and *Dermestes* (Coleoptera) larvae eat more food at low humidities, but it is clear that the bulk of their water is obtained as a result of the metabolism of this food rather than directly from its original water content (see below).

Many insects drink water if they are dehydrated. For example, locusts without food for 24 h or with access only to dry food, drink if they encounter free water, but turn away from it if they have had access to moist food (Bernays, 1977). Cockroaches, termites, beetles, flies, Lepidoptera and Hymenoptera are also known to drink (Edney, 1977).

The behaviour of some insects living in deserts is adapted to obtain water by condensation from fogs. The beetle *Onymacris*, from the Namib desert, is normally diurnal, but it emerges during nocturnal fogs and adopts a head-down posture on the tops of sand dunes. Water condenses on the body and trickles down to the mouth, so that insects may increase their weight by as much as 12 % overnight (Seely, 1976). *Lepidochora* (Coleoptera) constructs ridges of sand to trap moisture which it subsequently extracts (Seely and Hamilton, 1976).

The physiological control of drinking varies in different insects. In adult *Phormia* (Diptera) blood volume is important, but in adult *Lucilia* (Diptera) the concentration of chloride ions in the haemolymph governs drinking. In *Locusta* the tendency to drink is induced by a low blood volume, while a sudden drop in haemolymph osmotic pressure signals water satiation and switches off drinking behaviour (Bernays, 1977).

Uptake of water through the cuticle of the general body surface may occur in some insects, although this has not been proved (Edney, 1977), but some insects have special structures which are concerned with the absorption of water. The larva of *Epistrophe* (Diptera) can evert an anal papilla into a drop of water and absorb it. In Collembola the ventral tube (Noble-Nesbitt, 1963) and in *Campodea* (Diplura) the eversible vesicles on the abdomen have this function ((Drummond, 1953).

A few insects, when desiccated, can obtain water from water vapour in the air. Larval *Tenebrio* and *Chortophaga* (Orthoptera) can remove water from the atmosphere at relative humidities above 90%, while *Thermobia* (Thysanura) and the prepupa of *Xenopsylla* (Siphonaptera) can obtain water at any humidity above 50%. The more the insect is desiccated the faster it gains moisture until it reaches a characteristic equilibrium with the ambient humidity and then it maintains a steady weight, water uptake matching water loss. Since the haemolymph is normally in equilibrium with a relative humidity of approximately 99%, the movement of water from a lower humidity into the insect must be an active process involving the expenditure of energy. In *Tenebrio* and *Thermobia* water uptake occurs in the rectum, air entering through the open anal opening (Noble-Nesbitt, 1975), but in *Arenivaga* two vesicles associated with the hypopharynx are responsible (see O'Donnell, 1981). The apical membranes of the rectal cells of *Thermobia* are produced into deep, closely packed folds occupied by long, rod-like mitochondria and it is probable that this structure is associated with active transport from the lumen of the rectum.

Water is an end-product of oxidative metabolism and the water so produced is probably normally made use of by the insects; some are dependent on this water for survival. The amount of metabolic water produced depends on the amount and nature of the food which is utilised and from this point of view fat is a more satisfactory substrate than carbohydrate since it produces more water per unit weight. The complete combustion of fat leads to the production of a weight of water greater than the weight of fat from which it is derived (100 g of palmitic acid give 112 g of water; 100 g of glycogen only 56 g of water).

The larvae of *Tribolium* (Coleoptera) and *Ephestia* (Lepidoptera) normally obtain much of their water from the oxidation of food, especially at low humidites. In order to produce this water these insects eat and metabolise greater quantities of food at the lower humidities (Fraenkel and Blewett, 1944). Metabolic water is also of particular importance to starved insects and it enables them to survive where otherwise they would die from desiccation.

Water balance

Water balance is the net result of the various gains and losses experienced by the insect. A net gain is necessary for normal growth; a net loss, if sustained, will lead to death. The balance will vary with the quality of food, the environmental conditions, and the physiological capabilities of the insect. Two examples, showing extreme conditions, are shown in Table 7.

Gain of water by the locust normally depends on food intake; metabolic water produces only an insignificant amount. However, with dry food and reduced food intake, metabolic water provides the greater part of the water gained. Under these conditions dry faeces are produced and loss through the spiracles is minimised, but the insect still experiences a net loss of water.

Arenivaga is a desert-living cockroach. It has the capacity to absorb water vapour from moist air and this provides the biggest proportion of water gained. At the same time loss by transpiration through the cuticle and spiracles is reduced in moist air, so that the insect achieves a net gain of water.

Table 7

Water balance sheet for a locust and *Arenivaga* under different conditions
(expressed as mg water/100 mg/day) (from Edney, 1977)

	Locust		Arenivaga	
	fresh food	dry food	dry air	88 % R.H.
Gain				
food	76·05	0·3	0·22	0·44
metabolism	0·9	0·9	0·87	0·87
vapour absorption	0	0	0	2·14
total	76·95	1·2	1·09	3·45
Loss				
faeces	32·4	2·4	0·19	0·19
cuticle	6·3	6·3 ⎫	5·43	0·65
spiracles	7·35	2·4 ⎭		
total	46·05	11·1	5·62	0·84
Net change	+ 30·9	− 9·9	− 4·53	+ 2·61

In the case of starved *Tenebrio* larvae, defaecation does not occur and, since fat is metabolised and the respiratory quotient is low, loss in weight due to respiration is very slight. Hence any change in weight largely represents a balance between the metabolic water produced and water lost by transpiration and in respiration. At low temperatures and humidities water loss exceeds the water gained from metabolism and so the larvae lose weight, but in moist air at 30°C the weight of water lost by transpiration is less than that produced in metabolism and so the larvae gain weight and their water content increases (Mellanby, 1932).

25.5.2 Freshwater insects

In insects living in fresh water the problems of salt and water regulation are quite different from those of terrestrial insects. Since the haemolymph is hypertonic to the water there is a tendency for water to pass into the insect through the cuticle, the permeability of which varies in different species. The cuticle of adult water beetles and aquatic Heteroptera is relatively impermeable. *Sialis* (Megaloptera) larva also has a relatively impermeable cuticle, and in these insects the osmotic uptake of water is not excessive, about 4 % of the body weight per day. The majority of aquatic larval forms, however, have highly permeable cuticles without a lipid layer. Often the gills are even more permeable than the rest of the surface and in *Aedes aegypti*, where the anal papillae are very permeable, the osmotic uptake of water amounts to about 30 % of the body weight per day. Some water is probably also taken in with the food, but there is no evidence that drinking substantially increases the amount of water taken in under normal conditions. *Sialis* larvae do drink if their haemolymph volume is artificially reduced.

This uptake of water by freshwater insects is offset by the production of a copious urine. Presumably relatively little water is resorbed in the rectum.

25.5.3 Salt-water insects

Insects living in salt water are subject to the osmotic loss of water to the medium because the haemolymph is often hypotonic to the medium. More water is lost in the urine, but, as in terrestrial insects, some of this is resorbed in the rectum, so that a hypertonic urine is produced. The water lost is replaced by controlled drinking and absorption in the midgut, which in these species, but not in freshwater species, is able to withstand high salt concentrations without damage. The larva of *Philanisus* drinks about 25 % of its own weight of sea water per day (Leader, 1972) and the subsequent absorption of water in the midgut is probably linked to the uptake of salt (Stobbart and Shaw, 1974).

25.6 Other functions of the Malpighian tubules

In a few insects the Malpighian tubules are modified for functions other than excretion. The tubules of larval *Chrysopa* (Neuroptera) become thickened distally and the nuclei of the cells become branched after the second instar. These regions produce silk which is used to form the pupal cocoon. Before this the tubules produce a proteinaceous substance which acts as an adhesive during locomotion and may, at the same time, be an excretory end product. Uric acid is stored in the cells of the fat body (p. 583) (Spiegler, 1962). Myrmeleontid larvae also produce silk in the Malpighian tubules and store it in the rectal sac. Chrysomelid beetles produce a sticky substance in the Malpighian tubules for covering the eggs.

Amongst cercopids (Homoptera) the proximal region of the larval tubules is enlarged, consisting of large cells with large nuclei, but without a brush border. These cells produce the spittle within which the larvae live (Marshall, 1964a). Some other cercopids build tubes, that of *Chaetophyes compacta* being conical and attached to the stem of the host plant. The proximal part of the Malpighian tubules in this insect is divided into two zones. Adjacent to the gut is a zone of cells which produce the fibrils forming the basis of the tube. The fibrils pass from the Malpighian tubules and out through the anus and are laid down by characteristic semicircular movements of the tip of the abdomen accompanied by radial pushes from the inside which push the tube into its polygonal form. More prolonged deposition at the corners produces protuberances in these positions. Other organic and inorganic material is deposited on the meshwork so formed (Marshall, 1965). The more distal zone of the proximal region of the Malpighian tubules produces spittle, which is secreted at the mouth of the tube when the insect moults and in which the process of ecdysis is carried out (Marshall, 1964b).

In the larva of the fly *Bolitophila luminosa* the enlarged distal ends of the Malpighian tubules form luminous organs (p. 121).

REFERENCES

BEAMENT, J. W. L. (1959). The waterproofing mechanism of arthropods. I. The effect of temperature on cuticle permeability in terrestrial insects and ticks. *J. exp. Biol.* **36**: 391–422.

BEAMENT, J. W. L. (1964). The active transport and passive movement of water in insects. *Adv. Insect Physiol.* **2**: 67–130.

BERNAYS, E. A. (1977). The physiological control of drinking behaviour in nymphs of *Locusta migratoria*. *Physiol. Ent.* **2**: 261–273.

BERRIDGE, M. J. (1965). The physiology of excretion in the cotton stainer, *Dysdercus fasciatus* Signoret III. Nitrogen excretion and excretory metabolism. *J. exp. Biol.* **43**: 535–552.

BERRIDGE, M. J. (1970). Osmoregulation in terrestrial arthropods. *in* Florkin, M. and Scheer, B. T. (eds.), *Chemical Zoology*. vol. 5. Academic Press, New York.

BRADLEY, T. J. and PHILLIPS, J. E. (1977a). Regulation of rectal secretion in saline-water mosquito larvae living in water of diverse ionic composition. *J. exp. Biol.* **66**: 83–96.

BRADLEY, T. J. and PHILLIPS, J. E. (1977b). The effect of external salinity on drinking rate and rectal secretion in the larvae of the saline-water mosquito *Aedes taeniorhynchus*. *J. exp. Biol.* **66**: 97–110.

CHAPMAN, R. F. (1957). Observations on the feeding of adults of the red locust (*Nomadacris septemfasciata* (Serville)). *Br. J. Anim. Behav.* **5**: 60–75.

CLEMENTS, A. N. (1963). *The physiology of mosquitoes*. Pergamon Press, Oxford.

COCHRAN, D. G. (1979). Uric acid accumulation in young American cockroach nymphs. *Entomologia exp. appl.* **25**: 153–157.

CROSSLEY, A. C. (1972). The ultrastructure and function of pericardial cells and other nephrocytes in an insect: *Calliphora erythrocephala*. *Tissue & Cell* **4**: 529–560.

DRUMMOND, F. H. (1953). The eversible vesicles of *Campodea* (Thysanura). *Proc. R. ent. Soc. Lond.* A, **28**: 145–148.

EDNEY, E. B. (1977). *Water balance in land arthropods*. Springer-Verlag, Berlin.

FOSTER, W. A. and TREHERNE, J. E. (1976). Insects of marine saltmarshes: problems and adaptations. *in* Cheng, L. (ed.), *Marine insects*. North-Holland Publishing Co., Amsterdam.

FRAENKEL, G. and BLEWETT, M. (1944). The utilisation of metabolic water in insects. *Bull. ent. Res.* **35**: 127–139.

HARMSEN, R. (1966). The excretory role of pteridines in insects. *J. exp. Biol.* **45**: 1–13.

LEADER, J. P. (1972). Osmoregulation in the larva of the marine caddis fly, *Philanisus plebeius* (Walk.) (Trichoptera). *J. exp. Biol.* **57**: 821–838.

MACHIN, J. (1979). Atmospheric water absorption in arthropods. *Adv. Insect Physiol.* **14**: 1–48.

MADDRELL, S. H. P. (1964). Excretion in the blood-sucking bug, *Rhodnius prolixus* Stål. II. The normal course of diuresis and the effect of temperature. *J. exp. Biol.* **41**: 163–176.

MADDRELL, S. H. P. (1971). The mechanisms of insect excretory systems. *Adv. Insect Physiol.* **8**: 200–331.

MADDRELL, S. H. P. (1978). Physiological discontinuity in an epithelium with an apparently uniform structure. *J. exp. Biol.* **75**: 133–145.

MADDRELL, S. H. P. and GARDINER, B. O. C. (1974). The passive permeability of insect Malpighian tubules to organic solutes. *J. exp. Biol.* **60**: 641–652.

MADDRELL, S. H. P. and GARDINER, B. O. C. (1975). Induction of transport of organic anions in Malpighian tubules of *Rhodnius*. *J. exp. Biol.* **63**: 755–761.

MADDRELL, S. H. P. and GARDINER, B. O. C. (1976). Excretion of alkaloids by Malpighian tubules of insects. *J. exp. Biol.* **64**: 267–281.

MARSHALL, A. T. (1964a). Spittle-production and tube-building by cercopoid nymphs (Homoptera). 1. The cytology of the Malpighian tubules of spittle-bug nymphs. *Q. Jl microsc. Sci.* **105**: 257–262.

MARSHALL, A. T. (1964b). Spittle-production and tube-building by cercopoid nymphs (Homoptera). 2. The cytology and function of the granule zone of the Malpighian tubules of tube-building nymphs. *Q. Jl microsc. Sci.* **105**: 415–422.

MARSHALL, A. T. (1965). Spittle-production and tube-building by cercopoid nymphs (Homoptera). 3. The cytology and function of the fibril zone of the Malpighian tubules of tube-dwelling nymphs. *Q. Jl microsc. Sci.* **106**: 37–44.

MARSHALL, A. T. and WRIGHT, A. (1974). Ultrastructure changes associated with osmoregulation in the hindgut cells of a saltwater insect, *Ephydrella* sp. (Ephydridae: Diptera). *Tissue & Cell* **6**: 301–318.

MELLANBY, K. (1932). The effect of atmospheric humidity on the metabolism of the fasting mealworm (*Tenebrio molitor* L., Coleoptera). *Proc. R. Soc.* B, **111**: 376–390.

MOLOO, S. K. (1973). Accumulation and storage sites of uric acid in the developing egg of *Schistocerca gregaria* (Forskål) (Orthoptera: Acrididae). *J. Ent.* A, **48**: 85–88.

MULLINS, D. E. and COCHRAN, D. G. (1973). Nitrogenous excretory materials from the American cockroach. *J. Insect Physiol.* **19**: 1007–1018.

NIJHOUT, H. F. (1975). Excretory role of the midgut in larvae of the tobacco hornworm, *Manduca sexta* (L.). *J. exp. Biol.* **62**: 221–230.

NOBLE-NESBITT, J. (1963). A site of water and ionic exchange with the medium in *Podura aquatica* L. (Collembola: Isotomidae). *J. exp. Biol.* **40**: 701–711.

NOBLE-NESBITT, J. (1975). Reversible arrest of uptake of water from subsaturated atmospheres by the firebrat, *Thermobia domestica* (Packard). *J. exp. Biol* **62**: 657–669.

O'DONNELL, M. J. (1981). Frontal bodies: novel structures involved in water vapour absorption by the desert burrowing cockroach, *Arenivaga investigata*. *Tissue & Cell* **13**: 541–555.

PROSSER, C. L. and BROWN, F. A. (1961). *Comparative animal physiology*. Saunders, Philadelphia.

RAMSAY, J. A. (1958). Excretion by the Malpighian tubules of the stick insect, *Dixippus morosus* (Orthoptera: Phasmidae): amino acids, sugars and urea. *J. exp. Biol.* **35**: 871–891.

RAMSAY, J. A. (1964). The rectal complex of the mealworm *Tenebrio molitor* L. (Coleoptera: Tenebrionidae). *Phil. Trans. R. Soc.* B, **248**: 279–314.

RAZET, P. (1956). Sur l'élimination simultanée d'acide urique et d'acide allantoïques chez les insectes. *C. r. hebd. Séanc. Acad. Sci., Paris.* **243**: 185–187.

ROTH, L. M. and DATEO, G. P. (1965). Uric acid storage and excretion by accessory sex glands of male cockroaches. *J. Insect Physiol.* **11**: 1023–1029.

SAINI, R. S. (1964). Histology and physiology of the cryptonephridial system of insects. *Trans. R. ent. Soc. Lond.* **116**: 347–392.

SAVAGE, A. A. (1956). The development of the Malpighian tubules of *Schistocerca gregaria* (Orthoptera). *Q. Jl microsc. Sci.* **97**: 599–615.

SEELY, M. K. (1976). Fog basking by the Namib Desert beetle, *Onymacris unguicularis*. *Nature, Lond.* **262**: 284–285.

SEELY, M. K. and HAMILTON, W. J. (1976). Fog catchment sand trenches constructed by tenebrionid beetles, *Lepidochora*, from the Namib Desert. *Science* **193**: 484–486.

SHAW, J. and STOBBART, R. H. (1963). Osmotic and ionic regulation in insects. *Adv. Insect Physiol.* **1**: 315–399.

SPIEGLER, P. E. (1962). Uric acid and urate storage in the larva *Chrysopa carnea* Stephens (Neuroptera: Chrysopidae). *J. Insect Physiol.* **8**: 127–132.

STADDON, B. W. (1955). The excretion and storage of ammonia by the aquatic larva of *Sialis lutaria* (Neuroptera). *J. exp. Biol.* **32**: 84–94.

STADDON, B. W. (1959). Nitrogen excretion in nymphs of *Aeshna cyanea* (Mull.) (Odonata: Anisoptera). *J. exp. Biol.* **36**: 566–574.

STOBBART, R. H. and SHAW, J. (1974). Salt and water balance; excretion. *in* Rockstein, M. (ed.), *The physiology of Insecta.* vol. 5. Academic Press, New York.

TREHERNE, J. E. and WILLMER, P. G. (1975). Hormonal control of integumentary water-loss: evidence for a novel neuroendocrine system in an insect (*Periplaneta americana*). *J. exp. Biol.* **63**: 143–159.

WAKU, Y. and SUMIMOTO, K.-I. (1971). Metamorphosis of midgut epithelial cells in the silkworm (*Bombyx mori* L.) with special regard to the calcium salt deposits in the cytoplasm. I. Light microscopy. *Tissue & Cell* **3**: 127–136.

WATERHOUSE, D. F. and DAY, M. P. (1953). Function of the gut in absorption, excretion, and intermediary metabolism. *in* Roeder, K. D. (ed.), *Insect Physiology*. Wiley & Sons, New York.

WHARTON, G. W. and RICHARDS, A. G. (1978). Water vapor exchange kinetics in insects and acarines. *A. Rev. Ent.* **23**: 309–328.

WIGGLESWORTH, V. B. (1931). The physiology of excretion in a blood-sucking insect, *Rhodnius prolixus* (Hemiptera: Reduviidae). *J. exp. Biol.* **8**: 411–427.

WIGGLESWORTH, V. B. (1965). *The principles of insect physiology*. Methuen, London.

WIGGLESWORTH, V. B. and SALPETER, M. M. (1962). Histology of the Malpighian tubules of *Rhodnius prolixus* Stål (Hemiptera). *J. Insect Physiol.* **8**: 299–307.

SECTION E

The Nervous and Sensory Systems

CHAPTER XXVI

THE NERVOUS SYSTEM

The nervous system is a conducting system ensuring the rapid functioning and co-ordination of effectors, modifying their responses according to the input of peripheral sense organs. The basic elements in the nervous system are nerve cells which are produced into long processes, or axons, along which nerve impulses are conducted. The bodies of the nerve cells are aggregated to form ganglia while bundles of axons form the nerves. Within the nervous system the nerve cells are accompanied by other elements concerned with their nutrition and mechanical support. The central nervous system consists of a brain situated dorsally in the head and a ventral chain of segmental ganglia from which nerves run to the peripheral sense organs and muscle systems. A stomatogastric system, consisting of a number of small ganglia connected to the brain and their associated nerves, controls the movements of the alimentary canal.

Conduction along a nerve axon is an electrochemical process which is influenced by the composition of the fluid bathing the axons. However, the axons do not form a continuous system and successive axons are separated by small gaps. Transmission of an impulse across a gap to the next axon involves the movement of a chemical. Impulses may arise as the result of sensory stimulation or presynaptic activity of another neurone, but some neurones exhibit spontaneous activity which is modified by different inputs.

The nervous system is not a simple relay, it also integrates the many activities of the body. The brain plays an important part in this, while at the cellular level the pathways and connections of axons within the system and the physiological and anatomical characteristics of the synapses are of great importance. Integration may involve inhibitory as well as stimulatory effects.

Finally, the central nervous system is concerned with learning, but very little is known of the central processes involved.

A general review of the insect nervous system is given by Horridge (1965). Aspects of anatomy, fine structure and physiology are reviewed by Lane (1974), Callec (1974), Howse (1975), Pichon (1974), Treherne (1974) and Treherne and Pichon (1972), while neural integration and its relation to behaviour are discussed by Burrows (1975), Hoyle (1970), Huber (1974) and Miller (1974). Alloway (1972) and Eisenstein (1972) review aspects of learning in insects.

26.1 Structure of the nervous system

26.1.1 Nerve cell

The basic element in the nervous system is the nerve cell, or neurone. This consists of a cell body containing the nucleus and long cytoplasmic projections which extend to make contact with other neurones. The cell body is known as the soma or perikaryon, while the projections are known as axons. Frequently the axon has branches, collaterals, and ends in a terminal arborisation. Nerve impulses are conducted from one cell to the next along the axons. Part of each neurone is specialised for the reception of the stimuli which initiate conduction in the axon. This part, which is known as the dendrite, may arise directly from the perikaryon or represent the distal endings of an axon in which case there is no anatomical differentiation between axon and dendrite. The site at which neurones are closely apposed so that the activity of one is influenced by the other is called the synapse.

Most insect neurones are monopolar, having only a single projection from the perikaryon (Fig. 391A). This projection, or neurite, subsequently branches to form the axon and dendrite. The peripheral sense cells are bipolar with a short distal dendrite receiving stimuli from the environment and a proximal axon extending to the central ganglia (Fig. 391B). Some multipolar cells (Fig. 391C) occur in the hypocerebral and frontal ganglia and are also associated with stretch receptors (p. 728).

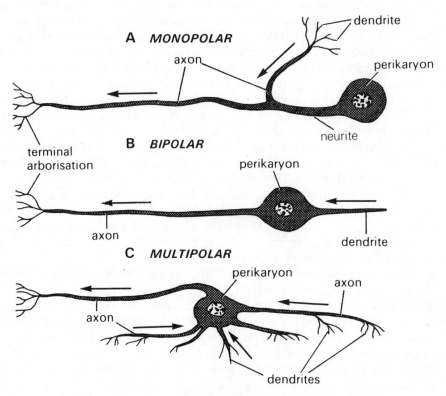

Fig. 391 Diagrammatic representations of the different types of neurone found in the insect nervous system. Arrows indicate the direction of conduction

The sense cells concerned with the perception of stimuli are mostly peripheral with dendritic processes extending to the cuticle (see following chapters) and axons which conduct towards the central nervous system and hence are called afferent or sensory axons. The axons from most insect sensilla are believed to extend to the ganglia of the nerve cord without synapses. Other axons conduct from the central nervous system to the effector organs and are called efferent or motor fibres. Their perikarya lie within the ganglia of the central nervous system. Afferent fibres may synapse directly with efferent fibres, but more frequently one or more neurones, known as interneurones, are interpolated between the two.

The neurones do not occur singly, but are aggregated to form the nervous system comprising the central nervous system with its peripheral nerves and the stomatogastric nervous system. Most adult insects, having a hard external cuticle, have no subepidermal nerve plexus, but in *Rhodnius* (Heteroptera), at least, neurosecretory axons from the ventral ganglionic mass run to the abdominal wall and penetrate the basement membrane of the epidermis. A subepidermal plexus does occur in soft-skinned larvae, where it is formed from the fibres of multipolar neurones.

26.1.2 Central nervous system

The perikarya of motorneurones and interneurones are aggregated to form ganglia within which they are grouped peripherally. The centres of the ganglia are occupied by the neuropile, a complex of afferent, internuncial and efferent fibres and their supporting glial elements (p. 622). Within the neuropile groups of fibres may be similarly orientated so as to form fibre tracts, or they may branch extensively (arborise), so that the axons of different cells are complexly interwoven. It is here that synapses occur. There are no cell bodies in the neuropile (Fig. 392A).

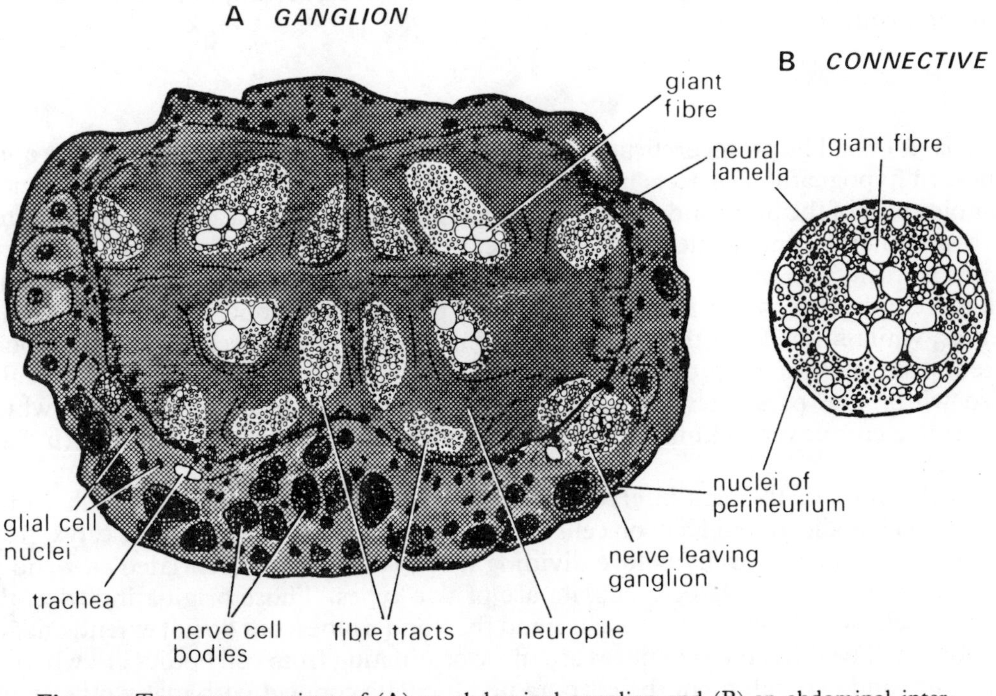

Fig. 392 Transverse sections of (A) an abdominal ganglion and (B) an abdominal interganglionic connective of *Periplaneta*. Not to same scale (after Roeder, 1953, 1963)

In many embryonic insects there is a paired ganglion in each segment of the body, but these always show some degree of fusion before the insect emerges from the egg. The most anterior ganglion is the brain or cerebral ganglion lying dorsal to the oesophagus in the head. It includes one or more segmental ganglia, how many is the subject of controversy, fused together with the primitive presegmental archecerebrum. From the brain the circumoesophageal connectives pass, one on either side of the oesophagus, to the first of a chain of ganglia lying ventrally in the haemocoel.

The ganglia are joined to each other longitudinally by connectives made up only of axons and supporting cells (Fig. 392B), while extending from each ganglion to the peripheral sense organs and effectors are the peripheral nerves. These are usually aggregations of both motor and sensory fibres (see Fig. 396) and in some cases, at least, the dorsal part of each nerve root contains only motor fibres, while the ventral part contains sensory fibres. A few nerves, such as that from the last abdominal ganglion to the cercus in the cockroach, contain only sensory fibres.

Brain

The brain is the principal association centre of the body, receiving sensory input from the sense organs of the head and, via ascending interneurones from the more posterior ganglia. Motor output from the brain supplies the antennal muscles and passes via descending premotor interneurones to the other ganglia, controlling the activities of the rest of the nervous system to some extent (p. 634). It also regulates many long-term organised behaviour patterns and governs their modification by learning (p. 635).

Three regions are recognised in the brain, a protocerebrum, deutocerebrum and tritocerebrum (Fig. 393).

Protocerebrum. The protocerebrum is bilobed and is continuous laterally with the optic lobes. In hypognathous insects it occupies a dorsal position in the head. It is the most complex part of the brain and, as with other ganglia, the perikarya are largely restricted to a peripheral zone while the central region is occupied by neuropile (p. 623). Anterodorsally, on either side of the midline, is a mass of cells forming the pars intercerebralis (Fig. 394). The anterior cells of the pars contribute fibres to the ocellar nerves, while fibres from the more lateral cells enter the protocerebral bridge (pons cerebralis), a median mass of neuropile connecting with many other parts of the brain. Also within the pars intercerebralis are neurosecretory cells, the axons of which decussate, cross over, within the brain and extend to the corpora cardiaca (p. 822; Fig. 546).

At the sides of the pars intercerebralis are the corpora pedunculata, each with a group of cell bodies called Kenyon cells over a flattened cap of neuropile, the calyx, from which a stalk runs ventrally before dividing into two lobes, differentiated as α and β. The fibres in the corpora pedunculata are of two types. Those originating from the Kenyon cells send branches to the calyx and the α and β lobes, but do not extend outside the corpus. The other types of fibres are those originating from cell bodies elsewhere in the brain, and through them the corpora pedunculata connect with many other parts (Howse, 1974, 1975). The connections to the calyx and α lobe may be largely sensory,

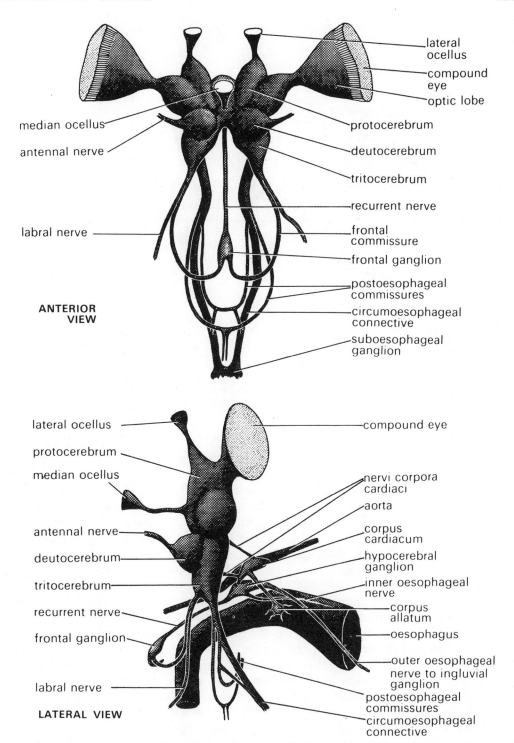

Fig. 393 Anterior and lateral views of the brain and stomatogastric nervous system of *Locusta* (Orthoptera) (after Albrecht, 1953)

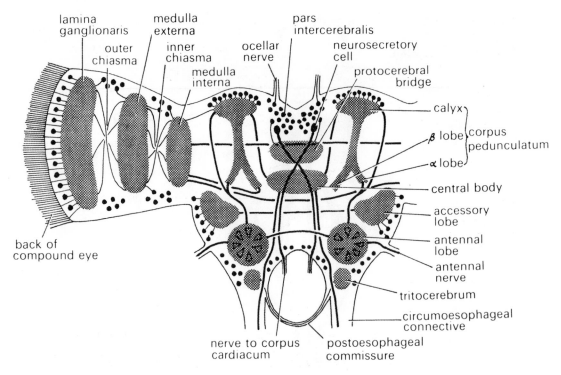

Fig. 394 Diagram of the brain showing the more important areas of neuropile (hatched) and a few of the main connections between these areas. Black dots represent zones containing perikarya

while the endings in the β lobe may synapse with premotor fibres, that is, with interneurones which conduct to motor fibres.

The relative size of the corpora pedunculata is related to the complexity of behaviour shown by the insects. They are small in Collembola, Heteroptera, Diptera and Odonata, of medium size in Coleoptera, Orthoptera, Dictyoptera, Lepidoptera and solitary Hymenoptera, and most highly developed in social insects (Fig. 395). In termites the volume of the peduncle and α and β lobes is large, but the calyx may be little better developed than in *Schistocerca*. In social Hymenoptera the calyx is large and has a very complex structure.

The corpora pedunculata have an important role in visual integration in social Hymenoptera, but in other insects they are relatively unimportant in this respect. It is probable that they are concerned with the selection and sequential organisation of behaviour patterns (Howse, 1974, 1975).

In the centre of the protocerebrum a mass of neuropile forms the central body. The volume of the central body is proportional to the size of the insect and it has a comparable structure in insects exhibiting different levels of behavioural complexity. In *Schistocerca* the arrangement of axons within it is well-ordered. One conspicuous feature is a fan-like arrangement of 64 axons which arise from perikarya in the protocerebrum and run in bundles through the central body. These axons arborise extensively in the protocerebral bridge and in the ellipsoid body, which is closely

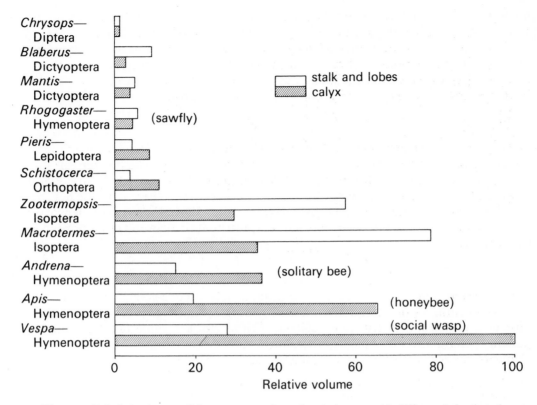

Fig. 395 Relative volumes of the corpora pedunculata in insects with different behavioural repertoires. The size is expressed relative to the volume of the central body in each species
(after Howse, 1974)

associated with the central body. Other fibres arborise in the central body itself and others, which run transversely through the body, probably extend to the lateral parts of the brain. There are no direct connections with the corpora pedunculata, or the optic or antennal lobes and Howse (1974) suggests that a principal role of the central body is to generate arousal—the readiness to respond (p. 634).

Optic lobes. The optic lobes are lateral extensions of the protocerebrum to the compound eyes. Each consists of three neuropile masses, known as the lamina ganglionaris, medulla externa and medulla interna, together with their associated perikarya and connections (Fig. 394). Axons of the retinula cells pass through the basement membrane at the back of the eye and into the lamina ganglionaris, where they synapse with large monopolar neurones, the axons of which extend to the medulla externa (Fig. 419).

Some fibres, which may be the axons of mechanoreceptors on the surface of the eye, pass directly from the lamina ganglionaris to the protocerebrum, but the majority pass to the medulla externa, crossing over each other to form the external chiasma between the two neuropile layers. A second crossover, the internal chiasma, lies between the medulla externa and the medulla interna. Cell bodies, supplying axons to these systems, lie peripherally and in a group on the outside of the medulla externa.

Fibres from the medulla interna, which is divided into two parts in Lepidoptera and Diptera, pass to the protocerebrum, and anterior and posterior tracts connect the optic lobes of the two sides. Other axons pass directly to the ventral cord via both the ipsilateral and contralateral circumoesophageal connectives.

Deutocerebrum. The deutocerebrum contains the antennal lobes which are divided into dorsal sensory and ventral motor areas. The antennal nerves, which enter this part of the brain and contain both sensory and motor elements, are similarly divided. The sensory neuropile typically contains a number of dense areas (Fig. 394), the neuropiles of the two sides being connected by a commissure. Fibre tracts, both sensory and motor, connect the antennal lobes with the corpora pedunculata and other fibres pass to the tritocerebrum.

Tritocerebrum. This is a small part of the brain consisting of a pair of lobes beneath the deutocerebrum. From it the circumoesophageal connectives pass to the suboeso-phageal ganglion and the tritocerebral lobes of either side are connected by a commissure passing behind the oesophagus. Anteriorly nerves containing sensory and motor elements connect with the frontal ganglion and the labrum.

Ventral nerve cord

The first ganglion in the ventral chain is the suboesophageal. This is a compound ganglion, lying ventrally in the head, arising from the fusion of the ganglia of the mandibular, maxillary and labial segments. It sends mixed, motor and sensory, nerves to the mandibles, maxillae and labium and an additional one or two pairs to the neck and salivary glands. Typically there are three thoracic ganglia, each with some five or six nerves on each side which innervate the muscles and the sensilla of the thorax and its appendages (Fig. 396). The arrangement of nerves varies considerably, but usually the last nerve of one segment forms a common nerve with the first nerve of the next.

The largest number of abdominal ganglia occurring in larval or adult insects is eight, as in Thysanura, male *Pulex* (Siphonaptera) and many larval forms (Fig. 397A), but the last ganglion is always compound, being derived from the ganglia of the last four abdominal segments. In the majority of adult insects some further degree of fusion, particularly of the abdominal ganglia, occurs and in the extreme cases all the ventral ganglia may be fused together into one large ganglionic mass as in *Musca* (Diptera) (Fig. 397B).

The abdominal ganglia are smaller than those of the thorax and, in general, fewer peripheral nerves arise from each of them than arise from the thoracic ganglia. In addition, the branching of the nerves is less diverse and variable, reflecting the relative simplicity of the abdominal musculature (Schmitt, 1962). In most cases the muscles of a segment are innervated by fibres from the ganglion of the same segment, this being related to the overall autonomy of each segment, but some innervation by axons arising

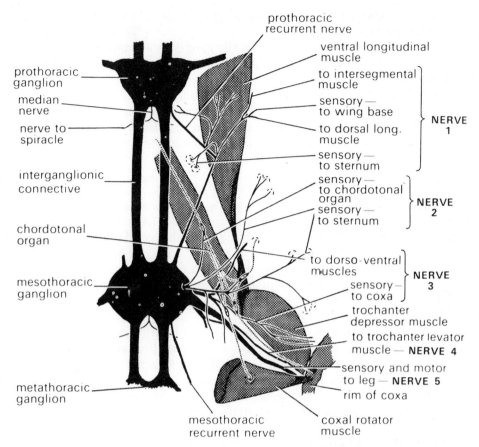

Fig. 396 Ventral view of part of the central nerve cord in the thorax of *Locusta* showing some of the nerves of the mesothoracic segment (after Campbell, 1961)

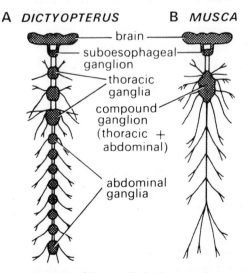

Fig. 397 Two extreme arrangements of the ganglia in the central nervous system showing (A) minimal and (B) maximal degrees of fusion (from Horridge, 1965)

in neighbouring ganglia also occurs (Fig. 355). Some afferent fibres may also be intersegmental (see below).

Between the paired connectives joining the ganglia is a small median nerve which runs from the back of each ganglion and branches transversely to the spiracles and some ventilatory muscles (Fig. 396). In the thorax the median nerve does not extend beyond the origin of its lateral branches, but in the abdomen it forms a complete connective extending from one ganglion to the next. In the larva of *Aeschna* (Odonata) the median nerve contains four axons, two motor and two sensory. Each axon divides where the nerve branches, so that each side of the body is innervated by each axon (Fig. 355).

Motorneurones

In each segmental ganglion are the perikarya of motorneurones concerned with control of muscles primarily, but not only, in the same segment. The number of motorneurones in each ganglion is relatively small, corresponding with the relatively small number of muscle units which insects possess, and probably does not exceed 200 in any one ganglion, though there may be more where fusion of ganglia takes place.

The perikarya (somata) of motorneurones are relatively large and in the locust metathoracic ganglion they range from about 20 to 90 μm in diameter. They are roughly constant in position and Fig. 398 maps the positions of the perikarya of some motorneurones with axons in the lateral nerves of the metathoracic ganglion of *Schistocerca*. The perikarya on the two sides of a ganglion are placed more or less symmetrically. There is a tendency for the perikarya of axons running within a single nerve to be grouped together, but even those running to the same muscle may be widely separated. For instance, the perikarya of the fast and slow axons to the metathoracic extensor tibiae muscle are widely separated and their axons run in different nerve branches.

The neurite of each motorneurone increases in diameter on entering the neuropile, within which it gives rise to many branches (Fig. 399). The shape of this dendritic tree is characteristic of each motorneurone and, in the locust at least, it is confined to the same half of the ganglion as the perikaryon. There is apparently no intermingling of dendrites of bilaterally homologous neurones (Burrows, 1975).

The complexity of these dendritic fields is an indication of the complexity of the synaptic connections which occur with other neurones. The response of a neurone will depend on the integration of inputs via these various connections, which may be both excitatory and inhibitory.

Interneurones

Some direct contacts are known to occur between afferent, sensory, fibres and motorneurones (p. 233), but these monosynaptic pathways are unlikely to occur commonly because such an arrangement does not allow any variability of response (Burrows, 1975). In general, interneurones are interpolated between sensory and motorneurones, and most of the neurones in the central nervous system are interneurones.

Many interneurones are confined to individual ganglia. The best known of these are in the brain, in the optic lobes (Fig. 395) and corpora pedunculata, but intraganglionic

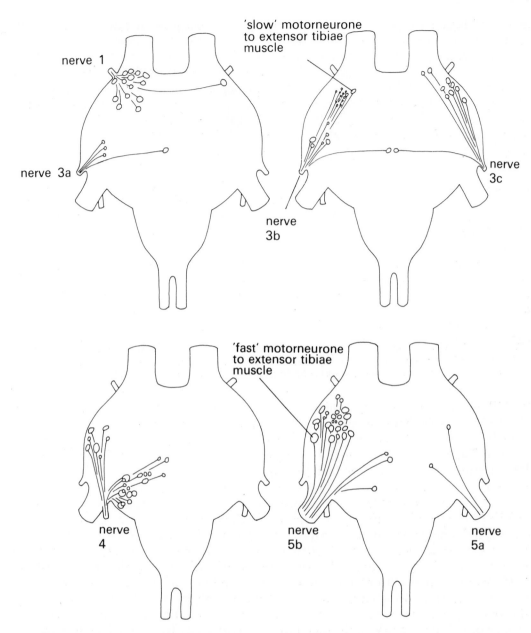

Fig. 398 Maps of the metathoracic ganglion of *Schistocerca* showing the distribution of perikarya of motorneurones associated with different peripheral nerves. Nerve 3 has three main branches. The 'axon pathways' are entirely diagrammatic and are intended only to indicate the association of the perikarya with particular nerves. For a representation of some of the true axon pathways see Fig. 399 (after Burrows, 1975)

interneurones are also common in other ganglia. For instance, it is estimated that there are approximately 1500 intraganglionic interneurones in the mesothoracic ganglion of *Periplaneta*, compared with 300 motorneurones and 200 interganglionic interneurones.

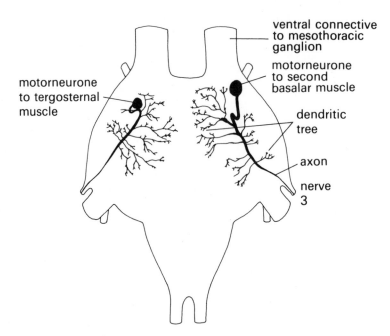

Fig. 399 Representation of two motorneurones with their dendritic branches in the metathoracic ganglion of a locust: *left*, fast motorneurone to a tergosternal muscle; *right*, fast motorneurone to the second basalar muscle (after Burrows, 1977)

Many, perhaps all, of these intraganglionic neurones do not produce action potentials and they are called non-spiking neurones. Similar neurones are known to occur in the thoracic ganglia of *Schistocerca* and *Teleogryllus*, and it is suggested that, since they are relatively short, slow changes in the resting membrane potential are adequate to achieve neural transmission; spike production is unnecessary.

Non-spiking neurones have low resting potentials, of about -30 to -50 mV, compared with spike-producing neurones (about -70 mV). Postsynaptic potentials are produced by these neurones by the release of a chemical synaptic transmitter just as in spiking neurones and in some cases the resting membrane potential is sufficiently low to produce a tonic postsynaptic potential. This may be depolarising so that the postsynaptic fibre fires tonically, or hyperpolarising so that the activity of the postsynaptic fibre is inhibited. Changes in the membrane potential of the non-spiking neurone lead to graded changes in the postsynaptic potential and hence to changes in the rate of spike production in the postsynaptic fibre (Fig. 400). An experimental change of as little as 2 mV in the membrane potential may have such an effect and it is known that in the course of normal activity changes of up to 15 mV may occur. All the motorneurones in the metathoracic ganglion of the locust which are involved with jumping are known to be associated with non-spiking neurones and it may be that these interneurones have an important role in the coordination of many activities (Pearson, 1977; Burrows and Siegler, 1978).

Interganglionic interneurones also occur. It is these which transmit command information from the brain and which coordinate the activity of different ganglia as in respiration. One of the most thoroughly studied interganglionic interneurones is the

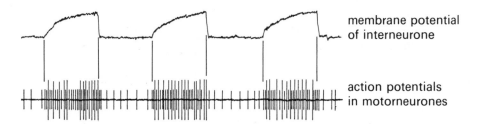

membrane potential
of interneurone

action potentials
in motorneurones

Fig. 400 Changes in the membrane potential of a non-spiking interneurone in the meta-thoracic ganglion of *Periplaneta* inducing action potentials in the motorneurones of the leg flexor muscles (after Pearson, 1977)

descending contralateral movement detector (DCMD) of the locust. There is one DCMD in each connective of the nerve cord, running from the brain to the metathoracic ganglion. The perikaryon is on the posterior face of the protocerebrum. Within the brain the axon swells to form an integrating segment from which six or more major dendrites diverge so that their fine branches occupy a sphere about 200 μm in diameter. It is in this region that the neurone receives input from other neurones.

In particular, it receives information about small-scale movements in the visual field. Beyond the integrating segment the axon crosses to the contralateral side of the brain and then passes down the connectives to the metathoracic ganglion. It gives rise to a single branch in the prothoracic ganglion, and to three main branches in the mesothoracic and metathoracic ganglia. These give rise to further branches, but do not form extensive arborisations like the dendritic fields of the motorneurones with which they connect. Electrophysiological evidence shows that in the metathoracic ganglion these branches make bilateral synaptic contact with a number of motor-neurones concerned with the control of muscles during jumping (Fig. 401) (O'Shea *et al.*, 1974).

Giant fibres are interneurones which have much greater diameters than other interneurones in the nerve cord. Within the ventral nerve cord of cockroach, various Orthoptera, dragonfly larvae, *Drosophila* (Diptera) and possibly in all other insects are a number of axons which are much bigger than the majority, some being as much as 60 μm in diameter compared with a normal diameter of less than 5 μm (Fig. 392). In the cockroach there are six to eight giant fibres, 20–60 μm in diameter, in each connective as well as 10 to 12 medium sized axons between 5 and 20 μm in diameter. Each giant axon in *Periplaneta* (Dictyoptera) arises from a perikaryon in the last abdominal ganglion.

Giant fibres run for considerable lengths of the nerve cord without synapses. In *Periplaneta* the biggest fibres extend from the last abdominal ganglion to the suboesophageal ganglion, but are greatly reduced in diameter as they pass through the thoracic ganglia (Spira *et al.*, 1969). Within the terminal abdominal ganglion each giant fibre has an extensive dendritic arborisation within which synapses are made with the afferent fibres from the cercal nerve (Fig. 407). Different giant fibres arborise in different parts of the ganglion suggesting that they receive input from different groups of sensilla (Milburn and Bentley, 1971).

The giant fibres have generally been considered to play an important role in evasive behaviour, providing direct fast conducting links between sensilla and effectors. It is

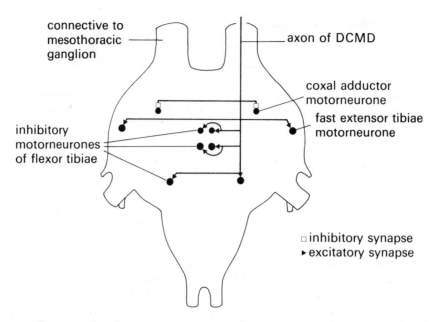

Fig. 401 Diagram of the metathoracic ganglion of *Schistocerca* showing the synaptic links of the descending contralateral movement detector (DCMD) interneurone with various motorneurones controlling the muscles of the hind leg. Synapses occur in the neuropile, not directly with the perikarya (after O'Shea *et al.*, 1974)

now clear, however, that while they may contribute to such behaviour, this is also induced, at least in the cockroach, via much smaller interneurones and the specific role of the giant fibres remains unknown (Parnas and Dagan, 1971).

Neurosecretory cells

Neurosecretory cells are present in all the ganglia of the insect central nervous system. Their distribution and functions are considered in Chapter XXXIV. Neurosecretory cells can be regarded as specialised neurones which, instead of releasing a transmitter substance at a synaptic gap, release a chemical into the haemocoel. In this way the effects of the cells are transmitted to widely dispersed effectors leading to their co-ordinated activity, and the period over which the activity is sustained is relatively long compared with the periods of activity of normal motorneurones.

Sensory cells

The perikarya of sensory cells occur peripherally in association with different types of sensilla (see Chapters XXVII–XXX). Their axons pass without synapsing to the central nervous system. Very little is known of the location and physiology of sensory fibres within the central nervous system, but it is assumed that they form synapses with interneurones in the neuropile of the relevant ganglia.

26.1.3 Stomatogastric nervous system

The stomatogastric nervous system consists of a number of small ganglia and their associated nerves. Above the oesophagus in front of the brain is the frontal ganglion, which is connected by a nerve to the tritocerebral lobe on either side. Sometimes a median frontal nerve extends forwards from the ganglion to the wall of the pharynx and posteriorly a median recurrent nerve runs along the oesophagus beneath the brain, joining the hypocerebral ganglion just behind the brain (Fig. 393). Laterally the hypocerebral ganglion connects with the corpora cardiaca and axons pass to it from the brain via the nervi corpora cardiaci. It is sometimes also connected by a nerve to the suboesophageal ganglion and, in addition, one or two nerves leave it posteriorly running backwards over the surface of the alimentary canal to the ingluvial ganglia on the posterior end of the foregut. From the ingluvial ganglia and the nerves running to them other nerves spread over the surface of the foregut and extend to the midgut (p. 58). In *Locusta* (Orthoptera) these nerves include three neurosecretory axons which probably have their origins in the brain (Strong, 1966).

The frontal ganglion contains the endings of axons from the brain and from the recurrent nerve and sends motor axons to the muscles of the gut wall. Thus it acts as a motor relay centre, co-ordinating local sensory input with premotor excitation from the brain. The frontal ganglion may control swallowing movements, but most of the movements of the foregut and midgut are directly controlled by the ingluvial ganglion. In *Locusta*, and probably in other insects, the stomatogastric system is concerned in controlling the release of secretion by the corpora cardiaca following distension of the foregut (Bernays and Chapman, 1972).

26.1.4 Histology of nervous elements

The same basic units occur throughout the nervous system and so a detailed description of a segmental ganglion (Fig. 402) suffices for the whole system. Receptors are dealt with separately (Chapters XXVII, XXIX and XXX).

Nerve sheath

The whole of the central nervous system is clothed in a non-nervous sheath, which is differentiated into a non-cellular neural lamella and a cellular perineurium. This sheath extends over the larger peripheral branches.

The neural lamella consists of an amorphous layer of neutral mucopolysaccharide and mucoprotein. Except in the outermost layer collagen-like fibrils are present within this matrix. They lie parallel with the surface, but otherwise are randomly orientated. The neural lamella is probably secreted by cells of the perineurium, although other cells may contribute to it (Lane, 1974). It provides mechanical support for the central nervous system, holding the cells and axons together while permitting such flexibility as is necessitated by the movements of the insect. It offers no resistance to diffusion of material from the haemolymph into the nerve cord.

The perineurium is a layer of cells beneath the neural lamella. The cells are separated from each other externally by long, tortuous intercellular spaces continuous with the space beneath the perineurium, but more centrally they are held together by tight junctions and septate desmosomes. On the inner side, the cells have relatively extensive processes which penetrate between the glial cells to a depth of about 10 μm. Some cells may contain extensive deposits of glycogen (Maddrell and Treherne, 1967).

The perineurium has a trophic function, passing nutrient from the haemolymph to the nervous tissue. It may also be an effective blood/brain barrier which regulates the chemical environment in which the nerve cells function (p. 629).

The finer branches of peripheral nerves lack a sheath formed by the perineurium. The axons are wrapped round by glial cells with a basement membrane on the outside.

Glial cells

Each neurone is almost wholly invested by one or more glial cells, which form an insulating, protective sheath round it. In the ganglia some of the glial cells are closely associated with the perikarya. The cell bodies of others are at the surface of the neuropile and, from these, processes extend inwards to invest the axons. The sheath which they form round an axon may consist of a single fold or the fold may coil round several times so that there are several layers forming the envelope (Fig. 402, axon A). This spiral arrangement of a glial cell round an axon is called a mesaxon. The same effect may be achieved by several overlapping cells, while, in the case of small axons, several may be enclosed within one glial fold (Fig. 402, axon B). Glial cells may be bound together by desmosomes and tight junctions.

The glial cells probably serve to insulate the axons from each other and it is believed that synapses only occur where glial folds are absent, although the absence of a glial fold does not necessarily indicate a synapse. In addition, the glial cells pass nutrient materials to the neurones, this being facilitated by finger-like inpushings into the neurones.

Between the glial cells are extracellular spaces. These are extensive peripherally, but much more restricted within the neuropile, where they are continuous with the narrow spaces between the glial folds. These spaces show periodic lacunae, which are characteristic of insect nerves (Fig. 402). The fluid in the extracellular spaces bathes the nervous elements directly and is therefore of great importance in nervous conduction (p. 629). It differs in composition from the haemolymph, the concentrations of sodium and potassium being higher and that of chloride lower than in the haemolymph (Table 8).

Neurones

The cell bodies, perikarya, of the neurones are situated near the periphery of the ganglion, close beneath the perineurium. They are often large with voluminous nuclei and contain extensive rough endoplasmic reticulum, abundant mitochondria and ordered associations of membranes known as dictyosomes. These are often crescent-shaped and are associated with small vesicles. They may be concerned with the elaboration of cellular materials and secretions.

There is an abrupt change in the internal organisation of the neurone at the origin of the axon. The axoplasm contains mitochondria, but no dictyosomes or ribosomes, while in addition, it contains neurofilaments. These are about 20 nm in diameter, sometimes appearing tubular, and they may form a link between the distal extremities of the axon and the perikaryon.

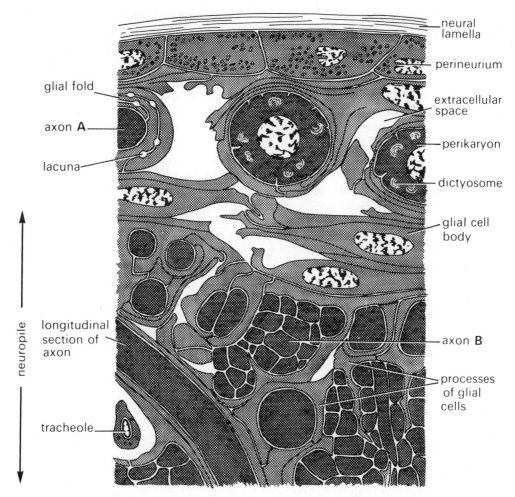

Fig. 402 Diagrammatic cross-section of part of an abdominal ganglion showing the arrangement of the various tissues (after Smith and Treherne, 1963)

Neuropile

The neuropile consists of a mass of axons of all types and particularly their terminal arborisations, together with their investing glial elements and fine branches of the tracheal system. The glial material is reduced in the body of the neuropile and may be absent altogether so that adjacent axons are in contact with each other. It is believed the most, or perhaps all, synapses occur in the neuropile. Altman (1981) describes the functional differentiation of the neuropile in the locust mesothoracic ganglion.

Synapses

Synapses occur where glial cells are absent and the axons lie very close together, their membranes being separated only by a narrow synaptic gap. Synapses are believed to be characterised by foci of electron dense material in areas 150–500 μm long close to the cell membrane where the two axons are adjacent. These foci are found particularly in what is presumed to be the presynaptic fibre. Also indicative of a synapse, although occurring elsewhere, are small synaptic vesicles, again usually found in the presynaptic fibre. These vesicles are of two types, some about 20 to 50 nm in diameter, which tend to aggregate in clusters and may contain the transmitter substance (p. 630), and others up to 100 nm across which resemble neurosecretory droplets. Mitochondria are most abundant in axons where synaptic vesicles occur.

Synapses of another type, perhaps involving electrical rather than chemical transmission, occur between the perikarya in the corpora pedunculata of *Formica* (Hymenoptera). There are gaps in the glial cells surrounding the perikarya, so that the membranes of adjacent cells approach each other very closely, perhaps forming a compound membrane, but no accumulations of vesicles are present in the adjacent cytoplasm (Landolt and Ris, 1966).

Nerve muscle junctions

The motor nerve supplying an insect muscle makes contact with each muscle fibre at a number of points (p. 247). The nature of the ending varies considerably. In the simplest form, such as occurs, for instance, in the flight muscles of Diptera, the fine nerve branches pass longitudinally over the surface of the muscle or sometimes, as in *Tenebrio* (Coleoptera), the terminal axon is completely invaginated into the muscle fibre so that it makes contact with the muscle all round its circumference. In Orthoptera the axon divides at the surface of the muscle and the branches, with their sheaths, form a claw-like structure (Fig. 403). Each junction may contain only one axon, as in *Tenebrio*, or more than one, as in *Blatta* (Dictyoptera). There is no known difference between the junctions of fast and slow axons (p. 255) and it is probable that multiaxonal junctions include both.

The fine structure appears to be similar in all these forms (Fig. 404). Glial cells are lacking along the nerve/muscle interface, so that the axon and muscle fibre plasma membranes are close together, separated only by a synaptic gap of about 10 nm. The terminal axoplasm contains synaptic vesicles some 25–45 nm across (Smith, 1965).

26.2 Physiology of the nervous system

Stimuli may be perceived in a number of ways depending on the nature of the stimulus and the characteristics of the sense organs. The energy received by the sense cell as a result of stimulation is then transformed (transduced) to electrical energy and this leads to the production of a nerve impulse which travels along the nerve axon to the central nervous system. Here the impulse crosses a synapse and, directly or via one or more interneurones, continues along a motorneurone, crossing a final synapse before producing some response in an effector organ, usually a muscle.

26.2.1 Reception and transduction of the stimulus

Different types of stimuli, mechanical, chemical or visual, are perceived in different ways and involve different sense organs. Mechanical stimuli appear to cause some mechanical distortion of the receptor dendrite (p. 707); chemical stimuli may act in a

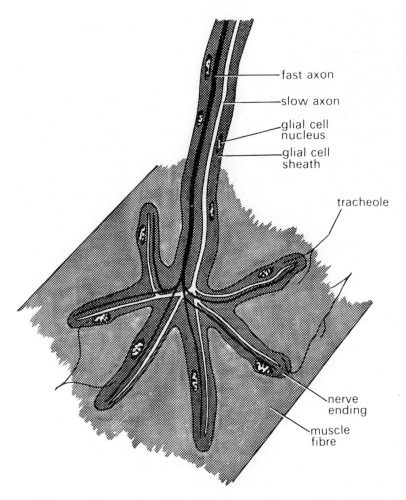

fast axon

slow axon

glial cell
nucleus

glial cell
sheath

tracheole

nerve
ending

muscle
fibre

Fig. 403 Diagram of a nerve/muscle junction in an orthopteran (after Hoyle, 1965a)

number of unknown ways, but it is suggested that sugars form complexes with specific receptor molecules at the receptor site (p. 749); while visual perception involves the breakdown of some light sensitive pigment (p. 653). Whatever the method of perception, the energy received by the sense cell is transformed to electrical energy. In some way not understood the stimulus affects the permeability of the plasma membrane of the dendrite so that it becomes depolarised (see below).

The potential produced in the dendrite by this depolarisation is called a receptor potential. It varies in size, or is graded, according to the strength of the stimulus, a weak stimulus producing only a weak receptor potential. The receptor potential leads to the development of a generator potential, although it is probable that in insects these are often not differentiated from each other. The generator potential is believed to arise in the region of the perikaryon. Like the receptor potential it is graded and if it exceeds a certain threshold value it triggers off the production of the all-or-none nerve impulse in the initial segment of the axon (Davis, 1961).

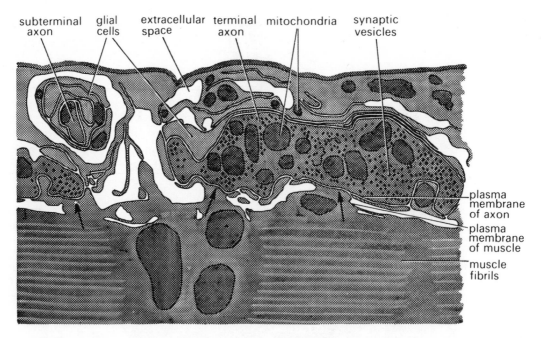

subterminal   glial   extracellular   terminal   mitochondria   synaptic
axon   cells   space   axon   vesicles

plasma
membrane
of axon

plasma
membrane
of muscle

muscle
fibrils

Fig. 404 A neuromuscular junction in *Apis* coxal muscle, from an electron micrograph. Arrows indicate points of apposition between neurilemma and sarcolemma (after Smith and Treherne, 1963)

26.2.2 Nerve impulse

The production and conduction of a nerve impulse in insects is not fully understood, but it appears to be similar to the process in other animals (Pichon, 1974). The account of the theory of conduction is therefore based to a large extent on the general concepts of nervous conduction (see *e.g.* Hodgkin, 1958; Keele and Neil, 1961).

Membrane potential

The ionic concentrations within an axon differ from those in the adjacent extracellular fluid despite the fact that the plasma membrane is freely permeable. Sodium is actively pumped out of the axon so that its concentration inside is much lower than outside and this movement is linked with an inward movement of potassium ions. Ionic movement is also influenced by large indiffusable organic anions within the axon and a Donnan equilibrium is set up across the plasma membrane with a high concentration of potassium ions inside the axon and a high concentration of chloride ions outside. As a result of the equilibrium the inside of the axon becomes negatively charged with respect to the outside and the potential produced in this way is known as the membrane, or resting, potential. Its magnitude varies, but commonly nerve axons have a membrane potential of about $-70\,\mathrm{mV}$.

Action potential

Unlike the generator potential, which may vary in amplitude, the action, or spike, potential is of constant amplitude. It arises from a depolarisation of the axon membrane associated with a change in permeability. When a nerve impulse is initiated the change in permeability is produced by the generator potential, but as the impulse passes along the axon the change is self-regenerative.

The first change which occurs is a brief, but very marked, increase in permeability to sodium, as a result of which sodium ions flow into the axon down the concentration gradient. This produces a rapid positive swing in the charge on the inside of the membrane, amounting to 80–100 mV in the cockroach, representing the rising phase of the action potential (Fig. 405). Adjacent areas of axon are negatively charged, so that a current flows in a local circuit away from the point of depolarisation inside the axon and towards it on the outside (Fig. 406). Where this current reaches an area of resting membrane it produces a slight depolarisation, of the order of 20 mV, so that the permeability to sodium rises and the charge on the inside of the fibre swings towards positive, becoming increasingly permeable as it does so. In this way a wave of increased permeability, and hence a nerve impulse, is propagated along the fibre without decrement.

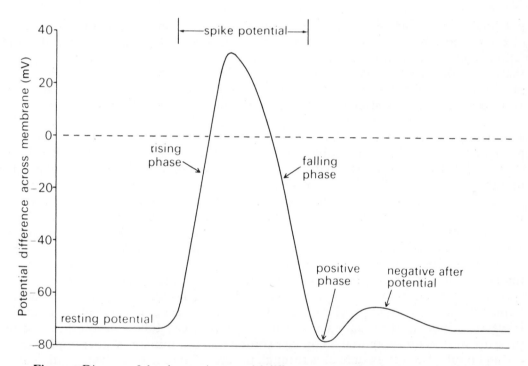

Fig. 405 Diagram of the changes in potential difference across the plasma membrane of an axon occurring during the passage of an impulse

The period of permeability to sodium is short-lived and is followed by a period of increased permeability to potassium, as a result of which potassium flows out of the fibre, which again becomes negatively charged on the inside. This is the falling phase of the action potential. Thus the total duration of the spike or action potential is very brief, only one or two milliseconds.

After the potential has returned to its resting level it overshoots slightly because of the high permeability to potassium. This is known as the positive phase and after it the

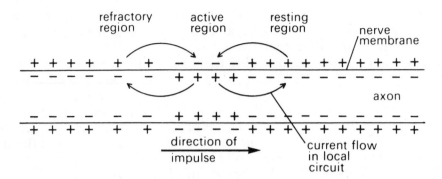

Fig. 406 Diagram of impulse conduction along a nerve axon. Conduction does not occur towards the left because the membrane is in a refractory state due to the recent passage of the nerve impulse (after Narahashi, 1965)

potential swings back again to a level slightly higher than normal (Fig. 405). This phase, the negative after-potential, results from the potassium which is released in the falling phase of the action potential accumulating just outside the axon membrane so that the tendency for potassium to move out is reduced. The negative after-potential persists for several milliseconds, but finally the membrane potential returns to normal. In insects the negative after-potential is short-lived compared with vertebrates.

Following the development of an action potential the ionic composition within the axon is altered, the sodium concentration has increased and the potassium concentration decreased. The ionic quantities involved are very small and it has been estimated that an axon 500 μm in diameter loses about a millionth of its potassium ions in the passage of one impulse. Nevertheless, if the axon is to continue functioning over long periods a recovery mechanism is required to bring the ionic concentrations back to their original values. This involves the sodium pump, which actively extrudes sodium ions, probably in exchange for potassium. In this way the concentration of sodium is slowly lowered, while that of potassium is raised to its original level.

Normally the stimulation of a nerve does not lead to the production of one nerve impulse, but of many. Since these are all of the same amplitude, information concerning the stimulus can only be conveyed in the number and frequency of the impulses, the latter being proportional to the size of the generator potential. There is, however, a limit to the frequency at which impulses can follow each other. In the presence of an action potential no further stimulation can initiate another impulse, nor can an impulse from elsewhere pass through the area. The period for which this is true is known as the absolute refractory period; it lasts for two or three milliseconds. Immediately after this an impulse can be produced, but only by a very strong stimulus and as the nerve recovers progressively weaker stimuli serve to produce impulses until the level of excitation returns to normal. This relative refractory period lasts for 10–15 ms.

The velocity of conduction in a nerve fibre is proportional to its diameter. Giant fibres, with diameters of 8–50 μm, have conduction speeds of 3–7 m/s; fibres of about 5 μm diameter conduct at speeds of 1.5–2.3 m/s. The velocity of conduction varies with temperature.

Effect of haemolymph composition on conduction

Since the passage of impulses in the nerve involves the movement of ions into and out from the axon it follows that this movement, and hence the impulse itself, is influenced by the concentration of ions in the medium bathing the axon (Treherne, 1965). If the level of potassium in the external fluid is raised there is less tendency for potassium to flow out of the axon and hence the membrane potential is reduced. Similarly a low level of sodium in the external medium reduces the height of the action potential.

In many insects the concentration of sodium in the haemolymph is high, while the concentration of potassium is low (p. 806), but in some, particularly in herbivorous insects such as *Carausius*, the converse is true and there is much more potassium than sodium. It might be supposed that this would influence nervous conduction in some way, but this is not so because the concentrations of ions in the extracellular fluid within the nerve sheath are quite different from those in the haemolymph (Table 8). Even in *Periplaneta*, where there is more sodium than potassium in the haemolymph, the ionic concentrations within the nerve sheath are different. Thus the nervous tissue lies in its own micro-environment, which resembles in ionic composition the body fluids of other animals.

Table 8

Ionic concentrations (in mM/kg tissue) in the nerve cord and haemolymph of some insects

(after Treherne, 1974)

		Na	K	Ca	Mg
Periplaneta					
	haemolymph	156	8	4	5
	nerve cord	76	132	—	—
Romalea					
	haemolymph	56	18	—	—
	nerve cord	69	89	—	—
Carausius					
	haemolymph	15	18	7	53
	nerve cord	64	313	30	22

This constant environment within the nervous tissue is maintained by the so called 'blood–brain barrier', though the barrier exists round all parts of the central nervous system, not just round the brain. The tight junctions between the cells of the perineurium provide an effective intercellular barrier, but there is a rapid flux of inorganic ions through the cells of the perineurium (Treherne and Pichon, 1972; Treherne, 1974; Schofield and Treherne, 1978). The sodium concentration surrounding the axons is kept constant by sodium pumps which, as well as maintaining the differential between haemolymph and nervous tissue concentrations, also regulate the concentrations in the immediate vicinity of the axons. Because the space between an axon and its ensheathing glial cell is so narrow, sustained nervous activity could result in a change in the ionic environment of the axon. This is prevented by active regulation by the glial cells (Bennett *et al.*, 1975).

Calcium is essential for efficient nerve conduction, being bound to molecules on the nerve membrane. When the calcium is displaced, as it is temporarily on stimulation, the permeability of the membrane increases. The calcium in the membrane is in equilibrium with that in the surrounding medium and lowering the level of external calcium results in progressive depolarisation of the membrane and complete nerve block. Thus calcium is an essential constituent of the extra-axonal fluid.

In *Carausius* magnesium is also an essential constituent of this fluid possibly being able to replace sodium to some extent in the development of an action potential. In other species high concentrations of magnesium block conduction.

26.2.3 Transmission at the synapse

When an impulse has passed along an axon it must cross a synapse in order to effect a response in another neurone or an effector. This effect may be excitatory or inhibitory. Transmission across the synapse involves a chemical which is stored in the presynaptic fibre in the synaptic vesicles. On the arrival of an impulse the membranes bounding the vesicles fuse with the cell membrane so that the transmitter substance is released into the synaptic gap. This process resembles the release of neurosecretory material from neurosecretory axons (p. 825). The transmitter substance becomes attached at receptor sites on the postsynaptic membrane and, through a change in permeability, causes it to become depolarised if the synapse is excitatory or hyperpolarised if it is inhibitory. The magnitude of the depolarisation or hyperpolarisation is presumed to be proportional to the number of vesicles released. Some vesicles are released in small numbers even in the absence of a nerve impulse. They produce very small changes in potential of the postsynaptic dendrite, but these miniature potentials, which in insect muscle average only 0·25 mV (Usherwood, 1963), are too small to evoke a response in the postsynaptic nerve fibre or effector. The arrival of a nerve impulse causes a large number of vesicles to be released simultaneously, so that a big change occurs in the postsynaptic membrane and a response is initiated. The change in the postsynaptic fibre is only short-lived because the chemical transmitter is rapidly hydrolysed by an appropriate enzyme.

At excitatory synapses within the central nervous system the chemical transmitter is acetylcholine, but at nerve/muscle junctions this is replaced, probably by L-glutamate (p. 252). Acetylcholine is destroyed postsynaptically by the enzyme acetylcholine esterase; it is synthesised in the presynaptic fibre in a two-stage reaction, the second involving the acetylation of choline from acetyl coenzyme A in the presence of choline acetylase.

At inhibitory synapses γ-aminobutyric acid is probably the transmitter which leads to hyperpolarisation of the postsynaptic fibre (Callec, 1974). Other transmitter substances may also occur in specific neurones. For example, monoamines are present in parts of the brain (Howse, 1975), and some fibres in the thoracic ganglia of *Schistocerca* produce octopamine. It is suggested that the general effect of octopamine is to modulate the effects of other neural inputs at nerve/muscle junctions (Evans and O'Shea, 1978).

The time taken for a transmitter substance to pass across a synapse and initiate an impulse in the postsynaptic fibre is long relative to the rate of conduction in the larger nerve axons. The delay in transmission at a synapse may be one or two milliseconds.

The postsynaptic receptor sites of insects appear to be less sensitive than those of other animals, requiring much higher concentrations of transmitter substances to effect transmission. This may reflect the high amino acid content of the extracellular fluid. Amino acids exert both inhibitory and excitatory effects on synapses and it is essential that transmission should only be effected by postsynaptic changes greater than those produced by the amino acids normally present (Treherne, 1966).

Electrotonic coupling

There is some evidence that direct electrical interactions may occur between neurones without involving chemical transmission at a synapse. Such electrotonic coupling may occur between the Kenyon cells of the corpora pedunculata and between some motorneurones which act synergistically on the same muscles. The effect of such coupling is to produce precisely synchronised electrical effects in the two neurones (Huber, 1974).

26.2.4 Spontaneous discharge

The production of an impulse in a nerve fibre normally results from stimulation of receptors, but many axons also discharge spontaneously in the absence of any such input. This discharge may be increased or decreased by neural input, or it may remain unaffected, continuing in intermittent bursts over long periods. In some cases this spontaneous discharge may be concerned with the maintenance of muscle tonus, but in general its effect is probably to maintain the system in a highly active state so that it reacts readily to input and is more easily excited. Stimuli which would be subthreshold in an unexcited fibre may produce a response in a fibre already discharging spontaneously (Roeder, 1963).

The rate of spontaneous discharge varies with temperature. For instance the output from an isolated ganglion of the cockroach increases with temperature up to a maximum and then falls off. The temperature at which the maximum occurs depends on the temperature to which the insects have been exposed previously, and the ganglia of insects kept at 22°C have a maximum output at 22°C, while in insects kept at 31°C the maximum is at 31°C. Sudden changes in temperature produce different effects in different fibres (p. 757).

26.3 Integration in the nervous system

The nervous system does not in general act as a simple relay between receptors and effectors (but see p. 233), it integrates the activities of different parts of the body so that appropriate behavioural responses and internal regulating changes are made. Thus, although the segmental ganglia are largely autonomous in their regulation of such activities as walking (p. 176) and respiration (p. 548), their output is modified by the input which they receive from other parts of the body and in this way the activities of the body as a whole are coordinated (Huber, 1974; Miller, 1974).

26.3.1 Integration at the synapse

Some measure of integration is achieved by individual interneurones as a result of the diversity of inputs which they receive from elsewhere, and the diversity of effector units which they supply. For instance, Fig. 407 shows some of the known inputs to one of the giant fibres in the terminal abdominal ganglion of the cockroach. These include the input from mechanoreceptors some of which exhibit a purely phasic input while others are tonic or phasic/tonic. There are also inhibitory fibres from the cercus which act via inhibitory interneurones, and there is input from both ipsilateral and contralateral cerci. Any one or all of these input routes may be in action at the same time and it is assumed that all this information is integrated and leads to the production of spikes at the narrow point on the axon. The number or frequency of spikes will vary with the overall input.

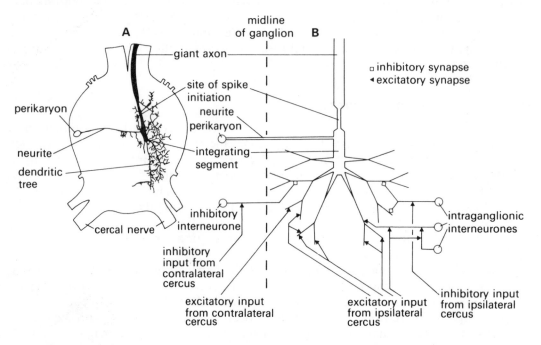

Fig. 407 A. Terminal abdominal ganglion of *Periplaneta* showing the origin of one of the giant fibres. B. Diagram showing the diverse sensory input to a giant fibre from both ipsilateral and contralateral sensilla and interneurones (after Callec, 1974)

Fig. 401 shows in comparison the motor connections of the DCMD interneurone in the metathoracic ganglion of *Schistocerca*. These include excitatory synapses with the motorneurones of the extensor tibialis muscles and inhibitory units of the flexor neurone. Contact is made with both ipsilateral and contralateral neurones, so that the activity of all these muscles is to a large extent coordinated by the activity of a single interneurone.

Further modulation is achieved at the effector muscles by the integration of activity of the various motorneurones. For instance the rapid relaxation of leg muscles during walking and jumping may be achieved by the action of an inhibitory neurone which supplements the effect resulting from the inactivity of excitatory fibres. Stronger contractions are produced by double firing in the motorneurones and additional muscle units may be recruited to produce more rapid or powerful movements (p. 686).

The physiological state of a synapse may also influence integration. For instance, the postsynaptic potential produced by the arrival of a single impulse at a synapse may not be big enough to initiate a postsynaptic impulse and will slowly decay. If, however, a second impulse arrives at the synapse and causes a further depolarisation of the postsynaptic fibre before the first potential has completely decayed the total potential resulting from the two successive depolarisations may exceed the threshold and initiate a postsynaptic impulse (Fig. 408). This phenomenon is known as temporal summation.

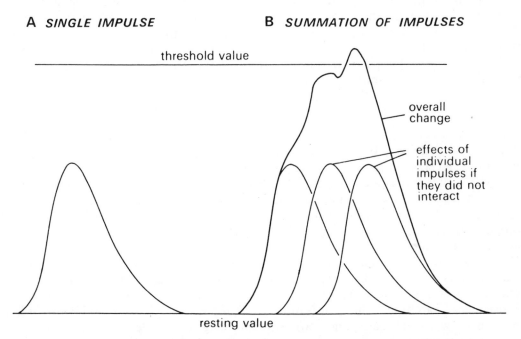

A *SINGLE IMPULSE*   **B** *SUMMATION OF IMPULSES*

threshold value

overall change

effects of individual impulses if they did not interact

resting value

Fig. 408 Diagram illustrating the changes in potential of a postsynaptic membrane. A. A single impulse in the presynaptic fibre produces a rise in the postsynaptic potential, but this does not reach the threshold value and so no action potential is produced. B. The increases in potential produced by three impulses arriving in rapid succession are summed so that a large overall increase is produced, exceeding the threshold and leading to the development of an action potential

Conversely depression of the activity of a synapse can occur as a consequence of previous activity. It appears that depression results from a decrease in the quantity of transmitter substance available in the presynaptic nerve ending (Callec, 1974).

26.3.2 Integration in the ganglion

The programmes of activity of motorneurones which result in particular behaviour patterns are commonly built-in to the appropriate ganglia. As a consequence, patterns of motor output may be recorded even from experimentally isolated ganglia. Such built-in programmes are known to occur in the control of walking (p. 176), flight of locusts (p. 232) and ventilation (p. 547). In such cases an interneurone with an oscillating output is connected via other interneurones to the motorneurones controlling the appropriate muscles. In all these cases, however, the central pattern is subject to modulation by the input from peripheral sensilla (see *e.g.* Huber, 1974; Miller, 1974).

26.3.3 Role of the brain

The role of the brain is not well understood. An important function is certainly the integration of the input from various sensory systems, the antennae and eyes, chemoreceptors on the mouthparts, proprioceptors in the wall of the gut and so on, so that appropriate behaviour patterns are expressed. The appropriate motor systems are then activated via interneurones from the brain to the segmental ganglia. The corpora pedunculata may be particularly important in switching on appropriate motor programmes and determining the sequence in which they occur.

Arousal

The central body may be concerned with regulating arousal (Howse, 1975). Insects vary in the level of expression of behaviour even under apparently constant conditions and with constant peripheral stimulation. Such differences in overt behaviour are said to reflect differences in the state of arousal of the insect (see *e.g.* Miller, 1974). For example, soon after feeding locusts are quiescent and are not responsive to plant odours, but as the period without food is extended they respond to odours more readily and move about even in the absence of new stimuli. Such insects vibrate their palps so that the terminal chemoreceptors come into contact with the substrate and this behaviour is such that they appear to be searching for food. If the insect briefly encounters a small quantity of food, insufficient for it to feed to repletion, its subsequent 'searching' behaviour is much more intense for a brief period before it falls back to a lower level again (Fig. 409). Similar changes in the level of arousal occur in other insects and in relation to other behaviour patterns.

The level of arousal must ultimately depend on some central nervous phenomenon which, perhaps, facilitates the activity of command interneurones from the brain. There is evidence, however, that the overall level of arousal is sometimes regulated by a hormone from the storage lobes of the corpora cardiaca. In *Phormia* (Green, 1964) and *Locusta* release of the hormone is induced when the foregut is distended with food. This hormone may act directly on the central nervous system. In *Locusta* it also reduces the potential input from peripheral chemoreceptors by reducing the extent to which the dendrites are exposed to the environment (Bernays and Chapman, 1972). However, the state of arousal is also related to the level of sensory input: an increase in sensory stimulation can raise the level of arousal. This is illustrated at the neuronal level by the DCMD, which habituates to repeated stimulation of the eye, but shows a short-lived increase in responsiveness to the same stimulus if the insect is subjected to any one of a variety of other stimuli (Rowell, 1974).

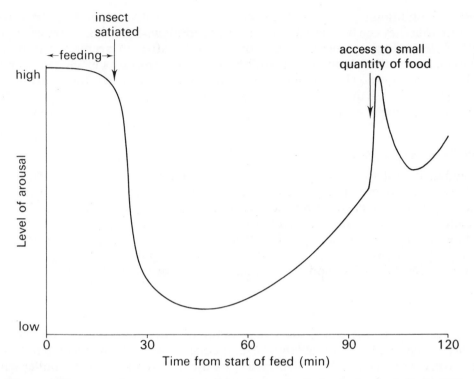

Fig. 409 Diagrammatic representation of the changes in the level of arousal of a locust in relation to feeding

26.4 Learning

Learning by insects is most apparent in social insects, but may also be well-developed in long-lived non-social species. The adults of *Heliconius* (Lepidoptera), for example, live for about six months. They feed on pollen from flowers of particular vines and they learn the positions of the flowers which are visited daily. Even short-lived insects may learn and a few examples are given in the different categories of learning.

Habituation

Habituation is the term employed for a progressive decrease in the magnitude or frequency of occurrence of a response as a result of its frequent elicitation by a particular stimulus. *Nemeritis* (Hymenoptera), for instance, moves away from the smell of cedarwood oil, but if it is continually exposed to the smell it learns to tolerate it. If a cockroach is continually disturbed it ultimately learns to tolerate the disturbance without trying to escape from it, and a mantis which displays at potential predators ceases to display if the predator reappears repeatedly (Barrós-Pita, 1974).

Conditioning

An animal may learn to respond to a stimulus which was previously ineffective if the stimulus occurs repeatedly in the presence of an effective stimulus. The process is known as conditioning. For instance, bees do not usually respond to the smell of coumarin, but they can be trained to associate the odour with feeding by exposure to the smell while feeding on sugar water. Subsequently, after an average of only seven training periods, the odour alone is sufficient to elicit proboscis extension. Similarly newly emerged *Plusia* (Lepidoptera) locate the flowers on which they feed by scent only, but after a few experiences of feeding they learn to associate the appearance of the flower with feeding and subsequently employ both vision and olfaction in food finding.

Trial-and-error learning

An animal is said to learn by trial-and-error when a particular stimulus becomes associated with a motor action as a result of reinforcement in some subsequent behaviour. For instance, *Leptinotarsa* (Coleoptera) is at first not at all discriminating in selecting a mate. It does not differentiate members of other genera from its own species or differentiate head from tail. It recognises only the long axis of the body. Subsequently, however, as a result of various attempted copulations it learns to distinguish head from tail and also to pick out its own species.

Latent learning

Latent learning is the association of stimuli or situations having no particular significance and without any obvious or immediate reward. In insects latent learning often involves the recognition of landmarks by the insect in becoming familiar with its territory. *Philanthus* (Hymenoptera), for instance, learns the position of its nest by the landmarks surrounding it. These are learned on an orientation flight lasting about six seconds which the insect makes on leaving the nest. On returning, after an interval of perhaps 90 minutes, the insect recognises the landmarks and finds its way to the nest. If the landmarks are displaced it continues to orientate to them and is unable to find the nest. Recognition depends on the configuration of the landmarks rather than on their precise nature and number.

    Apis (Hymenoptera) also learns to recognise the features of its home locality. In addition, the forager learns the position of the sun through the perception of polarised light (p. 663) and orientates the straight run of its dance appropriately on returning to the hive. Other workers in the hive learn the orientation of the dance and when they go out to forage base their subsequent orientation to polarised light on this knowledge (von Frisch, 1950).

Time sense

The ability to learn time has been most fully investigated in *Apis*. Individual bees can learn to come to food at particular times of day and to go to different localities at different times. They can also remember the times at which the food had particular qualities or was associated with a particular odour or visual stimulus. Thus a bee which learns that food is associated with geraniol at a particular time of day will visit geraniol sources at the same time on the next day, but will tend to ignore the odour at other times. A bee can remember and separate up to nine separate timed events in the course of a 9-hour day (Koltermann, 1974). The significance of this to the insect in natural conditions is that it is enabled to exploit nectar and pollen sources, which tend to occur at particular times of day, with the greatest efficiency. This is probably also true of *Heliconius*, which is known to visit particular flowers at particular times of day (Gilbert, 1975).

26.4.1 Neural basis of learning

Very little is known about the neural processes involved in the different types of learning. Most work has been concerned with habituation and learning by isolated ganglia.

The DCMD interneurone of the locust habituates if the insect is repeatedly presented with the same visual stimulus (a black disc moved backwards and forwards at the side of the head). The effect is to produce a progressive reduction in the number of action potentials elicited in the DCMD (Fig. 410). However, stimulating another part of the eye or changing the state of arousal of the insect by other stimuli results in a complete recovery to the original rate of firing. This indicates that the effect was not in the DCMD itself, but at an earlier stage in the neural pathway between the eye and this interneurone. The most probable mechanism to account for the process is depletion of synaptic transmitter of one of the neurones leading to the DCMD. Essentially similar neuronal changes associated with habituation have been recorded in the cockroach (Huber, 1974; Miller, 1974; Rowell, 1974).

Some degree of learning can occur in isolated segmental ganglia (Eisenstein, 1972). Thus headless *Periplaneta* can learn to keep a leg flexed so as to avoid electrical shocks.

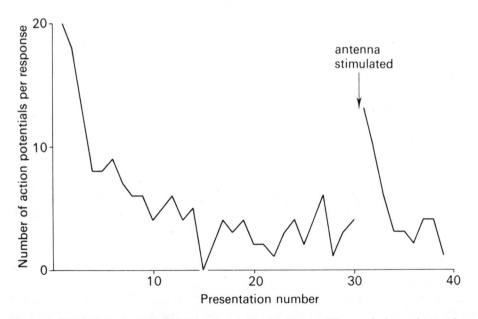

Fig. 410 Habituation in the DCMD interneurone of the locust. The graph shows the number of action potentials produced in the interneurone by repeated visual stimulation by a moving black disc. Successive presentations were made at 8 s intervals. Short-lived dishabituation occurred after the antennae were stimulated electrically (after Rowell, 1974)

The raising is produced by the contraction of a number of muscles, but the coxal levators are of particular importance. Pinching the foot or an electric shock applied after a drop in the frequency of discharge to the muscle produce a maintained increase in the frequency of impulses in the motor nerve so that the muscle contracts and the leg is raised. By gradually increasing the level of discharge at which a shock is given a 300 % increase in the motor frequency can be induced (Fig. 411). It is suggested as a generalisation that a burst of impulses in a sensory nerve following a change in rate of firing in a motorneurone induces a prolonged alteration in the output of the motorneurone in a direction counter to the original change so that further stimulation is avoided (Hoyle, 1965b).

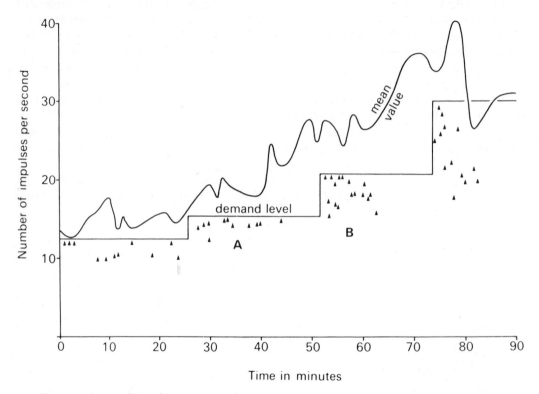

Fig. 411 A recording of the number of impulses per second arriving at the coxal adductor muscle of *Schistocerca*. Whenever the frequency fell below the arbitrarily fixed demand level the muscle was given an electric shock as indicated by the triangles. After a group of shocks, as at A and B, the frequency of impulses rose and remained high (modified after Hoyle, 1965b)

In terms of the leg movement this means that a reduction in the nervous discharge to the adductor muscle leads to a reduction in muscle tension so that the leg drops. As a result it touches the surface of a liquid and receives a shock. The increased input due to the shock leads to an increased discharge in the motor nerve and so muscle tension increases and the leg is raised. Maintenance of the high rate of discharge in the motor nerve keeps the leg raised so that further shocks are avoided. Input from the proprioceptors of the leg is apparently of no signficance in the response.

It is clear from this that the frequency of impulses to the coxal adductor muscles is determined in the metathoracic ganglion and that lasting changes of adaptive significance can occur in response to external events. The changes are readily reversed if the relationship to the environment changes.

Chen *et al* (1970) showed that while isolated ganglia did learn, they retained the information for only a short period. The brain and suboesophageal ganglion were necessary to develop long-term memory, but having once acquired the information the head was no longer essential, the segmental ganglia retaining the appropriate information derived from that processed in the head.

Within the brain the development of the corpora pedunculata is greatest in the social insects (Fig. 395), which show the most complex behaviour patterns of any insects. It is probable that they are associated with learning processes and Menzel *et al.* (1974) showed that bees were unable to associate odours with feeding if the α-lobes of the corpora pedunculata were inactivated for a short time after the training stimulus.

REFERENCES

ALBRECHT, F. O. (1953). *The anatomy of the migratory locust.* Athlone Press, London.

ALLOWAY, T. M. (1972). Learning and memory in insects. *A. Rev. Ent.* **17**: 43–56.

ALTMAN, J. (1981). Functional organisation of insect ganglia. *Adv. Physiol. Sci.* **23**: 537–555.

BARRÓS-PITA, J. C. (1974). Massed training and latent habituation of the deimatic response in the mantid, *Stagmatoptera biocellata. in* Browne, L. B., (ed.), *Experimental analysis of insect behaviour.* Springer-Verlag, Berlin.

BENNETT, R. R., BUCHAN, P. B. and TREHERNE, J. E. (1975). Sodium and lithium movements and axonal function in cockroach nerve cords. *J. exp. Biol.* **62**: 231–241.

BERNAYS, E. A. and CHAPMAN, R. F. (1972). The control of changes in the peripheral sensilla associated with feeding in *Locusta migratoria* (L.). *J. exp. Biol.* **57**: 755–763.

BURROWS, M. (1975). Integration by motoneurones in the central nervous system of insects. *in* Usherwood, P. N. R. and Newth, D. R. (eds.), *'Simple' nervous systems.* Edward Arnold, London.

BURROWS, M. (1977). Flight mechanisms of the locust. *in* Hoyle, G. (ed.), *Identified neurons and behaviour of arthropods.* Plenum Press, New York.

BURROWS, M. and SIEGLER, M. V. S. (1978). Graded synaptic transmission between local interneurones and motor neurones in the metathoracic ganglion of the locust. *J. Physiol.* **285**: 231–255.

CALLEC, J.-J. (1974). Synaptic transmission in the central nervous system of insects. *in* Treherne, J. E. (ed.), *Insect neurobiology.* North-Holland Publishing Co., Amsterdam.

CAMPBELL, J. I. (1961). The anatomy of the nervous system of the mesothorax of *Locusta migratoria migratorioides* R. & F. *Proc. zool. Soc. Lond.* **137**: 403–432.

CHEN, W. Y., ARANDA, L. C. and LUCO, J. V. (1970). Learning and long- and short-term memory in cockroaches. *Anim. Behav.* **18**: 725–732.

DAVIS, H. (1961). Some principles of sensory receptor action. *Physiol. Rev.* **41**: 391–416.

EISENSTEIN, E. M. (1972). Learning and memory in isolated insect ganglia. *Adv. Insect Physiol.* **9**: 111–181.

EVANS, P. D. and O'SHEA, M. (1978). The identification of an octopaminergic neurone and the modulation of a myogenic rhythm in the locust. *J. exp. Biol.* **73**: 235–260.

FRISCH, K. von (1950). *Bees. Their vision, chemical senses and language.* Cornell University Press, New York.

GILBERT, L. E. (1975). Ecological consequences of a coevolved mutualism between butterflies and plants. in Gilbert, L. E. and Raven, P. H. (eds.), *Coevolution of animals and plants*. University of Texas Press, Austin.

GREEN, G. W. (1964). The control of spontaneous locomotor activity in *Phormia regina* Meigen—II. Experiments to determine the mechanism involved. *J. Insect Physiol.* **10**: 727–752.

HODGKIN, A. L. (1958). Ionic movements and electrical activity in giant nerve fibres. *Proc. R. Soc. B*, **148**: 1–37.

HORRIDGE, G. A. (1965). The Arthropoda. in Bullock, T. H. and Horridge, G. A. *Structure and function in the nervous systems of invertebrates*. Freeman, San Francisco.

HOWSE, P. E. (1974). Design and function in the insect brain. in Browne, L. B. (ed.), *Experimental analysis of insect behaviour*. Springer-Verlag, Berlin.

HOWSE, P. E. (1975). Brain structure and behaviour in insects. *A. Rev. Ent.* **20**: 359–379.

HOYLE, G. (1965a). Neural control of skeletal muscle. in Rockstein, M. (ed.), *The physiology of Insecta*. vol. 2. Academic Press, New York.

HOYLE, G. (1965b). Neurophysiological studies on "learning" in headless insects. in Treherne, J. E. and Beament, J. W. L. (eds.), *The physiology of the insect central nervous system*. Academic Press, London.

HOYLE, G. (1970). Cellular mechanisms underlying behaviour—neuroethology. *Adv. Insect Physiol.* **7**: 349–444.

HUBER, F. (1974). Neural integration (central nervous system). in Rockstein, M. (ed.), *The physiology of Insecta*. vol. 4. Academic Press, New York.

KEELE, C. A. and NEIL, E. (1961). *Samson Wright's applied physiology*. Oxford University Press, London.

KOLTERMANN, R. (1974). Periodicity in the activity and learning performance of the honeybee. in Browne, L. B. (ed.), *Experimental analysis of insect behaviour*. Springer-Verlag, Berlin.

LANDOLT, A. M. and RIS, H. (1966). Electron microscope studies on soma-somatic interneuronal junctions in the corpus pedunculatum of the wood ant (*Formica lugubris* Zett.). *J. Cell Biol.* **28**: 391–403.

LANE, N. J. (1974). The organization of insect nervous systems. in Treherne, J. E. (ed.), *Insect neurobiology*. North-Holland Publishing Co., Amsterdam.

MADDRELL, S. H. P. and TREHERNE, J. E. (1967). The ultrastructure of the perineurium in two insect species, *Carausius morusus* and *Periplaneta americana*. *J. Cell Sci.* **2**: 119–128.

MENZEL, R., ERBER, J. and MASUHR, T. (1974). Learning and memory in the honeybee. in Browne, L. B. (ed.), *Experimental analysis of insect behaviour*. Springer-Verlag, Berlin.

MILBURN, N. S. and BENTLEY, D. R. (1971). On the dendritic topology and activation of cockroach giant interneurons. *J. Insect Physiol.* **17**: 607–623.

MILLER, P. L. (1974). The neural basis of behaviour. in Treherne, J. E. (ed.), *Insect neurobiology*. North-Holland Publishing Co., Amsterdam.

NARAHASHI, T. (1965). The physiology of insect axons. in Treherne, J. E. and Beament, J. W. L. (eds.), *The physiology of the insect central nervous system*. Academic Press, London.

O'SHEA, M., ROWELL, C. H. F. and WILLIAMS, J. L. D. (1974). The anatomy of a locust visual interneurone; the descending contralateral movement detector. *J. exp. Biol.* **60**: 1–12.

PARNAS, I. and DAGAN, D. (1971). Functional organizations of giant axons in the central nervous systems of insects: new aspects. *Adv. Insect Physiol.* **8**: 95–144.

PEARSON, K. G. (1977). Interneurons in the ventral nerve cord of insects. in Hoyle, G. (ed.), *Identified neurons and behaviour of arthropods*. Plenum Press, New York.

PICHON, Y. (1974). Axonal conduction in insects. in Treherne, J. E. (ed.), *Insect neurobiology*. North-Holland Publishing Co., Amsterdam.

ROEDER, K. D. (1953). Electric activity in nerves and ganglia. in Roeder, K. D. (ed.), *Insect physiology*. Wiley and Sons, New York.

ROEDER, K. D. (1963). *Nerve cells and insect behaviour*. Harvard University Press, Cambridge, Mass.

ROWELL, C. H. F. (1974). Boredom and attention in a cell in the locust visual system. *in* Browne, L. B. (ed.), *Experimental analysis of insect behaviour*. Springer-Verlag, Berlin.

SCHMITT, J. B. (1962). The comparative anatomy of the insect nervous system. *A. Rev. Ent.* 7: 137–156.

SCHOFIELD, P. K. and TREHERNE, J. E. (1978). Kinetics of sodium and lithium movements across the blood–brain barrier of an insect. *J. exp. Biol.* 74: 239–251.

SMITH, D. S. (1965). Synapses in the insect nervous system. *in* Treherne, J. E. and Beament, J. W. L. (eds.), *The physiology of the insect central nervous system*. Academic Press, London.

SMITH, D. S. and TREHERNE, J. E. (1963). Functional aspects of the organisation of the insect nervous system. *Adv. Insect Physiol.* 1: 401–484.

SPIRA, M. E., PARNAS, I. and BERGMANN, F. (1969). Histological and electrophysiological studies on the giant axons of the cockroach, *Periplaneta americana*. *J. exp. Biol.* 50: 629–634.

STRONG, L. (1966). On the occurrence of neuroglandular axons within the sympathetic nervous system of a locust, *Locusta migratoria migratorioides*. *J. R. microsc. Soc.* 86: 141–149.

TREHERNE, J. E. (1965). The chemical environment of the insect central nervous system. *in* Treherne, J. E. and Beament, J. W. L. (eds.), *The physiology of the insect central nervous system*. Academic Press, London.

TREHERNE, J. E. (1966). *The neurochemistry of arthropods*. Cambridge University Press.

TREHERNE, J. E. (1974). The environment and function of insect nerve cells. *in* Treherne, J. E. (ed.), *Insect neurobiology*. North-Holland Publishing Co., Amsterdam.

TREHERNE, J. E. and PICHON, Y. (1972). The insect blood–brain barrier. *Adv. Insect Physiol.* 9: 257–313.

USHERWOOD, P. N. R. (1963). Spontaneous miniature potentials from insect muscle fibres. *J. Physiol. Lond.* 169: 149–160.

CHAPTER XXVII

THE EYES AND VISION

Light is perceived by insects through a number of different sense organs, but the most important are the compound eyes. These consist of groups of units each of which is made up of a lens system and a small number of sense cells. The lens system focuses light on to a photosensitive element and the output from the sense cells travels back to the optic lobe of the brain. Here there are complex interconnections with other nerve cells having a wide variety of characteristics and the integrated signals are then fed back to the brain and ventral nerve cord.

The insect eye is well adapted to perceive movement, but complex form perception is also possible. The eye is not equally sensitive to all wavelengths, and further, its sensitivity varies under different conditions. Some species can discriminate between different colours, and some can perceive the plane of vibration of polarised light and may use this in navigation.

In addition to the compound eyes adults and larval hemimetabolous insects typically have three simple eyes, called ocelli, while larval holometabolous insects have no compound eyes, but have simple stemmata on the sides of the head. The function of the ocelli is obscure; possibly they have a general stimulatory effect on the nervous system. Stemmata permit a limited amount of form perception.

General reviews of the structure and physiology of insect eyes are given by Carlson and Chi (1979), Goldsmith and Bernard (1974), Horridge (1965, 1975a) and Wehner (1972). Goodman (1970, 1975) reviews knowledge of the ocelli.

27.1 Occurrence and structure of compound eyes

Most adult insects have a pair of compound eyes, one on either side of the head, which bulge out to a greater or lesser extent (Fig. 2) so that they give a wide field of vision in all directions. In some insects, such as Anisoptera and male Tabanidae and Syrphidae, the eyes extend dorsally and are contiguous along the midline, this being known as the holoptic condition.

The compound eyes are strongly reduced or absent in parasitic groups, such as the Siphunculata and Siphonaptera, and in female coccids and this is also true of cave-dwelling forms. Amongst Apterygota fully-developed compound eyes are present only in Machilidae. The Lepismatidae have 12 ommatidia on each side and Collembola have up to eight widely spaced ommatidia. Compound eyes are not present in Protura or Diplura.

Each compound eye is an aggregation of similar units known as ommatidia, the number of which varies from one in the worker of the ant *Ponera punctatissima* to over

10 000 in the eyes of dragonflies. When only a few ommatidia are present, the facets which they present to the outside are separated from each other by narrow areas of cuticle and are round; more usually, with larger numbers, the facets are packed close together and assume a hexagonal form (Fig. 412).

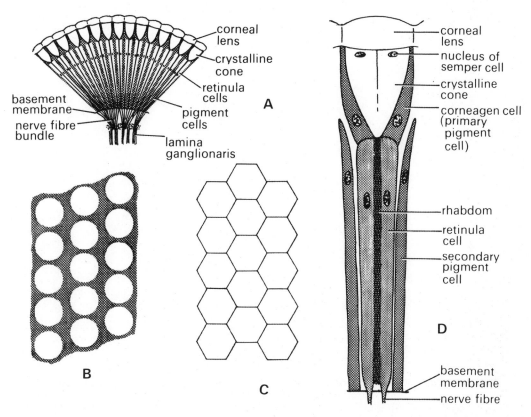

Fig. 412 Diagrams illustrating the structure of the compound eye. A. Section through part of an eye showing the arrangement of ommatidia. B. Surface view of part of the eye of an aphid, which consists of a small number of ommatidia, showing the facets well separated by unmodified cuticle. C. Surface view of part of the eye of a syrphid, which consists of a large number of ommatidia with the facets crowded together. D. Detail of a single ommatidium

Ommatidia vary in size from insect to insect and within the Hymenoptera facet size is proportional to the square root of the height of the eye (Fig. 413). Variations also occur within one eye. In *Apis* the facets in the centre of the eye are about 22 μm in diameter whereas those at the top of the eye are about 17 μm in diameter (Barlow, 1952), and in dragonflies the dorsal facets may have twice the diameter of the ventral ones. In some other species the eye is sharply differentiated into a region with relatively large facets and another with much smaller facets, as in the male of *Bibio*. This separation is complete in the male of *Cloeon* (Ephemeroptera), where each eye is in two parts quite separate from each other. Not only are the ommatidia in these two parts different in size, they are also different in structure. Those of the dorsal part are relatively large and of the clear-zone type (p. 646), while in the lateral part the ommatidia are smaller and of the apposition type (p. 646). The eyes are also divided into two in the aquatic beetle *Gyrinus* (Coleoptera), where the dorsal eye is above the surface film when the insect is swimming and the ventral eye is below the surface.

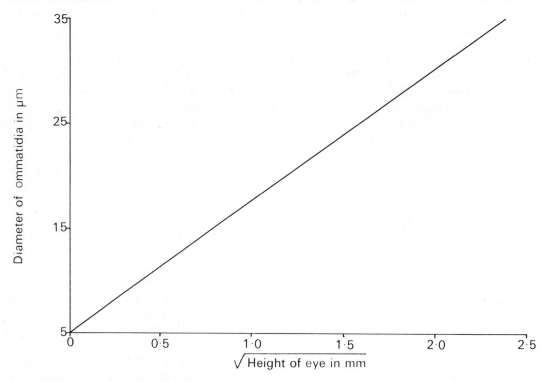

Fig. 413 The relationship between ommatidial diameter and the size of the eye in Hymenoptera (after Barlow, 1952)

27.1.1 Structure of an ommatidium

Each ommatidium consists essentially of an optical, light-gathering part and a sensory part, perceiving the radiation and transforming it into electrical energy.

The optical part of the system usually consists of two elements, a cuticular lens and a crystalline cone. The cuticle covering the eye is transparent and colourless and usually forms a biconvex corneal lens at the outer end of each ommatidium (Fig. 412D). It is these lenses which in surface view form the facets of the compound eye. In *Aleyrodes* all the lenses are not colourless, but each colourless one is surrounded by six yellow lenses. Some insects have the outer surface of the corneal lens produced into minute conical nipples about 0.2 μm high arranged in a hexagonal pattern with a 0.2 μm spacing. It is supposed that these projections decrease reflection from the surface of the lens and so increase the proportion of light transmitted through the facet. The cornea, like the rest of the cuticle, is secreted by epidermal cells, each lens being produced by two cells, the corneagen cells, which later become withdrawn to the sides of the ommatidium and form the primary pigment cells.

Beneath the cornea are four cells, the Semper cells, which, in most insects, produce the crystalline cone. This is a hard, clear intracellular structure bordered laterally by the primary pigment cells. Eyes in which the crystalline cone is present are called eucone eyes (but see below).

Immediately behind the crystalline cone in eucone eyes are the sensory elements. These are elongate nerve cells known as retinula cells, in each of which the margin nearest the ommatidial axis is differentiated to form a rhabdomere which extends the whole length of the cell. Primitively each ommatidium probably contained eight retinula cells arising from three successive divisions of a single cell. This number is found in some insects, such as *Periplaneta*. The cytoplasm of the retinula cells contains pigment granules, which are especially concentrated at the edge of the rhabdomere, but these granules do not contain the visual pigment. Arising from each cell is a nerve axon which passes out through the basement membrane at the back of the eye into the optic lobe.

The rhabdomere consists of close-packed microvilli about 50 nm across. They are round to hexagonal in cross-section and extend towards the central axis of the ommatidium at right angles to the long axis of the retinula cell. The microvilli of each retinula cell are all parallel with each other and roughly aligned with those of the retinula cell opposite, but they are set at an angle to those of adjacent retinula cells (Fig. 414). In *Drosophila* each rhabdomere is 60 μm long and 1.2 μm in diameter (Wolken *et al.*, 1957), while in *Sarcophaga* their diameter is only about 0.5 μm (Goldsmith and Philpott, 1957).

Collectively the rhabdomeres of each ommatidium form the rhabdom. In Diptera the individual rhabdomeres remain separate, grouped round a central matrix, which may have a fluid consistency (Fig. 414A). Other insects have the rhabdomeres so closely apposed that they are said to form a fused rhabdom, though the cells remain distinct (Fig. 414B). Clear-zone eyes always have a fused rhabdom.

The retinula cells are shrouded by 12 to 18 secondary pigment cells, which isolate each ommatidium from its neighbours (Fig. 412). Tracheae pass between the ommatidia proximally in some species.

27.1.2 Modifications of the ommatidial structure

The same basic elements are present in the compound eyes of all insects, but the precise arrangement shows considerable variation between species and also in respect of the degree of light- or dark-adaptation of the insect. The following descriptions relate to light-adapted eyes.

Variation in the lens system

The form of the corneal lens varies from convex–concave to biconvex with a long cone-shaped projection on the inside (Fig. 418B). With the latter development, which occurs in Elateridae and Lampyridae, the Semper cells do not form a crystalline cone, but extend inwards to the retinula cells as slender refractile strands. This is known as the exocone condition.

There are also various modifications of the crystalline cone which is produced by the Semper cells. In most insects it is intracellular and conical, but in some groups, and

A *DROSOPHILA*   B *APIS*

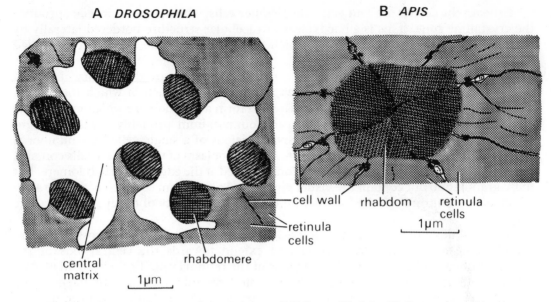

Fig. 414 Cross-section through the rhabdom of (A) *Drosophila* (after Wolken *et al.*, 1957) and
(B) *Apis* (after Goldsmith, 1962)

notably in Collembola and Thysanura, it is more or less spherical. Arthropleona
(Collembola) have an extracellular crystalline cone.

In a few beetles, some Odonata and most Diptera the Semper cells secrete an
extracellular cone which is liquid-filled or gelatinous rather than crystalline. Ommatidia with this type of lens are called pseudocone ommatidia. Finally there are eyes in
which the Semper cells do not produce a separate lens, but have a clear cytoplasm and
occupy the region normally filled by the cone (Fig. 418A). These acone eyes are present
in various families of Coleoptera, for example Coccinellidae, Staphylindae and
Tenebrionidae, in some Diptera and in Heteroptera.

Variation in the retinula cells

The arrangement of the retinula cells falls broadly into two classes: those in which the
rhabdom extends to the crystalline cone, and those in which there is a clear zone
between the cone and the rhabdom. Eyes with the latter arrangement are now
distinguished as clear-zone eyes; they were previously known as superposition eyes, on
the basis of their presumed manner of functioning (Horridge, 1975b). Eyes in which the
rhabdoms reach the crystalline cones are called apposition eyes. They are found in
diurnal insects; clear-zone eyes are, in general, in crepuscular and nocturnal insects.

The manner in which the space between the lens system and the rhabdom is bridged
in clear-zone eyes is very variable. In beetles with exocone eyes the Semper cells form a
thin strand about 5 μm in diameter, called the crystalline tract, across the clear zone to
the rhabdom (Fig. 418B). The retinula cells are restricted to a basal position in the
ommatidium. Some Lepidoptera, Bombycoidea and Hesperioidea, have a similar
crystalline tract, but it is formed by the retinula cells; these insects also have a

crystalline cone. In many other Lepidoptera and Coleoptera the retinula cells extend to the crystalline cone as a broad column, but the rhabdom is restricted to the basal region (Fig. 418C), or, as in Carabidae and Dytiscidae, one of the retinula cells also has a short distal rhabdomere just below the cone.

The arrangement of the rhabdomeres which collectively comprise the rhabdom varies considerably. In *Periplaneta* there are eight retinula cells of more or less equal length, but their contribution to the rhabdom varies at different levels in the ommatidium. In *Apis* eight cells have more or less similar rhabdomeres distally, but proximally two of the cells do not contribute to the rhabdom while a short, ninth cell is added (Fig. 415A). The retinula cells of *Apis* are twisted round each other (p. 663). Many other insects have retinula cells of different lengths so that they have a tiered arrangement, as in *Lepisma* (Fig. 415B), or as in *Spodoptera* (Fig. 415C). Many other arrangements are known (Goldsmith and Bernard, 1974; Paulus, 1975).

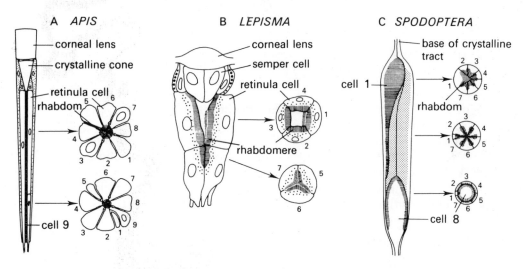

Fig. 415 Different arrangements of the retinula cells and their associated rhabdomeres. A. *Apis*, eucone eye with nine retinula cells, which are twisted round each other. B. *Lepisma*, acone eye with seven retinula cells in two tiers. C. *Spodoptera*, clear-zone eye with eight retinula cells (only basal part of eye shown). Numbering of retinula cells is arbitrary with no special significance (after Gribakin, 1975; Paulus, 1975; Langer et al., 1979)

Tapetum

In Noctuidae and some other moths with clear-zone eyes tracheae run through the eye parallel with the ommatidia and form a layer round each one (Fig. 416). This layer, known as the tapetum, reflects light back into the ommatidium.

27.1.3 Changes associated with dark adaptation

The eyes of insects adapt to darkness in two ways. Anatomical changes can reduce the amount of light which is absorbed before reaching the receptors, and changes can occur in the sensitivity of the receptors due to differences in the amounts of photopigment

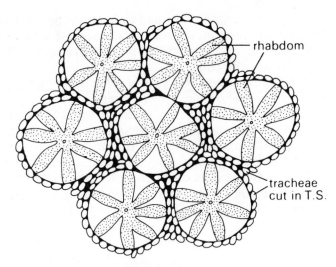

rhabdom

tracheae
cut in T.S.

Fig. 416 Cross-section of a group of ommatidia of a moth showing the interommatidial
spaces packed with tracheae (from Imms, 1957)

present (p. 658). Different anatomical changes occur in different types of eye, often
taking 15–20 minutes to develop completely (Fig. 427).

In light-adapted eucone apposition eyes, granules of a screening pigment are
usually present close to the inner ends of the microvilli of the rhabdomeres (Fig. 417).
In the dark, large vesicles develop in the endoplasmic reticulum so that a clear space is
formed round the rhabdom and the pigment granules in the retinula cells occupy a
more peripheral position. The clear region is known as the palisade. These changes are

LIGHT-ADAPTED   DARK-ADAPTED

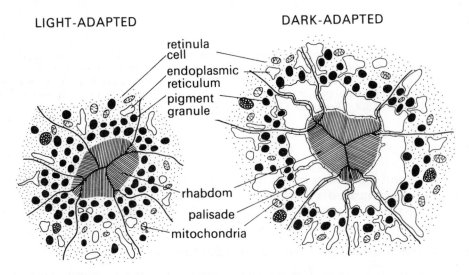

retinula
cell
endoplasmic
reticulum
pigment
granule

rhabdom
palisade
mitochondria

Fig. 417 Diagrams of cross-sections of the rhabdom and parts of the retinula cells from an
ommatidium of *Periplaneta* in the light-adapted and dark-adapted states (after Snyder and
Horridge, 1972)

produced by the light falling on the individual retinula cells and probably involve the visual pigment. As a consequence cells which are sensitive to different wavelengths adapt differentially according to the wavelength of the light falling on the eye (Walcott, 1975).

In the acone eyes of many Diptera and Heteroptera the retinula cells extend in the dark, carrying the distal end of the rhabdom to a more peripheral position and at the same time causing the Semper cells to become shorter and broader (Fig. 418A). This may involve the rhabdom in a movement of 15 μm or even more. At the same time the primary pigment cells are displaced laterally so that the aperture of the optic pathway is increased.

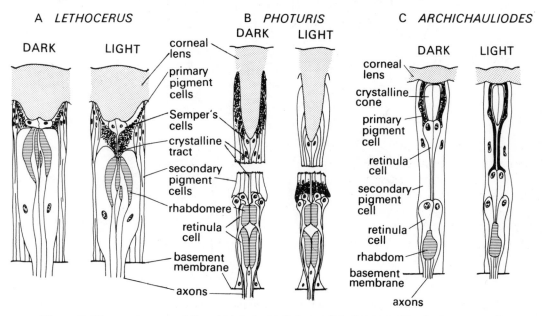

Fig. 418 Changes in ommatidia associated with light- and dark-adaptation. A. Acone eye of *Lethocerus*. B. Exocone eye of *Photuris*. C. Eucone eye of *Archichauliodes* (after Walcott, 1975)

In clear-zone eyes with a crystalline tract connecting the lens system with the rhabdom, the pigment in the pigment cells of the light-adapted eye effectively screens each rhabdom from light from neighbouring ommatidia. In the dark the pigment is concentrated between the lenses so that lateral movement of light within the eye is possible (Fig. 418B).

Finally, in clear-zone eyes where the retinula cells form a broad column to the lens, dark adaptation results in an extension of these cells, compression of the lens and restriction of the pigment to the most peripheral parts of the eye (Fig. 418C).

27.1.4 Nervous connections from the eye

In *Apis* the axons of the retinula cells which are sensitive to blue and green light extend only as far as the lamina ganglionaris (Fig. 419, short fibre), but the fibres from the cells responding to ultraviolet light pass to the medulla externa (Fig. 419, long fibre) (Menzel and Blakers, 1976).

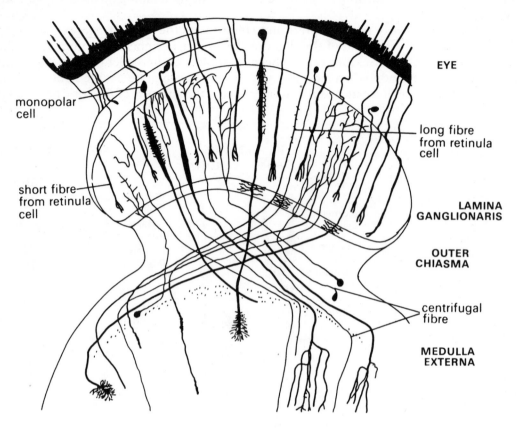

Fig. 419 Section through the back of the eye and part of the optic lobe of *Apis* illustrating some of the nervous pathways (from Goldsmith, 1964)

In the lamina the axons of retinula cells are grouped together with neurones originating in the lamina and in the medulla externa to form cartridges (Fig. 420). In the centre of each cartridge in the fly are two large axons with cell bodies more peripherally in the lamina (Fig. 419, monopolar cell). Grouped around these are the axons of six retinula cells; each of these axons comes from a different ommatidium, but from retinula cells with the same field of view. They make repeated synaptic contact with the large central axons. In addition, the two retinula axons (R7 and R8) from the ultraviolet-sensitive cells pass through the cartridge with only limited synaptic contact in the bee and with none at all in the fly. A number of small monopolar neurones, three in the fly, run outside the other fibres and connect with one or two retinular axons and also may make contact with adjacent cartridges. Finally, fibres which arise in the medulla externa run across the outer chiasma and synapse with the axon terminals of the retinula cells. Because they run outwards from their perikarya these are called centrifugal fibres (Fig. 419), but whether or not they conduct centrifugally is unknown

(Laughlin, 1975). Each group of fibres is enclosed within a glial cell to form the discrete cartridge and the number of cartridges equals the number of ommatidia in the eye.

The group of fibres emerging from a cartridge in the lamina crosses the outer chiasma and enters another synaptic region in the medulla without divergence. Within the medulla they remain associated in columns which include the retinal cell fibres R7 and R8, the fibres of the monopolar cells arising in the lamina, and numerous others with perikarya in the medulla externa or the medulla interna. Every column in the medulla contains a minimum of 46 fibres, and the number of columns is equal to the number of ommatidia and cartridges, although they are not bounded by a glial cell and so are less clearly defined than the cartridges. In addition, some fibres form strata at right angles to the columns and presumably information is passed laterally as well as inwards towards the brain (Campos-Ortega and Strausfeld, 1972).

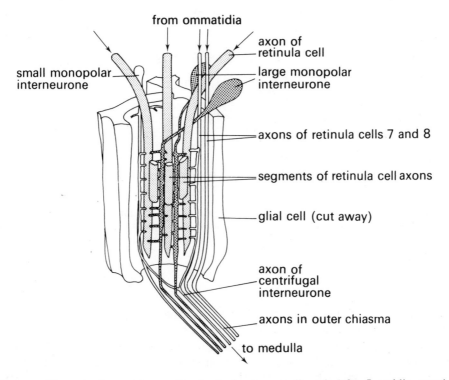

Fig. 420 Diagram of an optic cartridge in the lamina ganglionaris (after Laughlin, 1975)

27.2 Reception of light

If the insect is to do more than differentiate between light and dark, that is, if it has any degree of form vision, it must possess an optical system capable of forming a suitable image and a series of receptors capable of perceiving the image.

27.2.1 Image formation by the optical system

Lens system

Image formation depends on the optical properties of the corneal lens and the crystalline cone. Refraction of light will occur at any interface with a difference in refractive index on the two sides. Consequently light is refracted where it enters the corneal lens, unless it is normal to the surface of the lens, and also where it leaves the apex of the crystalline cone or its equivalent. In some insects refraction also occurs within the dioptric system because there are gradients of refractive index within one or both components. For instance in the thick corneal lens of the water beetle *Cybister* the refractive index increases from the outside towards the centre; there is a similar arrangement in the crystalline cone of *Toxidia* (Lepidoptera) (Fig. 421). Some degree of inhomogeneity within the lens system is probably common in the ommatidia of clear-zone eyes, but in contrast the crystalline cone in apposition eyes is probably always homogeneous (Horridge, 1975b; Meyer-Rochow, 1975).

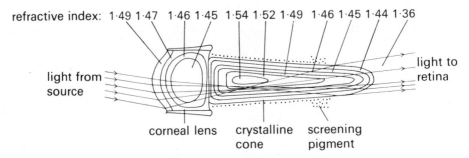

Fig. 421 Diagram of the lenses in an ommatidium of *Toxidia* showing the changes in refractive index in the corneal lens and crystalline cone, and the paths of rays striking the cornea at 10° to the long axis of the ommatidium (after Horridge, 1975b)

Light guides

The crystalline tract of clear-zone eyes acts as a light guide across the space between the apex of the crystalline cone and the rhabdom. This is true in both the light- and the dark-adapted eye, although its function in the two conditions differs. In the light-adapted eye the narrow wave guide is closely surrounded by pigment so that there is no other path by which light can reach the rhabdom. As a result, the effective apperture of the ommatidium is small and a sharp image is formed; any stray light is absorbed. The mechanism ensures that the high light intensity reaching the outside of the eye is attenuated so that the intensity of light reaching the rhabdom is within the range of sensitivity of the retinula cells. The extension of the cone which occurs when some eyes become light-adapted (Fig. 418C) also contributes to this same function.

In the dark-adapted clear-zone eye the crystalline tract is surrounded by material of low refractive index and internal reflection of light within it is enhanced. Consequently, in contrast to the situation in the light-adapted eye, a high proportion of the light entering the wave guide distally is transmitted to the rhabdom. However, in the dark-adapted eye much of the light leaving the lens system does not enter the wave guides at all, but reaches the rhabdoms after traversing the clear zone obliquely (p. 656).

The rhabdomeres themselves act as dielectric wave guides (Snyder, 1975). In apposition eyes changes in the development of the palisade occur with light adaptation (Fig. 417). In the light, pigment close to the rhabdomeres absorbs stray light and increases the refractive index of the surrounding cytoplasm and so reflection at the boundary of the rhabdomere is low; in the dark, the palisade provides a zone of relatively low refractive index round the rhabdom and the internal reflection of light is enhanced. As a consequence the absolute sensitivity and angular sensitivity of the retinula cell are increased when the eye is in the dark-adapted condition (Snyder and Horridge, 1972). In fact, as a result of the cross-sectional area of the rhabdomere being so small, light intensity is not uniformly distributed across it because of interference effects. Instead the light is transmitted in patterns known as dielectric waveguide modes.

27.2.2 Receptor processes in the rhabdom

The rhabdom is the site of photoreception. Within the membrane of the microtubules of the rhabdomeres is the visual pigment. This is a chromoprotein consisting of retinene, the aldehyde of vitamin A, conjugated with a protein and belonging to a group of chromoproteins known as rhodopsins. Insects with colour vision often have three different visual pigments which are sensitive to light of different wavelengths (p. 659), but only one pigment occurs in any one retinula cell. When light of the appropriate wavelength is absorbed by a molecule of visual pigment, the molecular configuration of the pigment is altered with the release of energy which results in the development of a receptor potential. The energy required to start this process by bleaching the pigment is derived from the light; within the spectral range even a single quantum of light has a high enough energy content to initiate bleaching.

In insects, rhodopsin is bleached to an isomer called metarhodopsin, which is itself a photopigment. In *Deilephila* (Lepidoptera) it maximally absorbs light with wavelengths between 450 and 500 nm, in the blue part of the spectrum. The energy derived from this light causes the reconversion of the molecule to the original isomer: thus rhodopsin is reconstituted very rapidly, since blue light is a major component of daylight. Metarhodopsin has the same maximum absorption irrespective of whether it is derived from the ultraviolet-sensitive or the green-sensitive rhodopsin (Hamdorf *et al.*, 1972).

27.2.3 Electrical activity resulting from excitation

Responses of the eye as a whole are measured extracellularly, the recording being known as an electroretinogram. This is the sum of potentials arising in the eye and optic lobe and in these records the cornea is negative with respect to the retinula cells. Typically, when the eye is illuminated, the cornea rapidly assumes an even higher negative potential and this persists, declining slowly, throughout the period of illumination (Fig. 422C). This potential is derived from the retinula cells and probably represents the receptor potential. Superimposed on this may be a slight positive 'on' effect, that is, a short-lived change in potential when the eye is first illuminated, which probably arises in the neurones of the lamina ganglionaris, and a negative 'off' effect, that is, a transient change when illumination stops. The height of the 'on' effect varies with the intensity of stimulation and the level of adaptation of the eye.

On the basis of the electroretinogram eyes may be classified into two types (Autrum, 1958), although not all authors regard the differences as being real (Dethier, 1963). In Orthoptera and Lepidoptera, relatively slow-flying insects, the electroretinogram is a sustained, slowly decaying response to illumination (Fig. 422C). These insects have poor discrimination of flicker (p. 667) with a flicker fusion frequency of about 40–50 per second. An eye with these characteristics is termed a slow eye. On the other hand in Diptera and Hymenoptera, fast-flying insects, there is a sharp positive 'on' effect, sometimes preceded by a slight negative potential, and then the potential returns to about the resting level except for a negative swing when the light is turned off (Fig. 422B). These eyes are less sensitive than slow eyes, but their flicker fusion frequency is about 300 per second. Eyes of this type are called fast eyes. It is suggested that the positive 'on' potential arising in the lamina ganglionaris of fast fliers prevents sustained depolarisation of the retinal cells so that they can respond to a much more rapid sequence of images than would be possible if they underwent a sustained depolarisation as in slow eyes.

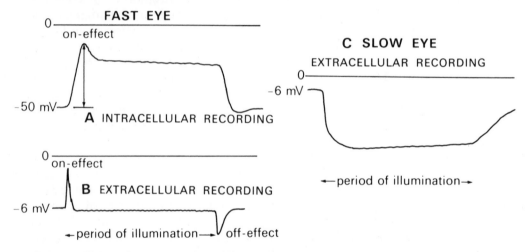

Fig. 422 Electrical responses of the eye. A. Intracellular recording in a retinula cell of *Calliphora*. B. Extracellular recording, electroretinogram, of same response. C. Electroretinogram from the eye of *Tachycines*. Notice that vertical scales differ in each case (modified after Autrum, 1958)

The individual retinula cell has a potential of 25–70 mV, the inside being negative with respect to the outside. Light falling on the cell decreases the potential and, in the worker of *Apis*, the reduction in potential persists throughout the period of illumination. The degree of depolarisation increases with the intensity of illumination and at higher light intensities the cell is strongly depolarised at first so that the potential may at first fall almost to zero and then be maintained 20–30 mV below the resting potential (Fig. 422A).

The sustained potential is regarded as the receptor potential, which may arise in the rhabdom and then spread across to the cell body, or the excitation of the rhabdom may be transmitted in some way to the cell body and the first change in potential may then take place. Action potentials are not produced by the retinula cells and the depolarisation is transmitted along their axons by passive conduction.

Depolarisation of the retinula cell axons leads to hyperpolarisation of the large monopolar cells in the optic cartridge. The degree of hyperpolarisation is proportional to the light intensity. At levels just above threshold the response is irregular, but at higher intensities it consists of a transient 'on' effect, a sustained plateau and a transient 'off' effect. A small depolarisation of the retinula cell produces a much larger hyperpolarisation in the monopolar cell so that there is some amplification in the system.

There is also some inhibition of the response of large monopolar cells by fibres from adjacent cartridges. Different cartridges have inputs from retinal cells with different visual fields and lateral inhibition by cartridges associated with adjacent visual fields can result in an effective increase in angular sensitivity of the eye. For example the angular sensitivity of retinula cells of *Calliphora* is 11°, but lateral inhibition between the cartridges effectively reduces this to 3°. This results in an increase in visual acuity (Laughlin, 1975).

The large monopolar cells conduct information to the medulla electrotonically; action potentials have not been recorded within their axons. However, within the outer chiasma of the optic lobe are axons which produce normal action potentials. Some are 'on–off' units with brief discharges at the onset and termination of a stimulus, others have a sustained discharge during the period of illumination. More centrally, there is considerable diversity in the way in which neurones respond to illumination. For example, the descending contralateral movement detector (DCMD) responds to small movements of images in the contralateral eye. Its activity is affected by inputs from other sensory systems and it makes synaptic connections distally with the motor-neurones of muscles involved in jumping (Fig. 401).

27.3 Functioning of the eye

27.3.1 Image formation

In apposition eyes and in many light-adapted clear-zone eyes each ommatidium is so completely surrounded by pigment that the rhabdom can only receive light from its own dioptric system. Each ommatidium has a limited visual field, its sensitivity falling off sharply as the angle of incidence of the light diverges from the long axis of the ommatidium. In the light-adapted eye of *Periplaneta* the relative sensitivity of the retinula cells is less than 50% of the maximum when the light diverges by more than 1.2° from the ommatidial axis; the angle of acceptance at this 50% level is thus 2.4° (Butler and Horridge, 1973). The degree of overlap in the visual fields of adjacent ommatidia depends on the interommatidial angle (Fig. 423), but in many positions in most eyes the degree of overlap will be small, so each ommatidium will tend to respond to light from a separate part of the object. In the apposition eye each dioptric system is capable of forming an inverted image on the rhabdom. This image may have some significance, but Kuiper (1962) suggests that the function of the lens system is to concentrate the light into a narrow beam. The light reaching the rhabdom in each ommatidium has an overall intensity which varies from one ommatidium to the next depending on the amount of light reflected by the object, and collectively the ommatidia produce a mosaic of spots of light of different intensities, which form an image of the object.

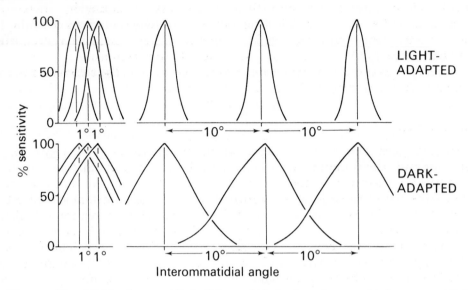

Fig. 423 Visual fields of ommatidia in light- and dark-adapted eyes, with interommatidial angles of 1° (left) and 10° (right) (after Butler and Horridge, 1973)

Dark-adapted clear-zone eyes

The intensities of moonlight and sunlight differ by a ratio of about $1:10^7$. Many insects have the capacity to respond over a large part of this range. This demands a very high

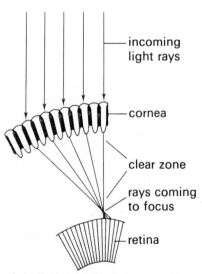

Fig. 424 The manner of formation of a superposition image in a clear-zone, well-focused eye (after Horridge, 1975b)

level of sensitivity at the low intensities with maximum use made of the available light. Dark adaptation involves the movement of pigment so that absorption of light is reduced to a minimum, but in apposition eyes the ommatidia still remain isolated from each other by pigment and light passing obliquely through the eye is absorbed. In clear-zone eyes this is not the case; the pigment is withdrawn so that light from any of the lens systems can pass obliquely through the eye and may reach rhabdoms of a number of ommatidia (Fig. 424). Some light still reaches the rhabdoms through their individual crystalline tracts, but the proportion which does so in the fully dark-adapted eye is probably small.

This system increases the sensitivity of the eye, but at the expense of visual acuity. The extent to which it does so varies in different insects. In *Toxidia* (Lepidoptera) the lens system focuses the light so that a well-focused image is formed on the retina (Fig. 424). This is a true superposition image and comparable well-focused images are formed by the eyes of many large moths and Neuroptera. The tapetum is an essential feature of these eyes since the tracheae serve to isolate the rhabdoms of adjacent ommatidia as well as reflecting light back into the receptor columns. As a result, each receptor column receives light from a wide aperture but without further loss of acuity due to light scattering at the level of the rhabdoms.

In other species the degree of focusing is relatively poor and so the image formed on the retina is very indistinct (Horridge, 1975b).

27.3.2 Sensitivity

The sensitivity of the insect eye depends on the characteristics of the visual pigment, the nervous interconnections behind the eye and the extent to which the eye is adapted to the prevailing light conditions.

In order to produce a response from the eye, sufficient light must be absorbed by the visual pigment to generate an action potential in the postretinal nerve fibres. For flashes of very short duration, up to 0·08, the photochemical effect of light is proportional to its total energy, that is, its intensity and duration, but over longer periods of illumination only the intensity is important and so the 'on' potential in the retinula cell is proportional to intensity (Fig. 425).

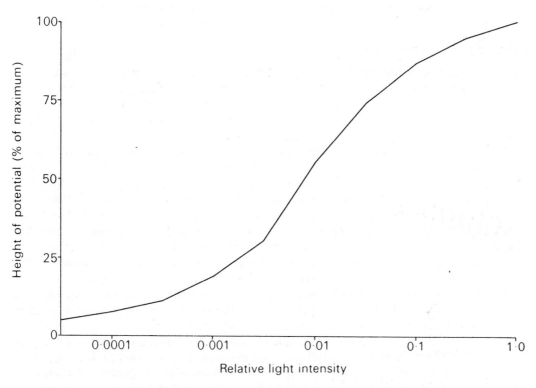

Fig. 425 The relationship between the intensity of white light and the height of the intracellular peak 'on' potential in Fig. 422A (after Burkhardt, 1962)

Clearly, only those wavelengths which are absorbed will have this effect and most insects respond to a range which extends from the near ultraviolet, 300–400 nm up to a maximum of 600 nm. Some butterflies and the firefly, *Photinus*, have a higher maximum, up to about 690 nm, but the sensitivity of these species at the ultraviolet end of the spectrum has not been examined.

Sensitivity is not the same throughout the range and if the intensities of all the wavelengths are kept constant some wavelengths will appear brighter to the insect than others. Most insects have two peaks of maximum sensitivity, one in the near ultraviolet at about 350 nm and a second in the blue–green, about 500 nm, although the peaks tend to be flattened at higher intensities. The sensitivity to different wavelengths reflects the absorption charactersitics of the visual pigments and in well-lit cells this is not influenced by the screening pigment (Burkhardt, 1962). On the other hand, weakly illuminated cells of *Calliphora* have a third peak of sensitivity at 616 nm, which probably does result from the characteristics of the screening pigments.

Adaptation

The sensitivity of the eye varies, depending on whether the insect has recently been in the light or in the dark. After a period of illumination the eye is said to be light-adapted and it becomes progressively less sensitive. In the dark, however, the eye becomes more sensitive as it becomes dark-adapted until a maximum sensitivity is reached. Thus in *Apis* there is a 1000-fold increase in sensitivity in the first 20 minutes in the dark, most of the increase occurring in the first minute (Fig. 426), but the longer the period of exposure to light the longer it takes for the insect to become fully dark-adapted. A dark-adapted insect is much more sensitive to light of low intensities than a light-adapted insect. This adaptation may involve a variety of different factors including the availability of the visual pigment, cytological changes in the eye and movements of the screening pigments. Adaptation may also occur within the nervous system.

The visual pigment is broken down in daylight as quickly or more quickly than it is produced, so that after a period in the light an increasingly strong stimulus is required to maintain a given level of response: the insect is becoming light-adapted. In the dark, on the other hand, sensitivity increases as the visual pigment accumulates: the insect becomes dark-adapted.

In addition, cytological changes occur in the eye as a result of which the effectiveness of the rhabdom as a light-guide is enhanced (p. 652) and an increase occurs in the angle of acceptance of the retinula cells and the ommatidia. In the light-adapted eye of *Periplaneta* the angle of acceptance is only about 2·4° compared with 6·7° in the dark-adapted eye. Consequently more of the available light reaches the retinula cells in the dark-adapted eye (Fig. 423).

Adaptation of clear-zone eyes also involves movements of the screening pigments between the ommatidia (Fig. 418) and so dark adaptation occurs in two phases. When first put in the dark there is a rapid increase in sensitivity due to the accumulation of the visual pigment then, beginning rather later, there is a further slow increase in sensitivity as the pigment moves to the dark-adapted position (Fig. 427 and see Dreisig, 1981).

In nocturnal moths there is a rhythmical movement of the eye pigments. Thus the eye of the codling moth normally starts to become light-adapted about half-an-hour before sunrise and dark-adapted just before sunset, the process taking about an hour to

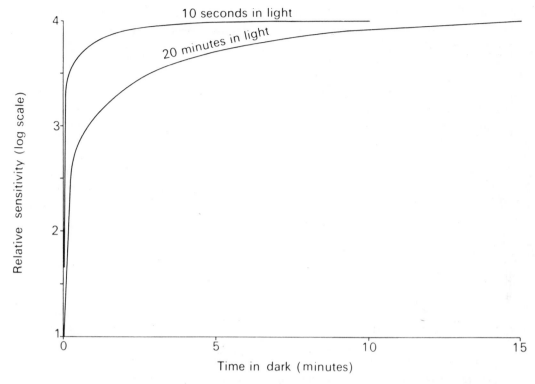

Fig. 426 Dark adaptation of the eye of *Apis* after different periods of light adaptation (from Goldsmith, 1964)

complete. This rhythm continues for a time if the insects are kept in complete darkness and may be part of a general diurnal rhythm of activity. The factors controlling pigment movement are not understood. They do not appear to be hormonal, but may involve a nervous mechanism (Day, 1941).

There is also a rhythm of sensitivity in the eye of *Dytiscus* (Coleoptera), but this is not wholly due to the movement of pigment. Thus the dark-adapted night eye is 1000 times more sensitive than the dark-adapted day eye although the distribution of pigments is the same, and similarly the light-adapted day eye is more sensitive than the light-adapted night eye.

27.3.3 Wavelength discrimination

Colour vision has been shown behaviourally to occur in a number of species belonging to the orders Hymenoptera, Diptera, Coleoptera, Lepidoptera, Neuroptera, Heteroptera, Homoptera and Orthoptera. The ability to discriminate between light of different wavelengths depends on the possession of photopigments with maximum sensitivity to light of different wavelengths. In the moth *Deilephila* two pigments have been demonstrated, one absorbing maximally in the ultraviolet part of the spectrum and one absorbing maximally in the green. It is probable that many insects possess a third, absorbing maximally in the blue region, while a few Lepidoptera have a fourth

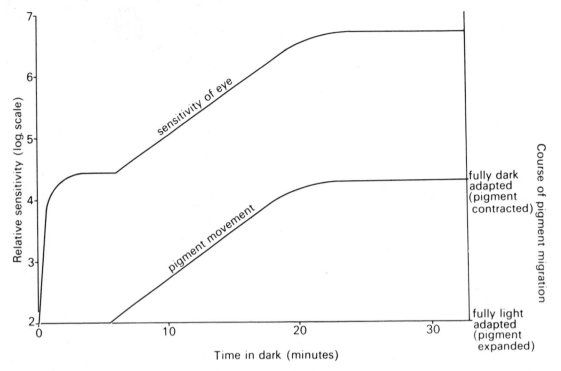

Fig. 427 Dark adaptation of the eye of *Cerapteryx* (Lepidoptera) showing the initial increase in sensitivity due to the accumulation of visual pigment and a further increase as the screening pigments migrate to the dark adapted condition (modified from Goldsmith, 1964)

pigment absorbing red light. In *Spodoptera exempta* this fourth pigment has an absorption maximum at 560 nm (Fig. 428) (Langer *et al.*, 1979), while in a number of butterflies the maximum is at 610 nm (Bernard, 1979).

Although the spectral sensitivity of each retinula cell depends primarily on the photopigment in the rhabdomere, other elements in the ommatidium may affect the wavelength of the light which reaches the cell. In most insects the lens system does not produce any change in the wavelength of light, but in some Diptera there is evidence that the cuticular facets act as filters and only transmit light over a limited waveband (Menzel, 1975). Where a tapetum exists it reflects light of certain wavelengths and as this light passes through the rhabdom twice the response of the retinula cells is differentially increased in this part of the spectrum.

In *Calliphora* and *Drosophila* the screening pigments in the eye do not absorb light with wavelengths much above 600 nm and so such light is transmitted with less attenuation than the shorter wavelengths. This has the effect of increasing the apparent sensitivity of the retinula cells to red light.

The retinula cells within an ommatidium may interact. Distal rhabdomeres function as filters for those situated more proximally and this will be most significant in ommatidia with tiered retinula cells. For instance in the fly it is probable that cell 7 filters out a high proportion of the ultraviolet and blue light, so that cell 8, which is proximal to it, receives a relatively high proportion of longer wavelengths and

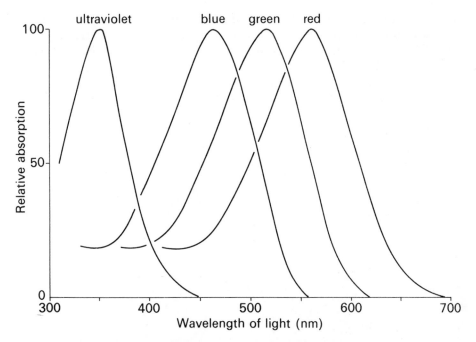

Fig. 428 Absorption of light of different wavelengths by the four visual pigments present in the eye of *Spodoptera*. The absorption by each pigment is expressed as a percentage of the maximum for that pigment (after Langer *et al.*, 1979)

consequently appears to be more sensitive to them. Adjacent retinula cells may also interact electrically so that the stimulation of one cell with light of a given wavelength may produce an effect in another even though the second cell lacks the appropriate photopigment. It is probable that this effect is not of great significance (Menzel, 1975).

The electrical response of the individual retinula cell depends on all these factors, but primarily on the particular photopigment which it contains. Retinula cells with different photopigments occur within one ommatidium. For instance in the ant *Formica* each ommatidium contains two ultraviolet-sensitive cells and six green-sensitive cells; *Apis* workers have three ultraviolet-sensitive cells, two green-sensitive, and in some ommatidia four blue-sensitive or additional green-sensitive cells; *Spodoptera* has six green-sensitive cells, one red-sensitive and one ultraviolet- or blue-sensitive. In some cases these cells are anatomically differentiated. For example, in *Apis* the short basal cell is one of the ultraviolet-sensitive cells and in *Spodoptera* the basal cell (cell 8) is red-sensitive and the distal cell (cell 1) ultraviolet- or blue-sensitive (Fig. 415).

The distribution of cells with different wavelength sensitivities may vary in different parts of the eye. For instance, the upper part of the eye of *Ascalaphus* (Neuroptera) contains more ultraviolet-sensitive receptors than other parts; and the ventral part of the eye of the drone bee has more green-sensitive cells than other parts. On the other hand, in *Periplaneta* ommatidia in all parts of the eye have three ultraviolet-sensitive cells and five green-sensitive cells.

Apis can discriminate a wide range of wavelengths, but this ability is greatest in the violet and blue–green regions, where it can differentiate between wavelengths differing by as little as 8 nm. The colours discriminated by the bee can be arranged in pairs of complementary colours to produce 'white' or uncoloured light for the bee (Fig. 429). It appears that the trichromatic theory of colour is valid for the bee, the sensation elicited by any single spectral colour also being elicited by an appropriate mixture of the three primary colours, which in this case are ultraviolet, blue and yellow.

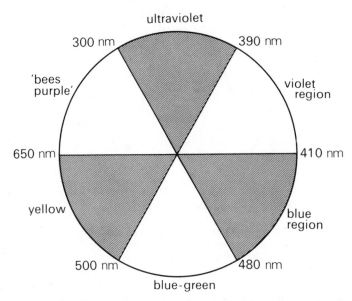

Fig. 429 Colour circle showing the colours which are differentiated by *Apis*. Hatched areas are primary colours (from Burkhardt, 1964)

Within the optic lobes, interneurones respond in different ways to stimulation of the different colour-sensitive cells. Some respond to inputs from any of the retinula cells with sustained excitation or inhibition; their response changes with intensity without any differential colour effects. Other cells respond to all three colour-types, but show differential effects with different wavelengths. In addition, there are interneurones which are associated with only one type of colour-sensitive cell or which are linked positively to one type and are inhibited by another. For example, some interneurones show an increased rate of firing when green-sensitive receptor cells are stimulated, but are inhibited by stimulation of the ultraviolet receptors; ultraviolet-sensitive inter-neurones are inhibited by wavelengths greater than 420 nm. These cells provide the neural mechanism for colour coding (Kien and Menzel, 1977).

Colour is important in the lives of those insects which possess colour vision. Most flower-visiting insects, such as *Apis* and *Eristalis* (Diptera), exhibit preferences for blue or yellow and where red flowers are visited this may be because, as with the poppy, large amounts of ultraviolet light are reflected. It is also significant that the majority of flowers in the temperate zones, where the flowers are insect pollinated, are blue or yellow, with few pure reds, while in the tropics, where birds are common pollinators, red flowers are common. New Zealand, with a sparse insect fauna, is poor in indigenous coloured flowers. Colour is also important in the feeding of leaf-eating species, *Chrysomela* (Coleoptera) and various caterpillars being attracted to green.

The reactions of an insect to colour may vary depending on its physiological state. Thus female *Pieris* at first show a preference for blue, purple and yellow, the colours of the flowers from which they feed, but when they are mature the preferred colours are green and green–blue, corresponding with the tendency to oviposit on leaves. *Macroglossum* (Ledpidoptera) females show a similar change of preference.

Colour vision also plays a part in the courtship behaviour of some insects (p. 146) and probably in the choice of backgrounds in cryptically coloured insects (p. 143).

27.3.4 Discrimination of the plane of vibration

Light waves vibrate in planes at right angles to the direction in which they are travelling. These planes of vibration may be equally distributed through 360° about the direction of travel, or a higher proportion of the vibrations may occur in a particular plane. Such light is said to be polarised and if all the vibrations are in one plane the light is plane polarised.

Light coming from a blue sky is polarised. The degree of polarisation and the plane of maximum polarisation of light from different parts of the sky varies and is correlated with the position of the sun (Wehner, 1976). Consequently it is possible to determine the position of the sun, even when it is obscured, from the composition of polarised light from a patch of blue sky. Certain insects are able to make use of this information in astrotaxis. It is particularly important in the homing of social Hymenoptera, and is best known in *Apis*, where the communication dances of workers may be orientated with respect to the sun even when the sun is obscured (see *e.g.* von Frisch, 1950). In other insects where the ability to perceive polarised light exists it probably enables them to maintain a constant and steady orientation.

Detection of the plane of polarisation is possible because the molecules of the photopigment are preferentially orientated along the microvilli of the rhabdomere and maximum absorption occurs when light is vibrating in the same plane as the dipole axis of the pigment molecule. In order to navigate, at least two receptors absorbing maximally in different planes are necessary and in addition it is necessary to be able to distinguish changes in input from the receptors due to changes in the plane of polarisation from changes in the intensity or wavelength of the light.

In ants and bees sensitivity to polarised light is restricted to the ultraviolet receptors. In these insects the retinula cells are twisted round each other in a spiral with a turn of 1° per micron of length. The rhabdomeres of the long retinula cells are twisted through 180° and so are effectively insensitive to the plane of polarisation. The two long ultraviolet-sensitive cells consequently provide a reference of changes in the intensity of ultraviolet light. It is the short, ninth, cells which give information about the plane of polarisation. These cells are also twisted, but because they are short they twist by only 40° and so respond differentially to the plane of polarisation. The retinula cells may be twisted clockwise or anticlockwise and the two arrangements occur randomly across the eye. Consequently the short cells of adjacent ommatidia are likely to be twisted in opposite senses and so their rhabdomeres will have different overall orientations even though they have the same orientations at their distal ends. Hence by the interaction of cells in two ommatidia the insect can orientate itself accurately. In ants, navigation is

dependent on a small group of ommatidia in the antero-dorsal part of the eye and it has
been shown that accurate navigation can be achieved with only 10 ommatidia in this
region (Wehner, 1976; Wehner *et al.*, 1975).

27.3.5 Field of view

Insects with well-developed compound eyes generally have an extensive field of view.
For instance, in the horizontal field *Periplaneta* has vision through 360°, with binocular
vision in front and behind the head (Fig. 430). In the vertical plane the visual fields of
the two eyes overlap dorsally, but not ventrally (Butler, 1973). Even in Collembola with
only a few ommatidia, the field of each eye is about 140°, but this is due to each
individual ommatidium having a wide angle of acceptance and the ommatidia being
orientated at different angles. As a result visual acuity is poor.

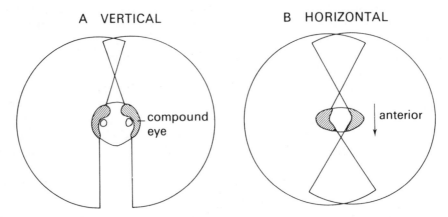

Fig. 430 The visual field of *Periplaneta* in (A) the vertical and (B) the horizontal planes. The
fields of the two eyes overlap above, behind and in front of the head (after Butler, 1973)

Distance perception

The ability to judge distances depends on binocular vision and if one eye is damaged the
power is lost. Errors can arise in the estimation of distance due to the size of the
interommatidial angle, since this is important in determining acuity. Fig. 431 shows
the error of estimation which might arise if the interommatidial angle was 2° and bigger
interommatidial angles will result in bigger errors. Related to this is the fact that
dragonfly larvae and mantids have smaller ommatidia on the inside of the eye. These are
the ommatidia used in judging the distance of the prey. Errors will also be larger if the
distance of the insect from its prey is long relative to the distance between the eyes
(Fig. 431), and in many carnivorous insects which hunt visually, such as mantids and
Zygoptera, the eyes are wide apart.

Insects, such as grasshoppers, which jump and need to judge distances accurately,
make peering movements while looking at their proposed perch. Peering movements
are side to side swayings of the body with the feet still and the head vertical, but moving
through an arc extending 10° or more on either side of the body axis. It is suggested that

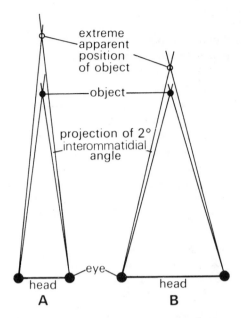

Fig. 431 Diagram to illustrate how a wider head with greater separation of the eyes improves the estimation of distance. If the supposed interommatidial angle is 2°, an object stimulating a single ommatidium might lie anywhere between the open circle and the black spot so that there could be a considerable error in distance estimation. In B the head is twice as wide and the possible error greatly reduced

distance in this case is estimated by the extent of movement over the retina; big movements indicate that the object is close to the insect, while small movements show that it is at a greater distance (Wallace, 1959).

27.3.6 Resolving power

Behavioural experiments suggest that the insect eye is capable of resolving two objects with an angular separation of about 1°. Objects closer together than this are not differentiated from each other and the smallest resolvable angular separation is known as the minimum visual angle. Hence the minimum visual angle is a measure of the ability of the eye to separate two objects close together.

Recording the nervous output from the eye in the optic ganglion or the ventral nerve cord indicates, however, that both *Locusta* and *Calliphora* are capable of differentiating objects with an angular separation of only 0·3°, although the insects do not respond behaviourally to such a separation.

The resolving power of the compound eye is reduced at low light intensities, partly because of the increased overlap of the visual fields of individual ommatidia (Fig. 423) and, in clear-zone eyes, because the quality of image produced on the rhabdoms is poor.

The quality of information transferred to the central nervous system from the optical system may be enhanced by lateral inhibition between optic cartridges in the lamina ganglionaris (p.420) (Wehner, 1975).

Form perception

Behavioural responses indicate that insects are able to separate objects with an angular separation of 1 or 2° and it follows that larger objects should be clearly visible to most insects. *Locusta* responds to a pattern of black stripes on a white ground, being attracted to the edge of the stripe where white and black adjoin. Vertical stripes are preferred to oblique or wavy-edged lines and taller figures are preferred to short ones. If no vertical stripes are presented the more complex figure is preferred (Wallace, 1958). Such behaviour would be relevant to the locust in food finding. The ability to follow stripes is best developed in phytophagous insects.

Apis responds to shapes and can be trained to come to any mark which contrasts with the background. Solid figures of different shapes are not differentiated from each other, nor are broken figures, but *Apis* readily differentiates between solid and broken patterns (Fig. 432), showing a preference for broken figures which is not overcome by training. The number of visits paid by bees to a particular pattern is proportional to the length of its contour, suggesting that the choice depends on the frequency of change of retinal stimulation as the bee moves, that is, on the flicker effect which the pattern produces in the eye. Related to this, it is found that the settling of bees on flowers is improved if the flowers are moving slightly (Wehner, 1975).

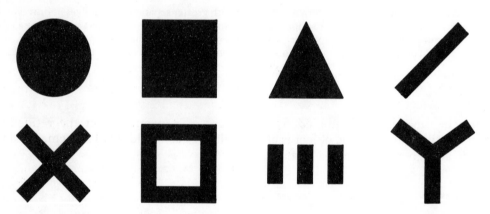

Fig. 432 Different symbols used in experiments on form perception by *Apis*. The shapes in the top row are not distinguished from each other, but are readily distinguished from those in the second row (from Wigglesworth, 1965)

At least some insects, particularly hunting insects, must have rather better vision than this suggests. For instance, the spider-hunting wasp *Sceliphron* must be able to recognise spiders from some distance, although olfaction is probably also important at close quarters. *Philanthus* (Hymenoptera) recognises landmarks, such as pine cones, in the vicinity of its nest and the removal of such landmarks makes it difficult for it to find the nest. Its vision must presumably be of a high order for it to recognise such landmarks.

Movement perception

The insect eye appears to be better adapted for movement perception than for form perception (Burtt and Catton, 1962). The system of small units, either ommatidia or rhabdomeres, which constitute the compound eye lends itself to the perception of changes in stimulation resulting from small movements of the object or the eye. Hence bees respond more readily to moving flowers than to stationary ones, dragonfly larvae respond to moving prey and, in experiments, most insects show a preference for more complex shapes causing more flicker.

However, if an object vibrates too quickly its movement may not be observed because the sensory units need time in which to recover from the previous stimulus. The stimulation of the eye by a succession of stimuli is called a flicker effect and the highest number of separate stimuli which the eye can differentiate in unit time as the flicker threshold or the flicker fusion frequency. The flicker threshold varies with the type of eye. In slow eyes (p. 654) the threshold value lies between about 20/second in *Tachycines* (Orthoptera) and 60/second in *Aeschna* larva, while in the fast eyes of *Apis* and *Calliphora* the threshold frequency approaches 300/second, the value varying with the light intensity. A high flicker threshold is well suited to a fast-flying insect since it facilitates the perception of features of the terrain passing rapidly beneath it.

Optomotor reaction

The optomotor reaction is a behavioural response to a pattern of stimulation moving over the eye. In experimental work the pattern usually consists of moving vertical stripes to which the insect responds by a turning movement tending to keep the images in the eye as stationary as possible. In the field the reaction is brought about by the apparent movement of environmental features as the insect moves. The passage of images across the eye from behind forwards indicates to the insect that it is moving backwards, while image movement from front to back indicates forward movement.

A flying insect appears to prefer images to pass over the eye from front to back at a certain moderate speed, it has a preferred retinal velocity. Often if an insect flies downwind this velocity will be exceeded and so it turns and flies into the wind. An upwind orientation in maintained so long as it is able to make headway against the wind. If, however, the wind is too strong and the insect is carried backwards, as indicated by the forward movement of images in the eye, it lands (Kennedy, 1951). Hence orientation with respect to the wind involves an optomotor reaction, although stimuli other than visual ones may also be important.

Some stream-dwelling insects hold their position in the current by an optomotor reaction. *Notonecta*, for instance, orientates upstream and swims strongly as the current tends to drift it downstream, so it tends to keep its visual field constant and as a result maintains its position. In a tank without any landmarks, or if the eyes are blackened, *Notonecta* is unable to keep station and is swept downstream.

Movement-sensitive interneurones

Movements of an object in the visual field are detected as a result of the successive stimulation of a number of retinula cells; this is true whether the object actually moves or whether it apparently does so as a result of the movement of the insect itself. The separation of such movements by the insect depends on integration in the optic lobes and brain; a number of interneurones with different characteristics have been recognised (Collett and King, 1975; Kien, 1975).

Some interneurones are sensitive to movement in any direction across the eye. They usually habituate quickly to a particular movement, but may then respond again if the same movement stimulates a different set of retinula cells. It has been suggested that an important function of these units is the maintenance of a high level of arousal (p. 634). The descending movement detectors (p. 619) also respond to movement in any direction, but they tend to be most sensitive to movements of small objects which contrast with the background. Consequently they tend to be unaffected by movements of the whole visual field such as result from movements of the insect.

Other interneurones in the optic lobes respond to movement in only one direction; the spontaneous rate of firing is increased by movement in the preferred direction and decreased by movement in the opposite direction. The unidirectional units in the medulla have a relatively narrow receptive field of about $50°$; more central units in the optic lobes have wide fields. These cells respond preferentially to either vertical or horizontal movement, so they can give information about the movement of the insect in space.

27.4 Dorsal ocelli

Dorsal ocelli are found in adult insects and the larvae of hemimetabolous insects. Typically there are three, forming an inverted triangle antero-dorsally on the head (Fig. 2), although in Diptera and Hymenoptera they occupy a more dorsal position on the vertex. The median ocellus shows evidence of a paired origin since the root of the ocellar nerve is double and the ocellus itself is bilobed in Odonata and *Bombus* (Hymenoptera). Frequently one or all of the ocelli are lost and they are often absent in wingless forms.

A typical ocellus has a single thickened cuticular lens (Fig. 433), but in other cases the cuticle is transparent, but not thickened, the space immediately beneath the cuticle being occupied by transparent cells. This is the case in *Schistocerca* and *Lucilia*. Pigment cells may form a ring round the outside of the ocellus, as in *Schistocerca*, or invest the whole ocellus, as in *Cloeon* (Ephemeroptera), but in some species, like the cockroach, pigment is lacking. At the back of the receptor cells may be a reflecting tapetum, probably consisting of urate crystals in a layer of cells.

Each ocellus contains a large number of retinula cells closely packed together; in the locust ocellus there are 800–1000 retinula cells. A rhabdomere is formed on at least one side of each retinula cell, and the rhabdomeres of from two to seven cells combine to form rhabdoms. The structure of the rhabdomeres is the same as in the compound eye (p. 645). Proximally each retinula cell gives rise to an axon which passes through the basement membrane of the ocellus and, in the adult locust, terminates in a synaptic plexus immediately behind the eye (Fig. 434A). In larval locusts some receptor cell axons pass directly to the brain, but these are apparently not present in the adult (Goodman *et al.*, 1979). The retinula cell axons synapse repeatedly and reciprocally with each other and with the interneurones in the ocellar nerve which extends from each ocellus to the protocerebrum.

Extending to the synaptic plexus from the brain are a small number of giant interneurones and a larger number of small ones; in the median ocellar nerve of *Schistocerca* there are seven giant fibres about 10 μm in diameter and 78 smaller interneurones. The giant fibres have extensive arborisations in the synaptic plexus and synapse repeatedly with many of the sensory axons. Four of those in the median ocellar nerve of *Schistocerca* also pass to the lateral ocelli, where they arborise again and

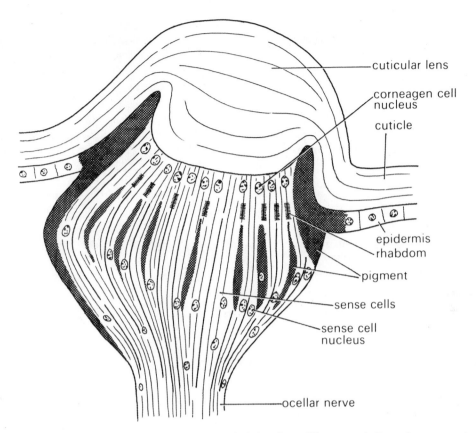

Fig. 433 Section through a dorsal ocellus of *Aphrophora* (Homoptera) (from Imms, 1957)

synapse with the lateral ocellar sensory axons (Fig. 434B). These cells connect with other giant fibres in the ocellar nerves, but have no extensive branches in the brain. The three other large interneurones pass back to the brain and form a dendritic field on each side to which giant fibres from the ipsilateral ocelli also contribute. Some of the smaller interneurones probably connect with more proximally extending retinula cell axons (Fig. 434A, fibres c and d). They have much more restricted dendritic fields than the giant axons. In the brain some of these fibres associate with the optic tracts and others may enter the nerves to the corpora cardiaca. Third order interneurones pass to the ventral nerve cord both ipsilaterally and contralaterally.

Illumination produces a sustained depolarisation of the retinula cell which is proportional to the intensity of light. In dragonflies there is also a sharp 'on-effect', but this does not occur in locusts. No action potentials are produced in the retinula cells; the graded receptor potential is transmitted along the axons to the synapses.

The second order giant interneurones are hyperpolarised by illumination of the retinula cells. At high light intensities a short-lived 'on-effect' is followed by a sustained hyperpolarisation until light-off, which produces a sharp depolarisation with a slow return to the resting level (Patterson and Goodman, 1974). The amplitude of the response in these second order cells is greater at low light intensities than that in the

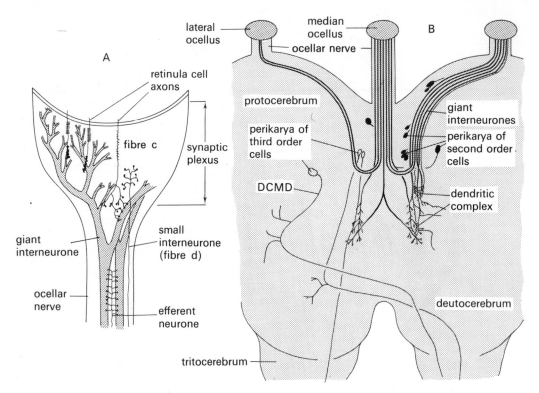

Fig. 434 A. Diagram showing the arrangement of retinula cell axons and interneurones in the synaptic plexus of the median ocellus of *Schistocerca*. B. Diagram showing the arrangement of some ocellar interneurones in the brain of *Schistocerca* (after Goodman, 1975)

receptor cells; a similar amplification occurs in the optic cartridges associated with the compound eye (p. 651). It is believed that the second order cells transmit information electrotonically to the brain, but very little is known about the smaller second order units in the ocellar nerve. Third order, spike-producing interneurones extend from the brain into the ventral nerve cord. They respond in a variety of different ways to ocellar illumination (Goodman, 1975).

The functions of ocelli remain uncertain. Although an image is produced by the lens it is not in focus on the retina. In addition, the extensive convergence of retinula cells on to a small number of interneurones indicates that form perception could at best be of an extremely crude nature. The structure and physiology of the ocellus, with a tapetum and neural convergence, seems adapted for the concentration of light and perception of intensity, and they are sensitive to light of low intensities. It is certain that in *Locusta* and *Gryllus* the ocelli influence the orientation of the insect with respect to a light source; it is possible that they also exert some general kinetic effect on activity (Goodman, 1970).

27.5 Stemmata

Stemmata are the only visual organs of larval holometabolous insects. They are sometimes called lateral ocelli, but this term is better avoided since it leads to confusion with the dorsal ocelli. They occur laterally on the head and vary in number from one on each side in tenthredinid larvae to six on each side in lepidopterous larvae (Fig. 435).

In *Isia* (Lepidoptera) each of the stemmata has a cuticular lens formed largely of endocuticle (Fig. 435B). It is secreted by three epidermal cells and may show indications of its origins in consisting of three small, separate facets forming a tripartite lens. Beneath the cuticle is a crystalline lens secreted by three cells and this again may have a tripartite structure. Each lens system has seven heavily pigmented sense cells associated with it, three arching over distally to form a distal rhabdom and four proximal cells which form a proximal rhabdom. Round the outside of the sense cells is a thin cellular membrane, which in turn is shrouded by an envelope formed by the extremely enlarged corneagen cells. The nerve fibres from the sense cells pass to the optic lobe of the brain (Dethier, 1942).

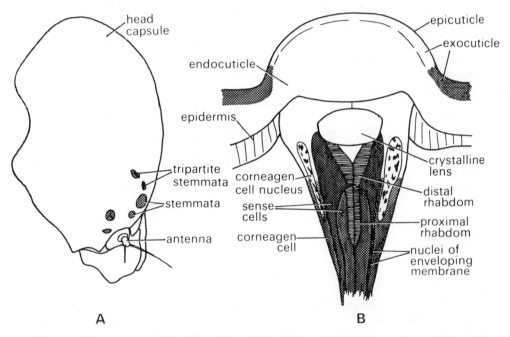

Fig. 435 A. Lateral view of the head of a caterpillar showing the positions of the stemmata. B. Section of a stemma (after Dethier, 1942, 1943)

A good deal of variation from this basic form occurs. In tenthredinid larvae the stemmata are more like dorsal ocelli, each containing numerous groups of sense cells and lacking a crystalline lens. In its place is a group of long, cylindrical, transparent corneagenous cells (Meyer-Rochow, 1974). *Dytiscus* and *Sialis* (Megaloptera) larvae have similar stemmata, but with a crystalline lens. Finally, larval Cyclorrhapha have lost all external trace of the stemmata, but there are light-sensitive spots, which are probably derived from the stemmata, internally on each side of the pharyngeal skeleton.

The lenses of the stemmata produce images which fall on the rhabdoms. In *Isia* if the object is closer to the eye than about 0·08 mm. the image falls on the proximal rhabdom, but if the object is any farther away than this the image is formed on the distal rhabdom (Dethier, 1943). Thus most objects will fall on the distal rhabdom and since this is only formed from three cells image perception by individual stemmata cannot be very efficient. Each of the stemmata receives light from the area at which it is directed and, since the fields of adjacent stemmata do not overlap, a caterpillar with six stemmata on each side will perceive 12 points of light from different parts of the visual field. Hence it perceives a coarse mosaic, which is improved by side-to-side movements of the head enabling it to examine a larger field. It is known that caterpillars can differentiate shapes and orientate towards boundaries between black and white areas.

The situation is different in tenthredinid larvae, which have only a single stemma. Here the lens has two layers of differing refractive index and produces a relatively sharp image on the retinula cells in the centre of the group, but towards the edges this sharpness falls off. This type of eye is capable of form perception. In *Perga* (Hymenoptera), pigment movements occur in the retinula cells in relation to light and dark adaptation. In the dark, pigment granules move radially away from the rhabdom and after a period become concentrated at the proximal end of the retinula cells. As a result of these pigment movements the dark-adapted cells are 500 to 1000 times more sensitive than fully light-adapted ones (Meyer-Rochow, 1974).

Larval *Neodiprion* (Hymenoptera) and tortricid caterpillars respond to the plane of polarisation of light. This response is presumably mediated via the stemmata.

27.6 Dermal light sense

A number of insects, such as *Tenebrio* larvae, still respond to light when all the known visual receptors are occluded. The epidermal cells apparently are sensitive to light. This is also suggested by the pigment movements which occur in isolated epidermal cells of some insects (p. 843). The production of growth layers in the cuticle (p. 505) is also apparently controlled by some light-sensitive response of the epidermal cells (Neville, 1975).

REFERENCES

AUTRUM, H. (1958). Electrophysiological analysis of the visual systems in insects. *Expl Cell Res. suppl.* **5**: 426–439.

BARLOW, H. B. (1952). The size of ommatidia in apposition eyes. *J. exp. Biol.* **29**: 667–674.

BERNARD, G. D. (1979). Red-absorbing visual pigment of butterflies. *Science* **203**: 1125–1127.

BURKHARDT, D. (1962). Spectral sensitivity and other response characteristics of single visual cells in the arthropod eye. *Symp. Soc. exp. Biol.* **16**: 86–109.

BURKHARDT, D. (1964). Colour discrimination in insects. *Adv. Insect Physiol.* **2**: 131–174.

BURTT, E. T. and CATTON, W. T. (1962). A diffraction theory of insect vision. I. An experimental investigation of visual acuity and image formation in the compound eyes of three species of insects. *Proc. R. Soc.* B, **157**: 53–82.

BUTLER, R. (1973). The anatomy of the compound eye of *Periplaneta americana* L. 1. General features. *J. comp. Physiol.* **83**: 223–238.

BUTLER, R. and HORRIDGE, G. A. (1973). The electrophysiology of the retina of *Periplaneta americana* L. 1. Changes in receptor acuity upon light/dark adaptation. *J. comp. Physiol.* **83**: 263–278.

CAMPOS-ORTEGA, J. A. and STRAUSFELD, N. J. (1972). Columns and layers in the second synaptic region of the fly's visual system: the case for two superimposed neuronal architectures. *in* Wehner, R. (ed.), *Information processing in the visual systems of arthropods*. Springer-Verlag, Berlin.

CARLSON, S. D. and CHI, C. (1979). The functional morphology of the insect photoreceptor. *A. Rev. Ent.* **24**: 379–416.

COLLETT, T. and KING, A. J. (1975). Vision during flight. *in* Horridge, G. A. (ed.), *The compound eye and vision of insects*. Clarendon Press, Oxford.

DAY, M. F. (1941). Pigment migration in the eyes of the moth, *Ephestia Kuehniella* Zeller. *Biol. Bull. mar. biol. Lab., Woods Hole* **80**: 275–291.

DETHIER, V. G. (1942). The dioptric apparatus of lateral ocelli. I. The corneal lens. *J. cell. comp. Physiol.* **19**: 301–313.

DETHIER, V. G. (1943). The dioptric apparatus of lateral ocelli. II. Visual capacities of the ocellus. *J. cell. comp. Physiol.* **22**: 115–126.

DETHIER, V. G. (1963). *The physiology of insect senses*. Methuen, London.

DREISIG, H. (1981). The dynamics of pigment migration in insect superposition eyes. *J. comp. Physiol.* **143**: 491–502.

FRISCH, K. von (1950). *Bees. Their vision, chemical senses, and language*. Cornell University Press, New York.

GOLDSMITH, T. H. (1962). Fine structure of the retinulae in the compound eye of the honey-bee. *J. Cell Biol.* **14**: 489–494.

GOLDSMITH, T. H. (1964). The visual system of insects. *in* Rockstein, M. (ed.), *The physiology of Insecta*. vol. 1. Academic Press, New York.

GOLDSMITH, T. H. and BERNARD, G. D. (1974). The visual system of insects. *in* Rockstein, M. (ed.), *The physiology of Insecta*. vol. 2. Academic Press, New York.

GOLDSMITH, T. H. and PHILPOTT, D. E. (1957). The microstructure of the compound eyes of insects. *J. biophys. biochem. Cytol.* **3**: 429–438.

GOODMAN, L. J. (1970). The structure and function of the insect dorsal ocellus. *Adv. Insect Physiol.* **7**: 97–195.

GOODMAN, L. J. (1975). The neural organization and physiology of the insect dorsal ocellus. *in* Horridge, G. A. (ed.), *The compound eye and vision of insects*. Clarendon Press, Oxford.

GOODMAN, L. J., MOBBS, P. G. and KIRKHAM, J. B. (1979). The fine structure of the ocelli of *Schistocerca gregaria*. The neural organisation of the synaptic plexus. *Cell Tissue Res.* **196**: 487–510.

GRIBAKIN, F. C. (1975). The functional morphology of the compound eye of the bee. *in* Horridge, G. A. (ed.), *The compound eye and vision of insects*. Clarendon Press, Oxford.

HAMDORF, K., PAULSEN, R., SCHWEMER, J. and TAEUBER, U. (1972). Photoreconversion of invertebrate visual pigments. *in* Wehner, R. (ed.), *Information processing in the visual systems of arthropods*. Springer-Verlag, Berlin.

HORRIDGE, G. A. (1965). The Arthropoda. *in* Bullock, T. H. and Horridge, G. A., *Structure and function in the nervous systems of invertebrates*. Freeman, San Francisco.

HORRIDGE, G. A. (ed.) (1975a). *The compound eye and vision of insects*. Clarendon Press, Oxford.

HORRIDGE, G. A. (1975b). Optical mechanisms of clear-zone eyes. *in* Horridge, G. A. (ed.), *The compound eye and vision of insects*. Clarendon Press, Oxford.

IMMS, A. D. (1957). *A general textbook of entomology*. 9th edition, revised by Richards and Davies. Methuen, London.

KENNEDY, J. S. (1951). The migration of the desert locust (*Schistocerca gregaria* (Forsk.)). *Phil. Trans. R. Soc.* B, **235**: 163–290.

KIEN, J. (1975). Motion detection in locusts and grasshoppers. *in* Horridge, G. A. (ed.), *The compound eye and vision of insects*. Clarendon Press, Oxford.

KIEN, J. and MENZEL, R. (1977). Chromatic properties of interneurons in the optic lobes of the bee I. Broad band neurons. *J. comp. Physiol.* **113**: 17–34.

KUIPER, J. W. (1962). The optics of the compound eye. *Symp. Soc. exp. Biol.* **16**: 58–71.

LANGER, H., HAMANN, B. and MEINECKE, C. C. (1979). Tetrachromatic visual system in the moth *Spodoptera exempta* (Insecta: Noctuidae). *J. comp. Physiol.* **129**: 235–239.

LAUGHLIN, S. B. (1975). The function of the lamina ganglionaris. *in* Horridge, G. A. (ed.), *The compound eye and vision of insects.* Clarendon Press, Oxford.

MENZEL, R. (1975). Colour receptors in insects. *in* Horridge, G. A. (ed.), *The compound eye and vision of insects.* Clarendon Press, Oxford.

MENZEL, R. and BLAKERS, M. (1976). Colour receptors in the bee eye—morphology and spectral sensitivity. *J. comp. Physiol.* **108**: 11–33.

MEYER-ROCHOW, V. B. (1974). Structure and function of the larval eye of the sawfly, *Perga. J. Insect Physiol.* **20**: 1565–1591.

MEYER-ROCHOW, V. B. (1975). The dioptric system in beetle compound eyes. *in* Horridge, G. A. (ed.), *The compound eye and vision of insects.* Clarendon Press, Oxford.

NEVILLE, A. C. (1975). *Biology of the arthropod cuticle.* Springer-Verlag, Berlin.

PATTERSON, J. A. and GOODMAN, L. J. (1974). Intracellular responses of receptor cells and second-order cells in the ocelli of the desert locust, *Schistocerca gregaria. J. comp. Physiol.* **95**: 237–250.

PAULUS, H. F. (1975). The compound eyes of apterygote insects. *in* Horridge, G. A. (ed.), *The compound eye and vision of insects.* Clarendon Press, Oxford.

SNYDER, A. W. (1975). Optical properties of invertebrate photoreceptors. *in* Horridge, G. A. (ed.), *The compound eye and vision of insects.* Clarendon Press, Oxford.

SNYDER, A. W. and HORRIDGE, G. A. (1972). The optical function of changes in the medium surrounding the cockroach rhabdom. *J. comp. Physiol.* **81**: 1–8.

WALCOTT, B. (1975). Anatomical changes during light adaptation in insect compound eyes. *in* Horridge, G. A. (ed.), *The compound eye and vision of insects.* Clarendon Press, Oxford.

WALLACE, G. K. (1958). Some experiments on form perception in the nymphs of the desert locust, *Schistocerca gregaria* Forsk. *J. exp. Biol.* **35**: 765–775.

WALLACE, G. K. (1959). Visual scanning in the desert locust *Schistocerca gregaria* Forskål. *J. exp. Biol.* **36**: 512–525.

WEHNER, R. (ed.) (1972). *Information processing in the visual systems of arthropods.* Springer-Verlag, Berlin.

WEHNER, R. (1975). Pattern recognition of insects. *in* Horridge, G. A. (ed.), *The compound eye and vision of insects.* Clarendon Press, Oxford.

WEHNER, R. (1976). Polarized-light navigation by insects. *Scientific American.* **235**: 106–115.

WEHNER, R., BERNARD, G. D. and GEIGER, E. (1975). Twisted and non-twisted rhabdoms and their significance for polarization detection in the bee. *J. comp. Physiol.* **104**: 225–245.

WIGGLESWORTH, V. B. (1965). *The principles of insect physiology.* Methuen, London.

WOLKEN, J. J., CAPENOS, J. and TURANO, A. (1957). Photoreceptor structures. III. *Drosophila melanogaster. J. biophys. biochem. Cytol.* **3**: 441–447.

CHAPTER XXVIII

SOUND PRODUCTION

Sounds are produced by many insects using a variety of mechanisms. Some sounds, such as that resulting from the vibration of the wings in flight, may be adventitious and of no particular value to the insect, but usually they have some significance and special mechanisms are developed for their production. In many instances sounds are produced by scraping a ridge over a series of striations on some other part of the body, which is thus caused to vibrate. Such frictional mechanisms are well known in Orthoptera and Coleoptera. In some Homoptera and Lepidoptera a specialised membrane is caused to vibrate by the direct action of a muscle.

The sounds produced by many insects appear to have some warning significance for other insects or perhaps serve to alarm a potential predator. In the latter case they often form part of a display which also involves the colour and movement of the insect. Sounds of this sort are irregular and extend over a wide range of frequencies.

Sounds which are of intraspecific significance are much more highly organised consisting of bursts of sound repeated in a regular manner. Some species have a number of different songs characterised by differences in the timing of the sounds and these are used in different situations. Intraspecific sounds are commonly used in courtship, but they may also be involved in sexual isolation, aggregation, and, in social insects, other behaviour which involves communication.

Insects only produce sounds under particular environmental conditions, the internal environment possibly being regulated by hormones. Given suitable conditions sound production is under nervous control, centres in the brain co-ordinating sensory input and signalling to centres in the segmental ganglia so that the appropriate songs are produced.

Sound production generally is reviewed by Haskell (1961, 1974) and Dumortier (1963a, b). Aspects of the nervous control of sound production are dealt with by Huber (1963) and Loher and Huber (1966), while Elsner (1975) describes the muscular mechanisms used by grasshoppers in stridulation. The behavioural significance of sound production is reviewed by Alexander (1967).

28.1 Mechanisms and the sounds produced

Sound with reference to insects may be defined as any mechanical disturbance which is potentially referable by the insect to an external and localised source (Pumphrey, 1950). Hence it includes not only vibrations carried through the air or water, but also vibrations transmitted through the substratum. Sufficient energy must be imparted to the medium for the sound waves to be transmitted to the recipient insect and stimulate

675

its receptors, and because of the small size of insects they are unable to produce low frequency sounds of sufficient power for them to be transmitted through the air. For this reason, the effective sound emissions of insects are in the kHz range (Michelson and Nocke, 1974). Low frequency vibrations can be transmitted through solids, although their intensity declines rapidly with increasing distance from the source.

The characterisation of the sounds produced by insects is difficult and there is much confusion in the literature (for discussion of terminology see Broughton, 1963). The sound may be continuous, as in the case of the noise produced by the vibration of the wings, but more usually it consists of discrete sounds separated by intervals of silence. The unitary sound perceived by the human ear is called a chirp and this may consist of a single pulse or, as in the cricket, of a series of pulses, a pulse being defined as a discrete train of sound waves. The sound produced by a single contraction and relaxation of the operating muscles is called a syllable and this may consist of one or more pulses. Finally the basic grouping of syllables is known as an echeme (Fig. 436) (Broughton, 1976).

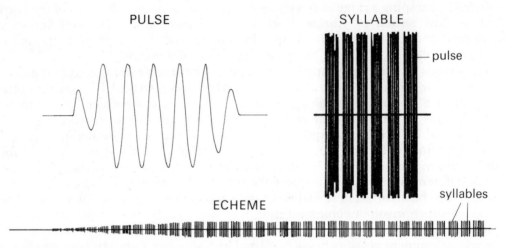

Fig. 436 Diagrammatic representation of some terms employed in describing insect sounds. A pulse is a discrete train of sound waves; a syllable is the sound produced as the result of a single cycle of contraction and relaxation of the sound-producing muscles; an echeme is the basic grouping of syllables

Many insects produce sounds and these may be divided into five categories according to the method used:
    sounds produced as a by-product of some other activity;
    sounds produced by the impact of some part of the body against the substratum;
    sounds produced by frictional methods, rubbing two parts of the body together;
    sounds produced by a vibrating membrane;
    and sounds produced by a pulsed air stream.
The term stridulation is used in many ways. Most often it is applied to sound production by the friction of one part of the body against another (Michelson and Nocke, 1974). It is in this sense that it is used here.

28.1.1 Sounds produced as a by-product of some other activity

Many sounds are produced by insects when they are feeding, cleaning or copulating, but there is no evidence that any of these sounds has any particular significance. Sounds produced in flight, however, may have some significance.

The vibration of the wings in flight causes waves of compression and rarefaction in the air and so produces a noise the fundamental frequency of which is the same as the frequency of the wingbeat (Sotavalta, 1963). However, other components may be added to this fundamental frequency as a result of the varied structure of different parts of the wing and the vibration of the thorax and so the overall sound produced is complex and its frequency may bear no simple relationship to the wingbeat frequency.

In insects such as Lepidoptera with a very low wingbeat frequency, of the order of 20 Hz, the sound produced is inaudible to man, but insects with a faster wingbeat produce clearly audible sounds. The flight tone of *Apis* is about 250 Hz and that of culicine mosquitoes from 280 to 350 Hz. The frequency is relatively constant for a particular species, but it may vary with temperature, age and sex (p. 223), while in general smaller species have a higher wingbeat frequency and flight tone than larger species. Hard bodied insects usually produce a higher intensity of sound than soft bodied insects.

The flight noise of a single locust (*Schistocerca*) is a complex sound with frequencies extending from 60 to 6400 Hz although mainly falling between 3200 and 5000 Hz. Pulses of sound are produced at the rate of 17–20 per second, corresponding with the wingbeat frequency. A swarm of *Schistocerca* produces a sound with a widely spread spectrum resembling random noise (Haskell, 1957b).

Sounds are also produced by the wings of certain insects when they are not flying. *Bombus* produces a high frequency sound when it is collecting pollen and *Sceliphron* (Hymenoptera) makes a similar noise when collecting mud to build its nest. These noises are made by very small amplitude movements of the wings when they are folded.

28.1.2 Sounds produced by the impact of part of the body against the substratum

Various insects produce sounds by striking the substratum, mostly without any related structural modifications, although female *Clothilla* (Psocoptera) have a small knob on the ventral surface of the abdomen with which they tap the ground. The death watch beetle, *Xestobium*, produces tapping sounds by bending its head down and banging it against the floor of its burrow in the wood seven or eight times a second. The sounds are produced when the insects are sexually mature. The grasshopper *Oedipoda* drums on the ground with its hind tibia at a rate, in the male, of about 12 beats per second. The female drums more slowly.

Some termites produce sounds by banging parts of the body against the substratum. Soldiers of *Zootermopsis* make vertical oscillating movements using the middle legs as a fulcrum so that the head rocks up and down banging the tips of the mandibles on the floor and, less frequently, the top of the head against the roof. Usually two or three taps are produced successively followed by an interval of about half-a-second before the taps are repeated. Workers and larvae produce a lower intensity sound by hitting their heads on the roof in similar vertical oscillating movements. The sound is produced as a result of outside stimulation, in particular vibration of the substratum, and leads to the release of oscillating movements and tapping by other individuals, so that the behaviour is prolonged and spreads through the colony. The predominant frequency of the sound is about 1000 Hz but this must vary to some extent according to the nature of the wood in which the termites are living (Howse, 1962).

28.1.3 Sounds produced by frictional mechanisms

Many insects produce sounds by rubbing a roughened part of the body against another part. Often it is possible to distinguish a long ridged or roughened file (strigil) from a single scraper (plectrum). Movement of the scraper over the file causes the membrane to which the file is attached to vibrate so that a sound is produced. Frictional mechanisms for sound production are employed by many different orders of insects, but are particularly associated with Orthoptera, Heteroptera and Coleoptera, and in one insect or another almost every part of the body has become modified to produce sound in this way.

Orthoptera

In Orthoptera two main methods of stridulation are employed: elytral stridulation in Grylloidea and Tettigonioidea and femoro-elytral stridulation in Acridoidea. The more unusual methods of sound production are reviewed by Kevan (1955).

In male Grylloidea each elytron has a cubital vein near the base on its underside modified to form a toothed file while on the edge of the opposite elytron is a ridge forming the scraper. The right elytron overlaps the left so that only the right file and left scraper are functional. In producing the sound the elytra are raised at an angle of 15–40° to the body and then opened and closed so that the scraper rasps on the file causing the elytron to vibrate and produce a sound. Sound is produced on closure of the elytra, not when they are opened, each impact between the scraper and a tooth causing the elytral membrane to vibrate. In *Gryllus campestris* the tooth impact rate is about 4 kHz and this corresponds with the natural frequency of the harp, an area of thin, smooth cuticle on the elytra. Hence the sound generated by the tooth impact rate is enhanced and the predominant frequency component of the calling song is at 4 kHz (Fig. 437), but there is an additional component at about 14 kHz which presumably arises from the vibration of some other part of the elytron at its natural frequency. In the courtship song 14 kHz is the principal frequency, corresponding with a higher tooth impact rate, but there are additional components with much higher frequencies (Nocke, 1972). Sound is produced by both elytra, each wing closure producing a single pulse of sound.

The calling songs of all the crickets studied have principal components of relatively low frequency, between 2 and 10 kHz (Walker and Carlysle, 1975), and presumably in all cases this represents the tooth impact rate enhanced by the corresponding natural frequency of some part of the elytra.

Each species of cricket has a number of different songs used in different situations (p. 698). These songs can be differentiated by the rate at which pulses of sound are produced, the pulse repetition frequency (Fig. 438), and by the frequency of the sounds although both of these parameters increase with temperature (Fig. 439). The increase in pulse repetition frequency with temperature may result solely from a more rapid opening of the elytra so that more sound-producing closures are possible in unit time as

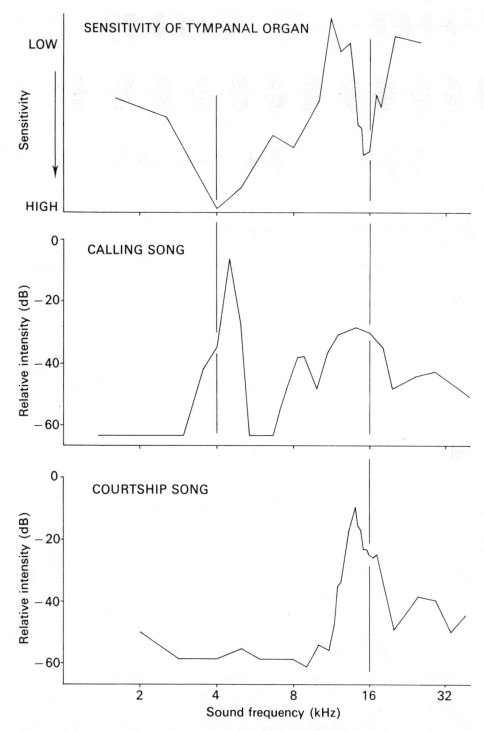

Fig. 437 Frequency spectra of the calling and courtship songs of *Gryllus campestris* and the sensitivity of the tympanal organs (after Nocke, 1972)

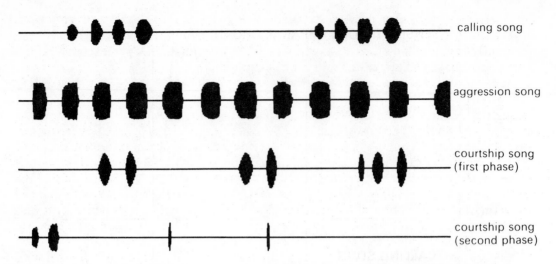

Fig. 438 Oscillograms of different songs of *Gryllus campestris* (from Haskell, 1974)

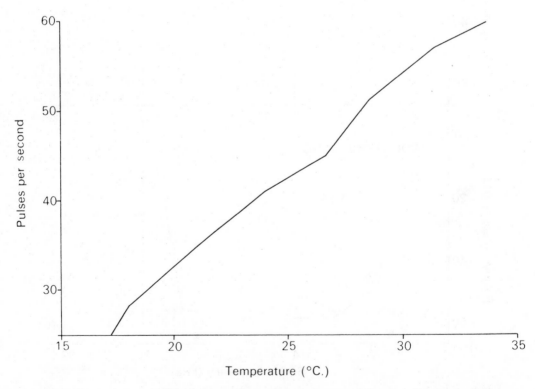

Fig. 439 Relationship between temperature and the pulse rate of the song of *Oecanthus* (after Walker, 1962)

in *Oecanthus*, or they may also involve a reduction in the number of file teeth employed so that short, rapid closing strokes of the elytra occur as in *Gryllus rubens*.

Female gryllids do not usually possess stridulatory apparatus, but male larvae of the later instars have the apparatus and may stridulate.

Some gryllids have developed mechanisms by which the low frequency sounds that they produce are amplified. *Oecanthus burmeisteri* emits a sound with a frequency of about 2000 Hz and a wavelength of 170 mm. The sound producing membrane on the wings is only 3·2 mm in diameter, so it is not an efficient radiator of such low frequency sound because the waves of compression and rarefaction of the air on the two sides of the membrane largely cancel each other out. The efficiency of sound production is increased by the use of a baffle which effectively separates the air on the two sides of the membrane. The insect cuts a small hole in a leaf and when singing it sits with its head projecting through the hole and its elytra tightly pressed against the leaf surface. It uses leaves ranging in size from 70 × 80 mm to 170 × 300 mm, so that even the smallest forms an efficient baffle (Prozesky-Schulze *et al.*, 1975).

Gryllotalpa vineae digs a singing burrow in the form of an exponential horn with two openings (Fig. 440). The dimensions of the horn are such that when the forewings are raised in the singing position they form a diaphragm across it. The sound produced by the wings, with a fundamental frequency of 3·5 kHz, is amplified and muscular energy is converted to acoustic power with very great efficiency. As a result the sound

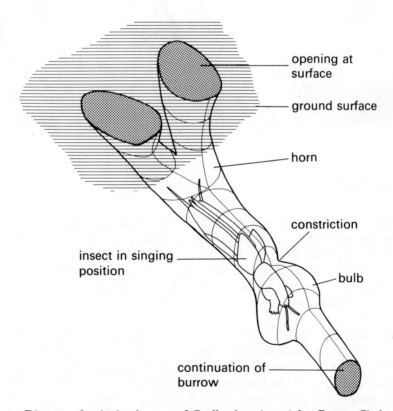

opening at surface

ground surface

horn

constriction

insect in singing position

bulb

continuation of burrow

Fig. 440 Diagram of a singing burrow of *Gryllotalpa vineae* (after Bennet-Clark, 1970)

carries over great distances, up to 600 m, and because of the tuning of the burrow the song is purer than when the insect is removed from the burrow. The sound is beamed in an arc by the arrangement of the openings of the burrow (Bennet-Clark, 1970).

The stridulatory apparatus of Tettigonioidea is similar to that of gryllids, but the left elytron overlaps the right and, in most fully-winged forms, only the left file and the right scraper are present. In some species, however, in which the hind wings are absent and the elytra are short and rounded (Fig. 441), being retained only for the production of sound, a file and scraper are present on each elytron, although only the left file is functional. Close to the stridulatory apparatus on one or both elytra is an area of thin, clear cuticle known as the mirror and this may be surrounded by other areas of thin cuticle.

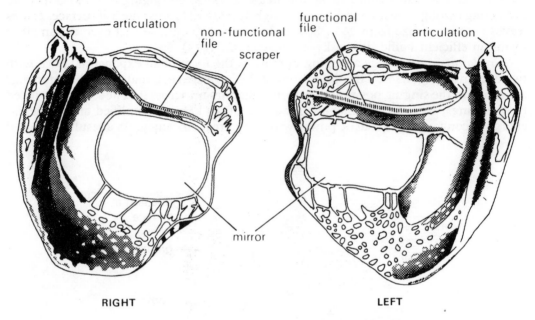

Fig. 441 Elytra of male *Ephippiger* from the ventral surface (after Dumortier, 1963a)

As in gryllids, sound is generally produced on wing closure, but sometimes, as in some individuals of *Platycleis intermedia* and in *Ephippiger* (Fig. 442), a pulse of sound is also produced on wing opening. Not all the file teeth are employed in producing a pulse. *Platycleis intermedia* has, on average, 77 teeth on the file and produces a syllable of three pulses, one pulse on opening the wings and two on subsequent closures. These pulses employ, respectively, only 31 %, 41 % and 67 % of the file teeth (Samways, 1976).

In tettigoniids each tooth impact causes the elytron to vibrate. Different parts vibrate with their own natural frequencies, so the sounds produced extend over a wide range of frequencies (Fig. 443). In *Platycleis intermedia* the main component of the song is in the range 15–30 kHz, but frequencies as high as 120 kHz have been recorded and a lower frequency component, modulating from 500 Hz to 1500 Hz and back, probably derives directly from the tooth impact rate. The main sound radiator in *Ruspolia* is the frame of the mirror. The distal part of the frame is surrounded

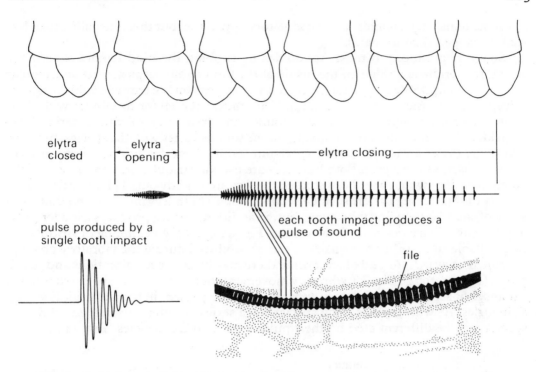

Fig. 442 Stridulation in *Ephippiger* showing the movements of the elytra in relation to sound production; detail of part of the left elytron showing the file and an oscillogram of a short train of sound waves (a pulse) produced by a single tooth impact (modified after Pasquinelly and Busnel, 1955)

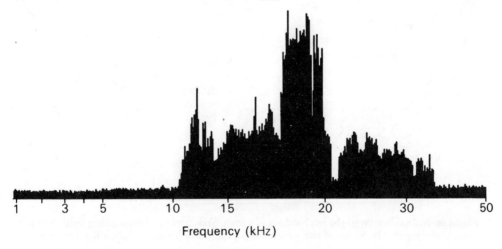

Fig. 443 Frequency spectrum of the song of *Ephippiger* (after Dumortier, 1963b)

by thin cuticle and so is free to vibrate at its natural frequency of 16 kHz producing the principal component of the song. The membrane of the mirror hardly emits any sound (Bailey, 1970). In *Conocephalus*, on the other hand, the mirror does play some part in sound radiation. Only the right elytron of *Ruspolia* is involved in sound radiation.

Some female tettigoniids have stridulatory apparatus, but this is usually much less well developed than in males.

Sound is produced in most Acridoidea by rubbing the hind femora against the elytra. In Acridinae a ridge on the inside of the hind femur rasps against an irregular intercalary vein, while in Gomphocerinae a row of pegs on the femur is rubbed against ridged veins on the elytron (Fig. 444). This causes the elytra to vibrate with their natural frequency and so produce a sound, the frequency of which varies from 2–50 kHz. To some extent the frequency of the sounds varies with the species, but even in a single insect a wide frequency spectrum results from the different resonances of different parts of the elytra. Both hind legs are used in stridulation, but in most of the Gomphocerinae which have been studied the legs are slightly out of phase and produce slightly different song patterns. In *Chorthippus mollis* both legs move up and down in a series of sound-producing vibrations, but, in addition, one leg produces a louder pulse of sound by a sharp downward movement (Fig. 448). At the beginning of stridulation each syllable consists of 10–12 pairs of pulses produced during the vibratory phase of movement; towards the end of an echeme there may be 26–28 leg vibrations and sound pulses (Elsner, 1974). Similar vibratory movements of the femur have been recorded in a number of acridids. Stridulatory apparatus is often present in female acridids as well as in males. As with gryllids, each species has a series of different songs and different species may be differentiated by their pulse repetition frequencies (Fig. 445).

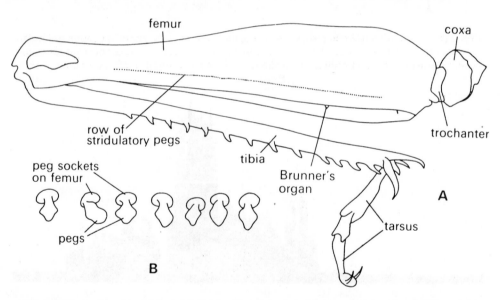

Fig. 444 A. Inside view of the left hind leg of a male *Stenobothrus* showing the position of the stridulatory pegs. B. Some of the stridulatory pegs much enlarged (after Roscow, 1963)

Many other stridulatory mechanisms occur in other Acridoidea and a single example from the Pneumoridae is given. Here the file consists of a series of radial ribs on the side of the third abdominal segment (Fig. 446). This is rubbed by a row of denticles on the inside of the hind femur, the dilated abdomen of these grasshoppers possibly acting as a sounding box and amplifying the sound (Kevan, 1955).

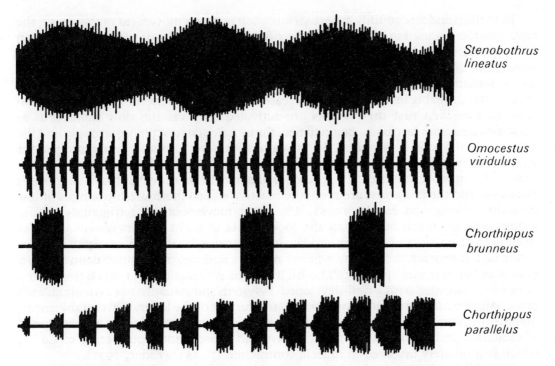

Fig. 445 Oscillograms of the calling or normal songs of the males of four common British grasshoppers. The oscillogram of *Chorthippus parallelus* represents one phrase of the song, which is made up of a series of such phrases. Time scale for each trace about three seconds (after Haskell, 1957a)

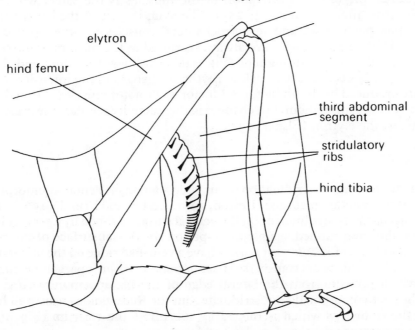

Fig. 446 Lateral view of the left side of the base of the abdomen of a male *Pneumora* showing the stridulatory apparatus (from Kevan, 1955)

In gryllids and tettigoniids, where stridulation involves movement of the wings, the same muscles are used in both flight and stridulation. Wing closure during stridulation by a cricket is produced by the indirect dorso-ventral muscles which produce the upstroke in flight (p. 217); wing opening, the equivalent of the downstroke, involves the dorsal longitudinal muscles and the direct wing muscles. The intensity of sound produced is probably increased by an increase in activity of all the muscles (Bentley and Kutsch, 1966). At first the muscles are activated only via the slow axons, but as excitation increases fast axons begin to fire, the muscles contract more strongly and the intensity of the song is increased. In the aggressive song excitation is maintained for longer than in calling by the presence of the intruding male, so that each chirp consists of a greater number of pulses. The presence of a female, on the other hand, suppresses excitation and the fast axons are normally inactive and so the courtship song is of low intensity (Ewing and Hoyle, 1965). The wing movements of tettigoniids during stridulation are much faster than the movements in flight and in *Neoconocephalus robustus* the frequency of opening and closing may exceed 200/s. This activity is under direct neural control, though most insect muscles undergo a sustained contraction if stimulated at this rate (p. 261). The high rate of contraction and relaxation of the muscles is associated with a well-developed T-system and sarcoplasmic reticulum, each muscle fibril being surrounded by a perforated curtain of the latter. This arrangement, together with the small size of the fibres, minimises the time taken for the inward spread of excitation and facilitates the rapid release and subsequent sequestering of Ca^{++}, which is intimately involved in muscle contraction (p. 253) (Elder, 1971).

In acridids, where stridulation is produced by movements of the femora, muscles at the pleurocoxal and coxotrochanteral joints are involved. Some of these muscles have a dual function, since they also move the wings during flight. In all the grasshopper species studied the order of activation of the muscles is the same, with fast units becoming active after slow units (p. 255). The main levator of the leg is a tergocoxal muscle, while pleurocoxal and tergotrochanteral muscles are the main depressors (Fig. 447). These three muscles are always recruited at the beginning of stridulation and are phasically active throughout (Fig. 448). Additional levators and depressors may subsequently become active, while rhythmic changes in the intensity of the song pattern are produced by the abductor, adductor and rotator muscles of the coxa. These are tonically active throughout, but changes in their activity regulate the pressure of the femur against the elytron (Elsner, 1975).

Heteroptera

Frictional mechanisms of stridulation occur widely amongst Pentatomomorpha, where 15 different methods are recorded (Leston, 1957; Leston and Pringle, 1963). The most common mechanisms involve a file on the ventral surface rubbed by a scraper on the leg or a file on the wing rubbed against a scraper on the dorsal surface of the body. For instance, both sexes of *Kleidocerys resedae* have a vein-like ridge on the underside of the hind wing. This ridge bears transverse striations about 1·7 μm apart and is rubbed on a scraper which projects from the lateral edge of the metapostnotum (Fig. 449). In general the Cimicomorpha do not stridulate, but the Reduvioidea nearly all have a file between the front legs which is rasped by the tip of the rostrum (Fig. 450). This apparatus is present in males, females and larvae.

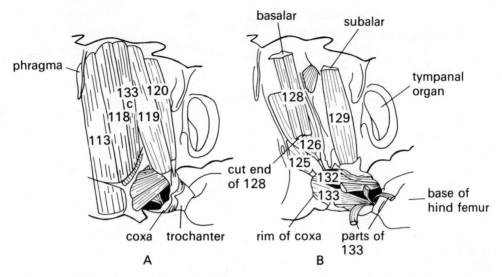

Fig. 447 The muscles used in stridulation by a grasshopper: A. the indirect flight muscles; B. the direct flight muscles. Numbers of muscles correspond with those shown in Fig. 448

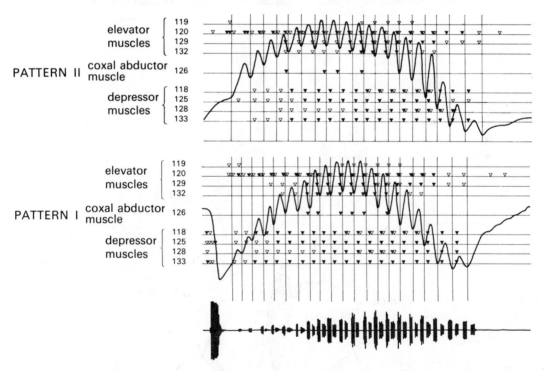

Fig. 448 Stridulation by *Chorthippus mollis*. The heavy line represents the movements of the femora during one complete up and down stroke. Pattern I is produced by one leg and pattern II by the other. Each triangle represents the recruitment of the muscle indicated. ▼ represents recruitment of all fast units; ▽ represents recruitment of some fast units or of slow units only (after Elsner, 1975)

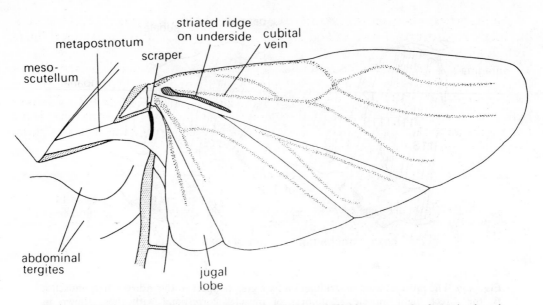

Fig. 449 The wing and part of the thorax and abdomen of *Kleidocerys resedae* from the dorsal surface showing the stridulatory apparatus (modified after Leston, 1957)

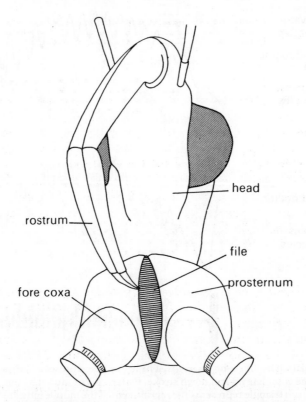

Fig. 450 Ventral view of the head and prosternum of *Coranus* (Heteroptera) showing the tip of the rostrum rasping against the intercoxal file (from Dumortier, 1963a)

Amphibicorisae are not known to stridulate, with the possible exception of Veliidae, but many Hydrocorisae, *Corixa* and *Notonecta*, for instance, are known to stridulate both in air and water.

The sounds produced by reduviids are of an irregular, unorganised nature (Fig. 451), but in other Heteroptera the songs are organised and show specific differences. Some, such as *Sehirus*, are known to have different songs with different pulse repetition frequencies. The fundamental frequency of the sound produced is the same as the natural frequency of the cuticular structure excited and the pulse repetition frequency equals the impact frequency of the file teeth.

Fig. 451 Oscillogram of the sound produced by a fourth instar larva of *Coranus*. Total trace lasting about 0.7 seconds (after Haskell, 1961)

Amongst Homoptera frictional methods of stridulation occur in *Toxoptera*, an aphid, and most Psyllidae.

Coleoptera

Stridulation using a frictional mechanism occurs in many beetles, especially amongst Carabidae, Scarabaeidae, Tenebrionidae and Curculionidae. Many different parts of the body are used to produce sounds in different species, but most commonly the elytra are involved. In *Oxycheila*, for instance, there is a striated ridge along the edge of the elytron which is rubbed by a ridged area on the hind femur.

Larval Lucanidae, Passalidae and Geotrupidae also stridulate, rubbing a series of ridges on the coxa of the middle legs with a scraper on the trochanter of the hind leg. In larval passalids the hind leg is greatly reduced to function as a scraper and is no longer used in locomotion (Fig. 452).

Lepidoptera

Some adult Lepidoptera, such as *Nymphalis io*, produce a grating sound when at rest by rubbing the veins on the wings together (p. 145). The sound lasts for about 100 ms and has a broad frequency spectrum. This species also produces high intensity clicks lasting only 30–100μs with a frequency of 30–60 kHz. Apparently the sound is produced by rubbing the base of the subcostal vein against the body (Mohl and Miller, 1976). *Heliothis* also makes ultrasonic clicks lasting up to 400 μs when the tips of the wings make contact with each other at the top of the upstroke during vigorous flight (Agee, 1971). *Thecophora* has a specialised vein on the hind wing which is rasped by the modified tarsus of the hind leg, and various other forms of stridulatory apparatus occur.

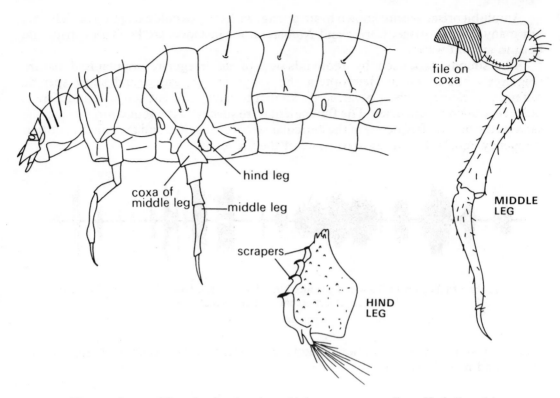

Fig. 452 Larva of *Passalus* showing the stridulatory apparatus (from Haskell, 1961)

Three main types of stridulation occur in lepidopterous pupae, excluding the probably adventitious sounds produced by the movement of the pupa in the cocoon (Hinton, 1948). In ten families, notably the Hesperiidae, Papilionidae, Lymantriidae and Saturniidae there are coarse transverse ridges on the anterior edges of certain abdominal segments against which fine tubercles on the posterior edges of the preceding segments are rubbed by movements of the abdomen. In Noctuidae the pupa may have rough areas on the head, thorax and abdomen which are rubbed against the inside of the cocoon or the inside of the cocoon itself may be ridged so that wriggling movements of the pupa produce a scraping sound. The pupa of *Gangara thyrsis*, a hesperiid, has a pair of transverse ridges on either side of the ventral midline of the fifth abdominal segment. The long proboscis extends between and beyond these ridges and is itself transversely striated, so that when the abdomen contracts it rubs against the ridges and produces a hiss.

Other groups

Relatively isolated instances of frictional stridulation are widespread in other groups of insects. A few examples will be given.

The larva of *Epiophlebia* (Odonata) has lateral ridged areas on abdominal segments three to seven. These are rubbed by the ridged inner side of the hind femur to produce a sound. Similarly, larval *Hydropsyche* (Trichoptera) have ridges on the side of the head and a scraper on the front femur (Johnstone, 1964). Amongst ants stridulation occurs in Ponerinae, Dorylinae and primitive Myrmicinae, striations at the base of the gaster being rubbed by a ridge on the petiole (Fig. 453). Finally in the Tephritidae (Diptera) stridulation is probably widespread. In the male of *Dacus tryoni* the cubito-anal area of each wing vibrates dorso-ventrally across two rows of 20–24 bristles on the third abdominal segment, thus producing a noise.

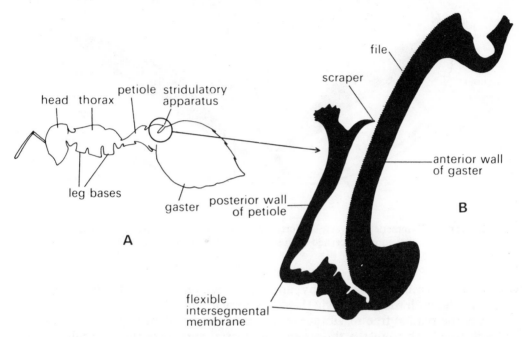

Fig. 453 A. Outline drawing of *Myrmica* showing the position of the stridulatory apparatus. B. Diagrammatic sagittal section through the cuticle of the stridulatory apparatus, highly magnified (from Dumortier, 1963a)

28.1.4 Sounds produced by a vibrating membrane

Sounds produced by the vibration of a membrane driven directly by muscles are common amongst Homoptera and also occur in some Heteroptera, Pentatomidae, and some Lepidoptera, Arctiidae. The mechanism is most fully studied in Cicadidae (Pringle, 1954), where it is normally restricted to the males, but is sometimes also functional in females.

In the dorso-lateral region of the first segment of *Platypleura* (Cicadidae) there is on each side an area of very thin cuticle supported by a thick cuticular rim and a series of dorso-ventral strengthening ribs. This area of cuticle forms the tymbal (Fig. 454) and it is protected by a forward extension of the abdomen forming the tymbal cover. Internally a cuticular compression strut runs from the ventral surface to the posterior edge of the supporting rim and a fibrillar tymbal muscle (p. 251), running parallel with the compression strut, arises ventrally and is inserted into an apodeme attached to the

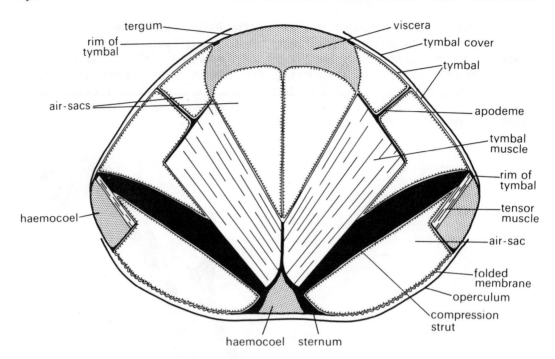

Fig. 454 Diagrammatic transverse section of the first abdominal segment of a cicada showing the main structures concerned with sound production (based on Pringle, 1954)

tymbal. The tymbal is backed by an air-sac which surrounds the muscle and communicates with the outside via the metathoracic spiracle. The presence of the air-sac leaves the tymbal free to vibrate with a minimum of damping.

Projecting back from the thorax on the ventral surface is the operculum, which encloses a cavity containing the tympanum (p. 721) and an area of thin, corrugated cuticle, the folded membrane, which separates the air-sacs from the cavity beneath the operculum. When the abdomen is raised the membrane is stretched.

Sound is produced when the tymbal muscle contracts, pulling on the tymbal so that it buckles inwards producing a click as it does so. On relaxation of the muscle the tymbal returns to its original position by virtue of the elasticity of the surrounding cuticle and so produces a second click. Thus, under experimental conditions, a double click of sound is produced by each muscle contraction (Fig. 455), although the amplitude of the IN click is much lower than that of the OUT click. Under normal conditions, however, this is altered by changes in the tension of the tymbal so that the IN click becomes much stronger and the OUT is lost in the sound of the IN.

The tymbal muscle contracts myogenically (p. 261), so that stimulation by a single nervous impulse produces a series of contractions and hence a series of sound pulses, the repetition frequency of which equals the frequency of muscle contraction. In *Platypleura capitata* a stimulus frequency of 120/s produces a pulse repetition frequency of 390/s.

The frequency of the sound produced is determined by the natural frequency of the tymbal, which in the case of *P. capitata* is about 4500 Hz, and in some species there are

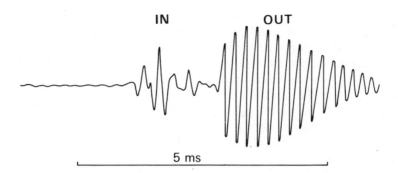

Fig. 455 Double click produced under experimental conditions by an IN-OUT movement of
the tymbal of a cicada (after Pringle, 1954)

harmonics due to the complexity of the membrane. The air-sacs are approximately
resonant to the frequency of the tymbal so that the intensity of the sound produced is
increased.

The mechanism is similar in all the species studied, but each has a different
repetition frequency due to differences in the tension of the tymbal. Running from a
backwardly projecting knob on the metathorax to the anterior rim of the tymbal is the
tensor muscle. When this contracts it pulls the rim of the tymbal so that the curvature of
the latter is increased; this has the effect of raising the amplitude of the sound produced
but lowering the pulse repetition frequency. Contraction of the tensor muscle or of
certain accessory muscles also raises the abdomen, stretching the folded membrane and
increasing the space between the abdomen and the operculum. This alters the resonant
frequency of the air-sacs so that they can be roughly tuned to the tymbal to increase the
intensity of sound. Each species apparently has a characteristic and inherent pattern of
activity of these different muscles and so despite the possession of similar organs each
species produces its own characteristic song.

The two tymbals work synchronously. In the first instance this must be due to
simultaneous nervous stimulation of the muscles, but they also remain in phase during
the myogenic contractions of the tymbal muscles. Possibly this is a mechanical effect
arising from the close proximity of the ventral attachments of the tymbal muscles of the
two sides. While the insect is singing certain ventral muscles running to the sternum
contract so as to crease the tympanum. In this way damage to the auditory system by the
high intensity of sound is avoided.

Contraction of the tymbal muscles is not myogenic in all cicadas: in *Magicicada* and
in *Fidicina* it is purely neurogenic. *Fidicina* produces 400–600 clicks/s and this high
rate is achieved by the tymbals of the two sides being out of phase. The tymbal muscles
contract about 100 times/s with separate clicks in the IN and OUT movements of the
tymbal. The sequence is thus:

$$\text{IN}_{\text{LEFT}} - \text{OUT}_{\text{LEFT}} - \text{IN}_{\text{RIGHT}} - \text{OUT}_{\text{RIGHT}} - \text{IN}_{\text{LEFT}} -$$

There is no change in the contraction rate of the tymbal muscles in different songs, but
the intensity of the sound produced is varied by changes in the tension of the tensor
muscles (Aidley, 1969).

Amongst other Homoptera a tymbal mechanism is present in the males of all the
Auchenorrhyncha examined and in both sexes of many families. In these insects the

tymbals are not backed by air-sacs and so damping of the tymbals is very high and the intensity of sound produced very low (Ossiannilsson, 1949).

The tymbals of Pentatomidae are membranes on the dorso-lateral surfaces of the fused first and second abdominal terga with an air-sac beneath. Each tymbal is buckled by the contraction of a dorso-ventral muscle producing a click which, in *Carpocoris*, has a frequency of 150–200 Hz, and a pulse repetition frequency of 9–12/sec. The tymbals usually occur in both sexes, although often only those of the male are functional.

A comparable mechanism exists in some Arctiidae (Lepidoptera) where the tymbal is formed by a thin area of cuticle on the side of the metathorax (Fig. 456) (Blest *et al.*, 1963). This is covered in scales posteriorly, but anteriorly has a band of parallel horizontal striations, which vary in number in *Melese* from 15 to 20. In other species there may be as many as 60 striations. The main effector muscle is the coxo-basalar

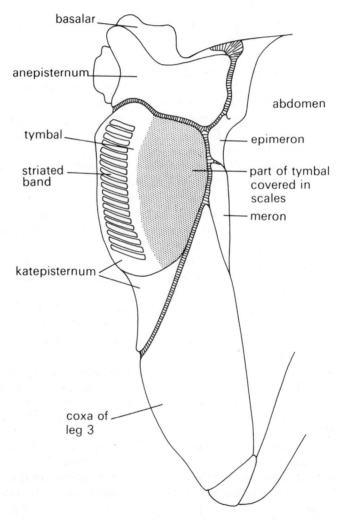

Fig. 456 Diagram of the left side of the metathorax of *Melese*, showing the position of the tymbal relative to the adjacent sclerites (after Blest *et al.*, 1963)

muscle. When this contracts the tymbal buckles inwards, starting dorsally and proceeding along the length of the striated band, each stria being stressed to the point of buckling and then suddenly giving way. Thus each stria acts as a microtymbal and the buckling of each produces a pulse of sound, so that the tymbal as a whole produces a sequence of 12–20 pulses. When the muscles relax the tymbal springs out due to the elasticity of the surrounding cuticle and a further series of pulses is produced. The sounds produced on the IN movement show a progressive fall in frequency, those on the OUT movement a progressive rise (Fig. 457). Such cycles of modulation occur in bursts of 1 to 20 with an average of 2·4 bursts per second. Most of the sound produced lies within a range of frequencies from 30–90 kHz, but the overall spectrum extends from 11 to 160 kHz.

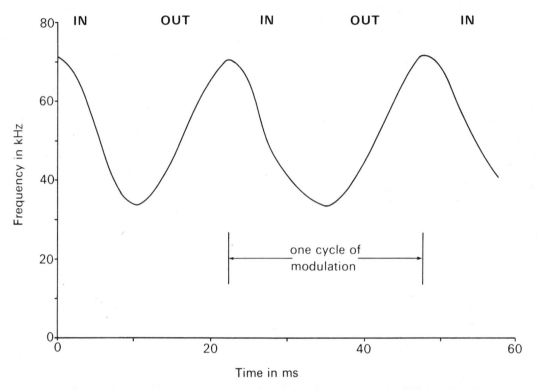

Fig. 457 Graph showing the cycles of modulation of the principal frequency component of the song of *Melese*. Each cycle is produced by an IN-OUT movement of the tymbal (after Blest *et al.*, 1963)

In quite a different category is the piping of queen bees. This sound is probably produced by vibration of the thoracic sclerites (Wenner, 1964) and so may be regarded as a vibrating membrane mechanism. The sound is only produced by virgin queens, the tendency to pipe being lost as the eggs mature, or by queens which are no longer ovipositing. The piping of free virgin queens consists of a phrase starting with a long pulse of sound followed by a series of short pulses with a fundamental frequency of 500 Hz together with harmonics. Queens still enclosed in their larval cells also pipe, but their piping consists only of short pulses at a lower frequency.

28.1.5 Sound produced by a pulsed air stream

The only well documented example of a sound produced by a pulsed air stream is the stridulation of *Acherontia* (Lepidoptera). Air is sucked through the proboscis by dilation of the pharynx causing the epipharynx to vibrate and create a pulsed air stream (Fig. 458A). In this way a sound with a frequency of about 280 Hz is produced. Contraction of the pharynx with the epipharynx held erect expels the air producing a high-pitched whistle (Fig. 458B). These sequences are repeated rapidly. The cockroach *Gromphadorhina* produces a hiss by forcing air out through the spiracles.

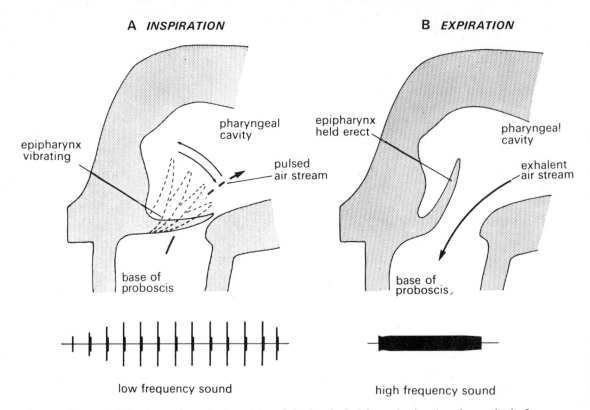

Fig. 458 Diagrammatic sagittal sections of the head of *Acherontia* showing the method of sound production, and oscillograms of the sound produced on inspiration and expiration (from Dumortier, 1963a)

28.1.6 Intensity of the sound produced

Relatively little work has been carried out on the intensities of the sounds produced by insects, but as some measure of this the distance over which a sound can be heard can be used. This distance will vary according to the sensitivity of the receiver, but the human ear can detect acridids at a distance of one or two metres, *Nemobius sylvestris* (Orthoptera) from eight metres, *Tettigonia viridissima* (Orthoptera) from 100 m and *Gryllotalpa* (Orthoptera) from 600 m.

28.2 Significance of the sounds produced

The sounds produced by insects can be classified according to whether they represent signals to other species, that is they are extraspecific, or whether they are signals to other members of the same species, that is they are intraspecific.

28.2.1 Sounds having extraspecific significance

Sounds having extraspecific significance are usually unorganised sounds having no regular pulse repetition frequency (Fig. 451) and covering a broad spectrum of frequencies. Usually they are produced by both males and females and sometimes also by the larvae. Sounds of this type, which include, for instance, the stridulation of reduviids, beetles and lepidopterous pupae, are presumed to be concerned with defence and warning, perhaps alarming a potential predator or warning other members of the species of the presence of a predator.

Sometimes warning stridulation accompanies other types of display as in the hissing noise produced by the opening of the wings of the peacock butterfly to display the eyespots (p. 145). Similarly in Arctiidae sound production is associated with a display of warning colours. These are distasteful species and it is generally true that sounds are more readily elicited from the less distasteful species amongst them, these being the forms which most need to reinforce their display if predators are to learn to avoid them. Noises associated with visual display are also produced by some mantids and grasshoppers.

There is also the suggestion that sound mimicry occurs. Not only do certain syrphids look like bees, they also sound like them (Sotavalta, 1963), and Lane and Rothschild (1965) suggest that the sounds produced by *Necrophorus* when it is disturbed are similar to those of a torpid bumble bee, to which the beetle also bears a superficial visual resemblance.

It is suggested that the sounds produced by the tymbals of Noctuidae (p. 694) are added to the echoes of the sounds made by bats and so have the effect of disrupting the echolocation systems of the bats while they are hunting for moths (Blest *et al.*, 1963).

28.2.2 Sounds having intraspecific significance

Sounds having intraspecific significance are organised sounds with a regular pulse repetition frequency. Often they are concerned with courtship and in many of these cases only the males stridulate.

Courtship

The role of song in insect courtship has been most fully studied in Orthoptera, but is also important in Heteroptera and Cicadidae. The Orthoptera have five main classes of song concerned with calling, courtship, copulation, aggression and alarm, and differing from each other in the pulse repetition frequency and the form of the pulse (Fig. 438). In the grasshoppers the female responds to the male only at certain times depending on her state of physiological development. She is not responsive until she is sexually mature or for a period of some 24 h before oviposition, but the responsive state is regained soon after oviposition. Responsiveness is also inhibited by copulation, perhaps through some chemical factor associated with the sperm, but is recovered after an interval of some days. Responsiveness finally disappears a few days before death. The female only stridulates when she is in the responsive state.

The sexual behaviour of *Chorthippus brunneus* is fairly characteristic of that of the British grasshoppers. If a female in the responsive state hears the song of a male she sings in reply, her song being similar to the male's calling song. The two insects orientate and move towards each other, stopping to sing at intervals and thus carrying out a mutual search which eventually leads to their becoming visible to each other. When the male sees the female he starts to sing his courtship song, but if a second male intervenes during this period they sing an aggressive rivals song until one of the contestants leaves. During the courtship song the male makes hopping movements, finally hopping on to the female and attempting to copulate with her. If he is not accepted he starts the courtship song again. If the female becomes disturbed or starts to move during copulation the male sings his copulation song, which has the effect of quietening her.

Other groups, such as the Pentatomomorpha and Tephritidae, are similar in that the song leads to a meeting of the sexes, but usually there is no female stridulation, only the male singing so that the female moves towards him. In mosquitoes the converse is true. The male of *Aedes aegypti* responds to the flight tone of the female and is attracted to her as a result. Immature females are not attractive, having a lower flight tone, but this reaches the attractive pitch as the female matures and subsequently she remains attractive for the rest of her life. The male can distinguish the female flight tone from a high level of background noise.

The knocking of *Xestobium* and the clicks of male *Oedipoda* in flight are also sexual signals.

Sexual isolation and aggregation

The different songs of different species of grasshoppers, crickets and cicadas have the effect of enhancing the isolation of species due to other factors. Usually, it is believed, the difference in song has arisen after species have become morphologically isolated, but in the two grasshoppers *Chorthippus brunneus* and *C. biguttulus* it is believed that the differences in song are of major importance in isolating the species from each other. These two species are very similar to each other and are only separated morphologically by a few small non-overlapping characters. They are not separated ecologically and have the same mating behaviour, so that crossing readily occurs in the laboratory with the production of viable offspring. There is thus no morphological incompatibility, but very little crossing occurs in the field. The major difference between the species is in their songs, which have a stimulating and orientating influence specific to their own species. For instance, in the presence of its own specific song a male moves faster and makes more attempts at copulation while a female is more ready to copulate than in the presence of the song of the other species. These behavioural factors result in an effective isolation of the two species (Perdeck, 1958).

In some insects sounds lead to aggregation. This occurs in cicadas which have one song leading to aggregation of males and females and resulting in a clumping of the species within a habitat so that particular trees may be occupied by a particular species. Thus in North America three species of *Magicicada* occur in the same habitat. In the laboratory interspecific crossing frequently occurs, but this is not the case in the field, where aggregation of each species occurs as a result of their different songs and the tendency for the different species to sing in chorus mainly at different times of day (Fig. 459). In this way interspecific contacts are reduced and sexual isolation is achieved (Alexander and Moore, 1962). The cicadas of Ceylon have in general only one song, which is concerned with aggregation, but the North American species also have a courtship song.

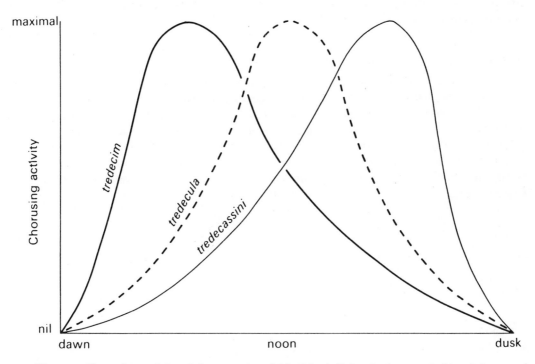

Fig. 459 Chorusing activity of three species of *Magicicada* living in the same habitat (after Alexander and Moore, 1962)

The songs of grasshoppers also lead to aggregation. If a male or female is isolated for 24 h it orientates and moves towards a source emitting its own song, continuing to move until it is within sight of the singing group (Haskell, 1957a, 1958).

Aggressive stridulation

Aggressive stridulation is well illustrated by crickets. Each male of *Oecanthus* has a territory of some 50 cm² in which he sings his normal song. If another cricket intrudes the male sings an aggressive song quite distinct from other songs (Fig. 438) and the intruding male replies. Fighting may occur, the males lashing each other with their antennae, sparring and biting until one male retires. The dominant males in a colony stridulate more in aggression than others less high in the hierarchy and at the end of an encounter the dominating male may continue to stridulate (Alexander, 1961). Larval passalids also exhibit aggressive stridulation (Alexander *et al.*, 1963).

The rivalry song of grasshoppers is also aggressive and in the course of this the two males commonly chirp alternately in a regular manner. Such distinct alternation results from the song of one male temporarily inhibiting, and therefore delaying, the song of the other, whose song in turn delays the next chirp of the first individual. In this way the alternating chirps become clearly separated and follow each other in a regular manner (Jones, 1966).

Aggressive stridulation probably has the effect of spacing the males over the largest possible area and at the same time reduces interference during mating (p. 359). The alternation of singing in some species may help an approaching female to locate the male by minimising background noise.

Sound communication in social and semi-social insects

In some social and semi-social insects sounds may be concerned in aspects of communication other than courtship and successful mating. *Apis* workers, for instance, produce a pulsed sound during the straight run of their dance and the number of pulses and total period of sound production is proportional to the distance from the food (Fig. 460). These sounds may be used, perhaps together with the number of waggles in the straight run, to indicate the distance of the food to other members of the colony. Sound might be more important than vision in the dark of the hive and since other workers tend to touch the thorax of the dancing bee they may be perceiving vibrations

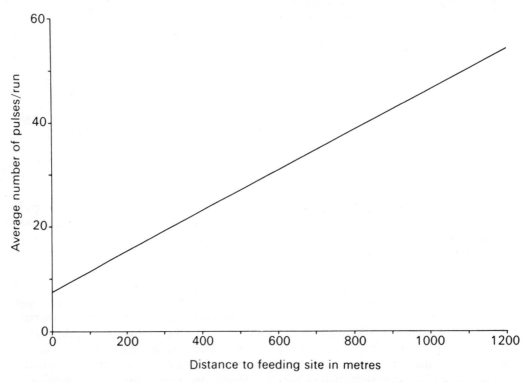

Fig. 460 Relationship between the average number of pulses produced by bees during the straight run of their dance and the distance of the feeding station from the hive (after Wenner, 1962)

of the thorax which are perhaps concerned with sound production (Wenner, 1962, 1964).

Returning foragers of *Melipona* produce a characteristic buzz when they are given syrup and when they return to the hive. This sound might stimulate other bees not in physical contact with the returning forager. It may be perceived through vibration of the substratum rather than carriage through the air and experimental colonies in sound-proofed hives in which vibration was eliminated soon died out. This suggests that the sounds are playing an essential role in the transmission of information within the colony.

The piping of queen bees may be important in informing the colony of the presence of a virgin queen in the colony and indicating whether she is free or still enclosed within the cell.

In locusts the flight noise may be of some social significance. For instance, the noise of a passing swarm of *Schistocerca* may stimulate other, settled locusts to take off. Once in the air the swarm noise might have some effect in maintaining flight and possibly also in the maintenance of swarm cohesion. If a locust tends to stray away from the swarm it soon passes beyond the range, about five metres, at which it can hear the rest of the swarm. Unequal stimulation might result in the locust turning back towards the noise and so back into the swarm, but there is no doubt that other stimuli are also important in swarm cohesion (Haskell, 1957b). The noise of an individual locust is audible to others from a distance of two or three metres. Locusts in swarms seem to fly at a preferred distance from their fellows and it is possible that the sound of another individual locust might have a repelling effect and so stop locusts getting too close to each other.

The sounds produced by *Zootermopsis* (p.677) are important as a warning to other members of the colony, being initiated by any disturbance and especially by vibration of the substratum. The sound leads to the retreat of other members of the colony to the remoter parts of the nest (Howse, 1962).

28.3 Control of sound production

Insects start to stridulate as a result of a balance between external and internal stimuli. The external stimuli include the physical factors of the environment. Temperature may be limiting; grasshoppers only sing when the air temperature is high or the solar radiation intense (Richards and Waloff, 1954). Light is also important in some species: some species of tettigoniid are nocturnal, others diurnal. Stridulation tends to be restricted to certain times of day in both North American and Sri Lankan cicadas (Fig. 459) and a rhythm may appear in the time of singing which, although not directly related to the environmental conditions, is derived from them.

Within the limits set by the physical environment biological factors are of great importance in initiating song. The most important external biological stimuli are visual, auditory and tactile. The sight or sound of another member of the species may lead to singing, the type of song, whether courtship or aggression, depending on the situation and sexes of the insects. Tactile stimuli are important in eliciting the warning stridulation of bugs and beetles.

Internal factors are also of great importance. Male grasshoppers only sing when they are sexually mature and there is a brief interruption of singing after copulation. In

Ephippiger the interruption is much longer, lasting three to five days, while male *Gryllus campestris* only sing when they are carrying a spermatophore. After copulation, when the spermatophore is transferred to the female, singing stops until a new spermatophore is passed into the spermatophore sac.

Female grasshoppers only sing when they are in a responsive state. Possibly this is under hormonal control since the removal of the ovaries of a mature female results in a loss of responsiveness, but responsiveness is restored following the injection of blood from another responsive female (Haskell, 1960). In *Gomphocerus* a secretion from the corpora allata regulates responsiveness.

REFERENCES

AGEE, H. R. (1971). Ultrasound produced by wings of adults of *Heliothis zea. J. Insect Physiol.* **17**: 1267–1273.

AIDLEY, D. J. (1969). Sound production in Brazilian cicada. *J. exp. Biol.* **51**: 325–337.

ALEXANDER, R. D. (1961). Aggressiveness, territoriality, and sexual behaviour in field crickets (Orthoptera: Gryllidae). *Behaviour* **17**: 130–223.

ALEXANDER, R. D. (1967). Acoustical communication in Arthropods. *A. Rev. Ent.* **12**: 495–526.

ALEXANDER, R. D. and MOORE, T. E. (1962). The evolutionary relationships of 17-year and 13-year cicadas, and three new species (Homoptera, Cicadidae, *Magicicada*). *Misc. Publs. Mus. Zool. Univ. Mich.* no. 121, 59 pp.

ALEXANDER, R. D., MOORE, T. E. and WOODRUFF, R. E. (1963). The evolutionary differentiation of stridulatory signals in beetles (Insecta: Coleoptera). *Anim. Behav.* **11**: 111–115.

BAILEY, W. J. (1970). The mechanics of stridulation in bush crickets (Tettigonioidea, Orthoptera). I. The tegminal generator. *J. exp. Biol.* **52**: 495–505.

BENNET-CLARK, H. C. (1970). The mechanism and efficiency of sound production in mole crickets. *J. exp. Biol.* **52**: 619–652.

BENTLEY, D. R. and KUTSCH, W. (1966). The neuromuscular mechanism of stridulation in crickets (Orthoptera: Gryllidae). *J. exp. Biol.* **45**: 151–164.

BLEST, A. D., COLLETT, T. S. and PYE, J. D. (1963). The generation of ultrasonic signals by a New World arctiid moth. *Proc. R. Soc. B,* **158**: 196–207.

BROUGHTON, W. B. (1963). Method in bio-acoustic terminology. *in* Busnel, R.-G. (ed.), *Acoustic behaviour of animals.* Elsevier, Amsterdam.

BROUGHTON, W. B. (1976). Proposal for a new term 'echeme' to replace 'chirp' in animal acoustics. *Physiol. Ent.* **1**: 103–106.

DUMORTIER, B. (1963a). Morphology of sound emission apparatus in Arthropoda. *in* Busnel, R.-G. (ed.), *Acoustic behaviour of animals.* Elsevier, Amsterdam.

DUMORTIER, B. (1963b). The physical characteristics of sound emissions in Arthropoda. *in* Busnel, R.-G. (ed.), *Acoustic behaviour of animals.* Elsevier, Amsterdam.

ELDER, H. Y. (1971). High frequency muscles used in sound production by a katydid. II. Ultrastructure of the singing muscles. *Biol. Bull.* **141**: 434–448.

ELSNER, N. (1974). Neuroethology of sound production in gomphocerine grasshoppers (Orthoptera: Acrididae). I. Song patterns and stridulatory movements. *J. comp. Physiol.* **88**: 67–102.

ELSNER, N. (1975). Neuroethology of sound production in gomphocerine grasshoppers (Orthoptera: Acrididae). II. Neuromuscular activity underlying stridulation. *J. comp. Physiol. A,* **97**: 291–322.

EWING, A. and HOYLE, G. (1965). Neuronal mechanisms underlying control of sound production in a cricket; *Acheta domesticus. J. exp. Biol.* **43**: 139–153.

HASKELL, P. T. (1957a). Stridulation and associated behaviour in certain Orthoptera. 1. Analysis of the stridulation of, and behaviour between males. *Anim. Behav.* **5**: 139–148.

HASKELL, P. T. (1957b). The influence of flight noise on behaviour in the desert locust *Schistocerca gregaria* (Forsk.). *J. Insect Physiol.* **1**: 52–75.

HASKELL, P. T. (1958). Stridulation and associated behaviour in certain Orthoptera. 2. Stridulation of females and their behaviour with males. *Anim. Behav.* **6**: 27–42.

HASKELL, P. T. (1960). Stridulation and associated behaviour in certain Orthoptera. 3. The influence of the gonads. *Anim. Behav.* **8**: 76–81.

HASKELL, P. T. (1961). *Insect sounds*. Witherby, London.

HASKELL, P. T. (1974). Sound production. *in* Rockstein, M. (ed.). *The physiology of Insecta*. vol. 2, Academic Press, New York and London.

HINTON, H. E. (1948). Sound production in lepidopterous pupae. *Entomologist*. **81**: 254–269.

HOWSE, P. E. (1962). Certain aspects of intercommunication in *Zootermopsis angusticollis* and other termites. Ph.D. Thesis, University of London.

HUBER, F. (1963). The role of the central nervous system in Orthoptera during the coordination and control of stridulation. *in* Busnel, R.-G. (ed.), *Acoustic behaviour of animals*. Elsevier, Amsterdam.

JOHNSTONE, G. W. (1964). Stridulation by larval Hydropsychidae, (Trichoptera). *Proc. R. ent. Soc. Lond.* A, **39**: 146–150.

JONES, M. D. R. (1966). The acoustic behaviour of the bush cricket *Pholidoptera griseoaptera*. 1. Alternation, synchronism and rivalry between males. *J. exp. Biol.* **45**: 15–30.

KEVAN, D. K. McE. (1955). Méthodes inhabituelles de production de son chez les Orthoptères. *in* Busnel, R.-G. (ed.), *Colloques sur l'acoustique des Orthoptères*, Paris, 1954: 103–141. *Annls. Épiphyt. fasc. hors série*.

LANE, C. and ROTHSCHILD, M. (1965). A case of Müllerian mimicry of sound. *Proc. R. ent. Soc. Lond.* A, **40**: 156–158.

LESTON, D. (1957). The stridulatory mechanisms in terrestrial species of Hemiptera Heteroptera. *Proc. zool. Soc. Lond.* **128**: 369–386.

LESTON, D. and PRINGLE, J. W. S. (1963). Acoustic behaviour of Hemiptera. *in* Busnel, R.-G. (ed.), *Acoustic behaviour of animals*. Elsevier, Amsterdam.

LOHER, W. and HUBER, F. (1966). Nervous and endocrine control of sexual behaviour in a grasshopper (*Gomphocerus rufus* L., Acridinae) *Sym. Soc. exp. Biol.* **20**: 381–400.

MICHELSON, A. and NOCKE, H. (1974). Biophysical aspects of sound communication in insects. *Adv. Insect Physiol.* **10**: 247–296.

MØHL, B. and MILLER, L. A. (1976). Ultrasonic clicks produced by the peacock butterfly: a possible bat-repellent mechanism. *J. exp. Biol.* **64**: 639–644.

NOCKE, H. (1972). Physiological aspects of sound communication in crickets (*Gryllus campestris* L.). *J. comp. Physiol.* **80**: 141–162.

OSSIANNILSSON, F. (1949). Insect drummers. *Opusc. ent. suppl.* **10**: 1–146.

PASQUINELLY, F. and BUSNEL, M.-C. (1955). Études preliminaires sur les mécanismes de la production des sons par les Orthoptères. *in* Busnell, R.-G. (ed.), *Colloques sur l'acoustique des Orthoptères*, Paris, 1954: 145–153. *Annls Épiphyt. fasc. hors série*.

PERDECK, A. C. (1958). The isolating value of specific song patterns in two sibling species of grasshoppers (*Chorthippus brunneus* Thunb. and *C. biguttulus* L.). *Behaviour* **12**: 1–75.

PRINGLE, J. W. S. (1954). A physiological analysis of cicada song. *J. exp. Biol.* **31**: 525–560.

PROZESKY-SCHULZE, L., PROZESKY, O. P. M., ANDERSON, F. and van der MERWE, G. J. J. (1975). Use of a self-made sound baffle by a tree cricket. *Nature, Lond.* **255**: 142–143.

PUMPHREY, R. J. (1950). Hearing. *Symp. Soc. exp. Biol.* **4**: 3–18.

RICHARDS, O. W. and WALOFF, N. (1954). Studies on the biology and population dynamics of British grasshoppers. *Anti-Locust Bull.* no. 17, 182 pp.

ROSCOW, J. M. (1963). The structure, development and variation of the stridulatory file of
    Stenobothrus lineatus (Panzer) (Orthoptera: Acrididae). *Proc. R. ent. Soc. Lond.* A, **38**: 194–
    199.
SAMWAYS, M. J. (1976). Song modification in the Orthoptera. I. Proclamation songs of
    Platycleis spp. (Tettigoniidae). *Physiol. Ent.* **1**: 131–149.
SOTAVALTA, O. (1963). The flight-sounds of insects. *in* Busnel, R.-G. (ed.), *Acoustic
    behaviour of animals*. Elsevier, Amsterdam.
WALKER, T. J. (1962). Factors responsible for intraspecific variation in the calling songs of
    crickets. *Evolution, Lancaster, Pa.* **16**: 407–428.
WALKER, T. J. and CARLYSLE, T. C. (1975). Stridulatory file teeth in crickets: taxonomic
    and acoustic implications (Orthoptera: Gryllidae). *Int. J. Insect Morphol. & Embryol.* **4**:
    151–158.
WENNER, A. M. (1962). Sound production during the waggle dance of the honey bee. *Anim.
    Behav.* **10**: 79–95.
WENNER, A. M. (1964). Sound communication in honey bees. *Scient. Am.* **210**: 116–124.

CHAPTER XXIX

MECHANORECEPTION

Treated in a broad sense mechanoreception includes the perception of any mechanical distortion of the body. This may result from touching an object or from the impact of vibrations borne through the air, water or the substratum, and thus mechanoreception includes the sense of hearing. It also includes distortions of the body which arise from the attitude of the insect and from the force exerted by gravity, so that some mechanoreceptors are proprioceptors, others gravity receptors. To carry out this variety of functions a number of different sensilla are involved.

Many of the hairs on the insect body are tactile organs and they may respond only during deformation or they may continue to respond throughout the period for which they are bent. The latter type commonly function as proprioceptors.

A second important class of mechanoreceptors are the chordotonal organs. These consist of single units or groups of units and occur in many parts of the body, recording changes in the positions of segments and also responding to vibrations from the environment. Associated with a tympanic membrane which is free to vibrate, these form the complex hearing organs found in a number of insects.

Campaniform sensilla respond to stresses in the cuticle, while internal proprioceptors are present in the form of stretch receptors.

General reviews of mechanoreceptors are given by Horridge (1965), McIver (1975) and Schwartzkopff (1974), while Thurm (1968, 1974) discusses transduction and associated processes. The structure and functioning of chordotonal organs is reviewed by Howse (1968) and of stretch receptors by Osborne (1970). Haskell (1961) describes tympanal organs and their functions and Michelsen and Nocke (1974) discuss some biophysical aspects of hearing.

29.1 Mechanoreceptor neurones

29.1.1 Structure

Mechanoreceptor neurones in insects are of two types: bipolar neurones with the dendrite more or less directly associated with the cuticle, and multipolar neurones associated with muscle and connective tissue. These are sometimes called, respectively, type I and type II neurones and the latter are described in Section 29.5.

Bipolar mechanoreceptor neurones usually have the dendrite divided into three sections. The proximal section arising from the perikaryon is commonly 1–2 μm in diameter and contains mitochondria. Some distance beneath the cuticle this narrows abruptly to the ciliary region (Figs. 461, 462), which contains a ring of nine doublets of

705

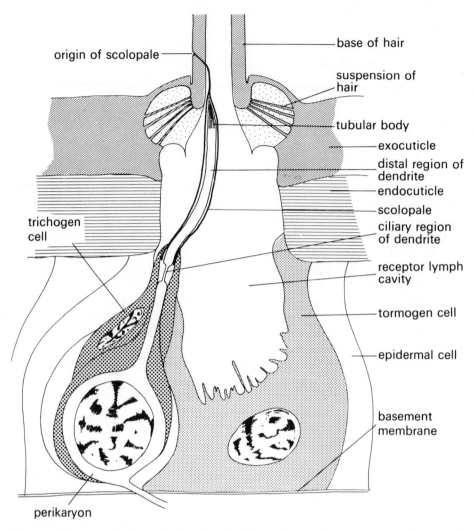

Fig. 461 Diagram showing the basal articulation of a mechanoreceptor hair and the arrangement of the associated cells

neurotubules but usually lacks the central tubules commonly present in motile cilia. The tubules arise from a basal body from which rootlets extend into the proximal region of the dendrite. The cilium is often enclosed in a basal cavity formed by a sheath cell.

After a short ciliary region the dendrite widens again. In this distal region the neurotubules increase in number, but no other organelles are present. At the extreme tip of the dendrite is a dense mass of microtubules. This is a common feature of trichoid and campaniform sensilla and is known as a tubular body. The whole of the distal part of the dendrite is enclosed in a sheath of cuticle-like material, which is attached to the cuticle of the body surface. This sheath, the scolopale, passes through an extracellular cavity bounded by the tormogen cell, the surface of which is thrown into folds or

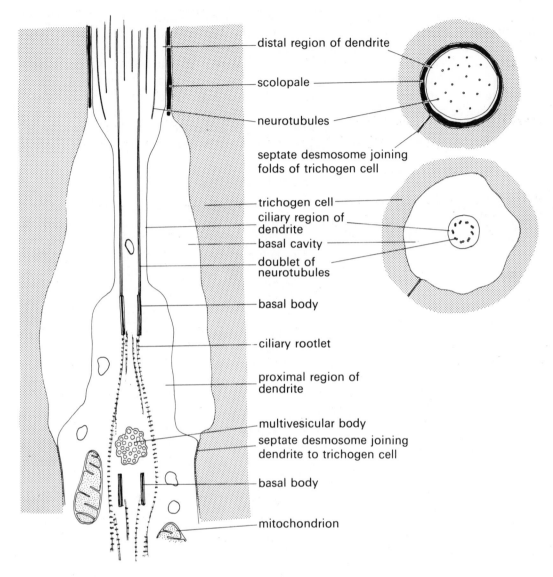

distal region of dendrite

scolopale

neurotubules

septate desmosome joining folds of trichogen cell

trichogen cell
ciliary region of dendrite
basal cavity
doublet of neurotubules

basal body

ciliary rootlet

proximal region of dendrite

multivesicular body
septate desmosome joining dendrite to trichogen cell

basal body

mitochondrion

Fig. 462 Diagram of the ciliary region of a mechanoreceptor dendrite. *Left*, longitudinal section; *right*, transverse sections at different levels

microvilli. The tormogen cell is tightly bound to adjacent cells by desmosomes, so that the receptor lymph cavity is isolated from the haemolymph. There is evidence of secretion from the tormogen cell into the cavity and it is probable that potassium is actively pumped into it (Küppers, 1974).

29.1.2 Transduction

The transduction process by which mechanical energy is transformed to electrical energy involves the deformation of the dendrite and production of a receptor potential.

It is probable that the tubular body plays an essential role in the process, deformation of the cuticle at the point of attachment producing compression of the tubular body, which in some way leads to an increase in the permeability of the membrane of the dendrite (Thurm, 1968). In some mechanoreceptor dendrites, however, a fully developed tubular body is not present and it has been suggested that bending the dendrite causes its outer membrane to be stretched leading to a change in membrane capacitance or conductance (Rice *et al.*, 1973). Development of the generator potential is associated with a fall in the potential across the epidermis between the haemolymph and the receptor lymph cavity (Thurm, 1974; Thurm and Küppers, 1980).

29.2 Trichoid sensilla

A trichoid sensillum is a hair-like projection of the cuticle articulated with the body wall by a membranous socket so that it is free to move. The hair is produced by a cell, the trichogen cell, and the socket by another, the tormogen cell, lying in the epidermis (Fig. 461). Associated with each hair is one or more nerve cells. Hairs concerned only with mechanoreception have only one or two neurones but chemosensory hairs with a number of neurones (Fig. 500) also often function as mechanoreceptors. In some hairs, such as those along the edge of the prothorax of *Schistocerca*, a potential is produced when the hair is bent in any direction, but others, such as those in the hair plates (Fig. 465) on the face, only respond when they are bent in certain directions (Fig. 463).

The receptor potentials produced in the distal part of the dendrite differ in different types of hair. In the majority, a potential only develops during movement of the hair, bending or straightening (Fig. 464A), a phasic response, but in others the potential is maintained all the time the hair is bent, adapting only very slowly (Fig. 464B). This is known as a tonic response.

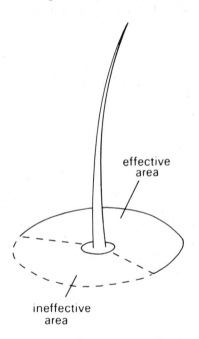

effective area

ineffective area

Fig. 463 Diagram to illustrate the directional sensitivity of a trichoid sensillum. Only bending towards the effective area leads to the development of a nervous impulse (after Haskell, 1960)

Phasic receptors

Hairs showing phasic responses function as tactile receptors, occurring particulary on the antennae, the tarsi and wherever the insect touches the substratum. They may also respond to vibration of the substratum and in some cases to sounds carried through the air, if these are of high intensity.

Hairs responding to sounds in the range 32–1000 Hz occur over the body of caterpillars and stimulation by high intensity sounds causes convulsive contractions of the longitudinal muscles so that the insects make writhing movements with their heads. Similar hairs are present on the ventral surface of the abdomen and on the cerci of

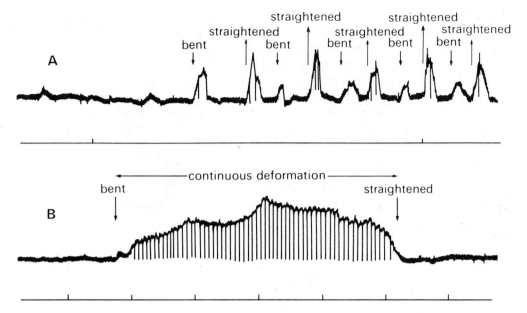

Fig. 464 Oscillograms of the responses to deformation of two types of mechanosensory hairs. A. On the wing of *Sarcophaga* responding only to movement of the hair. B. On the clasper of a male *Phormia* giving a continuous response to continuous deformation. Time marker 0.2 seconds (after Wolbarsht, 1960)

grasshoppers, while the cercal hairs of *Periplaneta* respond to frequencies up to 3000 Hz. At low frequencies the impulses in the cercal nerve of *Periplaneta* are synchronous with the stimulus frequency, but they become completely asynchronous at a stimulus frequency of about 800 Hz. It is doubtful if the cercal hairs of grasshoppers are of any importance in perceiving stridulation, but the hairs on the abdomen might be important when the intensity of sound is high, as during the later stages of courtship with the insects only a few centimetres apart.

Apart from sounds, air moving at only 4 cm/s is sufficient to stimulate the cercal hairs of the locust. The cockroach, but not the locust, makes rapid evasive movements when these hairs are stimulated by a puff of air.

Tonic receptors

Hairs which exhibit a tonic response to bending occur between the joints of the legs, on the prothorax and genitalia, and in many other situations on the body, often associated with joints. They serve different functions according to their positions, but, since their output adapts only slowly and so provides continuous information, they are often proprioceptors. Sometimes these hairs are grouped together to form hair beds. These occur on the face of the locust (Fig. 465), on the cervical sclerites, at the junction of the coxa with the thorax and the trochanter with the coxa, at the joints of the palps, at the base of the abdomen and elsewhere (see *e.g.* Markl, 1962). They serve different functions according to their positions.

The facial hair beds of the locust are stimulated by air blowing on to the face at speeds of 2 m/s or more. They show directional sensitivity and are orientated so that

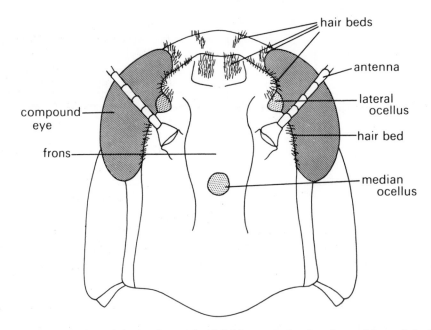

Fig. 465 Frontal view of the head capsule of *Schistocerca* showing the positions of the hair beds (after Weis-Fogh, 1949)

they respond to air passing along the axis of the insect. Thus they enable the insect to orientate to wind while on the ground and help to control yaw (p. 238) while it is flying, since asymmetrical stimulation of the hair beds of the two sides leads to variable oscillation of the wings. Stimulation of the facial hair beds also initiates a flight reflex resulting in the drawing up of the legs into the flight position and the maintenance of flight (p. 232).

Where hair beds occur at joints in the skeleton they are stimulated by contact with adjoining surfaces (Fig. 466) so that they function as proprioceptors. The hair beds on the first cervical sclerite, for instance, provide the insect with information on the position of its head. This is important in the mantis during feeding and aids the stability of the locust in flight when the head is orientated by a dorsal light reaction and the thorax is aligned with the head (p. 236).

Hair beds are also important in orientating to gravity. The ability to orientate to gravity must be important to most

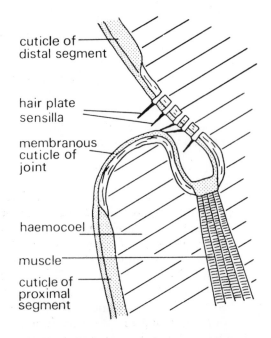

Fig. 466 Diagram to show the manner in which the sensilla of a hair plate are stimulated by coming into contact with adjacent cuticle

insects, but is particularly important in the communication dances of *Apis*. The head of *Apis* is suspended from the thorax by two cuticular processes which extend forwards from the episterna and articulate with the occipital condyles. There is a hair bed on the outside of each of these processes so placed that when the bee is standing on a horizontal surface the hairs are in even contact with the head capsule. The centre of gravity of the head is below its point of articulation with the thorax, so that when the bee crawls upwards the head nods down and the ventral hairs of the cervical hair beds are stimulated more strongly than those dorsally in the group. On a less inclined slope the forces acting on these hairs are reduced, while on crawling downwards the ventral part of the head hangs down, away from the thorax and the dorsal hairs of the hair beds are stimulated more strongly than the ventral ones. Side to side turning on a vertical surface will be indicated by forces of different intensity acting on the two sides. Other setal fields on the petiole, the antenna and elsewhere also play a part, but are less important. The response to gravity is a response to the combined output of these receptors, individually the hair beds function as proprioceptors (Lindauer, 1961).

The larger tactile setae on the legs of *Periplaneta*, and possibly of other insects function in an entirely different way from typical trichoid sensilla. At the base of each seta, where it joins the membrane of the socket, is a single campaniform sensillum 10–15 μm across. Movement of the hair is unlikely to deform the sensillum because of the flexibility of the socket membrane, but possibly the movement causes the membrane to fold up and press on the sensillum so that it is stimulated (Chapman, 1965).

29.3 Campaniform sensilla

Campaniform sensilla are areas of thin cuticle, domed and usually oval in shape, with a long diameter commonly 20–30 μm (Fig. 467). In *Blaberus* the dome of thin cuticle consists of an outer homogeneous layer and an inner lamellar layer, into which is

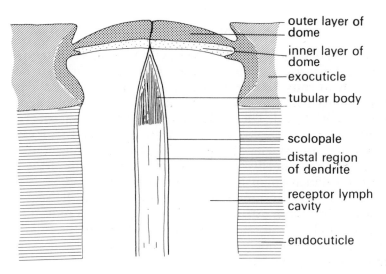

Fig. 467 Diagram of the cuticular elements and dendrite insertion in a campaniform sensillum

inserted the single dendrite enclosed within the scolopale. The dendrite ends in a tubular body. Cell structure and arrangement is similar to that of trichoid sensilla (Fig. 461).

Campaniform sensilla often occur in groups, all those within a group having the same orientation so that they function as a unit. They occur in all parts of the body subject to stress and are concentrated near the joints as at the base of the wing or the haltere in Diptera (Figs. 129, 130). On the leg of the cockroach there are four groups on the trochanter, each containing 15–20 sensilla, one at the base of the femur, another at the base of the tibia and one on each of the tarsal segments.

In the insect skeleton all stresses can be expressed as shearing stresses in the plane of the surface. Such stresses produce changes in the shape of the campaniform sensilla and, compression forces along the length of the sensillum raise the dome while extension in the same direction lowers the dome. The nerve is stimulated when the dome is raised, that is by compression forces along the length of the sensillum and, for instance, most or all of the campaniform sensilla on the leg are so orientated that they are stimulated when the foot is on the ground and the leg bears the weight of the insect. The longer the axis of the dome the greater the sensitivity of the sensillum and in groups of campaniform sensilla there is usually a range of sizes, perhaps giving a range of sensitivity (Pringle, 1938b).

The response of campaniform sensilla is determined by the properties of the cuticle: its elasticity, thickness and curvature; by the forces exerted on the cuticle by muscles; and by the pattern of forces due to gravity or inertia. They thus function as proprioceptors, but, unlike vertebrate proprioceptors, they do not respond to the movements of individual muscles, but to the resultants of a variety of contending strains on the cuticle. Thus some campaniform sensilla monitor the movements of the wings and halteres, others are concerned in the control of leg movement as, for instance, in *Periplaneta*, where the leg depressor reflex is initiated by stimulation of the campaniform sensilla of the trochanter. Like all proprioceptors they are slow adapting (Fig. 468).

29.4 Chordotonal organs

Chordotonal, or scolopophorus, organs consist of single units or groups of similar units called scolopidia. They are subcuticular, often with no external sign of their presence, and are attached to the cuticle at one or both ends. Each scolopidium consists essentially of three cells arranged in a linear manner: the neurone, an enveloping, or scolopale cell, and an attachment, or cap cell. The scolopidia in the locust tympanal organ also possess a fibrous sheath-cell round the base of the dendrite (Fig. 469). In this case, the dendrite ends in a cilium-like process containing a peripheral ring of nine double filaments and with roots extending proximally within the dendrite. The tip of the cilium lies in a hollow of the extracellular scolopale cap. In other cases the dendrite dilates distal to the cilium as in most other mechanoreceptors (p. 707). Within the scolopale cell is the tubular scolopale. In *Locusta* this is made up of five to seven rods of fibrous material arranged in a ring and enclosing an extracellular space round the cilium. The contents of the extracellular space are not known. The attachment cell connects the sensillum to the epidermis (Gray, 1960).

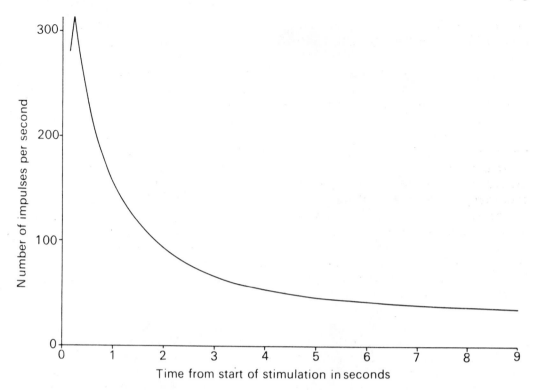

Fig. 468 The frequency of impulses in the nerves from a group of campaniform sensilla on the maxillary palp of *Periplaneta* showing the initial high level followed by a long period during which the frequency of impulses is maintained at a lower level with very little adaptation (after Pringle, 1938a)

Chordotonal organs occur throughout the peripheral regions of the body of the insect. In larval *Drosophila* there are 90 such organs, each containing from one to five scolopidia, arranged in a segmental pattern and suspended between points on the body wall so that they function as proprioceptors (Fig. 470). In *Melanoplus* (Orthoptera) there are 76 pairs. In the thorax of many insects there are large chordotonal organs, containing about 20 scolopidia; these record the movements of the head on the thorax. Others in the wing bases of some insects record some of the forces which the wings exert on the body. In *Apis* there are three such organs, each with 15–30 scolopidia, at the base of the radial and subcostal veins and in the lumen of the radial vein.

Typically four chordotonal organs occur in each leg. The first is attached proximally within the femur and distally is inserted into the knee joint. In *Machilis* this organ contains seven scolopidia; in grasshoppers there are about 300. Proximally in the tibia is the subgenual organ (see below) and distally another chordotonal organ, which in *Apis* contains about 60 scolopidia, arises in the connective tissue of the tibia and is inserted into the tibio-tarsal articulation. Finally, a small organ with only about three scolopidia extends from the tarsus to the pretarsus. These organs function as proprioceptors monitoring the positions of the leg joints.

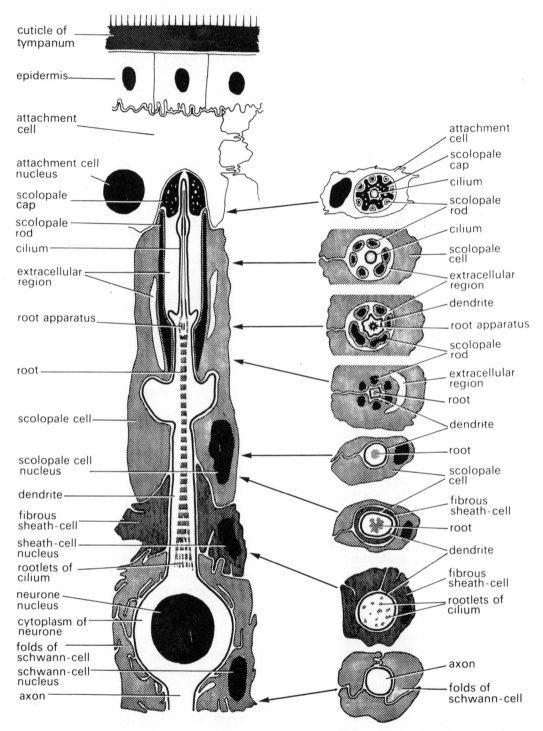

Fig. 469 Diagrammatic longitudinal section through a scolopidium from the tympanum of *Locusta* with transverse sections at the levels indicated (after Gray, 1960)

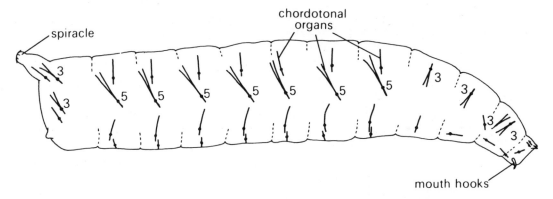

Fig. 470 Diagram of *Drosophila* larva showing the arrangement of chordotonal organs. The numbers indicate the number of scolopidia in each sense organ; those not numbered have one (from Horridge, 1965)

29.4.1 Subgenual organs

The subgenual organ is a chordotonal organ in the proximal part of the tibia, usually containing between 10 and 40 scolopidia. It is not associated with a joint. Processes from the accessory cells at the distal ends of the scolopidia are packed together as an attachment body, which is fixed to the cuticle at one point, while the proximal ends are supported by a trachea (Fig. 471). Often the organ is in two parts, one more proximal,

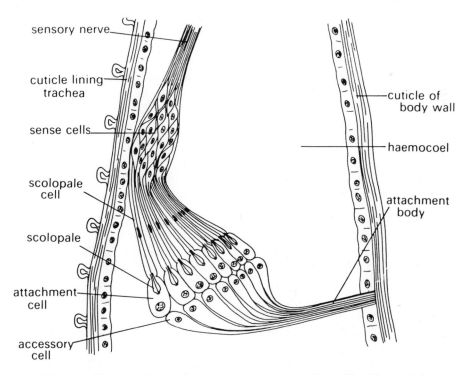

Fig. 471 Diagram of the subgenual organ of an ant (from Horridge, 1965)

called the true subgenual organ by Debaisieux (1938), and the other slightly more distal. Both are present in Odonata, Dictyoptera and Orthoptera. In Tettigonioidea and Grylloidea the distal organ probably gives rise to the intermediate organ and the crista acoustica (p. 719). In Homoptera, Heteroptera, Neuroptera and Lepidoptera only the distal organ is present, while in *Machilis*, Coleoptera and Diptera no subgenual organ is present at all (Debaisieux, 1938).

The subgenual organs are sensitive to vibrations of the substratum and to airborne sounds if these are of sufficiently high intensity to cause the leg or substratum to vibrate. They are extremely sensitive and in *Periplaneta*, for instance, respond to a displacement of only $10^{-9}–10^{-7}$ cm. The subgenual organs of *Periplaneta* are sensitive to vibrations at frequencies up to 8 kHz with an optimum at 1500 Hz. *Calliphora*, which has no subgenual organs, on the other hand, only responds to displacements greater than 10^{-5} cm within the frequency range 50–1000 Hz. In this case the sensilla which respond to vibration are the tibio-tarsal chordotonal organ, the tarsal hairs and hair beds between the joints of the legs.

The response of the subgenual organs of *Periplaneta* is synchronous with the stimulus at frequencies up to 50 Hz (Howse, 1964), but at higher frequencies it is asynchronous. In nature it is unlikely that pure tones occur, rather the insect is subject to pulse-like vibrations transmitted through the substratum and including the high frequencies as transients. Hence it is important that the organs should be able to perceive the high frequencies. Substrate vibration is important in sexual recognition in delphacids and may also be important in some tettigoniids (Kühne *et al.*, 1980). It is probable that such vibration is perceived via the subgenual organs.

The mechanism by which the subgenual organs are stimulated is not understood. Possibly vibrations of the leg create vortices in the haemolymph within the leg and these move the chordotonal organ so that the sense organ is stimulated. Alternatively, the vibrations of the leg may cause the organ to vibrate with its own natural frequency, but, because the attachment cells are bound together and attached to the cuticle, they have a different natural frequency from the scolopale cells, which are relatively free. Hence the proximal and distal parts of the organ will vibrate at different frequencies, so that rapid and complex changes occur in the forces acting at the junction between the two parts and these rapid changes serve to stimulate the sense cells (Howse, 1962).

29.4.2 Johnston's organ

Johnston's organ is a chordotonal organ lying in the second segment of the antenna with its distal insertion in the articulation between the second and third segments. It occurs in all adult insects but not in Collembola or Diplura, and, in a simplified form, is present in many larvae. It consists of a single mass or several groups of scolopidia and is most highly developed in the Culicidae and Chironomidae, where the pedicel is enlarged to house the organ. In Culicidae the base of the antennal flagellum forms a plate from which processes extend for the insertion of the scolopidia (Fig. 472). The latter are arranged in two rings all round the axis of the antenna and in addition there are three single scolopidia which extend from the scape to the flagellum.

Johnston's organ perceives movements of the antennal flagellum. In *Calliphora* most of the sensilla comprising the organ give phasic responses, potentials only developing during and immediately after the movement, so that a single to and fro

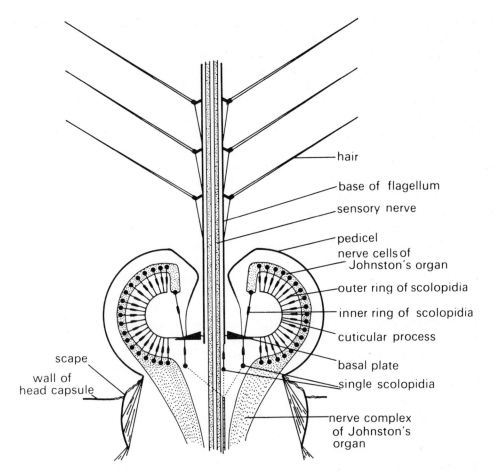

hair

base of flagellum

sensory nerve

pedicel

nerve cells of
Johnston's organ

outer ring of scolopidia

inner ring of scolopidia

cuticular process

basal plate

single scolopidia

nerve complex
of Johnston's
organ

scape

wall of
head capsule

Fig. 472 Diagram of the basal part of the antenna of a male mosquito showing Johnston's organ (from Autrum, 1963)

movement of the flagellum produces an 'on' and an 'off' response. The amplitude of the 'on' response increases with stimulus intensity due to different units having different thresholds and, if the stimulus is of very short duration, the 'off' response may be completely suppressed. Hence at high frequencies of stimulation small changes in stimulus pattern may produce major changes in excitation. Some of the sensilla respond to movement in any direction, others only if they are moved in a particular direction, stretching being the effective stimulus (Burkhardt, 1960). Since movement of the flagellum may result from a number of causes Johnston's organ may serve a variety of functions in any one insect.

In *Calliphora* Johnston's organ acts as a flight speed indicator and is concerned with the maintenance and control of flight speed. Wind blowing on the face causes the arista to act as a lever, rotating the third antennal segment on the second (Fig. 8D). This stimulates Johnston's organ, which because of the phasic nature of most of the sensilla responds primarily to changes in the degree of rotation of the third segment. Even in a steady airflow the antenna trembles, perhaps because of the setting up of eddies, and Johnston's organ is stimulated. With different angles of rotation more or different scolopidia are stimulated so that Johnston's organ can give a measure of the degree of static deflection of the third antennal segment as well as changes in its position (Burkhardt, 1960; and see p. 241).

Johnston's organ also perceives sounds carried through the air to *Calliphora* and in *Drosophila melanogaster* wing vibration by the male during courtship causes the arista of the female to oscillate and, by moving the third antennal segment, to stimulate Johnston's organ (Burnet *et al.*, 1971). In Chironomidae and Culicidae the males locate females by their flight tone (p. 677). The males of these insects have plumose antennae with many fine, long hairs arising from each annular joint. These hairs are caused to vibrate by sound waves and their combined action produces a movement of the flagellum. The amplitude of flagellar movement is greatest near its own natural frequency which approximately corresponds to the flight tone of the mature female and stimulation at this frequency leads to the seizing and clasping response in mating. *Aedes aegypti* males are most readily induced to mate by frequencies between about 400 and 650 Hz, but the limits to which they respond become wider as the insect gets older and are wider in unmated than in mated males. Sounds at other frequencies and high intensities produce a variety of reactions: cleaning movements, jerking, flight or freezing (Roth, 1948).

In order to find the female, the stimulated male must be able to determine the direction from which the sound is coming. This is possible with only one intact antenna and it is presumed that asymmetrical movements of the flagellum produce differential stimulation of the scolopidia in different parts of Johnston's organ.

The dominant forces acting on the antenna of ants are perceived by Johnston's organ, as presumably they are in any insect, and this may play a part in their orientation to gravity.

Johnston's organ is concerned with the orientation of *Notonecta* in the water. An air bubble extends between the head and the antenna so that when the insect is correctly orientated on its back the antenna is deflected away from the head. If, however, the insect is the wrong way up the antenna is drawn towards the head and Johnston's organ registers the position. Gyrinid beetles are able to perceive ripples on the water surface, apparently due to displacements of the antennal flagellum, so that they are able to avoid collisions with other insects and, by echolocating using their own ripples, also avoid the sides of their container. In order to do this the insect must also be able to detect the direction from which the ripples are coming.

Where Johnston's organ is well developed other chordotonal organs are absent from the antennae, but in most insects additional organs occur in the basal and terminal antennal segments, where they function as proprioceptors.

29.4.3 Tympanal organs

Structure and occurrence of tympanal organs

Tympanal organs are specialised chordotonal organs. Each consists of a thin area of cuticle, the tympanic membrane, which is generally backed by an air-sac so that it is free to vibrate. Attached to the inside of the membrane or adjacent to it is a chordotonal organ, which contains from one scolopidium in *Plea* (Heteroptera) to about 1500 in Cicadidae. Tympanal organs occur on the prothoracic legs in Grylloidea and

Tettigonioidea, on the mesothorax of some Hydrocorisae, such as *Corixa* and *Plea*, on the metathorax in Noctuoidea, and on the abdomen in Acrididae, Cicadidae, Pyralidoidea and Geometroidea (Lepidoptera).

In Acrididae there is a tympanum in a recess on either side of the first abdominal segment. The tympanum of *Locusta* is about $2 \cdot 5 \times 1 \cdot 5$ mm^2 in area and at the front edge is a spiracle which leads into the air-sac beneath the tympanum (Fig. 473). The chordotonal organ, attached to the centre of the tympanic membrane, is complex, containing about 80 neurones with the cell bodies aggregated into a ganglion (Fig. 474). From the ganglion the sensory units connect with the tympanum in four separate groups, which are attached to thickenings or invaginations of the cuticle. The scolopidia are joined to the epidermis by the attachment cells (Fig. 469). The whole chordotonal organ and the auditory nerve which runs from it to the metathoracic ganglion are enclosed in folds of the air-sacs which are continuous right across the body (Fig. 473). Tracheoles extend to the epidermis and attachment cells, but none occurs in the body of the ganglion. Two muscles are attached to the edge of the tympanum, but their function is unknown.

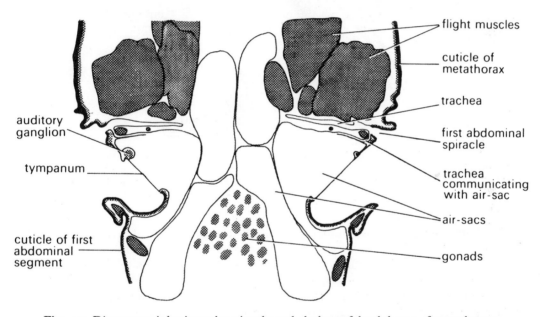

Fig. 473 Diagrammatic horizontal section through the base of the abdomen of a grasshopper, *Oedipoda*, showing the positions of the tympanic membranes, the air-sacs and the associated spiracles (after Schwabe, 1906)

The tympanal organs of Grylloidea and Tettigonioidea are similar to each other, being stituated in the base of the fore tibia, which is slightly dilated and typically has a tympanum on either side. Often the outer tympanum is bigger than the inner one and sometimes, as in *Gryllotalpa*, only the outer organ is present. In most Tettigonioidea the tympanic membranes are protected by forwardly projecting folds of the tibial cuticle (Fig. 475). The whole cavity of the leg between the two tympanic membranes is occupied by a trachea divided into two by a rigid membrane, the blood space of the leg being restricted to canals anteriorly and posteriorly.

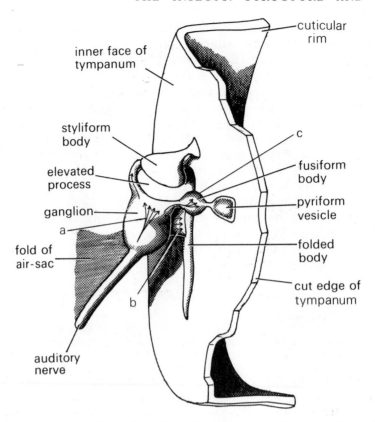

Fig. 474 Diagram to show the method of attachment of the auditory ganglion to the inner surface of the tympanum of *Locusta*. The folded body, styliform body and elevated process are cuticular structures. The orientations of the scolopidia are indicated by the arrows (compare Fig. 480) (after Gray, 1960)

In tettigoniids the trachea runs proximally through the femur without branching and suddenly widens into a vestibule which opens at the prothoracic spiracle. The cross-sectional area of the trachea from tibia to spiracle approximates to that of an exponential horn and there is no spiracular closing mechanism. The threshold sensitivity of the tympanal organs is lower for sound entering via the spiracle than for sound entering via the tympanic cavities (Lewis, 1974a) suggesting that this is the principal method by which stimulation occurs.

The chordotonal organs associated with the tympanal organs are in the anterior haemocoelic space of the tibia. The main organ, the crista acoustica, in *Decticus* contains 40 scolopidia. The more proximal seven of these are associated with the intermediate organ, another chordotonal organ (Fig. 476), but the remainder lie parallel with each other in a vertical row, the sensilla becoming progressively smaller towards the distal end. In *Teleogryllus* they are within a tent-like membrane which extends along the tympanal organ between the wall of the trachea and the dorsal (anterior) wall of the tibia (Young and Ball, 1974). The perikarya lie on the wall of the trachea and the dendrites project into the cavity of the tent. More proximal scolopidia are attached to large accessory cells within the tent, but, more distally, long attachment

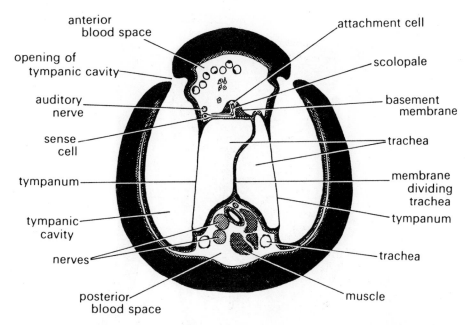

anterior blood space

opening of tympanic cavity

auditory nerve

sense cell

tympanum

tympanic cavity

nerves

posterior blood space

attachment cell

scolopale

basement membrane

trachea

membrane dividing trachea

tympanum

trachea

muscle

Fig. 475 Transverse section through the base of the fore tibia of a tettigoniid, *Decticus*, showing the arrangement of the tympanal organs (after Schwabe, 1906)

cells extend directly to the tibial epidermis (Fig. 477). The significance of the intermediate chordotonal organ is unknown. In these insects, as in the Acrididae, tympanal organs are present in all the instars, but they probably only become functional in the later larval instars and adults.

The tympanal organs of the Noctuoidea occupy the posterior part of the metathorax (Fig. 478) and the tympanic membrane faces into a cavity between the thorax and abdomen roofed over by the alula of the hind wing. Lateral to the tympanum and separated from it by a sclerotised ridge, the epaulette, is a soft white membrane, the conjunctiva, while medially there is a second membrane, resembling the tympanic membrane, but without a sense organ. This second membrane is the counter tympanic membrane, which is probably an accessory resonating structure. The sense organ, which is attached to the back of the tympanum, contains only two scolopidia, supported by an apodemal ligament and an invagination of the tympanal frame known as the Bügel (Roeder and Treat, 1957).

In cicadas the two tympanic membranes are situated ventro-laterally on the posterior end of the first abdominal segment behind the folded membrane (p. 692) and beneath the operculum. The air-sacs by which they are backed are continuous right across the abdominal cavity. Each chordotonal organ contains about 1500 scolopidia enclosed in a cuticular tympanic capsule and attached to the posterior rim of the tympanum by an apodeme.

In *Chrysopa* the tympanum is on the ventral side of the radial vein of the forewing. Near the base this vein has a bulbous swelling, thick walled and rigid above, but with the thin tympanum below. Unlike most other tympanal organs, the tympanum is in direct contact with haemocoel: it is not backed by an air-sac. About 28 scolopidia are associated with the tympanum (Miller, 1971).

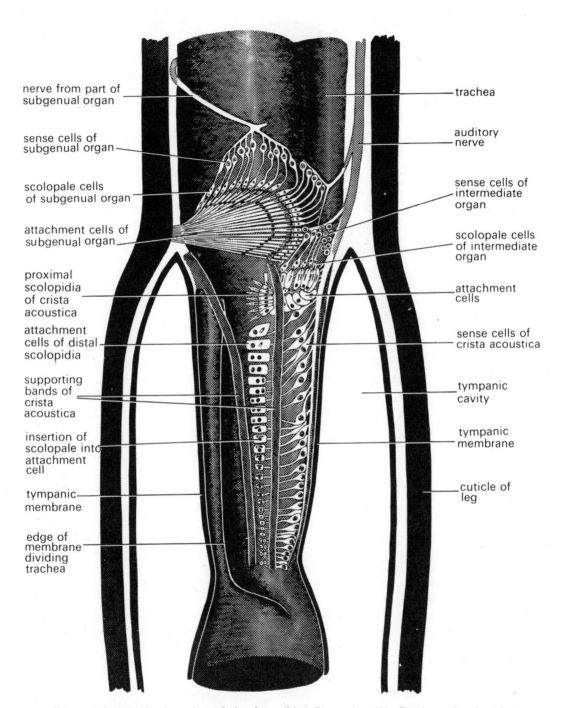

nerve from part of subgenual organ

sense cells of subgenual organ

scolopale cells of subgenual organ

attachment cells of subgenual organ

proximal scolopidia of crista acoustica

attachment cells of distal scolopidia

supporting bands of crista acoustica

insertion of scolopale into attachment cell

tympanic membrane

edge of membrane dividing trachea

trachea

auditory nerve

sense cells of intermediate organ

scolopale cells of intermediate organ

attachment cells

sense cells of crista acoustica

tympanic cavity

tympanic membrane

cuticle of leg

Fig. 476 Longitudinal section of the fore tibia of a tettigoniid, *Decticus*, showing the arrangement of the tympanal organs and associated chordotonal organs (after Schwabe, 1906)

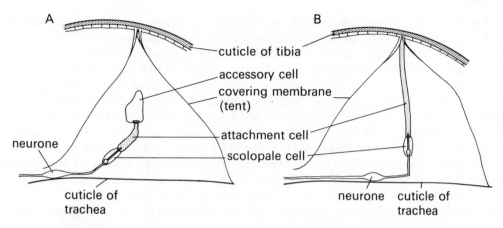

Fig. 477 Diagrammatic cross-sections of part of the tibia showing the forms of the scolopidia in the tympanal organ of *Teleogryllus*. A. A scolopidium from the proximal part of the organ. B. Scolopidium from distal part (after Young and Ball, 1974)

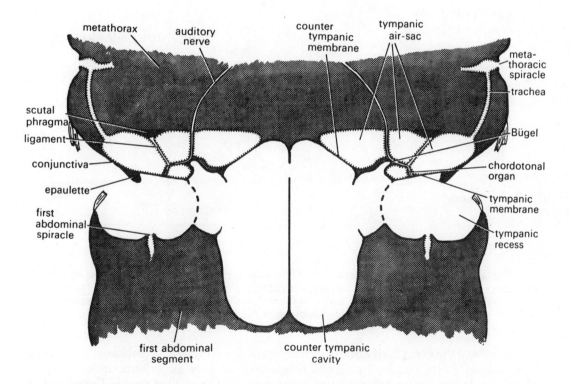

Fig. 478 Diagrammatic horizontal section through the metathorax and base of the abdomen of a noctuid moth showing the tympanal organs (modified after Roeder and Treat, 1957)

Functioning of the tympanal organs

Auditory receptors may function by perceiving the pressure pulses which emanate from the sound source or by perceiving the displacements of the air which its vibration causes. The former are called pressure or pressure-gradient receivers, the latter movement receivers (Michelsen and Nocke, 1974). Trichoid sensilla, which are sensitive to sound, are movement receivers, tympanal organs are pressure or pressure gradient receivers. In a pressure receiver sound impinges only on the front of the tympanum while in a pressure gradient receiver sound also reaches the back of the membrane via the air-sacs or through the tissues of the insect. The locust tympanum acts as a pressure receiver above 10 kHz, but as a pressure gradient receiver below this.

Sound impinging on the tympanic membrane causes it to vibrate. The amplitude of the vibrations varies with the frequency of the sound and with the structure of the membrane. In the locust, for instance, part of the tympanum is much thicker than the rest and marked differences in amplitude of vibration occur in different regions (Fig. 479). Vibration is also affected by the degree of damping of the tympanum. In most insects this damping is reduced to a low level by the air-sacs which back the tympanum, but the sensitivity of locust tympanal organs is reduced by extensive development of fat.

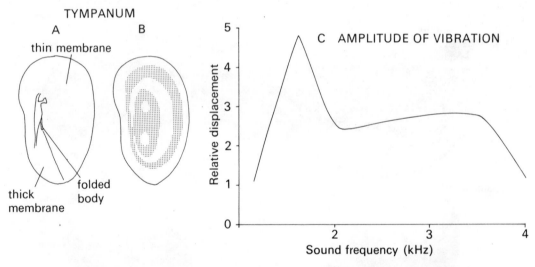

Fig. 479 The tympanum of a locust. A. The arrangement of the chordotonal organ on the inner face (see also Fig. 474). B. Vibration at 3 kHz, 112 dB, shaded areas indicate areas with equal amplitude of vibration. C. Changes in the amplitude of vibration in relation to frequency at a point near the folded body (after Michelson and Nocke, 1974)

Because of the complexity of the vibrations of the tympanic membrane, attachment areas within a few hundred microns of each other may experience quite different vibrations. It is suggested that the tympanal sensilla of the locust respond to vibrations perpendicular to the membrane in their immediate neighbourhood, but in addition respond to variations in tensile strain set up by vibrations in other parts of the tympanum (Michelsen and Nocke, 1974).

The tympanal organs of different groups of insects respond to a wide range of frequencies. Acrididae respond to sounds with frequencies from 100 Hz to 50 kHz, tettigoniids from 1 to 100 kHz, gryllids from 200 Hz to 15 kHz, noctuids from 1 to 240 kHz, and cicadas from 100 Hz to 15 kHz. Within these ranges sensitivity is generally greatest over a more limited range corresponding with the frequencies of the sounds to which they are adapted, commonly the sound produced during stridulation (Fig. 437).

Some degree of frequency discrimination is possible through the different sensitivities of the receptor cells. In locusts the cells in different parts of the auditory organ have different thresholds (Fig. 480) and the tympanal organ of *Gampsocleis* (Orthoptera) has two types of neurones with maximum sensitivity to different frequencies (Katsuki and Suga, 1960). Discrimination may also be achieved by differences in the responsiveness of different organs. In *Gryllus* the small tympanum produces a maximum response when stimulated by sound at 14 kHz, while the large tympanum has a maximum at 4 kHz. These two maxima correspond with maxima in the songs (Fig. 437) (Nocke, 1972). In the grasshopper *Oxya* the cercal hairs have a maximal response to stimulus frequencies of about 500 Hz, while tympanal organs respond maximally from two to 15 kHz (Fig. 481) (Katsuki and Suga, 1960). There is no evidence that frequency discrimination alone is of particular importance to the insect. It seems very likely that the discrimination allows the insect to tune in to stimuli of an appropriate wave length, but that further recognition depends on other characteristics of the sound.

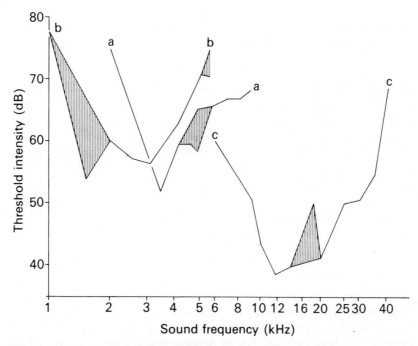

Fig. 480 Threshold sensitivites of scolopidia in the locust ear. Letters correspond with groups of cells shown in Fig. 474. Cross-hatched areas show the range of sensitivities of different cells within the same group (after Michelson and Nocke, 1974)

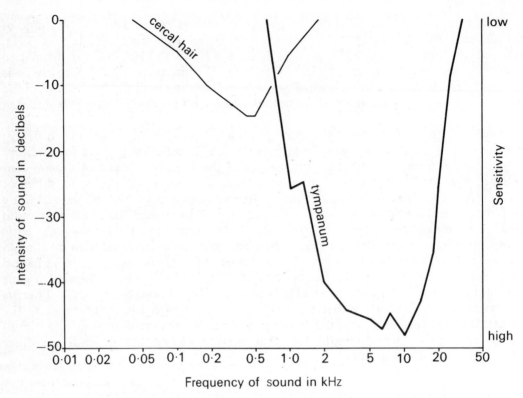

Fig. 481 The intensity of sound at different frequencies necessary to produce a response in the nerves from the cercal hairs and tympanal organs of *Oxya* (after Katsuki and Suga, 1960)

The amplitude of the impulses in the auditory nerve is proportional to the intensity of sound since the scolopidia have a range of thresholds at which they respond and the greater the intensity of sound the more scolopidia are stimulated. Following from this, it is found that insects can perceive amplitude modulations. Volleys of spikes occur in the auditory nerve synchronous with pulses of sound and hence the pulse repetition frequency of insect songs is probably an important factor in their recognition (p. 678). It is also possible that transients, sudden changes in intensity, are important in song recognition (for discussion and references see Haskell, 1956, 1961) and the output of the auditory nerve of *Tettigonia* can follow transients up to a frequency of 400 per second. The steeper the transient, the greater the response in the nerve.

Functions of tympanal organs

The tympanal organs play an important part in mating behaviour in insects which stridulate, auditory stimuli serving to locate and signal to the opposite sex (p. 697). They are also important in the aggregation of Acrididae and Cicadidae (p. 698). These activities require the recepient insect to orientate and move towards the source of sound. The female *Scapsipedus* (Orthoptera), for instance, is attracted to the male by his song. She moves in short bursts of about 400 ms duration between the chirps of the male which are produced at 1·6 s intervals. The female starts to respond within 350 ms of the beginning of a chirp, turning towards the source and then running in a straight line. Reorientation only occurs when the female is stationary and she has the capacity to discriminate between sounds coming from either side and, probably, from front or behind; more precise localisation of the sound apparently does not occur (but see Bailey and Stephen, 1978). The insect compares the sound reaching the tympanal organs on the two sides and if one tympanum is damaged the insect is unable to orientate. There is no evidence that the intensity of sound reaching the two sides is different when the sound source is on one side, but it is possible that the difference in arrival time of the signal at the two sides might provide a mechanism for directional discrimination (Murphey and Zaretsky, 1972). On the other hand, in *Ruspolia* the sound intensity reaching the tympanal organs on the two sides from a unilateral sound source is markedly different and does provide a means by which the insect could determine the approximate position of the sound source (Lewis, 1974b).

Differences in stimulation of the two legs are enhanced by a central contrast mechanism in *Gampsocleis*. Impulses in the auditory nerve evoke spikes in a large interneurone which extends from the metathoracic ganglion to the head, a continuous train of impulses from the tympanum producing only an 'on' response in the interneurone. Stimulation of the tympanum of one side excites the ipsilateral interneurone, so that the number of spikes produced is increased, but inhibits the contralateral fibre. As a result, any asymmetrical stimulation of the tympanal organs of the two legs is accentuated in the central nervous system. In addition, the discharge in the ipsilateral interneurone is synchronous with the sound pulses, but there is a delay in spike production in the contralateral fibre. In this way the information about the sound source received by the insect is increased (Suga and Katsuki, 1961).

Noctuids are able to locate a source of high frequency sound when they are flying and so they have the problem of localisation in a vertical as well as a horizontal direction. At low intensities of sound there is a difference in the response from the two tympanic membranes when they are asymmetrically stimulated, so that a basis for horizontal location of the source is available. In addition, the wings tend to screen the tympani, so that there is a marked difference in the responses of the two organs to asymmetrical stimulation when the wings are raised, but when the wings are in the lower half of their beat there is little difference between the two sides. There are thus cycles of sensitivity to asymmetrical sound stimulation and this may serve to assist in the location of the source (Roeder, 1965). Vertical localisation of the sound source also appears to depend on cyclical changes in the sensitivity of the tympanal organs in the course of a wing beat. Thus when the wings are down the insect is more sensitive to sounds coming from below it than to sounds from above, and a sound coming from below and in front would appear to be increasing in intensity during the downstroke.

During flight the auditory input from low intensity sounds of high frequency will thus vary cyclically and in different ways according to the position of the sound source. When the source is immediately behind the moth, however, no cyclical changes occur because the wings do not screen the tympanal organs, and this might provide a basis for the observed movements of moths away from low intensity sound sources (Roeder and Payne, 1966).

One of the functions of the tympanal organs of Lepidoptera is the detection of the sounds produced by bats. Insectivorous bats, such as *Myotis*, produce very short pulses of sound, about 0·5 ms duration separated by intervals of 5–6 ms, when they are hunting. The frequency of each pulse is modulated, starting at about 100 kHz and falling to 30 kHz or below (Griffin *et al.*, 1960). The tympanal organ of noctuids is sensitive over the whole of this range with a maximum sensitivity between 15 and 60 kHz. Unlike the tympanal organ of Orthoptera, it adapts rapidly to a continuing stimulus and has an after discharge which has the effect of amplifying any stimulus of short duration, so it is well suited to the reception of the sounds produced by bats.

Moths can detect bats about 30 m away and at such distances, where the intensity of stimulation is low, tend to turn away from the source of sound (see above). At high intensities of sound, such as would occur when the bat was within about 5 m of the moth, the response from the two tympanal organs is such that location of a sound source could not occur and at these intensities the moth takes violent evasive action. It may close its wings and drop to the ground, or power dive to the ground, or follow an erratic, weaving course. This behaviour is probably elicited by a time interval of less than 2·5 ms between the impulses produced in the auditory nerve. The frequency of impulses increases with the intensity of sound, so that as the bat approaches the impulse frequency in the auditory nerve increases, until finally the impulses are so close together that the moth is stimulated to take avoiding action. It has been shown that this avoiding action has survival value (Roeder, 1965; Roeder and Treat, 1961).

The tympanal organs of a moth also respond to the sound of the wingbeats of another moth if this is within a few feet, but whether or not this has any significance for the moth is not known.

The tympanal organs of *Chrysopa* also appear to function as bat detectors. They have a maximum response to frequencies in the range 40–50 kHz and a pulse of sound is followed by a twitch in the forewing flexor muscles of the flying insect so that the wings partly close. This flexion is maintained for several hundred milliseconds and probably leads to a sudden loss of height in a free-flying insect (Miller, 1971).

29.5 Stretch receptors

Stretch receptors differ from other insect sensilla in consisting of a multipolar neurone with free nerve endings, while all the others contain a bipolar neurone with a dendrite associated with the cuticle. There are no special structures in the endings of the dendrite comparable with the tubular body.

Stretch receptors occur in connective tissue or associated with muscles. In *Periplaneta* there is a pair in the dorsal region of each of abdominal segments two to seven above the bands of longitudinal muscle. The neurone is embedded in fibrous connective tissue which is connected to an intersegmental membrane at one end and to the dorsal body wall and the dorsal muscles at the other. In *Blaberus* (Dictyoptera) the ends of the dendrites inside the connective tissue are not sheathed in glial cells, as is the rest of the neurone, and are only 0·1–0·2 μm in diameter. The connective tissue consists of a matrix with fibrils embedded in it, but without any limiting membrane, so that it is in direct contact with the haemolymph and plasmatocytes (p. 797) are closely applied to the surface. The inelastic fibrils serve to support the neurone and, perhaps, prevent it from being stretched too far (Osborne, 1963).

Acrididae also have stretch receptors dorsally in the abdomen, but the dendritic endings are associated with a slender muscle fibre which runs from the anterior end of one segment to the anterior end of the next, forming a part of the dorsal longitudinal muscles. Stretch receptors associated with muscles also occur in Lepidoptera larvae, pupae and adults, and in Trichoptera and Neuroptera, but here the muscle strand is separated from the other muscles and has a separate innervation. It contains typical muscle fibrils, but these are sparse in the centre of the fibre, which contains a large amount of sarcoplasm and a giant nucleus (Fig. 482). Attached to the muscle and partly embedded in it is a tube of connective tissue known as the fibre tract, which contains reinforcing fibres set in a matrix. These fibres are secreted by the tract cell, which lies within the connective tissue and also has a giant nucleus. The neurone gives rise to two to four main dendrites, which run along the length of the fibre tract, remaining free at the centre but bound to the tract by connective tissue at the ends. From these main dendrites side branches, which at the tips are not clothed in glial cells, pass to the outside, and insinuate their way inside the fibre tract (Osborne and Finlayson, 1965).

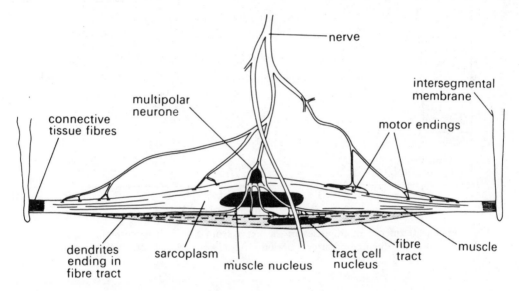

Fig. 482 Diagram of a stretch receptor from the larva of *Antheraea* (based on Finlayson and Lowenstein, 1958)

Larval *Antheraea* (Lepidoptera) have a pair of stretch receptors in the first nine abdominal segments just above the dorsal longitudinal muscles. At metamorphosis the dorsal longitudinal muscles of larval Lepidoptera disappear, but, except for those in the eighth and ninth abdominal segments, the stretch receptors persist. They do undergo a metamorphosis which involves dedifferentiation and subsequent redifferentiation of the associated muscles (Finlayson and Mowat, 1963).

These sensilla are proprioceptors and are stimulated by stretching. In the complete absence of tension there is no output, but under normal tension an output of 5–10 impulses per second is maintained for hours. With further stretching the impulse frequency rises and the adapted frequency is proportional to the length of the receptor. The muscle thus has a tonic response, but superimposed on this is a phasic response which appears while the length of the receptor is changing. The impulse frequency increases with the velocity of stretch and, in addition, a burst of spikes is produced by any acceleration of stretching, either at the start or in the course of stretch. When stretching is complete the impulse frequency falls to its new tonic level (Fig. 483).

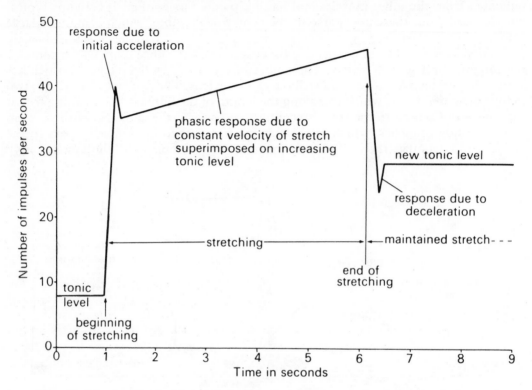

Fig. 483 The frequency of impulses in the nerve from a stretch receptor in the larva of *Antheraea* before, during and after a period of steady stretching (after Weevers, 1966a)

The stretch receptor can thus, through its tonic output, provide information on the position of one part of the body with respect to another, while the phasic response signals changes in these positions. Since at low frequencies, up to about five per second, the output is synchronised with stretching, these receptors may also monitor relatively slow rhythmic movements such as ventilatory movements (p. 546) (Osborne, 1963).

The frequency with which the receptor responds to cyclical stimulation may be limited by the viscosity of the connective tissue matrix in which the dendrites end, but the muscle associated with the lepidopteran stretch receptor may offset this effect to some extent by taking up the slack when the receptor is suddenly released. Relaxation causes a drop in the output of the receptor and this leads to a brief increase in the frequency of impulses to the muscle so that it contracts. Conversely, when the stretch receptor is stimulated the tonic stimulation of the muscle is inhibited so that it relaxes. This perhaps has the effect of preventing overstimulation of the receptor during rapid stretching (Weevers, 1966b).

29.6 Statocysts

Well-developed statocysts are unusual in insects, but in *Dorymyrmex* (Hymenoptera) there is a statocyst on the metathorax just above the coxa. It consists of an invagination of the cuticle lined with tactile hairs. Within the cavity are one or two sand grains which become supported by two cuticular projections in such a way that, although they cannot make large movements, they are free to move if the insect changes its orientation. As a result of a change in orientation they press on some of the hairs, different hairs being stimulated with different orientations so that the organs function as gravity receptors. Comparable organs occur in the head of *Anoplotermes* (Isoptera), and another, but with a cuticular statolith instead of a sand grain, on the prosternum of *Dorymyrmex* (Marcus, 1956).

An organ, known as Palmen's organ, which may function as a statocyst, occurs in the head of larval and adult Ephemeroptera. This consists of a cuticular nodule at the junction of four tracheae mid-dorsally behind the eyes. No special innervation of this organ is known, but behaviour is disturbed if it is destroyed.

Gravity receptors on the cerci of *Arenivaga* are described by Walthall and Hartman, 1981.

29.7 Pressure receptors

Most aquatic insects are buoyant because of the air which they carry down under the water when they submerge, but *Aphelocheirus* (Heteroptera), living on the bottoms of streams and respiring by a plastron, is not buoyant. Although the plastron can withstand considerable pressures (p. 564) it only functions efficiently in water with a high oxygen content, such as normally occurs in relatively shallow water. Hence some mechanism of depth perception is an advantage to *Aphelocheirus*, although it is unnecessary in the majority of other, buoyant insects.

On the ventral surface of the second abdominal segment of *Aphelocheirus* is a shallow depression containing hydrofuge hairs which are much larger than the hairs of the plastron. They are inclined at an angle of about 30° to the surface of the cuticle and dispersed amongst them are thin-walled sensory hairs (Fig. 484). The volume of air trapped by these hairs depends on the balance between the pressure of air inside and the

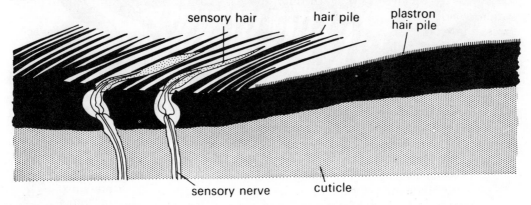

Fig. 484 Section through the edge of a pressure sense organ of *Aphelocheirus* (after Thorpe and Crisp, 1947)

pressure of water outside. If the insect moves into deep water the increase in water pressure reduces the volume of air so that the hairs are bent over, carrying with them the sensilla, which are thus stimulated. The insect responds to such an increase in pressure by swimming up, but there is no response to a decrease in pressure.

Changes in the gas tension in the water, by influencing the exchange of gases, may also influence the pressure in the tracheal system and hence could affect the volume of air trapped by the hydrofuge hairs. However, it is possible that such small changes may be damped out by compensating expansion or contraction of an air-sac on the trachea near the spiracle leading into the depression housing the receptor (Thorpe and Crisp, 1947).

Pressure receptors are also present in *Nepa* (Heteroptera), which has a pair on the sterna of each of abdominal segments three to five. Each consists of a number of mushroom-shaped plates enclosing an airspace (Fig. 485). Nerve endings occur in the plates, and sensory papillae on the inner wall of the airspace are stimulated by the plates pressing on them. A spiracle opens into the space so that the spaces in the three organs of one side are connected through the tracheal system. The receptors give no general response to an increase in pressure, but differential stimulation of the organs of one side produces a response. If the head is tilted upwards the air in the system of pressure receptors tends to rise towards the head end and as a result the anterior mushroom-shaped plates will tend to be pushed out while those on the posterior organ will collapse against the papillae so that the organ is stimulated (Fig. 486). The converse is true if the head is tilted downwards and in this way the insect obtains information on its orientation (Thorpe and Crisp, 1947).

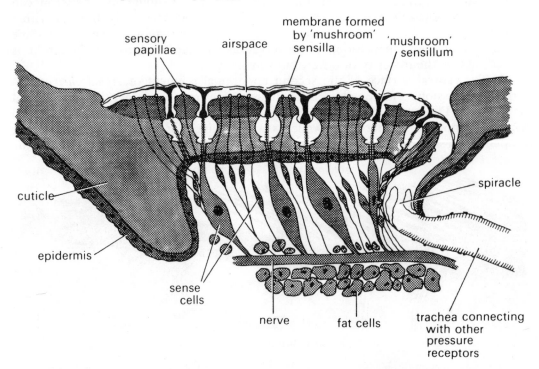

Fig. 485. Section of a pressure sense organ of *Nepa* (after Thorpe and Crisp, 1947)

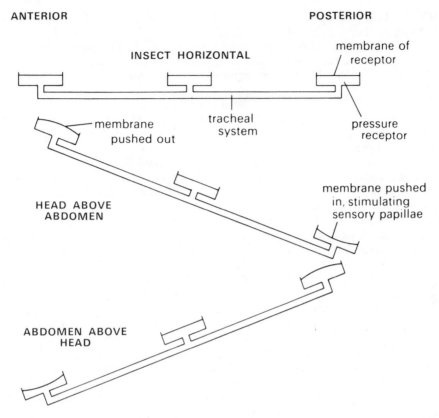

ANTERIOR

POSTERIOR

INSECT HORIZONTAL

membrane of receptor

membrane pushed out

tracheal system

pressure receptor

HEAD ABOVE ABDOMEN

membrane pushed in, stimulating sensory papillae

ABDOMEN ABOVE HEAD

Fig. 486 Diagram to show the principle of action of the pressure receptors of *Nepa* (after Thorpe and Crisp, 1947)

REFERENCES

AUTRUM, H. (1963). Anatomy and physiology of sound receptors in invertebrates. *in* Busnel, R.-G. (ed.), *Acoustic behaviour of animals*. Elsevier, Amsterdam.

BAILEY, W. J. and STEPHEN, R. O. (1978). Directionality and auditory slit function: a theory of hearing in bushcrickets. *Science* **201**: 633–634.

BURKHARDT, D. (1960). Action potentials in the antennae of the blowfly (*Calliphora erythrocephala*) during mechanical stimulation. *J. Insect Physiol.* **4**: 138–145.

BURNET, B., CONNOLLY, K. and DENNIS, L. (1971). The function and processing of auditory information in the courtship behaviour of *Drosophila melanogaster*. *Anim. Behav.* **19**: 409–415.

CHAPMAN, K. M. (1965). Campaniform sensilla on the tactile spines of the legs of the cockroach. *J. exp. Biol.* **42**: 191–203.

DEBAISIEUX, P. (1938). Organes scolopidiaux des pattes d'insectes. *Cellule* **47**: 77–202.

FINLAYSON, L. H. and LOWENSTEIN, O. (1958). The structure and function of abdominal stretch receptors in insects. *Proc. R. Soc.* B, **148**: 433–449.

FINLAYSON, L. H. and MOWAT, D. J. (1963). Variations in histology of abdominal stretch receptors of saturniid moths during development. *Q. Jl microsc. Sci.* **104**: 243–251.

GRAY, E. G. (1960). The fine structure of the insect ear. *Phil. Trans. R. Soc.* B, **243**: 75–94.

GRIFFIN, D. R., WEBSTER, F. A. and MICHAEL, C. R. (1960). The echolocation of flying insects by bats. *Anim. Behav.* **8**: 141–154.

HASKELL, P. T. (1956). Hearing in certain Orthoptera. II. The nature of the response of certain receptors to natural and imitation stridulation. *J. exp. Biol.* **33**: 767–776.

HASKELL, P. T. (1960). The sensory equipment of the migratory locust. *Symp. zool. Soc. Lond.* **3**: 1–23.

HASKELL, P. T. (1961). *Insect sounds.* Witherby, London.

HORRIDGE, G. A. (1965). The Arthropoda. *in* Bullock, T. H. and Horridge, G. A., *Structure and function in the nervous systems of invertebrates.* Freeman, San Francisco.

HOWSE, P. E. (1962). The perception of vibration by the subgenual organ in *Zootermopsis angusticollis* Emerson and *Periplaneta americana*. *Experientia* **18**: 457–458.

HOWSE, P. E. (1964). An investigation into the mode of action of the subgenual organ in the termite, *Zootermopsis angusticollis* Emerson, and in the cockroach, *Periplaneta americana* L. *J. Insect Physiol.* **10**: 409–424.

HOWSE, P. E. (1968). The fine structure and functional organization of chordotonal organs. *Symp. zool. Soc. Lond.* **23**: 167–193.

KATSUKI, Y. and SUGA, N. (1960). Neural mechanism of hearing in insects. *J. exp. Biol.* **37**: 279–290.

KÜHNE, R., LEWIS, B. and KALMRING, K. (1980). The responses of ventral-cord neurons of *Decticus verrucivorus* L. to sound and vibration stimuli *Behav. Process* **5**: 55–74.

KÜPPERS, J. (1974). Measurements on the ionic milieu of the receptor terminal in mechanoreceptive sensilla of insects. *in* Schwartzkopff, J. (ed.), *Symposium: mechano-reception.* Opladen, Westdeutscher Verlag. Abhandlungen der Rheinisch-Westfälischen Akademie der Wissenschaften.

LEWIS, D. B. (1974a). The physiology of the tettigoniid ear. I. The implications of the anatomy of the ear to its function in sound reception. *J. exp. Biol.* **60**: 821–837.

LEWIS, D. B. (1974b). The physiology of the tettigoniid ear. IV. A new hypothesis for acoustic orientation behaviour. *J. exp. Biol.* **60**: 861–869.

LINDAUER, M. (1961). *Communication among social bees.* Harvard Univeristy Press, Cambridge, Mass.

MARCUS, H. (1956). Uber Sinnesorgane bei Articulaten. *Z. Wiss. Zool.* **159**: 225–254.

MARKL, H. (1962). Borstenfelder an den Gelenken als Schwaresinnesorgane bei Ameisen und anderen Hymenopteren. *Z. vergl. Physiol.* **45**: 475–569.

McIVER, S. B. (1975). Structure of cuticular mechanoreceptors of arthropods. *A. Rev. Ent.* **20**: 381–397.

MICHELSEN, A. and NOCKE, H. (1974). Biophysical aspects of sound communication in insects. *Adv. Insect Physiol.* **10**: 247–296.

MILLER, L. A. (1971). Physiological responses of green lacewings (*Chrysopa*, Neuroptera) to ultrasound. *J. Insect Physiol.* **17**: 491–506.

MURPHEY, R. K. and ZARETSKY, M. D. (1972). Orientation to calling song by female crickets, *Scapsipedus marginatus* (Gryllidae). *J. exp. Biol.* **56**: 335–352.

NOCKE, H. (1972). Physiological aspects of sound communication in crickets (*Gryllus campestris* L.). *J. comp. Physiol.* **80**: 141–162.

OSBORNE, M. P. (1963). An electron microscope study of an abdominal stretch receptor of the cockroach. *J. Insect Physiol.* **9**: 237–245.

OSBORNE, M. P. (1970). Structure and function of neuromuscular junctions and stretch receptors. *Symp. R. ent. Soc. Lond.* **5**: 77–100.

OSBORNE, M. P. and FINLAYSON, L. H. (1965). An electron microscope study of the stretch receptor of *Antheraea pernyi* (Lepidoptera: Saturniidae). *J. Insect Physiol.* **11**: 703–710.

PRINGLE, J. W. S. (1938a). Proprioception in insects. I. A new type of mechanical receptor from the palps of the cockroach. *J. exp. Biol.* **15**: 101–113.

PRINGLE, J. W. S. (1938b). Proprioception in insects. II. The action of the campaniform sensilla on the legs. *J. exp. Biol.* **15**: 114–131.

RICE, M. J., GALUN, R. and FINLAYSON, L. H. (1973). Mechanotransduction in insect neurones. *Nature New Biology.* **241**: 286–288.

ROEDER, K. D. (1965). Moths and ultrasound. *Scient. Am.* 212, no. 4: 94–102.

ROEDER, K. D. and PAYNE, R. S. (1966). Acoustic orientation of a moth in flight by means of two sense cells. *Sym. Soc. exp. Biol.* **20**: 251–272.

ROEDER, K. D. and TREAT, A. E. (1957). Ultrasonic reception by the tympanic organ of noctuid moths. *J. exp. Zool.* **134**: 127–157.

ROEDER, K. D. and TREAT, A. E. (1961). The detection and evasion of bats by moths. *Am. Scient.* **49**: 135–148.

ROTH, L. M. (1948). A study of mosquito behaviour. *Am. Midl. Nat.* **40**: 265–352.

SCHWABE, J. (1906). Beiträge zur Morphologie und Histologie der tympanalen Sinnesapparate der Orthopteren. *Zoologica, Stuttg.* no. 50, 154 pp.

SCHWARTZKOPFF, J. (1974). Mechanoreception. *in* Rockstein, M. (ed.), *The physiology of Insecta.* vol. 2. Academic Press, New York and London.

SUGA, N. and KATSUKI, Y. (1961). Central mechanism of hearing in insects. *J. exp. Biol.* **38**: 545–558.

THORPE, W. H. and CRISP, D. J. (1947). Studies on plastron respiration. III. The orientation responses of *Aphelocheirus* (Hemiptera, Aphelocheiridae (Naucoridae)) in relation to plastron respiration; together with an account of specialised pressure receptors in aquatic insects. *J. exp. Biol.* **24**: 310–328.

THURM, U. (1968). Steps in the transducer process of mechanoreceptors. *Symp. zool. Soc. Lond.* **23**: 199–216.

THURM, U. (1974). Basics of the generation of receptor potentials in epidermal mechanoreceptors of insects. *in* Schwartzkopff, J. (ed.), *Symposium: mechanoreception.* Opladen, Westdeutscher Verlag. Abhandlungen der Rheinisch-Westfälischen Akademie der Wissenschaften.

THURM, U. and KÜPPERS, J. (1980). Epithelial physiology of insect sensilla, *in* Locke, M. and Smith, D. (eds.), *Insect biology in the future.* Academic Press, New York.

WALTHALL, W. W. and HARTMAN, H. B. (1981). Receptors and giant interneurons signalling gravity orientation information in the cockroach *Arenivaga. J. comp. Physiol.* A, **142**: 359–369.

WEEVERS, R. de G. (1966a). The physiology of a lepidopteran muscle receptor. I. The sensory response to stretching. *J. exp. Biol.* **44**: 177–194.

WEEVERS, R. de G. (1966b). The physiology of a lepidopteran muscle receptor. II. The function of the receptor muscle. *J. exp. Biol.* **44**: 195–208.

WEIS-FOGH, T. (1949). An aerodynamic sense organ stimulating and regulating flight in locusts. *Nature, Lond.* **164**: 873.

WOLBARSHT, M. L. (1960). Electrical characteristics of insect mechanoreceptors. *J. gen. Physiol.* **44**: 105–122.

YOUNG, D. and BALL, E. (1974). Structure and development of the auditory system in the prothoracic leg of the cricket *Teleogryllus commodus* (Walker). I. Adult structure. *Z. Zellforsch.* **147**: 293–312.

CHAPTER XXX
CHEMORECEPTION

Stimulation by chemicals can occur in different ways. First, if the chemicals are present in a gaseous state in relatively low concentrations they may be perceived as smells and the mechanism of perception is known as olfaction. Second, they may be perceived as a result of direct contact if they are present in the liquid state or in solution at relatively high concentrations. This is known as contact chemoreception and it is not clearly separated from olfaction. Finally, insects have a common chemical sense by which they perceive high concentrations of irritant substances such as ammonia.

The sensilla concerned with chemoreception are widespread, but are particularly abundant on the antennae, mouthparts and legs, and they are characterised by having fine nerve endings exposed through gaps in the cuticle. Olfactory receptors often have many sense cells each of which responds to a range of substances and which are sometimes specialised for the perception of chemicals of particular importance to the insect. Contact chemoreceptors often have a smaller number of sense cells.

The perception of chemicals is important in many aspects of the life of insects. For instance, smell may assist insects in finding food or a mate, while contact chemoreception may be of importance in final recognition of the food, an oviposition site or a mate.

Chemoreception in general is reviewed by Hodgson (1974) and the structure of chemoreceptors by Lewis (1970), Slifer (1970), Altner and Prillinger (1980) and Zacharuk (1980). Dethier (1976) reviews work on the structure and functioning of sensilla in *Phormia*, and Schoonhoven (1972a, 1972b) discusses chemoreception in caterpillars. The physiology of olfactory processes in insects is reviewed by Kafka (1971, 1974) Kaissling (1971, 1974), Steinbrecht and Kasang (1972) and Steinbrecht and Müller (1971).

30.1 Olfaction

30.1.1 Structure of receptors

The essential feature of insect olfactory sensilla is the possession of one or more neurones associated with a cuticular structure containing large numbers of small pores through which molecules may enter to stimulate the dendrites. The cuticular structures have a wide variety of forms: long slender hairs on the antennae of male *Bombyx*, short hairs or pegs (basiconic pegs) on the antennae of locusts, or flat plates on the antennae of bees and aphids (Figs. 487, 488; Table 9). They may stand above the surface of the cuticle, or be sunk beneath its surface, singly as in the coeloconic pegs of the locust (Fig. 489) or in pits containing large numbers of sensilla such as occur on the antennae of flies (Fig. 490) and on the labial palps of Lepidoptera and Neuroptera. In *Sarcophaga*

736

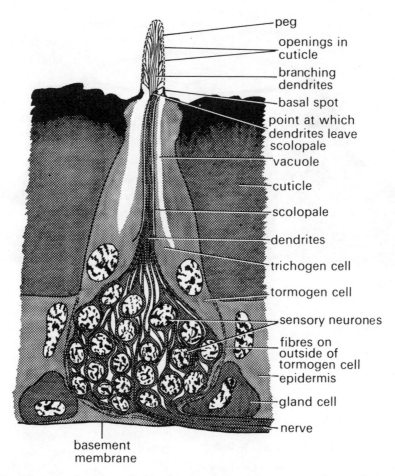

peg

openings in
cuticle

branching
dendrites

basal spot

point at which
dendrites leave
scolopale

vacuole

cuticle

scolopale

dendrites

trichogen cell

tormogen cell

sensory neurones

fibres on
outside of
tormogen cell

epidermis

gland cell

nerve

basement
membrane

Fig. 487 Diagram of a thin-walled basiconic peg from the antenna of a grasshopper (after Slifer *et al.*, 1959)

there are about 50 of these olfactory pits on each antenna of the male, but over 250 on each in the female; in *Phormia* there are 9–11 in males and 11–16 in females. The entrance to each pit is guarded by spines which prevent the entry of dust and the larger pits in *Sarcophaga* contain 200–300 sensory pegs. The pits on the median and dorso-lateral faces of the antenna contain mainly bottle-shaped pegs about 8 μm long (Fig. 490).

It is often true that olfactory sensilla with a large surface area have only a few neurones, but when the surface area is small there may be 40 or more neurones in a single sensillum (Table 9).

An olfactory neurone is similar in structure to a mechanoreceptor neurone (Figs. 461, 462), but lacks the specialised tubular body; there is no known structural modification of the neurone specifically associated with olfaction. The dendrite is enclosed within a scolopale, but close to the surface of the cuticle it passes out into the receptor lymph cavity. In the long trichoid sensilla of *Bombyx* the two dendrites continue unbranched to the tip of the hair (Fig. 487), but in the large basiconic sensilla

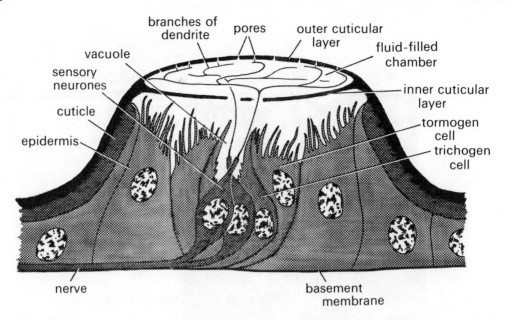

Fig. 488 Diagram of a plate organ from the antenna of an aphid (after Slifer *et al.*, 1964)

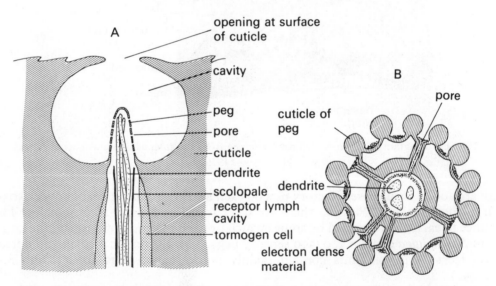

Fig. 489 Coeloconic sensillum of *Locusta*. A. Vertical section through the cavity and peg. B. Transverse section of peg (partly after Kafka, 1971)

of the same insect the dendrites of the three neurones divide into a number of fine branches which continue into the peg (Steinbrecht, 1973).

The pores in the cuticle vary in diameter from 10 to 100 nm in different sensilla. On the trichoid hairs of *Bombyx* there are 2 to 7 pores/μm^2 of cuticle surface, on the coeloconic pegs of *Bombyx* there are 20/μm^2, and on the plate organs of *Apis*, where they occur in radial rows, there are 125/μm^2. In coeloconic pegs the pores are between

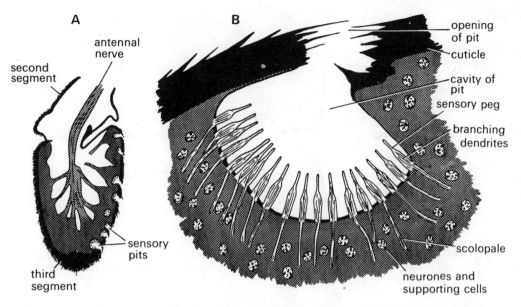

Fig. 490 A. Diagrammatic longitudinal section of the antenna of *Sarcophaga* showing the positions of the sensory pits. B. Detail of a single sensory pit (based on Slifer and Sekhon, 1964)

Table 9

Some characteristics of olfactory sensilla
(after Kaissling, 1974)

Insect	Type of sensillum	Length (μm)	Surface area (μm²)	Pores/μm²	Number of pores/ sensillum	Number of cells
Antherea	trichoid	300	3000	6	18 000	3
Bombyx	trichoid	100	600	3–8	2500	2
Necrophorus	basiconic	40	150	100	15 000	1
Locusta	basiconic	10	150	20	3000	35
Apis	plate	flat	40	125	5000	18

the ribs in the cuticle (Fig. 489). From the ends of the pores fine pore tubules, 10–20 nm in diameter, pass into the lumen of the peg and make contact with the dendrite endings (Fig. 491).

As in mechanoreceptors, the neurones are sheathed proximally by trichogen and tormogen cells. The trichogen cell secretes the cuticle of the peg, the scolopale and the pore tubules. The tormogen cell secretes the cuticle of the socket and bounds the receptor lymph cavity.

Olfactory sensilla are concentrated on the antennae and are known to occur in all the major orders of insects.

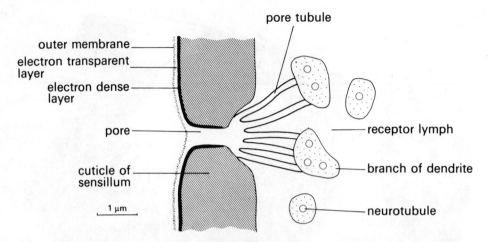

Fig. 491 Diagrammatic section through the wall of a basiconic sensillum showing a single pore and connections with the terminal branches of dendrites (after Steinbrecht, 1973)

30.1.2 Reception of odours and generation of nerve impulses

Since the molecules producing odours are present in relatively low concentrations in air, efficient olfactory reception requires a large surface area on which the odorous molecules can be captured. In species such as *Bombyx* where the female is detected by her scent, the male antennae have a large surface area and many olfactory sensilla (p. 13). The male has 17 000 long trichoid sensilla on each antenna compared with only 6000 in the female. Each sensillum has a surface area of about 600 μm^2 and together these sensilla comprise 14 % of the total surface area of the antenna, but they capture a disproportionately large number of the odour molecules which impact on the antennae.

The whole surface of the sensillum is involved in the capture of molecules and it is probable that an outer coating of polymerised lipid is involved in this. The layer consists of a thin outer membrane about 2·5 nm thick, a layer of electron transparent material 7·5 nm thick, which extends into the pores, and an electron dense layer (Fig. 491). This material is not confined to the sensilla, but also occurs elsewhere on the cuticle. When a molecule impacts on this surface it diffuses laterally in the surface layers and it has been calculated that, on a trichoid sensillum of *Bombyx*, this would bring any molecule on the surface to a pore within 2 ms of impaction. Subsequently the molecule would diffuse in through the pore, reaching the dendrite membrane in a further 1 ms (Fig. 492) (Steinbrecht and Kasang, 1972). Such molecular capture is probably not specific, molecules with low stimulating effect being collected as readily as molecules to which the sensillum is highly sensitive (Kaissling, 1974), but Kasang *et al.* (1974) suggest that there may be some degree of selection of the molecules collected.

On reaching the membrane of the dendrite a stimulating molecule becomes bound to a specific acceptor site, causing a change in membrane potential. This leads to an ionic flux across the membrane and the development of the receptor potential, which spreads proximally along the dendrite and results in the generation of nerve impulses. The stronger the stimulus, the shorter the reaction time between the arrival of the

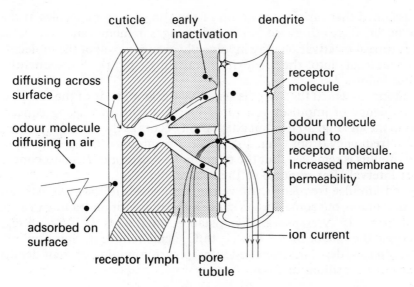

Fig. 492 Diagram of the capture and reception of an odour molecule on an olfactory receptor (after Kaissling, 1974)

stimulating material at the sensillum and the initiation of nerve impulses (Fig. 493A). This probably results from a larger number of molecules reaching acceptor sites simultaneously and causing a more rapid build-up of the receptor potential. In *Bombyx* it has been calculated that a single molecule of the female attractant pheromone is sufficient to generate a nerve impulse in a male receptor cell.

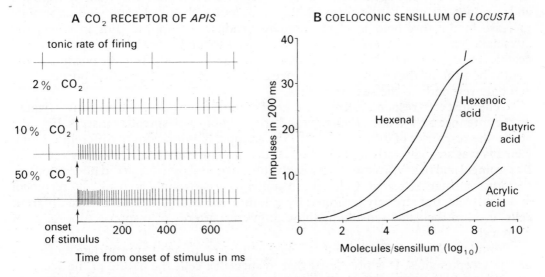

Fig. 493 Responses of olfactory receptors to stimulation. A. The CO_2 receptor of *Apis* showing the higher rate of firing at higher concentrations and progressive adaptation with continued stimulation. B. Changes in the rate of firing of a coeloconic sensillum of *Locusta* in relation to concentration of stimulus and with different stimulating chemicals. Rate of firing in first 200 ms of stimulation (after Kaissling, 1971)

It is assumed that early inactivation of the stimulating molecules at the acceptor sites must occur, since otherwise continued changes in membrane permeability would follow. The initial inactivation may involve physical removal of the molecules into the receptor lymph or into the dendrite (Kaissling, 1974). Subsequently enzymic degradation follows.

With odours to which the insect is sensitive the amplitude of the receptor potential and the frequency of impulses generated increase with increasing concentration of molecules in the air (Fig. 493B), but adaptation occurs as the stimulus continues and so the impulse frequency drops (Fig. 493A). Very commonly, firing stops as soon as the source of stimulus is removed, but the pheromone receptor of *Bombyx* continues to fire for a short interval after removal of the source.

Increased impulse frequency, above the tonic level, follows depolarisation of the dendrite membrane, but some odours cause hyperpolarisation leading to a reduction in the rate of firing. In *Necrophorus*, for instance, fatty acids with five to eight carbon atoms increase the rate of firing, but C_2 to C_4 acids reduce it. Some amines produce opposite responses, depolarisation and hyperpolarisation, in different dendrites in the same coeloconic sensillum of *Locusta*.

30.1.3 Sensitivity to odours

The sensitivity of individual chemoreceptor neurones to different odours is very variable. Some are highly sensitive to one odour and relatively insensitive to all others; these are known as specialist olfactory cells. Other neurones are sensitive to a wide range of different chemicals and are known as generalist cells.

The best known specialist cells are the pheromone receptor cells of some male moths. These cells are specifically tuned to perceive the female attractant pheromone and a minor change in the form of the stimulating chemical causes an enormous increase in the threshold level required to produce a response. For instance, the attractant pheromone of *Trichoplusia ni* is *cis*-7-dodecanyl acetate. *Trans*-7-dodecanyl acetate is 300–2000 times less effective as an attractant, while shifts in the position of the double bond along the chain further reduce effectiveness. For all practical purposes the cell only responds to the sex attractant.

Generalist cells respond to a wide range of odours. Such cells have been investigated on the antennae of *Apis* and *Antheraea* and are probably widespread in insects. Fig. 494 shows the responses of different cells in the antenna of *Antheraea* to different odours. Cell 27a was strongly activated by phenyl ethyl acetate and geraniol, weakly activated by terpineol and benzyl acetate, and weakly inhibited by isosafrole; it did not respond to the other substances tested. Cell 27b, in contrast, was strongly activated by terpineol and isosafrole, but strongly inhibited by geraniol and benzyl acetate. Hence different cells, even in the same sensillum, show different patterns of response to a range of chemicals.

Stimulation of an olfactory cell depends on the reception of appropriate molecules on the acceptor sites. It is presumed that in specialist cells the nature of the acceptor sites is such that they form bonds only with molecules having very specific characteristics. Among these characteristics are the stereochemical form of the molecule, the positions of double bonds and the presence and position of certain functional chemical groups. According to Wright (1977) specificity may depend on the far-infrared vibrational frequencies of organic molecules.

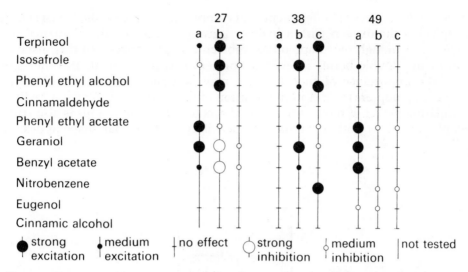

Fig. 494 Reactions of single cells from a basiconic sensillum of *Antheraea* to different odours. Each vertical line represents one cell; each group of three represents a different sensillum (after Kaissling, 1971)

Specificity of receptor cells in the coeloconic sensillum of *Locusta* has been studied by Kafka (1970, 1971). These cells are maximally stimulated by compounds with a chain length of six carbon atoms (Fig. 495); 2-oxohexanoic acid, *trans*-3-hexenoic acid and *trans*-2-hexenoic acid are the most effective (Fig. 496). Absence of the carbonyl

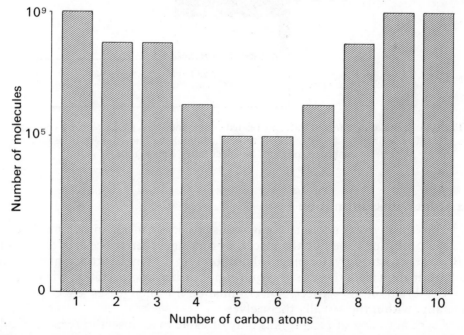

Fig. 495 Response of single cells in a coeloconic sensillum of *Locusta* to stimulation by n-acids with different numbers of carbon atoms. The response is measured as the number of molecules per pit required to produce an increase of 30 impulses/second in the firing rate (after Kafka, 1971)

group markedly reduces the effectiveness of compounds acting on the locust sensillum, while replacing the oxygen with a hydroxyl group almost totally eliminates activity (Fig. 496) even though the shape of the molecule is unchanged. In this instance the position of the double bond, or even its presence, is not critical. In other species, however, the importance of such features may be quite different. For instance, in *Acosmetia* (Lepidoptera) a shift in the position of the double bond can markedly affect the stimulating power of mono-unsaturated acetates (Fig. 497). This is also true with the sex pheromones of other moths and specificity of molecular shape appears to be critically important.

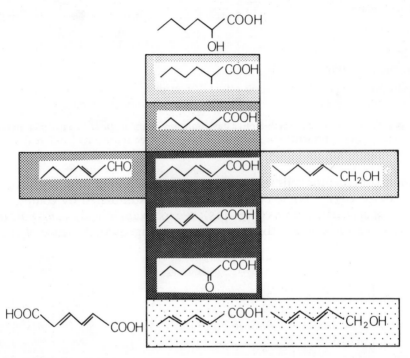

Fig. 496 Stimulating effect of different related compounds on a single receptor cell from a coeloconic sensillum of *Locusta*. Intensity of shading shows the strength of stimulation; unshaded indicates no effect (after Kafka, 1971)

30.1.4 Odour discrimination

The specific sensitivity of odour specialist cells provides a mechanism by which certain odours can be distinguished by the insect. For instance, certain cells in the sensilla of male *Bombyx* respond only (for practical purposes) to the female attractant pheromone. Hence information from these cells requires no further interpretation when transmitted to the brain of the insect. Discrimination in such cases effectively occurs peripherally, within the sensilla themselves.

Such special tuning of receptors is only of value to an insect in respect of odours which are encountered consistently and predictably and which have some special significance in its biology. However, all insects will periodically encounter other

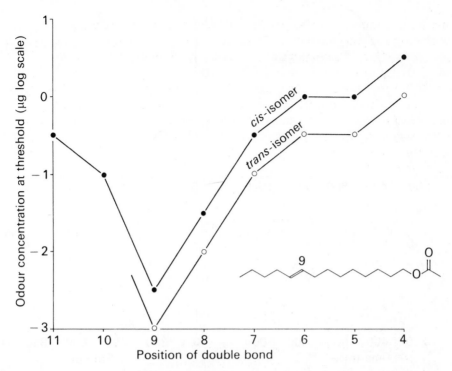

Fig. 497 Concentrations of mono-unsaturated acetates with the double bond in different positions required to produce a standard electroantennagram in male *Acosmetia*. Concentration was measured in terms of the load of the odour at source. Inset shows the structure of the most highly stimulating compound (after Kaissling, 1974)

odours, the recognition of which may be biologically important, but whose occurrence is variable and unpredictable. *Apis*, which has been most fully studied behaviourally, can differentiate an essential oil derived from oranges from many other scents including other oils derived from citrus fruits, although it does confuse the citrus oils to some extent. It can also detect very small changes in scents. Thus bees trained to the odour of benzyl acetate can separate this from a mixture containing 119 parts of benzyl acetate to one part of linalool (Ribbands, 1955).

This type of odour discrimination is facilitated by the generalist odour cells. Dethier and Schoonhoven (1969) showed that the pattern of response of four different cells on the antenna of *Manduca* larvae to different odours varied in respect of the rate of firing, the latency of response and the rates of increase in firing and of adaptation (Fig. 498). These differences provide a basis for discrimination between different substances within the central nervous system. In this case it is presumed that information coming to the brain from all the receptor cells is used in interpreting the nature of the stimulating material and an appropriate behavioural response follows. It is probable that differentiation of different odours by *Periplaneta* also occurs centrally, though some degree of peripheral discrimination by different sense cells also occurs (Sass, 1976).

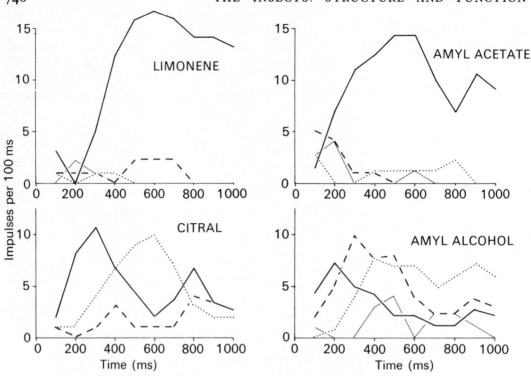

Fig. 498 The pattern of discharge from four cells in a basiconic sensillum on the antenna of larval *Manduca* in response to four different odours. Each cell is represented in the same way in all the diagrams (after Dethier and Schoonhoven, 1969)

30.1.5 Significance of odour perception

The effect of stimulation by odours is to promote activity; some substances attract insects, some lead to a rejection or an attempted avoidance of the stimulus, while in some cases the response varies with the concentration of the odour.

Whether a stimulating odour is attractive or repellent is determined by the genetic constitution of the insect. Hence carrion feeders react positively to the smell of ammonia which is associated with decaying meat, and female blowflies, which oviposit on meat, are more strongly attracted than males. Many insects, on the other hand, are repelled by ammonia at all concentrations. Similarly the specific response of male insects to female scents is genetically controlled.

Apart from the influence of the intrinsic make up of the insect, responsiveness is affected by its physiological state. For instance, blowfly larvae are attracted by the smell of ammonia during their feeding period, but when feeding ends in the third instar, at a time when the larvae normally leave the food in order to pupate, the response to ammonia is reversed. The state of feeding also influences the response of *Schistocerca* larvae to the smell of food. Fully fed larvae do not respond to food smells, but after being starved for a few hours they make directed movements towards the source of smell (Haskell *et al.*, 1962).

Further, the response varies with the concentration of the stimulating odour. In general the intensity of response, either attraction or repulsion, increases with the concentration, but some substances which are attractive at low concentration are rejected when their concentration becomes too high (Fig. 499). Other behavioural changes may result from increased concentrations of odour and, for instance, the pheromone from female *Bombyx* evokes an orientation response from the male at low concentrations, but at high concentrations it causes the male to make mating responses.

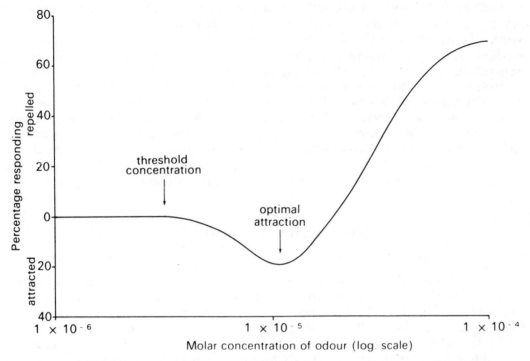

Fig. 499 Changes in the response of adult *Musca* (Diptera) to different concentrations of the odour of iso-valeraldehyde. Concentrations are low to the left of the figure (from Dethier, 1963)

Olfactory stimulation is of considerable importance to many insects in locating their food. Carrion-feeding species such as *Necrophorus* (Coleoptera) are attracted by the smell of ammonia. Unfed adult *Leptinotarsa* (Coleoptera) are attracted by the odour of species of Solanaceae, several of which are eaten, but not by most other plant species (Visser and Nielsen, 1977). *Philanthus* (Hymenoptera) only responds to insects having the smell of bees (p. 28). In *Apis*, flower scents on the bodies of returning foragers help other workers to recognise the source of food and this is further facilitated by the habit of marking the flowers which are visited with the colony odour.

Some plant odours repel insects and prevent them from feeding. The failure of *Schistocerca* to feed on lavender leaves is probably due to the presence of such repellent odours. The odour of α-pinene is known to repel insects of a number of species, and nepetalactone, the chemical giving a characteristic odour to catnip, repels a number of phytophagous Homoptera and Coleoptera (Eisner, 1964).

Female insects are commonly attracted to suitable oviposition sites by smell. Fertilised females of *Lucilia sericata* (Diptera) are attracted by the smell of wool. This species commonly oviposits on live sheep, but the related *L. caesar*, *L. illustris* and *Calliphora vomitoria*, which do not normally attack sheep in Britain, are not attracted to wool to any marked extent (Cragg and Cole, 1956). The parasite *Rhyssa* (Hymenoptera) is able to detect the larva of its host *Sirex* (Hymenoptera) through several inches of wood as a result of olfactory stimulation.

Odours, in the form of pheromones, are of great importance in many species in promoting the meeting of the sexes (p. 859) and in some cases are important in the later stages of courtship. In social insects colony odour is important in recognition of members of the colony and the differentiation of intruders. The laying and following of odour trails is particularly well-developed in ants (p. 869) (Wilson, 1974).

There is no evidence that insects can follow gradients of smell and it is unlikely that, under natural conditions with air turbulence, such gradients can be stable over any but very short distances. Thus it is improbable that smell provides a directing influence, but it may stimulate the insect to orientate to some other factor. Thus *Schistocerca* larvae tend to drift slowly downwind, but when stimulated by the smell of food they orientate into the wind and so, by moving upwind, arrive in the neighbourhood of the source of smell. Moths and bees responding to sexual pheromones also orientate to the wind (p. 860).

30.2 Contact chemoreception

30.2.1 Structure of receptors

Contact chemoreceptors are more constant in their basic structure than olfactory receptors. Each consists of a cuticular peg through which the scolopale extends to open by a pore at the tip (Fig. 500). The peg varies from a simple dome, not rising above the level of the rest of the cuticle, to a long hair 300 μm or more in length. The scolopale may be free within the lumen of the peg or fused with one side. Each sensillum contains a small number of neurones, commonly four or five, with dendrites extending to the pore at the tip of the peg. The dendrites are not exposed at the tip, but are protected by a layer of viscous mucopolysaccharide, which is presumably secreted in the basal cavity and passes to the tip within the scolopale.

The basic structure of the dendrites is similar to that in olfactory receptors, although they do not branch distally and remain within the scolopale throughout their lengths. It is common for one dendrite in a contact chemoreceptor sensillum to end at the base of the peg and possess a tubular body at its distal end, indicating that it functions as a mechanoreceptor. The trichogen and tormogen cells are similar in form and arrangement to those of olfactory receptors.

Contact chemoreceptors may occur on all parts of the body, but they are concentrated on the tarsi and on the mouthparts (p. 23).

30.2.2 Functioning of contact chemoreceptors

Although contact chemoreceptors can be stimulated by odours they are generally stimulated by chemicals in aqueous solution or by chemicals distributed over solid surfaces. It is known, for instance, that a number of insects are stimulated by chemicals

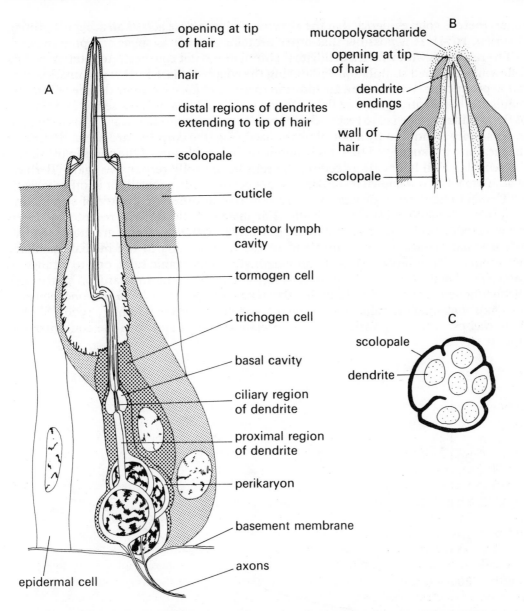

Fig. 500 Diagram of a contact chemoreceptor. A. Longitudinal section showing general structure. B. Longitudinal section of tip of sensillum showing detail of the structure. C. Transverse section through the scolopale in the receptor lymph cavity

in the dry wax on the surface of leaves (Chapman, 1977). In order to reach the dendrites, molecules diffuse through the plug of mucopolysaccharide at the opening of the scolopale. At the dendrite membrane the molecule binds to an acceptor site and, following an increase in membrane permeability, this leads to the development of a receptor potential. The acceptor sites are believed to be proteins and, in the case of sugar, there is good evidence that the enzyme α-glucosidase acts as an acceptor protein (Hansen, 1974). It is possible that other proteins also act as sugar acceptor sites.

The readiness with which a dendrite is stimulated is not constant. Adaptation occurs following sustained stimulation and during the adapted phase further stimulation may fail to produce nerve impulses. In addition there is, in *Locusta*, some degree of internal regulation of receptivity. Immediately following a meal, many of the sensilla on the tips of the maxillary palps fail to respond to normally stimulating chemicals. This reduction in sensitivity is induced by a hormone released from the corpora cardiaca at the end of the meal and it is suggested that it is brought about by a closure of the pores in the tips of the sensilla. Two hours after feeding the sensilla are fully responsive again (Bernays *et al.*, 1972). It is not known if similar changes occur in other sensilla or in other insects.

Contact chemoreceptor neurones are sensitive to different spectra of stimulating molecules. Some are relatively specific. For instance, the sinigrin receptor of *Pieris* larvae responds only to a few mustard oil glucosides. Other receptors are most sensitive to particular classes of compound and of the four sensilla in the medial maxillary sensillum of *Pieris* larva, two respond maximally to inorganic salts, one to a range of deterrent chemicals which inhibit feeding, and one to the mustard oil glucosides (Schoonhoven, 1972a). Similarly, in the tarsal receptors of *Phormia* one neurone responds maximally to salts, one to sugars, and one to water (Dethier, 1976). Within these classes, sensitivity varies with the precise chemical and with the concentration (Fig. 501).

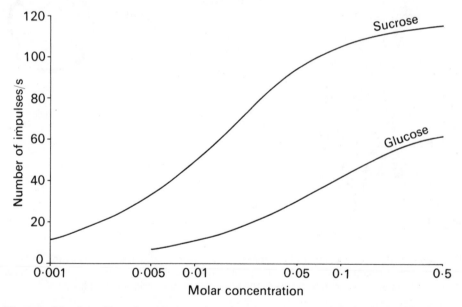

Fig. 501 Number of impulses per second produced in the styloconic sensillum on the maxilla of *Pieris* larva in response to different concentrations of two sugars (after Ma, 1972)

Some cells also respond to chemicals other than the classes to which they are particularly adapted and each cell probably has its own spectrum of activity which overlaps with, but is different from, that of other cells (van der Starre and de Jonge, 1973).

Hence a single sensillum with only five or six neurones can respond to many different chemicals. For instance, in *Locusta* one individual sensillum on the palp tip responded to inorganic salts, hexose, pentose and disaccharide sugars, amino acids, organic and dilute inorganic acids, a triterpenoid and an alkaloid (Blaney, 1974) and from behavioural studies sensilla in the same group are known to respond to waxes on plant surfaces.

Comprehensive studies have been made on *Phormia*, which responds to stimulation of the trichoid sensilla with sugar or water by extending the proboscis. The response varies with different sugars and in general the α-glucosides are the most stimulating. Thus in *Phormia* and *Calliphora* the lowest acceptance thresholds are for sucrose, maltose and trehalose of the disaccharides and fructose, fucose and glucose of the monosaccharides. Some sugars fail to stimulate altogether, while others have an inhibiting effect. Polysaccharides also fail to stimulate.

The response to water is most readily elicited by water free of salts. High osmotic pressure or the presence of inorganic electrolytes inhibit the response in varying degrees, and the effects of electrolytes are specific; calcium chloride, for instance, inhibits the response at lower concentrations than does sodium chloride.

Stimulation of the trichoid sensilla of *Phormia* with inorganic salts leads to proboscis withdrawal or the inhibition of extension. In general, inorganic cations are more effective if they have high ionic mobilities. Thus their stimulating or inhibiting power follows the series: $H^+ > NH_4^+ > K^+ > Ca^{++} > Mg^{++} > Na^+$. With anions the situation is more complex and is different for mono- and di-valent ions. In *Periplaneta* the stimulating power of anions follows the sequence: $OH > NO_3 > I' > Br' > Cl' = SO_4'' > Ac' > PO_4'''$. With organic electrolytes the hydrogen ions are important, but the anion also contributes to the stimulating power. Thresholds for stimulation are lower with longer chain lengths.

Similarly in any series of aliphatic organic compounds stimulating power is proportional to chain length, and thus to the boiling point, and inversely proportional to the vapour pressure. The relationship is not linear for any one series of compounds, but shows a sharp break in the region of a certain chain length which is characteristic for the series (Fig. 502). Replacement of the hydrogen atoms in the molecule by various other groups, such as chloride or a hydroxyl group, alters the stimulating power of the compound. It is suggested that surface energy relationships are involved in stimulation by these substances.

Where cells are not tuned to specific chemicals it is probable that discrimination between chemicals occurs in the central nervous system on the basis of all the information available, rather than peripherally on the basis of receptor specificity. This is probably the case with the palp tip sensilla of *Locusta* (Blaney, 1975) and may also be true in *Calliphora* (van der Starre and de Jonge, 1973).

Integration within the central nervous system is known to occur in co-ordinating the inputs from different sensilla. *Phormia*, for instance, responds to stimulation of the tarsal chemoreceptors with sugar by extending its proboscis, but it responds to lower concentrations of sugar if two tarsi are stimulated instead of one. Central integration is also suggested by the reduced response if one tarsus is stimulated with sugar and another with an unacceptable substance.

The rate at which impulses are produced is very high at the beginning of stimulation, but rapidly falls as adaptation occurs and most information is conveyed to

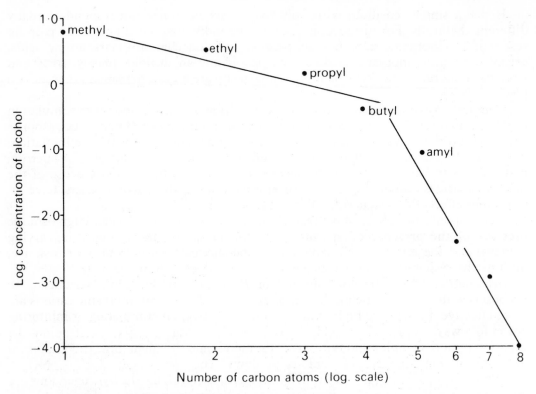

Fig. 502 Relationship between the number of carbon atoms in various primary alcohols and the concentrations required to cause rejection by 50 % of the flies tested. Concentrations are lowest at the bottom of the figure (from Dethier, 1963)

the central nervous system in the first 100 ms (Fig. 503A). In *Locusta* a more sustained flow of information is maintained from the sensilla on the tips of the palps as a result of the rapid vibration of the palps. This ensures that the sensilla make contact with the stimulating material for periods of less than 300 ms and during the intervals between successive contacts some disadaptation of the sensilla occurs (Fig. 503B) (Blaney and Duckett, 1975).

30.2.3 Significance of contact chemoreception

Contact chemoreception is of particular importance in the control of feeding. In *Phormia*, for instance, stimulation of the tarsi with sugar leads to proboscis extension. This brings the labellar hairs into contact with the food so that this is subjected to further monitoring. The labellar hairs are more sensitive than the tarsal hairs and so are able to detect substances, perhaps unsuitable, which are present in concentrations too low to stimulate the tarsal hairs. If the substance still proves to be suitable the labellar lobes are spread out and the insect starts to suck up the sugar. The entry of sugar into the pseudotracheal system immediately stimulates the interpseudotracheal pegs providing a final check on the suitability of the food. Continuous sensory input is necessary for feeding to continue (Dethier, 1976).

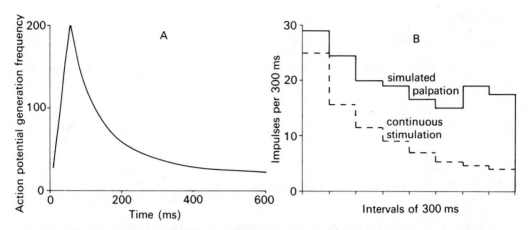

Fig. 503 Responses of a sensillum on the palp of *Locusta* to stimulation by 0.1 M NaCl.
A. The frequency with which action potentials are generated at different times after the onset of
stimulation. B. Adaptation of the response with continuous stimulation and with intermittent
stimulation such as occurs during palpation (after Blaney and Duckett, 1975)

Food selection by some insects is largely regulated by the presence of particular
chemicals in the food which stimulate specifically tuned receptors. For instance, *Pieris*
larva is stimulated to feed by mustard oil glucosides which occur in its host plants and it
has a neurone which responds specifically to these; the adult of *Chrysolina brunsvicensis*
is stimulated to feed by hypericin, found in the *Hypericum* on which it feeds, and it has a
tarsal neurone responsive to this substance (Rees, 1969). In other instances the picture
is quite different. Dethier (1973) has shown that, in a number of caterpillar species,
there is no consistent pattern of response in the medial and lateral sensilla to host or
non-host plants. No pattern is characteristic of acceptable plants or of unacceptable
plants and Dethier concludes that recognition depends on the overall pattern of
information reaching the central nervous system from all the sensilla. The evidence of
Blaney (1974, 1975) for *Locusta* and vander Starre and de Jonge (1973) for *Calliphora*
suggest that this type of food recognition, based on the sum of sensory inputs to the
central nervous system may be a common phenomenon in insects which are relatively
catholic in their choice of foods.

Contact chemoreception may also be important in the control of oviposition. Thus
Locusta, which oviposits in moist sand, digging a hole with the tip of the abdomen, can
detect various inorganic salts in the sand. If the concentration of salts is high the insect
withdraws its abdomen without ovipositing and the higher the concentration the more
often is the sand rejected as an oviposition site (Woodrow, 1965). Chemoreceptors on
the ovipositor are also important in parasitic insects.

30.3 Common chemical sense

Insects respond through the common chemical sense to high concentrations of irritant
substances such as ammonia, chlorine and essential oils by making avoidance reactions.
It is a characteristic of the sense that the sensilla by which it is mediated are widely
distributed over the insect and the response persists even after all the known olfactory
receptors have been destroyed.

REFERENCES

ALTNER, H. and PRILLINGER, L. (1980). Ultrastructure of invertebrate chemo-, thermo-, and hygroreceptors and its functional significance. *Int. Rev. Cytol.* **67**: 69–139.

BERNAYS, E. A., BLANEY, W. M. and CHAPMAN, R. F. (1972). Changes in chemoreceptor sensilla on the maxillary palps of *Locusta migratoria* in relation to feeding. *J. exp. Biol.* **57**: 745–753.

BLANEY, W. M. (1974). Electrophysiological responses of the terminal sensilla on the maxillary palps of *Locusta migratoria* (L.) to some electrolytes and non-electrolytes. *J. exp. Biol.* **60**: 275–293.

BLANEY, W. M. (1975). Behavioural and electrophysiological studies of taste discrimination by the maxillary palps of larvae of *Locusta migratoria* (L.). *J. exp. Biol.* **62**: 555–569.

BLANEY, W. M. and DUCKETT, A. M. (1975). The significance of palpation by the maxillary palps of *Locusta migratoria* (L.): an electrophysiological and behavioural study. *J. exp. Biol.* **63**: 701–712.

CHAPMAN, R. F. (1977). The role of the leaf surface in food selection by acridids and other insects. *Colloq. Int. C.N.R.S.* no. 265: 133–149.

CRAGG, J. B. and COLE, P. (1956). Laboratory studies on the chemosensory reactions of blowflies. *Ann. appl. Biol.* **44**: 478–491.

DETHIER, V. G. (1963). *The physiology of insect senses.* Methuen, London.

DETHIER, V. G. (1973). Electrophysiological studies of gustation in Lepidopterous larvae. II. Taste spectra in relation to food-plant discrimination. *J. comp. Physiol.* **82**: 103–134.

DETHIER, V. G. (1976). *The hungry fly.* Harvard University Press, Cambridge, Mass. and London.

DETHIER, V. G. and SCHOONHOVEN, L. M. (1969). Olfactory coding by lepidopterous larvae. *Entomologia exp. appl.* **12**: 535–543.

EISNER, T. (1964). Catnip: its raison d'être. *Science* **146**: 1318–1320.

HANSEN, K. (1974). α-glucosidases as sugar receptor proteins in flies. *in* Jaenicke, L. (ed.), *Biochemistry of sensory functions.* Springer-Verlag, Berlin.

HASKELL, P. T., PASKIN, M. W. J. and MOORHOUSE, J. E. (1962). Laboratory observations on factors affecting the movements of hoppers of the desert locust. *J. Insect Physiol.* **8**: 53–78.

HODGSON, E. S. (1974). Chemoreception. *in* Rockstein, M. (ed.), *The physiology of Insecta.* vol. 2. Academic Press, New York and London.

KAFKA, W. A. (1970). Molekulare Wechselwirkungen bei der Erregung einzelner Riechzellen. *Z. vergl. Physiol.* **70**: 105–143.

KAFKA, W. A. (1971). Specificity of odor-molecule interaction in single cells. *in* Ohloff, G. and Thomas, A. F. (eds.), *Gustation and olfaction.* Academic Press, London and New York.

KAFKA, W. A. (1974). Physicochemical aspects of odor reception in insects. *Ann. N. York Acad. Sci.* **237**: 115–128.

KAISSLING, K.-E. (1971). Insect olfaction. *in* Beidler, L. M. (ed.), *Handbook of sensory physiology.* vol. 4, Springer-Verlag. Berlin.

KAISSLING, K.-E. (1974). Sensory transduction in insect olfactory receptors. *in* Jaenicke, L. (ed.), *Biochemistry of sensory functions.* Springer-Verlag, Berlin.

KASANG, G., KNAUER, B. and BEROZA, M. (1974). Uptake of the sex attractant ^{3}H-disparlure by male gypsy moth antennae (*Lymantria dispar*) [= *Porthetria dispar*]. *Experientia.* **30**: 147–148.

LEWIS, C. T. (1970). Structure and function in some external receptors. *Symp. R. ent. Soc. Lond.* **5**: 59–76.

MA, Wei Chun (1972). Dynamics of feeding responses in *Pieris brassicae* Linn. as a function of chemosensory input: a behavioural, ultrastructural and electrophysiological study. *Meded. Landbouwhogeschool Wageningen* 1972, no. 11.

REES, C. J. C. (1969). Chemoreceptor specificity associated with choice of feeding site by the beetle, *Chrysolina brunsvicensis* on its foodplant, *Hypericum hirsutum*. *Entomologia exp. appl.* **12**: 565–583.

RIBBANDS, C. R. (1955). The scent perception of the honeybee. *Proc. R. Soc.* B, **143**: 367–379.

SASS, H. (1976). Zur nervösen Codierung von Geruchsreizen bei *Periplaneta americana*. *J. comp. Physiol.* **107**: 49–65.

SCHOONHOVEN, L. M. (1972a). Plant recognition by lepidopterous larvae. *Symp. R. ent. Soc. Lond.* **6**: 87–99.

SCHOONHOVEN, L. M. (1972b). Secondary plant substances and insects. *Recent Adv. Phytochem.* **4**: 197–224.

SLIFER, E. H. (1970). The structure of arthropod chemoreceptors. *A. Rev. Ent.* **15**: 121–142.

SLIFER, E. H. and SEKHON, S. S. (1964). Fine structure of the sense organs on the antennal flagellum of a flesh fly, *Sarcophaga argyrostoma* R.-D. (Diptera: Sarcophagidae). *J. Morph.* **114**: 185–207.

SLIFER, E. H., PRESTAGE, J. J. and BEAMS, H. W. (1959). The chemoreceptors and other sense organs on the antennal flagellum of the grasshopper, (Orthoptera: Acrididae). *J. Morph.* **105**: 145–191.

SLIFER, E. H., SEKHON, S. S. and LEES, A. D. (1964). The sense organs on the antennal flagellum of aphids (Homoptera), with special reference to the plate organs. *Q. Jl microsc. Sci.* **105**: 21–30.

STARRE, H. van der and DE JONGE, G. (1973). Salt–sugar interactions in tarsal taste hairs of the blowfly, *Calliphora vicina* Robineau-Desvoidy. *Netherlands J. Zool.* **23**: 215–221.

STEINBRECHT, R. A. (1973). Die Feinbau olfaktorischer Sensillen des Seidenspinners (Insecta: Lepidoptera). *Z. Zellforsch.* **139**: 533–565.

STEINBRECHT, R. A. and KASANG, G. (1972). Capture and conveyance of odour molecules in an insect olfactory receptor. *in* Schneider, D. (ed.), *Olfaction and taste* IV. Wissenschaftliche Verlagsgesellschaft, Stuttgart.

STEINBRECHT, R. A. and MÜLLER, B. (1971). On the stimulus conducting structures in insect olfactory receptors. *Z. Zellforsch.* **117**: 570–575.

VISSER, J. H. and NIELSEN, J. K. (1977). Specificity in the olfactory orientation of the Colorado beetle, *Leptinotarsa decemlineata*. *Entomologia exp. appl.* **21**: 14–22.

WILSON, E. O. (1974). *The insect societies*. Harvard University Press.

WOODROW, D. F. (1965). The responses of the African migratory locust, *Locusta migratoria migratorioides* R. & F., to the chemical composition of the soil at oviposition. *Anim. Behav.* **13**: 348–356.

WRIGHT, R. H. (1977). The olfactory transmission of information. *Colloq. Int. C.N.R.S.* no. 265: 61–71.

ZACHARUK, R. Y. (1980). Ultrastructure and function of insect chemosensilla. *A. Rev. Ent.* **25**: 27–47.

CHAPTER XXXI

TEMPERATURE AND HUMIDITY

Water forms a large proportion of insect tissues and survival depends on the ability to maintain the balance of water in the body (p. 592); enzymes function efficiently only within a limited range of temperatures and for these reasons environmental humidity and temperature are of great importance in the lives of all insects. Relatively little is known about the receptors involved with the perception of these phenomena, but since insects are poikilothermic, their temperatures approximating to and varying with ambient temperature, the nervous system must be directly influenced by changes in body temperature. In general, body temperature is probably more important than ambient temperature in controlling insect behaviour since it influences the nervous system and enzyme activity directly. It represents a balance between the heat gained from metabolic activities and from the environment and the heat lost by evaporation and convection.

There is little physiological control of body temperature, but behavioural adaptations tend to maintain the temperature as near to an overall optimum for metabolic activity as environmental conditions allow. Responses to humidity also tend to keep the insect within an optimal range and in both cases the response may vary according to the previous treatment of the insect.

Insects develop only within a limited range of temperature which is characteristic of the species and they are killed by temperatures outside this range. There is no limiting range of humidity and most insects can develop at any humidity provided they are able to control their water balance. A few insects are known which can withstand complete desiccation of all or some of their tissues.

The general effects of temperature and humidity on insect physiology, behaviour and development are reviewed by Bursell (1974a, 1974b) and Wigglesworth (1972). Howe (1967) discusses temperature in relation to embryonic development and Heinrich (1973, 1974, 1981) and May (1979) review temperature regulation in insects. Asahina (1969) and Salt (1969) review aspects of cold hardiness in insects.

31.1. Temperature

31.1.1 Temperature reception

Insects have specialised temperature receptor neurones. Sometimes a temperature sensitive neurone is present in an olfactory sensillum along with olfactory neurones, but in a number of cases special thermo- and hygrosensitive sensilla are present. These lack pores in the cuticle and often contain one temperature sensitive and two hygrosensitive neurones. The dendrites of two of the neurones branch extensively within the peg, but the third does not enter the peg, ending in a complexly folded structure (Altner and Prillinger, 1980).

The caterpillar of *Dendrolimus* has one cell in the maxillary palp and three in the antenna which respond to a sharp fall in temperature with a rapid, short-lived increase in the rate of firing (Fig. 504). A rise in temperature causes a small reduction in the tonic firing rate (Schoonhoven, 1967).

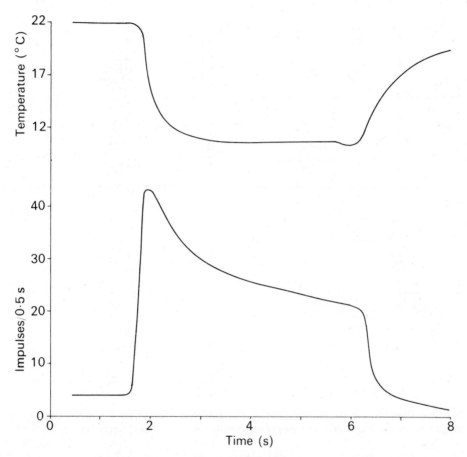

Fig. 504 Response of a cold receptor of *Dendrolimus* to changes in temperature (after Schoonhoven, 1967)

These cells are true peripheral receptors of temperature change. In addition, the firing rate of chemoreceptors and mechanoreceptors is affected by temperature, although they are not true temperature receptors. For instance, the firing rate of the labellar chemoreceptors of *Phormia* is not affected by variation in the temperature at the tips of the sensilla, but is affected by the temperature of the cell bodies (Dethier, 1976).

Since insects are poikilothermic the central nervous system itself is subject to temperature changes and the spontaneous output from the ganglia varies with temperature. In *Periplaneta* the units in the central nervous system fall into four categories with respect to their responses to temperature. In the first type, output is directly proportional to temperature (Fig. 505A). The output of the second type is also directly proportional to temperature, but in addition shows a transient decrease in output when the temperature rises and a transient increase when the temperature falls (Fig. 505B). The third type of unit is a 'cold receptor', being more active at low than at high temperatures (Fig. 505C) and, finally, the output of the fourth type is uninfluenced by temperature (Fig. 505D).

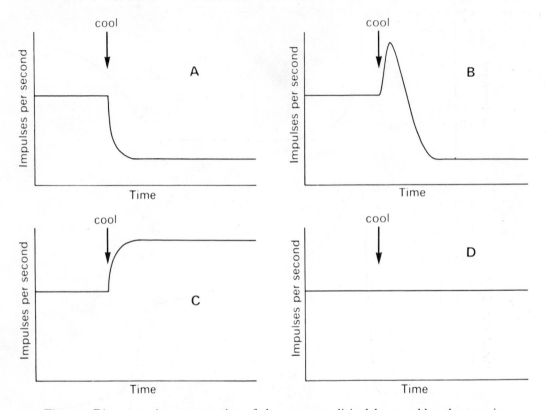

Fig. 505 Diagrammatic representation of the response elicited by a sudden decrease in temperature from four different types of nerve cells in the cockroach nerve cord (after Kerkut and Taylor, 1958)

Thus the response of the insect as a whole is determined by the external temperature influencing the sensory input and by the body temperature, which modifies the output from the central nervous system. Changes in internal body temperature will be slower than peripheral changes and so the central nervous system will usually only be affected by relatively persistent changes in the outside temperature.

There is little evidence that insects are able to perceive or orientate to radiant heat. This is true even in blood-sucking species, in which temperature is important in host-finding, but in *Melanophila* (Coleoptera) sensory pits on the underside of the mesothorax are reported to be sensitive to infrared radiation (Evans, 1964). See also Callahan (1965a, 1965b).

Insects can perceive small differences in air temperature. *Cimex* (Heteroptera), for instance, is sensitive to changes of less than 1°C, and bees can be trained to select one of two temperatures differing by only 2°C.

31.1.2 Body temperature

While some behaviour is probably a straightforward response to environmental temperature, the body temperature of the insect is of great importance because of its effect on metabolism and its direct effect on the central nervous system. In general, the body temperature is close to the ambient temperature, but the precise relationship varies, being a balance between the heat lost and gained by the insect (Fig. 506). As a result of differences in this balance, body temperature may differ widely from air temperature.

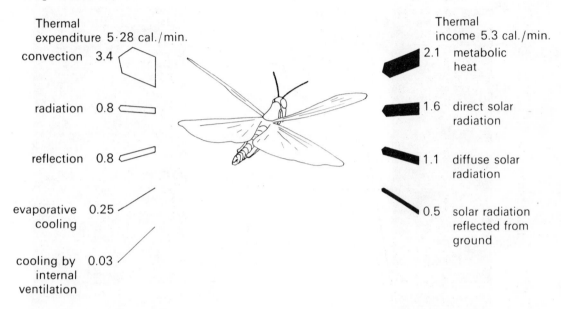

Thermal
expenditure 5·28 cal./min.

convection   3.4

radiation   0.8

reflection   0.8

evaporative   0.25
cooling

cooling by   0.03
internal
ventilation

Thermal
income 5.3 cal./min.

2.1   metabolic
heat

1.6   direct solar
radiation

1.1   diffuse solar
radiation

0.5   solar radiation
reflected from
ground

Fig. 506 Thermal balance of a flying locust (after Rainey, 1974)

Heat gain

The heat produced by metabolic activities, and especially by muscular activity, increases the body temperature, so that individual insects tend to be slightly warmer than their environment, especially at high humidities where evaporative cooling is reduced. Flight, which may involve a 50-fold increase in the metabolic rate (p. 115), is particularly important in this respect and the thoracic temperature of a moth in flight may be more than $10°C$ above ambient. Since the thorax is largely isolated from the head and abdomen in many insects, it is much hotter in flight than the rest of the body and in *Bombus* the thorax may be $10°C$ hotter than the abdomen, only $5-15\%$ of the heat generated being conducted to the head and abdomen (Church, 1960). This insulation of the thorax is important in maintaining the temperature of the flight muscles which only function efficiently within a limited range of temperatures (and see p. 274).

A second factor tending to raise the body temperature above ambient is solar radiation. A locust larva in the shade is much cooler than another fully exposed to the sun (Fig. 507), the amount by which the body temperature exceeds air temperature, the temperature excess, being directly proportional to the intensity of radiation. For a given size of insect the temperature excess in the thorax of Hymenoptera and Diptera, in which conduction to the head and abdomen from the thorax is reduced by the narrowness of the connections, is greater than in Orthoptera (Digby, 1955). The temperature excess is reduced in high winds because of the increase in evaporation and convection (see below).

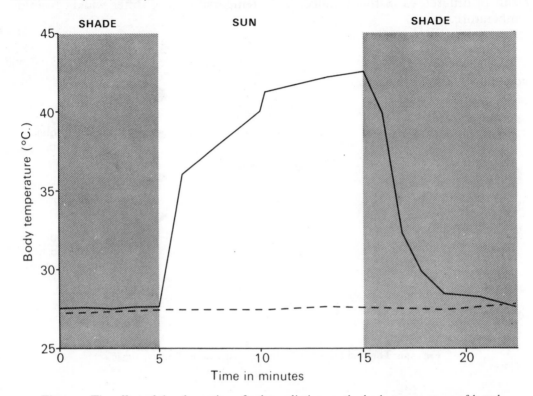

Fig. 507 The effect of the absorption of solar radiation on the body temperature of larval *Locusta*. Full line indicates the temperature of a larva at first in the shade, then in sunlight and then in shade again; broken line the temperature of a larva in continuous shade (from Uvarov, 1948)

Colour affects the amount of radiation absorbed: in bright sunlight gregarious locust larvae, which are black and orange in colour, may be 6°C hotter than green solitary larvae, although the differences are often much less marked than this (Stower and Griffiths, 1966).

If the insect is cooler than its immediate environment it may also gain some heat by long wave radiation from the surroundings.

Heat loss

Evaporation has the effect of cooling because the latent heat of vaporisation is withdrawn from the body. In stationary insects this is the most important source of heat loss and, for instance, in the range 10–30°C some 80–100% of the heat lost by *Anomala* (Coleoptera) is lost through evaporation. Hence factors affecting evaporation will also affect heat loss.

The rate of evaporation from a body is limited by the humidity of the immediate environment. If environmental humidity is high little evaporation occurs, so there will be little heat loss by this route. In dry air, on the other hand, evaporation is much faster and the body temperature of an insect in dry air may be 3–4°C below ambient. Evaporation may be reduced by local accumulations of water vapour round the body and this effect may be enhanced by hairs and scales which tend to hold a layer of still air adjacent to the body. Similarly, closure of the spiracles, by restricting evaporation from the tracheal system, tends to maintain the body temperature. In *Glossina* (Diptera), for instance, the body temperature with the spiracles open averages 0.6°C lower than that of insects with the spiracles closed. Air movement tends to remove local accumulations of water vapour and so to increase evaporation. Thus at higher wind speeds body temperature is reduced.

Evaporation is generally slight at low air temperatures, so that even in the absence of radiation body temperature slightly exceeds air temperature because of the heat produced by its metabolism. At higher temperatures evaporation is increased and body temperature falls below ambient. For instance, in *Gastrimargus* (Orthoptera) at a constant relative humidity of 60% the temperature excess at 10°C is 0.6°C, at 20°C it is 0.4°C, while at 30°C body temperature is 0.2°C below ambient.

Heat loss by convection through the spiracles is probably negligible, but convection from the body surface may be a major source of heat loss, as in larval *Schistocerca* and adult locusts in flight. In the latter, 60–80% of the heat loss results from convection, less than 10% from evaporation and about 10% by long wave radiation (Fig. 506). Convection is increased at higher wind speeds.

Conduction is probably unimportant as a means of heat loss or gain except in the transfer of heat between the body and the layer of air immediately adjacent to it.

Heat loss from the body is reduced by insulation at the surface. The hairs and scales of *Bombus* and *Noctua* (Lepidoptera) hold an insulating layer of air adjacent to the body and the same effect is achieved in dragonflies by a layer of air-sacs at the surface of the thorax. The effectiveness of the insulation depends on the density of hairs, but in general the temperature excess of flying insects is increased by 50–100% by their insulation, amounting to about 9°C in a hawk moth.

31.1.3 Temperature control

The control of body temperature by insects generally involves some behavioural mechanism. Extreme temperatures are avoided. At temperatures over 44°C, approaching the upper lethal temperature, *Schistocerca* larvae become highly active. Similarly, movement into an area of low temperature promotes a brief burst of activity. This activity is undirected, but may tend to take the insect out of the immediately unfavourable area so that it is neither killed by extreme heat nor trapped at temperatures too low for its metabolism to continue efficiently (Chapman, 1965).

Within the normal range of temperature insects have a preferred range in which, given the choice, they tend to remain for relatively long periods. The preferred temperature range is towards the upper end of the normal range of temperatures and in

Schistocerca, for instance, extends from 35 to 45°C with a peak at 40–41°C (Fig. 508). The tendency to remain still in this preferred range may be regarded as a mechanism tending to keep the insects within a range of temperatures which is optimal for most metabolic processes.

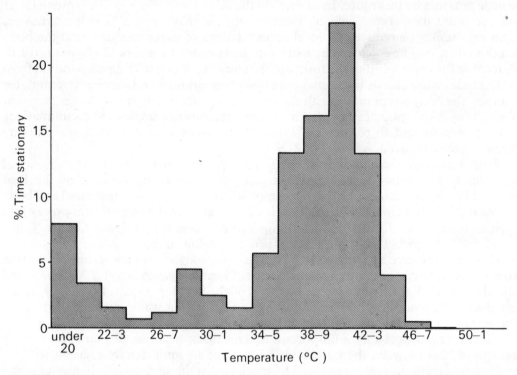

Fig. 508 The temperature preference of *Schistocerca* as shown by the amount of time spent stationary at different temperatures (after Chapman, 1965)

In the field behaviour may be varied so as to keep the body temperature within the preferred range. Thus at low temperatures *Schistocerca* sits broadside to the sun and, if it is on the ground, it lies over on its side so that its lateral surface is perpendicular to the sun's rays, exposing the maximum surface area. When the body temperature is within the range 39–43°C the insect turns to face the sun, so exposing a smaller surface. In a larval locust the ratio of the surfaces exposed in these two positions, known as flanking and facing, is 6 : 1 and as a result of this change in position the temperature excess of the body is reduced. At still higher temperatures the legs are extended so as to raise the body off the ground into the stilted position (Fig. 509). This permits a free circulation of air all round the body and at the same time avoids the excessive temperatures at the surface of the ground. For example, on one occasion with a ground temperature of 56°C, air temperature at 6 mm was only 40°C and the body temperature of a stilting locust 43°C. If temperatures on the ground become excessive the locust climbs up the vegetation, where it may be shaded and where convective and evaporative cooling by the wind are increased. This effect may be further increased by orientating across the

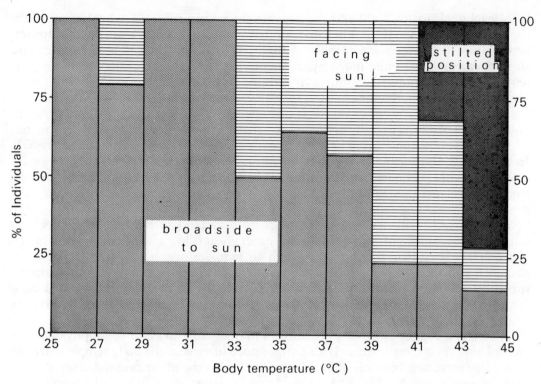

Fig. 509 The orientation of *Schistocerca* with respect to the sun at different body temperatures (based on Waloff, 1963)

wind. In the evening as temperature falls the locust crouches close to the ground, gaining heat by conduction (Waloff, 1963). The effect of these various activities is to keep the body temperature between 35 and 41°C for as long as possible, employing methods of warming at lower temperatures and cooling at higher temperatures.

Other insects show comparable behaviour. *Argynnis* (Lepidoptera), for instance, spreads its wings and orientates to the sun so that it may achieve a temperature excess of as much as 17°C. It varies the degree of opening of the wings to maintain a body temperature of 32–37°C and if the temperature becomes too high it closes its wings over its back and ultimately retreats to the shade (Vielmetter, 1958).

Many insects, such as locusts and moths, are able to raise the temperatures of their bodies by fanning, fluttering the wings without flight. This behaviour is most frequently observed if the insects are disturbed at temperatures suboptimal for flight and the increase in temperature produced may be such that flight becomes possible. In *Saturnia* (Lepidoptera), for instance, fanning can increase the body temperature to 26°C at an air temperature of 18°C.

In *Apis* and *Bombus* the thoracic temperature can be increased by oscillation of the flight muscles without moving the wings. Under these conditions the metabolic rate of the muscles is directly related to the frequency of nerve impulses reaching them, and the antagonistic flight muscles contract synchronously although in flight they function alternately (p. 274). The metabolic rate of the stationary insect may approach the high level obtained in flight and the heat produced can raise the temperature of the thorax of *Bombus* to 36°C when the air temperature is only 2°C. At this muscle temperature the insects are capable of flight. When flight occurs at these very low air temperatures it is punctuated by frequent visits to flowers during which the body temperature is maintained by muscular activity. At higher air temperatures less time is spent on the flowers (Heinrich, 1973, 1974; and see p. 274).

Reduction in body temperature is also generally achieved behaviourally. At the hottest times of day, especially in the tropics, many insects move into the shade and may occupy windy positions so that heat loss due to evaporation and convection is increased. In contrast, the butterfly *Precis villida* appears to reduce body temperature by flying for most of the time when its temperature is high. Apparently the heat lost by convection from this relatively small insect more than compensates for the metabolic heat produced during flight and so the insect does not overheat (Heinrich, 1972).

Large insects with well-insulated thoraces may tend to become excessively hot during continuous flight. In *Manduca* this excess heat is lost via the abdomen, which is less well insulated than the thorax. At high air temperatures heat is transferred to the abdomen and the thoracic temperature stablizes at 40–42°C, but at low air temperatures this transfer of heat does not occur. It is probable that the transfer of heat is regulated by changes in the blood circulation produced by changes in the activity of the heart (Heinrich, 1971).

There is a suggestion that some insects may be able to exert some physiological control over their temperature. If air temperature increases, the body temperature of a locust also increases, but only after a short time lag, so the insect becomes a little cooler than its environment (Fig. 510, stage I). After this, in a fully fed insect, body temperature increases at about the same rate as air temperature so that the difference between the two remains roughly constant (Fig. 510, stage II), but after a time it starts to increase more rapidly and so the difference between the two is reduced (Fig. 510, stage III). Finally, when the air temperature stops rising body temperature continues to rise until it is higher than ambient (Fig. 510, stage IV). In starved locusts, on the other hand, the body temperature does not increase as rapidly as air temperature and the difference between the two steadily increases. Further, when the air temperature stops rising body temperature does not overshoot it. It is suggested that normally the stimulation of peripheral receptors leads to the release of a substance into the haemolymph which stimulates some metabolic processes so that the temperature of the insect increases more rapidly than if it depended only on conduction from the air. This mechanism brings the insect into equilibrium with its environment more rapidly than would otherwise be the case and also enables it to make the maximum use of transient temperature increases. In starved locusts the metabolic process is disturbed and the insect is unable to maintain its temperature (Clarke, 1960).

Physiological regulation of temperature may also occur in *Kosciuscola* (Orthoptera) as a result of colour changes. At low temperatures the insects are darker and so they absorb more radiation (p. 141).

Temperature regulation is most highly developed in social insects. Ants, for instance, carry their larvae about the nest to the most favourable situations. On warm days in summer the older larvae are brought near to the surface, while in winter they may be a foot or more below the surface so as to avoid frosts. On hot days *Formica* (Hymenoptera) blocks the entrance to its nest with nest materials so as to stop the entry of warm air.

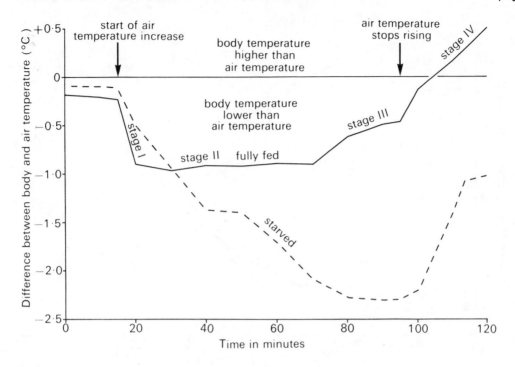

Fig. 510 The difference between the body temperature of *Locusta* and air temperature when air temperature is steadily increased from 20 to 35°C (after Clarke, 1960)

Temperature control is well known in *Apis*. At high temperatures workers stand at the entrance of the hive fanning with their wings so as to create a draught through the nest. This is sufficiently effective to keep the temperature of the brood down to 36°C when the hive is heated to 40°C. Water may also be carried in to help cool the hive by evaporation and at excessively high temperatures the bees leave the combs and cluster outside so that further heating due to their metabolism is avoided. On the other hand in winter when there is little or no brood the bees cluster together on and between a small number of combs. This behaviour is seen when the temperature drops below 15°C and the heat of their metabolism maintains the inside of the cluster at 20–25°C. By packing closer when the temperature is very low and spreading out when it is higher, the bees are able to regulate this temperature.

In addition, individual bees at low temperature increase their metabolic rate, and so increase heat output by contracting the flight muscles without moving the wings.

31.1.4 Metabolism

Within the wide limits set by the upper and lower lethal temperatures, enzyme regulated metabolic processes can proceed. The metabolic rate, as measured by oxygen consumption, increases with temperature up to an optimum (Fig. 511) and the various devices employed by insects to regulate their body temperatures effectively extend the periods of optimal metabolism. At high temperatures, still within the upper lethal limit, metabolic rate is reduced, presumably because enzymes are destroyed rapidly.

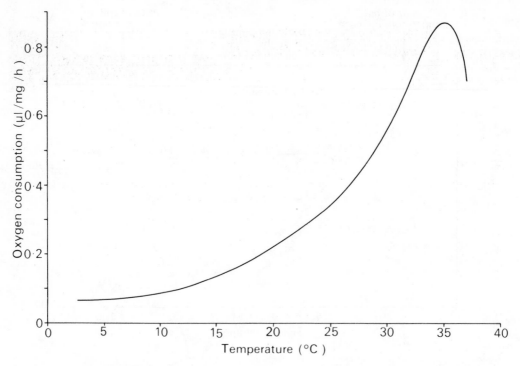

Fig. 511 The oxygen consumption of *Periplaneta* at different temperatures (from Keister and Buck, 1974)

The normal increase in metabolic rate with increasing temperature is reflected in an increased rate of development. Thus the larval development of *Locusta* occupies 40 days at 27°C, but only 20 days at 43°C, and the pupal period of *Tenebrio* lasts for 320 hours at 21°C, but only 140 hours at 33°C. The range in which development occurs varies, being 5–28°C in *Ptinus* (Coleoptera) and 15–40°C in *Tribolium* (Coleoptera), while in *Astagobius*, a cave-dwelling beetle, the environmental temperature ranges from only 1·0 to −1·7°C. The metabolic rate of the stationary insect is, however, not wholly temperature dependent and during diapause oxygen consumption may be very low at all temperatures. The optimum temperature range for diapause development is much lower than that for morphogenesis, and in many temperate species which overwinter in a state of diapause the completion of development only occurs at temperatures below 10°C (Fig. 512).

There is a general tendency for insects to be more active at higher temperatures as in *Nomadacris* larvae, which spend some 5% of their time in activity at 16°C, but about 15% at 34°C (Fig. 513). The effects of temperature changes and temperature preference are superimposed on this general tendency.

Most processes have an optimum temperature at which they proceed most favourably or most rapidly, falling off at higher and lower temperatures, but it is possible to base the optimum on a number of different criteria. For instance, it is possible to regard as optimal the temperature at which the least fuel consumption occurs in the completion of a certain stage of development. Thus in the pupa of *Glossina* (Diptera)

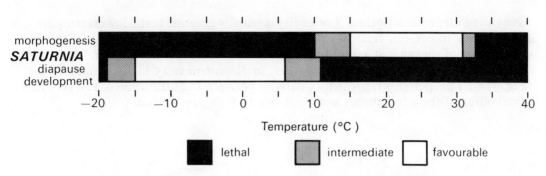

Fig. 512 The thermal requirements for morphogenesis and diapause development in a Palaearctic moth (*Saturnia*) (adapted from Lees, 1955)

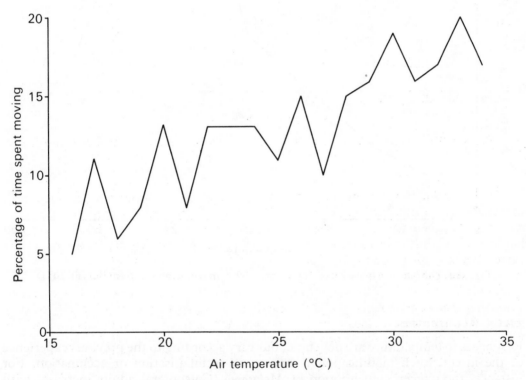

Fig. 513 Showing the increase in the activity of solitary larvae of *Nomadacris* at higher temperatures (after Chapman, 1959b)

least fat is utilised at 22–24°C. At higher temperatures the consumption of fat is increased without any corresponding reduction in the pupal period, while at lower temperatures there is a great lengthening of the pupal period with no corresponding decrease in fat consumption. Alternatively the temperature at which development is most rapid or that at which the largest number of insects successfully complete their development may be regarded as optimal. In adults, longevity and egg production also have their independent optima. Longevity is usually greatest at the lowest temperature at which an insect can feed normally; presumably at such temperatures the basic expenditure of energy is at a minimum. Egg production is mostly maximal at about the middle of the normal range of temperature, in *Toxoptera* at 25°C in a range of 5–35°C (Fig. 514). This perhaps represents a balance between the utilisation of reserves in the metabolism of the adult insect and their use in yolk production.

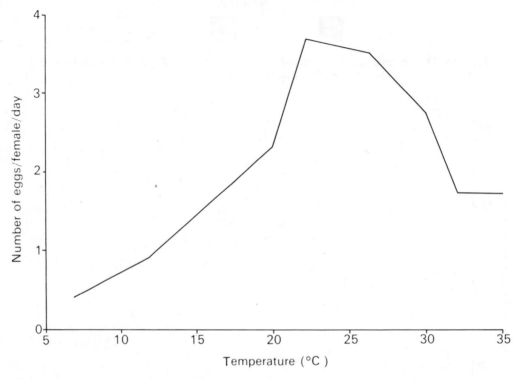

Fig. 514 The rate of oviposition of *Toxoptera* at different temperatures (from Bursell, 1974a)

31.1.5 Acclimation

Responses to temperature are not static, but vary according to the previous experience of the insect. Such modification is known as acclimatisation or acclimation. For instance, the oxygen consumption of *Melasoma* (Coleoptera) adults increases with temperature, but the level of consumption depends on the temperature at which the insects were kept before the experiment and for any given temperature, the oxygen consumption is higher in insects acclimatised to lower temperatures (Fig. 515). The temperature at which maximum oxygen consumption occurs is also lower in the insects preconditioned at the lower temperature. Similarly the spontaneous output from the central nervous system is related to preconditioning temperature (Kerkut and Taylor, 1958) as is the level of activity of the whole insect. Thus, adults of *Ptinus* previously maintained at 15°C are less active at all temperatures than others previously maintained at 28°C (Gunn and Hopf, 1942). Not all insects are so adaptable and some species of

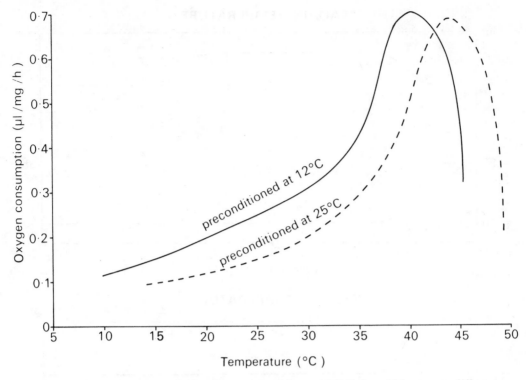

Fig. 515 The effect on oxygen consumption of preconditioning *Melasoma* at different temperatures (from Wigglesworth, 1972)

Drosophila which are restricted in distribution do not acclimate to different rearing temperatures (Hunter, 1966).

An increase in activity occurs after a change in temperature from that to which the insect is acclimatised, irrespective of whether the temperature increases or decreases. These increases in activity are only transient and subsequently activity returns to a level appropriate to the final temperature (Fig. 516). For instance, *Nomadacris* (Orthoptera) is stimulated to take off by the sun appearing from behind a cloud thus increasing its temperature, or by gusts of cold wind before a dust storm lowering its temperature. In the first case the insect may keep flying, but in the second it lands after a few minutes (Chapman, 1959a). Corresponding transients occur in the activity of the central nervous system (Fig. 505).

Acclimation is a continuous process and in the field its importance lies in tending to fit the insect to the prevailing conditions. The process continues at the extremes of the temperature range which may be extended as a result (see below).

31.1.6 Upper lethal temperature

At the upper end of the temperature range, above the preferred temperature, insects show a sharp rise in activity. At still higher temperatures this is followed by an inability to move, a phase known as heat stupor, and then by death. The temperature at which

FALL IN TEMPERATURE

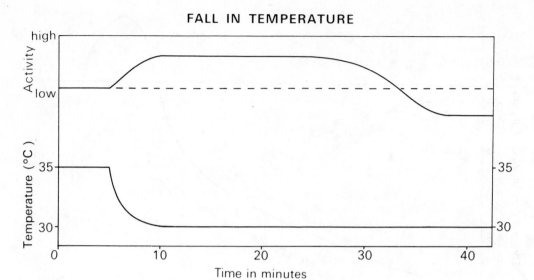

Time in minutes

RISE IN TEMPERATURE

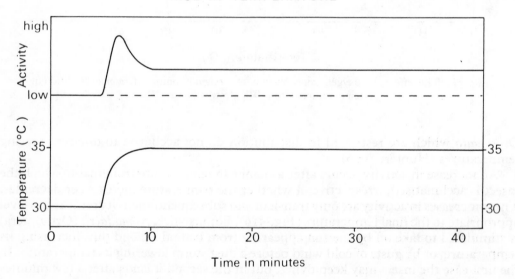

Time in minutes

Fig. 516 Diagram of the effect on activity of a sharp change of temperature (after Kennedy, 1939)

death occurs depends on the species, the duration of exposure and interaction with other factors, in particular with humidity.

Large insects are cooled by evaporation, so that for short periods of exposure of an hour or so they can withstand higher air temperatures if the air is dry. *Periplaneta*, for instance, dies at 38°C at high humidities, but can survive up to 48°C if the air is dry.

For long-term exposures humidity has the opposite effect because at low humidities the insects die from the effects of desiccation. Thus *Blatta* can survive for 24 h at 37–39°C if the air is moist, but dies as a result of similar exposure in dry air. In small insects such as lice, the humidity does not affect the lethal temperature since the volume of water available for evaporation is small while the surface taking up heat is relatively large.

For many insects the lethal temperature for short-term exposures is within the range 40–50°C, but for insects from particular habitats lethal temperatures may be very different. Thus *Grylloblatta* (Grylloblattodea), living at high altitudes in the Rocky Mountains, dies at 20°C, *Thermobia* (Thysanura), the fire brat, at 51°C, and in chironomid larvae living in hot springs at 49–51°C the lethal temperature must be even higher.

Some modification of the upper lethal temperature occurs, depending on the previous experience of the insect. Thus *Drosophila* reared at 15°C and maintained at 15°C as adults, survive for about 50 minutes in dry air at 33·5°C, but if they are maintained at 25°C beforehand they survive for about 130 minutes. If the larvae are also reared at the higher temperature the period of exposure which they can survive is still further increased to 140 minutes in adults maintained at 15°C and to 180 minutes in adults maintained at 25°C. Thus two types of acclimation can be recognised: long lasting acclimation due to conditions during development and short-term physiological acclimation depending on the more immediate conditions and easily reversible. The effect of physiological acclimation is more marked in dry conditions than in wet, indicating that this type of acclimation gives increased resistance to desiccation rather than to higher temperatures (Maynard Smith, 1957).

Death at high temperatures may result from various factors. Proteins may be denatured or the balance of metabolic processes may be disturbed so that toxic products accumulate. Thus blowfly larvae kept at high temperatures accumulate organic and inorganic phosphates and adenyl pyrophosphate in the haemolymph. In some cases food reserves may be exhausted and *Pediculus* (Siphunculata), for instance, survives better at high temperatures if it has recently fed. Sometimes, particularly over long periods, death at high temperatures may result from desiccation.

31.1.7 Lower lethal temperature

At temperatures below the preferred range insects become increasingly less active until finally they are unable to move, or do so only with difficulty. They may remain alive under these conditions for a considerable time, but if they are unable to feed they ultimately starve to death. This is the case, for instance, with *Locusta*, which does not feed below about 20°C. At lower temperatures death occurs much more rapidly from other causes, but in different insects the lower lethal temperature varies considerably (Salt, 1961).

Insects from warm environments often die quite quickly even at temperatures above freezing. *Glossina*, for instance, survives for only a few hours at 5°C. This may result from the accumulation of toxic products or some other metabolic disturbance. In *Apis* the absorption of sugars from the gut, where they are stored, is prevented below 8°C, so that the insects effectively starve. Some acclimation occurs in these insects. Thus *Blatta* reared at 30°C goes into a state of cold stupor at 7·5°C and soon dies at − 5°C, but after 20 hours at 15°C they are active down to 2°C and survive for nine hours at − 5°C.

At temperatures below freezing the majority of insects die as a result of the tissues freezing. The temperature at which this occurs is usually well below 0°C because the freezing point is lowered by the electrolytes in the haemolymph and tissues (p.806), but also because supercooling occurs. The temperature to which insects supercool is not fixed, but is influenced by many factors controlling the production of ice crystals. Crystals start to form round a nucleus and once this happens the whole of the body rapidly freezes. Food in the gut may provide such a nucleus, so feeding insects are much less cold-hardy than non-feeding insects and the supercooling point of *Ephestia* larvae is lower during the period of the moult when they contain no food. The greater hardiness of diapausing and hibernating insects also results partly from the absence of food in the alimentary canal.

Water droplets on the outside of the insect may also form nuclei for ice crystal formation, while, on the other hand, body fluids with a high viscosity tend to inhibit nucleation by reducing molecular travel. Viscosity increases as the temperature gets lower. Increased cold hardiness is often associated with some degree of desiccation of the tissues and in *Popillia* (Coleoptera) hardiness increases as the water content is lowered. This is not always true, however, and the apparent correlation could be fortuitous.

Many insects in which the supercooling point is low have glycerol in the haemolymph, sometimes in high concentrations. Thus in the hibernating stages of *Bracon cephi* (Hymenoptera) glycerol accounts for 25 % of the fresh weight and forms a 5 M solution in the haemolymph. This lowers the freezing point of the haemolymph to about − 15°C. It also greatly increases the viscosity, and the supercooling temperature of the insect may be as low as − 47°C, but factors other than the glycerol are also involved in this.

Glycerol is commonly formed only immediately before or during hibernation and disappears again afterwards. This is illustrated in the larva of *Monema* (Fig. 517), where the glycerol is produced from glycogen in the autumn and remains at a constant level throughout the winter. Synthesis of glycerol occurs optimally at 10°C, none is produced at 20°C. This could account for the fact that in some insects mild chilling often improves cold hardiness; perhaps during chilling conditions favour the synthesis of a protective substance (Asahina, 1969).

Cold hardiness is particularly important in hibernating insects in temperate and subarctic regions where they must survive long periods below 0°C. In many of these the supercooling temperature is about − 30°C, but the temperature at which freezing of the tissues occurs tends to rise the longer the period of exposure. Once the tissues freeze the insects die. The causes of death are not certainly known, but probably involve mechanical damage to the tissues by the ice crystals, especially if they are intracellular, an increase in the concentration of electrolytes so that they become lethal, and possibly also dehydration.

A few insects can tolerate ice formation provided this is restricted to the extracellular fluids. They are mostly lepidopterous larvae and pupae which hibernate in localities where the air temperature falls below the limit of supercooling. Intracellular ice formation destroys the cells, and if many cells are affected the insect dies when it thaws. In avoiding intracellular freezing any mechanism which reduces the rate of cooling at the surface of the cells is important. Thus the freezing of a large amount of the extracellular body fluids beforehand is beneficial and layers of blood containing high concentrations of salts round the ice crystals may limit the propagation of freezing and

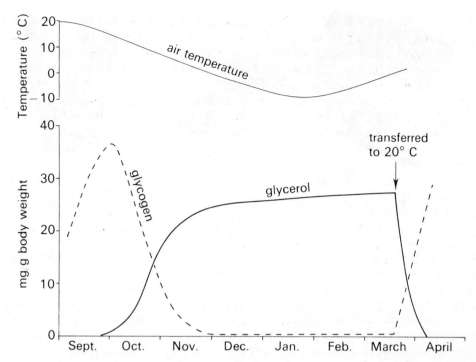

Fig. 517 Seasonal changes in glycerol and glycogen content of larval *Monema* (after Asahina, 1969)

prevent the contact of the crystals with the cell surfaces. The ability to withstand extracellular freezing may involve partial dehydration of the tissues or the production of a protective substance such as glycerol, but these are not the only factors and resistance may also involve some structural change in the cytoplasm. Prolonged extracellular freezing kills even these frost-resistant insects, perhaps due to some metabolic imbalance occurring below a certain temperature (Asahina, 1969).

31.2 Humidity

31.2.1 Humidity receptors

Receptors which respond to changes in relative humidity have been identified in a few insects. In *Tenebrio* and some other beetles they are thin-walled basiconic pegs (p. 736) and in *Tribolium* they are branched hairs (Fig. 518). In *Aedes* cells responding to humidity occur in olfactory sensilla in which other cells respond to odours (Kellogg, 1970). In *Locusta* two cells in some coeloconic sensilla which lack pores (Altner and Prillinger, 1980) respond to changes in humidity, one by a phasic-tonic increase in the rate of firing following an increase in humidity, the other by increasing its rate of firing when humidity decreases. The two cells respond antagonistically to each other following a change in humidity, but their rate of tonic firing is not directly related to the relative humidity. As in other coeloconic sensilla of *Locusta* which respond to odour (p. 742), the sensilla containing the humidity receptors have three neurones; the third is sensitive to temperature changes. These sensilla are morphologically indistinguishable

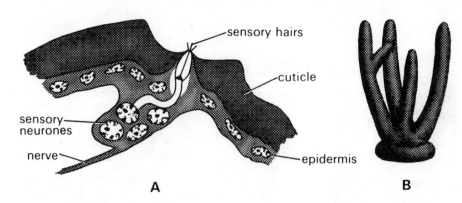

Fig. 518 A. Tuft organ from the antenna of *Pediculus*. B. Branched humidity receptor from the antenna of *Tribolium*

from the olfactory coeloconic pegs, but they are functionally separate (Waldow, 1970). Relative humidity changes as small as 2 % induce a response in the humidity receptors of *Aedes*.

In most cases the humidity receptors have been identified on the antennae, but the palps are also sometimes implicated and in *Drosophila* larvae the receptors are on the underside of the anterior body segments. In *Glossina* the guard hairs of the spiracles are sensitive to humidity and, because of their position, they are influenced not only by the ambient humidity, but also by the humidity of the air leaving the spiracles. Impulses from these receptors produce central inhibition of locomotion (Bursell, 1957).

The mode of functioning of humidity receptors is not understood, but various possibilities exist. They may respond simply to water molecules impinging on the surface in the same way that chemoreceptors are presumed to act. Alternatively they may function as hygroreceptors, containing some substance with hygroscopic properties which absorbs water in proportion to the amount of water vapour in the atmosphere. Finally, water loss from the sensillum may produce temperature differences due to evaporation or it may change the internal environment of the receptor cell, altering the chemical composition and osmotic pressure of the cytoplasm, as a result of which the cell initiates an impulse.

31.2.2 Responses to humidity

Humidity may affect the metabolism and hence the rate of development of insects. For instance, *Ptinus* eggs take 15 days to develop at 20°C and a relative humidity of 30 %, but at 90 % humidity the incubation period is reduced to 10 days. Similarly the rate of oviposition of most insects increases at high humidities. The low metabolic rates at low humidities implied by these differences may result from an increased water loss leading to a generally low water content. In some cases, however, humidity does not have this effect. The eggs of *Cimex* and other insects living in dry environments are not influenced by humidity, while in *Locusta* larval development is fastest at about 70 % relative humidity, being slower at lower and higher humidities.

Humidity also affects behaviour, most insects having a range of preferred humidities in which they are relatively inactive, while outside this range they become more active. In *Schistocerca* larvae the preferred zone is between 60 and 70 % relative humidity. Adult *Tenebrio* on the other hand, always choose the driest of two humidities even showing a slight, but distinct, preference for 5 % over 10 % relative humidity (Pielou and Gunn, 1940). Conversely, *Agriotes* (Coleoptera) larvae choose the wettest parts of the ranges. These differences reflect differences in the degree of waterproofing of the insects' cuticles; that of *Tenebrio* is relatively impermeable, while the cuticle of *Agriotes* larvae is freely permeable to water.

The intensity of reaction to different humidities varies in different parts of the range, but most insects have the greatest sensitivity at high humidities. For instance, although *Tenebrio* always shows a preference for the drier of any two humidities to which it is exposed, below 70 % relative humidity the intensity of the reaction is slight even when the two humidities differ by as much as 40 %. Above 70 % relative humidity, however, the reaction becomes much more marked and differences of 5 % and less produce very strong reactions. In the upper part of the range *Agriotes* larvae respond to differences of 0·5 % relative humidity.

The preferred range of humidity of any one insect may vary due to differences in its water content. Thus *Tribolium* normally has a preference for dry conditions, but after three or four days without food or water a preference for higher humidities develops, the speed of the change in preference being related to the rate of water loss.

Some insects, such as *Tribolium*, make directed movements towards areas of high humidity and others perform avoidance reactions when they pass out of the favourable zone. Thus *Tenebrio* on passing from the drier to the wetter side of a choice chamber sometimes stops and makes movements with its antennae and then turns back into the drier zone. *Agriotes* larvae make avoidance reactions in passing from wet to dry conditions.

Reactions of this type will tend to keep the insect within its preferred range of humidities and will account to some extent for the micro-environments occupied by the insects in the field. Other than in the soil, where, apart from the upper layers, humidity is fairly high and uniform, there are big differences in humidity between different micro-environments and there may also be marked temporal fluctuations (see *e.g.* Cloudsley-Thompson, 1962; Lewis, 1962).

31.2.3 Humidity and survival

The time of survival at different relative humidities depends largely on the ability of the insect to maintain its water content. If this falls too low the insect dies, although there are exceptions to this (see below). If, as in the egg and pupa, the insect is unable to replenish its water the duration of survival is inversely proportional to the rate of water loss and hence, roughly, to the saturation deficit. (Saturation deficit is the difference between the water vapour pressure in air at a given temperature and the saturation vapour pressure at the same temperature.) The more permeable the cuticle, the lower the saturation deficit at which the insect will die. For instance, the puparium of *Glossina brevipalpis* loses water at the rate of 10·2 mg/cm^2/h/mmHg and mortality is high in a saturation deficit of 5 mmHg (Fig. 519). The puparium of *G. swynnertoni*, on the other hand, loses water much more slowly, 1·6 mg/cm^2/h/mmHg, and mortality is slight even at a saturation deficit of 20 mmHg.

When the insect can replace the water which it loses it can usually withstand

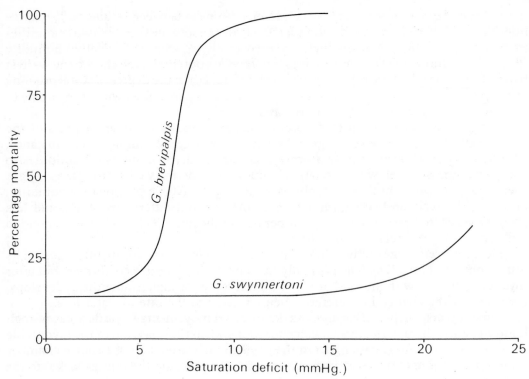

Fig. 519 The effect of saturation deficit on pupal survival in *Glossina brevipalpis* and *G. swynnertoni* (from Bursell, 1974b)

extremes of humidity. Thus there is no range outside which the insect cannot survive as there is with temperature. However, there may be mortality at low humidities even with an ample supply of water, possibly because the energy expended in maintaining the water content exerts a metabolic strain on the insect. Similarly death may occur at excessively high humidities because the insect is unable to get rid of its excess water quickly enough. This apparently occurs with *Tenebrio* at humidities over 70 % and temperatures over 30°C.

31.3 Cryptobiosis

Cryptobiosis is the term used to describe the state of an organism when it shows no visible signs of life and metabolic activity is brought reversibly to a standstill. The only insect in which this is known to occur is the larva of *Polypedilum* (Diptera), a chironomid living in pools on unshaded rocks in Nigeria. In the dry season these pools dry up and the surface temperatures of the rock probably reach 70°C. Active larvae of *Polypedilum* die after an exposure of one hour at 43°C, but if they are dehydrated so that their water content is less than 8 % of its original value they can survive extreme temperatures for long periods. Some recovery occurs even after one minute at 102°C or several days in liquid air at − 190°C. At room temperatures larvae can withstand total dehydration for three years and some showed a temporary recovery after ten years (Hinton, 1960).

There is some evidence that the larva of a species of *Sciara* (Diptera) and some ceratopogoniid larvae also exhibit cryptobiosis and other insects may possess some tissues which exhibit the phenomenon, although the insect as a whole may not. For instance, the blood cells in the gills of *Taphrophila* (Diptera) pupae (p. 567) and *Sialis* larvae can be desiccated for long periods, but when rehydrated show some vital activities such as clotting.

REFERENCES

ALTNER, H. and PRILLINGER, L. (1980). Ultrastructure of invertebrate chemo-, thermo-, and hygroreceptors and its functional significance. *Int. Rev. Cytol.* **67**: 69–139.

ASAHINA, E. (1969). Frost resistance in insects. *Adv. Insect Physiol.* **6**: 1–49.

BURSELL, E. (1957). The effect of humidity on the activity of tsetse flies. *J. exp. Biol.* **34**: 42–51.

BURSELL, E. (1974a). Environmental aspects—temperature. *in* Rockstein, M. (ed.), *The physiology of Insecta*. vol. 2. Academic Press, New York and London.

BURSELL, E. (1974b). Environmental aspects—humidity. *in* Rockstein, M. (ed.), *The physiology of Insecta*. vol. 2. Academic Press, New York and London.

CALLAHAN, P. S. (1965a). Intermediate and far infrared sensing of nocturnal insects. Part I. Evidences for a far infrared (FIR) electromagnetic theory of communication and sensing in moths and its relationship to the limiting biosphere of the corn earworm. *Ann. ent. Soc. Am.* **58**: 727–745.

CALLAHAN, P. S. (1965b). Intermediate and far infrared sensing of nocturnal insects. Part II. The compound eye of the corn earworm, *Heliothis zea*, and other moths as a mosaic optic-electromagnetic thermal radiometer. *Ann. ent. Soc. Am.* **58**: 746–755.

CHAPMAN, R. F. (1959a). Observations on the flight activity of the red locust, *Nomadacris septemfasciata* (Serville). *Behaviour* **14**: 300–334.

CHAPMAN, R. F. (1959b). Field observations on the behaviour of hoppers of the red locust (*Nomadacris septemfasciata* Serville). *Anti-Locust Bull.* no. 33, 51 pp.

CHAPMAN, R. F. (1965). The behaviour of nymphs of *Schistocerca gregaria* (Forskål) (Orthoptera: Acrididae) in a temperature gradient, with special reference to temperature preference. *Behaviour* **24**: 283–317.

CHURCH, N. S. (1960). Heat loss and the body temperatures of flying insects. II. Heat conduction within the body and its loss by radiation and convection. *J. exp. Biol.* **37**: 186–212.

CLARKE, K. U. (1960). Studies on the relationships between air temperature and the internal body temperature of *Locusta migratoria*. *J. Insect Physiol.* **5**: 23–36.

CLOUDSLEY-THOMPSON, J. L. (1962). Lethal temperatures of some desert arthropods and the mechanism of heat death. *Entomologia exp. appl.* **5**: 270–280.

DETHIER, V. G. (1976). *The hungry fly*. Harvard University Press, Cambridge, Mass., and London.

DIGBY, P. S. B. (1955). Factors affecting the temperature excess of insects in sunshine. *J. exp. Biol.* **32**: 279–298.

EVANS, W. G. (1964). Infra-red receptors in *Melanophila acuminata* DeGeer. *Nature, Lond.* **202**: 211.

GUNN, D. L. and HOPF, H. S. (1942). The biology and behaviour of *Ptinus tectus* Boie. (Coleoptera: Ptinidae), a pest of stored products. II. The amount of locomotory activity in relation to experimental and to previous temperatures. *J. exp. Biol.* **18**: 278–289.

HEINRICH, B. (1971). Temperature regulation of the sphinx moth, *Manduca sexta*. II. Regulation of heat loss by control of blood circulation. *J. exp. Biol.* **54**: 153–166.

HEINRICH, B. (1972). Thoracic temperatures of butterflies in the field near the equator. *Comp. Biochem. Physiol.* 43A: 459–467.

HEINRICH, B. (1973). Mechanisms of insect thermoregulation. *in* Weiser, W. (ed.), *Effects of temperature on ectothermic organisms.* Springer-Verlag, Berlin.

HEINRICH, B. (1974). Thermoregulation in endothermic insects. *Science* 185: 747–756.

HEINRICH, B. (ed.) (1981). *Insect thermoregulation.* Wiley, New York.

HINTON, H. E. (1960). Cryptobiosis in the larva of *Polypedilum vanderplanki* Hint. (Chironomidae). *J. Insect Physiol.* 5: 286–300.

HOWE, R. W. (1967). Temperature effects on embryonic development in insects. *A. Rev. Ent.* 12: 15–42.

HUNTER, A. S. (1966). Effects of temperature on Drosophila—III. Respiration of *D. willistoni* and *D. hydei* grown at different temperatures. *Comp. Biochem. Physiol.* 19: 171–177.

KEISTER, M. and BUCK, J. (1974). Respiration: some exogenous and endogenous effects on rate of respiration. *in* Rockstein, M. (ed.), *The physiology of Insecta.* vol. 6. Academic Press, New York and London.

KELLOGG, F. E. (1970). Water vapour and carbon dioxide receptors in *Aedes aegypti. J. Insect Physiol.* 16: 99–108.

KENNEDY, J. S. (1939). The behaviour of the desert locust (*Schistocerca gregaria* (Forsk.)) (Orthopt.) in an outbreak centre. *Trans. R. ent. Soc. Lond.* 89: 385–542.

KERKUT, G. A. and TAYLOR, B. J. R. (1958). The effect of temperature changes on the activity of poikilotherms. *Behaviour* 13: 259–279.

LEES, A. D. (1955). *The physiology of diapause in arthropods.* Cambridge University Press.

LEWIS, T. (1962). The effects of temperature and relative humidity on mortality in *Limothrips cerealium* Haliday (Thysanoptera) overwintering in bark. *Ann. appl. Biol.* 50: 313–326.

MAY, M. L. (1979). Insect thermoregulation. *A. Rev. Ent.* 24: 313–349.

MAYNARD SMITH, J. (1957). Temperature tolerance and acclimatization in *Drosophila subobscura. J. exp. Biol.* 34: 85–96.

PIELOU, D. P. and GUNN, D. L. (1940). The humidity behaviour of the mealworm beetle, *Tenebrio molitor* L. I. The reaction to differences of humidity. *J. exp. Biol.* 17: 286–294.

RAINEY, R. C. (1974). Biometeorology and insect flight: some aspects of energy exchange. *A. Rev. Ent.* 19: 407–439.

SALT, R. W. (1961). Principles of insect cold-hardiness. *A. Rev. Ent.* 6: 55–74.

SALT, R. W. (1969). The survival of insects at low temperatures. *Symp. Soc. exp. Biol.* 23: 331–350.

SCHOONHOVEN, L. M. (1967). Some cold receptors in larvae of three Lepidoptera species. *J. Insect Physiol.* 13: 821–826.

STOWER, W. J. and GRIFFITHS, J. F. (1966). The body temperature of the desert locust (*Schistocerca gregaria*). *Entomologia exp. appl.* 9: 127–178.

UVAROV, B. P. (1948). Recent advances in acridology: anatomy and physiology of Acrididae. *Trans. R. ent. Soc. Lond.* 99: 1–75.

VIELMETTER, W. (1958). Physiologie des Verhaltens zur Sonnenstrahlung bei dem Tagfalter *Argynnis paphia* L.—I. Untersuchungen im Freiland. *J. Insect Physiol.* 2: 13–37.

WALDOW, U. (1970). Elektrophysiologische Untersuchungen an Feuchte- Trocken- und Kälterezeptoren auf den Antenne der Wanderheuschrecke *Locusta. Z. vergl. Physiol.* 69: 249–283.

WALOFF, Z. (1963). Field studies on solitary and *transiens* desert locusts in the Red Sea area. *Anti-Locust Bull.* no. 40, 93 pp.

WIGGLESWORTH, V. B. (1972). *The principles of insect physiology.* Chapman and Hall, London.

SECTION F

The Blood, Hormones and Pheromones

CHAPTER XXXII

THE CIRCULATORY SYSTEM

Insects have an open blood system in which circulation is produced by the activity of a dorsal longitudinal vessel comprising a posterior heart and an anterior aorta. When the heart relaxes blood passes into it through valved openings, while waves of contraction, which normally start at the back, pump the blood forwards and out through the aorta. The heart is usually cut off from the major part of the body cavity by a muscular diaphragm, while in some insects a second diaphragm overlies the nerve cord. These diaphragms, together with accessory pulsatile organs associated with the appendages, supplement the activity of the dorsal vessel.

The frequency with which the heart contracts varies in different species, but also with the stage of development and physiological condition of the individual insect. Sometimes the contractions may start at the front instead of the back of the heart, or it may stop beating altogether for short periods. In some cases the activity of the heart is myogenic, but in most insects it is uncertain whether the beat is myogenic or neurogenic. Possibly a myogenic beat is modulated by the nervous input. Extrinsic activities, such as feeding, may modify the frequency of the heartbeat through the release of a hormone from the corpora cardiaca.

Jones (1977) gives a detailed account of the circulatory system, and specific aspects of the structure and physiology are reviewed by Davey (1964), Jones (1964, 1974), McCann (1970), Miller (1974), Richards (1963) and Wigglesworth (1972).

32.1 Structure

Insects have an open blood system with the blood occupying the general body cavity, which is thus known as a haemocoel. Blood is circulated mainly by the activity of a contractile longitudinal vessel which opens into the haemocoel and which usually lies in a dorsal pericardial sinus, cut off by a dorsal diaphragm from the perivisceral sinus which contains the viscera (Fig. 520A). Sometimes there is also a ventral diaphragm above the nerve cord which cuts off a ventral perineural sinus from the perivisceral sinus. The perineural sinus is normally only a small part of the haemocoel, but in Ichneumonidae it may form half the body cavity because the sterna, to which the ventral diaphragm is attached, are extended upwards (Fig. 520B).

32.1.1 Dorsal Vessel

The dorsal vessel runs along the dorsal midline, just below the terga, for almost the whole length of the body. Anteriorly it leaves the dorsal wall and is more closely

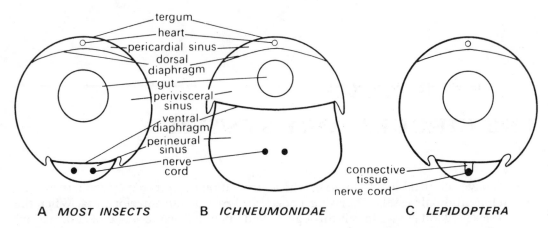

Fig. 520 Diagrammatic cross-sections of various insects showing the main sinuses of the haemocoel and the positions of heart, alimentary canal and nerve cord (after Richards, 1963)

associated with the alimentary canal, passing under the cerebral ganglion just above the oesophagus. The dorsal vessel is divided into two regions: a posterior heart in which the wall of the vessel is perforated by incurrent and sometimes also by excurrent ostia, and an anterior aorta which is a simple, unperforated tube (Figs. 521, 522). It is open anteriorly, but closed posteriorly except in Ephemeroptera nymphs, where three vessels diverge to the caudal filaments from the end of the heart.

The wall of the dorsal vessel is contractile and consists of a single layer of visceral muscle cells with a circular or spiral arrangement. In Heteroptera longitudinal muscle strands are also present, especially along the aorta. The muscles are linked together by intercalated discs which, in the 20–55 nm gap between the cells where the thin muscle filaments end, consist of an electron dense material. Elsewhere, where the intercellular space is only about 7 nm, the intercalated disc consists of septate desmosomes. In *Hyalophora* the Z bands of the heart muscles are unusual in consisting of discontinuous dense bodies. The thick filaments can pass through the gaps between these bodies and this arrangement is possibly an adaptation which allows the muscles to contract even when their total length is greatly reduced by shortening of the abdomen (McCann, 1970). There is no evidence that other types of cell occur in the wall of the dorsal vessel, and the muscle cells are bounded on both sides by a homogeneous membrane. On the outside there is also usually some connective tissue, and a network of tracheoles is often present, especially round the posterior part of the heart.

Heart

The heart is often restricted to the abdomen, but may extend as far forwards as the prothorax as in Dictyoptera. In orthopteroids it has a chambered appearance due to the fact that it is slightly enlarged into ampullae at the points where the ostia pierce the wall (Nutting, 1951). These ampullae are often more prominent in the thorax. In the larvae of Odonata and *Tipula* (Diptera) the heart is divided into chambers by valves in front of each pair of incurrent ostia and in other cases, as in *Cloeon* (Ephemeroptera) larvae, the

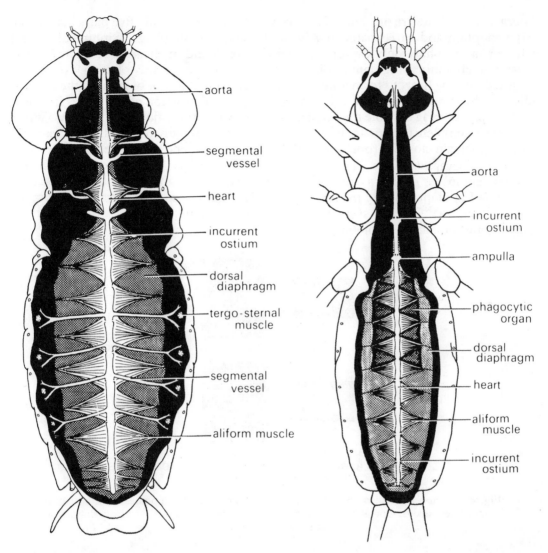

Fig. 521 Ventral dissection of *Blaberus* to show the dorsal and segmental vessels. The dorsal diaphragm and aliform muscles are continuous over the ventral wall of the heart and vessels, but are omitted from the diagram for clarity (after Nutting, 1951)

Fig. 522 Ventral dissection of *Gryllotalpa* to show the dorsal vessel and phagocytic organs. The dorsal diaphragm is continuous over the ventral wall of the heart, but is omitted in the diagram for clarity (after Nutting, 1951)

ostial valves themselves are so long that they meet across the lumen. The heart may be directly bound to the dorsal body wall or suspended from it by elastic filaments.

Incurrent ostia

The incurrent ostia are vertical, slit-like openings occuring laterally in the heart wall. There may be nine pairs of incurrent ostia in the abdomen and up to three pairs in the thorax. All 12 pairs are present in Dictyoptera, but there are only five pairs in aculeate Hymenoptera and three pairs in *Musca* (Diptera). Mallophaga, Siphunculata and Geocorisae also have only two or three pairs of ostia and the heart is restricted to the posterior abdominal segments. The anterior and posterior lips of each ostium are reflexed into the heart to form a valve which permits the flow of blood into the heart at diastole, but prevents its outward passage at systole. The action of the valves is shown in Fig. 523. During diastole the lips are forced apart by the inflowing blood (A). When diastole is complete the lips are forced together by the pressure of blood in the heart (B) and they remain closed throughout systole. Towards the end of systole the valves tend to become evaginated by the pressure (C), but they are prevented from turning completely inside out by a unicellular thread attached to the inside of the heart. In *Bombyx* (Lepidoptera) only the hind lip of each ostium is extended as a flap within the heart (Fig. 524). During systole this is pressed against the wall of the heart so preventing the escape of blood.

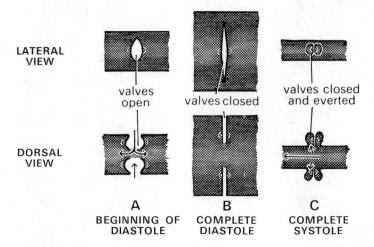

Fig. 523 Incurrent ostial valves in the larva of *Chaoborus* at different phases of the heartbeat. Lateral view above, dorsal below. Arrows indicate the directions of blood flow (from Wigglesworth, 1972)

Excurrent ostia

Nutting (1951) has described excurrent ostia in the orthopteroids and also in Thysanura. These are usually paired ventro-lateral openings in the wall of the heart without any internal valves. The number of excurrent ostia varies, but Acridoidea have two thoracic and five abdominal pairs. Externally each opening is surrounded by a papilla of spongiform multinucleate cells which expands when the heart contracts, so that blood passes out, and contracts when the heart relaxes, so that the entry of blood is prevented. The excurrent ostia of Phasmida open into the pericardial sinus, but in Acridoidea the papillae penetrate the dorsal diaphragm so that the ostia open into the perivisceral sinus (Fig. 525). In Tettigonioidea the ostia open between two layers of the

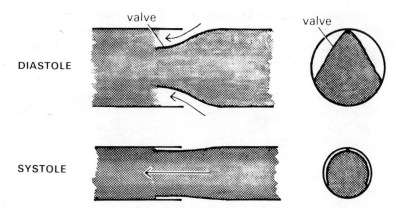

Fig. 524 Diagrammatic representation of the incurrent ostial valves as found in *Bombyx* seen in horizontal (left) and transverse (right) sections of the heart. Arrows indicate the direction of blood flow

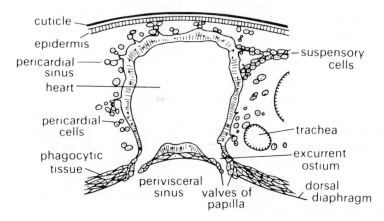

Fig. 525 Transverse section of the heart of *Taeniopoda* showing the excurrent ostia opening directly to the perivisceral sinus (after Nutting, 1951)

dorsal diaphragm, so that blood leaving the heart is channelled laterally before it enters the general body cavity. There are unpaired excurrent ostia in the heart of Plecoptera and Embioptera.

Segmental vessels

Most Dictyoptera have no excurrent ostia, but there are definite segmental vessels by which the blood leaves the heart (Fig. 521) (Nutting, 1951). In Blattaria there are two thoracic and four abdominal vessels, but only the latter are present in Mantodea. They pass out between the aliform (alary) muscles, branching distally and disappearing as fine ramifications in the fat (Fig. 526). At the origin of each vessel is a group of loosely packed cells which functions as a valve permitting only the outward flow of blood from the heart. The walls of the vessels are non-muscular.

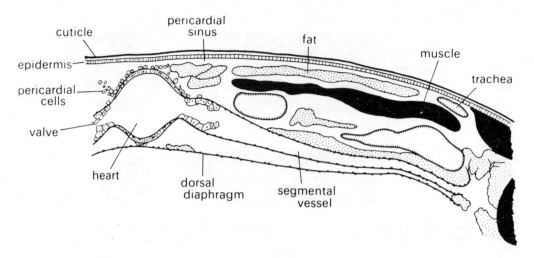

Fig. 526 Transverse section through the pericardial sinus in the abdomen of *Blaberus* showing a segmental vessel arising from the heart and discharging into fatty tissue distally (after Nutting, 1951)

Aorta

In front of the heart the dorsal vessel continues as the aorta. This is a simple tube without ostia, but in Odonata, Orthoptera, Coleoptera and Lepidoptera there may be diverticula extending from it dorsally. These diverticula are often connected with the pulsatile organs which are concerned with blood circulation through the wings. The aorta of orthopteroids extends below the cerebral ganglion as an open gutter; in other groups it ends more abruptly either discharging into the body cavity or, in *Rhodnius* (Heteroptera), into a sinus which runs forwards beneath the brain. In *Bombyx* the aorta dilates into a sac in front of the brain and from this vessels diverge to the maxillae, antennae and eyes (Gerould, 1938).

32.1.2 Aliform muscles and dorsal diaphragm

Closely associated with the heart are the aliform, or alary, muscles. These stretch from one side of the body to the other just below the heart or, as in *Hyalophora*, are directly connected to the muscles of the heart by intercalated discs (Sanger and McCann, 1968). Like the heart muscles, these are visceral muscles with 10 to 12 thin filaments to every thick filament. Usually they fan out from a restricted origin on the tergum, the muscles of each side meeting in a broad zone at the midline (Figs. 521, 522), but sometimes, as in Acridoidea, the origin of the muscles is also broad. In most orthopteroids, at least, only the proximal part near the point of origin is contractile, the rest and greater part of the 'muscle' being made up of bundles of connective tissue which branch and anastomose. Some of the connective tissue fibres form a plexus which extends to the heart wall, but in some insects, such as dipterous larvae, the aliform muscles are inserted directly into the walls of the heart instead of meeting beneath it. Orthopteroids may have as many as ten abdominal and two thoracic pairs of aliform muscles, but in other insects the number is reduced. Geocorisae, for instance, have from four to seven pairs.

The aliform muscles form an integral part of the dorsal diaphragm which spreads between them as a fenestrated connective tissue membrane. It is usually incomplete laterally, so that the pericardial sinus is broadly continuous with the perivisceral sinus in this region. The lateral limits are often indefinite and are determined by the presence of muscles or tracheae or the origins of the aliform muscles.

32.1.3 Ventral diaphragm

The ventral diaphragm is a horizontal septum just above the nerve cord cutting off the perineural sinus from the main perivisceral sinus (Fig. 520). It is present in both larvae and adults of Odonata, Orthoptera, Hymenoptera and Neuroptera, but is only found in adults of Mecoptera and the lower Diptera (Richards, 1963). No ventral diaphragm is present in the other orders of insects except in Lepidoptera, where it is unusual in having the nerve cord bound to its ventral surface by connective tissue (Fig. 520C). Laterally it is attached to the sternum, usually at only one point in each segment and so there are broad gaps along the margins where perivisceral and perineural sinuses are continuous, but in the Lepidoptera there are several points of attachment in each segment.

In several orders the ventral diaphragm is restricted to the abdomen, but in Orthoptera it is also present in the thorax. Posteriorly it does not extend beyond the posterior end of the nerve cord.

The structure of the ventral diaphragm varies. For instance, in the thorax of grasshoppers it is a delicate membrane with little or no muscle, but in the abdomen it becomes a solid muscular sheet. Its structure may also vary with age and in *Corydalis* it forms a solid sheet in the larva, but a fenestrated membrane in the adult.

The contractions of the ventral diaphragm are probably myogenic and are propagated by tension, while nervous inhibition reduces the frequency with which contractions occur.

32.1.4 Accessory pulsatile organs

In addition to the dorsal vessel there are often other pulsating structures connected with the haemocoel which are concerned with maintaining a circulation through the appendages. In the mesothorax and sometimes also in the metathorax there is a pulsatile organ concerned with the circulation through the wings. The veins of the posterior part of the wing connect with a blood space beneath the tergum via the axillary cord. In Odonata (Whedon, 1938) the blood space, or reservoir, opens through a terminal ostium into an ampulla at the end of a dorsal diverticulum of the aorta (Fig. 527). Contraction of this ampulla drives blood into the dorsal vessel; when it relaxes the ostium opens, drawing blood in from the reservoir beneath the tergum and hence, indirectly, from the wings. In many Lepidoptera the dorsal vessel itself loops up to the dorsal surface of the thorax and forms the so-called pulsatile organ (Fig. 528). A reservoir is cut off beneath the tergum by a muscular membrane and this connects with the heart by a pair of ostia at the top of the loop. At diastole blood is drawn into the heart from the reservoir, while at systole it is pumped forwards in the normal way and at the same time the muscular diaphragm falls, drawing in a fresh supply of blood from the wings and thorax. Gerould (1938) maintains that the muscular membrane moves

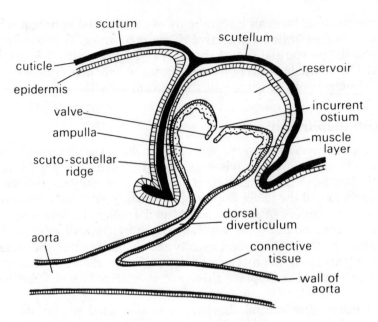

Fig. 527 Sagittal section of the mesothorax of *Anax* showing the pulsatile organ (after Whedon, 1938)

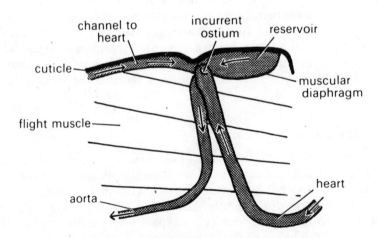

Fig. 528 Sagittal section of the mesothorax of *Bombyx* showing the dorsal loop of the heart resembling a pulsatile organ (after Gerould, 1938)

passively, but Brocher (1919) regards the membrane as actively forcing blood through the ostia.

The circulation of blood through the wings is also often aided by pulsatile membranes in the veins. For instance, in each wing of *Drosophila* there are four such membranes in the veins which conduct centripetally and one in a vein conducting centrifugally. The structure and mode of action of these membranes is not understood, but their activity is probably dependent on the activity of the thoracic pulsatile organ (see Jones, 1964).

Orthoptera and probably many other insects have a small ampulla at the base of each antenna. This communicates with the haemocoel by a valved opening and extends as a vessel into the antenna. When the ampulla expands, blood is drawn into it from the haemocoel; when it contracts, blood is forced into the antenna. Other pulsating organs occur in the legs of Heteroptera.

32.1.5 Innervation of the heart

In some insects, such as *Anopheles*, the heart is entirely without any nerve supply although there are segmental nerves to the aliform muscles (Jones, 1954). On the other hand, the heart of *Periplaneta* is innervated from two sources. Nerves from the corpora cardiaca and from the segmental ganglia combine to form a longitudinal nerve on either side of the heart, from which nerve endings ramify in the wall of the heart and the aliform muscles. The lateral nerve contains neurosecretory and non-neurosecretory axons. In addition, there may be sensory axons which join the nerves in the dorsal body wall as shown in Fig. 529, but the presence of these axons in *Periplaneta* has been questioned (Jones, 1977). Between the extremes represented by *Anopheles* and *Periplaneta* are various intermediate degrees of innervation. *Spodoptera*, for instance, has only segmental nerves.

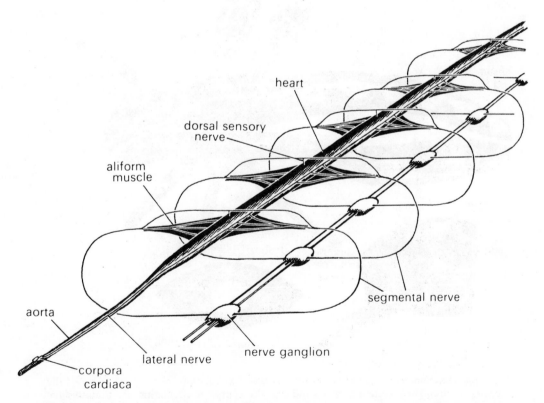

Fig. 529 Diagrammatic representation of the innervation of the heart in an insect, such as *Periplaneta*, with a well-developed innervation

In the cockroach, and probably most other orthopteroids, scattered nerve cells, known as ganglion cells, occur along the lateral heart nerves, but these are not always present in other insects.

32.2 Circulation

32.2.1 The course of circulation

In normal circulation the blood is pumped forwards through the heart at systole, passing out of the heart via the excurrent ostia and, anteriorly, from the aorta (Fig. 530). The valves on the incurrent ostia prevent the escape of blood through these openings. The blood driven forwards by the heart increases the blood pressure anteriorly in the perivisceral sinus, so that in this sinus blood tends to pass backwards along a pressure gradient. Blood percolates down to the perineural sinus, where it is agitated by movements of the ventral diaphragm which assist the blood supply to the nervous system and possibly produce a backward flow of blood. The dorsal diaphragm is usually convex above, so contraction of the alary muscles tends to flatten it. This flattening

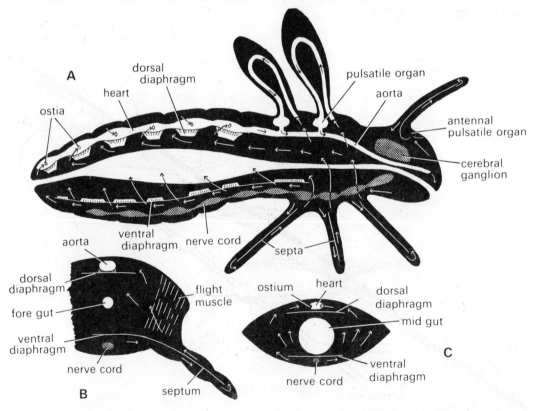

Fig. 530 Diagrammatic representation of the blood circulation in an insect with a fully developed circulatory system. Arrows indicate the course of circulation. A. Longitudinal section. B. Transverse section of thorax. C. Transverse section of abdomen (from Wigglesworth, 1972)

increases the volume of the pericardial sinus at the expense of the perivisceral sinus; as a result, blood passes up into the pericardial sinus and then at diastole is drawn into the heart through the incurrent ostia.

Many insects have a well-defined, but variable, circulation through the wings, although in some, apparently, circulation only occurs in the young adult. Normally blood passes out along the anterior veins, back to the posterior veins via cross veins and smaller tissue spaces and then back to the body via the posterior veins and the axillary cord. Changes in pressure modify the wing circulation by pumping blood into spaces which were previously empty or stagnant, but the general course of the circulation remains the same. If, however, the pressure changes in the thorax are very marked the direction of blood flow along the veins may be reversed, particularly in the anterior veins.

The flow at the base of the wings is directed by the fusion of the dorsal and ventral articular membranes so that the space between them is largely occluded. Anteriorly the membranes are held apart by the axillary sclerites and enclose a space, the anterior sinus (Fig. 531), which is continuous anteriorly with the perivisceral sinus. Behind the axillary sclerites the membranes are fused except for a few small, irregular channels, so blood from the anterior sinus is mostly directed back to the perivisceral sinus or out along the anterior veins. Posteriorly the anal veins connect with the axillary cord via channels between the two fused membranes and from here it is aspirated by the

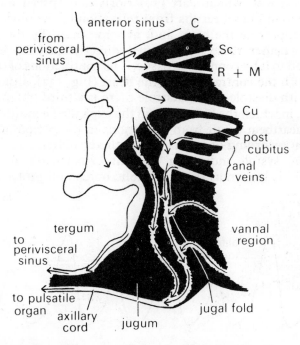

Fig. 531 Diagrammatic representation of the circulation in the base of the fore wing of *Blattella*. Areas in which the two membranes of the wing are fused together are black. Well-defined channels between the membranes, *e.g.* veins, have a regular outline, less definite channels have an irregular outline. Axillary sclerites are omitted (after Clare and Tauber, 1942)

pulsatile organ in the thorax (Clare and Tauber, 1942). In this way the normal circulation in the wings is maintained, although in *Anopheles* the contractions of the pulsatile organ are very irregular (Jones, 1954). The circulation is reduced when the wings are folded because of the occlusion of the channels in the articular membrane. In the absence of the wing circulation the tracheae in the wings of *Blattella* collapse, and the wing structure becomes dry and brittle.

Pulsatile organs also pump blood into the antennae and in Heteroptera serve to aspirate blood from the legs. In most insects the cavity of the legs is divided into anterior and posterior channels by a longitudinal septum. Blood passes down the posterior channel from the perineural sinus and up the anterior channel to the spaces between the wing muscles in the perivisceral sinus. It is thought that pressure differences between these two sinuses maintain the direction of flow.

The circulation is affected in an irregular manner by movements of the alimentary canal and by respiratory movements. Any activity which tends to induce pressure differences in different parts of the body must affect the circulation. In the cockroach transport of material in the blood to all parts of the body probably takes about five minutes (Miller, 1974).

32.2.2 Heartbeat

Systole, the contraction phase of the heartbeat, results from the contractions of the muscles in the heart wall which start posteriorly and spread forwards as a wave. Diastole, the relaxation phase, results from relaxation of the muscles assisted by the elastic filaments supporting the heart and, in some cases, by the contraction of the aliform muscles, whether these are inserted directly into the heart wall or only indirectly connected to it by connective tissue. The contractions of the aliform muscles are in antiphase with the contractions of the heart (Fig. 532), although they may not coincide exactly with diastole. After diastole there is a third phase in the heart cycle, known as diastasis, in which the heart rests in the expanded condition. Increases in the frequency of the heartbeat result from reductions in the period of diastasis.

In a mechanical recording of heart activity there is often a slight dip in the trace immediately before systole indicating a slight expansion before the contraction (Fig. 533). This dip is known as the presystolic notch and probably results from an

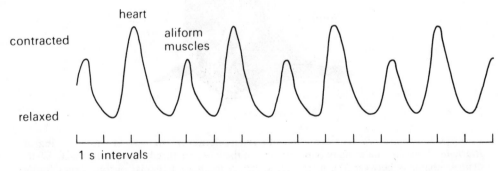

Fig. 532 A mechanical trace showing the alternating contractions of heart and aliform muscles in the larva of *Cossus cossus* (after de Wilde, 1947)

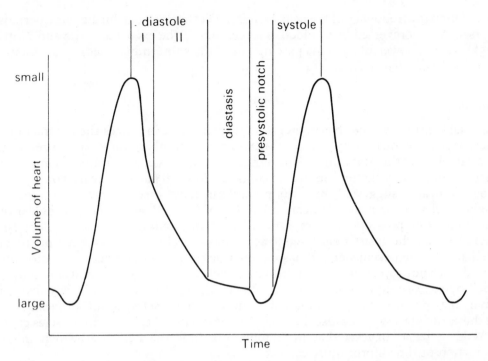

Fig. 533 Changes in volume of a section of the heart during beating as indicated by a mechanical trace. The first phase of diastole results from the elasticity of the heart wall, the second phase from contraction of the aliform muscles

increase in hydrostatic pressure within the heart due to the start of systole in the more posterior segments.

Rate of heartbeat

The frequency with which the heart contracts varies considerably. In general the frequency of beating is higher in early than in later instar larvae and also depends on the age within an instar, becoming very low just before moulting. In the larva of *Sphinx* (Lepidoptera) the rate drops from over 80 beats per minute in the first instar to less than 50 in the fifth; just before moulting it drops to 30 per minute and in the pupa is only about 22 beats per minute. The heart of the young pupa of *Anopheles* sometimes stops beating altogether and in old pupae no beating is observed (Jones, 1954). The heart beats faster in the adult than in immature stages: 150 beats per minute compared with 100–130 in *Anopheles*. Other factors also affect the rate of heartbeat; high temperature and activity increase it, strong movements of the gut may slow it or even stop it for short periods. In general, the heart stops beating at temperatures below 1–5°C, or above 45–50°C, but it is interesting that the heart of *Periplaneta* continues to beat when the insect is in a state of cold stupor.

The heart may undergo periodic reversals in which contractions start at the front and move backwards. This occurs particularly in late larval instars, pupae and adult insects, and in female *Anopheles* 31 % of the beats start at the front of the heart (Jones,

1954). Often the frequency of the heartbeat is lower than normal during these periods of reversal. With a reversed beat, blood is forced out of the excurrent ostia and Nutting (1951) records powerful currents passing out of the subterminal incurrent ostia in the heart of *Gryllotalpa* (Orthoptera).

Control of heartbeat

Since the heart sometimes has no nerve supply, in these instances the contractions of the heart muscle must be myogenic. Where a nerve supply to the heart is present it is not clear whether the beat is myogenic or neurogenic. Since, in a number of insects, the heart continues to beat after removal of connections to all parts of the nervous system a myogenic beat is suggested, but it is possible in these cases that there are intrinsic ganglion cells on or near the heart as in *Periplaneta*. Pharmacological evidence is conflicting, but possibly favours a neurogenic origin for the beat. Miller (1974) concludes that the heart muscle contracts myogenically, but may have neurogenic pacemakers. The pacemaker cell has cholinergic properties and acts via motor fibres with adrenergic properties. In turn the pacemaker cell may be stimulated and its output varied by sensory input from extrinsic fibres. When contraction is purely myogenic activity may be initiated by contraction of the aliform muscles, as in *Chironomus* larva, but this is not always so because the heart will beat with all the aliform muscles cut and de Wilde (1947) suggests that in Lepidoptera it is the heartbeat which initiates contraction of the aliform muscles.

The evidence for the control of the activity of the heart by neurosecretion is conflicting; secretions from the brain, the corpora cardiaca and the corpora allata have been recorded as accelerating the beat. In *Periplaneta* the corpora cardiaca release at least one neurohormone; when stimulated via the internal nerve to the corpus cardiacium. One of these accelerates the heartbeat (Gersch *et al.*, 1970). It is known to be released when the insect feeds on glucose, but probably also follows other activities. In *Locusta*, on the other hand, the heartbeat is accelerated by juvenile hormone from the corpora allata (Roussel, 1972). A beat can be initiated in any part of the heart (Beard, 1953), but normally contraction starts posteriorly and moves forwards. The direction of beat may be related to the distribution of blood pressures. If pressure at the front of the heart becomes so high that a back pressure is set up the heartbeat is reversed. The direction of beat after transection of the heart adds support to this suggestion and possibly the prevalence of a reversed beat in pupal insects results from the blockage of excurrent ostia by the abundant fat and histolysed tissue present at this time. In *Anopheles* the direction of heartbeat is sometimes correlated with abdominal ventilation. If ventilation starts posteriorly the heart beats forwards; if ventilation starts anteriorly the heart beats backwards. These changes might well be due to differences in pressure.

Alternatively, or additionally, the direction of heartbeat might be related to the availability of oxygen. In the absence of a good oxygen supply the rate of heartbeat is strongly reduced indicating the need for an adequate supply for normal working. The larva of *Bombyx* has a better tracheal supply to the posterior end of the heart than to the anterior end. Thus the posterior end has a better oxygen supply and so might be dominant, producing the normal forward heartbeat. If, however, the posterior spiracles are occluded so that the oxygen supply is reduced, the direction of heartbeat is reversed since the anterior part now has the better oxygen supply. In the pupa the tracheal system of the whole heart is poor and the rate of beating is low with reversals, while in the adult the tracheal system is dense both anteriorly and posteriorly and the heartbeat is rapid, again with reversals (see also discussion in Jones, 1964). McCann (1970) considers that reversal occurs as a result of changes in the timing of contraction of cells in different parts of the heart. These changes may be caused by any one of many different factors: differences in pressure, availability of oxygen, build up of CO_2 or changes in temperature, for instance.

REFERENCES

BEARD, R. L. (1953). Circulation. *in* Roeder, K. D. (ed.), *Insect physiology.* Wiley and Sons, New York.

BROCHER, F. (1919). Larves des Agrionides. *Ann. Biol. Lac.* **9**: 183–200.

CLARE, S. and TAUBER, O. E. (1942). Circulation of haemolymph in the wings of the cockroach *Blatella germanica* L. III. Circulation in the articular membrane: the significance of this membrane, the pteralia, and wing folds as directive and speed controlling mechanisms in wing circulation. *Iowa St. Coll. J. Sci.* **16**: 349–356.

DAVEY, K. G. (1964). The control of visceral muscles in insects. *Adv. Insect Physiol.* **2**: 219–245.

GEROULD, J. H. (1938). Structure and action of the heart of *Bombyx mori* and other insects. *Acta zool., Stockh.* **19**: 297–352.

GERSCH, M., RICHTER, K., BÖHM, G.-A. and STÜRZEBECHER, J. (1970). Selective Ausschüttung von Neurohormonen nach elektrischer Reizung der Corpora Cardiaca von *Periplaneta americana in vitro. J. Insect Physiol.* **16**: 1991–2013.

JONES, J. C. (1954). The heart and associated tissues of *Anopheles quadrimaculatus* Say (Diptera: Culicidae). *J. Morph.* **94**: 71–123.

JONES, J. C. (1964). The circulatory system of insects. *in* Rockstein, M. (ed.), *The physiology of Insecta.* vol. 3. Academic Press, New York.

JONES, J. C. (1974). Factors affecting heart rates in insects. *in* Rockstein, M. (ed.), *The physiology of Insecta.* vol. 5. Academic Press, New York and London.

JONES, J. C. (1977). *The circulatory system of insects.* Thomas, Springfield, Illinois.

McCANN, F. V. (1970). Physiology of insect hearts. *A. Rev. Ent.* **15**: 173–200.

MILLER, T. A. (1974). Electrophysiology of the insect heart. *in* Rockstein, M. (ed.), *The physiology of Insecta.* vol. 5. Academic Press, New York and London.

NUTTING, W. L. (1951). A comparative anatomical study of the heart and accessory structures of the orthopteroid insects. *J. Morph.* **89**: 501–597.

RICHARDS, A. G. (1963). The ventral diaphragm of insects. *J. Morph.* **113**: 17–47.

ROUSSEL, J.-P. (1972). Rythme et régulation du coeur chez *Locusta migratoria migratorioides* L. Acrida **1**: 17–39.

SANGER, J. W. and McCANN, F. V. (1968). Ultrastructure of moth alary muscles and their attachment to the heart wall. *J. Insect Physiol.* **14**: 1539–1544.

WHEDON, A. D. (1938). The aortic diverticula of the Odonata. *J. Morph.* **63**: 229–261.

WIGGLESWORTH, V. B. (1972). *The principles of insect physiology.* Chapman and Hall, London.

WILDE, J. de (1947). Contribution to the physiology of the heart of insects with special reference to the alary muscles. *Archs néerl. Physiol.* **28**: 530–542.

CHAPTER XXXIII

THE HAEMOLYMPH

The blood or haemolymph of insects consists of a fluid plasma in which nucleated cells are suspended. Several different types of blood cells occur and the number in circulation varies considerably, sometimes due to real changes in the numbers present, but also because they may adhere in large numbers to various tissues so that they do not circulate. Their functions include phagocytosis, wound healing and perhaps storage and intermediate metabolism.

Blood cells may be involved in connective tissue formation, but in many cases connective tissue is formed by the cells of other tissues. The functions of connective tissue include supporting and binding tissues together and in this the tracheal system may play an important role, but it is also possible that some connective tissue serves to conduct secretions from their origins to the target cells.

The volume of blood may vary at different stages in the life cycle and according to the physiological condition of the insect. The plasma contains various inorganic ions, of which sodium and chloride may be the most important, but insects differ from other animals in that other ions may be present in higher concentrations than these two. Organic substances are also present and in higher insects amino acids make a considerable contribution to the total osmolar concentration of the haemolymph. Proteins are also present and vary in concentration in the course of the life history. The concentrations of many haemolymph constituents are regulated about average values, but significant fluctuations from the average may affect the physiology and behaviour of the insects.

The plasma serves primarily as a means by which substances may be transported round the body, although it plays little part in respiration. It may also provide a store of substances such as sugars and proteins, while its water acts as a reservoir for the maintenance of the tissue fluids. The hydrostatic pressure of the haemolymph is important in the movements of soft-bodied larvae, in expansion and in other ways.

The structure and functions of the blood cells are reviewed by Arnold (1974), Crossley (1975), Gupta (1979) and Jones (1962, 1964), who also reviews haemopoiesis (Jones, 1970). Reactions to parasites are discussed by Nappi (1974) and G. Salt (1968, 1970), and coagulation by Grégoire (1971, 1974). The chemical composition, biochemistry and functions of the plasma are reviewed by Florkin and Jeuniaux (1974) and Jeuniaux (1971). Ashhurst (1968) reviews the structure and functions of connective tissue.

33.1 Haemocytes

The blood or haemolymph circulates round the body cavity between the various organs, bathing them directly. It consists of a fluid plasma in which are supended the blood cells or haemocytes.

33.1.1 Types of haemocyte

Many different types of haemocyte have been described, but a comprehensive classification is difficult because individual cells can have very different appearances under different conditions and a variety of techniques has been used in their study. Arnold (1974) attempts to equate the terminology of different authors. Jones (1962, 1964) recognises four main types of cell which have been distinguished in most of the insects studied:

1. Prohaemocytes (Fig. 534A) are small rounded cells with relatively large nuclei and intensely basophilic cytoplasm which contains large numbers of ribosomes but little endoplasmic reticulum. They divide at frequent intervals and give rise to other types of cell.

2. Plasmatocytes are frequently the most abundant cell type. They are variable in form with a basophilic cytoplasm containing many ribosomes, mitochondria and vacuoles of various sizes (Fig. 534B). They are phagocytic.

3. Granular haemocytes are also phagocytic but are characterised by the possession of acidophilic granules which are seen to be membrane bounded in the electron microscope (Fig. 534C). The cells also contain abundant rough endoplasmic reticulum.

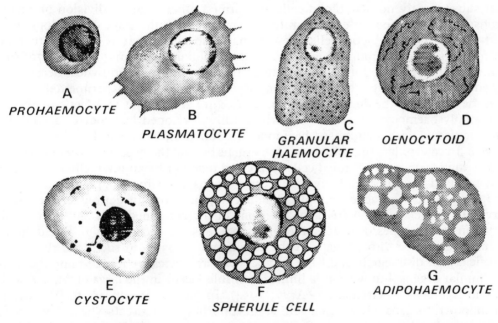

Fig. 534 Diagrammatic representation of various types of haemocyte as seen under phase contrast. All approx. × 2000. (A, D and G after Rizki, 1953; B after Jones, 1954; C and F after Jones, 1956; E after Grégoire, 1951)

4. Cystocytes (coagulocytes) when viewed with the phase contrast microscope have a small, sharply defined nucleus and a pale, hyaline cytoplasm containing scattered black granules (Fig. 534E), while other types of haemocytes have a larger, paler nucleus and

darker cytoplasm. The cystocytes are probably specialised granular haemocytes. These cells often possess phenoloxidases (Crossley, 1975).

In addition, there are other types of cell which only occur in certain insects. The commonest of these are oenocytoids, spherule cells and adipohaemocytes. Oenocytoids are found in Coleoptera, Lepidoptera and some Diptera and Heteroptera. They are usually large, thick, basophilic cells containing canaliculi, strands of granules or crystals (Fig. 534D) (Jones, 1962). Spherule cells, found in Lepidoptera and Diptera, are round or oval cells with large, non-refringent, usually acidophilic inclusions filling the whole cell (Fig. 534F). Adipohaemocytes (spheroidocytes) have been found in all the Lepidoptera and Diptera so far studied and in some representatives of various other groups. They are characterised by refringent fat droplets and other inclusions (Fig. 534G).

It is not clear if these different types of haemocyte represent different stages in the development of individual cells, but it seems probable that most of them are derived independently from prohaemocytes.

33.1.2 Origin of haemocytes

Haemocytes are derived from the embryonic mesoderm and in some insects it appears that subsequently no new blood cells are formed other than by division of existing prohaemocytes. The incidence of mitosis may vary with the stage of development so that the number of blood cells present may also change. It is possible that new haemocytes are also produced in specialised haemopoietic organs. Jones (1970, 1977) considers the evidence for haemopoiesis in these tissues to be equivocal because it is based only on histology, but Hoffmann (1972) presents good experimental evidence that the organs on the dorsal diaphragm of *Locusta* are true haemopoietic organs and not simply haemocytic reservoirs in which fully developed haemocytes accumulate. Similar tissue, with a supposed haemopoietic function, has been described in other insects. In caterpillars there are four such organs behind the prothoracic spiracles, each consisting of a mass of rounded cells connected together by an intercellular reticulum and enclosed in a capsule. They are discrete organs, not simply aggregations of cells, and have a discrete tracheal supply. The haemopoietic organs get bigger throughout larval life associated with frequent divisions of the contained cells and by the third larval instar all types of differentiating blood cells are recognisable. The definitive haemocytes escape through gaps in the capsule until finally, in the pupa, the haemopoietic organs disintegrate and large numbers of haemocytes are released into the blood.

Similar organs, but without a limiting capsule, occur in the larva of *Musca*, which has no free cells in circulation (Arvy, 1954). In general it appears to be true that haemopoietic organs release their cells at metamorphosis in insects where there are few or no cells already in circulation. Perhaps these cells assist in the histolysis which occurs at this time.

In *Gryllus* the phagocytic organs (p. 800) histologically resemble haemopoietic organs.

33.1.3 Numbers of haemocytes present

In general the density of blood cells ranges from about 25 000 to 100 000 per mm^3, but is possibly lower in adult Endopterygota and is very low, only about 100/mm^3 in some

Heteroptera. The total number cells obviously depends on the blood volume, but is about 15 000 000 in adult *Periplaneta* and just over 1 000 000 in last instar larvae of *Galleria*. Some insects, such as the larvae of *Musca* and *Chironomus plumosus*, normally have no haemocytes in circulation.

The number of haemocytes present in the blood fluctuates as the balance between production and cell death varies, but also because not all the cells are free in the circulation; many of them may adhere to the surfaces of tissues in the haemocoel, only appearing in the circulation at certain times. The number of circulating cells per unit volume of haemolymph often increases before a moult and decreases again after it. In *Sarcophaga* the blood cell count rises from about $800/mm^3$ in the larva to $34\ 000/mm^3$ just before pupation, possibly following the release of cells from the haemopoietic organs. In the early pupa the number drops to $12\ 000/mm^3$ probably as a result of many cells adhering to the tissues (Jones, 1956). These changes are largely due to alterations in the numbers of granular haemocytes, very few of which are present at the beginning of the last larval instar. Changes in haemolymph populations are controlled by hormones. In larval *Calliphora* the rise in the number of phagocytic cells in circulation before pupariation is controlled by ecdysone, which also governs the production of blood cells in fifth instar *Locusta*.

Differential changes in the types of cell present are common. Prohaemocytes are most abundant in the early instars. In *Sialis* granular haemocytes first appear in the last larval instar, reaching a peak and disappearing again before pupation (Selman, 1962). Similarly, the adipohaemocytes in *Prodenia* (Yeager, 1945) and the spherule cells in *Sarcophaga* reach a peak in numbers just before pupation. In *Prodenia* the most abundant cell types vary throughout the life of the insect and in holometabolous insects generally many of the cells break down at pupation and a new generation arises in the adult by division of the prohaemocytes.

33.1.4 Functions

Phagocytosis

An important function of haemocytes is phagocytosis of foreign particles, micro-organisms and tissue debris. Various types of cells are capable of phagocytosis but probably the plasmatocytes are most important. In older larvae of *Drosophila* and *Galleria* over 90 % of the circulating cells are phagocytic. Injection of micro-organisms sometimes results in an increase in the numbers of free blood cells and these often confer some degree of non-specific immunity on the insect. In the habitual host, phagocytosis of protozoans and fungi is not normally successful, but these organisms rarely survive in unusual hosts. The reaction against bacteria depends on the condition of host and parasite, any factors adverse to the insect tending to the success of the bacterium, and probably, in general, the plasma is more important than the haemocytes in combating bacteria.

The increase of phagocytes which occurs at metamorphosis may be associated with the phagocytosis of tissue debris, but this is not always true since in *Rhodnius*, for instance, phagocytosis does not occur at this time. Phagocytosed material may be digested in the cell or fully laden phagocytes may be encapsulated by other phagocytes. In some insects phagocytes aggregate to form well-defined phagocytic organs.

Phagocytic organs

The phagocytic organs are found in the anterior part of the abdomen of Tettigonioidea and Grylloidea. They are flattened triangular sacs opening ventro-laterally from the heart by narrow connections, at which there are excurrent valves, and then fanning out between the aliform muscles (Fig. 522). Two to four pairs may be present. The ventral wall of these organs is formed by the dorsal diaphragm, the dorsal wall by phagocytic cells which are multinucleate and occupy part of the lumen of each sac (Fig. 535). These organs appear to act as filters removing dyes and particles from the blood which is forced into them; the blood itself is presumed to percolate through the dorsal diaphragm.

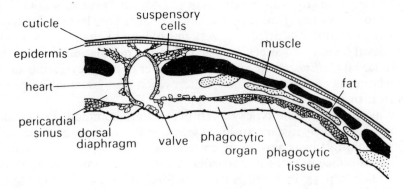

Fig. 535 Transverse section through the pericardial sinus in the abdomen of *Gryllotalpa* showing a phagocytic organ and phagocytic tissue. Pericardial cells form supporting elements (suspensory cells) for the heart dorsally (after Nutting, 1951)

Encapsulation

Particles such as metazoan parasites which are too large to phagocytose are encapsulated by large numbers of haemocytes. Blood cells start to accumulate over the surface of any foreign body soon after it enters the haemocoel. Whether they are attracted to it or simply come into contact accidentally in the course of circulation is uncertain (Nappi, 1974; G. Salt, 1970). Other cells adhere to the outside of the clump so that the foreign object is surrounded by a capsule many cells thick, the cells producing material containing an acid mucopolysaccharide which probably results in adhesion. At the same time cells in the middle layers of the capsule start to flatten and a cell originally about 6 μm in diameter may become a flattened disc 20–30 μm across. The flattened cells become joined by desmosomes and come to form a continuous layer, so that at this stage the capsule consists of an inner layer of unmodified cells, about 10 cells thick in *Ephestia* (Lepidoptera), a middle layer of flattened cells, and an outer layer of more or less unmodified cells about five cells deep (Fig. 536).

The inner cells secrete material into the intercellular spaces and subsequently become necrotic. Melanin is produced in this layer. Larval *Drosophila* contain a class of haemocytes, called lamellocytes, which typically are very flattened. These cells adhere directly to foreign objects and so development and form of the capsule is slightly different in this case. Subsequently many of the cells in the outer layer return to the

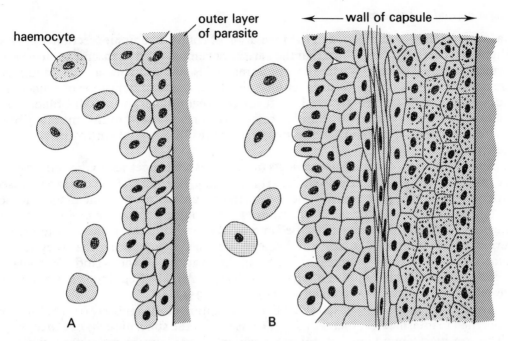

Fig. 536 Response of haemocytes to a relatively large parasite. A. Haemocytes aggregating on the outside of the parasite. B. Haemocytes compacted to form a capsule with distinct inner, middle and outer layers. Inner cells contain numerous cytolysomes (based on G. Salt, 1970)

circulation, so the capsule becomes smaller. For instance, the capsule formed round the larva of *Nemeritis* (Hymenoptera) by larval *Diataraxia* (Lepidoptera) shrinks to about one tenth of its original size and mass movements of the cells may change the shape of the capsule. Ultimately all that remains is a relatively thin envelope surrounding the foreign body. Whether this envelope consists wholly of fibrous connective tissue secreted by cells or whether it continues to contain some cells is uncertain.

Encapsulation normally occurs if the parasite is in an unusual host and generally the parasite dies through lack of oxygen. In an habitual host, encapsulation may or may not occur. Some parasitic Hymenoptera are able to resist encapsulation by making vigorous movements and older tachinid larvae have a respiratory funnel connected to the host tracheal system so that encapsulation does not impair their respiration. Some parasites, such as encysted metacercariae, are unaffected by encapsulation, apparently because of their low oxygen requirements. The majority of Hymenoptera in their habitual hosts do not evoke encapsulating behaviour by the haemocytes.

G. Salt (1970) considers that all foreign objects in the haemolymph are phago-cytosed or encapsulated unless they possess surface characteristics which are similar in some way to those of the insect's own connective tissue and so do not evoke a response. It is not known what features are important in this specific recognition, but mucopolysaccharides are possibly involved. Other possibilities are that successful invaders which are not phagocytosed or encapsulated inhibit the reaction of the host's haemocytes, or that foreign objects produce chemicals which attract haemocytes (see discussion in Nappi, 1974; G. Salt, 1970).

Secretion and metabolism

Haemocytes may be concerned in the formation of connective tissue (section 33.2) and Wigglesworth (1956) has shown that they are important in normal basement membrane formation in *Rhodnius*. When the epidermal cells are growing at the moult the haemocytes spread underneath the epidermis. They contain inclusions of mucopolysaccharide and these are secreted to form the membranes, while the blood cells themselves may break down. Similar cells may form sheaths round muscle fibres, insinuating themselves between the fibres and spreading over them before secreting their products.

There is evidence that in some insects haemocytes are concerned in the activation of the prothoracic glands before moulting. If the phagocytes of *Rhodnius* are immobilised experimentally before the critical period of the moult the prothoracic glands do not become fully activated for the production of the moulting hormone and moulting is delayed. Normally the phagocytes become associated with the gland at the critical period and they increase in size and become vacuolated, suggesting that they secrete some material which is necessary for full activation of the gland. Vacuolated haemocytes are also found in the corpora cardiaca of *Mimas* (Lepidoptera) when these are releasing neurosecretory material (Highnam, 1958).

Some haemocytes may be involved in the formation of the fat body (p. 101) and are concerned in intermediate metabolism. This is true of the spherule cells of *Sarcophaga*, which are most abundant just before pupation. They contain tyrosinase, which is important in the hardening and darkening of the larval cuticle to form the puparium (p. 475). Before the moult the level of tyrosinase builds up rapidly in the cells which aggregate beneath the epidermis and along the tracheae. Then they break down, releasing the tyrosinase into the plasma. The enzyme does not, however, immediately react with the tyrosine already present, apparently because it is inhibited by the low redox potential of the haemolymph. At the time of pupation the redox potential increases sharply. Jones (1962), however, has shown that the spherule cells are not essential for normal hardening and darkening of the puparium to occur.

Haemocytes are probably involved in other aspects of intermediate metabolism as yet unknown. They are also concerned in the transfer of nutrient materials round the body. Glycogen builds up in these cells in larval *Prodenia* (Lepidoptera), but is depleted at metamorphosis when it is utilised. Fat inclusions also occur if the insect is fed on a fatty diet.

In some instances the cells themselves break down to provide nutriment for other tissues and Jones (1956) accounts for the disappearance of granular haemocytes from the pupa of *Sarcophaga* in this way. In *Ephestia* blood cells adhere in large numbers to the membranes of the developing wings and the cell contents pass into the epidermal cells, providing nutriment.

Wound healing and coagulation

The blood cells are concerned in wound healing. Damaged tissues are phagocytosed and the plasmatocytes extend processes which join with those of other cells to form a cellular network. The plasma may coagulate in this network so that the wound is effectively plugged until the epidermis regenerates.

Two types of coagulation occur, both being variations of the same process and involving the cystocytes (Grégoire, 1971, 1974). In *Gryllotalpa* and many other insects when the blood is exposed the cystocytes stop moving and their cystoplasm expands rapidly and becomes vacuolated. Round each cystocyte a thin fog of particles appears in the plasma (Fig. 537A), progressively increasing in amount and density. This material coagulates so that the cystocytes are surrounded by areas of coagulation in which other types of haemocyte may become trapped. The second type of coagulation occurs, for instance, in many lepidopteran larvae and Scarabaeidae. Here there are no islands of coagulation, but the cystocytes send out straight, thread-like pseudopodia which stick to interfaces and foreign particles, forming a meshwork of threads (Fig. 537B). Slowly the fluid contained within the meshes becomes jelly-like and coagulates. Other types of haemocytes may stick to the pseudopodia or become trapped during coagulation. This reaction has more widespread effects than the first. In some Coleoptera and Hymenoptera, coagulation is a combination of these two types. It is not known if the cystocytes which produce these different reactions belong to the same category. The differences may result from the release of larger or smaller amounts of the substance

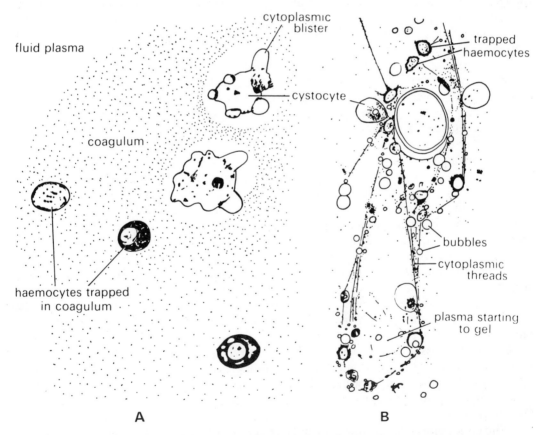

Fig. 537 A. Coagulation in *Gryllotalpa*. The coagulum (dotted) round two cytoscytes has trapped three other haemocytes. B. Coagulation in *Cychrus*. The cystocytes have produced a meshwork of cytoplasmic threads to which other haemocytes and foreign bodies adhere. Between the threads the plasma gels (after Grégoire, 1951)

inducing coagulation or they might reflect differences in the composition of the coagulating plasma. The blood of some insects amongst the Ephemeroptera, Homoptera, Heteroptera, Coleoptera and Diptera does not show any sign of clotting when it is exposed.

Commonly the cystocytes constitute 50 % of the blood cells, but the numbers vary and, in general, reflect the readiness with which the plasma coagulates. However, cystocytes are present in the blood of many Heteroptera and adult Diptera which does not coagulate. Haemocytes aggregate at a wound in the integument of *Rhodnius* within 12 h of the wound occurring. Within 24 h the cells become linked by zonulae adherens and subsequently tight junctions and septate desmosomes are formed, so that the haemocytes become bound together as a continuous tissue (Lai-Fook, 1970).

33.2 Connective tissue

Insect connective tissue is present as a basement membrane underlying the epidermis and other tissues, and as strands suspending other tissues in the body cavity, although the tracheal system is of major importance in this respect. Most basement membranes are less than 0·5 μm thick, but in some regions they are more strongly developed. This is especially true of the neural lamella (Fig. 402), which is 2–10 μm thick, and in adult Lepidoptera it is thickened dorsally and serves for the attachment of the muscles of the ventral diaphragm (Fig. 520) (Ashhurst, 1968).

The connective tissue bounding different organs is often continuous. For instance, the basement membrane of the epidermis is continuous with the sarcolemma surrounding the muscles, and the sarcolemma is continuous with the neurilemma where the muscles are innervated.

In many cases the connective tissue is a secretion of the underlying cells. This is true, for instance, of the neural lamella, which is secreted by the perineurium (p. 621), but in some cases, at least, plasmatocytes add mucopolysaccharide to the substance of the membrane. This has been observed to occur at the basement membrane of the epidermis and the sarcolemma of developing muscles. In *Rhodnius* material added to the epidermal basement membrane by plasmatocytes more than doubles its thickness from 0·2 μm to 0·4 μm (Wigglesworth, 1973). Collagen may also be produced in haemocytes (Crossley, 1975).

A neutral mucopolysaccharide forms a major part of the connective tissue and sometimes embedded in this are collagen fibres. These occur in the neural lamella, in the connective tissue of the auditory ganglion of *Locusta*, and sometimes in the basement membrane of the Malpighian tubules. A lipid is also present in the neural lamella of Lepidoptera.

Connective tissue membranes break down in the pupa, and in the neural lamella of *Galleria*, at least, this process is aided by haemocytes (Shrivastava and Richards, 1965). The connective tissue membranes of the adult are not produced until the underlying tissues are complete and they are characteristically absent from dividing tissues (Whitten, 1962).

The commonest functions of connective tissue are those of supporting and binding tissues together. Wigglesworth (1973) suggests that the thickening of the epidermal basement membrane which occurs just before apolysis in *Rhodnius* enables it to serve as a base for the forces used in moulding the new cuticle. The elastic properties of the tunica propria assist ovulation (p. 345), while in the larvae of higher Diptera and in *Leucophaea* the connective tissue membranes may serve to conduct secretions from their sites of origin to the target organs. For instance, in the larva of *Sarcophaga* the pericardial cells are attached to the heart by strands of connective tissue. Fine channels run through these strands, originating as a series of converging channels in the limiting membrane of the pericardial cells and running to the wall of the heart (Fig. 538). Probably the substance concerned in the control of the heartbeat (p. 794) is conducted to the heart in this way. Similar channels connect the ring gland (p. 823) with the heart, suggesting that the products of the former may be conducted to the heart so that they are distributed round the body with the blood with a maximum of efficiency. Channels are also present in some other membranes, but are absent from the majority, apparently occurring only where secretory cells are present. Such a system facilitates the rapid and uniform transport of secretions to their target organs (Whitten, 1964).

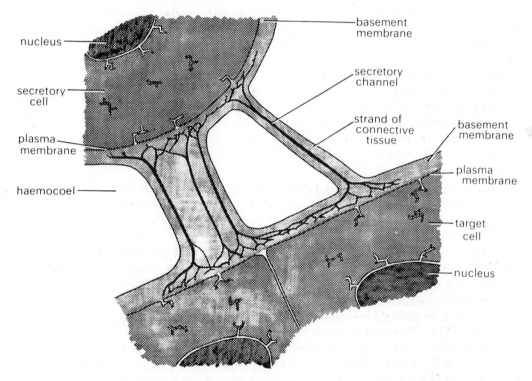

Fig. 538 Diagram showing the channels in connective tissue running from a secretory cell to target cells (after Whitten, 1964)

33.3 Plasma

33.3.1 Blood volume

About 90% of the insect blood is water, but the volume of water varies. Just before a moult the blood volume increases, partly because less water is excreted and partly by the removal of water from the tissues. Afterwards the volume decreases again (Fig. 539)

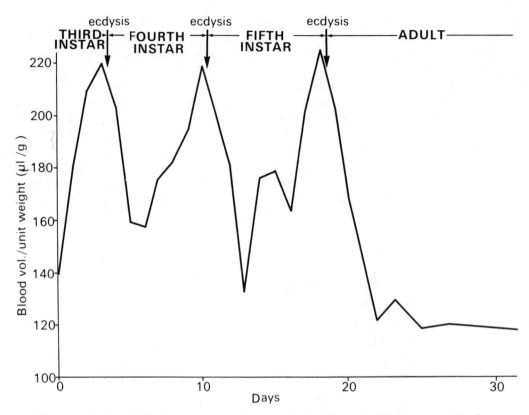

Fig. 539 Changes in the haemolymph volume during the life cycle of *Schistocerca* (after Lee, 1961)

water being returned to the actively growing tissues and some being excreted (Lee, 1961). The reduction after the moult is necessary because too high a blood volume during active periods would be a hindrance by creating too high a turgor pressure and so damping movements of the appendages.

Shorter-term changes in volume may also occur and there is probably a daily cycle related to feeding behaviour and the amount of desiccation. Thus, *Nomadacris* adults contain very little blood on a hot afternoon, but in the evening after feeding the blood volume increases and remains high until the following morning (Chapman, 1958).

Various inorganic and organic substances are dissolved in plasma (Wyatt, 1961).

33.3.2 Inorganic constituents

Chloride is the most abundant inorganic anion in insect blood. The concentration of chloride is high in Apterygota and hemimetabolous insects, but is characteristically low, usually amounting to less than 10% of the total osmolar concentration, in holometabolous forms (Sutcliffe, 1963). Other inorganic anions present are carbonate and phosphate, but these are rarely found in any quantity. Phosphates are important in *Carausius* and *Anabrus* (Orthoptera).

The most abundant cation is usually sodium, although the amount varies with the taxonomic position of the insect and its diet. Phytophagous insects have low concentrations of haemolymph sodium compared with predators, although locusts and grasshoppers have higher levels than other leaf eaters (Table 10). On the other hand, potassium and magnesium levels tend to be higher in the phytophagous groups. *Cimex* (Heteroptera) and *Stomoxys* (Diptera), both feeding on mammalian blood, have remarkably similar sodium and potassium concentrations in the haemolymph.

Table 10

Concentrations, in milli-equivalents/litre, of the major inorganic cations in the haemolymph of different insects

(from Florkin and Jeuniaux, 1974)

Feeding habit	Insect species	Order	Cation			
			Na	K	Ca	Mg
Phytophagous	*Locusta*	Orthoptera	60	12	17	25
	Carausius	Phasmida	9	27	16	142
	Bombyx larva	Lepidoptera	15	46	24	101
	Leptinotarsa larva	Coleoptera	2	55	43	147
	Pteronidea larva	Hymenoptera	2	43	17	61
Predaceous	*Aeschna* larva	Odonata	145	9	7	7
	Tettigonia	Orthoptera	83	51	—	—
	Myrmeleon larva	Neuroptera	143	9	12	31
	Dytiscus	Coleoptera	165	6	22	37
Blood-sucking	*Cimex*	Heteroptera	139	9	—	—
	Stomoxys	Diptera	128	11	—	—

Although cation concentrations are regulated, fairly wide variations about a mean value may occur. For instance, in *Periplaneta*, sodium concentration is consistently higher in haemolymph from the antenna than from the dorsal vessel and the ventral thorax (Pichon, 1970) and the potassium concentration in *Leucophaea* varies diurnally and has peaks in the light and dark periods (Fig. 540) (Lettau *et al.*, 1977). Changes also occur in relation to starvation and, in locusts, the potassium concentration increases markedly before moulting. These changes may affect the behaviour of the insect since neuromuscular junctions are directly exposed to the haemolymph and a low concentration of potassium raises the muscle resting potential. Changes in haemolymph potassium concentrations are also known to cause the release of neurosecretion from neurohaemal organs.

The concentration of magnesium in the blood is often relatively high. In phytophagous insects this to some extent reflects the high level of magnesium in the diet, since it is a constituent of chlorophyll, and in Lepidoptera the level in the blood falls when the larvae stop feeding. A good deal of magnesium still occurs, however, and all insects appear to concentrate this metal. Calcium is often present in lower concentrations than other metallic elements (Table 10).

In many insects the ionic concentrations in the blood are roughly similar in larval and adult stages, although adult Lepidoptera have less magnesium than the larvae (see

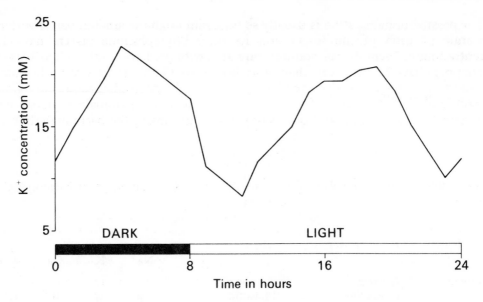

Fig. 540 Diurnal changes in potassium concentration in the haemolymph of *Leucophaea*
(after Lettau *et al.*, 1977)

above). There is relatively little information, however, on different stages of holometabolous insects and in *Vespula* the concentrations change markedly between the pupal
and adult stages, the sodium concentration increasing, while all the other cations
decrease (Table 11).

Various metallic trace elements are also found in the blood. The most frequent are
copper, which is a constituent of tyrosinase, iron, present in the cytochromes, zinc and
manganese.

Table 11

Concentrations, in milli-equivalents/litre, of the major inorganic cations in the
haemolymph of two insects in different stages of development
(from Florkin and Jeuniaux, 1974)

Insect	Stage	Cation			
		Na	K	Ca	Mg
Bombyx	larva	15	46	24	101
	pupa*	11	41	24	69
		22	55	29	87
	adult	14	36	14	47
Vespula	larva	26	56	19	24
	pupa	23	61	11	19
	adult*	93	18	2	3
		153	22	2	1

* estimates by different authors

It is possible that the metallic elements do not exist wholly as free ions, but that a proportion is bound in organic complexes. In species so far examined the amount of ion binding is small (Florkin and Jeuniaux, 1974).

33.3.3 Organic constituents

Insect blood is characterised by the very high level of amino acids present in the plasma, constituting 33–65 % of the non-protein nitrogen present. Most of the known amino acids have been recognised in various insects, but they vary considerably both qualitatively and quantitatively from one species to another and in different stages of the same species. To some extent the amino acids present depend on those available in the food.

In Exopterygota the total amino acid concentration is generally lower than in Endopterygota the various amino acids present in similar amounts. In Endopterygota, on the other hand, glutamic acid and proline are usually present in much higher concentrations than the others. Arginine, lysine and histidine are also sometimes present in relatively high concentrations.

The concentrations of amino acids may change at different stages in the life cycle. Tyrosine, for instance, commonly accumulates before each moult and then decreases sharply as it is used in tanning and melanisation of the new cuticle (p. 522). Similarly in the larva of *Bombyx* the amino acids, such as glutamic acid and aspartic acid, which are concerned with silk production fall to a very low level while the larva is spinning its cocoon, increasing again when this is complete (Fig. 541). Others, such as methionine, are not concerned with silk production, but increase at the time of the pupal moult as a result of the histolysis of the larval tissues (but see p. 489). In *Rhodnius*, however, the amino acid concentration in the haemolymph rises after feeding, but then remains constant right through the period of moulting. It appears that in this insect the utilisation of amino acids is offset by the slow, continuous digestion of the stored blood meal (Coles, 1965).

Other non-protein nitrogen in the plasma is mainly in the form of the end products of nitrogen metabolism. Uric acid is always present and in addition there may be allantoin, urea and ammonia. Apart from metabolic end products, amino sugars and peptides occur, the former sometimes constituting half the total carbohydrate in the blood.

Numerous proteins are present in the haemolymph; 19 are recorded from *Drosophila* and 21 from *Locusta*. They are not all present at the same time, but there are progressive changes through the life cycle of the insects. For instance, the first instar larva of *Locusta* emerges from the egg with seven different haemolymph protein fractions (Fig. 542). Within a day or two more fractions (16 and 17 in Fig. 542) have developed and these increase in concentration, but before the end of the instar four of the original fractions have disappeared (1, 4, 6 and 11 in Fig. 542). These probably represent the remains of yolk proteins which are being utilised (McCormick and Scott, 1966a). Another protein band regularly reaches a maximum at the time of moulting and then disappears again (14 in Fig. 542) (McCormick and Scott, 1966b; and see Chen and Levenbook, 1966).

The amount of protein in the haemolymph varies during development. In fifth instar *Locusta*, for instance, the total amount remains low over the first four days of

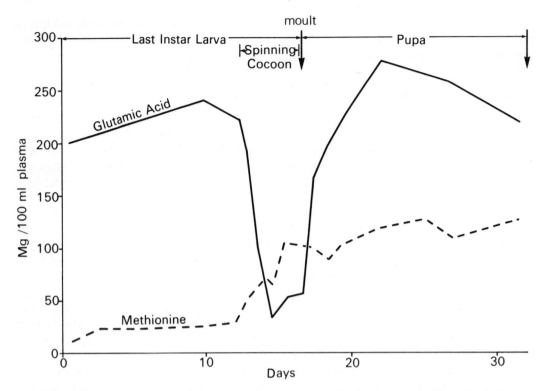

Fig. 541 Changes in the concentrations of two amino acids during cocoon formation and metamorphosis of *Bombyx*. Glutamic acid is involved in silk production, methionine is not (from Florkin and Jeuniaux, 1974)

development, but subsequently rises to over three times the original level and falls sharply at ecdysis (Fig. 543). The concentration in the haemolymph results from a balance between synthesis of more protein and sequestration in the tissues. Synthesis of blood proteins is high in mid-instar and at the same time these are actively taken up into the tissues, where they are either immediately degraded or are sequestered in a modified form. At the end of the instar, when protein is withdrawn from the blood at the time of the moult, relatively little synthesis occurs (Tobe and Loughton, 1969) (and see p. 489).

In female insects a sex specific protein appears in the haemolymph early in adult development, or in the pupa of some endopterygote insects. The concentration of this protein increases rapidly as it is synthesised and released from the fat body, but subsequently it is absorbed by the developing oocytes and forms the principal yolk protein. This type of protein is known as a vitellogenin. Vitellogenin production is regulated by juvenile hormone (Buhlmann, 1976) (p. 339).

The haemolymph proteins include a number of enzymes. Amongst these are trehalase and other carbohydrases (Florkin and Jeuniaux, 1974). Just before puparium formation in *Sarcophaga* the enzyme tyrosinase is released into the plasma from the blood cells.

Organic acids may be present in some quantity in the plasma. Citrate is usually present in high concentration, although this varies considerably from one species to

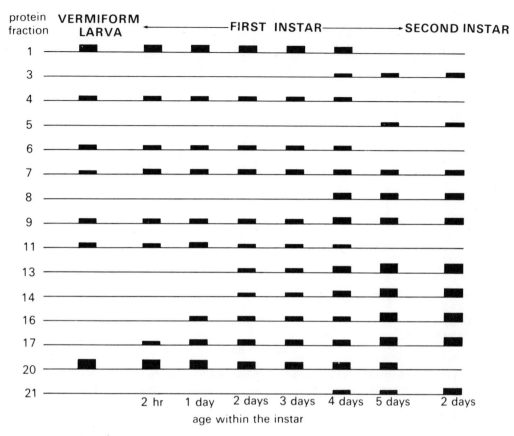

Fig. 542 Diagrammatic representation of an electropherogram showing the proteins present in the haemolymph of *Locusta*. The intensity of staining of the bands, which is influenced by the concentration of protein, is represented by their thickness in the diagram (after McCormick and Scott, 1966a)

another, and there is consistently more in the larva than in the adult. In *Prodenia* the level of citrate is not markedly affected by diet, so it must be endogenous in origin (Levenbook and Hollis, 1961). The organic phosphate concentration in insect blood is also usually high and in *Hyalophora* α-glycerophosphate and phosphocholine, in particular, contribute to this.

There is characteristically a high concentration of trehalose, a nonreducing disaccharide, in insect blood. Trehalose is a source of energy and so its level in the blood is reduced by starvation and also by activity, such as flight (Howden and Kilby, 1960), but it is increased after feeding because other sugars are converted to it (p. 103). *Apis* and *Phormia* are exceptional in having high concentrations of glucose and fructose in the blood.

Glycerol, or some equivalent, is probably always present, sometimes in very high concentrations, in insects which are able to tolerate freezing (p. 772) (R. W. Salt, 1961).

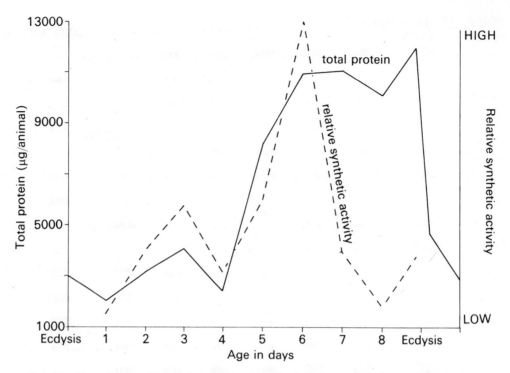

Fig. 543 Changes in total haemolymph protein and relative rate of synthesis of protein from amino acids in the haemolymph during the fifth instar of *Locusta* (after Tobe and Loughton, 1969)

The concentration of lipid in the haemolymph varies from about 1·5 to 5 %. Marked increases may occur during development or flight, when lipids in the fat body are mobilised as fuel for the flight muscles (p. 264). In *Pyrrhocoris* triglycerides and diglycerides form the bulk of haemolymph lipids.

33.3.4 Variations in plasma in different insect orders

Sutcliffe (1963) groups the plasma of pterygote insects into three broad categories:
1. Sodium and chloride account for most of the osmolar concentration (Fig. 544A). This is probably the basic type of insect blood and is similar to that in most other arthropods. This type occurs in Ephemeroptera, Odonata, Plecoptera, Orthoptera and Homoptera.
2. Chloride is low relative to sodium, which constitutes 21–48 % of the total osmolar concentration (Fig. 544B). Amino acids are also present in high concentration. This type is found in Trichoptera, Diptera, Megaloptera, Neuroptera, Mecoptera and most Coleoptera.
3. Amino acids account for about 40 % of the total osmolar concentration (Fig. 544C). There is a large unknown factor, but none of the other substances accounts for more than 10 % of the total. Lepidoptera and Hymenoptera have this type of blood.

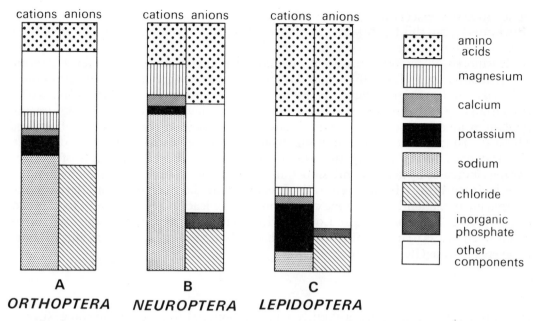

Fig. 544 Osmotic components of the haemolymph in different groups of insects expressed as percentages of the total osmolar concentration. Each vertical column represents 50 % of the total concentration (after Sutcliffe, 1963)

33.3.5 Pigments

Apart from *Chironomus* larvae, in which haemoglobin is present in solution in the plasma, respiratory pigments do not occur in insect blood. The blood may, nevertheless, assume a variety of colours due to various pigments. Commonly the blood is green due to the presence of insectoverdin, a mixture of carotenoid and bile pigment. Insectoverdin is present in the blood of Lepidoptera and in solitary locusts, but in locusts it becomes altered with starvation as the pigments are metabolised and if the insects are crowded together the insectoverdin is replaced by blue mesobiliverdin (Nickerson, 1956). In the blood of *Bombyx* larva carotene, xanthophyll and flavines are present; in the pupa of *Hyalophora* are α-carotene, taraxanthin, riboflavine and chlorophyll. Aphids frequently have a purplish-red pigment in the blood in large quantities, up to 2 % of the wet weight. This pigment is protoaphin belonging to a class of pigments, the aphins, so far found only in members of the Aphididae and the genus *Adelges* (Cromartie, 1959) (p. 138).

33.3.6 Properties of the plasma

Osmotic pressure

Although there may be active regulation of water movement between the blood and the tissue fluids, osmotic pressures also influence this movement. Hence the osmotic pressure of the blood is important in controlling the water content of the cells. It is generally believed that the osmotic pressures of blood and tissue fluids are roughly the same. In many insects the osmotic pressure of the blood is about 300–400 mOsmol (Buck, 1953), but this figure varies in different stages of development and in xerophytic insects is often higher, over 500 mOsmol.

Haemolymph osmotic pressure is maintained at a relatively constant level (Florkin and Jeuniaux, 1974). Even after eight days without water when haemolymph volume is reduced to half its original value, the haemolymph osmotic pressure of *Periplaneta* only rises from 413 to 459 mOsmol. This regulation is achieved by removal of sodium and potassium ions from the haemolymph and their storage in the fat body (Hyatt and Marshall, 1977). Short-term variations from the average osmotic pressure do occur. For instance, during feeding the osmotic pressure of the haemolymph of *Locusta* nymphs increases by about 50 mOsmol but returns to its original level in about an hour. The increase results from a removal of water from the haemolymph (Bernays and Chapman, 1974a) and under some conditions it may lead to a reduction in food intake (Bernays and Chapman, 1974b). Locusts which have been deprived of water will drink when given access to it, stopping when the haemolymph osmotic pressure falls to about its average value (Bernays, 1977).

pH

In most insects the blood has a slightly acid reaction, pH 6·0–7·0, but in some, such as *Chironomus*, it is distinctly alkaline, pH 7·2–7·7. There is usually a slight rise in pH at moulting.

Most enzymes only work efficiently within a limited range of pH and so its control is important. During normal activity there is a tendency for the blood to become markedly acid due to the liberation of acid metabolites, including carbon dioxide. This tendency to change is offset, or buffered, by substances in the blood. The buffering capacity of insect blood, that is, its ability to prevent change of pH, is minimal in the normal physiological range, but increases sharply on either side of this range. Levenbook (1950b) suggests that this arrangement is associated with tracheal respiration. Carbon dioxide passes from the tissues to the tracheae via the blood and if the insect is active it accumulates in the blood. This accumulation leads to opening of the spiracles and ventilatory movements, but the carbon dioxide only diffuses slowly from the blood to the gas phase because there is no carbonic anhydrase in insects to catalyse the reaction. This inefficiency of the system could result in very large changes in pH, but as the buffering capacity of the blood increases as the pH varies from the normal range these changes will be limited.

Within the normal physiological range bicarbonates and phosphates are the most important buffers. On the acid side of this range the carboxyl groups of organic acids such as citric acid are important while on the alkaline side the amino groups of various amino acids are most significant. Proteins buffer over a wide range of pH.

33.3.7 Functions of the plasma

Plasma is important in the transport of various materials about the body. Nutritive materials are carried from the alimentary canal and storage tissues to the sites at which they are to be metabolised, excretory products from their places of origin to the Malpighian tubules, and hormones from the endocrine organs to their sites of action.

The blood is normally unimportant in the transport of oxygen to the tissues because these are supplied directly by the tracheae. It normally contains much more carbon dioxide than oxygen. This partly reflects the much greater solubility of carbon dioxide, but the carbon dioxide in solution only accounts for about 20 % of the total in the blood. The remainder is bound in some form, mainly as bicarbonate (Levenbook, 1950a). Oxygen is only present in solution. The much greater affinity of the blood for carbon dioxide than for oxygen is probably important in the cyclic release of carbon dioxide which occurs in some insects (Buck, 1958) (p. 549).

The plasma acts as a store for some substances, although sometimes only for relatively short periods. Trehalose is present as a source of energy and the supply can be replenished relatively rapidly from the fat body. The levels of amino acids and proteins present at any one time are the result of a balance between synthesis and utilisation in different parts of the body.

Water storage is also important and by drawing on the plasma an insect can maintain the level of its cell fluids if the food is dry (Lee, 1961). The water itself also functions as a hydrostatic skeleton in forms, such as many larvae, where the cuticle is soft and provides little support for the insect. At moulting the hydrostatic properties are used in the expansion of the appendages and the ptilinum in cyclorrhaphous Diptera, while the amount of fluid present at this time can influence the ultimate size of the insect. Larval *Lucilia* with access to more moisture produce bigger adults, and wing size in *Orgyia* is greater if the emerging adult has a greater blood volume (Mellanby, 1939). Increases in hydrostatic pressure as a result of muscular activity are also responsible for the eversion of various organs such as the penis in male insects and the osmeterium, a fleshy, bifurcate defensive device, on the prothoracic segment of larval Papilionidae.

Reflex bleeding also results from an increase in hydrostatic pressure. In this case plasma is forced through weak spots or pores in the cuticle and in species exhibiting this behaviour the blood always contains some caustic or repellant substance, so this is presumed to be a defensive mechanism. In the grasshopper *Dictyophorus* the blood is mixed with air as it is forced out so that it produces a nauseous froth on the outside of the insect. In the bloody-nosed beetle, *Timarcha*, the red blood is forced out round the mouth. In general the blood is not lost to the insect, but the bulk is withdrawn into the haemocoel when the pressure is relaxed.

REFERENCES

ARNOLD, J. W. (1974). The hemocytes of insects. *in* Rockstein, M. (ed.), *The physiology of Insecta.* vol. 5. Academic Press, New York.

ARVY, L. (1954). Données sur la leucopoïèse chez *Musca domestica* L. *Proc. R. ent. Soc. Lond.* A, **29**: 39–41.

ASHHURST, D. E. (1968). The connective tissue of insects. *A. Rev. Ent.* **13**: 45–74.

BERNAYS, E. A. (1977). The physiological control of drinking behaviour in nymphs of *Locusta migratoria. Physiol. Ent.* **2**: 261–273.

BERNAYS, E. A. and CHAPMAN, R. F. (1974a). Changes in haemolymph osmotic pressure in *Locusta migratoria* larvae in relation to feeding. *J. Ent.* A, **48**: 149–155.

BERNAYS, E. A. and CHAPMAN, R. F. (1974b). The effect of haemolymph osmotic pressure on the meal size of nymphs of *Locusta migratoria* L. *J. exp. Biol.* **61**: 473–480.

BUCK, J. B. (1953). Physical properties and chemical composition of insect blood. *in* Roeder, K., *Insect physiology.* Wiley and Sons, New York.

BUCK, J. (1958). Cyclic CO_2 release in insects. IV. A theory of mechanism. *Biol. Bull.* **114**: 118–140.

BUHLMANN, G. (1976). Haemolymph vitellogenin, juvenile hormone, and oöcyte growth in the adult cockroach *Nauphoeta cinerea* during first pre-oviposition period. *J. Insect Physiol.* **22**: 1101–1110.

CHAPMAN, R. F. (1958). A field study of the potassium concentration in the blood of the red locust, *Nomadacris septemfasciata* (Serv.), in relation to its activity. *Anim. Behav.* **6**: 60–67.

CHEN, P. S. and LEVENBOOK, L. (1966). Studies on the haemolymph proteins of the blowfly *Phormia regina*—I. Changes in ontogenetic patterns. *J. Insect Physiol.* **12**: 1595–1609.

COLES, G. C. (1965). Haemolymph proteins and yolk formation in *Rhodnius prolixus* Stål. *J. exp. Biol.* **43**: 425–432.

CROMARTIE, R. I. T. (1959). Insect pigments. *A. Rev. Ent.* **4**: 59–76.

CROSSLEY, A. C. (1975). The cytophysiology of insect blood. *Adv. Insect Physiol.* **11**: 117–221.

FLORKIN, M. and JEUNIAUX, C. (1974). Hemolymph: composition. *in* Rockstein, M. (ed.), *The physiology of Insecta.* vol. 5. Academic Press, New York.

GRÉGOIRE, C. (1951). Blood coagulation in arthropods. II. Phase contrast microscopic observations on haemolymph coagulation in sixty-one species of insects. *Blood* **6**: 1173–1198.

GRÉGOIRE, C. (1971). Haemolymph coagulation in arthropods. *in* Florkin, M. and Scheer, B. T. (eds.), *Chemical zoology.* vol. 6, part B. Academic Press, New York.

GRÉGOIRE, C. (1974). Haemolymph coagulation. *in* Rockstein, M. (ed.), *The physiology of Insecta.* vol. 5. Academic Press, New York.

GUPTA, A. P. (ed.) (1979). *Insect hemocytes. Development, forms, functions and techniques.* Cambridge University Press.

HIGHNAM, K. C. (1958). Activity of the corpora allata during pupal diapause in *Mimas tiliae* (Lepidoptera). *Q. Jl microsc. Sci.* **99**: 171–180.

HOFFMANN, J. A. (1972). Modifications of the haemogramme of larval and adult *Locusta migratoria* after selective X-irradiations of the haemocytopoietic tissue. *J. Insect Physiol.* **18**: 1639–1652.

HOWDEN, G. F. and KILBY, B. A. (1960). Biochemical studies on insect haemolymph— I. Variations in reducing power with age and the effect of diet. *J. Insect Physiol.* **4**: 258–269.

HYATT, A. D. and MARSHALL, A. T. (1977). Sequestration of haemolymph sodium and potassium by fat body in the water-stressed cockroach *Periplaneta americana*. *J. Insect Physiol.* **23**: 1437–1442.

JEUNIAUX, C. (1971). Hemolymph-Arthropoda. *in* Florkin, M. and Scheer, B. T. (eds.), *Chemical zoology.* vol. 6. Academic Press, New York.

JONES, J. C. (1954). A study of mealworm hemocytes with phase contrast microscopy. *Ann. ent. Soc. Am.* **47**: 308–315.

JONES, J. C. (1956). The hemocytes of *Sarcophaga bullata* Parker. *J. Morph.* **99**: 233–257.

JONES, J. C. (1962). Current concepts concerning insect hemocytes. *Am. Zoologist* **2**: 209–246.

JONES, J. C. (1964). The circulatory system of insects. *in* Rockstein, M. (ed.), *The physiology of Insecta.* vol. 3. Academic Press, New York.

JONES, J. C. (1970). Hemocytopoiesis in insects. *in* Gordon, A. S. (ed.), *Regulation of hematopoiesis.* vol. 1. Appleton-Century-Crofts, New York.

JONES, J. C. (1977). *The circulatory system of insects.* Thomas, Springfield, Illinois.

LAI-FOOK, J. (1970). Haemocytes in the repair of wounds in an insect (*Rhodnius prolixus*). *J. Morph.* **130**: 297–313.

LEE, R. M. (1961). The variation of blood volume with age in the desert locust, (*Schistocerca gregaria*. Forsk.) *J. Insect Physiol.* **6**: 36–51.

LETTAU, J., FOSTER, W. A., HARKER, J. E. and TREHERNE, J. E. (1977). Diel changes in potassium activity in the haemolymph of the cockroach *Leucophaea maderae*. *J. exp. Biol.* **71**: 171–186.

LEVENBOOK, L. (1950a). The physiology of carbon dioxide transport in insect blood. Part I. The form of carbon dioxide present in *Gastrophilus* larva blood. *J. exp. Biol.* **27**: 158–174.

LEVENBOOK, L. (1950b). The physiology of carbon dioxide transport in insect blood. Part III. The buffer capacity of *Gastrophilus* blood. *J. exp. Biol.* **27**: 184–191.

LEVENBOOK, L. and HOLLIS, V. W. (1961). Organic acid in insects—I. Citric acid. *J. Insect Physiol.* **6**: 52–61.

McCORMICK, F. W. and SCOTT, A. (1966a). Changes in haemolymph proteins in first instar locusts. *Archs. int. Physiol. Biochim.* **124**: 442–448.

McCORMICK, F. W. and SCOTT, A. (1966b). A protein fraction in locust hemolymph associated with the moulting cycle. *Experientia* **22**: 228–229.

MELLANBY, K. (1939). The functions of insect blood. *Biol. Rev.* **14**: 243–260.

NAPPI, A. J. (1974). Insect hemocytes and the problem of host recognition of foreignness. *in* Cooper, E. L. (ed.), *Contemporary topics in immunology*. vol. 4. Academic Press, New York.

NICKERSON, B. (1956). Pigmentation of hoppers of the desert locust (*Schistocerca gregaria* Forskål) in relation to phase colouration. *Anti-Locust Bull.* no. 24, 34 pp.

NUTTING, W. L. (1951). A comparative anatomical study of the heart and accessory structures of the orthopteroid insects. *J. Morph.* **89**: 501–597.

PICHON, Y. (1970). Ionic content of haemolymph in the cockroach, *Periplaneta americana*. *J. exp. Biol.* **53**: 195–209.

RIZKI, M. T. M. (1953). The larval blood cells of *Drosophila willistoni*. *J. exp. Zool.* **123**: 397–411.

SALT, G. (1968). The resistance of insect parasitoids to the defence reactions of their hosts. *Biol. Rev.* **43**: 200–232.

SALT, G. (1970). *The cellular defence reactions of insects*. Cambridge University Press.

SALT, R. W. (1961). Principles of insect cold-hardiness. *A. Rev. Ent.* **6**: 55–74.

SELMAN, B. J. (1962). The fate of the blood cells during the life history of *Sialis lutaria* L. *J. Insect Physiol.* **8**: 209–214.

SHRIVASTAVA, S. C. and RICHARDS, A. G. (1965). An autoradiographic study of the relation between hemocytes and connective tissue in the wax moth, *Galleria mellonella* L. *Biol. Bull. mar. biol. Lab., Woods Hole.* **128**: 337–345.

SUTCLIFFE, D. W. (1963). The chemical composition of haemolymph in insects and some other arthropods, in relation to their phylogeny. *Comp. Biochem. Physiol.* **9**: 121–135.

TOBE, S. S. and LOUGHTON, B. G. (1969). An investigation of haemolymph protein economy during the fifth instar of *Locusta migratoria migratorioides*. *J. Insect Physiol.* **15**: 1659–1672.

WHITTEN, J. M. (1962). Breakdown and formation of connective tissue in the pupal stage of an insect. *Q. Jl microsc. Sci.* **103**: 359–367.

WHITTEN, J. M. (1964). Connective tissue membranes and their apparent role in transporting neurosecretory and other secretory products in insects. *Gen. Comp. Endocrin.* **4**: 176–192.

WIGGLESWORTH, V. B. (1956). The haemocytes and connective tissue formation in an insect, *Rhodnius prolixus* (Hemiptera). *Q. Jl microsc. Sci.* **97**: 89–98.

WIGGLESWORTH, V. B. (1973). Haemocytes and basement membrane formation in *Rhodnius*. *J. Insect Physiol.* **19**: 831–844.

WYATT, G. R. (1961). The biochemistry of insect haemolymph. *A. Rev. Ent.* **6**: 75–102.

YEAGER, J. F. (1945). The blood picture of the southern armyworm (*Prodenia eridania*). *J. agric. Res.* **71**: 1–40.

CHAPTER XXXIV

THE ENDOCRINE ORGANS AND HORMONES

The endocrine organs produce hormones which travel, usually in the blood, to various organs of the body, co-ordinating their longer term activities. The endocrine system is thus complementary to the nervous system.

Endocrine organs are of two types: neurosecretory cells in the central nervous system, and specialised endocrine glands. The neurosecretory cells may be modified motorneurones. Both types of organ produce hormones which are generally released directly, or indirectly via storage organs, into the blood, but in some instances the hormones produced by neurosecretory cells are conveyed to the target organs along the axons of the cells. Nervous stimuli commonly lead to the release of the hormones. In some cases it is fairly certain that the hormones act directly on the nuclei of the target cells so that appropriate biochemical changes occur in the cells, but in other instances the effects of the hormones are indirect.

The hormones of insects are many and various in their effects and even hormones from a single organ may have a variety of effects. Among others, activities which are affected by hormones are moulting, metamorphosis, oocyte production and colour change.

Highnam and Hill (1977) and Wigglesworth (1970) give general reviews of insect hormones. Specific aspects are reviewed as follows: neurosecretion by Maddrell (1974) and Goldsworthy and Mordue (1974); control of metabolism by Steele (1976); control of growth and moulting by Willis (1974); control of the visceral organs by Miller (1975); control of reproductive physiology by Engelmann (1968); control of aspects of behaviour by Barth and Lester (1973), Pener (1974) and Truman and Riddiford (1974a) and control of juvenile hormone titre (Kort and Granger, 1981).

34.1 Endocrine organs

The endocrine organs of insects are of two types: neurosecretory cells, mainly within the central nervous system, and specialised endocrine glands, such as the corpora cardiaca, corpora allata and prothoracic glands.

34.1.1 Neurosecretory cells

Neurosecretory cells normally occur in the ganglia of the central nervous system. They generally resemble typical bipolar nerve cells, but are characterised by showing cytological evidence of secretion. The secretion is granular and under the electron microscope appears as membrane bound, electron-dense particles 100–300 nm across. The granules are synthesised in the cell bodies and pass down the axons. Several types of cell can be differentiated by their staining reactions, but these types are not always comparable in the works of different authors and may sometimes represent successive stages in a cycle of secretion (Delphin, 1965). It is probable that the visible secretion is only a carrier, possibly a large protein molecule, to which the smaller hormone molecule is attached. When the hormone is finally released it becomes separated from the carrier and is then free to enter the blood. It is assumed that whenever the carrier is visible it is accompanied by the hormone (Schreiner, 1966).

The amount of granular material in a cell at any one time is the result of a balance between its rate of production and the rate of dissipation. Some authorities regard a cell full of granular material as actively secreting, while others regard such a cell as an inactive one accumulating material. It is probable that both points of view could be correct under different circumstances.

The endocrine activity of neurosecretory cells may take one of two forms: the cells may either produce hormones which act directly on effector organs or they may act on other endocrine organs, which, in turn, are stimulated to produce hormones. In this case the neurosecretory cells act as intermediaries between the nervous system and the endocrine glands, responding to the overall situation perceived and analysed by the nervous system (Scharrer, 1959).

Large numbers of neurosecretory cells may be present in the nervous system, but it is possible that they do not all produce hormones.

It is almost certain that neurosecretory cells do conduct electrical impulses, but the action potentials last longer than those in normal neurones, about 5 ms compared with 1 ms (Maddrell, 1974).

Neurosecretory cells of the brain

Typically there are two groups of neurosecretory cells on each side of the brain. One group is in the pars intercerebralis, near the midline. The axons from these cells pass backwards through the brain and some or all of them cross over to the opposite side, emerging from the brain as a nerve which runs back to the corpus cardiacum. Most of the fibres end here, but a few pass through the corpus cardiacum to the corpus allatum and, in the locust, to the foregut and ingluvial ganglion (Strong, 1966) (Fig. 545). In most Apterygota these median neurosecretory cells are contained in separate capsules of connective tissue, known as the lateral frontal organs, on the dorsal side of the brain, but in Machilidae the cells are usually intercerebral as in Pterygota. *Petrobius* occupies an intermediate position with some neurosecretory cells in the lateral frontal organs and others in an adjacent frontal zone of the brain (Watson, 1963).

The second group of cells is variable in position. Sometimes it is medial to the corpora pedunculata, sometimes between the latter and the optic lobes. In some Diptera and Hymenoptera the cells corresponding with these are grouped with the other neurosecretory cells in the pars intercerebralis. From these cells a second axon tract passes through the brain to the corpus cardiacum and in *Schistocerca* some fibres also extend to the corpus allatum (Highnam, 1964).

The products of the neurosecretory cells of the brain pass along the axons, usually to the corpora cardiaca or allata. Here they may be stored or released, or it is suggested that

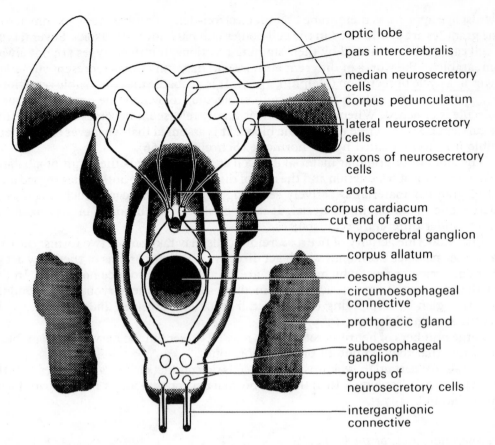

optic lobe
pars intercerebralis
median neurosecretory cells
corpus pedunculatum
lateral neurosecretory cells
axons of neurosecretory cells
aorta
corpus cardiacum
cut end of aorta
hypocerebral ganglion
corpus allatum
oesophagus
circumoesophageal connective
prothoracic gland
suboesophageal ganglion
groups of neurosecretory cells
interganglionic connective

Fig. 545 Diagrammatic representation of the relationships of the main endocrine organs

they may provide the raw materials from which specific hormones are produced in the various organs. In *Locusta* the axons of the median protocerebral cells loop through the neuropile of the brain and follow a spiral path (Fig. 546). They provide a reservoir of neurosecretion in addition to that in the corpora cardiaca. Some of the looping axons pass from one side to the other, so that neurosecretion reaches the corpus cardiacum of each side from both ipsilateral and contralateral protocerebral cells (Highnam and West, 1971).

The secretions of the neurosecretory cells in the pars intercerebralis promote the functioning of the prothoracic glands, stimulate protein synthesis and possibly control water loss, oocyte development and activity. It is not known whether these different effects are all produced by a single hormone or whether there are a number of separate hormones, but there are a number of different neurosecretory cell types, suggesting that several different secretions are possible.

Neurosecretory cells of other ganglia

Large numbers of neurosecretory cells occur in the ventral ganglia of the nerve cord. In *Bombyx* there are more secretory cells in the ventral ganglia than in the brain, but this is

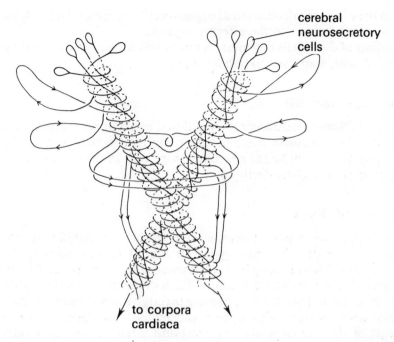

Fig. 546 Diagram showing the arrangement of the major axon tracts of the protocerebral neurosecretory cells leading to the corpora cardiaca of *Locusta* (after Highnam and West, 1971)

not true in *Schistocerca* (Delphin, 1965). Different cell types are widely distributed in different ganglia (Fig. 547), but some types are restricted to particular ganglia. The secretions from these cells can pass along the interganglionic connectives in either direction and also outwards along the peripheral nerves. The secretory products are

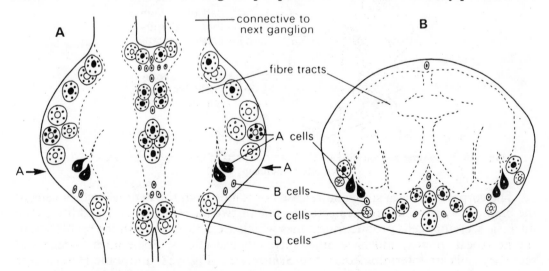

Fig. 547 Distribution of different types of neurosecretory cells in the third abdominal ganglion of *Schistocerca*. A. Dorsal view. B. Transverse section at AA (after Delphin, 1965)

liberated into the blood via neurohaemal organs on the peripheral nerves, but they may sometimes be carried direct to the effector organs.

The functions of these cells in general is unknown, but in some cases they are known to be concerned with water regulation (p. 843).

Peripheral neurosecretory cells

In *Carausius* and *Phormia* neurosecretory cell bodies occur on some peripheral nerves in the abdomen. In *Carausius* there are 22 peripheral neurosecretory cells in each abdominal segment and, unlike the neurosecretory cells in the central nervous system, they are multipolar cells (Maddrell, 1974).

34.1.2 Corpora cardiaca

The corpora cardiaca are a pair of organs often closely associated with the aorta, and forming part of its wall (Figs. 545, 548). In higher groups such as Lepidoptera, Coleoptera and some Diptera they become separated from the aorta. Corpora cardiaca are not known to be present in Collembola. Each organ contains the endings of axons from cells in the brain and other axons passing through to the corpora allata. In addition there are glial cells (p. 622) with a clear vacuolated cytoplasm, nerve cells, which constitute part of the stomatogastric system, and intrinsic secretory cells with long cytoplasmic projections extending towards the periphery of the organ. The projections probably serve for the release of secretions into the blood.

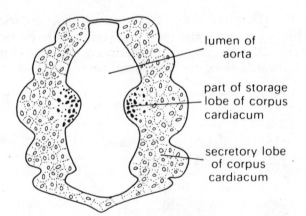

lumen of
aorta

part of storage
lobe of corpus
cardiacum

secretory lobe
of corpus
cardiacum

Fig. 548 Transverse section through the posterior parts of the corpora cardiaca of *Schistocerca* (after Highnam, 1961)

The corpora cardiaca store and release hormones from the neurosecretory cells of the brain, to which they are connected by one or two pairs of nerves. In addition, the intrinsic secretory cells produce hormones which are concerned with the regulation of the heartbeat (p. 794) and have other physiological effects. Sometimes storage and secretory cells are intermingled, but in *Schistocerca* (Fig. 548) and some Heteroptera one part of the corpus cardiacum is concerned with secretion and another part with storage (Cazal, 1948).

34.1.3 Corpora allata

The corpora allata are glandular bodies, usually one on either side of the oesophagus (Fig. 545) although they may be fused to a single median organ as in higher Diptera. Each is connected with the corpus cardiacum of the same side by a nerve which carries fibres from the neurosecretory cells of the brain. In addition, a fine nerve connects each corpus allatum with the suboesophageal ganglion. This is a major nerve in Ephemeroptera, where the nerve from the corpus cardiacum is absent. In Thysanura, the corpora allata are in the bases of the maxillae and in addition to a fine nerve direct from the suboesophageal ganglion they are innervated by branches from the mandibular and maxillary roots of the suboesophageal ganglion.

In Thysanura and Phasmida the corpora allata are hollow balls of cells, with gland cells forming the walls. Elsewhere they are solid organs of glandular secretory cells, often with lacunae between the cells. The secretory cells in the inactive gland of *Leucophaea* (Dictyoptera) are stellate with processes at right angles to the periphery, but in the active gland the cell membranes tend to straighten out.

The corpora allata produce juvenile hormone regulating metamorphosis (p. 830) and yolk deposition in the eggs (p. 838). Changes in the volume of the corpora allata or in the sizes of the cells within the gland are not necessarily correlated with juvenile hormone activity in the haemolymph (Johnson and Hill, 1973).

34.1.4 Prothoracic glands

The prothoracic, or thoracic, glands are a pair of diffuse glands at the back of the head or in the thorax (Fig. 545), but in Thysanura they are in the base of the labium. Each gland has a rich tracheal supply and often a nerve supply, but this is absent in some Heteroptera and Coleoptera.

The glands show cycles of development associated with secretion. At rest the nuclei are small and oval, but in the active gland they become enlarged and lobulated and the cell has more extensive and deeply staining cytoplasm. The numbers of mitochondria round the nucleus also increase and the endoplasmic reticulum becomes more extensive. At first intense RNA synthesis takes place in the nucleus and subsequently the RNA passes into the cytoplasm, where protein synthesis occurs. This presumably reflects the production of enzymes engaged in the synthesis of ecdysone (p. 827). Towards the end of a cycle the nuclei become small again.

The prothoracic glands produce moulting hormone, ecdysone (p. 828), and, except in Thysanura, which moult as adults, and in solitary locusts, the prothoracic glands break down soon after the final moult to adult.

There is evidence that in a number of insects ecdysone may also be produced in the abdomen, possibly by oenocytes. This ecdysone may be particularly important in regulating the pupa–adult moult (Hsiao *et al.*, 1975). In some flies, at least, ecdysone is also produced by the ovary (Hagedorn and Kunkel, 1979).

34.1.5 Ring gland

In the larvae of cyclorrhaphous Diptera the ring gland surrounds the aorta just above the brain (Fig. 549). It is formed from the corpora allata, corpora cardiaca and

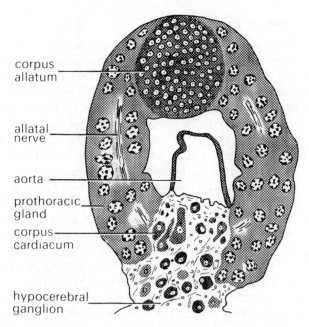

corpus
allatum

allatal
nerve

aorta

prothoracic
gland

corpus
cardiacum

hypocerebral
ganglion

Fig. 549 Ring gland from the early pupa of *Eristalis* (Diptera). Here the ring gland is fused
with the hypocerebral ganglion, but this is not always the case (after Cazal, 1948)

prothoracic glands all fused together, although the component elements can still be
identified. The ring gland is connected to the brain by a pair of nerves and it also has a
connection with the recurrent nerve.

The larvae of Nematocera have completely separate endocrine glands, but larval
Brachycera approach the cyclorrhaphan condition, although the corpus allatum tends
to be separated from the rest as a single median lobe.

34.2 Dispersal of hormones

Hormones produced in the neurosecretory cells pass along the axons of these cells as a
result of the intra-axonal flow of cytoplasm or possibly along minute tubules which run
the length of the axon. In this way the hormones may pass directly to their target organs
or they may ultimately be released into the blood.

Direct transfer of neurosecretion to specific target organs is probably widespread.
In aphis, for instance, two large neurosecretory cells in the protocerebrum have
extensive branching axons which pass to various parts of the body (Fig. 550), including
the hind-gut. Neurosecretory axons pass directly to the salivary glands in *Carausius*,
the spermatheca of *Periplaneta*, the Malpighian tubules of *Rhodnius* and the somatic
muscles in several species (Maddrell, 1974). It is presumed that in these cases the
neurosecretion regulates the activities of the target organs without dispersal in the
haemolymph; this type of control is sometimes differentiated as neurosecretomotor
control.

Where the hormones are released into the blood, specialised neurohaemal organs
are involved. For instance, the corpora cardiaca serve for the release and sometimes for

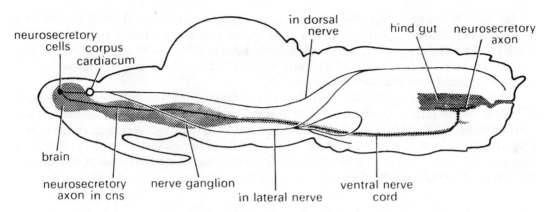

Fig. 550 Pathways of axons which carry neurosecretion from the brain and corpora cardiaca in the aphid *Drepanosiphum* (Homoptera) (after Johnson, 1962)

the storage of the brain hormone, and the position of these organs adjacent to the aorta may facilitate dispersal of the hormone. Other neurohaemal organs are present in the abdomen, and commonly the thorax as well, on the nerves of the peripheral nervous system. In these organs the neurosecretory axons branch profusely and the axon endings are devoid of a glial sheath so that they are in direct contact with the haemolymph. Fat body is absent round the neurohaemal organs and so haemolymph can circulate freely over them.

Hormone is released from the axon endings when the membrane of a neurosecretory vesicle fuses with the axon membrane (Fig. 551). This process is known as exocytosis and may occur when action potentials reach the axon ending. Exocytosis results in a temporary increase in the surface membrane of the axon, but subsequently membrane is retrieved by micropinocytosis. The small size of the vesicles cut off from the plasma membrane, about 40 nm diameter, ensures that only a minimum amount of extracellular fluid is taken up for a relatively large retrieval of membrane. Presumably the small vesicles are broken down and the material re-utilised.

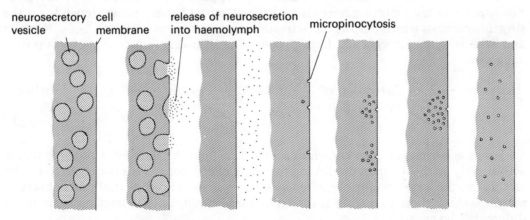

Fig. 551 Diagrammatic representation of the discharge of neurosecretion from an axon terminal and subsequent membrane retrieval by micropinocytosis (after Maddrell, 1974)

Juvenile hormone is lipophilic and is distributed in the haemolymph bound to a specific water-soluble lipoprotein. Whether or not it is sometimes released from the corpora allata in the lipoprotein complex is not known (Whitmore and Gilbert, 1972), but in *Schistocerca* it is released in simple form. Ecdysone is water-soluble and is released directly into the haemolymph.

Whitten (1964) suggests that some hormones may be transported from their organ of origin to the target organs or site of release in channels in the connective tissue membrane (p. 805). There are, for instance, channels in the basement membrane of the ring gland in larval *Sarcophaga* which connect with other channels in the connective tissue so that secretions are carried directly from the ring gland to the heart and so into the blood at a point where they are most readily dispersed.

34.3 Mode of action of hormones

The manner in which hormones produce their effects is not well understood. Ecdysone (p. 828) rapidly accumulates in the nuclei of epidermal cells and it is probable that it acts directly on the nuclei. In the giant chromosomes of dipterous larvae characteristic swellings (puffs) occur which appear to indicate activity of particular genes. When the larva of *Chironomus* moults to a pupa a new puff appears on one chromosome and another disappears. The injection of ecdysone into a larva between moults has the same effect, the first puff appearing within about 15 minutes of the injection and reaching a maximum in about two hours. A little later a second puff forms and two or three days later another characteristic pattern of puffs appears. This suggests that the changing biochemical activities in cells at the time of moulting may be initiated by ecdysone.

Under normal conditions the genes are not actively producing RNA because their activity is inhibited by repressors, possibly the histone with which the DNA of the gene is associated. The effect of the hormone is to free the gene from this repression so that specific messenger RNA is produced. This passes into the cytoplasm and protein synthesis follows.

Not all the gene activity which follows the activity of ecdysone results from such direct action, however. Some of the puffs which appear later in the puffing pattern are not specific to the moulting periods and the activity of these genes depends on the protein synthesis which follows the activation of the first genes (Clever, 1965; Karlson and Sekeris, 1966; Kroeger and Lezzi, 1966). The following sequence of events is thus suggested:

$$\text{Ecdysone} \rightarrow ? \rightarrow \begin{array}{c}\text{Activation of}\\\text{specific genes}\end{array} \rightarrow \text{mRNA} \rightarrow \begin{array}{c}\text{Protein}\\\text{synthesis}\end{array} \rightarrow ? \rightarrow \begin{array}{c}\text{Further}\\\text{genes}\\\text{activated}\end{array}$$

Juvenile hormone is also known to act at the cellular level and it is possible that it acts directly on the nucleus, modifying the effect of ecdysone. This is suggested by the fact that in the larval moults of *Chironomus* the first two chromosomal puffs observed are the same as those occurring at the larva–pupa moult, but the later puffs are quite different (Clever, 1965).

Whether or not the hormones act via the genes their effect is often to promote the synthesis or activity of proteins. Ecdysone, for instance, initiates the *de novo* synthesis of DOPA decarboxylase and also activates the enzyme which catalyses the synthesis of a phenol oxidase from its proenzyme. Thus essential enzymes for tanning the cuticle are made available (Karlson, 1963). In other cases hormones appear to be directly concerned with the activation of phosphorylases.

34.4 Chemical nature of hormones

Neurosecretory hormones are small proteins or peptides. The locust adipokinetic hormone, which is a peptide, has been completely characterised by Stone *et al.* (1976):

pyrrolidone carboxylic acid-leucine-asparagine-phenylalanine-threonine-proline-asparagine-tryptophan-glycine-threonine-amide

with a molecular weight of 1158. The brain hormone, bursicon and the diapause hormone of *Bombyx* are probably small proteins. Bursicon has a molecular weight of about 40 000. The hyperglycaemic hormone and the eclosion hormone are probably peptides (Highnam and Hill, 1977; Truman, 1980).

Ecdysone is commonly present in two forms, α-ecdysone and β-ecdysone (also known as 20-hydroxyecdysone). α-ecdysone is converted to β-ecdysone and in *Manduca* to 20,26-dihydroxyecdysone. Insects are unable to synthesise steroids and ecdysone is probably derived from cholesterol or some related steroid obtained with the diet.

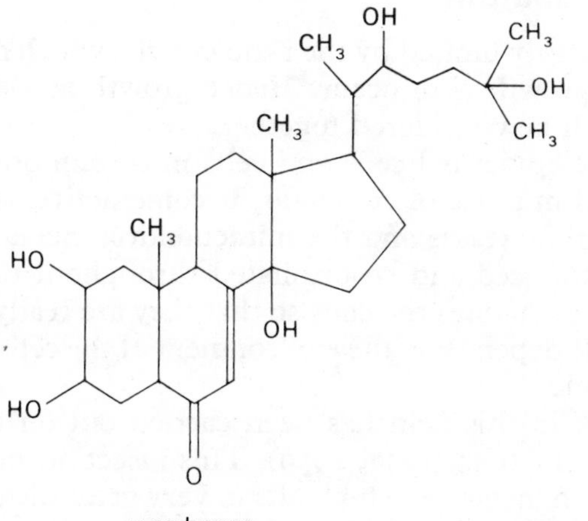

α-ecdysone

Juvenile hormone is a sesquiterpene. Three slightly different forms, known as JHI, II and III and containing 18, 17 and 16 carbon atoms respectively, have been isolated. JHI and II both occur in *Hyalophora*; JHIII has been found in *Periplaneta*, *Schistocerca*, *Manduca* and *Melolontha*. Juvenile hormones can be rapidly degraded by enzymes to inactive compounds and excreted, but they are not affected by enzymes when bound to lipoprotein.

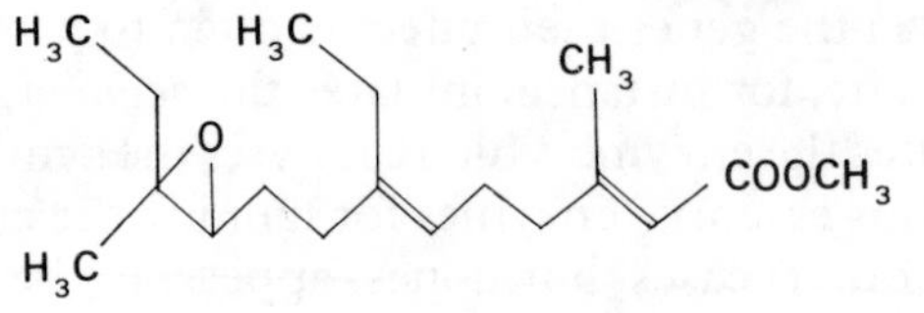

H$_3$C, H$_3$C,   CH$_3$

    O   COOCH$_3$ JH I   18 carbon atoms

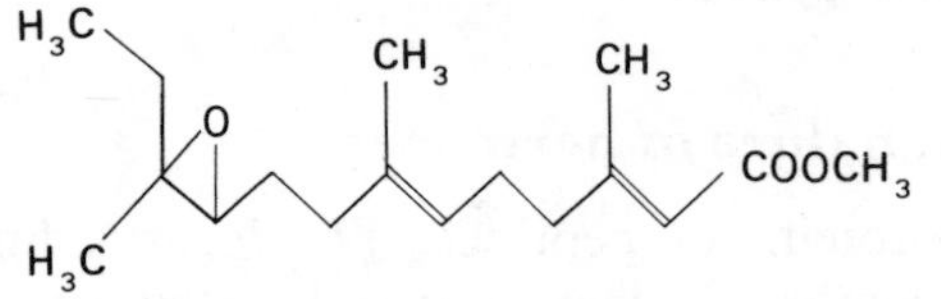

H$_3$C

H$_3$C,   CH$_3$ CH$_3$

    O   COOCH$_3$ JH II   17 carbon atoms

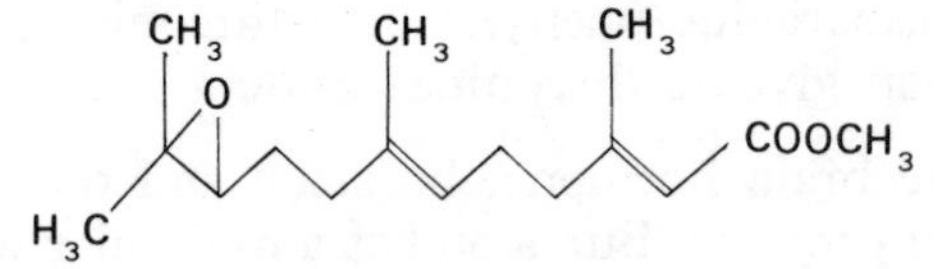

H$_3$C

CH$_3$ CH$_3$ CH$_3$

    O   COOCH$_3$ JH III 16 çarbon atoms

H$_3$C

34.5 Hormones and their functions

Insect hormones are at present receiving a great deal of attention by many workers and so this study is in a state of flux and is correspondingly complex. The following account is consequently extremely simplified and selective.

34.5.1 Growth and moulting

Growth in insects is largely limited by the rigid cuticle, which must be shed from time to time if continued growth is to occur. Hence growth and moulting must be very closely related and will be considered together.

Before a moult the epidermal cells and cells in certain other tissues, such as the sternal intersegmental muscles of *Rhodnius,* become active. Their nucleoli enlarge, RNA in the cytoplasm increases and the mitochondria increase in size and number. These changes are produced and co-ordinated throughout the body by a hormone which at the same time activates the cells so that they are ready to divide. Whether or not they do then divide depends on the environment of the cells; the hormone does not cause the cells to divide.

Much of the work in this field has been carried out on the blood-sucking bug *Rhodnius* (Wigglesworth, 1954, 1957, 1959). This insect normally takes only a single large blood meal in each instar, which results in very great distension of the abdomen. The changes described above start in the cells within six hours of feeding and moulting follows about 15 days later.

The changes are initiated by a secretion of the prothoracotrophic hormone from the median neurosecretory cells. This passes to the corpora cardiaca and then is liberated into the blood. The secretion stimulates the prothoracic glands to produce the moulting hormone, ecdysone, which initiates changes in the cells concerned with moulting (Fig. 552). The brain factor does not have a simple triggering effect on the prothoracic glands, but its continuous presence is necessary for two-and-a-half to three days for the continued activity of these glands; possibly it contributes some essential component to

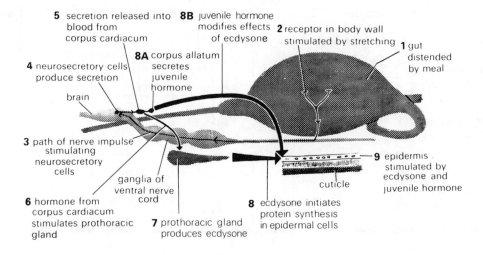

5 secretion released into blood from corpus cardiacum

8B juvenile hormone modifies effects of ecdysone

2 receptor in body wall stimulated by stretching

1 gut distended by meal

8A corpus allatum secretes juvenile hormone

4 neurosecretory cells produce secretion

brain

3 path of nerve impulse stimulating neurosecretory cells

ganglia of ventral nerve cord

6 hormone from corpus cardiacum stimulates prothoracic gland

7 prothoracic gland produces ecdysone

8 ecdysone initiates protein synthesis in epidermal cells

cuticle

9 epidermis stimulated by ecdysone and juvenile hormone

Fig. 552 Diagrammatic representation of the sequence of events leading to stimulation of the epidermis and moulting in *Rhodnius*. At the final moult to adult, juvenile hormone (stages 8A and 8B) would be absent

the ecdysone. The period for which the brain hormone is necessary is known as the critical period and its removal during this period, as by decapitation, results in a failure to moult. Decapitation after the critical period does not inhibit moulting. An essentially similar sequence of events occurs in other insects. Ecdysone regulates chitin synthesis as well as initiating moulting (Farkovich *et al.*, 1981).

In *Rhodnius*, the initial secretion of the brain factor is caused by the distension of the abdomen which results from feeding. The distension stimulates receptors in the wall of the abdomen and these stimulate the neurosecretory cells via the nerve cord. At the same time impulses, at the rate of about three per second, pass down the previously silent nerves to the corpora cardiaca, possibly leading to the release of neurosecretory material. At the end of the critical period the release of neurosecretory material is inhibited by feedback from ecdysone (Steel, 1975).

In other insects which feed continuously the control of prothoracotrophic hormone release appears to be rather different. Its secretion in larval *Manduca* is inhibited by juvenile hormone, but the juvenile hormone titre in the haemolymph falls rapidly when the last instar larva reaches a weight of 5 g. Release of prothoracotrophic hormone occurs in the next photophase (light period) and this leads to the secretion of ecdysone (Fig. 553). This takes place at the end of the larval feeding phase and induces gut purging; the larva wanders off the food in order to pupate and a further release of prothoracotrophic hormone and ecdysone lead to apolysis (Nijhout and Williams, 1974a; Truman and Riddiford, 1974b).

Apart from Thysanura, adult insects do not moult and the prothoracic glands degenerate. In *Rhodnius* degeneration starts within 24 h of the final moult and is complete within 48 h. In other insects the process takes rather longer. Degeneration occurs if the gland has passed through a moulting cycle in the absence of the juvenile

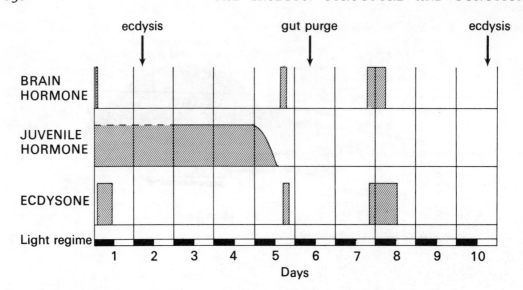

Fig. 553 Hormonal changes during the fifth larval instar of *Manduca* (after Nijhout and Riddiford, 1974; Truman and Riddiford, 1974b)

hormone (p. 832). In other words the gland itself must undergo some sort of metamorphosis.

Hardening and darkening of the cuticle following ecdysis are controlled by a hormone, bursicon. This has been demonstrated at the time of adult emergence in insects of several orders and also at hatching in locusts; it has not yet been shown to function in larval holometabolous insects (Fraenkel and Hsiao, 1965). In adult *Manduca* the release of bursicon from abdominal neurohaemal organs is a step in a sequence of behavioural acts initiated by the eclosion hormone (p. 495). Release of bursicon is delayed by sensory input until the wings start to expand (Truman, 1973).

Newly hatched larvae of *Schistocerca* worm their way to the soil surface (p. 452) and newly emerged flies use the ptilinum to burrow through the substrate; in both cases the cuticle remains flexible during the escape and hardens only when they are free. In newly hatched *Schistocerca* the release of bursicon occurs within 3 s of the embryonic cuticle starting to split (p. 454), the horizontal displacement of the cuticle along the body probably providing the stimulus. Maximum melanising activity in the haemolymph occurs within about 5 minutes of hatching and then slowly declines over the next 3 or 4 h (Fig. 554). The hormone is released from neurohaemal organs in the lateral abdominal nerves (Padgham, 1976).

Bursicon probably affects protein synthesis in the fat body and is involved in the hydroxylation of tyrosine to dopa (p. 523).

34.5.2 Metamorphosis

When a hemimetabolous insect moults it may moult to another, essentially similar larval form or it may undergo a more complete change in body form, usually associated with the development of wings, to become the adult insect. Wigglesworth (1961) regards the progressive development of larval characters and the final metamorphosis

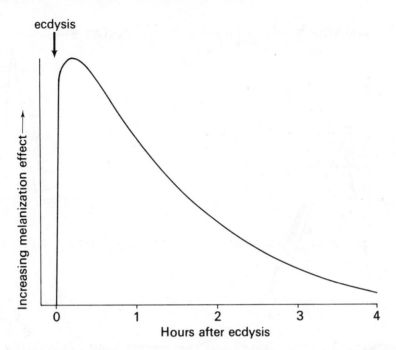

Fig. 554 Melanising activity of blood from newly ecdysed first instar larvae of *Schistocerca* (after Padgham, 1976)

to adult as two distinct types of differentiation. The first only takes place in the presence of the juvenile hormone which is normally secreted throughout all the larval instars except the last and which is responsible for the retention of larval characters. Differentiation of larval characters occurs at a certain rate, so that the changes occurring at successive moults are controlled by the timing and quantity of moulting hormone secreted.

Other authors regard the stages of development as resulting from a progressive reduction in the concentration of juvenile hormone. Although the corpora allata increase in size throughout larval development they do so more slowly than the body as a whole and this suggests that the concentration of juvenile hormone will be much lower in later larval instars than in the early instars. For a consideration of this point of view see Novak (1966).

Metamorphosis to the adult differs from larval development in that the moult takes place in the absence of juvenile hormone. It is thus believed that the effect of juvenile hormone is to modify the reaction of the target cells to the moulting hormone. Probably in its presence one set of genes, giving rise to larval characters, is activated, while in its absence a second set, producing adult characters, is activated. The juvenile hormone by itself has no effect.

Fig. 555 shows the changes in levels of ecdysone and juvenile hormone which occur in the last two larval instars of locusts. Ecdysone reaches a peak about 80 % of the way through each instar. During the fourth instar the level of juvenile hormone is always relatively high, but in the fifth instar no juvenile hormone is present in the haemolymph until after the peak of ecdysone. As a consequence, the larva moults to another larva in

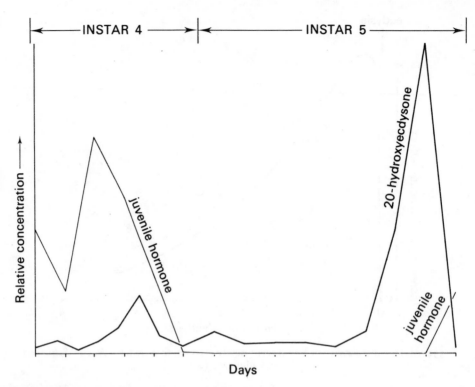

Fig. 555 Relative concentrations of 20-hydroxyecdysone and juvenile hormones during the fourth and fifth instars of a locust (after Johnson and Hill, 1973; Morgan and Poole, 1976)

the first case, but to an adult in the second (Johnson and Hill, 1973; Morgan and Poole, 1976).

In holometabolous insects the position is believed to be similar except that an intermediate concentration of juvenile hormone leads to the activation of a third group of genes, which produce pupal characteristics. The most extensive studies have been concerned with Lepidoptera. Hsiao and Hsiao (1977) showed that the moult to the final instar larva occurred in the presence of high levels of juvenile hormone (Fig. 556). In the middle of the final larval stage both juvenile hormone and ecdysone were absent, but both were produced towards the end of the instar. At this time the concentration of juvenile hormone was relatively low and a moult to the pupa occurred. Early in the pupal period a further increase in ecdysone in the complete absence of juvenile hormone led to the apolysis of the pupal cuticle and the development of adult characters (and see Bollenbacher *et al.*, 1981; Sehnal *et al.*, 1981).

The release of juvenile hormone is probably regulated by neurohaemal and neural activity from the brain. During the early larval instars of *Galleria* it is supposed that the corpora allata are activated by a neurohormone, possibly from the neurosecretory cells of the pars intercerebralis. In the last instar larva nervous inhibition of the activity of the corpora allata 48–60 h after the previous ecdysis leads to a reduction in secretion and this effect is reinforced by a decrease in the activity of the neurosecretory cells (Granger and Sehnal, 1974).

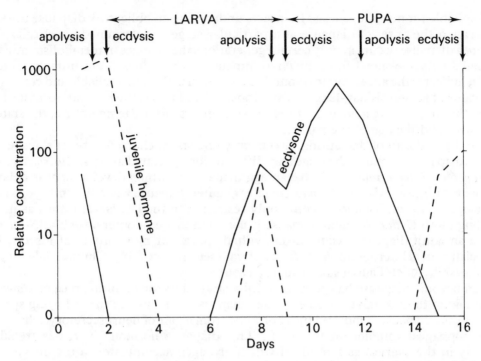

Fig. 556 Relative concentrations of ecdysone and juvenile hormone in the haemolymph of male *Galleria* during the final larval instar and pupal period (after Hsiao and Hsiao, 1977)

If the corpora allata are removed during the critical period so that they do not produce any juvenile hormone an insect will undergo a precocious metamorphosis at the next moult. The degree of perfection of the adult structures formed depends to some extent on the competence of the tissues to produce them at this time. Some organs, such as the genitalia, may be well developed, but in *Rhodnius* the wings are not well formed in a precocious adult because they contain too few cells to produce the extensive wings of the adult. Other organs vary in their ability to form precocious adult structures.

34.5.3 Diapause

One of the major functions of insect hormones is the control of morphogenesis and, if their production or release is retarded, delays in development result. The delay may be a direct consequence of prevailing adverse environmental conditions, when it is known as quiescence, or it may be an adaptive phenomenon which enables the insect to survive regularly occurring adverse conditions. In this case the delay in development is not immediately referable to the prevailing conditions and is known as diapause. In temperate regions diapause is generally concerned with survival during the cold winters when normal growth is not possible; in the tropics it may facilitate survival during a dry season which is characterised by lack of moisture and food.

Before diapause begins most insects lay down increased reserves in the fat body. This, as well as the onset of diapause itself, occurs while the prevailing conditions are still suitable for morphogenesis. In insects undergoing an obligatory diapause in every generation the onset of diapause at a particular stage is determined genetically, but where a diapause occurs in only certain generations the changes in metabolism must be initiated by some signal from the environment which, although not unfavourable in itself, indicates the advent of unfavourable conditions. The most reliable and consistent indicator of seasons is day-length or photoperiod and this is the most important of the sign stimuli initiating diapause. Other possible indicators are temperature, the state of the food, and the age of the parent.

In the majority of diapausing insects only one stage, characteristic of the species, enters diapause, although the stage may differ in closely related insects. *Austroicetes* and *Melanoplus differentialis* both have an egg diapause in which development is delayed before katatrepsis. *Melanoplus mexicanus* eggs enter diapause when the embryo is fully developed. Larval diapause is commonly restricted to the last larval instar, as in the codling moth *Cydia*. A pupal diapause is common in Lepidoptera, such as *Saturnia*, while an adult diapause occurs in individual species of most orders of insects, but especially in Heteroptera and Coleoptera (see reviews by Chippendale, 1977; Danilevskii, 1965; Tauber and Tauber, 1976).

Embryonic diapause has been most fully studied in the bivoltine race of *Bombyx*. Eggs laid in the autumn have an extended diapause and hatch in the following spring. In this case diapause is induced by a hormone from a pair of neurosecretory cells in the suboesophageal ganglion of the adult. This diapause hormone increases trehalase activity in the ovaries, as a result of which glycogen accumulates in the oocytes. In addition, the hormone results in a low level of an esterase (esterase A) in the eggs. This enzyme is abundant in non-diapause and postdiapause eggs, where its function is to facilitate yolk mobilisation by lysis of the yolk cell membranes. In diapause eggs the yolk cells are rigid with distinct cytoplasmic membranes and it is possible that the low level of esterase A is a critical factor resulting in diapause (Kai and Hasegawa, 1973). The activity of the suboesophageal neurosecretory cells is controlled by the brain, which inhibits their activity in adults laying non-diapause eggs but stimulates it in adults which lay diapause eggs. The occurrence of diapause depends on the temperature and light conditions experienced by eggs of the previous generation. Exposure of the eggs to long photoperiods and high temperatures leads to the production of diapause eggs; short photoperiods and low temperatures are followed by development with no delay.

Diapause in the larval or pupal stage results from the failure of the median neurosecretory cells of the brain to produce the prothoracotrophic hormone so that the prothoracic glands remain inactive and no ecdysone is released. Injection of ecdysone into the diapausing pupa of *Hyalophora* leads to a resumption of growth and the emergence of the adult moth.

In at least some larval Lepidoptera the corpora allata remain active during diapause and Nijhout and Williams (1974b) have shown that the effect of juvenile hormone is to inhibit the release of the prothoracotrophic hormone from the neurosecretory cells. As a result the insect fails to moult, but moulting follows when juvenile hormone secretion comes to an end.

Diapause in adult insects manifests itself in a failure to mature. This results from the inactivity of the corpora allata, which are normally responsible for maturation (p. 838).

34.5.4 Polymorphism

Wigglesworth (1954) suggests that larva, pupa and adult represent different forms of a polymorphic organism, and that polymorphism in adult insects may be similarly determined by differences in balance between ecdysone and juvenile hormone.

Imbalance of these hormones can arise in two ways. Either the influence of the juvenile hormone may be excessive, in which case juvenile characters will persist in the adult (metathetely or neoteny) or the influence of the juvenile hormone may be depressed, leading to a precocious development of adult characters in the larva (prothetely or paedogenesis). Metathetely in particular often results in the failure of the wings to develop fully and brachypterous adults are formed. This is the case in *Gryllus campestris* (Orthoptera), where the short wings are the result of a slight predominance of juvenile hormone in the later stages. Experimental adjustment of the hormone balance in favour of ecdysone leads to the development of fully winged forms. Conversely in *Locusta* (Orthoptera) prothetely may occasionally occur, resulting in a fourth instar larva with incomplete adult characters and which is sexually mature.

The hormone balance may be disturbed by a variety of external factors. In aphids winged and wingless forms (alatae and apterae) occur, the wingless forms being more juvenile in appearance with less sclerotisation of the thorax and fewer sense organs on the antennae. This appearance and the lack of wings is the result of an excess of juvenile hormone. In *Megoura* the activity of the corpora allata is regulated in the late embryo, and this determines the type of development which will follow. If the parent is in a crowd a hormone from her head activates the corpora allata of the embryo so that no wings develop, but if the parent is isolated the embryonic corpora allata are not activated and the offspring develops wings. In other species, such as *Macrosiphum* and *Aphis*, winglessness is determined later, crowding or isolating the early instars having a direct effect on wing development (Lees, 1966, 1967).

Wigglesworth (1954) found that low temperature upsets the hormone balance slightly in favour of the juvenile hormone whereas high temperature slightly favours ecdysone. If *Rhodnius* is bred at low temperatures it is slightly neotenous whereas at high temperatures it exhibits slight prothetely. Southwood (1961) has suggested that brachyptery in Heteroptera may arise from breeding at relatively low temperatures. This could be true of montane forms, since temperature is lower at higher altitudes, and in the first generation of bivoltine species, where this generation is subjected to lower temperatures during its development than is the second. On the other hand *Dolichonabis limbatus* has only four larval instars although most Heteroptera have five and Southwood suggests that in this case brachyptery arises as a result of prothetely.

Termite castes

Caste determination in termites is more complex, but is also under hormonal control with the juvenile hormone probably playing an important part (Lüscher, 1960). In a colony of *Kalotermes* a number of different forms occur: larvae of various instars, pseudergates (a larval form functionally equivalent to the worker caste in other species), nymphs (the conventional term for termite larvae with obvious wing buds), white soldiers or presoldiers, soldiers and a king and queen, the only reproductive stages. In the absence of the king or queen, replacement reproductives develop and at certain seasons immature, winged reproductives (imagos) are produced. The relationships of these forms are shown in Fig. 557. The pseudergate is a central form from which various others can be derived and which can also undergo stationary moults, retaining its form. Nymphs may undergo regressive moults, changing back into pseudergates.

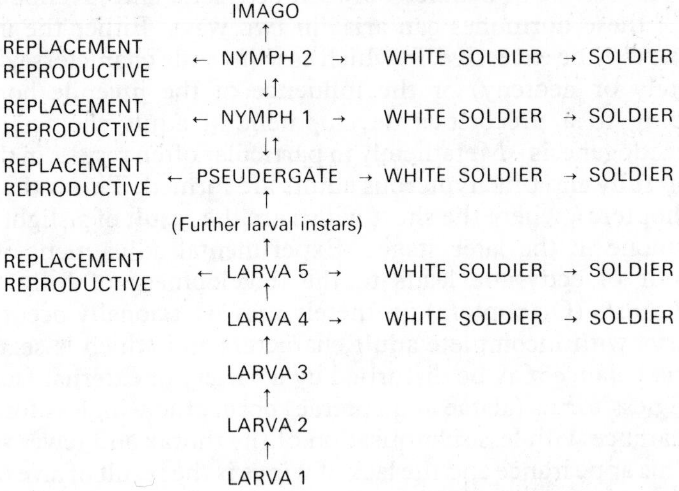

```
                                    IMAGO
                                      ↑
REPLACEMENT              ← NYMPH 2 →      WHITE SOLDIER → SOLDIER
REPRODUCTIVE                        ↓↑
REPLACEMENT              ← NYMPH 1 →      WHITE SOLDIER → SOLDIER
REPRODUCTIVE                        ↓↑
REPLACEMENT          ← PSEUDERGATE → WHITE SOLDIER → SOLDIER
REPRODUCTIVE                        ↑
                        (Further larval instars)
                                      ↑
REPLACEMENT              ← LARVA 5 →      WHITE SOLDIER → SOLDIER
REPRODUCTIVE                        ↑
                        LARVA 4 →        WHITE SOLDIER → SOLDIER
                                  ↑
                        LARVA 3
                                  ↑
                        LARVA 2
                                  ↑
                        LARVA 1
```

Fig. 557 The course of development of *Kalotermes flavicollis* (after Lüscher, 1960)

The development of the various castes is controlled so as to meet the needs of the colony by a series of pheromones (p. 874) produced by the reproductive and soldier castes. The pheromones act via the endocrine system and Lüscher (1960) supposes that they inhibit secretion by the brain neurosecretory cells. In the absence of pheromones the neurosecretory cells activate the prothoracic glands so that the insect moults. The result of this moult depends in part on the existing stage of development and in part on the timing of the moult relative to the secretory cycle of the corpora allata.

The corpora allata are presumed to show two peaks of secretion during a cycle (Fig. 558), the first bringing the insect into a state of competence to differentiate and the second leading to the retention of more juvenile characters in the usual manner of the juvenile hormone. In the complete absence of pheromone due to the absence of the king and queen, the neurosecretory cells of a pseudergate become active and ecdysone is secreted at an early stage during the first phase of corpus allatum activity. This leads to the secretion of a gonadotrophic hormone, supposedly distinct from juvenile hormone, with the result that the pseudergate moults to a replacement reproductive (Fig. 558B). Under more normal conditions in the presence of the king and queen the pseudergate might receive some gonadotrophic hormone from them in the course of trophallaxis. If this occurs during the first phase of activity of the corpora allata these glands stop producing juvenile hormone and produce gonadotrophic hormone instead. At the next moult a white soldier is produced (Fig. 558C).

If, in the presence of the king and queen, the pseudergate does not receive any gonadotrophic hormone its development at the moult depends on the amount of juvenile hormone produced during the second cycle of activity and this is related to nutrition. In the presence of abundant food the amount of juvenile hormone produced is reduced and the pseudergate moults to a nymph (Fig. 558D), but if food is scarce the corpora allata become active and the insect undergoes a stationary moult to another pseudergate (Fig. 558A). The moulting of nymphs is controlled in a similar way. With abundant food, corpus allatum activity is completely suppressed and the insect becomes a winged imago (Fig. 558E), but with little food a good deal of juvenile hormone is produced and the insect may undergo a regressive moult back to pseudergate (Fig. 558F).

Termites belonging to the family Termitidae are less flexible in their ability to differentiate into different morphs, but it is probable that caste formation is regulated in a similar way by the titre of juvenile hormone (Lüscher, 1976).

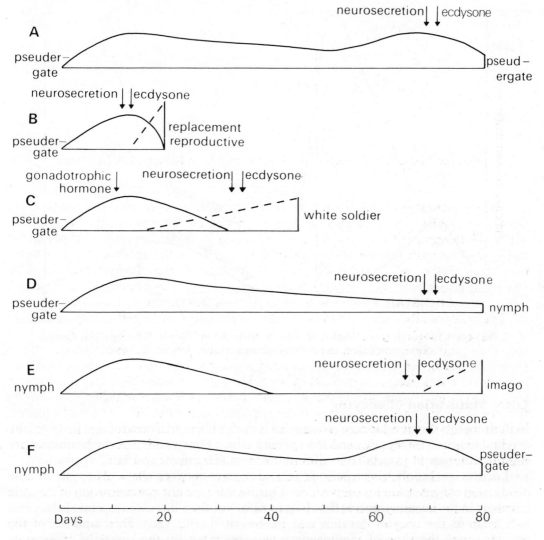

Fig. 558 The supposed activities of hormones in caste differentiation in *Kalotermes*. The continuous curves represent the juvenile hormone titre; the broken lines indicate production of gonadotrophic hormone by the corpora allata (after Lüscher, 1960)

Locust phases

Locusts exist in two extreme phases, the solitary and gregarious phases, which differ from each other in behaviour, appearance and morphometrics (Uvarov, 1966). The differences arise as a result of differences in sensory stimulation which affect the endocrine system via the cerebral neurosecretory system (Joly, 1972). The titre of juvenile hormone in the haemolymph of solitary locusts is higher than in gregarious insects of similar age (Fig. 559) (Joly *et al.*, 1977). Juvenile hormone is known to induce green colour in nymphs and to influence wing length in adults, two of the features which distinguish solitary from gregarious insects.

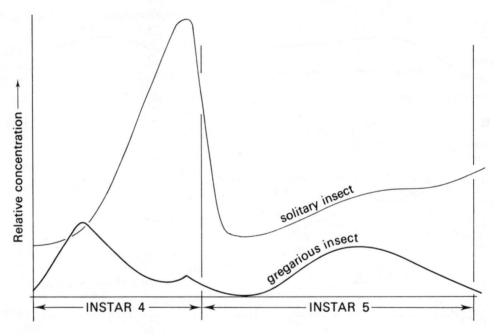

Fig. 559 Changes in concentration of juvenile hormone in solitary and gregarious *Locusta* during the fourth and fifth larval instars (after Joly *et al.*, 1977)

34.5.5 Maturation of oocytes

In most insects the development of oocytes is under hormonal control and involves the cerebral neurosecretory cells and the corpora allata, but the roles of the hormones are slightly different in insects from different orders (Highnam and Hill, 1977).

Locusts commonly have a period of about 20 days between the final ecdysis and the production of eggs ready for oviposition. During this time the concentration of juvenile hormone in the haemolymph at first falls to zero, but then increases to a maximum and falls again as the oocytes develop and are ovulated (Fig. 560). Development of the oocytes up to the time of vitellogenesis is accelerated by the presence of juvenile hormone, though it may not be entirely dependent on it. Subsequently, however, juvenile hormone is necessary to induce vitellogenin synthesis in the fat body and to facilitate the uptake of vitellogenins by the oocytes. In the latter instance it acts as a gonadotrophic hormone. The cerebral neurosecretory cells activate and maintain the secretion of juvenile hormone by the corpora allata (McCaffery, 1976), and are themselves stimulated by mating and some plant odours (Fig. 561).

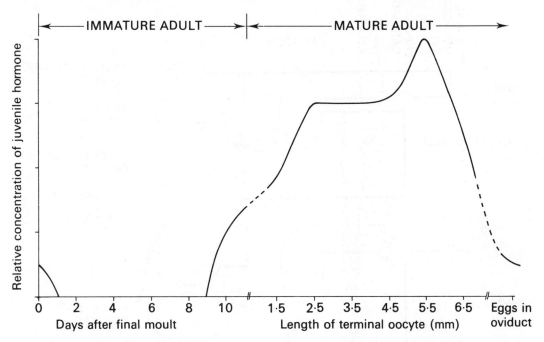

Fig. 560 Changes in the concentration of juvenile hormone in the haemolymph of an adult female *Locusta* in relation to maturation (after Johnson and Hill, 1975)

In *Rhodnius* a batch of eggs is laid following each blood meal, the number of eggs laid depending on the size of the meal. One effect of feeding is to initiate the secretion of juvenile hormone, which as in the locust regulates vitellogenin production; it also acts as a gonadotrophic hormone stimulating previtellogenic development of the oocytes and vitellogenesis (Fig. 561). In the latter case, at least, it acts on the follicle cells causing them to separate slightly from each other so that proteins in the haemolymph have free access to the oocytes. It is suggested that fully developed oocytes in the ovarioles cause some part of the reproductive tract to secrete an antigonadotrophin which blocks vitellogenesis in younger oocytes (Pratt and Davey, 1972). The cerebral neurosecretory cells have no direct role, although they are concerned, following mating, with producing a hormone which regulates oviposition.

Mosquitoes provide an example of another type of control. Here too oviposition follows blood-feeding which results in the release of neurosecretion stored in the corpora cardiaca. This hormone acts on the ovaries, which in turn produce ecdysone and it is this which initiates vitellogenin synthesis in the fat body (Fig. 561). Juvenile hormone acts early in oogenesis, stimulating previtellogenic development of the oocytes (see Hagedorn and Kunkel, 1979).

Many insects lay their eggs in batches, necessitating the synchronised development of oocytes in a series of cycles. The first cycle may be initiated by stimuli arising from

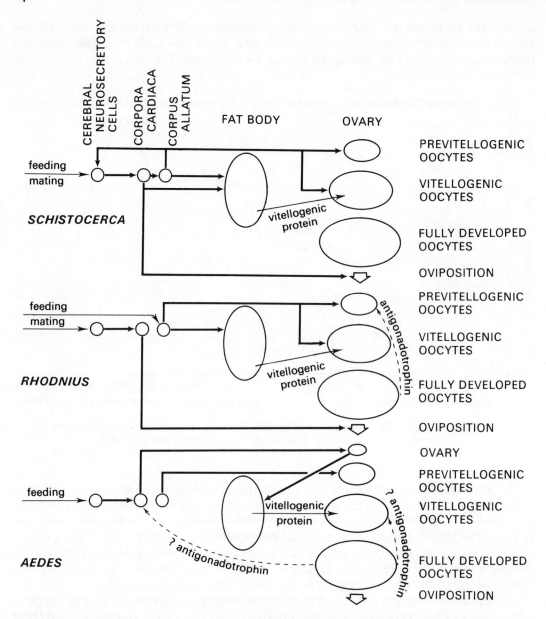

Fig. 561 Diagrammatic representation of the endocrine control of oogenesis in *Schistocerca*, *Rhodnius* and *Aedes* (after Highnam and Hill, 1977)

the food in locusts, or by a blood meal in mosquitoes. It is likely that feed-back from mature oocytes inhibits further development in some way. In locusts the titre of juvenile hormone in the haemolymph is reduced as the oocytes become mature and pass into the oviducts (Fig. 560). The effect of this is to reduce vitellogenin production and prevent its further uptake by immature oocytes. Oviposition stimulates the neuro-secretory cells so that a new cycle of corpus allatum activity is initiated and a second wave of vitellogenin production follows.

In *Diploptera* and some other cockroaches the eggs are retained in the uterus during the period of embryonic development. The wall of the brood sac is stretched by the ootheca and receptors in the wall are stimulated. These act via the central nervous system to inhibit the corpora allata so that no hormone is produced and no more oocytes mature. During gestation the receptors in the wall of the brood sac or interneurones in the central nervous system slowly become adapted, so that by the time of parturition the inhibition of the corpora allata has been almost completely lifted and more oocytes start to mature. In this way cycles of development of the oocytes are produced at the shortest possible intervals (Fig. 562).

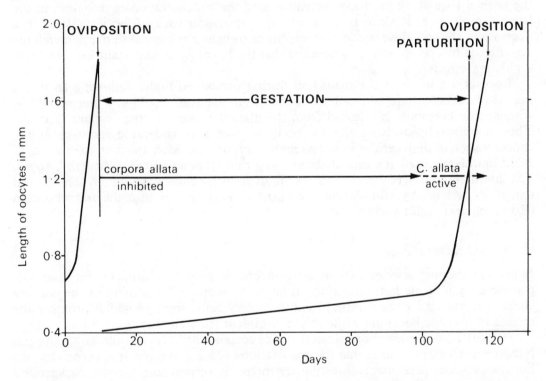

Fig. 562 Development of the oocytes in *Diploptera*, a viviparous cockroach (after Roth and Stay, 1961)

In many Lepidoptera the oocytes mature during the pupal stage and are ready for oviposition immediately after ecdysis and the control of oogenesis differs from most other insects. Juvenile hormone is essential for egg maturation in *Manduca*, but it affects some developmental process other than vitellogenin synthesis or uptake (Nijhout and Riddiford, 1974). It may be that in other species of Lepidoptera in which the eggs mature in the adult the corpora allata play a part comparable with that in other insects.

Carausius is parthenogenetic and eggs are laid singly, a situation which possibly does not require humoral regulation. The corpora allata are not essential for oocyte development; on the contrary, juvenile hormone can prevent vitellogenesis in the distal oocytes (Socha and Gelbič, 1973).

34.5.6 Other functions of hormones

Regulation of carbohydrate and lipid metabolism

In many insects extracts from the corpora cardiaca produce an increase in the concentration of trehalose in the haemolymph. Locusts produce two hyperglycaemic hormones, one in the neurosecretory cells of the brain and another in the intrinsic gland cells of the corpora cardiaca. Their effect is to activate the phosphorylase catalysing the production of trehalose from glycogen in the fat body. The functions of these hyperglycaemic hormones in the intact insect are unknown. Possibly they form part of the normal regulatory mechanism maintaining the concentration of trehalose in the haemolymph (p. 811) since removal of the corpora cardiaca of locusts results in a decrease in the trehalose concentration. Since trehalose is central to many metabolic activities in insects (p. 103) it is possible that the hormone is important in its indirect regulatory effects.

Locusts use lipids as the main fuel during prolonged flight, following an initial period of carbohydrate metabolism (p. 266). At the start of flight a hormone, the adipokinetic hormone, is released from the glandular lobes of the corpora cardiaca. This mobilises lipids from the fat body so that a considerable increase in the concentration of diglycerides in the haemolymph occurs. After the first 30 minutes of flight lipid is oxidised at a rate of about 85 μg/min (Jutsum and Goldsworthy, 1976). The hormone also acts directly on the flight muscle, enhancing the switch to lipid oxidation perhaps by stimulating the entry of acyl groups into the mitochondria (Robinson and Goldsworthy, 1977).

Colour and colour change

Many grasshopper species exhibit a green/brown polymorphism. Green colour is produced by juvenile hormone at the time of the moult. The activity of the corpora allata is regulated by the cerebral neurosecretory cells, some of which promote the release of juvenile hormone while others inhibit it (Rowell, 1971).

In locusts a neurosecretion released via the corpora cardiaca controls darkening and Nickerson (1956) postulates that the colouration of locust nymphs is governed by two hormones. One, presumably juvenile hormone, is responsible for the background colour, producing green when in high concentration and yellow when in low concentration; the other is responsible for the pattern, the amount of black pigment increasing with the concentration of hormone. Hence the green solitary form results from a high titre of background (juvenile) hormone and a low titre of pattern hormone; the gregarious form results from a decrease of background hormone and an increase of pattern hormone.

Physiological colour change (p. 140) may also be regulated by hormonal activity. Brown specimens of the stick insect, *Carausius* (Phasmida), become black at night, resuming their brown colour in daylight. The change results from movements of pigment granules in the epidermal cells and in particular from the movement of large brown-black granules. In the light these granules are concentrated in the lower parts of the cells, in the dark they move up close to the surface above the yellow-orange pigment in the middle of the cell (Fig. 563). This causes the insect to get darker. These changes are controlled by a secretion from neurosecretory cells in the tritocerebrum which

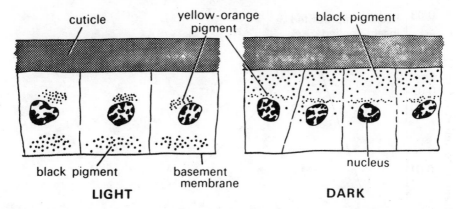

Fig. 563 Diagrammatic representations of the distribution of yellow-orange and black pigments in the epidermis of *Carausius* in the light and in the dark (after Dupont-Raabe, 1957)

passes back along the nerve cord to be liberated into the haemolymph, mostly from the suboesophageal ganglion. The corpora cardiaca also release a substance which causes moderate pigment migration with the development of intermediate colouration. This substance is probably derived from the brain secretion (Dupont-Raabe, 1957).

Water balance

Most insects take in relatively large amounts of water with their food and, in order to prevent undue dilution of the haemolymph, a diuretic regulatory mechanism probably exists in most insects. The problem is most acute in fluid-feeding insects. In *Rhodnius* feeding stimulates the release of a hormone from neurosecretory cells in the posterior part of the fused ventral ganglionic mass. The hormone enters the haemolymph via the neurohaemal organs in the lateral abdominal nerves and greatly enhances the rate at which fluid is secreted via the Malpighian tubules. Diuresis begins about 30 seconds after feeding and the effect is mimicked experimentally by injecting haemolymph from an insect which has recently fed, and so contains the diuretic hormone, into one which has not fed (Fig. 564).

Locusts, too, produce a diuretic hormone following feeding, but in this case the hormone is produced in the cerebral neurosecretory cells and released into the haemolymph via the corpora cardiaca. The hormone reduces resorption in the rectum as well as increasing the rate of secretion by the Malpighian tubules, and as a consequence more water is excreted.

An antidiuretic hormone has been reported in a number of insects, but no extensive studies have yet been carried out on its normal role.

Hormones and behaviour

Truman and Riddiford (1974a) classify hormones which effect behaviour as releasers and modifiers. A releaser hormone is one which triggers a response within a short time of its entering the haemolymph; no other stimuli are necessary to elicit the response.

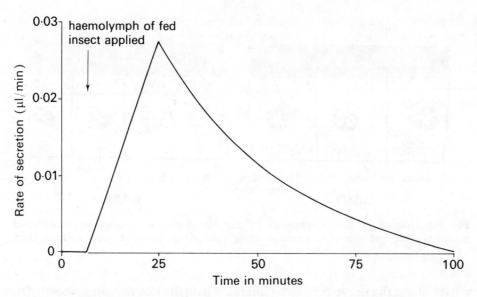

Fig. 564 Rate of secretion of urine by an experimental preparation of the Malpighian tubules of *Rhodnius*, showing the marked increase when blood from a newly fed insect, containing diuretic hormone, was applied (after Highnam and Hill, 1977)

Modifiers affect the responsiveness of the nervous system so that the response of the insect to a given stimulus is altered.

Pre-eclosion behaviour and calling by the female *Hyalophora* are triggered by releaser hormones. The eclosion hormone is a product of the neurosecretory cells of the brain; it switches on a sequence of activities regulated by the abdominal ganglia. Within 30 minutes of injecting the hormone into a pharate moth it begins a series of abdominal rotations. After about half-an-hour the insect becomes quiescent and then starts a series of peristaltic waves along the abdomen, which would normally lead to eclosion (p. 495, and see Truman, 1980).

Modifier effects of hormones are common and a good example is the change in responsiveness of female *Gomphocerus* following injection or normal production of juvenile hormone (see below). Juvenile hormone causes larvae of *Mimas* to respond negatively to gravity. As the titre decreases towards the end of the last instar the larvae become positively geotactic and crawl down to the ground to pupate. The response is reversed by the implantation of active corpora allata.

In regulating sexual behaviour, hormones serve to coordinate behaviour with the physiological state of the insect. For instance, an immature female grasshopper, *Gomphocerus*, responds to a courting male by making escape movements, but as the insect becomes sexually mature she responds positively to the male and allows him to mount and copulate. The change in behaviour and sexual maturation are regulated by juvenile hormone. Juvenile hormone also controls receptivity in female *Aedes*, but in female cockroaches it has less effect and neuroendocrine activity may have a major influence (Barth and Lester, 1973). Following mating there is a loss of receptivity, which sometimes results from loss of juvenile hormone, but may involve other factors.

Sexual receptivity is often associated with the production of pheromones signalling the state of readiness to the opposite sex. Pheromone production may again be controlled by the corpora allata, as in female *Byrsotria*, which produce a pheromone during the preovulation period and after parturition, but not during the period of pregnancy.

Endocrine control of male sexual behaviour is less well understood. The situation in Acrididae is reviewed by Pener (1974). In *Locusta migratoria* the median neurosecretory cells have a direct effect on sexual behaviour and also activate the corpora allata. The latter have some additional influence on behaviour and induce the yellow colour of the integument of mature locusts. In other species the balance between the neurosecretory cells and corpora allata is different.

Hormones may regulate behaviour by switching on specific motor sequences in the central nervous system when they act as releasers. In most other cases, however, they probably facilitate specific sensory–motor pathways in the insect nervous system. Sometimes a general effect on the activity of the nervous system may be involved. Following feeding, locusts become relatively inactive and unresponsive and this change in behaviour is associated with the release of hormone from the corpora cardiaca (Bernays and Chapman, 1974). In *Periplaneta* a homogenate of the corpora cardiaca reduces the spontaneous activity in the isolated nerve cord (Ozbas and Hodgson, 1958). Haskell and Moorhouse (1963) suggest that the relative inactivity of solitary locusts may be due to general hormonal effects on the nervous system. Ecdysone increases the spontaneous discharge in the central nervous system, but reduces the discharge in the motor nerves.

Finally, it is possible that hormones influence behaviour by regulating the input from peripheral sense organs. In *Locusta* a hormone from the corpora cardiaca causes the sensilla on the maxillary palps to become unresponsive after feeding (Bernays *et al.*, 1972). This is probably not the primary cause of the changed behaviour, but it is a contributing factor.

34.5.7 Sex hormones

There is no evidence that the gonads of insects produce hormones which affect the secondary sexual characters (Novak, 1966), but there are a few instances in which a hormone from the gonads appears to influence behaviour or some physiological process. For instance, ovariectomy of female grasshoppers leads to a failure to respond to male singing, but the response reappears following the injection of blood from a normal female. Presumably a factor in the blood produced by the ovaries is responsible for this. The behaviour of male grasshoppers, however, is not affected by castration (Haskell, 1960). In *Rhodnius* mature oocytes produce an antigonadotrophin which inhibits the development of younger oocytes (Pratt and Davey, 1972), and there is growing evidence that ecdysone is produced in the ovaries of a number of insects (de Loof, 1981).

34.5.8 Hormones and embryogenesis

In the embryo of *Locustana* (Orthoptera) the separation of the embryonic cuticle from the epidermis is apparently controlled by the neurosecretory cells and prothoracic glands (Jones, 1956a), but Micciarelli and Sbrenna (1972) have shown that the apolysis occurs in isolated abdomens of *Schistocerca* and so is independent of the prothoracic glands. The hormone from these glands stimulates the pleuropodia to produce the enzymes which digest the serosal cuticle before hatching (Jones, 1956b). Lagueux *et al.* (1979) have shown that ecdysone titres reach a peak in association with the production of each successive cuticle (serosal, embryonic and first instar, p. 424) in the embryo of *Locusta*, suggesting that cuticle production is controlled hormonally.

In the embryo of *Periplaneta* neurosecretory cells first appear in the brain about 12 days before hatching. Subsequently neurosecretion accumulates in the cells and then is lost before hatching. A similar cycle occurs in the corpora cardiaca, but in the corpora allata the accumulation of neurosecretory material is maximal at hatching and then declines in the newly hatched larva. There is thus a phase of neurosecretion before hatching, suggesting some similarity between hatching and moulting (Khan and Fraser, 1962).

34.6 The rabbit flea and hormones

The ovaries of the rabbit flea, *Spilopsyllus cuniculi*, only mature if the insect feeds on a pregnant female rabbit or a nestling rabbit less than a week old. In fleas feeding on rabbits in other stages, development of the ovaries does not occur. This effect is due to several of the host hormones produced during pregnancy acting directly on the flea. The most important of these hormones are the corticosteroids from the adrenal glands. Apart from maturation of the ovaries, the salivary gland and alimentary canal enlarge and the rate of defaecation increases, indicating an increase in feeding. The male is also affected, although the production of sperm is not controlled by the host hormones.

Fleas tend to mass on a pregnant doe rabbit and do not readily detach or move to another host, but a few hours after the young rabbits are born the fleas become active and move on to the young ones. This activity is probably initiated by a change in the hormonal balance of the female rabbit. On the young rabbits, which also have a high level of corticosteroid in the blood, feeding and copulation occur and the fleas leave the host to lay eggs in the nest, which is fouled by the blood defaecated by the parent fleas. This blood provides an important source of food for the larvae. As the level of hormone in the host blood declines the fleas stop laying eggs and the ovaries regress until another pregnant host is found (Rothschild, 1965).

Mead-Briggs (1964) suggests that the rabbit hormones lead to the release of hormone from the median neurosecretory cells in the brain of the flea. This activates the corpora allata and so leads to the laying down of yolk in the oocytes, while at the same time enzyme activity is stimulated so that more metabolites are available for vitellogenesis.

REFERENCES

BARTH, R. H. and LESTER, L. J. (1973). Neuro-hormonal control of sexual behaviour in insects. *A. Rev. Ent.* **18**: 445–472.

BERNAYS, E. A. and CHAPMAN, R. F. (1974). The regulation of food intake by acridids. *in* Barton Browne, L. (ed.), *Experimental analysis of insect behaviour*. Springer-Verlag, Berlin.

BERNAYS, E. A., BLANEY, W. M. and CHAPMAN, R. F. (1972). Changes in chemorecep-tor sensilla on the maxillary palps of *Locusta migratoria* in relation to feeding. *J. exp. Biol.* **57**: 745–753.

BOLLENBACHER, W. E., SMITH, S. L., GOODMAN, W. and GILBERT, L. I. (1981). Ecdysteroid titer during larval-pupal-adult development of the tobacco hornworm, *Manduca sexta*. *Gen. Comp. Endocr.* **44**: 302–307.

CAZAL, P. (1948). Les glandes endocrines rétro-cérébrales des insectes (étude morphologique). *Bull. biol. Fr. Belg. suppl.* **32**: 227 pp.

CHIPPENDALE, G. M. (1977). Hormonal regulation of larval diapause. *A. Rev. Ent.* **22**: 121–138.

CLEVER, U. (1965). The effect of ecdysone on gene activity patterns in giant chromosomes. *in* Karlson, P. (ed.), *Mechanisms of hormone action*. Academic Press, London.

DANILEVSKII, A. S. (1965). *Photoperiodism and seasonal development of insects*. Oliver and Boyd, Edinburgh.

DELPHIN, F. (1965). The histology and possible functions of neurosecretory cells in the ventral ganglia of *Schistocerca gregaria* Forskål (Orthoptera: Acrididae). *Trans. R. ent. Soc. Lond.* **117**: 167–214.

DUPONT-RAABE, M. (1957). Les mécanismes de l'adaptation chromatique chez les insectes. *Arch. Zool. exp. gén.* **94**: 61–294.

ENGELMANN, F. (1968). Endocrine control of reproduction in insects. *A. Rev. Ent.* **13**: 1–27.

FERKOVICH, S. M., OBERLANDER, H. and LEACH, C. E. (1981). Chitin synthesis in larval and pupal epidermis of the Indian meal moth, *Plodia interpunctella* (Hübner), and the greater wax moth, *Galleria mellonella* (L.). *J. Insect Physiol.* **27**: 509–514.

FRAENKEL, G. and HSIAO, C. (1965). Bursicon, a hormone which mediates tanning of the cuticle in the adult fly and other insects. *J. Insect Physiol.* **11**: 513–556.

GOLDSWORTHY, G. J. and MORDUE, W. (1974). Neurosecretory hormones in insects. *J. Endocr.* **60**: 529–558.

GRANGER, N. A. and SEHNAL, F. (1974). Regulation of larval corpora allata in *Galleria mellonella*. *Nature, Lond.* **251**: 415–417.

HAGEDORN, H. H. and KUNKEL, J. G. (1979). Vitellogenin and vitellin in insects. *J. Insect Physiol.* **24**: 475–505.

HASKELL, P. T. (1960). Stridulation and associated behaviour in certain Orthoptera. 3. The influence of the gonads. *Anim. Behav.* **8**: 76–81.

HASKELL, P. T. and MOORHOUSE, J. E. (1963). A blood-borne factor influencing the activity of the central nervous systems of the desert locust. *Nature, Lond.* **197**: 56–58.

HIGHNAM, K. C. (1961). The histology of the neurosecretory system of the adult female desert locust, *Schistocerca gregaria*. *Q. Jl microsc. Sci.* **102**: 27–38.

HIGHNAM, K. C. (1964). Endocrine relationships in insect reproduction. *Symp. R. ent. Soc. Lond.* **2**: 26–42.

HIGHNAM, K. C. and HILL, L. (1977). *The comparative endocrinology of the invertebrates*. Edward Arnold, London.

HIGHNAM, K. C. and WEST, M. W. (1971). The neuropilar neurosecretory reservoir of *Locusta migratoria migratorioides* R. & F. *Gen. comp. Physiol.* **16**: 574–585.

HSIAO, T. H. and HSIAO, C. (1977). Simultaneous determinations of molting and juvenile hormone molting titers in the greater wax moth. *J. Insect Physiol.* **23**: 89–93.

HSIAO, T. H., HSIAO, C. and de WILDE, J. (1975). Moulting hormone production in the isolated abdomen of the Colorado beetle. *Nature, Lond.* **255**: 5511.

JOHNSON, B. (1962). Neurosecretion and the transport of secretory material from the corpora cardiaca in aphids. *Nature, Lond.* **196**: 1338–1339.

JOHNSON, R. A. and HILL, L. (1973). The activity of the corpora allata in the fourth and fifth larval instars of the migratory locust. *J. Insect Physiol.* **19**: 1921–1932.

JOHNSON, R. A. and HILL, L. (1975). Activity of the corpora allata in the adult female migratory locust. *J. Insect Physiol.* **21**: 1517–1519.

JOLY, P. (1972). The hormonal mechanism of phase differentiation in locusts. *in* Hemming, C. F. and Taylor, T. H. C. (eds.), *Proceedings of the International study conference on the current and future problems of Acridology*. Centre for overseas Pest Research, London.

JOLY, L., HOFFMANN, J. and JOLY, P. (1977). Contrôle humoral de la différenciation phasaire chez *Locusta migratoria migratorioides* (R. & F.) (Orthoptères). *Acrida* **6**: 33–42.

JONES, B. M. (1956a). Endocrine activity during insect embryogenesis. Function of the ventral head glands in locust embryos (*Locustana pardalina* and *Locusta migratoria*, Orthoptera). *J. exp. Biol.* **33**: 174–185.

JONES, B. M. (1956b). Endocrine activity during embryogenesis. Control of events in development following the embryonic moult (*Locusta migratoria* and *Locustana pardalina*, Orthoptera). *J. exp. Biol.* **33**: 685–696.

JUTSUM, A. R. and GOLDSWORTHY, G. J. (1976). Fuels for flight in *Locusta. J. Insect Physiol.* **22**: 243–249.

KAI, H. and HASEGAWA, K. (1973). An esterase in relation to yolk cell lysis at diapause termination in the silkworm, *Bombyx mori. J. Insect Physiol.* **19**: 799–810.

KARLSON, P. (1963). Chemistry and biochemistry of insect hormones. *Angew. Chem. internat. Edit.* **2**: 175–182.

KARLSON, P. and SEKERIS, C. E. (1966). Ecdysone, an insect steroid hormone, and its mode of action. *Recent Prog. in Hormone Res.* **22**: 473–493.

KHAN, T. R. and FRASER, A. (1962). Neurosecretion in the embryo and later stages of the cockroach (*Periplaneta americana* L.). *Mem. Soc. Endocr.* **12**: 349–369.

KORT, C. A. D. DE and GRANGER, N. A. (1981). Regulation of the juvenile hormone titer. *A. Rev. Ent.* **26**: 1–28.

KROEGER, H. and LEZZI, M. (1966). Regulation of gene action in insect development. *A. Rev. Ent.* **11**: 1–22.

LAGUEUX, M., HETRU, C., GOLTZENE, F., KAPPLER, C. and HOFFMANN, J. A. (1979). Ecdysone titre and metabolism in relation to cuticulogenesis in embryos of *Locusta migratoria. J. Insect Physiol.* **25**: 709–723.

LEES, A. D. (1966). The control of polymorphism in aphids. *Adv. Insect Physiol.* **3**: 207–272.

LEES, A. D. (1967). The production of the apterous and alate forms in the aphid *Megoura viciae* Buckton, with special reference to the rôle of crowding. *J. Insect Physiol.* **13**: 289–318.

LOOF, A. DE (1981). New concepts in endocrine control of vitellogenesis and in functioning of the ovary in insects. *Proc. 3rd. Cong. Europ. Soc. comp. Physiol. Biochem.* Pergamon Press, Oxford.

LÜSCHER, M. (1960). Hormonal control of caste differentiation in termites. *Ann. N.Y. Acad. Sci.* **89**: 549–563.

LÜSCHER, M. (1976). Evidence for an endocrine control of caste determination in higher termites. *in* Lüscher, M. (ed.), *Phase and caste determination in insects.* Pergamon Press, Oxford.

MADDRELL, S. H. P. (1974). Neurosecretion. *in* Treherne, J. E. (ed.), *Insect neurobiology.* North-Holland Publishing Co., Amsterdam.

McCAFFERY, A. R. (1976). Effects of electrocoagulation of cerebral neurosecretory cells and implantation of corpora allata on oöcyte development in *Locusta migratoria. J. Insect Physiol.* **22**: 1081–1092.

MEAD-BRIGGS, A. R. (1964). A correlation between development of the ovaries and of the midgut epithelium in the rabbit flea *Spilopsyllus cuniculi. Nature, Lond.* **201**: 1303–1304.

MICCIARELLI, S. B. and SBRENNA, G. (1972). The embryonic apolyses of *Schistocerca gregaria* (Orthoptera). *J. Insect Physiol.* **18**: 1027–1037.

MILLER, T. A. (1975). Neurosecretion and the control of visceral organs in insects. *A. Rev. Ent.* **20**: 133–149.

MORGAN, E. D. and POOLE, C. F. (1976). The pattern of ecdysone levels during development in the desert locust, *Schistocerca gregaria. J. Insect Physiol.* **22**: 885–889.

NICKERSON, B. (1956). Pigmentation of hoppers of the desert locust (*Schistocerca gregaria* Forskål) in relation to phase colouration. *Anti-Locust Bull.* no. 24, 34 pp.

NIJHOUT, M. M. and RIDDIFORD, L. M. (1974). The control of egg maturation by juvenile hormone in the tobacco hornworm moth, *Manduca sexta*. *Biol. Bull.* **146**: 377–392.

NIJHOUT, H. F. and WILLIAMS, C. M. (1974a). Control of moulting and metamorphosis in the tobacco hornworm, *Manduca sexta* (L.): growth of the last-instar larva and the decision to pupate. *J. exp. Biol.* **61**: 481–491.

NIJHOUT, H. F. and WILLIAMS, C. M. (1974b). Control of moulting and metamorphosis in the tobacco hornworm, *Manduca sexta* (L.): cessation of juvenile hormone secretion as a trigger for pupation. *J. exp. Biol.* **61**: 493–501.

NOVÁK, V. J. A. (1966). *Insect hormones*. Methuen, London.

OZBAS, S. and HODGSON, E. S. (1958). Action of insect neurosecretion upon central nervous system in vitro and upon behaviour. *Proc. natn. Acad. Sci. U.S.A.* **44**: 825–830.

PADGHAM, D. E. (1976). Control of melanization in first instar larvae of *Schistocerca gregaria*. *J. Insect Physiol.* **22**: 1409–1419.

PENER, M. P. (1974). Neurosecretory and corpus allatum controlled effects on male sexual behaviour in acridids. *in* Browne, L. B. (ed.), *Experimental analysis of insect behaviour*. Springer-Verlag, Berlin.

PRATT, G. E. and DAVEY, K. G. (1972). The corpus allatum and oogenesis in *Rhodnius prolixus* (Stål.) III. The effect of mating. *J. exp. Biol.* **56**: 223–237.

ROBINSON, N. L. and GOLDSWORTHY, G. J. (1977). A possible site of action for adipokinetic hormone on the flight muscle of locusts. *J. Insect Physiol.* **23**: 153–158.

ROTH, L. M. and STAY, B. (1961). Oocyte development in *Diploptera punctata* (Eschscholtz) (Blattaria). *J. Insect Physiol.* **7**: 186–202.

ROTHSCHILD, M. (1965). The rabbit flea and hormones. *Endeavour* **24**: 162–167.

ROWELL, C. H. F. (1971). The variable coloration of the acridoid grasshoppers. *Adv. Insect Physiol.* **8**: 145–198.

SCHARRER, B. (1959). The role of neurosecretion in neuroendocrine integration. *in* Gorbman, A. (ed.), *Comparative endocrinology*. Wiley and Sons, New York.

SCHREINER, B. (1966). Histochemistry of the A cell neurosecretory material in the milkweed bug, *Oncopeltus fasciatus* Dallas (Heteroptera: Lygaeidae), with a discussion of the neurosecretory material/carrier substance problem. *Gen. comp. Endocrin.* **6**: 388–400.

SEHNAL, F., MAROY, P. and MALA, J. (1981). Regulation and significance of ecdysteroid titre fluctuations in Lepidopterous larvae and pupae. *J. Insect Physiol.* **27**: 535–544.

SOCHA, R. and GELBIČ, I. (1973). Stages in the differentiation of ovarian development in *Dixippus morosus* as revealed by the effects of juvenoids. *Acta Entomol. Bohemslov.* **70**: 303–312.

SOUTHWOOD, T. R. E. (1961). A hormonal theory of the mechanism of wing polymorphism in Heteroptera. *Proc. R. ent. Soc. Lond.* A, **36**: 63–66.

STEEL, C. G. H. (1975). A neuroendocrine feedback mechanism in the insect moulting cycle. *Nature, Lond.* **253**: 267–269.

STEELE, J. E. (1976). Hormonal control of metabolism in insects. *Adv. Insect Physiol.* **12**: 239–323.

STONE, J. V., MORDUE, W., BATLEY, K. E. and MORRIS, H. R. (1976). Structure of locust adipokinetic hormone, a neurohormone that regulates lipid utilisation during flight. *Nature, Lond.* **263**: 207–211.

STRONG, L. (1966). On the occurrence of neuroglandular axons within the sympathetic nervous system of a locust, *Locusta migratoria migratorioides*. *J. R. microsc. Soc.* **86**: 141–149.

TAUBER, M. J. and TAUBER, C. A. (1976). Insect seasonality: diapause maintenance, termination and post diapause development. *A. Rev. Ent.* **21**: 81–107.

TRUMAN, J. W. (1973). Physiology of insect ecdysis III. Relationship between the hormonal control of eclosion and of tanning in the tobacco hornworm, *Manduca sexta. J. exp. Biol.* **58**: 821–829.

TRUMAN, J. W. (1980). Cellular aspects of eclosion hormone action on the CNS of insects. *in* Sattelle, D. B., Hall, L. M. and Hildebrand, J. G. (eds.). *Receptors for neurotransmitters, hormones and pheromones in insects.* Elsevier/North Holland Biomedical Press, Amsterdam.

TRUMAN, J. W. and RIDDIFORD, L. M. (1974a). Hormonal mechanisms underlying insect behaviour. *Adv. Insect Physiol.* **10**: 297–352.

TRUMAN, J. W. and RIDDIFORD, L. M. (1974b). The physiology of insect rhythms III. The temporal organization of the endocrine events underlying pupation of the tobacco hornworm. *J. exp. Biol.* **60**: 371–382.

UVAROV, B. P. (1966). *Grasshoppers and locusts.* vol. 1. Cambridge University Press.

WATSON, J. A. L. (1963). The cephalic endocrine system in the Thysanura. *J. Morph.* **113**: 359–373.

WHITMORE, E. and GILBERT, L. I. (1972). Haemolymph lipoprotein transport of juvenile hormone. *J. Insect Physiol.* **18**: 1153–1167.

WHITTEN, J. M. (1964). Connective tissue membranes and their apparent role in transporting neurosecretory and other secretory products in insects. *Gen. comp. Endocrin.* **4**: 176–192.

WIGGLESWORTH, V. B. (1954). *The physiology of insect metamorphosis.* Cambridge Univeristy Press.

WIGGLESWORTH, V. B. (1957). The action of growth hormones in insects. *Symp. Soc. exp. Biol.* **11**: 204–226.

WIGGLESWORTH, V. B. (1959). *The control of growth and form.* Cornell University Press, Ithaca.

WIGGLESWORTH, V. B. (1961). Some observations on the juvenile hormone effect of farnesol in *Rhodnius prolixus* Stål (Hemiptera). *J. Insect Physiol.* **7**: 73–78.

WIGGLESWORTH, V. B. (1970). *Insect hormones.* Oliver and Boyd, Edinburgh.

WILLIS, J. H. (1974). Morphogenetic action of insect hormones *A. Rev. Ent.* **19**: 97–115.

CHAPTER XXXV

EXOCRINE GLANDS, PHEROMONES AND DEFENSIVE SECRETIONS

Hormones are concerned with regulation within the organism. Other chemical substances are concerned with communication with other individuals of the same species, when they are called pheromones, or with other species; in the latter instance they often take the form of defensive secretions. Most pheromones and defensive secretions are produced by ectodermal glands secreting to the outside of the body, exocrine glands. The basic structure of these glands is similar irrespective of whether they produce pheromones or defensive chemicals, but defence glands are usually associated with a reservoir while pheromone glands are not.

Most known pheromones influence the behaviour of other individuals, but some affect physiology. In many species one sex, often the female, produces a pheromone attracting the opposite sex from some distance away; other pheromones may regulate reproductive behaviour when the sexes are close together. Pheromones have many different functions where coordination of behaviour or physiology of individuals is necessary. They are particularly important in social insects, where they are concerned in communication and in the maintenance of colony structure. Particular glands may secrete a complex of chemicals, the combination of which may be important in conferring specificity on the pheromone.

Defence against enemies often involves the use of chemicals which are toxic or deterrent. The chemicals produced are often effective against a range of potential parasites and predators, both invertebrate and vertebrate.

The structure of exocrine glands is reviewed by Noirot and Quennedey (1974), while Percy and Weatherstone (1974) give an account of pheromone glands. Insect pheromones are reviewed by Birch (1974a), Jacobson (1972, 1974), Shorey (1973) and Shorey and McKelvey (1977). Reviews relating to more restricted aspects of pheromones are cited in the relevant sections. Weatherstone and Percy (1970) give an account of the chemicals used as defensive secretions, and Staddon (1979) reviews the structure and functions of the scent glands of Heteroptera.

35.1 The nature of exocrine secretions

Exocrine glands secrete material to the outside of the insect, in contrast to the endocrine glands, which produce secretions internal to the body. The exocrine glands of insects are produced from the epidermis. They include the salivary glands and rectal glands as well as other glands on various parts of the insect (p. 878). Salivary glands are dealt with in Section 3.7 (p. 60); in this chapter the functions of exocrine glands as producers of pheromones and defensive secretions is considered. In most cases these two functions are quite separate, but there are some examples of a single chemical from a single gland performing both functions. The formic acid produced by some ants is in this category.

Pheromones are substances which are secreted to the outside by animals and which, if passed to another individual of the same species, cause it to respond in a particular manner (Karlson and Butenandt, 1959). They are thus concerned with the co-ordination of individuals and are, therefore, often important in sexual behaviour and in regulating the behaviour and physiology of social and subsocial insects.

Some pheromones, such as sexual attractants in Lepidoptera, are perceived as scents by olfactory receptors and affect the recipient via the central nervous system. In other cases the pheromones are ingested by the recipient. These may be perceived by the sense of taste, exerting their effects via the central nervous system, or the pheromone, once ingested, may be absorbed and play some part in a biochemical reaction within the recipient. Pheromones which affect behaviour directly through the nervous system are called releaser pheromones; those that affect metabolism are known as primer pheromones.

Defensive secretions are produced by insects to deter potential predators or parasites and are sometimes classified as allomones—chemicals which are adaptively favourable to the producer. They are usually produced in larger quantities than pheromones.

Although in both types of secretion single chemicals may predominate and be very important, critical chemical analysis often reveals the presence of a number of chemicals. In such cases different components of the system may exert different effects, or the proportions of different components may confer specificity on the mixture.

35.2 Structure of exocrine glands

Exocrine glands may be composed of single gland cells, but more usually they comprise aggregations of such cells to form a discrete structure. Where isolated gland cells exist they are usually scattered through the epidermis as in the case of the epidermal glands involved in cuticle production (p. 522) or the pheromone glands of *Schistocerca* (p. 854). Multicellular aggregations of glands are developed on various parts of the body appropriate to their function.

Two principal types of epidermal gland cells occur: the class 1 cells of Noirot and Quennedey (1974), which are in direct contact with the cuticle which they secrete, but have no discrete duct leading through the cuticle (Fig. 565A); and class 3 cells, which are separated from the cuticle by epidermal cells and connect with the exterior via a duct (Fig. 565B). Noirot and Quennedey (1974) also describe class 2 cells, which have no direct contact with the cuticle, and also have no associated duct. This type of gland cell is only known from the sternal glands of termites.

The outer plasma membrane of class 1 cells is produced into microvilli or parallel lamellae, which may abut directly onto the cuticle but are often separated from it by a space in which it is presumed the secretion accumulates. The cuticle above the gland cells is usually unmodified and it is presumed that the secretion reaches the external surface of the cuticle via the pore canals and epicuticular filaments (p. 509).

Class 3 cells are always associated with one or more other cells to form the glandular unit. The surface of the gland cell is developed into microvilli which surround a cavity.

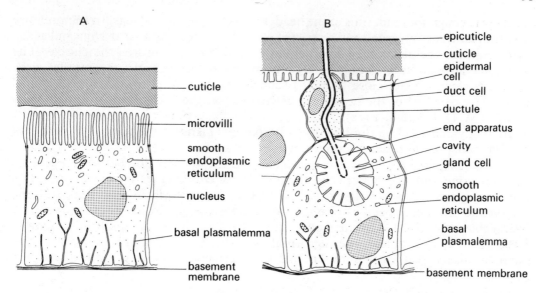

Fig. 565 A. Diagrammatic representation of Class 1 gland cell. B. Diagrammatic representation of Class 3 glandular unit (based on Noirot and Quennedey, 1974)

This cavity is extracellular and therefore not strictly a vacuole, though it is often referred to as such. Within the cavity is a structure called the end apparatus, which consists of a relatively electron-dense layer forming the initial part of the duct with a fibrillar region outside it. The dense layer is perforated and is continuous with the ductule formed by a separate duct cell. The ductule is formed of epicuticle and is continuous with the epicuticle on the outside of the body. Sometimes an additional cell is interpolated between the gland cell and the duct cell.

In most cases smooth endoplasmic reticulum is present in relatively large amounts in either a tubular or a vesicular form. This is presumably associated with the synthesis of the secretions. Mitochondria are usually abundant and the basal plasma membrane is strongly infolded, increasing the surface area available for uptake of material from the haemocoel.

Where glandular units are aggregated to form discrete glands they open into a reservoir in the case of defensive secretion, but usually there is no reservoir associated with pheromone glands. This reflects the greater volumes of secretion employed for defensive purposes compared with those used as pheromones. The manner of dispersal of the secretion also varies according to the nature of the secretion. Most pheromones are dispersed simply by exposure of the area of cuticle which covers the glands; defensive substances on the other hand are often forcibly ejected from the reservoir and this may involve a specific muscular development.

35.3 Pheromones

35.3.1 Distribution of pheromone glands and dispersal structures

In most insects pheromones are produced by glandular epidermal cells concentrated into discrete areas beneath the cuticle, but in male *Schistocerca* class 3 gland cells are scattered through the epidermis of the head, thorax, abdomen and legs. In an immature male the gland cells are small and restricted to the basal part of the epidermis, but as the insect matures the gland cells enlarge and extend distally towards the cuticle. The cytoplasm at this stage contains large numbers of electron-dense granules with numerous clear vesicles close to, and probably discharging into, the large terminal cavity. The contents of the cavity are discharged on the surface of the cuticle via a ductule (M. D. Kendall, 1972).

In many female Lepidoptera the pheromone glands producing the male sex attractant are present beneath an intersegmental membrane of the posterior abdominal segments. *Anagasta Küehniella* has the gland on the ventral side between segments eight and nine, but in other species the glands are lateral (Fig. 566), or dorsal. The individual gland cells are of class 1 type (p. 852) with no associated duct. Release of the pheromone involves a specific behaviour pattern resulting in exposure of the region of cuticle above the gland. This may be achieved by depressing the tip of the abdomen, if the gland is in a dorsal intersegmental memebrane, or through eversion of the gland by haemolymph pressure. In this case retraction involves specific retractor muscles.

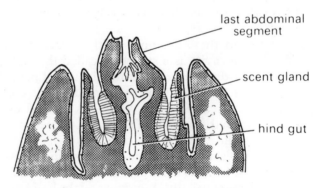

last abdominal segment

scent gland

hind gut

Fig. 566 Horizontal section through the tip of the abdomen of the female *Plodia* showing the integumental scent glands (from Wigglesworth, 1972)

Other insects have glands which underly abdominal sternites or tergites and are not eversible. Termites, for instance, have glands beneath sternites IV or V in which the trail pheromone is produced. Except in Rhinotermitidae these glands have no ducts, the pheromone diffusing through the cuticle. Male cockroaches have glands beneath the tergites of certain abdominal segments which produce an aphrodisiac pheromone (p. 863). The individual gland cells open at the surface of the cuticle through small ducts, sometimes in association with tufts of long setae which possibly assist in dispersal of the pheromone produced by the cells.

Many male Noctuidae produce an aphrodisiac pheromone in special glands, Stobbe's glands, in the second abdominal segment, which is dispersed by a brush of hair-like scales. The gland consists of a number of glandular cells which are greatly enlarged in the pharate adult, each enclosing a large central cavity continuous with the

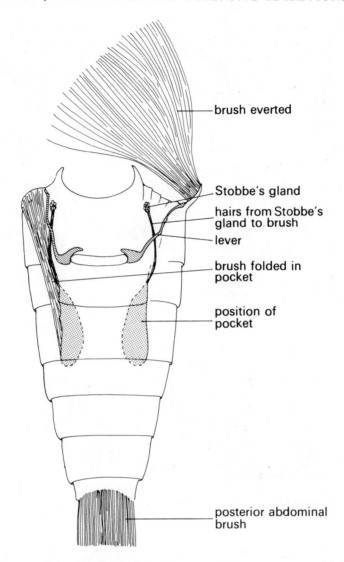

Fig. 567 Diagram of the abdomen of male *Phlogophora* from the ventral surface showing one brush folded in its pocket of cuticle (left) and the other everted (right) (from Birch, 1970)

base of a hair. After emergence of the moth the fluid in the cavity is discharged into the hair, which is tubular and ends at the base of a brush. The brushes, one on each side of the body, consist of a number of hairs mounted on a hinged lever (Fig. 567). Normally they are housed in longitudinal pockets extending back to sternite V; being enclosed in this way limits evaporation of the pheromone. In other species they occur at the tip of the abdomen (Fig. 568). During courtship the brushes are everted by muscular action so that pheromone is dispersed from the hairs. The structure of the hairs is such that evaporation from the distal ends is facilitated. In *Phlogophora* the basal part of each hair

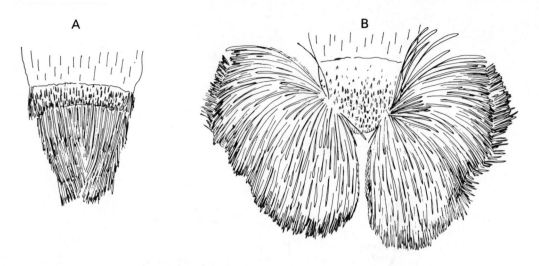

Fig. 568 Diagram of the scent brushes on the tip of the abdomen of male *Spodoptera littoralis*: A, retracted; B, expanded as in courtship (courtesy D. Windsor)

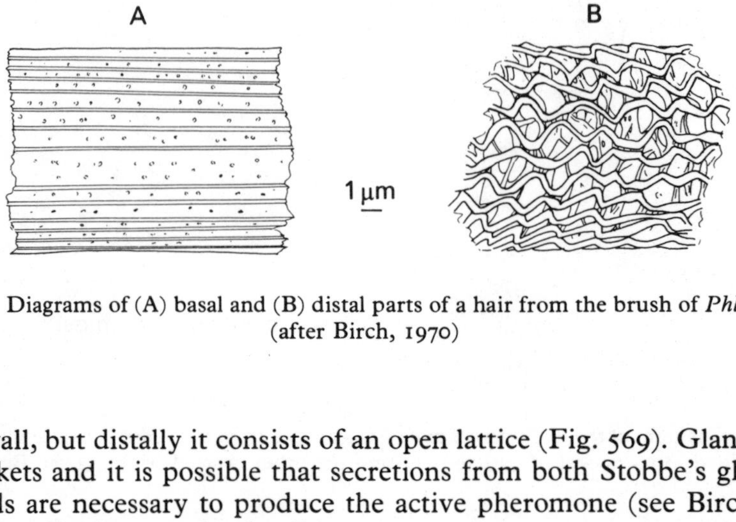

Fig. 569 Diagrams of (A) basal and (B) distal parts of a hair from the brush of *Phlogophora* (after Birch, 1970)

has a solid wall, but distally it consists of an open lattice (Fig. 569). Glands also open into the pockets and it is possible that secretions from both Stobbe's gland and the pocket glands are necessary to produce the active pheromone (see Birch, 1970 and Corbet and Lai-Fook, 1977 for details).

Male Danaidae have similar hairpencils or brushes which can be extended from the tip of the abdomen but they also have a glandular area, sometimes forming a pocket, on the surface of each hindwing. The hairpencils are introduced into the pockets and it has been shown in one species that contacts between hairpencil and pocket are a prerequisite for the biosynthesis of a pheromone component. In danaids the male pheromone is disseminated on minute particles of cuticle, pheromone transfer particles. These are produced in different ways in different species and in *Danaus formosa* they are formed inside the alar pockets, from which they are transferred to the hair pencils. The particles, with the pheromone, are dusted on to the female, including her antennae, during courtship (see Boppré, 1978, for references).

Other male Lepidoptera produce aphrodisiac pheromones from glands associated with scales. These scales, known as androconia, often occur on the wings, as in Pieridae, and they may be either scattered or grouped together. Scent scales often have an elongated form and terminate in a row of process or fimbriae (Fig. 570). Glandular cells in the wing membrane are presumed to connect with the base of the scale, but it is not clear how the scent is discharged from the scale. Bourgogne (1951) says that the products of the glands pass into the cavity of the scale and either diffuse out or pass through small terminal openings in the fimbriae, but Dixey (1932) does not consider that these terminal openings exist. Dickins (1936) is unable to decide whether or not pores are present. Alternatively, the glandular product may simply spread over the surface of the scale (Bourgogne, 1951), presumably from a basal pore. In any case, the effect of the frilled margin of the scale will be to increase the surface area from which evaporation occurs. Comparable scales may occur on the legs or abdomen.

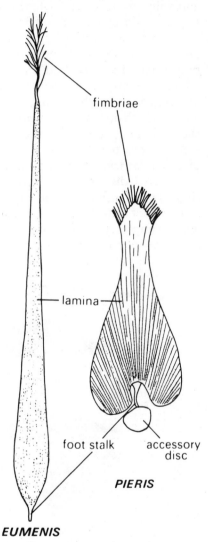

Pheromone glands of Hymenoptera

Honey bees have two important glands producing pheromones: the mandibular glands in the head and Nassanoff's gland in the abdomen.

The mandibular gland is sac-like with an epithelium of secretory cells lined by a thin cuticular intima. The duct from the gland opens at the base of the mandible into a groove which runs into a depression on the inner face of the mandible (Fig. 571). These glands are well developed in the queen and worker, but greatly reduced in the drone. They are present in nearly all Hymenoptera.

Fig. 570 Scent scales from the wings of *Eumenis* (from South, 1941) and *Pieris* (from Imms, 1957)

Nassanoff's gland is beneath the intersegmental membrane between abdominal tergites six and seven (Fig. 572). It is made up of a number of large cells, each of which has a narrow duct leading to the exterior through the cuticle. Normally the gland is concealed beneath tergite six, but it can be exposed by depressing the tip of the abdomen. Nassanoff's gland is well developed in workers but absent from drones, and opinions differ as to whether or not one is present in queens (Snodgrass, 1956).

Ants have mandibular glands similar to *Apis*. Other sources of pheromone are the poison gland and Dufour's gland, both of which are absent in males since they are associated with the sting, and Pavan's gland, which opens on the ventral surface of the abdomen above the sixth abdominal sternite. The poison gland consists of a pair of glandular tubules which unite to form a convoluted duct opening into a reservoir (Fig. 573). Dufour's gland opens into the poison duct near the base of the sting. It is a small, simple sac with thin glandular walls and a delicate muscular sheath.

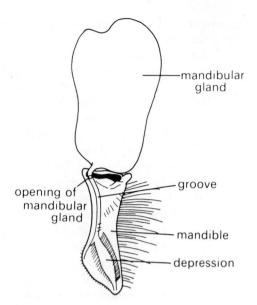

Fig. 571 Inner view of the mandible and mandibular gland of a worker honey bee (after Snodgrass, 1956)

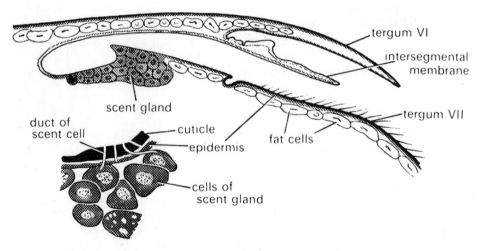

Fig. 572 Longitudinal section through the base of tergum VII of the abdomen of a worker honeybee showing the position of the scent gland. Enlargement showing a group of scent cells and their ducts (after Snodgrass, 1956)

35.3.2 Origins of pheromone chemicals

Pheromones are generally produced *de novo* in the glandular cells, but some instances are known where pheromone production is only possible if appropriate precursors are obtained in the food. This is the case with the aphrodisiac pheromone of male Danaidae (p. 863), and in *Dendroctonus*, where verbenone is considered to be an oxidation

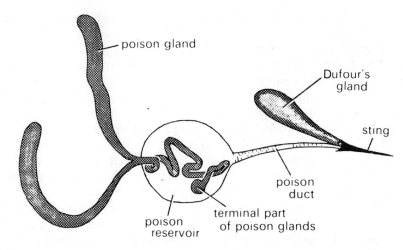

Fig. 573 Poison glands and Dufour's gland of a worker ant (after Wheeler, 1926)

product of pinene from the host tree. In *Reticulitermes* an unsaturated alcohol, *cis*-3, *cis*-6, *trans*-8-dodecatrienol, which occurs in wood infected with the fungus *Lenzites*, is used as a trail pheromone (Moore, 1974).

35.3.3 Pheromones affecting behaviour

Releaser pheromones which affect the behaviour of other members of the species are known to occur in many different insect orders. They are commonly involved in various aspects of sexual behaviour, but also occur in relation to other aspects of behaviour necessitating communication between insects of the same species.

Pheromones as sex attractants

Pheromones are employed by a large number of insects in bringing the sexes together for mating. These pheromones are known as sex attractants. They are widespread amongst the Lepidoptera and are also known to occur in some Dictyoptera, Coleoptera, Hymenoptera and some other orders (Jacobson, 1972). In most cases the pheromone is produced by the female to attract the male, while less frequently a male pheromone attracts the female, or both sexes may be lured by the odour.

Usually the glands in the female producing the sex attractant are between the more posterior segments of the abdomen, and the insect regulates the release of the scent by exposing or covering the glands by movements of the abdomen, or by everting and retracting the glands if they are of the eversible type. The sex attractant pheromone is only released when the surface of the pheromone gland is exposed. The rate of release in *Trichoplusia ni* is about 7 ng/min over a 10-minute period, but is probably higher in the first minute. The gland has no reservoir and the rate of release is governed, initially at least, by the amount of pheromone on the surface of the gland. Normally scent is only released at particular times of day which are characteristic for the species. For instance, males of *Lobesia* (Lepidoptera) are only attracted by the female from about 21.00 hours to midnight, while *Heliothis* (Lepidoptera) males are attracted to the females from

04.00 hours to daylight. Other species, such as *Ephestia*, however, appear to release the pheromone at any time.

Commonly females do not release the pheromone for a day or two after emergence and then they produce it until they are mated. Sometimes, however, the attractant is produced before the female emerges and males of *Megarhyssa* (Hymenoptera) may congregate on the tree trunks occupied by females, waiting for them to emerge. They are attracted by the female pheromone despite the fact that she has not yet emerged from the host in which she pupated. After mating the attractiveness of the female wanes in many species. This is the case in *Bombyx*, for instance, which only mates once, although the precursor of the pheromone is still present in the cells of the glands (Schneider, 1966). In other species, such as *Trichoplusia*, which mate several times the release of pheromone may continue undiminished after mating.

The scent is perceived by olfactory receptors on the antennae of the male and the antennae of many male Lepidoptera which are attracted by scent are strongly pectinate with large numbers of sensilla (Fig. 8C). Stimulation of the antennal sense organs by the female scent produces a characteristic pattern in the output from the antennal nerve even in very low concentrations. The effect of the scent is to excite the male and to promote take-off. In the case of *Trichoplusia ni* and *Bombyx* it has been estimated that a concentration of at least 10 molecules/mm^3 is necessary to produce take off. The insect then flies upwind commonly following a zigzag course with the lateral displacements becoming smaller as the insect approaches the source (Fig. 574). It is most likely that the upwind orientation involves an anemotactic response (Marsh *et al.*, 1978), although Farkas and Shorey (1974) suggest that the insect might be responding to increases in the average odour concentration as it gets closer to the source. It has been calculated, on the basis of pheromone release rates, male response thresholds and molecular dispersion in air, that a male *Trichoplusia ni* might be attracted from a distance of up to 100 m in a wind of 50 cm/s. Much greater distances, sometimes of several kilometres, are quoted in the literature, but it is difficult to assess whether the males are attracted from these distances or if they simply fly upwind and are only attracted by the pheromone when relatively close to the source.

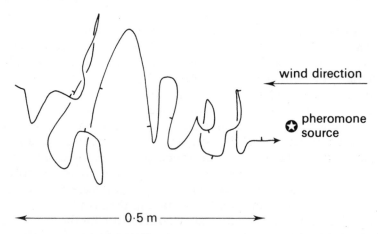

wind direction

pheromone source

0·5 m

Fig. 574 Track of a male *Plodia* flying towards a source of female pheromone in a wind tunnel. Marks on track at 1 s intervals (after Marsh *et al.*, 1978)

Landing is induced by high concentrations of the pheromone, in some cases at least with visual stimuli directing the male over the last few centimetres (Farkas and Shorey, 1974).

There are some instances of males producing sexual attractants. This is true of the beetle *Anthonomus* and of *Harpobittacus* (Mecoptera). In the latter, after the male has caught his prey and started to feed, two vesicles are everted from between the posterior abdominal tergites. These vesicles are expanded and contracted and the scent released in this way attracts the female. On her approach the male copulates with her and presents her with the remains of his prey (Shorey, 1973).

Attraction to a feeding site

The bark beetles, Scolytidae, aggregate in large numbers on host trees selected for attack and many species are known to produce attractant pheromones. Initial invasion is directed by odours from the host plant. In *Dendroctonus*, which is monogamous, the females invade first; in *Ips*, which is polygamous, the males start the attack. When a female *Dendroctonus* bores into the phloem of a host tree she produces a pheromone called *exo*-brevicomin. This is released in the faeces and is attractive to both sexes and so more beetles invade the tree. The males, when they arrive, produce a closely related pheromone, frontalin, which, together with the volatile myrcene from the tree itself, enhances the effect of the *exo*-brevicomin so that more and more beetles arrive at the tree. As the male beetles enter the female galleries they stridulate and this, in addition to causing the females to produce attractant pheromones also results in the release of

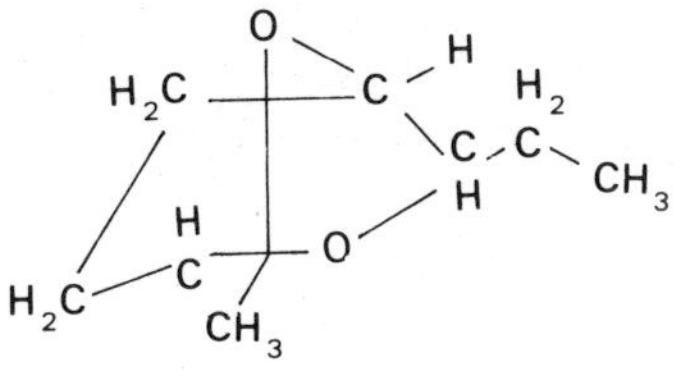

exo-brevicomin

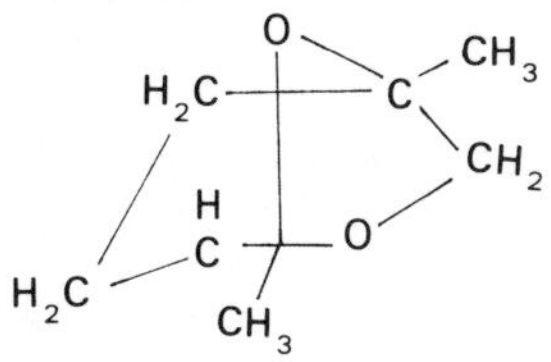

frontalin

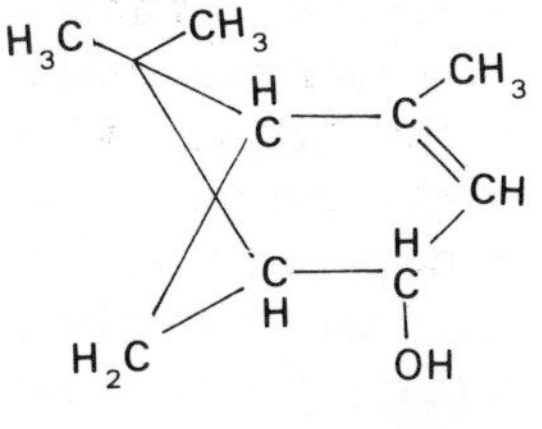

trans-verbenol

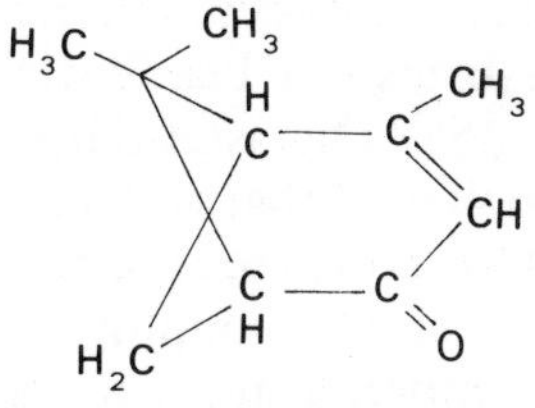

verbenone

pheromones which reduce the attractant response. These 'antiaggregative' pheromones are trans-verbenol, verbenone and others. The female stridulating in response
to the male chirp also promotes pheromone release by the males (Fig. 575) (Rudinsky
and Ryker, 1977; Wood, 1973).

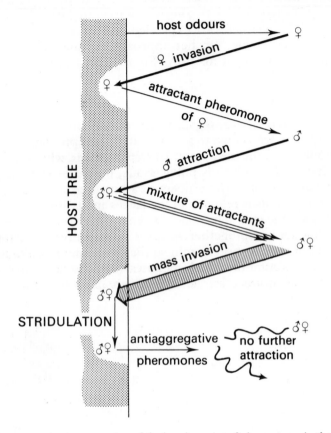

Fig. 575 Diagrammatic representation of the involvement of pheromones in the invasion of a
host tree by *Dendroctonus* (partly after Rudinsky and Ryder, 1977)

Attraction for defence

The male *Lycus loripes* (Coleoptera) emits a scent which attracts other beetles of both
sexes with the result that aggregations are formed on the flowers of the food plant
Melilotus. Mating occurs in these groups, but grouping is important for another reason.
Lycus is a distasteful beetle with a yellow colour which birds learn to avoid (Eisner and
Kafatos, 1962). Distasteful insects with aposematic colouration frequently form groups
and it is believed that as a result of grouping, which makes them more conspicuous,
predators learn to avoid them more quickly and wastage of the population is reduced. In
this case, at least, grouping is promoted by a pheromone. Scent also plays a part in
producing hibernating swarms of Coccinellidae in which mating subsequently occurs
before the insects disperse.

Aphrodisiac pheromones

This term is used with respect to pheromones which facilitate copulation after the two sexes have come together. In Danaidae the males are visually attracted to the females and fly in pursuit. When a male *Danaus gilippus* overtakes a female he extrudes his hair pencils and dusts her with pheromone transfer particles. These carry the pheromone, which stimulate via the olfactory sensilla of the antennae and induce the female to land. The male may then hover over the female, continuing to dust her with pheromone particles, until finally he lands and copulates.

A major component of the pheromone, present in a number of species of Danaidae, is the ketone 6, 7-dihydro-1-methyl-5H-pyrrolizine-7-one, sometimes referred to as danaidone.

Other related compounds may also be present. The production of the pheromone is dependent on the adult male having access to pyrrolizidine alkaloids. Normally the insects are attracted to plants containing these chemicals and after making contact with the plant surface with their antennae they secrete a droplet of fluid and then reimbibe it. In this way they obtain the alkaloid; if they do not have access to such plants they are unable to synthesise the pheromone (Boppré, 1978).

The brushes of male Noctuidae are used in an essentially similar way, being everted just before copulation when courtship is already in progress. The associated release of pheromone is essential for copulation to occur. The pheromones involved are of low molecular weight, commonly volatile terpenoids, or other aromatic compounds, or carboxylic acids (Birch, 1974b), but they are produced in larger quantities than the attractant pheromones produced by females. For instance, the male *Leucania impura* produces more than 5 μg of benzaldehyde from each brush, compared with a total of only 600 ng in the mature gland of a female of *Trichoplusia ni*. In most species more than one chemical has been identified from the brushes.

Other Lepidoptera produce aphrodisiac scents from androconia on the wings. For instance, in *Eumenis semele* the male follows the female visually, and ultimately, if she is a virgin, the female lands. The male has scent scales in a patch on the upper side of the fore wing and courtship is completed by the male standing in front of the female and bowing towards her with the wings partly open so that the female's antennae come into contact with the scent areas (Fig. 576). The female then allows the male to move round and copulate. Males with the scent scales removed have great difficulty in acquiring a mate.

Glands which may produce aphrodisiac scents also occur in various Neuroptera, Trichoptera, Diptera and Hymenoptera, sometimes in the male, sometimes in the female. Some male cockroaches produce a substance from a dorsal abdominal or thoracic gland which is fed on by the female and induces her to mount on the back of the male, so facilitating copulation (p. 363).

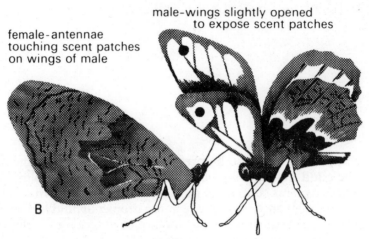

Fig. 576 A. Male *Eumenis semele* showing the position of the scent patches on the upper side of the fore wings. B. Male bowing towards the female during courtship so that the female's antennae touch his scent patches (after South, 1941; Tinbergen, 1951)

Other pheromones affecting behaviour

There is a considerable diversity of pheromones performing different functions in non-social insects and only a few examples can be given.

Females of *Schistocerca* tend to aggregate to lay their eggs and the most powerful stimulus leading to the cohesion of these groups is a pheromone. It is produced by both sexes, whether they are mature or immature and is important mainly as a contact stimulus (Norris, 1963). Female *Culex tarsalis* aggregate at water in which oviposition has occurred previously and as a consequence more eggs tend to be laid in the same place (Osgood, 1971).

An opposite effect, of oviposition being prevented, is known from some parasitic insects. For example, *Telenomus sphingis* is an egg parasite of *Manduca sexta*, but females generally avoid ovipositing in an egg which has already been parasitised. After ovipositing, a female backs over the host egg, twisting her abdomen from side to side so that the moist ovipositor is rubbed across the surface. This activity lasts for about 1·5 minutes and a chemical, presumed to be a pheromone, is left on the surface. A female of *Telenomus* subsequently contacting the egg touches it with her antennae, and commonly goes away without laying an egg. As a result, superparasitism is avoided (Rabb and Bradley, 1970).

The larvae of the flour moth, *Anagasta*, produce a pheromone from their mandibular glands when they encounter other larvae of the same species. This pheromone causes increased wandering, later pupation and ultimately results in smaller pupae. Consequently the moths emerging are also smaller and, since fecundity is proportional to size, fewer eggs are laid and population density is reduced (Corbet, 1971).

Variations in response

Pheromones may exert no effect at all, or may produce different types of behaviour in the recipient in different environmental conditions or in different concentrations. For instance, male moths which are normally nocturnal do not respond to the sex attractant of females in daylight. The trail pheromone of minor workers of *Pheidole* generally leads to recruitment of more minor workers to a food source; relatively few major soldiers are recruited. However, if a minor worker makes contact with an individual of *Solenopsis*, many more major soldiers are recruited as a result of its trail laying and instead of following the trail they rush out with their jaws wide open. This qualitative difference in response is probably produced by the trail pheromone in the presence of the odour of *Solenopsis*, which becomes transferred to the original minor worker (Wilson, 1976).

The sex attractant pheromones of many moths induce upwind flight by the male when they are present in low concentrations; in high concentrations the males attempt to copulate. Citral, which at low concentrations is the major component of the trail pheromone of *Trigona* (p. 871), functions as an alarm pheromone in high concentrations.

Inhibitory pheromones

A number of pheromones are known which mask or inhibit the response to other pheromones produced by the same species. Verbenone, for instance, reduces the response of *Dendroctonus* to its attractant pheromones so that excessive aggregation of insects leading to overcrowding on the host is avoided. Inhibitory pheromones which mask the attractant pheromone are also produced by a number of female moths; in experimental situations their effect is to reduce the effectiveness of attractant pheromone sources (Campion, 1976). The natural role of such inhibitors is not known. In *Spodoptera littoralis cis*-9-tetradecen-1-yl acetate is the inhibitory pheromone, while *cis*-9, *trans*-11-tetradecen-1-yl acetate is the attractant. It is not known if the inhibitors work by competing with the attractant pheromones for receptor sites on the dendrites or if they stimulate different dendrites and the insect responds to the total integrated input.

Specificity of pheromones

The function of pheromones is to produce communication between individuals of a species. It is important that an individual should not divert energy by responding to inappropriate signals from other species, and consequently pheromones should be species specific. Some measure of specificity may result from the ecological separation of species. The spatial separation of *Bombus* scent trails is an example of this (p. 869). However, within a habitat specificity must depend on chemical differences between the pheromones of different species.

The sex attractants of Lepidoptera are not always species specific; they may be group specific. In Saturniidae, for instance, all the species in a genus respond equally well to the attractant of one species. Members of some closely related genera also make a full response, but in others the response is less marked. More distantly related genera make no response at all (Fig. 577). This pattern of responses also occurs in other families (Schneider, 1966).

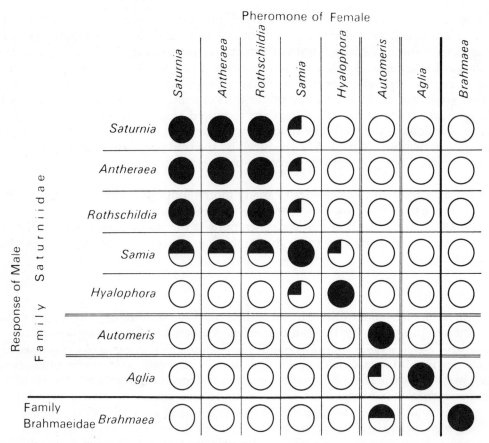

Fig. 577 Diagram to illustrate the specificity of the sex attractants of female Saturniidae, based on the electroantennogram responses of the males. Black disc indicates maximal response to the pheromone of the species indicated; white disc, no response; partially blackened disc, intermediate response (from Schneider, 1966)

The appropriate degree of specificity can only be achieved with relatively large molecules which permit some degree of variation. With a small molecule only a very limited number of variations is possible. At the same time, an essential feature of a sex attractant is that it should be volatile and volatility falls off with molecular weight. Hence molecular size of the sex attractant pheromones will represent a balance between these two opposing requirements, while a limit will also be set by the ability of the insect to synthesise the molecule (Wilson, 1963). All the sex attractant pheromones of Lepidoptera so far known are aliphatic compounds containing from 12 to 21 carbon atoms and the majority are acetates with 14, 16 or 18 carbon atoms and molecular weights between 182 and 308 (Table 12) (Tamaki, 1977). In several cases, as with *cis*-9, *trans*-12-tetradecadienyl acetate, the same compound is produced by a number of different species. However, in such cases it is probable that specificity is achieved by the production of a number of chemicals. Such multicomponent systems are known to occur in a number of species (illustrated by *Diparopsis* in Table 12) and in some cases, at least, the proportions of different chemicals are important. For instance, *Adoxophyes fasciata* and *A. orana* both produce *cis*-9- and *cis*-11-tetradecenyl acetates; males fail to respond to either chemical alone, but are attracted by a mixture. Optimal attraction of *A. fasciata* is obtained with *cis*-9- and *cis*-11-tetradecenyl acetates present in the ratio 60 : 40; *A. ovana* responds optimally to a 90 : 10 mixture (Tamaki, 1977).

Table 12

Chemicals identified as female sex attractant pheromones in some Lepidoptera
(partly after Tamaki, 1977)

Chemical	Formula	Species
trans-10, *cis*-12-hexadecadienol	$CH_3(CH_2)_2CH=CHCH=CH(CH_2)_9OH$	*Bombyx mori*
cis-9-tetradecenal	$CH_3(CH_2)_3CH=CH(CH_2)_7CHO$	*Heliothis virescens*
trans-9-dodecenyl acetate	$CH_3CH_2CH=CH(CH_2)_8OCOCH_3$	
11-dodecenyl acetate	$CH_3(CH_2)_{11}OCOCH_3$	*Diparopsis castanea*
trans-9,11-dodecadienyl acetate	$CH_2=CHCH=CH(CH_2)_8OCOCH_3$	
cis-9, *trans*-12-tetradecadienyl acetate	$CH_3(CH_2)_3CH=CH(CH_2)_8OCOCH_3$	*Anagasta kuehniella* *Cadra cautella* *Plodia interpunctella* *Spodoptera eridania* *Spodoptera littoralis*

Specificity also depends on the sensitivity of the receptors of the receiving individual. Male moths are known to possess receptor neurones in the olfactory sensilla of the antenna which respond to much lower concentrations of key pheromone chemicals than of other closely related compounds or even of stereoisomers. For instance, the male *Trichoplusia* is 2000 times less sensitive to *trans*-7-dodecenyl acetate than it is to the female pheromone *cis*-7-dodecenyl acetate (Table 13, and see p. 745).

The need for specificity will normally counteract any tendency to variability within a species, but such variability does occur. *Ostrinia nubilalis* is widespread in Europe and North America and its sex attractant, 11-tetradecenyl acetate, exists as two geometric isomers. Insects from some parts of Europe respond most readily to one isomer, while those from other areas are most sensitive to the other isomer (Klun *et al.*, 1975).

Table 13

Relative concentrations of female sex attractant and related compounds required to produce a response in male *Trichoplusia*

(from Kaissling, 1971)

Compound	Relative effective concentration
cis-7-dodecenyl acetate (the pheromone)	1
trans-7-dodecenyl acetate	2000
cis-7-dodecenyl propionate	40 000
cis-7-dodecenyl butyrate	40 000
cis-7-tetradecenyl acetate	100 000
cis-9-dodecenyl acetate	100 000
cis-6-dodecenyl acetate	inactive
cis-5-dodecenyl acetate	100 000

35.3.4 Pheromones affecting physiology

Most instances of pheromones affecting physiology are in relation to social insects, but some examples are also known in non-social insects.

Mature male *Schistocerca* accelerate the maturation of other, less mature locusts of either sex. The pheromone responsible for this is produced in the epidermal glands (Loher, 1960). Other individuals may perceive the pheromone either as a scent or by bodily contact, the latter being more effective. The mode of action of the pheromone is not understood, but its effect is to stimulate the activity of the corpora allata. This leads to maturation of the gonads and to some synchronisation of maturation throughout the population (Amerasinghe, 1978).

There is also evidence that immature adult locusts, females less than eight days old for instance, retard maturation in others. A retarding pheromone is suggested, although none has been isolated. This, with the accelerating pheromone, results in the synchronisation of maturation (Norris, 1962).

Both sexes of *Tenebrio* produce a pheromone which accelerates oogenesis in isolated females and also causes them to produce and release more attractant pheromone. The males are more effective than females in inducing these responses (Happ *et al.*, 1970).

35.3.5 Pheromones of social insects

The social insects possess pheromones comparable with those of other insects, but in addition pheromones have particularly important roles in effecting communication between workers and in the maintenance of colony structure. Some selected topics are considered below. Pheromones produced by ants are reviewed by Parry and Morgan (1979).

Sexual attraction

The queen of *Apis mellifera* attracts males by a pheromone, the principal component of which is 9-oxodecenoic acid, produced in the mandibular glands. In the absence of stimulation the males fly about randomly, but when stimulated by the attractant they fly upwind to the vicinity of its source, the queen. This attraction only occurs from 20–

30 metres (Butler, 1964a) and when the queen is more than 15 feet above the ground; below this males are not attracted to her. Having arrived close to the queen as a result of her scent, the final approach is probably visual. Sometimes males overshoot the queen on their upwind flight. In this case they fly on for 20–30 feet and then fly round at random with the result that they may soon reappear on the lee side of the queen and are able to reorientate to her.

It is possible that sexual attraction in *Bombus* involves pheromones, but here it takes a different form from that recorded in other insects. In *B. terrestris*, for instance, the male has a definite circuit round which he continually flies (Free and Butler, 1959). At intervals the route is marked by a scent produced in the mandibular glands. This is applied by the bee, which grasps the object to be marked in the mandibles and gnaws at its surface. Marking is carried out once in the morning and the scent then persists for the rest of the day while the male flies round the circuit. Each time he comes to a marked point he hovers for a short period before flying on to the next point. Females are said to be attracted by the scent so that they fly into the region of the circuit and the frequent passage of the male ensures that he will meet any female arriving (but see Butler, 1967).

The lengths of such circuits vary, and larger, stronger bees tend to have longer circuits. One recorded circuit of *B. terrestris* was 275 m long with 27 visiting places. The male flew round this circuit 35 times in 90 minutes. The same circuit is retained on successive days, but in the morning when the route is re-marked some previous stopping points may be omitted and new ones included. The circuits of different males of the same species may overlap so that several males may use one marked stopping point.

The scents used to mark these circuits are species specific and this specificity is enhanced by the tendency of different species to fly at different heights. *B. lapidarius* makes its circuit at tree-top level, *B. agrorum* about six feet above the ground and *B. terrestris* two to three feet above the ground. Comparable scent routes are also made by male *Psithyrus* and *Anthophora*.

Trail following

Most social insects lay trails which facilitate food-finding by other members of the colony. The persistence of such trails depends on the number of individuals depositing the pheromone, the nature of the pheromone and the substrate on which it is laid, as well as the prevailing environmental conditions. The trail laid by a single individual is relatively short-lived and it is by constant reinforcement that more persistent trails are produced (see below).

Probably all termites produce a trail pheromone from a gland on the ventral surface of the abdomen. In most species the pheromone is produced continuously so that a drop is deposited each time the abdomen touches the surface. In a number of instances a constituent of the food forms one component of the pheromone system (p. 859) and specificity is probably achieved through the presence of minor constituents of greater volatility (Moore, 1974).

Ants lay scent trails by which they are able to find their way about. The scent is produced in Dufour's gland or the poison gland in Myrmicinae, from Pavan's gland in Dolichoderinae, and from the hind gut in Ponerinae, Dorylinae and Formicinae. Hence it may be dispensed via the sting, the edge of abdominal sternite 6, or the anus. *Crematogaster* is unusual in having glands on the metathoracic tibiae which open proximally to the unguitractor plate of the pretarsus. In this genus the pheromone is applied to the substratum by the tarsi.

In most ants the trail initially consists of a series of scent spots produced by a worker ant touching the ground with its abdomen as it runs along. In *Solenopsis* these spots are not visible, but in *Lasius fuliginosus* visible drops of fluid are deposited. Subsequently, if the trail is used by many ants, the spots which they produce may merge into a continuous streak.

Some trails are concerned in exploration, others in the recruitment of workers to a source of food. Exploratory trails are produced by army ants (Ponerinae, Dorylinae) and are laid more or less continuously by the blind workers as they forage. These species do not have permanent nests, but form temporary bivouacs from which they forage in columns. The scent trail laid by the individual is insignificant, but the accumulated trail of a whole column of ants is considerable and may last for several weeks in dry conditions. By means of the trails foragers are able to find their way back to the bivouac with food and it is also suggested that the male after its initial flight is able to to find a trail and follow it to a bivouac where the new queens, which in these species are wingless, occur.

Recruitment trails are only laid by workers returning to the nest after finding a source of food or a more suitable nest site. These trails are laid by some members of the Myrmicinae, Dolichoderinae and Formicinae and, unlike the exploratory trails of army ants, are ephemeral, depending on constant use for their maintenance.

If a worker of *Solenopsis* finds food which it cannot carry, it returns to the nest laying a trail (Wilson, 1962). On encountering a fellow worker it rushes towards the second ant and may briefly climb on it, apparently bringing the trail substance to its attention. Such recruited workers follow the trail, usually back towards the food, although directions to and from the nest are not indicated by the trail and workers may follow it in either direction. If the food is within 50 cm of the nest the recruited workers may reach it, but if it is at a greater distance the first laid parts of the trail may have evaporated before the workers get to the end (Fig. 578). Feeding elicits trail laying, so any recruits which do reach the food deposit pheromone on their way back to the nest and the original trail is reinforced. The pheromone itself is sufficient to elicit the following response in other workers and so if the food is close to the nest a rapid build up of foragers at the feeding site occurs. As the food supply diminishes fewer workers lay trails as they return to the nest, less recruits are obtained and finally the trail fades out altogether.

At greater distances, although part of the initial trail evaporates, workers reaching the end of the trail continue searching and many rediscover the food. In this way a series of tracks are laid which, as more and more foragers are attracted, build up into a definite trail. Thus trails to more distant food depend on numbers of workers for their establishment because of the volatility of the pheromone. Related to this it is found that the distance foraged depends on the number of workers available; large colonies are able to find food more rapidly and at greater distances than small ones and there is a maximum distance beyond which a colony of a given size will not be able to produce a lasting trail.

Workers of *Solenopsis* often excavate along their trails and form irregular roofs over

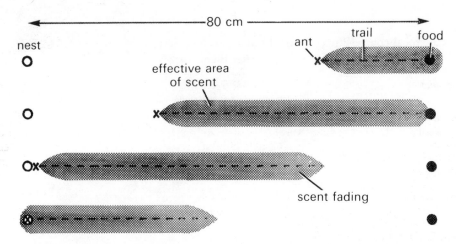

Fig. 578 Diagrammatic representations at successive time intervals of an ant laying a trail from a food source to the nest. The effective area of the scent is the area over which the scent is attractive to other ants (after Wilson, 1963)

them so that trails to old food finds may be maintained over long periods. In this way the foraging field of a colony may be enlarged.

The chemicals used by ants in making trails have been identified in a few species. In *Atta*, where the chemicals come from the poison gland, the pheromone contains volatile and non-volatile components; the volatile component is methyl 4-methylpyrrole-2-carboxylate (Tumlinson *et al.*, 1971). Where trail pheromones are produced in poison glands they constitute only a minor fraction of the venom, which is composed principally of proteins and amino acids (Blum, 1974). The trail pheromone of *Lasius* is produced in the hindgut and it contains a range of organic acids from hexanoic to dodecanoic acid as well as other substances in small amounts (Huwyler *et al.*, 1975).

Chemical trails are also utilised by some bees, though here the trail is followed in flight. Males of *Bombus* follow a discontinuous trail when ready to mate (p. 869), but in the stingless bees of the genus *Trigona* this type of trail is used to mark the route to a food source. A worker bee who has located a suitable food source marks it by biting and depositing the pheromone from the mandibular glands. Further odour spots are made at intervals of 1–5 m back to the nest and recruited workers follow the succession of odour spots to the food source (Blum *et al.*, 1970). Citral constitutes 95% of the pheromone from the mandibular glands of *T. subterranea*, but in some other species alcohols and ketones are amongst the major constituents (Blum, 1974).

The importance of chemical mixtures in conferring specificity on the signals provided by pheromones is illustrated by members of this genus. *Trigona postica* is unable to follow the trails of either *T. spinipes* or *T. xanthotricha*, but *T. xanthotricha* can follow the trail of *T. postica*. All these species produce 2-heptanol as a major component of the trail pheromone, but in *T. spinipes* there are only three known components compared with at least ten in the other two (Table 14). The differences in complexity may prevent confusion of the *T. spinipes* trail with those of other species, while quantitative differences in specific components presumably facilitate differentiation of the trails of *T. postica* and *T. xanthotricha* (Blum, 1974).

Table 14

Chemical composition of mandibular gland secretions of three species of *Trigona*
(after Blum, 1974)

Compound	Species		
	T. postica	*T. xanthotricha*	*T. spinipes*
2-heptanone	+ +	+ +	−
2-heptanol	+ + +	+ +	+ +
2-nonanone	+	−	−
2-nonanol	−	+	+
2-undecanone	+	+	−
2-undecanol	+	−	−
2-tridecanone	+ + +	+ + +	−
2-tridecanol	+	+ +	+
2-pentadecanone	+ +	+ +	−
2-pentadecanol	+	−	−
2-heptadecanone	+	−	−
2-heptadecanol	+	−	−
tetradecenyl acetate	+ + +	+	−
hexadecenyl acetate	+ + +	+ + +	−
benzaldehyde	+ +	+ +	−

+ indicates present, − absent

Alarm pheromones

Alarm pheromones are produced when a social insect is threatened in some way. The
response varies according to the species, but commonly involves attraction of other
workers or soldiers and the adoption of aggressive postures with the head raised and
jaws wide apart. Alarm pheromones are highly volatile and so they are quickly
dissipated; if this was not the case colonies might be in an almost continually disturbed
state. Sometimes the pheromone also functions as a defensive substance. This is the
case with the formic acid produced by *Formica*, but in most cases defensive substances
and pheromones are quite different.

When the termite *Drepanotermes* is disturbed it makes oscillatory movements
with its abdomen and at the same time releases limonene from its cephalic gland.
This causes a brief period of biting activity by other soldiers. The frontal gland
secretion in *Trinervitermes* serves as an alarm pheromone as well as for defence
(p. 878).

In ants the secretions of the mandibular glands are the principal alarm pheromones,
though secretions from other glands may function in the same way. Colony defence in
Oecophylla is undertaken by the major workers. The secretions from their mandibular
glands contain at least 33 components with hexanal, 1-hexanol and 2-butyl-2-octenal
as major fractions. It appears that these different components produce a sequence of
activity in a recipient soldier. Hexanal is the most volatile, so that the area over which it
spreads rapidly increases in size. It alerts other soldiers, who raise their heads and open
their jaws. Hexanol is rather less volatile and spreads more slowly; at low concentrations it stimulates movement towards the site of release. The third component,
2-butyl-2-octenal is only effective over a short distance and it, probably with some of
the minor components, induces biting (Fig. 579) (Bradshaw *et al.*, 1975). Ketones and

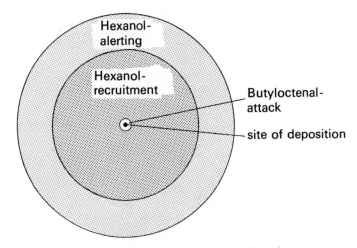

Fig. 579 Active spaces of mandibular gland pheromone components following their deposition by a major worker of *Oecophylla* (after Bradshaw *et al.*, 1975)

aldehydes are common components of ant alarm pheromones, but in members of the subfamily Ponerinae some quite different compounds occur (Table 15). The response of *Ponera* to its alarm pheromone, 2,5-dimethyl-3-isopentylpyrazine, is unlike that of other ants since the insects disperse rather than adopting an aggressive stance (Duffield *et al.*, 1976).

Table 15

Some chemicals functioning as alarm pheromones in ants
(partly after Blum, 1974)

Subfamily	Genus	Chemical	Chemical Class
Dolichoderinae	Iridomyrmex	2-heptanone	ketone
	Dolichoderus	4-methyl-2-hexanone	,,
	Tapinoma	6-methyl-5-heptene-2-one	,,
		2-methyl-4-heptanone	,,
Myrmicinae	Manica	4-methyl-3-hexanone	,,
		3-decanone	,,
		4,6-dimethyl-4-octen-3-one	,,
	Myrmica	3-octanone	,,
	Crematogaster	6-methyl-3-octanone	,,
		2-hexenal	aldehyde
Formicinae	Acanthomyops	citronellal	,, (monoterpene)
		citral	,, (,,)
		n-undecane	alkane
	Formica	formic acid	carboxylic acid
	Camponotus	*n*-decane	alkane
		n-dodecane	,,
Ponerinae	Paltothyreus	dimethyldisulphide	organic sulphide
		dimethyltrisulphide	,, ,,
	Odontomachus	2,5-dimethyl-3-isopentylpyrazine	nitrogen heterocyclic compound
		2,6-dimethyl-3-*n*-pentylpyrazine	,, ,, ,,
		2,6-dimethyl-3-*n*-butylpyrazine	,, ,, ,,
	Ponera	2,5-dimethyl-3-isopentylpyrazine	,, ,, ,,

The alarm pheromone of the bee *Trigona* is also produced by the mandibular glands. At least some of the chemicals which are used in trail laying also function in producing alarm, the nature of the response depending on the situation. An alarm pheromone is produced in the mandibular glands of *Apis*, and another is released via the sting chamber. Guard bees at the entrance to a hive use this to mark intruders and to stimulate aggressive activity by other bees.

Maintenance of colony structure

The differentiation of castes in termites appears to be regulated by a series of pheromones, although the pheromones have yet to be isolated. Most work has been carried out on *Kalotermes* (p. 835) (Lüscher, 1961).

Regulation in the numbers of a particular caste is brought about by the production and elimination of members of the caste concerned. For instance, in the absence of the king and queen, replacement reproductives are produced within a week. Usually an excess of replacements is produced and these are eaten by the pseudergates so as to leave only one pair. All this is believed to be controlled by pheromones produced by the reproductives.

Normally a queen *Kalotermes* produces a substance which inhibits the further development of female pseudergates (Fig. 580A). In the absence of this substance any female pseudergates that are competent to do so become replacement reproductives (p. 835). The male produces a comparable pheromone which inhibits the development of male pseudergates (Fig. 580B) and the production of this pheromone is stimulated in some unknown manner by the presence of the queen (Fig. 580C). The production of inhibitor by the queen is stimulated by the male to a lesser extent (Fig. 580D). These inhibitory pheromones are produced in the head or thorax and then pass via the alimentary canal to the anus. They are picked up by some pseudergates as a result of proctodaeal feeding and then passed on to others during mutual feeding. If a female pseudergate receives the female inhibiting substance it is believed that this is absorbed, but if she receives male inhibiting substance this is passed on unchanged to other members of the colony (Fig. 580E). Conversely males absorb male inhibiting substance, but merely serve to distribute the female inhibitor (Fig. 580F). This is important because the pheromones, as in the bees, are only active for a short time and so must be continually circulating round the colony in order to prevent the development of replacement reproductives.

The male produces a further substance which, in the absence of the female inhibitor, stimulates the production of females (Fig. 580G). If a comparable substance is produced by the queen it is very weak. Finally, the behaviour of the pseudergates is affected by other pheromones which lead the insects to eat any excess replacement reproductives which may be produced. The male produces a substance leading to the elimination of excess males (Fig. 580H), the female one leading to the elimination of excess females (Fig. 580J). These pheromones are possibly secreted through the cuticle and stimulate the pseudergates via their antennae. As a result of this complex of substances the colony is maintained with one male and one female reproductive.

The production of soldiers is probably controlled in a similar way. This is suggested by observations on colony structure. In large colonies of *Kalotermes* there are, on the average, three soldiers for every 100 individuals in the colony. If soldiers are removed others develop in their place. Conversely when a colony is producing alates the number

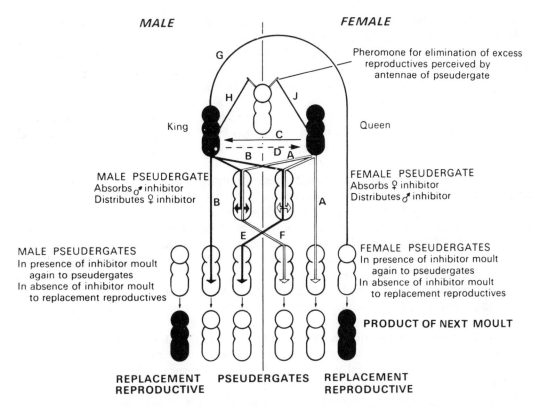

Fig. 580 Tentative representation of pheromone actions controlling the production and elimination of replacement reproductives in *Kalotermes*. Reproductives are shown in black, pseudergates in white. For explanation of the lettering see text (after Lüscher, 1961)

of individuals and hence the number of soldiers increases, but when the alates swarm the population of the colony suddenly decreases leaving an excess of soldiers. The excess is eliminated, being eaten by the pseudergates.

The pheromones in some way act on the nervous system, which in turn produces changes in the endocrine system leading to moulting and differentiation (p. 835).

The queen honey bee produces several pheromones which play a part in controlling the social structure of her colony. If a queen is removed from a colony her absence is very soon perceived by the workers, who become restless within about 30 minutes of her removal. A few hours later they start to build emergency queen cells, worker cells which are enlarged and reshaped so that the larvae within them can, with appropriate feeding, develop into queens. In the presence of the queen this behaviour is inhibited by a pheromone, known as queen substance, produced in her mandibular glands. The major component of the queen substance is 9-oxodecenoic acid, which is also the principal component of the sex attractant (p. 868). As with the termites, it is essential for the pheromone to be continually circulated round the colony in order to inhibit emergency queen-cell building and again mutual feeding amongst the workers is involved. From the mandibular glands the pheromone becomes distributed over the whole body of the queen and is licked off by the workers. Mutual feeding is a common occurrence in *Apis* colonies, but workers who have recently licked the queen are even more ready to offer food to other workers than is usually the case. As a result the substance is very quickly distributed round the colony.

Emergency queen-cell production is also inhibited by a volatile scent which acts with 9-oxodecenoic acid. The combined effect of the two substances in experiments is still less than that of a live queen, so in all probability at least one other inhibiting substance is involved.

Young virgin queens are unable to inhibit queen rearing. At first they produce no 9-oxodecenoic acid, but even after the first week, when this substance is formed, inhibition is poor, probably due to the absence of the inhibiting scent (Butler and Paton, 1962).

Queen rearing may take place in colonies with mature queens if the workers do not receive sufficient inhibitor. This can occur in two ways: the output of pheromone by an ageing queen may be reduced or, alternatively, if a colony becomes very large and crowded the distribution of the pheromone may become inefficient so that some workers do not receive an adequate amount. In either case queen cells may be built and queen rearing follows. Such behaviour will result in the development of more queens and subsequently in the supersedure of the existing queen by one of the new ones, or in a part of the colony leaving the hive as a swarm. In a small colony whether supersedure or swarming occurs depends, at least to some extent, on the prevailing environmental conditions.

In the absence of the queen the ovaries of some of the workers develop, this depending in part also on adequate amounts of protein and carbohydrate in the diet. Ovary development is normally inhibited by the pheromones inhibiting queen-cell building, but in this case scent is less effective.

Another pheromone produced by the mandibular glands is 9-hydroxydecenoic acid. This is a scent which is attractive to workers and plays a part in the maintenance of swarm clusters (Gary, 1974).

In ants there is some evidence for a substance comparable with queen substance since, at least in *Formica pratensis* and *Myrmica rubra*, the queen inhibits queen production.

On the other hand, the failure of worker ovaries to develop in bumblebees, wasps and some other ants is apparently not due to pheromones. It is possible that the insect with the best developed ovaries, normally the queen, so harrasses the others that development of their ovaries is retarded (Butler, 1964b).

35.3.6 Adverse effects of pheromones

Pheromones may serve to advertise the presence of an insect to another individual of the same species; they may also advertise the insect to potential parasites and predators and a few cases are known of such insects which respond to host pheromones. The clerid beetle, *Thanasimus dubius*, is a predator of *Dendroctonus*. It locates its host by responding to the pheromone frontalin, so that large numbers of predators arrive at a tree at the same time as the *Dendroctonus*. The response also brings the sexes together so that mating is facilitated (Vité and Williamson, 1970).

The pheromone produced by larvae of *Anagasta* induces the parasite *Venturia* to make probing movements with its ovipositor and so the chances of a larva being parasitised are increased (Corbet, 1971).

35.4 Defensive secretions

35.4.1 Structure of defence glands

Defence glands in general differ from pheromone glands in the possession of a reservoir in which the defensive material is stored for use, because the quantities of chemicals involved are much greater than those employed as pheromones. Most defence glands develop as invaginations of the epidermis and are lined by cuticle, the obvious exception being salivary glands which produce defensive substances. The glands can be grouped into those which are not everted, but from which the defensive chemicals are expelled more or less forcibly, and those which can be everted and from which the defensive material diffuses away or is effective only on contact.

In most cases of non-eversible glands which have been described, type 3 gland cells secrete directly into a reservoir which is lined by cuticle (Fig. 581). The opening of the reservoir is closed by the elasticity of the surrounding cuticle and fluid is forced out either by the contraction of a layer of muscles surrounding the epithelium of the gland, as in the stick insect *Extatosoma* (Strong, 1975), or by pressure developed by contraction of muscles of the body wall acting on the gland via the haemolymph, as in some beetles (D. A. Kendall, 1974). The metathoracic glands of the waterbug *Ilyocoris* are more complex, with a pair of tubular glands opening into a median reservoir formed from non-glandular epithelial cells. The reservoir discharges laterally on the metathoracic segment via a pair of channels in the cuticle (Staddon and Thorne, 1973).

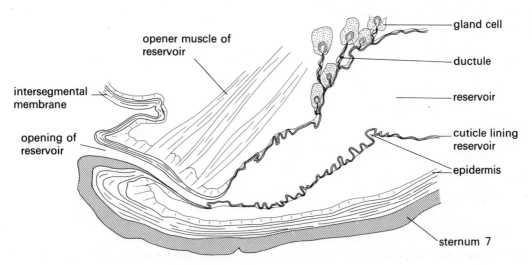

Fig. 581 Longitudinal section through part of the reservoir of the defensive gland in the abdomen of *Tribolium*, showing the opening at the posterior end of sternite 7 (after D. A. Kendall, 1974)

Eversible defensive glands are described from only a few species, the osmeterium of *Papilio* larvae being an example. The whole structure is normally completely inverted within the body, just behind the head, but when the larva is disturbed the osmeterium is everted by haemolymph pressure. It consists of two tubular arms lined by epidermis which, near the base of each arm, forms a glandular area of about 300 type 1 gland cells.

The cuticle above the gland cells is modified, apparently to facilitate the outward movement of secretions, while over most of the osmeterium it is produced into numerous papillae. The glands have no discrete reservoir (Crossley and Waterhouse, 1969). Some grasshoppers, such as *Acrotylus*, have glands which are everted from behind the pronotum (Uvarov, 1966).

35.4.2 Distribution of defence glands

Defence glands are known to occur in many orders of insects and occur on virtually all parts of the body. A few examples are given to illustrate this variety. The soldiers of some Termitidae have the salivary glands modified for defence, the reservoir occupying the front half of the abdomen, with the secretion being ejected from the mouth as a result of abdominal contraction (Noirot, 1969). Many termites also have a frontal gland in the head which discharges its secretion through a median anterior pore. The gland is well-developed in major soldiers of *Macrotermes subhyalinus* (Prestwich *et al.*, 1977), and in Nasutitermitinae the front of the head forms a rostrum with the gland opening at the tip (Fig. 582).

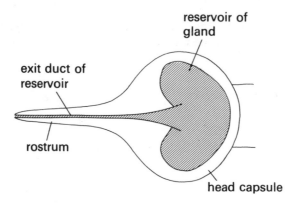

Fig. 582 Dorsal view of the head of a soldier *Trinervitermes* showing the frontal gland (after Noirot, 1969)

Some stick insects have glands opening on the thorax just behind the head (Strong, 1975), while in the bug *Ilyocoris* the gland opens ventrally on the metathorax. Some grasshoppers of the family Pyrgomorphidae have a gland which opens dorsally between the first and second abdominal tergites (Uvarov, 1966), and many beetles belonging to the families Tenebrionidae and Nilionidae have a pair of glands opening on the posterior border of abdominal sternite 7 (D. A. Kendall, 1974). The defensive secretions of bombardier beetles are produced in glands which open at the tip of the abdomen (Eisner *et al.*, 1977).

35.4.3 Chemicals used in defence

Many chemicals which are repellent or toxic to other organisms have been isolated from insects (Schildknecht, 1977; Weatherstone and Percy, 1970) and in some instances their use as defensive substances has been confirmed. In most instances the chemicals are secreted in the form which has a directly adverse effect on potential parasites or predators, but in some cases a chemical reaction occurs at the time of release to produce the active principle.

Volatile terpenoids are produced by many social insects for defence, a mixture of chemicals being secreted, as is commonly the case also with many alarm pheromones. In major soldiers of *Trinervitermes* the secretion of the frontal gland constitutes 8 % of the body weight with 250 μg of diterpenes and 65 μg of monoterpenes. α-pinene is the most abundant monoterpene, while in the minor soldier β-pinene and camphene are also present in large amounts (Prestwich, 1977). The phasmid *Anisomorpha* produces the terpene dialdehyde anisomorphal as a defensive spray. The secretions from the prothoracic defensive glands of the water beetle *Ilybius* contain a range of sesquiterpenes, such as γ-muurolene and δ-cadmene, and steroids as well as alkaloids. Sesquiterpenes and steroids are also found in other water beetles (Schildknecht, 1977).

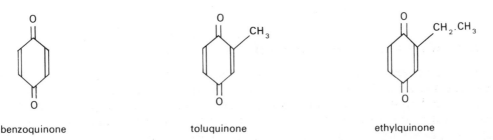

γ-muurolene δ-cadmene

Quinones are employed by other insects. *Odontotermes* employs a secretion which includes both benzoquinone and protein from the salivary gland reservoir. The contents of this reservoir when it is full make up 10 % of the body weight of the soldier termite (Wood *et al.*, 1975). In tenebrionids the supposed defensive secretions are complex mixtures of quinones often with other compounds, particularly 1-alkanes. Toluquinone and ethylquinone are produced by all the species examined, but vary in their relative proportions in different species (Tschinkel, 1975). Bombardier beetles from various subfamilies produce a quinonoid spray which is generated from hydroquinones (see below).

benzoquinone   toluquinone   ethylquinone

Phenolic compounds are produced by the pygidial glands of water beetles. The pygidial glands of *Platambus* produce *p*-hydroxybenzaldehyde, benzoic acid, *p*-hydroxybenzoic-acid-methyl-ester and hydroquinone (Schildknecht, 1977), while the scent glands of the water bug *Ilyocoris* contain *p*-hydroxybenzaldehyde and methyl-*p*-hydroxybenzoate.

p-hydroxybenzaldehyde   benzoic acid

In addition to these major classes of substances which are commonly identified in supposed defensive secretions, there is a variety of chemicals belonging to other chemical classes. The main components of the defensive secretion of workers of *Macrotermes subhyalinus* are hydrocarbons (Table 16) (Prestwich *et al.*, 1977), while in *Poekilocerus* cardiac glycosides form a significant component of the secretion.

Table 16

Major components of the frontal gland secretion of
Macrotermes subhyalinus
(after Prestwich *et al.*, 1977)

Component	Relative abundance (%)
n-tricosane	4·5
n-tetracosane	0·6
n-pentacosane	9·2
pentacosene	0·5
3- and 5-methylpentacosane	3·8
hexacosene	0·6
n-heptacosane	1·0
9-heptacosene	22·0
3-,5- and 7-methylheptacosane	11·0
9-octacosene	1·8
9-nonacosene	40·0
9-hentriacontene	5·0

35.4.4 Synthesis of defence chemicals

In most cases defensive chemicals are presumably synthesised *de novo* by the insect, but these substances may be toxic to the producers themselves and there is some evidence that their final production occurs extracellularly. For instance, the quinones produced by tenebrionids are probably derived from phenol glucosides by hydrolysis followed by oxidation. Happ (1968) suggests that these processes take place in the end-apparatus of the cell, which is extracellular. Consequently the cytoplasm is never exposed to the toxin. In this case the precursor and enzymes are all produced by the same cell.

An extreme example of the extracellular production of the active component occurs in the bombardier beetles. Quinones are generated explosively by the oxidation of hydroquinones so that they are ejected as a spray through the openings of the pygidial glands. The hydroquinones are stored with hydrogen peroxide in the glands, but at the moment of discharge these chemicals are mixed with catalases and peroxidases from an accessory chamber. This causes the sudden decomposition of the hydrogen peroxide and oxidation of the hydroquinones so that the quinones are forcibly ejected with an audible explosion and the generation of temperatures up to 100°C (Schildknecht, 1977). The same basic reaction occurs in beetles belonging to several different tribes (Eisner *et al.*, 1977).

As with some pheromones, the production of some defensive chemicals is dependant on their availability in the diet. Thus although *Poekilocerus* has the capacity to synthesise cardiac glycosides and secrete them into the dorsal defence gland, these are commonly derived directly from its foodplant *Calotropis* (Rothschild, 1973). Many insects sequester plant toxins, which have a protective role when associated with aposematic coloration; the chemicals are not secreted as defence chemicals, but are usually retained within the body and so they are effective only when the insect is tasted by a predator. In a few cases, however, the chemicals are separated from the food during ingestion and are subsequently used to repel attackers. Larvae of *Perga* feed on *Eucalyptus*. On the ventral side of the foregut they have a diverticulum in which *Eucalyptus* oils are sequestered; very little oil reaches the midgut and in the last instar larva the full gland may make up 20 % of the body weight. The oils are discharged if the larva is attacked and both birds and ants are repelled by them (Morrow *et al.*, 1976). Similar adaptations occur in larvae of *Neodiprion* feeding on *Pinus* (Eisner *et al.*, 1974) and in larvae of *Myrascia* (Lepidoptera) feeding on Myrtaceae (Common and Bellas, 1977).

35.4.5 Functions of defensive chemicals

Only in a few cases have functions of presumed defensive chemicals been proved by observation and experiment. The main functions are the incapacitation of potential parasites or predators, repulsion of potential parasites or predators, and protection against micro-organisms.

Enemies may be incapacitated by the physical nature of some secretions. The secretion of the frontal glands of nasute termites hardens to a sticky thread in air. It is ejected on contact with predators such as ants, but then its irritant action, which results from the presence of α- and β-pinene, causes the ant to preen and so the entangling material is spread even more. Some compounds of the secretion also act as an alarm pheromone attracting other soldiers from up to 30 cm away (Eisner *et al.*, 1976). The ants may die if they are unable to free themselves of the sticky substance. In *Macrotermes subhyalinus*, on the other hand, the secretion from the frontal glands of the soldiers apparently kills ants by preventing wound healing following a bite. The oily secretion in this case oozes from the gland and coats the surface of the head of the termite so that it is transferred to the enemy during combat (Prestwich *et al.*, 1977).

Repellent effects are recorded in a number of insects. *Anisomorpha* directs the spray from its thoracic glands at enemies. Predatory ants and beetles elicit this response if they bite any part of the stick insect; blue jays, on the other hand, are sprayed before they touch the insect and a single experience of the spray is sufficient for a bird to learn to avoid the insect subsequently. An adult female *Anisomorpha* can produce up to five discharges in a short time, but it then takes up to 15 days for the store of deterrent to be replenished; when its store is depleted it is susceptible to attack (Eisner, 1965). *Poekilocerus* secretions, which can be ejected for up to 40 cm, are also effective in repelling vertebrate predators. In this insect, too, the store of repellent is exhausted after about five expulsions (Abushama, 1972; Qureshi and Ahmad, 1970). *Neodiprion* larvae emit a drop of fluid from the foregut reservoir when attacked. The fluid remains on the mouthparts and repels ants and birds; the vapour also has some effect at a distance (Eisner *et al.*, 1974).

It is suggested that the phenolics from the metathoracic gland of *Ilyocoris* and the quinones of tenebrionids have an antibiotic function (Staddon and Thorne, 1973; Tschinkel, 1975).

The defensive functions of haemolymph and of venoms injected by stinging are considered on pages 815 and 34.

REFERENCES

ABUSHAMA, F. T. E. (1972). The repugnatorial gland of the grasshopper *Poecilocerus hieroglyphicus* (Klug). *J. Ent.* A, **47**: 95–100.

AMERASINGHE, F. P. (1978). Pheromonal effects on sexual maturation, yellowing, and the vibration reaction in immature male desert locusts (*Schistocerca gregaria*). *J. Insect Physiol.* **24**: 309–314.

BIRCH, M. C. (1970). Structure and function of the pheromone-producing brush-organs in males of *Phlogophora meticulosa* (L.) (Lepidoptera: Noctuidae). *Trans. R. ent. Soc. Lond.* **122**: 277–292.

BIRCH, M. C. (ed.) (1974a). *Pheromones*. North-Holland Publishing Co., Amsterdam.

BIRCH, M. C. (1974b). Aphrodisiac pheromones in insects. *in* Birch, M. C., (ed.), *Pheromones*. North-Holland Publishing Co., Amsterdam.

BLUM, M. S. (1974). Pheromonal sociality in the Hymenoptera. *in* Birch, M. C. (ed.), *Pheromones*. North-Holland Publishing Co., Amsterdam.

BLUM, M. S., CREWE, R. M., KERR, W. E., KEITH, L. H., GARRISON, A. W. and WALKER, M. M. (1970). Citral in stingless bees: isolation and functions in trail-laying and robbing. *J. Insect Physiol.* **16**: 1637–1648.

BOPPRÉ, M. (1978). Chemical communication, plant relationships, and mimicry in the evolution of danaid butterflies. *Entomologia exp. appl.* **24**: 264–277.

BOURGOGNE, J. (1951). Ordre des Lépidoptères. *in* Grassé, P.-P. (ed.), *Traité de Zoologie*. vol. 10. Masson et Cie, Paris.

BRADSHAW, J. W. S., BAKER, R. and HOWSE, P. E. (1975). Multicomponent alarm pheromones of the weaver ant. *Nature, Lond.* **258**: 230–231.

BUTLER, C. G. (1964a). Recent work on the swarm cluster and on the behaviour of honeybee drones in the field. *Proc. R. ent. Soc. Lond.* C, **29**: 12–13.

BUTLER, C. G. (1964b). Pheromones in sexual processes in insects. *Symp. R. ent. Soc. Lond.* **2**: 66–77.

BUTLER, C. G. (1967). A sex attractant acting as an aphrodisiac in the honey-bee (*Apis mellifera* L.) *Proc. R. ent. Soc. Lond.* A, **42**: 71–76.

BUTLER, C. G. and PATON, P. N. (1962). Inhibition of queen rearing by queen honey-bees (*Apis mellifera* L.) of different ages. *Proc. R. ent. Soc. Lond.* A, **37**: 114–116.

CAMPION, D. G. (1976). Sex pheromones for the control of lepidopterous pests using microencapsulation and dispenser techniques. *Pestic. Sci.* **7**: 636–641.

COMMON, I. F. B. and BELLAS, T. E. (1977). Regurgitation of host-plant oil from a foregut diverticulum in the larvae of *Myrascia megalocentra* and *M. bracteatella* (Lepidoptera: Oecophoridae). *J. Aust. ent. Soc.* **16**: 141–147.

CORBET, S. A. (1971). Mandibular gland secretion of larvae of the flour moth, *Anagasta kuehniella*, contains an epideictic pheromone and elicits oviposition movements in a hymenopteran parasite. *Nature, Lond.* **232**: 481–484.

CORBET, S. A. and LAI-FOOK, J. (1977). The hairpencils of the flour moth *Ephestia kuehniella* (Lep., Phycitidae). *J. Zool.* **181**: 377–394.

CROSSLEY, A. C. and WATERHOUSE, D. F. (1969). The ultrastructure of the osmeterium and the nature of its secretion in *Papilio* larvae (Lepidoptera). *Tissue & Cell* **1**: 525–554.

DICKINS, G. R. (1936). The scent glands of certain Phycitidae (Lepidoptera). *Trans. R. ent. Soc. Lond.* **85**: 331–362.

DIXEY, F. A. (1932).The plume-scales of the Pierinae. *Trans. ent. Soc. Lond.* **80**: 57–75.

DUFFIELD, R. M., BLUM, M. S. and WHEELER, J. W. (1976). Alkylpyrazine alarm pheromones in primitive ants with small colonial units. *Comp. Biochem. Physiol.* 54B: 439–440.

EISNER, T. (1965). Defensive spray of a phasmid insect. *Science* **148**: 966–968.

EISNER, T. and KAFATOS, F. C. (1962). Defence mechanisms of arthropods. X. A pheromone promoting aggregation in an aposematic distasteful insect. *Psyche, Camb.* **69**: 53–61.

EISNER, T., JOHNESSEE, J. S., CARRELL, J., HENDRY, L. B. and MEINWOLD, J. (1974). Defensive use by an insect of a plant resin. *Science* **184**: 996–999.

EISNER, T., KRISTON, I. and ANESHANSLEY, D. J. (1976). Defensive behaviour of a termite (*Nasutitermes exitiosus*). *Behav. Ecol. Sociobiol.* **1**: 83–125.

EISNER, T., JONES, T. H., ANESHANSLEY, D. J., TSCHINKEL, W. R., SILBERGLIED, R. E. and MEINWALD, J. (1977). Chemistry of defensive secretions of bombardier beetles (Brachinini, Metriini, Ozaenini, Paussini). *J. Insect Physiol.* **23**: 1383–1386.

FARKAS, S. R. and SHOREY, H. H. (1974). Mechanisms of orientation to a distant pheromone source. *in* Birch, M. C. (ed.), *Pheromones*. North-Holland Publishing Co., Amsterdam.

FREE, J. B. and BUTLER, C. G. (1959). *Bumblebees*. Collins, London.

GARY, N. E. (1974). Pheromones that affect the behavior and physiology of honey bees. *in* Birch, M. C. (ed.), *Pheromones*. North-Holland Publishing Co., Amsterdam.

HAPP, G. M. (1968). Quinone and hydrocarbon production in the defensive glands of *Eleodes longicollis* and *Tribolium castaneum* (Coleoptera: Tenebrionidae). *J. Insect Physiol.* **14**: 1821–1837.

HAPP, G. M., SCHROEDER, M. E. and WANG, J. C. H. (1970). Effects of male and female scent on reproductive maturation in young female *Tenebrio molitor*. *J. Insect Physiol.* **16**: 1543–1548.

HUWYLER, S., GROB, K. and VISCONTINI, M. (1975). The trail pheromone of the ant, *Lasius fuliginosus*: identification of six components. *J. Insect Physiol.* **21**: 299–304.

IMMS, A. D. (1957). *A general textbook of entomology*. 9th edition revised by Richards and Davies. Methuen, London.

JACOBSON, M. (1972). *Insect sex pheromones*. Academic Press, New York.

JACOBSON, M. (1974). Insect pheromones. *in* Rockstein, M. (ed.), *The physiology of Insecta*. vol. 3. Academic Press, New York.

KAISSLING, K.-E. (1971). Insect olfaction. *in* Beidler, L. M. (ed.), *Handbook of sensory physiology*. vol. 4. Springer-Verlag, Berlin.

KARLSON, P. and BUTENANDT, A. (1959). Pheromones (ectohormones) in insects. *A. Rev. Ent.* **4**: 39–58.

KENDALL, D. A. (1974). The structure of defence glands in some Tenebrionidae and Nilionidae (Coleoptera). *Trans. R. ent. Soc. Lond.* **125**: 437–487.

KENDALL, M. D. (1972). Glandular epidermis on the tarsi of the desert locust, *Schistocerca gregaria* Forskål. *Acrida* **1**: 121–147.

KLUN, J. A. and COOPERATORS (1975). Insect sex pheromones: intraspecific pheromonal variability of *Ostrinia nubilalis* in North America and Europe. *Envir. Ent.* **4**: 891–894.

LOHER, W. (1960). The chemical acceleration of the maturation process and its hormonal control in the male of the desert locust. *Proc. R. Soc.* B, **153**: 380–397.

LÜSCHER, M. (1961). Social control of polymorphism in termites. *Symp. R. ent. Soc. Lond.* **1**: 57–67.

MARSH, D., KENNEDY, J. S. and LUDLOW, A. R. (1978). An analysis of anemotactic zigzagging flight in male moths stimulated by pheromone. *Physiol. Ent.* **3**: 221–240.

MOORE, B. P. (1974). Pheromones in the termite societies. *in* Birch, M. C. (ed.), *Pheromones*. North-Holland Publishing Co., Amsterdam.

MORROW, P. A., BELLAS, T. E. and EISNER, T. (1976). *Eucalyptus* oils in the defensive oral discharge of Australian sawfly larvae (Hymenoptera: Pergidae). *Oecologia* **24**: 193–206.

NOIROT, C. (1969). Glands and secretions. *in* Krishna, K. and Weesner, F. M. (eds.), *Biology of termites*. Academic Press, New York.

NOIROT, C. and QUENNEDEY, A. (1974). Fine structure of insect epidermal glands. *A. Rev. Ent.* **19**: 61–80.

NORRIS, M. J. (1962). Group effects on the activity and behaviour of adult males of the desert locust (*Schistocerca gregaria* Forsk.) in relation to sexual maturation. *Anim. Behav.* **10**: 275–291.

NORRIS, M. J. (1963). Laboratory experiments on gregarious behaviour in ovipositing females of the desert locust (*Schistocerca gregaria* [Forsk.]). *Entomologia exp. appl.* **6**: 279–303.

OSGOOD, C. E. (1971). An oviposition pheromone associated with egg rafts of *Culex tarsalis*. *Ann. ent. Soc. Am.* **64**: 1038–1041.

PARRY, K. and MORGAN, E. D. (1979). Pheromones of ants: a review. *Physiol. Ent.* **4**: 161–189.

PERCY, J. E. and WEATHERSTONE, J. (1974). Gland structure and pheromone production in insects. *in* Birch, M. C. (ed.), *Pheromones*. North-Holland Publishing Co., Amsterdam.

PRESTWICH, G. D. (1977). Chemical composition of the soldier secretions of the termite—*Trinervitermes gratiosus*. *Insect Biochem.* **7**: 91–94.

PRESTWICH, G. D., BIERL, B. A., DEVILBISS, E. D. and CHAUDHURY, M. F. B. (1977). Soldier frontal glands of the termite *Macrotermes subhyalinus*: morphology, chemical composition, and use in defense. *J. Chem. Ecol.* **3**: 579–590.

QURESHI, S. A. and AHMAD, I. (1970). Studies on the functional anatomy and histology of the repellent gland of *Poekilocerus pictus* (F.) (Orthoptera: Pyrgomorphidae). *Proc. R. ent. Soc. Lond.* A, **45**: 149–155.

RABB, R. L. and BRADLEY, J. R. (1970). Marking host eggs by *Telenomus sphingis*. *Ann. ent. Soc. Am.* **63**: 1053–1056.

ROTHSCHILD, M. (1973). Secondary plant substances and warning colouration in insects. *Symp. R. ent. Soc. Lond.* **6**: 59–83.

RUDINSKY, J. A. and RYKER, L. C. (1977). Olfactory and auditory signals mediating behavioural patterns of bark beetles. *Colloq. Int. C.N.R.S.* no. 265, 195–209.

SCHILDKNECHT, H. (1977). Protective substances of arthropods and plants. *Pont. Acad. Sci. Scripta Varia* **41**: 59–107.

SCHNEIDER, D. (1966). Chemical sense communication in insects. *Symp. Soc. exp. Biol.* **20**: 273–297.

SHOREY, H. H. (1973). Behavioral responses to insect pheromones. *A. Rev. Ent.* **18**: 349–380.

SHOREY, H. H. and McKELVEY, J. J. (eds.) (1977). *Chemical control of insect behaviour. Theory and application.* Wiley and Sons, New York.

SNODGRASS, R. E. (1956). *Anatomy of the honey bee.* Constable, London.

SOUTH, R. (1941). *The butterflies of the British Isles.* Warne and Co., London.

STADDON, B. W. (1979). The scent glands of Heteroptera. *Adv. Insect Physiol.* **14**: 351–418.

STADDON, B. W. and THORNE, M. J. (1973). The structure of the metathoracic scent gland system of the water bug *Ilyocoris cimicoides* (L.) (Heteroptera: Naucoridae). *Trans. R. ent. Soc. Lond.* **124**: 343–363.

STRONG, L. (1975). Defence glands in the giant spiny phasmid *Extatosoma tiaratum. J. Ent.* A, **50**: 65–72.

TAMAKI, Y. (1977). Complexity, diversity, and specificity of behaviour-modifying chemicals in Lepidoptera and Diptera. *in* Shorey, M. M. and McKelvey, J. J. (eds.), *Chemical control of insect behaviour. Theory and Application.* Wiley and Sons, New York.

TINBERGEN, N. (1951). *The study of instinct.* Oxford University Press.

TSCHINKEL, W. R. (1975). A comparative study of the chemical defensive system of tenebrionid beetles: chemistry of the secretions. *J. Insect Physiol.* **21**: 753–783.

TUMLINSON, J. H., SILVERSTEIN, R. M., MOSER, J. C., BROWNLEE, R. G. and RUTH, J. M. (1971). Identification of the trail pheromone of a leaf-cutting ant, *Atta texana. Nature, Lond.* **234**: 348–349.

UVAROV, B. (1966). *Grasshoppers and locusts.* vol. 1. Cambridge University Press.

VITÉ, J. P. and WILLIAMSON, D. L. (1970). *Thanasimus dubius*: prey perception. *J. Insect Physiol.* **16**: 233–239.

WEATHERSTONE, J. and PERCY, J. E. (1970). Arthropod defensive secretions. *in* Beroza, M. (ed.), *Chemicals controlling insect behaviour.* Academic Press, New York.

WHEELER, W. M. (1926). *Ants. Their structure, development and behaviour.* Columbia University Press, New York.

WIGGLESWORTH, V. B. (1972). *The principles of insect physiology.* Methuen, London.

WILSON, E. O. (1962). Chemical communication among workers of the fire ant *Solenopsis saevissima* (Fr. Smith) 1. The organization of mass-foraging. *Anim. Behav.* **10**: 134–164.

WILSON, E. O. (1963). The social biology of ants. *A. Rev. Ent.* **8**: 345–368.

WILSON, E. O. (1976). The organization of colony defense in the ant *Pheidole dentata* Mayr (Hymenoptera: Formicidae). *Behav. Ecol. Sociobiol.* **1**: 63–81.

WOOD, D. L. (1973). Selection and colonization of ponderosa pine by bark beetles. *Symp. R. ent. Soc. Lond.* **6**: 101–117.

WOOD, W. F., TRUCKENBRODT, W. and MEINWALD, J. (1975). Chemistry of the defensive secretion from the African termite *Odontotermes badius. Ann. ent. Soc. Am.* **68**: 359–360.

TAXONOMIC INDEX

Page numbers in bold denote illustrations. The major orders are omitted.

SUBJECT INDEX

Page numbers in bold refer to a major reference or an illustration.